ENCYCLOPEDIA
OF HISTORICAL
ARCHAEOLOGY

ENCYCLOPEDIA OF HISTORICAL ARCHAEOLOGY

Edited by Charles E. Orser, Jr

London and New York

First published 2002
by Routledge
11 New Fetter Lane, London EC4P 4EE

Simultaneously published in the USA and Canada
by Routledge
29 West 35th Street, New York, NY 10001

Routledge is an imprint of the Taylor & Francis Group

© 2002 Routledge

Typeset in Baskerville by Taylor & Francis Books Ltd
Printed and bound in Great Britain by TJ International,
Padstow, Cornwall.

British Library Cataloguing in Publication Data
A catalogue record for this book is available from the British Library

Library of Congress Cataloging in Publication Data
Encyclopedia of historical archaeology / edited by Charles E. Orser Jr.
p. cm.
Includes bibliographical references and index.
ISBN 0–415–21544–7
1. Archaeology and history–Encyclopedias. 2. Excavations (Archaeology)–
Encyclopedias. 3. Historic sites–Encyclopedias. I. Orser, Charles E.

CC77.H5 E53 2002
930.1–dc21   2001048416

ISBN 0–415–21544–7

Contents

Editorial Team

Illustrations

List of contributors

Jonathan Adams
Southampton University, UK

Jim Allen
La Trobe University, Australia

S. Jane Allen
AMEC Earth and Environmental, USA

Steen W. Andersen
Vejle Museum, Denmark

Hans Andersson
University of Lund, Sweden

Anders Andrén
University of Lund, Sweden

Jette Arneborg
National Museum, Denmark

Grenville Astill
University of Reading, UK

David Barker
Potteries Museum and Art Gallery, Stoke-on-Trent, UK

Sherene Baugher
Cornell University, USA

Timothy Baumann
University of Missouri–St Louis, USA

Mary C. Beaudry
Boston University, USA

Marshall Joseph Becker
West Chester University, USA

Nancy L. Benco
George Washington University, USA

Simon Blatherwick
Rose Theatre Trust, UK

Julian M.C. Bowsher
Museum of London Archaeology Service, UK, and Greenwich Historical Society, UK

Alasdair M. Brooks
University of York, UK

Ronald C. Carlisle
Brown and Carlisle Associates, Inc., USA

Lynda Carroll
Binghamton University, SUNY, USA

Eleanor Conlin Casella
University of Manchester, UK

Thomas H. Charlton
University of Iowa, USA

Neil J. Christie
University of Leicester, UK

Matthew D. Cochran
Maryland – National Capital Park and Planning Commission, USA

M. Patricia Colquette
Louisiana State University, USA

David L. Conlin
National Park Service, USA

Graham Connah
Australian National University, Australia

Melissa Connor
Forensic and Archaeological Services, Lincoln, USA

Robert Cowie
Museum of London Archaeology Service, UK

Aron L. Crowell
Arctic Studies Center, Smithsonian Institution, USA

Peter Davies
La Trobe University, Australia

Christopher R. DeCorse
Syracuse University, USA

James A. Delle
Franklin and Marshall College, USA

Margarita Díaz-Andreu
University of Durham, UK

David Divers
Pre-Construct Archaeology Ltd, UK

Christopher Dobbs
Mary Rose Trust, UK

Terrence W. Epperson
Independent scholar, Philadelphia, USA

Susan Toby Evans
Pennsylvania State University, USA

Charles R. Ewen
East Carolina University, USA

Paul Farnsworth
Louisiana State University, USA

Alaric Faulkner
University of Maine, USA

Roland Fletcher
University of Sydney, Australia

William R. Fowler, Jr
Vanderbilt University, USA

Maria Franklin
University of Texas at Austin, USA

Pedro Paulo A. Funari
Universidade Estadual de Campinas, Brazil

David R.M. Gaimster
British Museum, UK

Jerzy Gawronski
Atdeling Archeologie, dienst Amsterdam Beheer, Netherlands

Lorinda B.R. Goodwin
Boston University, USA

Adrian Green
University of Durham, UK

Mark D. Groover
Augusta State University, USA

Byron Hamann
University of Chicago, USA

Scott Hamilton
Lakehead University, Canada

Gitte Hansen
Bergen Museum, Norway

Donald L. Hardesty
University of Nevada, USA

Edward Cecil Harris
Bermuda Maritime Museum, Bermuda

Donald P. Heldman
Zooarch Research, USA

Sue Hirst
London, UK

Audrey J. Horning
Queen's University of Belfast, Northern Ireland

Paul R. Huey
New York State Office of Parks, Recreation and Historic Preservation, USA

N. James
Freelance archaeologist, UK

Stephen R. James, Jr
Panamerican Consultants, Inc., USA

Stacey C. Jordan
Rutgers University, USA

Jon K. Jouppien
Heritage Resource Consultants/Society for Historical Archaeology, Canada

Kenneth G. Kelly
University of South Carolina, USA

Margaret A. Kennedy
University of Saskatchewan, Canada

Bas Kist
Hollandia Consultancy, Netherlands

Terry Klein
SRI Foundation, USA

Olga Klimko
Ministry of Sustainable Resource Management,
Victoria, Canada

Elizabeth Kryder-Reid
Indiana University – Purdue University, Indianapolis, USA

David B. Landon
University of Massachusetts, Boston, USA

Paul J. Lane
British Institute in Eastern Africa, Kenya

Susan Lawrence
La Trobe University, Australia

Mark P. Leone
University of Maryland, College Park, USA

Donald W. Linebaugh
University of Kentucky, USA

Barbara J. Little
National Park Service, USA

Jane Lydon
La Trobe University, Australia

Bonnie G. McEwan
Florida Bureau of Archaeological Research, USA

Larry McKee
TRC Garrow Associates, Nashville, USA

Heather McKillop
Louisiana State University, USA

Kaname Maekawa
Toyama University, Japan

Teresita Majewski
Statistical Research Inc., USA

Antonia Malan
University of Cape Town, Republic of South Africa

Christopher N. Matthews
Hofstra University, USA

Luciano Migliaccio
University of São Paulo, Brazil

Adrian Miles
Museum of London Archaeology Service, UK

Stephen A. Mrozowski
University of Massachusetts, Boston, USA

Paul R. Mullins
Indiana University – Purdue University, Indianapolis, USA

Larry E. Murphy
National Park Service, USA

Fraser D. Neiman
Monticello, Charlottesville, USA

Jessica L. Neuwirth
Historic Deerfield, Inc., USA

Martin K. Nickels
Illinois State University, USA

Ivor Noël Hume
Williamsburg, USA

Francisco Noelli
Universidade Estadual de Maringá, Brazil

Charles E. Orser, Jr
Illinois State University, USA

David T. Palmer
University of California at Berkeley, USA

Matthew Palus
Columbia University, USA

Alistair Paterson
University of Western Australia, Australia

Ana C. Piñón
Universidad Complutense de Madrid, Spain

Peter E. Pope
Memorial University of Newfoundland, Canada

Margarete Prüch
DAI, Germany

Włodzimierz Rączkowski
Adam Mickiewicz University of Poznań, Poland

Gilson Rambelli
Museu de Arqueologia e Etnologia da Universidade de São Paulo, Brazil

Víctor Revilla Calvo
University of Barcelona, Spain

Prudence M. Rice
Southern Illinois University, USA

Neville A. Ritchie
Department of Conservation, New Zealand

Timothy James Scarlett
University of Nevada, USA

Peter Schmid
Lower Saxony Institute for Historical Coastal Research, Germany

James Schoenwetter
Arizona State University, USA

Douglas D. Scott
Midwest Archeological Center, Lincoln, USA

Elizabeth M. Scott
Zooarch Research, Missouri, USA

Maria Ximena Senatore
University of Buenos Aires, Argentina

Paul A. Shackel
University of Maryland, USA

Russell K. Skowronek
Santa Clara University, USA

Barney Sloane
Museum of London Archaeology Service, UK

Angèle P. Smith
University of Northern British Columbia, Canada

Steven D. Smith
South Carolina Institute of Archaeology and Anthropology, USA

Suzanne M. Spencer-Wood
Harvard University, USA, and Oakland University, USA

Jörn Staecker
University of Lund, Sweden

Edward Staski
New Mexico State University, USA

Ian B. Straughn
University of Chicago, USA

Christopher Thomas
Museum of London Archaeology Service, UK

Sarah Peabody Turnbaugh
University of Rhode Island, USA

Diana diZerega Wall
City College of the University of New York, USA

Mark S. Warner
University of Idaho, USA

Gregory A. Waselkov
University of South Alabama, USA

Priscilla Wegars
University of Idaho, USA

Brent R. Weisman
University of South Florida, USA

Thomas R. Wheaton
New South Associates, Inc., USA

Carolyn L. White
Boston University, USA

Laurie A. Wilkie
University of California at Berkeley, USA

Susan M. Wright
University of Reading, UK

Rebecca Yamin
John Milner Associates, USA

Amy L. Young
University of Southern Mississippi, USA

Andrés Zarankin
PREP-CONICET, Argentina

W. Haio Zimmermann
Lower Saxony Institute for Historical Coastal Research, Germany

Thomas A. Zoubek
Yale University, USA

Introduction

The field of archaeology is eminently suited to presentation in an encyclopedic format. Archaeological data is by nature detailed, amenable to cataloguing and vast. The information gathered by archaeologists is also infinitely expandable. Archaeologists broaden our understanding of the past every time they turn a new shovelful of earth or sift another bucket load of soil. The boundaries of archaeological knowledge are constantly being pushed forward and something new is learned with every excavation. Historical archaeology is one kind of archaeology that is doing much to increase our understanding of the past, and, at the beginning of the twenty-first century, the field is adding fresh information to our storehouse of knowledge at an unprecedented rate.

Historical archaeology is an inherently interesting field from a purely intellectual point of view because it can be defined in two, somewhat distinct, ways. It can be defined as the archaeological investigation of any past culture that has developed a literate tradition; or it can be viewed as the study of the 'modern world', the historical and cultural conditions that have shaped our world since about AD 1500. These definitions of historical archaeology coexist and are not mutually exclusive, and both are widely used by the archaeologists of history.

Under the first definition, eighteenth-century France, nineteenth-century Australia, the fifteenth-century Maya and the first-century BC Greeks would all fall within the purview of historical archaeology because each culture had a tradition of writing. It does not matter methodologically whether the 'text' is a handwritten letter, a typeset legal document or an inscription chiselled onto stone. The important thing is that the 'text' has the ability to supplement and to complement archaeologically derived information. Archaeologists who use this definition of historical archaeology tend to be interested both in the cultures they study and in the wider questions of how archaeological (largely artefactual) data and written information can be united in the meaningful study of the past. The combination of 'historical' and 'archaeological' information has been a constant topic within historical archaeology, and it is something that historical archaeologists of many backgrounds continue to explore.

The second definition of historical archaeology tends to be used by archaeologists who live and work in those parts of the world that were colonised by Europeans during their so-called Age of Exploration. These archaeologists, who are also deeply interested in the union of excavated materials and written texts, tend to focus on several broad themes that have been important during the past 500 years. These themes involve the material aspects of colonialism, the creation of gender roles, the use of racial theories, the interaction of indigenous peoples with foreign invaders, the rise and growth of capitalism and many other topics.

An important disciplinary difference has often distinguished 'second-definition' historical archaeologists from those who tend to use the first definition. 'Second-definition' historical archaeologists are generally trained in anthropology and see historical archaeology largely as an anthropological pursuit. Though this distinction is a bit facile, many 'first-definition' historical archaeologists tend to view their field as essentially historical in focus, and they are usually somewhat less interested in the topics that fascinate anthropologists. However, we must be clear that historically minded and anthropologically minded historical archaeologists have much to teach one another, and a great deal of cross-fertilisation of ideas occurs in the discipline. It would be too simplistic to argue that these groups are well defined or entirely separate.

Historical archaeology, as a distinct kind of archaeology with that identifiable name, largely developed in the USA during the late 1960s. The apparent distinction between historical archaeologists who see themselves as historians and those who view themselves as primarily anthropologists served to confuse the field during its earliest days of formulation. Part of the reason for the confusion developed because historical archaeologists in Great Britain – who called themselves 'post-medieval archaeologists' – generally perceived their work as largely historical in orientation. They generally did not have the anthropological background of historical archaeologists trained in the USA, and many of them saw little need for an anthropological perspective in historical archaeology. Under a purely 'historical' definition of the field, however, one can see the beginnings of historical archaeology much earlier in the work of classical and Near Eastern archaeologists. These pioneering archaeologists used texts all the time, even though they seldom considered themselves to be 'historical' archaeologists. Using this definition, the roots of historical archaeology extend into the seventeenth century.

As historical archaeology enters the twenty-first century, its practitioners are no longer concerned with making distinctions between themselves. Most historical archaeologists today can accept that they need both anthropology *and* history (and many other disciplines, as well) to allow them to provide the most insightful interpretations of the past. At the same time, they also realise that they share the same methodological concerns as Mayanists, Egyptologists and classical archaeologists as they wrestle with the union of 'archaeological' and 'historical' information.

The differences of opinion about historical archaeology that have existed over the years mean that historical archaeology is a diverse and broad field. Historical archaeologists can make detailed studies of nineteenth-century glass buttons and then turn immediately to consider the theoretical nuances of cultural evolution. They can investigate the construction methods of eighteenth-century forts in Canada, and then consider the cultural impact of the Aztec conquest. Today's historical archaeologists view their vast latitude within the field as immensely positive. They correctly believe that their research is deeply important to the understanding of both local and world history, and that they can make significant contributions on many different geographical scales, extending from the household to the international level.

Historical archaeology has grown tremendously since the 1960s. Only fourteen individuals founded the (largely North American) Society for Historical Archaeology in 1967. Today, the Society has well over 2,000 members, as does its European counterpart, the (United Kingdom's) Society for Post-Medieval Archaeology. Societies dedicated to historical archaeology either now exist or are being created on all continents and in most countries, and historical archaeologists are conducting exciting, new excavations in every corner of the globe. The future of the discipline is exceptionally bright, indeed.

Given the breadth of historical archaeology and the rapid pace with which it is growing, readers of this encyclopedia should think of this book as a guide or an introduction to the field rather than as a definitive source or final word. Readers should use the entries in this book as a starting point to learn about various aspects of historical archaeology, understanding that their own, further reading will provide even more insights and greater information.

As we compiled this encyclopedia, we tried to keep our readership firmly in mind. We knew that archaeology students, both undergraduate and postgraduate, as well as our disciplinary colleagues would have recourse to use its information. Its concise overviews are ideal for students seeking to learn the basics of the many complex subjects investigated by historical archaeologists. We also felt confident that this work would have great relevance to students and scholars outside archaeology, those studying and working in the related fields of anthropology, history, geography, folklore, architecture and all the other disciplines that historical archaeologists regularly consult. We also imagined that men, women and pre-university students, having just discovered historical archaeology, could consult this book to learn more about it. Many of these potential readers may have encountered the discipline at the growing number of outdoor museums and historical parks that are being created with the assistance of historical archaeologists. They may have even seen historical archaeologists at work and become intrigued by the field. In the end, we hope that the material in this encyclopedia stimulates and informs all those who consult it.

Coverage and contributors

The creation of the headword list was a difficult and ongoing process. The general editor compiled the original list and then shared it with the associate editors. Each associate editor made several additions to the list and significantly strengthened it. The general editor was delighted that many of the contributors also made suggestions about additional headwords. Their additions improved the coverage of the book and made it a truly collaborative effort. This encyclopedia thus reflects what practising historical archaeologists view as important at the start of the twenty-first century.

We have tried to provide a balance between the two ways that historical archaeology has traditionally been defined and to provide an accurate representation of the field as it stands in 2001. We have adopted a balanced approach to indicate the intellectual breadth of the field and to illustrate the vast range of topics that historical archaeologists can conceivably investigate. This inclusive approach presented several difficult decisions concerning the amount of coverage to allocate to other kinds of archaeology, especially those that have long used written information in conjunction with archaeological excavation. For example, classical archaeology, the archaeology of the Maya, maritime archaeology and industrial archaeology all rightly stand as individual pursuits on their own. However, at the same time, each one can be perceived as a kind of historical archaeology. We believe that anyone wishing to know more about maritime archaeology, for instance, should begin here but then read more detailed accounts in books dedicated specifically to that subject. The same can be said for all the other kinds of 'historical' archaeology. Our goal here is to provide an introduction only, a signpost to further information.

Careful readers will note that we have not included any specific entries about individual archaeologists. The decision to exclude such entries was a difficult one that the editors discussed at great length. Reasonable pros and cons were voiced on both sides of the issue, but, in the end, we decided not to include such entries because most practising historical archaeologists, even many of the pioneering founders of the field, are still alive. We did not wish to be selective with the list and face the possibility of having excluded someone of importance. Readers will find the names of the most significant individuals within individual entries, and discerning readers can develop their own perspectives on any individual's importance to the discipline.

We have been particularly fortunate in having been able to gather together an impressive list of contributors, all of whom are experts in their particular areas of study. The editors discovered, when they sent out the first calls for contributions, that the overwhelming majority of the archaeologists we contacted immediately agreed to participate. We were heartened by their positive response, and we viewed their willingness to assist us as a sign of the growing importance of historical archaeology around the globe, their eagerness to promote the important research of the field and the need for this book. We did not always find it easy to identify the most noted scholars in a particular area of study because a growing number of individuals can justifiably lay claim to the title. In any case, all contributors were gracious enough to take valuable time away from their busy research, teaching and writing schedules to provide entries. We hope that we have not overlooked any major areas of study within historical archaeology, but we realise that oversights are possible, especially given the field's rapid growth. We especially hope that we have not ignored the archaeologists in those regions that are just developing an interest in historical archaeology but have yet to publicise their findings.

We have been somewhat limited by restricting the language of this volume to English. This restriction was practical and necessary, and we have tried to remedy its selectivity by including entries from non-English-speaking areas. We hope that these entries will encourage readers to explore the important works prepared in those places, and to learn from the indigenous scholars in every country. Only through such personal effort will readers discover the true richness of historical archaeology as it is practised everywhere today. It is clearly not an 'English-only' enterprise.

Historical archaeology is happily now a global pursuit, and we want this encyclopedia to have world-wide value. We apologise for any topic or region we may have inadvertently overlooked. Rather than being embarrassed by our failure to include everything, however, we are encouraged that historical archaeology continues to expand beyond limits that even we recognise. We understand – and in fact revel in the idea – that this book is not complete. That no single encyclopedia of historical archaeology could ever be finalised is a healthy sign for the field indeed.

Charles E. Orser, Jr

Acadian sites

As a geopolitical entity, 'Acadia' denotes a portion of north-eastern Canada and the USA that was nominally under French control from its first settlement in 1604 until the Acadian Expulsion of 1755–1764. The fluid boundaries of Acadia extended from the Gaspé Peninsula of Quebec south-westerly to the eastern two-thirds of the coast of the state of Maine in the USA, encompassing the Canadian maritime provinces of Nova Scotia, New Brunswick and Prince Edward Island. The majority of this region was taken by Britain in 1710 and formally ceded to them in 1713 by the Treaty of Utrecht. This left only Île Royale (Cape Breton, Nova Scotia), Île St-Jean (Prince Edward Island) and the Chignecto region of New Brunswick in French Acadian hands. By 1755, the entire region was controlled by the British, who forced most ethnic Acadians into hiding or exported them to other French colonies, especially Louisiana. In subsequent years, many returned to French Canada, where their descendants still consider themselves to be 'Acadian'.

With a few notable exceptions, archaeology of Acadian sites has been conducted for government agencies managing national and provincial parks. These sites fall into three groups. Seventeenth-century establishments were predominantly small, fortified outposts of traders and missionaries, and were generally situated at the mouths of the major drainage systems. Then, in the late seventeenth and early eighteenth centuries, modest agricultural communities, together with their dike systems, expanded rapidly through the low-lying basins of Nova Scotia and New Brunswick. Finally, following the British takeover of 1713 and prior to the 1755 Acadian Expulsion, defended settlements developed to protect the remaining, isolated French enclaves.

Initial settlements and fortified outposts

The first attempted Acadian settlement was also the site of the earliest government-sponsored 'archaeology'. In 1604, entrepreneur Pierre de Monts, with Samuel de Champlain's assistance, led a failed attempt to place a colony on an island at the mouth of the St Croix River to expand his fur trade. In 1797, working for a commission to establish a boundary between Canada and the USA, surveyor Thomas Wright verified the location of this early French claim using Champlain's plans and descriptions. Here Wright discovered substantial ruins of two stone foundations and yellow-brick chimney rubble with trees 18–20 inches in diameter growing within. In 1950, the United States Park Service commissioned excavations by Wendell Hadlock that were extended in 1968–9 by Jacob Gruber. This led to the rediscovery of the ruins of the 'storehouse', and the exhumation of twenty-three burials of the thirty-five known to have perished in de Monts's party. Gruber's unpublished report describes the distinctive Norman **stoneware** that characterises this early assemblage. St Croix Island has since become an international archaeological landmark on the boundary between Maine and New Brunswick.

After a disastrous year at St Croix, the De Monts colony departed across the Bay of Fundy to found Port Royal in the Minas Basin of Nova

Scotia. Archaeological excavations in 1938 were unsuccessful in verifying the location; nevertheless, near the presumed location Parks Canada maintains a living history replica constructed from the plans of Champlain and descriptions of the colony leader Lescarbot.

Subsequent settlements of the 1630s are better understood archaeologically, and most are comprised of small, fortified outposts. These were constructed by various French entrepreneurs, generally of minor nobility, who competed fiercely with each other to control the rich natural resources: fish, fur, timber and coal. Their complement seldom numbered more than a few dozen soldier-employees, craftsmen and sometimes clerics, and the fortifications served as much to defend these rivals against each other as against onslaughts from other European colonies or Native Americans. A pioneering description of one such outpost was conducted by Norman Barka in the early 1960s at Fort Saint Marie in modern St John, New Brunswick, the principal holding of Acadian Charles de La Tour, which stood from *c.* 1631 to 1645. Barka was the first to describe the footprint of one of these compact outposts, and to identify the distinctive ceramics from the Saintonge region of France that characterised the assemblage and have since helped to identify French colonial settlement elsewhere.

Fort Pentagoet in Castine, Maine, in the USA was constructed by La Tour's arch rival, Charles d'Aulnay, on the site of a former English trading post operated at the behest of the Plymouth colonists. This compact fortification has been extensively excavated and reported by Alaric and Gretchen Faulkner. Pentagoet defended the southwestern boundary of Acadia with New England between 1635 and 1654, and again from 1670 until its destruction by Dutch raiders in 1764. During its first French occupation, it served to protect d'Aulnay's private interests, primarily the trading of furs with the native Wabakai groups that regularly frequented the Penobscot River. Thereafter, in its second French occupation, it became the administrative capital of Acadia, defending against the neighbouring New Englanders to the south-west, who by this time far outnumbered the Acadians. In addition to extensive analysis of the footprint and architecture of the fort, the Faulkners

describe the changes in French ceramics, foodways and smoking habits of the enclave over these occupations. They also investigate the supply and maintenance requirements of the fort reflected in the products and by-products of the smithy/workshop.

Brigetta Wallace has tested Nicolas Denys's Fort Saint Pierre (1636–69) in St Peters, Nova Scotia, the operation of another rival pioneer. Denise Hanson has reported on a small sample of ceramics and other artefacts from this site consistent with the larger assemblages at Forts St Marie and Pentagoet.

By the last quarter of the nineteenth century, most of these outposts had been destroyed, abandoned or, as was the case of Fort Pentagoet, replaced by the more undefended enterprise of a lone trader. Jean Vincent de St-Castin's habitation in Maine, excavated by Alaric Faulkner between 1983 and 1993, was comprised merely of a modest dwelling and a storehouse/workshop, where St-Castin and his family traded powder, shot and tobacco to the local Wabanaki.

Eighteenth-century Acadian agricultural settlement

The eighteenth century saw great growth in the permanent residents of Acadia, the population doubling every twenty years and reaching a maximum of 10,500–12,000 by 1755. These agricultural settlements were concentrated in the principal basins of Nova Scotia: Beaubassin, Minas and Belleisle. Here Acadian farmers used their systems of dikes, originally developed for salt production, to produce rich farmland on the salt marshes. Since 1983, more than a hundred Acadian house depressions, along with their associated dikes, have been identified in this region. These were one-room wooden structures, with central cellars. The chimney was located on the gable end, and an exterior bread oven generally abutted it. The best recorded of these was the House 1 at Belleisle excavated by David Christianson in 1983, which measured 11.5 by 7.5 m and featured an abutting, circular bread oven, all set on a low, fieldstone foundation. On the inside, walls were apparently finished with a red, straw-tempered clay that was apparently whitewashed with a fine white slip and showed the impressions of the wooden lath to which it was attached. A similar structure has also been excavated at the Melanson Settlement near Annapolis. On western Prince Edward Island, Rob Ferguson successfully used electrical-conductivity surveying, a type of **remote sensing**, to locate a house very similar to the Belleisle construction. This was the homestead of Michel Haché-Gallant, the first Acadian settler of Prince Edward Island, and ancestor to many of the modern Acadian residents.

Further suggestions of how such houses were constructed come from above-ground archaeology. In the late 1970s, a nineteenth-century shopfront in Annapolis, Nova Scotia, was found to contain an earlier late eighteenth-century Georgian structure. While 'restoring' the latter as a historic showpiece, it was discovered that it in turn contained a smaller, mud-walled structure, probably constructed by Acadians early in the eighteenth century. Unlike the interwoven branches that characterise English wattle-and-daub construction, the framework for these walls were lath sprung between cracks in the uprights at about 10 cm intervals, a construction reminiscent of seventeenth-century English and Dutch **architecture**. The walls were clearly white-washed on the interior, like the structure at Belleisle. Subsequently, Barry Moody, historian at Acadia University, Wolfville, Nova Scotia, has identified three similar standing structures within the region.

Eighteenth-century Acadian fortifications and fortified settlements

The **Fortress of Louisbourg** was built on Île Royale, today's Cape Breton, Nova Scotia, one of the last French holdings in the region after the 1713 Treaty of Utrecht. Louisbourg was not an ethnic Acadian settlement, but rather a French mercantile 'city'. It was built from scratch, beginning in 1719, at the behest of Louis XIV to maintain a last vestige of French control in this region against further English incursion. The city was taken by British and New England forces in 1745, restored to France the following year, and finally retaken and its fortifications demolished in 1755. Louisbourg was the site of massive excavation and restoration between 1961 and 1979, and has been open ever since as a major living-history museum, on a scope comparable to **Colonial**

Williamsburg in Virginia. The assemblages recovered, which represent the local French trading sphere in the eighteenth century, have provided vast type collections against which collections from true Acadian sites are often measured.

Other archaeological sites associated with the defence of the last remnants of Acadia include Port La Joye, located on Île Saint-Jean (Prince Edward Island) and Fort Beauséjour, which defended the last Acadian holdings in the Chignecto region of New Brunswick.

Foodways and dress

The data from these Acadian excavations have been incorporated into a number of studies dealing with lifeways in Acadia and New France. Alaric Faulkner has documented the surprising measures taken by seventeenth-century French entrepreneurs and their followers to maintain the appearance of gentility, even in the most remote, unpopulated regions of frontier Acadia. Similarly, using ceramic and documentary evidence from the Roma settlement on Prince Edward Island and the Fortress of Louisbourg in Nova Scotia, Jean-François Blanchette has traced the transition from medieval cooking practices to the oven-to-table presentation reflected in the adoption of brown faience, a type of tin-glazed **earthenware**, during the mid-eighteenth century.

Further reading

Blanchette, J. (1981) 'The role of artifacts in the study of foodways in New France, 1720–1760', *History and Archaeology* 52, Ottawa: Parks Canada, pp. 1–184.

Christianson, D. (1984) 'Belleisle 1983: Excavations at a pre-expulsion Acadian site', *Curatorial Report* 65, Halifax: Nova Scotia Museum, pp. 1–97.

Faulkner, A. (1989) 'Gentility on the frontiers of Acadia, 1635–1674: An archaeological perspective', in P. Benes (ed.) *New England/New France, 1600–1850, The Dublin Seminar for New England Folklife Annual Proceedings*, Boston: Boston University Press, pp. 82–100.

Faulkner, A. and Faulkner, G. (1987) *The French at Pentagoet, 1635–1674: An Archaeological Portrait of the Acadian Frontier*, Augusta: The New Brunswick

Museum and The Maine Historic Preservation Commission.

Ferguson, R. (1990) 'The search for Port La Joye: Archaeology at Île Saint-Jean's first French settlement', *The Island Magazine* 27: 3–8.

Fry, B.W. (1984) '"An appearance of strength": The fortifications of Louisbourg', *Studies in Archaeology, Architecture and History*, vol 1, pp. 1–214, vol 2, pp 1–212, Ottawa: Parks Canada.

Lavoie, M.C. (1987) 'Belle Isle Nova Scotia 1680–1755: Acadian material life and economy', *Curatorial Report* 65, Halifax: Nova Scotia Museum, pp. 1–32.

ALARIC FAULKNER

acculturation

Acculturation is a term from **sociocultural anthropology** that refers to the process of cultural change which results when groups of people from different cultures come into prolonged face-to-face contact. The degree and intensity of the change is based on numerous factors, including the length and circumstances of contact, the number of individuals involved, the technological sophistication of the peoples involved and even the amount of cultural difference between the peoples.

Anthropologists use several specific terms to refer to the changes that can occur in an acculturative process:

- *substitution*, where one or both cultures in contact replaces an element from their culture with one from the foreign culture, with only a minor change in their traditional cultural pattern;
- *syncretism*, or incorporation, where people blend elements from the new culture with those from their traditional way of life;
- *compartmentalisation*, where a people keep separate the disparate elements of the two cultures;
- *origination*, or innovation, where a people create new cultural features to adapt to their changing situation;
- *deculturation*, or **assimilation**, where a significant part, or even all, of a culture loses its identity as the result of contact;
- and *rejection*, or **resistance**, where a large number of people within a culture in a contact situation resist the changes and attempt to maintain their traditional way of life.

The anthropological literature on acculturation is vast, but many anthropologists now consider the various forms of acculturation to be somewhat idealised. Anthropologists know that most culture contact situations are extremely complex, and it is often difficult to assign neat categories to describe the changes that have occurred or are in the process of occurring. Some anthropologists would be reluctant under any circumstances to assign specific terms to a particular contact situation, because doing so may suggest that all culture contact situations should be similarly portrayed. For them, too much local variation exists for such characterisations. Some anthropologists would not even use the term 'acculturation' at all, because it implies that cultures act monolithically with little room for individual action or personal motivation.

The study of acculturation has played a large role in much historical archaeology, even though the use of the concept is problematic. Most importantly, historical archaeologists have used acculturation models in their investigations of the contact situations that occurred because of the worldwide spread of European colonists after about AD 1500. The historical archaeologists' interest in the process of acculturation has stemmed largely from the belief that artefacts can be perceived as surrogate measures of the degree or intensity of culture change. This understanding of acculturation was particularly prevalent in the historical archaeology practised before the 1990s.

In the early 1950s, George Quimby and Alexander Spoehr, two US anthropologists working with Native American cultural history (see **Native Americans**), proposed that a past culture's degree of acculturation could be understood in a systematic manner by examining the artefacts found at the sites the people once occupied. In their scheme, the varieties and nature of the artefacts found could provide important clues about the process of acculturation. In other words, the artefacts functioned as tangible evidence of the acculturative process. A European artefact with no native counterpart – like a glass bottle – could be used to suggest a relatively high degree of acculturation, because in using the bottle the natives would have had to incorporate a wholly new object into their traditional culture. An even higher degree of acculturation could be indicated by objects that demonstrated the use of European materials and techniques, but which were actually made by native craftpeople. Artefacts that mimicked traditional artefacts, but which were made with new materials – like an arrowhead made from a piece of a European glass bottle – indicated a relatively low degree of acculturation.

Quimby used these ideas to construct an acculturative history of the Native Americans who lived in the western Great Lakes of North America between the years 1610 and 1820. As a basis of his interpretation, Quimby employed a typology (see **typologies**) or classification of artefacts that consisted of seven types, extending from 'new types of artifacts received through trade or other contact channels' to 'old types of artifacts modified by the introduction of a new element of subject matter'. The first category included all those artefacts that were new to the Native Americans, such as guns and steel traps. The second category encompassed old cultural elements modified with new ideas, such as rock paintings depicting Europeans or European objects. All other excavated objects would fall somewhere in between. Quimby used this framework to identify three historical periods in western Great Lakes Native American history: the Early Historic Period (1619–70), the Middle Historic Period (1670–1760) and the Late Historic Period (1760–1820). Each period in the sequence was characterised by greater acculturation and, because more European artefacts appeared at the sites of the last period, the Native Americans who lived then were judged to have experienced more acculturation than those who had lived in the earlier two periods.

Acculturation is a theoretically sound idea, and Quimby's use of the concept has a certain validity. Peoples in contact do undergo cultural change, particularly in situations where one culture has technological superiority and the desire to change the other's culture, such as occurred in historic North America. Archaeologists readily accept that **material culture** has the ability to alter a people's way of life. However, historical archaeologists who have examined acculturation in detail have come to realise that the process of cultural contact is too complex to permit easy understanding. The process is so complicated that some archaeologists would argue that, except in the most basic of terms, acculturation is a process best understood in particular places at specific points in time. General elements of acculturation may be consistent throughout the world in an idealised sense, but the precise way in which the process occurs varied over time and across space. Archaeologists cannot assume that the process has occurred the same way everywhere.

Many factors may account for the diversity in the acculturative process, but one of the most important elements is unquestionably the way in which the cultures each adapt to the contact situation. One problem with the acculturation model is that it contains the implied assumption that all peoples react to culture change in the same way. In truth, many cultures have found creative ways to resist acculturation while accepting the artefacts of the newly introduced culture. The use of a strict model of acculturation that relies on the examination of artefacts must also assume that the use, function and meaning of an artefact remained constant over time. This assumption is easy to refute. A new copper kettle, for example, could be used by Native Americans to cook their meals shortly after they received it. After a few years, the owners of the kettle could have cut it into many pieces to make triangular dress ornaments. These objects – the whole kettle and the pieces of the kettle – would have had completely different meanings within the Native American culture, depending upon the moment upon which they were observed. The archaeologist does not see the native men and women actually using the objects, and does not know that the small copper ornaments were ever used as a kettle. When an archaeologist encounters the objects, he or she concludes that they served as decorations and had meanings possibly relating to beauty, fashion and perhaps even social standing.

The acculturation concept can also be viewed as problematic by descendant communities: those men and women who count themselves as the relatives of the people whose settlements are being excavated. For some people, the word 'acculturation' conjures up images of surrender or cultural capitulation rather than the resistance that may be required to maintain a treasured way of life.

The concept of acculturation is clearly a difficult one for historical archaeologists to apply. Nonetheless, the concept still has validity because cultures do change over time when they come into prolonged contact with other cultures. Most archaeologists working in the year 2000 would use the concept cautiously and downplay the older ways of examining it. By understanding the complexity of the culture contact, historical archaeologists have learned that they must combine acculturation with resistance – in what is often a cultural give-and-take – and most would agree that much of the tangible evidence for acculturation may be subtle.

Further reading

Quimby, G.I. (1966) *Indian Culture and European Trade Goods: The Archaeology of the Historic Period in the Western Great Lakes Region*, Madison: University of Wisconsin Press.

—— (1939) 'European trade articles as chronological indicators for the archaeology of the historic period in Michigan', *Papers of the Michigan Academy of Science, Arts, and Letters* 24: 25–31.

Quimby, G.I. and Spoehr, A. (1951) 'Acculturation and material culture – I', *Fieldiana: Anthropology* 36: 107–47.

CHARLES E. ORSER, JR

aerial photography

Aerial photography, also termed 'high-altitude imagery' or 'overhead photography', refers to images of archaeological sites or areas taken from above. Aerial photography constitutes an indispensable tool for archaeologists for at least two important reasons: it provides an additional method of record keeping during an excavation, and it serves as a type of **remote sensing**, which can help archaeologists locate cultural features that they may not be able to see from ground level.

The use of aerial photography in archaeology began in the early 1890s when a British archaeologist tied a camera to a balloon to get a better view of a site he was excavating in India. Since then, archaeological practice has kept pace with the development of new technologies, and today's archaeologists can use photographs taken from satellites and even from the space shuttle.

Not all aerial photographs, however, must be made with the assistance of aircraft because many archaeologists have employed cleverly designed bipods and tripods to take pictures from above the ground. Archaeologists have been able to produce useful images of their sites by simply raising their cameras several metres off the ground with the aid of these instruments. Some archaeologists also still make use of balloons to take pictures from the air, and archaeologists excavating in urban areas can often take 'aerial' pictures from a nearby tall building.

Photographs taken from the air help archaeologists to document their findings. Archaeologists often excavate large sites or buildings that cannot be properly appreciated from a ground-level perspective alone. Aerial photographs help archaeologists to assess the spatial extent of the site or building, and provide an important additional method of keeping a record of the progress of the excavation. Aerial photographs of entire sites can also be used by future archaeologists to indicate the extent of a past excavation.

The use of aerial images to discern cultural features is particularly noteworthy. An aerial perspective often makes it possible to perceive the outlines of relict buildings, the routes of disused roads and trails, the position of old fence and lot lines, and shallow depressions that may otherwise be overlooked. When used in this manner, aerial photography is both a remote-sensing tool that can help to guide an archaeologist to an undiscovered site, and a research tool that provides new information.

Aerial photography is especially important for archaeologists interested in large-scale settlement patterns or landscape features, instances where a view from above the earth's surface offers a unique perspective. The use of high-altitude images assists archaeologists working in rural Europe, for example, to document the locations of old field boundaries, abandoned villages and military fortifications. Aerial photography used in this manner helps an archaeologist to 'read the landscape' in ways that would otherwise be impossible.

CHARLES E. ORSER, JR

Africa, maritime archaeology

Maritime archaeology is a distinct and emerging field within the broader discipline. It is primarily concerned with the documentation, investigation and recovery of the material remains and physical traces of maritime communities, technologies and practices. Such remains can take a wide variety of forms, ranging from, most obviously, **shipwrecks** and their contents, to such diverse features as tidal mills, fish traps, harbour installations, naval defences, coastal settlements, inundated sites and submerged landscapes. Unlike 'nautical archaeologists', whose principal interests are restricted to the study of different types of sea-going vessels and the techniques and practices associated with their construction and use, 'maritime archaeologists' take a more holistic approach that encompasses the full range of maritime activities, and not just those related to seafaring. By the same token, 'maritime archaeology' is not simply an alternative term for 'underwater archaeology', since, given its holistic stance, it is as equally concerned with the archaeological remains found on the foreshore and intertidal zones as with those that occur on the sea-bed.

Although the specific emphases of different maritime archaeology projects vary, the use of the sea for subsistence, trade, industry, defence, exploration and/or communication tends to be the principal concern. Anthropological studies of maritime societies have also emphasised the symbolic and/or religious importance that the sea and its associated resources can have. All of these different facets of maritime culture can receive material expression, and are thus amenable to archaeological investigation. When linked with other types of historical sources, such as documentary records, maps, oral traditions and pictorial evidence, the potential for studying changes and continuities within maritime societies over extended periods becomes considerable.

In sub-Saharan Africa, the practice of under-water, let alone *maritime*, archaeology is very much in its infancy. This is partly due to factors of cost and inadequate training, but it is also due to a general lack of appreciation of the research potential of maritime environments and the importance the sea had to many African societies. Such attitudes are common among land-based archaeologists throughout the globe, and are by no means unique to Africa. However, in the absence of a well-trained cadre of specialists, adequate funding and access to suitable equipment, the challenge of integrating a maritime perspective to better-established land-based approaches is especially great. This is unfortunate, given the rich potential offered by the continent's extensive coastline, the regular exploitation of maritime resources by its indigenous populations and the complex patterns of their interaction with other parts of the world.

Despite the long history of engagement with Europe and the Americas, an extensive documentary record and the existence of several protected landings along the coast, maritime archaeology is least well developed in West and West-Central Africa. Thus, for instance, there have been no systematic, scientific surveys of either the inshore waters off the main landfalls or any of the clusters of offshore archipelagos, such as the Cape Verde Islands, for shipwrecks. There are also numerous remains of British, Dutch, French, Portuguese and Danish forts along the Atlantic seaboard, and of trading posts and towns of mixed African and European composition. Extensive archaeological investigations by Christopher DeCorse at the Gold Coast town of **Elmina** in southern Ghana, and Kenneth Kelly at Siva on the former 'Slave Coast', in the Republic of Benin, have been particularly informative, especially with regard to the changing dynamics of culture contact, the archaeological record of European expansion and the impact of the Atlantic slave trade. Unfortunately, despite their proximity to the sea, archaeological research at these sites has provided only minimal insight into the specifically maritime aspects of these communities.

Rather more maritime archaeology has been conducted further south on the Namibian and South African coasts. Whipped by fierce storms coming in off the South Atlantic and prone to strong currents, the dangers to shipping along the

Namibian coast are well known. The remains of many wrecks can be seen at several points on the shore, most famously along the stretch known as the 'Skeleton Coast'. Despite featuring in many popular books, these and other traces of maritime activity have yet to be seriously studied, with the important exception of Jill Kinahan's survey of nineteenth-century fisheries around Sandwich Harbour. The archaeological remains here include those of an iron barque, deliberately beached so as to provide a storeroom, as well as traces of former fishing sheds and houses, and at least one sizeable midden. Comprising mostly the remains of different species of fish and shellfish, this probably represents the debris generated by commercial processing of fish catches, prior to curing and crating for onward shipping to Mauritius via Cape Town. Ships' registers, charts lodged with the British Hydrographic Department, the report from a joint Commission of Enquiry by the South West Africa and Cape Colony governments, and an aquarelle by the renowned artist Thomas Baines, among other historical sources, provide vivid insights into the life of this community and identify the remains as belonging to two different commercial enterprises.

Further south, near Saldanha Bay, South Africa, lie the remains of an early **Dutch East India Company** (VOC) outpost, founded in 1669. Now known as **Oudepost I**, extensive excavation here has provided important insights into the often complex relationships between the indigenous Khoisan populations of the Western Cape, Dutch settlers and Europe's metropolitan centres. The chance discovery, on the adjacent beach, of the only significant subsistence remains left by the fort's occupants underlines the importance of integrating survey work in the intertidal zone with land-based investigations when dealing with sites in a maritime setting.

The most import Dutch settlement was, of course, the revictualling station established for the VOC by Jan van Riebeeck in 1652 beside Table Bay, which later developed into the colonial city of **Cape Town**. Somewhat surprisingly, despite the growth in importance of the settlement, no formal harbour facility was built here until the mid-nineteenth century. The problem was brought to a head in July 1831, when no less than ten separate

vessels ran into difficulties during fierce winter storms. Of these, five were stranded on the beach and one was wrecked. The following year, the building of a stone jetty was authorised, but it was not until 1839 that work actually began on what became Cape Town's North Wharf. Rescue excavations in this area during the 1990s, in advance of redevelopment, uncovered the remains of parts of this structure, providing additional information about its construction to that gleaned from archival sources.

Over the centuries, many other ships were wrecked in Table Bay. Of these, the wreck of the VOC ship *Oosterland*, which sank on 24 May 1697, has been the most systematically investigated. Located in the eastern part of the bay, some 280 m offshore, and in 5–7 m of water, debris from the wreck covers an area of at least 14,000 m^2. Within this general scatter, most finds are concentrated in a 45 m^2 area, which has been the subject of detailed survey and test excavations. Material recovered from the site included numerous types of Chinese and Japanese **porcelain** bowls, plates, vases and figurines. Available documentary sources indicate that, between 1694–9, VOC merchants only rarely acquired porcelain for the company, suggesting that the Oosterland assemblage may have been an illicit cargo purchased for private resale.

The Dutch were not the first Europeans to reach Southern Africa, however. The Portuguese had preceded them by over 150 years (unless one accepts the claims made by Herodotus in Book 4 of his *Histories*, concerning the circumnavigation of Africa by the Phoenicians). Portuguese ships, under the command of Bartolomeu Dias, first rounded the Cape in 1487. A decade later, a second expedition, led by the navigator and explorer Vasco de Gama, pushed further up the East African coast, reaching Mombasa in April 1498. The arrival of Vasco da Gama's fleet marked the beginning of a new era of European exploration, commercial exploitation and colonial expansion, which had profound consequences for Africa and numerous other lands, including the Indian subcontinent and the Moluccas (Spice Islands). Inevitably, shipwrecks occurred, and there are many documentary sources concerning these (and those of other European vessels), sometimes written by survivors. As well as indicating the approximate location of wrecks around the shores of South Africa, Mozambique and Madagascar, these accounts also contain valuable information about the local inhabitants of these areas in the sixteenth and seventeenth centuries.

Archaeological traces of these catastrophes are less numerous. The remains of a camp left by the survivors from the wreck of the *Sao Goncalo*, which sank in 1630 in Plettenberg Bay, South Africa, have been excavated, and at least two Portuguese wrecks located, one in the Seychelles, and one in Mombasa harbour, Kenya. The latter vessel, the *Santo António de Tanná*, was originally a forty-two-gun frigate built in Bassein, north of Bombay, in 1681. At the time of its sinking off Fort Jesus, towards the end of 1697, the *S. António*, now carrying fifty guns, headed a small fleet sent by the Viceroy of Goa to relieve the town, which had been under siege by Omani-led forces since the previous year. The underwater excavations, directed by Robin Piercy, were the first to be conducted in East Africa. All of the surviving hull was exposed and recorded *in situ*, before being reburied. Over 6,000 artefacts and fittings were recovered, including part of a rare type of blunderbuss, several Far Eastern storage jars made up to 400 years before the vessel sank, and quantities of African ebony. As with the *Oosterland* **ceramics**, the latter may have been part of a private cargo.

A well-preserved series of wall paintings depicting Portuguese ships, groups of men, fish, animals and other features also survives on one of the bastion walls within Fort Jesus (built 1593–4). These have yet to be studied in detail, although at least one can be linked to a named ship, the *S. Agostinho da . . .*. Several depictions of earlier, non-European vessels, such as dhows and *mtepe* (a type of sewn boat), are known from various Swahili settlements along the Tanzanian and Kenyan coasts. These range widely in date, from the charcoal drawings of eighteenth-century *dau la mtepe* from the Captain's House at Fort Jesus, to earlier engravings on the plastered walls of elite houses and mosques of the great fifteenth-/sixteenth-century Swahili coastal trading centres, such as those of Kilwa, Ras Mkumbuu (Pemba Island, Tanzania), Gedi and Takwa (both Kenya). The engravings provide some of the best evidence,

until such time as actual shipwrecks are recovered, of the range of vessels plying the trade routes of the western Indian Ocean before the arrival of the Portuguese. They also complement existing documentary sources concerning the vessels used in this trade, especially the reference in the mid-first-century AD text, *The Periplus of the Erythraean Sea*, to the use of sewn boats on the East African coast.

A further value of the *Periplus* is that it includes a description of a sea voyage along the coast from a trading emporium known as Opone just south of the Somali Peninsula, to the ancient town of Rhapta. The latter is described as the principal, and most southerly, harbour of the Azanian (i.e. East African) coast. Despite its alleged importance, and the growing number of finds of Roman imports from mainland coastal sites and the offshore islands, the site of Rhapta has yet to be located. The settlement of Opone, on the other hand, was possibly situated on Ras Hafun (Somalia), where traces of two coastal settlements containing Roman, Egyptian, Mesopotamian and other imported ceramics, spanning the last century BC to the fifth century BC, have been excavated. Detailed study of these imports has provided an indication of the shifting patterns of trade over these centuries between Africa's Red Sea ports, such as Berenike (Egypt) and Adulis (Eritrea), and those of the Persian Gulf, Cambay and southern India. The discovery of a shipwreck containing Roman/Byzantine amphorae off Assarca Island, Eritrea, dated to between the fourth and seventh centuries AD adds to this picture. Also adding to this picture, once they have been fully studied, will be the mass of imported finds and *c.* 400 texts in nine different languages recovered from Berenike.

See also: Aksum; East Africa; Portuguese colonialism

Further reading

Gilbert, E. (1998) 'The Mtepe: Regional trade and late survival of sewn ships in East African waters', *International Journal of Nautical Archaeology* 27: 43–50.

Kinahan, J. (1991) 'The historical archaeology of nineteenth century fisheries at Sandwich Harbour on the Namib Coast', *Cimbebasia* 13: 1–27.

Lynch, M. (ed.) (1991) 'The Mombasa wreck excavation', *Institute of Nautical Archaeology Newsletter* 18(2): 2–29.

Pedersen, R.K. (2000) 'Under the Erythraean Sea: An ancient shipwreck in Eritrea', *Institute of Nautical Archaeology Quarterly* 27(2/3): 3–13.

Smith, A.B. (1986) 'Excavations at Plettenberg Bay, South Africa of the camp of the survivors of the wreck of the *Sao Goncalo*, 1630', *International Journal of Nautical Archaeology* 15: 53–63.

Smith, M.C. and Wright, H.T. (1988) 'The ceramics from Ras Hafun in Somalia: Notes on a classical maritime site', *Azania* 23: 115–41.

Werz, B.E.J.S. (1999) *Diving up the Human Past*, Oxford: British Archaeological Reports, S749.

PAUL J. LANE

African American archaeology

The study of the African **diaspora** is a well-established research priority in historical archaeology. Originally conceived to reveal the unrecorded aspects of black history, Theresa Singleton describes the discipline as the study of the formation and transformation of the New World by Africans. African American archaeology is an important part of diasporic research. Archaeologists who are interested in African American archaeology have focused their research on a variety of settings that reflect the diversity of the African American experiences on colonial, antebellum and postbellum plantations, farms, maroon communities, urban house lots of enslaved and free, and black churches, just to name a few.

Plantation studies

The greatest majority of African American archaeology has centred on slave and tenant house sites on plantations, since the quarter community is viewed as the place where African American culture was born. Archaeological data are crucial elements for the interpretation of the formation of African American culture and the everyday lives of slaves and black sharecroppers, because of the paucity of accounts written by African Americans on plantations. The multidisciplinary anthropological approaches used by archaeologists in this endeavour incorporate traditional archaeological data with information from **historical documents**, **ethnography**, ethnohistory and architectural studies. Motivated by black activism, the 1960s and 1970s investigations of African American archaeology set out to tell the story of Americans forgotten or underrepresented in the written record. From modest beginnings searching for 'survivals' of African traditions in African American material culture recovered from slave/tenant quarter sites, archaeological research at plantation sites has developed over several decades and branched out to cover several major themes: power and resistance, ethnic identity and our relationship with the past.

The complex, dynamic, reciprocal, but unbalanced, relationship between plantation owner and plantation labourer is a key element in plantation studies. For example, archaeological studies of slave housing that blend archaeological, architectural and documentary data suggest that dwellings were small and humble to maintain the subordinate position of the inhabitants, but snug enough to support stable slave family life (which was in the planter's best economic interest). Charles Orser's spatial analyses of slave/tenant houses at **Millwood Plantation** highlights how the plantation hierarchy was maintained by the owner through the use of house types and their placement on the landscape, and how the slaves/tenants may have challenged or disregarded hierarchy through the manipulation of their material world. Larry McKee's analysis of faunal remains (**zooarchaeology**) recovered from various slave house sites indicates that slaves were not mere recipients of rations, but were active participants in their food procurement (see **food and foodways**) and made a series of rational choices about the source and types of food consumed in the quarter community. For example, enslaved African Americans had to choose how much time to invest in hunting or gardening by considering the returns and risks involved in food production and collection. Amy Young's study of hunting at Saragossa, the antebellum plantation and the modern-descendant African American rural community, indicates that hunting was much more than a food procurement behaviour. As a group activity, it functioned to bind the community together and provide means for men to contribute important resources (meat) to the community. Choices in game and hunting styles were and continue to be important.

Another key component is the study of ethnic identity, looking especially for the continuities of practices (especially building and religious practices) identified in slave and tenant quarter communities with antecedent communities, particularly those in West (see **West Africa**) and Central Africa. Leland Ferguson (1992) demonstrates continuity in South Carolina slave communities with Bakongo (Central African) traditions through the continued use of the Bakongo cosmogram found on the base of slave-made colonoware pots (see **colonoware pottery**). He also argues that the small colonoware pots reflect the persistence of African foodways in slave communities. Archaeologists have suggested that early houses in the South Carolina low country (for example at Yaughan and Curriboo plantations) were built in the West African wattle-and-daub style. Other evidence of ethnic identity in the form of charms such as pierced coins for healing and conjuring has been recovered from numerous plantation sites in the New World. The use of magical charms does not merely signify continuity with African religious traditions, but that African Americans found new ways to express their religious values. The religious practices reflected in the artefacts recovered from various archaeological sites were not static but were transformed through time. Archaeologists continue to consider the cultural processes of syncretism and **creolisation** to understand these transformations.

Beyond the plantation

A number of very interesting studies of African American life outside of the plantation context present important and significant advances to our understanding of the breadth of the African American experience. Such studies have primarily focused on free black rural settlements and free black and enslaved urban communities. In many ways, the themes of this research are similar to those within plantation contexts.

For example, several studies conducted as part of the Archaeology in **Annapolis**, Maryland, pro-

gramme are concerned with the diversity among African Americans, recognising that African American culture is not monolithic. These studies explore how **capitalism** and **consumer choice** in the acquisition and use of ceramic (see **ceramics**) types was a factor in how African Americans defined economic and social distinctions within the black community. African Americans of the late nineteenth century also exercised their consumer choices and used objects like dishes and knick-knacks to distance themselves from the racial stereotypes that white Americans had constructed. These important studies show how much archaeologists can learn about the relationship between racial perceptions and material objects.

J.W. Joseph, in various **cultural-resource management** studies conducted in the southeast, has examined antebellum African American communities. He argues that for those Africans able to escape the bonds of the plantation, both enslaved and free, southern cities provided a set of experiences and opportunities that were distinct from those available in rural locations. He suggests that African Americans were able to make use of liminal and marginal areas in towns and cities (plots of land where ownership was contested and plots that were flood-prone, for instance) to establish communities, and thus access the opportunities afforded by city life. Liminal and marginal areas, by their very nature, were more accessible to African Americans during the antebellum period, who were usually denied land ownership.

Excavations at the Wayman African Methodist Episcopal (A.M.E.) church in Bloomington, Illinois, show how this site had dual functions in the black community in the late nineteenth and early twentieth century. In addition to serving as a religious centre, the church was also a medical facility, an important health care centre at a time when blacks were denied access to white hospitals and clinics. The abundance of medicine bottles and other medicinal objects highlights the fact that the black community did not passively accept the inferior health care that was characteristic of this era in American history.

The archaeology of maroon communities is in early developmental stages. Kathleen Deagan and others investigated **Fort Mose** in Spanish Florida, which was established in 1738 by black settlers who

Figure 1 African American house and yard near Charleston, South Carolina, 1938
Source: Library of Congress

fled the enslavement of British colonies. The research at Fort Mose illustrates the dynamic character of power and resistance. The Spanish granted the settlers of Fort Mose freedom in return for their help in defending Spaniards from the British. The actions of the occupants of Fort Mose were both resistance to slavery in British colonies, and an accommodation to Spanish hegemony. Maroon communities appear to have been rare in the USA. However, work on maroon communities outside our boundaries is examining how these dynamic and influential groups were connected with the outside world. Preliminary work at **Palmares**, a series of seventeenth-century maroon villages in north-eastern Brazil, hints at the economic and social interactions of African, Native South American, Dutch and Portuguese societies, highlighting the fact that African and African American communities were not isolated but inextricably linked to the global economy.

African American archaeology does not occur in a vacuum and archaeologists are becoming increasingly aware of how their research affects the public, especially descendant communities. Reactions of African American communities to archaeological investigations at the **African Burial Ground** in New York City highlighted the need for archaeologists to work closely with descendant communities. The general public's opinions about uncovering 420 burials of enslaved colonial-era Africans, the largest and earliest collection of African and African American remains, ranged from basic distrust of white archaeologists' abilities to interpret the remains, to the feeling that white bureaucrats with little insight into African American history and spiritual sensitivities were making crucial decisions about the remains of ancestors. For example, a reference to the cemetery as a 'potters' field' divorced the remains from their African origins and diminished the importance of the burials, which outraged the African American community. There was also an expressed belief that the bones were being mishandled and destroyed. While the overall reaction was negative, the incident highlighted the importance of African American archaeology in obtaining information about the past where documents were scarce. A consensus arose among archaeologists that it is crucial to work with descendant communities, keeping non-professionals informed of finds and research, consulting them concerning interpretations and especially involving the descendant communities in initial stages of research.

African American archaeology is an exciting endeavour in historical archaeology. The relatively few sites that have been intensively investigated, however, hindered broad interpretations. African American archaeology has been labelled as data rich but theory poor. However, the strong emphasis on resistance and power has greatly expanded our understanding of the African American experience in many times and places, and is a great step forward in theory building. Because African diasporic communities were connected with the outside world, archaeologists need to focus attention on understanding the extent and intensity of this interaction. Furthermore, we need to spend more time investigating the internal dynamics of black American communities, recognising the diversity within these communities whether they are plantation slave quarters, maroon villages or urban house lots and neighbourhoods. Truly, to gain a coherent understanding of African American life, it is necessary to think globally and dig locally.

See also: plantation archaeology

Further reading

Cabak, M.A., Groover, M. and Wagers, S. (1995) 'Health care and the Wayman A.M.E. Church', *Historical Archaeology* 29(2): 55–76.

Ferguson, L. (1992) *Uncommon Ground: Archaeology and Early African America, 1650–1800*, Washington: Smithsonian Institution Press.

McKee, L. (1992) 'The ideals and realities behind the design and use of 19th century Virginia slave cabins', in A.E. Yentsch and M.C. Beaudry (eds) *The Art and Mystery of Historical Archaeology: Essays in Honor of James Deetz*, Boca Raton: CRC Press, pp. 195–214.

Mullins, P.R. (1999) *Race and Affluence: An Archaeology of African America and Consumer Culture*, New York: Plenum Press.

Orser, C.E., Jr (1988) *The Material Basis of the Postbellum Tenant Plantation: Historical Archaeology in the South Carolina Piedmont*, Athens: University of Georgia Press.

Singleton, T.A. (1999) 'An introduction to African-American archaeology', in T.A. Singleton (ed.) *'I, too, am America': Archaeological Studies of African-American Life*, Charlottesville: University Press of Virginia, pp. 1–17.

Singleton, T.A. and Bograd, M.D. (eds) (1995) *The Archaeology of the African Diaspora in the Americas*, Tucson: Society for Historical Archaeology.

AMY L. YOUNG

African Burial Ground

The African Burial Ground – located in lower Manhattan, New York City – is an **African American archaeology** project that combines a state-of-the-art scientific programme with an active **public outreach and education** programme to analyse the earliest and largest African-descent cemetery excavated in North America.

Although **slavery** is popularly thought of as a southern US institution, New York City had the largest enslaved urban population outside of Charleston, South Carolina. Thousands of African-descent people were buried at the northern edge of settlement during the colonial period. Excavations initiated in 1991 prior to construction of a US Government office tower revealed that subsequent landfilling had protected many of the burials from nineteenth- and twentieth-century impacts. Over 400 individuals were exhumed before outrage from the African American community forced a halt to the excavations and a project redesign that would leave the remaining burials in place.

The original **human osteology** research was predicated on a bio-genetic conception of **race** that many African Americans believed was antithetical to both their cultural concerns and the tenets of appropriate scientific analysis. Because of continuing community pressure, the primary responsibility for research was transferred to the Cobb Laboratory at Howard University, under the direction of Michael L. Blakey. The original research design has been supplanted by a more inclusive **biological anthropology** approach that includes DNA analysis to determine genetic affinities between the African Burial Ground population and people now living in Africa and the diaspora. Four primary research questions are addressed by the ongoing analysis:

1 What are the cultural and geographical roots of the individuals interred in the African Burial Ground?
2 What was the physical quality of life for Africans enslaved in New York City during the colonial period and how was it different from the quality of life in their African homeland?
3 What biological characteristics and cultural traditions remained unchanged and which were transformed during the creation of African American society and culture?
4 What were the modes of resistance and how were they creatively reconfigured and used to resist oppression and to forge a new African American culture?

At the end of 1999, the archaeological, historical and biological anthropology analyses were still ongoing and plans were being developed for a permanent memorial at the site. The human remains and associated artefacts are currently scheduled for reinterment in the year 2001.

Further reading

Blakey, M.L. (1998) 'The New York African Burial Ground Project: An examination of enslaved lives, a construction of ancestral ties', *Transforming Anthropology* 7(1): 53–8.
Epperson, T.W. (1999) 'The contested commons: Archaeologies of race, repression, and resistance in New York City', in M.P. Leone and P.B. Potter (eds) *Historical Archaeologies of Capitalism*, New York: Plenum, pp. 81–110.
Harrington, S.P.M. (1993) 'Bones and bureaucrats: New York's great cemetery imbroglio', *Archaeology* 16(2): 28–38.
LaRoche, C.J. and Blakey, M.L. (1997) 'Seizing intellectual power: The dialogue at the New York African Burial Ground', *Historical Archaeology* 31(3): 84–106.
Perry, W.R. (1999) 'Archaeology as community service: The African Burial Ground Project in New York City', *North American Dialogue* 2(1): 1–5.

TERRENCE W. EPPERSON

Aksum, Ethiopia

Situated in the Tigray region of northern Ethiopia, the ancient town of Aksum rose to prominence in the first century AD as a regional trading centre, capital of the Aksumite kingdom, and subsequently as the ecclesiastical centre of the Ethiopian Orthodox Church. The precise origins of the town and kingdom are somewhat obscure, partly because the archaeology of the pre-Aksumite period is poorly known. On present evidence, a number of localised chiefdoms had emerged in the Tigray highlands around 1000 BC. By about 700/600 BC, at least one kingdom, known from epigraphic sources as D'MT (or Da'amat), was centred around Yeha in western Tigray, where the remains of a large temple still stand. The limited physical remains associated with this kingdom indicate close links with the contemporary Saba kingdom of southern Arabia. By about 300 BC, Da'amat's influence was waning, and it was probably during this phase that the social and economic foundations of the Aksumite kingdom were established.

The period from *c*. AD 100–400 witnessed the initial expansion of the kingdom across the eastern plateau in what is now central Eritrea. During this phase, trading networks were consolidated. With the decline of the Roman Empire from the third century, Aksum took control of the Red Sea trade, exploiting its intermediary position between the Indian Ocean and Mediterranean/Nile Valley circuits. Exports included various luxury goods made of ivory and tortoise shell, and raw materials such as emeralds and obsidian. These were shipped via Adulis (Eritrea) on the coast, in exchange for ceramics, wine, glass and precious metals among other goods. This era of rapid economic growth also saw the issue of a tri-metallic (gold, silver and copper) coinage. Aksum reached its peak between

AD 400–700, and began to decline thereafter, partly as a consequence of shifts in the pattern of Indian Ocean trade and the related expansion of Islam.

Aksum is best known for its series of carved stone stelae used as grave markers during the pre-Christian period. The most impressive, and probably latest, examples are up to 33 m tall and depict the façades of multi-storeyed buildings. The stelae were laid out in four main areas that flank the modern town. Whereas the central stelae area served as an elite burial ground, research has shown that the Gudit Stelae Field, on the western side of the town, was for lower-status individuals. Here, graves consisted of a simple pit marked with a roughly hewn stela. Other monumental architecture includes massive, multi-roomed palaces, some of which, such as the Enda Mika'el, may have been three storeys high.

Monophysite Christianity was introduced in the mid-fourth century, probably as a result of contact with Syrian Christians, and quickly adopted as the state religion. Later liturgy and certain architectural traditions also indicate links with the Alexandrine, Coptic sphere and with Judaism. The church of Maryam Tsion, in the eastern part of the town, became the focal point of the metropolis after the fifth century, and shrines and chapels were established throughout the kingdom. After the collapse of the state, Aksum continued as a religious centre, and the two Cathedrals of St Mary of Zion, rebuilt in the seventeenth century, are believed to house the Ark of the Covenant.

See also: Africa; gravestones; maritime archaeology

Further reading

Connah, G. (1987) *African Civilizations*, Cambridge: Cambridge University Press.

Munro-Hay, S. (1991) *Aksum, an African Civilisation of Late Antiquity*, Edinburgh: Edinburgh University Press.

Phillips, J. (1997) 'Punt and Aksum: Egypt and the Horn of Africa', *Journal of African History* 38: 423–57.

Phillipson, D.W. (2001) *Archaeology at Aksum, Ethiopia, 1993–7*, London: British Institute in Eastern Africa, Memoir 17.

PAUL J. LANE

almshouses

Relatively few almshouses, or poorhouses, were excavated by archaeologists prior to the 1980s. In analysing almshouses, archaeologists have evaluated the **architecture**, the **material culture**, the foodways and even the landscape design in order to understand the institutionalised care of the poor. The almshouse has existed since medieval times. The almshouse as a charitable institution (see **institutions**) has undergone a great variety of transformations over the centuries, from a home for the poor in pre-industrial times, to a nineteenth-century workhouse, to a contemporary homeless shelter.

Almshouses first developed as rooms in medieval monasteries where the homeless could spend the night after receiving alms (food, wood, clothing or cash) 'at the gate' of the monastery. A sixteenth-century almshouse at Glastonbury Abbey in Somerset, **England**, has been excavated.

Church giving of alms continued through the eighteenth century in Roman Catholic countries. In Protestant countries church parishes that were synonymous with townships taxed all citizens to provide alms to the poor in their homes, called 'outdoor relief'. In addition, Protestant churches sometimes founded almshouses, such as the Dutch Reformed Church almshouse in Albany, New York, founded in *c*. 1652. British archaeologists have excavated the seventeenth-century St Nicholas Almshouse in Bristol, and the remains of the Monoux Almshouse in London, founded in 1527. Combined archaeological and historical research have revealed that almshouses were often complexes of buildings around a rectilinear enclosed yard.

Since the sixteenth century, the number of vagrants increased due to wars, the agricultural revolution and the Industrial Revolution. As the population of poor vagrants in cities increased, their needs could no longer be met solely by church-organised charities. Secular public institutions for the poor developed first in Europe and later in the USA. Institutions for the poor were first divided into almshouses for the 'deserving' poor, who were physically or mentally unable to work, versus houses of correction, bridewells, workhouses or town farms for the 'undeserving' or able-bodied vagrant poor. In the mid-sixteenth century, the Protestant abolition of monasteries led to the first European public institutions for the poor, called 'houses of correction' in the Netherlands and 'bridewells' in England. In the eighteenth century, English law required each county to establish a workhouse. British archaeologists have excavated seventeenth-century workhouses in Gloucester, in Barnstaple, Devon, and in Wymondam, Norfolk.

In the USA, **New York City** was unusual in founding both a large publicly supported almshouse in 1735 and a separate bridewell nearby in 1775. However, most towns founded only one institution for the poor in the nineteenth century, calling it a poorhouse or almshouse when considering the 'deserving' poor it housed, and calling it a workhouse or town farm to specify its function in putting the 'undeserving' poor to work.

The able-bodied poor were considered lazy, dissolute criminals because they were able to work and supposedly chose not to because of their 'vicious habits'. Institutions for the 'undeserving' poor were designed to reform them into hard-working citizens by teaching them 'habits of industry' through regular menial labour, which could even be meaningless and punitive, such as breaking rocks or walking on an endless tread-wheel. Even in almshouses for the deserving poor, inmates were usually required to work as much as they were able in order to raise money for the support of the almshouse. In the seventeenth-century Albany, New York, almshouse, evidence of wampum manufacturing was found by archaeologists. In New York City the inmates in the eighteenth-century almshouse made clothes for sale, and archaeologists found remains of their homemade bone buttons, button blanks and straight pins. In the nineteenth-century Falmouth, Massachusetts, workhouse, inmates made a variety of predominantly agricultural products for sale, as well as picking oakum, the onerous picking apart of salt- and tar-encrusted marine ropes to make hemp-caulking material. Picking oakum was the

Figure 2 New York City almshouse, 1722–44, by cartographer David Grim, 1813

most lucrative work traditionally required of inmates in European houses of correction. However, in some institutions, documents reveal the ideal requirement of work was not actually put into practice.

Archaeology has provided insights about the lifeways of inmates, including the extent to which ideal reform practices were followed. Excavations at US almshouses in New York City, Albany, New York, Falmouth, Massachusetts, and Smithfield, Rhode Island, have recovered artefacts indicating a frugal but not harsh existence, maintained in part through donated food, clothing and supplies including dishes. The variety of decorated ceramic tablewares shows that eighteenth- and nineteenth-century US almshouses did not necessarily follow the ideal reform practice of providing undecorated tableware. The poverty of the inmates, as they were called, is evident from the lack of grave goods found in excavations of pauper cemeteries associated with almshouses in Uxbridge and Marlboro, Massachusetts. Yet, archaeological evidence at the

Falmouth almshouse indicates that inmates were not required to wear uniforms and surrender their personal possessions as they were required to do at the Destitute Asylum in Adelaide, **Australia**, which followed ideal reform practices.

In the seventeenth, eighteenth and nineteenth centuries a diversity of private institutions developed for the 'deserving' or 'worthy' poor, including poor houses for those no longer able to work. Some of these institutions were founded by a variety of different occupation groups, and others by wealthy benefactors. Some of these institutions were established by a fund set up in a will, such as Robert Roger's Almshouse (1604) in Poole, Dorset, England, for poor couples with a preference given to those 'decayed by the sea'. Lady Katherine Leveson's Almshouse (1674) in the hamlet of Temple Balsall, Warwickshire, England, was for poor, aged women. Also, Robert Randall's Sailors' Snug Harbour (1830) on Staten Island, New York, was for aged and injured seamen. Archaeologists have excavated material from these three charitable institutions.

Documents show that most almshouses followed the ideal English workhouse practice by, to some extent, segregating inmates by gender, age and condition, such as insanity or illness. In addition, by the nineteenth century, separate institutions for the poor were founded for different age groups, races and sexes. Separate old-age homes and homes for unemployed women of colour, men of colour, white women and white men were established. Separate orphanages were founded for boys and girls. Archaeologists have evaluated the care of children, playtime and children's **toys** in the Schuyler Mansion Orphanage in Albany, New York.

Were the poor treated differently in private institutions versus public institutions? Archaeologists have found that some private institutions, such as the Sailors' Snug Harbour in Staten Island, New York, and Sir Martin Noel's almshouse in Staffordshire, England, provided quality housing and accommodations, whereas some of the public facilities such as the destitute asylum excavated in Adelaide, Australia, were crowded and frugal. Some archaeologists have also addressed **gender** and **power** roles within the almshouses, including the destitute asylum of Adelaide, Australia, and the poorhouses of Smithfield, Rhode Island, and

Marlboro and Falmouth, Massachusetts, in the USA.

Archaeologists are just beginning to uncover the wealth of information about the so-called underclass. Almshouses provide unusual opportunities to research the lifeways of the poor and class relations in small towns as well as large cities. Hopefully, as more almshouses are excavated and more cross-site comparisons are made, we may be able to analyse if there are differences in the treatment of men and women, young and old, as well as the insane and ill. Archaeologists could address to what extent almshouses followed ideal English workhouse practices. Also, were almshouses used as a means of forced **assimilation** for non-Western peoples? These questions remain to be answered by twenty-first-century archaeologists.

Articles on almshouse excavations can be found in the following journals: *Historical Archaeology, International Journal of Historical Archaeology, Northeast Historical Archaeology* and *Post-medieval Archaeology.*

Further reading

Baugher, S. and Spencer-Wood, S.M. (eds) (2001) 'The archaeology of institutions of reform II: colonial-era almshouses', *International Journal of Historical Archaeology* 5: 115–202.

Feister, I. (1991) 'The orphanage at Schuyler Mansion', *Northeast Historical Archaeology* 20: 27–36.

Garman, J.C. and Russo, P.A. (1999) 'A disregard of every sentiment of humanity': The town farm and class realignment in nineteenth-century rural New England', *Historical Archaeology* 33(1): 118–35.

Spencer-Wood, Suzanne M. (1999) sections titled 'Site interpretations' and 'Comparative sites', in A.E. Strauss, and S.M. Spencer-Wood (1999) *Phase II Archaeological Site Examination at the Artists' Guild/Old Poor House Building in Falmouth, Massachusetts*, Boston: Massachusetts Historical Commission.

Spencer-Wood, S.M. and Baugher, S. (eds) (2001) 'The archaeology of institutions of reform I: asylums', *International Journal of Historical Archaeology*, 5: 1–114.

SHERENE BAUGHER AND
SUZANNE M. SPENCER-WOOD

Amsterdam, Netherlands

The introduction of archaeology in Amsterdam coincided with the development of **medieval archaeology** and **post-medieval archaeology** in Holland. One of the aims of the Amsterdam urban archaeological programme (see **urban archaeology**) has been thematic studies of pre-modern material culture in international perspective.

In 1972, Amsterdam became the second Dutch city (after Rotterdam) with a department for archaeology. In 1954, the Institute for Pre- and Proto-historical Archaeology of the University of Amsterdam had already begun systematic excavations in the historical town centre. In the past forty-five years, more than seventy sites have been investigated. The excavation policy was defined by a scientific programme of cultural heritage management as well as **rescue archaeology** triggered by construction development. The 'real-life' data presented by the material culture from this urban archaeological context produced, together with historical sources, new views on the town's development at the mouth of the river Amstel.

The first written record dates from 1275 and the available archaeological data points to 1200 as the beginning of the early pre-urban settlement. The archaeological research covers the complete medieval and post-medieval period of urban development, which was characterised by explosive growth. A small-scale settlement of 1,000 inhabitants in 1300 was transformed into a global trading metropolis of 200,000 inhabitants by 1700. Crucial was the shift as a shipping centre from a regional European level (Atlantic, Baltic) to an intercontinental level (Asia, Americas), based on the activities of the **Dutch East India Company** (VOC) and West India Company (WIC).

The excavations provided rich data on a variety of urban structures, varying from houses to churches, chapels, monasteries, hospitals, ramparts, the city gate, weigh-houses, warehouses, shipyards and even a castle. Initially, the archaeological research focused on the topography of the pre-urban location and the origin of the medieval town. Gradually, attention shifted towards an analysis of the role of material culture in trade and industry during this **urbanisation** process, touching upon features such as market economy, specialisation, social differentiation, **consumption** and **gender**. The increasing complexity of the town's material culture was studied by combining typological, socioeconomic and cultural aspects, producing for example a functional classification of red and grey ceramics, or monographs on import ceramics such as Italian majolica and faience, Portuguese faience or Japanese porcelain. Typo-chronological classifications of specific material categories, which could be developed on the basis of a large series of dated cesspits, proved useful for dating and identifying archaeological finds from other Dutch towns. Because of Amsterdam's global role in shipping, its material culture is an archaeological reference of intercontinental nature, relevant for sites in former contact areas, such as South-east Asia, Japan, the USA and the Caribbean.

Further reading

Baart, J.M. (1997) 'Amsterdam', in M. Gläser (ed.) *Lübecker Kolloquium zur Stadtarchäologie im Hanseraum I: Stand, Aufgaben und Perspektiven*, Lübeck: Amt für Archäologische Denkmalpflege der Hansestadt Lübeck, pp. 87–94.

——(1996) 'History and archaeology of Amsterdam', in *Unearthed Cities: Edo, Nagasaki, Amsterdam, London, New York*, Tokyo: Edo-Tokyo Museum, pp. 206–12.

Baart, J., Krook, W., Lagerweji, A., Ockers, N., van Regteren Altena, H., Stam, T., Stoepker, H., Southart, G., ver der Zwan, M. (eds) (1977) *Opgravingen in Amsterdam. 20 jaar stadskernonderzoek*, Haarlem.

JERZY GAWRONSKI

Amsterdam, shipwreck

The *Amsterdam* was a ship of the **Dutch East India Company** (VOC) that ran ashore at Hastings in southern **England** on 26 January 1749. The *Amsterdam* became internationally renowned as the best-preserved VOC wreck to be discovered. Its hull, which slightly protrudes from the sand and is exposed during low tides, is a coherent structure (50 m long, 12 m wide, buried approximately 6 m deep) with its original contents virtually untouched. Nevertheless, the wreck is degrading because of dynamic wave action and sediment erosion. The *Amsterdam* played an important role in the scientific development of underwater and ship archaeology in the 1970s and 1980s, contributing to the discussion on various matters, including legislation, conservation (see **conservation, underwater**), fieldwork techniques and historical archaeological integration.

Archaeological research was triggered by a preliminary survey by the British archaeologist Peter Marsden in 1969–70 following treasure-hunting activities. In 1974, the VOC-ship Amsterdam Foundation was established in Holland, which initiated plans for a dry-land excavation and subsequent salvage of the hull. In the beginning of the 1980s, the research programme shifted towards underwater archaeology. Three large-scale excavation campaigns were organised in 1984, 1985 and 1986 by Jerzy Gawronski (University of Amsterdam) and Jonathan Adams (University of Southampton). In view of the difficult working conditions on this shallow site and the complex three-dimensional structure of the wreck, strong emphasis was put on development of methods and techniques for survey, excavation, registration and conservation in order to ensure the highest possible archaeological data output.

The excavation was limited to the stern section, where the lower deck at a depth of 2–3 m under the sea-bed has been uncovered over a length of 15 m. The dense *in situ* deposit on the deck proved to be of great archaeological potential and contained a large variety of well-preserved artefacts and ecological components, like insects and botanical and faunal material. The finds were related to different spaces in the stern area, like the captain's cabin on the upper deck and the constable's room and the sick bay on the lower deck. They covered a number of functional topics, such as ship's equipment, armament, cargo, provisions for overseas settlements, personal belongings, nutrition, health, state of technology and environmental and living conditions on board.

The *Amsterdam* not only represents an outstanding archaeological site, but its historical significance is also considerable. The ship was, like the **Hollandia**, newly built in Amsterdam and dated from a period that was essentially the technical and organisational peak of the VOC. In concordance with the archaeological investigations,

an extensive archival and historical research programme was organised in the late 1980s and 1990s to develop a coherent frame of reference about the manufacture and supply system of the company. This historical data served as a basis for an integrated analysis and interpretation of the material culture of VOC ships. Simultaneously, an archaeological programme of the complete site was not realised after the three trial excavations because of a lack of national funding.

See also: Dutch colonialism

Further reading

Gawronski, J. (1996) *De Equipagie van de Hollandia en de Amsterdam. VOC-bedrijvigheid in 18de-eeuws Amsterdam*, Amsterdam: de Bataafsche Leeuw.

—— (ed.) (1985, 1986, 1987) *Annual Report of the VOC-ship Amsterdam Foundation 1984, 1985, 1986*, Amsterdam: VOC-ship Amsterdam Foundation.

Marsden, P. (1985) *The Wreck of the Amsterdam*, London: Hutchinson.

Rooij, H. van and Gawronski, J. (1989) *East Indiaman Amsterdam*, Haarlem: Gottmer/Becht.

JERZY GAWRONSKI

Angkor, Cambodia

Angkor, the most extensive, low-density, dispersed pre-industrial city on earth, is located just to the north of the Tonle Sap, a great lake that is fed by the Mekong River. The basis of the economy was rice and fish. Between the ninth century AD and its problematic demise in the fifteenth to sixteenth centuries, Angkor was capital of the Khmer state. At its inception the state religion was Hinduism.

Basic socioeconomic characteristics of Angkor remain in dispute. Population estimates range up to the 'popular' one million. The workings of the economy and its related water-management system are also a matter of confused dispute – split between the functionalists and the cosmologists who diverge about the degree to which irrigation was used. Estimates of its extent have ranged from the central 200 km^2 to more than 1,000 km^2. Research by Christophe Pottier, of the École Française d'Extrême Orient, on the southern half

Figure 3 Angkor Wat, Cambodia
Source: Photo: C. Wu

of Angkor has shown that occupation was scattered in patches throughout the urban area, far beyond the central enclosures and temples. Exploratory coring work has also shown that people lived along the canals and the great road embankments. Most of the inhabitants lived in timber and thatch houses raised on stilts, in marked contrast to the immense and beautiful stone and brick temples for which the city is world famous.

By the mid-ninth century AD, a capital was established at Hariharalya, just to the south-east near the lake. In the late ninth century, Yasovarman I shifted the capital to a new state temple, built on the hill of Phnom Bakheng in central Angkor. Contrary to the standard maps of Angkor, this urban centre did not have a moat. From the tenth until the late twelfth century, successive rulers built their state temples and great reservoirs (*barays*) at a variety of locations spread across an area of more than 100 km². Early temples were built substantially of brick with stone foundations, usually of laterite, with a gradually increasing use of sandstone for decorated surfaces. A great transition in temple architecture, to entirely stone constructions with a predominant use of sandstone,

occurred in the late tenth/early eleventh century with the incomplete Ta Keo, the state temple of Jayavarman V.

The justly famous Angkor Wat, one of the world's greatest architectural achievements, and the largest single religious monument on earth, was built for Suryavarman II between 1113 and 1150. The complex covers almost 200 ha. The outer boundary of the moat is 1.5 km from east to west and 1.3 km north to south. It is worth noting, however, that this temple is not the most massive construction in Angkor. That accolade would go to the west *baray*. One of two giant reservoirs, it is over 8 km long and about 2 km wide. It contains 55 million cubic metres of water held in by banks over 100 m wide and up to 15 m high.

In the late twelfth century, a significant cultural transition began in Angkor. During a complex period of the internecine succession wars from which the Khmer empire suffered, Angkor appears to have been sacked by forces from the Cham region, in what is now Vietnam. At the end of a conflict in which Khmer forces opposed each other and some were allied with the Chams, Jayavarman VII came to power. He is famous for taking

Buddhism, which was already present in Southeast Asia, and making it the new state religion in a syncretic association with Hinduism. During his reign, a massive building programme commenced. He created the first walled centre for the city, Angkor Thom, and a large number of temples, including his state temple, the Bayon in the centre of Angkor Thom and two temple monasteries, the Preah Khan and the Ta Prohm. A particular architectural innovation of his reign was the famous face towers that stand over each gate into Angkor Thom and make the Bayon such an extraordinary monument. Some of the construction work was completed in the reign of his successor, Indravarman II. Unusually for the inclusive tendencies of Hinduism, a return to the traditional state religion in the reign of Jayavarman III (1243–95) included iconoclastic destruction of almost all the Buddhist images and wall carvings of the two previous rulers.

When seen by Chou Ta-Kuan, a Chinese envoy, in 1295–6, Angkor appeared to be wealthy and powerful, even though threatened by the Thai from the west. Few new temples were built after the early thirteenth century. The last Angkorean style temple, Mangalartha, was completed in 1295. Thereafter, the monuments are Buddhist-style platforms. The factors involved in the demise of Angkor are a subject of dispute. It is no longer assumed, for example, that Angkor was irretrievably sacked by the Thai in 1431. Even in the mid-sixteenth century, the wall friezes of Angkor Wat were being finished according to designs prepared 400 years earlier. However, by the seventeenth century, Angkor was abandoned and its only link to the past was the continuing use of Angkor Wat as a Buddhist monastery.

The site was brought to the attention of the West by Mohout in the nineteenth century. The French began the reconstruction work at Angkor. This is now an enterprise of many nations. Angkor is a World Heritage Site managed by APSARA, an agency of the Royal Cambodian government.

Further reading

Chou Ta-Kuan (1992) *The Customs of Cambodia*, trans. from the Shuo-fu (Pelliot and then d'Arcy Paul), Bangkok: Siam Society.

Fletcher, R.J. (2001) 'Seeing Angkor: New views on an old city', *Journal of the Oriental Society of Australia* 320–33: 1–27.

Higham, C. (1989) *The Archaeology of Mainland Southeast Asia: From 10,000 BC to the Fall of Angkor*, Cambridge: Cambridge University Press.

Jacques, C. and Freeman, M. (1997) *Angkor: Cities and Temples*, London: Thames & Hudson.

Mabbett, I. and Chandler, D. (1996) *The Khmers*, Oxford: Blackwell Publishers.

ROLAND FLETCHER

Annapolis, Maryland, USA

Annapolis, a small city located on the west bank of the Chesapeake Bay in Maryland (see **Chesapeake region**), was first historically settled in 1649. After being selected to be the new capital of Maryland in 1694, the population, wealth and social diversity of the city grew. The city was redesigned following baroque fashion with circles built around the State House and the Anglican Church, and radiating streets connecting these to each other, the harbour and the rest of the settled area. Set amid a tobacco plantation economy, early attempts at industry faired poorly. Instead, beginning after 1763, the city was turned over to the politicians who led Maryland into and through the American Revolution.

By the end of the eighteenth century, Annapolis saw this 'Golden Age' pass. Instead of growth, the city slumbered with a relatively stable population of families with ties to southern Maryland's plantation belt. In 1845, after twenty years of wooing the federal government, Annapolis was chosen to be the site of the US Naval Academy. The Academy brought welcome attention to the small town but demanded much in return. Over the next several decades, Annapolitans carefully balanced the construction of a modern identity that could both accommodate the Academy as well as maintain what was true to Annapolis. By 1900, this work supported the symbolic identification of Annapolis as a colonial city. In the 1920s, the city was home to one of the earliest historic preservation organisations in the US. Revived in the 1950s, the effort to preserve historic Annapolis remains ongoing.

Though archaeology was included in the

Figure 4 The eighteenth-century William Paca
house in Annapolis, Maryland
Source: Photo S. Baugher

preservation effort in Annapolis as early as the 1960s, only in 1980 did a formal archaeological research programme begin. 'Archaeology in Annapolis', a joint archaeological research and public education programme run by the University of Maryland, College Park and the Historic Annapolis Foundation, Inc., has excavated over twenty sites in the city, ranging from formal gardens to city streets, from colonial brick mansions to early twentieth-century alley dwellings, and from the homes of the city's diverse elite to the residences of slaves to the houses of working- and middle-class blacks and whites. This diversity of work has followed a singular research design that seeks to understand the city as a single archaeological site. Research has placed emphasis on the contextual reconstruction of the city for a variety of time periods and from a diversity of perspectives. In particular, the project has aimed to use archaeology as a means to understand the development of the

culture of capitalism from its origins to the present day. Of these studies, three in particular stand out.

Focusing on class formation during the eighteenth century, Mark Leone, Paul Shackel and Barbara Little have explored the archaeological record of the transformation of everyday life resulting from the introduction of capitalist work-discipline. At the beginning of the century, probate records show that wealth disparities in Annapolis were minimally pronounced, yet by the end of the colonial period the wealthiest 20 per cent of population controlled 85 per cent of the wealth. Pairing this finding with the material record of the era, Leone and Shackel show that with increased wealth disparities there came an increase in the presence of clocks and scientific and musical instruments recorded in the probate inventories as well as an increase in sets of dishes, eating utensils and hygiene equipment in both the probates and the archaeological record. These studies argue that these objects were used as part of an extended ideological apparatus produced over the century as the wealthiest group asserted the legitimacy of its rank.

During the 1720s, a decline in the international tobacco market drove the first wedge in wealth disparity as the poorer population suffered disproportionately through the depression. At this time the use of scientific instruments and clocks as symbolic markers of wealth may have been reformulated to show that their owners were educated, refined and masters of the tenets of natural law. These tenets not only established society as a natural phenomenon knowable through empirical observation, but also elaborated the notion of the individual. Individuals in society were the cogs in a machine-like world, or, following the designs of the instruments being consumed, components of society like the degrees of a compass or the notes of a musical scale. To understand how to behave appropriately, the elite may have demonstrated the strict rules and routines involved with the correct use of the instruments. Such demonstrations, based in universally applicable standards and backed by the authority of wealth, metaphorically mechanised everyday experience as a sequential set of individual performances.

Such an understanding of the way material items may act back on their users, that is, how material culture is recursive in its essence, allowed archaeologists in Annapolis to expand on the formulation of the **Georgian Order**. Previous work showed that, during the eighteenth century, material forms grew increasingly standardised and more focused on the individual consumer. The development of the Georgian Order in Annapolis coincided with the growth in wealth disparity; thus, it was hypothesised that such standardisation and individuation of material culture may also have served to legitimise social inequality. Focusing on ceramics, Shackel shows that standardisation in individual place settings first appeared among the wealthy and then spread to the rest of Annapolitan society by the mid-nineteenth century. These place settings, like scientific instruments, were associated with rules of appropriate use. Yet, until one learns how to appropriately use scientific instruments they remain foreign; however, in the case of place settings, the rules are much more arbitrary. While anyone physically capable can drink from a cup and cut food with a knife, with the new place settings there also came new rules of etiquette that showed how to do just these sorts of things appropriately. Perhaps the most powerful common thread to the new etiquette rules was their reproduction of the same sorts of segregated instructional steps for using a sextant in the segregated individual place settings that marked the segregated phases of food consumption. We can read from this that through the medium of ceramics people could learn, first, that they were different from others as distinct individuals, and, second, that activities in life should proceed through orderly stages following the rules of appropriate behaviour.

By the end of the eighteenth century, this segregation of activities into rule-bound ordered steps was found in a diverse array of social locations. Its most obvious illustration was in the development of factories in which production passed from craft-oriented piecework to industrial wage work. Little has shown how this process was elaborated in the Green print shop and household in Annapolis. The Green site was the location of a printing business as well as a residence from 1745 until 1839. Excavation revealed the print shop to have been a separate structure behind the house. An analysis of ceramics shows a steady increase in the standardisation of consumption following the

expected pattern for increased individual discipline through time. A more interesting data set consists of the surviving issues of the *Maryland Gazette*, which was printed weekly by the Greens. Looking at the form of printing (e.g. columns, sections separated off from others, etc.) shows that the newspaper became increasingly consistent in form through time. The Green printing enterprise seems to have followed the same patterns of standardisation and segmentation found in other cultural facets from eighteenth-century Annapolis.

A careful analysis of the Green site data, however, has allowed Little to clarify one of the major points of contention that have developed from this research. Many have argued that the findings in Annapolis at best tell one side of the story and at worst disempower subordinate groups who appear duped into accepting the dominant order and thus their powerlessness. At the very least, the work in Annapolis has been based on the belief that the ideological constructions of the Annapolis elite have been conceived during moments of class conflict. It is important to remember, though, that this does not mean we can simply turn the tables to ask new questions of the data from another perspective. The archaeological signature of 'muted' groups was not the focus of the work reviewed here thus far because, as Little has argued, the muted groups have little choice but to express themselves through the ideology of the dominant group or risk ostracism, condemnation or belittlement.

Rather, to expand the picture, the effort in the archaeology of Annapolis has been to look at new arenas where the discourse between classes and interest groups has been played out. At the Green site Little shows that changes made by Anne Catherine Green while she ran the press after her husband Jonas's death reflect an alternative approach to production. While Jonas Green built a segregated structure for the printing press where he stored all of the material related to the business, Anne Catherine Green built a hyphen connecting the press structure to the house and kept printing materials in the main house. Also, while Jonas kept a clock in the press building, Anne did not. These subtle changes reflect that Anne Catherine Green de-emphasised the segregation of domestic from public space and in so doing may have relaxed the disciplinary structures that her husband embraced. Given authority over her life Anne Catherine Green chose to diverge from the dominant mode. Her choice can be seen as a domestication of the print shop, a process typical of women of the time and one that revived the craft ideals of the past. The question remains, as Little shows, whether this was an active form of resistance to progress or whether this rearticulation of space was a feminine expression formed more by the structural habit of Enlightenment culture to leave women left behind. In the latter case, the space is as much a product of the dominant mode as if she had followed the pattern of her husband. Clearly, more work needs to be done to understand the areas where the textures of social life are less clear.

Archaeology in Annapolis has worked to understand the archaeological record of capitalism by exploring its origins and development through the meanings and uses of material culture. The emphasis has been on understanding the city as a whole and in so doing has led to understanding how material culture is bound to the social process of class formation, power relations and identity negotiation within a single community. This work has revealed multiple expressions of domination that have moulded culture and individuals into modernity as they embraced, rejected and negotiated the structures of authority that developed. Ultimately, the project has created archaeologies that are useful in that they provide an understanding of how the ideologies of capitalism originated and persist.

See also: urban archaeology

Further reading

Leone, M.P. (1988) 'The Georgian Order as the order of merchant capitalism in Annapolis, Maryland', in M.P. Leone and P.B. Potter, Jr (eds) *The Recovery of Meaning: Historical Archaeology in the Eastern United States*, Washington, DC: Smithsonian Institution Press, pp. 235–63.

Little, B.J. (1994) '"She was…an example to her sex": Possibilities for a feminist historical archaeology', in P.A. Shackel and B.J. Little (eds) *Historical Archaeology of the Chesapeake*, Washington, DC: Smithsonian Institution Press, pp. 189–204.

—— (1988) 'Craft and culture change in the eighteenth-century Chesapeake', in M.P. Leone and P.B. Potter, Jr (eds) *The Recovery of Meaning: Historical Archaeology in the Eastern United States*, Washington, DC: Smithsonian Institution Press, pp. 264–92.

Potter, P.B., Jr (1994) *Public Archaeology in Annapolis: A Critical Approach to History in Maryland's Ancient City*, Washington, DC: Smithsonian Institution Press.

Shackel, P.A. (1993) *Personal Discipline and Material Culture: An Archaeology of Annapolis, Maryland, 1695–1870*, Knoxville: University of Tennessee Press.

Shackel, P.A., Mullins, P.R. and Warner, M.S. (eds) (1998) *Annapolis Pasts: Historical Archaeology in Annapolis, Maryland*, Knoxville: University of Tennessee Press.

Yentsch, A.E. (1994) *A Chesapeake Family and Their Slaves: A Study in Historical Archaeology*, Cambridge: Cambridge University Press.

CHRISTOPHER N. MATTHEWS

Antarctica

Historical archaeology in Antarctica started in the 1980s, but since the 1960s there had been an interest in the conservation of historical sites (see **conservation, terrestrial underwater**, **conservation, terrestrial**). Given the particular geopolitical context of Antarctica as International Territory, historical archaeology at first played a specific role as a means of contrasting, enlarging or supporting the different historical versions related to the claims of sovereignty of some countries. Nevertheless, as time went by archaeological research offered new perspectives to inquire into the history of this region, as shown by such subjects as underwater archaeology, archaeology of **capitalism** and conservation of materials.

Antarctica was the last continent to be discovered, in the early nineteenth century, largely because of its remote location. It consists of a continental area and adjacent islands. There are several versions of its discovery, involving different dates and protagonists, but it is generally accepted that it was reached in 1819. Since then, companies from various countries began the seasonal exploitation of sea mammals, but historical information about their occupations is limited to logbooks. Several scientific expeditions were conducted during the nineteenth and twentieth centuries, evidence for which appears in documents and in the remains of the structures these explorers built. Some of this **architecture** has been restored by different countries, including New Zealand, the USA, the UK and Argentina.

Archaeologists working in Antarctica have developed most of their research in the South Shetland Islands, focusing on the nineteenth century. In the 1980s, a Chilean group directed by R. Stehberg tried to demonstrate the participation of South American Indians as a workforce for seal-hunting companies. This hypothesis was developed from the discovery of Native American projectile points and human remains (see **Native Americans**). In addition, archaeologists excavated several huts made of rocks. In the 1990s, Spanish archaeologists directed by M. Martín Bueno joined the Chilean team and widened

the scope of the initial project. Underwater research was conducted to locate the wreck of a Spanish vessel, the *San Telmo*, closely associated with the European discovery of Antarctica. Off-coast surveying revealed the presence of several **shipwrecks**, though no firm identifications have been made.

Since 1995, the Argentinian archaeologists M. Senatore and A. Zarankin have been investigating the occupation of Antarctica as part of the capitalist expansion towards marginal or unknown areas. They were initially interested in defining the economic strategies used in Antarctica, at a regional scale. They registered and excavated about twenty seasonal camps – consisting of structures containing living areas and productive spaces used for the exploitation of sea resources – along the Byers Peninsula (Livingston Island). The artefacts they found dated from the late eighteenth and early nineteenth centuries. The use of local and non-local resources for food, shelter and fuel was established as well. In the late 1990s, Zarankin

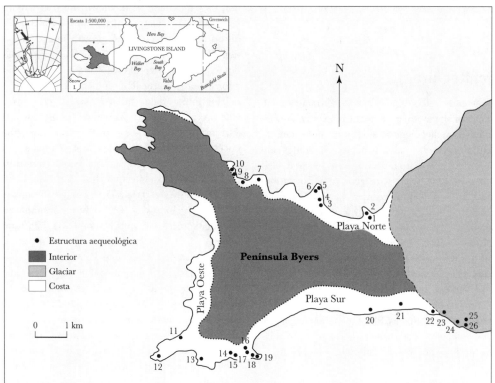

Figure 5 Byers Peninsula, Livingston Island, Antarctica, showing location of archaeological sites
Source: A. Zarankin and M.X. Senatore

and Senatore started considering ideological (see **ideology**) and symbolic variables in the practices of the settlers' **everyday life**, studying such issues as the organisation of space and the use of material culture.

Further reading

Martín Bueno, M. (1995) 'Arqueología Antártica: el proyecto San Telmo y el descubrimiento de la Terra Australis Antartica', in *Actas del V Simposio de Estudios Antárticos*, Madrid: Comisión Intermin- isterial de Ciencia y Tecnología, pp. 421–8.

Senatore, M.X. and Zarankin, A. (1999) 'Arqueo- logía histórica y expansión capitalista. Prácticas cotidianas y grupos operarios en Península Byers, Isla Livingston de las Shetland del Sur', in A. Zarankin and F. Acuto (eds) *Sed Non Satiata*, Buenos Aires: Tridente, pp. 171–88.

Stehberg, R. and Cabeza, A. (1987) 'Terra Australis Incognita: Una ruta de investigación arqueoló- gica', *Revista Chilena de Antropología* 6: 83–111.

MARIA XIMENA SENATORE

architecture

Architecture refers to the built environment and consists of all the structures that can exist at a once-occupied archaeological site, including houses, sheds, barns and all other structures. Buildings can have both above-ground and below-ground ele- ments, both of which archaeologists can study. Above-ground features consist of the buildings themselves, ornamental constructions – such as fountains – and building ruins. Below-ground features include foundations, post-holes, wall trenches and cellars. Much **industrial archae- ology** incorporates the study of architecture as well.

Architecture began to appear in history as soon as humans discovered the need to shelter them- selves from the elements. Since the initial invention of purposefully built shelters, humans have built structures out of many materials, ranging from grass to steel.

Archaeologists have a strong interest in archi- tecture for several important reasons. First, build- ings are the places where men, women and **children** conduct their daily activities. In the course of the day, people drop things around their houses, use their yards for specialised activities and storage, lose things through the floor-boards and deposit artefacts around their buildings in countless other ways. As a result, archaeology conducted around past buildings, both standing and relict, has the potential to provide information about numer- ous aspects of a past people's daily lives. Second, architecture does not simply 'happen'. People build structures in prescribed ways, with certain rules in mind to make them conform to their cultural ideas of how buildings should look and function. The buildings they construct reflect the construction methods they have designed to help them to survive in the environment. An analysis of a building's construction techniques and mode of design can thus provide unique cultural informa- tion. Third, the nature of archaeological research means that archaeologists have the potential to provide information about construction techniques that may otherwise be unknown. Even at famous buildings, like Thomas Jefferson's **Monticello**, historical archaeologists can provide new informa- tion about the architectural character of the old house. The presentation of new architectural information is particularly important, however, in helping to document the lives of men and women who are poorly known in written history, such as African American slaves. At the same time, the documentation of past architectural techniques can have a significant impact on **reconstruction** projects, where architectural historians simply do not know how a certain building may have looked in the past. In such cases, only excavation can provide the necessary information for architectural features that are otherwise hidden from view. Fourth, because architecture constitutes the con- struction of physical spaces, buildings have the potential to modify the ways in which people interact and even the ways in which they perceive the world around them. Living in a house with abundant windows provides a different perspective on the world than does life in a house with no view to the outside. Finally, people can use architecture to signify or express their position in society. When viewed in this manner, architecture represents a kind of communication that can be used to express an opinion or project a social image. Architecture perceived in this manner plays an active social role.

Architecture is divided into formal and **vernacular architecture**, and historical archaeologists have examined both types. 'Formal' architecture refers to construction according to accepted patterns or design books, with the buildings being designed by trained architects and often built under their direct attention. Examples of such buildings would be plantation mansions, governmental state houses, public buildings and **fortifications**. 'Vernacular' architecture refers to construction according to cultural designs, using methods that have either been passed down through the generations or else devised 'on the spot' to conform to a new natural environment. The rules of vernacular architecture are seldom committed to writing, and would be seldom, if ever, formally taught to architects.

Historical archaeologists have contributed much to the study of historical architecture, having conducted both surveys of vernacular architecture and detailed examinations of specific structures. Linda Worthy's survey of nineteenth- and twentieth-century, above-ground structures in the Richard B. Russell Reservoir area in South Carolina and Georgia, USA, is an example of an architectural survey with an archaeological dimension. An archaeological example of the study of a particular, still-extant building is Lynne Lewis's study of Drayton Hall, an eighteenth- and nineteenth-century plantation mansion near Charleston, South Carolina.

In addition to conducting their own investigations, historical archaeologists find detailed studies by architectural historians of particular interest because they often provide important information about building styles, construction techniques and architectural changes through time using a technical language that may be new to many archaeologists. An excellent example of the archaeological relevance of such works is N.W. Alcock's study of housing in Warwickshire, England, in which he provides a detailed examination of numerous buildings from the 1500–1800 period.

Historical archaeologists have explored many topics related to architecture, but perhaps three topics have attracted the most attention: the archaeology of colonial architecture, the archaeology of subordinate architecture and the archaeology of architectural meaning. Historical archaeologists around the world continue to conduct research on these topics.

The archaeology of colonial architecture

Historical archaeologists have played a large role in documenting the architecture built by colonial Europeans who travelled the world beginning in the late fifteenth century. Research on colonial architecture has been important because of the frequent lack of written information about the ways in which the earliest European settlers created a built environment.

Historical archaeologists working in Virginia have been particularly successful in providing information about colonial architecture. For example, Ivor Noël Hume, working at Martin's Hundred, a seventeenth-century English settlement near Williamsburg, Virginia, USA, discovered the remains of a semi-subterranean house, called a 'cellar house', which was constructed with an A-frame roof. His interpretation of the building was that carpenters, planning to construct more conventional structures later, built the house as a temporary shelter.

Archaeologists excavating at **Jamestown**, also in Virginia, have documented more conventional English housing in that settlement. They have shown that, during the second half of the seventeenth century, English colonists built urban row houses. The architects of these pieces of formal architecture modelled them after the houses of affluent urbanites in England, probably in an effort to construct a built environment with which they were comfortable.

In other parts of North America, historical archaeologists have provided information about the colonial settlements of Spanish, French and Dutch settlers. These archaeologists have investigated domestic, religious and military architecture. Archaeologists working in colonial New Spain – in the south-eastern and south-western regions of the USA and the Caribbean – have found abundant evidence of colonial Spanish architecture, extending from tiny huts to complex forts. Archaeologists working around the world have made similar finds at other colonial sites.

Military architecture is another kind of colonial

architecture, and research on fortifications has played a significant role in much historical archaeological research. Forts were some of the first places excavated in many parts of the world, and excavations at **Fort Michilimackinac** (Michigan), Fort Necessity (Pennsylvania), Fort Orange (New York), Oudepost I (South Africa), the fort in Buenos Aires (Argentina), **Fortress of Louisbourg** (Nova Scotia) and elsewhere have provided often-unknown architectural details that are important in the physical reconstruction of these historical sites. In addition to providing architectural information useful for reconstruction purposes, historical archaeologists have also produced information about the role of the built environment in structuring military life in the past as well as providing unique anthropological insights on the interactions between military personnel and indigenous peoples.

The archaeology of subordinate architecture

Subordinate architecture, as the term is used here, refers to buildings constructed by men and women who were not in positions of power in a society, and who may or may not have been able to control the kind of structures they built. Archaeology often provides the best information about this kind of architecture because it is often undocumented in written records.

Many groups of people may be considered to have constructed subordinate architecture, and historical archaeologists have studied many of them. Perhaps their greatest contributions to date, however, have been made in the examination of Native American and African American slave architecture.

In dealing with both groups of people, archaeologists have been able to document changes in house form, construction materials and location over time. The changes occurred in many cases because of culture contact and **acculturation**. Archaeologists have also been able to document the architectural elements of **resistance**, when indigenous peoples refuse to adapt their traditional housing to the ideals of another culture. One example comes from excavations at the Yaughan and Curriboo plantations in South Carolina, where early eighteenth-century slaves built houses that resembled African-style structures they knew from the Caribbean and ultimately from Africa. Other African-style houses

have been identified at other plantations, and the development and continued use of the shotgun house – a long, linear house – is an example of an African-style architectural tradition that is still used today in Louisiana and the Caribbean.

Archaeologists often find it difficult to discern the motives behind the construction of subordinate architecture. They do not know, for instance, whether the prevalence of African-style housing at a plantation site was the result of the slaves' retention of African designs or whether it represents the planter's acquiescence to traditional building techniques. The solution to questions such as this will often help archaeologists to conceptualise the social dynamics of the past, and help to provide a more complete contextual understanding of history.

The archaeology of architectural meaning

Historical archaeologists have also been involved in important studies into the meaning of architecture. Archaeologists with these interests attempt to unravel the messages that may be contained within architecture and to discover how architectural design can shape behaviour and perception.

Much of the archaeological interest in the meaning of the built environment began with Mark Leone's critical examination of William Paca's garden, an eighteenth-century formal garden in **Annapolis**, Maryland. Leone showed how the carefully designed garden was more than simply a functional place to enjoy greenery. Instead, the garden was planned in a way that presented a certain image of daily life, a way of segmenting nature from culture, the wild from the refined. Thus, the garden was really a metaphor for the US society that was in the process of then being created.

Many archaeologists have followed Leone's lead and have delved into the meaning of past architecture. In an interdisciplinary study of traditional architecture in western Suffolk, England, Matthew Johnson examined the transition between the late medieval and the early modern periods. This time in history witnessed a number of significant social and cultural changes in England and the world, not the least of which was the rise of global **capitalism**, as represented by the spread of European culture in places it had never been before. Johnson used the architecture of the Suffolk region to gain insight into the process of social and cultural change. Relying on a concept of 'closure' – the separation of public and private spheres of action within a structure – he demonstrated that the domestic architecture of the area underwent a fundamental transformation between the fifteenth and the seventeenth centuries. Changes in house layout and decoration, for instance, were related more to societal changes than strictly to economics. In another important study, Heather Burke used nineteenth- and twentieth-century architecture in Armidale, New South Wales, Australia, to investigate the use of capitalist ideology in building design. Her findings indicate that architecture, rather than being a passive bystander in social life, actually constitutes an active way for people to construct their identities. Architecture is thus expressive and meaningful on many different levels. In another study, Ross Jamieson examined the meaning of colonial architecture in Ecuador, specifically in Cuenca, a town that was initially an Inca centre but which became a Spanish outpost in 1557. Jamieson showed how the town's colonial architecture was used to negotiate power by the men and women who lived there, and how they assigned multiple, often complex, meanings to buildings.

Further reading

Alcock, N.W. (1993) *People at Home: Living in a Warwickshire Village, 1500–1800*, Chichester: Phillimore.

Burke, H. (1999) *Meaning and Ideology in Historical Archaeology: Style, Social Identity, and Capitalism in an Australian Town*, New York: Kluwer Academic/ Plenum.

Jamieson, R.W. (2000) *Domestic Architecture and Power: Historical Archaeology of Colonial Ecuador*, New York: Kluwer Academic/Plenum.

Johnson, M. (1993) *Housing Culture: Traditional Architecture in an English Landscape*, Washington, DC: Smithsonian Institution Press.

CHARLES E. ORSER, JR

Asia

In Asia, history is part of most archaeology, because written texts appeared in China by 3000

BP and in India by 3000–2000 BP. South-east Asian, Arabic, and Western texts all became available between AD 200 and 700. Historical archaeology has been conducted in East, South-east, and South Asia, as well as in the United Arab Emirates and Turkey.

East, South-east and South Asia

In China, Francis Allard and Yun Kuen Lee, working independently, analysed **historical documents** and archaeological evidence concerning an outlying polity at Dian in Yunnan. As briefly described in official Han histories, Dian was a large state with a king and 20,000–30,000 soldiers. Descriptions of groups nearby suggested that Dian's people were rice farmers with domesticated animals, and used cowries for currency. Archaeological evidence from burial grounds confirmed significant status differences, with sophisticated bronzes in wealthy graves. A seal referred to the King of Dian. Cowry shell containers depicted human sacrifices, battle scenes and groups of important persons. Agricultural tools, representations of domesticated animals, and weapons all confirmed and expanded on the scant information left historically concerning this outlying polity.

Several studies in China involved extensive excavation at walled and gridded cities such as Chang'an and Luoyang, the capital cities of the Han (206 BC–AD 220), Sui (AD 581–618) and Tang (618–907) Dynasties. Tang Chang'an was also the eastern terminus of the Silk Road, the main overland network of routes followed in the east–west **trade** since ancient times. Silks from Han dynasty China were recovered as far west as a tomb between Palmyra, Syria, and Antioch, Turkey. Porcelains (see **porcelain**), invented in China in the late sixth or seventh century AD, were recovered in large numbers at sites in West Asia.

In Japan, Yamato, studied by Gina Barnes, was the capital of a fifth- to sixth-century state in the Nara basin. Yamato's elites co-ordinated commoner labour to produce luxury items including **beads**, ceramics and iron artefacts for exchange with elites in Japan, Korea and China. Yamato possessed a military, complex burials, centralised settlements with palaces and rectangular pit and pillared commoner houses, canals and fields.

Monumental tombs produced **stoneware**, and iron tools and weapons imported from Korea. The nature and duration of Korea's relationships with Yamato, whose settlement was once attributed to 'horse riders' from Korea, remains one of the most provocative historical archaeological questions in the two areas.

In Okinawa, Richard Pearson and Hiroto Takamiya independently analysed archaeological evidence from the period between AD 1200 and 1609 for increasing centralisation: fortification (see **fortifications**) of cut-stone residences (*gusuku*); ceramic production at kilns eventually administered centrally; agricultural intensification; and maintenance of a flourishing extra-regional trade that supported Okinawa's city states. Imports included Japanese iron farming tools, Chinese porcelains and coins, celadonic wares from South-east Asia, Korea (*koryo* wares) and China, and Korean roof tiles. Most Okinawan exports were perishable (and archaeologically invisible), but historical documents describe dyes, silk floss and other fibres. Records also establish that Ryukyuan traders stayed in compounds at fifteenth-century Melaka (Malaysia) and other South-east Asian ports. Okinawa's success in trade helped it to remain autonomous while tributary to China, and even after the nineteenth-century Japanese takeover.

In Korea, Sarah Nelson and Kim Won-Yong, independently studied plundered and vulnerable tombs dating to between AD 300 and 668 to learn what their contents revealed about sociopolitical developments in three important states – Koguryo, Paekche and Silla – which unified most of the peninsula. Koguryo, with social stratification (see **stratification, social**), had fortified cities and a military that emphasised soldiers on horseback, and was supported in part by tribute from conquered peoples. Paekche, with twenty-two administrative districts, maintained contacts with southern China and with Japan, to which it exported a monumental tomb style. Silla's elite tombs produced gold jewellery, horse trappings that indicated the continued importance of horses, Chinese ceramics, Roman **glass**, Mediterranean beads and a silver Persian bowl (possibly imported from China). A Scythian bronze jar from a tomb in a fourth polity, Kaya, along with evidence for the continued importance of horses, suggests long-standing relationships with nomadic areas to the north-west.

In the Philippines, Karl Hutterer and Masao Nishimura evaluated evidence for elite control of trade goods at Cebu, a major fourteenth- to sixteenth-century trade centre. Laura Junker and Lis Bacus analysed evidence for elite control throughout the regional networks centred, respectively, on twelfth- to sixteenth-century Tanjay (Bais), Yap and Unto (Dumaguete), and Negros Oriental. At the main centres, prestige goods including Chinese porcelains and local decorated wares concentrated in elite-associated contexts, as did evidence for iron manufacture, suggesting elite control over exchange and local production. Inland settlements in Bais and Dumaguete became more regularly spaced through time; inland finds included imports and other items probably exchanged from the coast. Shortly before Spanish contact in AD 1521, lesser centres began to receive prestige goods, suggesting growing tiers of competing elites. Warfare increased in Tanjay after 1521, possibly to ensure access to prestige items under the Spanish monopoly.

European colonialism is often cited as the main stimulus for the current global economy. In the Philippines, however, Chinese expansion exerted profound influences for 500 years before Spanish contact. Russell Skowronek found that Spanish colonial patterns in the Philippines are very different from those left in the New World. Residences in Manila, behind Spanish façades, were organised for Asian, not European, life. Archaeological sites produced enormous quantities of Chinese ceramic wares, but few Spanish wares. These and other patterns revealed the importance of China in the development of an earlier global economy.

In Kedah, Malaysia, Jane Allen conducted a geoarchaeological survey in an area focused on two coastal centres that conducted exchange with China, India, the South-east Asian polities and the Middle East between *c.* AD 500 and 1500. Imports occurred in large numbers in areas interpreted as occupied by elites, suggesting elite control. Shrines at the coastal centres suggested foreigner compounds like those documented historically for fifteenth-century Melaka, further south. Most exports were perishable forest goods;

rare finds at downstream sites included tree resins. The importance of forest goods for export is suggested by the fact that the coastal centres moved, when their estuaries silted in, to maintain stream transportation corridors to inland areas. After AD 1200, over-use of hill slope fields produced soil erosion and increasing siltation at the coast; both centres are now landlocked several kilometres inland.

In historical Bali, where small temples held important places in decentralised political units, Vernon Scarborough, John Schoenfelder and Stephen Lansing conducted another geoarchaeological study, analysing evidence for a water management system operated and maintained by local rice field co-operatives working closely with one such local temple. At Sebatu, water first supplied temple baths and other ceremonial features, and then entered tunnels and ditches to feed extensive irrigated fields downslope. Botanical evidence indicated that extensive landscape change here began c. AD 1445, when the forest that had covered the area was replaced by agricultural fields, dams, weirs and bunds. Since AD 1445, nearly 3 m of sediments have been deposited at the temple.

In Cambodia, Miriam Stark conducted excavations at Angkor Borei, which was probably an inland capital of Funan, a polity described by third-century AD Chinese visitors as having walled settlements, palaces, libraries and a taxation system based on prestige items. Although the absence of new inscriptions after the seventh century suggested that Funan had ceased to exist, Stark's research established that at least one brick structure was occupied between the eighth and tenth centuries. The main site component overlay fourth- or third-century BC components that suggested early developments paralleling those at moated sites in north-eastern Thailand and possibly sites in the Chao Phrya valley.

David Welch studied evidence for the pre-Khmer period (pre-AD 1000), the Angkorian period (AD 1000–1300) and the post-Khmer period (AD 1300–1600) at sites in north-east Thailand. During the earliest period, political control was exerted by moated regional centres; temples were not yet administrative centres. Small villages, some fortified, occupied arable lower alluvial terraces. During the Angkorian period, temple hierarchies became major integrative forces in political and economic life, with large temples like Phimai's incorporated in administrative centres, and smaller temples participating in clearing and planting fields. Villages were no longer fortified, suggesting decreasing unrest. The post-Angkorian period produced no known inscriptions and no monumental buildings around Phimai, and little is known about the period until the seventeenth century, when Thais based at Khorat controlled the area.

An important issue in South and South-east Asia concerns whether sociopolitical developments between c. AD 1 and 1500 were local or imposed from outside – from Rome in the Indian case, from India in the South-east Asian case. Himanshu Ray and Ashok Datta, independently studying sites in east India and Bangladesh, established that developments there were local. In the Ganges area, settlements shifted towards the coast for access to maritime routes, ceramic production intensified, tanks and wells were constructed, and the sites became increasingly involved in a flourishing external exchange focused not on Rome but on South-east Asia. Similarly, evidence studied by Hermann Kulke did not support claims for Indian domination of South-east Asia. Eastern Indian polities during the first millennium AD were small and localised, lacking state-level administrations. They and the South-east Asian polities with which they regularly exchanged goods and ideas developed along convergent lines.

Further south in India, Kathleen Morrison surveyed the area around Vijayanagara, a fourteenth- to sixteenth-century city that required an elaborate system of water-retention features, with reservoirs, wells, terraces and canals to ensure urban and agricultural water supply. Historical evidence indicates that, while most canals were controlled by the king, large reservoirs were controlled locally by temples. Small reservoirs may have been family enterprises. These features, intricately interrelated, played a critical role in Vijayanagara's development into an urban centre that eventually controlled most of south India.

West Asia

In the United Arab Emirates, John Hansman

recovered evidence at Julfar, an Islamic port, for intense involvement in the east–west maritime trade between the fourteenth and seventeenth centuries. Ceramics recovered included, among others, Chinese, Vietnamese and Siamese porcelains and porcellaneous stoneware, south-west Indian **earthenware** and Persian and north-west African ware. Julfar's peak trade period, during the Portuguese colonial era, included the sixteenth and seventeenth centuries. Omanis drove the Portuguese out of Julfar in 1633, and its trade collapsed.

In Turkey, Uzi Baram interpreted the many clay smoking pipes (see **pipes, smoking**) and ceramic **coffee** cups that appear at Ottoman Empire sites as signs of a new, sixteenth-century pattern of leisure **consumption** of tobacco and coffee by commoner groups including soldiers, urban workers and guild members. Three centuries later, the Empire was in decline, and these same luxuries became old-fashioned vestiges of an out-of-date empire.

Lynda Carroll examined changes in elite-associated ceramics in sixteenth- to late eighteenth-century Ottoman Turkey. Elites controlled access to Chinese imports as long as they could. When Chinese wares became hard to acquire, elites supported and controlled local production of ceramics at kilns like Iznik, which produced wares that were uniquely Turkish but included Chinese motifs. By the mid-sixteenth century, Chinese wares were again easy to acquire, elites lost interest in local wares and the Ottoman kilns marketed increasingly to commoners and to Europeans, who considered their products prestigious Oriental wares. The global economy in which the Empire participated now began to shift emphasis from China and East Asia to Europe.

See also: architecture; destruction, site; landscape studies

Further reading

Barnes, G.L. (1988) *Protohistoric Yamato: Archaeology of the First Japanese State*, Ann Arbor: Museum of Anthropology, University of Michigan.

Hansman, J. (1985) *Julfar, an Arabian Port: Its Settlement and Far Eastern Ceramic Trade from the 14th to the 18th Centuries*, London: Royal Asiatic Society of Great Britain and Ireland.

Morrison, K.D. (1993) 'Supplying the city: The role of reservoirs in an Indian urban landscape', *Asian Perspectives* 32(2): 133–51.

Nelson, S.M. (1993) *The Archaeology of Korea*, Cambridge: Cambridge University Press.

Stark, M.T. and Allen, S. J. (eds) (1998) 'The transition to history in Southeast Asia', *International Journal of Historical Archaeology* 2: 163–348.

S. JANE ALLEN

assimilation

Assimilation is a process that reduces or, if it runs its complete course, removes the need for ethnic group identification. Ethnic groups are comprised of people who share common values, beliefs, attitudes, behavioural ideals and representative symbols, both abstract and material. Ethnic groups are distinguished from other social groups because they serve two related functions: they provide members with an identity that is recognised as both 'ascriptive' and 'exclusive', and they allow members to establish primary relationships with others who share that identity. If completed, the process of assimilation dispels the need for and operation of these two functions.

Ascriptive means that members must be born into the group, while exclusive means that group membership is fixed. In groups that are strongly ascriptive and exclusive (castes, for example), the criteria that determine membership are tangible, and not easily manipulated by individuals. Such groups have clear boundaries, and attempts to move from one group to another under discouraging social or cultural conditions often prove futile. The ascriptive and exclusive qualities of ethnic groups are strictly symbolic, however. Individuals can change the group with which they are identified, by manipulating the symbols of **ethnicity**. The group often remains resilient in spite of this manipulation, because of the continuing perception that membership is ascriptive and exclusive. Yet, since this is only a perception, the potential for significant assimilation is always present.

Primary relationships are those that are personal, intimate, informal and face-to-face. They require the involvement of the entire personality. Identification with an ethnic group directs these relationships towards those who claim the same identification, an adaptive strategy that increases social integration, provides economic and psychological support, and sustains traditional culture, religion, language and a sense of common origin among participants. This unique function of ethnic groups can be particularly important in the modern world, where various social and cultural systems are impersonal and assuming global proportions. Assimilation nevertheless overwhelms this contribution of ethnicity, under certain conditions.

The words assimilation and **acculturation** are often used interchangeably, though it is useful to define the latter as merely one aspect of the former. Acculturation is that part of the assimilation process which eliminates particular behavioural and material patterns that symbolically distinguish those people who are members of an ethnic group from those who are not. The balance of the assimilation process involves social and ideational changes necessary to meaningfully alter the way one interacts with others and conceptualises such interactions; included is the pivotal process of structural assimilation, which results in the re-arrangement of primary relations.

Historical archaeologists have focused on acculturation because of its behavioural and material qualities. This is, of course, a logical strategy, given the strengths and weaknesses of archaeological method and theory. Studying patterns of behaviour and patterns of material culture is, after all, what archaeologists do. Acculturation, however, is not the most significant part of assimilation, either to the people undergoing the process or to others interacting with them in the context of culture contact and change. Strategies for studying the totality of assimilation must be developed. This is particularly true of structural assimilation, during which members of ethnic groups enter institutions of non-members (usually of host societies) through alterations in their primary group relationships.

Acculturation generally precedes structural assimilation, although the occurrence of the former does not necessarily induce the latter. History is replete with examples of 'acculturation only'. In contrast, when structural assimilation occurs it results inevitably in the complete disappearance of ethnic identity (and sometimes the disappearance of entire ethnic groups), brought about by a series of ideational changes among group members that lead them to mentally disassociate themselves from the group. In more general terms, changes in social organisation result in important changes in cultural identity. How might historical archaeologists investigate these important, related transformations?

The obvious answer derives from the unique ability of historical archaeologists to directly glean changing social and ideational patterns from **historical documents**. Written records of various kinds can reveal aspects of the human experience that are not easily recovered from the archaeological record; social and ideational trends are examples. Social trends, in the case of assimilation changes in primary relationships, are recorded in various archives reporting births, deaths, marriages and familial characteristics, among others (the Census is an obvious example). Ideational trends, more specifically, in this case, changes in ethnic group identification, are recorded in various documents revealing aspects of self-identification (diaries, letters and responses to questionnaire surveys, to name a few). Historical archaeologists depend upon such data to comprehend the total assimilation process.

We might not be limited to documents when investigating structural assimilation, however. Indeed, certain research suggests that patterns of structural assimilation might be difficult but not impossible to observe in patterns of material culture. It appears that the relevant social and ideational trends might correlate to other, patterned changes, such as economic trends, which leave more obvious traces in the material realm. Archaeologists should continue to explore the nature of this possible correlation, in order to enhance their contribution to scholarship.

Describing the assimilation process is only part of the equation, of course. There also remains the challenge of explaining why it occurs to varying degrees among different groups of people living under different circumstances. There is no scholarly consensus here. This inability to explain the patterns of assimilation might seem discouraging at times. It nevertheless also serves as a stimulus for more rigorous research from a wide variety of scholarly perspectives, including historical archaeology.

See also: acculturation; ethnicity; historical documents

Further reading

McGuire, R.H. (1982) 'The study of ethnicity in historical archaeology', *Journal of Anthropological Archaeology* 1: 159–78.

Staski, E. (1990) 'Studies of ethnicity in North American historical archaeology', *North American Archaeologist* 11(2): 121–45.

EDWARD STASKI

Audley End, England

P. J. Drury applied archaeological techniques to the standing buildings of Audley End in Essex. This research linked the phasing of the building's stratigraphy to documentary records, in keeping with one of the primary methods of historical archaeology.

King Henry VIII dissolved Walden Abbey (founded *c.* 1140), granting the property to his Lord Chancellor, Thomas Audley, in 1538. Audley converted the buildings into a courtyard house, on the site of the cloisters, dividing the church into three storeys. Thomas Howard, Lord Treasurer to James I and Earl of Suffolk, rebuilt the house *c.* 1605–16. The hall remained in the west range, with first-floor state apartments to the north and the south, and the earl and countess's apartments beneath. A long gallery occupied the east range, accessing the chapel and council chamber. The second phase of building (begun *c.* 1608) created a house fit to receive the royal court. Twin projecting porches were added to either end of the hall (providing separate access to the king and queen's apartments) and an outer court was built onto the west front to create a palatial appearance and accommodate the family during royal visits. James I thought Audley End 'too large for a king, but might do for a Lord Treasurer'.

In 1667, Charles II purchased the house, and occupied the 'queen's apartments' in the north range; the superior staircase to these apartments overrode their otherwise inferior position (at the low-end of the hall, overlooking the great kitchen). Charles's catholic queen converted the council chamber into her own chapel. After 1670, Audley End was rarely used as a royal palace and was sold back to the Suffolks in 1701.

The great kitchen and north and south ranges of the outer court were demolished by the architect John Vanbrugh (1708–13). The eighth Earl of Suffolk (inherited 1724) planned a formal garden within the outer court, and demolished the chapel and council chamber of the main house. After 1752, the Countess of Portsmouth demolished the east range (containing the outmoded Jacobean long gallery), creating a U-plan house. In the late eighteenth century, Robert Adam redesigned the interiors and Capability Brown landscaped the gardens. Lord Braybrook restored the Jacobean character of the house in *c.* 1825–30.

Excavation of a 1763 floor in the south wing revealed oak framing over shallow brick vaults (to control dampness), with a boarded floor designed to exaggerate the proportions of the Adam interior. Archaeological dating of the plasterwork has distinguished the original early seventeenth-century work from eighteenth–nineteenth century restoration.

See also: architecture; dating methods

Further reading

Drury, P. J. (1984) 'Joseph Rose Senior's site workshop at Audley End, Essex: Aspects of the development of decorative plasterwork technology in Britain during the eighteenth century', *The Antiquaries Journal* 64(1): 62–83.

—— (1982a) 'Walden Abbey into Audley End', in S.R. Bassett (ed.) *Saffron Walden: Excavations and Research 1972–80*, London: CBA Research Report 45, pp. 94–105.

—— (1982b) 'A mid eighteenth-century floor at Audley End', *Post-medieval Archaeology* 16: 125–40.

—— (1980) '"No other palace in the kingdom will compare with it": The evolution of Audley End, 1605–1745', *Architectural History* 23: 1–39.

ADRIAN GREEN

Australasia

In contemporary usage this term refers jointly to Australia and New Zealand. Meaning 'southern Asia', in the past it has been used broadly to encompass South-east Asia, including Papua New Guinea and Australia, and narrowly to include only the continent of Australia. It was first used by French explorers in the seventeenth century. In its present form it enjoyed widespread popularity in the late nineteenth and early twentieth centuries. This reflected what many believed were the shared destinies of Australia and New Zealand, and the possibility that New Zealand would join the Australian colonies when they federated in 1901. The term has been incorporated into the titles of many organisations with both Australian and New Zealand members. One of these is the **Australasian Society for Historical Archaeology** (ASHA), formerly the Australian Society for Historical Archaeology.

See also: Australia; New Zealand

SUSAN LAWRENCE

Australasian Society for Historical Archaeology

The Australasian Society for Historical Archaeology (ASHA) is an association of professional and avocational historical archaeologists primarily working in Australia and New Zealand, but with some membership outside of those countries. It aims to provide a forum for the discussion of relevant issues and current research, to promote the interests of historical archaeology and to encourage the dissemination of information about the material culture of the post-contact period in Australia and New Zealand. It began in Sydney in 1971 as the Australian Society for Historical Archaeology. The name was changed to 'Australasian' (see **Australasia**) in 1992 to reflect the increasing participation by members in New Zealand. The Society publishes a quarterly newsletter, a journal, *Australasian Historical Archaeology* (formerly *Australian Journal of Historical Archaeology*) and a series of special publications. It holds an annual conference, hosted each year by a different city in one of the two countries.

See also: Australia; New Zealand

SUSAN LAWRENCE

Australia

The post-contact history of Australia began with Dutch voyages of exploration in the seventeenth century and was followed much later by permanent British settlement at **Sydney** in 1788. In the last thirty years, terrestrial and maritime archaeologists have begun to investigate the material record of post-contact Australia and vital and dynamic fields of research have emerged. The archaeology of the post-contact period is typically called 'historical archaeology', although '**contact archaeology**' and '**Australian Aboriginal historical archaeology**' are terms used to describe the archaeology of Aboriginal people during the same period.

Substantial research began during the 1960s when a number of early colonial sites were investigated, including **Port Essington** in the Northern Territory and **Wybalenna** in Tasmania. In the same decade, sport divers in Western Australia discovered the wreck sites of **Dutch East India Company** (VOC) ships, among them the *Batavia* and the *Vergulde Draeck*, and maritime archaeology in Australia began. Researchers came from a number of different academic backgrounds, most notably prehistoric, classical and Near Eastern archaeology, history and geography. The wide-ranging and multidisciplinary nature of historical archaeology in Australia was thus established from the outset. In 1971, these efforts culminated in the formation of the Australian (now **Australasian) Society for Historical Archaeology**, while the Australian Institute of Maritime Archaeology formed in 1982.

Archaeological sites and artefacts are protected under both state and federal legislation. All states have heritage departments that administer the legislation, and most of these departments employ historical and maritime archaeologists. Federally, the Australian Heritage Commission maintains a register of nationally significant sites. Since the

1970s, historical archaeologists have been increasingly involved in cultural heritage management, and most archaeologists are employed in this area. Historical archaeology is taught at university level in all states and territories with the exception of Tasmania. Maritime archaeology is taught at Curtin University (Perth), Flinders University (Adelaide) and James Cook University (Townsville).

Theoretical perspectives

Early historical archaeology in Australia was strongly influenced by the traditions of British approaches to prehistory and by classical and Near Eastern archaeology. At the University of Sydney and the University of New England these departments became the institutional homes of the first historical archaeology courses taught. The discipline has been less influenced by anthropology than was the case in North American historical archaeology. Much emphasis has been (and continues to be) placed on excavation and site description, with considerably less attention given to material-culture studies or to broader interpretation. Historical geography, however, has been very influential, and landscape approaches have long been a staple.

Explicit theoretical stances were for the most part lacking in the first decades, but, beginning in the 1980s, debate on theoretical issues began to appear in the literature. Tim Murray and Jim Allen were important leaders here, while the 'Swiss Family Robinson' colonisation model proposed by Judy Birmingham and Dennis Jeans was perhaps the first attempt at large-scale integration and interpretation. Discussion of this model and of theoretical issues in urban archaeology, and attempts to articulate the general goals and approaches of Australian historical archaeology, were among the subjects canvassed and influenced by first processual, and then post-processual, debates elsewhere.

The influence of the anthropological orientation of North American historical archaeology began to be more apparent in the 1990s, when resistance theory was applied to the study of the Aboriginal historical archaeological site of Wybalenna and later to the **Ross Female Factory convict site**. Feminist and post-colonial theory has also been influential in shaping studies such as Jane Lydon's work on the Chinese in the **Rocks**, while Grace Karsken's work in the Rocks has been influenced by ethnographic history, as has Susan Lawrence's work on the **Dolly's Creek goldfield**. Heather Burke's analysis of architecture in Armidale, New South Wales, represents the most fully articulated application of Marxist theory yet seen in Australian historical archaeology.

Results

Archaeological research on convict life has produced many insights. The excavation of convict huts in Parramatta, New South Wales, provided evidence of some of the earliest European structures in the Sydney region. When the huts were built in the 1790s, small groups of convict men were housed in one-room wattle-and-daub structures located near their places of work, or in their own homes in neighbourhoods like the Rocks. By the 1820s, the colonial government was attempting to centralise accommodation, and built the four-storey brick Hyde Park Barracks in Sydney.

Excavations of the sub-floor deposits revealed clothing and personal artefacts used by the male convicts and their successors in the building, female migrants and office workers. Survey along the Great North Road, built by convicts in the 1820s to link Sydney and Newcastle, demonstrated the work practices of convict gangs with varying skill levels. Unskilled labourers were employed on the flat sections of the road, while more highly skilled convict masons and engineers were employed on the steep and winding grades through the mountains, where more complex construction methods were required. Outside of the Sydney region, work has been done on the convict accommodation at the Fremantle Gaol in Perth, Western Australia, on Norfolk Island, and on many sites in Tasmania. There, the largest and best-known site is Port Arthur, but work has also been done on smaller sites. Most research has emphasised male convicts, but recently historians and archaeologists have begun to explore the experiences of female convicts. The excavation of Ross Female Factory, Tasmania, is an important example of this work.

Research on pastoralism has ranged from the architecture and lifeways at big station houses such as those in New South Wales at Glen Innes, Winterbourn, and Kinchega, to the technology used in the pastoral industry and the conditions of labour. For example, Michael Pearson has documented the technology used in cleaning or 'scouring' the wool after shearing, which revolutionised the industry in the 1890s. Isolated shepherds' huts, such as that at Burghley, Tasmania, illustrate working conditions and conflict with Aboriginal people. On many outback stations Aboriginal people were forced into employment when their land was taken over. **Contact archaeology** is increasingly investigating this process, particularly in Western Australia, the Northern Territory and Queensland.

There has been a considerable amount of research done on the great houses of the elite in both rural and urban settings. Some of the earliest historical archaeology in Australia was at Elizabeth Farm, near Sydney, home of the MacArthur family, who were important figures in the introduction of merino sheep into Australia. Regentville, New South Wales, and Viewbank, near **Melbourne**, Victoria, were also homes of wealthy settlers. In Sydney, the **First Government House** site, home of the early colonial governors, provides the earliest evidence of building in the colonies, and also documents the lives of the governors' families and their servants.

The urban poor have also been the subject of research. Most work has been done in Sydney because of the extent of recent development there and the well-developed cultural heritage management industry. Sites such as Cumberland/Gloucester Streets and Cadman's Cottage in the Rocks, Pitt Street and Paddy's Market provide evidence from the earliest convict period through the rapid expansion of Sydney later in the nineteenth and twentieth centuries. In addition to convicts, these sites and others like them were often home to inner-city working people and non-English-speaking groups such as the Chinese. Infrastructure was equally important in the growth of Sydney, and archaeologists have documented the development of water and sewerage systems, rubbish collection and city parks. The excavation of part of the cemetery associated with the Randwick Destitute Children's Asylum has produced a wealth of data comparable to that of **Spitalfields** in England.

While less abundant elsewhere, urban sites in Melbourne, Hobart, Adelaide, Perth and Brisbane have also contributed to understandings of the archaeology of cities. At Little Lon in Melbourne, a collaboration between archaeologist Tim Murray and historian Alan Mayne has sought to explicitly challenge 'slum' stereotypes, and has resulted in reinterpretations of the kinship networks and shared material culture of a dynamic inner-city neighbourhood.

Industrial archaeology has long been a significant research area. There have been detailed studies of particular industries, such as salt production, flour milling and timber-getting, in addition to considerable work on the archaeology of **whaling**, mining (see **mining archaeology**) and pastoralism. The various branches of mining industry have together constituted the largest area of study. Australia has been a major minerals exporter since the 1840s, and extraction and processing sites have been recorded and in some cases excavated in every state and the Northern Territory. Hard-rock mining and its associated technology, including ore-crushing, roasting, and smelting complexes, have received the most attention, although there has also been some study of alluvial mining. The hard-rock studies have indicated the diversity of approaches used, and the adoption of expedient techniques and recycled equipment as a means of dealing with difficult local terrains and isolation. As Peter Bell has shown on the Palmer Goldfield in north Queensland, over-capitalisation was often the norm, and when the yields were insufficient to pay the incurred debts, machinery was abandoned on site, too expensive to remove. Like industrial archaeology in Britain, on which it is modelled, much of this research has been descriptive and atheoretical, and oriented towards technological rather than social questions. However, Kate Holmes's work at Arltunga, Northern Territory, and numerous studies of the Chinese on the goldfields are important examples of the social context of mining. The predilection for technological description has also been challenged by recent work such as Barry McGowan's use of landscape and community studies approaches in his research on the Shoalhaven goldfields in New South Wales, and by Lawrence's excavation of the settlement at Dolly's Creek, Victoria.

Until after the Second World War the vast majority of migration to Australia was from the UK, and as a result there has been limited investigation of the archaeology of minority groups. Important exceptions were the large numbers of Chinese men who participated in the nineteenth-century gold rush. Justin McCarthy and Peter Bell are among those who have done studies of Chinese goldfields camps. In most of this work the emphasis has been on identifying and describing traits of the Chinese community, but Jane Lydon's study of the Chinese merchants and labourers in Sydney's Rocks utilised material culture to explore the fluid process of identity creation and negotiation. The other large group of non-English-speaking migrants in nineteenth-century Australia were the German people who settled in the Barossa Valley region of South Australia in the 1840s. The distinctive landscape of village plans and architectural forms derived from Germany has been documented by Gordon Young.

Aboriginal contact archaeology began as the study of European missions that were established in order to assimilate Aboriginal people into white Australian culture. Judy Birmingham's work at Wybalenna was the earliest work on missions. In the 1990s, research broadened to include a variety of post-contact sites, from traditional rock shelters and shell middens containing artefacts of European origin, to sites such as Burghley, Tasmania, abandoned by English-speaking shepherds but reoccupied by Aboriginal people, to pastoral stations where Aboriginal men worked as stockmen and Aboriginal women worked as housemaids, cooks and nannies. Much of the work on pastoral stations and later mission sites has been done in collaboration with Aboriginal communities and has incorporated oral history as a fundamental aspect of the research. This has led to more complex interpretations of the sites, and of the continuities manifested within contemporary Aboriginal culture.

See also: Melbourne; Rocks, the; Sydney; Tasmania

Further reading

Birmingham, J., Bairstow, D. and Wilson, A. (eds) (1988) *Archaeology and Colonisation: Australia in the World Context*, Sydney: Australian Society for Historical Archaeology.

Birmingham, J., Jack, R.I. and Jeans, D.N. (1979) *Australian Pioneer Technology: Sites and Relics*, Richmond, Victoria: Heinemann.

Burke, H. (1999) *Meaning and Ideology in Historical Archaeology: Style, Social Identity, and Capitalism in an Australian Town*, New York: Kluwer Academic/Plenum Press.

Connah, G. (1988, 1993) *The Archaeology of Australia's History*, Cambridge: Cambridge University Press.

Karskens, G. (1999) *Inside the Rocks: The Archaeology of a Neighbourhood*, Sydney: Hale and Iremonger.

Lawrence, S. (2000) *Dolly's Creek: An Archaeology of a Victorian Goldfield Community*, Melbourne: Melbourne University Press.

Lydon, J. (1999) *'Many Inventions': Historical Archaeology and the Chinese on the Rocks, Sydney, 1890–1930*, Melbourne: Monash Publications in History.

SUSAN LAWRENCE

Australian Aboriginal historical archaeology

The antiquity of Australian Aboriginal occupation of the Australian continent extends beyond 50,000 years BP, and much archaeological inquiry is directed towards the timing and organisation of ancient Aboriginal society. Another important research area for archaeologists is more recent Aboriginal life, particularly interactions between Aboriginal and non-Aboriginal peoples. The historical archaeology of Aboriginal Australia studies the interactions between indigenes and European settlers and how and why Aboriginal people came to be involved in (or not, as the case may be) colonial society.

Early encounters between predominantly Dutch and English explorers and Australian Aboriginal people began in 1606 at Cape Keerweer between the crew of Willem Jansz's *Duyfken* and Torres Strait Aboriginal people (it is conjectured yet unproven whether the highly secretive Portuguese crews had visited Australia in the 1500s). During the seventeenth and eighteenth centuries, crews of exploring

Dutch, Spanish, French and English vessels, including occasional shipwreck survivors, encountered Aboriginal people. European colonisation of the continent eventually followed with the English penal settlement at Botany Bay in 1788.

In the western Torres Strait Islands, interaction between people of northern Cape York Peninsula and Papua New Guinea – separated by 90 miles of water – had already forged a distinctive Torres Strait Islander society. Cultural practice and belief, and items of material culture such as outrigger dugout canoes suggest interaction between Melanesian and Cape York Peninsula Aboriginal peoples.

Other encounters between Aboriginal Australians and outsiders may have preceded European arrival. Seasonal visitors from eastern Indonesia – commonly from Macassar (Udjung Pandang) in southern Sulawesi – would sail praus on the monsoon to northern Australia, and return to Indonesia with the south-east trade winds. Remains of Macassan camps across northern Australia, especially Arnhem Land and offshore islands, are testimony to the commercial processing of trepang (sea cucumber), highly valued by the Chinese. Archaeological evidence for trepang processing sites includes stone bases for hearths in which large cauldrons boiled the trepang following harvesting from shallow coastal waters. Rattan matting and structural remains reveal wooden smokehouses. Pottery and glass artefacts litter the village sites where Aboriginal people interacted with the Macassans, often trading turtle shell, cypress pine timber and bull horn (after the European introduction of that species) with the visitors for metal hatchets and knives, glass, tobacco, alcohol and foreign foods, such as rice. The Australian government banned Macassan traffic in 1906, yet Macassan influence in Aboriginal society is seen in art, language and stories.

The British colonists spreading out from early settlements such as Sydney and Hobart encountered Aboriginal nations. The variety of indigenous societies revealed a range of human adaptations to environment and the diversity of Aboriginal languages and culture.

European settlement was at first largely focused in south-eastern Australia, then at remote settlements which would eventually become regional capitals such as Adelaide, Melbourne, Perth and Brisbane. The occupation of the more remote and semi-arid regions, away from the coast and Murray-Darling river system of eastern Australia, would follow almost a century after the settlement at Botany Bay. In general terms, Aboriginal people close to modern regional capitals and in south-eastern Australia inevitably suffered a greater disturbance to traditional life than in more remote and later colonised regions, yet throughout Australia the results of European colonisation have had grim consequences for Aboriginal peoples. One of the challenges for historical archaeology in Australia is to interpret the continent-wide transformation from hunter-gatherer to capitalist settler societies, and the resulting social, physical, economic and environmental indicators of this transition.

The study of mission settlements and government institutions is a significant area of archaeological research into Aboriginal society. Missions were a corollary to colonisation, and the organisation and success of missions is an important research issue. As an example, the short-lived **Wybalenna** Mission on windswept Flinders Island in the Bass Strait (1833–47) represents a sad chapter in the history of Tasmanian Aboriginal people. The residents, who represented most of the last full-blooded Tasmanian Aboriginals, had been persuaded to leave Tasmania by George Augustus Robinson – an evangelical colonist who travelled among the remote Tasmanian communities between 1827 and 1832. Archaeological excavations of the mission provide an important insight into the settlement. Robinson's journals as Wybalenna's Commandant and historic images of the settlement describe a transplanted British ideological system and an ordered lifestyle, emphasising how Aboriginal people benefited from church attendance, work and educational programmes. The archaeological record indicates ways in which the Tasmanians accommodated British ideology and goods while at the same time maintaining aspects of their own society. Analyses of faunal records indicate the maintenance of hunting for traditional food sources. The spatial distribution of artefacts – clay pipes, marbles, food refuse, **bottles**, clothing parts – and evidence for dogs suggest the differential resistance to Europeanising activities such as cleaning and dietary regimes.

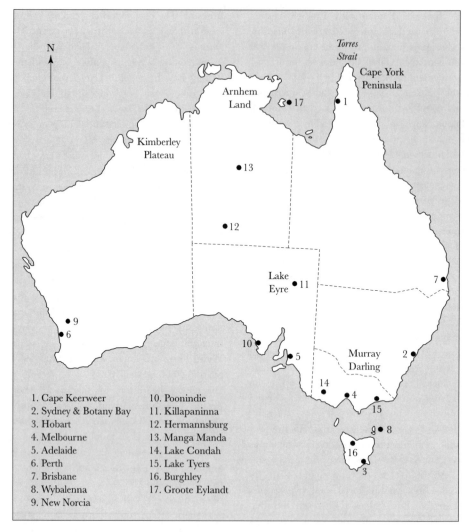

Figure 6 Australian locations referred to in text
Source: A. Paterson

Other missions throughout Australia have been the subject of analysis including: a Benedictine New Norcia Mission in Western Australia (1846 onwards), the Poonindie Native Institution (1885–94) on Eyre Peninsula in South Australia, Lutheran Killapaninna Mission (Bethesda) on Cooper Creek in Central Australia (1865–1914), Hermannsburg Lutheran Mission (1877–1982) near Alice Springs and Manga Manda (1945–55) in the Northern Territory. Also, in Victoria Lake, Condah, Ebenezer, Coranderrk and Lake Tyers communities

provide insight into Aboriginal and European interaction.

Resistance to the Europeans, and European practices, was more extreme in certain contexts. Archaeological evidence for warfare and resistance has been very difficult to obtain, and this is an area for future research. It is clear that in some places in colonial Australia European settlers met Aboriginal resistance and Aboriginal people suffered atrociously because of Europeans. Another important issue is the introduction of pathogens following

European arrival, which, like elsewhere in the world, caused some depopulation and spread of sicknesses among people with little natural resistance to new diseases.

Studies of places of interaction between Aboriginal people and others provide an understanding into the shared history of colonial Australia, much of which is unrecorded in documentary sources. At Burghley, a small cottage in the hills of north-western Tasmania, archaeological excavation of a stock camp established by the Van Dieman Land Company during the 1820s revealed Tasmanian Aboriginal occupation of the cottage after its abandonment by European shepherds, at a time characterised by massive upheaval in Tasmanian Aboriginal society. In such studies a range of different evidence – in this case stone and glass tools, eyewitness accounts and documentary sources – is used to provide a synthetic analysis.

Some regional approaches to archaeological investigations have explained cultural interaction in terms of longer trajectories of cultural transformation. For example, on Groote Eylandt in Northern Australia Aboriginal life since European arrival is studied in relation to longer archaeological records extending throughout the Holocene and Pleistocene. In the Kimberley region of northern Western Australia archaeologists study how evidence of recent cultural behaviour such as trading routes, settlement patterns or religious belief may have far more ancient precedents. These are stories of continuity of practice and attachment to place during the great disruption accompanying the arrival of Europeans.

Historical archaeology chronicles the role of Aboriginal people in colonial society, challenging the perception that pioneering was the exclusive achievement of European settlers. This is apparent when considering the pastoral industry, which has been an important economic activity in Australia since early European settlement. Research into the organisation of pastoralism is now indicating how, in certain contexts, Aboriginal peoples contributed labour and knowledge that were essential for the inception and survival of industry. In places such as the Lake Eyre Basin in Central Australia, there is evidence that the pastoral system sometimes formed an essentially stable domain with co-operation between some Aboriginal people and pastoralists.

The results were mutual: the pastoralists had access to an inexpensive labour pool, and were keyed into a much wider network of knowledge regarding available resources in the environment. Aboriginal people were provided with a colonial-period enclave, in which they had access to rations (food, tobacco and clothes) and opportunities to maintain connections with country and members of Aboriginal society outside of the pastoral domain. This is an ongoing story and in contemporary Australia many Aboriginal people remember pastoral work proudly. The evidence of campsites, outstations and work sites documents a period during which elements of Aboriginal attachment to land in colonial contexts was negotiated and redefined.

An important issue for archaeologists has been how to identify material expressions of Aboriginal practice in the historic period. Certain elements of hunter-gatherer life continue into the historic period, but with access to new materials. Examples of such continuity are glass, flaked tools. Aboriginal people throughout Australia have been making tools from a range of material for millennia. Following European arrival Aboriginal people made flaked tools using glass and ceramics, most commonly from bottles. Research into these artefacts has identified reduction sequences, consisting of quarrying, primary and secondary reduction, and use. In a similar fashion archaeologists are learning how mundane items from everyday life such as metal tools, food cans, toys and clothing (to name some examples) have been employed in Aboriginal society.

Increasingly, a range of Aboriginal historic places are being recognised, interpreted and protected for future generations. This is an essential part of the contemporary construction of identity that is important to Australian Aboriginal peoples and other parts of Australian society.

Australia as a nation is currently tackling indigenous rights to land and self-determination, and our understanding of colonial interaction has implications for these issues. Studies of cultural interaction realise the potential of historical archaeology to bridge gaps in knowledge concerning the histories of both literate *and* non-literate people in the historic period.

See also: Australia; Tasmania

Further reading

Birmingham, J. (1992) *Wybalenna: The Archaeology of Cultural Accommodation in Nineteenth Century Tasmania*, Sydney: Australian Society for Historical Archaeology.

Clarke, A. (2001) 'Time, tradition and transformation: The negotiation of cross-cultural engagements on Groote Eylandt, northern Australia', in R. Torrence and A. Clarke (eds) *The Archaeology of Difference: Negotiating Cross-cultural Engagements in Oceania*, London: Routledge, pp. 142–81.

Harrison, R. (2000) '"Nowadays with glass": Regional variation in Aboriginal bottle glass artefacts from Western Australia', *Archaeology in Oceania* 35: 34–47.

Head, L. and Fullagar, R. (1997) 'Hunter-gatherer archaeology and pastoral contact: Perspectives from northwest Northern Territory, Australia', *World Archaeology* 28: 418–28.

Macknight, C. (1972) 'Macassans and Aborigines', *Oceania* 42: 283–321.

Mulvaney, D. J. (1989) *Encounters in Place: Outsiders and Aboriginal Australians, 1606–1985*, Brisbane: University of Queensland Press.

Murry, T. (1993) 'The childhood of William Lanne: Contact archaeology and Aboriginality in Tasmania', *Antiquity* 67: 504–19.

Paterson, A. (2000) 'Situating belonging: The role of historical archaeology in locating cultural relationships using examples from Australian pastoral domains', *Balayi: Culture, Law and Colonialism* 2: pp. 109–31.

ALISTAIR PATERSON

Aztec archaeology

Aztec archaeology includes the pre-contact period of the Basin of Mexico from the fall of Tula around AD 1150–1200 until the arrival of the Spaniards in AD 1519 and the conquest of the Aztecs in AD 1521. It also includes the post-conquest cultural and demographic continuities until AD 1620–50, by which time the indigenous population had decreased to about 10 per cent of the pre-conquest total, had been relocated into a few centres and had been integrated into the lowest level of the Hispanic world-wide Empire in New Spain.

The Aztecs, Mexica or Tenochca of Tenochtitlan, in AD 1519, were the dominant power of a Triple Alliance that included the Tepaneca of Tlacopan and the Acolhua of Texcoco. Together these three city-states controlled substantial regions of central and southern Mesoamerica as a tributary empire. The Aztecs, however, were only one of several Nahuatl-speaking migrating ethnic groups mentioned in pre-conquest historical documents, and in accounts set down after the conquest as entering the Basin of Mexico during the first century after the collapse of Tula. Here I extend the term 'Aztec' to include all peoples in the Basin of Mexico following the demise of Tula, associated with specific Aztec ceramic complexes, but not all being ethnic Aztecs. An alternative term to use would be 'Nahuas'.

Although native historians are of use in reconstructing dynastic and migratory historical sequences, there are difficulties in correlating them directly with archaeological data. Such correlations that have been attempted usually try to link historically reconstructed pre-conquest cultural developments with archaeological data, with varying degrees of success.

Based on archaeology alone, there are two major Aztec pre-conquest periods in the Basin of Mexico, Early Aztec (AD 1150/1200–1428) and Late Aztec (or AD 1428–1519/1521) (Charlton 2000). Using historical data there are three distinct sub-periods within the Early Aztec period. These sub-periods are:

1 AD 1150/1200–1250, Migrations	Before and After the Collapse of Tula;
2 AD 1250–1350	City-State Consolidation: Limited Warfare; and
3 AD 1350–1428	Initial Expansionist Policy: Petty States on a Grander Scale.

They complement the Early Aztec period archaeological data.

Although it is not possible to identify migrating peoples archaeologically, the lack of continuity in settlement location suggests that intrusive new populations did appear. It is possible to define a situation of small, conflict-prone city-states, succeeded by large conflict-prone city-states, ultimately ending in the two major tributary states, that of the Acolhua on the east and that of the Tepaneca on the west side of the Basin. The Tepaneca took control of the entire Basin towards the end of the period. The settlement patterns described for the Early Aztec period correspond well with the political situation historically described for the end of the period.

During the period, political fragmentation was associated with local production of ceramics (Aztec I and II) but the import and general distribution of non-local goods, such as obsidian and cotton, indicated economic integration. Solar market systems probably functioned to move goods with city-states or confederacies of city-states, and were linked with other systems whereby regionally restricted goods were put into general circulation.

Once the Tepaneca had conquered the Acolhua (AD 1418) there was a falling-out with their reliable and increasingly more powerful tributary, the Tenochca of Tenochtitlan. This, coupled with a succession crisis among the Tepaneca, led to the Tenochca's conquest of the Tepaneca in alliance with Tepaneca from Tlacopan and the Acolhua of Texcoco, forming the Triple Alliance. This conquest formed the basis for the final pre-conquest period, AD 1428–1519: Triple Alliance Imperial Expansion.

This was accomplished in part by the direct access of the nobles to lands taken from Azcapotzalco and the reorganisation of the succession to leadership, making it more stable. Impressive archaeological data are available for this period in the Basin of Mexico including chinampa excavations, rural households, regional adaptations, craft production, irrigation systems, elite residential areas and the urban centres of Tenochtitlan and Tlatelolco. The associated ceramic complex is Aztec III. Linked with this period is a major population growth from c. 250,000 to between 800,000 and 1,200,000, with Tenochtitlan–Tlatelolco being an urban complex of 200,000 people and the top of the Mesoamerican world system.

The Early Colonial period in the Basin of Mexico began with the military conquest of Tenochtitlan in AD 1521 and ended with the *Congregaciones* ordered in AD 1603 and substantially implemented by AD 1620. During the same time, the indigenous population declined due to the introduction of exotic European diseases against which resistance was virtually non-existent. The reduction in numbers of tributaries was instrumental in the development of the *Congregaciones* to relocate the remaining population into fewer centres, where church and civil authorities could control them. At the same time, the Basin of Mexico became reoriented economically and politically from being the top of the Mesoamerican world system to being a lower-level node within the Hispanic world-wide imperial system centred on Madrid and encompassing the globe. Material culture changes are few in rural areas and more pronounced in the urban zones where most Spaniards lived.

See also: Mexico City; Spanish colonialism; world(-)systems theory

Further reading

Charlton, T.H. (2000) 'The Aztecs and their contemporaries: The central and eastern Mexican Highlands', in R.E.W. Adams and M.J. MacLeod (eds) *The Cambridge History of the Native Peoples of the Americas, Volume II, Mesoamerica, Part 1*, New York: Cambridge University Press, pp. 500–41.

—— (1986) 'Socioeconomic dimensions of urban–rural relations in the colonial period Basin of Mexico', in R. Spores and P.A. Andrews (eds) *Handbook of Middle American Indians, Supplement 4, Ethnohistory*, Austin: University of Texas Press, pp. 122–33.

Sanders, W.T., Parsons, J.R. and Santley, R.S. (1979) *The Basin of Mexico*, New York: Academic Press.

Smith, M.E. (1984) 'The Aztlan migrations of the Nahuatl Chronicles: Myth or history?', *Ethnohistory* 31: 153–86.

Vaillant, G.C. (1938) 'A correlation of archaeological and historical sequences in the Valley of Mexico', *American Anthropologist* 40: 535–73.

THOMAS H. CHARLTON

B

backyard archaeology

Backyard archaeology does not refer to casual digging by avocational archaeologists. It was a term coined by the late Charles Fairbanks in 1976 at the seventeenth annual **Conference on Historic Site Archaeology**. Backyard archaeology refers to the subject matter of historical archaeology: an investigation of the everyday life of average individuals.

Though historical archaeology has only really functioned as a recognised sub-discipline since the 1960s, it has followed the same recent general trends observed in archaeology. It was during the 1960s that a paradigm shift occurred in archaeology where questions concerning cultural processes replaced the descriptive, particularistic work that preceded it. Historical archaeology under the leadership of Stanley South adopted an explicitly scientific approach that differed from the humanistic approach characterised by the work of Ivor Noël Hume, the first archaeologist at Colonial Williamsburg, Virginia, USA. Debates raged as to whether the rightful home of historical archaeology was in departments of history or anthropology. The subject matter seemed historical, yet most archaeologists had received their training in anthropology. It was out of this milieu that 'backyard archaeology' was conceived.

Historical archaeology had initially focused on architectural questions and functioned primarily as an aid to the reconstruction of historic structures. Most of these structures were associated with the rich and famous individuals of the past. Historical archaeology was, essentially, a 'handmaiden to

history', providing anecdotal information to augment the historical record.

The rise of **processual archaeology** and the embracement of historical archaeology by the rest of the archaeological profession shifted the research focus from reconstructing past lifeways (though this has never been truly abandoned) to understanding how those past lifeways came to be by studying such cultural processes as **acculturation** and sociopolitical class formation (see **class, social**).

Charles Fairbanks, one of the pioneers of historical archaeology, embraced the **New Archaeology** for his own research agenda. As he put it, the conduct of historical archaeology largely followed the lead of prehistoric archaeology by turning away from a preoccupation with the monumental remains of the past and towards the examination of the commonplace. Fairbanks believed that historical archaeologists should investigate commonplace remains, such as trash dumps.

Fairbanks's own research concerned the Spanish colonial period in Florida. He noted that, since most of the activity in Spanish colonial households took place in the rear portions of the lots in patios or open areas, it was inevitable that excavations there would reveal more about household activities than would excavations of the structure itself. Only by excavating the areas of activity adjacent to the houses would archaeologists recover the sorts of information sought by anthropologists – about subsistence, status, ethnicity and acculturation. Hence his term 'backyard archaeology' was born. He not only applied this strategy to his own work but later to his students who carried on his approach in their work in **St Augustine** and on slave-holding plantations in Florida and Georgia.

The term 'backyard archaeology' has come to signify the shift in historical archaeology from an historical orientation to one more concerned with answering anthropological questions. This shift is very evident in the types of projects which historical archaeologists undertook and the literature they produced. On plantations (see **plantation archaeology**), the focus shifted from the gentry in the owners' mansions to slave cabins and their occupants. In urban settings, investigations of colonial governors' palaces and military **fortifications** began to share journal space with studies of middle-class houses and factories. A preoccupation with the chronological context of artefacts gave way to a concern with their behavioural context. Thus, historical archaeology was redefined.

The perception of historical archaeology, both in the profession of archaeology and among the general public, shifted from 'the most expensive way to find out about something we already know' to a realisation that history was mostly about the lifestyles of people not like us, and that archaeology provides the only way to learn about the lives of common men and women. Specifically, the backyard approach to historical archaeology fills gaps in the historical record. It studies what most of the people were doing most of the time. It corrects errors in the historical record, such as errors in perception (there is a camp in social science that claims there is no objective reality), sins of omission and flat-out lies. It can test archaeological concepts. Work on documented sites can establish patterns that can help us understand undocumented sites (e.g. social stratification (see **stratification, social**), site function and seriation). Taking an anthropological perspective, the backyard approach investigates *why* things happen. History tends to focus on *what* happened, *when* it happened and *who* did it. What seem like the obvious questions that current students of historical archaeology are taught to ask were actually an innovation in the mid-1970s.

See also: behavioural historical archaeology; history of historical archaeology; Spanish colonialism

Further reading

Cleland, C.E. (ed.) (1993) 'The Society for Historical Archaeology and its first twenty-five years', *Historical Archaeology* 27(1): 3–43.

Fairbanks, C.H. (1983) 'Historical archaeological implications of recent investigations', in R. Newman (ed.) *Geoscience and Man*, Baton Rouge: Louisiana State University School of Geoscience, pp. 17–26.

—— (1977) 'Backyard archaeology as research strategy', *The Conference on Historic Site Archaeology Papers 1976* 11: 133–9.

Johnson, K., Leader, J. and Wilson, R. (eds) (1985) *Indians, Colonists and Slaves: Essays in Memory of Charles H. Fairbanks*, Florida Journal of Anthropology Special Publication No. 4, Gainesville: University of Florida.

Schuyler, R. (ed.) (1978) *Historical Archaeology: A Guide to the Substantive and Theoretical Contributions*, Farmingdale, NY: Baywood.

CHARLES R. EWEN

Basing House, England

The ruins of Basing House in Hampshire, site of the longest siege of the English Civil War, have been extensively excavated since the nineteenth century. Roman and Saxon remains indicate a Roman site possibly succeeded by a manorial property. In the eleventh century, a Norman castle was constructed. Basing House was extensively rebuilt in the sixteenth century by William Paulet, Marquess of Winchester. The 'Old House' was constructed in brick around 1532 on medieval foundations within the earthworks of the circular castle enclosure, entered through a double gatehouse with corner towers, on the foundations of a medieval gateway. Around 1560, the more magnificent 'New House' (reputedly with 380 rooms) was built to the east, again of brick, around a courtyard. The Marquesses of Winchester were prominent courtiers under the Tudor and Stuart monarchs and Basing House was an important royalist stronghold during the English Civil War (1642–8).

Repeatedly under siege between 1643 and 1645 (earthwork defences survive to the south), Basing House witnessed some of the most brutal fighting of the war. A decapitated skull with a sword cut on its crown, recovered from the postern gate connecting the Old and New Houses, is regarded as testimony to the violence of Oliver Cromwell's successful assault in October 1645. The brick mansion was severely damaged in 1645 and parliament subsequently encouraged the removal of building materials to erase this monument to royalist resistance. Sixteenth-century brick was reused in the **vernacular architecture** of Basing village.

After the Restoration of the monarchy in 1660, the Paulet family commemorated their loyalty to the king by creating a garden in the ruins of the house and erecting a separate mansion to the north (known as 'the Grange' or 'New Place'). The site of Basing House was landscaped, making good the 6 m high earthwork bank and ditch around the circular citadel, and creating a parterre on the site of the Old House reached by brick steps on the site of the citadel gateway. Celia Fiennes observed the vineyard and park in the 1690s. Two pairs of late seventeenth-century gate piers (with very fine moulded brickwork) indicate the location of the New Place, next to the surviving early sixteenth-century brick Great Barn.

Between 1875 and 1908, Lord Bolton sought to uncover the plan of the Old and New Houses, and Sir Charles Peers reported on these excavations in 1909. Stephen Moorhouse published the finds in 1970–1 (mainly seventeenth-century finds, mostly redeposited after the Civil War). David Allen has provided a full report on excavations undertaken since 1978 and summarises the earlier excavations.

Further reading

Allen, D. and Anderson, S. (1999) *Basing House, Hampshire: Excavations 1978–1991*, Hampshire Field Club and Archaeological Society Monograph 10.

Moorhouse, S. (1971) 'Finds from Basing House, Hampshire c1540–1645: Part 2', *Post-medieval Archaeology* 5: 35–76.

—— (1970) 'Finds from Basing House, Hampshire c1540–1645: Part 1', *Post-medieval Archaeology* 4: 31–91.

Peers, C.R. (1909) 'On the excavation of the site of Basing House, Hampshire', *Archaeologia* 61(2): 553–64.

ADRIAN GREEN

Battle of the Little Bighorn, Montana, USA

The date 25 June marks the anniversary of the Battle of the Little Bighorn, the anniversary of the day George Armstrong Custer led approximately 210 men to their deaths in the Montana wilderness. Since that day, the story of Custer and the Battle of the Little Bighorn has assumed legendary, if not mythological, proportions in US culture.

The battle epitomises the clash of cultures – the Native American (see **Native Americans**) and the Euro-American – that is so much a part of US heritage. These two cultural systems clashed in terms of hundreds of ideological and practical concepts – in ideas of land ownership, treaties and boundaries, leadership structure, even concepts of how to fight a war. At the Battle of the Little Bighorn, these cultural differences produced a conflagration that has illuminated the distinction between Native Americans and the non-Indian, US public from 1876 to the present.

A literal conflagration in August 1983 produced an opportunity to examine the battlefield in a new way when a wildfire scorched the Little Bighorn Battlefield National Monument, administered by the US National Park Service. Recently, a series of multidisciplinary studies have combined to provide fresh interpretations of the battle and its significance in US history. Archaeological investigations have used physical evidence – artefacts – to interpret specific elements of the battle. In turn, the archaeological studies spurred historians and other researchers to re-evaluate the documentary record, Native American oral tradition and ethnohistorical accounts.

The results of this combined study provide a significant reinterpretation of the battle events. Some of the reinterpretation is particularistic in nature, literally following combatant movements across the field or revealing physical evidence that, when combined with oral tradition, identifies the site and occupants of a previously unknown Lakota camp circle on the west side of the Little Bighorn River. Other elements allow a broader re-evaluation of the events.

In an attempt to make the battlefield speak for itself, archaeological procedures were applied during the summers of 1984, 1985, 1989, 1993, 1994 and 1996. This programme of investigation has resulted in the accumulation of over 5,000 artefacts, and much new data on the battle. The multidisciplinary work clearly demonstrates that Custer divided the Seventh Cavalry into three elements during the early phases of the battle and then sub-divided his immediate command into wings. This division of his troops in the face of an overwhelming number of Native Americans may not have been his best decision, but it was an accepted and field-tested military tactic that was successful until this battle.

The Lakota and Cheyenne warriors, although surprised by the army's attack, quickly rallied and put all elements of the Seventh Cavalry's attack on the defensive. The Native Americans fought in a prescribed cultural manner as is demonstrated both by the oral tradition and the physical evidence. Ramifications of the event aside, it is clear from the newly reinterpreted multidisciplinary sources that the Lakota and Cheyenne warriors outnumbered, outgunned and outfought the soldiers of the Seventh Cavalry, giving the army its worst defeat of the entire Indian Wars.

The project archaeologists chose to view the battlefield as a crime scene and, by using a combination of forensic techniques such as studies of firing-pin marks on cartridge cases and rifling marks on bullets, and standard archaeological field, laboratory and analytical techniques, they have been able to determine the variety of weapons used by the various participants. By combining crime lab methods with the archaeological constructs of spatial patterning and individual-artefact analysis, they have been able to discover evidence for the movement of individual firearms over the field of battle, verify cavalry positions and define previously unknown Native American fighting areas. Forensic studies on the human skeletal remains have revealed information about the wounds the men received, as well as their general health and condition at the time of death.

Human remains consistent with those of a minimum of forty-four individuals were uncovered during the archaeological investigations. The combination of skeletal and artefactual material reveals some of the most poignant pictures of the battle. The examinations revealed that the men had poor dental health as a rule, although one man had several gold and tin fillings, indicating that the quality of dental care available in the 1870s was generally good when people went to the dentist. The soldiers' teeth also revealed the widespread use of coffee and tobacco. Other skeletal elements demonstrate broken bones, as well as significant back problems. The bones demonstrate that these men led a rugged life, certainly not the romantic one so often portrayed in books and on film.

See also: battlefield archaeology

Further reading

Fox, R.A., Jr (1993) *Archaeology, History, and Custer's Last Battle: The Little Big Horn Reexamined*, Norman: University of Oklahoma Press.

Scott, D.D. (ed.) (1991) *Papers on Little Bighorn Battlefield Archaeology: The Equipment Dump, Marker 7, and the Reno Crossing*, Lincoln, NB: J & L Reprint Company.

Scott, D.D., Fox, R.A., Jr, Connor, M.A. and Harmon, D. (1989) *Archaeological Perspectives on the Battle of the Little Bighorn*, Norman: University of Oklahoma Press.

DOUGLAS D. SCOTT

battlefield archaeology

The term 'battlefield archaeology' refers specifically to the investigation of sites associated with military operations. The study of military and battlefield sites can provide an important means of analysing the behavioural patterns and cultural expressions of status of a society. Because military sites are easily defined archaeologically, and are usually relatively compact social, cultural and physical units, they are ideal for intensive survey and excavation. The archaeological analysis of military sites can also offer unique perspectives on the behavioural aspects of cultures in conflict.

Military sites, particularly forts and **fortifications**, have long been of interest to historical archaeologists. There is a plethora of published site reports detailing the results of investigations at military sites. The investigations have often been conducted as ancillary studies to preservation, restoration, **reconstruction** or interpretation efforts of local, state or national agencies. Recently, another type of military site, the battlefield, has become the subject of archaeological investigations.

While the archaeological investigation of battlefield sites was once considered useful only for locating the opposing armies' cannon positions or recovering war relics for museum displays, recent battlefield archaeology at sites dating from the mid-1600s to the late nineteenth century has demonstrated a far wider usefulness of battlefield archaeology.

Battlefield research

Until recently, battlefield archaeology concentrated on uncovering or tracing fortifications, particularly earthworks. Archaeological investigations by Lee Hanson in 1968 of the US Civil War Water Battery at Fort Donnelson, Tennessee, USA, was oriented towards the identification of gun emplacements, including determining what type of guns were placed at each embrasure. Another US Civil War earthwork, at Causton's Bluff, Georgia, revealed, through archaeological work by Lawrence Babits in 1986, otherwise unknown details of the construction of bomb-proof shelters.

The first intensive archaeological study of an open battlefield site took place from 1985 to 1996 at the Little Bighorn Battlefield National Monument in south-eastern Montana, USA. The site yielded thousands of cartridge cases, bullets, army equipment, clothing fragments, Sioux and Cheyenne artefacts, and some skeletal remains of the soldiers who died on 25 June 1876. The computer-assisted analysis of the distribution of artefacts on the battlefield yielded information about how the combatant groups utilised the terrain. Firearms identification analysis (see below) of thousands of recovered bullets added substantial knowledge about the role of firearms in the battle. The archaeological investigations demonstrated in con-

siderable detail how George Custer's Seventh Cavalry was outnumbered, outgunned and outfought by Native American adversaries.

Since the completion of the Little Bighorn investigations, several other battlefield sites have been studied using metal-detecting techniques (see **metal detectors**) and artefact-patterning analysis. Sites studied include the English Civil War site of Naseby investigated by Glenn Foard. Charles Hacker's 1993 investigations of the 1846 Mexican–American War site of Palo Alto, Texas, succeeded in finding the battlefield, which was believed lost, and he definitively located both US and Mexican troop battle lines. His findings have modified the traditionally held historical view of a Mexican rout, with the archaeological data clearly showing it was a pitched battle with extensive movement by the Mexican troops. The defeated Mexican army left behind a wealth of uniform and equipment artefacts that archaeologically demonstrate a valiant fight by a poorly armed and badly equipped army facing a much better equipped and armed US Army.

Several US Civil War battlefields have also been investigated with the metal-detecting technique. William Lees has completed the most intensive studies to date. One of his projects was located at the Honey Springs, Oklahoma, battle (1863) that pitted Federal African American, Native American and white troops against Confederate Native American and white troops. A second project occurred at Mine Creek, Kansas, the site of an 1864 battle during Confederate general Sterling Price's raid into Missouri. The Mine Creek investigations show that historians have incorrectly identified the battle site. Lees's work defined much of the actual battle site and determined positions and movement of both combatant groups, which was unrecorded or poorly documented in the historical record. Another US Civil War battle site, recently investigated by Douglas D. Scott, is Monroe's Crossroads, North Carolina. Because this 1865 cavalry battle is little recorded in the historical record, archaeological investigation was the primary means to recover the site's history. The battle site, located within the boundaries of modern-day Fort Bragg, is used by the US Army for small-unit leadership training exercises. Other US Civil War battlefields are under investigation by Stephen

Potter and Clarence Geier at Manassas, Virginia, and Anteitam, Maryland.

Aside from the Little Bighorn, other US Indian War battlefields have also been investigated. Douglas D. Scott studied the 1877 Nez Perce War battle site of Big Hole, Montana. Archaeology there revealed information that supported Nez Perce **oral history** and interpretation of the battle events, and demonstrated that the US Army battle accounts were somewhat exaggerated. Several other US Army posts in Texas, Arizona, and New Mexico are currently undergoing multiphased investigations by various researchers.

Battlefield theory

Because of the structured and ranked nature of military forces, battlefields have proved to be excellent locales for finding archaeologically definable behavioural patterns. Those who engage in combat usually fight in the established manners and patterns in which they have been trained. It is precisely this training in battlefield or combat behaviour that results in the deposition of artefacts that can be recovered by archaeological means and interpreted with an anthropological perspective.

Although interest in behavioural dynamics is not new in historical archaeology, battlefield archaeology is a relatively new area of study. The battlefield model developed by Richard Fox and Douglas Scott (1991) asserts that individual, unit and battlefield movements can be reconstructed using pattern-recognition techniques. The model also predicts certain types of depositional patterns depending on the culture, training and organisation of the combatant groups.

Battlefield studies can yield information on combatant positions used during the course of the battle as well as details of dress, equipage and, in some cases, individual movements. Archaeological investigations can also retrieve information on troop deployments, firing positions, fields of fire and the types of weapons present. Studies of artefact patterning can also reveal unit or individual movement during the battle, weapon trajectory and range of firing by determining forces of projectile impact. Viewed in an anthropological

context, battlefields are the physical and violent expression of the culture or cultures in conflict.

Battlefield recovery and analytical techniques

Archaeological remains of military equipment and firearms are among the most important classes of battlefield evidence. The ability to translate patterning of these artefacts into behavioural dynamics, however, particularly through the use of modern firearms identification procedures, constitutes an important advance over the traditional, non-systematic recovery of battlefield relics.

The comparative study of ammunition components, known as firearms identification analysis, was first developed by law-enforcement agencies as an aid in solving crimes. Firearms, in their discharge, leave behind distinctive metallic 'fingerprints', or signatures, on the ammunition components. These signatures, also called 'class characteristics', allow the determination of the types of guns used in a given situation. Further, this analytical technique allows the identification of individual weapons by comparing the unique qualities of individual firearm signatures. This capability is important because, coupled with the precise artefact locations, identical individual characteristics can be used to identify specific areas of firearms use and individual movement. Analysis of a series of individual movements can, in turn, define unit deployment, and a series of unit deployments can be used to determine overall combatant tactics and the application of battle doctrine.

It is not enough to know where artefacts are found on a battlefield; archaeologists must also determine where they are not found. A primary goal of most battlefield research is therefore to define the limits of the battlefield. Faced with examining a large area, and assuming that most artefacts of war are either metallic or associated with metal, metal detectors have been successfully employed to define the full extent of the battlefield. As was the case at the Little Bighorn Battlefield National Monument (see **Battle of the Little Bighorn**), the use of metal detecting by experienced operators proved its value. It enables archaeologists to uncover artefacts with minimal disturbance and to point-plot each artefact location for precise mapping. Precise artefact location information is essential to revealing the behavioural patterns that are crucial to understanding the combat events.

Battlefield archaeology is a relatively new field of study, yet it has demonstrated its utility in correcting errors in the historical record and in adding new information. Recovered battlefield artefacts, as the physical evidence of the event, are also useful for interpretive purposes. More importantly, the artefactual data and the archaeological context provide new and independent sources of evidence for analysis of conflict situations and the broader study of the anthropology of war.

See also: fortifications; metal detectors; remote sensing

Further reading

Fox, R.A., Jr and Scott, D.D. (1991) 'The post-Civil War battlefield pattern: An example from the Custer battlefield', *Historical Archaeology* 25(2): 92–103.

Scott, D.D. and Connor, M.A. (1986) 'Post-mortem at the Little Bighorn', *Natural History* 95: 46–55.

Scott, D.D., Fox, R.A., Jr, Connor, M.A. and Harmon, D. (1989) *Archaeological Perspectives on the Battle of the Little Bighorn*, Norman: University of Oklahoma Press.

Snow, D.R. (1981) 'Battlefield archaeology', *Early Man* 3: 18–21.

DOUGLAS D. SCOTT

beads

Beads are small ornamental objects that people use to adorn themselves. Beads can be used individually or in groups strung on a line, they can be sewn on clothing in decorative patterns, they can be used in tandem with certain household items (such as counter-weights on nineteenth-century European lace bobbins) and they can be used in religious ceremonies, such as in rosaries. Archaeologists often find beads in cemeteries because of the use of beads on clothing and religious objects.

People in the past have made beads from many different materials, including fossils, stone (crystal, amber, garnet, jet and carnelian), shell, bone, ivory, horn, metal and glass. The earliest known beads, made from ivory and appearing at a burial context, come from the palaeolithic era, and date to around 75,000 years ago.

Historical archaeologists have been interested in beads since the earliest days of their field, largely because they have found hundreds of examples of glass trade beads at the Native American sites they have excavated (see **Native Americans**). Historical archaeologists find beads made of many different materials, but glass is without question the most common material of manufacture for the historic period. Christopher Columbus is credited with introducing glass beads to the indigenous peoples of the New World in 1492, but Portuguese traders are known to have traded in glass beads with Africans before this date. Most European countries produced glass beads to some extent, with Venice and **Amsterdam** being perhaps the most important centres of production during the historic period.

Historical archaeologists find glass beads because native peoples around the world readily accepted beads as trade items, and traders found the eagerly sought-after beads easy to transport over long distances. Since tiny beads were often traded by weight, hundreds of beads could change hands in a single transaction. Beads were also given as gifts, and they could also be used as currency (such as the wampum, or shell, beads of colonial New England).

Glass-bead manufacturers used two major methods for making the glass beads of the post-Columbian era: the 'hollow-cane' or 'drawn' method, and the 'mandrel-wound' or 'wire-wound' method. In the first method, glass blowers made a long, hollow tube of glass that, once cooled, they broke into short sections that they then smoothed and polished. These short tubes were the beads themselves. Bead producers made mandrel-wound beads individually by winding a thread of molten glass around a revolving wire mandrel until a bead was fully formed. Bead makers could also produce beads using moulding techniques, although these types seem to be less common on historic-period archaeological sites.

Archaeologists have described glass beads as either 'simple' (composed of a single mass of glass), 'compound' (composed of two or more concentric layers of glass, one on top of the other) and 'complex' (made in such a way that decorative designs were impressed in the glass to make intricate patterns, stripes and other elements). Archaeologists also divide glass beads into at least seven different shapes (although other shapes are possible as well): spheroidal, round, olive-shaped, elongated olive-shaped, barrel-shaped, doughnut-shaped and tubular. Archaeologists have also found glass beads in a variety of colours, including – but certainly not limited to – red, blue, caramel-coloured, black, white, frosted, white with blue stripes, solid red with a white or green interior, solid yellow with blue stripes, white with red and blue stripes and solid blue with white stripes. The 'chevron' beads (or *millefiori*) common on Spanish colonial sites (see **Spanish colonialism**) in the New World are distinctive because their pattern, when viewed from the end of the bead, resembles a multisided, many-coloured star. These beads can be composed of as many as seven layers of differently coloured glass. Other beads can have squared sides or be made with knobs to resemble raspberries.

The wide variety of possible bead styles has spurred some archaeologists to create complex **classification** systems to describe bead variation. These archaeologists typically use observable bead characteristics to separate the beads into discrete groups. The most widely used attributes are manufacturing technique, shape, colour and complexity. Faced with a large collection of beads from an archaeological site, an archaeologist could use the classification system to facilitate the description and interpretation of the collection.

In addition to finding whole beads traded to indigenous peoples, archaeologists also sometimes uncover situations where native peoples used European trade beads to produce glass pendants and other objects, like animal effigies, which appear distinctly 'non-European'. For example, the nineteenth-century Arikara Indians, who lived along the Missouri River in the central USA, made triangular-shaped, blue and white pendants by crushing, melting and recasting European trade beads. These pendants, though made of imported

materials, were clearly of native design and meaning. Some cultures in West Africa are also reported to have crushed and recast some of the foreign beads they received in trade.

Archaeologists who have made intensive studies of beads have also realised that some beads can be used for relative dating purposes. The technology of bead design changed over time, and various colours and styles became popular for a while and then were phased out of production. Chevron beads provide a good example. Glass blowers in the sixteenth century made these beads using seven layers of glass, but in the seventeenth century they used only five layers. By the eighteenth century, they dropped to only four layers of glass. Archaeologists have also noticed observable changes in bead frequencies over time. In the western Great Lakes of North America, for instance, the number of polychrome, or multicoloured, beads tends to decrease from the seventeenth to the early nineteenth centuries.

Historical archaeologists can also use beads found in cemeteries to help frame interpretations about past religious **belief systems**. For example, archaeologists excavating at the colonial Spanish mission site of Santa Catalina de Guale, in Georgia, USA, have found thousands of glass beads in the burials, mixed among Native American objects and Christian medallions. The close relationship of these diverse items implies that the Native Americans who were in contact with the mission were blending elements of the introduced religion with parts of their traditional culture.

Further reading

Karklins, K. (1985) '*Glass beads: The Levin catalogue of mid-19th century beads, a sample book of 19th century Venetian beads, and guide to the description and classification of glass beads*', Ottawa: National Historic Parks and Sites Branch.

Karklins, K. and Sprague, R. (1980) *A Bibliography of Glass Trade Beads in North America*, Moscow, ID: South Fork Press.

Kidd, K.E. and Kidd, M.A. (1970) 'A classification system for glass beads for the use of field archaeologists', *Canadian Historic Sites: Occasional*

Papers in Archaeology and History 1, Ottawa: National Historic Sites Service, pp. 45–89.

Spector, J.D. (1976) 'The interpretive potential of glass trade beads in historic archaeology', *Historical Archaeology* 10: 17–27.

CHARLES E. ORSER, JR

behavioural historical archaeology

Behavioural archaeology is a kind of archaeology that was created in the 1970s, during the development of **processual archaeology**, when many archaeologists were attempting to make their discipline more scientific and more overtly anthropological. Behavioural archaeology differs from earlier perspectives because it downplays the role of **culture** in favour of behaviour. It is fair to state, however, that behavioural archaeology is not a unified way of looking at the past, but rather a set of interrelated principles, methods and theories. Behavioural archaeology was created largely to help interpret prehistoric sites, and its ideas have not been widely used in historical archaeology. Examples of behavioural historical archaeology, however, do exist.

The proponents of behavioural archaeology have argued that their project of creating a new way of thinking about the past has also required them to redefine archaeology itself. For them, archaeology offers a way to investigate the specific relationships between humans and their artefacts, everywhere in the world and during every period of human history. Having redefined archaeology in this manner, behavioural archaeologists realised that they would have to create new ways of examining these human–artefact relations, since they found all of the current methods to be lacking in rigour. Before behavioural archaeology was created, archaeologists often made vague associations between the artefacts they unearthed and the past 'culture' they were investigating. Behavioural archaeologists judged these vague statements to be unscientific and intellectually unsatisfying. Rather than to focus on the workings of 'culture' broadly defined, they proposed that the true emphasis of behavioural archaeology was on events and processes of everyday behaviour. Behavioural archaeologists realised at the same time that they would need to know something about processes that had nothing to do with humans at all. Such natural processes, like weathering and erosion, could affect and alter archaeological deposits once they were laid down in the earth. The natural processes were as important as the conscious cultural processes such as refuse disposal practices. Behavioural archaeologists refer to all the processes that affect the creation, preservation and eventual character of archaeological sites as 'formation processes'.

Because behavioural archaeologists seek to create a new way of looking at the past, their work is often replete with jargon that is often specific to their research. Much of this jargon is necessary because behavioural archaeologists need to know, in often intimate detail, how humans have interacted with artefacts, during use, abandonment and discard. In many cases, terms did not exist in archaeology to explain or to illustrate the ways behavioural archaeologists were thinking about artefacts and human behaviour.

One of the most explicit usages of behavioural archaeology in historical archaeology is Stanley South's application. Like all behavioural archaeologists, South believes that historical archaeology is ultimately a science, and that its practitioners, working as scientists, should be interested in examining and elucidating the processes involved in the conduct of past social and cultural life. South also believes, like other behavioural archaeologists, that the final goal of archaeology should be to understand past human behaviour through the lens of culture. South's efforts largely revolve around the creation of artefact patterns from which elements of this past behaviour could be inferred. His examples mostly derived from the sites he excavated in the US South. South's basic argument was that various behaviours – by British colonists, German-American settlers, merchants and others – produce regular patterns that archaeologists can identify in the remains of the sites they excavate. Thus, a distinct group of men and women who exhibit the same behaviours, because of their cultural perceptions, attitudes and understandings, can be expected to discard their rubbish in just about the same manner. The idea behind this formulation is that people who share culture will also share many behaviours.

Other historical archaeologists have also used behavioural archaeology. Edward Staski, for example, used the principles of behavioural archaeology to examine the correlation between the distribution of artefacts and the structure of hierarchical power at Fort Fillmore, New Mexico, a mid-nineteenth-century installation near the USA–Mexico border. The initial analysis of the ceramic sherds (see **ceramics**) from the fort suggested that more locally made vessels were present near the quarters associated with the officers when compared against those from the enlisted men's housing. After considering the site formation process, namely 'trampling behaviour', Staski concluded that the greatest number of locally made vessels actually occurred near the enlisted men's quarters. In this particular case, an analysis rooted in behavioural archaeology showed that site formation processes – specifically, the tramping feet of enlisted soldiers – can have a dramatic impact on a site's characteristics. These characteristics will directly influence the way in which an archaeologist interprets the site's history

In another study, Lester Ross used the ideas of behavioural archaeology in the examination of sixteenth-century Basque barrel making. Using a 'flow model diagram' designed to infer a barrel's 'life history', Ross explored the 'life cycle' of the casks from their 'natural context' – as trees – to their 'cultural context' – first as containers of whale oil and then as refuse – and finally to their 'archaeological context' – as artefacts. This use of behavioural archaeology enabled Ross to demonstrate that the barrels were part of a living, changing culture. The barrels were not simply tangible, static pieces of culture, they were actively engaged in the life of people whose behaviours directly affected the barrels' 'life histories'.

Behavioural archaeologists are constantly refining their methods and perspectives, mostly because human behaviour is a complex subject, even among living peoples. The study of behaviour in the past is especially difficult because the behaviours cannot be directly observed. Behavioural archaeologists work to devise new ways to gain insight into human behaviour, always with an eye towards archaeological analysis.

In 1999, Michael Schiffer, the most important proponent of behavioural archaeology, published an archaeological model that can be used to investigate human communication, which he considers to be tightly associated with behaviour. Whereas almost all communication theories start with the sender of messages, Schiffer's theory begins with the receiver. Most important from an archaeological standpoint, however, is Schiffer's contention that all communication theories have seriously downplayed or even overlooked the role of artefacts in the human communication process. As a result, the behaviours represented during communication are mediated by artefacts. The artefactual basis of communication means that archaeologists have a significant role to play in contributing to our knowledge about human behaviour. This contribution extends far beyond archaeology. Consistent with this view of behavioural archaeology's broad applicability is one of the behavioural archaeologists' main contentions: that archaeology is a discipline which has insights to offer to all social sciences. Behavioural archaeologists work diligently to prove the general relevance of archaeology.

See also: processual archaeology

Further reading

Orser, C.E., Jr (1995) 'Is there a behavioral historical archaeology?', in J.M. Skibo, W.H. Walker and A.E. Nielsen (eds) *Expanding Archaeology*, Salt Lake City: University of Utah Press, pp. 187–97.

Schiffer, M.B. (1999) *The Material Life of Human Beings: Artifacts, Behavior, and Communication*, London: Routledge.

—— (1987) *Formation Processes of the Archaeological Record*, Albuquerque: University of New Mexico Press.

—— (1976) *Behavioral Archaeology*, New York: Academic Press.

South, S. (1977) *Method and Theory in Historical Archaeology*, New York: Academic Press.

CHARLES E. ORSER, JR

belief systems

Belief systems concern what some people may tend to think of as the intangible part of human culture. Belief systems are composed of cogent thoughts, attitudes and ideas that groups of men and women hold in common. Though belief systems do involve the cognitive processes of living human beings, archaeologists have learned that belief systems do leave archaeological traces.

In the first half of the twentieth century, most archaeologists had greatest interest in the cultural histories of human groups, and they used the artefacts they found at archaeological sites to establish group identities and to chart the migrations and contacts of different groups of people through time. With the advent of **processual archaeology** in the 1960s – as an overt kind of anthropological archaeology – many archaeologists expanded their interests beyond culture history and began to examine the ways in which human groups adapted to their environments. As archaeologists began to envision adaptation as something brought about by **culture**, they started to speak of three elements, some would say 'levels', of culture: the technological (dealing with ecological adaptation and subsistence), the social (having to do with organisation and interaction) and ideational (involving belief systems). Archaeologists were slowest to develop an interest in the study of belief systems, but, by the year 2000, many archaeologists had begun to focus their attention on these ideational systems. Understanding a past group's beliefs is always a daunting archaeological task, but historical archaeology is particularly well suited to investigate the nature of past belief systems because of the presence of **historical documents** that archaeologists can use to identify, to describe and even to help explain the belief systems that may be no longer practised.

When we think today about belief systems, we often first think about religion. Religion is, of course, a ubiquitous and fascinating element of human culture, and it is not surprising that archaeologists would be interested in this subject. Belief systems, however, are not limited to religion, but can also consist of political ideas and even pernicious beliefs, such as racism, superiority and bigotry.

Many historical archaeologists have studied religious beliefs, and the number of archaeologists with interests in religion is growing. Archaeologists have been particularly interested in African American religious observance, specifically as it pertains to the religions of African American slaves. Historians and anthropologists agree that religion was a belief system that helped slaves, as individuals and as communities, to sustain themselves in the face of enforced degradation and humiliation. The belief systems practised by African slaves in the New World, however, were complex and multifaceted because they could include elements of traditional African religions, Christianity, Islam, many combinations of these and even new forms created in the New World.

Given the complexity of belief systems among living men and women, archaeologists have discovered that **cemeteries** often provide good locales in which to gain insight into past religious practices. For example, archaeologists excavating at a seventeenth-century slave cemetery associated with a British sugar plantation (see **plantation archaeology**) in Barbados discovered the remains of an old man who had been interred with numerous objects. Some of the objects were commonplace – copper bracelets, white metal rings and a metal knife – whereas other objects were more exotic, such as a necklace composed of seven cowrie shells, twenty-one drilled dog canines, fourteen glass **beads** of various sizes and colours, drilled vertebrae from a large fish and one large carnelian bead. After combing the historical literature for information about African belief systems, the archaeologists decided that these grave objects probably meant that the old man had been an 'Obeah' practitioner. The documents revealed that Obeah men were folk doctors who were highly regarded in the slave communities for their powers of healing and divination. Similarly, a burial of a 40–49-year-old male uncovered during a salvage excavation in New Orleans, Louisiana, USA, contained a white metal rosary made of sixty-three black wooden beads, two silver medallions embossed with Christian symbols and a glass and metal medallion containing the etched image of the Virgin Mary. The presence of these items in this burial, which dated to about 1800, suggests that the African American man had converted, or at least had pretended to convert, to Christianity before burial.

Other archaeological sites associated with African Americans contain objects that undoubtedly relate to belief systems, but which are much more difficult to interpret. For instance, some pieces of colonoware pots (see **colonoware pottery**) found in South Carolina and Virginia, USA, exhibit incised 'X' designs on their bases and sometimes on their inside bottoms. These symbols may represent simple **makers' marks** or family identifiers or they could have religious meaning. Pots with similar marks are known from **West Africa**, where they are associated with healing and the belief in supernatural forces. Other items that probably relate to an African American belief system are the fist amulets found at the **Hermitage Plantation** in Tennessee, USA, the historic home of President Andrew Jackson. These tiny metallic objects (roughly 1 x 2 cm in size) are similar to the *figas*, or good-luck charms, which are today popular in parts of Latin America. *Figas* are thought to represent the hand of God grasping the souls of the saved, and their wearers tend to believe that the amulets protect them from the evil eye and make them impervious to bullets. Archaeologists have found *figas* at the Spanish colonial site (see **Spanish colonialism**) of **Santa Elena** in South Carolina, USA. Because the fist amulets do not precisely resemble true *figas*, no one is absolutely certain of their meaning. It does seem clear, however, that these tiny objects relate to a past belief system of some sort.

Belief systems are not just about religion, and many people can hold political and even social attitudes that they may consider part of their belief system. Archaeologist Paul Mullins has demonstrated – using archaeological remains from **Annapolis**, Maryland, USA – that racism and white supremacy were belief systems that had archaeological manifestations. Settlement patterns and the use of public spaces provide arenas in which archaeologists can see the effects of such belief systems.

See also: African American archaeology; history of historical archaeology; ideology

Further reading

Mullins, P.R. (1999) *Race and Affluence: An Archaeology of African American and Consumer Culture*, New York: Kluwer Academic/Plenum.

Orser, C.E., Jr (1994) 'The archaeology of African-American slave religion in the antebellum South', *Cambridge Archaeological Journal* 4: 33–45.

CHARLES E. ORSER, JR

Benin City, Nigeria

Benin City, the centre of a complex Edo polity in western Nigeria, entered into the consciousness of Europeans with the arrival of Portuguese mariners in 1486. As an important trading centre during the early period of European contact, it is one of the few African cities (another is Loango) that is depicted with some accuracy in contemporary engravings published by Dapper in 1686. After the initial Portuguese contact Benin City was little visited by European traders despite its size and importance in the regional economy and politics of the region, in large part because it lay nearly 100 km inland, in the forested region where travel was difficult and dangerous for European traders. It remained an important settlement in West Africa until the 1890s when the British conquered and sacked it as they struggled to consolidate control over what became the colony of Nigeria. Much of what is known about Benin City in the pre-European contact and early historical periods derives from archaeological research that has been informed by sources such as oral traditions, or other non-documentary sources.

Benin City is well known in international circles for the so-called Benin bronzes. These extraordinary examples of lost wax casting are among the most well known and emblematic icons of West African art. However, most of these were not recovered archaeologically, but were instead the booty of war, from the 1897 British campaign of conquest. No significant archaeological studies occurred at Benin City until the 1950s, under the auspices of the British colonial administration.

The best known archaeological studies at Benin

City were those undertaken by Graham Connah in the early 1960s. These studies consisted of the identification and mapping of a series of large-scale ditch and wall complexes surrounding the old city, test cuttings through several sections of the wall and excavations at several locations within the bounds of the old city itself. Among other distinctive finds identified were extensive potsherd pavements predating European arrival, and trade goods dating from both before and after the Portuguese visit. Several aspects of the archaeological excavations, including the massive wall system that surrounds the city and extends at least 20–30 km beyond the city boundaries, as well as the evidence of an apparent sacrifice of at least forty-one women, suggest the degree of political power enjoyed by the leader of the Benin polity.

Since Connah's work, various other archaeologists, both foreign and Nigerian, have continued to investigate the site. Much of the more recent work has been limited to surveys of the surrounding region, and small-scale test excavations. Unfortunately, excavations of the scale undertaken by Connah have not been repeated more recently, particularly in light of the rapid population growth of the modern city, which is the most serious threat to further understanding of the past of Benin City and its surrounding hinterland as the archaeological resources are damaged or destroyed by urban sprawl.

See also: Portuguese colonialism; West Africa

Further reading

Connah, G.E. (1975) *The Archaeology of Benin*, London: Oxford University Press.
Darling, P. J. (1998) 'A legacy in earth – ancient Benin and Ishan, southern Nigeria', in K.W. Wessler (ed.) *Historical Archaeology in Nigeria*, Trenton, NJ: Africa World Press, pp. 143–97.

KENNETH G. KELLY

Bergen, Norway

According to saga tradition, Bergen was founded *c.* 1070 by the Norwegian king Olaf Kyrre. Located on Norway's west coast, the town is sited around the bay of Vågen. The bay is flanked to the north by the Holmen promontory, where the royal and ecclesiastical centre (Bergenhus) lay, and to the south by the Nordnes Peninsula, where two monasteries and the archiepiscopal estate were to be found. The early medieval town occupied most of the bay's northern shoreline, with settlement first expanding into the area at the head of the bay and, by the fourteenth century, into parts of Nordnes as well. By the thirteenth century, Bergen had become western Norway's main administrative, ecclesiastical and commercial centre.

Archaeological investigations have been carried out in Bergen since the middle of the 1800s. Historical archaeology in the nineteenth century was synonymous with the study of monumental architecture, which served as an important symbol for the re-emerging Norwegian nation. Excavations were carried out on several ecclesiastical and royal monuments and ruins in Bergen, most often as part of restoration work on the standing buildings, but also as regular scientific excavations. Several individuals were involved from the 1840s until the turn of the century, but none was an archaeologist by profession. The monuments were studied singly, and were used as topographical fixed points in connection with the writing of local or national histories.

In the early twentieth century, local historian Christian Koren-Wiberg started to record vernacular building remains, and used them to reconstruct the town's medieval topography. Study of historical documents helped him locate several previously undiscovered buildings, whose ruins were subsequently unearthed. These results were published in his popular historical surveys of Bergen.

From 1929 until the 1950s, architect Gerhard Fisher carried out excavations and building-history investigations in the town area and the Archbishop's Palace. His main efforts, however, were directed at the royal and ecclesiastical centre on Holmen, and his work provided much new technical and architectural information about the buildings.

In 1955, a fire destroyed an area of *c.* 6,000 m^2 in the northern part of the old town, and ushered in a new era in **urban archaeology**. Starting that year, the extensive 'Bryggen excavations' were carried out continuously until 1968, thereafter intermittently until 1979. This was Norway's first large-scale urban excavation. It was directed by Asbjørn E. Herteig, who, a prehistorian by training, brought with him new methodological approaches to historical archaeology. Stratigraphic excavation, with buildings as the principal elements in the stratigraphy, was introduced, the cultural deposits were excavated in mechanical layers and artefacts were collected and recorded in relation to either structures or fire-layers. As a methodological principle, Herteig was determined not to rely on the written sources while interpreting the archaeological material, which was instead to be allowed to speak for itself without bias from 'prior knowledge' about the town. This showed a new confidence in material culture as a primary source of information about medieval history. Besides its methodological contributions, the Bryggen excavations provided new insights into the topography of the early medieval town and particularly the development of the waterfront area from c. 1150 onwards. Herteig's interpretations and dating of the stratigraphy and settlement structure were published in 1990 and 1991.

In 1980, in response to the revised Cultural Heritage Act of 1978, the Central Office for Monuments and Sites (Riksantikvaren) set up an excavation unit in Bergen, with a new generation of archaeologists taking over the fieldwork. In 1994, the excavation unit's field archaeologists were transferred to the Norwegian Institute for Cultural Heritage Research (NIKU), which assumed responsibility for all archaeological investigations within the medieval town. In the 1980s, the unit concentrated on refining its excavation and documentation methods; culture-layers were now viewed as fossilised traces of activity, and interpretation of the excavated material was rooted in the precise analysis of individual layers. Some 250 investigations, ranging from minor watching briefs to major systematic excavations, were carried out from 1980–99, and many have been published in reports now available from NIKU. Most of the larger investigations have been planned and carried out as interdisciplinary projects involving the participation of principally botanists and historians, with other specialists consulted where appropriate.

From the 1950s to the 1990s, Bergen archaeology's greatest advances were in methodology and the identification and exploration of new archaeological sources. Coping with the challenges of rescue archaeology meant that research work beyond the level of report writing was sparse. During the last two decades, however, several artefact groups from the original Bryggen excavations have been published in *The Bryggen Papers*, *Main Series* and *Supplementary Series*; the latter also provides a forum for the discussion of methodological issues connected with Bergen archaeology. Three volumes in the monograph series *Norges Kirker* (The Churches of Norway) present a comprehensive survey of Bergen's churches.

In 1994, the University of Bergen created a chair in medieval archaeology at the Department of Archaeology, and since the same year the various institutions comprising the historical archaeology community have been gathered together under one roof at Bryggens Museum, which makes for a fruitful working environment. Prior to 1994, research theses concerning material found in Bergen were relatively few and far between, but this is no longer the case. With an emphasis on broader perspectives, the huge body of material from 150 years of archaeology in Bergen now serves as a basis for research at all levels.

Further reading

The Bryggen Papers Main Series (1985–91), vols 1–4, Bergen: University of Bergen.

The Bryggen Papers Supplementary Series (1984–98), vols 1–4, A. E. Herkeig (ed) Bergen: University of Bergen.

Golembnik, A. (1995) 'Stratigraphic reconstruction of the urban deposits at the sites of Finnegården 3A, Dreggsalmenning 14–16 and Skostredet 10 in Bergen', in W. Hensel, S. Tabaczynski and P. Urbanczyk (eds) *Theory and Practice of Archaeological Research* 2: 301–28, Warszawa.

Lidén, H.-E. and Magerøy, E.M. (1980, 1983, 1990) *Norges kirker, Bergen*, Oslo: Riksantikvaren.

Øye, I. (1997) 'State, tasks and outlook for archaeology in Bergen', in M. Gläser (ed.) *Lübecker Kolloquium zur Stadtarchäologie im Hanseraum I: Stand, Aufgaben und Perspektiven*, Lübeck: Verlag Schmidt Römhild pp. 441–54.

GITTE HANSEN

Bertrand, steamboat

The steamboat *Bertrand* sank on 1 April 1865, in the Missouri River in the central USA, after hitting a snag. The wreck site was approximately 40 km north of Omaha, Nebraska. Treasure salvors originally found the wreck in 1968 by using newspaper accounts, old maps, land abstracts and a magnetometer (a **remote-sensing** tool). The wreck was buried in 8.5 m of silt and clay underneath the water table. The salvors were interested in finding the wreck because local legend stated that it has been loaded with fabulous wealth at the time of its sinking. Archaeologists systematically excavated the wreck in 1968–9.

The *Bertrand* is an important find for historical archaeology because it was laden with foodstuffs, clothing and mining and agricultural supplies for the settlers living in the Montana Territory, far to the north of St Louis, Missouri, the boat's point of origin. The items on board were the items the settlers and miners would have used in their everyday lives, and the finds from the *Bertrand* offered a rare glimpse into this **material culture**. At the same time, the archaeologists were able to collect detailed information about the architecture and design of the ship, and they were even able to obtain data on artefact conservation (see **conservation, underwater**) by studying the time it took to dry the waterlogged wood.

The ship's cargo was vast, amounting to roughly 283 cubic m. About half of the cargo had been crushed by the weight of the mud on top of it, but the artefacts recovered provide a remarkable catalogue of the materials used in the USA during the mid-nineteenth century. Archaeologists found many of the objects in their original shipping boxes, with some of them carrying the stencilled name of the manufacturer or merchant burned on their sides. Archaeologists recovered over 6,000 **bottles** alone, some of which still had their paper labels affixed to them. The bottles were commonly used during the mid-nineteenth century, but today most are extremely rare.

Included in the collection are food items (including dried and salted beef, mutton and pork, oysters, pepper sauce, strawberries, peaches and peanuts), liquor bottles (bourbon whiskey, brandy and brandied cherries), patent-medicine bottles, textiles and wearing apparel (including gloves, hats, trousers and coats), household goods (including mirrors, candle moulds, clocks, combs and whiskey glasses), mining supplies (blasting power, pickaxes and shovels) and hardware, tools and building supplies of all descriptions. Also included were a number of miscellaneous items, including bull-whips, cartridges, and cigars. Some items were marked with the names of their owners and so can be associated with specific individuals, a rare occurrence even in historical archaeology.

The finds from the *Bertrand* provide important and unique information about the transportation of goods up the Missouri River during an important period of US expansion into the western USA. The finds offer information about both the *Bertrand* specifically and about other steamboats as well. In addition, the diversity of the collection means that the artefacts can serve as an important study collection for other archaeologists conducting research on the mid-nineteenth century.

CHARLES E. ORSER, JR

biblical archaeology

Biblical archaeology, established during the nineteenth century, has an exceptional place among the disciplines aimed at studying the civilisation of the ancient Near East. The exceptional nature of biblical archaeology is due to its relationship with the Holy Bible, a collected corpus of texts that has suffered from complex elaboration and which is considered both a historical document (see **historical documents**) and a divine revelation. At the same time, biblical archaeology shares several theoretical and methodological problems with other disciplines, most of them originating from its own formative stage.

During the second half of the nineteenth century, biblical archaeologists had clearly defined their discipline's geographical area and purpose of study: the Syria–Palestine region, and the Hebrew civilisation as described in the Old Testament. Because the political history of the Bronze and Iron Ages was often affected by and related to it, this frame of reference was occasionally extended to include Egypt and Mesopotamia (from Assyria to

Babylonia). As a matter of fact, the beginnings of Mesopotamian archaeology and Egyptology (and their acceptance by a curious public) were encouraged by the possibility that the discovery of Assyrian and Egyptian texts referring to monarchs, events and places could be used to confirm the historical accuracy of the chronicles appearing in the Old Testament.

The relationships among the different disciplines had been favoured by the '*de facto*' identification of ancient civilisations with biblical history until last century. In many cases, this history was fabricated and manipulated by outsiders. It must be remembered that direct documented sources for the study of Egyptian, Assyrian, Hittite, Babylonian and Persian civilisations were non-existent until the nineteenth century. Even though hieroglyphs and cuneiform documents were known to Europe as early as the seventeenth century, they could not be deciphered until the nineteenth century. At the same time, the control of the Turkish Empire, over wide areas of the Near East, kept European investigators far from the monumental (urban and architectural) and artistic materials of ancient Mesopotamian culture. So, direct observation and **classification** were limited, and the disciplines dedicated to a critical analysis of documented sources – such as palaeography, sigillography and heraldry – were enhanced during the sixteenth and seventeenth centuries, becoming the real basis for European historical research. This proximity to the past and its monuments, together with the perception of a major cultural identity, also stimulated the development of archaeology and the study of classical art away from the antiquarian point of view.

The outset of Oriental studies, which included from the biblical world from the beginning, is parallel to the political penetration of European states in the Near East. The coincidence between scientific interest and political activity was a constant issue for pioneers such as P.E. Botta and H. Layard. Their activities attracted the attention of the public and opened the way for the creation of scholarly societies during the nineteenth century, most of which were academically focused: the Palestine Exploration Fund, the Society for Biblical Archeology and the Egypt Exploration Society.

As is true of other disciplines focusing on the Near East, biblical archaeology is closely associated with philology. In fact, of all the disciplines, philology has had the strongest and most stable interdisciplinary linkage with archaeology. The close link between philology and archaeology in both Orientalistic archaeology and Egyptology occurs because of the almost constant discovery of new texts, both literary and historical, in archaeological deposits. The advantage of continuously incorporating new historic-cultural references – and with it, the possibility of rewriting certain periods of history – have also had a negative side: an excessive devotion to political history and the consequent subordination of archaeology to history. This subordination made archaeology merely a tool for obtaining new texts and, more generally, as a method for confirming historical questions about such things as battles and destruction, invasions and migrations.

Together with those coincidences, biblical archaeology excels as an area of original knowledge, a development that has been specially conditioned to certain non-archaeological factors, including religious and political needs. Central among these factors are the competence of the three major, monotheistic religions to control certain holy places and sacred traditions, and which would allow for the implementation of historical rights. The establishment of the State of Israel in 1948, with its intentions of historical and political legitimisation, are an outcome of this process. Much of this legitimisation rests on key passages in the Old Testament (such as the conquering of the Promised Land) compared to a relative uninterest in the New Testament. Without any doubt, many of the political rights of the region relate to theological issues concerning Christianity. Many of these issues were developed in the context of a different and much bigger historical scene: the Roman Empire.

Other factors, both theological and methodological, follow scientific criteria, but many have also been polluted by the special status attributed to biblical texts. The basic problem involves the relationship between **material culture** and literary texts.

In order to understand the origin and development of biblical archaeology, it has to be remembered that, during its creation in the nineteenth century, the biblical narration – considered holy history – was the essential frame of reference used to organise human history. Ancient history was, from the days of the **Renaissance**, concentrated on the study of the great political and cultural problems of Greece and Rome. The Bible gave a chronology (beginning with world origin as the result of God's creation) and a meaning to the chain of events and empires as a drama scenario (Redemption) managed by God's will. At the time, biblical texts were the only way to approach the Egyptian and Mesopotamian states. The characters, scenarios and episodes, considered as human behavioural archetypes, were particularly useful for understanding the relationship between the Chosen People and divinity.

It was in this context that the biblical archaeology appeared to be the complement and the confirmation of the biblical text and it is not a question of chance. Its formation in Protestant Anglo-Saxon ambiences was never tied to university education. Rather, its importance was affirmed in the context of a polemical defence of the Christian sense of history that, during the nineteenth century, had to reject both geological and biological points of view. The development of those sciences, based on the works of Charles Lyell (such as *The Principles of Geology*, published in 1833) and Charles Darwin (*The Origin of Species*, 1859, and *The Descent of Man*, 1871), established new ideas that broke with the creationists' schemes. The final outcome of the controversy resulted in an alteration of the traditional position of human beings as superior and perfect beings compared with the rest of nature. This position upset the chronological framework of rigidly dogmatic Christian history. The relationship of biblical archaeology with a historical-religious tradition and a concerned polemic has conditioned its use and explains its dependence on literary texts, even to a greater extent than many other archaeologies, including **classical archaeology**.

During the second half of the nineteenth century and the first decades of the twentieth century, biblical archaeology was first of all a tool that pretended to confirm the validity of the Bible's texts, and its essential historical validity was never questioned. Successive researchers only had to profile and clarify this question by paying special attention to certain important facts. At the same time, they slowly contributed to the development of biblical archaeology as an archaeological discipline. Its scientific basis, however, was not completely reached until later. W.F. Allbright, the leading biblical archaeologist of the central decades of the twentieth century, is perhaps the best example of the limits and merits of this situation. His efforts were based on the problems and historical epochs considered central: the Patriarchs' age (for which he proposed the integration to the Middle Bronze Age), and the reaching of the Promised Land (Later Bronze Age). From this perspective, the archaeology – as represented by the material culture – could be considered to be the complement needed to identify historical facts (such as migrations and battles) as well as socioeconomic characteristics of historically known cultures. At the same time, however, the new perspective tried to refine both excavation techniques and archaeological documentation procedures.

The traditional subordination of biblical archaeology to historical reconstruction based on an often indisputable textual authority has many consequences. One consequence is the circular relationship that is established between the evidence and the text. The evidence may confirm the historical veracity of a certain fact as related to the correspondent biblical reference (assuming it could be verified). Another consequence is the difficulty of correctly estimating the originality of the Hebrew culture in the Near Eastern context.

This subordination has, at the same time, meant a rather slow progress in methodology, and it has also limited the archaeologists' interest to certain topics: biblical topography and ancient-town exploration (mainly those mentioned in the Old Testament), monumental art and models and evolution of religious and palatial **architecture** within the Syria–Palestine area. It is significant that some of the main protagonists of Palestinian archaeology – Flinders Petrie, Leonard Woolley and Kathleen Kenyon – had their origins in other study areas and that they maintained a certain hesitancy to get involved with the archaeological verification of historical facts.

The impact of new theoretical tendencies developed in Anglo-Saxon countries during the last decades of the twentieth century has greatly affected research in biblical archaeology. The research designs of the **New Archaeology** are of special importance. The precedence for this **processual archaeology** rested to some extent on the innovative studies developed during the 1930–50 period in the Near East. These pioneering works asked important questions related to the development of complex societies, the fashioning of urban society and the development of the state in the context of Palestine. Those works had theoretical and methodological consequences quite important to the history and the archaeology of the area, but, at the same time, they could also be easily positioned on the margins of the biblical scholarship.

The main result of the new theoretical currents has raised questions about the traditional relationship between archaeology and the biblical texts. Of particular importance is whether the dependence on written texts has to be maintained. This dependence on the part of archaeology significantly limits its role merely to confirming or disconfirming questions related to history.

During the last two decades of the twentieth century, many archaeologists have changed their perspective about the historical studies in the Near East. This new understanding could bring a certain autonomy to biblical archaeology. Attention has focused on the cultural procedures that involve a global analysis of societies and that have particular rhythms. The so-called *longue durée* of the *Annales* School is considered to be the opposite of the vision of history based on facts and characters. This perspective forces biblical archaeology to be interdisciplinary. Indeed, certain intellectual and religious sectors maintain their tendencies to consider the archaeological task in Palestine to be a complement to the Biblical exegesis. This situation holds the danger of not only provoking disciplinary divisions but also may lower the scientific status of the discipline.

See also: processual archaeology

Further reading

Aharoni, Y. (1982) *The Archaeology of the Land of Israel*, London: SCM Press.

Aviram, J. (ed.) (1985) *Biblical Archaeology Today: Proceedings of the International Congress of Biblical Archaeology, Jerusalem, April, 1984*, Jerusalem:

Israel Exploration Society and Israel Academy of Sciences and Humanities.

Dever, W.G. (1990) *Recent Archaeological Discoveries and Biblical Research*, Seattle: University of Washington Press.

Kenyon, K.M. (1979) *Archaeology in the Holy Land*, fourth edn, London: Methuen.

Moorey, P.R.S. (1991) *A Century of Biblical Archaeology*, Cambridge: Lutterworth Press.

VÍCTOR REVILLA CALVO

biological anthropology

Biological anthropology is a relatively recent name preferred by some for what is more traditionally known as 'physical anthropology'; the terms are essentially interchangeable. 'Physical' refers to the biological make-up and natural history of humans, with a strong emphasis on comparing and contrasting one human population to another. The domain of biological anthropological research encompasses the study of the fossil and genetic evidence relating to human evolution; the genetic diversity of, and relationship between, existing and recent modern human populations; the anatomical, skeletal and physiological aspects of human adaptation to various environments; the nutritional, dietary and growth and developmental aspects of human biological variation and adaptation; and all of these same areas as they apply to non-human primates. One speciality area within biological anthropology of special note is **forensic anthropology**. The biological anthropological study of humans developed during the eighteenth and nineteenth centuries, along with the development of the rest of anthropology as part of the period of European exploration and colonisation of the world, and the resulting European fascination with human cultural and biological diversity.

History

George Louis Leclerc, the Count de Buffon (1707–88), first categorised the growing interest in the natural history and variation of humans into the study of humanity's natural history, the comparison of humans to non-humans and the study of the present-day 'races' of humans. Remarkably, these are still the three principal areas of physical or biological anthropology: palaeoanthropology, primatology and modern human variation and adaptation.

The often designated 'father' of physical anthropology was Johann Friedrich Blumenbach (1753–1840). A German physician, Blumenbach's 1775 publication *De Generis Humani Varietate Nativa* (*On the Natural Variations in Humankind*) is traditionally considered a landmark or seminal work. Blumenbach's principal interest was in comparative anatomy (especially cranial comparisons) and, more broadly, the physical ('racial') variation of modern human populations. He introduced and insisted on the meticulous scientific measurement of subjects, be they living or dead, for the purposes of classification. His own classification of modern humans into five races in the 1781 edition of his book was based strictly on **human osteology** (primarily craniological) information. This approach differed notably from earlier classifications by Carolus Linnaeus (1707–78) and Buffon, who had each included behavioural attributes in their schemes. Blumenbach's choice of 'Caucasian' to refer to most Europeans is one of the more enduring historical legacies of racial studies.

By the twentieth century, the physical anthropological study of humans was firmly established. Then, there were two principal concerns of physical anthropologists: the study of modern human physical variation and the study of human fossils. Training and schooling was primarily in human and comparative anatomy. Physical anthropologists typically worked in medical schools. The emphasis, if not obsession, was the measurement of one's subjects – fossils, skeletons or living subjects – for the purpose of proper taxonomic classification. Whether one was dealing with extinct or extant specimens, the goal was to construct a classification scheme that most reflected evolutionary and biological reality. The racial classifications published prior to the last half of this century are almost too numerous to count. There were virtually as many different classification schemes as there were classifiers. It was not until the 1950s that physical anthropologists began to incorporate a more explicit genetic and evolutionary perspective that de-emphasised the static nature of both fossil forms

and modern human populations. Physical anthropologists finally began to despair of both the virtual impossibility of agreeing on the criteria to be used in distinguishing between human races and the equally difficult task of disentangling social, ethnic, linguistic, religious, economic and political factors from the 'strictly' biological and genetic in the construction of racial classifications. Collectively horrified at the way 'scientific' racial classification had been used in Nazi Germany to justify the most atrocious acts of mass murder and torture, physical anthropologists basically abandoned both the 'race' concept as applied to humans and the practice of seeking the ultimate, all-inclusive classification of modern human populations.

In 1951, Sherwood Washburn published an essay entitled 'The new physical anthropology', in which he characterised the difference between the 'old' and the 'new' disciplines. He described the 'old' physical anthropology as being principally a technique involving the taking of measurements and the computation of indices and a variety of statistics. However, according to Washburn, the 'new' physical anthropology was more an area of interest, with the goal being to understand better primate evolution and human variation using whatever techniques are most appropriate. Such techniques clearly involve more focus on evolutionary processes and genetics than mere measurements of bones.

Human variation

The pivotal concept referred to by Washburn is the new emphasis on 'process' rather than just pattern, as had been the case previously. The European fascination with human physical variation did not, of course, begin with Blumenbach, but his scientific approach to studying it embodied the traditional approach of dealing with the phenomenon by attempting to discover all of the human races that it was presumed must exist. The effort was one essentially of classifying for the sake of classification. The goal of scholars became one of describing and defining each and every human race that one could find. A virtual deluge of studies and books proposing how human races should be classified and categorised followed. It was not until the middle of the twentieth century when enhanced understanding of the genetic basis of biological variation became more prevalent that physical anthropologists began to abandon their attempts to discover the 'real' classification of races.

By explicitly including genetic and evolutionary processes as essential to understanding both human natural history and present-day variation, physical anthropologists replaced the age-old question of 'How many humans races are there?' with the more scientific one of 'How have human populations adapted to the variety of environments they now inhabit?' Rather than being concerned, for example, with just how many different human skin colour categories existed and how these could be used to define racial groups, physical anthropologists asked what the range of human skin colour variation was, what its genetic and developmental basis was and how such variation reflected different adaptive responses to different environmental conditions. The incorporation of, first, the growing body of knowledge pertaining to human genetic variation of an ever-growing number of biochemical systems with, second, the amassed knowledge of human physical (i.e. external in this sense) variation led to new insights.

The concept of populations as dynamic 'pools' of genes, in the sense that numerous processes continually act to alter them over time, is not really compatible with the idea inherent in the traditional race concept that races are fixed or stagnant in their make-up. Physical anthropologists increasingly recognised the futility of finding consistent and meaningful correlations between the traditional anatomical and skeletal attributes they had been using to describe populations and the genetic patterns characteristic of those same populations. There is, for example, no correlation between the geographical or populational distribution of ABO blood group frequencies and either skin colour or stature or cranial shape. Given the inevitable occurrence of genetic mutations, there can be no such thing as a 'pure' race in the sense of a population that has maintained its original genetic make-up unchanged over time. Additionally, the 'flow' or admixture of genes between human populations over at least the past several hundred years has greatly accelerated as a result of both forced and unforced population movements and migrations. This has reduced the number of genetic differences existing between populations and increased their genetic similarity to one another. Efforts to track such population movements and genetic admixture in prehistoric and historic populations has included the analysis of both metric and non-metric osteological traits in human skeletal series, with varying degrees of success.

Primatology

The study of the biological and behavioural variation and evolutionary history of the approximately 200 living primate species has also been of interest to physical anthropologists. Long recognised as the most human-like non-human animals on earth, the study of primates provides essential information about the biological origin and evolution of humans. Thomas Henry Huxley's (1825–95) *Zoological Evidence as to Man's Place in Nature* (1863) provided extensive anatomical evidence for the close similarity of humans to the only two African apes known at the time, the gorilla and chimpanzee. Darwin used this information in *The Descent of Man* (1871) as justification for predicting that fossils of the earliest human ancestors would most likely be found in Africa. His prediction came true over fifty years later with the discovery of the first such fossil in 1924 at Taung in South Africa, *Australopithecus africanus*.

In the last half of the twentieth century, genetic and biochemical research into primates and humans has provided spectacular verification of the especially close similarity of humans to the gorilla, chimpanzee and the bonobo. Indeed, comparisons of chromosomes, DNA, mitochondrial DNA and dozens of proteins and enzymes have indicated an unexpectedly high degree of similarity between the African apes and humans: e.g. over 98 per cent DNA similarity between humans and chimpanzees and bonobos.

Further insights into human prehistory have come from the ability of molecular biologists to calculate rates of evolutionary change for various molecules, by combining dates obtained from palaeontological studies of fossils with knowledge about the extent of molecular differences existing between modern species. Application of these rates of molecular evolutionary change has led to calculations that humans and apes (especially chimpanzees and bonobos) probably last shared a common evolutionary ancestor about 4–6 million years ago. These dates have been corroborated by the discovery of the earliest human-like fossils at about 4–5 million years ago in Africa (discussed below).

The convergence of two independent lines of evidence – the palaeontological and the molecular – resulting in congruent 'windows' of geological time for the origin of human-like creatures on earth is one of the more compelling justifications for accepting the accuracy and validity of the biological theory of evolution, in general.

Human natural (evolutionary) history

One of the greatest successes of biological anthropology in the last half of the twentieth century has involved the study of the human evolutionary past. The number and nature of fossil discoveries of earlier human-like forms that represent our natural historical past has been nothing less than stunning, and continues to intrigue and fascinate both the scientific community and the general public. The discovery of 4 to 5-million-year-old hominids (human-like forms) with clearly ape-like attributes in East Africa has firmly rooted our evolutionary 'tree' on that continent. This has been followed by numerous discoveries of a succession of African hominids up to and including the earliest members of our own genus *Homo*. Fossil discoveries support the conclusion that some members of *Homo* migrated out of Africa by 1.7 million years ago and moved into Eurasia. Beginning by about 125,000 years ago, the fossil record is even more extensive and indicates a biological diversity. Scholars are still trying to understand the evolutionary significance of this diversity. Specifically, the relationship between largely European Neanderthal populations and more modern-looking forms is an ongoing area of vigorous – and occasionally contentious – research and dispute. The addition of genetic studies (particularly of mitochondrial DNA), which have been widely interpreted as indicating a relatively recent single origin of modern humans in Africa, to the ever-growing body of fossil evidence continues to spark lively debate on this issue.

Further reading

Ciochon, R.L. and Fleagle, J.G. (1993) *The Human Evolution Source Book*, Englewood Cliffs, NJ: Prentice-Hall.
Dolhinow, P. and Fuentes, A. (1999) *The Nonhuman Primates*, Mountain View, CA: Mayfield.
Jones, S., Martin, R. and Pilbeam, D. (1992) *The Cambridge Encyclopedia of Human Evolution*, Cambridge: Cambridge University Press.
Lewontin, R. (1995) *Human Diversity*, New York: Scientific American Books.
Washburn, S.L. (1951) 'The new physical anthropology', *Transactions of the New York Academy of Sciences*, Series II, 13: 298–304.
Wolpoff, M.H. (1999) *Paleoanthropology*, second edn, Boston, McGraw-Hill.

MARTIN K. NICKELS

Black Death

The 'Black Death' is the common term for the eruption of bubonic plague in Europe in 1347–50. It is a disease caused by the bacillus *Yersinia pestis*, which affects wild rodents, principally rats, and is transmitted to humans through fleas. It originated in China, entered Western Europe in 1347 and became endemic until the late seventeenth century. It killed a sizeable percentage of the European population and caused massive social, religious and economic upheaval.

One site related to the Black Death that archaeologists have investigated is in London. The plague arrived in London in September 1348. Initially, the London dead were probably buried in existing churches and churchyards, but two new **cemeteries** were quickly established on the northern and eastern outskirts of the city, at West Smithfield and East Smithfield, to cope with the emergency. Excavations in 1986 by the Museum of London revealed a substantial sample of the East Smithfield burial ground. Finds of coins definitively dated the cemetery to between 1344 and 1350. The cemetery, surrounded by a stone wall, was carefully laid out, and did not suggest a panicked response to the plague. Bodies were interred in two discrete burial areas, and were laid out in north–south rows. To the west, burials took place in two mass burial trenches, a mass burial pit and individual graves, all laid out in eleven parallel north–south rows. The trenches measured about 2 m wide by over 1 m deep. The larger of the trenches yielded 242 skeletons. The corpses had been carefully placed rather than thrown in. They were packed densely and laid up to five deep. Children often filled small spaces between adults. Many were buried in coffins, some lined with charcoal. Shroud buckles were also recovered. The smaller trench held fifty skeletons. The remainder of the burial rows were occupied by 262 individual graves. A number of the graves were in the same row as the mass burial pit and the small mass burial trench. Almost half were in coffins. One individual was buried with a belt purse containing a large coin hoard dated to 1344–51.

The eastern section of the cemetery comprised one mass burial trench and four north–south parallel rows of individual graves. The long burial trench was possibly in excess of 125 m long, about 2 m wide and 0.75 m deep. One hundred and two corpses were recovered from this trench.

The majority of those interred in the cemetery were probably from the lower strata of society. The probable original total of burials at the East Smithfield cemetery was around 2,400, based on the dimensions of the cemetery and the density of surviving burials. The cemetery was probably planned to accommodate more burials but the plague seems to have passed before the space was needed. The total estimated figure of about 12,400 burials in the West and East Smithfield cemeteries based on size of cemetery is significantly lower than previous estimates, and may indicate that some historical accounts of the mortality rate were exaggerated.

Further reading

Grainger, I., Hawkins, D. and Waldron, T. (forthcoming) *Excavations at the Black Death Cemetery, East Smithfield, London*, London: Museum of London Archaeology Service.

Hawkins, D. (1990) 'The Black Death and the new London cemeteries of 1348', *Antiquity* 64: 637–42.

Kelly, M. (forthcoming) *A History of the Black Death in Ireland*, Stroud: Tempus.

Platt, C. (1997) *King Death: The Black Death and Its*

Aftermath in Late-Medieval England, London: University College London Press.

BARNEY SLOANE

Boott Mills, Lowell, Massachusetts, USA

Sponsored and funded by the US National Park Service (NPS), excavations at the Boott Mills boarding houses in 1985 and 1986 were part of an interdisciplinary study of the Boott Mills industrial complex (1835–1957) and associated housing for mill workers, the earliest of which was completed in 1842, and agents' housing, erected in 1845. The industrial complex was investigated by Thomas Mahlstedt and Douglas George for the Denver Service Center of the NPS. The study of the residential complexes was carried out jointly by the North Atlantic Regional Office of the National Park Service and Boston University, under the direction of Stephen A. Mrozowski (NPS) and Mary C. Beaudry (Boston University). The latter project was a case study in **contextual historical archaeology**, combining extensive documentary research, environmental reconstruction and analysis of site formation processes with interpretations of excavated data. Excavations were conducted in the back lots of three sorts of residences: a 'typical' boarding house; a tenement for skilled workers; and an agent's duplex. Agents and supervisory personnel tended to be native New Englanders, and initially the boarding-house residents were Yankee 'mill girls' from farming communities throughout New England. After *c.* 1850, however, Yankee workers were replaced by immigrants, at first Irish and French Canadians, later Eastern Europeans. Comparative analysis of the three types shed light upon differences in **consumer choice** based on income and household type; the boarding houses were female-headed 'corporate' households that differed in composition from the family-occupied tenement and agent's house. Each type of household produced a distinctive material signature. Evidence from **palynology**, phytoliths and macrofossils revealed that conditions in the back lots of the company-run boarding house and tenement deteriorated over

time, while the agent's lot was carefully maintained. The boarding house was run according to
strict rules, although finds from the back lot
revealed frequent flouting of company policy,
especially regarding alcohol consumption. Ceramics and glassware were plain, serviceable and
bought in bulk by the keeper, whereas families had
greater variety of vessel forms, with more decorated wares. Few dietary differences were detected,
but, at the boarding house, artefacts of personal
adornment and leisure revealed efforts by mill-
workers to construct not just working-class identities but also distinctive individual identities within
the corporate system.

See also: consumption; household archaeology;
institutions; urban archaeology

Further reading

Beaudry, M.C. and Mrozowski, S.A. (eds) (1989)
*Interdisciplinary Investigations of the Boott Mills,
Lowell, Massachusetts. Volume III: The Boarding
House System as a Way of Life*, Cultural Resources
Management Series 21, Boston: National Park
Service, North Atlantic Regional Office.
—— (1987) *Interdisciplinary Investigations of the Boott
Mills, Lowell, Massachusetts. Volume I: Life in the
Boarding Houses: A Preliminary Report*, Cultural
Resources Management Series 18, Boston:
National Park Service, North Atlantic Regional
Office.
—— (eds) (1988) *Interdisciplinary Investigations of the
Boott Mills, Lowell, Massachusetts. Volume II: The
Kirk Street Agents' House*, Cultural Resources
Management Series 19, Boston: National Park
Service, North Atlantic Regional Office.
Mahlstedt, T.F. and George, D. (1988) *Boott Cotton
Mills, Lowell National Historic Park, Lowell, Massa-
chusetts: Archeological Data Section of the Historic
Structures Report*, draft, Denver, CO: Denver
Service Center, National Park Service.
Mrozowski, S.A., Ziesing, G.H. and Beaudry, M.C.
(1996) *'Living on the Boott': Historical Archaeology at
the Boott Mills Boardinghouses in Lowell, Massachu-
setts*, Amherst: University of Massachusetts Press.

MARY C. BEAUDRY

Bordesley Abbey, England

Bordesley Abbey was a (royal) Cistercian abbey
founded around 1140 and dissolved in 1538, after
which most of the site was deserted. Few of the
monastery's records exist, but the whole monastic
complex survives as a complicated set of earthworks extending over 35 ha. Running for more
than thirty years, the Bordesley Abbey Project is
one of the most sustained, interdisciplinary, research programmes on a European monastery. The
site is owned and maintained as an amenity by the
Borough of Redditch; a visitor centre adjacent to
the precinct displays and interprets some of the
major finds.

The heart of the project has been the abbey
church. Here there is an exceptionally well-
preserved succession of floors and construction
levels within the 2 m high remains of its walls:
seven separate floor levels and intermediate make-
up and builders' layers, extending from the twelfth-
century preparatory building operations to the final
floor and destruction debris from the Dissolution.
The archaeological stratification and material
assemblage can be related to the architectural
remains to give a detailed history of the building
and its use in a way that is rarely equalled.

Investigations have extended beyond the abbey
church and the cloister, with its associated buildings
and cemeteries, to the gateway chapel (with its
unusual seventeenth- to nineteenth-century grave
markers from the time when it was used as a parish
church) and the precinct boundary. The watermills
and industrial workshops (operating from the twelfth
to fourteenth century) on the precinct's periphery
have also been excavated, giving the earliest
evidence for water-powered metalworking in the
country. The network of farms (granges) is now being
examined through documentary and archaeological
fieldwork to investigate Bordesley's economy and its
relationship with the West Midlands.

Orthodox archaeological techniques have been
enhanced by geophysical and geochemical surveys
in the outer court, and by macrobotanic analysis,
which demonstrated the transformation of a
wooded, poorly drained valley into a place for
permanent occupation, testifying to the dramatic
impact of the Cistercians on the Arrow valley.
Dendrochronology has not only provided accu-

rate dating for the mills, drainage systems and a grave cover, but also illustrated woodland management. Scientific analysis has established the sources of ceramic building materials.

The project has continued to develop and to test its hypotheses and methodologies. The multidisciplinary approach remains, however, central and has developed important research themes: the sequence and technology of stone and timber buildings; the use of space that informs liturgical change and decorative schemes (through **architecture**, window **glass**, tiles and painting); patronage and its expression in building schemes, gifts or burial; and medieval technology and industry. Bordesley has the capacity not only to increase our knowledge of monasticism, but also of wider aspects of the medieval world because of the exceptional preservation of its archaeological deposits.

See also: England; gravestones; industrial archaeology

Further reading

Astill, G. (1993) *A Medieval Industrial Complex and Its Landscape: The Metalworking Watermills and Workshops of Bordesley Abbey*, York: CBA Research Report 92.

—— (1989) 'Monastic research designs: Bordesley Abbey and the Arrow Valley', in R. Gilchrist and H. Mytum (eds) *The Archaeology of Rural Monasteries*, Oxford: BAR British Series 203, pp. 277–93.

Astill, G., Hirst, S. and Wright, S.M. (2000) 'Bordesley Abbey' (http://www.reading.ac.uk/bordesley).

Astill, G.G. and Wright, S.M. (1993) 'Perceiving patronage in the archaeological record: Bordesley Abbey', in M. Carver (ed.) *In Search of Cult: Archaeological Investigations in Honour of Philip Rahtz*, Woodbridge: University of York Archaeological Papers and the Boydell Press, pp. 125–37.

Hirst, S.M., Walsh, D.A. and Wright, S.M. (1983) *Bordesley Abbey II: Second Report on Excavations at Bordesley Abbey, Redditch, Hereford-Worcestershire*, Oxford: BAR British Series 111.

Hirst, S.M. and Wright, S.M. (1989) 'Bordesley Abbey church: A long-term research excava-

tion', in R. Gilchrist and H. Mytum (eds) *The Archaeology of Rural Monasteries*, Oxford: BAR British Series 203, pp. 295–311.

Rahtz, P. and Hirst, S. (1976) *Bordesley Abbey, Redditch, Hereford-Worcestershire: First Report on Excavations 1969–73*, Oxford: BAR British Series 23.

GRENVILLE ASTILL, SUE HIRST
AND SUSAN M. WRIGHT

bottles

Bottles constitute one of the most important and abundant kinds of **material culture** studied by historical archaeologists. Like **ceramics**, bottles can be examined to yield important information about the technological, social and economic characteristics of history. Some bottles are made of ceramics, but most of the bottles studied by historical archaeologists are made of glass. As may be expected, bottles can be produced in many shapes, sizes and colours. They can be painted or labelled with the name of the liquid they contain. Bottles can contain alcoholic and non-alcoholic beverages, medicines (both prescription and proprietary), chemicals, foodstuffs, fruit and many other materials.

Glass bottles

Ancient Syrians probably developed the world's first bottles around 1500 BC by wrapping strands of molten glass around forms made of straw, mud and animal dung. Around about 300 BC, the Syrians also developed a method of producing glass bottles by using a blow pipe, a method that remained essentially unchanged until the mid-nineteenth century. Overall, however, the methods for producing glass bottles have changed throughout history, from complete mouth blowing ('free blown') to mouth blowing in a mould (beginning in the late seventeenth century) and eventually to the fully machine-made bottle (in the early twentieth century).

Historical archaeologists can examine glass bottles to date archaeological sites and soil strata (see **stratification, soil**) by recognising the clues the bottles contain. When archaeologists examine bottles they break the bottle down into a series of elements, which are, from top to bottom: the finish (composed of the bore (or mouth)), the lip (the first ring of glass under the bore) and the string rim (a second ring of glass that, if present, appears just beneath the lip); the neck; the shoulder; the body; the heel (the very bottom of the bottle); the resting point (the part on which the bottle actually sits) and the base (the entire bottom, including resting point). Some bottles also contain an area on the base that is pushed up into the bottle's body, thereby reducing the amount of liquid a bottle can hold but also providing greater stability for the bottle. Bottle experts refer to this depressed area as the 'push up', 'kick up' or sometimes merely the 'kick'. Great variety can exist in the design of the elements that can appear on any one bottle. For instance, archaeologists have identified several different kinds of bottle lips, including but not limited to forms that are straight, flanged, flattened, rounded and V-shaped. Bottle bodies, when viewed from the shoulder down towards the base, can be circular, oval, kidney-shaped, square, round with flat sides, triangular and many other shapes. Some bottles have even been made in the shape of log cabins or have been elongated so that their flat, side panels represent pointed cathedral windows.

Mouth-blown bottles contain a tell-tale mark on their bases called a 'pontil scar' or 'pontil mark'. The pontil is a long iron rod that the glass blower attached to the base of the newly made bottle while the glass was still hot. A mark was left in the glass on the bottle's base when the glass blower removed the pontil. Pontil marks can be either 'unfinished' (leaving rough and sometimes sharp edges), 'roughly ground' (where the glass blower partially smoothed the pontil scar) and 'finished' (where the glass blower has smoothed the rough glass completely away, leaving a shallow, round mark on the base). Pontil marks can be found on mouth-blown bottles made from Roman times until the invention of bottle-making machines in the late nineteenth century. 'Empontilling' is still present wherever mouth-blown bottles are made.

Historical archaeologists also examine the bottles and bottle sherds they find for evidence of seams, because these features convey information about the technology used in a bottle's manufacture and hence relative date. Only bottles made in moulds will exhibit seams. Thus, completely mouth-blown bottles have no seams. The exception to this rule is those bottles produced in 'dip moulds'. In this technique, the glass blower would stand above the mould, sometimes on a raised platform, and, using a blow pipe, blow the bottle into the mould. The resultant bottle would have the shape of the mould, but it would be essentially mouth-blown. Bottle makers used the dip-moulding technique throughout the eighteenth century, and in some places until the mid-nineteenth century.

Bottles blown into 'two-piece moulds' contain mould seams that start beneath the finish, run down the body, extend diagonally across the base and then run up the other side of the bottle. The seam does not extend to the bottle's lip because the bottle makers used a hand tool to make the finish. Bottle specialists have established that bottles made with two-piece moulds date from about AD 1750 to about 1880. Some two-piece moulds are called 'vertical body moulds' because bottle makers employed a separate base part that leaves a seam mark around the heel of the bottle. Manufacturers produced bottles made in two-piece moulds from the mid-nineteenth century until well into the twentieth century.

Bottle makers also used 'three-piece moulds'. These moulds were composed of a dip mould for the bottle's body and two matching halves for the shoulder and neck segments. The use of a three-piece mould leaves a seam line running around the bottle's shoulder. Bottle manufacturers used three-piece moulds from about the 1820s until the 1920s.

In the late nineteenth century, several bottle makers began to experiment with methods of producing bottles with the aid of machines. Inventors patented semi-automatic bottle-making machines in the USA in 1881 and in England in 1886, with France following in 1897, and Germany in 1906. Some of the machines were of limited use, only having the ability to produce certain kinds of vessels like wide-mouthed jars, and bottle manufacturers also often faced the opposition of glassblowers' labour unions who could foresee the loss of their jobs with the widespread use of machines. Michael Owens invented the first fully automatic bottle-making machine around 1903, and within a few years bottle companies were moving rapidly to replace their glass-blowing workforce with fully automatic machines. Bottles made by semi-automatic and fully automatic machines look similar. They can exhibit 'ghost' mould seams around the lip, around the neck just under the finish, on the body around the heel and vertically up the side of the body. The most telling seam line, however, is the line that runs vertically up the entire height of the bottle from the base to the lip. Archaeologists finding bottles with a seam line that extends up the entire surface of the bottle can feel confident that the bottle was made after about 1903.

Many machine-made glass bottles carry the name of their manufacturer embossed or stamped on their bases. Using books of **makers' marks**, archaeologists can use these tell-tale symbols to identify the maker and to date the bottles they find during excavation. For example, the Illinois Glass Company of Alton, Illinois, operated from 1873 until 1929. Before about 1880, the company stamped its products with a simple 'I G'. From about 1880 to 1900, they used 'I G Co', and, from about 1900 to 1916, they placed 'I G Co' inside an elongated diamond. Their last symbol was a simple 'I' inside the diamond. Thus, an archaeologist finding a bottle base marked 'I G Co' would know that it had been manufactured by the Illinois Glass Company some time between about 1880 and 1900.

Another important element of glass bottles is the closure. Throughout the history of bottle manu-facture, bottle makers had to invent ways to ensure that the contents of their bottles stayed inside and free from contamination. Bottle makers worried about closure design because, unlike **ceramics**, consumers bought bottles, not for the bottle itself, but for what it contained. The producers of foodstuffs, medicines, inks and other liquids would do business with bottle makers who could ensure a secure closure. Corks were some of the earliest and the most widely used bottle stoppers, having been used as early as the sixteenth century. Bottles that used cork stoppers would be made with straight or gently sloping bores into which the cork would snugly fit. Some bottles, such as those containing pepper sauce, had a metal sprinkler top affixed to the top of the cork, but the bottle's bore would still be straight. Other bottles, also with straight or gently sloping bores, could have glass stoppers inserted in them.

Bottle makers became interested in new closure designs during the nineteenth century with the invention and marketing of a wide array of new products, many of which contained gas. Many inventors obtained patents for their new closure forms. Some of these inventions required the use of new bottle designs. For example, Englishman Hiram Codd invented a complex stopper in the early 1870s that involved the use of a marble as a stopper. His idea was that the gas from the carbonated beverage would keep the marble firmly against the inside the neck and thus make a firm seal. To employ this stopper design, however, bottle makers had to produce bottles that had a flattened neck (to hold the marble in place) and two glass ledges inside the neck (to keep the marble from plugging up the bore). Without question, the crown finish, invented by American William Painter in the early 1890s, was the most effective closure for carbonated drinks. Characterised by the famous crimped bottle cap, this closure is still widely used today.

Many bottles, of course, carry labels on them that describe their contents. A great many other bottles, however, had messages embossed directly on their surfaces. Nineteenth-century medicine bottles were usually made in a rectangular shape so that they could be embossed with information – product name, location of business, flavour and so forth – on their front, back and side panels. Some of them were even embossed with a human organ, like a kidney, to show what ailment they were intended to cure. Other bottles, like the famous Coca-Cola bottle, have both a distinctive emboss-ing design and a unique and readily identifiable shape. In the twentieth century, some bottle makers used combinations of embossing and painting.

Ceramic bottles

Not all bottles were made of glass. During the nineteenth century, for example, some producers of ale, stout and beer began to market their products in heavy, ceramic bottles. One of the first to use this method was the William Younger Company of Edinburgh, Scotland, around 1805. Archaeologists working on nineteenth-century sites often find examples of these bottles because, like most ceramics, these bottles survive well in the ground. Ale, stout and beer bottles were usually made of wheel-thrown salt-glazed **stoneware**. The bodies and bases of these bottles were often cream-coloured (and usually referred to as 'Bristol' glazed) and have a tan wash that extends from the shoulder to the lip. Many of them were stamped with the manufacture's name on their base and sometimes on their heel. Some stoneware bottles may also be stamped with the name of their contents, like 'ROOT BEER', though ceramic soft-drink bottles were not as common as ale, stout and beer bottles.

Bottle makers in the rest of Europe also made stoneware bottles for ale and other alcoholic drinks. Unlike the other forms, which generally mirrored the shapes of glass bottles, some bottles were usually tall and cylindrical in shape with a short neck, a narrow bore and a rounded, globular finish. These bottles often had a small, loop handle attached to one shoulder, and they were often stamped with the city of their origin, such as **Amsterdam**.

In addition to ceramic bottles for alcoholic beverages, bottle makers also produced stoneware bottles for ink. These bottles were usually somewhat squat in appearance, often brown in colour and sometimes they would exhibit a tiny spout pressed into the edge of the lip. These bottles could also be impressed with the name of ink they contained.

Further reading

Fike, R.E. (1987) *The Bottle Book: A Comprehensive Guide to Historic, Embossed Medicine Bottles*, Salt Lake City: Gibbs M. Smith.

Jones, O. and Sullivan, C. (1985) *The Parks Canada Glass Glossary for the Description of Containers, Tablewares, Flat Glass, and Closures*, Studies in Archaeology and History, Ottawa: National Historic Parks and Sites Branch, Parks Canada.

Ketchum, W.C., Jr (1975) *A Treasury of American Bottles*, Indianapolis: Bobbs-Merrill.

Toulouse, J.H. (1971) *Bottle Makers and Their Marks*, New York: Thomas Nelson.

CHARLES E. ORSER, JR

Brazil

The study of archaeology in Brazil began in the mid-nineteenth century, sponsored by the Brazilian Institute for History and Geography, at Rio de Janeiro, but historical archaeology in the region has only developed in earnest since the 1980s. This late development is due to several reasons, not least of which is the fact that the country experienced military rule from 1964 to 1985, hindering the free search for the historical past. Given the history of archaeology in Brazil, the field is usually conceived as being divided into prehistory, historical archaeology and **classical archaeology**. Prehistory deals with remains of indigenous peoples up to AD 1500, historical archaeology covers the period after the arrival of the Portuguese in 1500 and classical archaeology studies the ancient civilisations of Greece and Rome. Historical archaeology is divided further into urban archaeology, the archaeology of Roman Catholic missions (see **mission sites**), maroon archaeology, heritage and educational approaches and **rescue archaeology**. Publications in historical archaeology and the preparation of graduate dissertations are increasingly visible in the academy and in the society at large.

Brazilian archaeologists usually say that 'history' began on 22 April, AD 1500, when Pedro Álvares Cabral arrived with his expedition on the Brazilian coast. The historical period is usually divided into three periods: colonial (AD 1500–1822), Independent Imperial (1822–1889) and Independent Republican (1889 onwards). The study of the **material culture** of historical sites in Brazil began in the 1930s with architects interested in preserving buildings and working in heritage institutions. It was at this time that the first laws regarding the protection of historical sites were enacted. Archaeologists, however, would only turn to historical subjects later, in the 1960s, when Brazilian archaeologists started a well-established tradition of studying classical archaeology. Classical archaeology has also been contributing to the spread of methodological and theoretical interpretive frameworks among historical archaeologists dealing with Brazilian sites. Historical archaeology properly developed as a minor concern for archaeologists trained as prehistorians, in the

1960s and 1970s, but the interest in the field has grown continuously since the mid-1980s.

The study of Roman Catholic missions in the south of Brazil was the first area of concentration to be established by archaeologists using a historical approach. Jesuit missions were established in areas inhabited by Guarani Indians and they lived almost independently from the Spanish authority. When the Jesuits were expelled in the eighteenth century and colonists from the Portuguese colony (Brazil) settled in the surrounding areas, the missions were left in ruins. In the 1980s, archaeologists from Rio Grande do Sul State in southern Brazil decided to develop a long-term archaeological project about the missions. Due to the rich documentary evidence available and to the institutional links with the discipline of history, archaeological fieldwork has been carried out in order to supplement information to a documentary history of the sites.

Elsewhere in the country, **urban archaeology** has been developing, largely as a result of major city development projects, notably in Rio de Janeiro, São Paulo, Belo Horizonte and other metropolises. Rural-settlement historical archaeology is still rare, but maroon archaeology has been attracting archaeologists concerned with exploitation and ethnic issues. Eighteenth-century runaway settlements in Minas Gerais State, in the south-east of the country, and most notably the huge seventeenth-century maroon settlement of **Palmares**, in the north-east, studied by Brazilian and foreign archaeologists, emphasise a growing interest in a historical archaeology engaged in exploring racial and social themes, particularly those that are relevant both to society at large and to other social sciences and the humanities.

Rescue archaeology has been a major force in promoting fieldwork in Brazil, as both private and public companies are bound by law to fund salvage surveys and excavations. Historical archaeology has also benefited, mostly in urban redevelopment, as surveys and excavations revealed remains of vernacular buildings (see **vernacular architecture**) in different areas. The rescue survey at the site of the rebellion of ordinary backlands followers of Antônio Conselheiro, in the so-called Canudos revolt of the late nineteenth century, is another example of the search for non-elite remains.

Several historical archaeology projects, be they rescue or research-driven, have been mindful of the educational aspects of archaeology, as well as of the related heritage management implications of any archaeological endeavour. Since the 1990s, public archaeology has been considered by many archaeologists as a necessary development, as is the growing dialogue with historians, anthropologists and other academics studying similar subjects.

The study of artefacts, like ceramics, pottery and bottles, is still rare, largely because there is a lack of publication of scholarly corpuses of material that could enable more interpretive studies to be proposed. On the other hand, graduate courses in historical archaeology, even when they are situated within a history, anthropology or general archaeology framework, are spreading, and there are in the late 1990s historical archaeology master's and doctoral dissertations being written. Some are even published as journal articles. The outlook of the discipline is bright, considering its growing insertion in a world context and the interest of the new generations of students.

See also: classical archaeology; South America

Further reading

Funari, P.P.A. (1997) 'Archaeology, history, and historical archaeology in South America', *International Journal of Historical Archaeology* 1: 189–206.

—— (1997) 'European archaeology and two Brazilian offspring: Classical archaeology and art history', *Journal of European Archaeology* 5: 137–48.

—— (1996) 'Historical archaeology in Brazil, Uruguay, and Argentina', *World Archaeological Bulletin* 7: 51–62.

Orser, C.E., Jr (1996) *A Historical Archaeology of the Modern World*, New York: Kluwer Academic/Plenum Press.

Prous, A. (1994) 'L'Archéologie Brésilienne aujourd'hui. Problèmes et tendances', in P. Lévêque, J.A. Dabdab Trabulsi and S. Carvalho (eds) *Recherches brésiliennes: Archéologie, histoire ancienne et anthropologie*, Paris: Les Belles Lettres, pp. 9–43.

PEDRO PAULO A. FUNARI

Brunswick Town, North Carolina, USA

Brunswick Town, North Carolina, USA, was a colonial outpost built around 1725 and destroyed in 1776. The town was excavated from 1958 to 1968 under the direction of Stanley South. It is an important site in historical archaeology not only because it provides information about a colonial, North American settlement but also because it figures prominently in South's many theoretical works.

Brunswick Town was settled as a British colony on the banks of the Cape Fear River in southern North Carolina. Spanish raiders sacked the town in 1748. In an effort to build the fortunes of Brunswick Town in the 1750s, a group of gentlemen of the town asked the royal governor to establish his home there, which he did in 1758. By the 1770s, after the governor had moved away, many of the residents of the town, including the King's collector of customs, began to express their support for the American separatists' cause. As a result of this apparent disloyalty, the British Army attacked the town and destroyed most of it in April 1776. Two people continued to live in Brunswick Town until 1820, but after that date it was never reoccupied. Local preservationists became interested in the town ruins in 1909. Archaeologists discovered that some of the town was located underneath the remains of Fort Anderson, an earthen fortification (see **fortifications**) built around 1862 by the Confederate States of America. A detailed map, drawn in 1769, helped to guide the archaeological research and provided a valuable tool for interpreting the remains.

South completely excavated the town, including the Hepburn-Reonalds House, the Public House–Tailor Shop, the Moore House (including its well, detached kitchen and smokehouse) and Russellborough, the royal governor's mansion. In the first detailed theoretical work in historical archaeology, *Method and Theory in Historical Archaeology*, South used the remains of Brunswick Town to illustrate his ideas about constructing a fully scientific historical archaeology. As part of this work, he introduced the 'Brunswick Pattern of Refuse Disposal' using the information he had collected at the Brunswick Town site. South recognised this pattern as rooted in the idea that British-Americans living in the eighteenth century deposited their rubbish at the entrances and exits of their residences, retail shops and military installations. Because South could demonstrate the widespread validity of this finding, he proposed that the Brunswick Pattern of Refuse Disposal provided a way to predict the location of refuse deposits at other eighteenth-century sites occupied by British-Americans. His idea was based on the anthropological concept that men and women exhibit behaviour that is consistent with their cultural norms and mores.

See also: behavioural historical archaeology; history of historical archaeology; processual archaeology

Further reading

South, S. (1977) *Method and Theory in Historical Archaeology*, New York: Academic Press.
—— (1967) 'Russellborough, the royal governors' mansion at Brunswick Town', *The Conference on Historic Site Archaeology Papers*, 1: 111–22.
—— (1962) 'Interpreting the Brunswick Town ruins', *The Florida Anthropologiest*, 17(2): 56–62.

CHARLES E. ORSER, JR

Buenos Aires, Argentina

Traditionally, American archaeology as a branch of anthropology has focused its interest on the 'cultural other', that is to say in the pre-European past. In this way, archaeology and prehistory have generally been considered as synonyms. This conception is one of the reasons why the archaeology of historical sites has been slow to develop in Argentina.

In Argentina, as in almost all Latin American countries, there were no systematic projects in historical archaeology before the 1980s, except for some isolated works done either by prehistoric archaeologists, by professionals related to the field of history or even by amateurs. Since then, and with increasing force, investigators have begun to develop studies in this field, approaching diverse themes from different theoretical frameworks.

In 1983, when democracy returned to Argentina, excavations in **urban archaeology** began to appear and this development gave impetus to the growth of historical archaeology. Appearing first in Buenos Aires, this tendency soon spread to cities such as Rosario, Mendoza, Cordoba and Tucumán, among others. Investigations in abandoned urban Spanish colonial centres such as Santa Fe la Vieja (1573), Nombre de Jesus (1580), Concepción del Bermejo (1585) and Ibatín (1565), among others, also boomed. In general, archaeologists pursued aims that were intended to supplement information present in written sources. Some of the most frequently conducted analyses were centred on elaborating **typologies** of archaeological materials, either to study the Native Hispanic contact from normative conceptions – for instance, the '**acculturation** process' – or as a way to reconstruct periods of history. **Mission sites**, operated both by the Franciscans and the Jesuits, are extremely important, but they have not yet been studied in depth.

Since 1990, studies have been developed that are specifically focused on the nineteenth and twentieth centuries. Some of the topics examined include: military settlements; the processes of incorporating new territory into the nation; the extermination of Indians; European immigration processes, which developed during the last part of the nineteenth and first decades of the twentieth centuries; **industrial archaeology**, the archaeology of **capitalism** and underwater archaeology.

Buenos Aires was founded by the Spanish Crown in two attempts. The first attempt was made by Pedro de Mendoza in 1536. Because of isolation, lack of resources and aboriginal hostility, the settlement had to be abandoned. Juan de Garay made the second colonising attempt in 1580, this time on the de la Plata river. This is the settlement that persists today. The physical structure of Buenos Aires corresponds to the typical pattern of the Hispanic American city, consisting of a large square, around which religious and administrative buildings are located. The growth of the city kept relatively steady until the end of the nineteenth century, when it experienced a rapid growth due to the arrival of European immigrants.

Since then, Buenos Aires started an intense process of expansion and transformation that is still underway.

Historical archaeology started in Buenos Aires in the mid-1980s when different locales inside the city were excavated under the supervision of architect Daniel Schávelzon. These excavations were largely works of archaeological rescue, which resulted in the publication of several reports mainly focused on the typological description and classification of the excavated materials. These works generated inferences on various cultural aspects of Buenos Aires society. One of the members of Schávelzon's team, Mario Silveira, is developing studies on historical fauna with the aim of achieving an understanding of the eating habits of the residents of Buenos Aires.

A series of researchers have begun to explore other problems using new theoretical frames of reference, many especially linked to the archaeology of the modern world or of **capitalism**. Thus, Buenos Aires has become a city site, which allows archaeologists to work from an approach that integrates information within a large-scale perspective. Among other topics, Maria Senatore is working on the local production and supply of ceramics, Marcelo Weissel is conducting research on the immigrant working classes in La Boca neighbourhood and Andrés Zarankin is analysing the transformation of the city's spaces and its architectural (see **architecture**) changes through time.

See also: South America

Further reading

Funari, P.P.A. (1997) 'Archaeology, history and historical archaeology in South America', *International Journal of Historical Archaeology* 1: 137–48.

Morresi, E.S. and Gutierrez, R. (1983) *Presencia Hispánica en la Arqueología Argentina*, Resistencia, Museo de Antropología 'Juan A. Martinet', Instituto de Historia, Facultad de Humanidades, Universidad Nacional del Nordeste (UNNE).

Schávelzon, D. (1991) *Arqueología Histórica de Buenos Aires, la Cultura Material Porteña en los Siglos XVIII y XIX*, Buenos Aires: Corregidor.

Zarankin, A. and Senatore, M.X. (1996) 'Reseña

crítica sobre la arqueología colonial en la Argentina', *Páginas sobre Hispanoamérica Colonial, Sociedad y Cultura*, 3: 123–41.

ANDRÉS ZARANKIN

buttons

Buttons are the most common **dress**-related artefact recovered on archaeological sites. Archaeologists study buttons as a class of material culture and use buttons to enhance site interpretation. Buttons reflect styles of dress, modes of production, availability and popularity of materials, and can be used to assess status. Archaeologists classify buttons by material and form, and – since buttons changed gradually through time and reflect changes in manufacturing techniques – use buttons as diagnostic artefacts.

Sculptural evidence in the twelfth century provides the first European evidence of buttons; documentary references exist from *c.* 1300. Excavations by the Museum of London recovered buttons from the medieval period that consist mainly of plain metal buttons thought to be worn by people of low socioeconomic levels. It was not until the sixteenth century, however, that buttons became common clothing fasteners. Buttons were manufactured on a small scale by craftspeople until the mid- to late eighteenth century, when button manufacture expanded. In the nineteenth century, the button industry continued to grow with technological developments, datable by patent registrations, allowing for increasingly rapid production. Until the nineteenth century, buttons were used mainly to fasten men's garments.

Documentary records, such as account books, business records and advertisements, and visual records, such as portraits, prints and photographs, have been employed to define button types, cost and availability in different regions of the world. Buttons were used as fasteners on every manner of clothing. Coat, jacket and vest buttons are decorative types used to fasten these garments. Sleeve buttons consist of a set of linked buttons used to fasten one cuff to another. Sleeve buttons are a special class of buttons, commonly decorated, and the shape of the links can be used to date the buttons. Buttons were also used to fasten shirts, breeches and trousers, boots and shoes, undergarments and gloves. The size and material used to make a button aids archaeologists in identifying a button's use, since these vary according to placement and cost. The kinds of materials used in the manufacture of buttons can be employed to interpret the kinds of clothing worn by individuals at a given site, and to assess the socioeconomic status of these same individuals.

Stanley South developed the first archaeological typology (see **typologies**) of buttons using the sites of **Brunswick Town** and Fort Fisher. This typology described manufacturing techniques, materials, design and other details to aid in identifying buttons from the seventeenth to nineteenth centuries. It remains a useful guide to button identification. Other researchers have developed different typologies and, along with the research conducted by button collectors, provide a comprehensive overview of button types.

Researchers also use buttons to enhance interpretations of archaeological sites. On African American sites, buttons are used to explore the retention and transmutation of West African beliefs by enslaved African Americans. William Kelso proposed that the high frequency of buttons found on African American sites is a product of quilt making, a tradition traced back to West Africa. Enslaved African Americans used pieces of discarded cloth to make quilts, and the buttons were cut from the cloth. Alternatively, Patricia Samford suggested that the high frequency of buttons on African American sites may be because they were strung on gourds, replacing cowrie shells, to make a *shekere*, a West African musical instrument

Uniform buttons, particularly military buttons, have been studied more than any other type of button. The dates of manufacture of different button forms and button images and symbols associated with groups of armed forces are known, making buttons instrumental as an aid to identify battle participants and to further understand the lives and conditions of military encampments.

Buttons are generally classified by material; the material and form of the button can provide information on the mode and date of manufacture. Buttons are made of all types of metal – silver, **pewter**, ferrous metals, copper, brass and steel.

Metal buttons are identifiable according to their form, size, material and, most importantly, type of shank. Metal buttons are recovered on archaeological sites from all periods, but, along with buttons made of organic materials, were among the first kinds of buttons to be made. Metal buttons were manufactured on a small scale in the seventeenth and eighteenth centuries. In the mid- to late eighteenth century, a thriving industry grew in Birmingham, England, which produced metal buttons of all sorts, followed by major technological advancements in the nineteenth century.

Glass buttons were mainly manufactured in the nineteenth and twentieth centuries, though metal buttons set with cut glass were made in the eighteenth century. Black glass buttons were popular in the nineteenth century as imitation jet.

Ceramic buttons were made by **porcelain** companies in the eighteenth and nineteenth centuries; at this time they were an expensive luxury item. Beginning in 1840, porcelain buttons were manufactured using the patented Prosser method whereby powdered clay was pressed into dies, allowing for mass production. White utilitarian ceramic buttons are common archaeological finds. Other types of ceramics were also used to make buttons, though these are rare.

Organic buttons are made of bone, horn, wood and shell; those of bone, horn and wood are among the oldest buttons known. Bone and wood were also used as core materials for metal and fabric buttons. Evidence of bone-button manufacture is often found on household sites, revealing a small-scale level of manufacture. Shell buttons were made in the eighteenth century and mass-produced in the nineteenth century.

Synthetic buttons are made of celluloid, casein, rubber and plastic. The form of synthetic buttons ranges widely. These buttons are easily datable; beginning dates for the production of synthetic materials are generally known.

See also: African American archaeology; battlefield archaeology

Further reading

Albert, A.H. (1976) *Record of American Uniforms and Historical Buttons*, Boyertown, PA: Boyertown Publishing Company.

Egan, G. and Pritchard, F. (1991) *Dress Accessories c.1150–c.1450: Medieval Finds from Excavations in London: 3*, London: The Stationery Office.

South, S. (1964) 'Analysis of the buttons from Brunswick Town and Fort Fisher', *Florida Anthropologist*, 17(2): 113–33.

White, D.P. (1977) 'The Birmingham button industry', *Post-medieval Archaeology* 11: 67–79.

CAROLYN L. WHITE

C

Canada, western

The formative years of historical archaeology in western Canada were without question dominated by fur trade investigations. Fur trading posts across the west became the focus of large-scale excavation and reconstruction projects, particularly in the 1960s and 1970s when they were seen as a vehicle by which to manifest a growing pride in national identity. Several archaeologists in western Canada, however, have examined sites that are not strictly 'fur trade' sites.

Although related to the fur trade, the Métis, descendants of Euro-Canadian fur traders and native women, have been studied archaeologically with approaches not usually employed in standard fur trade investigations. Their distinctive ethnic origins and cultural development have encouraged archaeologists to explore aspects of culture change and adaptation, especially when Métis buffalo hunters of the nineteenth century are considered. Archaeologists have conducted numerous investigations into Métis sites across the prairie west, with the earliest taking place in 1967 when wintering village sites were recorded and excavated in the Cypress Hills region of south-eastern Alberta. Further work on more cabin clusters in this area was summarised in a master's thesis by Jack Elliott in 1971, and this work provided a comparative base for future research. The Provincial Museum of Alberta sponsored excavations between 1970 and 1983 at Buffalo Lake, a large late nineteenth-century wintering village in central Alberta, and, in 1986, a large multifaceted research project representing the first extensive examination of Métis wintering village sites in Saskatchewan was undertaken (Burley *et al.* 1992). This effort focused on culture change as observed in spatial organisation and lifeways. The publication from this research stands as a model example of successful synthesis of anthropological principles and archaeological and historical approaches in Métis studies.

The largest archaeological project developed around the Métis in western Canada was the multi-year study at Batoche, Saskatchewan, a permanent village site occupied after the abandonment of the buffalo-hunting life. The first of three major field seasons began in 1976 (and continued in 1977 and 1978) and smaller-scale excavations have been conducted on a specific-need basis in subsequent years. The original project goals were to research settlement patterns, to assess the presumed archaeological distinctiveness of a Métis community and to discover socioeconomic differences within the village. To deal with the very large collection of artefacts and spatial information, a computerised system for recording, processing and analysing site data was developed in 1976. The artefact coding system was an especially important element of the Batoche project and contributed to succeeding historical archaeological analyses in the Parks Canada western region. Archaeologists in the Red River (Winnipeg) region of Manitoba have conducted a large number of studies into the lifeways and residential patterns of agricultural Métis settlers.

The near extinction of buffalo and the removal of native people to reserves in the 1870s marked a dramatic change in human history on the western plains. The North West Mounted Police acted as a vanguard of incoming Euro-Canadian settlement and were important in the transition to sedentary life for native people. Since this era of western history was seen to contribute to the same sense of developing national character as did the fur trade, it is little surprise that a number of North West Mounted Police posts were selected for reconstruction and public interpretation by federal, provincial and municipal agencies, particularly during the 1970s. Historical archaeology was thus performed on a largely 'mission-oriented' basis, in which information on building location and external features was gathered prior to site development. Fort Walsh in the Cypress Hills is one of the best known examples among at least six forts explored archaeologically. In 1973, a four-season programme was initiated by Parks Canada to investigate Fort Walsh and the town that had grown up around it in the 1870s. The purpose of the excavations was to provide information to guide development and interpretation within the park. Most of the reporting that ensued through the *Parks Canada Manuscript Report Series* (on the **material culture** of Fort Walsh, including **ceramics**, container glass, faunal remains, metal and glass **bottles**) was strictly analytical in scope, but higher-level questions were addressed in a master's thesis by Jeff Murray in 1985. Murray sought to discern social relations within the material and spatial elements of the Fort Walsh built environment.

Large-scale ranching endeavours occupied the western plains in the 1880s and 1890s, prior to the era of concerted homesteading. Two examples, one with extant buildings and the other with archaeological remains only, have been the focus of excavations prior to interpretive development.

A fair amount of attention in western Canadian historical archaeology has been paid to the remains of the homesteading and settlement era of the late nineteenth and early twentieth century. At the beginning of the twentieth century, the Canadian government actively solicited in Europe, particularly Eastern Europe, for farming folk who could be moved to the unoccupied western plains and parklands in large numbers. As a result, the social fabric of western Canada is distinctively multicultural. As part of the information-gathering process prior to developing a park comprised of restored Ukrainian farm buildings east of Edmon-

ton, Alberta, a number of Ukrainian homesteads were excavated in 1984 and structural and material culture characteristic of early Ukrainian farm lifeways was collected. In Saskatchewan, an early twentieth-century Doukhobour village was excavated as part of mitigation activities when a major highway realignment exposed it. In a master's thesis based on the excavations and the large artefact and faunal assemblages, Stacy Kozakavich explored the relationship of **ethnicity** and **consumer choice** among the inhabitants of Kirilowa village. Her conclusions were that these Doukhobour farming folk cannot be simply defined in terms of ethnicity, but rather a complex interrelationship of group philosophy, ethnic, economic and geographic factors must be considered.

Homestead sites on the prairies are seldom regarded as significant resources as they are thought to be ubiquitous, but modern development is erasing them quickly from the landscape. They have received some attention through mitigation activities at large dam and reservoir projects in the west, since such site types are commonly represented in the rural area under impact. In one such project, the Souris–Alameda reservoir project, **oral history** was fruitfully combined with archaeology to shed light on regional community structure and organisation. Examples of other early settlement archaeology include Cannington Manor, a village established in 1882 to service British immigrants in southern Saskatchewan, and Motherwell Homestead, a large farm established by a noted politician and agriculturalist in southern Saskatchewan. Both site excavations were mission-oriented; i.e. the objectives were set by historians, architects and engineers involved with developing each site for public interpretation.

Chinese Canadian lifeways in British Columbia have been the focus of research by Imogene Lim of University-College in Nanaimo. Along with Stan Copp of Vancouver's Langara College, she undertook excavations at Canton Alley in Vancouver's Chinatown, in deposits preserved under paved parking lots. It was the first **urban archaeology** in that city and allowed the establishment of a database for comparison with other Chinese urban sites in Canada as well as access to a piece of little-studied western Canadian history. One highlight of the project was the recognition by the city's planning department that heritage went beyond standing buildings and lay in the ground beneath.

As part of her doctoral research at Simon Fraser University, Ying ying Chen investigated the Chinese population at Barkerville, an 1860s gold-mining boomtown in the Cariboo region of British Columbia. Working outwards from the townsite for a radius of some 50 km, Chen conducted an archaeological survey of outlying Chinese mining settlements and camps. She integrated this settlement information with results of archaeological excavation of the Chih Kung T'ang building in Barkerville (conducted under the supervision of Phil Hobler in 1993) and the data she had collected on the building itself during a detailed architectural study in 1991. She discovered a settlement system among the Chinese in which smaller outlying settlements were linked with the larger Chinatowns – an economic and mercantile structure with roots in China itself.

Church missions have received a fair amount of archaeological work in western Canada, usually as part of interpretive development. In these instances, research often explores the nature of culture contact with native populations, and the adaptive process undergone by both native and white communities through the presence of the mission.

Natural resource exploitation, such as logging, mining (coal, silver–lead–zinc, clay and other materials) and fishing, has been a vital part of the economic growth of western Canada. Although the physical remains of such historic activities usually fall within the field of **industrial archaeology**, the associated residential areas are frequently regarded as a more accessible avenue by which to explore what can typically be large, complex and dangerous industrial sites. Thus, the study of workers' housing, for example, tends to be conducted within historical rather than industrial archaeological parameters. Case studies include investigation of various coal-mining townsites such as Lille, Passburg and Pocohantas in the Rocky Mountains (including excavations at brothel sites in the coal-mine towns of south-western Alberta) and residences associated with the Gulf of Georgia Cannery, the Britannia Ship Yard and the McLean lumber mill, all three on the Pacific coast and being developed by Parks Canada.

A large proportion of the historical archaeology undertaken in western Canada has been driven by management needs whenever a site was selected for public interpretive development. This has produced a vast body of data and some pre-eminent work in material culture studies. The dominance of **cultural-resource management** (CRM) as the main venue for modern archaeology is resulting in a paradox: many more historical sites are being encountered under historical resource assessment activities, but few receive more than cursory treatment, such as mapping and recording. Research-oriented historical archaeology is now best found in the universities of western Canada.

Further reading

Burley, D.V., Horsfall, G.A. and Brandon, J.D. (1992) *Structural Considerations of Métis Ethnicity: An Archaeological, Architectural and Historical Study*, Vermillion: University of South Dakota Press.

Doll, M.F.V., Kidd, R.S. and Day, J.P. (1988) *The Buffalo Lake Métis site: A Late Nineteenth Century Settlement in the Parkland of Central Alberta*, Edmonton: Alberta Culture and Multiculturalism.

Kennedy, M. (1995) 'Industrial archaeology in western Canada', *Manitoba Archaeological Journal* 5(2): 86–104.

—— (1989) 'Houses with red lights: The nature of female households in the sporting subculture community', in S. MacEachern, D. J.W. Archer and R.D. Garvin (eds) *Households and Communities. Proceedings of the 21st Annual Chacmool Conference*, Calgary: The Archaeological Association of the University of Calgary, pp. 93–100.

Klimko, O. (1998) 'Nationalism and the growth of fur trade archaeology in western Canada', in P. J. Smith and D. Mitchell (eds), *Bringing Back the Past: Historical Perspectives on Canadian Archaeology*, Ottawa: Canadian Museum of Civilization, pp. 203–13.

Klimko, O. and Taft, M. (1990) 'A sense of place: A preliminary report on an experiment in historic archaeology, folklore and oral history', *The Western Canadian Anthropologist* 7(1–2): 139–55.

MARGARET A. KENNEDY

Cannon's Point Plantation, Georgia, USA

Cannon's Point Plantation was a late eighteenth- and early nineteenth-century, long-staple cotton plantation located on St Simons Island, Georgia, USA, on the Atlantic coast. Historical records indicate that John Couper, originally from Scotland, was the owner and builder of the plantation. Couper and his family moved to Cannon's Point in 1796 and established the slave-holding estate. At the time of the plantation's creation, long-staple cotton enjoyed a brisk world market and generally brought a good price because it was used for making lace and fine thread. During the antebellum, or pre-US Civil War era (1800–60), many prominent people, including the world-renowned geologist Charles Lyell, visited the plantation and recorded their observations of it. One visitor even left a detailed account of slave life on the plantation, a somewhat rare occurrence at the time. The plantation continued to operate in one fashion or another until 1890, when a fire destroyed the mansion and the site was largely abandoned.

In 1972, a development corporation purchased the Cannon's Point Plantation property with the intention of building a residential subdivision in this now highly sought-after location. The developers contacted the late Charles Fairbanks, then professor of anthropology at the University of Florida and the founder of **plantation archaeology**, and asked him to consider conducting excavations there. Fairbanks, along with his students, received several grants to complete this research programme.

Cannon's Point Plantation is important within historical archaeology for several reasons, most of them related directly to the research and writing of one of Fairbanks's students, John Otto. Much of the early, anthropologically focused plantation archaeology in the USA was geared towards the examination of the settlements of African American slaves, but Cannon's Point Plantation offered an opportunity to investigate habitation sites that had been home not only to slaves, but also to owners and overseers. The spatial layout of the plantation made this kind of study possible because

each settlement area was distinct. The planters' house and complex was located on the extreme northern tip of the island, with slave cabins (probably intended for house servants) placed nearby to the south. The overseer's cabin was situated further south, and beyond it was another group of slave dwellings. This physical arrangement meant that excavations could occur within each discrete occupation zone, with the implication being that any differences in the artefacts could be attributable to the different social positions of each group (planter, overseer, slave). In this sense, the excavations at Cannon's Point Plantation served as a test case for examining the differences in the **material culture** of the various groups of men and women who lived on slave plantations.

Another important aspect of Otto's research at Cannon's Point Plantation was that he was one of the first historical archaeologists to write specifically about **race**. While race and racial identification was a central element of life in the antebellum US South, archaeologists before Otto had scarcely mentioned it. However, Otto proposed that race, as a social if not biological factor, should have certain archaeological correlations. He posited that slaves – people who were judged by US society to be black and enslaved – would have had a different access to artefacts than those men and women who were perceived as white and who were essentially free.

So, while the research at Cannon's Point Plantation demonstrated the value and potential of plantation (see **plantation archaeology**) and African American archaeologies in general, it also provided information that proved central to the theoretical maturation of historical archaeology. Otto's research at the plantation, though somewhat dated by the year 2000, stands nonetheless as a major achievement in the field.

See also: African American archaeology; history of historical archaeology; plantation archaeology

Further reading

Orser, C.E., Jr (1988) 'The archaeological analysis of plantation society: Replacing status and caste with economics and power', *American Antiquity* 53: 735–51.

Otto, J.S. (1984) *Cannon's Point Plantation, 1794–1860: Living Conditions and Status Patterns in the Old South*, Orlando: Academic Press.

—— (1977) 'Artifacts and status differences: A comparison of ceramics from planter, overseer, and slave sites on an antebellum plantation', in S. South (ed.) *Research Strategies in Historical Archaeology*, New York: Academic Press, pp. 91–118.

CHARLES E. ORSER, JR

Cape Town, South Africa

Cape Town is situated at the extreme south-western corner of Africa, where a temperate Mediterranean-type climate with winter rainfall distinguishes this region from the rest of South Africa. The **Dutch East India Company** (VOC) established an outpost there in 1652 at which fresh food and water and hospital facilities were provided for crews and passengers on ships sailing between Europe and the East.

Table Bay is open to winter storms and many vessels came to grief on its shores, including the VOC *Oosterland*, which sank in 1697 on its way home to the Netherlands. This was the first shipwreck in the bay to be excavated under the direction of a maritime archaeologist. Artefacts from the cabins, galley and cargo holds included metal and wood objects, clay tobacco pipes (see **pipes, smoking**), money cowries, basketry and cordage, peppercorns and indigo. There were ceramic items (see **ceramics**) used on board and being privately shipped to Europe, including ornaments and tableware of Asian porcelain and Yixing (dry red stoneware) tewares.

A substantial stone-walled fortification (Castle of Good Hope) (see **fortifications**) with five bastions was built after the original earthen fort kept collapsing. A section was excavated through the moat and part of the internal structures of the earthen fort but the rest remains buried beneath a parking lot. Excavations at the Castle tracked extensive changes that took place in and around the structure from 1660 to the present. The archaeological record is rich. Deep trenches beneath the Granary reached pre-colonial beach sands containing artefacts of the Later Stone Age

and they were capped by nineteenth-century brickwork. Outside the Castle entrance, excavations revealed layers of debris deposited in the moat by the barrow-load between 1740 and 1760. Disused wells in the kitchen floors of the Captain's Quarters were filled with discarded objects from the eighteenth century. A huge cache of **bottles** was discovered in the courtyard.

There were extensive stone-built fortifications extended around the town and the peninsula over three centuries as a result of fluctuating periods of war and peace between the Dutch and other European powers. At Table Bay, the Chavonnes Battery (1715), believed destroyed during harbour developments in the 1860s, was discovered beneath a modern fish factory in 1999, and the Amsterdam Battery (1781) and later British fortifications have also been investigated. These structures at times also acted as prisons, barracks and slave quarters.

The VOC established a string of outposts. An early one in False Bay (Muizenberg) comprised a three-roomed structure with an open hearth set on the floor. At Paradise, the post holder was also in charge of surrounding timber resources, and excavations at his homestead revealed a sequence of architectural developments between 1720 and 1800.

Unlike other VOC posts in the Indies, there was no indigenous agriculture at the Cape, so Commander Van Riebeek was ordered to plant a 'garden'. The present suburb of Gardens, however, refers to market gardens owned by free-burgher and free-black colonists that supplemented Company produce and supplied visiting ships and inhabitants of the town with fresh food until the late nineteenth century.

Various edifices were built on Company Garden land through the centuries, including Bertram House (1835), a rare remaining face-brick Georgian dwelling. Beneath Bertram House, and at other sites on the slopes of Table Mountain, archaeologists have found extensive traces of open irrigation systems that were channelled, piped and covered as **urbanisation** sprawled outwards and upwards. The entire Castle moat and VOC-period canals were filled in the late nineteenth century because of their unsanitary state. Refuse was dumped in waterways and on the shores of Table

Bay throughout Cape Town's history; these areas provide rich pickings for historical archaeologists.

Enslaved men, women and children imported from Africa and Asia supplied labour for Company officials, townspeople and farmers alike. Convicts and political exiles were banished to the Cape by authorities at the VOC headquarters in Batavia. Slaves soon outnumbered their owners in Cape Town, while some were freed and settled as colonists. The indigenous Khoi and San populations were assimilated into powerless servitude. The archaeology of specific sites of **slavery**, however, is problematic. The problems are partly due to the close relationships between soldier, sailor, slave and colonist in a small-scale settlement, but also because of spatial integration at the household level. Family, servants, slaves and business shared premises.

A vernacular language (Afrikaans) and style of **architecture** developed during the eighteenth century. Urban renewal has destroyed most traces of earlier period structures, though a handful of official buildings and examples of elite domestic architecture remain from the late eighteenth century. Work on **probate inventories** taken room-by-room has enabled archaeologists to re-create house layouts and room functions for buildings that no longer exist.

Due to the complex nature of **urban archaeology** sites and the virtual absence of discrete waste pits, there is a lack of archaeological sites associated with individual households in Cape Town. Artefacts excavated from a well in Barrack Street that could be correlated with the archival records of particular property owners proved a welcome exception. The three layers of debris also illustrated the transition from VOC to British **material culture**, particularly the declining proportions of Asian porcelains to British refined/industrial wares.

Apart from locally produced low-fired coarse **earthenware**, akin to European styles, all ceramics, glass, metal and textiles were imported from Europe or Asia. Cape Town's ceramic assemblages (see **ceramics**) were dominated by Asian porcelains in the eighteenth century and Staffordshire wares in the nineteenth century. Because the Cape

is situated at the halfway point between East and West, ceramic studies based on European models do not fit. There is no comparable historical archaeology being carried out in other Asian colonial sites. Jane Klose has developed a system of **classification** and typology (see **typologies**) for ceramics that is designed for the Cape. A series of neighbourhood 'dump' sites (Bree Street, Sea Street, Tennant Street and Harrington Street) provided comparative ceramic type collections covering the mid-eighteenth to late nineteenth centuries.

The expansion of the city across its Dutch-period borders has been tracked through excavations and archival research into house and street histories. Hotel extensions in Hof Street allowed archaeologists to record the architectural history of buildings in the block from the elite market-garden estate homestead of the 1790s, through early Cape Georgian styles to the Gothic middle-class villa.

Working-class districts suffered from extensive 'slum' clearance during the twentieth century, when inhabitants were removed under the notorious apartheid Group Areas Acts. Some areas were demolished (District Six), others were partially gentrified (Woodstock) or 'improved' (Bo-Kaap). The archaeology of District Six has included archival research and excavations in Horstley, Stuckeris and Tennant Streets. These sites cover the development of rented housing, changing land ownership and occupants from the 1840s onwards and provide material evidence of daily life up to the very moment of demolition in 1970.

Further reading

Hall, M. and Markell, A. (eds) (1993) 'Historical archaeology in the western cape', *The South African Archaeological Society Goodwin Series* 7.

Worden, N., van Heyningen, E. and Bickford-Smith, V. (1998) *Cape Town, the Making of a City: An Illustrated Social History*, Claremont: David Philip.

ANTONIA MALAN

capitalism

Among historical archaeologists, capitalism typically encompasses an economic system, several types of general theory and a specific historical process. These aspects of capitalism provide enhanced understanding of both the larger social systems in the historic past that structured **everyday life** and the actual people who created the archaeological record. Scholars usually view capitalism from one of two theoretical perspectives. Mainstream economists and economic historians regard capitalism to be the primary concept behind the free market system. The free market system is composed of producers and consumers within industrialised and developing nations. Among economists, the capitalist-based market economy is considered to be a positive catalyst of progress and development. During the late eighteenth century, this perspective was first proposed by Adam Smith, a political economist, in the book, *The Wealth of Nations*. Natural resources, the means of production, such as factories, the transportation system required to distribute commercial goods and consumers form the basis of the free market economy defined by Smith and later economists. The objective of capitalists is to use material wealth or capital to create more wealth. Private ownership of the means of production, profit accumulation, free competition in a market economy and limited government regulation are four of the main economic principles of capitalism.

In contrast to the standard definition of capitalism advanced by mainstream economists, social scientists and humanists influenced by historical materialism and Marxian thought have critiqued capitalism as an exploitative economic system. German social theorist Karl Marx first presented this perspective in the middle of the nineteenth century. Marx argued that capitalism is a pernicious economic system that dehumanises workers. It also creates polarised, industrial societies that contain pronounced wealth disparities between different economic classes. Several influential scholars during the second half of the twentieth century have further expanded the critique of capitalism on a much larger scale than originally presented by Marx. Historical sociologist Immanuel Wallerstein, for example, developed

world-systems theory in the 1970s. A neo-Marxian approach, this perspective emphasises that the modern global economy is composed of wealthy industrialised nations that benefit from unequal exchange relations with politically weaker, developing nations. Similarly, cultural anthropologist Eric Wolf, in the influential book *Europe and the People Without History*, relied upon Marxian-influenced theory to explore the impact of European nations upon pre-industrial cultures across the globe.

Paralleling the interrelated influences of **postprocessual archaeology**, **Marxian approaches**, world-systems theory and the *Annales* School of French social historians, capitalism is a concept that has gained widespread use in historical archaeology since the 1980s. Besides being merely an economic system, historical archaeologists also view capitalism as a powerful and dynamic historical process. For better or worse, this ongoing process was first set in motion 500 years ago and continues to influence the development of the modern world. The history of capitalism is usually divided into two periods. Mercantile capitalism first appeared in the late 1400s and continued through the 1800s. This initial form of capitalism was eventually replaced by industrial capitalism. Industrial capitalism began in late eighteenth-century Great Britain with the onset of the Industrial Revolution. Subsequently transplanted to other nations across the globe, industrial capitalism matured between the 1800s and 1900s. Persisting without abatement into the twenty-first century, industrialisation has exerted long-term cultural repercussions among seemingly disparate cultures.

Commencing in the 1400s, early mercantile capitalists established the first long-distance trading monopolies. The effort to establish long-distance trade relations with distant cultures and governments was also the main catalyst that spurred the expansion of European nations into previously unexplored parts of the globe. During the 1500s, Spain and Portugal began systematically to establish colonies in the New World. By the 1600s, the Netherlands, Great Britain and France were likewise competing to establish colonies in the Americas. Backed financially by private investors and merchants with commercial interests, the purpose of exploration was to claim new territories for settlement. Political rulers and merchants also viewed recently established colonies as potential sources of wealth and as markets for trade goods produced in Europe.

In eastern North America, daily life at many of the colonial-period sites inhabited between the sixteenth and eighteenth centuries was directly or indirectly structured by mercantile capitalism. Historical archaeologists often study the influence of mercantile capitalism at colonial-period sites by first identifying the types of economic activities that were conducted by different households. Historical archaeologists are also interested in understanding how economic activities influenced the material culture used by Native Americans, enslaved Africans and European settlers. Along the southern colonial frontier, or backcountry, extending from the Shenandoah Valley of Virginia, to the Georgia Piedmont, USA, for example, economic activities occurred in a sequence or progression of specific types as the colonial period waxed and waned between the late seventeenth and eighteenth centuries. Specific economic activities in turn often produced distinctive sites and artefact assemblages.

Under the protection of soldiers at fortified posts, deerskin traders, a form of frontier merchant, were some of the first Europeans to reside in the backcountry. Forts inhabited by deerskin traders are a prevalent type of colonial-period site investigated by historical archaeologists. George Galphin, for example, operated a lucrative trading post at Silver Bluff, located adjacent to the Savannah River near Augusta, Georgia, between *c*. 1750 and 1780. Galphin exchanged deerskins obtained by Creek and Chickasaw hunters for trade goods manufactured in Europe. Since the early 1980s, several episodes of site investigations have been conducted at Silver Bluff. These field efforts suggest Galphin's trading post was a large, rectangular compound enclosed by a tall, defensive wooden wall, or palisade. The compound contained several wooden-frame structures. A storehouse for trade goods and the residences of the trader and slaves were probably located within the palisaded compound.

The deerskin trade conducted during the seventeenth and eighteenth centuries established strategic economic footholds along different parts of the frontier in eastern North America. Trading companies were also an important middle link between frontier residents and markets in Europe. Trading companies and merchants acquired animal skins from Native Americans and agricultural products from colonists. In turn, traders and merchants supplied settlers and Native Americans with manufactured items essential for daily life. Merchants were also the source for luxury goods that influenced the development of popular culture and consumerism in the Americas.

In the southern backcountry, frontier traders were subsequently followed by cattle herders, subsistence-level farmers and small-scale planters who owned enslaved labourers from West Africa. During the eighteenth century, traders, herders, farmers and planters all participated in mercantile capitalism to varying degrees by acquiring or producing items for exchange within the market economy. In turn, frontier residents, despite substantial geographic distances, often obtained consumer goods manufactured in Britain, ranging from ceramic tableware, personal items and furnishings like clocks and musical instruments, to books containing the latest works of literature.

Artefacts recovered from the backcountry residences of cattle herders, farmers and small-scale planters typically possess a distinctive quality, underscoring the pluralistic, multiethnic character of frontier life. Despite the pervasive influence of mercantile capitalism and formative consumerism, backcountry material culture often reflects the different folk-based ethnic groups that occupied a specific site. Multiethnic sites that were occupied by both enslaved African Americans and European Americans, for example, often exhibit a fascinating fusion of folk- and industrially based material culture. Earthfast timber-frame dwellings, industrially manufactured consumer goods, **colonoware pottery** (a type of locally produced ceramic) and distinctive faunal assemblages composed of substantial proportions of wild game, like deer, rabbit, turkey and different varieties of fish, are usually encountered at backcountry sites. Between the 1970s and 1980s, historical archaeologists in eastern North America sometimes simplistically equated **vernacular architecture**, locally produced ceramics and reliance on wild game with material impoverishment. Further inquiry since the 1980s demonstrates that, during the eighteenth century, a distinctive, pre-industrial standard of living was prevalent in many frontier contexts, despite the presence of economic activities that were clearly embedded within the formative commercial system. At backcountry sites investigated in South Carolina, researchers are often confronted with seemingly contradictory historical and material contexts. This situation is best described as an example of cultures in flux or transition between pre-capitalist material and social forms and fully developed, industrially based material conditions.

Backcountry residences occupied by affluent households, for example, are often investigated archaeologically. Beginning in the 1750s, the Catherine Brown site was inhabited by cattle raisers who were among the upper segment of wealth holders in the region. Likewise, the de la Howe site, occupied by a French physician, was investigated in McCormick Country during the 1990s. Despite substantial wealth, frontier residents like the Brown and de la Howe households often chose to reside in modest timber-frame dwellings beside enslaved African Americans. Archaeological research conducted in the southern colonial backcountry likewise reinforces similar conclusions drawn in other regions of the USA. Local, regionally specific cultures persisted for much of the eighteenth century. In turn, the full brunt of formative capitalism was not experienced materially among most households until the ensuing nineteenth century with the advent of industrialisation.

During the end of the eighteenth century, as frontier conditions diminished in eastern North America, the Industrial Revolution first gained momentum in Great Britain. Technological developments in mechanical engineering and energy-capture devices, such as the steam engine, coupled with the concept of standardised production, encouraged the growth of industrialisation. The manufacturing of standardised parts and consumer goods was a central, innovative concept during the Industrial Revolution. Mass production in turn was one of the main factors responsible for the development of consumerism.

By the end of the 1820s, industrial manufacturing was developing in the USA at a rapid tempo. The cultural landscape of the North-east and Mid-west became punctuated with carefully planned and regulated mill towns as these regions became leading manufacturing centres. At the end of the nineteenth century, the USA had the fastest growing economy among all industrialised nations. Industrial capitalism exerted a profound effect upon several domains of daily life among North Americans. The effects of industrialisation were particularly pronounced in the areas of work, household-level social relations and consumerism.

In the USA, industrial capitalism accelerated the transition from an agrarian culture to an industrially based society. As farm residents migrated to urban centres, commodified labour, where a monetary value is placed upon a worker's time, replaced kin-based labour systems characteristic of rural groups. Rural labour systems among households operated according to reciprocity and delayed compensation in the form of inheritance. At the household level, as industrialisation gained momentum, the nuclear family replaced the extended family. Industrial capitalism likewise encouraged the increasing use of manufactured goods. This process eventually created a society composed exclusively of consumers that are dependent upon manufactured goods and commercially produced food.

The culture of consumption wrought by industrial capitalism is particularly accessible through historical archaeology, which places emphasis upon the study of **material culture**. Archaeologically, this transition to industrialisation is illustrated by artefact-abundant yet mundane refuse deposits that are encountered at most nineteenth-century residences. Nineteenth-century artefact assemblages usually contain a substantial amount of glass container fragments, such as glass canning jars, ceramic tableware sherds and a noticeable range of personal items like coins, pocket knives, metal harmonica reeds and children's toys made from cast metal. Most of these consumer items were produced within the Manufacturing Belt of the USA, located in the North-east and Mid-west. When quantified by decade intervals at individual sites like the Gibbs farmstead in East Tennessee, it becomes apparent that the substantial amount of items discarded by households accelerated dramatically during the second half of the nineteenth century, underscoring the origins of disposable consumer culture prevalent during the twentieth century. These admittedly subtle trends are none-theless significant archaeological portents of sub-sequent developments within industrial capitalism, which profoundly shaped the character of material life during the twentieth century.

Further reading

Dunaway, W.A. (1996) *The First American Frontier: Transition to Capitalism in Southern Appalachia, 1700–1860*, Chapel Hill: University of North Carolina Press.

Kulikoff, A. (1992) *The Agrarian Origins of American Capitalism*, Charlottesville: University Press of Virginia.

MARK D. GROOVER

Caribbean archaeology

Historical archaeology in the Caribbean, which traditionally examines the post-Columbian occu-pation of the region, has focused primarily on the experiences of Europeans and enslaved and freed African peoples. Although research began in the late 1960s, historical archaeology in the Caribbean took off in the 1980s as **African American archaeology** stimulated interest in sites associated with members of the African **diaspora**. Archae-ological investigations in the Caribbean have been conducted on numerous islands, and have concen-trated on various kinds of sites. The range of sites investigated in the Caribbean includes late fif-teenth-century Spanish fortified settlements, later Dutch and English urban settlements, plantation sites associated with the production of **sugar** and **coffee**, and maroon villages (see **maroon sites**).

Early European settlements

With the exception of Norse settlement in coastal Canada at sites like **L'Anse aux Meadows**, the Caribbean is the location of the earliest known European settlements in the New World. In the 1970s, the late Charles Fairbanks and his students and colleagues – including Kathleen Deagan, Bonnie McEwan and Elizabeth Reitz, among others associated with the University of Florida

and the Florida Museum of Natural History – began an extensive investigation of the site of **Puerto Real**, Haiti. This large urban site was inhabited by Spanish colonists, as well as indigen-ous Taino people and Africans, from 1503 to 1578. In examining the faunal remains and artefacts recovered from the site, the Puerto Real team was able to provide a vivid interpretation of what life was like for colonist and Indian alike during the very first years of European presence in the New World. Deagan in particular has followed this work up with excavations at Concepcion de la Vega and **La Isabella**, settlements directly associated with Columbus. The earliest known Spanish settlement on Jamaica, located at Nuevo Seville, near **Seville Plantation**, has been the focus of much research since the 1980s, most recently by Robin Wood-ward. Diana Lopez has led a long-term study of the Spanish colonial occupation of urban San Juan, Puerto Rico.

Early colonies settled by Northern Europeans have also been investigated by historical archae-ologists. **Port Royal**, the first British capital of Jamaica, may perhaps be the most extensively studied Caribbean site. As a result of an earthquake that shook the island in 1692, just less than half of the city literally fell into the sea; fortunately for archaeologists, the so-called sunken city of Port Royal lies beneath only ten feet of water, making underwater investigations of Port Royal quite possible. Preliminary investigations at Port Royal were conducted in the late 1960s by Bob Marx; in a much more thorough investigation, Donny Hamilton of Texas A. & M. University led a multi-year project at Port Royal that concluded in the early 1990s. Hamilton's team recovered a stunning array of artefacts from houses, workshops and other structures, virtually in the same positions they were left at the time of the earthquake. The ongoing analysis of this material is shedding significant light on the seventeenth-century lifeways of both British colonists and enslaved Africans in an urban Caribbean setting; for example, Dorrick Gray, of the Jamaica National Heritage Trust, analysed craft workshops from the sunken city. In the 1980s and early 1990s, Norman Barka led a multi-year project on the Dutch island of **St Eustatius**; the heart of Barka's project was the excavation and interpretation of sites on a quarter-mile stretch of beach along which some 600 ware-houses once stood. These warehouses were the centre of activity of St Eustatius as a colonial entrepôt and smuggling port in the eighteenth century.

Plantation archaeology in the Caribbean

Although the Caribbean was a locus of intensive trading activity, as revealed in the mercantile nature of places like Port Royal and St Eustatius, the production of plantation agricultural commodities – primarily sugar, but including tobacco, cotton and **coffee** – has dominated the political economy of the region for most of its post-contact history. There has long been an interest in examining the everyday lives of enslaved African peoples held captive in the Caribbean. In the 1970s, Jerome Handler and Frederick Lange demonstrated the potential of Caribbean archaeology through their excavations at **Newton Plantation** in Barbados. Because the area of the slave village was heavily disturbed, Handler and Lange initially focused their investigation on burials located in a slave cemetery associated with Newton Plantation. Written at the height of the hegemony of **New Archaeology**, which at its extreme called for the virtual abandonment of documentary research, Handler and Lange demonstrated the necessity of merging archaeology and history into what they called an 'ethnohistorical approach'. At the time Handler and Lange were running their investigations in Barbados, the historian Barry Higman began a series of excavations at Montpelier Plantation, in Jamaica, which demonstrated that slave housing could be identified and excavated.

Soon after the appearance of Handler and Lange's monograph on Newton Plantation, excavations began at a number of other plantation sites throughout the Caribbean. In the early 1980s, Lydia Pulsipher and Conrad Goodwin began publishing the results of investigations they had conducted at Galways Plantation in Montserrat. Initially focusing on the visible monumental architecture of the plantation's industrial works, this investigation led Pulsipher to consider how garden spaces may have been used by enslaved labourers in the Caribbean, a focus of her later work.

In the later 1980s and early 1990s, Douglas Armstrong directed two projects on sugar plantation sites on Jamaica's North Coast, at Drax Hall and Seville Plantation, respectively. In both cases, Armstrong focused on the spatial organisation of slave villages. At Drax Hall, Armstrong was able to identify and excavate a number of house areas, including house yards. In the Caribbean in general, and Jamaica in particular, the exterior spaces around the house were as important, if not more so, to the inhabitants of the village; these spaces were important materially – as they were used for the production of garden vegetables, animal husbandry and food preparation – and socially – as they were the location of much social activity in the village. Armstrong followed this project with a multi-year investigation at Seville Plantation, where he was able to investigate two separate slave villages, one dating from the early eighteenth century, the other from the later eighteenth century. In comparing the organisation of these two villages, Armstrong concluded that the linear organisation of the earlier village was most likely imposed on its inhabitants by the planters, while the more nucleated structure of the later village may have been constructed at a time when the planters' strategies of **domination** were temporarily relaxed. This later argument is supported by architectural evidence that the planter's great house was severely damaged and rebuilt at approximately the same time that the first village was abandoned, and the second village was established; all of these events may have been related to the plantation being damaged by a severe storm or hurricane in the late eighteenth century. While plantation archaeology has focused primarily on sugar plantations, by the mid-1990s archaeologists began to consider other types of plantation contexts. Matthew Reeves, a student of Armstrongs, conducted a dissertation project in which he compared the material assemblages associated with enslaved peoples from both sugar and coffee plantations located in the Juan de Bolas region of central Jamaica. Simultaneously, James Delle initiated a long-term project focused on the analysis of spatial dynamics on Jamaican coffee plantations. In the first phase of this project, Delle examined the cartographical, documentary and architectural remains of a number of coffee plantations located in the Blue Mountains of eastern Jamaica. In doing so, he was able to analyse how space, both materially and cognitively constructed, was an active force in the negotiation of power between planter elites and workers of African descent. In the late 1990s, Delle initiated excavations at an African Jamaican village in central Jamaica, associated with Marshall's Pen, formerly a coffee plantation. His preliminary findings suggest that the village was organised into a series of compounds, each containing a number of houses, and sharing yard spaces and animal pens. The final component of Delle's work considers how geographic information systems (GIS) technology can be applied to analyse the regional settlement patterns of coffee plantations in the Negro River Valley of eastern Jamaica.

Numerous other plantation studies were conducted or initiated in the 1980s and 1990s. Jay Haviser has conducted investigations of plantation sites in St Maarten and other islands in the Netherlands Antilles. Jean Howson has examined plantation sites in Montserrat; a number of graduate students studying with Norman Barka at the College of William and Mary have examined various elements of a variety of sugar plantations on St Eustatius. In the late 1990s, several Canadian and French archaeologists initiated investigation of sugar plantations in the French Antilles and Guyana, Theresa Singleton initiated a collaboration with local archaeologists on plantation sites in Cuba, Dan Mouer worked in Barbados and excavations were conducted by US and British scholars in Nevis, Barbuda and the Bahamas.

Regional settlement patterns in the Caribbean

As it is an archipelago of geographically bounded islands linked together historically, the Caribbean is an ideal location to examine how local settlement patterns are impacted by changes in the global economy. In the late 1980s, James Delle conducted a plantation settlement pattern study as part of Barka's St Eustatius project. Coming from a perspective influenced by **world systems theory**, Delle concluded that both the distribution of plantations across the island and the internal

arrangement of plantation physical plants changed as a direct result of shifts in the European world economy. A similar study was conducted in the early 1990s by Chris Clement on Tobago. Clement argued that the location of sugar plantations in Tobago, particularly the placement of planters' great houses in elevated positions, was a key to understanding how plantations worked as socio-spatial entities. According to Clement, visual communication among plantations, and between plantation houses and urban settlements, was necessary for the minority planters to control the majority enslaved labourers. This line of argument has been taken up by Delle in his GIS project in the Negro River Valley of Jamaica.

Maroon archaeology

From at least the early seventeenth century, there were independent settlements in the interior of the larger Caribbean islands, inhabited primarily by escaped slaves, but also by the remnants of the indigenous population that was largely decimated in the sixteenth century. The inhabitants of these independent settlements are known as 'maroons'. Kofi Agorsah has been a pioneer in excavating maroon sites, and has conducted investigations at a variety of sites in Jamaica, including Accompong and **Nanny Town**; Agorsah has also conducted studies on maroon sites in Surinam, on the mainland of South America. His excavations at Nanny Town, a very remote location deep in the mountains of Jamaica, revealed that the settlement was more ancient than traditionally believed, undoubtedly predating the conquest of Jamaica by the British from the Spanish in the 1650s. According to Agorsah, the presence of artefacts associated with the indigenous people of Jamaica suggests one of two things: either that the black maroons escaping first from the Spanish and later the British were accompanied by surviving Taino Indians, or else the settlement was established first by Tainos fleeing the Spanish. In either event, there seems to have been interaction between the two groups, perhaps reflecting a process of **creolisation** far removed from the European-dominated lowlands. Excavations at maroon sites may provide significant data to interpret such social phenomena.

Other archaeological studies in the Caribbean

A variety of other kinds of studies have been conducted by historical archaeologists in the Caribbean. Several islands, including Tobago, Puerto Rico and Jamaica, are currently struggling with incipient **cultural-resource management** programmes. Several scholars, including Barbara Heath and Mark Hauser, have examined locally produced earthenwares. Following the completion of the Seville Plantation project, Armstrong initiated excavations at a free-black settlement, dating to the late eighteenth century, in St Johns, US Virgin Islands. A number of themes remain virtually unexplored, including sites associated with indentured labourers from the Far East and the Indian sub-continent. Unfortunately, many sites are quickly being destroyed as tourist development expands in the Caribbean.

See also: African American archaeology; plantation archaeology

Further reading

Armstrong, D.V. (1990) *The Old Village and the Great House: An Archaeological and Historical Examination of Drax Hall Plantation, St. Ann's Bay, Jamaica*, Urbana: University of Illinois Press.

Deagan, K. (ed.) (1995) *Puerto Real: The Archaeology of a Sixteenth-century Spanish Town in Hispaniola*, Gainesville: University Press of Florida.

Delle, J.A. (1998) *An Archaeology of Social Space: Analyzing Coffee Plantations in Jamaica's Blue Mountains*, New York: Kluwer Academic/Plenum.

Handler, J.S. and Lange, F.W. (1978) *Plantation Slavery in Barbados: An Archaeological and Historical Investigation*, Cambridge, MA: Harvard University Press.

Haviser, J. (ed.) (1999) *African Sites Archaeology in the Caribbean*, Amsterdam: Markus Wiener.

Higman, B.W. (1998) *Montpelier, Jamaica: A Plantation Community in Slavery and Freedom, 1739–1912*, Kingston: University of the West Indies Press.

Howson, J. (1995) 'Colonial goods and the plantation village: Consumption and the internal economy of Montserrat from slavery to freedom', doctoral dissertation, New York University, New York.

JAMES A. DELLE

Carter's Grove, Virginia, USA

Carter's Grove is an eighteenth-century plantation located on the James River, in Virginia, USA, eight miles south-east of Williamsburg. The site is important for historical archaeology because of the excavations carried out there, and because the property today includes an innovative living museum (see **living museums**) based on the African American slave experience.

Carter Burwell, the son of a wealthy Virginia family, began to have the plantation's impressive mansion built in a series of stages that ended in 1755. So intent was Burwell on having a grand estate that in 1752 he paid the transatlantic passage money for an English joiner and his family. This skilled craftsman built the intricate, beautiful woodwork that visitors to the mansion can still see today. In addition, Burwell paid to have 540 window panes glazed. The mansion house is an excellent example of Georgian formal **architecture** and includes five connected brick sections. The house has had a colourful history, including the late nineteenth-century red, white and blue painting of the intricate woodwork. In 1969, the then-owners deeded the property to the Colonial Williamsburg Foundation for preservation (see **preservation legislation**) and protection.

Systematic archaeology was first conducted at Carter's Grove in the early 1970s by Ivor Noël Hume and William Kelso. The excavations revealed the presence of a dairy building, the fence lines of eighteenth-century gardens and African American slave dwellings. The presence of slave cabins at the estate was not completely unexpected because the plantation was at one time home to about 1,000 slaves. Archaeologists also found the remains of an earlier, seventeenth-century settlement called '**Martin's Hundred**'.

As a living museum, the Carter's Grove complex is today reached via a winding country road that runs from Williamsburg. The complex includes a visitor reception centre, a reconstructed slave quarter, the mansion and a formal garden.

Archaeological excavations established the location of the slave quarters, and museum personnel used eighteenth-century techniques to reconstruct them at their original locations. The quarters consist of several dwellings and fenced garden areas. Site interpreters today strive to present an accurate picture of slave life to the estate's visitors by performing typical daily tasks, such as hoeing the garden plots, and by giving accounts of slave life gleaned from historical records and **oral history**.

Further reading

Epperson, T.E. (1990) 'Race and the disciplines of the plantation', *Historical Archaeology* 24(4): 29–36.
Noël Hume, I. (1979) *Martin's Hundred: The Discovery of a Lost Colonial Virginia Settlement*, New York: Alfred A. Knopf.

CHARLES E. ORSER, JR

cathedrals

The archaeological study of cathedrals is a multi-disciplinary analysis of the material and biological remains of great **churches**, and the churchyards and closes associated with them. Unlike parish churches, cathedrals are seldom declared redundant. Therefore, the opportunity to excavate usually occurs when repairs must be made or improvements added to the structures. Beginning in the 1960s, extensive excavations at York Minster and the Old Minster, Winchester, in the UK proved the feasibility of doing major archaeological work in the context of an active cathedral.

Particularly in Old World locations, a cathedral may sit atop the remains of two, three or more earlier ecclesiastical structures. A case in point is Wells Cathedral, **England**. Excavations in the cloister and gardens, between 1978 and 1993, revealed an intricate stratigraphy beginning with a late Roman mausoleum. On top of the mausoleum were several chapels and part of an Anglo-Saxon minster.

In 1999, excavations preparatory to replacing the 1786 floor in the nave and south-west transept of Canterbury Cathedral revealed a similarly complex stratigraphy. Directors Kevin Blockley and Paul Bennett reported that the earliest layer consisted of the remains of a Roman street and adjacent buildings. A scant 0.20 m beneath the 1786 floor, excavators found remains of various construction phases of an Anglo-Saxon cathedral. The structure is believed to have been one of the largest in England.

Because churches and cathedrals are often built on top of, or adjacent to, older ecclesiastical structures, the presence of an archaeologist while repairs are being made is vital. New work may compromise or destroy valuable pieces of the archaeological record. Sometimes this destruction is unavoidable. The archaeologist's job is to mitigate this damage through careful recording.

Multidisciplinary expertise for analysis of finds is important. Viewing remains from a variety of perspectives adds depth to the archaeological study. Art, **architecture**, **mortuary analysis**, biological analysis of past populations and settlement studies are only a few of the fields that can benefit archaeology. Cathedrals were the recipients of much of the art and architecture produced during the Middle Ages and the **Renaissance**. In addition, the presence of a cathedral was an important factor in the establishment of markets and the growth of towns.

Biological remains provide clues to **disease**, nutrition, social status and mortuary practices of the populations surrounding the cathedral. Graves are present either in the churchyard, in floor burials or in raised tombs. Excavation often reveals a sub-floor so honeycombed with burials that one is amazed that the floor did not fall in.

Although cathedral archaeology appears to be exclusively Old World, such studies are done in the New World, particularly in Latin America. However, most of this work, done in conjunction with repairing colonial-period cathedrals, is sadly not published.

Further reading

Rodwell, W. (2000) *The Archaeology of Wells Cathedral*, London: English Heritage.

M. PATRICIA COLQUETTE

cemeteries

Cemeteries provide historical archaeologists with the remains of specific individuals and their associated artefacts, which, together with documentary information, enrich interpretations about past peoples. Family plots and churchyard burials of European settlers to the Americas and elsewhere, burial grounds of enslaved Africans, military cemeteries, colonial graveyards and burial grounds of paupers yield rare glimpses about ethnicity, culture contact, gender and capitalism. Material remains include artefacts associated with the person and artefacts associated with the coffin, as well as gravestones.

Urban development in North America during the latter part of the twentieth century, along with **preservation legislation**, has meant that cemeteries have been legally excavated by contract archaeologists – either when the cemeteries were accidentally discovered during construction or when a cemetery was legally closed by its owner for re-use. Archaeologists also have excavated cemeteries previously closed but where some or all of the burials had not been removed. Cemetery excavations have elicited significant interest among the public, who are sometimes outraged that cemeteries can be legally closed. Some cemeteries have become catalysts for ethnic identity or cultural revival, as with the **African Burial Ground** in New York City. For that cemetery, African American researchers have argued that they are best suited to analyse the remains of that ethnic group.

Often, cultural, historical and biological information recovered from cemeteries is unavailable elsewhere. Cemeteries become demographic records, particularly for areas pre-dating census records or for marginal ethnic or lower-class groups for whom written records are poor. Archaeologists work in conjunction with researchers in **biological anthropology**, who study the health of past populations. Art historians and genealogists also contribute to research, although analyses of iconography and other information from gravestones often are carried out by historical archaeologists. The recovery of the material remains from the graves is evaluated in comparison with documentary, gravestone and biological information to evaluate common interpretations used in prehistoric and historical archaeology in mortuary analysis. Paramount among these is the relationship between the deceased person's social and economic status in life and their grave

furnishings – both personal belongings and the coffin itself. Historical archaeologists have found there is a complex relationship between the two, involving lower-class emulation of high-class funerals and the status of the deceased's family, among other factors.

Most archaeologically excavated cemeteries and research on historical cemeteries has been carried out in North America, although important studies have been done elsewhere, notably **Spitalfields**, London. Excavated cemeteries include ethnic diversity and reflect social history. They include mission sites where native people had church burials (Tipu, Belize), enslaved or free African burial grounds (African Burial Ground, **Millwood Plantation**, Georgia, and St Peter's Cemetery, New Orleans), family plots (Manassas, Virginia), churchyards (St Thomas Anglican Churchyard and Prospect Cemetery, **Ontario**, eastern Canada), military cemeteries (Snake Hill, Ontario) and poorhouse cemeteries (Highland Park, Rochester, New York, and Uxbridge, Massachusetts).

Early cemeteries of European settlers to the Americas consisted of small family plots on farms and churchyards in urban places. The nineteenth century marked a time of **urbanisation**, with concomitant overcrowding in cemeteries, along with a fear of disease spreading from corpses in the churchyards. Beginning in 1831 with Mt Auburn, located outside of Boston, the Rural Cemetery Movement placed cemeteries outside of cities in pastoral settings. This was the time when the Industrial Revolution marked a settlement shift from rural farming to urban factory work, as well as the development of the funeral industry and modern cemeteries. There was a romantic interest in the past when the family worked and lived together in a rural setting on farms. This interest is reflected in cemeteries by elaborate grave markers and coffin hardware with pastoral and romantic icons.

The development of the lawn cemetery movement at the turn of the twentieth century, with minimal gravestones and minimal funerary ceremony, reflected the public's 'denial of death' that became more pronounced with the growth of memorial park cemeteries that are devoid of upright markers and vegetation, and separated from church and community. Historical archaeologists have studied the markers and spatial layout of late twentieth-century lawn and memorial park cemeteries but not their underground graves.

With 579 coffin burials, St Thomas Anglican Churchyard is one of the largest cemetery excavations and has revealed significant information from abundant and diverse artefacts. Represented in smaller quantities at other excavated cemeteries, there were artefacts associated with the coffin, notably coffin handles, name plates, decorative domes and metal trim, wood, cloth, nails and viewing glasses. Artefacts associated with the person included buttons, shroud pins, cloth, boots, glasses and hair combs. The motifs on coffin handles were the same as those on nineteenth-century gravestones. There were differences between children's and adults' graves that could be used to distinguish them when no skeletal remains were present, including distinctive motifs on coffin handles, smaller and fewer handles, and smaller coffins or coffin stains. In addition, the motifs on the coffin handles and the separate treatment of children reflected Victorian concepts of **children**: they were most pure and therefore associated with heaven, untarnished by work or the outside world and therefore associated with romantic notions of home as heaven. Artefacts from St Thomas Churchyard – a large, white, middle- to upper-class cemetery – provide a standard for smaller cemeteries and cemeteries of lower classes and disenfranchised groups.

See also: churchyard archaeology; gravestones; mortuary analysis

Further reading

Harrington, S.P.M. (1993) 'Bones and bureaucrats: New York's great cemetery imbroglio', *Archaeology* 46: 28–38.

Little, B., Lanphear, K.M. and Owsley, D.W. (1992) 'Mortuary display and status in a nineteenth-century Anglo-American cemetery in Manassas, Virginia', *American Antiquity* 57: 397–418.

McKillop, H. (1995) 'Recognizing children's graves in nineteenth-century cemeteries: Excavations in St. Thomas Anglican churchyard, Belleville, Ontario, Canada', *Historical Archaeology* 29: 77–99.

Poirier, D.A. and Bellantoni, N.F. (eds) (1997) *In Remembrance: Archaeology and Death*, London: Bergin & Garvey.

Rose, J.C. (ed.) (1985) *Gone to a Better Land*, Arkansas Archeological Survey Research Series 25, Fayetteville, Arkansas: Arkansas Archeological Survey.

HEATHER McKILLOP

Central America

Although the historic period in Central America is well documented by historians, only since the 1970s have archaeologists turned their attention to historic sites in the area. This is partly due to archaeologists' emphasis on large prehistoric ruins of the Maya (see **Maya archaeology**) or **Teotihuacan** civilisations, but also to the focus, in Mexico in particular, on the tourism value of restored prehistoric sites and colonial buildings. Historical archaeology has been carried out to investigate the impact of missions (see **mission sites**) on native populations during the colonial period, with limited research on later historic settlements. This research includes locating historic missions and other sites, describing settlement patterns, assigning ages by ceramic (see **ceramics**) analysis, estimating **ethnicity** from **material culture** and placing sites within the broader world system. Most fieldwork has been carried out in Mexico and Belize, with limited research in Guatemala, Honduras, Nicaragua and Panama.

The colonial period

Beginning with the arrival of Hernan Cortez in Mexico in 1519 and subsequent travels by other Spanish explorers, the colonial period is marked by religious, economic and political changes imposed by the Spaniards that had devastating effects on indigenous populations. Native people were relocated to towns where Spanish churches were built, often on demolished indigenous temples. As part of the *encomienda* system, natives were required to pay tribute in labour and goods. Historians have documented the decimation of the native populations by European diseases including smallpox, measles and influenza, and the impact of relocation and tribute that resulted in the virtual elimination of the native groups in Costa Rica and dramatic diminution of their numbers elsewhere. The mission programmes of the Franciscans and Dominicans in Mexico and Belize and the Mercedarians in Honduras have been investigated by archaeological studies, aided by historic documents at Tipu and Lamanai in Belize and in Honduras. These studies reveal the impact of colonialism and missionisation on natives, processes not well documented by the Spaniards. Mexican churches have been mapped and investigated at Ek Balam by Craig Hansen, Dzibilchaltun by William Folan, and Xcaret by Anthony Andrews and E. Wyllys Andrews IV. Andrews summarises the distribution and styles of Franciscan churches in the Yucatan.

The historic mission at Tipu in western Belize, established on the Maya community of Negroman in 1544, was the political centre of the Dzuluinicob Province and grew cacao for trade and tribute. The site was discovered through archival research and fieldwork by Grant Jones. Robert Kautz found and partially excavated the church and mapped the surrounding area between 1980 and 1982. Elizabeth Graham's excavations in 1984–7 included mapping and excavation of the historic area, including almost 600 burials associated with the church.

The Tipu Maya accepted Christianity and maintained good relations with the visiting Franciscan friars until a rebellion in 1638. The continuation of Christian burials in the church indicates that Christianity made an impact on the indigenous religious practices. The historic **architecture** marked a dramatic change from the prehistoric styles. The prehistoric style of erecting buildings of stone or pole and thatch, on earth or rubble platforms, faced with stone around a plaza was replaced by historic buildings placed directly on the ground. Some historic structures were built on the demolished foundations of prehistoric platforms. Another departure was the use of cobblestone pavement for a plaza, walkways and by houses, perhaps with roofed patios. The church was a rectangular structure with a thatch roof and open sides typical of the earliest Yucatecan churches.

Few European goods were brought to Tipu, probably due to its remote, frontier location.

Majolica and **olive jar** sherds found around the church and plaza suggest they had restricted use by visiting friars or Christianised Maya of high status. There was a continuity of the prehistoric Maya ceramic tradition into historic times. Among European goods, silver earrings, rosary **beads**, metal needles and coffin **nails** were found. Silver earrings and beads recovered from **children**'s graves in the church suggested that children had been a focus of proselytising by the Franciscans, who had given them gifts.

A Franciscan mission established after 1544 at the Maya community of Lamanai was excavated during the 1970s and 1980s by David Pendergast. The community was a reduction centre where Maya were resettled from outlying areas. A small early church measuring 6 × 9 m, with a thatched roof, earth floor and partial masonry walls, was a blend of Spanish style and local building techniques. A later, larger church with a masonry chancel built in Spanish style reflects the growing role of Lamanai in the Spanish reduction system. The few European ceramics from excavations of a midden and historic building include olive jar and Columbia Plain sherds, and several majolica sherds, representing a virtual lack of Spanish tablewares. The Spanish colonial mission at Lamanai was successful in converting the Maya to Catholicism, but had little impact on the economy and politics of the community, which remained unchanged in settlement pattern beyond the church and associated warehouse or convent. After the 1638 uprising, visiting friars Fuensaldia and Orbita found, during their visit of 1641, the church and associated buildings burned and abandoned, marking the end of Spanish influence.

In addition to the excavations of mission communities at Tipu and Lamanai, a regional project carried out by John Weeks detailed the regional settlement patterning of Mercedarian missions in the Telcoa region of western Honduras occupied by the Lenca Indians. Using historic documents, he located and identified nine mission sites with churches and carried out excavations at a number of sites. Mission sites were located by their occurrence on prehistoric native communities. Initial churches of perishable materials were replaced by mortar and rubble churches. Ceramic analysis focused on identifying a sequence from prehistoric into colonial times.

In contrast to the remote frontier situation of the Belizean mission sites of Tipu and Lamanai, excavations at the native colonial community of Ocelocalco in the Soconusco region of Chiapas, Mexico, by Janine Gasco revealed greater access to European goods. The Soconusco region, famous prehistorically and in colonial days for its chocolate, was incorporated into the *encomienda* system. Ocelocalco was established in 1572 as part of a native relocation programme. Most of the artefacts were local utilitarian ceramics revealing a continuity from prehistoric to colonial times (as at Tipu and Lamanai), although majolica, lead-glazed **earthenware**, olive jars, Chinese **porcelain**, **creamware** and other European ceramics as well as metal objects were found. Gasco considered that the natives' lives remained little changed in the early colonial times, since most of the new artefacts simply replaced local versions.

Gasco also used Ocelocalco in a regional study locating colonial sites in the field from historic documents. The difficulty finding colonial sites in Soconusco was attributed to the small native population, in contrast to the larger native population in adjacent coastal Guatemala, where the Franciscans built more durable stone churches. In the Antigua area of Guatemala, Eugenia Robinson found cultural continuity in settlement location from the seventy protohistoric through early colonial sites found during her 1988–90 survey.

The limited historical archaeology in Mexico is accompanied by many restoration and consolidation projects of colonial architecture, involving the initial excavation or exposure of a building by archaeologists. Much of the work was in Mexico City and carried out by Mexican archaeologists, and often described in Mexican publications not cited by foreigners. Since the focus was architectural restoration, artefacts were not normally recovered nor was there an attempt to recover dietary or other anthropological information. Since the 1970s, Mexican archaeologists have directed research interest to historical archaeology, and some foreign researchers, notably Thomas Charlton, have also carried out historical archaeology. Fournier-Garcia analysed ceramics, focusing on consumer trends, class (see **class, social**) and ethnicity, noting that colonial class division between Spaniard and native was demarcated by greater access to majolicas by the former. Her research follows seminal studies by Florence and Robert Lister and Donna Seifert on majolica and other European ceramics in Mexico, and Thomas Charlton's work in central Mexico.

Judith Zeitlin and Lillian Thomas located and excavated the hamlet of Rancho Santa Cruz and the Dominican convent at Tehuantepec as part of a historical archaeological survey in Oaxaca in 1990. Excavations of a midden and house at Rancho Santa Cruz indicated an early indigenous occupation with a subsequent colonial occupation marked by European ceramics. The ceramics indicate a continuity of prehistoric traditions into colonial times, with Mexican-made majolicas, and the most common pottery a new local industry of Tablon Orange ceramics. They explain the greater access to majolicas by the native population than generally expected, as related to their entry into the market economy.

Unlike other historical archaeology projects that focused on Maya communities impacted by Spanish presence, Kira Blaisdell-Sloan examined a Spanish colonial community in southern Nicaragua. She examined the pottery recovered from earlier excavations and found a virtual absence of European ceramics – perhaps no more than the original settlers brought with them from Spain.

Post-colonial period

Limited attention has been directed to later archaeology in Central America. David Pendergast reported a nineteenth-century sugar mill and settlement at Lamanai. A regional survey and mapping project in the Yaxcaba Region of the Yucatan, Mexico, by Rani Alexander examined the surface evidence for the Spanish impact on native populations from 1750 until 1847, beginning with the population increase, associated with the introduction of large haciendas where Maya worked, to the Caste War of the Yucatan. She mapped a pueblo, hacienda and independent ranch to examine acculturation of Yucatec Maya.

Charles Cheek reported the ceramics found during the 1982–3 Proyecto Garifuna at Campamento,

Site 1 and Site 8, near Trujillo, Honduras. The area was dominated by the descendants of Garifuna or black Caribs, who had been deported by the British from St Vincent's Island in the Caribbean (see **Caribbean archaeology**) in 1799. A relatively high proportion of English teawares (see **tea/tea ceremony**) in the artefact inventories was attributed to the Garifunas' intent to identify ethnically with the British.

Fieldwork in the Port Honduras region of southern Belize by Heather McKillop revealed historic camps attributed to the nineteenth- and early twentieth-century mahogany industry in the Deep River area at Muschamp Creek and Pineapple Grove. In addition, a nineteenth- to twentieth-century fishing community was identified on the Maya site of Wild Cane Cay.

The burgeoning field of historical archaeology in Central America has focused since its inception in the 1970s on the colonial period, particularly the impact of missions on the native populations, which is not well articulated in Spanish documents. The archaeology of Central America will ultimately be better understood within a context of Spanish and British colonialism in the Americas.

See also: cemeteries; churches; South America

Further reading

Alexander, R.T. (1998) 'Community organization in the Parroquiade Yaxcaba, Yucatan, Mexico, 1750–1847', *Ancient Mesoamerica* 9: 39–54.

Andrews, A.P. (1981) 'Historical archaeology in Yucatan: A preliminary framework', *Historical Archaeology* 15: 1–18.

Cheek, C.D. (1997) 'Setting an English table: Black Carib archaeology on the Caribbean coast of Honduras', in J. Gasco, G.C. Smith, and P. Fournier-Garcia (eds) *Approaches to the Historical Archaeology of Mexico, Central, and South America*, Los Angeles: Institute of Archaeology, University of California, pp. 101–9.

Fournier-Garcia, P. and Miranda-Flores, F.A. (1992) 'Historic sites archaeology in Mexico', *Historical Archaeology* 26(1): 75–83.

Gasco, J. (1992) 'Material culture and colonial Indian society in southern Mesoamerica: The view from coastal Chiapas, Mexico', *Historical Archaeology* 26: 67–74.

Graham, E.A. (1991) 'Archaeological insights into colonial period Maya life at Tipu, Belize', in D.H. Thomas (ed.) *Columbian Consequences*, vol. 3, Washington, DC: Smithsonian Institution Press, pp. 319–35.

Pendergast, D.M. (1991) 'The southern Maya lowlands contact experience: The view from Lamanai, Belize', in D.H. Thomas (ed.) *Columbian Consequences*, vol. 3, Washington, DC: Smithsonian Institution Press, pp. 337–54.

HEATHER McKILLOP

ceramics

The term 'ceramics' refers to products made of clay mixed with various additives and hardened by applying heat. Types of ceramics range from structural (e.g. bricks, tiles, drainpipes) and decorative (e.g. vases, figures, artware) to useful (e.g. tableware, teaware, kitchenware), and are characterised by both coarse and refined varieties. This definition is more restrictive than materials science definitions but broader than that used in prehistoric archaeology, where the focus tends to be on pottery (**earthenware**) used for decorative and useful purposes. Being simultaneously fragile and durable, ceramic objects tend to enter the archaeological record frequently but survive for later recovery. Ceramics have long been favoured by both prehistorians and historical archaeologists as the primary material class used to establish site chronology and function, as well as the socioeconomic status and **ethnicity** of a site's occupants.

Disagreements among researchers about the **classification** of historical ceramics have led to the use of inconsistent nomenclature in the literature, which hinders the archaeologist's ability to compare ceramics found at different sites. Based on his work with British ceramics, George Miller contends that ceramics should be classified by decoration rather than ware type. He proposes referring to ceramics by the same terms used by potters, merchants and consumers of the period, rather than the terms coined by collectors and frequently adopted by historical archaeologists (e.g. 'white granite' versus '**ironstone**', 'china glaze' versus '**pearlware**'). Teresita Majewski and Michael J. O'Brien recommend categorising ceramics based on 'body type' and 'degree of vitrification'. Their scheme is equally applicable to all ceramics produced during the historical period, from **colonoware pottery** to tin-glazed earthenware to Chinese **porcelain**, a fact that helps the researcher understand the interconnectedness of global technological advances and stylistic movements. Miller focuses primarily on nineteenth-century ceramics, but Majewski and O'Brien, and later Majewski and Schiffer, extend the discussion into the twentieth century and integrate information on ceramics produced outside of Great Britain. For those interested in the development of eighteenth-century English ceramic technology, a key source is David Barker's work on the potter William Greatbatch, a contemporary of the famous Staffordshire potter Josiah Wedgwood.

Earthenware, **stoneware** and porcelain are the most common ceramic 'bodies'. 'Body' refers to what prehistorians call 'paste', and is roughly equivalent to 'ware' as understood by historical archaeologists (e.g. **creamware**, **redware** ceramics). Body can also be defined as the clay part of a pot as opposed to additional parts such as glazes, slips and colours. A 'glaze' is a coating fused to a ceramic body either to seal it against moisture, as with porous earthenwares, or to decorate it with a variety of colours and textures. A glaze can appear 'glassy' (e.g. on creamware or porcelain) or 'opaque' (e.g. on tin-glazed earthenwares, Bristol-glazed stoneware). A 'slip' is potter's clay mixed with water to form a smooth, creamy liquid used to decorate ceramics, such as slipwares. Colours used to decorate ceramics usually come from metallic oxides (e.g. cobalt oxide for blue, chromium oxide for green).

Degree of vitrification of the body is an objective means for sub-dividing historical ceramics into wares. Earthenware and porcelain lie at opposite ends of a continuum that is based on how absorbent, or porous, a body is. Most earthenware bodies are non-vitreous/fairly porous (e.g. redware, colonoware, tin-glazed earthenware, white-bodied earthenwares – creamware, pearlware, whiteware) but there are also semi-vitreous/moderately porous (e.g. ironstone, or more properly termed 'white granite') and vitreous/barely porous to non-porous (e.g. hotelware) bodies. Differences in clay mixtures and firing regimens can be used to separate stoneware and porcelain bodies, which are vitreous, from earthenware. The harder a ceramic body, the higher the temperature at which it was fired.

Technological and stylistic observations on underglaze and overglaze decorative treatments provide much of the temporal and cultural information used in historical ceramic identification. Miller contends that it is possible to date ceramics fairly accurately if one understands the relationship between decorative methods and the technological characteristics of specific ceramic bodies. Majewski, Majewski and O'Brien, and Samford add a consideration of 'style' to the equation. Particularly time-sensitive decorative methods include transfer printing and decaling.

Makers' marks – generally impressed, incised, transfer printed or painted on the bases of ceramic vessels – provide important information on manufacturer, date of manufacture, country of origin and marketing practices. Stanley South developed the **mean ceramic dating** method, which uses the median manufacturing date of certain ceramic types to arrive at a mean date for an assemblage.

While ceramics are often used primarily to establish site chronology and function, as a material class they offer almost limitless research possibilities beyond these traditional foci. Miller, for example, used documentary evidence to establish sets of price index values for nineteenth-century plates, cups and bowls. These 'index values' have been employed by Miller and others to compare expenditure patterns for ceramics from different archaeological assemblages and to hypothesise about the socioeconomic status of a site's prior inhabitants.

See also: class, social; consumer choice; consumption; dating methods; food and foodways; formula dating; Longton Hall; tea/tea ceremony

Further reading

Barker, D. (1990) *William Greatbatch: A Staffordshire Potter*, London: Jonathan Horne.

Figure 7 Transfer-printed plate, *c.* 1830, with '*Views in Mesopotamia*' pattern, attributed to James Keeling,
       Staffordshire, England
Source: W.E. Sudderth Collection, courtesy of T. Majewski and G.L. Fox; photo: T. Majewski

Majewski, T. (1996) 'Historical ceramics', in J.F.
    Burton, *Three Farewells to Manzanar: The Archeology
    of Manzanar National Historic Site, California*, Part 3,
    Tucson, Arizona: National Park Service, Wes-
    tern Archeological and Conservation Center,
    pp. 793–862 (Appendix D).

Majewski, T. and. O'Brien, M. J. (1987) 'The use
    and misuse of nineteenth-century English and
    American ceramics in archaeological analysis',
    in M.B. Schiffer (ed.) *Advances in Archaeological
    Method and Theory* 11, San Diego: Academic
    Press, pp. 97–209.

Majewski, T. and Schiffer, M.B. (2001) 'Beyond
    consumption: Toward an archaeology of con-
    sumerism', in V. Buchli and G. Lucas (eds)
    Archaeologies of the Contemporary Past, London:
    Routledge, pp. 26–50.

Miller, G.L. (1991) 'A revised set of CC index
    values for classification and economic scaling of
    English ceramics from 1787 to 1880', *Historical
    Archaeology* 25(1): 1–25.

—— (1980) 'Classification and economic scaling of
    19th century ceramics', *Historical Archaeology* 14:
    1–40.

Samford, P. (1997) 'Response to a market: Dating
    English underglaze transfer-printed wares', *His-
    torical Archaeology* 31(2): 1–30.

TERESITA MAJEWSKI

Chesapeake region, USA

The Chesapeake region was among the first areas in the US to receive serious attention by historical archaeologists. Beginning in 1897, the Association for the Preservation of Virginia Antiquities, which owns parts of James Island, uncovered foundations at **Jamestown**. Extensive excavation of colonial era remains began in the 1930s at **St Mary's City**, Williamsburg and **Mount Vernon**. Private and public entities were involved in this early archaeology. The Rockefeller Foundation created Colonial Williamsburg, the Mount Vernon Ladies Association sponsored work at George Washington's home and the National Park Service initiated its own excavations at Jamestown in 1934.

Large-scale excavations of the 1930s and earlier were concerned with gathering data for architectural reconstructions and served to strengthen an Anglo-American history concerned with the social and political elite. Historical archaeology has continued in the Chesapeake with each project providing new information.

Archaeologically, the Chesapeake region is thought of as the parts of Virginia, Maryland, Delaware and the District of Columbia within the Chesapeake Bay's watershed. The Spanish attempted settlements in the region and the English had attempted settlements before founding Jamestown in the southern Chesapeake in 1607. St Mary's City was founded in 1634. Other early settlements were **Martin's Hundred**, **Flowerdew Hundred Plantation**, Kingsmill Plantations, Virginia, Curles Plantation, Virginia – the home of Nathaniel Bacon of Bacon's Rebellion – and King's Reach, at Jefferson Patterson Park and Museum in southern Maryland. Settlers capitalised on the high price of tobacco in Europe and the tobacco economy encouraged a dispersed settlement pattern. During the seventeenth and eighteenth centuries, towns were rare and small. Plantations were the centres of the economy. Jamestown and St Mary's City served as capitals through the seventeenth century but both colonies moved their capitals in the 1690s to Williamsburg and **Annapolis**, respectively, when European settlement in the region shifted from frontier to settled community. In the nineteenth century, the capital of Virginia moved to Richmond and, while Annapolis retained its government functions, the economic centre of the state shifted to Baltimore.

Researchers investigating early settlement in the Chesapeake are interested in cultural contact between indigenous peoples, Europeans and Africans; self-sufficiency; and adaptation in a frontier. Early attempts at an iron industry challenged relations with the mother country. Impermanent architecture may be an indication of early colonists' intentions of making their fortunes and returning home.

Archaeology of the eighteenth century is concerned with subsistence and economic strategies, settlement patterns, group relations of class, race, ethnicity and gender, cultural and political tensions between the colonies and England, **Georgian Order** and world view, and slave resistance. Focus tends to be on cities in the eighteenth century because urban places, while still small, had then become more important in colonial political, economic, social and cultural structures. Landscape has been studied for expressions of ideals and ideology, and expressions of power over the natural and hence social environments. Mark Leone's influential study of **garden archaeology** at the William Paca Garden, in Annapolis, Maryland, provides an excellent example.

Plantations were vital parts of the economic and social landscape through the nineteenth century. Plantations varied greatly in size and structure. Tobacco was the original basis of wealth, although later economies were redirected to mixed grain. Plantations are places to study not only the economy of the Chesapeake but also influences on African American heritage and culture, and the institutionalisation of racism.

The archaeology of African Americans is not confined to the study of enslaved life on plantations. Paul Mullins investigates late nineteenth- and early twentieth-century African American consumer strategies as an explicit method of battling racism. Several caches of crystals and related materials, perhaps with magical or religious significance, have been discovered in urban contexts in pre-emancipation Annapolis. Archaeologists disagree about the source of **colonoware pottery** and whether it was made and used by African Americans or **Native Americans** in the region. The Chesapeake provides excellent data for the comparative study of plantation slavery with the south-eastern USA, which also has extensive colonoware.

During the nineteenth century, earlier small-scale manufacturing turns into full-blown industrial development. There is increasing commerce, industry, agriculture and regionalism with the pitting of Chesapeake states against each other during the American Civil War. In Washington DC, archaeologists investigate urban neighbour-hoods and alley dwellings from the nineteenth and twentieth centuries. Issues include **gender** rela-tions, **prostitution**, **ethnicity**, class (see **class, social**) and neighbourhood boundaries.

See also: African American archaeology; plantation archaeology; urban archaeology

Further reading

Leone, M.P. (1984) 'Interpreting ideology in historical archaeology using rules of perspective in the William Paca Garden in Annapolis, Maryland', in D. Miller and C. Tilley (eds) *Ideology, Power and Prehistory*, Cambridge: Cam-bridge University Press, pp. 25–35.

Mullins, P.R. (1999) *Race and Affluence: An Archaeology of African America and Consumer Culture*, New York: Kluwer Academic/Plenum Press.

Shackel, P.A. and Little, B.J. (eds) (1994) *Historical Archaeology of the Chesapeake*, Washington, DC: Smithsonian Institution Press.

Yentsch, A.E. (1994) *A Chesapeake Family and Their Slaves: A Study in Historical Archaeology*, Cambridge: Cambridge University Press.

BARBARA J. LITTLE

children

What constitutes a 'child' or 'childhood' is both biologically and culturally constructed. The role of children in society, children's responsibilities and the length of childhood have undergone important transformations during the past 200 years. These transformations have important implications for archaeological study.

Until the late eighteenth to early nineteenth centuries, children were perceived as 'little hands', or miniature adults who had labour responsibilities within the household. This corresponds to the period before the separation of the domestic and business spheres that characterised industrial **capitalism**. A typical household could be ex-pected to include biological kin and non-kin. Women's and men's labour were not necessarily spatially divided. Children laboured on household and business chores that were age-appropriate.

As **industrialisation** changed the organisa-tion of household labour, men's labour was increasingly spatially removed from the household, leaving women responsible for the domestic sphere. **Gender** roles were transformed, and the notion of the 'housewife' became naturalised. For middle-class families, elaboration of etiquette practices became a means of jockeying for enhanced social standing. The nineteenth century is characterised by a bevy of proscriptive literatures related to etiquette. The elaboration of entertaining and **domesticity** is seen archaeologically in rapid fashion shifts in ceramic styles and in increasing numbers of specialised vessels.

Childhood, too, was transformed by the separa-tion of the spheres. Proscriptive literature, such as that written by Lydia Child, explained to mothers the important stages of development for boys and girls. Children were no longer seen as little adults, but as constantly changing individuals with distinct developmental needs. A mother who ignored or did not properly nurture these needs bore the respon-sibility for any character flaws the child might develop. For middle-class children, the duration of childhood came to increase, with children staying in their natal home until their late teens. Age and gender-appropriate games, **toys**, tablewares, med-icines and food products became important ele-ments of household material culture that are found with great frequency archaeologically.

While childhood changed radically in the swelling ranks of the middle class, this was not the case for all families. Enslaved African American children were expected to labour for their owner by the time they were nine or ten years old. In her studies of **prostitution** in Washington, DC, Donna Seifert found that many of the prostitutes living in brothels were in their early teens. The **Boott Mills** also depended upon the labour of young teenaged girls in their factories.

Children and childhood have been an under-studied arena of historical archaeology. Children are usually discussed in the terms of presence or absence at a particular site, not as engaged social actors in their own right. The study of race- and class-based notions of children and childhood has great potential in the field, as well as implications for how social identities are instilled in children.

Further reading

Wall, D.D. (1994) *The Archaeology of Gender*, New York: Plenum Press.

Wilkie, L.A. (2000) 'Not merely child's play: Creating a historical archaeology of children and childhood', in J.S. Derevenski (ed.) *Children and Material Culture*, London: Routledge, pp. 100–13.

LAURIE A. WILKIE

China

The Chinese term for archaeology, *kaogu*, which means 'investigation of the past', originally had been used by Song dynasty (960–1279) antiquarians, but it was only in the twentieth century that the connotation of this word was used as a translation for 'Western archaeology'. While the Chinese have always been interested in the investigation of their past, especially true for their long tradition of written material, scientific archaeology only started in the beginning of the twentieth century. The focus then was on the early periods, including the palaeolithic (*c.* 100,000 BC), the neolithic (*c.* 5500–2000 BC), the beginning of the early historical dynasties (*c.* twenty-first century BC) and the imperial dynasties, starting with the Qin dynasty of the First August Emperor of China (221 BC).

Scientific research from the West was introduced into China at the beginning of the twentieth century. In 1920, the Swedish geologist Johan G. Andersson (1874–1960) did the first sustained modern fieldwork in China proper. Although not trained as an archaeologist, he excavated Zhou-koudian, a palaeolithic site near Beijing (Peking), where later the famous Peking man (*Sinanthropus pekinensis*) was found. He also discovered painted pottery in the small village of Yangshao in Henan province. Thus, the so-called 'Yangshao culture' marks the beginning of prehistory in China. In the 1930s, the Longshan culture with its characteristic black pottery had been identified, and, together with the Yangshao culture, was said to be the foundation of Chinese culture. At the same time, the discovery of the oracle bone inscriptions (written texts on animal bones) at the end of the nineteenth century led to the first independent scientific excavation made by Chinese archaeologists at the Shang dynasty (*c.* sixteenth–eleventh centuries BC) site of Anyang (Yinxu ruins). This marked the birth of field archaeology in China.

The Sino-Japanese war led to an interruption of archaeological work until the foundation of the People's Republic of China in 1949. From this point on, Chinese archaeology for a long time was based on Marxist theory associated with cultural patriotism, and was also greatly influence by Soviet archaeology. As a socialist country wherein the state owns all the land, China owns all antiquities found both on and under the ground. Archaeological research was therefore placed in a stable framework under the State Bureau of Cultural Relics (*Goujia wenwuju*), which controlled the administration of nationwide excavation and conservation of all relics. In 1950, the Institute of Archaeology (*Kaogusuo*) attached to the Academy of Social Science (*Shehui kexueyuan*) was named the premier organisation for conducting field excavations, with permanent archaeological stations all over the country. On the local level, each province slowly established a bureau for archaeology or cultural relics, and, since 1979, they have become full-fledged archaeological institutions.

The discovery of several Bronze Age sites in Erlitou in the late 1950s in the north of the country led to the assumption that the Shang dynasty was preceded by the so-called Xia dynasty. As of this date, no written records have been found and the existence of the Xia is one of the highly debated questions in Chinese archaeology.

Archaeological activities were almost stopped in the 1960s by the Cultural Revolution. Chinese archaeology only attained maturity in the 1970s and 1980s, with a period of increased excavation and a rise in site reports publication. Also during this period the first archaeological exhibitions were sent to foreign countries.

Xia Nai, director of the Institute of Chinese Archaeology for twenty years (1962–82), declared the years from the foundation of the People's Republic to the year 1979 as the 'Golden Age of Chinese Archaeology'. Altogether, the number of archaeological sites excavated since 1949 runs to over 10,000. Large-scale industrial or agricultural construction projects provided the opportunities for many of these discoveries, and, in this environment, archaeologists often had to conduct their work as salvage excavations.

From the palaeolithic period to the People's Republic

One of the main tasks of Chinese archaeology has been to investigate the origins of Chinese civilisation. Until about 1979, archaeological research was almost exclusively focused on the sites of the Yellow River valley, which long had been regarded as the cradle of Chinese civilisation. The palaeolithic (100,000 BC) remains discovered all over the country have evoked interest among international scholars engaged in the study of human evolution. For the neolithic period (10,000–2000 BC), a new framework has been established, splitting China into six great divisions: three facing the Eurasian landmass and three at the Pacific Ocean coast. This design is thought to represent the historical and structural foundation of China, with the focus on the formation of Chinese civilisation and agriculture. For example, more than 140 prehistoric sites have yielded remains of rice cultivation. The majority of these sites are found in the middle and lower reaches of the Yangzi River. In the northern and north-eastern regions, farming consisted mainly of a dry-land millet cultivation.

Many Chinese archaeologists are involved in the so-called 'Three Dynasty Project', covering the historical dynasties of Xia, Shang and Zhou. The existence of the Xia dynasty is highly debated in both China and abroad. Since the first discovery of a city-like wall structure and tombs with bronze artefacts in Erlitou, Henan Province, in the 1950s, a discussion arose as to whether this important

discovery could be proof of a state-level society preceding the Shang dynasty finds at Yinxu in the 1930s. Erlitou may have been the capital of the Xia (flourishing c. 2100–1600 BC), which would make it the first historical dynasty. No writing system has yet been discovered for the Xia.

For the Shang dynasty (sixteenth–eleventh centries BC) written sources prove the existence of a stable political-religious hierarchy administering a large territory from a central capital. Large **cemeteries** prove the existence of a dense population. In 1976, archaeologists discovered a pit tomb close to Anyang, which belonged to Lady Fu Hao, who died c. 1250 BC, and which had never been robbed. It was filled with ritual vessels, showing also a complete set of sacrificial bronze vessels. Inscriptions on the vessels marked the owner of the tomb. Human sacrifices followed Lady Fu Hao into death, a common practice during the Shang period. Archaeological excavations of this sort are important, because Lady Fu Hao, probably one of the king's wives, has also been mentioned in many oracle bone inscriptions. A discovery in 2000 of a large Shang city close to the old Yinxu walls shows that Yinxu did not appear without antecedent urban occupancy.

In about 1050 BC, the Shang had been defeated by the Zhou dynasty, which is divided into the Western (1050–771 BC) and the Eastern Zhou (770–256 BC). Texts exist for the early phase of the first period. Many of these texts were only accessible through excavation, such as the long inscriptions on bronze vessels explaining the battle with 'barbarians' as well as the deeds of and for the ancestors.

The intellectual foundations of Chinese civilisation were established in the Eastern Zhou, a period of political fragmentation. Smaller state units arose and gained power. The excavation of large cemeteries provides insight into contemporary life, still conducted in the tradition of their predecessors. The splendid furnishing of the tombs indicates that bronze, lacquer and silk production were important industries during this period. In the late Zhou period, iron casting was invented mainly for making tools and weapons. Archaeologists have also unearthed quite a few sets of instruments used in court performances of the Zhou. Key instruments were bamboo flutes, drums and bronze bells that had to be struck from the outside. The biggest cache of these instruments was unearthed in Hubei Province, in the tomb of Duke Yi from Zeng, dated to the year 433 BC. The complete orchestra shows that music had reached an advanced state by this date. Recent discoveries of tombs, such as the smaller sized tomb in Guodian, Hubei Province, also revealed philosophical texts written on bamboo strips, providing scholars with new material of the early versions of classical texts.

With the first imperial dynasty of the August Emperor of China, Qin Shihuangdi (reigned from 221–9 BC), the unification of the Chinese nation took place. While his tomb close to the city of Xi'an, Shaanxi Province, still awaits excavation, the side pits have been excavated and thousands of terracotta soldiers and horses were discovered from the first half of the 1970s to date. One of the main problems in China concerns whether or not to employ literary evidence in archaeological interpretation, but this necropolis provides a famous example of archaeological discovery correlating with contemporary written sources.

Within the following Han dynasty (206 BC–AD 220), the tombs of the local aristocracy, mainly relatives of the Emperor, have interested archaeologists for the last two decades. Since the spectacular discovery of the untouched Mawangdui tombs (dated 186–68 BC), belonging to one aristocratic family, archaeologists have also been focusing on this period and have been doing excavations all over the country. The necropolis of Mawangdui revealed that the Chinese were able to mummify a corpse. Wooden tomb constructions as well as cave tombs or brick tombs were in fashion at this time, and these have posed many questions about the ritual of burial, some of which are still unsolved.

Archaeologists have also conducted **urban archaeology**, mainly for the capital of the Tang dynasty (618–907) in Chang'an. These excavations provide an opportunity to examine the rectangular city structure, complete with districts for the different workshops, the market-places, the administration and the palace. Foreign influences entering the country from the Silk Road are still visible in some tomb furnishing. Silk, silver and gold were luxurious trade goods. Buddhism also found its way into China during this period. Excavations in

Buddhist monasteries and cave temples during the 1980s and 1990s shed new light on traditional **architecture** and also on the practice of storing valuable relics and Buddhist texts, like the 10,000 stone sutras in the Yunju temple close to Beijing. Some of these scientific projects are supported by foreign countries, who provide financial and technical aid.

Under the Mongols of the Yuan dynasty (1279–1368) sea-borne commerce had its heyday, though lots of ships sank before they reached their final destination. New fields such as underwater archaeology have been developed in China, focusing on **shipwrecks** and their valuable freight.

Royal tomb architecture has always been of special interest in Chinese archaeology. In the long tradition of rich burials for the Chinese emperors, the mausoleums of the Ming royalty (1368–1644) are outstanding. In the hilly terrain outside the capital of Beijing, thirteen Ming emperors are buried. Excavations started in the 1950s showed that most of the tombs had been robbed and only a few precious grave goods remained. **Looting** of graves has always been a major problem for Chinese archaeologists. The prevalence of site looting led to the creation of the Chinese Cultural Protection Law, finally ratified in 1982 with a major revision in 1991.

The Three Gorges Dam in the middle reaches of the Yangzi River will be finished in 2003. Chinese archaeologists have concentrated on excavations (mostly salvage excavations) in this region. Eighteen institutions have participated in the survey. Eight hundred sites have been discovered on the total area of 200,000 m^2. These discoveries provide scholars with new information on the continuous occupation of this region, starting in the neolithic age.

Further reading

Chang Kwang-chih (1986) *The Archaeology of Ancient China*, fourth edn, New Haven: Yale University.

Childs-Johnson, E. and Sullivan, L.R. (1996) 'The Three Gorges Dam and the fate of China's southern heritage', *Orientations*, July/August: 55–61.

Goujia wenwuju (1999) *Zhongguo wenwu shiye wushinian – China's Cultural Heritage 1949–1999*,

Discovery, Preservation and Protection, Beijing: Zhao-hua [in Chinese].

Keightley, D. (1983) *The Origins of Chinese Civilization*, Berkeley: University of California Press.

Ledderose, L. (1999) *Ten Thousand Things – Modul and Mass Production in Chinese Art*, Princeton, NJ: Princeton University Press.

Loewe, M. and Shaughnessy, E.L. (eds) (1999) *The Cambridge History of Ancient China: From the Origins of Civilization to 221 B.C*, Cambridge, Cambridge University Press.

Von Falkenhausen, L. (1995) 'The regional paradigm in Chinese archaeology', in P.L. Kohl and C. Fawcett (eds) *Nationalism, Politics and the Practice of Archaeology*, Cambridge: Cambridge University Press, pp. 198–217.

MARGARETE PRÜCH

Christianisation

Christianisation had its starting point in the theologically known and partly historically confirmed mission by the apostles after the death of Christ. Between the first and fourth centuries, the mission was limited to the territory within the Roman Empire. The number of Christian communities increased quickly in spite of the intense persecutions under the Roman emperors. For a long time, these communities centred on urban places. However, after the battle at the Milvinian bridge in AD 312, when the emperor Constantin decided to reunite the Western and Eastern Roman Empire under one ruler and one religion with one God, Christianity had its first breakthrough.

From the fourth century onwards, the term 'Christianisation' may be related to political, economic and cultural efforts to change society. It was part of an ideological concept where the rulers used the new religion and its monotheistic structure to destroy an indigenous pagan religion and a tribal community. This effort is clearly demonstrated by the introduction of the image of Christ. The depiction of Christ in Early Christian, Merovingian and Viking art (see **Vikings**) was in the form of the living and victorious Christ (*Christus vivus, Christus rex*). The passion of Christ and its main message in the New Testament was sub-ordinated to the aspect of Christ's victory against the devil. This aspect of victory made it possible for Germanic societies to accept the contradictory destiny of Christ. The moral and ethical values of Christianity were already integrated in Christian teaching (e.g. the *Heliand* or *Otfrid's Evangelistbok*), but they did not dominate as in the High and Late Medieval periods.

The mission of the initial phase of Christianisation can be divided into peaceful (with the book) and violent parts (with the sword). While most of the European countries in the first millennium AD accepted Christianity freely, a change of politics can be observed with the subjugation of the Saxons by Charlemagne and the mission of the Slavs and Balts by the Germans. This colonial way of thinking was subsequently reflected in the Christianisation of North America's **Native Americans** and indigenous peoples in East Asia and **Australia**. Missions (see **mission sites**) were especially successful when the Bible was translated into Gothic (Wulfila) or Slavonic (Kyrillos and Methodios). Missions were not successful in politically and economically well-organised and stable societies, such as the Chinese or Japanese cultures, which had their own religious images and beliefs, and the social hierarchy needed to defend them.

The process of Christianisation can be confirmed by history and archaeology, but quite often the latter plays a subordinate role. In cases with no written evidence to support an early mission, Christian symbols in graves, hoards and settlements are often interpreted as part of robbery, trade or gift-giving. The same problem has been discussed for the transition period between pagan and Christian religions. Graves furnished with Christian symbols but arranged in pagan tradition are often regarded as an expression of syncretic beliefs. The methodologically invalid approach of accepting Christian elements only in Christian contexts must be replaced by a different analysis of **material culture**. The transition period often starts much earlier and runs over a longer period of time than earlier believed. An indication of this time depth can be viewed in the increase of pagan symbols during a period when Christian symbols were still playing a minor role. After this initial phase, the material culture inspired by Christianity developed in the form of **churches**, the layout of churchyards (with Christian burials following the Christian norms) and the introduction of Christian art and **writing** (e.g. pottery with Christian symbols, erection of sarcophagi/runestones, individual Christian symbols, minting with Christian iconography and so forth).

The process of Christianisation mainly depended on the course of the mission. A violent mission resulted in instant change with the establishment of parishes and bishoprics. However, the missing transition period (see **transitional periods**) indicates a different attitude towards the new religion. This phenomenon could be observed for centuries after the official conversion. An analysis of a peaceful mission shows quite a different picture. Different phases can be observed in this case:

1 Contact with neighbouring Christian empires and cultural exchange led to an abandoning of cremation graves and an introduction of inhumation graves. In the beginning, the graves could be west–east or south–north oriented and single Christian symbols without Christian context could appear.

2 The first efforts of missionary activity started and resulted in the baptism of certain individuals. This is reflected by single Christian symbols in 'pagan' graves. At the same time, the first pagan symbols appeared, thus manifesting the indigenous pagan belief.

3 The missionary activity subsequently became more intense, as reflected in the conversion of the King and the nobility. Most graves became west–east oriented and only a minority were still completely furnished. Typical pagan grave goods like horses, food and drink disappear. Christian burials were established on separate parts of the pagan gravefields. The amount of Christian symbols in the graves was increasing while the amount of pagan symbols was reaching its maximum. The first chapels or simple churches were being built on private ground.

4 With the preliminary mission completed a massive baptism occurred in the urban centres and trading places. Churches with churchyards were founded and existed side by side with pagan gravefields in the rural landscape. These gravefields have graves with few grave goods. The foundation of private churches continued while some common churches were established. The mission was finally completed with the baptism of the rural society. The pagan gravefields were abandoned, a large number of churches were founded and the final phase of organisation with the foundation of an archbishopric, bishoprics and parishes started.

Further reading

Berschin, W., Geuenich, D. and Steuer, H. (eds) (2000) *Mission und Christianisierung am Hoch- und Oberrhein (6.–8. Jahrhundert). Archäologie und Geschichte*, Freiburger Forschungen zum ersten Jahrtausend in Südwestdeutschland Band 10, Stuttgart.

Mayeur, J.-M., Pietri, C.L., Vauchez, A. and Vernard, M. (eds) (1991) *Die Geschichte des Christentums*, Freiburg–Basel–Wien.

Müller-Wille, M. (ed.) (1997–8) *Rom und Byzanz im Norden. Mission und Glaubenswechsel im Ostseeraum während des 8.–14. Jahrhunderts*, Band I–II. Akademie der Wissenschaften und der Literatur. Abhandlungen der Geistes- und sozialwissenschaftlichen Klasse Nr. 3, I–II, Mainz.

—— (1993) *Death and Burial in Medieval Europe*, Lund: Scripta Minora, Regiae Societatis Humaniorum Lundensis.

Sawyer, B. (1990) 'Woman and the conversion of Scandinavia', in W. Affeldt (ed.) *Frauen in Spätantike und Frühmittelalter. Lebensbedingungen–Lebensnormen–Lebensformen*, Sigmaringen, pp. 263–81.

Staecker, J. (1999) *Rex regum et dominus dominorum. Die wikingerzeitlichen Kreuz- und Kruzifixanhänger als Ausdruck der Mission in Altdänemark und Schweden*, Lund Studies in Medieval Archaeology 23, Stockholm.

JÖRN STAECKER

churches

Church archaeology is the study of all material aspects associated with ecclesiastical buildings. Interest in church excavation runs the gamut from art and **architecture** to history and biology. Therefore, a multidisciplinary approach to the study is necessary. When buildings have been severely damaged, declared redundant or are to undergo alterations, archaeologists have the opportunity to conduct excavations.

Architecture and history are logical aspects of church excavations. Art history is also important. During the Middle Ages and the **Renaissance**, the church was a major sponsor for the arts and commissioned works, not only for cathedrals, but also for parish churches. The church is often one of the oldest structures in a community. Burials inside the church and in the surrounding churchyard give biological anthropologists (see **biological anthropology**) the opportunity to study earlier populations. Burials also provide information about mortuary practices.

Churches fall victim to war, vandalism, natural disasters and time. Studies of the remains of damaged buildings add to the archaeological record and, when repair is possible, provide a guide for duplicating missing pieces. Early churches may be renovated to add modern conveniences. No matter how practical the project, parts of the structure are still irrevocably altered. A church may

be declared redundant if membership drops below the level needed to provide support. Redundancy leaves three options. First, the church may be preserved as a monument. Second, the structure may also be converted to another use, such as a restaurant. Finally, the church may be demolished to make way for redevelopment or urban renewal. When alterations of any kind are to be made to structures, analysis should be done to mitigate the loss to the archaeological record.

The earliest studies of churches were conducted to record architectural forms. The records of John Leland, King's Antiquary, are some of the earliest examples. Leland's collection of records and drawings of monasteries, **cathedrals** and colleges could well be called **rescue archaeology**. Leland worked amid Henry VIII's destruction of the monasteries. Architectural history is still an important aspect of church archaeology.

Churches in Europe were often built on the foundations of earlier churches. In the early 1800s, Thomas Rickman observed that architectural stratigraphy could be found in the construction methods and materials used. Vertical wall grids and

Figure 8 The church of S. Giorgio al Velabro, Rome, seventh–thirteenth centuries
Source: Photo: N.J. Christie

photogrammetric recording are two valuable techniques for studying changes in construction methods over time.

The destruction of ecclesiastical structures in Europe during the First and Second World Wars provided an impetus in church archaeology. In the USA, most sites are mitigated by **cultural-resource management** companies. A few others are associated with studies of a larger area, such as **Jamestown** and Williamsburg, Virginia.

As all archaeology is destructive, the record of a site must be complete. It should include all periods of a church site's history. Each structure in some way reflects the population that built and used it. In terms of knowledge lost, Anglo-Saxon remains are no more valuable than the Victorian church standing on its foundations.

See also: Central America

Further reading

Rodwell, W. (1989) *Church Archaeology*, London: B.T. Batsford.

M. PATRICIA COLQUETTE

churchyard archaeology

The term 'churchyard' is often used as a contrast to pagan graveyards, but it does not include other burial sites (e.g. Jewish or Muslim communities). It illustrates the effort of the Church to keep the Christian community together in the hereafter, to exclude other members of society and to renounce paganism (like Charlemagne's *Capitulatio de partibus Saxoniae*). Only baptised individuals had a claim to a Christian burial and no strict claim could be allowed in the case of those who had not lived in communion with the Church. This was expressed in the maxim of Pope Leo the Great (448): 'we cannot hold communion in death with those who in life were not in communion with us'. By this definition the churchyard includes burials in consecrated ground for baptised men, women and children, and even for unbaptised children. The funeral of Christ created the Christian ideal of an inhumation grave in supine position without grave goods (*imitatio christi*). By an east–west

orientation of the grave where the head faced the east, the dead would be ready for the day of resurrection.

The establishment of a churchyard is often regarded as a clear sign of a successful mission, but this view does not take Christian burials outside this zone into account (such as village-graveyards in the Baltic countries and pagan graveyards with Christian symbols). Churchyard archaeology is not only the investigation of a yard, which is surrounding the church and limited in its extension by a ditch, a wall or a hedge. It should rather be defined as an archaeology including the Christian burial custom and its liturgy, e.g. church graves, tombstones inside and outside the church, epitaphs and **gravestones**. An important criterion is that the analysis of material culture must be seen in connection with historical anthropology. While there is commonly a spatial connection between church and burial site, this is not the case in Russia where the graves are situated in close distance to the church but not surrounding it. Churchyards did not only function as funeral places but were also meeting places and zones where the right of asylum was valid. With the Reformation, a change in this conception can be observed. The churchyards of the Protestants were no longer *res sacrae* and there was a tendency to move the funeral place outside the town.

The archaeological investigation includes the first Christian funerals in the Roman Empire (e.g. sarcophagi), medieval and post-medieval churchyards inside and outside towns (*intra* and *extra muros*), and in the rural landscape. Anthropological analysis has focused on aspects like age, sex, disease and ethnic origin. In combination with archaeology, where the position of the grave, its type and eventually grave goods have been analysed, emphasis has been put on social factors such as gender and regionality. The segregation in the churchyard according to sex and social class, also known from law texts (cf. the Norwegian *Borgarthings* and *Eidsivathingslaw*), and the spatial division inside the church can be observed in some parts of Europe. In Northern Europe, sex segregation with women on the north side and men on the south side of the churchyard existed until the thirteenth–fourteenth centuries. In many cases a clear distinction between church graves, graves under the roof of the church (*sub stillicidio*), graves in the middle of the churchyard and graves in the periphery can be registered. This social segregation lasted until the Reformation. Regional studies, where local traditions and deviations can be noticed (e.g. urban and rural churchyards; monastery and parish churchyards), are important. In addition to these aspects, recent research has focused on DNA analysis as a tool to investigate aspects like kinship and ethnic origin.

The level of research varies between Europe and its Christian colonies. Archaeology is still struggling with the basic problem of chronology. Stratigraphical analysis of the burials and dendrochronological or ^{14}C methods are other ways of securing the chronology. The change of burial rites with an introduction of a change of the position of the arms is one variation over time. Another method of dating is by grave goods. In spite of the normative behaviour (there were no laws), the custom of grave furnishing was frequently used among the nobility throughout history. Furnished graves can even be observed in lower social classes as expressions of different social structure or different strategies of mission.

As focus has been put on the graves of the nobility inside the church, the relation of these graves to the churchyard and its reflection of Christian society has often been neglected. Even the division into the disciplines of history, art history, heraldry, anthropology and archaeology has had a negative impact on research. The combination of epitaphs and church graves has not been investigated and the research of grave slabs has focused on iconographical aspects, but not on the epigraphy and iconography as an expression of **identity**. Aspects like the use of different formulae, languages, types of inscription and the choice of motives can be used in order to improve our knowledge of a society, which used the grave to send a message to the living world.

Further reading

Kieffer-Olsen, J. (1993) *Grav og gravskik i det middelalderlige Danmark – 8 kirkegårdsudgravninger*, Afdeling for Middelalder-arkæologi och Middelalderarkæologisk Nyhedsbrev, Ph.d. afhandling, Aarhus: Aarhus Universitet.

Müller-Wille, M. (1982) 'Königsgrab und Königs-grabkirche. Funde und Befunde im frühgeschichtlichen und mittelalterlichen Nordeuropa', *Berichte der Römisch-Germanischen Kommission* 63: 349–412.

Mytum, H. (1994) 'Language as symbol in churchyard monuments: The use of Welsh in nineteenth- and twentieth-century Pembrokeshire', *World Archaeology* 26: 252–67.

Parker Pearson, M. (1982) 'Mortuary practices, society and ideology: An ethnoarchaeological study', in I. Hodder (ed.) *Symbolic and Structural Archaeology*, Cambridge: Cambridge University Press, pp. 99–113.

Staecker, J. (2000) 'In atrio ecclesiae. Die Bestattungssitte der dörflichen und städtischen Friedhöfe im Norden', in M. Auns (ed.) *Lübeck Style? Novgorod Style? Baltic Rim Central Places as Arenas for Cultural Encounters and Urbanisation 1100–1400 AD*, Conference Taalsi 1998, Taalsi, pp. 187–258.

Thomas, D.H. (1991) 'The archaeology of mission Santa Catalina de Guale, our first fifteen years: The missions of Spanish Florida', *Florida Anthropologist* 44: 17–125.

Valk, H. (1999) *Rural Cemeteries of Southern Estonia 1225–1800 AD*, Tartu: University of Tartu Archaeology Centre.

JÖRN STAECKER

class, social

The study of material differences between individuals, households and social classes has been a prevalent topic in historical archaeology since the 1970s. Social scientists divide human groups into two general categories, composed of non-stratified and stratified societies. Non-stratified societies, like hunter-gatherers and subsistence-level farming cultures, lack centralised political control and formal leaders. Chiefdoms and states, examples of stratified societies, are characterised by centralised political authority, complex exchange economies and significant material disparities between social classes. Social classes are composed of individuals that possess the same general access to resources, power and prestige.

During the past 200 years, technological advances have dramatically transformed many agricultural states into industrial-level societies. The population of industrial states usually possesses several social classes. Within the USA, during the early twenty-first century, the upper class comprises less than 5 per cent of the population and controls the majority of resources and wealth in the nation. The middle class, consisting mainly of professionals and business people, represents approximately half of the population. The remaining half of the population, encompassing the working and lower classes, is composed of skilled and unskilled labour. Since the end of the nineteenth century, the middle class has expanded while the working and lower classes have proportionally decreased in size. Consequently, a larger proportion of people in the USA during the twentieth century experienced a middle-class standard of living than people during the nineteenth century. Family background, occupation, education, race, ethnicity and gender are variables that influence class membership in industrial states.

Historical archaeologists in North America mainly study the material remains of complex, stratified societies that developed between the sixteenth and twentieth centuries. Research focusing on social class first began in the early 1970s. These initial studies were not systematic, but merely emphasised that socioeconomic status might be defined with artefacts from historic sites. Socioeconomic status, an idea developed by sociologists and anthropologists, combines the variables of social and economic position. Several early historical studies attempted to identify relative social class at specific sites through analysis of ceramic tableware sherds (see **ceramics**). This strategy was used since ceramic sherds are very abundant at most sites, resist deterioration and possessed a wide range of cost. The underlying premise concerning status and ceramics is that affluent households expressed status through consumer goods such as expensive table services. In this context, ceramics were often used as status display items during meals while entertaining guests.

Concerning early ceramic studies, in 1970, J. Jefferson Miller and Lyle Stone, in the monograph *Eighteenth-Century Ceramics from Fort Michilimackinac* (a French and British colonial fortification located in the north part of Michigan, USA) noted that different-quality ceramics might be used to identify status differences among the inhabitants at the site. John Otto was one of the first archaeologists to effectively explore this suggestion in a detailed study of social class and material culture at **Cannon's Point Plantation** in coastal Georgia. Otto identified specific material differences between the planter, overseer, and slaves at the plantation, particularly in the areas of ceramic use and diet.

The study of socioeconomic status and ceramics in historical archaeology reached a plateau in the 1980s. George Miller, a ceramic specialist, developed a method of estimating the general economic cost of ceramic assemblages. The method provided a way of calculating ceramic cost indices for different sites. The indices could then be compared to determine the relative status of previous site inhabitants. By the late 1980s and early 1990s, several historical archaeologists, dissatisfied with ceramic and status studies, began to question the usefulness of inquiry that reinforced conclusions potentially accessible within the historical record. For example, everyone knew that slaves occupied lower social positions in the plantation system of the South and had limited access to food and household items, compared to planters and plantation managers. Demonstrating this fact archaeologically was beginning to be seen as a simplistic and circular endeavour. Archaeologists also critiqued the imprecise concept of socioeconomic status. In a 1988 article, Charles Orser proposed that plantation society should be considered from a perspective emphasising the interrelated variables of economics and power.

Since the early 1990s, historical archaeologists have further refined the study of social organisation and adroitly identified those domains that accurately reflect material differences between different social classes. Within the archaeology of rural contexts, several researchers studying farmsteads have independently concluded that household items – ceramics, personal objects and home furnishings – typically comprised a very small fraction of the total economic resources held by individual families. As revealed by analyses of probate inventories, household goods often comprised less than 10 per cent of a family's economic resources. Consequently, this discovery seriously questions the validity of inferring social class from ceramics, an artefact type that accounts for a very insignificant proportion of a household's financial resources. Archaeologists investigating rural contexts, have demonstrated   rather, that the built environment and means of production – dwelling size and style, number of outbuildings, types of farm equipment and landholdings – are a much more reliable indicators of rural social class than portable material culture. The next twenty-five years will undoubtedly witness the development of many new and exciting advances in the archaeological study of social class and material differences during the historic past.

See also: farmstead archaeology in Canada and the USA

Further reading

Cabak, M.A. and Inkrot, M.M. (1997) *Old Farm, New Farm: An Archaeology of Rural Modernization in the Aiken Plateau, 1875–1950*, Savannah River Archaeological Research Papers, Columbia: South Carolina Institute of Archaeology and Anthropology, University of South Carolina.

Friedlander, A. (1991) 'House and barn: The wealth of farmers, 1795–1815', *Historical Archaeology* 25(2): 15–30.

Horn, J.P. (1988) '"The bare necessities": Standards of living in England and the Chesapeake, 1650–1700', *Historical Archaeology* 22(2): 74–91.

Orser, C.E., Jr (1988) 'The archaeological analysis of plantation society: Replacing status and caste with economics and power', *American Antiquity* 53: 735–51.

Otto, J.S. (1977) 'Artefacts and status differences: A comparison of ceramics from planter, overseer, and slave sites on an antebellum plantation', in S. South (ed.) *Research Strategies in Historical Archaeology*, New York: Academic Press, pp. 91–118.

MARK D. GROOVER

classical archaeology

Classical archaeology, largely the archaeology of ancient Greece and **Rome**, is a most distinguished field of research, whose origins are to be found in the Renaissance. Some archaeologists consider classical archaeology to be historical archaeology because of the common use of written, textual materials in conjunction with archaeological data.

The collection of Greek and Roman works of art started in earnest in Italy in the early days of the 'modern' era, but it would be the eighteenth-century discovery of the ancient remains of Pompeii and Herculaneum that sparked the modern interest in antiquarianism. For centuries, the collection of works of art was considered a private activity, sponsored by the nobility and existing within the framework of the *ancien régime*. The new antiquarianism that resulted from the unearthing of the cities once located around Vesuvius introduced an interest in less impressive, 'high-art' subjects, like the more ordinary artefacts people used every day. German antiquarian Johann Joachim Winckelmann (1717–68) is regarded as the founder of classical archaeology as art history, and the German flavour of the discipline still exists, with its legacy being an overwhelming emphasis on detail and comprehensiveness.

From the end of the eighteenth century, antiquarianism was to be coupled with a new trend. The French Revolution and the spreading of the Enlightenment throughout Europe gave birth to a new science: 'philology', or the scientific study of language. Language was perceived by many to lie at the basis of history, and philology was to provide a scientific study of the past through the understanding of written documents. The first theoretical philologists searched for the Indo-European language and restated the supremacy of the Greek and Latin languages for the Western world, labelling Greek and Latin as the highest class, hence classical, literature. Since the seventeenth century, 'classical' was used to refer to Greek and Roman antiquities, but philologists would use the term to refer to the Greco-Roman world, as opposed to Egypt and the Mesopotamian antiquity, then for the first time studied directly through their written documents and monuments. Classics as an academic field soon included not only the core disciplines of Greek and Latin, but also comprised the history and archaeology of the 'classical world'.

Classical archaeology as a scholarly endeavour sprung from philology and was usually practised within institutions devoted to the classics. In several quarters, archaeology and art history were considered as twin subjects, as the study of the material remains of the ancient world was first concerned with high-style **architecture**, sculpture and painting. Classical archaeology was also directly linked to the imperial ambitions of the British, French and German states, as well as from the USA, and the result was the founding of important archaeological institutions in Athens and Rome, namely the British School, the École Française, the Deutsches Archäologisches Institut and the American Academy, from the mid-nineteenth century, followed by archaeological schools in several other classical sites. Classical archaeology was thus directly linked to imperialist policies.

Many debates have occurred about the definition and application of the term 'classical archaeology'. In several institutions – mainly through the influence of the original German definition of the field – classical archaeology is coupled with art history, as is the case in German-speaking countries and Italy, but also in institutions elsewhere, as in the USA. Almost everywhere, classical archaeology is linked to the study of Greek and Latin, but recently it has also been taught in archaeological, non-language-related institutions, as is the case in the UK. Another controversy involves the civilisations studied by classical archaeology, as sometimes the field can also include all those areas important for the constitution of a Western legacy, namely Egypt, the Near East, and the Aegean. Another dispute regards the chronological boundaries of classical archaeology, even for the majority who consider it to constitute the study of Greece and Rome. In general, 'Greece' includes pre-Hellenic Greece up to the Roman conquest in the second century BC, while 'Rome' began with protohistoric Italic sites and extends up to the Antonines in the second century AD, or even much later up to the settlement of large numbers of German peoples in the former Roman Empire, in the fifth century AD. Finally, the area comprised by classical archaeology varies according to the spreading of Greek and Roman remains, with its core in the Mediterranean but also reaching as far north as Scotland, briefly occupied by the Romans in the second century AD, as far south as Arabia and North Africa, as far east as Turkey and the Middle East and as far west as Wales and Portugal.

The term 'classical' is particularly ambiguous, for it can also refer to a specific period in time, an acme of civilisation, as in 'classical' Greece (fifth century BC) or Rome (late Republic and early Empire). Within archaeology, the term is also used to refer to zenith periods of different civilisations, as with the 'classic-period Maya' in the New World. The term 'classical' is also used by different disciplines to refer to different subjects, like classical music (i.e. a late eighteenth-century style) or classical style in general, as opposed to romantic.

Classical archaeology, as the archaeological study of Greece and Rome, is rooted in philology and its core methodology is philological. The definition itself of its subject is based on the written languages used, namely Greek and Latin. As it is linked to the study of these languages, the classical archaeologist must learn both Greek and Latin, but specialise in one of these two languages and cultural areas. Classical archaeologists are thus almost by definition Hellenists *or* Romanists, and the early specialisation in one of those fields is generalised. Underlying these features of the discipline is the assumption that archaeologists study different civilisations, a concept of German origin to refer to a rather ambiguous mix of customs, ethos and other subjective aspects of a common identity. As the discipline developed as a side-effect of the modern nation-state, its practitioners tended to interpret the ancient Greek and Roman worlds as homogeneous entities, like their modern counterparts. In the same direction, as the modern states considered that they were spreading superior Western civilisation to inferior colonised peoples, eager to adopt the more developed Western culture, classical scholars coined the terms 'hellenisation' and 'romanisation' to refer to the adoption of supposedly superior Greek and Roman traits, not least of which involved **material culture**.

Another feature associated with classical archaeology and rooted in its philological origins is the importance of written archaeological evidence, studied by archaeologists specialising in epigraphy and palaeography. The publication of inscriptions since the mid-nineteenth century has been an important aim of classical archaeologists, and the publication of a *corpus* of inscriptions served as the model for the scholarly publication of archaeological artefacts. The *Corpus Vasorum Antiquorum* and *Lexicon Iconographicon Mythologiae Classicae* are two distinguished examples of the philological model in the publication of archaeological iconography. Classical archaeology has also developed a wide variety of fields, from the study of coins, or numismatics, to the study of amphorae, all of them characterised by the publication of corpora of artefacts, usually with German-style comprehensive references.

Typological studies have also characterised the field, again inspired by philological models. This development is particularly clear in the study of Greek painted vases and Roman painting. In both cases, styles were defined following language analogies, and the typological method used throughout the discipline to study different categories of artefacts is rooted in historical philology, notably its interpretation of the entire cycle of existence of language and artefacts. Languages are considered to follow a biological cycle in the historical philology tradition from birth to adolescence, through maturity, decadence and decay up to death. This scheme is thus applied to material culture, with artefacts acquiring a life cycle.

Classical archaeology has also been split along Mediterranean and Northern European field techniques. In the Mediterranean, there has been a long tradition of unearthing large-scale architectural features, and this programme of action was as much the result of a lack of concern for small finds as to the splendour of finds on the shores of the Mediterranean. Even if isolated archaeologists introduced stratigraphic excavations, as was the case of Nino Lamboglia before the Second World War in Italy, the spread of excavation techniques was due to Northern European influences. Mortimer Wheeler first and Paul Courbin afterwards were responsible for the adoption of strict field methodology in classical archaeology. Wheeler's field strategy, inspired by strict military organisation, meant a revolution in excavation practices, because for the first time attention was paid to contextual evidence. Furthermore, after the war, classical archaeologists have been increasingly concerned with ordinary artefacts, from humble amphorae to bricks and bronze trinkets. In Mediterranean countries, the study of ordinary artefacts is known by the Latin expression *instrumentum domesticum*. Classical archaeology has

also been characterised by a huge multiplication of specialised fields.

In recent decades, several unresolved issues have been haunting classical archaeology. There has been an overall challenge to the relevance of the study of the ancient world in general. Latin and Greek were taught to pupils in elite schools and the classical world was idealised as a model for modern imperialist powers. However, the classics have been sidelined in society, empires are no longer in existence or are in fashion and classical archaeology has been challenged by fellow archaeologists who consider it a conservative discipline, largely out of touch with modern science. Classical archaeology has been slow to respond to the changes in the scholarly world, but it is increasingly re-evaluating its role in society. Classical archaeology almost missed the discussions of the **New Archaeology**, but classical archaeologists are now more actively interacting with post-processual trends (see **post-processual archaeology**), especially as the philosophical and discursive features of post-modern theories are rooted in common classical roots. It is not accidental that some of the most active theoretical archaeologists today are classical archaeologists.

The outlook for mainstream classical archaeology depends on its capacity to interact with the new realities. Several avenues are open, notably the co-operation with archaeologists working with other civilisations and periods. This trend is already noticeable in the Anglo-Saxon world. The development of traditional areas of study will continue, as is the case with the sciences in general, but, increasingly, the relevance of classical archaeology will be judged by the ability of its practitioners to address a broad, scholarly audience. Classical archaeology has a long and rich scholarly tradition and its future is linked to the challenge of keeping this legacy and at the same time interacting with the contemporary scholarly discussions.

Further reading

Allison, P.M. (1995) 'House contents in Pompeii: Data collection and interpretive procedures for a reappraisal of Roman domestic life and site formation processes', *Journal of European Archaeology* 3: 145–76.

Bernal, M. (1987) *Black Athena. The Afroasiatic Roots of Classical Civilization*, New Brunswick, NJ: Rutgers University Press.

Fotiadis, M. (1993) 'Regions of the imagination: Archaeologists, local people, and the archaeological record in fieldwork, Greece', *Journal of European Archaeology* 1: 151–68.

Schnapp, A. (1993) *La Conquête du passé: aux origines de l'archéologie*, Paris: Éditions Carré.

Shanks, M. (1997) *The Classical Archaeology of Greece, Experiences of the Discipline*, London: Routledge.

PEDRO PAULO A. FUNARI

classification

The process of classification involves organising artefacts into standardised, hierarchically ordered descriptive systems. Complete systems of classification are called **typologies**. Unlike many used in prehistoric archaeology, the systems of classification used in historical archaeology often rely on more than descriptions of artefact form. With the help of historical documents like encyclopedias and **probate inventories**, historical archaeologists can categorise artefacts on the basis not only of their form, but also of their material, method of production and even function, depending on the aims of the researcher. Systems of classification allow archaeological data to be quantified, enabling intra- and inter-site comparisons. In classifying artefacts, historical archaeologists have an advantage over prehistorians in that many of the objects found on historical sites are familiar items, similar to ones used today.

Classification entails sorting artefacts into discrete units or classes on the basis of selected attributes. These attributes, or observable characteristics, may be formal, stylistic, technological, functional or chronological. Often in historical archaeology, the initial groupings in a classificatory system are based on material ('**glass** artefacts'). These classes are further sub-divided into types on the basis of more specific characteristics like method of production ('blown glass') or function ('drinking glasses'). Classes, then, are collections of artefacts that share some but not all of the attributes that define the constituent types. The resultant classificatory system or typology is hierarchically organised according to the relative significance given to the particular chosen attributes. While some archaeologists believe that artefact types are inherent, most recognise that artefact groups are constructed by researchers, who choose the particular descriptive features of artefacts that will be used in classification. The characteristics chosen to group artefacts within a system of classification should be suited to the questions being asked by the researcher. A typology of historical glass based on elements of technology and style, for example, may be more useful for answering questions regarding chronology than would one based on artefact function. With this in mind, different systems of classification may simultaneously be used to organise and analyse the same artefact collection depending on the aims of the archaeologists involved.

Historical archaeologists can use the documentary record to help understand how artefacts were classified in the past by the people who made and used them. Documents like potters' production records can provide a variety of information, including an artefact's range of production dates and the names employed by its makers. Other documents like probate inventories allow researchers to see how artefacts were named and used by people in everyday life. Some researchers emphasise the importance of employing these 'natural' or historical categories to reveal the perceptions of past people. Given the information provided to historical archaeologists by the documentary record, the categories employed in classificatory systems may be based on both empirical characteristics, such as the materials from which artefacts were made, and cultural characteristics, such as the activity domain like food preparation or personal ornamentation in which the objects were used.

Other archaeologists believe that classificatory systems need not correspond to those used by the producing society. To these researchers, classificatory systems are not intended to represent past reality. Instead, they are a framework for producing data relevant to specific issues of interest. This approach classifies archaeological data according to variables that may not have been significant to the artefacts' makers and users, but which answer particular questions posed by the archaeologist. An examination of the distribution of historical ceramics in trade networks, for example, may require a system of classification that relies on artefact attributes which were not part of past folk typologies. For an analysis such as this, classifying ceramic vessels according to the kind of temper included in the ceramic fabric may be more important than classifying them according to their past function.

The process of classification structures archaeological collections and allows systematised descriptions of artefact types. This enables researchers to process archaeological data in a standardised system, making possible the quantified study of artefacts and their relationships both within a single site and between sites over time and space. By organising data into systems of classification, archaeologists are able to compare the material record from different sites, recognise patterns of material culture in the archaeological record and measure the regularities and variations between assemblages. Stanley South, for example, used statistical analyses of artefact types to elucidate archaeological signatures like the 'Carolina' and 'frontier' patterns that correspond to particular site functions and activities.

Systems of classification are subject to refinement. They are the researcher's means of ordering archaeological data, but must be open to revision given new information. The process of classifying artefacts is only the beginning of artefact analysis. A classificatory system is a flexible framework for organising information and provides a researcher with a standardised system through which to compare, discuss and interpret archaeological collections and the past activities and meanings they represent.

See also: folk typology; pattern recognition

Further reading

South, S. (1977) *Method and Theory in Historical Archaeology*, New York: Academic Press.
Stone, L.M. (1970) 'Formal classification and the analysis of historic artifacts', *Historical Archaeology* 4: 90–102.
Walker, I.C. (1967) 'Historic archaeology: Methods and principles, *Historical Archaeology* 1: 23–34.

STACEY C. JORDAN

coffee

Coffee was one of several commodities produced in Caribbean plantation contexts during the eighteenth and nineteenth centuries using enslaved African labour. Unlike other tropical and semitropical agricultural commodities, coffee grows primarily in highlands. Many plantations are poorly represented archaeologically, as fragile features such as impermanent slave housing are subject to serious degradation from soil erosion and other depositional processes. While many studies have focused on sugar, tobacco and cotton plantations, relatively few have focused on coffee. Two dissertation projects occurred in the mid-1990s – conducted by James Delle and Matthew Reeves – that focused on Jamaican coffee plantations, and one **cultural-resource management** report was completed in Puerto Rico by Joe Joseph. Theresa Singleton initiated a coffee plantation project in Cuba in the late 1990s. Coffee plantation sites provide great potential to understand the African experience in highland settings in heretofore unstudied contexts in Jamaica, Haiti, the Dominican Republic, Cuba, the Lesser Antilles and the Central and South American highlands.

JAMES A. DELLE

cognitive archaeology

If cognition can be defined as the act or faculty of knowing or perceiving some thing, then cognitive archaeology is the study of past ways of perception and thought, or the function of cognition in the past, as seen in the material remains of a culture. Generally, the objective of such studies is to uncover cultural reasoning, human reasoning or the common sense of a culture. Through a variety of approaches, cognitive archaeology seeks to reconstruct the ways in which a culture understood its surrounding environment, processed sensory information, managed memory and communicated ideas through art, language and writing. Cognitive archaeology can also be seen as the study of past *mentalité*, or past cultural world view as seen in assemblage patterning, artefact design and decoration, and other data.

Cognitive archaeology grew out of a dissatisfaction with the Neo-Evolutionism and functionalism of the processual school of archaeology (see **processual archaeology**). It was in part a reaction against a subsistence-settlement orientation, which dominated archaeology in the 1960s and 1970s, and focused on human–environment interaction, cultural change as the result of environmental stress and the explanation of human behaviour. In terms of Julian Steward's divisions of culture into the technomic, socio-technic and ideo-technic, cognitive archaeology sought to leave the purely technological, adaptive and functional base of this hierarchy, and approach the higher questions of the superstructure (as opposed to the technical 'base'). In order to study the ideo-technic, cognitive archaeologists conceived of variation and pattern in the archaeological record as a reflection of how people think about, understand or view their world. The everyday functions of human life take place within a framework of cultural norms and beliefs; thus cognitive archaeologists look for evidence of this framework. The archaeological record is not just the result of human behaviour, but is evidence of human cognition, world view and ideological beliefs.

Currently, cognitive archaeology is more strongly associated with prehistoric archaeology than with historical archaeology. In prehistoric archaeology, which lacks many of the documentary materials available to historical archaeologists, cognitive archaeology operates from a grounded, scientific, empirical tradition of social research that has characterised processual archaeology since the 1960s. This school of cognitive archaeology seeks to expand the realm of processual research beyond the settlement-procurement focus of the New Archaeologists into the ideas and symbolic systems of past cultures, while maintaining a positivist epistemology. Patterns of cognition (and changes in cognition) are reflected in archaeological remains within sites as well as on the landscape. This style

of research has been termed the 'cognitive-processual' school by Colin Renfrew.

Among historical archaeologists, cognitive archaeology is most strongly represented by the work of archaeologist James Deetz and folklorist Henry Glassie. These scholars took a linguistic approach to understanding cognition, and their work was informed by the semiotic work of Noam Chomsky, and the structuralist anthropology of Lévi-Strauss. Glassie and Deetz sought to discover the basic cognitive units of culture through examination of surviving artefacts, and looked for evidence of deep structures of thought that organise cultural behaviour and material products. Such structures, whether hard-wired into the brain or simply learned ways of viewing the world, organise all human behaviour, including the material remains of any culture. These structures act like a grammar, and determine how people build their homes, live in those homes, cook and eat their food, conceive of the universe and so on. That is, the shape, decoration and design of artefacts are normative; people have an idea of what a plate should look like and how that plate should be used, taught to them by other members of the culture, and can only reproduce variations on that image. Thus, patterns in the archaeological record must reflect human behaviour, which in turn reflect or are patterned by deep cultural or human structures of thought. In this sense, artefacts are seen as reflections of the mental templates of the makers, and they allow archaeologists to understand the grammar that defined them to their makers.

Henry Glassie's study *Folk Housing in Middle Virginia* involved a detailed analysis of vernacular houses in Virginia. He examined window and door arrangements, room size and placement, and ratios of walls, windows and doors in an effort to discover the rules that guided the builders of these houses. Similarly, James Deetz's work on seventeenth- and eighteenth-century **New England** focused on both the type of artefacts and the total assemblage of artefacts commonly found in homes during that period. To Deetz, shifts in assemblage patterning from the seventeenth to the eighteenth centuries were representative of a substantial change in world view, from medieval and organic to ordered and **Renaissance**. Both studies recognised real change over time in artefact design, but suffered from the inability to account for that change. The focus on describing cultural structures of thought created a synchronic view of these societies, but not a diachronic picture of cultures.

Cognitive archaeology provided a starting point for symbolic, structural and post-structural archaeology, and has largely been subsumed into these areas of inquiry among historical archaeologists. For historical archaeologists working after the 1970s, cognitive archaeology contributed to a growing interest in recursivity and meaning in material culture. Cultural artefacts have come to be seen as evidence of past world view, and many researchers are now less interested in how artefacts reflected social norms or human cognitive faculties, and more interested in what artefacts meant to their makers and users, and how that meaning changed over time. This represents a shift away from an interest in systems of thought or human cognition, to an interest in how humans symbolically constituted their worlds in social action.

See also: history of historical archaeology

Further reading

Deetz, J. (1977) *In Small Things Forgotten: The Archaeology of Early American Life*. Garden City, NY: Anchor Press/Doubleday.

Glassie, H. (1975) *Folk Housing in Middle Virginia*, Knoxville: University of Tennessee Press.

Hodder, I. (ed.) (1982) *Symbolic and Structural Archaeology*, Cambridge: Cambridge University Press.

Renfrew, C. and Zubrow, E.B.W. (1994) *The Ancient Mind: Elements of Cognitive Archaeology*, Cambridge: Cambridge University Press.

JESSICA L. NEUWIRTH WITH
MATTHEW PALUS AND MARK P. LEONE

colonialism

Colonialism is a relationship of **power** between, on the one hand, a dominating element constituted by a group of people present, for purposes of economic exploitation, in a territory outside that of their origin, and, on the other, a dominated element, constituted by the native population. As a power relation, colonialism spans a broad time frame, having existed in different historical periods, for instance: Greek and Roman colonisation in classical antiquity; Spanish (see **Spanish colonialism**), Portuguese (see **Portuguese colonialism**) and British colonialism in the modern era, when the phenomenon was particularly pronounced in the Americas, and in the nineteenth and twentieth centuries, when it was pervasive in Africa and Asia.

A dialectical relationship exists between archaeology and colonialism that allows for two kinds of analysis. The first sees archaeology as an instrument of colonialism; the second, on the contrary, understands archaeology as an instrument for the study of colonialism.

The first approach emphasises the functional role of archaeology in the context of the economic, political and ideological **domination** that defines colonialism; it is owing to this domination that the discipline of archaeology begins to develop. From the fifteenth to the nineteenth centuries, archaeology is characterised by its ideological transposition of the relationship of economic domination between the coloniser and the colonised; that is, archaeological theory and praxis reflect that relationship of power. Thus, archaeology takes on the adjective 'colonialist', for it enacts a devaluation of the native culture and engages in the appropriation of the past of the native peoples by Western culture, which is essentially represented by European, white **ethnicity**.

In this sense, archaeology perpetuates colonialism through three primary processes: first, through selection of the objects of study, as it chooses those that can be useful for the specific purposes of domination and rejects those that cannot. This was the case, for example, at **Great Zimbabwe**. The second, concerning forms of interpretation, applies specific theories that represent cultural values more than theoretical systems, as in evolutionism and diffusionism, which were two main interpretative models in the history of colonialist archaeology. The third involves forms of dissemination of the object and the knowledge gained, as archaeology also adopted those that were favourable to exhibiting and exalting domination. Collections in the form of cabinets of curiosities first, and archaeological museums later, served as powerful tools for reproducing and displaying the superiority of the colonisers over the colonised. To cite only one example, we could mention the fact that, in **Brazil**, materials produced by indigenous populations were traditionally displayed in natural history museums, whereas European-style or colonial materials took on the status of civilised and were consequently exhibited in historical museums, due to their supposed distance from the state of nature ascribed to indigenous culture.

Therefore, the role of archaeology in the colonial period was to legitimise the dominant **ideology** by creating theories and interpretations about the past of the colonised that were distorted so as to be favourable to the coloniser. It also had three additional characteristics, namely: it was a field engaged in mostly by non-natives; it was closely linked to ethnography, thereby leading to a static view of the present population; and it generally used systems of interpretation that placed the indigenous population in a position of inferiority to Europeans. Unlike colonialism in classical antiquity, modern colonialism always bore an attitude of scorn towards the 'other', the colonised. The relationship of otherness, which was inevitable in the intercultural contact that usually accompanied the colonial process, loses its symmetry to the extent that the author of the scientific discourse is always a member of the colonising group, whereas the colonised is reduced to an object of prestige or of study.

The second form of analysing the relationship between colonialism and archaeology sees the latter as a method of building an analysis of colonialism, which leads us to a state of affairs that is utterly opposed to the prior one: archaeology becomes a useful instrument for criticising colonialism. This has happened precisely because, in studying colonialism, archaeology turns into a means of recovering the subjugated otherness. In other words, archaeology is capable of revising official history by the study of material remains of social and ethnic groups that were powerless and voiceless in the colonial relationship.

This task is undertaken mainly by historical archaeology by focusing on the relationship between the development of capitalism and forms of colonialism, and identifying both realities as crucial to the formation of European states, European and individual identity, and, ultimately, to modernity. In this way, historical archaeology exposes the role played by colonialism in the definition of a broad array of identities, and engages in self-criticism in order to evaluate its own contribution to this process, thereby freeing itself from the adjective 'colonialist'. Archaeology thus no longer ratifies the official history, and becomes a form of political resistance to domination and a path towards democratisation that adopts a view of the past as a common heritage, a change that is beginning to happen in countries like **South Africa**, **Brazil** and **Australia**.

To investigate colonialism, understood as one of the primary manifestations in the rest of the world of European capitalism, historical archaeology relies on sources such as **historical documents**, pictorial images, artefacts, settlement structures and **architecture**. Among these sources, the last two have traditionally carried more weight. Indeed, the study of architecture and architectonic structures is responsible for the close links between archaeology and the preservation of cultural memory and heritage.

Owing to the high symbolic value that society attaches to architectural remains recovered, studied and preserved, at times historical archaeology participates in the power relations born under colonialism. This is the case, for instance, when monuments or constructions that are representative of dominant groups tend to be valued and preserved. Investigation of Roman Catholic mission settlements (see **mission sites**) has been particularly useful for this purpose. In South America, investigation into this phenomenon has been on the rise in recent times, and countries such as Brazil, Argentina, Paraguay and Uruguay intend to create a common identity that sees the factor of European religion as the basis for their bond. Thus, in spite of the fact that Roman Catholic missions offer a wealth of possibilities for studying different indigenous responses to the new social and economic order brought by colonisers, some projects do no more than study specific architectural elements. This is manipulation of the past, for it transforms what was merely a microcosm of the colonial process in the Americas into an imaginary bond between elites seeking to forge economic unity (MERCOSUR) among the countries of the Southern Cone.

Furthermore, the excessive value attributed to a specific settlement type may hide a broader and more complex reality. Settlements established under European colonialism are diverse, and they follow different patterns according to the origin of the coloniser, or even the particular colonial agent under the same colonial power. Hence, in the Americas, settlement patterns differ, depending on whether settlements are British, Spanish or French; this variety extends even further, for it is also seen in different colonising social agents.

Bernard Fontana exhaustively studied and classified the types of settlements established under colonialism; his point of departure was the very diversity of settlements in the Americas. This lack of uniformity is a result of the fact that modern colonialism involves domination and the institution of a new ideological, economic and political order that did not spread under the same form or with the same intensity in all colonised territories; its development and progress were conditioned by the economic interests of the coloniser in specific geographic areas, interests which revolved around the resources or potential these areas offered. Thus, in the colonised world, archaeological sites can be seen that clearly reveal different stages of the colonial process. These settlements, clearly distinguishable from each other, are classified as follows: 'proto-historical settlements', where indigenous people has contact with European **material culture**, though they did not enter into direct contact with colonisers, and where colonisation and **acculturation** were consequently weaker; 'frontier settlements', where indigenous peoples lived in direct, frequent contact with colonisers; and, finally, settlements with the self-explicative names of 'contact settlements' and 'post-contact settlements'.

This varied **assimilation** and propagation of the new economic order and its material culture by the non-European world, that is, colonialism itself, is the very phenomenon that historical archaeology seeks to investigate and account for.

See also: Dutch colonialism; French colonialism; politics in archaeology

Further reading

Barringer, T. and Flynn, T. (eds) (1997) *Colonialism*

and the Object: Empire, Material Culture and the Museum, London: Routledge.

Bond, G.C. and Gilliam, A. (eds) (1997) *Social Construction of the Past: Representations as Power*, London: Routledge.

Gathercole, P. and Lowenthal, D. (eds) (1989) *The Politics of the Past*, London: Unwin Hyman.

Prakash, G. (ed.) (1995) *After Colonialism: Imperial Histories and Postcolonial Displacements*, Princeton: Princeton University Press.

Thomas, N. (1994) *Colonialism's Culture: Anthropology, Travel and Government*, Cambridge: Polity Press.

Trigger, B. (1984) 'Alternative archaeologies: Nationalist, colonialist, imperialist', *Man* 19: 355–70.

ANA C. PIÑÓN

colonoware pottery

By the early 1960s, archaeologists in the Chesapeake and other coastal areas of the south-eastern USA began to recognise a low-fired, unglazed, usually hand-modelled **earthenware** on historic sites dating primarily to the colonial period. In 1962, Ivor Noël Hume described such earthenware in the Virginia tidewater as being made by **Native Americans** for trade with European colonists, and he dubbed it 'Colono-Indian ware'. By the mid-1970s, archaeologists were recognising this pottery in the lowcountry of South Carolina – where they assumed it to be of Native American origin – and in the Caribbean (see **Caribbean archaeology**) – where archaeologists assumed it represented an African tradition.

Colonoware is found primarily in the Chesapeake, Carolina lowcountry and the Caribbean. Little has been found or recognised in North Carolina, Georgia, Florida or other parts of the US. It is commonly found on plantations or rural domestic sites, but has also been found in urban settings. In the Chesapeake, colonoware appears in the late seventeenth century, while in the lowcountry and Caribbean it seems to begin in the early eighteenth century. By the early nineteenth century, colonoware, and particularly the African American version, quickly decreased in importance in the Chesapeake and lowcountry, while the Native American version continued until the twentieth century. In the Caribbean, the African-influenced colonoware tradition is still alive on some islands at the end of the twentieth century.

Leland Ferguson, among others, began strongly to suspect that, at least in South Carolina, this ware was being produced and used by African Americans. Thus, he suggested changing the name of this ware from 'Colono-Indian' to 'Colono Ware', a loose term indicating locally made, non-European ceramics. Colonoware – as it is now known – has thus come to include all non-European ceramics made during the colonial period in European-dominated areas of the New World.

By the late 1970s, clear evidence was found for the manufacture of this ware by African Americans on Yaughan and Curriboo Plantations in South Carolina. By 1999, it had become generally accepted that colonoware was made and used primarily by African Americans and secondarily by Native Americans in the South Carolina low-country, and by African Americans in the Caribbean, while the question of attribution is still unclear in the Chesapeake. In Florida, it appears to be more closely associated with a Native American tradition during the Spanish period.

Colonoware has several characteristics that make it difficult to define types and varieties precisely. Not only was it made by a variety of Native American groups, but it was also made by Africans from a wide variety of cultures and by their descendants, who may have been influenced by other groups including Native Americans. Archaeologists have provided detailed physical descriptions of colonoware for the Chesapeake, the South Carolina lowcountry and the Caribbean.

The methods of manufacture and clay sources varied widely, often within a single site, so that the distinguishing characteristics of the various types of colonoware are generally form and decoration rather than paste and method of manufacture. Bowls and cooking jars are often the most common forms, but other forms, including European, occur and vary in proportions depending on the region, the time period and whether the site is rural or urban, among other factors.

Since the early 1980s, research has shifted away from descriptive studies of the ceramics and towards closer examination of what these ceramics imply about other aspects of culture. Being able to distinguish Native American and African American versions of the ware has allowed archaeologists to re-examine various issues of the plantation and African American experience in the New World. Defining the African American presence on both inter- and intra-site bases, and being able to examine other aspects of culture such as foodways, has provided insights into cultural continuity, **creolisation**, world view and **power** relationships within the plantation, as well as between rural and urban sites. In the 1990s, various aspects of surface decoration, including etched crosses and other symbols on the interior of bowls, coupled with similar symbols on spoons and other objects in an African American setting, and an increasing trend for researchers to look to Africa for ethnographic comparisons, has indicated that the study of colonoware will continue to produce insights into the process of creolisation of African, Native American and European cultures in the New World.

See also: plantation archaeology; slavery

Further reading

Ferguson, L. (1990) 'Lowcountry plantations, the Catawba nation, and river burnished pottery', in A.C. Goodyear and G.T. Hanson (eds) *Studies in South Carolina Archaeology, Essays in Honor of Robert L. Stephenson*, Columbia: South Carolina Institute of Archaeology and Anthropology, pp. 185–92.

Heath, B.J. (1988) 'Afro-Caribbean ware: A study of ethnicity on St. Eustatius, doctoral dissertation, Philadelphia: University of Pennsylvania.

Henry, S. (1980) 'Physical, spatial and temporal dimensions of colono ware in the Chesapeake, 1600–1800', master's thesis, Washington, DC: The Catholic University of America.

Mouer, D.L., Hodges, M.E.N., Potter, S.R., Renaud, S.L.H., Noël Hume, I., Pogue, D.J., McCartney, M.W. and Davidson, T.E. (1999) 'Colonoware pottery, Chesapeake pipes and "uncritical assumptions"', in T.A. Singleton (ed.) *'I, too, am America': Archaeological Studies of African-American Life*, Charlottesville: University Press of Virginia, pp. 83–115.

Noël Hume, I. (1962) 'An Indian ware of the

colonial period', *Quarterly Bulletin of the Archae-ological Society of Virginia* 17(1): 2–4.

Wheaton, T.R., Freidlander, A. and Garrow, P.H. (1983) *Yaughan and Curriboo Plantations: Studies in Afro-American Archaeology*, Atlanta: National Park Service.

THOMAS R. WHEATON

commodification

Archaeologists use the term 'commodification' in a broad way to describe the process by which an object is separated from the complex of meanings that inspired its original creation and use, and is ascribed with a new set of social meanings and values. This transformation can occur through time, across cultures (see **culture**) and, in the case of some economic systems, is an inherent aspect of the material world.

Michael Shanks and Christopher Tilley in *Re-Constructing Archaeology* offer a sustained discussion of how artefacts become commodified over time. They argue that the display of excavated materials within a museum setting (see **museums**) effectively strips objects of the meanings that informed their original production and use. Thus, a Greek statue, a Native American (see **Native Americans**) projectile point and a European chamber pot, under the careful lighting of their display cases, all become valued as aesthetic objects. Beneath the gaze of twentieth-century museum visitors, the vast differences in how these items were originally construed becomes irrevocably lost.

Time is not the only factor that alienates an object from its original constellation of meanings. A compelling illustration of commodification occur-ring cross-culturally took place within the various World's Fairs held in the USA during the late nineteenth and early twentieth centuries. As several scholars have argued, these fairs were not merely forms of entertainment, but implicitly celebrated the prowess of US beliefs and ideals. In his discussion of the 1893 Columbian Exposition, the historian Curtis Hinsley uses this cultural elitism as a starting point from which to assess the content of the Exposition. Specifically, he examines the popularity of displays that contained both materials and peoples from other parts of the world. These carefully contrived tableaux purportedly recreated cultures as disparate as the Kwakiutl (with a reconstructed village) to an Arab street scene replete with Egyptians who had been transported to the USA for the exhibition. Displayed side by side, Hinsley argues that the cumulative effect of such displays was to reduce these rich and varied cultures into merely a form of entertainment for the supposedly advanced tastes and sensibilities of the US public.

It should come as no surprise that these examples of commodification across time and across cultures should occur within capitalist societies. Indeed, the intellectual origins of the concept of commodification come from the works of scholars such as Karl Marx, Georg Simmel and Walter Benjamin. Their interest in capitalist societies stemmed from the fact that, within this socioeconomic system, almost all objects are separated from their original contexts and are given a uniform meaning, namely a monetary price. Thus, a book of poetry, which can clearly have deep personal meanings to both its author and reader, can cost the same as a cut of meat. In essence, the meat cut and the book, despite the differing contexts in which they were produced, come to be defined in the same manner within a capitalist economy. Benjamin offers a classic discussion of this reduction of material objects in his essay 'The work of art in the age of mechanical reproduction'. In this work, Benjamin explores the changes of meaning that result from the easy ability to reproduce art. Through the ability to reproduce art as well as the creation of new forms of art that can be simultaneously experienced by many (like photographs), art is separated from its original 'aura' (or context). Through being copied and broadly disseminated the art object is fundamen-tally transformed. Meaning is no longer based in its authenticity and uniqueness, but rather it becomes a commodity and equal in value to many other objects.

Given the multifaceted nature of commodifica-tion, it is not surprising that the concept has been somewhat inconsistently explored within historical archaeology. A considerable amount of work in historical archaeology essentially reinforces the commodification of artefacts through the development of scaling models for materials such as **ceramics** and faunal remains. These scales allow scholars to equate temporally and geographically differing assemblages with each other. In contrast to this approach other scholars have begun to explore the implications of commodification for particular groups of people. Archaeologist Paul Mullins, for instance, investigates how mass-produced bric-a-brac recovered from African American households represents an attempt by African Americans to participate in an overwhelmingly white consumer society – into which they were simultaneously incorporated and excluded. On the one hand, the bric-a-brac represented their abilities as consumers in white society, while on the other hand they were identifiers of their positions within African American society.

See also: capitalism; consumer choice; consumption; Marxian approaches; material culture; post-processual archaeology

Further reading

Appadurai, A. (1986) 'Introduction: Commodities and the politics of value', in A. Appadurai (ed.) *The Social Life of Things: Commodities in Cultural Perspective*, Cambridge: Cambridge University Press, pp. 3–63.

Benjamin, W. (1969) 'The work of art in the age of mechanical reproduction', in *Illuminations*, ed. H. Arendt, trans. H. Zohn, New York: Shocken, pp. 217–51.

Hinsley, C.M. (1991) 'The world as marketplace: Commodification of the exotic at the World's Columbian Exposition, Chicago, 1893', in I. Karp and S.D. Lavine (eds) *Exhibiting Cultures: The Poetics and Politics of Museum Display*, Washington, DC: Smithsonian Institution Press, pp. 344–65.

Mullins, P.R. (1999) '"A bold and gorgeous front": The contradictions of African America and consumer culture', in M.P. Leone and P.B. Potter, Jr (eds) *Historical Archaeologies of Capitalism*, New York: Kluwer Academic/Plenum Press, pp. 169–93.

Shanks, M. and Tilley, C. (1992) *Re-Constructing Archaeology: Theory and Practice*, second edn, London: Routledge.

MARK S. WARNER

computers

Computers are electronic devices used to store and process information, the latter by means of mathematical equations. Five elements compose the computer hardware: a central processing unit (CPU); input devices; memory storage devices; peripheral devices (such as a monitor); and a communications network. In turn, this hardware allows a series of programs – called software – to be run. The software provides a sequence of instructions for the computer to perform operations on given data.

Computers are an essential tool in modern archaeological work. Gradually incorporated into research beginning with the 1960s they have produced not only a technological but also a substantial mental change in the way archaeology is done. In the 1990s, the use of computers increased for the writing of texts, the storing and organising of databases, the processing of drawings and maps, and the making and delivering of presentations. They have also been widely applied in teaching and communication, including through electronic magazines and the Internet.

The incorporation of computers in archaeological work in the 1960s was related, on the one hand, to technological advances that produced a great reduction in the size of machines and an increase in the capacity and speed of information processing. On the other hand, there occurred at the time a great transformation in archaeology brought about by scientific or **processual archaeology**. Processual or 'New' archaeologists began to consider and to illustrate the value of quantitative and statistical analyses of archaeological data.

Computers opened a wide scope of possibilities in archaeological research. Nevertheless, the computer's potential was not achieved immediately, but was the result of a process lasting several years. One reason for the length of this process was that, in the early years of computer work, the computers themselves – being enormous in size and extremely complex to use – were operated by skilled technicians who were generally not archaeologists. In the early period, archaeologists mainly used computers to analyse the distribution of artefacts and to compare typological variables among different collections of artefacts. The study of an eighteenth-century cemetery in eastern Massachusetts, USA, conducted by Edwin Dethlefsen and James Deetz in 1967, provides a good example of this. The authors used the programme SYMAP, which had been developed by Harvard University, to make a series of correlations among the gravestones that allowed them to approach demographic problems in the past.

It was not until the 1980s and more definitely until the 1990s that computers became an essential and widely used tool for modern archaeologists. The use and handling of computers – which had dramatically decreased in size and could now be taken into the field – became part of the researcher's everyday work and had a great influence on the way archaeology was done and written. The impact of computers in archaeology could also be perceived by the appearance of different organisations and groups devoted to examining the value of using computers in archaeology. The Computer Applications and Quantitative Methods in Archaeology, for instance, is an international organisation in which archaeologists, mathematicians and computer experts try to develop new technological tools for archaeology.

The most frequently used programmes in historical archaeology are generally multiple-purpose programmes designed by large companies and adapted by archaeologists to their personal interests. Among the most widely used are Data Base and Excel to organise and store databases, Corel Draw and Computer Aided Design (Auto-Cad) to process drawings and maps, Word or WordPerfect to write texts and PowerPoint to make presentations. More complex programmes, such as Geographical Informations Systems (GIS) – used to examine different aspects of landscape change through time – and SYMAP and Surfer – used to correlate variables and build distribution maps – are becoming standard tools for archaeologists. Simulation programs are used to study the incidence of different variables on the archaeological record and even to create 3-D virtual-reality reconstructions. Programs specifically designed for archaeology, however, are rare. One archaeology program that appeared in the early 1990s was called Re:Discovery and was designed specially for historical archaeologists. It allowed users to have a

detailed record of materials as well as of museum collections, to write reports and presentations and to store the documentary database.

Computers offer enormous possibilities for the future of archaeology. Nevertheless, we must bear in mind that access to new technologies neither is nor will be egalitarian. Unfortunately, inequality of access, along with other variables, contributes to an increased gap between researchers in different countries and sometimes even within the same country.

See also: new technologies; remote sensing

Further reading

Andresen, J., Madsen, T. and Scollar, I. (eds) (1993) *Computing the Past. CAA 9: Computer Applications and Quantitative Methods in Archaeology*, Aarhus: Aarhus University Press.

Dethlefsen, E. and Deetz, J. (1967) 'Eighteenth century cemeteries: A demographic view', *Historical Archaeology* 1: 40–2.

Reilly, P. and Rahtz, S.P. (eds) (1992) *Archaeology in the Information Age: A Global Perspective*, London: Routledge.

Richards, J.D. (1999) 'Recent trends in computer applications in archaeology', *Journal of Archaeological Research* 4: 331–82.

Ryan, N.S. (1988) 'Bibliography of computer applications and quantitative methods', in S.P. Rahtz (ed.) *Computer and Quantitative Methods in Archaeology 1988*, Oxford: BAR, pp. 1–30.

ANDRÉS ZARANKIN

Conference on Historic Site Archaeology

Stanley South, excavator at **Brunswick Town**, North Carolina, and **Santa Elena**, South Carolina, USA, created the Conference on Historic Site Archaeology in 1960. South started the Conference as a venue for people interested in historical archaeology – often referred to as 'historic site archaeology' during its early history – to meet and discuss the common problems they faced and to present the results of their research.

Archaeological conferences at this time were overwhelmingly dedicated to prehistory, and the issues and artefacts of interest to historical archaeologists were seldom mentioned. The Conference largely grew out of the prehistory-focused Southeastern Archaeological Conference – which had been created in 1938 – but it was never a regional conference.

The first Conference was held in Gainesville, Florida, with the support of John Goggin, a pioneering historical archaeologist, especially well known for his early research on Spanish majolica **ceramics**. Presenters at the conferences discussed topics of both general theoretical interest to all historical archaeologists as well as subjects unrelated to the US South.

The publication of the *Conference on Historic Site Archaeology Papers* was a major feature of the Conference. The earliest conference papers appeared in *The Florida Anthropologist*, with the support of Charles Fairbanks, a pioneer in **plantation archaeology**. Fifteen volumes of the Conference *Papers*, however, were published independently (covering the conferences from 1965 to 1980). The Conference ceased to exist in 1982, after it was clear that historical archaeology had moved into the archaeological mainstream, and a separate conference was no longer needed.

CHARLES E. ORSER, JR

conservation, terrestrial

'Conservation' and 'preservation' are terms that are common in archaeological parlance. We preserve, that is, keep safe from decay or decomposition, our field notes, photographs and artefacts. Conservation is the planned management of a resource to prevent its destruction. Conservators are to archaeological sites what doctors are to patients. That is, they seek to save them from an untimely demise.

The by-products of behaviour – artefacts, ecofacts, features and structures – that are part of the living or systemic world are changed and sometimes destroyed through a number of chemical, mechanical and organic forces as a site becomes part of the archaeological context. Conservation of the surviving materials from a site is important because the objects and the patterns in which they are found are the basic units of archaeological study. Artefacts represent both the ideas and the activities of people, and as such they and their context are the prime resources of archaeological interpretation. Since the process of gathering artefacts destroys the physical contexts for future study, the relationships between artefacts, soil layers and other archaeological finds is preserved in notes, drawings and photographs. Artefacts thus represent the only truly tangible remains from the site itself. Encoded in these materials may be specific information regarding where and when they were made, such as dates or **makers' marks**, or general information about the technology used to fabricate them.

An artefact or ecofact (a 'natural' artefact, like a clam shell) is something modified by humans from a naturally occurring form. Through human agency, the mineral or organic material is transformed from its stabile or natural state into another form, and placed in another environment. This change may make the material unstable, or cause accelerated deterioration, unless it is protected using artificial means. An example from the systemic, or living, context is the maintenance of a firearm through washing, oiling and the application of grease to keep it from rusting or oxidising. Once an object passes from the systemic into the archaeological context, human intervention to preserve the item ceases, and it passes into a new, often hostile environment that accelerates its deterioration. Eventually, it will, if not destroyed, reach a point of some equilibrium or stability with its surrounding matrix or environment. When archaeologists recover an artefact, they remove it from the anaerobic situation in which it has stabilised, and reintroduce it into the aerobic systemic environment.

Until the 1960s, the majority of archaeological work in the US was conducted on prehistoric sites containing artefactual remains made of stone, bone, pottery and wood. Archaeologists saw these materials as largely unmodified from their natural state and therefore inert. They would carefully wash the materials in water, dry them in the direct sun and label them with pen and ink. Rare pieces of wood, bone, shell and copper would be handled separately, but bone from neutral basic soil and copper materials would frequently be similarly handled and labelled. If materials of shell and bone were recovered in good condition, the archaeologists would generally allow them to stay that way. The main reason for the inherent stability of these materials is that they are subtractive artefacts made from a single, naturally occurring material, such as bone, copper and stone.

When historical archaeology came into its own, most practitioners were trained by prehistorians and so all of these artefacts were handled, washed and labelled in the same way as those items from prehistoric sites. This process was especially true for metal artefacts. These items appeared solid and intact, wanting only for wire brushes, sandblasting, naval jelly or brasso to remove surface oxides. However, the cosmetic change that resulted was both deceiving and temporary, because the chlorides that caused the original corrosion were still present in the artefacts. Once returned to the systemic context, fluctuations in humidity caused them to oxidise again. The historical archaeologist must realise that the majority of the artefacts they deal with are additive in nature and are thus made up of several materials altered by humans. These include glazed ceramics (including clay, lead, tin and other materials), glass (composed of sand, potash and manganese), smelted copper and its alloys (such as brass and bronze), iron, steel and lead.

When cast into the ground – an anaerobic salt–ion atmosphere – an artefact is penetrated or infiltrated with these naturally occurring salts and they oxidise (corrode or patinate). In this setting, an equilibrium in temperature and moisture will be attained. Buried metals react with the surrounding environment to form stable minerals (iron oxides). This electrochemical corrosion occurs with the formation of an ion-conducting electrolyte solution of soluble salts (sodium chloride) on the outer surfaces of an artefact. These items corrode to reach a state of equilibrium with the surrounding atmosphere in the ground. This process is an aspect of the second law of thermodynamics, or the 'Law of Entropy' wherein there is a tendency for a system to move towards disorder or to an inert or natural state. When archaeologists recover artefacts from archaeological contexts, they place the object in a new atmosphere that, if conservation is lacking, may result in renewed oxidation and corrosion. Failure to control this renewed corrosion can result in the loss of the original surface, causing loss of important identifying marks and forms. We need only consider the spalling of a tombstone. Upon seeing one that has been weathered, we may recognise its form – and thereby its function – but we may not be able to read what was once written upon it.

A number of techniques have been developed for the conservation of archaeological materials over the past fifty years. An important aspect of these techniques is their reversibility, in case more effective techniques can be developed later. If anything has come from these conservation efforts it is a recognition that conservation needs must be addressed before the first shovel breaks the ground. Because archaeological remains are non-renewable resources, archaeologists have a responsibility to preserve as much of the archaeological record as possible or not to undertake the excavation in the first place.

See also: conservation, underwater; laboratory methods; restoration

Further reading

Cronyn, J.M. (1990) *The Elements of Archaeological Conservation*, New York: Routledge.

Fairbanks, C.H. (ed.) (1983) *The Conservation of Archaeological Materials: A Laboratory Manual for Prehistoric and Historic Collections*, Tallahassee: Florida Anthropological Society.

Pelikan, J.B. (1966) 'Conservation of iron with tannin', *Studies in Conservation* 11(3): 109–16.

Peterson, H.L. (1968) *Conservation of Metals*, Technical Leaflet 10, Nashville: American Association of State and Local History.

Plenderleith, H.J. and Werner, A.E. (1971) *The Conservation of Antiquities and Works of Art*, London: Oxford University Press.

Sease, C. (1994) *A Conservation Manual for the Field Archaeologist*, Los Angeles: Institute of Archaeology.

RUSSELL K. SKOWRONEK

conservation, underwater

Archaeological materials recovered from a fresh or salt water environment require special handling to ensure their long-term survival. Conservation is the planned intervention to effect this preservation. Depending on the environmental circumstances, items recovered may exhibit spectacular preservation or extreme deterioration. Ships and many other artefacts, such as muskets and clothing, are composite creations of both organic and inorganic materials. As long as they are part of the systemic, or living, environment they are purposely preserved by human intervention. Their preservation in the archaeological record, however, will depend upon the nature of this new environment and how they came to be deposited within it.

Water, salt water particularly, is a dynamic environment, with organic, mechanical and electronic action considerably affecting the objects. These natural processes come to bear on that most complex of historic artefacts – the ship. Three mechanical actions that cause ships to sink and cause damage to the vessel are foundering in storms, running onto shoals or other obstacles, and involvement in violent naval actions. In shallow waters, currents, surge and wave action will continue to batter the wreck and cause it to scatter across the tidal zone. Ships that settle in deep water will be less affected by mechanical processes and so will better maintain the spatial context of their contents.

Soon after submersion, wooden objects may be attacked by a number of biological organisms, including fungi, moulds, bacteria and molluscs such as *Teredo navalis*, the shipworm. These plant and animal life forms ingest organic materials, but they are sensitive to variations in the environment. For example, fungi only survive in temperatures between 76 and 86°F and shipworms only survive in salt water. The absence of shipworms in fresh and brackish water has resulted in spectacularly preserved ships. These wrecks include: the steamboat ***Bertrand***, lost on the Missouri River; the gunboat *Philadelphia*, lost in 1776 in Lake Champlain; the *Scourge* and *Hamilton*, lost in Lake Ontario during the war of 1812; and the oldest and most famous named intact vessel, the *Wasa*, lost in Stockholm harbour in 1628. One need only compare these vessels to the remains of the *Mary Rose*, HMS *Fowey* (see ***Fowey, HMS***) and the ships of the 1554 *flota* lost off Padre Island, Texas, USA, to understand the effect of biological organisms on submerged organic remains.

Immersion also brings about chemical and electronic changes to submerged artefacts. Salt water has a corrosive effect on most metals. Following the Law of Entropy, there is a tendency for a system to move towards disorder or to an inert or natural state. Iron changes to iron oxide, and silver, copper and copper alloys will oxidise or patinate. The process of deterioration is speeded up by galvanic currents. Because a shipwreck usually contains a variety of metals, a galvanic current is set up between the different metals. Precious metals, such as gold, are inactive in an electrolyte. Less noble metals and alloys will oxidise until the site reaches equilibrium. Equilibrium is reached when the site is either buried under sediments or when a crust of sand and other calcareous materials are cemented to the corrosion products. In some warm-water environments, the sites will become completely encased in living coral.

Organic materials, such as wood, that survive biological and mechanical decomposition processes are altered chemically. Waterlogging results in the dissolution of the cellulose in the cell walls of the wood. As long as it is wet, the pressure of the water in the decomposed cells will maintain the form of the object. In order to preserve the wood the water must be removed and replaced with a more stable substance. Pioneering work on the *Wasa* and the Roskilde Viking ships demonstrated that uncontrolled air drying of soft and hard woods would result in 1/10 to 1/3 shrinkage of the item. In order to conserve the items, a number of different techniques have been developed. They all involve de-watering the object and filling it with a substance that will not shrink and is not hygroscopic. Conservators first used potassium alum. They would head an object in a supersaturated solution of alum and glycerine. As the wood was de-watered, the alum penetrated and when cooled it crystallized. It was, however, hygroscopic and would, unless closely monitored, go into solution and cause the wood to collapse.

Scandinavian conservators pioneered the use of the synthetic material known as polyethylene glycol

(PEG). Depending upon its molecular weight, from 200 for a viscous liquid to 6,000 for a less hygroscopic, wax-like solid, PEG seemed to be ideal for the conservation of small items. Such artefacts could be submerged in baths of PEG or impregnated using freeze-drying or vacuum chambers. The problem has been in the penetration of large wooden items. For example, the *Wasa* could not be submerged after its raising in 1960. It was instead sprayed with a solution of PEG. During the first decade of the conservation project it was learned that this method had penetrated less than 3 mm into the *Wasa*'s timbers. As a result, this ship and, later, the *Mary Rose* have been sprayed with PEG for decades and each has had a temperature- and humidity-controlled structure constructed over them. With few exceptions, this type of preservation is economically unfeasible.

Whether in salt or fresh water, in seas, lakes or wells, if left undisturbed in these anaerobic conditions, archaeological materials will cease to decompose. It is imperative that sites not be disturbed unless an adequate conservation plan is in place and a trained conservator is part of the research team.

See also: *Bertrand*, steamboat; conservation, terrestrial; maritime archaeology; *Mary Rose*, shipwreck

Further reading

Barkman, L. and Franzen, A. (1972) 'The Wasa: Preservation and conservation', in *Underwater Archaeology: A Nascent Discipline*, Paris: UNESCO, pp. 231–42.

Hamilton, D.L. (1976) *Conservation of Metal Artifacts from Underwater Sites: A Study in Methods*, Austin: Texas Memorial Museum and Texas Antiquities Committee.

Pearson, C. (1987) *Conservation of Marine Archaeological Objects*, London: Butterworths.

Peterson, M.L. (1972) 'Materials from post-fifteenth-century sites', in *Underwater Archaeology: A Nascent Discipline*, Paris: UNESCO, pp. 243–9.

Schmidt, J.D. (1985) 'Freeze drying of historic/cultural properties', *Technology and Conservation* 9(1): 20–6.

Singley, K. (1988) *The Conservation of Archaeological Artifacts from Freshwater Environments*, South Haven, MI: Lake Michigan Maritime Museum.

Townsend, S.P. (1972) 'Standard conservation procedures', in *Underwater Archaeology: A Nascent Discipline*, Paris: UNESCO, pp. 251–6.

RUSSELL K. SKOWRONEK

Constantinople

Constantinople, also known as Istanbul, was the capital of the Byzantine Empire, and the last capital of the **Ottoman Empire**. Although the earliest settlements of the Istanbul Peninsula date to the third millennium BC, its major occupations date from AD 330 until the present day. Although Constantinople was one of the major cities of the eastern Mediterranean, relatively few archaeological excavations have focused on its recent past. Instead, historical archaeology in Constantinople usually focuses on the Greco-Roman period, and, to a lesser extent, the Byzantine period. An archaeology of Ottoman-period Constantinople (1453–1923) is not well developed. Several potential directions for archaeological study of this city's recent past include an archaeology of Constantinople's built environment, based on **landscape studies**, and examinations of ceramic production (see **ceramics**) and use in the city.

Constantinople as Ottoman capital

In AD 330, Constantine moved the seat of the Roman Empire from Rome to Byzantium. The Emperor created a new state and 'the city of Constantine' became its new capital. This city was also known as the 'Second Rome'. Constantinople flourished until the thirteenth century, when European Crusaders seized and sacked the city, thus leaving it weakened by the time of the Ottoman conquest.

The Ottoman state emerged after the late thirteenth century from a small principality of Turkish tribesmen organised along the frontiers of the Selcuk sultanate and Byzantine Empire in Asia Minor. After gaining much control over north-western Anatolia against the weakened Byzantine state, the Ottomans initially expanded through north-west Anatolia and the Balkans, concentrating on territories surrounding Constantinople. The city finally came under Ottoman control in 1453, when Mehmed the Conqueror captured the city. At that point, he made Constantinople the new Ottoman capital and named himself the latest Alexander the Great.

In the middle of the fifteenth century, the Ottomans initiated major restorations of the city. The goal was to revive the new Ottoman capital by promoting resettlement; the state encouraged migrations into the city, offered tax concessions for merchants and allowances for semi-autonomous religious communities. With the construction of the new Topkapi palace above the old acropolis, Constantinople became the home of the imperial household, and elite class of bureaucratic administrators and officials, and other Ottoman subjects. The capital remained a major centre for **trade**, controlling exchange between the Black Sea, the Sea of Marmara and the Mediterranean world.

Landscape studies

Although few archaeologists have focused specifically on Constantinople's recent past, geographers and art historians have examined this city's built environment, especially its **architecture** and city planning. In a study of Ottoman Constantinople, Zeynep Çelik uses historical documents, photographs and geography studies to examine the changing landscape of the city. The capital underwent major reconstructions in the nineteenth century, in the aftermath of a series of major fires that left much of the city in ruin. The rebuilding of the city was part of a larger effort to reorganise the urban environment based on Western models, including city planning based on a grid system, and a new imperial palace at Dolmabahçe, which was designed based on French Empire style. According to Çelik, changes in the Constantinople landscape also correspond to political and economic transformations of the nineteenth century, many of which were initiated as an attempt to restructure Ottoman state and society on a European model.

Ceramics

A significant body of literature exists concerning Ottoman-period ceramics, but most of this work examines ceramic consumption by the state and elite classes, or production as related to the imperial system. The relatively few archaeological studies focusing on Byzantine and Ottoman ceramic consumption deal mainly with expensive, highly decorated ceramics from wealthy households.

John Hayes examined pottery excavated from Saraçhane. This site was a relatively wealthy neighbourhood, which includes Byzantine and Ottoman occupations. While the household assemblages included expensive wares, they also included a wide variety of plain, **earthenware** vessels and storage containers. However, although elite household assemblages included expensive imports, as well as utilitarian wares, studies on Ottoman ceramics have focused mainly on the highly decorated types.

Many of the ceramics consumed in Constantinople were traded into the city. In the late fourteenth through seventeenth centuries, a large quantity of ceramic vessels came from Iznik, located approximately 100 km south-east of the capital. Iznik vessels were either commissioned, or generally sold in the open marketplace. These vessels were emulations and reinterpretations of Chinese export porcelains (see **porcelain**), in response to demand for these types of wares by elites. In 1582, the imperial household was able to purchase 541 plates, dishes and bowls from the bazaar for the fifty-two days of celebrations for Prince Mehmed's circumcision. Most of these wares were probably produced at Iznik.

Ceramic production also occurred within the capital city. For example, Tefkur Sarayi was a major ceramic production centre located in the city whose workshops supplied relatively expensive wares for elite consumption in the eighteenth century. In an attempt to revive the classical styles of Ottoman ceramic manufacturing of the sixteenth century, master potters were brought to the capital from Iznik.

Ceramic studies in Constantinople provide several possible venues for entering into archaeological studies of the capital city. In particular, historical archaeologists can examine the city's relationship with imperial and global trade networks, and how that affected local household consumption of ceramics. However, archaeological investigations of non-elite households in the city are necessary. In addition, a wide variety of **historical documents** about Ottoman state and society are housed in the Ottoman State Archives in Istanbul, including census data, probate records and price indices. There is a great potential to develop an **urban archaeology** of Constantinople, as well as a historical archaeology that combines Ottoman history with archaeological research.

See also: Crusades; maps; pictorial information; world(-)systems theory

Further reading

Çelik, Z. (1993) *The Remaking of Istanbul: Portrait of an Ottoman City in the Nineteenth Century*, Berkeley: University of California Press.

Hayes, J. (1992) *Excavations at Saraçhane in Istanbul. Volume 2: The Pottery*, Washington, DC: Dumbarton Oaks

LYNDA CARROLL

consumer choice

The study of consumer choice in historical archaeology provides a framework for addressing the decision-making processes and motivations behind **consumption**. In general, archaeologists who use consumer choice approaches argue that social and economic relationships can be evaluated based on the choices people make in acquiring **material culture**, and use the household as the primary unit of analysis. Two major approaches have been used by historical archaeologists to evaluate the choices that people in the past made in acquiring material culture. The first uses consumer choice as an analytical tool to infer social differentiation from artefact assemblages. Alternatively, the second approach focuses on the cognitive and symbolic meanings behind the choices people make in the act of consuming.

Consumer behaviour theory

Much of the work on consumer choice in historical archaeology expanded in the late 1980s, and echoed a growing interest in consumption through-

out the social sciences. Studies focusing on consumer choice stemmed out of discussions in cultural materialism, as well as economic and symbolic anthropology. Early approaches to consumer choice were aimed at explaining consumption as a reflection of social differentiation.

For many historical archaeologists, the first influential work on the subject came in 1987 with Spencer-Wood's edited volume *Consumer Choice in Historical Archaeology*. This collection of articles presented a number of variables that were considered to influence consumer decisions, including household income, artefact prices, ethnicity or race. Using complementary documentary sources, such as price indices or probate records (see **probate inventories**), historical archaeologists could compare the discard of relatively expensive versus inexpensive goods found in artefact assemblages in order to reconstruct the socioeconomic status of consumers.

In 1991, Klein and LeeDecker's special issue of *Historical Archaeology* entitled 'Models for the Study of Consumer Behavior' moved beyond the concept of consumer choice to create consumer behaviour models. These models focused on quantitative data and patterns of expenditure to interpret artefacts. Using flow charts and considering variables such as income, external influences and the psychological and physiological needs of consumers, consumer behaviour theory assumed that people would make purchases based on a number of prescribed conditions. During the early 1990s, the growth of consumer behaviour theory in historical archaeology relied heavily on economic theory and marketing research, and was known as consumer behaviour modelling. More generally, social and economic **identity** was seen as a way to predict patterns of consumer activity. For many, consumer choice approaches, and Klein and LeeDecker's consumer behaviour models in particular, represented a form of middle-range theory for historical archaeologists that linked artefacts and documents with social and economic status.

Households as units of analysis

Historical archaeologists often address consumer choice in terms of decisions made on behalf of a household. Archaeological assemblages from domestic sites are often considered to be the accumulation of consumption activities, and the result of disposal patterns, of households. In addition, **historical documents**, such as probate inventories, often focus on specific households, which makes them convenient units of analysis. Many historical archaeologists argue that consumer behaviour is related to gender, and often involves the acquisition of goods by women, usually on behalf of a household. Therefore, consumer choice models often consider women's roles in economic activity through consumer behaviour. In addition, since the acquisition of material culture is often assumed to be linked to income and wealth, consumer behaviour models are most widely used to determine the socioeconomic status of households.

In a study of seventeenth-century English settlers in the Chesapeake region of Maryland (see **Chesapeake region**), James Gibb argued that consumer choices were decisions made by households about the allocation of wealth. Gibb's study focused on two domestic sites. By examining buildings, ceramic (see **ceramics**) and **glass**, and **cemeteries**, Gibb assessed consumer behaviour and its relationship to wealth. Gibb argued that consumption and production are not mutually exclusive processes, and consumer choices are linked to production. During the seventeenth century, wealth in the Chesapeake was linked to a household's ability to grow tobacco. Thus, in order to produce wealth, households needed to obtain both land and labour. Consumer behaviour was linked to available labour resources, household production strategies and the ability to acquire productive land. Households made decisions to acquire land as a way to secure wealth, and invested in tools and animals in order to reproduce it. Other forms of material culture were used to make statements about social identity.

Consumer choice and industrialisation

Consumer choice in historical archaeology developed as part of an effort to examine the rise of industrial **capitalism** and the formation of consumer society. Archaeologists can easily note the escalation of material culture found since the Industrial Revolution, the resultant increase in commodities consumed in the late nineteenth century and the rise in consumerism and consumer ideologies in the twentieth century. Thus, consumer choice approaches are often linked to the changes in productive activities that emerged with **industrialisation** in the nineteenth century.

Traditional approaches to consumption argue that consumer behaviour results from the changing relationships between production, consumption and consumer choice, as people reacted to a market flooded with an increasing supply of consumer goods. In the 1990s, historical archaeologists used consumer choice approaches to re-evaluate the relationship between consumption and the means of production, using the assumption that consumer behaviour is not simply a reaction to industrialisation. Instead, consumer desire played a role in launching the Industrial Revolution by creating new demands for consumer goods. Consumption was put forward as a way that people actively participated in and directed transformations that led to the Industrial Revolution.

Consumer demand was traditionally seen as originating from within elite classes, by people who typically had access to the majority of goods available within a society. Thus, late nineteenth-century consumption patterns among non-elite groups were presented as reacting to the increased production of goods, and through emulating elite consumption. Since the 1990s, a growing number of archaeologists have begun to re-evaluate both the extent to which working classes (as well as ethnic and racial minorities) had active roles in their own consumption choices, as well as their roles in the increased demand for consumer goods.

Consumer choice and agency

In the late 1990s, consumer choice approaches began to address issues of human agency, based on the premise that people communicate ideas and information, especially related to their identities, using material culture. This perspective stemmed largely out of Bourdieu's perspective that consumption is a part of the process of communicating meaning. As a result, many historical archaeologists redirected their interest from assessments of socioeconomic stratification through consumer behaviours, to examinations of consumption as a way to examine human agency. The choices made by consumers were not simply a reflection on wealth and access to goods, but also had to take desire, socially defined needs and class relations into consideration.

Relying largely on the work of Daniel Miller, Cook, Yamin and McCarthy argued that consumption – or more specifically shopping – is an important social and economic activity. In a review of consumption studies in historical archaeology, these authors argued that, despite interest in consumption studies, much of the research described as consumer choice approaches ignores human agency and individual decision-making processes in the acquisition of material culture. According to these authors, most consumer choice approaches do not really look at the individual motivations of why people acquire goods. Consumption is a ritual activity, complete with symbolic meaning and shifting values. Consumer choices thus play a role in self-meaning and self-definition, as people use goods, and the rituals involved in their acquisition, to negotiate their social lives.

Material culture can be used as a way to negotiate identity between and within groups. In addition, commodities have symbolic meanings, and therefore are involved in the reproduction of social groups – at the individual as well as household level. As a negotiated process, the construction of identities is mediated through the use of material culture. Objects are not simply direct reflections of identity or status, but are used as symbols to actively negotiate social and economic relationships. According to this perspective, decisions made about the acquisition and use of material culture can be evaluated using socially defined meanings of material culture.

Paul Mullins examined the growth of consumer culture in **Annapolis**, Maryland, by looking at the use of material culture by African Americans between 1850 and 1930. According to Mullins, consumption was highly racialised; consumer space and material symbolism were constructed within contexts of white **domination**. While African Americans critiqued consumerism, they also participated in it, using consumer goods as one way to improve their lives. By acquiring commodities symbolically linked to dominant white society, they negotiated their identity and status within an emerging consumer society. The meanings behind material culture were used by people to negotiate power relationships and racial identity.

Critiques of consumer choice

A number of scholars have critiqued the use of consumer choice approaches in historical archaeology. Early approaches, such as consumer behaviour models, often emphasised socioeconomic status, but did not differentiate between social and economic status. These approaches conflated these terms, and assumed that status is mainly economic ranking. Consumer behaviour theory often emphasised wealth and economic status, and thus focused mainly on particular index artefacts that were expensive.

In a critique of consumer choice approaches, Wurst and McGuire argued that the proliferation of studies in historical archaeology that emphasise consumer choice and consumer behaviour models play upon and maintain consumer ideologies of late twentieth-century capitalism. By positioning the individual as an autonomous consumer, consumer choice approaches trivialise class, as well as social and economic, inequalities. According to Wurst and McGuire, consumer behaviours are restricted by social relationships of dominance and subordination. Consumer choice is not significant for most people. Instead, a more relevant issue for historical archaeologists is how do people produce and reproduce themselves and their social group within their everyday lives (see **everyday life**).

Debates about decision-making processes, and consumption as a form of self-expression and status negotiation, have become important in historical archaeology. However, these debates rely on concepts that were constructed and which gained importance in the late twentieth century, and are therefore not necessarily applicable to the past. One of the most important critiques has thus been whether consumer choice approaches can even be used to understand consumption in periods before the twentieth century, since the concept of consumer choice was constructed within the context of late capitalist culture and is heavily influenced by the political economy of mass production and twentieth-century consumer ideologies.

See also: class, social; commodification; household archaeology

Further reading

Cook, L. J., Yamin, R. and McCarthy, J.P. (1996) 'Shopping as meaningful action: Toward a redefinition of consumption in historical archaeology', *Historical Archaeology* 30(4): 50–65.

Gibb, J.G. (1996) *The Archaeology of Wealth: Consumer Behavior in English America*, New York: Kluwer Academic/Plenum Press.

Klein, T.H. and LeeDecker, C.H. (eds) (1991) 'Models for the study of consumer behavior', *Historical Archaeology* 25(2): 1–91.

Mullins, P.R. (1999) *Race and Affluence: An Archaeology of African America and Consumer Culture*, New York: Kluwer Academic/Plenum Press.

Spencer-Wood, S.M. (ed.) (1987) *Consumer Choice in Historical Archaeology*, New York: Plenum.

Wurst, L.A. and McGuire, R.H. (1999) 'Immaculate consumption: A critique of the "shop till you drop" school of human behavior', *International Journal of Historical Archaeology* 3: 191–9.

LYNDA CARROLL

consumption

Consumption denotes the destruction or using-up of utilities, through either physical destruction (eating food, burning petrol) or exploiting a good or service (visiting a dentist). Historical archaeologists use consumption to denote both the act of shopping and the conversion of resources into objects or actions (which produce features). In the materialist framework of archaeology, assumptions about consumption underlie most other subjects of study. The patterns in what people purchase or how they spend their resources is reflective of, influenced by, or constitutes each individual's **ethnicity**, **class, social**, **gender**, age, sexuality, socioeconomic status, their location in geographic space and so forth. In consumption-based studies, archaeologists make one of two assumptions about the relationship between people and material

things. These different approaches can be called the 'consumption as reflection' and the 'consumption as construction' perspectives.

Consumption as reflection

Members of the 'consumption as reflection' school assume that the decisions and behaviours of individuals reflect their background and identity. Therefore, when a person takes action to cook food, buy clothes or build a home, the artefacts and features they act upon reflect their identity. This is a systematic or structural view of humanity in which an articulated set of generalities exists that we can call 'middle class', 'feminine' or 'Chinese'. This structural or systematic understanding of consumption is rooted in Plato's theory of essences in classical philosophy.

In archaeology, the idea that patterns of consumption in material culture reflect group 'essence' was based upon the belief that sociocultural systems are static and bounded abstractions. A **culture** could be described by constructing a list of traits exhibited by each group. In 1947, Walter Taylor directed archaeologists away from the definition of culture-trait lists, geographic areas and chronologies. Archaeologists like Louis Binford, David Clarke, Stanley South and James Deetz followed Taylor's argument and focused upon the associations and relationships in human behaviour. 'New Archaeologists' moved away from studies of culture-history and trait-lists, but they maintained this essentialist view of culture when examining cultural patterns.

Essentialist philosophy accepts that cultural systems are relatively static sets or systems of meaning. For members of a group, the articulation between actions and these constructs are tacit, hidden deep within the unconscious organisation of thought in the brain. Therefore, groups of people sharing a culture will unintentionally consume clothing, architecture or food in a similar manner.

Archaeology is an excellent tool for discovering and measuring patterns in artefacts, features and landscapes. Any changes in measured patterns of consumption should reflect changes in the underlying structures or systems. Archaeologists found these assumptions articulated very well with biological and social science perspectives that sought to model, predict and explain changes in material patterns. Historical archaeologists used consumption patterns as the basis to study **assimilation**, ethnogenesis, blending and other products of migration and culture contact.

'Black Lucy's Garden' was a farmstead in nineteenth-century Andover, Massachusetts. Vernon Baker's 1978 study is a typical example where consumption was treated as a reflection of cultural systems. Vernon correlated a ceramic pattern centred on serving bowls rather than plates and a very high frequency of certain butchering methods on animal bones. He argued that these patterns of consumption reflected the consumption of stews in Lucy Foster's home, and could represent the maintenance of a traditional African foodway. He acknowledged that it was impossible to separate the influence of economic status from the cultural pattern of food consumption. In addition, while white neighbours had access to a nearly free market in which to make their decisions, Lucy Foster was poor, and cash and commodities were sometimes provided to her by the Overseers of the Poor and the South Parish Church.

'Consumption as reflection' evolved as archaeologists developed a more nuanced understanding of localised socioeconomic contexts. Studies of consumption diverged. Many scholars continued to examine consumption in relation to cultural systems of identity. Others focused on the relationship between status, household (see **household archaeology**) life cycle and patterns of commodity consumption, favouring questions of economics over identity. This style of scholarship became known as '**consumer choice**' analysis or 'consumer behaviour studies'. These scholars attempt to quantitatively link a calculated value for an archaeological assemblage with a measure of social and economic position. They drew inspiration from the literatures of market economics, sociology and psychology.

George Miller made a major contribution to this approach in 1980 when he introduced his ceramic price-scaling indices. Miller compiled data on the cost of various nineteenth-century ceramic forms and decorative techniques in relation to one another, and tracked the relationships as relative values changed through time. Archaeologists began to compare the mean values of ceramics from

excavated sites with documentary evidence for the socioeconomic status of the head of household, most often measured through the occupation. Parallel tools were developed in zooarchaeology, including the preference ranking of meat cuts, price scaling, measurements of biomass and meat weight. Specific methodologies of measurement proliferated.

Archaeologists had some success correlating mean price scales for a single artefact class with measures of socioeconomic status. When attempting to cross-correlate among artefact classes such as bones and ceramics, however, the strength of the statistical associations was sharply reduced. Archaeologists who study consumer behaviour are still struggling to resolve the complexity of shopping and decision-making processes. Various scholars are studying the relative importance of market access, supply–demand interactions, transportation networks, ethnicity, household size and composition, political status, class, religious affiliations, anticipations of permanence and mobility, and distribution systems. The evolving complexity of study in consumer choice analysis is making geographic information systems a very important tool.

Critics of this approach argue that 'consumption as reflection' reduces humans to the status of ants or robots simply programmed through enculturation to act in certain ways. The approach, critics assert, disguises variation within groups of individuals and systematically reinforces stereotypes along ethnic, gender and religious boundaries. It also minimises the significance of material culture as a symbolic area of human expression.

Consumption as construction

Henry Glassie and James Deetz were among the first to question the behavioural focus of consumer studies in historical archaeology. Deetz's 1977 study *In Small Things Forgotten* was an examination of how medieval European traditions were replaced by the rational values of the Enlightenment. Deetz argued that this shift in values was visible in the material culture: houses, pottery, food and gravestone iconography (see **gravestones**). Further, he argued that the penetration of Enlightenment ideals through time and space could be measured by examining the growth or decline in consumption of certain goods. While Deetz's work was focused upon cognitive meanings rather than behavioural process, his research gave primacy to stereotyped and idealised patterns.

Since 1990, a growing number of scholars have rejected the essentialist model of cultural systems. As a result, they also moved away from pattern analysis, consumer choice and behavioural models of explanation. These archaeologists have begun to examine consumption as an expressive act. Since patterns reflect the average behaviour within a group, they argue that analysis of those patterns creates the illusion of conformity and similarity. In symbolic consumption studies, consumers pick and choose from material culture while they construct their identity at both conscious and unconscious levels. The consumer is an active participant, negotiating their identity within contexts of power, ethnicity, class, gender or nationality.

These archaeologists imagine the consumer as a bricklayer who explicitly assembles his or her information about his or her identity utilising the symbols of artefacts and actions. Objects are analogous to words, which can be assembled into expressions that transmit information. Sets of symbols must then be 'read' by contemporaries in society (as well as archaeologists in the present). Rather than focus upon explanation of behaviour, these archaeologists sought to understand an individual's decisions and interpret the purposes behind them. This approach drew upon several literatures, including post-structural linguistics, post-Marxist hegemony and the **contextual historical archaeology** pioneered by Ian Hodder.

David Burley's early work demonstrated how Metis women used teawares (see **tea/tea ceremony**) to attract the courtship of white traders. Leslie Stewart-Abernathy studied changes in purchasing patterns among nineteenth-century rural consumers in the Ozark Mountains of Arkansas. He argued that residents were able to adopt modern industrial products like machine-made, glass canning jars, while assigning them new meanings as symbols of traditional rural life.

Mary Beaudry and Stephen Mrozowski led a study of the tenements and boarding houses of the **Boott Mills** in Lowell, Massachusetts. The occupants of company housing used **material culture**, including clothing, foodways and especially alcohol and tobacco as mediums to create and maintain **culture** and identity. In a similar way, the residents of the **Five Points** slum neighbourhood in **New York City** used material culture to create their own identity. They selected clothing, food and bric-a-brac to express their position between the European and American social and ethnic networks.

Paul Mullins completed a significant study detailing the emergence of consumer culture among African Americans in nineteenth- and early twentieth-century Annapolis, Maryland. Mullins described the objects purchased and the manner of their acquisition in terms of a multitude of conflicting and concurrent social debates. Purchase and display occurred within matrices of racist violence, new disciplines in hygiene and body management, marketing technologies and methodologies, shifting moralisation and stigmatisation of consumerism and labour, and intersected throughout with the relations of power, control, resistance and expression.

Critics of the 'consumption as construction' approach argue that, while these individual studies are interesting, the interpretations are specific to a certain time and place. As a result, the interpreter's conclusions cannot be used to generate general explanations of human behaviour. In addition, the results of these symbolic, contextual studies are generally not mathematically 'testable'. The debate between the 'consumption as reflection' and 'consumption as construction' scholars is symptomatic of the largest rift in historical archaeology. This conflict divides investigators who favour interpretative humanism approached through studies of the construction of emic meanings and those researchers who value the social and biological sciences and etic examinations of the repercussions of human behaviour.

See also: cognitive archaeology; consumer choice; pattern recognition; stratification, social

Further reading

Beaudry, M.C., Cook, L.J. and Mrozowski, S.A. (1991) 'Artifacts and active voices: Material culture as social discourse', in R.H. McGuire and R. Paynter (eds) *The Archaeology of Inequality*, Oxford: Blackwell, pp. 150–91.

Cook, L.J., Yamin, R. and McCarthy, J.P. (1996) 'Shopping as meaningful action: Toward a redefinition of consumption in historical archaeology', *Historical Archaeology* 30(4): 50–65.

Klein, T.H. and LeeDecker, C.H. (eds) (1991) 'Models for the study of consumer behaviour', *Historical Archaeology* 25(2): 1–91.

Miller, D. (1987) *Material Culture and Mass Consumption*, Oxford: Blackwell.

Miller, G.L. (1991) 'A revised set of CC index values for classification and economic scaling of English ceramics from 1787–1880', *Historical Archaeology* 25(1): 1–25.

Spencer-Wood, S.M. (ed.) (1987) *Consumer Choice in Historical Archaeology*, New York: Plenum Press.

Stewart-Abernathy, L.C. (1992) 'Industrial goods in the service of tradition: Consumption and cognition on an Ozark farmstead before the Great War', in A. Yentsch and M.C. Beaudry (eds) *The Art and Mystery of Historical Archaeology: Essays in Honor of James Deetz*, Boca Raton: CRC Press, pp. 101–25.

TIMOTHY JAMES SCARLETT

contact archaeology

The term 'contact archaeology' represents a particular topic of study rather than a sub-discipline within historical archaeology. The topic of interest concerns the interaction of men and women from different cultures, or, in other words, the process of cultural contact and exchange.

The term, however, is meant to imply that contact occurs at a specific point in history, and that the archaeologists' interest is on this period. The historical purview of any particular programme of contact archaeology can be short term or long term. The short-term contacts would involve the brief interaction of two distinct people (such as the meeting between Columbus and the Arawaks), whereas the more long-term, intensive contacts would involve the earliest years of Spanish–Native American contact throughout the Caribbean (see **Caribbean archaeology**) and the south-western and south-eastern portions of the

USA. As such, the archaeological period of study could be a few months or several decades.

Archaeologists often refer to the period within which cultural contact occurs as 'protohistory', or sometimes 'secondary prehistory'. The idea is that the contact period usually involves the interaction of two cultures, one of which is more technologically sophisticated than the other. In a post-AD 1500 context, this interaction would involve indigenous peoples and Europeans. Before the arrival of the Europeans, the indigenous people would be considered 'prehistoric'. The use of 'protohistory' or 'secondary prehistory' is meant to convey the idea that writing – for many, a hallmark of 'history' – is present but not widespread and often one-sided. In a European–Native American context (see **Native Americans**), for instance, one might find French colonial administrators using a written system of communication, but the Huron, with whom they were in contact, not using writing. For some archaeologists, this period is neither prehistory nor exactly history, and hence the use of the unique terms. Other archaeologists, however, would not make such distinctions, preferring to envision history as an unbroken flow of years with no artificial breaks.

Historical archaeologists have been interested in the history and cultural characteristics of contact for as long as the field has been practised. Their interest has been especially strong in North America, **South Africa** and **Australia**, where cultural contact has played an especially important role in history.

Historical archaeologists in the past may have often seen the role of contact archaeology merely to involve the analysis of the exchange of **material culture** from one culture to another. In this vein, their theoretical interests often rested in studies of **acculturation** and **assimilation**. They were interested in learning how artefacts and other pieces of material culture would indicate or reflect the contact process. Today's historical archaeologists, however, have learned that contact is a complicated process that involves more than simply the exchange of objects. Cultural contact also involves significant amounts of **ideology**, symbolism and other, less obvious, material elements.

The complex nature of cultural contacts, and the broad variation in the ways in which people can engage in **resistance** to assimilation, has revitalised the archaeologists' interest in contact archaeology. Several important studies were completed at the beginning of the twenty-first century, and many more can be expected in the future. These studies will help to refine our understanding of cultural contact and help to define contact archaeology.

CHARLES E. ORSER, JR

contextual historical archaeology

The construction of meaningful contexts lies close to the heart of debate in historical archaeology. Archaeologists often argue over whether one perspective or tool provides the best means for interpretation. These arguments concern the conception of archaeological data in two senses: broader sociocultural scopes of understanding *and* more specific and fine-grained analytical methods that squeeze ever more data from archaeological remains. The former resonates with the field's struggle with social theory while the latter relates to archaeological methods. It is important to recognise, however, that the desire for more and better tools of analysis typically results from the demand that archaeology work not merely towards site reporting, but towards the production of cultural interpretation. Developing contexts, in their temporal, spatial, cultural and critical senses, thus, is essential for archaeological studies of the development and cultural understanding of the modern world.

Temporal contexts

One serious debate in historical archaeology concerns the matter of time. At what point does the subject matter of the field become either too old or too new? At some point, the age of archaeological data reaches beyond the stated scope of historical archaeology and enters the realm of prehistory and thus becomes the responsibility of prehistorians. Likewise, the study of recent and extant material culture, as it fails to be of a certain age, is the responsibility of cultural

anthropologists, modern material cultural experts or other scholars of living culture.

While the line between living and archaeological cultures is somewhat easy to define, the issue of the prehistory–history divide in archaeology is a thorny one. For some, historical archaeology, if it means the archaeological study of groups with the presence of a literate population that inscribed their impressions and recorded the moments of their lives, stretches as far back as Mesopotamia, let alone the classical civilisations of the Mediterranean, the Far East and the Americas. To a certain degree this is correct, but in practice historical archaeology focuses on more recent times. James Deetz has defined historical archaeology as the archaeological study of European expansion around the globe since the fifteenth century and its effect on native people encountered along the way. The history–prehistory divide in this sense is marked by the first arrival of Europeans wherever the archaeology is being done. From this origin, so it seems, we can develop dates for historical archaeological sites.

Discovering this basis, however, actually does little to solve the problem of understanding the temporal context. Too much has happened, and at varying tempos and through multiple schemes, since the start of European colonialism to simply know that Europeans arrived and that history began, and then ask 'Where does a site fit in?' Determining temporal contexts requires a broader conception of the processes that drove the development of the modern world. A site can only be known when it is placed along a series of continua that are recognised as significant agents of historical change. Charles Orser has identified four of these as **capitalism**, **colonialism**, Eurocentrism and **modernity**. To these I add **urbanisation**, **industrialisation** and consumerism.

To establish the date of a site, then, an understanding must be made about when in contextual time the site was occupied or used. To know that the site was occupied from 1700 to 1750, for example, means very little on its own because it means quite different things whether the site is on the Pacific Coast or the lower Mississippi valley, or whether the site was a plantation or a frontier fort, or whether conditions were in a reputed period of prosperity or decline. This list could obviously go on. Temporal contexts thus need to be locally determined. The lives we wish to understand did uniformly pass through time, but the experience of that time was under the essentially unique sway of the dominant local conditions of everyday life.

Spatial contexts

Especially with the rise of **world systems theory** and the study of the development of a meaningful global entity, archaeologists have questioned the validity of understanding sites within *any* given spatial context. Multiple scales of inquiry have been studied, e.g. household, town, county, region, nation and global-system, and each of these scales has been found to have both shortcomings and advantages. Household studies, for example, allow the fine-grained archaeological record to be situated within its very maker's personal realm. These studies, however, often retain the bias of the small sample when more general abstractions regarding culture and society are made. The application of larger contexts has been used oftentimes as a successful remedy. Nevertheless, global-scale approaches, as they often draw on understandings of the vast exchange of commodities around the world, seem only to give an outsider's view as to how any particular archaeological record was made. It seems that meaningfully to merge the global perspective with the detail of the archaeological site something more must be done when the spatial context of an archaeological site is conceived.

The best route is to develop an understanding of the community or communities to which given subjects belonged. This means determining the variety of groups that intersected to bring the materials that we find to the site. A hypothetical example of foodways (see **food and foodways**) will illustrate. All people obtain the food they eat to live. This refers not only to food needed to meet the minimum caloric needs, but also food used for cultural reasons. Usually, at historical sites this food will be at least partly be produced agriculturally. To some degree, then, we can explore how these foods made it from the field to the table. To do this we need to find the human connections between the consumer and the multiple producers in the acquisition of seed or livestock, the wholesale

purchase of bulk food, the retail purchase of household needs and the division of labour in food preparation and storage within a household. Throughout these chains of connection we must also define the associated trades involved, such as the production and sale of agricultural equipment or food storage vessels. Also, this clearly idealised scheme of modern foodways can and should be modified to fit varying situations.

What is important is that communities are formed through exchanges like these of goods, services and ideas. Reading archaeological sites, both the materials and the texts, lets us recognise these communities and then determine the appropriate spatial context for interpretation. This approach is akin to working with multiple levels of spatial context at once, but it requires that the multiple levels be reduced to the one, essentially emic, level that was active in the lives of the people we are studying. Drawing from the above example, we have to see that though certain foods, for example **coffee** or **sugar**, may have been produced for a global market, whether this made a difference in the life of a given consumer is not simultaneously determined. Were the purchasers aware of the grand scale or were they perhaps more concerned with the actual availability of the foods where they lived? Global economies do not necessarily mean the existence of comparable levels of consciousness. To assume that they do is to overlook the everyday experience of culture and the spatial context of community.

Cultural contexts

Life is certainly more complex than the temporal and spatial confines in which it is contained. Humans are human because they have and employ **culture** to understand and manipulate the natural and social worlds in which they live. A contextual historical archaeology, thus, strives to determine the cultural contexts that the people we study were enmeshed in. To do this we have to employ the nodes of cultural life that most explicitly illustrate the human experience at a given time and space. These nodes are the points on which people hang their hats as they come to understand who they are: **race**, **ethnicity**, **gender** and class (see **class, social**).

Though lately couched as elements of identity politics, these means of self- and other-definition taken together build the social whole in terms of who makes up the cultures we study. If it is possible to let go of the essentialism found associated with the various expressions of these identities, then we can explore for different times and places how they were put together. Cultural context, thus, is a product of the times and places of daily life merged with the traditions and lands of history that people know and use as they encounter themselves and others every day.

How can archaeologists determine cultural contexts? I believe that the best method is to follow the route of our standard humanistic interpretive inquiry. The process of interpretation is commonly characterised as a circular movement of inquiry between nodes of significance until a coherent picture is produced. Though this is usually described as a method for research, it can be equally said to be true of how people know anything at all. This is especially the case when culture is given a high standing in the process of knowledge production. This perspective challenges experiential knowledge by arguing that humans know their world not through experiencing it, but through interpreting it. Thus, to develop cultural contexts for archaeology, we have to attempt to reconstruct past ways of knowing.

The handholds of race, ethnicity, gender and class allow historical archaeologists to do this sort of context building. Through the historical record we often have access to facts and patterns of behaviour that allow us to understand the social make-up of the communities we study, and how that diversity may have been understood. From this we can begin to assemble the possible sorts of interpretation for given people based on who they were and how they might socially know themselves because of it. Archaeologists benefit from this sort of process because the cultural contexts of the artefacts we find come through it. Artefacts are social clues for people. They bear and receive meanings based on how they become situated in the process of cultural interpretation. Archaeologists must use these clues to see how the cultural life of past people acted to produce the archaeological records we study.

One of the best examples of this sort of scholarship is Paul Mullins's study of the contradictory racial and consumer consciousnesses of middle-class African Americans in late nineteenth- and early twentieth-century **Annapolis**, Maryland. This study begins by establishing nodes of identity made real in American racism and consumer culture,, and then draws a portrait of the struggles black people had in merging these contradictory streams of cultural interpretation. Through the historical and archaeological records, Mullins demonstrates that African Americans actively used the equality espoused in consumer culture to combat the inequality of racial discrimination. Determining who they were and what that meant through an interpretive process allowed these men and women to subtly subvert racial inequality, ultimately leading towards the development of a distinctly American black consciousness (called a double consciousness by African American scholar W.E.B. DuBois) that eventually challenged much of the legitimacy of racism in America.

Critical contexts

Making meaningful contexts in historical archaeology cannot be done solely through passive observation. The meaning of archaeology in contemporary society also affects how archaeological contexts are made. Throughout this entry I have presented current approaches to contextual development; thus, I hope it reflects schemes that carry little of the effect of essentialist characterisations or other unreflective efforts at making history. More than dislodging bias, however, a critical contextual historical archaeology hopes to reveal how that bias, both today and in the past, has marginalised or made irrelevant certain factors in favour of others.

Asking that archaeologists develop, rather than assume, their temporal, spatial and cultural contexts is the first step towards doing critical archaeology. Developing the critical context will inadvertently follow because it will be evident in the research process that time, space and culture were always nodes of contested terrain. Not all members of past communities agreed on how these facts of cultural life should be interpreted, nor did divergent groups use or have the same tools for interpretation. Different ways of knowing have always existed within any community. To develop the critical context, historical archaeologists must recognise that the same lack of uniformity exists today concerning the meaning of what we find and how we interpret it. Making this part of the contextual development of research programmes allows the contested terrain of today, on the one hand, to make more sense as part of the continuum of history, and, on the other, to critically inform the process of our work. Archaeology is not just something that is done today, but an active and positive part of the construction and interpretation of contemporary society.

Further reading

Crumley, C.L. and Marquardt, W.H. (eds) (1987) *Regional Dynamics: Burgundian Landscapes in Historical Perspective*, New York: Academic Press.

Matthews, C.N. (1999) 'Context and interpretation: An archaeology of cultural production', *International Journal of Historical Archaeology* 3(4):261–82.

Mullins, P.R. (1999) *Race and Affluence: An Archaeology of African-America and Consumer Culture*, New York: Kluwer Academic/Plenum Press.

Orser, C.E., Jr (1996) *A Historical Archaeology of the Modern World*, New York: Kluwer Academic/Plenum Press.

Stahl, A. (1993) 'Concepts of time and approaches to analogical reasoning in historical perspective', *American Antiquity* 58: 235–60.

CHRISTOPHER N. MATTHEWS

Council for Northeast Historical Archaeology

One of the oldest professional organisations for historical archaeology is the Council for Northeast Historical Archaeology (CNEHA). It was founded in 1966, a year before the establishment of the **Society for Historical Archaeology**. CNEHA's geographic range is north-eastern North America, including the states and provinces of Connecticut, Delaware, District of Columbia, Maine, Massachusetts, Newfoundland and Labrador, New Brunswick, New Hampshire, New Jersey, New York, Nova Scotia, Ontario, Pennsylvania, Prince Edward Island, Quebec, Rhode Island, Vermont, Virginia and West Virginia. Initially, the organisation was called the Symposium on Historic Site Archeology but the board of directors quickly realised that its work involved more than organising conferences and hence the name was changed. CNEHA's goals are to encourage: the advancement and practice of historical archaeology; the preservation of archaeological sites; and the dissemination of knowledge through its publications (journal and newsletter) and its yearly fall conferences. Conferences are open to the public and at least one conference every three years is held in Canada. Professional archaeologists join with students, avocational archaeologists and colleagues in allied disciplines to discuss the latest issues in the field. Conference papers and journal articles cover the time period from the first contact between **Native Americans** and Europeans up through the multicultural diversity of the late nineteenth and early twentieth centuries. Papers with a north-east-based area focus cover diverse topics such as class (see **class, social**) and status, **ethnicity**, **gender**, **urban archaeology**, farmsteads, **industrial archaeology**, military-sites archaeology and landscape archaeology.

In the early years of CNEHA, the board recognised the need for a professional publication and the first issue of its journal *Northeast Historical Archaeology*, appeared in 1971 (in 1987 it became a refereed journal). The journal publishes field reports, technical and methodological studies, commentary and interpretive analyses, all with a focus on the north-eastern USA and Canada, plus a book review section. CNEHA has recently added a monograph series. The inaugural issue was Lynne Sussman's profusely illustrated, in-depth study of factory-made slipware. CNEHA also publishes a newsletter three times per year. The newsletter covers field reports, updates on excavations and commentary sections, plus information on conferences and other CNEHA-related business. CNEHA membership primarily includes archaeologists from Canada and the USA, with additional members in Europe and Australia. CNEHA encourages participation by **cultural-resource management** archaeologists and more than half of the members are affiliated with CRM firms.

Further reading

Huey, P.R. (1986) 'The beginnings of modern historical archaeology in the northeast and the origins of the Conference on Northeast Historical Archaeology', *Northeast Historical Archaeology* 15: 2–15.

Starbuck, D.R. (1986) 'A bibliography of northeast historical archaeology', *Northeast Historical Archaeology* 15: 19–99.

Sussman, L. (1997) 'Mocha, banded, cat's eye, and other factory-made slipware', *Studies in Northeast Historical Archaeology* 1: 1–102.

Wilson, B. (1986) 'The Council for Northeast Historical Archaeology: The early years', *Northeast Historical Archaeology* 15: 16–18.

SHERENE BAUGHER

creamware

Creamware is a modern term used to refer to the refined cream-coloured earthenware, or 'cream colour', which was made by Staffordshire potters from the 1740s. It was promoted by Josiah Wedgwood under the name 'Queen's ware' from 1765, after he had obtained the patronage of Queen Charlotte. 'Queen's ware' found favour among the nobility, gentry and affluent middle classes, becoming the fashionable tea and tableware of choice in preference to Chinese porcelain. The name subsequently came to be used by all manufacturers.

Creamware was made of white-firing ball clay from Devon and Dorset, with calcined flint added to the body for strength. After a biscuit firing of about 1,150 °C, vessels were dipped into a liquid lead glaze, dried and then given a second glost firing of 1,050 °C. The transparent glaze acquired an off-white or cream colour from the iron impurities in the clay body and glaze mixes. A gradual lightening of the colour by the early 1770s forms a general trend, with creamwares of the 1790s and later being almost white in colour.

A few known creamwares bearing dates in the early 1740s are unusual in that their underglaze painted decoration is reminiscent of contemporary delftwares. Typical Staffordshire creamwares of the late 1740s and 1750s are either undecorated or have all-over 'tortoiseshell' decoration, formed by sponging coloured metallic oxides onto the biscuit body. The first reference to tortoiseshell wares dates to 1749, with the style surviving into the 1770s. Tea and coffee wares and plates are the dominant forms, many of which had additional applied decoration of 'sprigged' or 'mould-applied' reliefs formed in plaster of Paris moulds or brass dies respectively. These were added to their unfired bodies in patterns of trailing vines, leaves, grapes and flowers.

Brightly coloured creamwares in ornate moulded forms proliferated around 1760. Vessels in the form of pears, apples, melons, cauliflowers and pineapples, covered with coloured glazes, were made by many factories and remained popular into the 1770s. However, from the mid-1760s more subtle painted and printed decoration gradually supplanted indiscriminate colour and the creamware glaze was an ideal surface for these decorations.

Painted decoration in enamel colours, used overglaze, became increasingly popular, as more factories employed decorators. Overglaze bat-printed decoration in black or red, with images transferred from an engraved copper plate by means of a glue 'bat', also became common. Printed designs were sometimes coloured by the addition of enamel colours. Decoration of any sort increased the cost of pottery to the consumer, overglaze decoration even more so as additional low-temperature firings were needed to harden on colours.

Around 1775 – contemporaneous with the introduction of **pearlware** – factories began to decorate creamwares underglaze, a method which was cheaper than the overglaze decoration. Chinese-inspired landscapes and other scenes were painted in blue in imitation of Chinese **porcelain**, and coloured slips were used to produce marbled patterns. However, both blue-painted and marbled slip decoration worked better when used on a pearlware body and increasingly it was pearlwares that were decorated in this way.

Creamware forms were thrown and turned, press-moulded or, less frequently, slip cast. Many of the wide range of tea, table, dessert and toilet wares are illustrated in catalogues of the late eighteenth and early nineteenth centuries, such as that produced by Charles and James Whitehead of Hanley, **Stoke-on-Trent**, in 1798.

From the 1760s until the early 1800s, creamware was the most significant product in almost every British pottery factory. Stoke-on-Trent had the largest concentration of factories making creamware, but the wares of Liverpool, Leeds, Swinton and Bovey Tracey are also well known. There was also a significant production in continental Europe. Few British factories marked their wares and it is therefore extremely difficult to distinguish between the wares of different factories or centres. Moreover, the products of most factories were effectively interchangeable, using identical production methods, and using types of decoration that were easily copied. Creamware was very widely used and was a major export of the British potteries to the rest of Europe and to the burgeoning North American market.

From the mid-1770s, creamware and pearlware co-existed, being made in the same factories and from the same moulds. Blue-tinted pearlwares added to the range of ceramics available, but gradually gained in popularity as a result of the greater variety of decoration that they carried, and by the early nineteenth century creamware had lost its fashionable status. The common perception is that creamware was replaced by pearlware. This was not so; it was replaced by decorated ware, which happened to be mainly pearlware.

Declining demand for creamware resulted in vessels becoming cheaper and, consequently, un-decorated. Henceforth, undecorated creamware was the cheapest type of tea and tableware. This loss of status also led to a narrower range of forms being available, the most common of which, by the 1800–20 period, were undecorated plates, baking dishes and toilet wares. By 1830, creamware in the eighteenth-century sense was no more, although the term 'CC' continued to be used until the end of the century for undecorated white earthenwares, which were still a major product of the Stafford-shire industry. Even the name 'Queen's ware' survived into the later part of the century.

Further reading

Barker, D. (1991) *William Greatbatch: A Staffordshire Potter*, London: Jonathan Horne.

Lockett, T.A. and Halfpenny, P.A. (1986) *Creamware and Pearlware*, Stoke-on-Trent: City Museum and Art Gallery.

Miller, G.L. (1991) 'A revised set of CC index values for classification and economic scaling of English ceramics from 1787 to 1880', *Historical Archaeology* 25(1): 1–25.

Miller, G.L., Martin A.S. and Dickinson, N.S. (1994) 'Changing consumption patterns. English ceramics and the American market from 1770 to 1840', in C.E. Hutchins (ed.) *Everyday Life in the Early Republic*, Winterthur: Henry Francis du Pont Winterthur Museum, pp. 219–48.

Whitehead, J. and Whitehead, C. (1798) *Designs of Sundry Articles of Earthenware*, undated reprint, *The Whitehead Catalogue 1798*, Milton Keynes: D.B. Drakard.

DAVID BARKER

creolisation

Creolisation refers to a process whereby men and women actively blend together elements of different cultures to create a new culture. Unlike the older term, **acculturation**, creolisation is perceived as a more active process and one that involves, by definition, a give and take between peoples of diverse cultural traditions. Social scientists became increasing interested in creolisation in the 1990s, and historical archaeologists have been particularly visible in this research effort. Many historical archaeologists find the anthropological significance of creolisation to be particularly interesting.

Scholars who have examined creolisation gen-erally think the word may have been created from two Spanish words, *criar* (to create, to establish) and *colono* (a colonist or founder). Individuals who study creolisation today generally follow three perspec-tives. Those who use a linguistic perspective stress the importance of an analogy with language and propose that creolisation is a cultural version of language blending. Different actors have essentially created a blended culture from elements of others in the same way that 'creolised' languages have been created. Scholars who subcribe to a second perspective generally perceive the process of creolisation to have resulted from a cultural adaptation to a new social, cultural and natural environment. These adaptations need not develop from the mixing of different populations as such, but rather can occur through contact alone. Cultural change occurs simply because of the interactions between the individuals. Investigators using a third perspective, which they consider to be largely biological, believe that creolisation is a process that involves cultural and biological mixing. The outcome of creolisation is a hybrid population, both culturally and physically.

Historical archaeologists have used all three perspectives in their research and have sometimes combined elements from all three perspectives to understand and interpret the interactions between specific past populations. Individual archaeologists have also viewed creolisation as a process having universal characteristics – aspects that are true for all times and places – and as a process that is uniquely case specific – being related to specific peoples, places and times.

Much of the creolisation research in historical archaeology has centred around the interactions of African American slaves with Europeans and indigenous peoples in the Caribbean and the US South, where 'creole' cultures still exist. Greater numbers of historical archaeologists, however, are expanding this research to other historical situations. By the year 2000, creolisation had become a major topic within much historical archaeology.

Further reading

Dawdy, S.L. (ed.) (2000) 'Creolization', *Historical Archaeology* 34(4): 1–133.

Ferguson, L. (1992) *Uncommon Ground: Archaeology and Early African America, 1650–1800*, Washington, DC: Smithsonian Institution Press.

CHARLES E. ORSER, JR

Crusades

The Crusades were, speaking very broadly, a political and religious movement of the Middle Ages that sought to conquer areas controlled by Islam and pagans on behalf of western Christianity. They are usually associated with Palestine, Syria and Egypt, but the Spanish *reconquista* and the conquests of the Teutonic knights along the shores of the Baltic Sea are also important to an understanding of the movement. The foundation of the Crusader states in Palestine and Syria from 1099 on may be seen as the founding roots of European colonialism. Further west, the Spanish *reconquista* ended in 1492, the same year Columbus set sail, and the expansionist militarism of early **Spanish colonialism** has direct roots in the centuries of warfare between Christian and Muslim Spain. Finally, the wars of the Teutonic knights had a tremendous impact on the development of the eastern Baltic Sea, and, while it would be easy to overplay the similarities, provided much of the mythic foundation of the *drang nach osten* of the Third Reich.

The Crusades began in 1095 when the Byzantine emperor Alexius I Comnenos appealed to western Christianity through Pope Urban II for mercenaries to help reconquer those areas of Anatolia lost to the Turks. Instead, Alexius found himself hosting a ragtag army dedicated to the reconquest of the Holy Land. Against all odds – and helped considerably by Islamic disunity – the First Crusade was spectacularly successful, resulting in the foundation of Crusader states that, in some form or another, were to last for nearly 200 years. These states, however, were on the defensive almost from the beginning, and, after Saladin's victories in 1187, were lucky to hang on as a string of coastal trading cities until the end of the thirteenth century. Visitors to 'Outremer' ('overseas'), as the colonies in Palestine were known, were shocked at the 'luxurious' and 'oriental' lifestyle of the descendants of the original Crusaders, and the culture of the Crusader states may be seen as Europe's earliest experience with colonial **creolisation**. The long-term impact of the doomed states of Outremer on European **material culture** was, however, arguably minimal, with the notable exception of the development of the castle, of which Krak des Chevaliers and Beaufort are among the finest surviving examples.

For a variety of reasons, the crusading movement eventually turned its attention to non-Christian areas of Europe, notably Muslim Spain and the pagan Baltic. These Crusades were arguably far more successful than their eastern counterparts, resulting in the permanent conquest of most of these areas for western Christianity. The final conquest of Granada in 1492 also left the Spanish warrior class without a local scope for conflict for the first time since the eighth century, and the discovery of the New World did much to channel their energies into a new, more overtly colonial, sphere.

In many ways, the Crusades were an unmitigated disaster: they led directly or indirectly to the sacking of **Constantinople**, the destruction of the Byzantine Empire, the near-annihilation of Muslim and Jewish culture in Spain, the widespread destruction of native peoples of the Americas and a hardening of the mutual intolerance between Islam, Judaism and Christianity that exists to this day. They nonetheless remain vital to an understanding of the forces of European colonialism that are so important to historical archaeology.

Further reading

Boas, A.J. (1999) *Crusader Archaeology: The Material Culture of the Latin East*, London: Routledge.

Runciman, S. (1978) *A History of the Crusades*, 3 vols, Harmondsworth, Middlesex: Penguin.

ALASDAIR M. BROOKS

cultural-resource management

Cultural-resource management (CRM) is a term used in the USA to denote the control and administration of traditional cultural properties (TCPs), buildings, engineering structures, objects, landscapes and archaeological sites, usually by a federal governmental agency. The purpose of CRM is to identify, evaluate and manage, for the public good, important resources and the cultural values and information they contain. In Europe and elsewhere, CRM is often referred to as **heritage management**, and it includes **rescue archaeology**.

Many archaeologists and preservationists have made the argument that CRM began in the

nineteenth century, when people recognised the need to protect buildings and sites important in US history. The 1906 Antiquities Act and the 1935 Historic Sites Act gave certain highly significant national landmarks and monuments special status and a certain level of protection; and, of course, people were hired to manage these resources. The Smithsonian Institution's River Basin Surveys in the 1950s, along with the 1960 Reservoir Salvage Act, helped to provide for the emergency salvage of endangered sites so that they could be recorded before they were destroyed.

In any case, the term *cultural resource*, and the beginnings of what is today commonly considered the *management* of cultural resources or CRM, began with the National Historic Preservation Act (NHPA) of 1966, and the reaction to it and to other environmental laws in the early 1970s. Archaeologists give varying explanations for the origin of the term, but most writers agree that the term 'cultural resources' was invented by archaeologists in the south-western USA in the early 1970s. Their purpose was to give to archaeology equal credibility with natural resources when obtaining federal funding for archaeological projects. Non-archaeologists, taking the term at face value, began to include all resources of a cultural nature within their purview. By the 1980s and early 1990s, **Native Americans** and other peoples had extended the meaning of the term to include places and objects that hold special meaning in the lives of cultural groups, or TCPs.

Cultural-resource management blossomed in the USA in the 1970s and 1980s as federal and state laws and regulations were developed to implement the NHPA and other laws affecting cultural resources; as federal and state agencies began to hire archaeologists and others to enforce the new regulations; and as archaeologists and universities scrambled to meet the growing need to locate and evaluate the rapidly increasing number of sites affected by federally controlled or funded projects.

Perhaps the two most important things at the federal level affecting CRM as it was known and practised in the year 2000 was the approval in the late 1970s of detailed regulations governing Section 106 of the National Historic Preservation Act (36CFR800) and the formation of the President's

Advisory Council on Historic Preservation (ACHP). The ACHP is mandated with interpreting and enforcing these regulations. The 36CFR800 regulations and subsequent modifications have effectively subsumed most of the previous, scattered and overlapping regulations developed since the 1906 Antiquities Act.

The most important non-governmental factor affecting CRM as it is practised in the USA was the development of private-sector consulting firms specialising in one or a variety of the cultural-resource disciplines. By the mid-1970s, universities were unable to meet the growing demand for timely and consistent CRM services, and private-sector cultural-resource consulting firms, modelled after engineering consulting firms, began to take over some of the burden. By the 1980s, the vast majority of CRM services were being provided by private consulting firms, and, in 1995, many of these private-sector firms joined in a national trade association – the American Cultural Resources Association (ACRA) – to promote their business interests and to stress the professionalisation of CRM generally.

CRM has matured to the point that clearly defined roles can be delineated for the federal agencies, state agencies and private-sector consulting firms. At the federal level, the lead agency takes responsibility for enforcing the NHPA and other regulations. The agencies are responsible for projects they fund, on property they own or manage, and on projects for which they grant permits. Federal agencies can therefore be the funding source for projects as well as the regulatory enforcer. The other major governmental entity in CRM in the USA is the State Historic Preservation Officer (SHPO). This is a federally mandated position at the state level. This person and his or her staff have the role of protecting the state's and the public's interests by reviewing projects on federal lands that use federal funds or that require federal permits. Similarly, Tribal Historic Preservation Officers (THPOs) have a review role on lands pertaining to Native American interests. The private-sector consultants are the primary providers of the basic information upon which the federal agencies and SHPOs/THPOs base their decisions. While these firms make recommendations about the resources found, and the SHPO/

THPO comments on those recommendations, the final decision on the fate of cultural resources and enforcement of the NHPA regulations is left up to the federal agency in charge of a particular project or to the ACHP if there is disagreement among the parties. Some states and localities have their own laws and regulations that deal with resources under their jurisdictions.

Taking archaeology out of the academy and into the everyday world has had profound implications for historical archaeology. The impact can be seen in the rapid and extensive development of sub-fields such as **African American archaeology** and **urban archaeology**, a proliferation in archaeological and other previously academic jobs, more efficient and effective field and analytical methods, and an increase in the public awareness of archaeology. In the future, several issues must also be resolved, including the cost to curate the vast number of artefacts and data recovered, decisions about what artefacts and data deserve to be curated for the long term, resolution of the uneven quality of the data collected, the evolving issue of TCPs and making the results of CRM accessible and useful to the public that pays for it.

Further reading

King, T.F. (1998) *Cultural Resource Laws and Practice, an Introductory Guide*, Walnut Creek, CA: Alta-Mira Press.

THOMAS R. WHEATON

culture

Anthropologically trained historical archaeologists are likely to use the word 'culture' with great regularity, but the definitions they associate with this term have varied greatly throughout the discipline's history. Ultimately, differences in definitions reflect debates within the broader disciplines of archaeology and anthropology, and arise from differing perspectives regarding the relationships between individuals and society and between individuals and **material culture**. A range of theoretical approaches has shaped the ways historical archaeologists define culture.

'Culture history' approaches characterised the intellectual state of much archaeological research in North America prior to the mid-1960s. Culture historians would define culture as the practices and beliefs shared by a group of people living together at a particular place and time. The archaeological focus of cultural historians was descriptive, resulting in discussions of artefact types and chronology. The influences of a cultural historical approach can be seen in the earliest historical archaeological pursuits, such as Ivor Noël Hume's research at **Martin's Hundred**, Virginia, USA, where emphasis was placed on the recovery of artefacts for museum display and to inform the reconstruction of historic structures.

Systems theory, as most prominently advocated by Stanley South in the 1970s, brought a new explanatory bent to historical archaeological definitions of culture. Influenced by the writings of prehistorian Lewis Binford, South adopted Binford's notion of culture as an extrasomatic means of adaptation. Humans were rational, efficient beings who used cultural systems as a means of adapting to their environments. Material culture was a passive reflection of the behaviours that shaped cultural systems. South introduced a number of analytical techniques that were intended to identify patterns of artefact distributions that could be used to identify site occupants based solely on the materials they used. The systems model of culture denied agency to individuals, instead viewing human behaviour as predictable and widespread.

Contrasting theoretically to South was the 1970s work of James Deetz, which employed a structuralist view of culture. Deetz defined culture as the socially transmitted rules for behaviour, ways of thinking about and doing things. These rules for behaviour created a series of mental templates. Unlike the processually minded South, Deetz argued that cultural practices were not necessarily rational, but needed to be understood within their cultural context. Material culture, using Deetz's definition, is the product of culture – the mental templates in physical form. Thus, like South, Deetz envisioned artefacts as passive by-products of human action.

Deetz's and South's views of culture and its relationship to material culture shaped much of historical archaeological practice in the 1980s, particularly research focused on **ethnicity**. Archaeologists tried to equate the presence of certain artefacts with the presence of particular ethnic identities. Studies focusing on cultural changes and continuities in societies in contact situations were popular. Evidence of traditional artefacts or architecture was viewed as evidence of cultural continuity, whereas the adoption of new materials was seen as evidence of cultural change or, in the case of Native American–European contact (see **Native Americans**), as evidence of **acculturation**. Still others looked for evidence of cultural blending, or **creolisation**, as evidenced through the creation of new artefact forms. Kathleen Deagan's pioneering research into the process of creolisation among the Spanish and Native American populations of **St Augustine**, Florida, is an excellent example of research from this time.

Ultimately, South's and Deetz's visions of culture and its relationship to material culture failed to account for the endless variety of human behaviours reflected at archaeological sites. During the late 1980s and 1990s, many archaeologists have recognised that the role of individual action and its impacts on the creation of material cultural assemblages must be considered in archaeological research.

Archaeologists have injected the issue of human agency into their notions of culture in a variety of ways. Following the lead of Charles Orser, who has been inspired by neo-Marxian theories, many archaeologists studying plantations have looked for artefactual evidence of agency in the form of African American resistance. Larry McKee, working at the **Hermitage Plantation**, Tennessee, has suggested that root cellars dug beneath dirt floors in slave cabins provided African Americans a hiding place for sacred traditional objects. Lu Ann DeCunzo has drawn upon the social theories of Pierre Bourdieu and Anthony Giddens in her study of life within the Philadelphia Magdalen Society. These theorists emphasise the importance of routines in the construction and maintenance of an individual's cultural identity. That which is routine becomes a person's understanding of culturally normative behaviour. The Magdalen societies, by enforcing a new everyday routine upon the 'fallen women', were attempting to counteract the routines (or culture) of everyday life that had led these women astray, and to introduce a more moral lifestyle. Kent Lightfoot, in his study of native Californian and Alaskan interactions at the Russian Fort Ross, in California, has also used the ideas of Bourdieu to understand cultural change and continuity after European contact by analysing household space.

Many archaeologists continue to use the idea of culture, while others have abandoned it entirely in favour of studies focusing upon class, race or gender. Some scholars have even argued that what archaeologists have called cultural is merely the by-product of individuals' attempts to negotiate their social position. Increasingly, descendants of the people historical archaeologists study are demanding that research illuminate their cultural heritages. As long as this is the case, and as long as archaeology in North America remains situated within the discipline of anthropology, culture is likely to remain a concept central to historical archaeological debate.

See also: cognitive archaeology; history of historical archaeology

Further reading

De Cunzo, L. (1995) 'Reform, respite, ritual: An archaeology of institutions; The Magdalen society of Philadelphia, 1800–1850', *Historical Archaeology* 29: 3.

Deetz, J. (1977) *In Small Things Forgotten: The Archaeology of Early American Life*, New York: Anchor/Doubleday.

Lightfoot, K., Schiff, A. and Wake, T. (eds) (1997) *The Archaeology and Ethnohistory of Fort Ross, California. Volume 2: The Native Alaskan Neighborhood, A Multi-ethnic Community at Fort Ross*, Berkeley: University of California Archaeological Research Facility.

Yentsch, A. and Beaudry, M. (eds) (1992) *The Art and Mystery of Historical Archaeology: Essays in Honor of James Deetz*, Boca Raton, FL: CRC Press.

LAURIE A. WILKIE

culture history

Culture history, the chronological description of a society's past, may be reconstructed using the techniques of archaeology independent of, or as a complement to, the historical record. Linking archaeological findings to relevant documents provides an exceptionally accurate view of a culture's past. The archaeological record also provides particularly long time depth, potentially extending the record back to the 'origins' of a culture. Archaeological descriptions of culture history reveal the roots of a society and enable us to recognise relationships with other cultures as well as shared derivations.

The detailed story of each culture, delineating its specific changes and descent, remains a primary goal of archaeological inquiry. Since the 1960s, archaeological research has become more theory driven. Concern with cultural processes and specific aspects of individual societies, as they might reveal anthropological rules that are applicable to **culture** in general, now dominate current research. These modern approaches have led to an intensification of attention to field methods and theory, and to a corresponding florescence in the numbers of other disciplines that have become allied to archaeology. New and detailed data recovery systems and traditional geological methods now are augmented by research in physics (^{14}C dating), plant biology (**dendrochronology**) and other disciplines to interpret and understand culture history in new and more specific ways. Dozens of other analytical techniques plus space age technology have been incorporated in studies of culture history.

The nineteenth-century founders of anthropology saw cultures as evolving from foraging societies around the world, with Western Europeans supposedly enjoying the most 'advanced' of these systems. Lewis Henry Morgan's *Ancient Society* provided data that applied Darwinian views to the study of human societies. Morgan's ideas regarding social evolution were rapidly accepted, in one form or another, by most archaeologists as well as by early social anthropologists. Morgan's construction of culture history also appeared to be of immense support to the materialist ideas of Karl Marx and Friedrich Engels, who projected these views of social evolution into their Utopian future. This view of social evolution, taken in a teleological sense, had once been accepted as the critical force in shaping the history of each culture. Despite the efforts of Franz Boas and Alfred Kroeber to understand each culture in its own unique context, Morgan's rigid evolutionary views concerning culture history lingered well into the second half of the twentieth century. The followers of Boas and Kroeber, conducting their research in the 'American Historical Tradition', continued to view each culture history as revealing a unique process not necessarily bound by rigid evolutionary rules.

Leslie White's 1959 publication of a controversial volume on culture change came only a few years after V. Gordon Childe's lectures describing an archaeological view of social evolution. White's work, which straddled the past and the future, used ethnography to augment the archaeological record. White recognised the value of studying the economies and behaviours of living societies to infer behaviours of past cultures. His awareness that these past systems often created the antecedents of present cultures offered an alternative to rigid evolutionary models of culture change and shifted the focus of research.

The long view of history provided by the archaeological record enables anthropologists to examine the record of each culture, linking the prehistoric past to evidence provided by written records. What is sought by modern archaeologists is more than the evidence for the material culture, or the bases for a specific economic system. The physical evidence that had formed the data sets for the early historical-materialist theorists became the starting point for a new approach to understanding culture histories. Placing basic excavation data within the theoretical context of the strongly anthropological **New Archaeology** has provided a much more rounded picture of past societies.

Culture history includes much more than an explication of the written record documenting the past of a society. Archaeology not only enables us to extend our view of the past far beyond the beginnings of a society's own record keeping, but it also clarifies the limited historical record and amplifies the many aspects of a society that never appear in written form. Assembling the historical documents together with the excavation evidence, and comparing the results with ethnographic analogies, reveals a continuous record of a society; one that often leads back to the origins of the earliest specific patterns that define their culture.

Further reading

Childe, V.G. (1951) *Social Evolution*, Cleveland: Meridian Books.

Harris, M. (1979) *Cultural Materialism: The Struggle for a Science of Culture*, New York: Random House.

Morgan, L.H. (1877) *Ancient Society or Researches in the Lines of Human Progress from Savagery through Barbarism to Civilization*, Chicago: Kerr.

White, L.A. (1959) *The End of Culture: The Development of Civilization to the Fall of Rome*, New York: McGraw-Hill.

MARSHALL JOSEPH BECKER

Cuzco, Peru

The city of Cuzco, a UNESCO World Heritage site (1983), lies 3,360–400 m above sea level in the Huatanay Valley of Peru's south-eastern Andes. Cuzco, meaning 'navel' in Quechua, the indigenous Inca language, was the capital of the Inca Empire of Tawantinsuyu (the Land of the Four Quarters). Although the city has gone through a number of episodes of rebuilding because of earthquake damage, in 1650 and 1950, and growing urban renewal and growth, many of the walls built by the Inca still exist.

According to historical records of the Spanish chroniclers, such as Guaman Poma de Ayala and Cieza de Leon, Cuzco was established in about AD 1200 by the legendary founder Manco Capac. Some maintain that Cuzco was reorganised by emperor Pachacuti (1438–70) in the shape of a puma in profile. The puma's head and jaws were formed by the cyclopean Saqsaywaman, which functioned as a sun temple. The puma's tail (*Pumachupan*) is formed by the convergence of the Huatanay and Tullamayo rivers that frame the core of the city.

Cuzco was conceptually divided into two parts at the Huakaypata Plaza, located between the puma's legs, which in Inca times was covered with sand brought from the Pacific shoreline. The upper (*hanan*) half of Cuzco contained Saqsaywaman and a number of royal palaces while the lower (*hurin*) half contained the Qorikancha or Temple of the Sun. The division of the city into two separate but unequal halves illustrates the importance of the

Andean concepts of duality and complementary opposition. It was from the plaza that four roads led out into the Inca domain dividing it into four unequal parts or *suyu*.

The Qorikancha was composed of six chambers surrounded by a curved enclosing wall, all built of the finest polished cut-stone masonry. During Inca times, the structures were covered in gold and silver, and dedicated to the various deities in the Inca pantheon. This temple served as the nexus of the Inca's radial organisation of space. From the Qorikancha radiated forty-one lines or *ceques* on which were located 328 shrines or *huacas*. Anthony Aveni and Tom Zuidema have suggested that the shrines marked the passage of time and rituals in a sidereal lunar calendar.

Following the conquest of Cuzco by Pizarro in 1533, the Spanish appropriated Inca sacred and royal enclosures, using them as the foundations for colonial buildings. The construction of the Spanish Convent of Santo Domingo directly over the Qorikancha is typical. Likewise, the Huakaypata Plaza was converted into the Plaza de Armas with a great cathedral built to dominate it.

The Cuzco region's archaeological importance first gained renown after the excavation of Machu Picchu, a royal estate, by Hiram Bingham of Yale University. In the 1940s, John Rowe helped to clarify pre-Inca and Inca occupations in Cuzco, and Brian Bauer, Ann Kendall and Gordon McEwan have carried on this work. Kendall's Cusichaca Project is particularly notable for having restored Inca terrace field systems and canals, resulting in a return to pre-Hispanic agricultural practices.

See also: preservation legislation; South America; Spanish colonialism

Further reading

Bauer, B.S. (1992) *The Development of the Inca State*, Austin: University of Texas Press.

Kendall, A. (1985) *Aspects of Inca Architecture: Description, Function and Chronology*, Parts 1 and 2, BAR International Series 242, Oxford: British Archaeological Reports.

Rostworowski de Diez Canseco, M. (1998) *The History of the Inka Empire*, Cambridge: Cambridge University Press.

Rowe, J.H. (1944) 'An introduction to the archaeology of Cuzco', *Papers of the Peabody Museum of American Anthropology and Ethnology* 27(2): 1–63.

Zuidema, T. (1990) *Inca Civilization in Cuzco*, Austin: University of Texas Press.

THOMAS A. ZOUBEK

D

dating methods

Historical archaeologists, like all archaeologists, rely on a number of methods to assign dates to soil layers, artefacts and sites. Dating methods fall into four gross categories: radiometric, geochemical, relative and **formula dating**. Historical archaeologists usually rely most strongly on relative dating methods, but many also use formula dating as well. Radiometric and geochemical dating are seldom used.

The radiometric dating techniques include all those highly scientific procedures that are intended to help date archaeological materials. These techniques include: radiocarbon, or carbon 14 (^{14}C), dating, potassium-argon (K-Ar) dating and fission track dating. These methods of dating archaeological deposits are seldom used in historical archaeology because they are mainly applicable to dating extremely old materials, including early-human fossil remains.

Archaeologists dealing with long time periods can also use geochemical dating methods. These include the analysis of varves (geologic deposits laid down by retreating ice sheets during glacial periods) and obsidian hydration, which involves the dating of geological materials – most notably obsidian – in terms of chemical weathering over time. Historical archaeologists generally cannot take advantage of these dating methods because of the short periods of time they study.

Relative dating techniques are by far the most important methods in historical archaeology. These methods, though not as scientifically based as the radiometric or geochemical methods, are, nonetheless, powerful and useful. Relative dating consists of methods that permit archaeologists to judge the date of a deposit, artefact or site by comparing it with other deposits, artefacts or sites. For example, historical archaeologists rely on classic archaeological methods when they use the relative placement of soil deposits to assign dates. Using the 'Law of Superposition', archaeologists know that in the absence of major disturbances of the land surface, the uppermost soil layers are the most recent in date. In keeping with this law, the deeper the deposit, the earlier the date. Accordingly, archaeologists know that artefacts near the surface are more recent in date than those found at deeper levels.

Historical archaeologists can also use the known dates of manufacture of artefacts for relative dating purposes. The industries of the post-Industrial Revolution era were businesses very much like those that operate today in that they designed, produced and marketed goods to the public. Like products today, the items sold in the fifteenth through nineteenth centuries were introduced, became popular and then, after a while, lost their appeal. As a result of this cycle, the artefacts studied by historical archaeologists have certain discrete dates of manufacture. Archaeologists can establish these dates through historical research – such as for English **ceramics** – and can apply this knowledge for relative dating. Archaeologists would know, for instance, that a kind of ceramic decoration, if manufactured only between 1820 and 1840, could not date before 1820. This ceramic design, then, would provide a relative date when compared with ceramic decorations know to have been used from 1860 to 1880.

Glass **bottles** often provide similar information about the dates of their manufacture. **Makers' marks** – which also appear on many nineteenth- and twentieth-century ceramics – as well as marks left from the manufacturing process, such as seam lines, can also indicate a relative date for an archaeological context by providing a range of manufacturing dates.

Historical archaeologists can also find relative dates from the shapes of the artefacts they study. The bowls of white clay smoking pipes (see **pipes, smoking**), for example, are known to have changed over time. In the late sixteenth century, when the practice of smoking was not widespread and tobacco was an expensive commodity, the bowls were quite small. Over time, pipe makers made the bowls increasingly larger, in response to the growth of the tobacco market and the demands of consumers. Archaeologists can use the size and shape of mass-produced objects, like white clay smoking pipes, to determine relative dates for archaeological deposits and features.

Relative dating is perhaps not as precise as some other methods of dating that involve the use of complex scientific principles. It can be a powerful tool, however, when used in conjunction with all the other sources of information available to historical archaeologists.

See also: formula dating; Harris matrix; stratification, soil

Further reading

Harris, E.C. (1979) *Principles of Archaeological Stratigraphy*, London: Academic Press.

Noël Hume, I. (1969) *A Guide to Artifacts of Colonial America*, New York: Alfred A. Knopf.

CHARLES E. ORSER, JR

dendrochronology

Dendrochronology, or tree-ring dating, is a dating method that involves the inspection of growth rings on wooden objects. As trees grow, particularly in environments with well-defined wet and dry seasons, their growth rings vary accordingly. An extremely wet season would cause a thick ring to develop, whereas a relatively dry season would produce a thinner ring. These rings tell the history of the tree's growth, and by extension reveal information about the surrounding environment.

Archaeologists can use dendrochronology as a dating method in locales where scientists have devised a master sequence of tree-ring growth. This master sequence, painstakingly constructed from numerous cross-sectioned samples, provides the standard against which wood specimens are compared. The master sequences for the US south-west and for parts of Europe, for example, extend back thousands of years. An archaeologist who finds a piece of wood that retains its ring pattern – a roof beam, for example – can compare the rings on the object with the master sequence, and therefore determine the object's date with some confidence.

Historical archaeologists have used dendrochronology at pueblo sites in the US South-west, such as Acoma Pueblo, New Mexico, and in Europe, such as at **Richmond Palace**, England.

Dendrochronology is not a foolproof dating method because people can reuse wood or replace rotten roof beams with new, more recent ones. By the same token, wooden artefacts found in an archaeological context, such as a house, may be either younger or older than the structure itself. Thus, a slavish devotion to dendrochronology can provide spurious dates. Historical archaeologists, however, because of the nature of their discipline, usually have the opportunity to correlate tree-ring dates with historical records, datable artefacts and other sources of information.

CHARLES E. ORSER, JR

Deptford Dockyard, London, England

The Royal Dockyard at Deptford was founded in 1513 by Henry VIII, although royal ships had been built there from the early fifteenth century in the reign of Henry V. Portsmouth is generally regarded as the earliest of the Royal Dockyards, founded by

Henry VII in 1496. Henry VIII favoured the Thames rather than the south-coast ports and founded dockyards at Woolwich and then at Deptford, where he built a storehouse and dry dock. The 1513 date was recorded on original masonry from the storehouse, much of which was demolished following Second World War bomb damage. In 1517, the old pond, in existence since the thirteenth century, presumably resulting from a breach in the river wall, was adapted as a basin to house several of the King's ships.

The Deptford yard became known as the King's Yard and was soon the most important of all the Royal Dockyards, employing large numbers of men and bringing wealth and prestige to the town. Soon, more storehouses were being rented, the dock was rebuilt and, by the end of the sixteenth century, the dockyard had been enlarged with additional wharfage extending 500–600 ft along the waterfront.

By the early seventeenth century, the growing importance of Chatham Dockyard, on the River Medway, had led to proposals to sell the Deptford yard. Despite this threat, the oak paling that had enclosed the yard was replaced by a brick wall, and then the construction of ten men-of-war in only five years appeared to prevent any further talk of closure. The yard continued to expand and, by the end of the seventeenth century, it contained more storehouses, several slipways, new mastponds, cranes, smiths, saw houses and many other facilities.

The early eighteenth century saw continued expansions: the Great Dock was lengthened and the yard was extended on two occasions. By the middle of the eighteenth century, the basin had been remodelled with several slipways and a second dry dock, complementing the earlier shipbuilding facilities that fronted onto the Thames.

Immediately upstream of the King's Yard, the Royal Victualling Yard was officially founded in 1742, but its origins probably lay in an old storehouse known as the Red House that had burnt down in 1639 and was rebuilt later that century. The Dockyard was soon extended into the Victualling Yard, allowing construction of a larger mastpond, masthouse and another shipbuilding slipway, all of which were enclosed by a brick wall.

This was the last major expansion of the dockyard, which was to only undertake maintenance work from 1821. Land was returned to the Victualling Yard and from 1830 the dockyard was only used for shipbreaking. Building of small warships recommenced in 1844 but the yard was finally closed in 1869. The Victualling Yard closed in 1961.

Trial excavations, prior to the redevelopment of the dockyard site, have revealed that most of the main features of the dockyard, the storehouses, dry docks, slipways, ponds and the basin, still survive below ground level.

DAVID DIVERS

Deptford, London, England

Deptford has played a major role in English maritime history, a history that has had implications around the globe. It was the starting point for many of the sixteenth- and seventeenth-century voyages of discovery and became known as the *Cradle of the Navy*.

Modern Deptford, a suburb of South-east London, has its origins in the deep ford where the London to Dover road crossed the River Ravensbourne, a tributary of the Thames. The ford probably had Roman origins dating from the first century AD. Archaeological excavations have revealed nearby evidence for Roman settlement and Saxon burials dating from *c.* seventh century AD. Pottery from these excavations suggests continuous occupation of this part of Deptford from the tenth century AD. A bridge had certainly been built here by the 1270s and Deptford became the last stopping place for London-bound coaches.

There is, however, evidence to suggest that the focus of settlement shifted towards the Thames. Deptford's medieval church of St Nicholas and the manor house (see **manor houses**) of Sayes Court were both established near the Thames, as was the medieval settlement of Deptford Strand. Its economy was probably based on fishing, the earliest references dating from the thirteenth century. Ships were certainly being built here by the early fifteenth century and the industry had become well established by the end of the century.

In 1513, Henry VIII established a Royal Dockyard at Deptford (see **Deptford Dockyard**), although ships continued to be built at privately owned dockyards along the waterfront.

Deptford's maritime connections were not limited to shipbuilding. *The Corporation of Trinity House of Deptford Strand*, formed by royal charter in 1514, probably evolved from a medieval seamen's guild based at Deptford. The Corporation's initial responsibilities included the pilotage of ships in the increasingly busy Thames, and the maintenance of a hall and almshouses, which have been investigated archaeologically. The Corporation soon became influential and prosperous, with increased responsibilities including the administration of ballast, beacons, buoys and lighthouses.

Francis Drake's ship, the *Golden Hind*, was put in dry dock on its return from circumnavigating the world in 1581 and remained an attraction until the 1660s. Archaeological attempts to find its remains have so far been unsuccessful.

The East India Company also had strong links with the town. Their first voyages set sail from Deptford in 1600 and the Company had established a dockyard there by 1614. Although their direct involvement did not last long, the yard continued building ships for the Company and the navy into the nineteenth century. Archaeological excavations have revealed timber river walls and slipways from the dockyard and shipbuilding waste.

Deptford was also a centre for the production of bricks, pottery and copperas, as well as being an important centre for market gardening. Excavations have revealed huge quantities of **redware** pottery wasters used for land reclamation during the eighteenth century. Despite the presence of the local brick industry, building surveys have shown that timber-framed traditions continued in Deptford into the eighteenth century when brick was favoured elsewhere.

DAVID DIVERS

deserted villages

Deserted villages are earthworks or ruins. The term connotes the remains of ordinary permanent nucleated settlements of various sizes, from hamlets to small towns. Research in Western Europe and the Americas has shown that settlements grow, contract and shift continuously. However, deserted villages are not shrunken settlements or settlements that have been left temporarily. By convention, desertion is defined in Britain as abandonment of all but three houses or less.

Most desertions were caused by changes of land use such as agricultural conversion, embarking or industrial relocation ('ghost towns'). Reservoirs and damming account for many recent desertions (inundated sites). Smaller villages were more susceptible. The causes varied in different periods and regions. In midland England, for example, many desertions were caused by conversion from arable to pastoral farming in the Tudor period, and the earthworks were then preserved by continued commitment to grazing. Along the border with Scotland, however, desertions were caused by war. The term 'deserted village' is not used for sites destroyed by natural disasters, although some desertions were prompted by the effects of epidemics, notably in early Spanish America.

In historical archaeology, deserted villages are commonly identified by combining archival and field evidence, but many are known from archaeological evidence supported only indirectly by documents. Others known from historical sources have yet to be traced on the ground. In certain terrains, decay of organic building materials has made the sites more difficult to find. Typical features include house platforms and associated plots (known as 'tofts' and 'crofts', respectively, in Britain), lanes ('holloways'), ditches and ponds, and churches or temples (which, along with their administrative boundaries, may long survive the last residents). It is estimated that there are at least 3,000 sites in England alone.

Comparative study (**settlement analysis**) has helped to elucidate the general history of settlement and landscapes, notably in England. Preserved layouts proved especially valuable. The research contributed greatly to the development of **landscape studies** throughout Britain. In turn, the sites are now being appraised in the context of other features such as isolated farmsteads, moats and field patterns. The research has broadened to embrace issues such as the long-term history of landownership and economic development.

Research was pioneered, in England, by W.G. Hoskins and, especially, Maurice Beresford, in the 1940s. It was through studying medieval fields, in the first place, that Beresford began to discover how many sites exist. In 1952, he and J.G. Hurst founded the Deserted Medieval Village Research Group, reorganised in 1986 as the Medieval Settlement Research Group. Systematic work has been carried out in districts throughout Britain and **Ireland**. There has also been considerable research in Italy, and some projects in other countries too. Deserted villages are recognised in the Americas but most research there treats them as evidence for other topics, less a subject in themselves.

See also: Wharram Percy

Further reading

Beresford, M. and Hurst, J.G. (eds) (1971) *Deserted Medieval Villages: Studies*, London: Lutterworth.

N. JAMES

destruction, site

Site destruction is both a part of normal archaeological practice and a significant challenge to the preservation of archaeological remains. The destruction of sites can be caused by both natural forces and human activity.

Site destruction by nature

Nature can play a significant role in causing the destruction of archaeological sites and deposits. When the inhabitants of settlements abandon them, they leave their houses, fields and other structures open to natural deterioration and even full-scale destruction. Major events, such as earthquakes and hurricanes, can play a dramatic role in destroying archaeological remains. The eruptions of Mount Vesuvius in AD 79, which buried Herculaneum and Pompeii, and the volcano of Santorini, which destroyed the ancient Minoan civilisation in the second millennium BC stand as classic examples of the devastating role nature can play in destroying archaeological sites. Surprisingly,

however, earthquakes can also preserve archaeological remains by covering them with thick layers of ash.

Violent storms also have the ability to destroy fragile archaeological remains and to mix and confuse soil deposits. The incredible force of high winds and rushing water can displace entire buildings, and forever alter the archaeological deposits with which they are associated. As might be expected, the temporary structures often built by European colonists, and the indigenous dwellings sometimes associated with them, suffer the most damage.

Other natural processes are less dramatic and more subtle, but archaeologists must still be aware of their abilities to destroy, or at least to alter, archaeological sites. These processes include erosion, the effects of burrowing and foraging animals on archaeological deposits (called 'faunalturbation'), the impact of root disturbance (called 'floralturbation'), the shrinking and swelling of clayey soils in dry and wet seasons (called 'argilliturbation'), the movement of soils as a result of the action of air (called 'aeroturbation') and the repeated action of freezing and thawing.

Field archaeologists have long experience with these processes, but it was not until Michael Schiffer called attention to their importance in moulding archaeological interpretation that archaeologists paid them serious attention. Today's archaeologists now know these processes as 'environmental formation processes'. When archaeologists excavate abandoned settlements they understand that the sites may have been affected by natural formation processes over many years. Nature does not stop having an impact on archaeological sites after they are abandoned, and archaeologists now realise the importance of nature in destroying and altering the deposits they study.

Site destruction by humans

Storms and earthquakes can have major, devastating impacts on archaeological sites, but perhaps the greatest threat to the world's archaeological resources comes from humanity. Site destruction caused by humans can be divided into three categories: scientific, unintentional and intentional.

All practising archaeologists know that when

they excavate a site they are in effect destroying it. Excavation forever mixes the soils, removes the artefacts, destroys the relationships between the artefacts and completely changes the character of a site's landscape. Site destruction is an unavoidable element of archaeological research. Archaeologists are well aware of this reality, and the destructive nature of excavation represents the main reason why they spend so much of their field time writing copious notes, drafting precise drawings and taking numerous pictures. One goal of the professional archaeologist is to provide as complete a record as possible of the site they have altered through excavation. With the advances being made in computer technology (see **computers**), archaeologists have begun to experiment with more sophisticated ways of collecting even more information from the sites they excavate.

The severe, destructive impact of excavation has led many archaeologists to develop ways to protect sites rather than to excavate them. Many archaeologists, stressing the monumental cultural and historical significance of some sites, have proposed 'saving' them until archaeological techniques get better. These forward-looking archaeologists acknowledge that future archaeologists will have even better methods of collecting information from fragile archaeological sites.

Many archaeological deposits can also be destroyed inadvertently by men and women who may live at a site after the earlier residents have moved away. At these 'multicomponent' (or multiple-occupation) sites, people of one historical period can dig pits, sweep the ground and even make collections of the ancient artefacts they find. These people do not set about consciously to destroy archaeological remains; they simply conduct their daily lives in ways that are familiar to them. When they need to dig a pit, they usually do it without a conscious regard for the archaeological deposits that may lie underneath. As a result, their actions can have a tremendous impact on the archaeological deposits on which they live. Nineteenth-century farmers who built their houses on ancient Native American mounds in the central USA (see **Native Americans**), or tenant farmers in **Ireland** who kept their cattle in ringforts (most of which date to the AD 600–900 period) provide excellent examples. Of course, it is quite possible

that the archaeologist investigating a multicomponent site may be interested in all the occupations, and then may be able to make a study of the processes of disturbance that have occurred. Archaeologists describe the effects of humans on sites as 'cultural formation processes'.

Without question, however, the purposeful destruction of archaeological sites is one of the most serious challenges to modern archaeology. The **looting** of important historical sites has an unfortunately long history that stretches back at least to the ancient robbing of Egyptian royal tombs. The looting of sites of interest to historical archaeologists occurs on both land and underwater.

Archaeological site destruction can be conducted by 'professional' looters, often called 'pot hunters' in the USA because of their desire to locate whole pieces of ancient pottery. These semi-professional looters often sell their finds to 'art' collectors, who then pass them on to eager buyers. Looters of this sort are not interested in the scientific value of the objects because they view them merely as commodities to be sold on the open market. Bottle hunters are perhaps the most prolific kind of looter to have an impact on nineteenth-century sites. These looters explore archaeological sites, often clandestinely, searching for privies; that may contain whole bottles that they can sell to antique dealers and collectors. These collectors use long metal probes to locate soft spots in the ground that may be buried prives and refuse pits. Once they find a soft spot, they dig for the bottles, in the process completely destroying the archaeological contexts and removing the artefacts.

In addition to looters who seek to sell their finds, avocational looters are also a problem. Many amateurs can be great assets to professional archaeologists because of their profound knowledge of an area or a region, and the best amateurs are committed to understanding archaeology and history. These concerned amateurs are generally motivated by a sincere desire to contribute to knowledge and to learn what they can about the past. Unfortunately, however, not all avocationalists are so nobly motivated. Others seek to obtain artefacts for their private collections. They use these 'buried treasures' to enrich their personal attachment to history, but in making these selfish collections they are destroying the archaeological remains, and removing valuable information. One of the ongoing challenges of professional archaeologists is to teach the looting avocational archaeologists that they are destroying sites for all time. Many professional organisations have joined with avocational groups to promote public education about archaeology.

Looting is, of course, also a major problem for underwater sites. Sport divers are always locating shipwrecks and, because it appears that no one actually owns them, it seems acceptable to 'salvage' their remains. Professional 'treasure salvors' constitute a major problem for underwater archaeologists because the salvors often have the financial resources and the time to locate and to loot important wreck sites. Many private investors, faced with the possibility of finding sunken treasure, are often eager to contribute funds to salvage operations in the hope that their investment may yield even greater riches. To combat the problem of underwater salvaging, some governments have developed underwater preserves, where it is illegal to remove objects from sunken ships. An example is the Fathom Five National Marine Park in Ontario, Canada, where twenty-two shipwrecks are protected.

Site destruction is also caused by the march of progress. As cities and towns expand, increasing numbers of archaeological sites are in danger of being destroyed by new construction projects. This kind of site destruction occurs both in urban contexts (as engineers building skyscrapers require extremely deep excavations for foundations) and in rural areas (as urban sprawl spreads in once-rural areas). Archaeologists involved in **cultural-resource management** face many of the challenges of progress on a daily basis, and through their efforts seek either to save as many sites as possible from the bulldozer or to recover as much information as possible before sites are destroyed forever.

Archaeologists must also contend with site vandalism. No easy answer exists either to explain or to discourage the senseless destruction of valuable cultural and historical sites and properties. Many professional archaeological societies have addressed the problem of vandalism, along with looting, and have generally decided that education provides the best cure for the problem. Many archaeologists around the world are experimenting with different ways to educate the public, including **museums**, **living museums**, site visits and educational programmes.

Further reading

Davis, G.E. (ed.) (1996) *Effects of Hurricane Andrew on Natural and Archaeological Resources: Big Cypress National Preserve, Biscayne National Park, Everglades National Park*, Denver: National Park Service.

Schiffer, M.B. (1987) *Formation Processes of the Archaeological Record*, Albuquerque: University of New Mexico Press.

CHARLES E. ORSER, JR

diaspora

'Diaspora' in simplest terms denotes the dispersion of people from their original homelands. Although the earliest use of the term generally referred to the dispersion and exile of Jews from biblical times and onwards, its application and definition have shifted significantly over the past twenty years. As diaspora-related scholarship continues to grow, competing conceptualisations of the diaspora have emerged. It is therefore difficult, if not impossible, to provide a single, overarching definition of diaspora that sufficiently encompasses all instances of the processes that lead to diasporic community formation. As a starting point, however, diaspora refers broadly to communities formed away from their homeland (whether real or imagined) through forced migration (for example refugee-ism, enslavement, exile or as a result of natural disasters or political upheaval) or voluntary migration. Many diasporic groups are further identified through their collective oppression and marginalisation in their new environments. Thus, the Jewish, African, Irish, Vietnamese, South Asian and Chinese dispersions, to name but a few examples, are referred to as 'diasporas' although their respective histories, experiences and reasons for migrating from their point of origin greatly differ.

Studies in disciplines such as anthropology, cultural studies, sociology and history on issues ranging from immigration to post-colonialism and transnationalism have added new dimensions to the concept of diaspora. In general, scholars use 'diaspora' in two ways: to define a displaced community or group using a series of traits, or to interpret the process by which diasporic groups form their own identities in response to a number of factors including racism, ethnocentrism, nationalism, cultural practices, locale, politics and their interactions with other groups. With regard to the first, in defining diasporic groups the following features are invariably used:

1 A collective memory and myths of their history of dispersal and of their homeland that is passed down to future generations.
2 A collective identity and recognition of a cultural heritage that is defined by their real or perceived relationships to their homeland.
3 a sense of alienation within the host society that serves as an impetus for group mobilisation, **resistance** and the maintenance of distinct identities.

Moreover, while diasporic groups variously recreate their cultures and traditions in their new settings, certain communities may envision an eventual return to their homeland, while more often than not many others forgo such a return. In contrast to this 'descriptive' approach of defining diasporic communities, others have considered the ways in which these groups have forged and reproduced ethnic, religious or racial identities within their host societies as a means to subvert their subjugation and exclusion.

Although historical archaeologists have not yet directly engaged in theorising about the formation of diasporic communities or the meaning of diaspora to any great extent, they have in fact researched various diasporic groups. Archaeological investigations of industrial complexes and boarding houses associated with European immigrant groups, African American-related sites and Chinese immigrant camps and neighbourhoods are some of the examples that could potentially contribute to diaspora studies.

Further reading

Orser, C.E., Jr (1998) 'The Archaeology of the African diaspora', *Annual Review of Anthropology* 27: 63–82.

MARIA FRANKLIN

disease

Diseases, or pathological conditions that adversely affect **health**, have been studied by historical archaeologists through several different lines of evidence. One of the primary means is through examination of human remains, especially skeletons. Excavations of **cemeteries** have been the main source of direct information about diseases in historic populations. Other lines of evidence used are documents, oral traditions and artefacts associated with disease. Research that focuses on skeletal evidence but uses all other available evidence to contextually interpret evidence of disease is called bioarchaeology. This approach is most associated with Clark Larsen.

The majority of disease research in historical archaeology has focused on the impacts of European-introduced Old World diseases on **Native Americans**. Archaeologists have found that, contrary to popular belief, the New World was not a disease-free paradise prior to European contact. Also, introduced diseases did not travel in unhindered waves across the continent, having uniform disastrous effects on all populations. The exact numbers of Native Americans who died as a result of introduced diseases is still being debated. It is clear from archaeological work done in the different regions of the USA that Native American responses to introduced disease were localised and variable, depending on such things as population density, sanitation and nutritional and overall health status prior to exposure.

Other archaeological research on disease in historic populations has looked at diseases and their impacts on Euro-American settlers and enslaved Africans. Although protected to a degree from some diseases because of previous exposure, Euro-American settlers and enslaved Africans also suffered and died frequently from diseases such as smallpox, yellow fever, malaria, cholera, pneumonia, tuberculosis and syphilis. Again, factors such as population density, sanitation and nutritional and overall health status greatly affected the degree of susceptibility to disease on the part of all of these populations.

Evidence of conditions such as osteoarthritis, syphilis (both congenital and venereal varieties), iron-deficiency anaemia, and non-specific infections (periosteal reactions) are often found in the skeletal remains of historic populations. Enamel hypoplasias, dental anomalies due to growth stoppage, are another direct indicator of past negative impacts on health. These are interpreted as a result of exposure to disease and/or inadequate nutrition during a period of the individual's life.

The presence or absence of skeletal evidence of disease is one way of assessing the health of a population. Ironically, deadly epidemic diseases, such as smallpox and plague, often do not leave direct physical evidence on the skeleton. This is because individuals do not live long enough for the disease to produce an impact on the skeleton. Instead of direct evidence on the skeletons of individuals, other evidence must be used to infer disease epidemics. Documents mentioning disease outbreaks, mass burials and unusual burial demographics are typical ways of inferring past epidemics. Other evidence of disease looked for by historical archaeologists includes parasites in human faeces recovered from privies, and artefacts associated with disease such as patent-medicine bottles, syringes and other medical or healing-associated artefacts.

Several issues complicate interpreting the disease responsible for outbreaks from documentary records. The symptoms described in accounts may fit several different known diseases. Also, the organisms that cause many diseases are subject to evolutionary forces, the same as any other living creature. Thus, a historically known disease may be an ancestral form of a modern disease, or even an entirely different disease organism unknown today. Descriptions themselves must be interpreted keeping in mind the differences in world view between today and the time the account was written. Details which a modern observer who follows the germ theory of disease spread would record, are likely to have been overlooked by an observer subscribing to the miasma theory or other theory of disease causation. Observers may also have only been on hand to record the events towards the end of an outbreak, and may apply moral or other interpretations of causality to the disease.

Some diseases, which are generally not fatal to modern industrial peoples, were deadly to historic populations. Lack of knowledge of effective treatments, inadequate nutrition and sanitation, lack of

care providers and even mental responses to disease such as depression contributed to mortality. Especially for Native American populations, population decline was an indirect as well as direct result of disease. Loss of food producers and providers, care givers and leaders, as well as, infertility are all effects of disease that impact those who managed to survive.

There are a few diseases found in archaeological sites that retain their virulence, requiring archaeologists to take precautions while excavating and handling site materials. Historical archaeologists working on privy sites, medical **institutions** and some cemeteries must take precautions against disease, especially if the sites are relatively recent. Other diseases that archaeologists must beware of while working in certain areas include valley fever, Hantavirus and Lyme disease.

Historical archaeology has added much to our knowledge of diseases and their impacts on past populations. With more data available from a broader range of sites and new analytical techniques becoming available, the future of this vein of research will bring even greater, more nuanced understanding.

Further reading

Kealhofer, L. (1996) 'The evidence for demographic collapse in California', in B.J. Baker and L. Kealhofer (eds) *Bioarchaeology of Native American Adaptation in the Spanish Borderlands*, Gainesville: University Press of Florida, pp. 56–92.

Larsen, C.S. (2000) *Skeletons in Our Closet: Revealing Our Past through Bioarchaeology*, Princeton: Princeton University Press.

—— (1994) 'In the wake of Columbus: Native population biology in the postcontact Americas', *Yearbook of Physical Anthropology* 37: 109–54.

DAVID T. PALMER

Dolly's Creek goldfield, Australia

Dolly's Creek is an abandoned goldfield west of Melbourne, Australia. Gold was discovered in the Australian colonies in 1851, triggering one of the world's largest gold rushes. One of the legacies of the gold rush, which eventually reached every

Australian state and territory, is a rich archaeological landscape of mine workings and deserted settlements. In the 1990s, Susan Lawrence conducted research at Dolly's Creek, which was settled during the 1860s.

The study combined traditional archaeological methodologies with approaches drawn from history, anthropology and geography. The resulting ethnographic history of the settlement highlighted lifeways on what contemporaries called a 'poor man's diggings', small fields where independent miners scratched a living without the need for large capital investment. While much work has been done on hard-rock mining sites and Chinese settlement sites on Australian goldfields, this study was one of the first to investigate English-speaking settlements and the archaeology of alluvial, or placer, mining, and the first to use gender as a major analytical category.

Four house sites were excavated during the fieldwork. The houses were one-roomed structures of canvas and bark with crude unshaped fireplaces of stone and mud mortar at one end. They were ephemeral dwellings, intended to be erected quickly on arrival at the field, and abandoned when a move to another field was necessary In contrast to the impermanent nature of the **architecture**, the interior fittings and **material culture** indicated that the homes were made as comfortable and respectable as possible. The fireplaces were coated with whitewash, and tables and mantelpieces were adorned with fashionable clocks and pressed glass dishes. Tablewares were a colourful collection of earthenware plates, teacups and saucers in a range of transfer-printed designs. Faunal remains suggested that a variety of meat was consumed, much of it probably raised locally.

The study revealed a subsistence mining strategy that was adopted not only at Dolly's Creek, but which also characterised other small Australian goldfields. This pattern of small-scale mining supplemented with income from other labouring jobs was reliant on the efforts of whole families. It succeeded because, unlike the North American goldfields where English-speaking women and children were rare, in Australia many families moved to the goldfields during and after the rush. At Dolly's Creek, over half the population were adult women and their young **children**. The

population structure resembled that of a modern, developing suburb, with many young families and few elderly people. With a 'Miner's Right', or licence, the holder was entitled to a small plot of land on which to build a house. On this land many women planted gardens of vegetables, fruit and flowers, raised chickens, goats and cows, and either sold or bartered any produce the family did not need itself. In this way the family's own diet was improved, and the income extended with the profits from the sale of the produce.

See also: Australia; mining archaeology

Further reading

Lawrence, S. (2000) *Dolly's Creek: An Archaeology of a Victorian Goldfield Community*, Melbourne: Melbourne University Press.

SUSAN LAWRENCE

domestic sites

Domestic sites are where people lived. A great deal of historical archaeology is devoted to the investigation of such sites in one form or another. Domestic sites might be contrasted with other types of sites such as military, industrial, commercial, institutional, landscape, transportation, cemetery or shipwreck sites. However, domestic sites are often closely associated with other types of sites. Military sites, for example, include domestic components, as do many industrial sites, particularly those of early or small-scale manufacturing. Analysis of activity areas is used to determine domestic spaces within working places like battlefield camps, farms and commercial waterfronts.

Some parts of landscapes, particularly utilitarian gardens, may be thought of as domestic spaces. Neighbourhoods as well as house lots may be appropriate scales for studying domestic life. Issues involve the use of space on domestic lots, including the placement of outbuildings and landscape features, and the separation or co-occurrence of work and domestic spaces within house lot, neighbourhood and community.

Domestic archaeological sites include the remains of residential occupations such as houses, outbuildings and associated privies, middens and sheet refuse deposits. Domestic sites, whether urban residence, rural village or farmstead sites, are pieces of a whole system that includes industrial sites and other locations of labour, military installations, institutions such as churches and schools, commercial sites and districts, and transportation networks. Looking at domestic sites as if they could stand alone diminishes their research value because the connections that could be made within local and regional economic and settlement systems are overlooked. Domestic sites are involved in most of historical archaeology's research domains: **ethnicity**; class (see **class, social**); **gender**; **health**; **food and foodways**; cultural contact, conflict and accommodation; **acculturation** and community studies. Questions of health, diet and **disease**, for example, may be investigated through analysis of parasites and seeds from the organic matter in privies as well as from artefacts such as patent-medicine **bottles**.

Domestic places are a logical place to investigate some manifestations of inequality. In a consumer society, the issues of consumer choice of goods and organisation of foodways are involved in the investigation of class and ethnicity. In **plantation archaeology**, domestic sites from big house to slave cabins are investigated for insight into economic and power relations among and between planters, overseers and the enslaved. Domestic spaces may serve both to control and to resist control, as described for a landscape of slavery by Terry Epperson. In many regions and time periods, domestic sites are the location of much of women's labour. Therefore, the issue of gender relations is often central, albeit not explicitly dealt with, at domestic sites. Issues of gender definition in the Victorian era have been addressed, for example, by Diana Wall for middle-class, domestic sites in New York City. Issues of workers' responses on the domestic front to the sweeping changes of the factory system have been investigated in both northern and southern settings in **Boott Mills** in Lowell, Massachusetts, and in **Harpers Ferry**, West Virginia.

Common types of artefact analysis have been developed for application to domestic sites, including the Miller index of economic scaling, which looks at relative costs of ceramics. Traditional expectations about **material culture** and status, that high status translates into more, or more expensive, household goods, are not always met, particularly when there are secondary economies that provide alternatives for the distribution of goods, or when mass-produced goods become so inexpensive that their cost becomes less meaningful. Historical archaeologists often use a straightforward but misleading correlation between status and the cost of goods, particularly ceramics. Especially with the mass production of ceramics, their cost is a minor part of a household budget and they are therefore not a clear indicator of socioeconomic status, which should be derived from other data.

Pattern recognition was conceived initially partly as a way to identify ethnic identities at domestic sites. In addition, the analysis of ceramics and other specific objects is frequently undertaken at domestic sites to find 'ethnic markers' for Chinese, African American, Spanish, Native American (see **Native Americans**), German, Dutch or other ethnicities. In some time periods and some places, material culture choices may be as poor an indicator of ethnicity as they are of social status. Access to national, regional and local markets can be revealed by household assemblages, but the mass-produced consumer goods present a difficult challenge for the archaeologist, who must try to decode subtle variations in the material record. One of the challenges for archaeologists working on domestic sites is to create methods for getting beyond stereotypical questions and analysis.

See also: backyard archaeology; consumer choice; consumption; domesticity; everyday life; food and foodways; household archaeology; ordinary people's culture; urban archaeology

Further reading

Epperson, T.W. (1990) 'Race and discipline of the plantation', *Historical Archaeology* 24(4): 29–36.

Rothschild, N.A. (1990) *New York City Neighborhoods, the Eighteenth Century,* New York: Academic Press.

Wall, D.D. (1994) *The Archaeology of Gender: Separating the Spheres in Urban America,* New York: Kluwer Academic/Plenum Press.

Wegars, P. (ed.) (1993) *Hidden Heritage, Historical*

Archaeology of the Overseas Chinese, Amityville, NY: Baywood.

BARBARA J. LITTLE

domesticity

Archaeological research on domesticity is a type of **gender** research analysing how material culture expressed nineteenth-century, middle-class gender ideologies that divided the world into woman's domestic sphere versus man's public sphere. The gender ideology of female domesticity in the private home began to develop in the early nineteenth century as middle-class men's workplaces became increasingly separated from homes.

In her 1994 book *The Archaeology of Gender: Separating the Spheres in Urban America*, Diana Wall used documentary and archaeological data to research whether middle-class women proactively developed the practices of domesticity as a source of female power *before* the increasing separation of men's workplaces from the home, or only later in reaction to this development. Wall researched this, feminist question with data on combined household and work sites of three middle-class families dating to the 1780s, *c.* 1805 and the 1820s in New York City. Wall found material evidence of ceramics involved in women's elaboration and ritualisation of meals and teas before men's workplaces were separated from the households at these three sites. Wall concluded that historic women were proactive in developing the practices of domesticity as a source of female power.

Feminist historians have found that in the first half of the nineteenth century most domestic manuals shifted from advocating patriarchal authority in the home to advocating that women rule the home using mother-love and women's higher morality. By 1850, domestic manuals written by middle-class men for the male head of household were eclipsed by the greater popularity of domestic manuals written by middle-class women for urban and suburban women aspiring to middle-class domesticity and gentility. Gender ideologies in domestic manuals written for women championed the importance of women's supposedly innate domestic roles and argued that the

'domestic sphere' should be controlled by women. In the dominant urban middle-class gender ideology, men were to have jobs in the public sphere that would support their families. Women were to stay home and raise children, clean, prepare meals and create a refuge for men after their day of work outside the home.

As women's domestic production for the market decreased due to the rise of factory production, especially of textiles and dairy products, nineteenth-century middle-class women developed a number of ideologies to raise the status of women's household maintenance, child-rearing and consumption roles. Women's domestic manuals championed a number of ideologies of domesticity that elevated women and their domestic sphere to a status equal to men and their public sphere. Feminist historians and historical archaeologists have researched domestic manuals and other literature to identify, define and find material expressions of the following major ideologies of domesticity: the 'Cult of True Womanhood' or 'Domesticity', the 'Cult of Republican Motherhood', the 'Cult of Real Womanhood', the 'Cult of Idle Domesticity', and 'Domestic Reform'. Each of these ideologies elaborated, changed the meaning of and elevated the status of some of women's domestic roles, and the domestic sphere. The Cult of Domesticity is related to the Cult of Gentility that prescribed ideal values and behaviours for genteel dining and social interaction.

The Cult of Domesticity or True Womanhood argued that women were innately more pious, pure and moral than men because women's domestic sphere of the home was separated from men's capitalistic, public sphere that condoned sinful practices such as usury. The belief in women's greater morality began to develop during the mid-eighteenth-century Great Awakening because women at home maintained traditional religious communitarian values and commandments such as 'neither a borrower nor a lender be', while most men drifted away from the church in developing conflicting capitalistic values that put individual competition for monetary success above the good of the community as a whole.

The dominant belief in women's superior morality increased during the second Great Awakening of the 1830s that transformed the puritan belief in women's original sinfulness (because Eve tasted and gave Adam the fruit of knowledge that led God to cast them out of Eden) into a Lockian belief in the original purity of children. In the dominant ideology espoused by the Cult of Domesticity of True Womanhood, true women retained their innate childhood purity, piety and morality in the domestic sphere of the home and did not directly participate in the sinful practices of men's capitalistic public sphere. When women went into the public sphere to buy household goods they were seen as carrying their purifying domestic influence into the public sphere.

Archaeologist Suzanne Spencer-Wood has researched how in their most popular mid-nineteenth-century domestic manual, Catherine Beecher and her famous sister Harriet Beecher Stowe used **material culture** to embody ideologies of domesticity and elevate the status of women's household roles to the equivalent of men's secular and religious careers. In their 1869 domestic manual, the Beecher sisters metaphorically raised the status of women to that of a 'sovereign of an empire', in analogy with Queen Victoria. This was a further development from an earlier domestic manual by Henry C. Wright that called the home 'the empire of the mother', as noted in Mary P. Ryan's 1982 book *The Empire of the Mother: American Writing about Domesticity 1830–1860*.

The Beecher sisters also made an analogy between housewives and ministers that was congruent with the Cult of Home Religion started by Reverend Horace Bushnell. In the Cult of Home Religion, the status of housework was elevated by viewing women as ministers of the home who attained high status through self-sacrifice in performing services for their family flock. In the Cult of Home Religion, women performed family religious services, ideally using a small round table and Bible in a cruciform-shaped house with gothic trimming, doors, furniture and niches for religious statues. The Cult of Home Religion was supported by the evangelical Christian belief that women were innately more pious and moral than men.

Catherine Beecher's domestic manual of 1837 elaborated and raised the status of child-rearing through the Cult of Republican Motherhood, which pointed to the critical importance of women as rearers of the next generation of leaders of the US republic. This ideology raised the status of child-rearing from a natural female role subsidiary to household production into a complex role that was analysed into scientific practices and material culture for producing higher achieving children.

Upper-class women developed the ideology of Idle Domesticity in which a woman's main role was as the manager of household servants and the decorative social secretary, displaying and promoting the high status of husband and family through elaborate dress and expensive china, displayed in elaborate multi-course Victorian dinners, ideally prepared and served by servants or slaves. Archaeologist Robert Jameson has researched the ideal prescribed material expressions of rules of etiquette for high-Victorian dinners in his chapter entitled 'Purity and power at the Victorian dinner party' in Ian Hodder's 1987 edited volume *The Archaeology of Contextual Meanings*.

Archaeologists have researched both how ideologies of domesticity were expressed through material culture, and to what extent actual material practices have differed from ideal behaviours prescribed in the dominant gender ideology. Diana Wall researched how mid-nineteenth-century middle-class women ideologically raised their status by materially elaborating their domestic roles. Diana Wall and Robert Fitts each found some diversity in the ways middle-class women materially expressed their domesticity. Some used expensive gilt- and floral-decorated porcelain tea sets for secular competitive status display, while others used white-panelled gothic ceramics that symbolised a religious orientation to communal family meals. Gothic ceramics expressing the sanctity of the home and religious communitarian values are both congruent with the Beecher sisters' elevation of women's status to ministers of the home in the Cult of Home Religion. Suzanne Spencer-Wood has discussed the possibility that floral-decorated porcelain tewares could symbolize women's closeness to nature and God that gave them their superior morality and status in the Cult of Domesticity. Spencer-Wood and Fitts have each suggested that flowerpots found by archaeologists may symbolize domestic sanctity, since potted plants were advocated in the Beecher sisters' domestic manual. Spencer-Wood also analysed how the Beecher sisters' manual used material culture with nature motifs as well as gothic motifs to symbolize the purity and sanctity of the domestic sphere and women's superior morality in their role as ministers in the Cult of Home Religion.

Further reading

Fitts, R.K. (1999) 'The archaeology of middle-class domesticity and gentility in Victorian Brooklyn', *Historical Archaeology* 33(1): 39–62.

Spencer-Wood, S.M. (1999) 'The world their household: Changing meanings of the domestic sphere in the nineteenth century', in P.M. Allison (ed.) *The Archaeology of Household Activities: Gender Ideologies, Domestic Spaces and Material Culture*, London: Routledge, pp. 162–89.

—— (1996) 'Feminist historical archaeology and the transformation of American culture by domestic reform movements, 1840–1925', in L.A. De Cunzo and B.L. Herman (eds) *Historical Archaeology and the Study of American Culture*, Knoxville: University of Tennessee Press, pp. 397–446.

Wall, D.D. (1994) *The Archaeology of Gender: Separating the Spheres in Urban America*, New York: Plenum Press.

—— (1991) 'Sacred dinners and secular teas: Constructing domesticity in mid-19th-century New York', *Historical Archaeology* 25(4): 69–81.

Young, L. (1998) 'The material construction of gentility: A context for understanding the role of women in early nineteenth-century sites', in M. Casey, D. Donlon, J. Hope and S. Wellfare (eds) *Redefining Archaeology: Feminist Perspectives*, Canberra: ANH University Publications.

SUZANNE M. SPENCER-WOOD

domination

Domination is one-half of a dialectic used to understand the material residues of the negotiation of **power** – its antithesis is **resistance**. This dialectic occurs in social contexts in which there is an inequitable distribution of resources; domination occurs when those agents within the system that control access to material goods use their social position to deny other agents access to such goods. Domination may be directly expressed materially through such phenomena as sumptuary laws restricting the **consumption** of specific goods or through the raw exercise of sanctioned violence through executions, mutilations, confinement in a variety of **institutions**, etc. Domination may also be expressed more subtly, through the construction and reproduction of ideologies (see **ideology**) that may mask or obfuscate the real nature of social relations.

Mark Leone was one of the first historical archaeologists to use the concept of domination directly in his work. In his famous study of the William Paca garden in **Annapolis**, Maryland, USA, Leone concluded that the manipulation of formal landscapes by elite members of society was part of a larger strategy of ideological domination, in which those elites reinforced their dominant position in society by demonstrating their ability not only to own land, but to manipulate that land using tricks of visual perspective. Leone later built upon this work to suggest that such seemingly disparate artefacts as garden landscapes, globes, clocks and other scientific instruments were used by elites to demonstrate that the natural world was hierarchically ordered, hence justifying the social hierarchy at which they stood at the apex. Randy McGuire and LouAnn Wurst have examined how grave markers in Broome County, New York, were similarly used to materially express ideologies of domination; McGuire's study expanded to include a consideration of how industrial and domestic architecture in Binghamton, New York, was incorporated into such an ideology.

A number of scholars have examined domination through the material processes by which societies have been fragmented into self-interested individuals. Following the ideas of the French philosopher Michel Foucault, historical archaeologists have examined this process through the creation of discipline, which is seen as a variant of domination. At the heart of this type of investigation is the examination of material cultures of surveillance, and how such material cultures create individuals who are constantly aware that they are under surveillance; thus, they will self-correct their behaviour in order to avoid possible corporal reactions from those in positions of authority. Terry Epperson has examined how panoptic surveillance was built into the landscapes of Virginia plantations; similar themes in a variety of contexts have been investigated by Paul Shackel (industrial Harpers Ferry), James Delle (Jamaican coffee plantations), Charles Orser (tenant farms in the US South), Paul Mullins (in the construction of African American consumer culture) and Elizabeth Kryder-Reid (in Chesapeake formal gardens). All suggest that domination is a key factor in the reproduction of capitalist social relations.

Further reading

Delle, J.A., Leone, M.P. and Mullins, P.R. (1999) 'Archaeology of the modern state: European colonialism', in G. Barker (ed.) *Companion Encyclopedia of Archaeology*, London: Routledge, pp. 1107–59.

Leone, M.P. and Potter, P.B. (eds) (1999) *Archaeologies of Capitalism*, New York: Kluwer Academic/ Plenum Press.

—— (eds) (1988) *The Recovery of Meaning: Historical Archaeology in the Eastern United States*, Washington, DC: Smithsonian Institution Press.

McGuire, R.H. and Paynter, R. (eds) (1991) *The Archaeology of Inequality*, Oxford: Basil Blackwell.

Paynter, R. (1989) 'The Archaeology of equality and inequality', *Annual Review of Anthropology* 18: 369–99.

JAMES A. DELLE

dress

Dress subsumes a range of garments and accessories under one general title. Since textiles do not preserve well in most archaeological contexts, archaeologists rely on other parts of dress to understand what people wore in the past. Archaeologists examine portions of garments or accessories that do survive. These other parts of dress fall into five basic categories: clothing parts, fasteners, jewellery, hair-related items and miscellaneous accessories. As a category of **material culture**, dress artefacts have not been widely investigated by historical archaeologists, though there are some notable studies, and there is great potential for further research.

Of all artefact classes, clothing artefacts – which include textiles, leather, metallic thread and hem weights – are the most direct evidence of garments worn in the past. Though complete garments rarely survive, textile fragments are occasionally preserved. Archaeologists use textiles and leather, along with thread and other trims, both to reconstruct entire garments and identify the status of the individual, his or her adherence to fashion ideals of the period and the availability and use of types of textiles in a given region.

Fasteners – buckles, **buttons**, cuff links, hooks and eyes, pins and studs – are the most frequently recovered dress-related artefacts on archaeological sites. Of these, buttons are the most common. Buckles were used to fasten shoes, breeches at the knee, stocks, gloves and other kinds of garments, and the form of the buckle varies accordingly. Hooks, eyes and pins were used for edge-to-edge closure on garments. Cuff links, or sleeve buttons as they were called in the seventeenth through early nineteenth centuries, were also used to close shirts at the wrist, and studs fastened clothing at the collar as well as down the front of shirts. All of these classes of artefacts change through time, as do the materials used to make them, and reflect the technology used in their manufacture and the status of site inhabitants.

The category of jewellery includes **beads**, bracelets, brooches, clasps, earrings, necklaces, pendants and rings, among other items. Often, jewellery parts – primarily links and clasps – are recovered archaeologically and identification of these components is difficult, as the basis for comparison tends to be confined to high-style objects in museum collections. Archaeological analysis is beginning to identify materials worn by varying socioeconomic classes.

Hair-related artefacts – including aigrettes, barrettes, bodkins, combs and wig accessories – remain the most ephemeral of the dress-related artefact classes, as they are often made of feathers, thin wire and other fine materials that degrade quickly in archaeological contexts. Combs, including those used to adorn the head and to maintain hairstyles and those used for grooming, and wig curlers, however, are frequently recovered. Bodkins – a type of sewing implement – were also worn as fancy head adornments. Excavated examples include a bodkin recovered at the late eighteenth- and early nineteenth-century Mill Pond site in

Boston, Massachusetts, USA, and one recovered at **Jamestown**, Virginia.

Many minor dress accessories do not fit into any of the aforementioned categories, including purses, fans, spurs, insignia, watches, watch fobs, watch keys and chatelaines. Watches and their associated accessories were fashionable luxury items in the seventeenth and eighteenth centuries, and became popular and widely available in the nineteenth century. Watch fobs were hung with accessories besides watches – keys, seals and small medals – all of which are recovered on archaeological sites. Similarly, women's chatelaines supported watches, sewing tools and accessories.

Dress has not been extensively explored by historical archaeologists, although there are some notable exceptions. Excavations by the Museum of London have annotated all manner of accessories of dress from the medieval period. Ivor Noël Hume employed dress accessories found at **Martin's Hundred**, Virginia, such as buttons and a wire head spring used to hold a linen cap in place, to identify and expand the profiles of individuals at the site.

Margaret T. Ordoñez and Linda Welters analysed textiles recovered from a seventeenth-century privy in Boston, Massachusetts. This study is one of few archaeological investigations to specifically examine dress. The classification of the textiles showed that the majority of the recovered fragments were high-quality materials – silk fabrics and ribbons. These fragments provided unusual information about seventeenth-century garment construction, particularly trims, edges and tailoring. The textiles provide insight into a variety of kinds of garments – hoods, dresses, undergarments, coats, breeches and stockings – worn in the seventeenth century. This study points to the utility and potential of such analysis of dress.

Jeffery A. Butterworth's analysis of shoes from Boston privies provided insight into common and uncommon types of footwear in the seventeenth, eighteenth and nineteenth centuries. His study of these shoes elucidated features of everyday footwear in colonial and post-colonial Boston and provides information about local shoe manufacture.

Grace Ziesing explored the kinds of clothing worn by workers at the **Boott Mills**, in Lowell, Massachusetts, by examining artefactual evidence of clothing. Her insightful analysis discussed the less expensive adornments worn by mill workers as they tried to emulate elite fashions. She presented the common forms of beads, buttons, studs, combs, jewellery and leather found in Lowell in nineteenth-century deposits.

In order to identify artefacts of dress on archaeological sites, archaeologists find evidence in a variety of sources. Comparative examples from museum collections are used extensively. Other sources include visual images from portraits, prints and retail catalogues, and documentary descriptions from wills, probate inventories, poetry, diaries and court records.

Further reading

Butterworth, J. (1998) 'Forming the past', *Historical Archaeology* 32(3): 91–8.

Egan, G. and Pritchard, F. (1991) *Dress Accessories c.1150–c.1450: Medieval Finds from Excavations in London: 3*, London: The Stationery Office.

Ordoñez, M.T. and Welters, L. (1998) 'Textiles from the seventeenth-century privy at the Cross Street back lot site', *Historical Archaeology* 32(3): 81–90.

Ziesing, G.H. (1990) 'Personal effects from the backlots of Boott Mills corporate housing in Lowell, Massachusetts: A gender study in historical archaeology', master's thesis, Boston University.

CAROLYN L. WHITE

Dutch colonialism

After 1585, the Dutch Republic soon controlled a **trade** empire from the West Indies to Indonesia. The **Dutch East India Company**, founded in 1602, established posts and settlements in the Moluccas and Java. In 1609, the Dutch claimed the Hudson Valley in North America, named New Netherland and administered by the West India Company chartered in 1621. Between 1630 and 1637, the Dutch acquired Brazil, Curaçao, St Eustatius and **Elmina**, Ghana. Settlement at the Cape of Good Hope, **South Africa**, occurred in 1652. Dutch 'colonies', however, varied from small communities of merchants and craftsmen in foreign cities to large areas over which political control was exercised.

In 1871, Norwegian Elling Carlsen discovered ruins of the wooden refuge constructed by the Barents and Van Heemskerck expedition on Nova Zembla during the winter of 1596 and 1597. Carlsen's collection of artefacts left by the explorers aroused great interest in **Amsterdam**. In 1993 and 1995, Pieter Floore and JaapJan Zeeberg returned to the site and retrieved artefacts that indicated a surprising degree of elegance and material comfort. Wooden timbers brought to Moscow in 1992 have been identified as a fragment of the Barents' ship.

In 1878, a Dutch expedition to the site of the Dutch whaling village of Smeerenburg (*c.* 1618–60) at the north-west corner of Spitsbergen found extensive evidence of the site and human remains. A century later, Bas Kist returned to survey what remained. Louwrens Hacquebord recorded a gun platform, seven tryworks and seventeen houses, of which seven were excavated. Well-preserved organic remains provide insight into how the Dutch adapted to the arctic environment. Further excavations in 1998 and 1999 elsewhere on Spitsbergen identified a 1618 Dutch whaling station site.

Excavation from 1984 to 1986 and in 1989 of Deshima, the community to which the Dutch were restricted at Nagasaki, Japan, between 1640 and 1854, defined site limits, revealed storehouse foundations and pits filled with debris from the great fire of 1798, and uncovered a ceramic kiln and many artefacts. **Ceramics** include Chinese and Vietnamese imports; some **porcelain** bears the East India Company VOC monogram. Minoru Nagamatsu of Nagasaki has reported this work.

Evidence of Dutch merchant and craftsman communities in other cities remains to be studied. Ceramic sherds unearthed between 1954 and 1961 in **Southwark** and illustrated and described by Ivor Noël Hume in 1977, for example, represent early seventeenth-century Dutch potters living in London. Tin-glazed majolica kiln wasters were made apparently by craftsmen using exactly the same technology, decoration and material as used in manufacturing majolica in the Netherlands.

While extensive terrestrial archaeological research on Dutch colonialism has occurred in Africa, North America and the West Indies, colonial sites exist elsewhere. Excavations as early as 1935 at Kota Linggi, a Dutch fort in Malacca (1757–9), produced East India Company artefacts. Much research has focused on Indonesian prehistory; some of this has generated collections useful in studying Dutch colonialism. From 1997 through 1999, Peter Lape studied pre-1621 village sites and settlement patterns in the Banda Islands. In 1999, he excavated in the courtyard of the former East India Company governors' residence in Banda Neira; in a well-stratified sequence, upper levels produced Dutch colonial material, while lower levels dated to the fifteenth and sixteenth centuries. In Jakarta, meanwhile, excavations in the Pasar Ikan (Fish Market) produced primarily nineteenth-century colonial material.

Pieter Floore and Carmel Schrire excavated on the Indian Ocean island of Mauritius in 1998 and 1999. At the site of Dutch Fort Frederik Hendrik (1638–1710), later occupied by a French structure, they uncovered a palisade trench with charred posts. Early in 2000, Ranjith Jayasena began excavations in Sri Lanka at Katuwana, a Dutch frontier fort (*c.* 1680–1803).

As early as the 1920s, artefacts were collected during building projects at **Cape Town**, South Africa. Dutch coffin burials, in the 1960s, and a portion of a buried eighteenth-century ship, in 1970, were excavated. Programmes for **rescue archaeology** and the study of Dutch colonists' domestic **culture** were initiated. In 1983, excavations near Cape Town Castle revealed part of the 1652 Dutch fort; in 1990 and 1991, work directed by Gabeba Abrahams produced many artefacts, in addition to a burial. Martin Hall, Antonia Malan and others excavated and analysed material from late Dutch colonial **domestic sites**, such as a Bree Street home in western Cape Town (1788–1817). Meanwhile, from 1984 until 1987, Carmel Schrire and Cedric Poggenpoel uncovered remains of the Dutch stone-walled fort **Oudepost** I (1669–1732), located at the tip of southern Africa.

In Ghana in 1975, Merrick Posnansky excavated the site of Fort Ruychaver, the only Dutch trading post established in the Gold Coast hinterland, confirming the temporary character of the fort (1655–9). Few European items were found. Near **Elmina** Castle, on the coast, David Calvocoressi in 1977 excavated one of several small, protective nineteenth-century Dutch forts. In 1986, Christopher DeCorse began excavations in the Old Town site adjacent to the Castle. Destroyed in 1873, the site produced a variety of local and imported artefacts, including ceramics, Dutch and English pipes (see **pipes, smoking**), and US medicine **bottles**. As in South Africa, excavations at Elmina have produced large amounts of Chinese porcelain.

Individuals including William Beauchamp began serious archaeological study of Dutch colonialism in New Netherland in the nineteenth century with research on European trade artefacts from seventeenth-century Indian sites. Charles Wray, Bert Salwen and others continued these studies in the twentieth century. Excavations in seventeenth-century Dutch domestic sites occurred as early as 1935, but documentary associations and dates were not established. Excavations commenced in Kingston, New York, originally a stockaded Dutch town laid out in 1658 near the Hudson River, when Paul Huey in 1969 excavated a 'mill house' site dating from 1661 at the corner bastion of the town stockade wall. In 1970, Bert Salwen and Sarah Bridges excavated an area containing Dutch artefacts and stockade post holes on the line of the east stockade wall. During 1970 and 1971 in Albany, Huey uncovered a portion of the site of Fort Orange, built in 1624, revealing the remains of four structures, the main entrance pathway and a cobblestone-lined moat. Astounding amounts of seventeenth-century Dutch material were retrieved, including majolica and faience, glass roemers and beakers, **beads**, gunflints and part of a wheel lock. There were also wampum beads and Indian pottery fragments. Wampum, made of shell and used as currency, was greatly valued for trade with the Native Americans. Excavations continued in the 1970s in Beverwyck (Albany), the town established near Fort Orange in 1652. Beyond Fort Orange and Beverwyck was the separate Colonie of Rensselaerswyck, an agricultural enterprise commenced in 1630. At least four seventeenth-century farm sites have been studied, including Crailo State Historic Site and the Schuyler Flatts site, under development by the Town of Colonie as a historic park. Major rescue excavations in the 1980s and 1990s in Albany revealed features and structures from pre-1664 Beverwyck.

In New Amsterdam (**New York City**), 150 miles to the south, Nan Rothschild and Diana Wall in 1979 and 1980 excavated the 1642 Stadt Huys site. Nearby, Joel Grossman in 1983 and 1984 uncovered foundations of a West India Company warehouse, a cistern built of yellow brick and mid-seventeenth-century privies. Many artefacts like those found at Fort Orange were retrieved, including notched pipe stems reworked to produce small whistles or flutes. Overall, ceramics recovered from Dutch sites in New Netherland represent a consumption pattern different from that at colonial sites of this period in South Africa. Rare in New Netherland, Chinese porcelain was common in South Africa. In South Africa, tin-glazed ceramics were relatively rare, while in South Africa but not in New Netherland fragments of oriental **stoneware** storage pots called martevans are common. The Cape settlement has abundant evidence, studied by Stacey Jordan, of coarse red-bodied utility **earthenware** pottery, locally manufactured by East India Company potters. Meta Janowitz in 1993 analysed dietary evidence in New Amsterdam, finding the diet remained largely traditional, with the addition of Indian items. Fort Orange occupants relied on venison traded by Indians, but in New Netherland, and especially at Fort Orange, the Dutch succeeded remarkably well at importing and re-establishing their rich material culture from home.

In **South America**, **Brazil** has many sites dating from the Dutch occupation (1630–54). Excavations occurred as early as the 1980s in the site of the Port of Nazaré da Capitania de Pernambuco, built after 1630. Excavations also occurred in the fort of Cabadelo in the State of Paraíba in north-east Brazil, a site greatly enlarged during Dutch occupation. Ulysses Pernambuco de Mello published information about clay pipes from these sites. Beginning in 1992, Pedro Paulo Funari and Charles Orser explored sites in **Palmares**, the north-eastern Brazilian runaway slave community adjacent to the area of Dutch control. Although the Dutch repeatedly attacked the settlements in the 1640s, Palmares was situated to maintain a constant interaction with Dutch colonials and others.

In the Caribbean, in 1981 Norman Barka and Edwin Dethlefsen began a long-term research programme on St Eustatius, locating Dutch colonial warehouse, residential and institutional sites, ruins of plantations (see **plantation archae-ology**) with slave sites and sugar mills, offshore submerged cobblestone quays and many other resources. Excavations were conducted in Oranjestad 'Lower Town' rubbish pits and warehouse sites. In the Upper Town, a building complex from the eighteenth and nineteenth centuries and, near Fort Oranje, three building foundations and deep basements filled with enormous quantities of eighteenth- and nineteenth-century artefacts and faunal material were excavated. In 1994, excavations began at Concordia, the eighteenth-century estate of a wealthy Dutch governor. In 1998, several structures were exposed, including remains of a large sugar-boiling house. Near another was a shallow late eighteenth-century midden, perhaps left by slaves.

Jan Baart, assisted by Meta Janowitz, excavated in 1989 at Fort Amsterdam on the island of St Maarten, a Dutch colony since 1648, revealing seventeenth-century Dutch as well as Spanish deposits. Clay pipes included a Dutch 'Sir Walter Raleigh' pipe and pipes crudely carved from red and yellow bricks. Excavating briefly in Philipsburg, Baart and Janowitz revealed an extensive nineteenth-century deposit with many fragments of ceramics produced by the Regout Aardewerkfabriek of Maastricht. Barka began surveys of eighteenth- and nineteenth-century sugar plantation sites on St Maarten in 1989 and completed in 1993 the first comprehensive island-wide report on sites visible above ground. In 1999, excavations in the sugar works and mill complex of Belvedere Plantation revealed fill deposits from as early as the mid-eighteenth century.

On the island of Curaçao in 1990, Jay Haviser and Nadia Simmons-Brito surveyed the downtown Punda district of Willemstad, uncovering ceramics and sequences of numerous yellow-brick floors. Excavations along the Handelskade during 1993 renovations uncovered many seventeenth- through nineteenth-century square glass bottles and other artefacts, while in St Anna Bay excavations have been carried out on the wreck of a Dutch frigate that sank in 1778.

Studies of East India Company shipwreck sites, scattered from Indonesia to the coasts of Great Britain, began in the 1960s. As of 1996, at least thirty-eight wreck locations dating between 1606 and 1795 had been found. Some of the most noteworthy are those of the *Batavia* (1629) and *Vergulde Draeck* (1656), both sunk off western **Australia** and both discovered in 1963, the *Mauritius* (1606), on the African coast, and the *Amsterdam* (1749), wrecked on the coast of England. The immense number of wrecks in the Straits of Malacca has been declared 'an archeological resource that is probably one of the largest in the world'. Other probable Dutch shipwrecks have been found in the western hemisphere. Jerome Hall excavated a 1650s wreck in the Dominican Republic, finding a cargo of Dutch faience and of clay pipes made in Amsterdam. In the seaport of Bahia, Brazil, Robert Marx found a wreck in 1981 he identified as the *Hollandia*, Piet Heyn's flagship sunk in 1624. Important artefacts were displayed in Rio de Janeiro, but the rest were sold at auction.

Further reading

Abrahams, G. (1985) *The Archaeological Potential of Central Cape Town*, as *Munger Africana Library Notes* 77/78, Pasadena: California Institute of Technology.

Falk, L. (ed.) (1991) *Historical Archaeology in Global Perspective*, Washington, DC: Smithsonian Institution Press.

Huey, P.R. (1988) 'The archeology of colonial New Netherland', in E. Nooter and P.U. Bonomi (eds) *Colonial Dutch Studies: An Interdisciplinary Approach*, New York: New York University Press, pp. 52–77.

Posnansky, M. and DeCorse, C.R. (1986) 'Historical archaeology in sub-Saharan Africa: A review', *Historical Archaeology* 20(1): 1–14.

Schrire, C. (1995) *Digging through Darkness: Chronicles of an Archaeologist*, Charlottesville: University Press of Virginia.

PAUL R. HUEY

Dutch East India Company

The Dutch East India Company (Verenigde Oostindische Compagnie, or VOC) was a private trading organisation with an intercontinental scope. For two centuries, from 1602 to 1795, the company developed and maintained a shipping network between Europe and **Asia** as well as shipping links within the intra-Asiatic trade. The VOC is of particular interest for historical archaeology. First, the activities of the VOC are related to the process of globalisation, which is an essential theme in studies of the pre-modern age. Second, the VOC offers a strong case of integrated historical and material culture studies.

Due to the geographical range of its long-distance trade, the company was structured in two entities. The largest was its overseas network of some 300 settlements in Africa, the Middle East and Asia with Batavia (Jakarta) as government centre. Many were trading stations with a local representative, but large-scale settlements were developed, which included **fortifications**, **churches**, hospitals, schools and other urban components. Personnel in Asia numbered about 25,000 in the eighteenth century. The smaller entity was its homeland where the VOC had branches ('chambers') in six cities (**Amsterdam**, Hoorn, Enkhuizen, Rotterdam, Delft and Middelburg). Each branch had its own administration, warehouses and shipyards, and followed an independent policy, but all were centrally managed by a board of seventeen directors, who also controlled all overseas activities. The most important branch was Amsterdam, where the company's headquarters were located.

The historiography of the VOC was formed under the influence of different prevailing ideologies regarding **Dutch colonialism**. Both the imperialistic and the anti-colonialist view in the nineteenth and twentieth centuries stamped a negative image of the role of the company in Asia. With the healing of the post-colonial trauma, however, attention shifted to the functioning of the VOC as an early example of intercontinental manufacture, trade and transport. Simultaneously, historians found the VOC archive to be a valuable source of information on the overseas societies where the company was settled. These Dutch historical accounts yielded rich data on the ethnography, anthropology, linguistics or natural and social history of the Asian territories and their indigenous populations.

Since the 1960s, the study of the VOC, which was traditionally based on written and iconographic sources, was stimulated by the availability of a new source of information, the shipwrecks of sunken Dutch East Indiamen. These **VOC shipwrecks** produced large quantities of material records directly reflecting the practical aspects of the shipping activities. By confronting archaeological finds and written sources from the company's archive, views could be developed that were not limited to the particular individual vessel, but that also touched upon more general subjects, such as the infrastructure for ship production and the intricate network of suppliers. Following the (underwater) archaeology of VOC wrecks, interest was sparked in the material remains of terrestrial settlements. The archaeology of fortifications and other VOC sites covers multiple aspects, for example military architecture, urban development and indigenous–European contact.

See also: Dutch colonialism

Further reading

Boxer, C.R. (1977) *The Dutch Seaborne Empire 1600–1800*, London: Hutchinson.

Bruijn, J.R., Gaastra, F.S. and Schöffer, I. (1987) *Dutch-Asiatic Shipping in the 17th and 18th Centuries*, vols 2 and 3, The Hague: Martinus Nijhoff.

—— (1979) *Dutch–Asiatic Shipping in the 17th and 18th centuries*, vol. 1, The Hague: Martinus Nijhoff.

JERZY GAWRONSKI

E

earthenware

Many European post-medieval ceramic (see **ceramics**) traditions were based upon earthenwares, which were fired at between 900–1,150 °C. Clays fuse at these temperatures, but do not completely vitrify, which means that earthenware pots are not impervious to liquids and, without the use of a glaze, will absorb any liquid contents. Vitrification will occur at 1,200–1,300 °C, resulting in a **stoneware** body that is impervious to liquid. Vitrification could occur unevenly in early kilns, and many earthenwares show signs of having been accidentally over-fired.

Every Western European country and every region had its own coarse earthenware traditions, producing utilitarian forms necessary for daily life. Dishes and milk pans, bowls, cups, jugs, porringers, chamber pots, storage jars and three-legged cooking pots known as pipkins were common types made primarily for a local market. Some well-situated industries secured an export trade, especially in those countries with colonial interests in the Caribbean (see **Caribbean archaeology**) and the Americas. Green-glazed earthenwares from northern France are commonplace in French colonies, while Dutch redwares were far more widely used. English coarse wares that reached North America during the seventeenth century included Border Wares, from the area around Farnborough, south of London, and gravel-tempered wares from Devon. Typical eighteenth-century English coarse wares included black lead-glazed storage jars, dishes, pans and jugs. These were made over much of the country, but those commonly found in the USA are thought to originate from the potteries of south Lancashire or Buckley in North Wales.

Other common seventeenth- and eighteenth-century English earthenwares include black lead-glazed drinking vessels and slipwares, both of which were made at many centres. Slipwares – slip-decorated earthenwares – were important products of major industries in Essex, north Staffordshire, Bristol, Donyatt and north Devon. The potters of Barnstaple and Bideford in Devon and Donyatt in Somerset mainly produced slipwares with sgraffito decoration, whereby a pattern is cut through a covering slip coat to reveal the clay body beneath. The others specialised in wares decorated with trailed slip. All of these centres exported their wares to North America.

Most coarse earthenwares had a lead glaze that derived its colour from iron in the pot's clay body, from an iron-rich slip coat, or from colorants – such as iron, manganese or copper oxides – deliberately added to the glaze. Most earthenwares were once-fired – that is, they were thrown, dried, decorated (if at all), glazed and fired without a separate biscuit firing. However, some of the European slipwares were twice-fired, a feature shared by the slipwares of north Devon. Significantly, most coarse earthenwares were made from local clays.

An important class of European earthenware, with its origins in the Middle Ages, was tin-glazed earthenware, 'majolica' or 'delftware'. This was a more refined earthenware, generally twice-fired, with a lead glaze opacified by the addition of tin oxide. The effect is of a fine ceramic with a good quality all-over glaze. Some sixteenth-century Italian majolicas achieved a high status on account of their elaborate painted decoration; Spanish majolicas were frequently decorated with metallic lustres. Dutch delftwares tended to have blue painted decoration, and a growing fashion for Chinese-style designs set the trend for 'delftware' decoration from the later seventeenth century. Delftwares were passable imitations of Chinese porcelain which was becoming fashionable during the later seventeenth century. In England, delftware manufacture had commenced by the 1620s. London was the main centre of delftware manufacture, but factories were established in Bristol, Wincanton, Liverpool, Dublin, Belfast and Glasgow.

Tin-glazed earthenwares were an important European export during the seventeenth and eighteenth centuries. French 'faience' and Spanish 'majolica' are mostly found in French and Spanish colonies, while Dutch and English wares were more widespread in the Caribbean and North America until the late eighteenth century. These wares were ideal vehicles for painted decoration, but had the disadvantages of not being hard wearing and not suitable for hot liquids; they occur frequently as pharmaceutical wares.

While delftwares satisfied a desire for white wares, the pottery factories of **Stoke-on-Trent** began to compete around 1720 with more durable white salt-glazed **stoneware** tea and table wares. At the same time, they introduced new refined earthenwares in a range of colours; these were wheel-thrown and lathe-turned, twice-fired and lead-glazed. The earliest of these – in production by the early 1720s – were glazed red earthenwares, misleadingly referred to as 'Astbury' wares after one of many Staffordshire manufacturers. Agate wares, with bodies formed of different coloured clays, were introduced around 1730, and after 1750 we find refined black glazed earthenware tea and coffee wares among most factories' products; the name 'Jackfield' ware, used for the black wares, is another misleading term.

By the 1760s, **creamware** had become the dominant earthenware, setting a fashion for white earthenwares that was to continue into the twentieth century. However, some refined earthenwares with coloured bodies remained in production throughout. Lustre decoration of 1800–50 is frequently on red-bodied wares, while black-glazed tea wares re-emerged in the late nineteenth century with overglaze painted decoration in aesthetic style; these, too, are referred to as 'Jackfield', although they were made at many British manufacturing centres. Yellow wares, with buff bodies, beneath a lead glaze became common in the 1820–60 period, especially as kitchen and toilet wares.

The need for domestic coarse earthenwares never disappeared, and manufacturers continued to meet these needs. Later coarse wares are little changed from their seventeenth- and early eighteenth-century predecessors. The export of these declined, however, as fine wares monopolised the trade, and as local needs were met by local manufacturers. In the USA, for example, red earthenwares developed a distinctive style, influenced greatly by the potting traditions of English, Dutch and German immigrants.

Further reading

Brears, P.C.D. (1971) *The English Country Pottery, Its History and Techniques*, Newton Abbott: David & Charles.

Coleman-Smith, R. and Pearson, T. (1988) *Excavations in the Donyatt Potteries*, Chichester, Sussex: Phillimore.

Grant, A. (1983) *North Devon Pottery: The Seventeenth Century*, Exeter: University of Exeter.

Grigsby, L.B. (1993) *English Slip-Decorated Earthenware at Williamsburg*, Williamsburg: The Colonial Williamsburg Foundation.

Hurst, J.G., Neal, D. and van Beuningen, H.J.E. (1986) *Pottery Produced and Traded in North-west Europe 1350–1650*, Rotterdam: Museum Boymans-van Beuningen.

Pearce, J. (1992) *Border Wares*, London: HMSO.

DAVID BARKER

East Africa

'Historical archaeology' is an ambiguous concept, particularly where it is applied to African contexts. In current practice, the term is rarely used outside of Southern Africa, even though one of the earliest uses of the term in the archaeological literature was with reference to sites and materials found along the East African littoral. The reasons for this reluctance to use the term are complex, and are due in part to the history of the discipline on the African continent, the pattern of European colonisation of Africa and current national and global contexts of archaeological and historical production in Africa and about past African societies. A further complicating matter arises from the range of historical sources that are potentially available to archaeologists, and the degree to which different scholars consider that by using these they are practising 'historical archaeology'. Thus, for instance, linguistic data are widely employed to develop models for the emergence and expansion of early farming communities across Eastern Africa some 2,000–2,500 years ago. Whether this can be termed 'historical archaeology', however, is something of a moot point, and it is much more usual to treat such reconstructions as being part of 'Iron Age' archaeology.

These observations notwithstanding, many archaeologists dealing with the material remains of East African societies of the last two millennia do make use of a variety of sources that can be broadly defined as 'historical', and in so doing have often enriched current understanding of the archaeology of the region. These sources range from linguistic data concerning the convergence and divergence of different languages and language families; the numerous myths, legends and oral traditions of the region's different ethnic groups; oral histories collected by professional historians from living informants; various early textual sources written in Greek, Arabic, Persian and Chinese; maps and other documents produced by Portuguese administrators, navigators and soldiers between 1498 and the late eighteenth century; and the countless nineteenth- and twentieth-century records and other documentary materials compiled by British, German and French officials, missionaries, traders, explorers and military personnel. Each of these has its own methodological strengths and weaknesses, and is applicable at different temporal and spatial scales. Thus, for instance, although the Greek, Arabic, Chinese and Portuguese documentary sources collectively span virtually all of the last two millennia, they are concerned, principally, only

with the communities that inhabited the East African littoral from the Somali Peninsula southwards as far as Cape Delgado in Mozambique. Conversely, whereas the records compiled by the various nineteenth-century European missions and colonising powers cover a much more extensive geographical area, they are of most relevance for understanding East African societies over only the last 200 years or so.

The manner in which archaeologists have used these disparate sources has also varied considerably. In coastal archaeology, for instance, emphasis has been placed on using the available texts as a means of locating and identifying different settlements, and as a source of information about particular events, individual rulers and the different groups living along and visiting the coast in connection with the Indian Ocean trade. Thus, for example, the earliest text, known as *The Periplus of the Erythrean Sea*, which has survived as copies transcribed in post-classical Greek during the Byzantine era, but probably dates to around AD 40, includes a description of a sea voyage along the East African coast from a trading emporium known as Opone, just south of the Somali Peninsula, to the ancient town of Rhapta. *The Periplus* also includes descriptions of various landmarks and other ports that lay along this route, and sketchy details of the local inhabitants. Some of the topographical features of the coast, such as the Lamu Archipelago and Mount Kilimanjaro, are readily identifiable from the descriptions, and using these in conjunction with the sailing directions provided, scholars have sought to link some of the known archaeological sites with the ports and other settlements named in *The Periplus*. However, few if any of these, including Rhapta, have been identified unambiguously, and the value of *The Periplus*, and other early texts such as Claudius Ptolemy's *Geography* (c. AD 150), lie in their testimony to the existence of long-distance trading links between East Africa and the Mediterranean world in the first few centuries AD, rather than as detailed guides to site locations.

Although the later texts, and especially the tenth-century accounts by the Arab geographer al-Mas'udi, contain significantly more detail, such as the range of materials being traded, the names of individual rulers, and descriptions of the customs and material culture of some of the local populations, there are also significant discrepancies, inaccuracies, omissions and, on occasion, outright fabrication. As an example, one might cite the fact that the important and sizeable town of Manda in the Lamu Archipelago, which is known from archaeological excavations to have been in existence by the ninth century AD, appears to have been overlooked by these authors for reasons that remain unclear, and the first textual reference to it occurs only in 1586.

Attempts to link the various oral traditions of communities occupying the East African interior with specific archaeological sites have encountered similar difficulties. The use of such traditions is a common component of most archaeological surveys, principally as a means of providing an overview of the more recent history of the area under investigation. It is rare, however, to find unequivocal confirmation of this information, and efforts at archaeological verification of oral traditions can often run into problems of circular argument. This happened, for instance, in connection with initial archaeological investigation of some of the sites in the Interlacustrine region associated with an elite known as the Bacwezi. According to at least one set of traditions, the Bacwezi had been the historical rulers of a large region centred in the lush grasslands of western Uganda, which, by calculating from genealogical data, would appear to have existed perhaps five to six generations ago. A number of extensive complexes of ditched earthworks, including the sites of Bigo, Munsa, Kibengo and Kasonko, are known from this area. During the 1950s–1960s, various archaeological campaigns were undertaken at the more impressive of these in an attempt to provide a clearer understanding of their date and function, and their link with the Bacwezi dynasty. The discovery at Bigo of an enclosure similar in form to that found at some of the later royal capitals in Uganda, and a suite of radiocarbon dates from the site suggesting occupation between the thirteenth and sixteenth centuries, led to the conclusion that Bigo was indeed the capital of the pastoral Bacwezi kingdom, and that the other sites were part of the same political system.

Recent reappraisals of these investigations, however, have called into question many of the historical interpretations that were used to guide the archaeological excavations and more general problems associated with trying to substantiate oral traditions archaeologically. Moreover, the results of recent field investigations by Peter Robertshaw at Munsa and Kibengo indicate that, despite some superficial similarities, these not only differ from one another but also from Bigo, in terms of their site inventories and material culture traditions. Thus, rather than belonging to a single state, Robertshaw suggests that each of these sites represents the centre of an independent polity that was in competition with its neighbours over resources and control of the local populace.

Using a different set of traditions, Peter Schmidt has argued that the Bacwezi 'myth' must be seen as a symbolically loaded, metaphorical account of trends in the region's history and changing power relations, rather than as a literal description of actual historical events and relationships. More specifically, Schmidt found during his research in the Kagera region of north-west Tanzania that oral traditions, as in Uganda, linked the more recent, immigrant Bahinda ruling dynasty with the Bacwezi, and that the power and authority of the Bahinda clans was generally associated with control over iron-working, rain-making and fertility rites. However, genealogical reckoning placed the period of Bacwezi rule up to twenty to twenty-five generations ago and thus significantly earlier than had been estimated from the Ugandan traditions. Moreover, excavations at Katuruka, the former capital of Rugamore Mahe, one of the Bahinda rulers of the Kiamutwara kingdom during the seventeenth century, led to the discovery of iron-smelting remains associated with the very beginnings of settled farming in the region and dating to around 500 BC. Although similar remains of early farming and iron-smelting communities were found at many of the other ritually important places within the historical topology of the Bahinda landscape, in other respects there was a lack of direct settlement continuity as evidenced by typological differences between Early Iron Age ceramics and those associated with the second-millennium kingdoms.

On the basis of this, Schmidt concluded that whereas the Bacwezi may have been indigenous rulers of small-scale polities during the first millennium AD or possibly earlier, later leaders, unconnected with Bacwezi, subsequently manipulated traditions and appropriated the archaeological remains of the Bacwezi's evident iron-smelting abilities to legitimise their own assumption to power.

Another strand of historical archaeology in Eastern Africa encompasses the issues of **colonialism** and **contact archaeology**. This can be approached either from the perspective of European expansion, conventionally taken as dating from the first appearance of the Portuguese on the East African coast in 1498, or, somewhat more radically, in terms of the rise of Omani mercantile capitalism and the establishment of a compradorial state, ultimately centred on Zanzibar, during the seventeenth to nineteenth centuries. This was an era of considerable political and economic change and social upheaval, and as a direct consequence the settlement geography of many areas was transformed. For example, caravan halts frequently developed into more permanent markets, and tracts of land were abandoned and agricultural production strategies changed to meet new, commercial demands. At the same time, inter-ethnic differences were often accentuated and 'tribal' boundaries solidified, with more frequent inter-community raiding leading to the emergence of new forms of defended settlement. Whereas this could have acted to reinforce material culture differences and encourage the use of artefacts to signal identity, there was also increased interaction between geographically distant communities with the result that new material traditions were introduced into virtually every region, thereby potentially blurring pre-existing stylistic boundaries.

Some aspects of these transformations to the material and architectural landscape have been investigated archaeologically. These include, in particular, James Kirkman's extensive excavations and recording at Fort Jesus, built in 1593 by the Portuguese to protect their provisioning station at Mombasa (Kenya) from Omani and Swahili incursions; and studies of various nineteenth-century sites in the interior associated with either the caravan trade (e.g. Tongwe Fort, Ngandu and Ngambezi in Tanzania) or European colonisation. There has also been some limited investigation of the **maritime archaeology** of the coast, including excavation of a seventeenth-century Portuguese frigate, the *Santo António de Tanná*, lost off Fort Jesus in 1697, and documentation of German and British First World War wrecks around the Rufiji Delta, Tanzania. In addition, there is a growing trend among researchers to document the emergence of local vernacular traditions (such as those of the Luo *ohingni* and Mijikenda *kayas* in Kenya), many of which were undoubtedly affected by the profound changes that occurred as the region was steadily drawn into the world capitalist system.

Yet, despite the enormous wealth of detail contained in the published and archival records of the last few centuries, the full potential for 'historical archaeology' as it is more conventionally understood has yet to be realised.

See also: capitalism; world(-)systems theory

Further reading

Horton, M.C. (1996) *Shanga: The Archaeology of a Muslim Trading Community on the Coast of East Africa*, London: British Institute in Eastern Africa.

Kirkman, J.S. (1974) *Fort Jesus, a Portuguese Fortress on the East African Coast*, Oxford: Clarendon Press.

—— (1957) 'Historical archaeology in Kenya 1948–1956', *Antiquaries Journal* 32: 168–84.

Lane, P. (1993) 'Tongwe Fort', *Azania* 28: 133–41.

Schmidt, P.R. (1990) 'Oral traditions, archaeology and history: A short reflexive history', in P. Robertshaw (ed.) *A History of African Archaeology*, London: James Currey, pp. 252–70.

Sheriff, A. (1987) *Slaves, Spices and Ivory in Zanzibar*, London: James Currey.

PAUL J. LANE

Elmina, Ghana

The African settlement of Elmina is located in the Central Region of coastal Ghana. Archaeological data indicate that the occupation of the site predates the arrival of the Portuguese on the coast in the late fifteenth century, but the town expanded rapidly after the founding of Castelo de São Jorge da Mina by Portuguese in 1482. The castle was a centre of European trade in **West Africa**, first under the Portuguese and, later, under the Dutch who captured the castle in 1637. Gold was initially the principal trade item. The castle later became important as one of the principal barracoons for enslaved Africans awaiting shipment to the Americas. Most of these individuals were not from Elmina or its environs but captive Africans purchased on other parts of the West African coast. The population of the African town at Elmina grew from a few hundred people in the fifteenth century to perhaps 20,000 inhabitants by the mid-nineteenth century. The castle was ceded to the British in 1872. The bombardment of the town and its subsequent abandonment marked the beginning of the British–Ashanti conflict of 1873–4.

A.W. Lawrence undertook restoration work and study of the castle's architectural history during the 1950s. Archaeological work on the associated African settlement was carried out by C.R. DeCorse between 1985 and 2000. The archaeological remains of the old settlement extend over 81 ha (200 a), though most concentrate on the 8 ha (20 a) located closest to the castle. Archaeological survey and excavation examined the entire area of the town site, making this one of the largest archaeological settlement studies undertaken in West Africa. Over 40 stone-walled structures were excavated. The nineteenth century, the time of the settlement's destruction, is best represented but archaeological materials span the pre-European contact period through the nineteenth century.

A particularly significant aspect of the Elmina excavations was the large amount of trade materials recovered compared to other African settlements of the period. The close chronological control afforded by these items facilitated the dating of associated African artefacts, including a wide variety of cast copper alloy and gold objects, **beads** and **ceramics**. Another distinctive aspect of the settlement was the large number of houses constructed using stone, a building technique that came to characterise the town beginning in the seventeenth century. While these changes in the material record attest to Elmina's connection with a world economy increasingly dominated by Europe, the use of the artefacts, their patterning and the world view they represent indicate continuities with African beliefs.

See also: West Africa

Further reading

DeCorse, C.R. (2001) *An Archaeology of Elmina: Africans and Europeans on the Gold Coast, 1400–1900*, Washington: Smithsonian Institution Press.

Lawrence, A.W. (1963) *Trade Castles and Forts of West Africa*, London: Jonathan Cape.

CHRISTOPHER R. DeCORSE

Elverton Street, near Westminster, England

This extensive and unparalleled horse burial ground, dated to the fifteenth and possibly sixteenth centuries, was excavated in the mid-1990s. Nearly 200 burial pits were recorded, but there may be many more in the locality. Although bone preservation was generally poor, the remains of seventy-six expertly dismembered horses survived in thirty-one pits. The horses appear to have been working animals near the end of their useful lives. There is no historical record of the burial ground, but it was presumably used by butchers from Westminster with permission of the landowner, which was Westminster Abbey until the Dissolution, and subsequently the Dean and Chapter of the Collegiate Church of St Peter, Westminster.

See also: England

Further reading

Cowie, R. and Pipe, A. (1998) 'A late medieval and Tudor horse burial ground: Excavations at Elverton Street, Westminster', *The Archaeological Journal* 155: 226–51.

ROBERT COWIE

England

English historical archaeology, or **post-medieval archaeology** to use the common local term, initially grew out of a need to study the increasing amount of finds – especially pottery – generated by sites with both medieval and post-medieval pottery. The **Society for Post-medieval Archaeology** (founded 1967) itself developed from the Post-medieval Ceramics Research Group, founded in 1964 to study ceramics dating between 1450 and 1750. The year 1450 traditionally marked the decline of medieval pottery traditions and the arrival of significant amounts of imported wares, while 1750 traditionally marked the beginning of English porcelain production. These dates would remain the defining dates of most post-medieval archaeology in England for the best part of the next three decades.

Post-medieval archaeology was in many ways the poor relation of British and English archaeology. As recently as the 1960s, many urban excavators would ignore the upper levels of a site in order to reach the Roman remains as quickly as possible, while to this day many English universities give at best cursory attention to anything post-dating the Norman Conquest of 1066. This omission only stresses the great richness of the English archaeological record, of which post-medieval archaeology is only one small part. Yet, despite post-medieval archaeology's relatively recent development as a respectable field of inquiry, its contributions to our understanding of the past have been significant. This is especially true given the undeniably important historical role of the British Empire within the post-medieval period. It is worth noting that the division of British post-medieval archaeology into sections on England, **Wales**, Scotland and Northern **Ireland** is highly artificial. There is inevitably considerable overlap, and the discussion of the development of post-medieval archaeology that follows is often relevant across the UK, hence the frequent references to 'Britain', rather than just 'England', in this entry.

The early years

Given the sub-discipline's roots, it is not surprising that many of · the earliest references to post-medieval finds in the British archaeological literature are references to pottery. The first known published description of post-medieval pottery dates to 1847: four sixteenth-century Tudor green jugs were illustrated in the 1847 volume of the *Archaeological Journal*. It was also in the mid-nineteenth century that William Chaffers formulated a theory of analysis for medieval pottery that was to become equally applicable to post-medieval pottery. Chaffers stated that medieval ceramics should be 'considered in regard to their utility and domestic economy, not to their elegance of form or fineness of material'. Years ahead of his time, Chaffers's work was the first coherent attempt to separate the archaeology of medieval (and, by association, post-medieval) pottery from a purely art-historical tradition.

A strong sense of continuity has always existed between the medieval and post-medieval periods in English archaeology, particularly in the early years of post-medieval archaeology's development. Early seminal figures in the development of medieval and post-medieval pottery, such as Gerald Dunning, John Lewis, John Hurst and Kenneth Barton, were perfectly happy to move between both worlds. The study of industrial ceramics, particularly the refined white-bodied wares, would eventually break down this continuity somewhat, but even in the mid–late nineteenth century it remains possible to see past traditions at work in the manufacture of folk pottery, such as the Ewenny potteries of Glamorgan, Wales.

Finds studies were far from the only element to contribute to post-medieval archaeology. These studies may have been a catalyst because, as a whole, the sub-discipline ultimately evolved from several separate post-medieval elements. The development of the post-medieval rural landscapes, urban development, **industrialisation** and **churchyard archaeology** have all been prominent in the development of the discipline. As with finds studies, these areas have a strong sense of continuity with earlier periods, yet also contain unique post-medieval elements of their own, such as the enclosure and improvement of the rural landscape, for example. Anything resembling a complete list of important relevant fieldwork would be beyond impossible in this short article, but significant work has included the excavation of the crypt of Christ Church, **Spitalfields**, the ongoing work on the factories of the Staffordshire potteries and the examination of the abandoned post-medieval village of Whelpington, Northumberland. Inevitably, London has cast a long shadow across post-medieval archaeology, and much vital work has taken place in the metropolis. The definitive survey of traditional work in these areas remains Crossley's *Post-Medieval Archaeology in Britain*.

A vitally important aspect of the post-medieval period is the rise of industrial Britain. The relationship between post-medieval and **industrial archaeology** in Britain has never been satisfactorily resolved, however. The division between the two fields has never been period-based. By 1970, the literature summary in the Society for Post-medieval Archaeology's journal was considering publications examining archaeology up to 1800 instead of the original 1750 date. Nonetheless, by the mid-1970s, calls for a separate Society for Industrial Archaeology reached fruition. As a result, while industrial sites post-dating 1750 produced a voluminous literature within the sub-discipline of industrial archaeology, non-industrial sites (rural farms, for example) post-dating 1750 often resided in an uncomfortable conceptual limbo – traditionally neither post-medieval nor industrial.

The advent of theory

Post-medieval archaeology has often been accused of being inherently atheoretical. While this may have been more true in the past, it was never an entirely fair charge. Certainly, post-medieval archaeology, unlike North American historical archaeology, remained largely unaffected by the processualist movement, especially the concept of archaeology as anthropology. This is not to say that wider British archaeology as a whole was not aware of, or failed to contribute to, a new paradigm. The first edition of David Clarke's *Analytical Archaeology* was published in 1968. Clarke advocated many of the same methodological positions as the processualists, such as the testing of predictions through empirical measurements. The recognition of a more analytical approach calls for more overt quantification in archaeological data and the exploration of mathematical approaches to culture change have all featured prominently in the wider British archaeological landscape.

Substantial differences remained, however, between quantitative approaches in Britain and North America. North American archaeology established strong disciplinary links with anthropology, to the extent that archaeology became an anthropological sub-discipline, taught almost exclusively in anthropology departments. British archaeology maintained a more distinct identity, and text-aided periods continued to have much stronger links to history than their North American counterpart. Furthermore, Clarke's quantitative methodology was much less dogmatic in intent than that of North American processualism. As demonstrated by Stanley South's conceptual 'pole-arm of archaeology', the processualists believed that they had reached the end of archaeology's theoretical development. Clarke was far more flexible.

The North American theoretical dogmatism and the insistence on archaeology as anthropology have been primarily responsible for the lack of processual models in English post-medieval archaeology. However, exceptions, such as studies of regional patterning in church archaeology, have been written from time to time. Yet these studies are usually recent and are the exception rather than the rule. Indeed, it is hard to disagree with Champion's observation that English and other British archaeologists felt that debates on the nature of explanation and explanation of processes of social change were irrelevant to periods with an established, documented narrative.

Despite the English and British rejection of processualism, many of the most lasting and influential contributions to post-processualism were British in origin, notably Ian Hodder's *Reading the Past*. Post-processualism's textual model of material culture and its rejection of a strictly objective paradigm has permeated archaeology on both sides of the Atlantic. In Britain, post-processualist archaeology led archaeologists in text-aided sub-disciplines to question the level of traditional disciplinary links with history – though by no means to the same extent as the North Americans. Champion in particular has written of the 'tyranny of the historical record', complaining that the programme of historic-period archaeology is set and indeed limited by the culturally biased 'historic vision', and suggesting that alternative conceptual frameworks be developed. Perhaps inevitably, the search for 'alternative frameworks' has led to the examination of strata of society that were under-represented in the past. In the context of Great Britain, particular attention has been paid to such communities in **Wales** and **Scotland** In England specifically, attention has turned towards the urban and industrial underclasses, such as Matthews's work on the lower social strata of urban Chester.

Away from a narrow focus on processualism and post-processualism, post-medieval archaeology briefly flirted with humanism. Indeed, Jenkins's paper in the 1968 edition of *Post-medieval Archaeology* anticipated many of the themes that would later inform James Deetz's humanist approach. Jenkins issued a plea to 'breathe life into the dry bones of cultures' and to use the possession of a material object as a starting point in the study of the 'lore, custom and language' affiliated therewith. Furthermore, Jenkins expressed the opinion that post-medieval archaeology could contribute to the study of the way of life of communities of any size, unaffected by industrialisation, strongly implying in the process that this was irrespective of the date of the community in question. It is to post-medieval archaeology's cost that the humanist thread was not as immediately influential as Deetz became in North America.

Despite these occasional interactions with theory, in practice, most English post-medieval archaeology has been atheoretical. Nonetheless, it should be stressed that a considerable corpus of work exists that considers wider issues of meaning and interpretation. While by no means can this work be considered to form an intentional coherent school of theory-informed analysis, its existence demonstrates that post-medieval archaeology considers issues of meaning and ideology far more frequently than some critics believe. In ceramics studies alone, examples include the Donyatt pottery report's discussion of social context and public mood and opinion, as evidenced through dishes that portray Siamese twins from Somerset, and Elizabeth Lewis's extensive work on the social backgrounds of the Blackwater potteries. Pottery analysis is by no means unique in this regard. Also, if none of this work is explicitly theoretical, it does prove that the necessary base for a wider, interpretive analysis does exist, and always has existed, within English post-medieval archaeology.

The present

Whatever the supposed sins of the past, post-medieval archaeology appears more exciting both in practice and theory today than at any time previously. This is as true of the popular imagination as it is of the professional mind. Popular archaeology television programmes such as Channel 4's *Time Team* actively include post-medieval sites, local archaeology units' occasionally cavalier attitudes towards the recent past are being replaced with a more sensitive approach, and the 1998 reorganisation of *Post-medieval Archaeology* promises a more inclusive approach within the sub-discipline's most important journal. Meanwhile, recent scholarship has sought to break down the artificial boundaries between post-medieval archaeology and other sub-disciplines, particularly medieval and industrial archaeology. Within this vibrant landscape, three recent publications in particular stand out: Johnson's *An Archaeology of Capitalism*, Gaimster's *German Stoneware 1200–1900* and the Tarlow and West edited volume *The Familiar Past?* These books are notable for their explicit considerations of ideology, meaning and social context in both multi-period and multi-national contexts while remaining firmly rooted in the traditional strengths of English, and indeed British, post-medieval archaeology. Indeed, as English post-medieval archaeology continues to develop theory-informed research agendas, it will inevitably go some way towards balancing the common North American misconception that 'archaeology is anthropology or it is nothing'.

See also: history of historical archaeology

Further reading

Champion, T. (1991) 'Theoretical archaeology in Britain', in I. Hodder (ed.) *Archaeological Theory in Europe: The Last Three Decades*, Routledge: London, pp. 129–60.

Crossley, D. (1994) *Post-medieval Archaeology in Britain*, Leicester: Leicester University Press.

Gaimster, D. (1997) *German Stoneware 1200–1900*, London: British Museum Press.

Jenkins, J.G. (1968) 'Post-medieval archaeology and folk-life studies', *Post-medieval Archaeology* 2: 1–9.

Johnson, M. (1996) *An Archaeology of Capitalism*, Oxford: Blackwell.

Reeve, J. and Adams, M. (1993) *The Spitalfields*

Project; Volume 1: The Archaeology; Across the Styx, York: Council for British Archaeology.

Tarlow, S. and West, S. (eds) (1999) *The Familiar Past? Archaeologies of Later Historical Britain*, London: Routledge.

ALASDAIR M. BROOKS

English colonialism

Although involved in wars of conquest in Great Britain for centuries, beginning in the middle of the sixteenth century the English began to expand overseas, ushering in the era of English colonialism. As a historical phenomenon, **colonialism** is much more than the establishment of new settlements on previously unoccupied territory, but involves the conquest and subjugation of indigenous peoples, the creation of new economic systems, the development of new social hierarchies and the concomitant development of colonialist ideologies, which more often than not justified English colonialism by denigrating the social and material worlds of the colonised. Archaeologists have studied these and other processes in a variety of contexts, notably in New England, the US southeast (particularly Virginia), **Ireland**, the Caribbean (see **Caribbean archaeology**) and, more recently, **South Africa** and **Australia**.

Conquest and subjugation

A common phenomenon to all European colonial expansion – whether on the part of the Spanish, French, Dutch or English – is the appropriation of land upon which to build settlements. This generally involves social conflict between the colonisers and the colonised, generally expressed through the dialectic of **domination** and **resistance**. Several historical archaeologists have considered how the English experimented with colonisation in Ireland, particularly through a phenomenon known as 'plantation', literally the planting of English colonists on appropriated lands in Ireland. This process began in the mid-sixteenth century through land seizures and the establishment of colonial outposts in central and western Ireland, particularly in the province of Munster.

James Delle has examined how English architectural styles were used as a tool of colonial domination in south-western Ireland and how this was resisted; Eric Klingelhofer has excavated sites associated with leading English colonists in Ireland, including Walter Raleigh and Edmund Spenser. Brooke Blades, Audrey Horning and Nick Brannon have conducted excavations on English plantation sites dating to the early seventeenth century in the province of Ulster, in modern Northern Ireland, while Charles Orser has examined how English colonialism impoverished millions in early nineteenth-century Ireland.

Early English colonial sites, particularly those dating from the sixteenth and seventeenth centuries, often prominently feature military fortifications, as evidenced through the appearance of star-shaped forts throughout Ireland in the seventeenth century. Early English colonies tended to be precarious settlements, and were often attacked and burned either by the displaced indigenous people, as happened in Ireland and probably in Raleigh's ill-fated Roanoke colony, or else by other colonial powers attempting to wrest control of colonies from the English. The assumed necessity of such fortifications is evidenced in early English colonies in Virginia, like **Jamestown**, excavated in the 1930s and 1950s by J.C. Harrington, and more recently by William Kelso. A more dramatic episode of resistance to English colonial incursions in Virginia was recorded by Ivor Noël Hume through his excavations at Wolstonholme Town, part of **Martin's Hundred**, destroyed in an attack by local indigenous people resisting the co-optation of their land, and its subsequent reapportioning to Englishmen by the King of England. In excavating this early seventeenth-century colonial site, Noël Hume revealed that colonialism was certainly a contested process.

English colonialists often took advantage of factionalism and political fragmentation among indigenous peoples, conflicts that both predated the English presence, and which arose as a direct result of colonial incursions. Such factionalism existed in seventeenth-century New England, and led to direct conflicts between the colonists and their colluding allied groups, on one hand, and those resisting or trying to better manipulate the emerging colonial order, on the other. Notable

New England events related to English colonialism include King Phillip's War and the attempted genocide of the Pequot; since the late 1980s, Kevin McBride has worked with the Pequot descendant community on excavating sites both pre-dating and post-dating the arrival of English colonialism in New England.

The creation of new economic systems

English colonialism was as much an economic phenomenon as it was a social one. An important economy that developed in North America as a result of English colonialism was the fur trade. Scott Hamilton has analysed the impact that the fur trade had on the indigenous economics of northern North America. The colonial settlement strategy of establishing permanent or semi-permanent fur-trading posts encouraged both the overexploitation of fur-bearing animals in the hinterlands directly around the post and the abandonment of the traditional mobile subsistence strategies previously employed by the indigenous peoples from whom the European traders procured their furs. The overexploitation of animals resulted in local extinctions of prized animals, forcing trappers deeper into interior North America. This development resulted in increased tensions between English (and French) traders and the local indigenous peoples, and provoked disputes among indigenous groups. As the fur trade penetrated into the interior, new economies of meat production developed, as local peoples hunted and processed foods to provision the trappers and traders. By examining faunal assemblages from fur-trading posts in Canada, Hamilton has demonstrated how food procurement economies shifted as both the fur-bearing and meat-producing animal populations declined.

At least equally important was the development of monocrop plantation economies, based alternatively on the production of tobacco, rice and **sugar**. Early English colonialism in North America was focused on the extraction of agricultural wealth. The development of plantation monoculture in the tobacco-growing regions of the Chesapeake (see **Chesapeake region**) tidewater resulted in the development of a marked colonial social hierarchy; the operation of this system has

been the focus of much historical archaeology in Virginia, Maryland, and both South and North Carolina. The development of this colonial system is evident at sites like **Monticello**, **Carter's Grove**, **Flowerdew Hundred Plantation**, **Martin's Hundred** and **Mount Vernon**, and resulted in the development of wealthy urban settlements like **Annapolis**, Maryland and Williamsburg, Virginia. Tobacco monocrop agriculture was so successful as a colonial economic system that the system was applied throughout the southern tier of English North American colonies, and adopted in the Caribbean. **Plantation archaeology** focuses on sites associated with the development of this system. While many people were incorporated into this system either willingly or coercively, many chose to resist the hegemony of the economic system. Such resistance is evident in the settlement of **maroon sites** by people fleeing slave labour in English colonies, who chose to create independent subsistence systems. Kofi Agorsah has excavated such a site at **Nanny Town** in Jamaica; Kathleen Deagan has examined the establishment of a free-black town at **Fort Mose**, originally settled by slaves seeking refuge from the English colonial system by living among the Spanish in Florida.

The construction of new social hierarchies

The development of new colonial economies expanding out of the conquest and subjugation of indigenous Native Americans and the enslavement of millions of Africans and their creole descendants resulted in the creation of new social hierarchies based on the accumulation of wealth and reinforced by a system of social segmentation, based not only on accumulated wealth, but on newly defined racial identities. Terry Epperson has analysed how seventeenth-century Virginia slowly developed a racial ideology that eventually resulted in a system of bondage through which the progeny of enslaved peoples would be bound to their mothers' enslavers in perpetuity; whiteness was concomitantly defined as a social identity for the first time. The result of this was an erosion of class solidarity that had developed between white and black servants as new racial and class structures simultaneously emerged. Perhaps the greatest social impact of English colonialism was the massive importation of captive Africans to work on New World plantations both in North America and the Caribbean; the resultant social structure created a racial hierarchy throughout the New World that privileged those who could claim white descent over those who could not.

Ideologies of domination

Many archaeologists studying English colonialism have argued that the resulting systems of economic and social inequality needed to be reinforced materially as well as ideologically. Mark Leone's work on the development of capitalist ideology in **Annapolis**, Maryland, is perhaps the best researched example of how colonial ideologies developed under English colonialism. Although Leone's thoughts on ideology have evolved over time, as he first applied the concept to Annapolis, Leone argued that ideology was not solely about world view or shared belief, but was a system of thought that both ordered nature and society, and masked inherent social disparities by incorporating them as a natural outcome of the social order. Leone analysed the William Paca garden in Annapolis as a material expression of this ideology of naturalising a constructed social hierarchy. Similarly, Paul Shackel has argued that such a process is evident in the construction of the city plan of Annapolis, in which the street plan was designed so that the state house and church were placed on high ground, visible from virtually every part of the city. This served to produce a landscape in which the hierarchical social order controlled by the political and religious elite was constantly visible, and absorbed by the residents of Annapolis through their daily interactions in the city.

As is evident in many historical museums and historic districts, the English colonial past, at least in North America, is often remembered with nostalgia for a simpler, kinder day. In looking at the history of the town of Deerfield, Massachusetts, Robert Paynter has analysed how the construction of pasts based on nostalgia is itself an ideological process. Paynter demonstrates that in constructing the early colonial history of this town, generations of scholars and laypeople alike have reconfigured the town's epic event, the 1704 attack on the town by the French and their Native American allies (see **Native Americans**). Although this was but one in a series of violent skirmishes in the long colonial struggle between the French and English for control over north-eastern North America, the event has become known as the Deerfield 'Massacre', primarily as part of the early twentieth-century wave of nostalgia known as the 'Colonial Revival'. This telling of the event has minimised the French presence, recasting the event as an Indian 'massacre' of innocent settlers. In constructing this heroic colonial past for the town, an ideology justifying English – and later American – occupation of the area was constructed, in which the dispossessed native peoples are depicted as the aggressors, and the colonialists who settled on appropriated lands appear as innocent victims.

While many historical archaeologists have worked on sites dating to the colonial period in North America, few have traditionally problematised the social and economic dynamics of English colonialism. As more historical archaeologists recognise colonialism as a contested social process, more interpretations of how new economic and social formations were developed will be proposed. Although archaeological studies of English colonialism have traditionally focused on North America, the scope of this research focus is increasing; as research develops in places like Australia, Ireland, Africa and India, the material dimensions of English colonialism as a global process will be better understood.

Further reading

Egan, F. and Michael, R.L. (eds) (1999) *Old and New Worlds*, Oxford: Oxbow.

Leone, M.P. (1984) 'Ideology and historical archaeology: Using the rules of perspective in the William Paca garden in Annapolis, Maryland', in D. Miller and C. Tilley (eds) *Ideology, Power, and Prehistory*, Cambridge: Cambridge University Press, pp. 25–35.

Noël Hume, I. (1982). *Martin's Hundred*, New York: Alfred A. Knopf.

Orser, C.E. (1996) *A Historical Archaeology of the Modern World*, New York: Plenum Press.

JAMES A. DELLE

environmental reconstruction

Environmental reconstruction involves a number of earth and life sciences. Environmental reconstruction is dependent upon proxy indicators, the presence, absence or relative abundance of which are used to infer past environments. The temporal resolution and spatial specificity of these interpretations may be quite coarse-grained. While more commonly used in prehistoric studies, under appropriate conditions the methods of environmental reconstruction are relevant in historical archaeology. In historical archaeology, historic records are also informative.

Micro-fossil remains

Palynology is the study of pollen grains and spores. Pollen grains are the microscopic containers of the male gametophyte of higher plants. The morphology and surface texture of pollen grains are species-specific, thereby enabling some level of taxonomic identification. As part of the plant reproductive cycle, pollen is dispersed into the air to fertilise the flowering (female) part of plants of the same species. The vast majority of the released pollen fails to pollinate, and may become part of the micro-fossil record. The outer shells of pollen grains are composed of a complex polymer called sporopollenin that resists biological and chemical degradation, particularly in anaerobic conditions. Palynology often involves extraction of sediment cores from water-saturated lakebeds and peat bogs representing the stratified accumulation of organic and inorganic particles. By sampling at intervals along the core, pollen deposited at various times can be extracted by selectively destroying all other particles, enabling the concentration of the chemically resistant grains. These pollen grains are speciated through microscopic examination. Measuring the relative abundance of each genus of species in successive samples enables reconstruction of past vegetative communities, and, by inference, past climatic conditions.

Phytolith analysis involves the interpretation of microscopic silica bodies found in plants, particularly leaves. Some phytoliths can be speciated on the basis of their size and morphology. While not as well developed as pollen analysis, phytolith studies offer great potential for environmental reconstruction because they appear to preserve well under diverse conditions, and are not as prone to aeolian redistribution. While phytoliths are attractive for measuring local vegetative conditions in terrestrial sites, valid interpretation is still dependent upon good stratigraphic control. In contrast to palynology, most phytolith research has focused upon hearths, storage pits and refuse middens, and tends to reflect human use of plants rather than directly documenting past environmental conditions.

Diatoms are microscopic algae that live in fresh water or marine situations, and survive in the micro-fossil record because of their silica cell walls. They are environmentally sensitive, with species representation varying with water salinity. By sampling lakebed sediment cores, shifts in the relative abundance of diatom species can indicate climatic conditions that affected the lake. For example, with Pleistocene climate shifts, the resultant changes in ocean salinity may be reflected in the fossil diatoms recovered from ocean cores. Shallow terrestrial lakes may yield datable cores containing shifting frequencies of diatom species, perhaps reflecting drought cycles.

Macro-fossil remains

The study of tree-growth rings, or **dendrochronology**, offers a method of absolute dating, and a means of inferring local climate. Dendrochronology is most effective in conditions where local seasonal climatic variations tend to be extreme, and where water supplies are minimal. It is least useful in situations of minimal seasonal climatic variation, or where micro-climate, water supply or sediment conditions vary locally. In situations of marked seasonality, trees annually lay down concentric rings composed of large thin-walled cells during the early growing season, and smaller thick-walled cells as the growing season ends. Variability in the size and density of these rings directly reflects the nature of successive growing seasons, and documents environmental events including climatic variability, severe drought, unseasonable frost, disease or fire damage. Reconstructing climatic conditions using annual growth rings is dependent upon developing a master tree ring chronology for the local area through cross-dating. Such a chronology requires a sequence of tree samples with overlapping lifespans whereby the climatic record can be absolutely dated. Fragments of ancient wood and charcoal can also be taxonomically identified, allowing reconstruction of tree cover in the study area.

Skeletal remains of animals and insects can indicate past environmental conditions, and the pace of biotic transformation in the recent past. When recovered from well-dated and stratigraphically secure contexts, remains of small animals and insects may indicate micro-environmental conditions, while bones from larger animals may document human hunting preferences. **Zooarchaeology** can also address changing environmental conditions, the consequences of over-hunting and the spread of exotic and domestic species released into North America, **Australia** and **New Zealand**.

Historical documents

Environmental reconstruction in historical archaeology can be facilitated using archival documents. Climate records and written narratives may indicate past weather patterns and precipitation. Archival maps may document prominent landmarks, hydrological systems and general vegetation patterns. Ethnohistoric syntheses, reminiscences and the 'oral tradition' are informative, as are legal survey records, sketches, drawings, paintings and early photographs. In north-western North America, Africa and Australia, such maps are seldom more than 150 years old, but remain useful since they predate dramatic twentieth-century ecological change. In such cases, they can be used to model earlier environmental configurations that can be tested using conventional environmental reconstruction methods.

The historic period is often characterised by colonial agricultural settlement, urbanisation and sedentism. Such processes caused rapid environmental change that utterly transformed the landscape. Deforestation, destruction of indigenous taxa, soil erosion and hydrological change were common consequences. These changes were so dramatic and pervasive that we may be unaware of the magnitude of recent change. By employing these and other environmental reconstruction methods, historical archaeologists may be able to document change, assess causality and provide insight into the consequences of future environmental transformation.

See also: environmental studies

Further reading

Dimbleby, G.W. (1985) *The Palynology of Archaeological Sites*, London: Academic Press.

Holliday, V.T. (ed.) (1992) *Soils in Archaeology*, Washington, DC: Smithsonian Institution Press.

Moore, P.D., Webb, J.A. and Collinson, M.E. (1991) *Pollen Analysis*, second edn, Oxford: Basil Blackwell.

Rapp, G. and Mulholland, S.C. (1992) *Phytolith Systematics: Emerging Issues*, New York: Plenum Press.

Schwengruber, F.H. (1988) *Tree Rings: Basics and Applications of Dendrochronology*, Dordrecht: Reidel.

SCOTT HAMILTON

environmental studies

Environmental archaeology encompasses a range of specialised research techniques that address the relationship between humans, their cultures and the environments within which they lived. This can involve **environmental reconstruction** using biological indicators such as pollen, phytoliths and diatoms, and macro-botanical, insect, invertebrate and vertebrate remains. Ancient wood can be subjected to dendrochronological analysis to infer when the timber was cut, and also micro-climatic conditions during the life of the tree. Soil analysis can involve pedological studies of sediment weathering, chemical analysis to assess soil enrichment or depletion, or particle size analysis to measure mechanisms of sediment accumulation or erosion. Stable carbon and nitrogen isotopes recovered from organic materials can be used to reconstruct human dietary choices. Oxygen isotopes recovered from glacial ice or foraminifera shells deposited in ocean basins can also be used to infer past global climatic conditions. Samples can derive from suitable deposits removed from the archaeological site (facilitating indirect environmental interpretation), or from within the archaeological site (enabling more comprehensive documentation of resource use or micro-environmental selection).

Palaeo-environmental data are often collected and interpreted for non-archaeological purposes, such as addressing long-term, global-scale, climatic and environmental change. Consequently, the interpretations offered are of coarse temporal and spatial resolution. Such macro-scale generalisations may provide limited insight regarding environmental conditions affecting specific human groups. Depending upon the materials examined, some environmental studies are geographically and temporally tightly focused, thereby enabling environmental contextualisation of archaeological deposits. However, the data may be insufficient to address the role of the environment in human socioeconomic adaptation, or the impact of human activities upon the physical environment. Such limitations reflect the nature and depositional context of the materials under study, or that samples are seldom collected and interpreted from tightly dated contexts expressly for archaeological interpretation. Site transformation and sample degradation (oxidisation, chemical corrosion, biological decay and soil leaching) can also affect the applicability of such studies.

Environmental studies in archaeology can involve the examination of materials transported by humans to habitation, processing or consumption sites, or, alternatively, specimens deposited by natural forces. In the former case, such specimens can be used to address prey selection, food processing, socially mediated redistribution of resources and waste-disposal behaviours. Such research reflects patterns of human resource selection, rather than directly documenting regional environmental conditions. Organic remains deposited through non-cultural agencies can be used to infer environmental conditions during the time of interest. Of particular value are species with a narrow range of environmental tolerance. For example, the recovery of specific species of land snails, insects and small rodents can suggest terrestrial climatic and local biotic conditions, while molluscs can indicate the nature of aquatic environments. In situations of good contextual control and fine temporal resolution, analysts can document short-term environmental perturbations, cultural responses to environmental change, or the

ecological impact of human landscape modification.

One would expect that environmental studies in historical archaeology involve conventional methodologies of palaeo-environmental interpretation, coupled with historic documentation. We might also expect that text-aided environmental study would be noted for its detail, and fine temporal and spatial resolution. A cursory review of historical-archaeology publications reveals surprisingly few examples of environmentally oriented research. Perhaps this is because conventional approaches to environmental reconstruction are too coarse in temporal resolution to be immediately useful in studying the recent past. Perhaps it is thought that environmental reconstruction in historical archaeology is unnecessary since such information can be derived through analogy to contemporary conditions, or by reference to historic climate or vegetation records. It may also reflect the theoretical orientation of historical archaeologists who are less often interested than prehistoric archaeologists in overtly materialist or cultural ecological research questions.

Developing an environmental approach in historical archaeology can offer significant insight. For example, environmental studies in historical archaeology might aid in addressing the timing and subtle impact of environmental change caused by colonial expansion, agricultural production and urbanisation. This includes examination of the introduction of exotic and domestic species, extinction of indigenous taxa and environmental degradation brought about by deforestation, soil erosion and declining groundwater deposits. While written documentation of some of these impacts exists, significant change often occurred prior to written records. As historical archaeology is strongly oriented towards the study of European colonial expansion, an overtly environmental approach may be valuable in addressing these phenomena when no records survive. For example, a detailed climate change model is valuable in assessing factors contributing to the failure of Norse settlement in North America and Greenland. Alternatively, an environmental perspective could offer valuable insight into the consequences for aboriginal populations of European colonial expansion in the Americas, **Australia** and Africa.

These disenfranchised, subordinated or subjugated populations are mute or underrepresented in the historical texts, and their history can often only be given voice through archaeological inference and the oral tradition.

Environmental studies can be used to assess the precision of historical records of past climate and biotic capacity, and provide baseline information of environmental conditions prior to recent landscape change. Such studies aid in critically evaluating the relationship between directly observed environmental conditions and proxy indicators of those conditions. This will be valuable in refining and validating palaeo-environmental methodologies used to interpret the more distant past. Studies of human-induced environmental change in the recent past may be valuable in predicting the consequences of contemporary environmental change.

See also: zooarchaeology

Further reading

Dincauze, D.F. (1987) 'Strategies for paleoenvironmental reconstruction in archaeology', in M.B. Schiffer (ed.) *Advances in Archaeological Method and Theory* 11, New York: Academic Press, pp. 255–336.

Evans, J.G. (1985) *An Introduction to Environmental Archaeology*, Ithaca: Cornell University Press.

Goldberg, P., Holliday, V.T. and Ferring, C.R. (ed.) (2001) *Earth Sciences and Archaeology*, New York: Kluwer Academic/Plenum.

Rapp, G. and Hill, C.L. (1998) *Geoarchaeology: The Earth-Science Approach to Archaeological Interpretation*, New Haven: Yale University Press.

Shackley, M. (1981) *Environmental Archaeology*, London: Allen & Unwin.

Waters, M.R. (1992) *Principles of Geoarchaeology: A North American Perspective*, Tucson: University of Arizona Press.

SCOTT HAMILTON

ethnicity

Studies of ethnicity in historical archaeology include all research into the nature, characteristics and dynamics of ethnic groups and ethnic identity. Archaeologists struggle to define terms like these in both meaningful and useful ways, given the constraints of archaeological methods and theories. They have found it more rewarding to study certain ethnic groups, settings and research topics rather than others, and have had some success in contributing to a scholarly understanding of ethnicity. This research nevertheless remains some of the most challenging in historical archaeology.

History of research on ethnicity

Cultural anthropologists, sociologists, historians and other scholars have been researching ethnicity for at least a century. Archaeologists, in contrast, have shown a serious interest in ethnicity for only about twenty-five or thirty years. At that time, ethnic studies in archaeology grew in number and impact at a remarkably rapid pace, so that today it is one of the more common research themes. This is particularly the case in historical archaeology. Other, related interests, including **urban archaeology**, **gender** studies and the archaeological investigation of social class (see **class, social**) and status, also grew remarkably during this time, and all of these developments emerged as a result of the rise of historical archaeology as a formal and recognisably legitimate field of study.

Despite its great popularity, or some might argue because of it, historical archaeologists have learned that studying ethnicity entails a number of compelling methodological and theoretical challenges. These challenges originate in the difficulty of simply defining ethnicity, ethnic groups and other related concepts (e.g. **acculturation** and **assimilation**). Even researchers who study living people, whose behaviours can be observed and whose thoughts can be recorded directly, disagree over the most appropriate definitions of these terms. Historical archaeologists face the additional challenge of finding meaningful definitions that also allow observation of pertinent variables in the material and documentary records.

Throughout the twentieth century, scholars have suggested various definitions of ethnic groups, stressing diverse factors. Depending on whose definition is chosen, members of ethnic groups are seen as: sharing some combination of traits, including a common psychological identification, a common history or presumed common history and a constellation of cultural, behavioural or physical characteristics; pursuing social and political power by capitalising on a recognisable identity; participating in ecological and economic interdependent relationships with the members of other ethnic groups, often under conditions where resources are scarce; or using ethnic identity to extend lines of relationship and altruistic behaviour to a greater number of individuals than kinship systems allow. A definition that works relatively well for archaeology is one that stresses ethnic-group distinctive patterns of behaviour and related patterns of material well preserved in the archaeological record.

Definitions for historical archaeology

In accordance with the previous discussion, an ethnic group is first defined as a particular kind of social group. Any social group consists of people who share common attitudes, values, beliefs, behavioural ideals and representative symbols, both abstract and material. What distinguishes an ethnic group from other social groups is that the former serves two related functions. First, ethnic groups provide members with an identity that is perceived to be both ascriptive and exclusive. Second, ethnic groups allow members to establish primary relationships with fellow members: others who share that identity.

Ascriptive means that movement into the group is not a matter of individual choice. Exclusive means that movement out of the group is just as impossible so far as individual motivation is concerned. True ascriptive and exclusive groups are very rare, if not non-existent (castes come close), and the ascriptive and exclusive qualities of ethnic groups are strictly symbolic. Thus, in reality individuals can change the ethnic group with which they are identified; it just does not seem as if they can. Primary relationships are those that are intimate, informal, deeply personal and face-to-face. They are experienced on a daily basis, and require the involvement of the entire personality.

Defining ethnic groups in this manner compels one to focus on function and process, and not on any artificial descriptive classification of ethnic-group traits, either material or otherwise. Thus, while not eliminating all methodological challenges for the archaeologist, the definition is nevertheless useful because it removes the temptation to simply equate ethnic groups with archaeological cultures, that is, distinctive collections of artefact forms, styles and types that recur together. It is widely understood that archaeological cultures do not adequately represent any social or cultural reality. Any similarly conceived definition of ethnic group would be equally useless.

Groups studied

In North America, historical archaeologists have selectively studied certain ethnic groups repeatedly, while almost completely ignoring others. The vast majority of research has concerned groups who, traditionally, have been pushed to the social and economic margins of society: African Americans, Hispanics and Asian Americans. Relatively little attention has been given to groups having European ancestry, whether this be Northern, Western, Eastern or Mediterranean Europe.

North American scholars have also studied various situations of culture contact and interaction between Westerners and indigenous North American peoples, though these studies are usually not included within the literature of ethnicity in historical archaeology. Rather, they most often fall under the rubric of ethnohistory, and are not considered here. This work is similar to the majority of historical archaeology that occurs outside both North America and Europe.

In Europe itself the situation is different. Historical archaeologists there do not observe circumstances of rapid, relatively short-term, but nevertheless consequential, contact between expanding European and indigenous peoples. Rather, the archaeological record reflects contact and interaction between diverse European populations over a relatively long period of time. It is nevertheless the case that those studying ethnicity there emphasise European groups once living on the geographic and political margins of the continent (e.g. Northern Irish, Scottish). This emphasis mirrors the choices of North American scholars who emphasise the socially and economically marginal.

There are a number of possible explanations for these patterns. For instance, the ethnic groups studied most have frequently been labelled racial groups as well. As such, they have been subject to extraordinary treatment by members of dominant groups (e.g. they have been subject to extreme discrimination and prejudice). This treatment has resulted in greater visibility in the archaeological record, and more feasible archaeological research. Second, those ethnic groups given most attention by historical archaeologists are also commonly the most poorly represented in the documentary record. Historical archaeologists have seen the greater need to study these people with archaeological means, and by doing so bring them into historical consciousness.

Settings studied

Historical archaeologists studying ethnicity focus on certain social and geographical settings, as well as certain time periods, while nearly ignoring others. Emphasis is given to those situations where ethnic groups experienced a relatively great degree of contact with one another, and with other social groups (including dominant groups). The theoretical assumption is that ethnicity will be most pronounced in such situations, either in the form of resistance to potential change or in the form of change itself by acculturation and assimilation. It is thought that the greater visibility of ethnic identity under such circumstances has both behavioural and material expression.

Social settings in which contact is great include cities, frontiers and other social and political boundaries. Ethnic studies in historical archaeology concentrate on places that exhibit a combination of contact-inducing characteristics (e.g. cities on frontiers or international borders).

Geographical locations and time periods explored are more reflections of the ethnic groups studied and the specific topics investigated. For example, in North America the majority of archaeological research on African Americans is conducted in the south-eastern United States and Caribbean, at the sites of antebellum and recently postbellum plantations where occupation was concentrated. The impacts and legacy of slavery are common topics of study. In contrast, archae-

ologists who study Hispanics concentrate on the south-eastern and south-western US, and Caribbean. Most of this research concerns the earlier, Spanish colonial period, with a topical interest in the experiences of Spanish colonists who came into contact with Native Americans. Finally, those who study Asian American ethnic groups concentrate their efforts on the western USA and Canada, and direct their attention to nineteenth- and early twentieth-century materials. A favourite topical interest concerns the seeming lack of acculturation and assimilation experienced by members of these groups, despite significant contact with non-Asian populations.

Outside North America and Europe, archaeologists studying ethnicity focus on locations where, and time periods when, contact between indigenous groups and Europeans was at its most extreme. Within Europe no comparable focus exists, although temporally there might be an edge given to post-medieval and industrial-age settings (i.e. **post-medieval archaeology** and **industrial archaeology**).

Theoretical concerns

The primary theoretical issue explored by historical archaeologists studying ethnicity concerns the nature of ethnic group maintenance and transformation under various conditions. In the face of culture contact and change, why do some ethnic groups survive, and sometimes even enhance their ability to persist, while others experience significant degrees of acculturation and assimilation to the point, in some cases, that they disappear? This is the primary theoretical question facing all historical archaeologists who study ethnicity.

Archaeologists confronting this complex issue do not seek out specific material symbols of ethnic identification, recognising that such objects are rare and not often committed to the archaeological record. Rather, there is an attempt to delineate patterns of more common material items that are thought to reflect patterns of behaviour distinctive to ethnic group members. Of these behaviours, much attention is given to the acquisition and use of consumer goods and, more specifically, the nature of foodways.

Studying foodways has resulted in some success.

Dietary patterns, as reflected in how foods are selected, prepared and consumed, seem to suggest ethnic-group affiliation more often and more clearly than other consumer patterns do. It has also been suggested that these dietary patterns more directly reflect ethnic identity than other social-group affiliation, such as class or status. Still, there is clearly no simple correspondence between foodways and ethnic identity. This problem is most obvious when the transformation of ethnic groups through acculturation and assimilation is being studied; degree of dependence on traditional ethnic foodways is no measure of degree of identity with an ethnic group.

Historical archaeologists are aware of this problem. Indeed, the primary methodological issue among those who study ethnicity concerns recognising and measuring ethnic-group characteristics in the archaeological record. Related to this issue is the challenge of defining ethnicity and related terms in ways that are meaningful and useful given the constraints of archaeology.

See also: acculturation; assimilation; class, social; gender; industrial archaeology; post-medieval archaeology; urban archaeology

Further reading

McGuire, R.H. (1982) 'The study of ethnicity in historical archaeology', *Journal of Anthropological Archaeology* 1: 159–78.

Penner, B.R. (1997) 'Old World traditions, New World landscapes: Ethnicity and archaeology of Swiss-Appenzellers in the colonial South Carolina backcountry', *International Journal of Historical Archaeology* 1(4): 257–321.

Shennan, S. J. (ed.) (1989) *Archaeological Approaches to Cultural Identity*, London: Unwin Hyman.

Staski, E. (1990) 'Studies of ethnicity in North American historical archaeology', *North American Archaeologist* 11(2): 121–45.

EDWARD STASKI

ethnoarchaeology

Ethnoarchaeology is a term that has evolved within archaeology since the late 1970s. When it was first widely used by archaeologists, the term had two meanings: one restrictive and one broad.

The most accepted use of the term refers to the conduct of ethnographic research for specific archaeological purposes. The key elements of ethnoarchaeology, when defined in this manner, are:

1 that an archaeologist must conduct the research;
2 that the questions posed by the investigator should have clear archaeological relevance;
3 that the research can be conducted among any living population, not just so-called 'primitive' or 'traditional' people; and
4 that the ultimate object of the research is to understand the past.

Ethnoarchaeology defined in this way emphasises archaeological goals, in that the investigator's observations are meant to reflect archaeologically inspired questions. For example, when James Skibo conducted ethnoarchaeological research among the Kalinga in the northern Philippines, his goal was to study how daily use affected and modified pottery. Working as an archaeologist within a living community, his goal was not to record the daily lives of the people themselves as would an ethnographer. As a result, his findings about the chemical and physical changes experienced by the pottery made and used by the Kalinga can be used to frame broadly applicable questions about the use-alteration of any pottery collection.

The first meaning of ethnoarchaeology is most widely used by archaeologists, but a few historical archaeologists have used the other, broader meaning of the term. When used in this way, 'ethnoarchaeology' refers simply to the union of archaeological data and historical sources of information. These 'historical' sources can include oral interviewing, personal observation and archival research. William Adams's study of Silcott, Washington, USA – an early twentieth-century farming community – provides a clear example of this meaning of ethnoarchaeology. In the course of his research, Adams combined the results of his archaeological excavations with personal interviews with some of the town's former inhabitants, period photographs showing daily activities in the community and **historical documents** about the town. Using this methodology, Adams produced a rich, humanistic picture of past life in Silcott.

The use of the second meaning of ethnoarchaeology has been more common in historical archaeology than in prehistoric archaeology, simply because more sources of information, such as documents, pictures and living informants, are available only for recent periods of history. As a result, historical archaeologists are more likely to envision their work as broadly defined 'ethnoarchaeology'. By the late twentieth century, however, most historical archaeologists had abandoned the second meaning of the term, preferring instead to see this kind of historical archaeology as merely conducted within the best multidisciplinary tradition of the discipline. Most archaeologists working in the year 2000 generally know 'ethnoarchaeology' as **ethnography** conducted for archaeological purposes.

See also: behavioural historical archaeology

Further reading

Adams, W.H. (1977) *Silcott, Washington: Ethnoarchaeology of a Rural American Community*, Pullman: Laboratory of Anthropology, Washington State University.

Gould, R.A. (1980) *Living Archaeology*, Cambridge: Cambridge University Press.

Kramer, C. (ed.) (1979) *Ethnoarchaeology: Implications of Ethnography for Archaeology*, New York: Columbia University Press.

Longacre, W.A. and Skibo, J.M. (1994) *Kalinga Ethnoarchaeology: Expanding Archaeological Method and Theory*, Washington, DC: Smithsonian Institution Press.

Skibo, J.M. (1992) *Pottery Function: A Use-Alteration Perspective*, New York: Plenum Press.

CHARLES E. ORSER, JR

ethnographic analogy

Ethnographic analogy is an interpretive tool that archaeologists use to assist in understanding archaeological information. The term refers to the use of ethnographic accounts of contemporary cultures that have been gathered by cultural anthropologists and are then used by archaeologists to explain excavated artefact assemblages. The assumption behind archaeological interpretations using ethnographic analogies is that observed behaviours can be relatively similar to past behaviours, and therefore it is appropriate to draw parallels between present and past behaviours.

The use of ethnographic analogy in archaeological interpretation became a significant area of research in the 1960s as part of the **New Archaeology**. More specifically, ethnographic analogy is associated with **ethnoarchaeology**, an avenue of inquiry that became popular among archaeologists in the 1960s and 1970s. During this time period, many archaeologists attempted to use material generated from ethnographies to explain their archaeological findings. Two of the best-known examples are the works by Lewis Binford and Richard Gould. Binford conducted an **ethnography** of the Nunamiut in Alaska, where he recorded what happened to animal bones as a result of the hunting, butchering and disposal practices of the Nunamiut. He conducted the study with three objectives in mind. The first objective was to use ethnographic information to assess the overall utility of several methods of analysis in **zooarchaeology**. His second objective was to develop new methods of faunal analysis. Finally, he used this ethnographic information in the analysis of artefact assemblages recovered from other parts of the world, a process that has been repeated by numerous other archaeologists.

Gould's use of ethnographic analogy in his work was somewhat different from Binford's. Gould began with an ethnography of Australian aborigines, where he examined their use of **material culture** (particularly the foods they ate and how they were prepared) and then immediately followed his ethnography with an excavation of former Aboriginal habitation areas. Gould's intent was to use the interplay of ethnographic information in corroboration of or in contrast to the excavated archaeological information to better understand the lifeways of the Aborigines, and to better understand the strengths and weaknesses of archaeological data.

With regard to historical archaeology, while the specific term 'ethnographic analogy' is used rather infrequently in the literature, there are many examples of the use of historical ethnographic accounts or oral-history information to help interpret archaeological data. An example of this approach was the excavation of a Dakota Indian village by Janet Spector. The village, known as 'Inyan Ceyaka Atonwan' (Village at the Rapids), was located in south-eastern Minnesota and had been occupied during the early to mid-nineteenth century, a period when the area had been regularly visited by fur traders and missionaries. The traders and missionaries who travelled through the region recorded fairly extensive descriptions of the Dakota Indians who lived in the region. When Spector excavated a village in the 1980s, she used these written accounts to interpret her archaeological data. Particularly compelling was Spector's use of a description of how women recorded their production of objects on their awls. Spector used this ethnographic vignette to explain the markings on the awl she excavated, as well as to create a richly textured account of the Dakota village.

While ethnographic analogies provide several different avenues of interpretation for both prehistoric and historical archaeologists, scholars have also expressed concerns with overextending these comparisons. They note that it is important to be mindful that cultures (see **culture**) change over time and that behaviours in one group are not necessarily the same from one region to another. It has also been argued that historical archaeologists in particular must be sensitive to the potential biases of the ethnographic, historical or oral-history data they gather to help explain the archaeological record. While ethnographic analogy can be a powerful interpretive tool for archaeologists, it should be noted that it is crucial to assess the suitability of such comparisons. Ethnographic analogies can help to explain past lifeways but also, when used indiscriminately, they can project behaviours on to past cultures that are not appropriately associated with that particular culture.

See also: cultural anthropology; ethnoarchaeology; ethnography; New Archaeology; oral history

Further reading

Adams, W.H. (1977) *Silcott, Washington: Ethnoarchaeology of a Rural American Community*, Pullman: Laboratory of Anthropology, Washington State University.

Binford, L. (1978) *Nunamiut Ethnoarchaeology*, New York: Academic Press.

Gould, R. (1980) *Living Archaeology*, Cambridge: Cambridge University Press.

Purser, M. (1992) 'Oral history and historical archaeology', in B.J. Little (ed.) *Text-Aided Archaeology*, Boca Raton, FL: CRC Press, pp. 25–35.

Spector, J.D. (1993) *What this Awl Means: Feminist Archaeology at a Wahpeton Dakota Village*, St Paul: Minnesota Historical Society Press.

MARK S. WARNER

ethnography

An ethnography is a detailed description of a society, produced by directly observing the daily lives of its members. Ethnographies are written by ethnologists who often, but not exclusively, focus upon familial and genealogical structure, social organisation, political economy, technology (means and mode of production) and spiritual structure.

Ethnographies are ideally based upon long-term field observation (participant observation) of comparatively small social groups. These observations are then extrapolated to offer generalisations about the whole society. Ethnographic studies have traditionally been normative, and focused on the integrative or systemic character of culture. They tend to focus on idealised behaviour, and emphasise social conventions that perpetuate the *status quo*. Less analytical attention is paid to individual action, or social discord and transformation. As **sociocultural anthropology** continues to evolve, these generalisations become less valid. Contemporary research addresses, for example, social deviance and conflict, gender studies, intragroup power relations and culture change. Since archaeological utilisation of ethnography is historically oriented, it tends to focus on the traditional ethnographic literature.

Early ethnologists frequently addressed non-Western cultures. The underlying rationale was the documentation of cultures that were subject to **acculturation** by Western (or colonising) societies. This reflects a 'salvage' orientation that followed the assumption that these societies were likely to disappear in face of **assimilation**.

Consequently, many older ethnographies are cast in the 'ethnographic present', an analytical construct whereby the idealised structure and operation of the society was presented as it was thought to exist prior to disruption by colonial contact.

While ethnographic studies provide intimate insight into the structure and dynamic operation of a society, their integration into historical analysis can be difficult. For example, does the ethnography reflect the observed conditions, or is it an extrapolation of what were thought to be traditional cultural values and social behaviour? Can such normative extrapolations be used for historical and archaeological analysis? The discipline of ethnohistory aids in addressing these issues. It represents the integration of ethnographic literature with historical text to document the direction of culture change. The ethnohistorian seeks to understand culture change by developing a temporal framework, and identifying pressures that contributed to change. Such an approach enables more credible use of ethnographic data, and permits informed analysis of the consequences of European **colonialism**. Thus, ethnohistorians are oriented to the study of social change, while traditional ethnologists sought to 'filter out' the disruptive effects of recent cultural transformation.

Historical archaeologists interested in Aboriginal societies often use ethnographic data to develop interpretative frameworks for archaeological data. This can range from providing a functional context for the material culture, through to aiding the reconstruction of belief systems, land use and the political economy. The ethnographic data may be used to deductively define an archaeological research problem, or aid in the *post hoc* interpretation of archaeologically observed patterns.

Ethnographic information is often used to develop analogies (see **ethnographic analogy**). Human activity is interpreted by comparing ethnographically documented objects and structures to archaeological phenomena that exhibit formal similarities. This might involve functional interpretation of archaeologically recovered objects by reference to ethnographic descriptions of similar objects in use. An example is Binford's (1967) functional interpretation of archaeologically observed shallow pits based upon comparison to ethnographically reported smudge pits. In this case,

no direct relationship is necessarily asserted between the ethnographically observed group and the archaeological site of interest. Instead, the ethnographic information provides a general interpretative frame for the archaeological data. Other types of analogy require that a direct relationship be demonstrated between the ethnographic and archaeological data. For example, interpretation of archaeologically observed sacred imagery might involve comparison to similar images noted in the ethnographic literature. This might require that a cultural link be established between the contemporary practitioners and the ancient artists. Demonstration of such a relationship would strengthen interpretative credibility. Such analogies might then be used to assert continuity of spiritual practice, patterns of population migration or, alternatively, continuity of occupation. Such direct historical analogies are difficult to develop, and risk tautology.

Historical archaeologists routinely synthesise historical and ethnographic information to contextualise archaeological data. When historical archaeologists address the more recent past, sometimes they solicit information directly from living informants. This might include direct memories of people who occupied the place of archaeological interest, or reminiscences passed down through the generations. At its most superficial, such research might address the physical layout, function and transformation of specific historic sites. At a more profound level, it might involve social, economic or spiritual issues that have relevance for the archaeological interpretation. The integration of **oral history** is particularly important when the archaeological study is focused on populations for whom written records are rare, or were exclusively written by outside observers. In such circumstances, the historical archaeologist may be able to contribute to historical revision that gives voice to historically subordinated or disenfranchised social groups. By combining oral history with archaeological data, new insights might develop that run counter to the received truths from the written record. This latter record may exclusively reflect the perspectives of the literate elite. While ethnographic and archaeological data have systematic biases, so too does the written record. The challenge is in comparing alternative information sources, and developing a new synthesis that accounts for the ambiguities that become apparent.

See also: ordinary people's culture

Further reading

Binford, L.R. (1967) 'Smudge pits and hide smoking: The use of analogy in archaeological reasoning', *American Antiquity* 32: 1–12.

Mrozowski, S.A. (1988) 'Historical archaeology as anthropology', *Historical Archaeology* 22(1): 18–24.

Orser, C.E., Jr (1972) 'Ethnohistory, analogy, and historical archaeology', *Conference on Historic Site Archaeology Papers* 13: 1–24.

Orser, C.E., Jr and Fagan, B.M. (1995) *Historical Archaeology*, New York: HarperCollins.

SCOTT HAMILTON

everyday life

Everyday life as a focus of historical archaeological research is as elusive to define as it is all-encompassing. At the same time that it includes consideration of those quotidian activities and behaviours that are so ubiquitous as to be hardly thought of, everyday life contains the essence of **culture**. The study of everyday life might include research into foodways (see **food and foodways**) and drinking, **architecture**, furnishings, **dress**, art and decoration, health and sanitation, manners, education, funerary practices, marriage and living arrangements, **leisure** and recreation, social organisation, religion and **folklore**, government, law, warfare, manufacture and crafts, farming and anything else that might come into view in the course of an ordinary day. It is more a focus on the cultural anthropological or ethnological rather than the historical, the ways in which people lived and interacted within a cultural context rather than in light of a particular historical event. It might be described as the study of those activities and behaviours that support survival, both biological and cultural.

Historical archaeologists became increasingly involved with the study of everyday life as part of a general move away from the discipline's roots in the study of sites associated with specific historic

events or significant players in those events: in short, sites associated with 'firsts', historic homes of famous figures, and battlefield sites. With increasing interest in widening the focus of historical research to include women and ethnic minorities in the late 1960s and early 1970s, the idea of using everyday life gained currency. Everyday life as a research focus is by nature inclusive in its subject matter: women, **children**, servants, enslaved people and those who would not ordinarily have constituted a part of earlier research are more often readily considered for inclusion in the study of everyday life. Most recently, this inclusive sort of study has been championed by post-processualist (see **post-processual archaeology**), Marxian (see **Marxian approaches**) and feminist researchers (see **feminist archaeology**).

With this definition in mind, the study of everyday life might reasonably be expected to exclude those situations where the subjects represented a small elite portion of the population or where there were extraordinary constraints (such as regulations imposed by prison or ecclesiastical orders, or other regulated institutions), but it would be erroneous to confine research to the households of 'ordinary folk'. While the analysis of abbey architecture or the design of a military encampment would not fit under this rubric, for example, a study of the structure of monastic life or how soldiers lived in a camp would be included as everyday life. The archaeology of everyday life is not restricted solely to the household or to domestic home life and does not necessarily exclude that which is extraordinary (such as holidays or rites of passage) because that both is created by and shapes the culture in addition to informing the researcher. The archaeological treatment of everyday life examines individuals or families or communities and how they interact with and within their culture. Thus, depending on the subject, that experience of everyday life may vary compared with others in a society.

Historical archaeology is particularly suited to the study of everyday life because the data are such that they often can be corroborated by other sources, and information can be recovered for a household or community even when it is not created by the subjects themselves. On the other hand, the evidence of activities found on a site might actually contradict what is found in the documentary record, informing the researcher what was publicly stated (or personally believed) and what was actually done.

James Deetz, in his groundbreaking volume *In Small Things Forgotten*, explicitly addressed some of the issues that historical archaeologists must consider when investigating everyday life. Stating that even the most insignificant items of **material culture** could reveal larger pieces of a culture – 'in the seemingly little and insignificant things that accumulate to create a lifetime, the essence of our existence is captured' – Deetz exhorted historical archaeologists to move beyond the simple recognition of the presence of artefacts on a site by situating these goods into their social and cultural milieux, considering the cultural processes that brought the artefacts to the site and the ones that governed their use and discard. Employing a structuralist approach, Deetz sought to identify large-scale social changes that occurred in colonial times through observations of quotidian objects recovered archaeologically. Artefacts bear a wealth of cultural symbolic meaning, and while individual objects are significant, it is through assemblages, sometimes *in situ*, that the most information can be extracted. Catastrophic events (such as shipwrecks, volcanic eruptions, fire or earthquake) that 'freeze' and preserve an assemblage in place often provide important data on everyday life.

Similarly, some very detailed illustrations (including Dutch and Flemish genre representations and prints or paintings by William Hogarth) often suggest how houses, rooms and outdoor spaces were organised, in addition to how (and in what contexts) specific artefacts or classes of artefacts were used. These illustrations are particularly useful when it comes to the study of **ceramics**, dress and foodways, as well as posture and gesture, but, as with every source available to the archaeologist, ought to be used carefully and with due consideration of the bias of the artist, as the items or situations depicted might be more a result of the preferences, ideas (political or fashionable or satirical) and what was available in the studio. Equally, the illustration might reflect the sitter's statements of social **identity** and taste rather than an absolutely accurate representation of daily life.

All manner of other sorts of documents – ranging from newspapers, to books, to insurance maps, photographs, tombstones, diaries, letters, tax documents, account books, censuses and city registers, probate records and wills, advertisements – can be used to learn about everyday life. Biases are also present in official or private records, whether through unwitting omissions or additions, prejudices, knowledge or point of view.

In addition to studying artefacts and documentary evidence, archaeologists also need to consider non-tangible behaviour. Social rituals, manners and religion are among those elements of culture that affect the shape of the archaeological record or its correct interpretation. Many of these things will be components of social identity and, while intangible, are key to understanding what objects found on a site meant or how they were used.

Living-history museums, particularly when supported in some way by archaeological or historical research, attempt to show the public how life might have looked at a given time or place and, in doing so, create a sense of place and community that puts actors in historical roles. More useful to the archaeological researcher is the ongoing experimentation in using items (such as tools or domestic equipment) or in trying to reconstruct structures or crafts, whereby the archaeological work and museum studies inform each other.

Very often, everyday life is examined exclusively at the household level; it is best understood at a larger community level and the approach to everyday life is properly an interdisciplinary one. In a carefully considered essay on the multidisciplinary study of the Bixby household in Barre, Massachusetts, John Worrell, Myron Stachiw and David Simmons utilised an archaeological survey of the neighbourhood of Barre Four Corners, an architectural survey of buildings belonging to the families associated with the Bixby family (including structural and decorative details, and site histories), and an intensive archaeological survey of the Bixby lot and structures. The archaeological study of the Bixby property included research into the architectural fabric of the family's house and other structures, the internal arrangement and decoration (including furnishings) of the house, the alteration of external spaces and the stratigraphic information, along with the documentary evidence.

An abrupt and seemingly inexplicable change in the family's account book work entries was revealed, where costly material improvements were made by the family coincident with an apparent decrease in the blacksmithing work. This change was explained in light of understanding the change to a cash-based exchange system (rather than indebtedness and the exchange of labour) and the use of female outwork to contribute to the household income. By examining the documentary and material data within increasingly large research units (from the household itself, through the neighbourhood level, regional level and national and international contexts), it was possible to see how the Bixby family and their neighbours responded to the dramatic social and economic changes that took place in early nineteenth-century **New England**.

Diana Wall's exploration of domestic sites in **New York City** at the turn of the nineteenth century reveals the active roles played by men and women in the separation of the home and workplace. Wall detected changes in the documentary and archaeological records that showed the close relationship between social behaviour and material culture, particularly where meals were concerned, between 1780 and 1840. She observed that the timing and service of meals (as well as the table settings used to shape these) was altered at the same time the workplace was removed from the home. The archaeological recovery of different sets of tablewares indicates the increased emphasis on family meals as rituals that established the centrality and sanctity of the family in what was perceived as an increasingly hostile and commercial world, an indication of how outside forces prompted significant reaction on the part of families that markedly altered their daily existence.

Another study noted for its treatment of everyday life is the **Boott Mills** research project in Lowell, Massachusetts. By examining the boarding house back lots of nineteenth-century textile mill workers, Mary Beaudry and Stephen Mrozowski observed the structure of corporate paternalism and how workers responded to that regulation with independent acts both open and covert. The archaeologists demonstrated the differences between what the management wanted and what workers actually did, by revealing the workers' aspirations to middle-class

gentility and respectability in choosing living situations that accommodated those aspirations and by indulging in behaviours, such as smoking and drinking, that were active responses to strict corporate regulation, poverty or expressions of individual or group identity. By using the mill regulations as a starting place and then observing in the archaeological record how that was challenged by the workers, Beaudry and Mrozowski were able to develop a vivid picture of life for the workers in the mill community.

Any study of everyday life must be sensitive to the cycles that govern the pattern of life at a particular place or time. The rhythm of seasons, agriculture, animal husbandry or tides dictates what will be required at a given time or place, particularly in non-industrial contexts, and artificially imposed calendars – such as economic years or fashion seasons – may need to be considered in industrial settings. Even the movement of an individual from birth through life to death within a society is important to understand, revealing how an individual might move or change status in a society.

See also: architecture; ceramics; food and foodways; identity

Further reading

Beaudry, M.C. and Mrozowski, S.A. (eds) (1989) *Interdisciplinary Investigations of the Boott Mills, Lowell, Massachusetts, Vol. III: The Boarding House System as a Way of Life*, Cultural Resource Management Study 21, Boston: National Park Service.

—— (1988) *Interdisciplinary Investigations of the Boott Mills, Lowell, Massachusetts, Vol. II: The Kirk Street Agents' House*, Boston: National Park Service.

—— (eds) (1987) *Interdisciplinary Investigations of the Boott Mills, Lowell, Massachusetts, Vol. 1: Life at the Boarding Houses: A Preliminary Report*, Boston: National Park Service.

Deetz, J. (1977) *In Small Things Forgotten: The Archaeology of Early American Life*, Garden City, NY: Anchor Press/Doubleday.

Wall, D.D. (1994) *The Archaeology of Gender: Separating the Spheres in Urban America*, New York: Plenum Press.

Worrell, J., Stachiw, M.O. and Simmons, D.M. (1996) 'Archaeology from the ground up', in L. De Cunzo and B.L. Herman (eds) *Historical Archaeology and the Study of American Culture*, Winterthur: The Henry Francis du Pont Winterthur Museum, pp. 35–69.

LORINDA B.R. GOODWIN

excavation methods, terrestrial

Archaeologists have a number of excavation methods they can use to investigate an archaeological site. The method chosen must conform to several conditions, including the amount of time and funds available, the size of the excavation crew, the purpose and goal of the excavation, the nature of the site itself and the natural environment within which the site exists. Archaeological excavation is a painstaking process that involves map drawing, measurement and photography, in addition to discovering and removing artefacts.

Archaeologists almost never have the opportunity to excavate all of a site, and so they must adopt a 'sampling strategy' that conforms to all the conditions mentioned above. Many archaeologists even prefer not to excavate an entire site, believing it best to leave some of it untouched for future investigators. Many varieties of **sampling** exist, which are grouped into 'non-probabilistic' and 'probabilistic' sampling. Non-probabilistic sampling is a non-mathematically-based method in which the archaeologist attempts to provide a qualitative assessment of a 'sampling universe'. Using this method, archaeologists can simply walk through an area looking for signs of past habitation. Probabilistic sampling is more scientific because the archaeologist imposes a grid over the sampling universe and then samples within the grid's units at a certain level (a 5 per cent sample, for example). When the archaeologist is finished with the survey, he or she can use statistical measures to assess the representativeness of the sample. Archaeologists use sampling both across entire regions and across individual sites.

Excavations at a site can take many different forms, from the smallest 'test pits' to large-scale 'block' excavation. Small test pits (also called 'shovel tests') usually consist of a shovel-sized excavation used to sample a site's deposits in a systematic manner. An archaeologist using test pits usually chooses to place them a set distance apart depending on the size of the site. Test pits are widely used in **cultural-resource management** because they can quickly provide information about the spatial extent, depth and integrity of a buried archaeological site. For example, an archaeologist working in an area several hectares in size that is suspected to have been the location of a single homestead would be wise to select test pits that are fairly closely spaced, lest the sampling completely miss the remains. Some test pits can be as large as 1 × 1 m or even 2 × 2 m. Beyond test pits, the excavations themselves can be almost any size, but archaeologists generally select the dimensions of the excavation units based on the size of the crew and the extent and nature of the site. Archaeologists can use 1 × 2 m or 2 × 2 m units for a single excavator, and can even string them together to create large blocks of excavation or even long trenches. They can use units of any size they deem reasonable. The important point is that the units must be carefully and systematically excavated to permit the collection of all possible information. It is for this reason that archaeologists excavate in such a way that their units have perfectly straight sides (often called 'walls'). The use of straight walls also makes it possible to produce precise drawings of the stratigraphy visible within the unit.

During excavation, archaeologists attempt to remove each soil layer individually, keeping all the artefacts from that layer together. Before the modern-day techniques of excavation were implemented, archaeologists often dug in artificial levels of 1 or 2 inches thick. These arbitrary excavation levels created a false impression of the site's stratigraphy and caused archaeologists to group artefacts from different soil layers in the same excavated level. Archaeologists will sometimes still excavate in artificial levels, but only within thick soil layers where removing the entire layer as a unit is impractical.

Historical archaeologists must be particularly conscious of 'microstratigraphy' at the sites they excavate. Microstratigraphy consists of a series of thin soil layers that are often difficult to discern individually. Prehistorians often encounter micro-stratigraphy when they excavate rockshelters and caves, but historical archaeologists frequently find them at residence sites that have been repeatedly occupied for short time periods, such as tenant farmer sites in the US South.

By the year 2000, most archaeologists used the metric system of measurement. Some historical archaeologists investigating sites associated with **English colonialism**, however, continue to use the English system of measurement, arguing that this usage provides excavation units that are consistent with the colonists' system. The use of the metric vs the English system is a minor matter because the most important consideration is the systematic nature of the excavation, regardless of what measurement system is used. It does explain, however, why historical archaeologists can be seen to work in both systems.

Most archaeological excavation is conducted with hand tools, with spades and trowels being the most commonly used implements. Archaeologists who have a huge area to examine or who know that their site is deeply buried sometimes use mechanised equipment to remove the 'over burden', the soil lying on top of the remains of interest. Machinery will speed the process of excavation but it must be done carefully by skilled operators. Excavated earth is usually sifted through screening material to facilitate the collection of small objects, like **beads**, coins and straight pins. Archaeologists usually collect some earth, particularly from human-built 'features' (hearths, storage pits, ash lenses), for flotation, a method in which the soil sample is washed through water to ease the collection of seeds and extremely small artefacts.

Further reading

Barker, P. (1982) *Techniques of Archaeological Excavation*, second edn, New York: Universe Books.

Hester, T.R., Shafer, H.J. and Feder, K.L. (1997) *Field Methods in Archaeology*, seventh edn, Mountain View, CA: Mayfield.

Joukowsky, M. (1980) *A Complete Manual of Field Archaeology: Tools and Techniques of Field Work for Archaeologists*, Englewood Cliffs, NJ: Prentice-Hall.

Wheeler, M. (1954) *Archaeology from the Earth*, Baltimore: Penguin.

Woolley, L. (1930) *Digging up the Past*, Harmondsworth, Middlesex: Penguin.

CHARLES E. ORSER, JR

excavation methods, underwater

Archaeological excavation underwater is the controlled dismantling of submerged deposits in order to reveal surfaces, structures, objects and materials relating to past human existence (Fig 9). In practice, underwater excavation entrains other activities such as recording, which together comprise the methodology of archaeology. Excavation is therefore an element in the process of archaeology beginning with the formulation of research goals in the context of existing knowledge, advancing through stages of data gathering, analysis and reconstruction, thereby building new interpretations.

Just as on land, underwater archaeological sites cannot be un-excavated; hence the process is inherently destructive and can only be mitigated through comprehensive recording and publication. The decision to excavate underwater is given additional gravitas because the conservation of materials from waterlogged and marine environments can be problematic and expensive. For all these reasons the archaeological profession regards excavation as a last resort in the investigation of a finite, non-renewable resource. The trend has therefore been towards policies of 'preservation *in situ*', especially as our ability to characterise sites using non-intrusive techniques has advanced significantly. In essence, therefore, excavation can only be justified in two ways: when research questions cannot be answered any other way and/or the site is under some sort of threat.

Underwater excavation, as on land, consists of two distinct procedures each of which has its associated tools: first, the actual digging to reveal archaeological material, and, second, the removal of 'spoil' – the unwanted sediments loosened in the process. Underwater deposits are generally less consolidated, which means that digging can sometimes be done with that most sensitive of instruments: the human hand. Otherwise tools are the same as those used on land: trowels, brushes, dental picks, etc. In contrast, spoil removal underwater is very different. Occasionally, the current alone is sufficient but normally suction devices are used, adapted from those first developed for industry.

The first to be drafted into archaeological service was the airlift, a rigid pipe into which compressed air is introduced at the lower end. As the air rises up the pipe it expands and accelerates, creating suction (see Fig. 10a). The power obtained is a function of the length of the pipe relative to the water depth and of the volume of air supplied by the compressor. They do not therefore work efficiently in very shallow water (< 2 m). Airlifts for archaeological purposes are commonly made from 75–150 mm diameter plastic soil-pipe (see Dean *et al.* 1992: 308–9).

An alternative is the water-dredge, variously known as a 'water-suction dredge' or 'induction dredge'. This produces a similar effect as the airlift but is powered by water from a pump. Introduced as a jet across the intake, a venturi action is produced creating suction (Dean *et al.* 1992: 310–12). Advantages over the airlift include the smaller power plant needed to produce the equivalent suction and that it can be used in any depth of water. It is used more or less horizontally, again appropriate for shallow water, the spoil being moved along the sea-bed rather than up into the water column. This has advantages for maintaining visibility on sites with little current.

Another power tool occasionally used is the water jet. This is simply high-pressure water released through various shaped nozzles at a volume and pressure appropriate for the task. The indiscriminate nature of a high-velocity jet of water, let alone its effect on visibility, limits its application on archaeological sites. Miniature versions run off a water-dredge, however, can be highly effective for delicate work (see Fig. 10b: inset). Rows of small water jets can also be used to induce an artificial current, e.g. in lakes.

All these devices can be highly efficient, indeed

Figure 9 Underwater archaeologists at work at Port Royal, Jamaica
Source: Photo: D. L. Hamilton

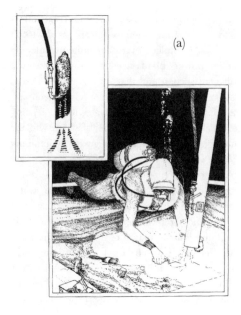

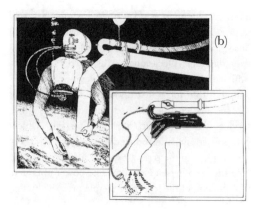

Figure 10 Underwater archaeologists at work
(10a) An airlift fitted with a quarter-turn valve within easy
reach. The operator holds it by the rim. This helps to
prevent the intake getting too near fragile material and
also enables buoyancy adjustment. (Drawing: J. Adams)
(10b) A water-dredge with control valve. It can be used in
various configurations. Floats are fitted to provide neutral
buoyancy. A small hose can be attached to the supply tube
to power a 'micro-jet' (inset), ideal for excavating delicate
materials. (Drawing: J. Adams)

too much so. One of the mistakes of some pioneers
was to treat underwater excavation as an engineering task rather than an archaeological one. On the
assumption that any equipment made for use by
divers must be indestructible, airlifts and dredges
were often over-engineered. However ingeniously
fabricated, such devices were cumbersome and
difficult to use with control. This was not seen as a
disadvantage as they were used as the actual digging
tool; in other words, the distinction between
excavating and spoil removal went unrecognised.
The operator dug directly into the sea-bed, indiscriminately sucking sediment and anything in it to
the surface or into a sieve. This technique was
fundamentally inappropriate for two reasons. First,
while some things may survive such conveyance,
fragile objects and organic materials in particular are
likely to disintegrate. As the preservation of organics
is one of the key advantages of underwater sites,
recovering them this way is utterly perverse. Second,
an object seen for the first time on the surface or
when collected from a sieve has been divorced from
its archaeological context. Yet it is in the relationships between objects, assemblages, structures and
landscapes that so much of archaeology's potential
lies, particularly so in 'closed finds' of which
shipwrecks are such a notable example.

This heavy-duty attitude to the 'mining' of
artefacts betrayed the object-oriented approach of
much early work. Interest was typically focused on
the intrinsic qualities of artefacts as things rather
than on their relationships and wider social contexts.
It was not that these aspects were regarded as
uninteresting, but the possibility they could be
recovered was not appreciated, an understandable
oversight when few archaeologists actually dived. A
shift in conceptual approach began to occur in the
late 1950s, crystallised in George Bass's excavation
in 1960 of the Bronze Age shipwreck at Cape
Gelidonya in Turkey. This was the first entirely
underwater excavation that in every aspect would
still satisfy modern professional codes of conduct.
Thereafter, steady advances were made, particularly
on those excavations that had to address the recovery
of thousands of well-preserved but fragile organic
objects and samples, e.g. wreck sites such as the *Mary
Rose*, Armada wrecks off Ireland, Canada's Red Bay
wreck, the VOC *Batavia* and submerged settlement
sites in Denmark, Scotland and Switzerland. On
these projects the aim was to achieve the same
standards as would be expected on land. It was soon
realised that there was a direct relationship between

the design of the various tools and the standard of excavation one could achieve when using them. The Mary Rose project, on which over 30,000 dives were made, saw each generation of airlift become simpler and lighter. Excavation was carried out with greater ease and, as a result, with greater *control*, the watchword of all excavation. In this mode the excavator dug with a tool appropriate to the deposit and the finds within it. Airlifts and dredges were relegated to removing spoil. In other words, the distinction between excavating and spoil removal was honoured and the inextricable link between practice and theory more sharply perceived.

With light, manœuvrable tools it was also possible for excavators to avoid resting themselves or their equipment directly on the deposit being dug. This may not be problematic on rocky sea-beds but on less consolidated sediments one can do untold damage to organic materials just below the surface, reducing visibility in the process. If the risk assessment allows, fins are often dispensed with for these reasons. Instead, a grid or similar framework is erected over the excavation area. With their feet on the grid, excavators hover over the trench, only touching the deposit with the tools selected, an ability that gravity denies to land diggers. *Mary Rose* workers practised a further refinement that utilised the increase in an airlift's buoyancy when the intake is partially obstructed. Holding the airlift by the rim, buoyancy is adjusted simply by opening one's fingers into the water flow. Excavators can lower and raise themselves into and out of sensitive areas of the trench with ease. For this reason, writers who have designated airlifts as the tool for heavy work and the dredge for delicate work are mistaken. Both can be used extremely delicately, allowing control over the rate at which archaeological material is revealed, and its primary recording to be carried out before removal. A useful maxim is that excavators should know, within reason, what is going up the pipe, otherwise they are excavating too fast or without proper control. Used thus, airlifts and dredges not only keep the visibility clear, they constitute another of the advantages of underwater excavation in being the all-in-one equivalent of the land excavator's dustpan, brush, bucket, wheelbarrow and conveyor-belt. They may also incorporate the land excavator's sieve, although where airlifts are concerned

this can be counterproductive because the additional mass restricts manœuvrability and thus ease of use. Sieves are easier to fit to various configurations of dredge, especially those incorporating a length of flexible exhaust hose. If sieves are used, they should function in the same way as they do on land sites, i.e. as a means of monitoring the general efficiency of excavation procedures and as a safeguard against the loss of unusually small or hard-to-see objects. If too much is found in the sieves, then techniques and procedures need to be modified and/or the pace of excavation slowed.

The other major constraint on the pace of excavation is conservation (see **conservation, underwater**). While research aims, resources and the capacity of the team constrain the overall scope and scale of the project, it is the capacity of the conservation staff and their facilities that will regulate the pace of excavation on a day-to-day basis. In keeping with the old maxim of 'if it's wet keep it wet...' etc., objects are often recovered with a certain amount of their surrounding sediment and taken ashore still within water, thus minimising the impact of their transition from an environment of relative stability.

The formation and stratification (see **stratification, soil**) of those same sediments are also of great concern to the underwater excavator, although much of what has been written on underwater stratigraphy implies it is of lesser importance, especially on shipwreck sites. While sequences on some sites may be relatively simple, the complex stratification one can meet in estuarine conditions or other deeply sedimented bedforms is ignored by excavators at their peril.

Safety

As already described, incorrect use of tools can be highly destructive to archaeological material but can also endanger the user. Proper instruction is always essential. Depth, current and visibility, etc., will all make their use more hazardous, hence codes of practice for archaeological diving should identify the minimum diving qualifications required in various conditions. However equipment is configured, there are some standard guidelines. Spoil-removing tools should not be excessively powerful and must have a control valve within easy reach of the operator. Airlifts should be rigged to prevent them rising to the surface if blocked. Diving equipment should be configured so that nothing is sucked into the intake. However experienced the operators may be, they should never work in circumstances where assistance cannot be rendered immediately.

Reference

Dean, M., Ferrari, B., Oxley, I., Redknap, M. and Watson, K. (eds) 1992.*Archaeology Underwater: The NAS Guide to Principles and Practice*, London: Nautical Archaeology Society.

Further reading

Green, J. (1990) *Maritime Archaeology, a Technical Handbook*, London: Academic Press.

Muckelroy, K. (1978) *Maritime Archaeology*, Cambridge: Cambridge University Press.

JONATHAN ADAMS

exploration

Much historical archaeology has concerned exploration in one way or another. During the initial years of the discipline, it was the early colonial sites associated with Europe's 'Age of Exploration' that attracted the attention of historical archaeologists all over the world. Military **fortifications** and colonial settlements were the places that historical archaeologists could examine the physical manifestations of exploration.

The topics historical archaeologists have found to be interesting about exploration generally relate to the characteristics of cultural contact – both as a general anthropological process and as the working out of this process at specific places – and to providing information about individual expeditions.

The excavations of historical archaeologists have provided new insights into specific explorations throughout the world. For example, archaeologists interested in **Spanish colonialism** in the New World have investigated remains associated with the expeditions of Columbus at Hispaniola,

Hernando de Soto in the US south-east and Vásquez de Coronado in the US south-west. Others have followed the path of Lewis and Clark into the US west. Archaeologists in other parts of the world have conducted similar studies of exploration.

One of the most thorough investigations of early European exploration in the New World has focused on the sixteenth-century expeditions of Martin Frobisher. Setting out in 1576, the English explorer made three expeditions to Baffin Bay, just west of Greenland, in his search for the North-west Passage. In 1981, 1990 and 1991, archaeologists led by William Fitzhugh of the Smithsonian Institution conducted a series of field investigations on Kodlunarn Island, the suspected site of Frobisher's blacksmith shop and iron-smelting operation. Showing the significance of **language** in historical archaeology, it is interesting to note that *kodlunarn* is a native word meaning 'white man'. Fitzhugh and his team mapped and examined seventeen structures, including dwellings, the smithy, the assay office and cache pits. In addition, his archaeologists found numerous sixteenth-century artefacts, including fragments of crucible cups, ceramic tiles (see **ceramics**), pieces of English flint, glass **beads** and scraps of iron. They also found the remains of several settlements of the Eastern Inuit, the men and women who met Frobisher's expedition. This research in the Arctic has provided important information about some of the first interactions between indigenous people and European explorers in the New World. In addition, this research, like all research of this nature, provides information about the creation and maintenance of social relations between disparate people, a topic that anthropologists and historians find relevant to their own research.

The search for the physical evidence of Frobisher's expeditions actually began in 1861 when Charles F. Hall attempted to reach the central Arctic in an effort to solve the mystery of the ill-fated Sir John Franklin expedition of 1845–8. Hall was unable to travel as far north as Franklin and his men had gone, so he turned his attention to Baffin Island, where he was the first to locate tangible evidence of Frobisher's expeditions. Hall published his findings – along with drawings of what he termed 'Frobisher relics' – in 1864, in one of the earliest writings in historical archaeology.

The fate of the Franklin expedition – which, like Frobisher's, also went in search of the North-west Passage – had been a profound and haunting mystery since 1848. Lady Jane Franklin spent the rest of her life working to discover the truth of her husband's disappearance, and fifty separate expeditions sailed in search of the expedition's resting place, with many of their participants undoubtedly interested in the £40,000 reward for concrete information. Traces of the Franklin expedition were first discovered in 1850, and scholars now know that Franklin's ships became icebound and that Franklin died on 11 June 1847. With his death, 105 survivors – out of the original 129 – left the stranded ships and trekked south, all to perish on the way.

The exact fate of the expedition was not known until 1984, when Canadian anthropologist Owen Beattie led his own expedition to the site of the Franklin disaster. Beattie's plan was to exhume a number of Franklin graves that had been discovered years before, with the goal of using his knowledge of **forensic anthropology** to provide an answer for what went wrong with the well-equipped expedition. Beattie and his team found and excavated the graves of Franklin crew members John Torrington, aged 20, John Hartnell, aged 25, and William Braine, aged 33, and removed tissue, hair and bone samples from each.

After a scientific analysis of these specimens, Beattie concluded that, in addition to exposure and undoubtedly fear, Franklin's men succumbed to lead and food poisoning as well as pneumonia. The poisoning had been inadvertently caused by the solder on the tin cans they carried with them. Not only did the solder leak a dangerous amount of lead, the poorly joined seams also allowed the food inside to spoil.

Historical archaeology has provided a great deal of concrete information about the extent, nature and activities of expeditions, both as anthropological examples of 'travelling' and as specific historical events. Every place historical archaeologists work is a potential place to discover new information about past expeditions.

Further reading

Beattie, O. and Geiger, J. (1987) *Frozen in Time: Unlocking the Secrets of the Franklin Expedition*, New York: Penguin.

Fitzhugh, W.W. (ed.) (1985) *Cultures in Contact: The Impact of European Contacts on Native American Cultural Institutions, A.D. 1000–1800*, Washington, DC: Smithsonian Institution Press.

Fitzhugh, W.W. and Olin, J.S. (eds) (1993) *Archaeology of the Frobisher Voyages*, Washington, DC: Smithsonian Institution Press.

CHARLES E. ORSER, JR

F

farmstead archaeology in Canada and the USA

Farmsteads constitute the most common type of historic site found in the USA and Canada. Archaeological investigations and analyses of these sites, however, have received little attention in the published literature. Information on farmstead archaeology is sporadic and generally is found only in **cultural-resource management** (CRM) reports and other special documents produced by state, provincial and federal agencies. There have been very few attempts to synthesise information on these sites. One notable exception is a comprehensive bibliography on the **architecture** and archaeology of farms written by Peggy Beedle and Geoffrey Gyrisco in 1996. This lack of readily available information and syntheses is troubling as urban and suburban areas expand into the countryside, resulting in the loss of more and more North American farmsteads to development.

Given the lack of information and synthesis, government historic preservation planners have no guidance on how to preserve these sites or even how to determine which ones are worthy of preservation. As John Wilson noted in 1990, some agencies even ask the question: 'Why study farmsteads, particularly those dating to the nineteenth and early twentieth centuries? They are so common and so well documented!' One compelling reason is that, between AD 1600 and 1900, a majority of the population of the USA and Canada were involved in farming. In order to understand local, state, provincial or regional history it is important to understand agrarian society. Further, the occupants of farms were diverse in terms of **ethnicity**, class (see **class, social**) and agricultural practices, all of which changed dramatically during this 300-year history.

During the colonial period, 90 per cent of the people lived in rural settings. Some were involved in small family subsistence farms, or practising what is known today as sustainable agriculture. The majority produced diverse foods both for their family and for the market-place, with some becoming cash crop farmers. Archaeological investigations of these early sites in the northern colonies focus on small farms owned and operated by families. For example, Mary Beaudry's research at the Spencer–Peirce–Little farm (1635–1986) in Massachusetts and research by archaeologists at Historic St Mary's City in Maryland show the transitions in farming and the diversity in research questions that can be applied to farmsteads. Large cash crop plantations developed in the southern colonies. Archaeological research on colonial and antebellum plantations (see **plantation archaeology**) is a specialised area separate from the investigation of small family-owned or tenant-occupied farmsteads.

In the nineteenth century, the Industrial Revolution and growth of cities in the US North, Midwest and West provided farmers with expanding urban markets for their produce. The nineteenth-century agricultural revolution brought scientific approaches to farming, changing the form, layout and appearance of farms. The material culture of agriculture and of farm households also changed with the mass manufacturing and marketing/advertising of goods, particularly during the late nineteenth and early twentieth centuries. Some archaeologists have uncovered material evidence of these dramatic changes, such as, Louis Berger and Associates' Fort Drum Cultural Resource Project, which examined many nineteenth-century farms in northern New York State.

What components of a farm are of interest to archaeologists? The key features include: the domestic buildings (owner's house, slave quarters, servants' quarters, tenant housing); the barns and stables; outbuildings (kitchens, dairies, outdoor ovens, spring houses, smoke houses); rubbish pits; sheet middens, dumps; wells; cisterns; privies; fences and walls. Landscape features such as the paths, lanes, roads, gardens, orchards and even drainage systems are also of interest. If the farm was quite large and self-contained it might also have a kiln, a saw mill, carpentry shop and a blacksmith shop. Most farms, even small farms, had family cemeteries.

What is the research focus of farmstead archaeology? Archaeologists have examined questions regarding status, class and the consumer behaviour of families living on farms – research questions that have also been applied to urban households. The diversity in these types of research questions can be seen in the CRM studies published by the Arkansas Archaeological Survey, the Illinois Historical Preservation Agency and South Carolina Institute of Archaeology and Anthropology.

Issues connected to ethnicity, race and religion also can be addressed within the context of both the lifestyle of the farmer and the operation and design of the farm including the placement of buildings, gardens, orchards, fields and wood lots. Excellent examples of the application of these types of research issues can be found in recent historical context publications and the CRM reports produced by the Delaware Department of Transportation and the Delaware State Historic Preservation Office.

By the late 1990s, papers on farmstead archaeology appeared more frequently at the **Society for Historical Archaeology** conferences and at regional, state and provincial conferences. Hopefully, this growing interest in the archaeology of farmsteads will generate new research and publications. Future research could focus on the rural/agricultural character and function of these sites, the impact of technology and increasing markets on farms and the transition from subsistence farming to market farming or from sustainable agriculture to cash crops.

Further reading

Baugher, S. and Klein, T. (eds) (2002) 'Archaeology and preservation of 19th-century farmsteads in northeastern United States and Canada', *Northeast Historical Archaeology* 30–31.

Beaudry, M. (1995) 'Scratching the surface: Seven seasons at the Spencer–Peirce–Little farm, Newbury, Massachusetts', *Northeast Historical Archaeology* 24: 19–50.

Beedle, P.L. and Gyrisco, G.M. (eds) (1996) *The Farm Landscape: A Bibliography of the Architecture and Archaeology of Farmsteads and Settlement in Wisconsin and in the Areas of Origin of its Settlers in the United States and Europe*, Madison: State Historical Society of Wisconsin.

Louis Berger and Associates (1994) *Cultural Resources of Fort Drum: Synthesis of Principal Findings*, report on file with the National Park Service, Philadelphia, Pennsylvania.

Wilson, J. (1990) 'We've got thousands of these! What makes an historical farmstead significant?', *Historical Archaeology* 24(2): 23–33.

SHERENE BAUGHER AND TERRY KLEIN

Fatherland site, Mississippi, USA

The Fatherland site is the archaeological name of what the colonial French referred to as the 'Grand Village of the Natchez'. Located at today's Natchez, Mississippi, along the Mississippi River, the 'Grand Village' was the main village of the Natchez culture, and home of the Great Sun, the revered leader of their chiefdom. The Natchez occupied this village before 1682 and until 1730. The Natchez culture was populous, socially stratified and highly complex, and their main village was characterised by the presence of two large flat-topped ('platform') mounds. The Great Sun's cabin sat on the summit of one of these mounds, and the other, situated across a broad, flat plaza, held the culture's sacred temple. One important feature of the Fatherland site is that it – and what the colonial French visitors said about it

– serves as a model for archaeologists who study the Mississippians, a prehistoric culture in the central USA that also built large platform mounds and had a stratified society.

The Fatherland site was excavated by James A. Ford in the 1930s and as a result represents an early example of historical archaeology in the central USA. His excavation recovered large quantities of glass trade **beads**. In the early 1940s, George Quimby, a pioneering historical archaeologist, made a thorough study of these beads, and compared them with those found at Fort St Joseph, a French fortification (see **fortifications**) in southern Michigan, USA, occupied from about 1700 to 1781. Quimby demonstrated that the French traded the same bead types in the Lower Mississippi River valley (where the Natchez lived) as in the Great Lakes region (where the French built Fort St Joseph). More important from an anthropological standpoint, however, was Quimby's contribution to the growing literature about the role of **material culture** in social and economic exchange, culture change and **acculturation**.

See also: French colonialism

Further reading

Ford, J.A. (1936) *Analysis of Indian Village Site Collections from Louisiana and Mississippi*, New Orleans: Department of Conservation, Louisiana Geological Survey.

Quimby, G.I. (1966) *Indian Culture and European Trade Goods: The Archaeology of the Historic Period in the Western Great Lakes Region*, Madison: University of Wisconsin Press.

—— (1939) 'European trade articles as chronological indicators for the archaeology of the historic period in Michigan', *Papers of the Michigan Academy of Science, Arts, and Letters* 24: 25–31.

CHARLES E. ORSER, JR

Feddersen Wierde, Lower Saxony, Germany

Between 1955 and 1963, the Lower Saxony Institute for Historical Coastal Research in Wilhelmshaven, Germany, excavated a prehistoric elevated village (*Wurt* settlement) for the first time. The excavation provided essential new insights into the methods of settlement and husbandry, the development of landscape and vegetation in marshes, as well as the social structures of their inhabitants in the first five centuries AD.

The Feddersen Wierde is one of eight settlements that were established at sea level after the ocean had withdrawn. They were built on the high terrain of a levee in the first century BC and then, with increasing oceanic flooding, artificially raised to become large villages. The settlements had approximately 2,400 ha of marshland for agricultural usage at their disposal, which indicates that each settlement had approximately 300 ha. Of these, only about 50 ha were suitable for tillage and 250 ha for pasture.

At the outset of the settlement the remains of five farms were found. Their main building is the byre-house complex, divided in three building parts. The living quarters are situated at one end of the house, with a central fireplace. Further on, there is a common kitchen area that can be accessed through two side entrances. Situated behind these is the byre, which could be of various sizes, with stalls for the animals at the side of the building. Two rows of paired pillars that serve as roof supports margin the middle section of the houses. The walls are made from wattle work. Whereas the average length of the houses is 18 to 22 m and the width 5 to 6 m, larger buildings also exist that are 30 m long and 7 m wide. In these, up to thirty-two large animals, mainly cattle, could be accommodated. Side buildings consist of smaller houses, often without byres, where craftsmen worked, and supply stores, raised on poles.

As early as the beginning of the first century AD, the type of long, linear, low-built village that accommodated eleven farming units was abandoned. With the onset of the building of elevated settlements, the design was altered to a circular arrangement of the houses with a central courtyard. A small hill (*Wurt*) was erected from soil and sods to accommodate the living quarters for each of the fourteen economic units that were first surrounded by a trench and later by a fence. These hills were further elevated and widened in seven phases altogether until the settlement was aban-

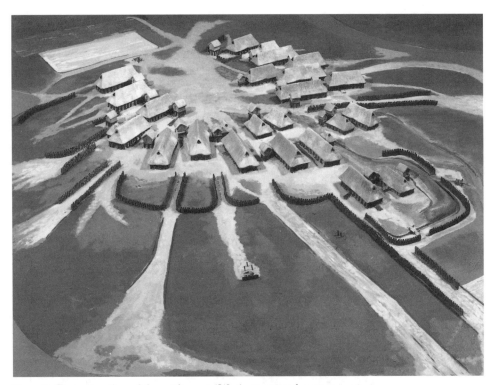

Figure 11 Reconstruction of the settlement (*Wurt*), AD second century
Source: Photo: P. Schmid

doned in the fifth century AD. During the third century, the individual settlements were growing into an interconnected living area of approximately 4 ha and with a height of 4 m, and accommodating about twenty-six farms. Because of the humidity of subsequently added layers of flooring, all organic matter from the settlement, such as the ground plans of the buildings, tools, plant rests, textiles and animal bones, was outstandingly well preserved.

Due to the relatively small area of surrounding land suited for farming, limits were set to the spatial extension of the settlements. Thus, during the prime time of the settlement in the third century, there were only about 300 ha of farmable acreage for twenty-six farms. At that time, the number of settlers had reached about 300, with 450 heads of heavy livestock. Despite the necessary limitation on the number of inhabitants, farm numbers increased from five to twenty-six over a span of approximately 250 years. This increase was only possible with the amalgamation of several

family farms into larger economic associations. Smaller enterprises of farm-oriented craftspeople associated with these larger farms; they performed the various craft jobs on the farms. Because these people lacked their own agricultural production they were provided with food from the larger farms of the association.

The economic base of the settlement thus remained agricultural, with a small portion of it being field farming, a fact shown by the remains of tilled plots at the base of the settlement. According to the findings of the botanical investigations of field crops, threshing and plants remains, barley and oats were cultivated predominantly, as well as horse beans, flax and gold of pleasure. Brought about by the marshland conditions, livestock farming played a significant role.

The zoological examination of approximately 50,000 animal bones proves that domesticated animals included horned cattle, and, in smaller numbers, sheep, horses and pigs. The determination of the animals' age at the time of slaughter sheds light on the difficult living conditions. Cattle dominated meat production, providing about 66 per cent of it, but 17 per cent of the young animals had to be slaughtered early, after their summer pasture.

A large number of utensils made from clay, wood, horn, antlers, bones and iron, and imported millstones, revealed the methods of processing of the agricultural products on the farms. Information on the wide range of skilled trades performed in the settlement was revealed by findings from work spaces designed for the textile and leather industry, woodturning and cartwright work, as well as for the processing of iron and non-ferrous metals. Raw materials such as wood and iron had to be imported from the neighbouring Pleistocene soils of the Geest, a sandy region in northern Germany. Findings of wood indicate that heavy, four-wheel carts with swivelling steering were used to transport goods overland for exchange. At the same time, the landing on a nearby river indicates coastal **trade** and fishery.

Several different groups of relics, such as domestic and Romanic **ceramics**, show the trade connections to both neighbouring and remote Germanic settlements or Roman provinces. Through these trade channels, materials and products, such as millstones manufactured from basalt lava from Eiffel, came to Feddersen Wierde. Other more sophisticated products such as Roman **glass**, **beads**, ornamental fibulas and metal vessels, as well as military-equipment components and coins, depending on the place and time of their origins, are assessed as evidence of diplomatic relations (tribute payments) or military events (service in the Roman army).

The organisation of activities that extended beyond local agriculture was probably in the hands of the inhabitants of a large farming alliance at the eastern border of the settlement. As early as the second century, this group of settlers possessed the largest farm in the area, with a substantial livestock population of at least thirty-two head of cattle, judging from the number of stalls in the byre. This large farm integrated several, apparently weaker, small farms into one large one, consisting of living quarters and byres of various sizes. They also built their own meeting hall protected by a strong palisade fence. Since some of the inhabitants of the

smaller farms were craftspeople, working especially with wood and metals, this farm provided a goal-oriented food supply in order to cover the rising demand for food. A larger area of storage buildings was erected on the premises as well as a second hall that was connected to an area for the drove of livestock. Evidence of cult-oriented animal burials in the house and on the outer edges of the farm grounds show that the hall was apparently used for both profane and cultic purposes by the entire population of the settlement.

With the organisation of the economic side of the settlement attained by the socially elated core farm, the livelihood of the settlers was secured over a longer period of time. In the fifth century, however, the maximum number of inhabitants the agricultural area could sustain was exceeded. This caused the economic system to collapse, and the Feddersen Wierde as well as the neighbouring villages were abandoned in the course of migratory movements to **England**.

Further reading

Haarnagel, W. (1979) *Die Grabung Feddersen Wierde. Methode, Hausbau, Siedlungs- und Wirtschaftsformen sowie Sozialstruktur*, Text- u. Tafelband. Feddersen Wierde 2. Wiesbaden.

Hayen, H., Ullemeyer, R., Tidow, K., Ruttner, F. and Institut für Härterei-Technik Bremen-Lesum (1981) *Einzeluntersuchungen zur Feddersen Wierde. Wagen, Textil- und Lederfunde, Bienenkorb, Schlackenanalysen*, Feddersen Wierde 3. Wiesbaden.

Körber-Grohne, U. (1967) *Geobotanische Untersuchungen auf der Feddersen Wierde*, Text- u. Tafelband. Feddersen Wierde 1. Wiesbaden.

Kossack, G., Behre, K.-E. and Schmid, P. (eds) (1984) *Archäologische und naturwissenschaftliche Untersuchungen an ländlichen und frühstädtischen Siedlungen im deutschen Küstengebiet vom 5. Jahrhundert v. Chr. bis zum 11. Jahrhundert n. Chr. Bd. 1. Ländliche Siedlungen.* Weinheim.

Reichstein, H. (1991) *Die Fauna des germanischen Dorfes Feddersen Wierde*. Text- u. Tafelband. Feddersen Wierde 4. Stuttgart.

Schmid, P. (1993) *Feddersen Wierde*, in J. Hoops (ed.) *Reallexikon der germanischen Altertumskunde* 8.

2.Aufl., 249–66, 7 Abb., 2 Taf. Berlin, New York.

PETER SCHMID

feminist archaeology

Although a few archaeologists were using feminist perspectives in the 1970s, it was not until the mid-1980s that feminist archaeology began to be articulated within the discipline, and not until the 1990s that it began to flourish. Several different theoretical approaches have been put forth and feminist archaeology has been conducted in all parts of the world.

Archaeological research about **gender** in the past may be, but is not necessarily, feminist research. Historical and post-medieval archaeologists (see **post-medieval archaeology**) have examined the material and documentary evidence of gendered activities in the past without then moving beyond mere recognition of men and women's presence in a past community. In addition, historical archaeologists often imply, uncritically, that gender roles and attitudes in the recent past were the same as those in present-day societies; they are thus talking about gender, but not investigating its role in society.

Feminist archaeology can be distinguished from the archaeology of gender in several ways. Feminist archaeologists often seek to correct male-centred reconstructions of past societies; that is, reconstructions in which the roles of men are assumed to have been the most important and are therefore emphasised. Thus, feminist archaeologists often focus on the importance of women's roles, thereby making women more visible and correcting previous, flawed pictures of the past.

Feminist archaeology is also closely tied to feminist struggles for political and economic equality in the present; a belief that gender roles are learned and not biologically determined is fundamental to much feminist archaeological research. Questioning inequalities between men and women in today's societies can logically lead to a questioning of the relations between them in the past. Because the past is often used to explain the present, feminist archaeologists try to uncover evidence of the variety of gender relations in past societies, revealing how we came to be the societies that we are today. Some feminist archaeologists focus only on women in the past, emphasising the importance of women's work and showing that women sometimes took on roles and duties that our present-day society relegates primarily to men. This research reveals that present assumptions about gender roles have not always been so, and therefore need not be so in the future.

In one study, Suzanne Spencer-Wood examined the domestic reform movement in Boston and the surrounding area during the nineteenth century. This movement brought women into the public arena through their reform activities in soup kitchens, schools of domestic science, housing for the indigent, co-operative communities and kindergartens, to name just a few. These structures and the artefacts of activities there are a material reminder on the urban landscape of the integral role domestic reform institutions played in nineteenth-century urban USA.

Donna Seifert and Charles Cheek have studied nineteenth-century working-class neighbourhoods in Washington, DC, that included brothels and houses of prostitution. They have been able to show variation in wealth between brothels and other working-class households, as well as ways in which changes in the profession of prostitution affected the well-being of women who were prostitutes. Their study combined artefacts and food remains from a variety of households with census data, city directories, maps and other archival data.

Other feminist archaeologists examine men, women and other gender categories in terms of the political, social and economic relations between them in the past. By showing how one's gender made a difference in these contexts, feminist archaeologists show how everyday life was shaped, in part, by gender. The features of everyday life can range from the gendered division of labour (who did what kind of work, and for whom) to the designation of special gendered statuses or roles (e.g. midwives, healers, shamans, doctors) to differences in the way members of particular gender groups were treated in death.

Historical archaeologists who employ a feminist perspective are often also interested in other aspects of identity in the past, such as **race**, **ethnicity** and economic class (see **class, social**), and in how these combined with gender to affect people's lives. Because historical and post-medieval archaeology has been primarily concerned with the period after AD 1400, when various European and Euro-American countries began colonising other parts of the world, it has primarily concerned the quite culturally diverse societies that resulted from that **colonialism**. Thus, feminist archaeologists also look at gender as one aspect of cultural diversity in the past.

Janet Spector studied a Native American community of the 1830s (see **Native Americans**), the Wahpeton Dakota, in what is now Minnesota. She used archaeological materials, ethnohistoric records, paintings and **oral-history** interviews to reconstruct life in the community, detailing the various tasks and activities that men, women and children carried out, and the ways in which this community coped with rapidly encroaching Euro-American society. This information was presented separately and also woven together in a literary, or narrative, story. Spector's study combined the perspectives of the descendant Wahpeton Dakota community, a feminist critique of traditional archaeological training and the material and documentary records to effectively illustrate an inclusive, feminist archaeological approach.

Elizabeth Scott's research into the eighteenth-century fur-trading community of **Fort Michili-mackinac**, in what is now northern Michigan, concerned a highly diverse settlement of men, women and children from several different classes and ethnic groups. Because of the cultural diversity, the variability of household composition (single male traders, soldiers, families, priests), and the combination of domestic and public space inside the household (when households were also work-places), she found that the association of household artefacts with particular genders was far from clear-cut.

Diana Wall studied several household sites in late eighteenth- and early nineteenth-century **New York City**, combining the archaeological data with maps, census records, city directories and other archival data. She revealed how both men and women were active participants in the separation of life into workplace and home – into domestic and public spheres – that occurred during the first half of the nineteenth century (see **domesticity**). Even the kinds of dinner ware and tea ware in the ceramic assemblage indicated changes in the function of dinners and teas among the city's middle-class and elite residents. This change coincided with changes in the capitalist economy, residence patterns and the demographic make-up of the city, all of which resulted in the creation of men's public and women's domestic spheres for the middle and upper classes.

Feminist archaeologists have also looked at gender roles and attitudes in all-male or predominantly male communities. One example is the work of Donald Hardesty at several mining camps, settlements and towns in the nineteenth-century western USA. He found that gender played a fundamental role in residential patterning as well as within the household; attitudes about gender roles were fundamental in shaping class and ethnic ideologies in these mining towns as well. Another example is the study by Elizabeth Kryder-Reid of an all-male religious community in nineteenth-century Maryland. She found that, in this single-sex community, the roles of both genders were nonetheless carried out, reflecting the gender system of the broader US culture at the time.

Feminist archaeologists who study the post-AD 1400 period have the advantage of utilising written, oral history and pictorial records in addition to the material, archaeological record. These sources allow us some understanding of past attitudes about gender roles and gender ideologies, and provide us with the perspectives of people from various gender, class and ethnic groups in the past. This information can then be combined with, and tested against, the material evidence for gender relations that is available archaeologically.

See also: mining archaeology; pictorial information; women in historical archaeology

Further reading

Hardesty, D. (1994) 'Class, gender strategies, and material culture in the mining west', in E.M. Scott (ed.) *Those of Little Note: Gender, Race, and Class in Historical Archaeology*, Tucson: University of Arizona Press, pp. 129–45.

Kryder-Reid, E. (1994) '"With manly courage"': Reading the construction of gender in a nineteenth-century religious community', in E.M. Scott (ed.) *Those of Little Note: Gender, Race, and Class in Historical Archaeology*, Tucson: University of Arizona Press, pp. 97–114.

Scott, E.M. (1991) 'A feminist approach to historical archaeology: Eighteenth-century fur trade society at Michilimackinac', *Historical Archaeology* 25(4): 42–53.

Seifert, D.J. (1994) 'Mrs. Starr's Profession', in E.M. Scott (ed.) *Those of Little Note: Gender, Race, and Class in Historical Archaeology*, Tucson: University of Arizona Press, pp. 149–73.

Spector, J. (1993) *What this Awl Means: Feminist Archaeology at a Wahpeton Dakota Village*, St Paul: Minnesota Historical Society Press.

Spencer-Wood, S. (1987) 'A survey of domestic reform movement sites in Boston and Cambridge, c. 1865–1905', *Historical Archaeology* 21(2): 7–36.

Wall, D.D. (1994) *The Archaeology of Gender: Separating the Spheres in Urban America*, New York: Plenum Press.

ELIZABETH M. SCOTT

feminist theory

The founding of feminist historical archaeology was influenced by political feminisms, feminist anthropology and prehistoric archaeology, and personal experiences of sexism in historical archaeology. In many countries some of the earliest feminist research in historical archaeology was concerned with the status of women in the field. Papers in a 1992 symposium at the American Anthropological Association meetings and other papers published as Number 5 of the AAA Archaeological Papers, entitled *Equity Issues for Women in Archaeology* (1994), edited by M.C. Nelson *et al.* reported research on gender inequities and discrimination against women in archaeology, including historical archaeology, in countries around the world. Inequities in historical archaeology were only separately addressed in three papers on the **Society for Historical Archaeology** (SHA) and its journal *Historical Archaeology*.

Starting in the 1970s, overtly feminist papers in historical archaeology were presented in conference symposia on more general topics such as **gender** research in anthropology, prehistory or history, or lifeways of a particular site or region. For instance, some of the earliest European papers on feminist gender research in historical archaeology were Liv Helga Dommasnes's study of late-Iron Age gender roles and Anne Stalsberg's interpretation of Viking women's artefacts (see **Vikings**) in Russia in the landmark 1979 Norwegian conference proceedings 'Were they all Men?' (1987). Some feminist research in historical archaeology has also been published in the proceedings of the Australian Women in Archaeology conference initiated in 1991 by Hilary du Cros and Laurajane Smith, and held biennially (ANH publications, RSPAS, Australian National University, Canberra).

A survey of feminist colleagues in the USA, Europe and Australia indicates that the first conference symposia devoted entirely to feminist gender research in historical archaeology were organised by Suzanne Spencer-Wood for the 1989 annual meetings of the SHA in the USA and for the international 1989 Chacmool conference in Canada. The Chacmool symposium was published in the ground-breaking conference proceedings entitled 'Gender in Archaeology' (1991). SHA conference symposia on gender research have been organised nearly every year since 1989, often sponsored by the women's caucus. A 1990 SHA gender symposium was published in 1991 as an issue of *Historical Archaeology* edited by Donna Seifert, one of the journal's editors. The 1992 SHA gender symposium was published as *Those of Little Note: Gender, Race and Class in Historical Archaeology* (1994), edited by Elizabeth Scott. In Australia, a 1991 session of four papers on gender research was organised at the seminar 'Historical Archaeology of the Rocks and Miller's Point' organised by Jane Lydon and partially published in the *Australasian Journal of Historical Archaeology*. In **classical archaeology**, a symposium entitled 'Feminist Approaches to Classical Art and Archaeology' was organised by the Women's Classical Caucus for the 1993 annual meetings of the Archaeological Institute of America. At the World Archaeological Congress, the first conference symposium on feminist historical archaeology was organised in 1994 by Suzanne

Spencer-Wood. Papers in this symposium addressed feminist historical archaeology in Australia, Britain, Italy, Spain and the USA by authors from those countries, as well as a paper on Korean gender research. The first conference symposium on Classical Mayan gender research was organised in 1994 at the American Anthropological Association.

Feminist theory in historical archaeology

Publications applying feminist theory in historical archaeology have drawn on prior publications applying feminist theory in prehistoric archaeology and in some cases on feminist history. Suzanne Spencer-Wood's theoretical papers in *The Archaeology of Gender* (1991) and in the proceedings of the 1990 conference 'Quandaries and Quests: Visions of Archaeology's Future' (1992) have argued that gender is a primary cultural construct structuring all aspects of society. All individuals in a society have gender, including men and children as well as women. Cultural ideology fundamentally structures ideal gender categories, roles and practices as well as individual identities, beliefs, relationships and behaviours. Gender is a complex dynamic cultural system that includes processes of creating, maintaining, renegotiating and changing gender ideologies that define the meaning of ideal behaviours in culturally constructed categories such as masculine, man, boy, feminine, woman, girl, heterosexual, bisexual, homosexual, gay, lesbian, transsexual or berdache. Gender categories are not universal, but vary among cultures. The cultural gender system also includes processes of maintaining and changing actual performances of gender identities and practices in human relationships. What people actually do in gender relationships, as well as in their gender beliefs and identities, may be congruent with or differ from ideal gender identities, roles and practices prescribed in the dominant cultural ideology.

Non-dominant social groups may reject the dominant gender ideology and construct an alternative gender ideology (or ideologies), which specifies non-dominant ideal gender identities, roles, relationships and behaviours. Gender is not just a series of categories but includes the processes by which the interrelated meanings of these categories are constantly socially renegotiated, as individuals and social groups change their identities in ways that can transgress or redefine culturally constructed gender categories and ideal behaviours assigned to them by the dominant gender ideology. Culturally dominant gender ideology and practices can be, and have historically been, transformed, sometimes purposefully, by alternative gender ideologies and practices of social subgroups. This is shown by Diana Wall's research on the 'Cult of **Domesticity**', and by Suzanne Spencer-Wood's research on domestic reformers who transformed US culture by redefining the dominant gender ideology to make it acceptable for middle-class women to have public professions.

Feminist theory has differentiated the cultural gender categories of man, woman, gay, etc., from the genetic/biological sex categories of male, female and hermaphrodite, which actually is composed of a variety of biological conditions. Research has shown that historic women's gender roles, such as producing textiles, butter and cheese, were not genetically determined, as is female biology. Basic aspects of female biology are universal while women's gender roles vary in different cultures and subcultures. For instance, although female biological lactation is genetically determined, in dominant Western ideology, since at least the seventeenth century, elite women's gender roles ideally prescribed not breastfeeding their own babies and instead hiring lower-class women as wet nurses. Yet, to members of a society, culturally prescribed gender roles usually appear natural because they have learned since infancy to associate cultural gender roles with the biological sexes. Cultural ideology and **language** legitimise and naturalise gender roles by making cultural gender categories such as 'man' and 'woman' synonymous with the biological sex categories 'male' and 'female'.

Waves of feminist theories

Feminist theory is concerned with power dynamics in gender relationships. A number of different feminist theoretical approaches have been applied simultaneously in gender research in historical archaeology, although they developed sequentially. Critical feminist theory began to develop by the fifteenth century in the French Querelles des

Femmes that critiqued learned men's misogynist characterisations of women. More recently, feminist standpoint theory has facilitated critiques of the western male-centred standpoint in historical records and archaeologies written about American Pueblo Indians and about Australian Aborigines. In a chapter in *Manifesting Power* (1999) Spencer-Wood critiques limited masculine hierarchical definitions of power as dominance and argues for the equal consideration of feminine forms of lateral co-operative power.

What is called the first-wave feminist movement for suffrage and equal rights, starting in the mid-nineteenth century, argued that women could be public citizens and have public professions equal in status to those of men. This egalitarian feminist theoretical approach sought evidence that women could perform the same public roles as men and that in many cultures a balance of power between women and men was maintained through complementary and interdependent gender roles.

Starting in the 1970s, the second wave of feminist theory uncritically accepted the dominant ideology that men and women were opposed homogenous categories and analysed cultural structures supporting supposedly universal male dominance and female subordination in actual gender practice. In a 1980 *Signs* article, feminist anthropologist Michelle Rosaldo critiqued her and Louise Lamphere's ground-breaking second-wave edited volume for projecting Victorian gender ideology onto other cultures to classify universally all men's roles as public and dominant and all women's roles as domestic and subordinate. In historical archaeology Yentsch (see **gender**) used second-wave theory to analyse how ceramics expressed the dominant eighteenth-century ideology of public dominant men and private subordinate women.

Marxist–feminist theory that developed in the 1970s was imported into historical archaeology by Elizabeth Scott in a paper presented at the 1990 SHA conference in a mini-plenary entitled 'Shaken, not Stirred'. In the introduction to her edited volume *Those of Little Note: Gender, Race and Class in Historical Archaeology* (1994) Scott discussed the application of the Marxist paradigm of domination and resistance to gender research, as well as to post-modern feminist theory.

In the 1990s, post-modern feminist theory developed as women of colour critiqued earlier essentialist feminist theory for portraying white middle-class women's ideology and experiences as universal. In historical archaeology Spencer-Wood's above-cited theoretical publications and her 1996 article in the *World Archaeological Bulletin* drew on post-modern feminist theory to critique binary structuralist constructions of gender, arguing instead for analyses of women as well as men as diverse social agents who shaped their own lives, creating variety and flexibility in historic women's and men's experiences, powers, gender ideologies, identities, roles, relationships and practices. Gender practices were differentiated from gender ideologies. Spencer-Wood proposed an inclusive both/and feminist theoretical approach and created continuum models of individual and group variation along different social dimensions. For instance, individual identities were modelled as a line ranging from the extremes of masculine and feminine at two ends with all the shades of grey in between. The race continuum encompassed the full range of variation between the poles of black and white. Intersections of continua for different social dimensions modelled the complex intersections among gender, sex, race, ethnicity and religion for individuals or groups.

Within post-modern feminist theory, queer theory developed to critique heterosexist biases in feminist theory and instead to ask questions about diversity in sexual orientations and bodily identities and concerns. In *Archaeologies of Social Life* (1999) Lynn Meskell argued that biological sex be considered as a continuum. Post-modern feminist theory has also led to theories and gender research on masculinity. A post-modern approach to researching historic masculinity/ies was advocated by Bernard Knapp in the proceedings of the 1995 'Australian Women in Archaeology' conference, entitled *Redefining Archaeology* (1998).

Feminism and methods in historical archaeology

Feminist theory in historical archaeology has critiqued and problematised male-biased methods in the field. In *The Archaeology of Gender* (1991) Spencer-Wood's paper addresses male biases in methods of classification. She critiqued the disappearance of women in male-defined categories, such as classes defined by men's occupations and households defined only by the male head. Further, she critiqued the consideration of brothels from a male-centred view as 'entertainment' sites, considering Lowell mill boarding houses (Massachusetts) as domestic sites rather than female-operated businesses, and for failing to consider the public economic functions of many domestic sites, from women's production of agricultural goods for sale in public markets to women entrepreneurs taking in laundry and boarders. In this paper and in a 1996 *World Archaeological Bulletin* article, Spencer-Wood critiqued the androcentrism in South's ungendered category of personal artefacts and his categorisation of all household ceramics in a kitchen artefact group.

Anne Yentsch's paper in *The Archaeology of Gender* further unpacked South's kitchen artefact group, showing that it lumped together in a meaningless category 'ceramics' used in very different gendered activities, including food storage, preparation and dining. She also critiqued South's androcentrism in interpreting excavated pins at a domestic site as evidence of the presence of a male tailor rather than women. Yentsch further connects such male biases in research with male dominance in the field of historical archaeology. In a 1991 *Historical Archaeology* article, Yentsch applied her critique of South's kitchen group to analyse excavated ceramics into more informative categories, including dairying. Mary Casey's 1999 comparative article in *Australasian Historical Archaeology* analysed locally produced ceramic vessel types used in dairying, food preparation, storage and dining at early colonial sites in Sydney. In documents women were listed as 'dairymaids' about five times more often than men were listed as 'dairymen' or 'milkmen'.

Feminist research in historical archaeology has corrected androcentric methods and created new methods to analyse gender without male biases. In a 1985 chapter in *Archaeology, Ecology and Ethnohistory of the Prairie–Forest Border Zone of Minnesota and Manitoba*, Janet Spector created a feminist task-differentiation method to break down ungendered artefact classifications and to analyse gender roles and relationships from ethnohistorical and archaeological data. This method was used by Elizabeth

Scott in a 1991 *Historical Archaeology* article to analyse eighteenth-century gender roles and relationships at **Fort Michilimackinac**. Cathy Blee's 1991 dissertation compared the statistical archaeological signatures of single-gender sites, such as mining camps or brothels, with mixed-gender sites such as hotels or domestic sites, including some in mining camps.

At a deeper level the connections between sexist language, analogies, theory and methods of observation have been exposed by Spencer-Wood in her 1991, 1992 and 1996 feminist theory publications, and by Louise Zarmati in her paper on 'Archaeospeak' in *Redefining Archaeology* (1998). In slightly different ways both authors point out how women become invisible in male nouns and pronouns that are claimed to be generic but linguistically support a male-centred view of the past. Both authors also critique the neglect of gender in the controlling male-centred archaeological paradigm, and the use of sexist analogies for excavation and museum displays. Spencer-Wood further showed how scientific methodology and language predominantly used in archaeology have misrepresented archaeological research as completely objective, masking the subjectivity and male bias involved in what research questions are considered important and the methods used to analyse data, both of which determine the conclusions. The use of the scientific omniscient third-person passive voice stating what the facts or data show masks the subjective processes of interpretation and inference, making them more difficult to challenge. Applying feminist theory, Spencer-Wood argued for and, when not prohibited from doing so by book editors, has used the first-person active voice to reveal the subjective processes and biases involved in archaeological interpretation. Janet Spector's *What this Awl Means* (1993) exemplified the value of the use of the first-person active voice by archaeologists and pioneered the constructions of narratives about people's lives in the past based on ethnohistorical and archaeological evidence about a nineteenth-century Dakota village in Minnesota called 'Little Rapids'.

Further reading

Meskell, L. (1999) *Archaeologies of Social Life: Age, Sex, Class, et cetera in Ancient Egypt*, Oxford: Blackwell.

Nelson, M.C., Nelson, S.M., and Wylie, A. (eds) (1994) *Equity Issues for Women in Archaeology*, Archaeological Papers of the American Anthropological Association 5, Washington, DC: American Anthropological Association.

Scott, E.M. (ed.) (1994) *Those of Little Note: Gender, Race, and Class in Historical Archaeology*, Tucson: University of Arizona Press.

Sweely, T.L. (ed.) (1999) *Manifesting Power: Gender and the Interpretation of Power in Archaeology*, London: Routledge.

Walde, D. and Willows, N.D. (eds) (1991) *The Archaeology of Gender: Proceedings of the Twenty-Second Annual Conference of the Archaeological Association of the University of Calgary*, Calgary: Archaeological Association of the University of Calgary.

SUZANNE M. SPENCER-WOOD

Ferryland, Newfoundland, Canada

Ferryland, located in today's Newfoundland, Canada, is the name of an English colonial settlement purchased by George Calvert (1579/80–1632), the first Lord Baltimore, in 1620. After twelve intrepid settlers established Calvert's colony in 1621, King James I awarded Calvert a larger parcel of land, which he called 'the Province of Avalon'. Historical archaeology has been conducted at Ferryland for about seventy years, with the current, long-term project beginning in 1992 by archaeologists from the Memorial University of Newfoundland.

The first settlers at Ferryland built several structures including a 'mansion house', tenements, a brewhouse, a forge and a defensive palisade. Thirty-two settlers lived at Ferryland by 1622 and the population quickly grew to over a hundred. Calvert, by this time a member of the Roman Catholic faith, visited the colony in 1627, bringing other Catholics with him. Ferryland thus became the first colony in British-controlled North America to be tolerant of Roman Catholics. By 1629, Calvert was forced to admit that environmental conditions at the outpost were harsher than he had expected, and so he decided to attempt to build another colony to the south. He died before he could realise this goal, but his descendants established **St Mary's City**, Maryland, in 1634.

Archaeology has always had an important place within the interpretation of the Avalon colony. The first archaeology was conducted in the 1930s, and archaeologists revisited the site in the late 1950s and again in 1968, before historical archaeology was a fully recognised discipline. In the mid-1980s, archaeologists began more extensive excavations, and, in 1992, the Canadian government made a long-term commitment to a multi-year, well-organised archaeological project at the site. Even though excavations have been conducted at Ferryland ever since, archaeologists have examined only about 5 per cent of the colony.

The Ferryland archaeologists have collected over 1 million artefacts as of this writing. Most of these artefacts derived from the years the colony existed, but many specimens are associated with the indigenous Beothuk Indians. The archaeologists at Ferryland have already investigated a small migratory fishing station (built in the early 1660s by European fishermen merely visiting the coast without intending to settle there), the forge built in 1622 (one of the first buildings the colonists constructed), the 'mansion house' (where Calvert and his family lived during the winter of 1628–9), a street of tight cobblestone paving (laid during the first year of residence and called by the colony's leader 'a prettie streete'), a section of the waterfront, including a seawall, a storehouse, a stone-lined privy (ingeniously designed to be flushed by the tide twice a day), a planter's house (that exhibited evidence of having been burned by the French attack in 1696), a stone-lined well that was 7.6 m deep (and which was filled in the late eighteenth century after a child had fallen in and drowned) and parts of the defensive ditch and palisade built around the initial settlement.

The breadth and scope of the Ferryland project, along with the commitment of the Canadian government to interpret its history and culture, make it one of the most significant archaeological projects of the early twenty-first century.

CHARLES E. ORSER, JR

firearms

Historical archaeologists have unearthed thousands of pieces of firearms during the course of their many and varied excavations. **Fortifications** are the most obvious place to find evidence of firearms, but domestic sites or any other place where men and women used firearms for protection or subsistence also yield the remains of firearms. In addition, firearms were important objects within the **trade** conducted between Europeans and indigenous people throughout the world. Firearms intended for trade were particularly important elements in the fur trade in Canada and the northern USA, and archaeologists in those places have found abundant evidence of their presence at both native and European sites. In fact, historical archaeologists find evidence of firearms at all the time periods they study, from isolated bullets to the remains of entire weapons.

The firearms artefacts found by historical archaeologists can be grouped into three general categories: parts of firearms, the projectiles fired by them and the objects associated with the weapons, such as gunflints. As may be expected, a large literature exists for each category, especially since the different kinds of firearms made over the years represent technological innovation and refinement. Specialists, both professionals and avocationalists, exist for each kind of artefact.

Historical archaeologists conducting excavations at colonial-period sites have found numerous examples of early gunlock designs. These clever mechanisms were needed to ignite the powder and cause the weapon to fire. Mid-seventeenth-century types include matchlocks, wheel locks and the snaphaunce, each of which was designed to be more reliable and easier to use than the type that preceded it. Gunsmiths developed the famous flintlock as an improvement on all these designs. The earliest examples of gun hardware were made of iron, but brass parts became more commonplace after the early eighteenth century. The elements historical archaeologists find are typically those made of metal, because in most cases the wooden stocks of the portable weapons and the wooden wheels and carriages of cannons have deteriorated. The elements of a typical flintlock that historical archaeologists commonly find include the entire firing mechanism, the trigger guard, the butt plate, the sideplate and even sections of barrel. Archaeologists working at sites dating to the post-flintlock period find examples of carbines and shotguns.

The projectiles fired by firearms that are often found at archaeological sites run the gamut from simple lead balls to pinfire shells to centre-fired shells. Brass cartridges made since the nineteenth century can provide important dating information because many of them carry headstamps that can be readily identified. These headstamps are **makers' marks** because manufacturers use them to identify their products. A cartridge stamped 'U.M.C.' was manufactured by the Union Metallic Cartridge Company, while one stamped 'W.R.A.Co.' was made by the Winchester Repeating Arms Company. Archaeologists, often using law enforcement manuals or information compiled by black-powder enthusiasts as guides, can separate the cartridges into calibres, and through these means determine the kinds and even numbers of firearms once present at a site. Archaeologists working at colonial, flintlock-period sites also find artefacts associated with lead shot, such as fragments of 'sprue', lead waste remaining from the casting of the shot and the bullet moulds themselves.

Historical archaeologists have also spent a great deal of time examining gunflints, those pieces of stone that were needed to fire a flintlock because they created a spark when they struck the metal of the lock mechanism. Great variation in gunflint design was of course possible because they were individually chipped by skilled artisans, but the two most important forms were the 'English' gunflint (generally rather squarish in form with a flat platform on top) and the 'French' gunflint (more rounded in form with a straight surface in front, a rounded back and a wedge shape in cross-section). The form of the flint was necessary to ensure that the flint would be firmly seated within the cock as the cock was released and the flint travelled forward to create the spark. English gunflints were typically made from a black or dark grey flint, whereas French flints were honey-coloured or brown.

Cannons, of course, have attracted great attention from both professional maritime archaeologists and by treasure salvors. Treasure hunters find cannons to be exotic, emotive artefacts that can carry a high market price. The size and weight of cannons help to protect them from salvors, and professional archaeologists and archaeological conservators have spent long hours on the recovery and examination of submerged cannons. In many cases, they have created new methods of preserving them.

See also: Battle of the Little Bighorn; US Civil War archaeology

Further reading

Hamilton, T.M. (1980) *Colonial Frontier Guns*, Chadron, NE: The Fur Press.
—— (1968) *Early Indian Trade Guns, 1625–1775*, Lawton, OK: Museum of the Great Plains.
Noël Hume, I. (1972) *A Guide to Artifacts of Colonial America*, New York: Alfred A. Knopf.
Witthoft, J. (1966) 'A history of gunflints', *Pennsylvania Archaeologist* 36: 12–49.

CHARLES E. ORSER, JR

First Government House, Australia

The site of First Government House symbolises the beginning of European settlement in Australia following the arrival of the First Fleet and its cargo of convicts in 1788, and its interpretation continues to focus debate regarding national and local identity. Its footings were laid by Governor Phillip on 15 May 1788, and it served as the seat of government of Britain's penal colony until its demolition in 1845. Its position overlooking Sydney Cove, the settlement's port, commanded all traffic with the outside world.

Excavation of the site began under the direction of Anne Bickford in February 1983, prior to construction of a forty-four-storey New South Wales government office tower. Finding sandstone and brick footings bonded with white pipeclay, which, as First Fleet diarists had noted, served in lieu of rock lime, the excavators knew that they had found the original building. Throughout the project, the government exerted pressure on the

archaeologists to conclude excavations quickly, but public interest in the site prompted demonstrations, the formation of the 'Friends of the First Government House Site' and a concerted campaign to allow full investigation and to preserve the remains of the site *in situ*, which was successful.

In 1987, artefact analysis was undertaken, demonstrating the colony's place within the British trading network, as well as its close links with Asia during its early years, and the rich lifestyle of the rulers of the settlement. However, its value for most Australians is as a tangible historical link with the nation's European origins, while to Aboriginal people it is a symbol of invasion.

The Historic Houses Trust of New South Wales was given the task of developing a museum on the site in 1991, and, reflecting contemporary notions of cultural diversity and reconciliation, it decided to explore the many different perspectives on the site's meaning; a major theme is the exploration of cultural exchange between white and Aboriginal people. This approach proved controversial, because many of the site's supporters resented what they perceived to be a diminution of the site's individual value, especially when its name was announced as the Museum of Sydney on the site of first Government House.

Using innovative interpretive and technological means, the museum, open since May 1995, abstains from delivering an authoritative narrative, instead aiming to trigger the visitor's imagination through presenting fragments, stories and multiple, competing versions of the past. This museological policy has also proved controversial among heritage professionals, including archaeologists.

See also: Rocks, the; Sydney

Further reading

McBryde, I. (1989) *Guests of the Governor: Aboriginal Residents of the First Government House*, Sydney: Friends of the First Government House Site.
Museum of Sydney (1996) *Sites, Nailing the Debate: Archaeology and Interpretation in Museums*, Sydney: Historic Houses Trust of New South Wales.
Proudfoot, H., Bickford, A., Egloff, B. and Stocks, R. (1991) *Australia's First Government House*,

Sydney: Allen & Unwin and the Department of Planning.

JANE LYDON

Five Points, New York City, USA

Five Points was, and still is, known as **New York City**'s most notorious nineteenth-century slum. Named for the intersection of three streets – Baxter (formerly Orange), Park (formerly Cross) and Worth (formerly Anthony) – the open area at the intersection was portrayed in period lithographs as throbbing with illicit activities, and contemporary writing characterised the inhabitants as prostitutes, drunkards and criminals. The construction of a federal courthouse at Foley Square in the 1990s required excavation of a block that abutted the Five Points intersection. The investigation of fourteen historic lots bound by Pearl, Park Row and Baxter Streets exposed former tenement foundations, cellar floors, courtyards and fifty backyard features. Artefacts were recovered from twenty-two of the features, most of which were either wood- or brick-lined privies. Several cisterns, a large cesspool and an icehouse were also found.

The interpretive artefact analysis, conducted by John Milner Associates under the direction of Rebecca Yamin, focused on assemblages that could be tied to lot occupants. The earliest assemblages, dating to about 1800, belonged to artisans – a baker, a carpenter, a coffin-maker – who lived and worked on their properties. Although the neighbourhood in this period was as industrial as it was residential, the artisans set their tables with Chinese **porcelain**, engraved Stiegel-like **glass** and hand-painted teawares. By the 1830s, many houses had been subdivided for tenants and most households included boarders. An assemblage from this period belonged to a household headed by Harris Goldberg, a rabbi, scribe and tailor. His synagogue met for a year in his house and the faunal remains indicate that the family kept kosher. No pork or hindquarters were present in the remains and two sets of well-used everyday dishes – one edge-decorated and one willowware – were probably used for milk and meat. Other Jewish tailors lived around the corner on Baxter Street in

the 1840s, but tucked among them was a brothel. The brothel assemblage included fancier teawares than found elsewhere on the block, many wine bottles and several female urinals, probably used when prostitutes were confined to bed with venereal disease.

By the late 1840s, there were five-storey tenements on Pearl Street built to accommodate the Irish who had fled the Great Famine. Several assemblages associated with the tenements provide insights into the newly arrived immigrants' lives. Individual households appear to have owned Staffordshire dinnerware and teasets in fashionable styles, they decorated their apartments with plants and figurines, and provided their children with didactic dishes meant to teach manners and pride in personal property. Following Irish custom, they ate more pork than other meat, although fish would have been a cheaper alternative. The motifs on the clay smoking pipes recovered suggest that the Irish avoided identifying with the patriotic imagery associated with the Nativist (Know-Nothing) Party, perhaps because the Nativists were so prejudiced against them. A unique and fascinating artefact from the Irish tenement at 472 Pearl Street was a teacup decorated with the image of Father Mathew preaching to an adoring flock. Father Mathew, a leader of the temperance movement in Ireland, made a trip to the USA in 1849, which may have included a visit to Five Points.

The archaeological investigations on the courthouse block confirmed that living conditions at Five Points were abysmally unsanitary and overcrowded. Front and back tenements on single lots left only tiny courtyards in between and the courtyards were filled with privies, cesspools and schoolsinks. The artefacts recovered, however, suggest that the people who lived in the tenements, and the artisan home-owners before them, attempted to live respectable lives. They spent some of their limited incomes on fashionable dishes, decorated their living spaces no matter how minimal and raised their children to have appropriate values. Additional documentary data show that Five Points residents saved money at the Emigrant Savings Bank, men worked at a variety of skilled and unskilled occupations and women added to household income by doing laundry, outwork for the garment industry and taking in boarders. Like other nineteenth-century working-class neighbourhoods Five Points' reputation as a slum was coloured by middle-class fears and prejudices. From the inside, it appears to have been a complex multi-ethnic neighbourhood where immigrants struggled to get a foothold in their newly adopted homeland.

See also: class, social; immigration; Ireland; urban archaeology

Further reading

Blackmar, E. (1989) *Manhattan for Rent, 1785–1850*, Ithaca: Cornell University Press.

Foster, G.G. (1990) *New York by Gas-Light and Other Urban Sketches*, Berkeley: University of California Press.

Mayne, A. (1993) *The Imagined Slum, Newspaper Representation in Three Cities, 1870–1914*, London: Leicester University Press.

Stott, R.B. (1990) *Workers in the Metropolis, Class, Ethnicity, and Youth in Antebellum New York City*, Ithaca: Cornell University Press.

REBECCA YAMIN

Flögeln, Lower Saxony, Germany

Flögeln, an interdisciplinary project of the Lower Saxony Institute for Historical Coastal Research in Wilhelmshaven, Germany, was supported by the German Research Council. Flögeln is situated on the 'Geest', the sandy Pleistocene bed near the clay district. The aim of the project was to investigate the evolution of the settlement and its economic background from neolithic times until the last centuries on an 'island' of 23 km² surrounded by bog. The archaeological field research was carried out from 1971 to 1986 with large-scale excavations. Some are already published. The evaluation of others is still ongoing.

The innovative idea behind the project was to study the five to six millennia of settlement in a naturally bordered area, a *Siedlungskammer*, an inhabited island. The interdisciplinary project was conducted by archaeologists, palaeoethnobotanists

(pollen analysis and macro-fossils), pedologists, historical geographers and others.

The team made important findings about the settlement structure and the development of building practices. From about 3500 BC to the first century AD, the settlements were dispersed. Small farms consisting of a longhouse, sometimes together with outhouses, were scattered widely, shifting after only a few decades to another location. Beginning with the early second century, settlement was concentrated in villages consisting of several farms. Difference in size, together with special buildings and finds, helps the archaeologists to recognise the farms belonging to chieftains. These villages periodically shifted only short distances. After a period of desertion in the late sixth and early seventh centuries, new habitation began, again with large villages. The main excavation of such a village was carried out in Dalem, dated to the seventh to the fourteenth centuries. Social stratification (see **stratification, social**) could be detected in this village.

Another primary topic of the project was the evolution of buildings with a wealth of new information on main houses and many types of outhouses, such as sunken huts, granaries and helms. During neolithic times, houses had two aisles, but they had three aisles from the Bronze Age to the late Migration Period (sixth century). Byres, under the same roof as the houses, were first introduced in the Bronze Age and remained until the sixth century. From the first to the sixth centuries, the main houses grew longer. (During the fifth century they were longer than 60 m.) The increasing length was the effect of adding new compartments of different functions to the earlier standard house (with only living space and byre). From the seventh to the tenth century onward, farms developed several outhouses, one of which was the byre. The main houses were first one-aisled but, from the ninth century, new side aisles were added. This development leads to the *Hallenhaus*, the prevailing farmhouse type of recent times. During high medieval times, houses were often 'ship formed', meaning that the long walls were curved outward.

Earthfast structures prevailed during prehistoric times, but construction on sills and/or post pads was already known in Europe since neolithic times. A shift away from earthfast buildings could be detected during the tenth to the fourteenth

Figure 12 Dalem, reconstruction of a sunken hut with warp-weighted loom and oven
Source: W. H. Zimmermann
Note: The rows of loom weights of several burnt down looms were found; the biggest loom was 4 m across. In several instances, an uncovered oven with small stones on top indicates the use of the sunken hut as a sauna too.

centuries. An early post-on-padstone construction in Flögeln dates to about AD 400.

Preservation at Flögeln is far inferior to that of the *Wurt* settlements, such as the **Feddersen Wierde** nearby, and so phosphate mapping was used to detect the functions of the different parts of the buildings. Investigation of the arable fields by excavation and pedological mapping – together with pollen analysis, evaluation of the macro-fossils and so forth – shows the evolution of agriculture. Until about the birth of Christ the fields were deserted after only short periods, and after that they become more and more permanent. This practice became possible because of manuring, the manure having been produced in the byres.

Further reading

Behre, K.-E. and Kucan, D. (1994) *Die Geschichte der Kulturlandschaft und des Ackerbaus in der Siedlungs- kammer Flögeln, Niedersachsen, seit der Jungsteinzeit,*

Probleme der Küstenforschung im südlichen Nordseegebiet 21, 1–240, Oldenburg.

Zimmermann, W.H. (2001) Phosphatkartierung mit großem und kleinem Probenraster in der Siedlungsarchäologie. Ein Erfahrungsbericht. '...Trans Albim Fluvium'. Forschungen zur vorrömischen, kaiserzeitlichen und mittelalterli- chen Archäologie. Festschrift für Achim Leube. Internationale Archäologie, Studia honoria, Bd. 10, 69–79, Rahden/Westf.

—— (1999) 'Why was cattle-stalling introduced in prehistory? The significance of byre and stable and of outwintering', in C. Fabech and J. Ringtved (ed.) *Settlement and Landscape*, Århus: Jutland Archaeological Society, pp. 295–312.

—— (1998) Pfosten, Ständer und Schwelle und der Übergang vom Pfosten- zum Ständerbau- Eine Studie zu Innovation und Beharrung im Haus- bau. Zu Konstruktion und Haltbarkeit prähis- torischer bis neuzeitlicher Holzbauten von den Nord- und Ostseeländern bis zu den Alpen.

Probleme der Küstenforschung 25, 9–241, Oldenburg.

—— (1994) Flögeln. Hoops, Reallexikon d. Germ.
Altertumskunde 8, 206–216, Berlin.

—— (1992) Die Siedlungen des 1. bis 6. Jahrhunderts nach Christus von Flögeln-Eekhöltjen,
Niedersachsen: Die Bauformen und ihre Funk-
tionen. Probleme der Küstenforschung im südlichen Nordseegebiet 19, 1–360, Hildesheim.

W. HAIO ZIMMERMANN

Flowerdew Hundred Plantation, Virginia, USA

Flowerdew Hundred is a plantation site located on
the banks of the James River in Virginia, about
half-way between Williamsburg and Richmond. Sir
George Yeardley, the first governor of Virginia,
created the 405 ha plantation and named it for his
wife, Temperance Flowerdew. The plantation is
noteworthy in the history of the Atlantic slave trade
because fifteen of the twenty African slaves first
brought to Virginia lived there. The plantation also
had the dubious distinction of having an inordinate
amount of US southern history swirl around it. For
example, it was the scene of a Powhatan Indian
attack in 1622, Revolutionary War gunboats
commanded by Benedict Arnold lobbed shells at
its buildings in the late eighteenth century and, in
1864, the Union Army under the command of
Ulysses S. Grant crossed the James River at the
plantation to outflank the Army of Northern
Virginia commanded by Robert E. Lee. Throughout all this national history, however, the diverse
men and women who lived at the plantation made
their own histories on a daily basis.

James Deetz, of the University of Virginia,
began to excavate the site in the 1970s. Deetz and
his crews excavated eleven separate buildings,
including an enclosed compound or palisaded
area, a stone foundation with nearby burials, an
icehouse and slave cabins. In addition to the
architectural remains, Deetz's archaeologists also
recovered important artefacts. The ceramic (see
ceramics) collection alone includes a number of
wares imported from **England**. Within this
collection are sgrafitto wares from North Devon-
shire, combed slipwares, Jackfield and Whieldon
wares, transfer-printed specimens and factory-
turned slipwares. Non-English ceramics include
sturdy brown stoneware bellarmine jars and
Westerwald stoneware mugs from Germany and
delicate export **porcelain** from China.

Archaeologists at Flowerdew Hundred also
excavated a number of interesting white-clay and
terracotta smoking pipes (see **pipes, smoking**).
These pipes are important because geometric
designs and patterns have been etched on their
bowls and stems. Archaeologists have discovered
similar seventeenth-century pipes on sites in the
northern Chesapeake (see **Chesapeake region**),
including at **St Mary's City**, Maryland, where an
extensive study of the pipes has been made.
Archaeologists do not currently know with cer-
tainty whether Native American or African slaves
inscribed these pipes or whether they represent a
form of **creolisation**, made and used by both
peoples.

Further reading

Deetz, J. (1993) *Flowerdew Hundred: The Archaeology of
a Virginia Plantation, 1619–1864*, Charlottesville:
University Press of Virginia.

CHARLES E. ORSER, JR

folk typology

Folk typology (also referred to as 'folk taxonomy' in
disciplines such as **folklore**) is the systematic
classification of objects, ideas or events according
to criteria that are meaningful to the local
population. All cultures organise their world in
particular ways, but the methods of organisation
can vary considerably from one culture to another.
Also, while some typologies may be recorded,
many, if never formally written down, are known
only through the collective memory of a population. An example of these differences occurring in
unrecorded typologies across different cultures is
the informal division of animals into categories
such as 'food' and 'pet'. For many in the USA and
Europe, a cow would be considered a potential
food source while a dog would be considered a

'pet'. In other parts of the world, however, these associations shift, with a dog in some cultures considered to be 'food' and a cow in other cultures considered to be a holy animal. Frequently, such broad divisions separate into more discrete categories, revealing even further cross-cultural or socioeconomic divisions. For instance, while the cow may generally be considered to be 'food' in the USA and Europe, upon further division only portions of the animal are considered to be 'food' while other portions would be considered 'waste'. Thus, a steak is food for many people, the stomach (tripe) is food for some people and waste for others, and brains are considered to be waste for many people, and possibly food for only a few people.

The identification and study of folk typologies is a well-recognised subject of study in two areas of scholarship, folklife studies and ethnobiology, with each discipline taking somewhat different approaches to research. Ethnobiology is a hybrid discipline of anthropology and biology. In ethnobiology, the intent is to explore similarities and differences in understanding plants and animals between differing groups of people. Typically, this involves the comparison of the typologies created by indigenous populations with taxonomies created through the logic of Western scientific methodology. A lengthy example of an ethnobiologist's use of folk typologies is the work of cultural anthropologist Brent Berlin. Berlin conducted extensive ethnographic work with three groups (two in Peru and one in Mexico). His work focused on understanding the ways that the three populations organised the plant and animal species in their environment. From there he attempted to build some cross-cultural parallels of systems of organisation to identify commonalities between indigenous populations, as well as in relation to Western **classification** systems.

In contrast to ethnobiology's comparative approach, the study of folk typologies in folklife studies is to identify typologies that are either unrecorded or unrecognised. A very well-known example of this type of research is the folklorist Henry Glassie's study of vernacular **architecture**. In 1966 and 1967, Glassie studied the layout of 338 houses that were built and owned by non-elite members of central Virginian society. Out of that sample he identified 156 houses constructed during the eighteenth and nineteenth centuries that used 'traditional' building designs passed on from builder to builder, rather than relying upon the plans in pattern books often used by the wealthy segments of society. From this assemblage of houses, Glassie identified the building typologies of these common farmers and labourers. Upon examining the characteristics of each of these types, Glassie found that over time the houses became more formal in organisation. He then argued that such a shift in this folk typology represented an attempt by this community to bring order to their built environment specifically at a time when their political and religious institutions were disintegrating.

As Glassie's work suggests, the importance of a folk typology for historical archaeologists is that a particular typology can present a sense of how a past population ordered their world. In other words, it allows for the scholar to reveal categories that are meaningful to the people who actually produced and utilised the materials (an 'emic' or insider's understanding) rather than attempt interpretations of past cultures through categories generated by the scholar (an 'etic' or outsider's understanding).

See also: environmental studies; folklore and folklife studies

Further reading

Beaudry, M.C. (1988) 'Words for things: Linguistic analysis of probate inventories', in M.C. Beaudry (ed.) *Documentary Archaeology in the New World*, Cambridge: Cambridge University Press, pp. 43–50.

Berlin, B. (1992) *Ethnobiological Classification: Principles of Categorization of Plants and Animals in Traditional Societies*, Princeton: Princeton University Press.

Deetz, J. (1977) *In Small Things Forgotten: The Archaeology of Early American Life*, Garden Ciry, NY: Anchor Press/Doubleday.

Dorson, R.M. (ed.) (1972) *Folklore and Folklife: An Introduction*, Chicago: University of Chicago Press.

Glassie, H. (1975) *Folk Housing in Middle Virginia: A Structural Analysis of Historic Artefacts*, Knoxville: University of Tennessee Press.

MARK S. WARNER

folklore

The field of folklore examines the expressive aspects of folk cultures. Folk cultures were pre-scientific societies that lived in different regions of the world. A folk culture shares the same language and traditions. Folk traditions are passed on to successive generations over long periods of time. Folklife studies originally developed during the middle of the nineteenth century in Europe with the advent of industrialisation. Folklife studies were subsequently established in North America during the late nineteenth and early twentieth centuries. Profound culture change during this period compelled early folklorists to document the rapidly disappearing lifeways of folk societies.

Folklore studies are not meant to be merely a catalogue of social customs, but rather illustrate the important function and vitality of culture among human groups. Providing rules for everyday life, folk culture reinforces norms, or those practices considered to be the right way of doing things. Likewise, folklife structures various cultures by providing meaning and purpose. Perhaps most importantly from an anthropological perspective, folk culture serves to construct and reinforce social and ethnic identity. Interestingly, the underlying cultural foundation of folk groups is not static, but, like all societies, is in a perpetual state of change. Despite the emphasis among folklorists upon conservatism and maintenance of traditional practices, folk cultures, due to culture contact and the spread of ideas and inventions, are constantly being remodelled and transformed. Unfortunately, however, folk cultures were much more prevalent before the twentieth century. Today, the homogenising effects of **globalisation** and consumerism, which are making all of the world's cultures more similar, are quickly eroding the distinctiveness of folk cultures.

Paralleling topics in cultural anthropology, folklore as a discipline investigates both non-material and material culture among groups in the recent past and present. Non-material culture encompasses a diverse range of practices and beliefs. Folk tales, superstitions, folk songs, proverbs and riddles are examples of non-material traditions studied by folklorists. **Material culture**, in contrast, includes all of the distinctive objects made and used by different societies in order to survive. Craft traditions and dwelling styles are two types of material culture frequently studied by folklorists. Craft traditions include utilitarian household items that serve everyday functional purposes among different cultures. Although their daily function is often mundane, craft traditions associated with specific cultures usually possess distinctive stylistic characteristics that identify the ethnic groups that produced the objects. Pottery and textile manufacture, woodworking and metallurgy are examples of craft traditions studied by folklorists. In addition to household objects, material-culture studies also focus on folk or vernacular architectural styles. Different folk groups typically constructed their houses in distinctive ways. Log houses built by European settlers and wattle-and-daub-thatched dwellings constructed by **Native Americans** in the US south-east illustrate the range of vernacular dwelling styles prevalent in North America.

The emphasis on material culture in folklore studies is particularly relevant to historical archaeology and has significantly influenced the discipline since the 1970s. James Deetz was one of the first historical archaeologists effectively to exploit the potential of folk culture by combining the ideas of folklorist Henry Glassie and cultural anthropologist Claude Lévi-Strauss. In the book *In Small Things Forgotten*, Deetz presented an eloquent interpretation describing the transition that had occurred materially among US colonial society between the seventeenth and eighteenth centuries. Illustrated in the seemingly unrelated domains of domestic **architecture**, gravestone art and foodways (see **food and foodways**), this important juncture was characterised by the shift from regionally specific and isolated folk societies to an integrated, national-level consumer culture. Deetz envisioned this transition as not only involving the adoption of new material culture by groups in colonial North America, but ultimately was due to a subtle yet profound change in cultural world view. This transition involved a shift from the communal orientation typical of folk cultures to the emergence of modern individualism that is highly valued by contemporary US society. Since the late 1980s and through the 1990s, historical archaeologists influenced by historical materialism and **Marxian approaches** have subsequently expanded Deetz's original interpretation. These scholars attribute the cultural juncture originally described by Deetz to the deepening of **capitalism** during the past 500 years.

Since the late 1970s, Deetz and his students have explored the British-based folk cultures that were transplanted and transformed in the New World during the colonial period. Beginning in the late 1980s, other historical archaeologists have drawn upon information preserved in folk studies to better understand the material culture and beliefs of non-Western groups, especially enslaved West Africans in the US South. This trend was first set in motion by Leland Ferguson in his influential study of **colonoware pottery** recovered from plantations in the South Carolina lowcountry. Colonoware is a type of unglazed, hand-built pottery that was manufactured by Native Americans and enslaved Africans during the colonial period in Virginia, South Carolina, Florida and the Caribbean (see **Caribbean archaeology**). Interestingly, colonoware sherds marked with large Xs are typical finds at lowcountry plantations, especially around river landings in underwater contexts. Originally thought to be merely owner's marks, after examining West African and African American ethnographic information, Ferguson presented the compelling interpretation that the inscribed sherds are probably the material remnants of West African-inspired religious practices. Used as ritual paraphernalia, specifically as containers for offerings to deities, vessels marked with Xs or swastika-like motifs were prevalent among the Bakongo, a West African group. This cultural practice and associated belief system were subsequently transplanted to the Caribbean and the coastal South by enslaved West Africans from the Kongo region. Since Ferguson's study of marked colonoware vessels first appeared in the early 1990s, other historical archaeologists have explored the material expressions of West African-inspired belief systems. After careful scrutiny of African American folklore, historical archaeologists excavating slave quarters realised that many seemingly mundane artefacts, such as glass beads, pierced coins, quartz crystals and brass charms, were central elements in the folk beliefs of enslaved African Americans.

See also: Native Americans; plantation archaeology

Further reading

Deetz, J. (1977) *In Small Things Forgotten: An Archaeology of Early American Life*, New York: Anchor/Doubleday.

Ferguson, L. (1992) *Uncommon Ground: Archaeology and Early African America, 1650–1800*, Washington, DC: Smithsonian Institution Press.

MARK D. GROOVER

folklore and folklife studies

'Folklore' usually refers to a body of stories and tales that are orally transmitted and that have some antiquity. As such, folklore represents an intangible element of human life. 'Folklife', on the other hand, typically refers to **material culture**, or the tangible aspects of human life. Both terms are historically associated with agrarian, or 'folk', culture, with the terms originally being created to distinguish between the 'real' or 'traditional' cultures of a region from the modern, 'artificial' urban cultures being built around the globe beginning in the late eighteenth century. The original users of 'folklore' and 'folklife' used the terms to evoke nostalgia for what they perceived as a fading way of life and to construct images of an idealised past that may never have existed. Used in this manner, these terms could also help to promote strong feelings of nationalism, as developing nations used stories of the past to foster within their citizens a sense of community and togetherness. They often used traditional material culture as powerful cultural symbols in conjunction with the folk tales.

Folklore and folklife have a somewhat tenuous, though expanding, association with archaeology, even though archaeology and folklore/folklife were historically linked through the practice of antiquarianism. When eighteenth-century antiquarians developed their initial interest in archaeology, they examined all sources of information and saw little difference between the poorly defined realms of folklore and archaeology. Archaeology and folklore were only defined as separate academic fields in the mid-nineteenth century. It was at this time that the practitioners of both fields went their individual ways, seldom joining forces thereafter. Some twentieth-century scholars, however, have attempted to link folklore and archaeology, as archaeologists – particularly historical archaeologists – have grown less concerned about maintaining stiff academic boundaries between disciplines. In the 1960s, for example, archaeologists in **Ireland**, led by E. Estyn Evans, made explicit calls for the union of archaeology and folklife, a combination that was to be constructed around an overt interest in geography and multidisciplinary research. The often rigid boundaries between the disciplines, however, worked to postpone or even to negate any real opportunities for collaboration. In historical archaeology specifically, the use of folklore/folklife information would only become important after the 1960s, when many historical archaeologists turned their attention to the common men and women of the past. Historical archaeologists investigating sites inhabited by African slaves or by peasant farmers quickly realised that they could develop new insights by paying attention to the stories and tales recorded among such peoples. Most historical archaeologists consider folklore akin to oral history, and so are not averse to using it in their research.

Archaeologists may have an easier time accepting folklife information than folklore because of the tangible nature of the folklife materials. A folklife study may involve the examination of a number of abandoned, standing buildings in a region, or the analysis of rural furniture styles found in several old, but still inhabited houses. These topics have recognisable archaeological correlates.

Historical archaeology is particularly applicable to assisting in the construction of **living museums** where old ways of doing things are on display or even demonstrated by actors. The first open-air museum dedicated to folklife was opened in Sweden in 1891. This facility included the reconstruction of folk **architecture** representing the various regions of Scandinavia, complete with the proper regional furniture. Interpreters demonstrated crafts and agricultural practices in and around the buildings using folklife objects. One of the first folklife museums in the US was Henry Ford's Greenfield Village in Dearborn, Michigan, opened in 1929. Here, Ford funded the reconstruction of buildings that were explicitly intended to evoke an image of a serene, pastoral US history, a past that he was paradoxically helping to destroy with his mass-produced automobiles. Folklife museums have since opened around the world, and thousands of tourists visit them every year.

The interpretation of folklife objects presents problems readily familiar to archaeologists because of their material qualities. Folklore, on the other hand, can present special problems that many archaeologists may have little experience of solving. Most notable among the potential problems involves deciding whether the information presented in a folk tale is accurate or even relevant to the archaeological situation under study. Oral traditions are known to change with time, and stories will often be told based on the circumstances of their telling. A story told to a group of children may be told differently to a group of men in a tavern. Some tales are known to migrate from country to country, taking on local or national flavour as the teller sees fit. Storytellers can take a tale from one place and add local place names to make the story more immediate and memorable to their audiences. Some traditions can be simply invented for political, social or cultural reasons. As these stories are repeatedly told, they can assume the character of cultural and national traditions.

Archaeologists using folklore information must be as adept as folklorists in knowing how to interpret the information they convey, or else they must collaborate with a trained folklorist who knows the pitfalls and promise of folklore. Catalogues of folklore motifs have been prepared by specialists to help scholars decide whether a tale is simply a local variant of a common, widely known story or whether the elements of a tale are unique. Many nations have collected their folklore materials in catalogued archives, and archaeologists can consult these collections as they would any other archival material. In other cases, no compiled archives may exist and the archaeologist may be compelled to conduct his or her own interviewing to acquire folklore.

Archaeologists can make valuable use of folklore/folklife information in numerous ways. For example, folklore can provide archaeologists with insights about a people's view of their past and their notions of what they view as most important within their culture. Archaeologists can also employ folklore to discover what a people thinks about ancient archaeological sites and monuments, how they perceive the past and how they conceptualise their environment and landscape.

See also: oral history

Further reading

Evans, E.E. (1973) 'Archaeology and folklife', *Béaloideas* 41: 127–39.

Gazin-Schwartz, A. and Holtorf, C.J. (eds) (1999) *Archaeology and Folklore*, London: Routledge.

Thomas, C. (1960) 'Archaeology and folk-life studies', *Gwerin* 3: 7–17.

CHARLES E. ORSER, JR

food and foodways

The study of food and foodways is an important theme in historical archaeology. Historical archaeologists study plant remains, animals remains, **ceramics**, glassware and other artefacts to reconstruct past diet and food practices, a central component of the archaeology of **everyday life**. Historical archaeologists also study broader questions about cultural aspects of past 'foodways'. James Deetz brought the concept of foodways into historical archaeology from Jay Anderson's work in folklife studies. Anderson defined foodways as the 'interrelated system of food conceptualization, procurement, distribution, preservation, preparation, and consumption'. Taking a foodways perspective helps archaeologists move beyond dietary reconstruction to interpretations that explore the many social, cultural and ideological uses and meanings of food.

Many common classes of archaeological finds relate to food and foodways. **Bottles**, glass tableware, ceramics, animal bones, plant remains, cutlery and a variety of other artefacts often provide direct information about past foodways. The form and decoration of ceramic and glass vessels are frequently indicative of function, which can be linked to interpretations of past food practices. **Zooarchaeology**, the study of animal bones from archaeological sites, can determine the variety of animal foods eaten, their relative dietary importance and how people butchered animals and prepared meals. Similarly, the study of plant remains from sites can show the range of species used and their role in the diet. Historic sources often provide a wealth of information on foodways systems: newspaper advertisements specify the price and availability of foodstuffs; **probate inventories** list stored foods and food preparation artefacts; accounts books record food exchanges; recipe books detail preparation; and period illustrations show kitchen scenes and food consumption. Historical archaeologists use all of these various data sources, often in combination, to derive interpretations of past foodways.

At the most basic level, archaeological studies of food and foodways involve the reconstruction of diet and dietary practices: what people ate in the past; how it was prepared; and how it was consumed. Archaeology has made significant contributions to our understanding of historic diet, especially for marginalised or oppressed groups of people. For example, archaeology gives a new view of the dietary practices of enslaved Africans and African Americans in the USA. Animal bones from plantation sites show that slaves hunted, fished and collected a wide variety of wild food resources in order to supplement inadequate plantation food rations. In South Carolina, forms of **colonoware pottery** vessels also suggest the continuation of African food preparation and consumption practices on early plantations.

Reconstructing past diet is logically linked to understanding food production and exchange systems. The presence of certain foods in an archaeological assemblage can give insight into the means of how food was acquired, whether from hunting, fishing, collecting, agriculture or some sort of exchange. For example, bottom-dwelling fish require certain fishing methods to be caught, and their presence in an assemblage informs interpretations of past fishing practices. Wild plant and animal foods in an archaeological assemblage provide insight into the environmental resources and zones people used. In some instances the use of wild foods followed a distinct seasonal cycle based on seasonal variation in the availability of wild resources, competing demands for labour and the availability of agricultural products. Assemblages dominated by the remains of domestic plants and animals can also provide information about food production systems, the uses of different agricultural products and their role in foodways systems.

Food practices encode many different culturally specific social and ideological meanings. Foodways tend to be a conservative part of culture, resistant to dramatic changes. Archaeologists study traditional cultural practices, be they Dutch, Chinese or Spanish, to characterise practices brought with immigrants to the Americas, to assess how foodways changed in new environments and to understand the emergence of distinctive regional or ethnic diets. In situations of cultural contact archaeologists have used food practices to study processes of **acculturation** or **creolisation**.

Archaeologists also study how foodways reflect and express aspects of social identity, such as social class (see **class, social**), religion, **ethnicity** or other social variables. Numerous factors structure access to, or choice of, certain types of foods. Simultaneously, the choice of certain foods or specific methods of preparation and consumption expresses identity. At **Cannon's Point Plantation**, John Otto compared the foodways of enslaved African Americans, a free white overseer and a wealthy, white plantation owner. These people varied in their race, social status and position in the plantation hierarchy. Their foodways also differed in important ways, as reflected in the bottles, ceramics and animal bones in the assemblages. The planter's household ate the most diverse range of foods from fancy decorated plates and platters. The slaves and the overseer used more bowls and hollow vessels. The slaves ate the most wild meat, augmented by the least desirable parts of the domestic animals butchered on the plantation. As all of these examples demonstrate, studies of past foodways offer insight into many important issues in the field of historical archaeology.

See also: tea/tea ceremony

Further reading

Anderson, J. (1971) 'A solid sufficiency: An ethnography of yeoman foodways in Stuart England', doctoral dissertation, Philadelphia: University of Pennsylvania.

Benes, P. and Benes, J.M. (eds) (1984) *Foodways in the Northeast*, Annual Proceedings Dublin Seminar for New England Folklife, Boston: Boston University Press.

Geismar, J.H. and Janowitz, M.F. (eds) (1993) 'Health, sanitation, and foodways in historical archaeology', *Historical Archaeology* 27(2): 1–111.

Gumerman, G. (1997) 'Food and complex societies', *Journal of Archaeological Method and Theory* 4: 105–39.

Landon, D.B. (1996) 'Feeding colonial Boston: A zooarchaeological study', *Historical Archaeology* 30(1): 1–153.

Scott, E.M. (1996) 'Who ate what? Archaeological food remains and cultural diversity', in E.J. Reitz, L.A. Newsom and S.J. Scudder (eds) *Case Studies in Environmental Archaeology*, New York: Plenum Press, pp. 339–56.

DAVID B. LANDON

forensic anthropology

Forensic science in general is the application of science to the investigation of possible criminal activity and the pursuit of justice. Forensic anthropology, specifically, is the application of the techniques for studying human skeletal and dental remains developed within **biological anthropology** in judicial investigations involving human skeletal and dental remains. Such investigations may be associated with either possible criminal activity or other mysterious and accidental death.

Beginning in the late nineteenth century, biological (physical) anthropologists initially specialised in and focused on the study of skeletal and dental variation in living and extinct humans. Using virtually nothing but osteological (the study of bones) measurements and observations, this early work was directed towards the construction of human racial classifications and the delineation of the differences between modern humans and either prehistoric forms or other primates. Consequently, biological/physical anthropologists developed an array of analytical techniques for studying human anatomical and osteological variation, as well as an extensive body of knowledge regarding such variation between the sexes and between different populations at different biological or developmental ages. Anthropologists also studied pathological and behavioural modifications of the skeleton and dentition, and thereby developed a database of indicators of osteological abnormalities. It is these techniques and this extensive database of population variation and skeletal abnormalities that are used in forensic anthropology.

Human identification

The two most important questions forensic anthropologists attempt to answer regarding the human skeletal and dental remains they deal with are 'Who is this?' and 'What can we tell about how the individual may have died?' Examination of prehistoric, historic or contemporary bones and teeth of humans is done first with the goal of determining the sex, age at death, stature, weight and possible population affinity of the remains. In addition, there is examination for evidence of any pathologies or trauma such as diseases, accidental injury or wounds, as well as specific individual characteristics (which may be especially useful in the forensic effort to establish the identity of the remains). Such examination is all directed to providing the maximum amount of knowledge possible about the individual being studied or investigated. The application of the techniques and evaluative criteria necessary for such an examination is the contribution biological/physical anthropology can make to criminal investigations.

Sex

One of the most basic aspects of human identification involves the determination of sex. Osteologically, the most important differences between males and females are found in the pelvis. Compared to adult males, adult females show a number of distinctive features reflective of the generally broader pelvis related to childbirth. Differences in the size and shape of various muscle attachment sites on the skeleton are also used as indicators of sex, although such size differences can be deceptive due to both individual variation between the sexes

within a population and the variation in overall male–female differences or sexual dimorphism found in different populations.

Age at death

As equally important as sexual identification is the determination of the developmental or chronological age of an individual at death. The most commonly used criteria for sub-adult individuals are the eruption sequences of the primary or deciduous teeth and the adult teeth, and the fusion sequence of epiphyses to the shafts of the long bones of the skeleton. (The approximately 206 bones of the adult human skeleton form from some 806 ossification centres. The growing shaft of a long bone is termed a 'diaphysis' and the ends and other protuberances on it are termed 'epiphyses'.) In adult individuals, the most reliable criteria involve sequential changes that transform the appearance of the pubic symphysis in the pelvis. Sequence standards for all of these criteria have been worked out for different contemporary populations and, where appropriate, males and females separately. Applying the appropriate population standards to the skeletal remains in question can be problematic if there is no reliable indication of the population affinity of the remains.

Stature estimation

It is possible to estimate the stature of an individual by inserting measurement data from selected long bones into regression formulae derived from examination of individuals of known height. The same caveats regarding the variation in ageing criteria between the sexes and within different populations apply here.

Population affinity or 'race'

The most problematic aspect of human identification involves the determination of an individual's population affinity or 'race'. It is understandable, perhaps, that forensic anthropologists are asked to provide racial information by law enforcement officials since such information is common in many forms of official identification. Nonetheless, it is also especially ironic since physical anthropologists have done as much or more to discourage the use of this concept in dealing with modern human variation. The principal difficulty, of course, is the lack of clearly discrete character states or dimensions that distinguish reliably and uniformly the members of one population from another.

Individual or idiosyncratic characteristics

Individual life experiences leave physical scars on many people. Developmental anomalies (e.g. unerupted or absent teeth), trauma (e.g. both healed and unhealed fractures), disease (e.g. syphilis), degenerative processes (e.g. occupational wear facets, osteoarthritis), nutrition and diet (e.g. anaemia, dental caries) are the more common sources for transforming and scarring the skeleton. Proper identification of as many individual aspects of skeletal remains as possible is frequently the key to the final identification of those remains.

DNA matching

Advancements in molecular biology have enabled scientists to match DNA samples extracted from human remains with known databases. Precise identification is possible if reference samples are available. The US military now obtains samples from its soldiers for future possible identification purposes. Such a practice is expected to resolve questions of the identity of human remains and prevent the need to inter any more 'unknown' soldiers.

Further reading

Bass, W.M. (1987) *Human Osteology: A Laboratory and Field Manual*, third edn, Columbia: Missouri Archaeological Society.

Krogman, W.M. (1962) *The Human Skeleton in Forensic Medicine*, Springfield, IL: Charles C. Thomas.

Stewart, T.D. (1979) *Essentials of Forensic Anthropology*, Springfield, IL: Charles C. Thomas.

MARTIN K. NICKELS

forensic archaeology

Forensic archaeologists are those who use both the paradigms and the methods developed in anthropological archaeology, in criminal investigations, and humanitarian exhumations of human remains. The use of archaeological techniques in forensic work started as the application of simple archaeological recovery techniques in death scenes involving a buried body or skeletal remains. It has expanded to include the application of archaeological paradigms (context, taphonomy), methods (excavation, surveying, cartography) and goals (the reconstruction of past events) for the purposes of a medico-legal or humanitarian forensic investigation. This differs from **forensic anthropology** in that the latter is the use of the methods of physical anthropology in forensic contexts.

The skills archaeologists bring to a medico-legal investigation are critical in site location, determining how a clandestine grave was dug, the way in which body disposal was carried out and in documenting physical evidence associated with the event, such as the locations of expended cartridge cases and bullets. Investigators seeking to reconstruct past events at a crime scene can use the evidence collected and documented by archaeologists.

To participate effectively in death investigations, archaeologists need forensic training in addition to extensive archaeological experience. This training includes becoming familiar with the protocols for crime scene processing, chains of custody and effective court testimony.

Further reading

Connor, M.A. and Scott, D.D. (eds) (2001) 'Archaeologists as forensic investigators: defining the role', *Historical Archaeology* 35(1): 1–104.

Morse, D., Duncan, J. and Stoutamire, J. (1983) *Handbook of Forensic Archaeology and Anthropology*, Tallahassee, FL: Bill's Bookstore.

MELISSA CONNOR

formula dating

Historical archaeologists, because they largely focus their activities on the past 500 years, occasionally have the opportunity to use dating methods that are rooted in the systematic changes in artefact design over time. Specifically, they have used formula dating to provide dates for collections of white-clay smoking pipes (see **pipes, smoking**) and English-made **ceramics**.

Pioneering historical archaeologist J.C. Harrington noticed that the holes, or 'bores', in the stems of the white-clay smoking pipes he excavated were about half the size in late eighteenth-century collections as they were in early seventeenth-century collections. Examining this phenomenon closer, he discovered that the bore diameters gradually grew larger as one progressed backward from 1750 to 1650. The regularity of this change inspired archaeologist Lewis Binford to devise a regression formula to illustrate the change and to make it possible to predict the dates of other large pipe stem collections based on bore diameter alone. Other archaeologists later realised that Binford's linear regression formula was a bit unrealistic (because the bore could never actually disappear) and they devised a more sensible curvilinear formula that showed that bore diameter could only grow so small before the pipe became useless.

Stanley South, after contemplating the known manufacturing dates of the English ceramics he collected at the sites he excavated, decided that it was possible to examine the date ranges for all the ceramics in any one collection, to calculate all the mean dates of manufacture for each ceramic type and then, from these means, to calculate a single 'mean ceramic date' for the entire collection. Historical archaeologists everywhere became interested in South's method after he demonstrated that his ceramic calculations generally came within a few years of the known mean occupation dates of the sites in his study. The implication of South's finding was that historical archaeologists could use the 'mean ceramic dating formula' to provide dates for a site that was otherwise undocumented.

See also: mean ceramic dating; pipe stem dating

CHARLES E. ORSER, JR

Fort Michilimackinac, Michigan, USA

Fort Michilimackinac was first established by the French on the south shore of the Straits of Mackinac in northern Michigan as a Jesuit mission and small fur-trading compound in about 1715. Within a high, protective, upright log palisade the earliest town contained French *poteaux-en-terre* (posts-in-ground) houses for priests, soldiers and fur traders. Immediately outside the west palisade, on an open and unprotected beach, Jesuits built their mission church to serve local **Native Americans**. Because 'Indian wars' had greatly diminished by 1717, the government in Versailles no longer viewed Native American alliance and religious conversion as major political objectives in New France and focused instead on the fur trade.

Indeed, the archaeological remains of palisades, houses and the mission church reveal that, by the early 1730s, Michilimackinac was completely rebuilt into a much larger and well-planned fur trade town. This rebuilding was to be the largest and most important in its history and, like most French-Canadian settlements in North America, Michilimackinac enjoyed economic prosperity until the close of the French and Indian War in 1759. Archaeological studies of the distribution of food remains and such artefacts as **ceramics**, glassware and jewellery reveal French social structure at Michilimackinac.

Within the 1730s, palisaded settlement houses numbered forty in all, comprising seven lengthy row houses along the four palisade walls. The parish Church of Ste Anne de Michilimackinac, built in 1741, was of *pièce-sur-pièce* (horizontal log) construction. A large semi-subterranean powder magazine was constructed within the south-east section of the fort; surrounding it was a neighbourhood known from artefact evidence to have been where poorer colonists resided.

Most building ruins found archaeologically at Michilimackinac date from the 1730s settlement. All constructions within palisades were aligned along a system of streets and lanes that are known by their French names. The most striking aspect of the 1730s town is its overall architectural symmetry, and this settlement plan changed little throughout the remaining history of the town, despite later British architectural additions and palisade expansions.

More than three decades of relative prosperity ended in the mid-1740s when France and Britain once again went to war. Within a decade, the fighting spread world-wide and resulted in the final collapse of French rule in North America. Nowhere is the French demise more evident than in the archaeological record for Michilimackinac between 1744 and 1761. Artefact studies reveal a shift to local cottage industry because of British blockades. By 1760, with the collapse of New France, British traders and soldiers moved westward to fill the vacuum left by the French-Canadians.

Historiographies, stratigraphic studies and a re-evaluation (and re-identification) of artefact functions all demonstrate status differences during both colonial occupations of Michilimackinac. Almost immediately upon the arrival of the British in the former French colony, however, relations with the Native Americans began to sour, primarily because of negative British racial and ethnic attitudes. Archaeological evidence of activity areas within the fort revealed **gender** and ethnic roles among the various social classes living there. By 1763, most British-occupied settlements in the Great Lakes region were attacked and captured by Native Americans during a well co-ordinated rebellion known as 'Pontiac's Uprising'. At Michilimackinac the entire military garrison was killed, and the town occupied by Native Americans and some remaining French-Canadians.

Thanks to almost half a century of continuous excavation, soil resistivity surveys and archaeometry studies, we know that virtually all structures at Michilimackinac were made of wood. When British forces returned to Michilimackinac in 1764 they found a dilapidated, tumbled-down settlement, where even a large portion of the palisades had been destroyed. The town was in total need of rebuilding and British authorities were determined to rebuild it along military lines. Because of a scarcity of suitable stone, rebuilding was done in wood.

By the mid-1760s, the British had expanded the north and south palisades outward to form a hexagonal enclosure in order to create more living space. They also erected a number of military buildings. These British changes in the settlement pattern (see **settlement analysis**) of the 1730s have been delineated successfully by archaeologists, both horizontally and stratigraphically, and allow a definition of actual neighbourhoods within the fort by social class.

By the mid-1770s, the outbreak of the American Revolution ultimately led British authorities to abandon their rebuilding efforts and move the entire garrison to nearby Mackinac Island, where they built a new fort of stone. Michilimackinac was burned to the ground in 1781, so that nothing was visible at the site of that fort when archaeologists first began excavations there in the late 1950s.

See also: fortifications; French colonialism

Further reading

Heldman, D.P. (1999) 'Euro-American archaeology in Michigan: The French period', in J.R. Halsey (ed.) *Retrieving Michigan's Buried Past: The Archaeology of the Great Lakes State*, Bloomfield Hills: Cranbrook Institute of Science, pp. 292–311.

—— (1991) 'The French in Michigan and beyond: An archaeological view from Fort Michilimackinac', in J.A. Walthall (ed.) *French Colonial Archaeology: The Illinois Country and Western Great Lakes*, Urbana: University of Illinois Press, pp. 201–17.

—— (1986) 'Michigan's first jewish settlers: A view from the Solomon-Levy trading house at Fort Michilimackinac, 1765–1781', *Journal of New World Archaeology* 6(4): 21–3.

—— (1980) 'Coins at Michilimackinac', *Historical Archaeology* 14: 82–107.

Heldman, D.P. and Grange, R.T., Jr (1981) 'Excavations at Fort Michilimackinac, 1978–1979: The Rue de la Babillarde', *Archaeological Completion Report* 3, Mackinac Island: Mackinac Island State Park Commission.

DONALD P. HELDMAN

Fort Mose, Florida, USA

Fort Mose, or Gracia Real de Santa Teresa de Mose, was the first free African American settlement legally created in the USA. Established about

3 km north of **St Augustine**, Florida, in 1738 by the colonial governor of Spanish Florida, Fort Mose was a sanctuary for slaves fleeing the plantations of English Carolina. In addition to being a constant reminder to the British of the fragile nature of their empire, the free inhabitants of Fort Mose also served in a militia that openly fought against their former enslavers. An important cultural element of the settlement was that its inhabitants blended aspects of their native African ways of life with the cultural traditions of the Spanish and the English. Fort Mose was abandoned in the late eighteenth century when Spain lost control of the region, and it is today a US National Historic Landmark.

Archaeologists under the direction of Kathleen Deagan excavated at the site of Fort Mose in 1987 and 1988. They collected hundreds of artefacts from the site, including **ceramics**, glass **bottles**, gunflints, smoking pipes (see **pipes, smoking**), **beads** and other objects associated with daily life. A detailed examination of the animal bones collected from the site reveals that the men and women who lived there had greater access to domestic meat than did the **Native Americans** in the area, but less access than the Spanish colonists living in St Augustine. The excavation of Fort Mose is important in historical archaeology because it has added to the growing literature on free African American lifeways and it has further documented one part of the African diaspora.

See also: creolisation; Spanish colonialism

Further reading

Deagan, K. and MacMahon, D. (1995) *Fort Mose: Colonial America's Black Fortress of Freedom*, Gainesville: University Press of Florida.

Landers, J. (1992) *Fort Mose: Gracia Real de Santa Teresa de Mose: A Free Black Town in Spanish Colonial Florida*, St Augustine: St Augustine Historical Society.

Reitz, E.J. (1994) 'Zooarchaeological analysis of a free African community: Gracia Real de Santa Teresa de Mose', *Historical Archaeology* 28(1): 23–40.

CHARLES E. ORSER, JR

Fort Necessity, Pennsylvania, USA

Fort Necessity, a National Battlefield Site maintained by the US Park Service since 1933, was the scene of a battle between British and French forces during the contest for empire waged between both their governments. A body of volunteers from Virginia under command of 22-year-old George Washington constructed the fort in 1754, but were soon defeated by a larger French force. J.C. Harrington, one of North America's first professional historical archaeologists, excavated the site of the makeshift fort in 1952 and 1953.

The association with George Washington gave the fort a national significance, and in 1816 a professional surveyor mapped the fort remains when they were still visible. His survey showed that Washington's men had built the fort in a triangular shape with a small, square projection extending from the triangle's base. Archaeologists first explored the area of the fort in 1931. This initial work was intended to establish the exact location and design of the stockade to aid the Park Service in planning their reconstruction of the fortification. Based on both the early survey and the rudimentary archaeology, the Park Service decided to reconstruct the fort as a triangle. Questions remained, however, as to whether this was the fort's proper shape or whether it had actually been constructed as a square. Harrington was called in as a trained professional to settle the design controversy and to collect artefacts for museum displays that could be used to interpret the site to the public.

Harrington's controlled excavations revealed that the fort was neither triangular nor square, but rather circular. His excavations uncovered the remaining stumps of the palisade's posts, preserved by water and still standing where Washington's men had placed them. Harrington's research also unearthed artefacts related to the fort's occupation. This collection includes iron bolts and spikes, glass **bottles**, military **buttons**, gunflints and lead shot.

Harrington's excavation at Fort Necessity is important to historical archaeology because it occurred early in the history of the discipline. The 1950s was still a time of uncertainty about the exact nature of historical archaeology and Harrington's research helped to define the utility of the field at least as far as history was concerned. More importantly, however, Harrington's project demonstrated the practical value of historical archaeology as an aid to physical reconstruction. He demonstrated that historical archaeologists, using a careful combination of excavation and historical research, could provide new information about the sites occupied in the past, including (and, at this time, especially) those associated with famous people and 'important' events.

See also: English colonialism; French colonialism; fortifications; history of historical archaeology

CHARLES E. ORSER, JR

Fort Union, North Dakota, USA

Fort Union Trading Post was constructed in 1828 by the American Fur Company as its headquarters for the lucrative bison-hide trade, principally with the Assiniboin, Crow and Blackfeet **Native Americans**. The builders of the post strategically situated it at the junction of the Missouri and Yellowstone rivers, in what is today extreme western North Dakota. The fort operated as a fur-trading station until 1867, when its owners sold it to the US Army, which was then attempting to establish dominance over the Native Americans in the area. The soldiers razed the fort the same year they purchased it, and used the materials to build a new fort, Fort Buford, approximately 3 km away. The US Congress designated Fort Union a National Historic Site in 1966, and in 1985 they passed a bill mandating its reconstruction. The reconstruction occurred from 1986 to 1989, with the goal of making the fort appear as it did in 1850–1. Information collected by historical archaeologists was central to the reconstruction effort.

Archaeologists for the US National Park Service conducted excavations at the site of Fort Union from 1986 to 1988, with their highest priority being the recovery of architectural information that could be used by the site's reconstructors. They excavated approximately 4,400 m^2 of the site, an area that encompassed the entire fort.

Though the research was largely guided by the needs of the reconstruction, significant information was also collected about the interaction between Native Americans and the fort's US fur traders. For example, in a pioneering study of cultural interaction, William Hunt examined the relationship between **firearms** and **ethnicity**. Rather than confine himself merely to studying the kinds of firearms available at the post and their periods of availability, as others have done, he wanted to know about the cultural side of the firearm trade. He wanted to know, for instance, whether the commonly held wisdom that Native Americans preferred smooth-bore muskets to rifles was actually true. His research suggested that this was in fact the case, and that the US traders preferred rifles. Hunt's research was limited to Fort Union, and it is impossible to know at this time whether the pattern he observed will be duplicated at other nineteenth-century fur-trade posts. What is important, however, is that he used the archaeological materials to examine an important period of cultural interaction.

See also: fortifications; fur trade archaeology in western Canada

Further reading

Hunt, W. J., Jr (1993) 'Ethnicity and firearms in the upper Missouri bison-robe trade: An examination of weapon preference and utilization at Fort Union Trading Post N.H.S., North Dakota', *Historical Archaeology* 27(3): 74–101.

CHARLES E. ORSER, JR

fortifications

The discovery and excavation of military fortifications has played a major role in the development of historical archaeology. Early historical archaeologists were originally drawn to fortifications because they were prominent places within a nation's ideology and because they were usually associated with people, typically men, who were important within a nation's telling of its history. At the same time, fortifications were often visible on the landscape, and, as such, may have been important in a region's oral traditions. Historical archaeologists, often in search of excavation funds, learned that the investigation of military sites could often obtain funds from government agencies intent on using fortification sites as tourist locales. For this reason, much of the earliest historical archaeology at fortifications was directed towards the collection of architectural details that could be used in larger **restoration** and **reconstruction** projects. Over the years, however, archaeologists engaged in fortification studies have shifted their attention from an almost exclusive interest in fort **architecture** and design to a broader, more anthropological understanding of the cultural interactions that occurred at fortifications and even to the symbolic role forts could play within diverse cultural and physical landscapes.

Historical archaeologists have discovered numerous examples of fortifications throughout the world, and the literature is too vast to enumerate. Suffice to say that Europeans built fortifications everywhere they went during their colonialist enterprises. Excavations have revealed that for-

tifications can be extremely small and constructed to protect a single dwelling, such as what archaeologist Frazer Neiman encountered at the seventeenth-century Cliffs Plantation, Virginia, or absolutely massive, such as the fortified cities of Europe or the eighteenth-century **Fortress of Louisbourg**, Cape Breton Island, Canada. Of course, the literature, and even popular culture, is replete with examples of fortified trading posts all over the world.

The history of fortifications stretches backward into prehistory, and every culture in history who has needed protection has devised some means of providing it through military engineering. The innovations in the design and construction of fortifications – and those that are of most concern to historical archaeologists – were made to keep pace with the technological design innovations of **firearms**, beginning in the sixteenth century. Defenders of cities and settlements found that they needed stronger and more complex fortifications as the enemies' weapons increased in destructive intensity. People facing a pitched battle with an

Figure 13 A section of reconstructed fortification wall at the Fortress of Louisbourg, Nova Scotia
Source: Photo: S. Baugher

army equipped with cannons simply needed different defences from those confronting an indigenous enemy armed with bows and arrows. Castles designed to defend against archers and catapults could not withstand the sustained assaults of weapons charged with gunpowder.

In the history of European fortifications, Sebastien Le Prestre de Vauban (1633–1707), a French 'general of fortifications', was perhaps the most influential. Vauban's *On Siege and Fortification* (written in 1705–6) was so important that it dominated military engineering for the next century. After Vauban had described his method of fortification, European military engineers worked to refine his methods. For example, John Muller's *A Treatise Containing the Elementary Part of Fortification, Regular and Irregular* was published in 1746 as a manual for British engineers. The wide acceptance of the designs promoted by Vauban and his followers is the reason that colonial forts of the eighteenth century look similar, or even identical. Thus, Fort Stanwix, built by the British in New York State in 1758, is almost identical in form to the Dutch-built, and Portuguese-occupied, Fortaleza de Santa Cruz de Itamaracá in north-east Brazil.

The fortifications designed by the formal, European military engineers of the eighteenth and early nineteenth centuries were characterised by the presence of 'bastions', or pointed projections that extended from the corners of the square box that formed the centre of the fort. These bastions were designed so that a fort's defenders could shoot down the length of the fort's walls, called 'curtains', from the bastions, leaving no blind spots for attackers to hide against the fort's walls. The job of the military engineer was to ensure that the fort was designed in such a way that all the wall angles permitted an adequate defence.

One reason that great variation exists in fortification design stems from the simple fact that people in different cultures have dissimilar ideas about how to defend themselves within the natural and cultural environments in which they live. For example, the designs used by European engineers were vastly unlike those used by their non-European counterparts. The fortification of Himeji Castle in Japan, initially built in 1346 and renovated in the early seventeenth century, re-

flected none of the elements promoted by Vauban. Instead, the fortification projected a thoughtful integration of technology and nature, employing high towers situated on hills inside the main, fortified enclosure. Three moats and 15-m-high, sloping, stone walls – which obscured the view of the main castle – completed a design that was intended to frustrate all attackers. Himeji Castle, though never the scene of hostilities, represented a formidable obstacle that would have been every bit as effective as Vauban's designs.

Historical archaeologists have done much to reveal how specific fortifications were built. Their efforts have enhanced the physical reconstruction of forts all over the world. An important aspect of the historical archaeology of fortifications, however, rests in its ability to document the deviations from the ideal. Historical archaeologists have repeatedly discovered in their excavations that the actual builders of fortifications often did not construct forts precisely as the engineer had designed them. The foundations may not be as deep or as thick as required, the bastions may have been oddly shaped or they may be entirely missing, or a fort's curtains could be too long.

Historical archaeologists will always play an important role in documenting the physical forms and design elements of fortifications but it is unlikely that they will ever again be content simply to provide details for architectural historians and restorationists. As historical archaeologists increasingly turn their attention to the symbolic role of fortifications in affecting local social relations and in changing and shaping individual and group perceptions, it is likely that their examinations of fortifications will become more sophisticated and more anthropologically rigorous and meaningful.

See also: Fort Michilimackinac; Fort Mose; Fort Necessity; Fort Union

CHARLES E. ORSER, JR

Fortress of Louisbourg, Cape Breton Island, Canada

French colonists began building the Fortress of Louisbourg in 1719 on the island they then called

'Isle Royale'. Following their loss of Acadia and Newfoundland with the Treaty of Utrecht (1713), the French established the massive fortification (see **fortifications**) to protect their claims to the cod fisheries of the Great Banks. They only completed the fortified town in 1745, immediately before the first siege by British forces from **New England**. The British assault was successful and they held the fort for three years, when it was returned to the French under terms of the Treaty of Aix-la-Chapelle. The British attacked again in 1758, again retaking the town. They finally demolished the walls of the fortress to ensure that it would never again be returned to the French. In 1961, the Canadian government announced their decision to reconstruct a sizeable portion of the old town as it looked in the 1740s before the first British attack, and it was in this environment that archaeologists began working at the site. Since then, their detailed research has contributed much information about the physical character of the fortress and about the daily lives of the men and women who lived there.

The research at Louisbourg is multidisciplinary in scope, and the scholars who work there have used many sources of information to aid in their interpretation. For example, archaeologists have unearthed millions of artefacts, the ruins of several fortification walls and the buildings within them, while historians have compiled hundreds of maps and well over a half a million documents from archives in Europe, Canada and the USA.

Archaeologists at Louisbourg spent much of the 1960s and 1970s providing architectural information that the restorers could use in their reconstruction. For example, in the early 1960s, they focused on the Royal Battery (located just north of the town) and on the King's Bastion, the Chateau St Louis (which included the Governor's Wing) and various casemates. These excavations revealed the thickness and design of both fortification and building walls, and provided key information for the reconstruction. More recently, the archaeologists have turned their attention to the roadways, conducting research along the Rue Royalle, one of

Figure 14 Reconstructed buildings and street at Fortress Louisbourg, Nova Scotia
Source: Photo: S. Baugher

the main streets in the reconstructed town. Their research has revealed precise information about the repair of the roadways and the construction of stone-capped drains.

The artefact collection from the Fortress of Louisbourg includes practically everything the colonial French used in the eighteenth century. These objects include glass **bottles**, faience dishes, coarse **earthenware** vessels, military buckles and accoutrements, gunflints and white-clay smoking pipes (see **pipes, smoking**). The archaeologists at Louisbourg have completed several important studies of these artefacts. These studies are extremely significant because the artefacts have often been found in tightly dated contexts, meaning that they provide specific information about the **material culture** of the French in the New World for certain, fixed periods. A study of clay pipes published by Iain C. Walker in 1971, for example, focuses on pipes found in contexts datable to 1700–50, 1749–55, 1755–60 and 1720–c.1732. These kinds of datable collections prove invaluable in helping archaeologists interpret life in short time periods.

CHARLES E. ORSER, JR

Fowey, HMS

Launched in 1744 in Hull, **England**, HMS *Fowey* was not yet four years old when it was 'holed' on a reef and sunk in what is known today as Legare Anchorage in Biscayne National Park, Florida, USA. Heavily armed with six, nine and eighteen pounder guns, and crewed with over 200 men *Fowey* was a formidable Royal Naval vessel.

During its short existence, *Fowey* was first active in the English Channel and the waters off Gibraltar. Later, in 1746, *Fowey* escorted troop transports to the recently captured **Fortress of Louisbourg**, Cape Breton in Nova Scotia. For the balance of its career, *Fowey* was assigned to a split duty station cruising the coast of North America from South Carolina to Boston during the summer and operating out of Port Antonio, Jamaica, and the Caribbean in the winter. In June 1748, *Fowey* captured a Spanish ship, the *St Judea*. It was while

escorting this 'prize' and two British colonial merchant vessels to its summer duty station off Virginia that the *Fowey* ran onto a reef and sank. The English crew crowded on to the merchant vessels and navigated the hostile waters of Spanish Florida to Charleston. The crew of the *St Judea* were given their parole and sailed for Havana, Cuba.

Two hundred and twenty-seven years would pass before the remains of the *Fowey* would be identified in 1975 by US National Park Service archaeologist George Fischer. Four years later, a sport diver from Miami requested title in Admiralty Court to a 'wrecked and abandoned sailing vessel with Legare Anchorage in Biscayne National Park'. At this time, the Abandoned Shipwreck Act was a decade in the future. The USA intervened in the lawsuit as the defendant seeking title, arguing that the shipwreck was public property in a national park and, as such, should be preserved as a part of the nation's patrimony. In 1983, the USA won the case. The court decision constituted a landmark in US historic shipwreck preservation case law. It stated that the remains of HMS *Fowey* were an archaeological site, not a ship in terms of Admiralty salvage; that the site was in no peril and did not need rescuing by the salvor; and that the site was public property and a part of the USA's heritage that ought to be managed in the best interests of the public rather than privately salvaged and sold for profit.

In the twenty-five years since the wreck was identified, HMS *Fowey* has been broadly studied in the surviving documentary records of the USA, Canada and Great Britain, and has been the subject of three National Park Service field projects. The largest and best documented of these was conducted in 1983. Evidence of the wreck's function as a Royal Naval vessel includes iron ballast blocks and guns, and copper gunpowder barrel hoops marked with the 'Broad Arrow' denoting ownership by the English Crown. Its cultural affiliation is further denoted by the presence of English-made pewter, glass and ceramic tablewares (see **ceramics**).

See also: shipwrecks

Further reading

May, W.E. (1958) 'The wreck of HMS Fowey', *Mariner's Mirror* 44(1): 320–4.

Skowronek, R.K. (1997) 'Hurricane uncovers 18th-century wreck', *Naval History* 11(1): 14.

—— (1985) 'Sport divers and archaeology: The case of the Legare Anchorage ship site', *Archaeology* 38(3): 22–7.

—— (1984) *Archaeological Testing and Evaluation of the Legare Anchorage Shipwreck Site, Biscayne National Park, Summer 1983*, Tallahassee, FL: National Park Service.

Skowronek, R.K., Johnson, R.E., Vernon, R.H. and Fischer, G.R. (1987) 'The Legare Anchorage shipwreck site – grave of HMS *Fowey*', *International Journal of Nautical Archaeology* 16: 313–24.

RUSSELL K. SKOWRONEK

French colonialism

Archaeological study of French colonialism has so far been limited essentially to North America, although glimmerings of interest are appearing in Guyana, the Caribbean islands of Martinique and Guadeloupe, and other former colonies of France across the globe. Within North America, the development of French colonial archaeology has taken somewhat divergent paths in Canada and the USA, due largely to differences in the nature of French colonial sites located in each country. Canadian archaeologists have concentrated on urban sites (Québec City, Montréal, and the **Fortress of Louisbourg**), military forts, **shipwrecks** and rural farmsteads (in Acadian Nova Scotia and the St Lawrence River valley). Archaeologists in the USA have investigated many outposts established principally for trade with **Native Americans**.

French colonisation in North America spanned more than two centuries, from Giovanni da Verrazano's exploratory voyage along the Atlantic coast in 1524 to the cession of French colonies by the Treaty of Paris in 1763. Early archaeological interest, beginning in the 1860s, tended towards searches for sites associated with famous colonists, such as investigations of Jacques Cartier's presumed anchorage at Montréal in 1535; initial

settlements by Samuel de Champlain on Ste-Croix Island (1604–5) and at Port Royal (1605–13); and the graves of numerous Jesuit missionaries, including that of martyred Jean de Brébeuf at Mission Ste-Marie.

Modern scientific archaeology at French colonial sites is often considered to have begun with Kenneth Kidd's excavations at Ste-Marie for the Royal Ontario Museum from 1941 to 1943. Investigation of this centre for Catholic missionisation among the Hurons inspired many subsequent excavations at sites of contact between French and Indians, both native villages and outposts, such as **Fort Michilimackinac**, which served as fur-trade entrepôts. This sustained archaeological interest in the subject of French–Indian contact reflects the importance placed by most French colonial officials themselves on maintaining good relations with key Indian allies.

French–Indian contact

Following Jacques Marquette's and Louis Jolliet's descent of the Mississippi River in 1674, Indian societies of the mid-continent developed particularly close economic, social and military ties with the French. One consequence was the adoption by the French of the calumet ceremony, a widespread native ritual of greeting involving the smoking of a pipe (calumet), which enabled travellers to cross tribal boundaries for purposes of diplomacy and trade. Calumet pipe bowls, made from a distinctive red stone quarried in Minnesota and Kansas, have been found at Indian sites throughout the region, as far north as **Marquette Mission** (1671–1705) and as far south as Old Mobile (1702–11), on the coast of the Gulf of Mexico.

Access to French traders offered Native Americans opportunities for the selective adoption of European manufactured goods, particularly firearms, tools and weapons of steel, cloth, copper kettles and personal adornments. Earlier in this century, anthropologists considered native acceptance of European technology as evidence of **acculturation**, the replacement of aspects of a traditional culture influenced by the presence of a dominant intrusive culture, a process that was thought frequently to lead to **assimilation**, the absorption of a traditional culture by a dominant

Figure 15 Early nineteenth-century Pierre Menard House in southern Illinois
Source: Photo: C.E. Orser, Jr

culture. Modern studies, however, document the resilience of traditional cultures and the many successful strategies devised by native peoples to cope with colonisers. Jeffrey Brain's research on the Tunicas, who occupied part of the lower Mississippi valley during the French colonial period, is an important case study of a small-scale Indian society that withstood severe acculturative pressures and survives today with a distinct ethnic identity.

Brain studied the 'Tunica Treasure', a collection of nearly 200,000 artefacts looted from graves at the Tunica village site of Trudeau, Louisiana, occupied between 1731 and 1764. Due to several factors – including their strategic location at the confluence of the Red and Mississippi rivers, their prominence in the colonial horse trade and their steadfast diplomatic attachment to the French – the Tunicas received great quantities of French goods in trade and as presents from colonial officials. The Trudeau assemblage includes French ceramics, iron hoes and adzes, pewter porringers, silver earbobs, copper kettles and brass bells, glass beads and bottles, gun parts and vermilion paint (to list just a portion of the European manufactured items), along with traditional Tunica pottery, shell beads, red stone pipes and cane basketry. The absence of stone arrow points and some other indigenous artefacts reflects a considerable degree of dependency on French trade goods. On the other hand, the exceptional range and volume of material wealth present at the Trudeau site testifies to the Tunicas' skill at manipulating French colonial officials eager to attract and retain anti-British allies.

Across the mid-continent, French and Indian interests coincided at numerous trading centres, nominal military posts where soldiers and their officers traded beside civilian merchants for furs and hides from native trappers and hunters. Among the best known archaeologically is Fort **Michilimackinac** (1715–61), overlooking the Straits of Mackinac between lakes Michigan and Huron. The scene of nearly continuous excavations for four decades, Fort Michilimackinac may be the most thoroughly investigated French colonial site in North America. In 1974, Lyle Stone published a catalogue of excavated artefacts, one of the earliest attempts at rigorous formal classification in historical archaeology. Successive archaeologists have uncovered over half of the fort's interior structures and produced a score of reports on such topics as French and British subsistence and architecture, indigenous craft industries and analyses of particular artefact categories (e.g. gunflints, lead seals for cloth, 'Jesuit' rings).

Archaeological studies that focus on the interface between French colonial and Indian cultures continue to be important because they contribute information frequently absent from written records of the colonial experience. Those records, of course, are heavily biased by the perceptions and preconceptions that French writers brought with them from Europe to the North American frontier. As a corrective, archaeologists apply anthropological methods of inquiry to evaluate the interactions of French and Indians, and the independent motivations of each society, as they negotiated the creation of a 'New World' during the colonial era.

French colonial life in North America

Despite the undeniable importance of Indian relations to the French in Acadia, Isle Royale, New France and Louisiana, the majority of colonists did not adopt native lifestyles, but rather endeavoured to transplant and maintain a semblance of European French culture in their new homes. Alaric and Gretchen Faulkner's excavations in the 1980s at Fort Pentagoet, an Acadian military and fur-trading outpost occupied intermittently between 1635 and 1674, revealed surprisingly strong ties to France. Not at all a frontier improvisation cobbled together by ill-supplied colonists, Fort Pentagoet was a French-style stone structure stocked with Old World provisions prepared and served in French fashion, and garrisoned by soldier-employees equipped and dressed according to the standards of their native country. Although trade for furs with the local Indians provided the post's economic rationale, these colonists resisted acculturation to Indian lifestyle as strenuously as Indians remained stead-fast to their own cultures. Interestingly, however, English artefacts are more abundant at Fort Pentagoet than objects of native manufacture, testifying to a surreptitious trade with New England merchants to the south.

Archaeology has proven particularly helpful in uncovering evidence of intercolonial smuggling and trade, practices that all colonial powers attempted to curb since they subverted the mercantilist premise of colonialism. Jean-Baptiste Colbert, King Louis XIV's chief minister during the late seventeenth century, developed his influential mercantilist theory for the economic administration of overseas colonies. According to Colbert, colonies should provide France with raw materials, thereby freeing the country from a dependence on foreign trade, and should also serve as markets for French manufactured goods. In France as well as her colonies, however, mercantilist trade restrictions invited smuggling in collusion with foreign merchants willing to evade embargoes and export/import taxes.

A decade of excavations by Gregory Waselkov at the town site of Old Mobile, original capital of French colonial Louisiana from 1702 until 1711, has uncovered abundant evidence of private trading with Spanish colonial merchants in Veracruz and Havana. Spanish silver coins and large quantities of Mexican majolica pottery testify to a lively exchange between the competing colonies. Mobile colonists even obtained Chinese **porcelain**, then still a rarity in France, from their trade contacts in Veracruz. Spanish officials eventually halted this particular avenue of intercolonial trade. However, excavations at the slightly later, nearby site of Port Dauphin (c. 1715–25) reveal that French colonists continued to trade surreptitiously with their neighbours, especially British colonists from South Carolina. Farther north, the colonists of New France, Acadia and Isle Royale (all in modern-day Canada) circumvented mercantilist tenets by trading with New England merchants, despite frequent wars in the region.

Judging from recent archaeological investigations underneath present-day Québec City and Montréal, and at the Fortress of Louisbourg, life at urban sites differed dramatically from the daily routine of existence experienced at the many isolated outposts of French North America. In a sophisticated comparison of mid-eighteenth-century households in Québec and Louisbourg, based on excavated artefact collections as well as historical **probate inventories**, Paul-Gaston L'Anglais demonstrates substantial differences in wealth and social display among the administrative and economic elite. At both locations, urban dwellers accumulated immensely more diverse assemblages of material wealth than did their rural and frontier counterparts, particularly in terms of decorated pottery and expensive glass tableware. Louisbourg's occupants had relatively unimpeded access to British trade goods, due to the geographical proximity of that fortress to British shipping routes, than did Québec's inhabitants, with their predominantly French possessions. However, the functional diversity of artefacts found at both town sites – including stemware and wine glass coolers, liquor bottles, perfume vials, tumblers, barbers' bowls, all sorts of plates, drinking cups, tea and chocolate pots, cooking pots, storage jars, platters, pitchers, vases and chamber pots – indicates how enthusiastically the wealthiest colonists participated in the growing materialism of the eighteenth century.

Marcel Moussette's recent interpretation of the Intendant's Palace site in Québec City provides another insight on French colonialism in an urban setting. A brewery built on that site around 1669 was later converted to serve as the home and offices of the intendant, chief financial officer of the colony. That building burned down in 1713 and was replaced by a new Intendant's Palace, while the ruins of the first palace were incorporated into the King's Stores, a group of storage buildings destroyed in 1759 during a battle between French and British armies. The site has remained continually in use to the present day. Moussette's analysis distinguishes between the site's structural evolution, along a path constrained and influenced by the brewery building that first occupied the spot, and its symbolic evolution, which changed as each occupant imposed a new identity on a location rich with historical precedents. Moussette's study exemplifies how the continuity of a Francophone population in Canada is contributing to our deeper understanding of some long-lasting implications of French colonialism in North America.

See also: contact archaeology; Fatherland site

Further reading

Brain, J.P. (1979) 'Tunica Treasure', in *Papers of the Peabody Museum of Archaeology and Ethnology, Volume 71*, Cambridge: Harvard University Press.

Brown, I.W. (1989) 'The calumet ceremony in the southeast and its archaeological manifestation', *American Antiquity* 54: 311–31.

Faulkner, A. and Faulkner, G. (1987) *The French at Pentagoet, 1635–1674: An Archaeological Portrait of the Acadian Frontier*, Augusta: Maine Historic Preservation Commission.

L'Anglais, P.-G. (1994) 'Les Modes de vie à Québec et à Louisbourg au milieu du XVIIIe siècle à partir de collections archéologiques', in *La Collection Patrimoines, dossier 86*, Québec: Ministère des Affaires culturelles.

Moussette, M. (1996) 'The site of the Intendant's Palace in Québec City: The changing meaning of an urban space', *Historical Archaeology* 30: 8–21.

Walthall, J.A. and Emerson, T.E. (eds) (1992) *Calumet and Fleur-de-lys: Archaeology of Indian and French Contact in the Midcontinent*, Washington, DC: Smithsonian Institution Press.

Waselkov, G.A. (1997) 'The archaeology of French colonial North America: English–French edition', in *Guides to the Historical Archaeological Literature 5*, Tucson: Society for Historical Archaeology.

GREGORY A. WASELKOV

fur-trade archaeology in western Canada

Although interest in fur-trade sites in western Canada (from north-western Ontario to British Columbia) can be documented as early as the late 1800s, systematic fur-trade archaeology did not begin in earnest until the 1960s. Prior to this time, interested scholars or avid non-professionals primarily focused on locating the large number of trading posts that represent the various phases of the fur trade. Fur trade archaeological studies tend to reflect the prevailing views, attitudes and methods in practice in the larger discipline of archaeology in the USA. This is not surprising considering Canada's close geographical proximity to the USA and comparatively small archaeological community.

The fur trade can be characterised primarily as an early European capitalist, exploratory and empire-building venture into North America to procure furs for the European market. However, towards the latter part of the nineteenth century, US 'whiskey traders' also expanded their fur-trading operations into western Canada. As a result of the different competing ventures, there are hundreds of fur-trade sites that include: small independent posts, mainly of the late eighteenth century; posts of the major companies, the Hudson's Bay Company (HBC) and the North West Company (NWC), during the competitive era from the 1780s to 1821; large administrative centres existing before and after the amalgamation of the HBC and NWC in 1821; and American 'whiskey' trading posts.

Early archaeological fur-trade studies were carried out by practitioners trained in prehistoric archaeology. Field research focused on surveys to locate sites to establish regional histories and excavations to retrieve architectural information often geared towards reconstruction. Although hundreds of sites were located and received some level of field investigation, only a few were excavated to any great extent. Examples of major excavations for site preservation, reconstruction, commemorative or tourism purposes in the western provinces include: Fort William in north-western Ontario, Lower Fort Garry and York Factory in Manitoba, Fort Carlton and Last Mountain House in Saskatchewan, Fort George and Fort Dunvegan in Alberta and Fort St James and Fort Langley in British Columbia. Most of these sites represent major HBC or NWC establishments.

The early fur-trade archaeologists encountered a rich, unknown archaeological resource base for which there was much documented historical information and great public appeal and interest. However, they lacked basic comparative data for historic material-culture analysis and had little input into site selection, which was influenced largely by commemorative or development interests of local, provincial or national heritage groups. These factors contributed to work that rarely progressed beyond the production of preliminary descriptive reports outlining fieldwork, site layout, building construction, feature descriptions and artefact typology and manufacture. These studies served an important purpose as they provided necessary baseline data on physical attributes, architectural details and artefacts from which to contemplate broader concepts. Unfortunately, this rudimentary descriptive focus has never completely disappeared. At times, archaeological excavations often become the tourist attraction, without reconstruction being an end goal.

The scientific approach advocated by processual or '**New Archaeology**' in the USA caught the attention of fur-trade archaeologists who attempted to go beyond site description to incorporate a problem-oriented approach into their studies. Researchers began to look at pattern recognition based on the quantification and distribution of artefact assemblages, as well as diet and subsistence strategies indicated by faunal data. For example, in his study of Pine Fort in southern Manitoba, Scott Hamilton looked at aspects of the inhabitants' behaviour by identifying activities within the fort. He accomplished this by grouping artefacts into functional categories and plotting their distributions. The analysis provided information on group activities, refuse discard and the sexual division of labour. Most importantly, the data confirmed that the fort represented a community and not just a commercial enterprise.

Fur-trade archaeological studies in the late 1980s and 1990s have expanded beyond the scientific problem-oriented approach to encompass a diversity of research interests. Identifying social organisation that incorporates social position within the fur trade has been attempted through the analysis of material culture and fauna. The hierarchical structure of the fur trade, well documented in the historical records, lends itself to entertaining questions on status and rank. The major premise directing these studies is that a higher proportion of better-quality material goods will be related to a higher-status group. By examining the variety, quality and quantity of material-culture items, archaeologists, such as Heinz Pyszczyk, have concluded that social position was maintained through differential access to and consumption of higher-quality items such as the possession of certain types of ceramics or glassware and greater quantities of preferred meat.

Another topical interest centres on non-verbal communication to examine how architecture and space played a role in reinforcing social information both within and outside the fort community. Employing historical documentation and archaeological data for the 1780 to 1821 time period, Scott Hamilton identified three types of posts based on their logistical role: large administrative headquarters, regional headquarters and wintering posts in remote areas. Comparisons showed that at all post types the principal trader and their assistants were segregated from the common labourers. Sometimes, in the more outlying wintering posts, social distance meant only a separate bedroom allotting more personal space to the principal trader. Where the head traders were housed in individual structures, these often had glass windows rather than parchment and more elaborately finished interiors such as wooden floors versus dirt floors.

Using comparative data from the above three site types, David Burley and Luke Dalla Bona challenged the popular image of frontier wilderness posts protected by palisades and bastions from hostile forces, human and natural. They discovered that while administrative and regional headquarters regularly had palisades with guard walks and corner bastions, the use of palisades at remote wintering posts was variable. As a defensive strategy most of these features would not withstand a concerted attack because logs making up the palisade could seldom stop a bullet and often were constructed with gaps between individual members. It appears that the construction of palisades and bastions, which required a heavy expenditure of labour, served non-defensive purposes such as controlling access to the post and creating a striking, powerful presence on the landscape.

Greg Monks limited his study to one particular site, the HBC administrative post of Upper Fort Garry. He provided information on how structures and space were used to constantly express and reinforce the quasi-military organisation of the HBC, as well as its dominant social and economic position within the rapidly growing agrarian-based Red River Settlement of the mid- to late 1800s. **Fortifications** incorporating bastions and rifle or cannon ports were erected, although the major threat to the fort was flooding. These fortifications, however, sent a message to the settlers that the HBC would use force to resist social or economic upheaval. Archaeological evidence confirms these walls were not very sturdy, but merely used for show, whereas the walls of the fur warehouse foundations were thicker, thus revealing the true priorities of the HBC. Likewise, the expansion of the post that doubled the interior space promoted a view of growing prosperity, even though the HBC was facing economic hardships due to US competition.

Some studies have looked beyond the post itself to document the long-range effects of the fur trade on animal populations within a region. Relying on major historical documentary research and archaeological excavations carried out at two posts in the Peace River region in north-eastern British Columbia, David Burley and Scott Hamilton discovered that, over a thirty-year period, there was a noticeable decline in certain animal species. In the early years, bison and wapiti (elk) were the primary food sources, with beaver being the most valued fur bearer. Due to the pressures of provisioning canoe brigades bison all but disappeared as a food source, resulting in an increased reliance on more elusive and solitary large game such as moose and small game such as hare. Also, the preference for beaver pelts dramatically affected the beaver population and hence their availability for trade.

Most archaeological studies have looked at the Euro-Canadian aspect of the fur trade. However, native people played an equally important and active role, although little attention has been directed at the archaeological evidence of their involvement. Lynda Gullason tackled this question by examining the archaeological record of the plantation at the Fort George-Buckingham House site complex in Alberta. The 'plantation' refers to the area in the immediate vicinity of the posts where Natives encamped while conducting their trading activities. Archaeological evidence for a historic Native presence in the form of features or artefacts is extremely scant, because of the transitory nature of these camps. The same situation is also encountered in the search for historic Native contact sites outside the immediate locality of the post. The latter exercise is further complicated by natural factors such as thick silt deposits on flood plains or lack of soil stratigraphy in forest environments.

In the latter half of the nineteenth century, US entrepreneurs crossed the International Border to establish a highly lucrative, although short lived, trade with the Native population by providing cheap trade goods and liberal amounts of alcohol in exchange for buffalo robes and other furs. Over forty-five posts were built in southern Alberta/south-western Saskatchewan. Throughout the 1980s, Margaret Kennedy directed many field projects and examined historical documents to locate, document and excavate whiskey-trading establishments in southern Alberta. These studies revealed that many posts were built on river bottoms and were oriented towards the rivers or river junctions. Also, the traders favoured certain localities in a region, as indicated by the clustering of post remains. As for the individual posts, their structure was based on a general plan equated with US fur forts that included tall wooden stockades, buildings located against the stockade, strong gates and bastions.

Further reading

Burley, D. and Dalla Bona, L. (1988) 'Palisades and function: Understanding construction variability in the western fur trade', paper delivered at the twenty-first Canadian Archaeological Association Meeting, Whistler, BC.

Burley, D.V., Hamilton, J.S. and Fladmark, K.R. (1996) *Prophecy of the Swan: The Upper Peace River Fur Trade of 1794–1823*, Vancouver: University of British Columbia Press.

Gullason, L. (1994) '"No less than 7 different nations": Ethnicity and culture contact at Fort George-Buckingham House', in J.S.H. Brown, W. J. Eccles and D.P. Heldman (eds) *The Fur Trade Revisited*, East Lansing: Michigan State University Press, pp. 117–42.

Hamilton, J.S. (2000) 'Dynamics of Social Complexity in Early Nineteenth-Century British Fur Trade Posts', *International Journal of Historical Archaeology*, 4: 217–73.

—— (1986) 'Pine Fort: A socio-economic analysis on the basis of the spatial distribution of activity-specific artifacts', *Manitoba Archaeological Quarterly* 10: 2–3.

Kennedy, M.A. (1997) *The Whiskey Trade of the Northwestern Plains: A Multidisciplinary Study*, New York: P. Lang.

Pyszczyk, H. (1989) 'Consumption and ethnicity: An example from the fur trade in western Canada', *Journal of Anthropological Archaeology* 8: 213–49.

OLGA KLIMKO

Fyrkat, Denmark

Fyrkat is a Viking-Age circular fortress of so-called Trelleborg-type close to Hobro, North Jutland, Denmark. The Danish National Museum excavated Fyrkat in the 1950s, shortly after they finished their examinations of the circular fortresses at Trelleborg, West Seeland.

Fyrkat is characteristic of the construction of other circular Viking fortresses in Denmark, which are known for their symmetry and precision. Fyrkat consists of a circular rampart with an internal diameter of 120 m and a width of almost 12 m. It was built as an earth-filled timber structure with inner and outer faces, and with four gates at the four points of the compass. Concentric with the rampart there were two smaller parts of a dry ditch with a V-shaped section at a depth of about 2 m. The interior of the fortress was divided into four sections by two linear streets connecting the four gates. In each section (only three of which have been excavated) there were four timber-built long houses, lying close to one another around a courtyard. Inside the courtyard was a rectangular house measuring about 5 by 10 m. The long houses had slightly bowed walls with almost straight gables. Their length was just over 28 m, with a width at the centre of just over 7 m, falling to 5 m at the gables. The walls consisted of a double row of posts and outside these, in a distance of 1 m, were rows of inclined posts. Each house had four doors, one on each long side and two in the centre of the gable ends. The long-side doors were provided with weather porches.

Archaeologists located a cemetery a short distance to the north-east of the fortress. This burial ground contained approximately thirty graves, all of which were oriented east-to-west.

The objects found at Fyrkat provide evidence for a large range of craft activities and various other everyday chores. In chronological terms the artefacts suggest the second half of the tenth century. This dating has been confirmed by dendrochronological investigations of oak posts found in the rampart. The fortress must have been built around 980 at the same time as Trelleborg. Finds of charcoal suggest that Fyrkat's functions came to an end with a fire. Archaeologists do not know the precise date of the fire, but it must have occurred a relatively short time after the buildings were completed. Nothing indicates that the fortress was in use after the year 1000.

No written sources mention the circular fortresses, but, because of size, archaeologists think that their owner must have been a king. The Danish King at this time was Harold Bluetooth, who died about 985. The purpose of these huge fortresses has been discussed since the excavation of Trelleborg. In the late 1990s, most scholars believed that the fortresses were part of King Harold's efforts to unite Denmark and to consolidate his personal power.

See also: cemeteries; dendrochronology; Vikings

Further reading

Olsen, O., Roesdahl, E. and Schmidt, H. (1977) *FYRKAT. En jysk vikingeborg* [English summary], Copenhagen: Det kgl.nordiske Oldskriftselskab.

STEEN W. ANDERSEN

G

Garbage Project

The Garbage Project, or 'Le Projet du Garbage', is an innovative and important use of archaeological methods and perspectives to investigate modern-day rubbish dumps. Begun in 1974 by archaeologists at the University of Arizona, led by William L. Rathje, the original goal of the research was to examine the quantitative correlations between social variables and the waste various social groups produced. The Garbage Project was developed to provide insights into topics having purely archaeological significance, including ways to interpret the relationship between **material culture** and behaviours that can be related to **ethnicity**, **race** and **gender**. Historical archaeologists have been

Figure 16 Excavation of an eighteenth-century landfill in New York City
Source: Photo: S. Baugher

particularly interested in the Project's findings because of the temporal similarity between modern-day rubbish deposits and the sites they regularly study. An important spin-off of the Garbage Project involves its ability to provide insights relating directly to modern waste-disposal practices. Archaeologists have learned, for example, that many products once considered to be biodegradable do not deteriorate in the airless environment of a modern rubbish dump. Such findings have been of immense interest both to local waste managers and to transnational corporations engaged in the safe disposal of modern waste. Though the Project was begun in Tucson, Arizona, with fairly modest goals, it soon developed an international reputation and importance. While being sceptically viewed by many professional archaeologists when it first began, the Garbage Project is now respected as a powerful example of a practical application of archaeological knowledge.

See also: behavioural historical archaeology

CHARLES E. ORSER, JR

garden archaeology

The archaeology of gardens is concerned first and foremost with the recovery of past landscapes, and more particularly those designed landscapes known in Western and non-Western cultures under a variety of terms that we translate today as gardens. These range from the small kitchen gardens invaluable for feeding a household to the extensive gardens of palaces, monasteries, asylums and elite residences. It is because of this juxtaposition of the latter sort of garden with significant architectural monuments that archaeologists have been called upon to recover and interpret the gardens associated with significant historical sites such as Hampton Palace and Painshill in England, **Monticello** and **Mount Vernon** in Virginia, Mission San Juan Capistrano in California, Madinat al-Zahra, an Islamic garden in Spain, and Pasagadae, the royal gardens of Cyrus the Great in Achaemenid Iran.

Garden archaeology is one of those rich specialities within historical archaeology that finds itself allied with a wide range of disciplines. Charged with the recovery and interpretation of past designed landscapes, it holds much in common, particularly its excavation and analytical techniques, with environmental studies. Collections such as *Archaeology of Garden and Field* attest to this mutual concern. The particular focus on the designed landscape means that garden archaeology is also part of the broader scholarship on the history and meanings of gardens. Both in publications and in team field projects, therefore, garden archaeologists often collaborate with art historians, landscape historians, cultural geographers, botanists, historic preservationists, landscape architects and historians.

One of the main challenges of the studying of past gardens is the scale of endeavour; a garden may encompass several acres or several hundred acres. Another challenge is the transience of the art form and the ephemeral nature of a garden's living material, i.e. its plants, shrubs and trees. Not only are gardens continuously transforming as trees mature, patterns of sun and shade shift, and scales of plant material change, but gardens are also subject to extensive redesign and reconfiguration as styles and tastes shift. A historic garden site may represent not just one garden, but a series of gardens superimposed on one another. It is not simply because of the economics of historic preservation that most garden excavations focus on the most elaborate gardens of their time – the ubiquitous dooryard gardens and vegetable patches created little impact on the landscape and are rarely manifest in the archaeological record as more than the occasional shovel divot, planting hole and humus-rich layer of soil. The more ornate and extensive gardens generally had more built architecture (bridges, walls, canals, summerhouses, greenhouses, orangeries, pavilions, temples, follies, fountains), more extensive earthworks (mounds, mounts, ha-has, terraces, slopes) and circulation routes (ramps, steps, drives, walks), all of which result in a much more visible archaeological footprint.

Archaeologists have therefore developed techniques suited to the data and scale of past gardens. A significant contribution to the field has been **remote sensing**, both the non-intrusive readings of sub-surface features, with techniques such as ground-penetrating radar, soil resistivity and magnetometer surveys, and aerial photography at a variety of scales and wavelengths. The sub-surface testing is particularly valuable for locating buried architectural features, such as foundations and brick walkways, although to date the technique has been less successful at identifying soil features such as paths and fill. Archaeologists have experimented with various forms of coring to reconstruct comprehensive views of topographic alterations to a garden – those major earth-moving episodes such as terraces and falls being carved out of hillsides, mounds created with the fill from cellar holes and ha-has dug at the edge of lawns to keep grazing cattle at bay.

Another major contribution to the technical analysis of past gardens has been floral analysis. The recovery of preserved botanical evidence such as seeds, pits and nuts through soil flotation is useful in reconstructing the plant material of the garden, particularly for sites such as Pompeii where the preservation is excellent. The study of micro-floral remains, such as **palynology** and phytolith analysis, holds much potential for garden archae-ology, although at present the typologies are so general that they rarely can identify the specific plants in the garden.

Mapping is a critical part of reconstructing past landscapes, and the advent of computer-assisted mapping (see **computers**) has been invaluable. Not only has it allowed more efficient and accurate means to measure the land, but it also has the capacity to depict and manipulate landscapes in three-dimensional perspective. This ability has been especially useful in understanding the visual logic of gardens and recreating the spaces as they may have been perceived by those who worked and played in them. What could formerly be created only through time-consuming perspectival drawings, as in Kath-ryn Gleason's 1994 reconstruction of the Porticus Pompeinana, the first public park in Rome, can now be achieved with computer-assisted drawing pro-grams, which use digitised or scanned maps, drawings, plans and photographs to create three-dimensional environments that can be rotated and analysed from a variety of vantage points.

Another visual tool in the recovery and inter-pretation of gardens has been the use of pictorial and photographic information. Gardens were recorded as dedicated subjects by landscape painters such as

Ralph Earl and Charles Fraser, and also on a wide variety of art forms such as textiles, prints, ceramics and furniture painting. Thomas Jefferson's extensive plans, diaries and sketches, for instance, have been instrumental in the reconstruction of gardens at Monticello, Virginia, USA. Some of the most useful visual records for archaeologists have come from the details of portraits in which the sitter's own garden is included in the background of the painting. It was through such an image, Charles Willson Peale's portrait of William Paca, that the Paca garden restorers were able to recreate the pavilion at the base of the garden and the Chippendale-style bridge across the fish pond. **Photographic information** has also been an essential tool in documenting the changes to a landscape over time. The photographic record at Gunston Hall in Virginia, home of George Mason, reveals a series of dramatic makeovers of the house and garden in the nineteenth and twentieth centuries. Unpeeling the history of those alterations has contributed to the understanding of the garden's original eighteenth-century design.

Garden archaeology tends to be far less artefact intensive than the excavations of more densely occupied spaces. Archaeologists must rely on subtle changes in soil colour and texture to identify remains of planting features such as planting holes and beds or the traces of ephemeral garden structures such as trellises, arbours, aviaries, fence lines and beeskeps.

It is perhaps because of these technical chal-lenges that garden archaeology is a fairly recent addition to the list of historical archaeology's specialities. Early work, such as Stanley South's excavations of the Paca House in Annapolis, Maryland, USA, Wilhelmina Jashemski at Pompeii and Audrey Noël Hume in Williamsburg, Virginia, demonstrated the potential of archaeology to locate and identify preserved garden features, but the value of examining 'the spaces between the places' was not widely capitalised on until the 1980s. The 1990 publication of *Earth Patterns* marks one of the first collections on the subject in North America, and since that time the literature has burgeoned.

Garden archaeology has become a valued tool in the study and restoration of numerous historic sites, and it has had a growing impact on the interpretation of the built environment. The interdisciplinary focus of landscape studies is also

Figure 17 The eighteenth-century William Pace
garden in Annapolis, Maryland
Source: Photo: S. Baugher

reflected in the range of interpretive approaches
within garden archaeology. Building on the work of
garden historians whose central concern has been
the attribution of stylistic analysis to garden
remains, archaeologists have questioned their sites'
relationship to trends in garden history, relating
their finds to styles, such as 'natural style',
picturesque, Dutch, French and Italian. Often,
the evidence on the ground refutes received history.
In contrast to the writings in garden treatises and
by some garden historians, recent studies by Tom
Williamson and others in **England** have revealed
how styles, once thought to be limited to certain
time periods, continued to be preserved and even
built because they appealed to their owners or, in
some cases, were less expensive to maintain than
the 'newer' styles.

Archaeology's attention to stratigraphy and therefore to the reconstruction of three-dimensional
space has called into focus the role of manipulating
optics or lines of sites in landscape gardens. This
work has been instrumental in reconstructing how
these landscapes were designed to be perceived,
such as where and how the intended audience was
to experience the landscape. It has also raised the
significance of the unintended audiences of the
gardens – those myriad servants, slaves, labourers,
passers-by and uninvited trespassers who possessed
the landscapes in their own ways. Understanding
the optics of a garden has suggested ways in which
some gardens, particularly those at slave-holding
plantations (see **plantation archaeology**) and
missions (see **mission sites**) using indigenous
labour, abetted the surveillance of the enslaved and
oppressed.

Archaeologists have been concerned with placing people in the garden in other ways. Studies
have examined the spaces from the vantage of how
gender relations are enacted in the landscape, how
notions of leisure and labour (and in particular the
machine in the garden) are negotiated in the design
of garden space and how gardens are made
meaningful and even sacred through ritual. Of
particular interest has been how gardens serve as
stages for self-presentation. In the early USA, the
history of gardens, at least of the more elaborate
landscape variety, is integrally tied to the planter
gentry who built formal gardens, with particular
reference to their elites who were likewise demonstrating not only botanical knowledge and design
acumen, but the ability to invest in immovable and
essentially ornamental spaces as complements to
their architectural showcases. Readings of these
gardens as ostentatious displays and ideological
statements have added yet another component to
the view of the intricate strategies these elites were
using to situate themselves socially, politically and
economically.

Other readings of the material culture of
gardens have also dealt with the ideology of their
design. If one reads past issues of publications such
as the *Journal of Garden History*, one will encounter
interpretations of the ideology of Nazi-era land-

scape architecture, the symbolism of African American yardscapes in the south, the religious meanings of Utopian community gardens and gardens as signifiers of empire building and colonial encounters. While these readings of the landscape are not necessarily based on archaeologically recovered remains, they are pertinent to garden archaeology as part of the broader endeavour of understanding past landscapes through a combination of documentary and material culture sources even if those sources are not known through excavations.

Another theme in the historical archaeology of gardens has been to deconstruct 'revival-style' gardens such as the Colonial Revival gardens at Williamsburg and the Mission Gardens of California. Understanding the meanings informing these often highly fictional 'reconstructions', which find their origins in the late nineteenth century, not only provides insight into the myth making of American historical memory, but also reveals the ongoing power of sites that continue to attract millions of visitors annually.

See also: environmental studies; palynology; photographic information; pictorial information; remote sensing; restoration

Further reading

Brown, A.E. (ed.) (1988) *Garden Archaeology: Papers Presented to a Conference at Knuston Hall, Northamptonshire, April 1988*, CBA Research Report 78, London: Council for British Archaeology.

Jacques, D. (ed.) (1997) 'The techniques and uses of garden archaeology', *Journal of Garden History* 17(1): 1–99.

Jashemski, W. (1979) *The Gardens of Pompeii: Herculaneum and the Villas Destroyed by Vesuvius*, New Rochelle, NY: Caratzas.

Kelso, W.M. and Most, R. (eds) (1990) *Earth Patterns: Essays in Landscape Archaeology*, Charlottesville: University Press of Virginia.

Kryder-Reid, E. and Ruggles, D.F. (eds) (1994) 'Site and sight in the garden', *Journal of Garden History* 14(1): 1–66.

Miller, N.F. and Gleason, K.L. (eds) (1994) *The Archaeology of Garden and Field*, Philadelphia: University of Pennsylvania Press.

Yamin, R. and Metheny, K.B. (eds) (1996) *Landscape Archaeology: Reading and Interpreting the American Historical Landscape*, Knoxville: University of Tennessee Press.

ELIZABETH KRYDER-REID

Geldermalsen, shipwreck

The *Geldermalsen* was a ship of the **Dutch East India Company** (VOC) that on 3 January 1752 hit a reef not far from present-day Singapore. The *Geldermalsen* is one of the recently discovered VOC ships that clearly exemplifies the rich cultural-historical potential of these wreck sites and the devastating effects of the activities of the international, commercial salvage network. This virtually intact wreck was destroyed in 1986 to recover **porcelain** for auction purposes.

The *Geldermalsen* was built in 1746 in the second biggest shipyard of the VOC at Middelburg. Here, as well as in **Amsterdam**, this largest type of VOC ship could be produced, measuring approximately 1,150 metric tons. Her first trip took the *Geldermalsen* to Java, then to China and India, and finally to Canton to take on board a cargo of tea (see **tea/tea ceremony**), porcelain and textiles destined for Europe. Apart from 239,200 pieces of porcelain the cargo list mentions 625 pieces of lacquerware, 5,240 pieces of silk textiles, 686,997 pounds of tea, sappan and caliatour wood, and a number of gold bars. After its departure from Canton in December 1751, the ship capsized a month later south-east of the Riau archipelago, now in Indonesian waters. Only thirty-two of the 112 people on board managed to save themselves in two open boats. The survivors arrived safely in Batavia (now Jakarta).

The records of their interrogations on the disaster still remain in the VOC archive in the Hague. These detailed historical documents enabled a consortium of treasure hunters to locate the wreck in 1985. The leader of the operation was Michael Hatcher, who had wide experience in salvage and treasure hunting in Asian waters. Upon his discovery, Christie's in Amsterdam launched a major publicity campaign in anticipation of an auction. In the meantime, Hatcher raised the porcelain cargo without paying any attention to the archaeological importance of the site. The ship's structure was apparently still intact, preserved from the orlop deck down. To remove the porcelain the ship's structure had to be demolished as well as the original packaging of the cargo. No proper recording procedures were followed because the operation was conducted under extreme pressure of time, without any official licensing or scientific archaeological support.

The salvage resulted in an enormous blue and white porcelain collection that was auctioned in Amsterdam in 1986 under the mystifying title 'The Nanking Cargo', achieving record-breaking prices. The events surrounding the salvage and sale of the porcelain cargo caused international indignation particularly in archaeological and cultural-heritage circles. A unique opportunity to record and study an intact eighteenth-century cargo including its packaging and stowage was lost.

Further reading

Christie's (1986) *The Nanking Cargo, Chinese Export Porcelain and Gold*, Amsterdam: Christie's Amsterdam, Auction Catalogue, 28 April–2 May.

Hatcher, M. (1987) *The Nanking Cargo*, London: H. Hamilton.

Jörg, C. J.A. (1986) *The Geldermalsen: History and Porcelain*, Groningen: Kemper.

JERZY GAWRONSKI AND BAS KIST

gender

Perhaps the earliest gender research in historical archaeology was a 1920 book *A Study of Women in Attic Inscriptions* by Helen McClees. Classical Roman gender research appeared in the 1960s, but the classics remain dominated by documentary research. In the 1983 book *Images of Women in Antiquity* five chapters include some archaeological data with documentary data in analysing women's roles and limited powers in ancient Greece, Egypt and Babylon. Classical Mayan gender research from texts and art was initiated by Titana Poskouriakoff's 1960s publications. Some of the

earliest gender research in US historical archaeology included: a 1963 study by James Deetz of material changes in Native American gender roles (see **Native Americans**) due to contact with the Spanish at **La Purisima Mission** in California; a 1979 article in *Man in the Northeast* on gendered differences in nineteenth-century gravestones by Lisa Poinset and Emme Bill; and parts of Kathleen Deagan's 1983 book *Spanish St. Augustine*, addressing how the Indian wives of Spanish colonists brought Indian foodways and material culture into Spanish households.

Starting in the 1980s, feminist gender research in historical archaeology was pioneered in the USA, Australia and Europe as feminists entered the field. In the USA, early feminist publications in historical archaeology appeared in general feminist journals, such as 'State formation in Sumer and the subjugation of women' by R. Rohrlich in *Feminist Studies* (1980). In 1987, *Historical Archaeology* published its first feminist article, Suzanne Spencer-Wood's 'A survey of domestic reform movement sites in Boston and Cambridge c.1865–1905'. The only feminist archaeology journal, *KAN* (translates as 'Women in Archaeology' in Norwegian), founded in 1985, includes some articles in historical archaeology. In classical Mayan archaeology, feminist-informed papers by Karen Bruhns and by Andrea Stone were published in proceedings of a 1985 conference symposium, *The Role of Gender in Precolumbian Art and Architecture* (1988). In 1988, Roberta Gilchrist's pioneering English feminist research on gendered spaces in medieval nunneries was published in the *Archaeological Review from Cambridge*. In 1990, the first feminist article in the *Australian Journal of Historical Archaeology*, by Pam Hourani, explored the relationships between changes in the size and arrangement of household rooms and gender power dynamics. In 2000, a landmark two-volume set from a conference, *Representations of Gender from Prehistory to the Present* and *Gender and Material Culture in Archaeological Perspective*, edited by Moira Donald and Linda Hurcombe, includes some historical archaeology.

Feminist theories applied to gender research in historical archaeology

As in feminist anthropology and prehistoric

archaeology, a variety of feminist theoretical approaches have been used in gender research in historical archaeology. These approaches have been used nearly simultaneously, although they will be discussed in the chronological order of the development of **feminist theory**. First-wave egalitarian feminist theory critiqued sexist claims of a biologically determined universal male dominance and female subordination. In contrast, archaeological research has demonstrated that historic women have held the same or similar public roles as men, from the most powerful positions of rulers and priests to warriors, business owners, merchants, entrepreneurs, craftswomen and owners and operators of farms and plantations. In her 1997 book *Gender in Archaeology: Analyzing Power and Prestige*, Sarah Nelson discusses historical archaeological research on Korean queens, Japanese queens, Germanic female prophets, female Chinese warriors and female priests in ancient Greece. Some of the earliest gender research in historical archaeology, starting in the 1970s, analysed texts and images on monuments to show that some elite Mayan women held high-status positions as rulers, spouses and mothers of ruling nobles. Kirsten Erskine's paper in the proceedings of the third (1995) 'Australian Women in Archaeology Conference' provided evidence of early medieval Scottish women who were scholars, nuns, princesses and possibly warriors. Anne Stalsberg's paper in *Social Approaches to Viking Studies* (1991) critiques the androcentric assumption that all Viking traders were men and provides documentary and archaeological evidence that some Viking women were traders. Carmen Weber's paper in the proceedings of the 1989 Chacmool conference 'The Archaeology of Gender' analysed a lineage of elite seventeenth- and eighteenth-century English and US women who gained status and prestige from their gardening expertise as much as elite men who were previously researched.

A legacy of first-wave feminism is an egalitarian feminist approach that asks if there is evidence that a balance of power between women and men developed through complementarity and interdependence of different gender roles. Documentary and archaeological evidence of complementary gender roles among the classic Maya has been discussed in Rosemary Joyce's paper in *Exploring*

Gender through Archaeology: Selected Papers from the 1991 Boone Conference (1992) and in Carolyn Tate's chapter in *Manifesting Power* (1999). In the same volume, another chapter by Geoffrey and Sharisse McCafferty provided evidence of symbolic equality between Aztec men's and women's different roles. Spencer-Wood's chapter in *The Archaeology of Inequality* (1991) provided evidence of material culture that women reformers used to symbolise and implement their argument that woman's domestic sphere should be equal in status to man's public sphere.

Drawing on the second-wave feminist anthropology of the 1970s, Anne Yentsch took a structuralist/essentialist approach to divide early eighteenth-century domestic sites and artefacts into opposed public/masculine versus private/domestic/feminine spaces and **ceramics** in her chapter in *The Archaeology of Inequality*. Essentialist feminist theory and research investigates sociocultural structures that maintain and enforce in actual practice a supposedly universal ideology of asymmetrical power in gender relations. Yentsch divided household space and pots into categories that she argued symbolically expressed and reinforced actual practice of the elite gender ideology identifying men with dominance in public/cultural/sacred rituals and spaces, while women were identified with secular/natural/subordinate activities in private spaces. She identified the elite household dining room and the white ceramics used there as *ipso facto* a masculine public domain because of their use for elaborate ritual dinners that displayed the male head of household's wealth to guests. She argued that men carefully selected their white ceramics from overseas. Further, she contended that elite women's access to men's public dining rooms was limited to subserviently displaying their husbands' wealth. Yentsch interpreted actual gender practices to conform to a construction of medieval courtly gender ideology in which men controlled not only the public sphere but the domestic sphere of the home to which women were limited.

However, Spencer-Wood's article in the *World Archaeological Bulletin* (1996) reported documentary evidence of elite women as well as men selecting Oriental armorial white porcelain for ceremonial dining, suggesting that elite women were sometimes at least as involved as men in the display of family wealth to guests in public dining rituals. In her paper in the 1989 Chacmool conference proceedings, *The Archaeology of Gender* (1991), Spencer-Wood also argued that women as well as men could display their own wealth in dining and tea rituals. In fact, women often brought inherited wealth or a dowry into a marriage. Further, Grauer's article in *The Archaeology of Gender* (1991) challenged essentialist/structuralist constructions of medieval women as limited to domestic roles controlled by men with evidence suggesting a number of single women had public occupations in cities following depopulation caused by the plague. In *Invisible People and Processes* (1997), edited by Jenny Moore and Eleanor Scott, a chapter on gender and medieval archaeology by Roberta Gilchrist critiqued universalising structuralist constructions of gender that limited women to peripheral household spaces used for food preparation while men supposedly controlled public central spaces inside and outside the house. Instead, documentary research by historians showed that the medieval manor as well as the peasant house, including central public areas, were identified with and used by women. In addition, women had a high degree of mobility both in the countryside and in towns.

In the 1970s, Marxist feminism emerged by making an analogy between the way the capitalist class underpaid the oppressed working classes and the ways men as a class benefited from women as a class because women were not paid for their domestic labour. In contrast to the essentialist/ structuralist analysis of dominant gender ideology as congruent with actual practice, Marxist feminist theory was concerned with women's actual gender practices that resisted the gender ideology of public men's dominance over subordinate domestic women. For instance, in a 1991 article Yentsch speculated that mid-nineteenth-century US women may have resisted when their household cheese production was usurped by male-run factories. This may have occurred in some cases, but a 1987 Berkshire Women's History conference paper by Sally McMurray found many nineteenth-century interviews of farm women documenting that they were eager to give up the exhausting work of producing cheese, which amounted to a form of family servitude.

Post-modern feminist theory critiqued essentialist constructions of gender in ahistorical structural dichotomies and instead analysed the diversity, flexibility and historical change in gender ideologies, identities, roles, relationships and powers. Gender ideology was differentiated from actual practices. Further, evidence was sought that women were social actors as much as men. Postmodern papers include: papers in the historical archaeology symposium of *The Archaeology of Gender* (1991), such as Elizabeth Scott's paper relating the variety of clothing items in documents at **Fort Michilimackinac**, Michigan, to the intersections between gender, race, ethnic and socioeconomic groups; Susan L. Cheney's paper on the power of women in the western USA to change men's recreational patterns; Western perceptions of, and interactions with, American Indians by Lee Fratt and by Carol Devens; *Historical Archaeology* (vol. 25, no. 4) articles on 1) diverse gender roles among Dakota Indians by Mary Whelan; 2) Spanish colonial women by Bonnie McEwan; 3) Native American, English and French interactions at Fort Michilimackinac by Elizabeth Scott; a chapter in *Manifesting Power* (1999) by Katharine Woodhouse-Beyer on the importance of Alaskan Indian women's economic roles in maintaining the Russian fur trade; a paper on gendered differences in Australian aboriginal responses to Western contact by Judy Birmingham in the proceedings of the first (1991) 'Australian Women in Archaeology Conference'; *Women in Archaeology: A Feminist Critique* (1993), edited by Hilary du Cros and Laurajane Smith; a chapter on changes in gender ideology and practices among immigrant Jewish communities in Boston, by Spencer-Wood in *Historical Archaeology: Back from the Edge* (1999); and most chapters in *Those of Little Note: Gender, Race and Class in Historical Archaeology* (1994).

Examples of post-modern approaches that contrasted singular ideal gender roles prescribed in dominant ideology with the actual diversity in gender practices include Linda Stine's paper in the symposium of *The Archaeology of Gender* (1991) on the flexibility in actual gender practices on southern US tenant farms compared with dominant gender ideology, and Penny Russell's 1993 article in *Australasian Historical Archaeology* discussing how public and private activities in the colony occurred in the same domestic spaces, in contrast to the separate gender spheres in Victorian gender ideology. Susan Lawrence-Cheney's paper in *Women in Archaeology* (1993) analysed ethnic variation in material expressions of the cult of domesticity or gentility. Margaret Purser's 1991 article in *Historical Archaeology* analysed women's economic importance and how they spread the material culture of domestic gentility in Californian mining towns and camps. In papers in *Redefining Archaeology* (1998) limited material expressions of gentility were found in mining camps in southern Australia (Lawrence), and in boarding houses in Sydney (Lydon).

In 1994, Roberta Gilchrist's book *Gender and Material Culture: The Archaeology of Religious Women* analysed women's social agency in creating gender identities of nuns and other kinds of medieval women's religious communities through architecture that had multiple possible symbolic interpretations. Gilchrist showed that the purposes of nunneries differed from monasteries and critiqued the male-biased assessments of nunneries as inferior according to the standard of men's monasteries.

In **classical archaeology**, chapters by Penelope Allison and by Marilyn Goldberg in *The Archaeology of Household Activities* (1999) challenge stereotypical gender attributions of classical Greek and Roman domestic spaces and artefacts as either female or male, with evidence of fluidity in the gendered use of domestic spaces and artefacts. Spencer-Wood's chapter provides documentary evidence of classical Greek gender ideologies and actual behaviours that differed from the dominant Greek ideology that was used by nineteenth-century classical archaeologists and historians to naturalise and legitimate the Victorian ideology of male dominance by tracing it back to the dawn of Western civilisation.

Spencer-Wood's post-modern gender research considers the polyvocal nature of culture and women's and men's actions in constantly renegotiating gender ideologies and actual gender practices. In her 1999 chapter, above, and in a 1994 chapter in *Those of Little Note*, Spencer-Wood showed that Victorian men sought to justify their dominance during a period when middle-class reform women were developing alternative gender

ideologies and actual gender practices that contested and changed the dominant Victorian gender ideology limiting women to a subordinate role in the home. Reformers redefined and expanded the meaning of women's domestic sphere in the dominant ideology by developing new ideologies of 'Domestic Reform', the 'Cult of Single Blessedness' and the 'Cult of Real Womanhood', which legitimated the creation of new gender practices in female public professions by claiming they were really domestic, or by sanctifying women who chose to work and not marry as analogues to the single blessedness of virginal nuns who married their calling.

Post-modern Marxist feminist approaches have rejected universalising theorisations to contextually analyse how specific groups of women resisted male dominance in particular situations. For instance, Eleanor Casella excavated evidence that women in a Tasmania, Australia, 'female factory' or prison took actions to resist their incarceration in solitary-confinement cells by destroying them with fire. She also found archaeological evidence that women successfully resisted prison prohibitions against inmates having money and other personal items by burying such contraband in the dirt floors. In another case study, Susan Piddock found evidence that inmates of the Adelaide Destitute Asylum, an almshouse, successfully resisted and evaded institutional rules against keeping personal items. These articles appear in the *International Journal of Historical Archaeology* vol. 5, no. 1 (2001).

A more recent post-modern feminist approach that includes queer theory is used by Lynn Meskell in *Archaeologies of Social Life: Age, Sex, Class, Et Cetera in Ancient Egypt* (1999). Meskell analysed the complexity of individual identities and social agency as well as sub-group and temporal variation along a number of intersecting social dimensions. She considered personal and emotive aspects of death and burial that archaeologists have avoided. Queer feminist theory led Meskell to critique and correct heterosexual assumptions and the neglect of sex and the body in archaeological analyses of ancient Egypt. A precedent to queer theory is 'Eros in love: Pederasty and pornography in Greece' by H.A. Shapiro and R.F. Sutton, in *Pornography and Representation in Greece and Rome* (1992). This feminist contextual analysis of Attic vase painting and texts revealed changing standards of sexual behaviour, attitudes towards homosexual and heterosexual roles and the relative power of men and women of different classes in sexual and romantic relationships.

Finally, feminist theory has led to the development of research on masculinity and men's identities, roles and relationships. Elizabeth Kryder-Reid's chapter in *Those of Little Note* (1994) pointed to the importance of men's studies and masculinist archaeology in researching how an all-male nineteenth-century religious community created an alternative masculinity for lay brothers who performed domestic tasks, idealising feminine virtues associated with the 'Cult of True Womanhood' or 'Domesticity'.

See also: Vikings

Further reading

Donald, M. and Hurcombe, L. (eds) (2000) *Representations of Gender from Prehistory to the Present*, New York: St Martin's Press.

Hurcombe, L. and Donald, M. (eds) (2000) *Gender and Material Culture in Archaeological Perspective*, New York: St Martin's Press.

Nelson, S.M. (1997) *Gender in Archaeology: Analyzing Power and Prestige*, Walnut Creek, CA: AltaMira Press.

Scott, E.M. (ed.) (1994) *Those of Little Note: Gender, Race, and Class in Historical Archaeology*, Tucson: University of Arizona Press.

Sweely, T.L. (ed.) (1999) *Manifesting Power: Gender and the Interpretation of Power in Archaeology*, London: Routledge.

Walde, D. and Willows, N.D. (eds) (1991) *The Archaeology of Gender: Proceedings of the 22nd* [1989] *Chacmool Conference*, Calgary: Archaeological Association, University of Calgary.

SUZANNE M. SPENCER-WOOD

genealogical research

Historical archaeologists must often engage in detailed genealogical research. The need for this kind of research exists because historical archae-ologists so often know the family name of the men, women and **children** who inhabited the sites they study. The use of genealogical information is somewhat unique in historical archaeology because archaeologists in other branches of the field study distant periods of time inhabited by people whose names have long been forgotten. Historical archaeologists have learned that understanding a family's genealogy can aid them in unravelling the nuances of family structure, living arrangements, the use of outbuildings as residences and other aspects of the past they may not have otherwise considered. Genealogies can occasionally provide information about cultural or even family-specific practices, and shed light on the idiosyncratic spatial arrangement of a site and even provide information about particular artefacts (such as monogrammed silver spoons). It is not unusual for historical archaeologists who have studied a family's history in intense detail to know more about a family they have never met than about their own family!

Historical archaeologists conduct genealogical research by examining several sources, both written and oral. Notable written information on historic individuals can be found in census records, immigrant ship manifests, **probate inventories**, newspaper accounts, personal letters, land deeds and court documents. Most practising historical archaeologists are familiar with all these sources, and have gained personal experience conducting genealogical research in many locales from local parish repositories to national libraries and archives. Much of this research is time-consuming and difficult because of the required close attention to detail. Some genealogical research is made even more tedious because many of the sources are available only on microfilm.

Many historical archaeologists have discovered that they must use oral interviewing techniques to acquire genealogical information. In fact, oral interviewing can often be the only way an archaeologist can develop a picture of a past family. The sort of information usually sought by archaeologists – mostly revolving around the mundane events of daily life – were never written down anywhere. Living ancestors are often the sole place to learn about the unrecorded elements of a family's life history.

Many excellent sources exist to inform historical archaeologists and others in the proper ways to undertake genealogical research. The World Wide Web has recently become a wonderful source of genealogical information as family researchers post their family's histories, and as men and women interested in genealogical research develop support networks that involve the sharing of information.

CHARLES E. ORSER, JR

Georgian Order

The concept of the 'Georgian Order' was invented by archaeologist James Deetz in the late 1970s to account for the unified, though unconscious, way of perceiving the world by Anglo-American men and women during the reign of Great Britain's King Georges (1714–1830). Because this time represents a period in the USA's colonial history, archaeologists working in the US East have used the concept most often where the earliest English colonial sites exist. Deetz referred to this single train of thought as a 'world view' or 'mindset', but archaeologists have generally preferred to use the term 'Georgian Order'. An important element of the concept is that, because it was a tacit perception held in the past, it helps archaeologists today to think explicitly about past thought processes, an area of study once viewed as impossible in archaeology.

Archaeologists' use of the word 'order' is not coincidental because the mindset adopted by Anglo-American men and women, and embodied by the concept, promoted neatness and symmetry. Thus, when archaeologists in the US East, particularly in the **Chesapeake region**, examined archaeological sites dating to the Georgian period, they discovered a distinct shift towards symmetrical order in **architecture** (both formal and **vernacular architecture**), **gravestones** and **material culture**. Houses began to be designed with symmetrical roofs and windows, and gravestones became squarer in shape. In terms of **ceramics**, the dedication to the 'Georgian Order' meant that the earthtone-coloured vessels were replaced with whiter pieces, usually designated by archaeologists as **creamware**, **pearlware** and whiteware. Archaeologists believe that whiter dishes were viewed as neater and more

orderly than the darker, earthier vessels of the Middle Ages and the Renaissance.

The Georgian Order concept, though widely used in the US East, is not without its critics. Some archaeologists believe that the concept is so broadly conceived that it can encourage facile interpretation. As a universalising concept, it has the potential to rob past historical actors of their agency, or ability to act as individuals. Rather than causing archaeologists to delve into the nuances of past behaviour, the Georgian Order has the potential to become the explanation for behaviour. In other words, it could be said that men and women in the past did some things simply because of the Georgian Order. Even though this potential exists, the Georgian Order is an important concept because it allows archaeologists to think about the mental elements of past life and to place a more human face on the men and women of the past.

CHARLES E. ORSER, JR

glass

Glass is essentially a melted combination of sand (silicon dioxide), soda (sodium oxide) or potash (potassium oxide), and lime (calcium oxide) or lead (lead oxide). Glass referred to as 'crystal' is made with fine lead or flint rather than common sand. During the twentieth century, glass manufacturers devised many highly specialised kinds of glass including sophisticated shock-resistant, photosensitive, fibre-optic and heat-conducting varieties. Historical archaeologists seldom encounter these more complex forms of glass, except at the most recent sites. At domestic sites, historical archaeologists mostly encounter container glass, whereas, at colonial-period Native American sites (see **Native Americans**), the most common glass artefact is the trade bead (see **beads**).

Ancient Egyptians and Mesopotamians manufactured the first glass containers some time around 1700–1500 BC, although glass was used at least one thousand years earlier as a glaze for ceramic vessels (see **ceramics**). Glass manufacture grew increasingly more sophisticated during the period of interest to historical archaeologists, and many archaeologists have made significant contributions to knowledge about this important class of artefacts.

Glass vessels were first produced by winding glass rods around moulds made of sand. The first great innovation in the manufacture of glass vessels occurred around 30 BC, when the blowpipe, or hollow rod, was invented. With this method, glassblowers could shape objects by using their own controlled airflow and, coupled with their skill as artisans, they could produce useful and even beautiful objects. With the developments of mass production and mass marketing, enterprising manufacturers invented ways to blow glass containers into moulds, thereby creating glass objects that were of standard size and shape. These improvements eventually led to the invention of a fully automatic bottle-making machine in 1904.

Archaeologists can usually determine how a glass object was manufactured by examining the object's surface. For example, the technique used to make a glass bottle can be discerned by the presence and location of seam lines. Fully mouth-blown bottles will have no seam lines whatsoever, whereas the most recent, fully machine-made bottles and jars will have a seam line running the entire length of the vessel from base to lip. Similarly, historical archaeologists can recognise how glass beads were manufactured by examining their surfaces. Drawn beads will exhibit straight or slightly twisted lines within the glass, but wound beads will contain thin striations around their circumferences. Many glass containers also carry **makers' marks** that archaeologists can use to identify their manufacturers.

Glass can be manufactured in many different colours, ranging from 'black' (extremely dark green) to clear (colourless). Some glass is manufactured as opaque white (called 'milk glass' or 'opal glass'), iridescent (called 'carnival glass') and marbled (called 'slag glass'). Some glass is clear when manufactured, but turns light purple (amethyst) after long exposure to sunlight because of the manganese (or 'glass makers' soap') in the formula. Archaeologists often refer to this kind of glass as 'polarised'.

Many different objects can be manufactured from glass, including **bottles** and other containers, medical and scientific equipment, health-related items (like eyeglasses), light bulbs, objects of personal adornment (like beads and **buttons**), toys (like marbles) and windows. Glass objects can be smooth and flat, or decorated with complex etched and pressed decorations. In addition, glass can be decorated with gilt, enamel and paint or impressed with flutes, panels, notches, cross-hatching, scallops and many other innovative patterns meant to interest consumers and, in the case of bottles, to showcase their contents.

Glass making was an important and widespread industry throughout the period of history studied by historical archaeologists. During the earliest days of Europe's colonial history, Venice was an important centre of glass production, but major industries also developed throughout the rest of Europe and elsewhere around the globe. The first glass-manufacturing industry in the USA was begun at **Jamestown**, Virginia in 1608.

Glass-making sites can be small, cottage industries or large, industrial concerns. When J.C. Harrington excavated the glass-making industry at Jamestown in the late 1940s, he discovered that the glasshouse had only been about 11 × 15 m in size. This seventeenth-century industrial building contained three furnaces and a pot kiln. The furnaces were built with small piles of stones within which a central, narrow chamber ran. As the manufacture of glass became more sophisticated, glass makers designed the 'English glass cone', a tall, conical funnel designed to increase the draught, making for a hotter fire. These cones could be quite tall. One at the Lemington glassworks in Newcastle-upon-Tyne, **England**, for example, was 33 m high.

See also: bottles; industrial archaeology

Further reading

Harrington, J.C. (1972) *A Tryal of Glasse: The Story of Glassmaking at Jamestown*, Richmond, VA: Dietz Press.

Jones, O. and Sullivan, C. (1985) *The Parks Canada Glass Glossary for the Description of Containers, Tableware, Flat glass, and Closures*, Ottawa: Parks Canada.

McKearin, G.S. and McKearin, H. (1989) *American Glass*, New York: Bonanza.

Noël Hume, I. (1969) *Glass in Colonial Williamsburg's*

Archaeological Collections, Williamsburg: Colonial Williamsburg.

CHARLES E. ORSER, JR

globalisation

Globalisation refers to a process that involves the world-wide spread of cultural elements, including **material culture**, from one place (sometimes called the 'core') to other parts of the world (sometimes called the 'periphery'). Globalisation is relevant to historical archaeologists because it was with the beginnings of determined European expansionism in the fifteenth century that European material objects, and the ideas they promoted, were carried around the world and introduced to cultures to whom the objects were completely foreign. Globalisation pursued since the 1940s is often referred to as 'Americanisation', as corporations based in the USA establish foreign subsidiaries.

The archaeological study of globalisation is somewhat unique to historical archaeology. Though numerous classical archaeologists (see **classical archaeology**) have explored the myriad characteristics of the expanding Roman Empire, empires do not have the same meaning in historical archaeology as globalisation. The Roman Empire – and other large, pre-modern polities – established ties with other cultures based largely on the Empire's well-defined political structure. In modern-era globalisation, however, the expanding powers created an overarching economic system that incorporated unequal, master–client social relations usually organised around the exchange of material things. Thus, modern-era connections are usually rooted in economics, though they may also incorporate a great deal of personal subjugation and wholesale culture change.

Historical archaeologists first developed an interest in the process of globalisation in the 1970s, when other social scientists, notably historical sociologists, began to explore the topic. It was not until the 1990s, however, that historical archaeologists began to devise specific perspectives for examining the material elements of the process.

An overt interest in globalisation grew as historical archaeology began to be practised around the world. A substantive concern for globalisation was not necessary when historical archaeology was practised only in the USA, Canada and Great Britain. Archaeologists interested in transoceanic linkages at this time had only to investigate Anglo-American contacts. With the rise of a more globally diverse historical archaeology, it became increasingly clear that the study of globalisation could be pursued in many parts of the world and within diverse cultural situations. Thus, archaeologists working, for example, in Portugal, Brazil and parts of Africa could begin to conceptualise the ways in which these diverse regions were really elements of a huge economic and cultural network. Artefacts found at colonial sites in Brazil resembled those found at comparably dated sites in Portugal because of globalisation; the artefacts may even have been manufactured in the same factory. As a result of this new understanding, historical archaeologists could begin to envision colonial-period villages as being linked together in complex, multifaceted ways.

Archaeologists who study globalisation do not bestow unlimited power on the European economic superpowers who came in contact with the world's indigenous peoples. Instead, one of the major challenges facing the archaeologists of globalisation is to develop ways of investigating native resistance and rebellion, and in finding ways to study how indigenous peoples changed the cultures of the economic superpowers. In other words, historical archaeologists interested in globalisation place great emphasis on the 'local', with the understanding that local sociocultural circumstances and history affected the specific ways in which any global network would be operated. The power of the 'local' is the reason that archaeological sites in South Africa, for instance, do not look exactly like those in the Netherlands, and why British-affiliated, colonial sites in the USA are not mirror images of English villages.

An illustrative example appears in Aron Crowell's study of the fur trade in one part of Russian America, the southern coast of Alaska. In the late eighteenth and early nineteenth centuries, Russian fur traders moved into the Aleutian Islands and Alaska because of the region's rich supply of fur-bearing animals. Establishing themselves at certain well-chosen camp sites and trading posts, the Russians set up extractive outposts from which they could harvest furs and subjugate the indigenous Qikertarmiut people. Excavating at Three Saints Harbour on Kodiak Island, Crowell demonstrated the complexities of globalisation when viewed from the perspective of the 'local'. The Russian fur trade was a hierarchically arranged organisation composed of capitalists, managers and workers. Some of the workers were foremen who oversaw the hunting activities of the indigenous people, many of whom had become 'debt slaves' to the company. The archaeological research indicated that the men in the upper levels of the organisation strove to maintain their Russian identity, whereas the men in the lower ranks were less concerned with being Russian. The lower ranks of the Russian organisation were materially similar to their indigenous workers, indicating that **acculturation** on the island was a two-way, complicated process.

The number of historical archaeologists around the world interested in globalisation was growing as of the year 2000, and it is expected that archaeologists in developing nations – just those places that experienced the brunt of colonial globalisation – will show increasing interest in the subject. Sophistication in understanding the material dimensions of globalisation will grow as the research develops.

See also: world(-)systems theory

Further reading

Crowell, A.L. (1997) *Archaeology and the Capitalist World System: A Study from Russian America*, New York: Plenum Press.

Falk, L. (ed.) (1991) *Historical Archaeology in Global Perspective*, Washington, DC: Smithsonian Institution Press.

Orser, C.E., Jr (1996) *A Historical Archaeology of the Modern World*, New York: Plenum Press.

—— (1994) 'Toward a global historical archaeology: An example from Brazil', *Historical Archaeology* 28(1): 5–22.

CHARLES E. ORSER, JR

Globe Theatre, London

The Globe Theatre, situated in the part of London known as **Southwark**, was constructed from timbers of the playhouse known as The Theatre in early 1599. Due to leasehold problems with the site of The Theatre in Shoreditch, Richard and Cuthbert Burbage contracted the carpenter Peter Street to dismantle The Theatre and carry the timbers south, across London Bridge. They re-erected the timbers on a site, leased from Nicholas Brend. Brend leased one moiety of his land (divided into two plots separated by a lane) to the Burbages and the other to William Shakespeare, John Hemings, Augustine Phillips, Thomas Pope and William Kemp. The annual rent for each plot was seven pounds and fifteen shillings with the lease granting right of access along the lane dividing the plots. The land was said to be subject to flooding as there was no embankment to keep the water out. The new playhouse was ready for occupation by the Chamberlain's Men in autumn 1599.

The Globe flourished, with its success possibly contributing to the demise of the **Rose Theatre**, but was destroyed by fire during a performance of *Henry VIII*, on 29 June 1613. Within a year, the theatre had been rebuilt, with the players also negotiating an extension on their original thirty-one-year lease. They now held the lease until Christmas 1644. During the English Civil Wars of the seventeenth century, plays were prohibited (not entirely successfully) by order of parliament. The Globe was apparently demolished (in the 1640s) and the site developed with tenement properties.

During the following 300 years, the location of the site of the Globe became shrouded by confusion – this being added to by the incorrect labelling on Wenceslaus Hollar's panoramic etching known as the *Long View of London from Southwark*. However, the work of W.W. Braines, at the beginning of the twentieth century, pinpointed the location of the Globe Estate.

It was this land that was subject to archaeological evaluation during 1989. Large parts of the Globe Estate had been truncated by later activity, particularly the foundations of the Barclay-Perkins Brewery, but, in the north-east corner of the site, remains interpreted as being part of the Globe

Theatre were discovered. The recorded remains consisted of a series of chalk and brick foundations representing the parallel walls of a polygonal structure, with a brick foundation (possibly a stair turret depicted by Hollar) to the east. The archaeological remains appear to continue under a Grade II Listed building to the west of the site.

Further reading

Blatherwick, S. (1997) 'The archaeological evaluation of the Globe Playhouse', in J.R. Mulryne and M. Shewring (eds) *Shakespeare's Globe Rebuilt*, Cambridge: Cambridge University Press, pp. 67–80.

Blatherwick, S. and Gurr, A. (1992) 'Shakespeare's factory: Archaeological evaluations on the site of the Globe Theatre at 1/15 Anchor Terrace, Southwark Bridge Road, Southwark', *Antiquity* 66: 315–33.

Braines, W.W. (1924) *The Site of the Globe Playhouse, Southwark*, London: Hodder & Stoughton.

SIMON BLATHERWICK

Göteborg (Gothenburg), Sweden

Göteborg, today the second largest city in Sweden and located on the west coast, was founded in 1619, but in practice it had a number of predecessors, all involved in some way in asserting Sweden's interests on the west coast. Until 1658, Göteborg lay in a narrow corridor of Swedish territory between the Danish province of Halland and the Norwegian province of Bohuslän. In 1658, however, the whole west coast became Swedish, thus completely changing the situation of the town of Göteborg. The oldest medieval town in the area was Gamla Lödöse, which archaeological investigation has shown to go back at least to the early twelfth century. Its international role was taken over at the end of the fifteenth century by Nya Lödöse, a newly founded town within the boundary of the present-day Göteborg. In principle these towns did not differ from the other medieval towns in Sweden. However, the first town bearing the name Göteborg, often called Karl IX's Göteborg after the king who founded it, was different. It was

constructed in 1607 by Dutch reformed dissidents as a part of the Swedish King's aspiration to use Dutch expertise to promote the copper trade. The town was burnt down in 1611 during warfare between Sweden and Denmark. When Karl IX's son Gustav II Adolf founded the new city of Göteborg, the Dutch were once again given a special role, and at the same time the tradition of the Swedish–German town of Nya Lödöse was continued.

The city plan of Göteborg, with canals and fortifications, was inspired by the Netherlands and may be compared with cities in the Dutch colonies, such as Jakarta, formerly Batavia. The Dutch influence was soon succeeded by German influence. In the eighteenth century, English contacts began to dominate. The East India Company, founded in Göteborg in 1731, was of crucial significance for the economic, industrial and social development of Göteborg for a long time to come.

Gamla Lödöse has yielded some of the best urban archaeological material in Sweden, the majority of it from the thirteenth and fourteenth centuries. It has been possible to reconstruct the medieval town plan. The material from Nya Lödöse consists mainly of a large number of artefacts, chiefly from the sixteenth century and later. Excavations have revealed the extent of the town, the harbour area and central parts including the church. From Karl IX's Göteborg there are very few finds; they comprise some building material, such as very small bricks corresponding to a kind known in Holland. Today, only a church foundation, probably once belonging to the town's reformed Dutch congregation, is visible above ground. Within the present-day Göteborg, considerable parts of the seventeenth-century town plan, the canal system and the fortifications survive. Since the town has been ravaged by fires on several occasions, the most serious one around 1800, very few of the oldest buildings are preserved. However, in the western part of the city centre the German Church, the auction hall of the East India Company (now the City Museum) and some cellars survive from the seventeenth and eighteenth centuries.

Archaeological investigation of the town began in the 1930s, which was early in terms of the study of remains from the beginning of the modern period. Archaeological work then mostly consisted of observing trenches dug by builders, but the material that was collected served as a basis for a couple of important essays about the history of faience in Göteborg and in Sweden. In recent decades, several major excavations have been conducted, yielding detailed new knowledge about the earliest development of Göteborg, including the original plot pattern and the character of the oldest houses. Several excavated wooden houses come from the earliest period in the history of the city. Important elements in the archaeological material are the so-called waste bins, which were evidently emptied now and then but which still preserved a considerable number of finds.

The East India Company is also manifested in the large quantities of finds discovered by marine archaeologists, especially Chinese **porcelain**, retrieved from one of the company's ships, the *Götheborg*, which was wrecked in 1745 just as she was about to put into her home port of Göteborg. The urban archaeological material is mostly stored in the Göteborg City Museum, apart from the finds from Gamla Lödöse, which are in Lödöse Museum and the Museum of National Antiquities in Stockholm. By Swedish standards, the amount of post-medieval archaeological material from Göteborg is unusually large.

See also: Dutch East India Company

Further reading

Andersson, H. (1972) 'Historisk arkeologi i Göteborg', in *Göteborgs Historiska Museum Årstryck, 1972*, pp. 39–55, Göteborg: Göteborgs Historiska Museum.

Andersson, S., Jönsson-Kihlberg, E. and Broo, B. (eds) (1986) *Livet i det gamla Göteborg*, vol. 2, Göteborg: Göteborgs Arkeologiska Museum.

Carlsson, K. and Ekre, R. (1980) *Gamla Lödöse*, Medeltidsstaden, vol. 21, Stockholm: Riksantikvarieämbetet.

Järpe, A. (1984) *Nya Lödöse*, Medeltidsstaden, vol. 60, Stockholm: Riksantikvarieämbetet.

Kjellberg, S.T. (1933) 'Fajansfynd i Göteborg', *Göteborgs Historiska Museum Årstryck* 1933, pp. 33–62. Göteborg: Götesborgs Historiska Museum.

Nilsson Schönborg, G. (2001) *Kinesiskt importporslin i*

Göteborg sett ur ett arkeologiskt perspektiv, Göteborg: Urbaniseringsprocesser i Västsverige.

Strömbom, S. (1923) *Forskningar på platsen för det forna Nya Lödöse (1915–1918)*. Skrifter utgivna till Göteborgs trehundraarsjubileum, vol. 5, pp. 1–300. Göteborg: Göteborgs litografiska aktiebolag.

Wästfelt, B., Gyllensvärd, B. and Weibull, J. (1991) *Porcelain from the East Indiaman Götheborg*, Höganäs: Wiken.

HANS ANDERSSON

Gotland, Sweden

The largest island in the Baltic Sea was politically dependent on Sweden from the Viking Age until 1361, when the island was conquered by the Danish King Valdemar Atterdag. It remained under Danish control until 1645, after which it became part of the Swedish realm again. Gotland's importance and wealth in the Viking Age and medieval period was based on the ideal condition for sea trade and a certain degree of political independence for the farmer-traders. During the Viking Age, six important trading places were known. The Gotlandic farmers had intense trading contacts with Eastern Europe, especially Novgorod. From the thirteenth century and onwards, this role was taken over by the Hansa town of Visby.

Historical archaeology has a long tradition on Gotland. Unique Viking Age material consisting of sixth- to ninth-century picture stones, enormous hoards with imported coins, hacksilver and jewellery (mainly reflecting contacts with the Eastern world), trading places and graveyards, has been investigated. The **material culture** changed radically after the Christianisation of the island between AD 1000–1100. Furnished graves in churchyards, cross-shaped churches, frescoes, cross-pendants and baptismal fonts demonstrate a unique identity and contacts with the Russian–Byzantine church. However, a mission from the East cannot be proved; the contact was mainly based on individual actions. Almost a hundred churches were erected before the middle of the fourteenth century with rich interior and exterior in Romanesque and Gothic style. Apart from early church archaeology, the archaeology of the battlefield of the Battle of Visby in 1361 was investigated in 1905. Urban and rural houses in stone have been investigated and preserved since the early twentieth century. An investigation of the landscape development has been carried out on the basis of excellent seventeenth-century maps. The difference between the rural and urban population was not only manifested in a civil war in 1288 – caused by the building of the town wall – and a badly equipped army in 1361, but was also demonstrated by the choice of motifs and language on medieval grave slabs. The military defeat of the farmers, the change of trading routes, the establishment of new markets for Hanseatic towns in the Baltic Sea (and the emigration of German citizens), the disappearance of weapon exports/crusading and the Black Death were all factors that helped to seal the end of a period, when Gotland was one of the richest and wealthiest islands of medieval Europe. The farmers lost their partial independence during the fifteenth century and Gotland turned back to agriculture and the limestone industry.

See also: churchyard archaeology

Further reading

Staecker, J. (1999) 'Dialog mit dem Tod. Studien zu den mittelalterlichen Grabplatten Schwedens im Spiegel der Europäisierung. Die Epigraphik', in N. Blomkvist and S.-O. Lindquist (eds) *Europeans or Not? Local Level Strategies on the Baltic Rim 1100– 1400 AD*, Symposium Kalmar 1998, CCC papers: 1, Stockholm: Almqvist and Wiksell, pp. 231–62.

Thordemann, B. (1939–40) *Armour from the Battle of Wisby 1361*, text and plates I–II, Kungl, Vitterhets-, historie- och antikvitetsakademien, Stockholm: Kungl. Vitterhets-, historie- och antikvitestakademien.

Yrwing, H. (1978) *Gotlands medeltid*, Visby: Gotlandskonst AB.

JÖRN STAECKER

gravestones

Gravestones constitute an important class of **material culture** studied by historical archaeologists. They can provide an abundance of intriguing historical, social and cultural information, some of which may not be available elsewhere.

Historical archaeologists have learned that gravestones can provide historical information because they exhibit both names and dates on their surfaces. The careful inspection of grave markers can provide important genealogical information, including birth and death dates, and often the name of a spouse. Archaeologists can use this information, in conjunction with written information, to compile family and community histories.

Historical archaeologists have also discovered that gravestones can often be dated by the style in which they were carved. In a seminal study on this topic, James Deetz and Edwin Dethlefsen demonstrated the rise and fall in popularity of three styles of gravestones used in Massachusetts, USA, from 1720 to 1820. By the 1720s, the area's stonemasons were making flat gravestones topped on the front side with an engraved 'death's head' motif, or a winged skull. By examining numerous graves, they discovered that this pattern had begun to lose favour by the 1770s, and that, by the 1790s, it was no longer widely used. Beginning in the 1760s, however, stonemasons began to replace the menacing skull design with a cherub motif, a more pleasantly faced winged image. The cherub design reached its peak of popularity in the 1780s, but, by the 1800s, it too was losing favour, and, by the 1810s, it had also disappeared. Deetz and Dethlefsen's research showed that, beginning in the 1770s, gravestone engravers began to use a second design, the 'urn and willow' motif, within which they replaced the skull and the cherub with a peaceful burial urn overarched by serene willow branches. The use of this new design grew in popularity, and in the 1810s it completely replaced the cherub pattern. Their analysis also illustrated an important characteristic of artefacts: that decorative patterns were created, grew in popularity and then slowly declined as people became interested in new designs. In the **New England** of 1770–80, all three grave motifs were used, but to varying amounts as one design replaced an earlier one.

Deetz and Dethlefsen's analysis also demonstrated that the patterns on gravestones migrated in

Massachusetts from east to west, carried along with migrating stone carvers. Following the movement of these carvers – through the evidence left behind on the grave markers they decorated – can provide large-scale information about cultural change (through the growth and decline of interest in specific patterns) as well as unique, particular information about how specific stonemasons handled the various design motifs through time.

An important element of the studies by Deetz and Dethlefsen that extends beyond historical issues concerns the deeper meanings of what the gravestone patterns represent. The different popularity of the decorative motifs indicates that they were not placed on gravestones without ideas attached to them. The usual interpretation is that the different motifs represent the changing ideas about death and the afterlife that circulated at different times among Protestants in New England. The realisation that gravestones could provide new insights into the non-material elements of past life dramatically opened new vistas of research within historical archaeology. By 2000, studies of **ideology** and meaning had become commonplace throughout archaeology, including in historical archaeology.

As interest in **ethnicity** and social inequality grew among historical archaeologists, many realised that gravestones could provide information about these important subjects as well. As a result, several historical archaeologists began to examine gravestones for information about ethnic boundary maintenance and class divisions (see **class, social**). Archaeologists discovered that gravestone carvers could use words and phrases from their native languages, as well as folk motifs, to promote the ethnic affiliation of the deceased. When gravestones decorated in culture-specific ways cluster in certain spots of a cemetery (see **cemeteries**), the percentages of specific motifs may provide information about the influx of immigrants into an area at certain points in time. In addition, the use of native words on the gravestones of first-generation immigrants and the lack of them on second-generation stones can provide information about **acculturation** and the social pressures immigrants faced in their new homes.

Historical archaeologists also learned that important class differences could be demonstrated by examining gravestones. The obvious differences between grand, ornate stones and simple, flat stones could be used to indicate the social distinctions that once operated in a region or city. Gravestone differences can also be used to show differences that existed between rural and urban dwellers.

Further reading

Deetz, J.F. and Dethlefsen, E.S. (1967) 'Death's head, cherub, urn and willow', *Natural History* 76(3): 29–37.

Dethlefsen, E.S. and Deetz, J.F. (1966) 'Death's heads, cherubs, and willow trees: Experimental archaeology in colonial cemeteries', *American Antiquity* 31: 502–10.

Mytum, H. (1999) 'Welsh cultural identity in nineteenth-century Pembrokeshire: The pedimented headstone as a graveyard monument', in S. Tarlow and S. West (eds) *The Familiar Past? Archaeologies of Later Historical Britain*, London: Routledge, pp. 215–30.

Wurst, L. (1991) '"Employees must be of moral and temperate habits": Rural and urban elite ideologies', in R.H. McGuire and R. Paynter (eds) *The Archaeology of Inequality*, Oxford: Blackwell, pp. 125–49.

CHARLES E. ORSER, JR

Great Zimbabwe, Zimbabwe

The site of Great Zimbabwe, located in south-central Zimbabwe, Africa, is not technically a historic site since it was occupied during the African Iron Age, approximately from about AD 1100 to 1500. Nonetheless, the site has important connections to historical archaeology, and some African archaeologists would even consider the site to be 'historic'.

Great Zimbabwe today consists of a series of impressive dry-stone ruins, all built without the use of mortar. In many places, the builders created decorations with the stones, such as chevrons near the tops of walls. One of the most striking structures is the Conical Tower, a building 5 m in diameter and 9 m tall. At its largest, between 12,000–20,000 people may have lived at Great

Zimbabwe, when the city was an important centre of trade within south-east Africa.

Sixteenth-century Portuguese explorers were the first non-Africans to see the ancient city, and they immediately concluded that it must have been built either by Prestor John, the mysterious Christian king of Ethiopia, or by the biblical King Solomon. Their biased attitude against the native Africans did not allow them to imagine that indigenous peoples had constructed the city. The site remained largely unknown to Europe until a German geologist visited the ruins in 1871. Roughly twenty years later, Cecil Rhodes, the diamond magnate, outfitted the first archaeological expedition to the site. Rhodes's team of archaeologists were also unable to convince themselves of the indigenous character of the site, and they concluded that the ancient Phoenicians must have built it. Archaeologists did not confirm the African origins of Great Zimbabwe until early in the twentieth century.

The importance of the site to historical archaeology stems from its colonial Portuguese connections and from the way pre-twentieth-century visitors interpreted the site. Archaeologists have used the example provided by Great Zimbabwe to demonstrate the danger of preconceived ideas in archaeological research, and to promote the understanding that an archaeologist's world view can have an impact on his or her interpretations.

CHARLES E. ORSER, JR

Greenwich Palace, England

The site of Greenwich Palace largely lay within the grounds of the former Royal Naval College but also extended south to the area now covered by the National Maritime Museum. The development of the palace is recorded in the substantial accounts of the *King's Works*. The earliest illustration of the palace, by Antony van den Wyngaerde in 1558, as well as later views and plans, also provided some detail of the palace layout. Greenwich was already a royal holding in Saxon times, but, to date, only burials of this period have been found to the south and south-east. However, a royal presence is attested since at least 1408, when Henry IV signed his will from his Manor of Greenwich.

It is probably this Manor that was uncovered in the lowest strata of excavations in the Grand Court of the College in 1970–71. This comprised chalk and limestone foundations of a rectangular building dated to the fourteenth century. This riverside structure was substantially rebuilt in brick in the early fifteenth century. This can safely be identified as the mansion known as Bella Court built by Humphrey, Duke of Gloucester (brother of Henry V) between 1426–34. Humphrey had been granted the Greenwich Manor in 1517 and was also responsible for enclosing the area later to become Greenwich Park and building a 'castle' on the site later occupied by the Royal Observatory. In 1447, the Humphrey estate reverted to the Crown and the riverside mansion became known as 'Pleasaunce' or 'Placentia'. Expenditure on the property throughout the rest of the fifteenth century was confirmed during the excavations, which revealed numerous additions and adaptations. It was in this building that Henry VIII was born in 1491.

This enlarged manor house was completely demolished at the end of the fifteenth century and Henry VII completed a new grandiose palace by 1506, which largely comprised four wings around a courtyard. The 1970 excavations revealed much of the north wing, including the riverside tower, and part of the west wing. Walls of the south wing were revealed during service trenching in the 1960s and a small part of the east wing was recorded in a watching brief of 1995. The east wing incorporated the great hall whose location is known since its undercroft, inserted in 1604, survives in the cellars of Wren's Queen Anne building. The eastern end of the complex contained a chapel, which survived until the 1690s. There may have been another court to the south of the chapel and east of the great hall, although plaster floor surfaces of probable Tudor date were found in this area (the courtyard of the Queen Anne building) in 1999.

In 1482, Edward IV gave a plot of land on the western side of the palace to the Observant Order of Greyfriars. This complex, largely lying beneath the King Charles buildings, is known to have included a church – seen on most contemporary illustrations, and cloister, frater, dorter, chapter house and cemetery. A wall, tentatively identified with the chapter house, was uncovered in excavations inside the King Charles building in 2000. To the south-east, burials found in 1963 were plausibly identified with the Friary. A landing stage or jetty to the north-west is known to have been rebuilt by Henry VIII and timbers on the foreshore uncovered in 1996 have been identified with it.

A number of outbuildings associated with the palace complex have been identified in the sources, but few have been revealed archaeologically. However, walls probably associated with the tilt yard and its adjacent banqueting chambers were revealed in an excavation in the lawns of the National Maritime Museum in 1993. The famous Greenwich Armoury, established by Henry VIII in 1514, lay just to the west of the Friary but it has not been found. Farther west, the location of a stable and a barn, built in 1510–11, survived long enough for their positions to be recorded; the stables under the present Mews and the barn just to the south, near the Dreadnought Hospital. On the eastern side of the palace was the Office of Works compound, which served construction programmes in the area until the 1730s, of which a couple of walls were identified in 1999. During the Tudor period, a number of important courtiers established mansions within the vicinity of the palace and one, Compton House, 150 m to the east of the palace complex, was excavated in 1997.

A late addition to the palace complex was the building of the Queen's House to the south. This masterpiece by Inigo Jones was begun in 1616 but only completed in the 1630s. Thereafter it underwent many alterations, and archaeological work in 1985 and 1999 in the cellars has defined a number of different phases. Traces of a planned addition to its south-east corner were also uncovered in 1988.

The main palace and the Friary were demolished in the 1660s and archaeological work throughout the site has uncovered demolition layers. However, a number of domestic structures grew up in the area from the mid-seventeenth century and traces of these have been found in watching briefs throughout the site. The most important development was the planned new palace started in 1664 by John Webb for Charles II. Only a west wing, now the King Charles Building, was finished and it has been described as the first baroque building in the country.

In the 1690s, Sir Christopher Wren began the construction of Greenwich Hospital, incorporating Webb's unfinished building. This magnificent complex survives today and numerous watching briefs associated with recent refurbishments have recorded its foundations, as well as traces of the earlier history of the site. The Hospital graveyard to the south has also been partially examined.

Archaeological work in the grounds of the National Maritime Museum has revealed boundary walls and a roadway of the seventeenth century; outbuildings associated with Greenwich Hospital of the eighteenth century; and nineteenth-century outbuildings associated with the development of the Greenwich Hospital School.

Further reading

Bold, J. (2000) *Greenwich: An Architectural History of the Royal Hospital for Seamen and the Queen's House*, New Haven: Yale University Press.

Bowsher, J.M.C. (1999) 'Recent archaeological work in Greenwich', *Journal of the Greenwich Historical Society* 2(2): 32–42.

Chettle, G.H. (1937) *The Queen's House, Survey of London*, vol. 14, London: HMSO.

Colvin, H.M. (ed.) (1963–82) *The History of the King's Works*, London: HMSO.

Dixon, P. (1972) *Excavations at Greenwich Palace*, London: Greenwich and Lewisham Antiquarian Society.

Milne, G. (1996) 'A Tudor landing stage at Greenwich', *London Archaeologist* 2(3): 70–4.

Museum of London archives; unpublished archaeological reports.

Thurley, S. (1993) *The Royal Palaces of Tudor England*, New Haven: Yale University Press.

JULIAN M.C. BOWSHER

H

Harpers Ferry, West Virginia, USA

Harpers Ferry developed as an armoury town at the confluence of the Potomac and the Shenandoah rivers in Virginia (what is now West Virginia), USA. Armourers produced the first guns by 1801 and they considered themselves craftsmen, knowledgeable in the production of the entire gun – 'lock, stock, and barrel'. The transformation to wage labour, where workers tended machines to create interchangeable parts, came with great difficulty. Finally in 1842, a military superintendent took control of the facilities and ordered the standardisation of labour.

Archaeological studies of households related to the armoury show how different groups reacted to the industrialisation process. For instance, one worker's domestic assemblage dating to the 1830s indicates the adherence to home industry, as it contained a large quantity of gun parts and tools. After 1841, tools and gun parts vanish from the archaeological record with the implementation of wage labour. The post-1841 household also used goods that were fashionable several generations earlier. This archaeological expression may indicate that women, who were in charge of the domestic sphere, had a role in protesting the conditions of the new industrial order.

At the outbreak of the US Civil War (1861), Virginian troops captured the town and they transported the armoury machinery to Richmond, Virginia, and Fayetteville, North Carolina. Harpers Ferry later served as Sheridan's staging ground for his march up the Shenandoah valley in 1864–5. Major archaeological surveys identified the Civil War fortifications and campgrounds on Maryland and Loudoun Heights, an area that served a strategic role in protecting Harpers Ferry. Archaeologists have also studied deposits related to a private boarding house that served transients, such as labourers and newspaper reporters, during Sheridan's campaign.

By the 1880s, northern entrepreneurs reinvested in the town's industry. Boarding houses developed and archaeologists have examined many of these late nineteenth-century assemblages. These finds illuminate the differences in material wealth and health conditions between classes in an industrialising society.

Virginius Island, an area incorporated into Harpers Ferry, developed in the 1840s with large-scale industries, like flour mills and textile mills. Women and children entered the workforce as unskilled or semi-skilled workers. The earliest excavation concentrated on these industries. More recently, domestic structures have been evaluated that had residents who cross-cut the social, cultural and economic structure of Virginius Island. Archaeology furnishes some important information about the lifeways and living conditions of entrepreneurs, craftsmen and wage labourers.

The archaeology at Harpers Ferry shows how industry affected both work and domestic life as well as the landscape and the built environment. As time discipline increasingly drove individuals' lives, they chose to either participate in these new cultural patterns, attempt to alter them or withdraw from them. The archaeology at Harpers

Ferry, a nineteenth-century industrial town, provides some interpretations of how people responded to the new industrial order.

Further reading

Gilbert, D. (1999) *Mills, Factories, Machines and Floods at Harpers Ferry, West Virginia, 1762–1991*, West Virginia: Harpers Ferry Historical Association.

Shackel, P.A. (1996) *Culture Change and the New Technology: An Archaeology of the Early American Industrial Era*, New York: Plenum Press.

Shackel, P.A. and Winter, S.E. (eds) (1994) 'An archaeology of Harpers Ferry's commercial and residential district', *Historical Archaeology* 28(4): 16–26.

Smith, M.R. (1977) *Harpers Ferry Armory and the New Technology: The Challenge of Change*, Ithaca: Cornell University Press.

PAUL A. SHACKEL

Harris matrix

Invented in 1973, the Harris matrix allowed archaeologists for the first time to 'see' the stratigraphic sequences of archaeological sites. It is a method that produces a calendar for the stratigraphic events on a site in relative time order. As time has no physical reality, it can only be seen by the use of diagrams, such as a clock face or an ordinary calendar. Each archaeological site has a unique sequence of events embedded in the development of its stratification. Each site, when excavated by the stratigraphic method, produces a unique calendar of events in relative time, inferred from the physical disposition of the individual soil layers, architectural structures such as walls and other features such as postholes.

Such calendars are known as stratigraphic sequences. Every sequence is unique and therein lies its value and that of the site itself to historical studies. The stratigraphic sequence of a site is the testing pattern against which nearly all other analyses of the site must be compared. As stratification (see **stratification, soil**) is a byproduct of cultural activity, stratigraphic sequences are an unbiased record of such past activity.

Prior to the Harris matrix as a way to see stratigraphic sequences, archaeologists relied on section drawings to demonstrate the evolution of a site. As they are only one-dimensional representations through the depth of stratification, section drawings are not stratigraphic sequences because the other three dimensions (length, width and time) cannot be shown. Harris matrix diagrams, on the contrary, are compiled from the stratigraphic data in all dimensions and show the entire stratigraphic sequence for any site, no matter its area or physical complexity.

All archaeological sites are four-dimensional entities, as they will contain at least two stratigraphic events that have the three physical dimensions of length, width and height (depth). As such events are archaeological entities, they contain elements of the fourth dimension, namely time. Length and width are interpreted and recorded by plan drawings, the height or depth by sections. Harris matrix diagrams illustrate the time relationships of all the stratigraphic units.

Before the Harris matrix, the stratigraphic paradigm in archaeology was one-dimensional, as it was based upon sections that show only the depth of stratification. The Harris matrix changed the paradigm of stratigraphic archaeology from a one-dimensional to a four-dimensional science. It did so by giving archaeology a universal method for seeing stratigraphic sequences in diagrams that combine the three physical dimensions of stratigraphic data with their properties in the fourth dimension of relative time.

The analysis of stratigraphic sequences is the foundation of archaeological research and the Harris matrix and its associated methodology are central to such studies. It is also universally applicable to the study of any archaeological phenomena that exhibit stratification, such as standing buildings, superimposed rock art paintings or shipwrecks.

See also: dating methods; stratification, soil

Further reading

Harris, E.C. (1989) *Principles of Archaeological Stratigraphy*, London: Academic Press.

Harris, E.C., Brown, M.B. and Brown, G.J. (eds)

(1993) *Practices of Archaeological Stratigraphy*, London: Academic Press.

EDWARD CECIL HARRIS

health

Historical archaeologists take several different approaches to the study of health, all of which are complementary in informing us about the lives of past people. Those using a bioarchaeology approach examine human skeletal remains for evidence of **disease**, life expectancy, frequency, type and degree of physical activity, diet and nutritional adequacy. Another approach common in historical archaeology is to examine the living and working environments of past people and the implications for maintaining bodily and mental health. A third approach is concerned with understanding the different ways people in the past have understood health and how best to maintain and restore it. Combinations of artefactual, documentary, ethnohistorical and ethnographic as well as oral history data are used with all of these approaches.

The bioarchaeology approach is most associated with Clark Larsen. Larsen's research into past health has provided much new information about the effects of European contact, and especially missionisation, on the lives of **Native Americans**. He has also written about the health status of frontier Euro-American settlers.

From skeletal evidence bioarchaeologists can determine several things about an individual's health status during life. One is workload and the types of frequent activities. For example, osteoarthritis and bone compression are evidence of overwork, while bone thickness and geometry can tell us if the overwork was from carrying, lifting, grinding, riding or other activities. Skeletal remains can also provide evidence about dietary sufficiency, health of the individual and general sanitary conditions in which an individual lived. Dental remains can inform specialists about dental hygiene, childhood illnesses and nutritional stresses, as well as the overall type of diet consumed by an individual.

Bone isotope analysis is another method of determining the predominant diet or foodways (see **food and foodways**) of an individual, and can also be used to find evidence of toxins, such as lead in the body, which may have impaired health. Fractured bones, and how well (and if) they healed, are another indicator of health, informing us of the degree of danger in an individual's life and quality and availability of any medical treatment and care. Demographic information, such as age at death, learned from burial populations and/or documents is another way of inferring the relative health of individuals or a population.

Diet (interpreted from bone chemistry and dental wear), height, iron deficiency, growth disruption, oral health and infection are parameters of health that were used by Larsen in a comparison of seventeenth-century and nineteenth-century frontier Euro-American populations from Maryland and Illinois. Oral health was very poor for both populations, due to lack of dental hygiene and dependence on a diet heavy on roughly processed maize. Iron-deficiency anaemia and growth disruptions were seen in both populations, also attributable to the over-dependence on maize. The nineteenth-century Illinois frontier adults were taller than their seventeenth-century Maryland counterparts, but shorter than today's average, another indication of less than ideal nutrition. Osteoarthritis and degenerative joint disease were present in the bones of adults of both sexes from these frontier populations, indicative of hard, frequent and heavy work. Life expectancy was much shorter than today for both populations, and infant mortality high.

Approaches focusing on the health environment of past peoples include studies of privies (outhouses), urban and rural sanitation regulations and their practice, **institutions** concerned with health and sometimes contradictions between official thought regarding health and its effectiveness. Archaeologists working at the **Boott Mills** boarding houses of Massachusetts, USA, for example, found evidence of several contradictions. They found that privies were still in use even though a city ordinance had mandated water closets, and that the privies were shallow and too close to wells. In addition, company policy emphasising painting of the boarding houses as a way to make them appear healthier resulted instead in toxic levels of lead being present in the houses and yards.

Theories of health and health maintenance and restoration from the time periods studied by historical archaeologists were varied and often contradictory. Dr Rush's so called 'heroic medicine' of the eighteenth century emphasised bloodletting as the way to restore health, while others in the eighteenth and nineteenth centuries preferred more moderate approaches such as homeopathy, herbal remedies and self-treatment with patent medicines. Differences in thought concerning health and its maintenance and restoration among ethnic groups has been found by historical archaeologists studying **ethnicity** and its reflection in artefacts.

Laurie Wilkie's study of traditional health practices of African American women at a nineteenth- and early twentieth-century Louisiana plantation is an example of this approach, emphasising the importance of context and using multiple lines of evidence. Maintaining proper blood balance was the theoretical basis of health treatment and maintenance for this population. Treatments prior to the twentieth century were frequently home-made, often from herbs dissolved in alcohol or prepared as teas. Tea cups (see **tea/tea cere-mony**) recovered archaeologically thus may be attributed to health practice in this context as well as to consumption of beverages. Artefacts from commercial preparations such as patent medicines and petroleum jelly were found to be more abundant in twentieth-century contexts. Wilkie's analysis determined that these commercially prepared products were functional substitutes for traditional preparations, and thus a continuation of the traditional health system.

See also: bottles; contact archaeology; ethnography; glass; mission sites

Further Reading

Beaudry, M.C. (1993) 'Public aesthetics versus personal experience: Archaeology and the interpretation of 19th-century worker health and well being in Lowell, Massachusetts', *Historical Archaeology* 27(2): 90–105.

Larsen, C.S. (2000) *Skeletons in Our Closet: Revealing Our Past through Bioarchaeology*, Princeton: Princeton University Press.

—— (1994) 'In the wake of Columbus: Native population biology in the postcontact Americas', *Yearbook of Physical Anthropology* 37: 109–54.

Wilkie, L.A. (1996) 'Medicinal teas and patent medicines: African-American women's consumer choices and ethnomedical traditions at a Louisiana Plantation', *Southeastern Archaeology* 15(2): 119–31.

DAVID T. PALMER

heritage management

Heritage management involves the protection, examination and preservation of archaeological sites, properties and monuments. It is an area of concern to archaeologists around the world, and most nations, and even some international bodies, have enacted laws that govern the use and protection of archaeological sites deemed important.

Decisions about what constitutes an 'important' archaeological site are complex and generally relate in some measure to a national perspective. For instance, in Great Britain, 'importance' (or **site significance**) is based on the following criteria: date of the site and its representation of a period of antiquity; rarity and diversity; degree of preservation and completeness; association with sites of similar period; potential to provide information about the past; and the amount of documentation about the site. Archaeologists in the USA are required to use four criteria to demonstrate that a site or property is important enough to be listed on the **National Register of Historic Places**. Criterion A holds that sites must be associated with broad patterns of national, state or local history; Criterion B relates to the association with famous people notable in history; Criterion C states that sites must represent a distinctive manner of construction or represent the work of a particular master; and Criterion D mandates that sites must have the potential to yield significant new information for scientific or scholarly research. Sites and properties can be deemed 'significant' under any of the criteria, and many archaeological sites are deemed 'important' under Criterion D.

Such definitions of what is deemed worthy of preservation, or, put another way, what is considered important to a nation's heritage, are coming under increasing scrutiny by indigenous peoples. Distinct cultural traditions can hold different ideas about what constitutes 'importance', and a colonised people may reject the heritage notions of a dominant culture (which established its towns and cities during a period of **colonialism**). Native peoples in North American and Australia have been particularly vocal about issues of heritage, but cultures around the world are also questioning other nations' views of significance.

Controversies over what is meant by 'importance' involve the larger issue of who owns a region's heritage. Individual interest groups may provide different answers, and national governments have not been the only bodies to express their ideas about what constitutes heritage. International organisations have also attempted to provide leadership in defining and designating heritage. The United Nations Educational, Scientific, and Cultural Organization (UNESCO) has been particularly active in matters involving heritage. Their *Convention Concerning the Protection of the World Cultural and Natural Heritage*, first published in 1972, defined 'cultural heritage' as 'monuments, groups of buildings and sites with historical, aesthetic, archaeological, scientific, ethnological or anthropological value'. One element of the *Convention* was the creation of the concept of the 'World Heritage Site', defined as a cultural property that has 'outstanding universal value'. Sites deemed to have global significance are recorded on the 'World Heritage List'.

Such regulations as the UNESCO *Convention* can be viewed both positively and negatively. Positively, they promote an ethic of preservation and study, but, negatively, they tend to solidify ideas about what constitutes 'heritage' based on the date on which they were written. Concepts of heritage management evolve over time like other concepts, and what is deemed unimportant today may be extremely important in the future. Nineteenth-century farmsteads in the US Mid-west provide a good example. In the late twentieth century, when hundreds of standing examples still existed, few heritage managers expressed much interest in saving them, and many were destroyed by new

highway construction and other public-works projects. At the dawn of the twenty-second century, when it is possible that almost all of these farmsteads may be destroyed, a desire may exist to preserve the sites before they are all lost forever. At this time, sites that were once considered unimportant become 'significant'.

Conservation and restoration constitute a major element in heritage management. These topics have also received international attention. The International Committee on Monuments and Sites (ICOMOS) codified an *International Charter for the Conservation and Restoration of Monuments and Sites* (1965) and the *Charter for the Protection and Management of the Archaeological Heritage* (1990). In addition to such broad international policies, some private concerns have been formed to protect archaeological sites by purchasing them. In the USA, for example, the Archaeological Conservancy, based in Albuquerque, New Mexico, has bought 170 archaeological sites in twenty-nine states since its founding in 1980.

One of the most difficult questions in heritage management concerns the preservation and use of sites deemed to be sacred. Indigenous peoples may discover to their outrage that they may no longer gain access to their sacred sites once heritage managers have deemed these sites to be 'significant'. The offended peoples are often forced to argue their cases in court, under the claim that their traditional religious rights have been abridged. In answer to this problem in the USA, some federally recognised Native American tribes have created their own criteria for defining heritage, and some of them, such as the Navajo, have their own staff of archaeologists and heritage managers.

Questions of religious freedom become especially complicated when New Age groups decide that a particular site or area is important within their belief system (see **belief systems**). Stonehenge provides a famous example as every year druids and others visit the site for religious observance, sometimes vying for control of the site. Other New Age groups may have particular political or ethnic causes, such as those espoused by Afrocentric scholars, who may claim an archaeological site in the New World to be associated with medieval West African seafarers, or pseudo-archaeologists, who claim a site to be associated with extraterrestrials.

The continuation of **looting** at archaeological sites, even those listed on preservation rolls, shows that the goals of heritage management are never truly reached. New challenges daily confront heritage managers and ideas about significance continue to change.

Further reading

Hardesty, D.L. and Little, B. J. (2000) *Assessing Site Significance: A Guide for Archaeologists and Historians*, Walnut Creek, CA: AltaMira Press.

Renfrew, C. (2000) *Loot, Legitimacy and Ownership*, London: Duckworth.

Skeates, R. (2000) *Debating the Archaeological Heritage*, London: Duckworth.

CHARLES E. ORSER, JR

Herjolfsnes, Greenland

Herjolfsnes, Greenland, is a Scandinavian farmstead with accompanying church and churchyard in the Norse Eastern Settlement located today in the municipality of Nanortalik. The farmstead was occupied from *c.* AD 1000 to *c.* 1450. The main archaeological investigation of the site took place in 1921, and most remarkable are the outstanding and well-preserved medieval garments that were found at the churchyard. Instead of coffins, the bodies were wrapped in discarded clothes, among which were about thirty dresses or parts of dresses, for both adults and children, about fifteen liripipe hoods, five caps and six hoses. The garments date from the fourteenth and the fifteenth centuries, and although of Greenlandic origin they reflect the latest European fashion of the time. The garments are kept in Copenhagen at the Danish National Museum.

See also: churchyard archaeology; dress

Further reading

Nørlund, P. (1924) 'Buried Norsemen at Herjolfsnes', *Meddelelser om Grønland* 67: 1–270.

JETTE ARNEBORG

Hermitage Plantation, Tennessee, USA

The Hermitage was the cotton plantation and home of Andrew Jackson (seventh president of the USA) from 1804 until his death in 1845. The property, located near Nashville, Tennessee, has been the site of archaeological research since the early 1970s. The work has focused on the site's mansion and its service buildings, the adjacent formal garden, the overall organisation of the plantation and especially on the archaeological record related to and created by the site's large community of enslaved African Americans. As at **Monticello**, **Mount Vernon**, Williamsburg and other museums sites, archaeology at the Hermitage serves as both an important research tool and a useful way of presenting the past to the visiting public.

Since 1889, the Ladies' Hermitage Association, a private, non-profit organisation, has owned and administered the Hermitage as a historic museum property. Its current holdings of 700 acres include the locations of all the plantation's original buildings and agricultural facilities.

The Hermitage's enslaved community numbered between 150 and 180 during the 1830s and 1840s. Excavation has occurred in three distinct slave-quartering areas on the property. The work has yielded extensive evidence on dwelling **architecture**, which ranged from log huts in the early 1800s to substantial brick structures from the 1820s. Archaeologists have discovered underground storage pits or 'root cellars' within ten of fourteen excavated dwellings. The variation of the features from household to household suggests that these pits were added after the construction of the buildings by residents making use of a loose, mental template in regard to size, placement and construction details.

Excavation has also produced substantial quantities of artefacts, revealing that Hermitage slaves had an unexpectedly rich material life. The evidence points to extensive foraging in the wilds for extra food, participation in the local cash economy and an active spiritual life separate from the mainstream Christianity encouraged by their owners. Comparisons of the assemblages from dwellings near the mansion with those from the distant field quarter show surprising similarities in terms of the quantity and variety of recovered items, challenging the standard assumptions about the different lives of house servants and field hands.

The archaeological record of the Hermitage slave community suggests these people achieved some level of autonomy and satisfaction for themselves and their families in spite of Andrew Jackson's plans for their efficient, minimally humane management and control.

See also: African American archaeology; garden archaeology; plantation archaeology; public archaeology; resistance; slavery

Further reading

McKee, L. (1996) 'The archaeology of Rachel's Garden', in R. Yamin and K.B. Metheny (eds) *Landscape Archaeology: Reading and Interpreting the American Historical Landscape*, Knoxville: University of Tennessee Press, pp. 70–90.
—— (1995) 'The earth is their witness', *The Sciences* 35(2): 36–41.
Russell, A.E. (1997) 'Material culture and African-American spirituality at the Hermitage', *Historical Archaeology* 31(2): 63–80.
Smith, S.D. (1977) 'Plantation archaeology at the Hermitage: Some suggested patterns', *Tennessee Anthropologist* 2(2): 152–63.
Thomas, B.W. (1998) 'Power and community: The archaeology of slavery at the Hermitage Plantation', *American Antiquity* 63: 531–51.

LARRY McKEE

Historic American Building Survey

The Historic American Building Survey (HABS) documents the architectural heritage of the USA. The National Park Service sets quality standards for documentation through measured drawings, large-format photography and written histories. The Library of Congress preserves the records and makes them available to the public through its

Prints and Photographs Division. All HABS records are archivally stable, reproducible and copyright-free. HABS records structures of all types from small utilitarian structures to monumental formal architecture. The HABS collection, which documents more than 32,000 structures in the USA and its territories, is one of the largest collections of architectural documentation in the world.

HABS was established in 1933 as a work relief programme for architects during the Great Depression and continues under the authority of the Historic Sites Act of 1935. The **Historic American Engineering Record** (HAER) was established in 1969 as a companion programme.

See also: Historic American Engineering Record

BARBARA J. LITTLE

Historic American Engineering Record

The Historic American Engineering Record (HAER) was established in 1969 as a companion programme to the **Historic American Building Survey** (HABS). HAER documents industrial, maritime and engineering history. The maritime programme, established in 1986, builds on the Historic American Merchant Marine Survey (HAMMS), which operated from 1936–7 under the Works Progress Administration (WPA). The National Park Service sets quality standards for HAER documentation through measured drawings, large-format photography and written histories. The Library of Congress preserves the records and makes them publicaly available through its Prints and Photographs Division. All HAER records are archivally stable, reproducible and copyright-free. Detailed written histories that accompany drawings and photographs document the development of industrial and engineering processes to interpret the significance aspects of a recorded property. HABS/HAER documentation is often required prior to the demolition of buildings or structures under Section 106 of the National Historic Preservation Act of 1966.

See also: Historic American Building Survey

BARBARA J. LITTLE

historical documents

The 'historical' in historical archaeology makes reference to the fact that the discipline encompasses the study of historic periods beginning at the point of European expansion and **colonialism**, within which a variety of textual and visual documents were produced. Thus, historical documents constitute a fundamental line of evidence in historical archaeological research.

Archaeologists seek out historical sources that relate to their archaeological investigations, whether they are tied to particular individuals, events or places. These 'primary sources' – or documents created by individuals contemporary to the time period under study, who witnessed first hand particular events and recorded them – may potentially aid in interpreting specific sites, or may help to construct a regional historical context for one's study. As with the archaeological record, the documentary record encompasses a multitude of diverse sources, each with the ability to provide unique kinds of information. These records of the past can be found left behind in attics or archived in churches, libraries, county courthouses and a number of other public and private institutions.

The range of historical documents

The type of historical document an archaeologist may seek out is often related to the kind of archaeological site under exploration, and how much previous information about the former occupants is known. For example, if one is excavating a late nineteenth-century, urban house site it is likely that there will be a title deed associated with the house lot that can be found at the county courthouse. The deed will contain the owner's name and this information can lead the archaeologist to other sources. Did the person attend a local church and is there a record of marriage, death or baptism? Perhaps the person is listed on a US census record. Are there descendants living in the area who may have an old photograph or other personal records, such as letters, passed down through the generations? Public and official documents, such as court records, deeds, city directories, wills, insurance plats and military census and tax records, may variously reveal facts about an individual's ethnicity, relative economic and social status, occupation and family lineage.

A number of sources will not be available for, or relevant to, many archaeological studies. For instance, a site may predate certain types of documentation (e.g. the US census was first conducted in 1790), or the records may be incomplete (e.g. a tenant farmer's name would not be recorded on property deeds). The study of colonial sites, for example, would require a shift in historical-research strategies.

Suppose one is investigating a slave quarter on a plantation site (see **plantation archaeology**) in colonial Virginia. With plantation-related sites, archaeologists often must rely on primary sources related to the slave owner to glean information about the plantation's enslaved community. **Probate inventories** have been helpful in such instances. Probate inventories are official documents listing an individual's property at the time of death, recorded for tax purposes and to ensure that one's heirs would receive their fair share of the estate. A court-appointed appraiser recorded the name, value, occupation, and often the age of each enslaved person. Given their detail, these documents can prove valuable for reconstructing enslaved family and household composition. As an economic enterprise, plantation records often included business-related documents regarding the management of enslaved labour, as well as the purchase and provisioning of food rations. It is therefore possible to begin to interpret the day-to-day living circumstances of the enslaved community using these sources. A number of slave owners, such as Thomas Jefferson and Landon Carter, also kept journals and wrote letters mentioning some of the daily interactions they had with their slaves. Such personal records often provide intimate details about the interactions between slave-owning whites and enslaved blacks, and can also present information about the prevailing racial ideologies and attitudes regarding slavery.

Newspapers often hold a wealth of information about life in the past. Paid advertisements hawking various goods for sale at local shops can reveal what was fashionable for the time, as well as the relative cost of specific items. Advertisements used in conjunction with store records or manufacturers' price lists can help to fine-tune cost estimates, market trends and even the dating of sites. The latter is clearly an important objective in archaeology. Historic sites are usually dated by using **ceramics** with known manufacturing dates obtained from records kept by manufacturers such as **England**'s Staffordshire potteries, which dominated the US market from colonial times through the nineteenth century. Yet certain ceramic types had varying availability in different locales, and ads can help to assess when a town or city actually had access to specific wares. By combining what we find in the ground with the evidence from historical documents archaeologists can actually refine dating techniques.

In addition to historical documents that are textual in form, others are visual in nature, such as photographs, paintings, pictures and maps. Historic maps have been essential to archaeological research in helping to locate sites, and to reconstruct historic landscapes and settlement patterns as people transform their environments and establish residences and towns. Period photographs, paintings and drawings offer us a glimpse of individual faces and personalities of the past, which are difficult to envision using the artefacts alone. Archaeologist Ivor Noël Hume often used early paintings of domestic life and portraits to provide a cultural and social context for how the bits and pieces of artefacts he recovered were potentially used and displayed.

It is easy to understand how a photograph or painting can be taken at face value to represent a factual, objective image of the past, but one must not assume that images are unbiased. A picture may be worth a thousand words, but the messages contained within it are in reality constructed from the point of view of the photographer or artist. In fact, caution must be exercised in using any historical document to interpret the past since they are inherently biased records of bygone events. Historical archaeologists in the past often fell into the trap of privileging written and visual texts as

factual evidence over the archaeological evidence. Their usage sparked a fierce debate over the relationship between history and archaeology, and of text versus artefact.

Critical analyses of historical documents

In the early years of their discipline, historical archaeologists often took it for granted that primary sources revealed truths about the past. Archaeologists collected historical documents that helped to interpret and explain what they uncovered archaeologically. If discrepancies were discovered between the historical and archaeological evidence, it was assumed that the historical record was accurate, leaving the impression that archaeology was in fact 'a handmaiden to history', a discipline with secondary importance that could best be used to substantiate historically based knowledge.

Historical documents, however, were purposefully created by people with all of the subjective biases that come with individual personalities, backgrounds and life experiences. Therefore, paintings and photographs captured images in ways that the artist felt was important and aesthetically pleasing. Slave owners left behind their impressions of enslaved individuals in words that reflected their feelings of racial superiority, and often neglected to record the elements of enslaved life that blacks themselves would have thought most important. Cartographers mapped those details that they felt were crucial to the task, in order to satisfy themselves or their intended audiences. For example, military maps highlight encampments, fortifications and enemy holdings, while often omitting residences and streets.

Even something as seemingly objective as a census or a probate inventory must be approached with a critical eye. A census taker may judge and record someone to be of a particular ethnic or racial background that conflicts with the individual's own judgement of their identity. Similarly, appraisers even within the same town all possessed varying levels of competence in judging an object's value and literacy in describing property, and exercised different approaches to categorising things. All of these factors contributed to the accuracy of probate inventories.

It is clear from the above examples that historical documents must be critically analysed and interpreted before their usefulness can be realised. We cannot simply peruse documents in search of 'isolated facts and descriptions' that fit our research objectives. A number of archaeologists have even argued that historical documents must be treated as a form of **material culture**, which requires thoughtful and rigorous analysis, and comparative study.

Using historical documents and archaeological evidence

Historical archaeologists generally agree that the most productive approach is to use multiple lines of evidence in conjunction with one another to arrive at meaningful interpretations. James Deetz's analysis of tobacco pipe stems (see **pipes, smoking**) from sites at **Flowerdew Hundred Plantation** in tidewater Virginia is a case in point.

Deetz argued for a multidirectional approach where one uses both archaeological and historical evidence by 'constantly refining and reformulating questions raised by one set of data by looking at it against the background of the other'. By plotting the distribution of dated pipe stem fragments recovered from seventeenth- to eighteenth-century sites across Flowerdew Hundred, Deetz delineated a three-phase settlement pattern. The earliest phase peaked between 1620–50 and abruptly fell off; the second phase had a more gradual rise over the second half of the seventeenth century before a plateau at the end of the century; and the sites of the final phase peaked during the middle of the eighteenth century.

Deetz looked to documents that helped to construct a regional historical context of the wider Chesapeake (see **Chesapeake region**) within which to understand Flowerdew Hundred's three fairly distinct settlement phases. The major forces shaping Chesapeake society from the 1620s to the 1750s were a tobacco economy and a shift in the labour force from white indentured servitude to enslaved African workers. Using these as tentative explanations for the settlement patterns, he then went back to the archaeological record for more site-specific data. He found a correlation between the first group of sites and earthfast (posts-in-the-ground) dwellings, the sites of the second group and more permanent **architecture** as well as the beginning of industrial production and a relation between the third group of sites and the initial appearance of slave-related pottery known as **colonoware pottery**. Once again, Deetz returned to historical documentation to examine the demographics for each time period and to judge the importance of tobacco farming to the economy. He was able to conclude that the first group of sites correlated with the region's initial tobacco boom and a 'get rich quick and get out' frame of mind, thus explaining the appearance of cheap, earthfast housing. The second group of sites, which exhibited a more dispersed settlement pattern across the plantation, were related to the growing trend of colonists to remain in Virginia and make an attempt to diversify the tobacco-based economy. Finally, the sites in the third group, which were largely located away from the fertile bottomlands along the James River, consisted of much larger holdings than in previous years. Planters had removed living spaces from the bottomlands in order to maximise agricultural space, and the presence of colonoware further indicated that the plantation system and slave-based labour were well entrenched. Deetz argued that he would never have been able to fully understand the archaeology of Flowerdew Hundred and its relationship to the events occurring in the broader Chesapeake had he not considered each body of data as complementary and unique in its own right, and moved back and forth from each to refine his research questions.

Further reading

Beaudry, M.C. (ed.) (1988) *Documentary Archaeology in the New World*, Cambridge: Cambridge University Press.

D'Agostino, M.E., Prine, E., Casella, E. and Winer, M. (eds) (1995) 'The written and the wrought: Complementary sources in historical anthropology', *Kroeber Anthropological Society Papers*, pp 1–241.

Deetz, J. (1993) *The Archaeology of Flowerdew Hundred*, Charlottesville: University of Virginia Press.

Little, B.J. (ed.) (1992) *Text-Aided Archaeology*, Boca Raton: CRC Press.

Ravn, M. and Britton, R. (eds) (1997) 'History and archaeology', *Archaeological Review from Cambridge* 14(1): 1–162.

Seasholes, N.S. (1988) 'On the use of historical maps', in M.C. Beaudry (ed.) *Documentary Archaeology in the New World*, Cambridge: Cambridge University Press, pp. 92–118.

MARIA FRANKLIN

history of historical archaeology

One's perspective on the history of historical archaeology depends upon how one defines the field. If historical archaeology is defined as any archaeology in which the practitioner uses a combination of archaeological sources (artefacts, soils, standing monuments and buildings) and 'historical' or textual sources (documents, stelae and inscriptions), then the field is as old as Egyptology, Assyriology and **classical archaeology**. If the field is defined in the most common, contemporary manner, however, then the history of historical archaeology begins with the initial interest of archaeologists in the post-Columbian world and the cultural interactions that occurred as part of that history. The first definition is used in places where a long literate tradition exists, such as **China**, whereas the second definition is used by archaeologists working in those parts of the world that were colonised by Europeans, beginning in the fifteenth century. Historical archaeology, as a named field of study, was originally designed by scholars interested in the second definition.

Beginnings

The first examples of what might be considered historical archaeology according to the second definition were characterised by the work of scholars who had developed a personal interest in one particular period of history or in a specific historical locale. These individuals had decided, probably both in response to the growing knowledge about archaeology in Western society in general and based on their own interest in history, that they might be able to locate buried deposits of past historical settlements if they actually looked for

them. Freeman Lewis's location and survey of **Fort Necessity**, Pennsylvania, in 1816, the cursory excavations of Jesuit Félix Martin at the Canadian mission site (see **mission sites**) of Sainte Marie I in 1855, and the excavations in 1856 by civil engineer James Hall at the home of English Pilgrim Miles Standish in Massachusetts provide examples of this initial research. These early cases of historical archaeology admittedly do not meet today's standards of professionalism, and so they can only be marginally considered to be 'archaeology' in the strictest sense. Any artefacts found were considered merely to be curios or relics of a bygone era. These rudimentary explorations, however, did illustrate at least two important points that would be relevant to the future of historical archaeology: that historic-period sites do exist, and that they can be investigated using archaeological methods. These findings, so obvious today, were a revelation at the time because, in those days, the word 'archaeology' was synonymous with classical Greece and Rome or dynastic Egypt.

The formative years

The formative years of historical archaeology can be considered to extend from the nineteenth century to the early 1960s. This period was characterised by a growing institutionalisation of the field, a greater application of controlled excavation at prominent historical sites and an overt interest in the great people (typically men) of history and the 'significant' places associated with them. During this period, pioneering historical archaeologists began to investigate the most well-known sites of history. In the USA, the sites of interest were places associated with the earliest European settlements, such as **Jamestown**, Virginia, or those having something to do with the early history of the nation, such as Williamsburg, Virginia. Some research was also directed to the study of the homes of prominent leaders, such as the archaeology conducted at Abraham Lincoln's home in Springfield, Illinois.

Much of the research during the formative period focused on **architecture**, with archaeologists working largely as technicians unearthing buried information that historical architects and restorationists could use in their physical reconstructions. In many cases, the finds recovered by archaeologists provided the only information available about the construction and size of building foundations, the sequence and dates of room additions and the precise placement of outbuildings and gardens. Those specialists engaged in presenting and interpreting historic sites to the public often found the archaeological information to be invaluable. One problem during this period, however, was that archaeologists seldom tried, or were kept from trying, to move beyond the collection of architectural detail.

One characteristic of the formative period – probably because of the strong role architectural information played – is that historical archaeologists as a body were uncertain as to the academic placement of their discipline. At this time in archaeological history, the primary job of the archaeologist was perceived as relating to the construction of large-scale cultural histories for prehistoric peoples. In theory, these 'prehistoric histories' could then be linked, at least conceptually, to the later sequences known from history (perceived as post-Columbian in time and present in written records). Within a framework in which prehistorians constructed regional sequences that often had great time depth – and generally terminating with the presence of Europeans in an area – no place existed for historical archaeologists within academic archaeology. As a result, most leading historical archaeologists of this period saw what they were doing as essentially a 'historical' endeavour, rather than one rooted in anthropology. The historical archaeologists' recovery of architectural details helped to define the field as a kind of history. In much of Europe, this tradition continues to hold sway, as historical archaeology is known as '**post-medieval archaeology**', a term that tends to stress the historical connections between the medieval era and the one that followed it.

Maturation

The maturation of historical archaeology as a discipline with its own perspectives and approaches is still an ongoing process at the beginning of the twenty-first century. This process of growth began in the mid-1960s, with the development of **processual archaeology** or **New Archaeol-**

ogy, and it continues to move forward as historical archaeologists experiment with innovative perspectives and new approaches. The tenets of the 'new', or overtly scientific, archaeology have been debated since it first emerged in the 1960s and, regardless of how one chooses to evaluate its perspective, it was a major boon to the development of historical archaeology. Processual archaeologists argued that, rather than concentrating on the construction of cultural histories as an end in itself, archaeologists should be working as anthropologists, examining cultural processes in all times and places. This position opened the door to the development of an anthropologically based historical archaeology, a field that strove for more than just the collection of architectural elements from the homes of the rich and the famous. In adopting a broad view of the role of archaeology in this endeavour, it was probably not an accident that Lewis Binford, one of the founders of processual archaeology, had early experience in historical archaeology at **Fort Michilimackinac**, Michigan, USA.

Though historical archaeologists could, and did, still study famous people and noteworthy places and recover architectural details after the 1960s, they nonetheless began to play more of a role in anthropological archaeology, particularly in the USA and increasingly in other places as well. Early studies by James Deetz, on the role of archaeology in the study of Native American (Arikara) kinship in the central USA (see **Native Americans**), and James Allen's investigation of colonialism in **Australia** demonstrated the promise of this new kind of historical archaeology. Historical archaeology, because of its use of many different kinds of information – including at a minimum both archival and archaeological sources – could provide special insights into the processes of past culture. In other words, historical archaeologists no longer had to operate as the 'handmaids of history' because they had the intellectual tools and the academic mandate to study the social and cultural dynamics of the past.

An overt interest in science helped historical archaeologists to strengthen their arguments and think about how they framed their interpretations. Stanley South was a pioneer in showing historical archaeologists ways to do this, particularly through his concept of **pattern recognition** and his **mean ceramic dating** formula.

As historical archaeology became a more sophisticated field of inquiry in the late 1960s and 1970s, several archaeologists – now more in tune with anthropological thinking – began to imagine the tremendous insights their field had to offer about all elements of past life. Specifically, many of them realised that historical archaeology provided a perfect way in which to study the lives of men and women who had been largely forgotten in history or who had been pushed aside as insignificant by past historical observers. Whereas early historical archaeologists concentrated many of their efforts on the famous names of the past, this new breed of archaeologist was more interested in learning about those hundreds of thousands of men and women who had toiled, often in desperation, to build cities, canals and wealth for others. As a result of this realisation, many historical archaeologists began intensive investigations of the lives and living conditions of plantation slaves, tenant farmers, factory workers, tenement dwellers and hard-scrabble miners. Since the late 1960s, then, historical archaeologists have been working diligently to provide a more realistic view of the past, one in which countless men and women worked in obscurity. At the beginning of the twenty-first century, this research continues to be one of the most important elements of modern historical archaeology.

At the same time that historical archaeologists began to investigate the hidden side of history, many of them began to examine the hidden, or symbolic, meanings of artefacts and large-scale landscape features, such as gardens (see **garden archaeology**). As they became conversant with the works of cultural anthropologists, literary critics and **material-culture** specialists, some historical archaeologists realised that any individual artefact can have many different meanings, depending upon who is perceiving it and in what social and cultural setting it is perceived. Whereas, in the USA, a Big Mac hamburger may be seen as just another kind of fast food, in a setting where McDonald's is perceived as an element of US expansionism, it may be seen as something quite different. Or, it can be seen as both by the same person. This kind of subtle nuancing is now

recognised by most historical archaeologists, and many are deeply engaged in unravelling the many social and cultural meanings of the artefacts they unearth.

Many historical archaeologists have also begun to think of their discipline as being able to make concrete and important statements about the historical nature of the crises and processes that affect the world today. Thus, some historical archaeologists have begun long-term examinations of **capitalism**, **colonialism** and imperialism, and its many local manifestations. These topics are never easy to understand, even in a living context, and historical archaeologists hope to provide insights that are available in no other sources.

At the same time, many historical archaeologists work in **cultural-resource management**, usually employed by engineering firms, construction companies or even their own archaeological consultancies. These archaeologists are engaged on a daily basis in retrieving information before it is lost forever beneath the bulldozer's blade or under the walls of a new housing development. Archaeologists working in this often fast-paced environment have collected information on thousands of archaeological sites around the world, many of them well within the purview of historical archaeology. Some of the most important theoretical advances in historical archaeology have come from data originally collected during a cultural-resource management project. Though some of this work suffers from limitations of time and funds imposed by the demands of construction schedules, historical archaeology as a discipline has exploded with the enactment of cultural-resource management based on laws intended to protect and preserve fragile archaeological remains. At the beginning of the twenty-first century, historical archaeology is indebted to these archaeologists working in the private sector.

Further reading

Orser, C.E., Jr and Fagan, B.M. (1995) *Historical Archaeology*, New York: HarperCollins.

South, S. (ed.) (1994) *Pioneers in Historical Archaeology: Breaking New Ground*, New York: Plenum Press.

CHARLES E. ORSER, JR

Hollandia, shipwreck

The *Hollandia* was a ship of the **Dutch East India Company** (VOC) that sank with no survivors west of the Scilly Isles off south-west England on 13 July 1743. The *Hollandia* belongs to the category of shipwreck sites where the ship's structure has disintegrated completely. Due to the wrecking process and environmental conditions, the ship's contents are widely scattered and artefacts are heavily damaged and fragmented. Nevertheless, this site yielded important data on the **material culture** of mid-eighteenth-century VOC ships. The vessel was newly built at the company's shipyard in **Amsterdam** and belonged to a new type of VOC ship; historically, the *Hollandia* is closely related to the ***Amsterdam***.

In 1968, the British shipwreck explorer Rex Cowan took the initiative to locate the wreck through documentary research and magnetometer surveys. After its discovery in 1971, excavation extended continuously throughout the 1970s, 1980s and the early 1990s. The site comprised three distinct clusters within an area of approximately 180 by 100 m. Its southern half contained remains from the lower part of the hull, including lead ingots, barrels of **nails**, iron bars and two bronze mortars, which had fallen to the sea-bed while the *Hollandia* was damaged and adrift after striking a rock. The ship itself fell apart in the northern section of the site with the stern facing south, creating two concentrations of debris of 40 by 30 m each. Artefacts settled in gullies in the rocky sea-bed and around the heaviest remains, consisting of five anchors and twenty-eight iron guns. The strong currents resulted in a random-find distribution that did not allow for a refined spatial reconstruction of the ship's layout. Interpretation of such a complex site was further hampered by the fieldwork methodology. The excavation during the 1970s reflected the early stage of the development of underwater archaeological standards in north-west Europe.

The archaeological catalogue comprised some 3,500 items, silver coins and lead ingots excluded. Although most finds were fragmentary and mainly consisted of durable materials, such as various metals and **ceramics**, they offered heterogeneous data, including some unique items, among which are the ship's fire engine, a printing press and a luxurious silver dinner set. Post-excavation artefact processing and analysis was enhanced by the acquisition of 80 per cent of the total collection in 1980 by the Rijksmuseum in Amsterdam. Research focused on the problem of functional classification of fragmented artefacts from a ship-wreck site. This research resulted in the *Hollandia Compendium* publication, a volume that combines a systematic archaeological catalogue with a lexicon of historical documentation on the construction and equipment of VOC ships around 1750.

Further reading

Cowan, R., Cowan, Z. and Marsden, P. (1975) 'The Dutch East Indiaman *Hollandia* wrecked on the Isles of Scilly in 1743', *International Journal of Nautical Archaeology* 4: 267–300.

Gawronski, J. (1992) 'Functional classifications of artifacts of VOC-ships: The archaeological and historical practice', in D. Keith and T. Carrell (eds) *Underwater Archaeological Proceedings from the Society for Historical Archaeology Conference 1992*, Tucson: Society for Historical Archaeology, pp. 58–61.

Gawronski, J., Kist, B. and Stokvis-Boetzelaer, O. (eds) (1992) *Hollandia Compendium. A Contribution to the History, Archaeology, Classification and Lexicography of a 150 ft. Dutch East Indiaman (1740–1750)*, Amsterdam: Elsevier.

JERZY GAWRONSKI

household archaeology

The majority of historical sites excavated throughout the world have been at least in part residential in nature, and in most cases investigators have focused on some aspect of the household as a social and economic unit in their analysis and interpretation of finds from domestic sites. The late US historical archaeologist Charles Fairbanks was convinced that historical archaeologists ought to be able to wrest information from household middens just as prehistorians did, and in the early 1970s he advocated that historical archaeologists target backyard middens as well as cellar holes and house foundations, and initiated his students into the skills of what he termed 'backyard archaeology'. Fairbanks and his students aimed to find patterns in the data so that they could make generalisations about other sites of the same culture and of roughly the same time period. Such an approach was typical of **processual archaeology** and its search for artefact patterns leading to broad generalisations about culture; quantification was adopted as the means for identifying such patterns.

Stanley South developed a set of broad artefact classes that continue in wide use in US historical archaeology today, especially in the south-east and among contract or consulting archaeologists. South's Brunswick pattern addressed households directly; it added the spatial dimension to artefact counts to delineate patterns of rubbish disposal at eighteenth-century British colonial sites in North and South Carolina. South also attempted to introduce Lewis Binford's notions of site structure into historical-sites analysis, but this aspect of South's work remained underdeveloped.

Processualist historical archaeologists devoted their attention to artefacts and faunal remains in and of themselves, independent of their contexts, characterising sites on the basis of percentages of recovered items, using sherd counts as opposed to vessel counts, with little attention given to site structure, site formation processes and contextual relationships among artefacts and soil strata. Consumer choice analysis is an outgrowth of pattern analysis that focuses on household economics; it relies upon the analysis of selected categories of household refuse in light of historical data on each item's relative cost. A household's investment in ceramics or meat is calculated in order to assess its relative socioeconomic status. In such studies the socioeconomic rank of the head of household is used to characterise the household as a whole. As a result, consumer choice studies often confirm what was already known about the economic standing of a given household from documents. Thus, there is a tendency to overlook the complexity and diversity of household make-up and to approach household consumption as a one-dimensional phenomenon. Many have noted that not all household members contribute equally to the household economy and that some goods in the

household context may have more to do with production than with consumption. Consideration must be given to variability in income strategies (e.g. domestic production for outside sale versus domestic production for internal household consumption and survival; piecework and outwork; taking in boarders; etc.) and the overall household economy, including contributions made by women, servants, slaves, boarders *and*, potentially, children. The household can also serve as a unit of employment; large households often provided long-term or temporary employment (as well as accommodation) for a wide range of individuals who possessed a variety of skills.

Kathleen Deagan has, since the mid-1970s, made tremendous contributions to our understanding of the effects of household composition on diet and material life in the early years of the sixteenth- and seventeenth-century frontier Spanish community of St Augustine, Florida. Indeed, Deagan's work on *mestizaje* – a process of cultural interaction and acculturation resulting from marriages of Spanish men to Indian women – demonstrated unequivocally that women's participation in household activities could be detected through careful analysis of household rubbish, especially food remains, ceramics and food preparation equipment. Deagan was the first historical archaeologist to derive from the archaeological record clear evidence of women's contribution to household economy and social dynamics.

A profitable approach to household archaeology takes into account the varying functions performed by the household and how household 'responsibilities' may or may not differ in urban versus rural settings. Stewart-Abernathy, for example, through his case study of early twentieth-century Washington, Arkansas, learned that in many early US towns and cities, house lots were in essence 'urban farmsteads' with the full complement of outbuildings and activity areas one might expect at a rural homestead. This of course is true of many other urban places throughout history, up to very recent times. Assemblages recovered from sites of the French regime in Canada have been the focus of 'lifestyle analysis' (*les modes de vie*). For example, Paul-Gaston L'Anglais used household analysis as a framework for his study of collections from Place Royal in Québec and from Fortress Louisbourg in

Nova Scotia; he sought to characterise every aspect of consumption and production in selected eighteenth-century households through the detailed analysis of complete assemblages.

At the Rocks in Sydney, Australia, archaeologists have explored house lots and house foundations quite literally quarried from Sydney's stony 'other side' by convicts and ex-convicts and their families, who established themselves as respectable householders well beyond the rules and regulations of the penal colony's government and police force. Interdisciplinary excavations along Cumberland and Gloucester Streets have revealed the hard work and pride that went into creating permanent dwellings, kitchen gardens and decent family life in this unlikely spot, and documentary analysis has linked the archaeological evidence with the life histories of the Rocks' earliest homemakers.

Other studies have used the framework of family history in interdisciplinary studies combining archaeology, **material-culture** analysis, family history and architectural analysis within a framework of anthropological theories about the household. Anne Yentsch, for example, used family reconstitution and other demographic techniques to trace the changing composition of households in her analysis of materials from the Narbonne House site in Salem, Massachusetts. Here she was able to link deposits found in the back lot to specific households that once occupied the house. Yentsch's subsequent work in Annapolis, Maryland, brought this approach to its full expression in the form of a historical ethnography of the Calvert family and their slaves. Such studies have demonstrated conclusively that features and their disposition in space are equally, if not more, telling than artefacts alone for household analysis.

In the 1980s, household archaeology emerged as a major research focus in all areas of archaeology, and theories and models from other disciplines were incorporated into archaeological studies. As archaeologists studying households began to be explicit in their use of theories about households drawn from anthropology and family history, they increasingly recognised the need to construct appropriate models for interpreting historical households in all their different forms and contexts. The **Boott Mills** boarding-houses (Lowell, Massachusetts) study is a good example; here it was

possible to construct a comprehensive and multi-layered model based on reconstitution of boarding-house demographics that aided in interpreting the corporate nature of the boarding household at different contextual levels.

Brothels constitute another form of alternative, corporate household, and several archaeological studies have taken an explicitly household archaeology approach to the interpretation of brothels. These recent studies of brothels have taken a **feminist-archaeology** perspective that examines the material culture of brothels as evidence for a special class of household and the world of the prostitute as constituting a distinctive sub-culture, and consider prostitution not as a source of entertainment for men but as a business or income strategy for women. The work of Donna Seifert in the area of Washington, DC, known in the nineteenth century as 'Hooker's Division' and of Julia Costello and Mary and Adrian Praetzellis in the nineteenth-century red-light district of Los Angeles, California, stand out in this regard.

Similarly, archaeologists studying religious communities and residential religious or civic institutions have recognised that it is critical to examine closely the ways in which the beliefs and principles espoused by religious and civic groups affect selection and use of material culture, residential accommodations, use of space and household economics. For example, David Starbuck examined how the composition of nineteenth-century Shaker households at Canterbury Shaker Village in New Hampshire was controlled by the Shaker belief system and was, in turn, reflected in architecture and material culture. Lu Ann De Cunzo, in her study of the nineteenth-century Magdalen Society of Philadelphia, Pennsylvania, outlined a contextual approach to the archaeological study of institutions that incorporates anthropological theories of ritual with documentary and material-culture analysis of the Magdalen Society's institutional structure and principles, and of its buildings and their furnishings. Missions, convents, orphanages, almshouses, dormitories and other sites of reform and religious institutions, therefore, can all be examined as specially constituted forms of the household.

Historical archaeologists increasingly have recognised that delineating the life history of a site is a first step towards interpretation and is vital for understanding households and their transformations. Archaeologists working at St Mary's City, Maryland, for example, by plotting the distribution of chronologically diagnostic artefact types and changing ratios of chemicals in plough zone contexts, have been able to identify the locations of middens over time and to trace changes in the use of space throughout the seventeenth century. In a similar vein, Kathleen Wheeler has analysed formation processes at a number of eighteenth- and nineteenth-century sites in Portsmouth, New Hampshire, demonstrating that households are only partly represented by downcutting features and that midden analysis can be more illustrative of the full range of material goods discarded by a given household.

Attempting to build upon the approaches outlined above, Mary C. Beaudry has been developing a way of deciphering complex site formation processes in order to correlate finds from sealed features as well as redeposited materials and the earth-moving episodes that created these secondary deposits with changing household composition, architectural renovations and landscape modification. Her work at the Spencer–Peirce–Little Farm (1630–1986) in Newbury, Massachusetts, makes use of developments that have demonstrated the value of viewing sites as complex matrices, whose sediments suspend not just artefacts but a vast array of data about past household activities. Deciphering site formation processes has been shown to be critical to the archaeology of households; so has the use of a combination of differing forms of contextual analysis – cultural and historical context as well as a close understanding of place derived from ecological data provide for a powerful interpretive framework.

US historical archaeologists have only recently begun to acknowledge that folk beliefs may have affected certain household practices. Archaeologists working in the UK have long acknowledged the significance of such enigmatic features, but US historical archaeologists, steeped in science and statistics, have tended to shy away from attributing anything but the most blatant of objects (e.g. crucifixes, holy medals, etc.) to religious beliefs or folk superstitions. Ritual protection of houses against witches, for instance, may have been responsible for the creation of some intriguing deposits, including a possible witch bottle pit at Julia King's excavations at seventeenth-century Patuxent Point in Maryland and a cat burial beneath the entryway to the house built in 1630 in Charlestown, Massachusetts, for John Winthrop, leader of the Puritan separatist group that founded Boston.

The archaeology of historical households is as varied in its research goals and analytical approaches as is the discipline as a whole. Analysis of middens and feature systems, as well as of artefacts linked to particular families and households, from a range of theoretical perspectives makes household archaeology a rich and continuously productive area of research.

See also: behavioural historical archaeology; consumption; contextual historical archaeology; cultural anthropology; domestic sites; domesticity; probate inventories; prostitution; settlement analysis

Further reading

Beaudry, M.C. (1999) 'House and household: The archaeology of domestic life in early America', in G. Egan and R. Michael (eds) *Old and New Worlds*, Oxford: Oxbow Books, pp. 117–26.

—— (1984) 'Archaeology and the historical household', *Man in the Northeast* 28: 27–38.

Karskens, G. (1999) *Inside the Rocks: The Archaeology of a Neighbourhood*, Alexandria, New South Wales: Hale & Iremonger.

MacEachern, S., Archer, D.J.W. and Garvin, R.D. (eds) (1989) *Households and Communities: Proceedings of the 21st Annual Chacmool Conference*, Alberta, Canada: The Archaeology Association of the University of Calgary.

Mrozowski, S.A. (1984) 'Prospects and perspectives on an archaeology of the household', *Man in the Northeast* 27: 31–49.

Stewart-Abernathy, L.C. (1986) 'Urban farmsteads: Household responsibilities in the city', *Historical Archaeology* 20(2): 5–15.

Wilk, R.R. and Rathje, W.L. (1982) 'Household archaeology', *American Behavioral Scientist* 25: 617–40.

MARY C. BEAUDRY

Huánuco Pampa, Peru

Huánuco Pampa (Huánuco Viejo) was a town founded by the Incas, around AD 1475, after conquering the surrounding region. An administrative and logistical centre along the imperial road from Cuzco, it witnessed critical manœuvres in the civil war (1532). It was deserted in 1541, after the initial Spanish Conquest. The well-preserved ruins comprise features known at similar but less investigated sites elsewhere in Peru. Archaeological and archival investigation here and in the hinterland illustrates Inca imperialism.

The main buildings are spread over 1.5 km^2. There are fourteen key features. The town was laid out in zones, two to either side of the road, around a square of 19 ha. Each zone seems to comprise three groups of buildings. Typical of Inca **architecture**, most buildings were rectangular, gathered around courts, but there were also many modest round buildings. Zone by zone, the rectangular buildings vary in size and/or associated finds: the main zone at the east, interpreted as a palace complex, includes features in metropolitan style; one zone is interpreted as a craftwork quarter, perhaps staffed by women; another was evidently residential but not palatial; and the proportions of crockery found in another zone are thought to indicate mass catering. Amid the square is a monumental platform. There were corrals for pack animals. Overlooking the town are warehouses. Most of the pottery is in the metropolitan style, unlike the regional industries. In the square are the distinctive remains of buildings from a brief early Spanish occupation.

The site is at high altitude. Contemporary settlements in the hinterland were lower. They shared little of the town's features except the round buildings. Yet, Spanish archives indicate that the Incas had required villagers to supply the town and even to work there for short stints (the amount of craft production is in doubt). This paradox and the features at Huánuco Pampa and, hence, at similar sites have been interpreted as follows.

Huánuco Pampa was the regional centre of Inca authority and a depot along the highway. The palace was for passing royalty. The square was for crowds from the surrounding valleys to gather around the monument. Local people trekked up regularly to supply the stores. Those working here were equipped, fed and housed in metropolitan style, at the state's expense. There were permanent residents, too (thought to number at least 5,000). Huánuco Pampa's plan – bipartite with four zones each divided in three – corresponded to the organisation of Cuzco. The town was intended to inculcate official **ideology** but the strategy was at odds with local tradition, hence little or no prior occupation, little diffusion of **material culture** beyond and rapid failure in the Spanish period.

See also: settlement analysis; Spanish colonialism; urban archaeology

Further reading

Morris, C. and Thompson, D.E. (1985) *Huánuco Pampa: An Inca City and Its Hinterland*, London: Thames & Hudson.

N. JAMES

human osteology

The study of all aspects of human skeletal remains has fascinated scholars for centuries and at one time was the principal focus of physical anthropology. The medieval interest in human biology used skeletal studies as the basis for understanding how the body worked in a mechanical way. The study of the human body became one of the basic aspects of anthropological inquiry in the nineteenth century. Anthropological interest in human skeletons developed from three distinct academic concerns, as a continuation of earlier studies that wanted to understand how the body worked. Modern anthropologists put these investigations into an evolutionary and comparative perspective. First, anthropologists want to study modern human skeletons for comparison with the fossil record in order to understand the process of human evolution and diversification. Second, human osteology is linked with primate osteology in order to trace origins of our nearest kin and also to establish the range of differences that separates us. Third, human osteology is an essential aspect of archaeological analysis. Macroscopic studies of human skeletal remains continue to provide the most efficient means of evaluating the ways in which ancient cemeteries were used, and to trace the kinds of disturbances commonly associated with burial areas and other parts of a community in antiquity.

The fundamental goals of human skeletal studies in association with archaeology remain the rapid ability to assess the age and sex of individuals recovered from cemetery contexts. This information enables the archaeologist to evaluate the complex cultural behaviours associated with funerary ritual, such as whether or not zones of a cemetery are segregated by sex or by age. By plotting the age and sex of individuals on a plan of a cemetery, archaeologists are also able to determine the presence of family burial plots, and to trace changes in social organisation at a site. This procedure enabled the excavator of Osteria dell'Osa, the burial zone of ancient Gabii near **Rome**, to understand the dynamics of settlement at an Italian Iron Age site that was the first territory to be absorbed by the developing Roman state.

Human osteological research also can detect variations in age clustering at a site, which reflects the users' views regarding birth and childhood. Each culture has its own understanding of how a newborn relates to the community. By evaluating the age of the individuals in a cemetery osteologists can detect specialised burial areas for perinatals and infants. Of considerable note is the finding that specialised locations within cemeteries, specifically for infants, was an ancient Etruscan custom that still survives throughout most of modern Italy.

Human osteologists can also reconstruct individual stature based on long-bone measurements. This aspect of research was developed in parallel with forensic specialists interested in identifying skeletalised corpses. Now this also can be used to infer diet and nutrition, and to recognise the differential status of individuals within a population. These status differentials often have behavioural differences that can be detected in the musculature as it is seen on the bones. Occupational differences often are inferred on the basis of the skeletal evidence.

Human osteology has become sub-divided into a vast range of specialised research areas. Human palaopathology evaluates diseases that leave their marks on the bone, and can be used to trace the origins and evolution of certain types of disorders. The evaluation of cremated remains continues to be a specialised area of research that is more of an art than a science, but has seen some significant successes in recent years. The study of human teeth was once a small part of osteological evaluation. Recently, many scholars have specialised in this part of the field, with their numbers continuing to grow. In addition to the development of this subspeciality, journals and books specific to dental anthropology are now common. The evaluation of human bone through chemistry also has become an important means by which scholars can explore the human past. The reconstruction of ancient diets tells us much about human adaptation, the development of agriculture and many other aspects of human behaviour. Today, there are considerable numbers of highly specialised aspects of human osteology that attract new scholars, and perhaps the fastest growing area of research involves DNA studies. The processes of extracting DNA from ancient bone is becoming more sophisticated each year. DNA has been isolated from bone up to 25,000 years old, with success using bones of greater antiquity being documented all the time. Many of the more basic tasks of the human osteologist, such as determining sex and racial affinities, may some day be achieved through DNA analysis. At present, human osteology continues to be an essential part of forensic science and physical anthropology.

Further reading

Kieser, J.A. (1990) *Human Adult Odontometrics: The Study of Variation in Adult Tooth Size*, Cambridge: Cambridge University Press.

Price, T.D. (1989) *The Chemistry of Human Bone*, Cambridge: Cambridge University Press.

Ubelaker, D.H. (1989) *Human Skeletal Remains: Excavation, Analysis, Interpretation*, second edn, Washington, DC: Taraxacum.

MARSHALL JOSEPH BECKER

identity

The recognition of social identity has become in many ways the holy grail of historical archaeology. Identity is a complex, multifaceted, dynamic and cultural construct, and is negotiated and recreated through language, **material culture** and other symbols. Elements of identity can be ascribed, assumed or achieved, and is therefore the most personal as well as the most private of individual or group statements, for identity can be enforced or prohibited by law or less formal constraints, resulting in a dissonance between how the actor views himself and how society views him; to a certain extent success in identity negotiation comes from how others accept it. Aspects of identity include: **gender**, **ethnicity** and/or **race**, religion, economic status, social status, prestige status, occupation or political affiliation. These may be quite consciously manipulated in response to outside circumstances or in pursuit of perceived benefit; the ability to create and modify identity is a significant form of **power**. It must also be remembered that each individual is made up of an array of identities, and the complexity of these as they are selectively brought into public or private cultural play is of great interest to the historical archaeologist. In historical archaeology, individual artefacts, assemblages, spatial organisation and a wide variety of **historical documents** all contain clues to identity; problems begin in identifying those clues and understanding what they mean. The importance of considering identity in US historical archaeology was first articulated in the late 1960s and 1970s with the civil rights movement and the women's movement, and was perhaps reinforced by a widespread reconsideration of US history with the US Bicentennial. Since that time, the study of identity has evolved from the simple recognition of identity markers on a site to an increasing emphasis on personal and group agency, and the complexity of social interaction through the study of identity construction, domination and **resistance**, and negotiation. These are questions of primary concern to post-processualist, feminist (see **feminist archaeology**) and Marxian researchers (see **Marxian approaches**).

The problem of identity in the past can be broken into two main issues: the recognition of elements of identity in the ground, in artefacts and in documentary sources, and the understanding of how those identities are viewed both by the actors and by the community around them, which has the potential to answer many questions about social interaction, site and artefact use, and cultural adaptation or persistence. While documentary data are often the best means to pinpointing and understanding cultural identity, the artefactual and stratigraphic records are frequently the only evidence that exists, especially for groups or individuals unable to leave their own record behind. The study of identity must be undertaken with an interdisciplinary approach; the most important contributions come from cultural anthropology, prehistoric research and **ethnographic analogy**, as well as sociology and psychology.

Historical archaeological research finds elements of identity in both the archaeological and documentary records. In the archaeological record, the presence of identity might be read in artefact styles, assemblages and their organisation on a site, and architecture. Additionally, specific artefacts or 'markers' might be understood to signal the presence of a member of a particular ethnic group, gender, religion or class on a site. The presence of women, for example, has often been associated with artefacts related to child-rearing, cosmetics and certain clothing; the presence of Africans or African Americans by blue **beads**, specially marked pottery or '**colonoware pottery**', and the presence of Roman Catholics by the location of a crucifix or rosary beads. Because mass-produced artefacts might be used in ways that are specific to some identity group, archaeologists may be more likely to observe the residue of activities associated with an identity, like foodways (see **food and foodways**), **ceramics** or **architecture**. Theresa Singleton and Mark Bograd, in discussing the African **diaspora**, point out that artefactual meaning is variable and non-discrete. They observe that objects associated with black sites may be derived wholly from African cultures, made by and used by blacks and whites but differently understood by blacks, or may show evidence of African labour. On the other hand, special or extraordinary deposits, like burials, can present superb evidence in isolating characteristics of identity.

The scale of research often determines what is visible and, generally speaking, the larger the sample of a site or a community or region, the better. In situations where there is a high degree of segregation or isolation from a wider community (as in religious enclaves, brothels, military installations, corrective **institutions**, work camps, boarding houses and slave quarters), there may be the potential for better clarity of identity, but the question of legal or social control over the community may be what determines what goes into the archaeological record.

In considering identity as seen in artefacts, it is imperative to consider whether artefacts left behind were the choices of the people who used them. For example, architecture might reflect the regional identity of the house's owner, but it might also represent the builder's knowledge of construction and design. Similarly, consumer availability of certain goods may have more to do with a site assemblage than identity (see **consumption**).

The documentary record is at once more direct and more biased; the former because it can contain direct references to identity (as in church records, diaries, letters, portraits, tax records and historical accounts) and the latter because, quite frequently, those who are disenfranchised, considered insignificant or illiterate are left out, given short shrift or misrepresented with no chance for expression or representation. Portraits or other pictorial representations are similarly problematic; although these commonly represent the elite, portraits are valuable because they represent identity through clothing, jewellery, setting, significant artefacts and even posture or gestures.

Gender, ethnicity, race and class

In a carefully considered essay addressing some of the most compelling and troublesome issues regarding the components in identity in historical archaeological research, Elizabeth Scott describes a 'triumvirate' of gender, race and class, and how each of these elements affects the other. She points out that no part of identity can be studied in isolation, and issues are further complicated by how the perception of these categories is altered by factors like age, sexual preference, religion or nationality. She cogently states a concern that the discussion of gender, race or class will only be applied to women, blacks and workers, because of the erroneous notion that these groups (respectively) have more gender, race and class than middle-class white males.

Rather than strictly falling along the lines of biological sexuality, gender is a cultural construction, observable in the differential participation of men and women in social, economic, political and religious institutions within a specific cultural setting. Margaret Conkey and Janet Spector note how many cultural factors influence the nature of relations between men and women, and that archaeologists should study where and how each group exerts power, in response to cultural and environmental situations.

The study of gender in historical archaeology does not refer solely to the presence of women, but to men and others, too, and it is important not to make assumptions about how gender might appear in the archaeological record. While artefacts that signal the presence of women are considered, assumptions too often leave the question of 'masculine' artefacts unaddressed. For example, if jewellery or cosmetic bottles mark the presence of women on a site, does this indicate that the entire remainder of the material-cultural universe is inherently masculine? The contextual definition of gender roles will greatly affect the interpretation of the archaeological record.

An ethnic group can be defined as an ascriptive and exclusive group, which persists because of an ethnic boundary maintained by manipulation and display of symbols, often material in form. Race, on the other hand, is closely related but more complicated by misuse and its understanding in the past. It can be broadly defined as a group of people sharing common ancestry, but the criteria for inclusion are culturally determined and vague. These two elements of identity are sometimes closely related and often affected by the same issues, although, depending on the cultural context (and as with any characteristic of identity), one may be more significant than the other.

Randall McGuire points out that a common theme in the study of ethnic difference is competition and power, where competition creates the motivation for ethnic identity, and power determines the nature of the relationship between ethnic groups. This implies a need for archaeologists to examine the degree of ethnic-boundary maintenance and understand the disparity of power between groups. Too often the act of identifying ethnic or racial markers in the archaeological record oversimplifies the problem, focusing on the presence of identity rather than the dynamic cultural processes that create, change or sustain that identity.

Class is often studied through money alone or exotic goods, or only as power, but with no further discussion of contemporary notions of social stratification. Class is not as simple as economic situation and is further complicated by occupation, gender, age, religion, ethnicity or race. LouAnn Wurst and Robert Fitts claim that class either has been overshadowed by other social considerations or that it has never been thoroughly considered by archaeologists. Examination of class or status is important, but it may 'blur' other parts of identity in the archaeological record; for example, if the occupants of a site are both poor and part of an ethnic minority, do the artefacts represent poverty or ethnicity? Similarly, social status comes into play, granting higher class status to revered members of the community, such as members of the clergy, who may not be wealthy.

Like other elements of identity, class can be manipulated and defined. Lorinda B.R. Goodwin, in considering the archaeological remains of colonial merchant sites in Massachusetts, USA, found that the elite members of the merchant community consciously manipulated material culture and mannerly behaviour to emulate the British nobility and reify their position at the apex of the colonial urban social structure.

There are issues of identity that come into play in the modern world, outside of archaeological consideration. The ways in which archaeologists study identity may reinforce stereotypes, or the modern experiences of researchers may shape their non-emic definitions of identity. On the other hand, historical archaeological research may help to empower those who are marginalised in the modern world.

See also: class, social; consumption; feminist archaeology; post-processual archaeology

Further reading

Beaudry, M.C., Cook, L. J. and Mrozowski, S.A. (1991) 'Artifacts and active voices: Material culture as social discourse', in R.H. McGuire and R. Paynter (eds) *The Archaeology of Inequality*, Oxford: Blackwell, pp. 150–91.

Conkey, M.W. and Spector, J.D. (1984) 'Archaeology and the study of gender', *Advances in Archaeological Method and Theory* 7: 1–38.

Goodwin, L.B.R. (1999) *An Archaeology of Manners: The Polite World of the Merchant Elite of Colonial Massachusetts*, New York: Kluwer Academic/Plenum Press.

McGuire, R.H. (1982) 'The study of ethnicity in historical archaeology', *Journal of Anthropological Archaeology* 1: 159–78.

Scott, E.M. (1994) 'Through the lens of gender: Archaeology, inequality, and those "of little note'"', in E.M. Scott (ed.) *Those of Little Note: Gender, Race, and Class in Historical Archaeology*, Tucson: University of Arizona Press, pp. 3–24.

Singleton, T.A. and Bograd, M.D. (1995) *The Archaeology of the African Diaspora in the Americas*, Tucson: Society for Historical Archaeology.

Wurst, L. and Fitts, R.K. (1999) 'Introduction: Why confront class?', *Historical Archaeology* 3(1): 1–7.

LORINDA B.R. GOODWIN

ideology

The term ideology has had a long and varied life within Western intellectual traditions, and carries distinctly different meanings when understood through Marxist traditions, as opposed to, for example, eighteenth-century idealist or twentieth-century post-modern traditions. However, in general, ideology can be defined as a body of socially constituted ideas, produced by, and typical of, any group within a society; a world view that is created and replicated in social action. Ideology can further be defined as the ideas and beliefs (whether true or false) that make sense of daily life and the social condition of particular social groups. The Marxist tradition emphasises that ideology describes the ideas and beliefs that dominant social groups use to facilitate and legitimate their power, at times through obscuring the social reality of oppressed groups, at times through gaining the co-operation of oppressed groups. In this sense, ideology can be seen as the misrepresentation of social reality; as used and usable descriptions of how the world should work that reinforce the current social order.

Karl Marx's insight into the ideological aspects of cultures has had a hand in shaping debate in sociology, anthropology, history and philosophy on this topic, and on topics like **power**, **resistance** and **domination**. To some degree, the idea that 'common-sense' views of the world are actually ideologies that shape and order our lives is the underlying premise of much of post-modern thought. Scholars as diverse as Bourdieu, Derrida, Foucault and de Certeau (to name only a few) are working from the premise that, while there are no 'deep structures' within cultures, ideologies and social order offer certain types of structure to the human experience, and to identity. The concept of ideology also continues to play a role in archaeological thought that deals with recursivity and linguistic models of culture. However, a shift away from a call to social action, and a lessening of the political nature of the critique of ideology, typical of Marxist approaches to ideology, characterise the late twentieth-century study of ideology.

Karl Marx and ideology

While the term ideology began its intellectual life during the Enlightenment, Karl Marx and Friedrich Engels transformed the term and our understanding of the social creation of reality, meaning and value. Marx's sense of ideology, society and the movement of history is inseparable from the development of **capitalism** that he chronicles. His works are among the great narratives of modernity in that they evoke a powerful picture of the creative destruction of capitalism. In this sense his work best expresses the workings of capitalist societies.

However, while Marx's ideas were born in the political and economic turmoil of the mid-1800s, his work is also embedded in the tail end of the Enlightenment. Marx held to the image of 'man' as the carrier of liberty through struggle, his theories are grounded in the positivism of the times and his materialism is a direct refutation of the idealism of some of the great late-Enlightenment thinkers such as Hegel and Kant. In an inversion of the idealist position, Marx argued that the ideal is a production of the real, rather than the real being a less perfect copy of the ideal. For Marx, the ideal, society's world view, for example, developed out of social reality and served purposes in everyday life. Nothing in capitalist society (for example the market, commodification or laws of profit maximisation) was natural or a result of human nature. Rather, all aspects of society were the creation of humans, and were thus capable of being changed. Indeed, the ideal often obscured the real circumstances of life (religion as the opiate of the masses is Marx's most famous example). To unmask the ideal as the real was to gain an understanding of the many ways that capitalism alienated and oppressed particular groups within society. Marx's political interests demanded that the insight gained through the unveiling of the illusions that masked social reality, through the critical examination of cultural world view (or ideology), had to be followed by social action.

For Marx, capitalism was not the natural expression of mankind's rational nature, but rather a social and economic system marked by a sharp dichotomy between capital and wage labour. Further, the practices and beliefs associated with capitalism tended to serve those in power. Marx's contention that economic systems and thought and religion are social products also underlies his concept of ideology. Ideology, for Marx, was the generally held and propagated sense of how the world should and does work; ideas that served the interests of capital masked the actuality of social relations, the alienation of labour, the workings of money and so on. Ideology (and human conscious-ness) was grounded in the material realities of daily life; ideology was produced and replicated in social action, and in specific historic circumstances. In this sense of the term, ideology can be seen as the meta-narrative of capitalist life that naturalised all activities of capitalism, and served the interests of those who controlled capital.

Frankfurt school

A number of European scholars of the early twentieth century occupied themselves with the critique of capitalist society, expanding upon Marx's ideas about the modern world and ideology. Working explicitly within a Marxist framework, the Frankfurt school explored such topics as how the ideology of the ruling classes became the controlling force within the lives of the oppressed, and maintained Marx's emphasis on seeking social action.

Antonio Gramsci, in particular, explored ideol-ogy as active struggle. Gramsci saw ideology not as a system of ideas that emanated from dominant social groups, but rather as social practice that was a part of everyone's daily life. Gramsci studied the ways that dominant social groups gained, main-tained and fought for power. In his view, dominant groups had to have more than an ideology to subjugate others; coercion, co-operation and phy-sical force played a role in the success of any social group and their ideology. Ideology was not necessarily forced upon society, but rather was something that had to be accepted by society at large, either by consent or by coercive means. Termed 'hegemony', ideology as social practice can be seen as a way in which moral, political and intellectual leadership in everyday life was estab-lished through the equation of dominant political interests with those of a broader society. Hegemo-nic forms created within society must be won, sustained, renewed and modified, taking into account the interests of the powerless. Hegemony can never entirely be achieved, but may be seen as a whole range of strategies for controlling and organising cultures through which the political interests of particular classes are met, legitimated and made to seem natural.

Building on an understanding of ideology as practice, Theodor Adorno and Herbert Marcuse, writing in the shadow of Nazi Germany, held a very pessimistic view of the ways in which ideology invaded the lives of citizens of the modern world. They took the idea that ideology informed daily life to an extreme, arguing that life is lived within a seamless web of the dominant ideology. The dominant ideology creates subjects who are often unaware that they are inculcated with beliefs that help to subjugate them. Hegemony is gained because ideology is insidious; that is, ideology is a part of people's thoughts, dreams and actions, all of which serve to replicate the social order. In a capitalist system, ideology manufactures the per-sonality and the soul of its citizens. The wants, needs and senses are conditioned by the capitalist system so that willing workers are created; workers who sublimate their needs during the week to become peaceful and productive workers, and become happy-go-lucky weekend warriors con-suming the products of capitalism. In this sense, ideology is a totalitarian system that maintains order by creating people in its own image.

Post-structuralism/post-modernism

Scholars of the mid- to late twentieth century have been greatly influenced by Marx's insight that ideology operates at the interface of power, authority, political discourse and class structure. For Michel Foucault, power or domination in a society works its way into every aspect of life and self so that there is nothing in life that is not in some way an expression of the system of domination. In this sense, ideology as the ideas and practices that legitimate and naturalise the social order dissolves into a generalised idea of all-pervasive power that writes itself on every aspect of society and citizens. Jean Baudrillard holds a similar view of ideology. Baudrillard, commenting from a point of view that can be seen as complete nihilism, challenges the basic premise of the definition of ideology, the belief that there is any reality within social relations to be found, let alone to be obfuscated. Baudrillard suggests that there is no longer such a thing as ideology, in that there is no longer such a thing as reality, only simulations of reality, replications of short-circuited societal referentials promoted through signs. Through the work of these theorists (and others working in the same vein), who generally reject the positivism of Marx and the Frankfurt school, the end of ideology has been declared.

Scholars such as Pierre Bourdieu and Michel de Certeau have not been so quick to discard the concept of ideology and continue to explore its ramifications in daily life. Bourdieu is interested in how the ideologies of dominant social groups play out in the daily life of the subjects. His work explores how ideology is transferred and promulgated through the minutiae of life such as school, work, play and common speech. De Certeau, who also examines how ideology is a part of common social practice, offers one of the few suggestions of how resistance to domination may occur through his examination of how people negotiate daily life. Ideology, or the words of 'priests and kings', offers one structure for life, while the daily actions of the common person rewrite and recreate those strictures. De Certeau thus argues for the possibility of autonomous action within the broader constraints of ideology.

Ideology in archaeology

An interest in both ideology and Marxism rose in the 1970s and 1980s out of, and as a reaction to, the **New Archaeology**. Proponents of the New Archaeology recognised that ideology (in a generalised sense) was a key component of culture, but focused much of their research on economic systems and on culture as humanity's extra-somatic means of adaptation. By the 1980s, archaeologists had turned back to consider humans as creators and users of symbols, and developed an interest in how different cultures thought about and understood their worlds. Symbolic and **cognitive archaeology** developed out of this interest.

Marx's understanding that ideology is grounded in the everyday historical circumstances of life has also influenced current material-culture theory. This key insight provides a way of exploring why ideology is important in the study of archaeology. Material objects create and are created by ideology; they act as recursive agents within cultures and as the building blocks of ideology. Material objects also take their form and meaning from ideology. Thus, within capitalist society, the operation of material objects is inseparable from the operations of ideology. Further, if we study culture, rather than simply human material remains, then the idea of ideology in any of its guises must be part of the inquiry. If culture is to be understood as more than an adaptation to the environment, then ideology, or the way that society and the world around one are culturally organised and replicated, must play a part. Further, because historical archaeologists are concerned with the cultural consequences of capitalism, the Enlightenment and their territorial expression, **colonialism**, we must of necessity be concerned with ideology as a typical operation of capitalist cultures.

See also: Marxian approaches

Further reading

Eagleton, T. (1991) *Ideology: An Introduction*, London: Verso.

Foucault, M. (1977) *Discipline and Punish: The Birth of the Prison*, New York: Pantheon.

Gramsci, A. (1971) *Selections from the Prison Notebooks*, eds. Q. Hoare and G. Nowell Smith, London: Lawrence & Wishart.

Marx, K. and Engels, F. (1972) *The German Ideology*, ed. C. J. Arthur, New York: International.

JESSICA L. NEUWIRTH WITH
MATTHEW D. COCHRAN AND MARK P. LEONE

immigration

Immigration is one form of migration, and involves the geographical movement of individuals or groups. Immigrants are usually individuals and their dependants who enter a new geopolitical location seeking employment that is either permanent, seasonal or temporarily residential. Historical archaeologists separate the study of immigration into areas: the immigration process and the resulting contact situations created by that process.

Migrations are internal or external; voluntary or involuntary; short term or long term; intracontinental or intercontinental; and conservative (preserving a way of life) or innovating (facilitating radical change). The term immigrant is never used to describe people who travel for pleasure (i.e. tourists), short-term business or academic study. In addition, it does not include any resident of a frontier or boundary area who crosses borders while undertaking normal social or economic activities. Generally, the term also excludes refugees. The rise of nation-states produced a need to measure populations, so governments began to require a periodic census. Once populations were measured, governments began to track migrations within their territories. Immigration and migration first came into common use in the late nineteenth century.

Immigration as process

Immigration plays a significant role in defining the structure of a settlement, and, as an ongoing process, it continues to shape life in a settlement over time. Immigrants sometimes move in a 'wave of advance', as Fredrick Jackson Turner viewed the Anglo settlement of western North America. Populations can also move from 'point-to-point', creating 'islands of urbanity' as demonstrated by Donald Hardesty.

Ken Fliess described the demographic evolution of Virginia City, Nevada, between 1860 and 1910. Like most settlements dedicated to the extraction of a natural resource, Virginia City's urban population underwent cyclical boom and bust periods where population shifts mimicked economic changes. Fliess used the US Federal Census to measure the change in Virginia City as it appeared in ten-year intervals. Besides examining changes in

Virginia City through time, Fliess also compared the population statistics with the entire USA. He concluded that, during the census years, Virginia City had a population with a high median age but a low dependency ratio. This structure existed because the process of immigration is a self-selecting force where older, single and childless people (in this case, primarily males) dominated the population structure. These statistics are important because they describe the context of the human lives in the city. Fliess used the demographic data to describe the condition of the 'marriage market'. Initially, the population contained many more males than females. The ratio tended towards balance through time, but never equalised. While males had a higher age at first marriage than females, both the male and female age at first marriage were lower than the national average. In a marriage market with a restricted number of females, it is normal for the average age at first marriage for females to be depressed. The depressed rate for males could have been due to two factors. First, the adult male population was younger on average than the USA as a whole, and this depressed the statistic. Alternatively, it is possible that younger couples self-selected to immigrate to the Comstock.

Immigration, therefore, had a powerful influence over marriages and families in Virginia City, contributing to the social matrix of settlement. Generally, demographic processes significantly shape communities. Immigration influences ethnic identity (see **ethnicity**) and boundary marking by creating pluralistic contexts; creates opportunities for economic networking; establishes vectors for the spread of diseases (see **disease**); and usually provides labour for the activities of mercantile or market **capitalism**.

Annalis Corbin was able to capture the process of immigration by studying archaeological remains from two steamboats that had sunk on the Missouri River. The *Arabia* and the ***Bertrand*** both sank while loaded with passengers' trunks. The contents of the trunks, called 'boxes', were time capsules containing the items that immigrants thought they would need in their new lives, but would be unable to obtain from the markets of the new locale. Besides providing a fascinating qualitative picture of travel, Corbin also developed and tested several hypotheses about the process of immigration. She transformed commonly held assumptions about immigration into explicit and testable assertions, such as 'single men will have a higher frequency of occupational-based items in their boxes and fewer personal effects and household items'. This hypothesis proved true, supporting assertions that single men were more mobile than family units in the westward migration of the USA.

Immigrant communities

Many more historical archaeologists study the result of the immigration process. While human populations have always moved about the earth, the past 500 years have experienced a dramatic increase in the rate, size and distance of population movements. Multiple forces have driven great migrations. Territorial, economic and ideological expansion created colonial relationships that brought the French to **Fort Michilimackinac**, the Spanish to **St Augustine**, the Dutch to **Oudepost I** and the English to **Plymouth** and **Jamestown**. Both voluntary and involuntary migrations have been caused by powerful articulations of capital and labour (Africans in **Port Royal** and **plantation archaeology**, overseas Chinese sojourners – see **overseas Chinese historical archaeology** – and mill workers at the **Boott Mills**). Migrations have been both the result of, and the cause of, biological epidemics and plagues (the **Black Death**, and the Irish at **Five Points**). Other immigrant communities are the result of racist oppression (Jews fleeing the Holocaust, the many peoples in **Palmares**). While immigrants settle either in urban environments or in borderlands and frontiers, the result is nearly always a rich area of culture contact marked by **creolisation**, **acculturation**, **assimilation**, hybridity, boundary marking and ethnogenesis.

See also: Christianisation; consumption; contact archaeology; English colonialism; household archaeology; political economy; Spanish colonialism

Further reading

Corbin, A. (2000) *The Material Culture of Steamboat Passengers: Archaeological Evidence from the Missouri River*, New York: Kluwer Academic/Plenum Press.

Fliess, K.H. (2000) 'There's gold in them thar – documents? The demographic evolution of Nevada's Comstock, 1860–1910, and the intersection of census demography and historical archaeology', *Historical Archaeology* 34(4): 65–88.

TIMOTHY JAMES SCARLETT

industrial archaeology

In a broad sense, industrial archaeology is the study of the causes, character and consequences of **industrialisation**. Industrial archaeology is based on the identification, recording, preservation and interpretation of the material remains of industry, in their cultural and historical contexts. In many respects, industrial archaeology is a subfield of historical archaeology, focused on a specific topic and time period. Many historical archaeologists study industrial sites – investigating past workplaces, the conditions of work and the domestic life of workers. At the same time, industrial archaeology differs from historical archaeology in important ways, especially the interpretive goals and the scale and nature of the material remains that comprise the archaeological record of industry. Industrial archaeologists are often interested in reconstructing the layout and organisation of past production processes, the work skills of past artisans and the decision making of entrepreneurs. They study defunct factory complexes, machinery, the products of factories and the wastes left by production processes. Industrial archaeology is interdisciplinary, sharing methods and goals not just with historical archaeology, but also with architectural history, economic history, the history of technology and museum studies. In the USA, the 'dirt-archaeology' component of industrial archaeology is relatively underdeveloped, and continued cross-pollination between historical archaeology and industrial archaeology will strengthen both fields.

Industrial archaeology was born with a concern for recording and preserving our vanishing industrial heritage. In both Great Britain and the

Figure 18 Ruins of nineteenth- and twentieth-century Pearle Mill, Georgia, before archaeologists
conducted excavations there
Source: Photo C.E. Orser, Jr

USA, the rapid pace of development in the second half of the twentieth century led to the loss of many early industrial sites. Avocational and professional interest groups formed to try to record and preserve key components of the industrial heritage. In the 1960s and early 1970s, these groups spawned ongoing professional societies that began publishing specialised journals in industrial archaeology. The USA-based Society for Industrial Archeology was launched in 1971, beginning publication of *IA: Journal of the Society for Industrial Archeology* in 1975. In Great Britain, the Newcomen Society, focused on the history of engineering and technology, launched the *Journal of Industrial Archaeology* in 1964. In 1973, a more specific Association for Industrial Archaeology was formed in Great Britain, beginning publication of *Industrial Archaeology Review* in 1976. The Society for Industrial Archeology and the Association for Industrial Archaeology are today the major professional organisations in the field.

In addition to the establishment of professional societies, other preservation efforts began in the 1960s. In 1969, the US National Park Service, the Library of Congress and the American Society of Civil Engineers together created the **Historic American Engineering Record** (HAER). HAER works on documenting and recording outstanding monuments of engineering and technology. HAER typically records sites through architectural drawings, historical documentation and photography. In Great Britain, in 1963, the Council for British Archaeology and the Ministry of Buildings and Public Works launched the Industrial Monuments Survey and established a National Record of Industrial Monuments (NRIM). The NRIM was folded into the Royal Commission on Historic Monuments of England in 1981, which was ultimately merged with English Heritage in 1999.

In some ways the early emphasis on preservation and recording individual monuments and sites has stayed with industrial archaeology, hampering its maturation. Avocational enthusiasts are a much more important constituency in industrial archaeology than in historical archaeology. In the past,

many archaeologists perceived industrial archaeology as perpetuating a fixation on objects and
structures with little interpretive emphasis. The
image of railway, bridge and steam engine buffs
engaged in local preservation efforts is partially
true, but forms an incomplete picture of the field.
Industrial archaeology is a growing part of
cultural-resource management projects,
many of which are engaged in survey and
evaluation of a wide variety of industrial sites.
Broader-scale and more interpretive studies are an
expanding segment of the literature, and the
opportunity for additional theoretically grounded
and contextual studies is great. Historical archaeologists have a role to play in the process by adding
their diverse interpretive perspectives to the study
of the industrial heritage.

Industrial archaeologists often modify traditional fieldwork techniques to deal with the nature
and scale of the archaeological record of industry.
Projects often focus on landscapes, transportation
networks, structures and machinery rather than
archaeological artefact assemblages. Landscape
studies require large-scale survey, mapping and
historic map research. Similarly, standing bridges,
factories and **windmills** require specific recording
methods. Many industrial archaeology projects use
architectural drawings and large-format photography to document standing structures. Excavation at
industrial sites, when it does take place, tends to
emphasise exposing large structural features to
interpret site layout, chronology and organisation.
The placement of machinery is interpreted from
footings and fittings, and combined with historical
information to reconstruct past production processes. As in historical archaeology, industrial
archaeologists use a complete array of historical
documents in their studies. For example, researchers use company payroll records to classify jobs and
pay rates, period technical literature to illustrate
machinery design, newspaper accounts to understand strikes and labour conflicts, and fire insurance maps to reconstruct factory layout.

Excavation at industrial sites often generates a
very different artefact assemblage than excavation
at other historical sites: the raw materials for
production; broken tools and machinery parts; and
the waste products and rejects left by specific
manufacturing processes. For example, the archae-

ological assemblages from many **iron production**
sites are dominated by remnants of iron ore,
charcoal or coal, and waste slag left from the
smelting processes. The study of most classes of
industrial artefacts is very underdeveloped, with
the notable exception of the **ceramics** industry.
Archaeologists have collected lots of information
about pottery kilns, production processes, kiln
furniture and wasters, in part to understand the
chronology and manufacture methods for ceramic
artefacts. Even basic typological information is
lacking for most other classes of industrial artefacts,
yet these artefacts do potentially contain significant
information. Manufacturing rejects tell of production failures or worker sabotage. Scientific analysis
of products, or even wastes, can tell about
production methods, the level of efficiency and
the skills of past artisans. These types of analysis are
too infrequently done at historic sites.

In the USA there continues to be a gap between
the main approaches of historical and industrial
archaeology. As a result of different developmental
trajectories historical archaeology is more closely
aligned with anthropology and prehistoric archaeology, while industrial archaeology is more closely
aligned with history and US studies. Historical
archaeologists typically study excavated assemblages of domestic artefacts to interpret lifeways,
while industrial archaeologists typically do little
excavation and study standing structures, historical
sources and museum collections to address questions about past industry. Part of the problem in the
USA rests with HAER. Despite the excellent
standard of much of HAER's work, the role of
archaeology in HAER projects is quite limited.
HAER has trained many architects, historians,
landscape architects and photographers, but very
few archaeologists. In Great Britain and other parts
of Europe, industrial archaeology is much more
closely linked to mainstream archaeology, and
survey and recording projects of industrial sites
are often run by archaeologists. Continued attempts to take an archaeological perspective, and
to bridge the gap between interests in ceramic
sherds and steam engine valves, will create a more
holistic archaeology of industrialisation.

Industrial archaeology can broaden our view of
past industrial sites. Our stereotypical picture
of many industries is based on the limited amount

of structural evidence that survives to the present. For example, historic smelting furnaces are a visible and frequently preserved remnant of the iron industry. Yet, in reality the furnace was only one component of a past iron-smelting site. The air-blast system, casting shed, charging deck, slag dumps, coal heaps and other ancillary structures need to be identified and interpreted to properly understand smelting sites. It is equally important to connect the smelting site to the iron workers' housing, linking the routines of home and work. In many instances the factories and industrial sites that survive to the present are from the most successful, well-capitalised and innovative companies. **Industrialisation** is equally a story of failed experiments, technological dead ends and misguided enterprise, all of which can be explored through the archaeological record of failed industrial sites.

Industrial archaeology can teach us much about historic technology and the skills and experiences of past industrial workers. Studying sites to recreate machinery design, factory layout and past production processes provides direct insight into past technology. In this instance, the archaeological record can show modifications from original designs and changes in processes through time. Many industries in the USA, Australia and other areas relied on the skills of European immigrants. For example, in the mid-nineteenth century, skilled Cornish miners and surface workers emigrated to many emerging mining districts. Studying the spread of Cornish mining and processing techniques gives insight into historic processes of technology transfer and the role of skilled Cornish immigrants in historic mining districts. Historic technology is also well suited for experimental archaeology. Recreating a historic charcoal burn or operating historic machinery shows the skills and work routines of past artisans. Finally, interpretations of past work should explore the social organisation of past production systems and past areas of labour conflict. Industrialisation changed many aspects of work. Studying the responses of people to the often oppressive conditions of work, and to the myriad economic and technological changes taking place, must remain an important goal of industrial archaeology.

Industrial archaeology can help us characterise processes of environmental change, providing a geographic and diachronic interpretation of the landscape wrought by industrialisation. The course of rivers and location of falls determined the distribution of water-powered industries. The distribution of timber, coal, iron ore and limestone shaped the growth of iron-production sites. Industry also altered the landscape. This took many forms, including large-scale deforestation for charcoal iron production and damming and changing river courses for transportation and water power. **Mining archaeology** projects have documented many environmental changes. Hydraulic mining technologies literally carved their signature in the landscape of the western USA. Poor rock piles mark shaft locations; ore processing has left extensive tailings piles; and leaching in underground works has created polluted mining landscapes. Ultimately, there is a strong potential for conflict between archaeological and environmental approaches to these landscapes. Environmental interests in cleaning up past industrial sites has the potential to sanitise our view of the past. Industrial archaeology has an important role to play interpreting past landscapes of industry.

Taking a broad view, industrialisation ranks as one of the most significant processes in human history. No change since the beginnings of agriculture has so profoundly altered human use of the planet's resources. We have reached the point where our technology and our pace of resource use threaten our own existence. Similarly, industrialisation has contributed to many important social changes, from urbanisation to the development of world systems (see **world(-)systems theory**). Industrial archaeology provides detailed case studies of specific industries and the life and work experiences of industrial workers. Through this information, an archaeology of industrialisation, properly conceived and executed, has much to tell us about the cultural and historical character of these significant transformations.

See also: Boott Mills; Harpers Ferry

Further reading

Alfrey, J. and Putnam, T. (1992) *The Industrial Heritage: Managing Resources and Uses*, London: Routledge.

Gordon, R.B. and Malone, P.M. (1994) *The Texture of Industry: An Archeological View of the Industrialization of America*, New York: Oxford University Press.

Kemp, E.L. (ed.) (1993) *Industrial Archaeology: Techniques*, Malabar, FL: Krieger.

Palmer, M. and Neaverson, P. (1998) *Industrial Archaeology: Principles and Practice*, London: Routledge.

Trinder, B.S. (ed.) (1992) *The Blackwell Encyclopedia of Industrial Archaeology*, Oxford: Blackwell.

DAVID B. LANDON

industrialisation

Industrialisation, or the 'Industrial Revolution', refers to recent broad-scale changes in the social and technological organisation of production. In **England**, the USA and many parts of Western Europe, the nineteenth century was the most intense period of industrialisation. Water wheels and steam engines began to power a diverse array of new machines, helping to usher in an era of increasingly factory-based production. Large numbers of men, women and children went to work in the new factories, earning wages rather than farming or producing their own goods. The mass-production methods initiated in the factories increased the range and availability of consumer products. Canals, roads, steamboats and **railways** connected larger areas, moving raw materials into the factories and taking finished products to an expanding market. New farm machinery decreased the need for farm labour, sending people into urban areas and factory jobs. All of these changes had profound social consequences that affected people quite differently based on their position and role in society. Archaeologists study industrialisation by investigating changes in industries, documenting historic technologies, tracing the spread of mass-produced consumer goods, examining the responses of workers to new modes of production and studying the social aspects of these changes for individuals and households.

Industrialisation began in Great Britain in the eighteenth century, especially with developments in coal mining, **iron production** and textile processing. Industrialisation in the USA began with attempts to copy or steal British technology. The US textile industry was aided by a British immigrant, Samuel Slater, who brought knowledge of water-powered machinery with him to New England. Similarly, several early US railroads relied on British locomotive engines for their designs. By the 1820s, some aspects of US industry took on unique patterns, notably the construction of steamboats, large infrastructure projects like the Erie canal and gun manufacturing. The US arms-manufacturing industry, centred in the National Armories at Springfield, MA, and **Harpers Ferry**, West Virginia, USA, developed new methods of standardised and mechanised production, and promoted the idea of interchangeable parts. Mechanised and standardised production methods spread to other industries, contributing to large-scale production of many late nineteenth-century consumer goods.

The study of industrialisation often links historical archaeology to the history of technology. The process of industrialisation was spurred on by many technological innovations such as the water-powered spinning frame, stationary steam engine and the railroad locomotive. However, industrialisation is not just a story of technological change, but also a story of environmental and cultural change. Industrialisation caused profound changes in the landscape. A new infrastructure of roads, canals and railways criss-crossed the countryside. Improved transportation decreased travel time, brought down the costs of transporting materials and increased the size of markets for factory-produced goods. Early factories often relied on water to power machinery. As a result, many industries spread along rivers, building dams and canals to run waterwheels or turbines. Good water power locations attracted rapid development, and the new factories, with adjacent worker housing, became budding urban centres. With the spread of stationary steam engines, the need for water power declined, and factories could be sited near sources of raw materials, good transportation routes, existing urban centres or other locations. Industrialisation also influenced the agricultural landscape. For example, the development of the cotton gin and the mechanisation of the textile industry encouraged the spread of cotton plantations in the southern USA. Cotton plantations exploited the labour of enslaved Africans and African Americans to produce inexpensive raw cotton, which in turn fed cotton textile factories in Great Britain and New England.

Industrialisation is also a story of change in the nature of work and society. The rise of factory production decreased the importance of craft production, as specialised machinery took over the work of skilled craftsmen. New factories and businesses became the primary workplaces, rather than the household. The separation of work from home profoundly altered conceptions of gender roles. Some working-class women took on factory jobs, especially in the textile and garment industries, while wealthier women tried to create idealised domestic environments. Some industrialists tried to take a paternalistic interest in their workers' welfare, building good housing and creating a moral work environment. However, in many instances the new work order included **domination** of the workers by the factory owners and **resistance** on the part of workers. The incredible wealth generated in the factories went disproportionately to the factory owners, increasing social stratification (see **stratification, social**).

Archaeologists study industrialisation in diverse ways. **Industrial archaeology** looks directly at many of these issues through studies of factories, technological change, industrial landscapes and industrial processes. Chronological information about technological change in production methods forms a basic dating method (see **dating methods**) for many common historic artefacts. Historical archaeologists work to interpret the social consequences of industrialisation for individuals or households, examining the spread of mass-produced ceramics, delineating patterns of **consumer choice** in a market economy and studying **ethnicity** among immigrant workers. Studies of workers' households at **Boott Mills** and **Harpers Ferry** examined how domestic **material culture** both expressed and shaped workers' responses to changes in work and society. Industrialisation followed diverse paths in different industries and regions, contributing to a variety of specific technological, environmental and social changes. Documenting these changes, examining their material manifestations and assessing their con-

sequences for individual households are important goals of historical archaeology.

See also: capitalism; commodification; globalisation; political economy

Further reading

Ashton, T.S. (1997) *The Industrial Revolution, 1760–1830*, Oxford: Oxford University Press.

Gordon, R.B. and Malone, P.M. (1994) *The Texture of Industry: An Archeological View of the Industrialization of America*, New York: Oxford University Press.

Hindle, B. (1986) *Engines of Change: The American Industrial Revolution, 1790–1860*, Washington, DC: Smithsonian Institution Press.

Licht, W. (1995) *Industrializing America: The Nineteenth Century*, Baltimore: Johns Hopkins University Press.

DAVID B. LANDON

institutions

Institutions is a large category that encompasses houses of worship, **almshouses** and workhouses; orphanages; hospitals; missions; 'homes' for a variety of social groups; schools; libraries; settlement houses; prisons, asylums; and reformatories. Most of these types of institutions were initially founded privately, and all except churches and settlements were later established as public institutions. Houses of worship and schools date from antiquity, while almshouses and hospitals have existed at least since medieval times. Since 1980, archaeologists have excavated an increasing number of these diverse institutions.

Archaeological research has been conducted in the yards or burial grounds of a few houses of worship. Excavations by Jeanne Ward and Cary O'Reilly at the site of a seventeenth-century Quaker Friends meeting house in Burlington, New Jersey, USA, showed that it had been symbolically built as a hexagon and meals had been eaten but not cooked in the building. In Philadelphia, archaeological research permitted comparison of elite burial customs followed at Anglican Old St Paul's Church with African

American burial customs representing African beliefs retained by the malnourished parishioners at the First African Baptist Church. Suzanne Spencer-Wood has researched how some Boston Jewish synagogues that used Protestant churches chose to adopt some key aspects of Protestant worship and material culture. Archaeological research has been less frequently conducted on monasteries or Spanish missions (see **mission sites**) to **Native Americans**.

Schools encompass a broad category from kindergartens to colleges. It is easiest for archaeologists to study school sites where deposits associated with classrooms and residential life can be separated. In schools where the student body resided in dormitories, archaeologists have been able to evaluate the material remains discarded by the students. For instance, David Singer's master's thesis at the University of Massachusetts at Boston analysed food remains excavated in the yards of eighteenth-century dormitories at Harvard University, which showed that students fished and otherwise supplemented food provided by the university. Excavations by John McCarthy and Jeanne Ward at the site of the mid-nineteenth-century, Methodist-sponsored Hamline University in Minnesota found evidence of alcohol consumption despite rules against it. Excavations directed by Stephen Pendery of the Lowell National Historic Park in Lowell, Massachusetts, USA, at the early nineteenth-century African American Phillips elementary school in Boston revealed the relocation of the girls' and boys' privies in the yard in order to prevent pollution of the water supply, which had made some students ill. At the mid-nineteenth-century John Quincy Adams Public School in Philadelphia, excavations revealed evidence that some students pulled pranks on others by dumping a writing set, a pocketknife and toys down the privy. By the late nineteenth century, schoolhouses were one of the most common public buildings on the landscape and James Gibb and April Beisaw have compared ideal reform-school designs by the state education department with excavated evidence of their implementation at the Oella School House site, in a *Maryland Archaeology* article (USA). In the nineteenth century, most academies and colleges were for only one **gender**.

In a 1994 *Landscape Journal* article, Suzanne Spencer-Wood describes her research on the landscape archaeology of public schools and kindergartens, including playgrounds and gardens (see **garden archaeology**). Nineteenth-century women reformers first privately founded kindergartens and playgrounds for neighbourhood children, often as part of missions or social settlements. Reformers persuaded male governmental officials to support their private neighbourhood playgrounds, including grading the land and planting trees and shrubs. Then reformers convinced city and town officials to adopt kindergartens and playgrounds as part of the public schools. School gardens developed at the same time as, and sometimes in conjunction with, playgrounds. School gardens were created to provide urban children with education that they would have received on the farm in rural areas.

The concept of industrial schools developed from the manual work required in eighteenth-century workhouses, which were also called 'Schools of Industry', because the work was considered training for manual occupations, often in textile production. Increasing immigration in the nineteenth century led to the establishment of industrial schools, sometimes in social settlements. Industrial schools were usually segregated by gender. In his chapter in *The Familiar Past?* (1999), Gavin Lucas researched the division of space in a workhouse girls' school, as well as the segregation by gender and disability in a workhouse complex in Southampton, England.

Social settlement houses were institutions co-operatively operated by reformers to assist in meeting the social needs of working-class neighbourhoods. The settlement movement was founded in the 1880s by male reformers in poverty-stricken East London and was spread to the USA by Jane Addams, who founded the Hull House settlement in 1890 in Chicago. Settlements offered a wide variety of programmes to assist the working poor and immigrants, including public libraries, health clinics, well-baby clinics, day nurseries, kindergartens, playgrounds and after-school clubs and classes to keep children off the streets and help immigrants become self-supporting citizens. In her chapter in *Those of Little Note* (1994), Suzanne Spencer-Wood researched negotiations between middle-class reformers and working-class participants over the material implementation of settlement programmes, including industrial classes in Boston.

During the nineteenth century, institutional 'homes' were founded by social reformers for an increasing variety of social groups, segregated by gender, **ethnicity**, age and condition. For instance, homes were founded for coloured aged women or men, intemperate men or women, and for working women who were African American, Roman Catholic, Protestant or Jewish.

Hospitals in medieval Europe were founded by churches to meet the needs of the poor. Hospitals became secular and public institutions in **England** after monasteries were abolished in the sixteenth century, and in eighteenth-century France as vagrancy increased with the breakdown of feudalism. In the US colonies, hospitals often evolved from almshouses. Bellevue Hospital in New York City began in 1739 as a part of the 1736 almshouse, a site excavated by Sherene Baugher. Benjamin Franklin helped found the first colonial hospital that was not associated with an almshouse: the Pennsylvania Hospital in Philadelphia, founded in 1751 and modelled after charity hospitals in London and Paris. Archaeologists at colonial Williamsburg have excavated the eighteenth-century Public Hospital for the Insane. British archaeologists have uncovered sixteenth-century deposits at the Whitgift Hospital in Croydon, Kent. The research focus for hospital sites has been on the quality of care provided for the patients. In the USA, archaeologists have focused less on public hospitals than on military hospitals, especially those associated with the US Civil War.

Many institutions developed as poverty and crime grew following the agricultural and industrial revolutions in Europe. Protestants argued that the traditional practice of public punishment for crimes and poverty was un-Christian and that the poor and criminals could be reformed by removal from society to institutions that required work to reform inmates into respectable hard-working citizens. Initially, many institutions were organisationally and physically modelled after the home. In the late eighteenth century, reformers proposed more effective punishment and reform of prison inmates through solitary confinement. A few reform penitentiaries were constructed, but most jails and prisons

punished inmates by depriving them of their freedom, food and other facilities.

Total institutions, including asylums, reformatories and prisons, removed inmates from society and completely controlled their lives in an effort to reform them. Archaeologists have seldom excavated these types of sites. Suzanne Spencer-Wood conducted an archaeological survey to identify and locate the unmarked burial ground of the Northampton, Massachusetts, State Asylum (later Hospital) for the insane. In excavations at Philadelphia's nineteenth-century Magdalen Asylum for women and girls who had 'strayed from the path of virtue', Lu Ann De Cunzo found evidence that a new 'home' was constructed following eighteenth-century ideals. Cheap ceramics were excavated that were probably used by the inmates, while excavated unmatched and possibly donated porcelain was probably used by the matron to host visiting benefactors of the institution. Research also revealed evidence of gender dynamics in relationships between inmates and reformers who ran the Asylum.

Penitentiaries or prisons developed in a 1770s English reform movement that combined the concept of a total institution, previously embodied in houses of correction and bridewells, with the concept of using a jail for punishment. Michael Ignatieff pointed out in his book *A Just Measure of Pain: The Penitentiary in the Industrial Revolution 1750–1850* that since the Middle Ages the main function of jails was not to punish inmates through imprisonment, but just to hold prisoners awaiting trial. Few prisoners were punished by being sentenced to jail, since, until the late eighteenth century, punishments were usually public and relatively quick, including warning out of town, whipping, tarring and feathering, stocks, cutting off body parts and hanging. Only a few prison sites have been excavated by archaeologists. In Philadelphia, excavations at the Walnut Street Prison site revealed a predominance of artefacts associated with food preparation and consumption similar to those found at lower-income domestic sites. However, remains were also found of work in the workshops that successfully reformed most prisoners, including hand-made **buttons** and button blanks of bone and shell, a large number of **nails** from the documented nail factory, and pins for sewing. British archaeologists have excavated the building that was the model for the Walnut Street Prison, the seventeenth-century bridewell in Symondham, Norfolk. In Tasmania, Australia, Eleanor Casella directed excavations at the rural **Ross Female Factory convict site** that showed this women's prison was built in the traditional form of a jail, in contrast to the octagonal structure of an urban female factory in Hobart that followed the latest prison reform designs. Casella also researched gender relations in the prison.

Archaeological excavations can provide information about actual institutional practices and the lifeways of inmates that is not available in documents. Documents provide information about the historical context that is crucial to understanding the meaning of material culture found by archaeologists. Documents often describe planned ideal institutional buildings and practices. In contrast, archaeological analyses may provide new insights about the actual material implementation of pre-twentieth-century reforms in education, health care, and prisons.

Further reading

Baugher, S. and Spencer-Wood, S.M. (eds) (2001) 'The archaeology of seventeenth- and eighteenth-century almshouses', *International Journal of Historical Archaeology* 5(2).

Cotter, J.L., Roberts, D.J. and Parrington, M. (1992) *The Buried Past: An Archaeological History of Philadelphia*, Philadelphia: University of Pennsylvania Press.

Spencer-Wood, S.M. (1999) 'The formation of ethnic-American identities: Jewish communities in Boston', in P.P.A. Funari, M. Hall and S. Jones (eds) *Historical Archaeology: Back from the Edge*, London: Routledge, pp. 284–307.

—— (1994) 'Turn of the century women's organizations, urban design, and the origin of the American Playground Movement', *Landscape Journal* 13 (2): 125–38.

Spencer-Wood, S.M. and Baugher, S. (eds) (2001) 'Gendering nineteenth century institutions for reform: Asylums and prisons', *International Journal of Historical Archaeology* 5(1).

SUZANNE M. SPENCER-WOOD
AND SHERENE BAUGHER

interdisciplinary research

Interdisciplinary research involves the close coordination of specialists from a variety of academic disciplines. Historical archaeologists have traditionally worked with specialists in **material culture**, architectural history, **folklore**, social history or **zooarchaeology**. Over the past twenty years, the scope of this kind of disciplinary collaboration has expanded greatly to include a number of specialists from the natural sciences including archaeobotanists, palynologists, phytolitharians, parasitologists, entomologists, soil chemists, dendrochronologists and micro-stratigraphers. Other forms of disciplinary collaboration involve humanist disciplines such as literary criticism, philosophy, environmental history, African and African American studies, US studies, Native American studies (see **Native Americans**) and women's studies

In contrast to most forms of multidisciplinary collaboration, interdisciplinary inquiry involves a greater degree of interaction and active participation on the part of specialists in the formulation of research agenda and sampling strategies. This model contrasts with that of British environmental archaeology where specialists have little or no input into the prioritisation of research problems or excavation strategies. In North American historical archaeology, interdisciplinary collaboration has led to a more sophisticated understanding of the role of material culture and biological forces like disease in the construction of cultural perceptions of race, class and gender. In this sense it represents a truly interdisciplinary enterprise that draws method, perspective and inspiration from both the biological and social sciences in the construction of richly textured portraits of the past.

Early examples of this kind of interdisciplinary collaboration include Kathleen Deagan, Elizabeth Reitz and Margaret Scarry's work in Florida, and palynologist and parasitologist Karl Reinhard, palynologist Kathleen Orloski and archaeologist and archaeobotanist Stephen Mrozowski's study of Newport, Rhode Island. Reitz and Scarry were able to provide a rare look at the biological dimensions of colonisation in their 1985 study of the subsistence practices of the sixteenth-century Spanish colonists of Florida. Despite the preparation of the Spaniards, the New World environment presented many challenges. They needed to re-place Old World cultigens with New World varieties and turned more to wild game then they had in either Spain or the Caribbean. They also needed to adapt some Old World plants to New World environments. All of these steps were clearly visible in the archaeological record, providing the authors with a wealth of information on the processes of adaptation that accompanied the Spanish colonisation of Florida.

The Newport research involved a multifaceted study of artisan and merchant households. Through a combination of historical, archaeological and biological information, the project partici-pants were able to facilitate comparisons across class and occupation lines. The artisan households presented evidence of a diversified economic strategy that involved blacksmithing, the keeping of borders, seamstressing and both gardening and animal husbandry. A heavy reliance on limited yard space for many of these activities resulted in poor sanitation and high levels of disease. This lifestyle contrasted with that portrayed in the image of a shaded, not intensively used yard of a merchant who appears to have spent much of his time entertaining. In their own way, the inter-disciplinary images that emerge speak to different economic strategies and different, materially con-structed identities.

The use of an interdisciplinary approach to examine the formation of cultural identity is also evident in the multi-year study of the **Boott Mills** in Lowell, Massachusetts, conducted by the US National Park Service and Boston University. In the same manner that the Newport study sought to provide detailed micro-environmental data on both health and hygiene, the Lowell study sought to examine the cultural and biological forces that shaped working-class identity. Combined with landscape data and material-culture analyses of ceramics, smoking equipment and personal items, the Lowell study was able to chronicle the growth of working-class consciousness in response to changing company attitudes about their commit-ment to the well-being of their workforce.

The growth of **landscape studies** has also fostered the development of interdisciplinary re-search. Two contrasting views of this approach are provided by Paul Shackel in his study of **Harpers**

Ferry, West Virginia, and Matthew Johnson's study of enclosure and early **capitalism** in Britain. Both published in 1996, these studies employed contrast-ing models of interdisciplinary collaboration. Shack-el's examination of the character of work at Harpers Ferry included a landscape component that em-ployed archaeobotanical, palynological and phyto-lith analysis to aid him in his reconstructions of the changing yardscapes of the community. Johnson drew instead from history, architectural history and landscape studies in his study of the effects of enclosure on the English countryside. Despite their contrasting approaches, both studies demonstrate the importance of reading the landscape in search of broader cultural changes.

Still another example of interdisciplinary colla-boration comes from **Jamestown**, Virginia, where the study of individual archaeological contexts linked their formation to broader political and economic changes. Collaboration between the archaeological team and tree-ring specialists also found evidence that the English arrived during one of the worst droughts of the past millennium. It may well be that these conditions contributed to the high mortality rates among Jamestown's early settlers.

Further reading

Johnson, M. (1996) *An Archaeology of Capitalism*, Oxford: Blackwell.

Kelso, G.K., Mrozowski, S.A., Currie, D.R., Ed-wards, A.C., Brown, M.R., Horning, A. J., Brown, G. J. and Dandoy, J.R. (1995) 'Differ-ential pollen preservation in a seventeenth-century refuse pit, Jamestown Island, Virginia', *Historical Archaeology* 29(2): 43–54.

Mrozowski, S.A. (1999) 'The commodification of nature', *International Journal of Historical Archaeology* 3: 153–66.

Mrozowski, S.A., Ziesing, G. H. and Beaudry, M.C. (1996) *'Living on the Boott' Historical Archae-ology at the Boott Mills Boardinghouses in Lowell, Massachusetts*, Amherst: University of Massachu-setts Press.

Reinhard, K.J., Mrozowski, S.A. and Orloski, K. (1986) 'Privies, pollen, parasites, and seeds: A bio-logical nexus in historical archaeology', *The MASCA Journal* 4(1): 31–6.

Reitz, E. J. and Scarry, C.M. (1985) *Reconstructing Historic Subsistence with an Example from Sixteenth-Century Spanish Florida*, Special Publication 3, Tucson: Society for Historical Archaeology.

Shackel, P.A. (1996) *Culture Change and the New Technology: An Archaeology of the Early American Industrial Era*, New York: Plenum Press.

STEPHEN A. MROZOWSKI

International Journal of Historical Archaeology

The *International Journal of Historical Archaeology* is a scholarly journal published quarterly by Kluwer Academic/Plenum Press. First published in 1997, it was created by Charles E. Orser, Jr, to provide a global outlet for international research in the field. The idea behind the journal was to create a forum for all historical archaeologists, particularly those who were living in and conducting research outside those regions traditionally served by *Historical Archaeology*, the journal of the North American **Society for Historical Archaeology**, and *Post-medieval Archaeology*, the journal of Great Britain's **Society for Post-medieval Archaeology**. The journal defines historical archaeology in broad terms and considers manuscripts from all theoretical perspectives. It also promotes communication among the diverse practitioners of the discipline through its 'Views and Commentary' section.

CHARLES E. ORSER, JR

Ireland

Archaeology in Ireland began in the 1830s, but historical archaeology has only developed in earnest since the 1980s. Given the history of political conflict since the late seventeenth century, Irish archaeology is usually conceived as being divided into research conducted in Northern Ireland (the six counties in the north-eastern part of the island) and in the Republic of Ireland (the remaining twenty-six counties). At the year 2000, historical archaeology is much more developed in Northern Ireland than in the Republic. Archaeological subjects include the English plantation era, **urban**

archaeology and the archaeology of rural settlement.

Irish archaeologists usually say that 'history', or the beginning of a written tradition, began in AD 431 when the pope sent a bishop to Ireland. Historians attribute two fifth-century manuscripts to St Patrick, Ireland's most famous missionary, but no solid documentation beyond this exists before the seventh century AD. Irish archaeologists usually refer to the period from about AD 450 to about 1100 as the 'Early Medieval Period', and the period from about 1100 to about 1500 as the 'Late Medieval Period'. The 'Early Modern Period' extends from about 1500 to about 1700. Archaeology conducted on sites dating after 1700 is usually termed 'Modern' or **industrial archaeology**. Many archaeologists in Ireland believe that the focus of historical archaeology begins with the Early Modern Period, with the beginnings of **capitalism**, and so define the archaeology of the pre-1500 period as **medieval archaeology**. In keeping with European tradition, most Irish-trained historical archaeologists refer to the archaeology of the post-1500 period as **post-medieval archaeology**, whereas non-Europeans working in Ireland refer to themselves as historical archaeologists. Thus, 'historical archaeology' and 'post-medieval archaeology' are used interchangeably in Ireland.

Northern Ireland

Many of the historical archaeologists working in Northern Ireland have been interested in the English 'plantations' in Ulster, Ireland's northern-most province. As used in this sense, a 'plantation' refers to the 'planting' of colonists in the early seventeenth century. Examinations of the English colonisation of Ireland have led to comparisons with the contemporaneous colonisation of North America. In his study of the 'Londonderry plantation' in County Derry, for example, Brooke Blades examined the ways in which English colonists sought to transform the Irish landscape in a manner that was comfortable to them. Understanding how English settlers built their houses and interacted with the indigenous Irish people provides insights for the particularities of English–Irish contact but also serves as a model for the archaeology focused on the interactions between English settlers and **Native Americans** in North America.

In a study similar to Blades's, Nick Brannon excavated at the Brackfield Bawn in County Derry, and provided detailed information about the construction of a plantation bawn, or fortified dwelling. An English planter family built the bawn in 1611. The only seventeenth-century artefacts Brannon found were a few crude bricks, an English roofing tile and a piece of an English dish. The excavation proved important, however, because Brannon used the archaeological findings in conjunction with **historical documents** to illustrate seventeenth-century construction techniques. Archaeological excavations of this sort are important because they help to document details of **vernacular architecture** that may otherwise be lost. Brannon was also able to demonstrate a common problem for archaeologists: that extensive reuse of the building after the seventeenth century had destroyed much of the site's earliest deposits.

Archaeologists have also conducted **urban archaeology** in Northern Ireland. Urban renewal activities in the centre of Belfast in the early 1980s gave archaeologists a rare opportunity to examine the archaeological deposits that remained sealed under the city's streets. Archaeology is especially valuable in Belfast because the city is poorly represented in historic **maps**. In 1984, archaeologists discovered a large, late seventeenth-century rubbish pit while excavating in the area of the old gardens that once stood at the back of High Street. Inside this pit they found **ceramics** from English and continental factories, **bottles**, hand-painted window glass, pieces of corroded metal and numerous animal bones. A careful examination revealed that the bones included the remains of domestic dogs and cats, as well as rats and sheep. The presence of bones from both medieval, native-Irish shorthorn cattle and from imported, longhorn cattle proved that the inhabitants of seventeenth-century Belfast ate sirloin and T-bone steaks and used beef skulls and toes for soups. The information gleaned from these animal bones has been invaluable in providing new information about Irish **food and foodways** in an important urban centre during the seventeenth century.

Further excavations in Belfast in 1990, along a street named Winetavern Street but popularly known as 'Pipe Lane', permitted a fuller understanding of the clay-pipe industry that once operated in the city. Archaeologists collected twenty-seven different types of pipes, including both plain and decorated varieties, manufactured from about 1813 to 1933. The pipe makers had decorated some of the pipes with Masonic symbols (compasses and plumb bobs) and others with political messages ('Home Rule' and 'Gladstone'). Historical accounts provide some information about the city's clay-pipe industry, but the archaeological discovery offers evidence about specific pipe shapes and decorations that may never have been committed to writing. In addition, the discovery of decorated pipes permits a view of what kinds of pipes people wanted – a **consumer choice** matter – and illustrates what political issues the public found important during various times in the past.

The Republic of Ireland

As is true in Northern Ireland, most historical archaeology in the Republic of Ireland has focused on the earliest years of the Early Modern Period. In 1989, for example, Eric Klingelhofer made a brief excavation at Dunboy Castle, overlooking the sea in west County Cork. Dunboy has an illustrious history, being the traditional seat of the Gaelic O'Sullivan family and later the site of a Cromwellian star-shaped fortification (see **fortifications**). It was also the last stronghold in the Province of Munster, the south-westernmost of Ireland's provinces, to resist the Elizabethan invasion of Ireland. Klingelhofer conducted an in-depth study of the arrangement and function of the Elizabethan defences. His discovery of a previously unknown stone wall convinced Klingelhofer that he had found the original wall of Elizabethan defence, a line that may have been constructed by a small Spanish force that had arrived in 1602 to assist the Irish in the defence of their homeland.

In a related project in 1993, Klingelhofer began a multi-year study of Kilcolman Castle, also in County Cork. This square castle is most famous for its renowned resident, Edmund Spenser. Kilcolman was probably built in the 1420s, but Spenser lived there from 1589 to 1598, spending some of his time composing his famous epic poem *The Faerie Queene*. Klingelhofer's efforts to understand the nature of **English colonialism** in Ireland before the institution of the English colonies in colonial Virginia led him to Kilcolman, and his excavations there unearthed pieces of Irish, English and German pottery, a **pewter** spoon, pins, the bronze tip of a dagger scabbard and metal furnishings from trunks or pieces of furniture. Klingelhofer also found plaster, stone, **nails**, burnt timber and window glass from the building itself. As is true of most historical archaeology associated with the homes and properties of famous people, Klingelhofer could find nothing that he could definitely associate with Spenser himself. Nonetheless, his research is important because it provides a further understanding of the living conditions experienced by some people in sixteenth-century Ireland.

Kilcolman Castle is an example of an Irish tower house. Usually rectangular in design and consisting of four or five storeys, tower houses were fortified private residences. Their builders usually outfitted them with numerous slits for archery and **firearms**, and they usually constructed one floor of stone to serve as a protection against fire. They usually built the other rooms with strong oak timbers. Tower houses were popular in Ireland from the fifteenth to the seventeenth centuries, and their remains still dot the Irish countryside.

In a broadly conceived study, James Delle sought to understand how the English used tower houses, like Kilcolman, as an element of their colonial presence in Ireland. Delle was interested in learning how the English specifically used the houses to solidify their control over their Irish subjects and to dominate the landscape by their very presence. Though he did not actually excavate a tower house, Delle adopted a methodology that is common to much historical archaeology: he studied documentary sources in conjunction with the physical remains of existing tower houses. Delle learned that the English developed tower houses as their seats of power by either occupying existing houses or building new ones. In response to this English redefinition of their traditional landscape, the native Irish sought to resist the encroachments by simply moving away. The strategy of self-preservation may have worked for the native Irish,

but it has had a lasting impact on archaeological research. By adopting a plan to keep moving, the Irish left only ephemeral traces on the landscape during the fifteenth to seventeenth centuries. As of 1999, the native Irish settlements have continued to elude archaeologists. On the other hand, the tower houses of the English, massive and stone-built, continue to survive as visible symbols of the English plantation on the Irish landscape.

The archaeological investigation of the nineteenth century only began in earnest in the 1990s. An archaeological study conducted by Theresa McDonald on Achill Island, County Mayo, has a nineteenth-century component. Achill Island, the largest island off the west coast of Ireland, has been continuously occupied for about 5,000–6,000 years, or extending back to the neolithic period. In 1991, McDonald began a multi-year study of the entire history of the island, including a village site known as the Deserted Village. This village is divided into three clusters of tiny, mostly single-room, dry-laid stone houses, about ninety of which still stand in ruins. McDonald's archaeological research is designed to accomplish three goals:

1 to provide a better understanding of the daily lives of the inhabitants of the village, including information about their food and foodways;
2 to document the building remains before they are destroyed by the elements or are the subject of destruction through other means (see **destruction, site**); and
3 to explore the feasibility of creating a visitor centre at the site that can provide public education (see **public outreach and education**) about the island's history and archaeology.

Another project focused on the nineteenth century is Charles Orser's study of rural life in County Roscommon from about 1800 to 1850. By 2000, Orser had excavated portions of three village sites: Gorttoose, Mulliviltrin and Ballykilcline. His research provides information about the way in which villagers were connected to one another, to other villages and to the outside world. At all three sites, Orser found several specimens of imported English-made and native, Irish-made ceramics. The Irish ceramics, or **redware**, provide evidence that the Irish villagers had contacts with a native pottery tradition that probably stretched back in time to the Middle Ages. At the same time, the presence of these wares in association with English wares indicates that the villagers did not entirely give up on their traditional ceramics just because new, imported wares were available.

See also: deserted villages

Further reading

Delle, J.A. (1999) '"A good and easy speculation": Spatial conflict, collusion, and resistance in late sixteenth-century Munster, Ireland', *International Journal of Historical Archaeology* 3: 11–35.

Donnelly, C. and Brannon, N. (1998) '"Trowelling through history": Historical archaeology and the study of early modern Ireland', *History Ireland* 6(3): 22–5.

Klingelhofer, E. (1999) 'Castle of the *Faerie Queene*: Probing the ruins of Edmund Spenser's Irish home', *Archaeology* 52(2): 48–52.

McDonald, T. (1998) 'The Deserted Village, Slievemore, Achill Island, County Mayo, Ireland', *International Journal of Historical Archaeology* 2: 73–112.

Orser, C.E. Jr (1997) 'Archaeology and nineteenth-century rural life in County Roscommon', *Archaeology Ireland* 11(1): 14–17.

CHARLES E. ORSER, JR

iron production

Historical archaeologists, particularly those working in **industrial archaeology**, have often examined locations associated with the production of iron. Though the first use of iron began some time during the second millennium BC, historical archaeologists usually confine their studies to more recent iron production, typically beginning with the Industrial Revolution in the eighteenth century.

Sites of iron production range from large, world-famous industrial centres, such as the eighteenth-century Darby Furnace in Ironbridge Gorge, Shropshire, **England**, to the small, nineteenth-century Jackson Forge in the Iron Range that runs through the State of Michigan's Upper Peninsula. Archaeologists have provided information about the colonial history of iron production, such as at the Saugus Iron Works in Massachusetts. In operation from 1646 to 1668, the Saugus works represented the first integrated ironworks in North America. Archaeologists interested in iron production also conduct research on the lives of the men and women who were associated with iron production and provide information that site interpreters can use to present information to the public about the history of iron manufacture and the social, political and environmental impacts of this production.

Archaeological research at the Fayette Historic Townsite in Michigan, USA, provides an excellent example of what historical archaeologists can offer to the study of iron production. Fayette, located on the southern coast of the Upper Peninsula at the northern tip of Lake Michigan, was an iron-producing boom town operated by the Jackson Iron Company from the 1870s to 1891. The State of Michigan in 1959 began a programme of restoration, preservation and interpretation, and today the town serves as a living museum (see **living museums**), containing numerous buildings, including labourers' log cabins, a blacksmith shop, boarding houses and a complete iron-producing industry composed of a blast furnace complex, charcoal and lime kilns, and a limestone quarry.

Excavations carried out during the 1980s at the town site revealed that the workers' families lived in a humble fashion in houses that contained just over 37 m^2 of living space and had few windows. Most of the **ceramics** used by the families were inexpensive, undecorated wares and the excavated animal bones reveal that they ate low- and medium-priced cuts of meat.

Archaeologist Peter Schmidt produced an innovative and important archaeological study of iron production in Tanzania, East Africa, in the 1970s. Schmidt, who was actually interested in the Iron Age in the Lake Victoria region (dating to about 500 BC–AD 500), termed his research 'historical archaeology' because he used oral tradition to determine the locations of Iron Age iron-smelting sites. This use of oral tradition is somewhat commonplace in historical archaeology and it demonstrates the importance of using many sources of information. Schmidt's innovation, however, was to use orally gathered information to examine a period of prehistory.

CHARLES E. ORSER, JR

ironstone

Ironstone or ironstone china was introduced by manufacturers in **Stoke-on-Trent** in the early nineteenth century, but it was neither china nor stoneware, and it did not contain iron. It was an earthenware originally developed as a durable, affordable alternative to – and copy of – Chinese porcelain, whose commercial importation into Britain all but ceased from the early 1790s.

Several leading manufacturers made ironstone bodies of a similar type. In 1800, William and John Turner of Longton applied for a patent for their body, known as 'Turner's Patent', while, from 1805, Josiah Spode of Stoke made a similar body under the name 'Stone China' or 'New Stone'. The best known of the ironstone chinas was Mason's Patent Ironstone China. Introduced by Charles James Mason of Fenton in 1813, it was to become the most successful of these new bodies and is still manufactured today.

Numerous recipes were used for ironstones, but all included significant proportions of china clay, china stone and calcined flint, together with other clays and other raw materials. The ware was thrown or moulded, twice-fired, lead-glazed and decorated in the manner of other contemporary refined earthenwares, although ironstone bodies appear more dense and more highly vitrified than earthenwares, and their glazes frequently have a blue tint.

The name 'ironstone china' came to be widely used; it suggested both strength and delicacy in the fine-quality wares, the most ornate and most expensive of which were lavishly decorated with printed and painted designs in Chinese and Japanese styles. The highly decorated ironstone chinas were mainly produced as dinner and dessert services, and as teawares, guaranteeing a market among the more affluent tradesmen and gentry classes. Quality ironstone china remained desirable throughout the nineteenth century.

Most British pottery manufacturers of this period produced an ironstone-type body. Trade names such as 'Stone China', 'Semi Porcelain', 'Granite China', 'Opaque China' and 'Semi China' were used, but these can be misleading as manufacturers frequently used the names on their standard earthenwares, thereby enhancing the status of their cheaper products. Indeed, many of the less elaborate ironstones of the middle decades of the nineteenth century are difficult to distinguish from standard earthenwares, whether pearlwares (see **pearlware**) or white wares, and a thicker body can be the only clue. All used identical printed decoration in blue, pink, purple, green and grey, and many vessel forms occur across the range of earthenware types. These single-colour printed wares were cheaper than the fine printed and painted ironstone chinas, and were widely used in Britain, the rest of Europe, North America and elsewhere. Two printed types that were made mainly for export, however, are the flow blue, and flow mulberry ironstones, which were not to British taste.

During the 1840s, the potters of Stoke-on-Trent began to produce undecorated wares in an ironstone-type body. 'White ironstone' was a deliberate attempt to secure a significant market in North America by catering for the North American taste for undecorated wares in the latest moulded shapes. The name 'White Granite' created a separate identity for this undecorated ironstone and became widely used for the exports to North America. James Edwards, potter of Dale Hall in Stoke-on-Trent, is generally credited with developing and promoting white granite, but, whether this is correct or not, the ware was to become the most significant of north Staffordshire's ceramics exports to North America during the period 1850–80.

White granite was available as tea (see **tea/tea ceremony**), table, kitchen and toilet wares. Vessels are mostly press-moulded and comprise either heavy lobed, faceted or ribbed forms, or else they have leaf, flower or wheat designs moulded in relief. Additional surface decoration is occasionally found, but is largely restricted to overglaze painted leaf or flower sprigs, painted bands of enamel colour or lustre, or applied moulded reliefs that may be lustred. The ware is blue-grey in appearance and has a similar appearance to more expensive French porcelain – fashionable in North

America at the time – whose elegant forms it imitated. Its relative low price and durability ensured its widespread use. Some contemporary commentators recommended it for hotel and steamboat use, while others regarded it as clumsy but durable. White granite, the undecorated ironstone preferred in North America, was not used in Britain; it was made solely for export.

Many potteries in Stoke-on-Trent, Scotland and north-east **England** were producing white ironstone wares for export, and a number of large north Staffordshire firms specialised in granite and other wares for the North American trade. Manufacturers often marked their wares with printed or impressed marks and many bear diamond registration marks, which give the date upon which forms were registered. White granite forms are therefore easily datable, providing valuable evidence in an archaeological context.

White ironstone remained an important export to the end of the nineteenth century, although after the mid-1870s there was a gradual decline in its popularity. Initially, white granite, while never expensive, was only slightly cheaper than printed wares. British potters began to experience competition in the market from US and Canadian factories, which began to produce white granite during the 1870s. However, neither rapidly increasing production in North America nor high import duties significantly affected the import of British-made white granite wares, which remained a significant item of consumption to the end of the century. Ironstone-type wares are still made today as the ubiquitous hotel wares of firms such as Dudson and Steelite.

Further reading

Ewins, N. (1997) '"Supplying the present wants of our Yankee cousins": Staffordshire ceramics and the American market, 1775–1880', *Journal of Ceramic History* 15: 1–154.

Godden, G.A. (1999) *Godden's Guide to Ironstone Stone & Granite Wares*, Woodbridge: Antique Collectors' Club.

Miller, G.L. (1991) 'A revised set of CC index values for classification and economic scaling of English ceramics from 1787 to 1880', *Historical Archaeology* 25(1): 1–25.

Stoltzfus, D. and Snyder, J.B. (1997) *White Ironstone: A Survey of Its Many Forms, Undecorated, Flow Blue, Mulberry, Copper Lustre*, Atglen: Schiffer.

Sussman, L. (1985) *The Wheat Pattern: An Illustrated Survey*, Ottawa: Parks Canada.

Weatherbee, J. (1996) *White Ironstone: A Collector's Guide*, Dubuque: Antique Trader Books.

DAVID BARKER

J

Jamestown, Virginia, USA

Jamestown Island, Virginia, is situated approximately 45 km (30 mi) inland from the Chesapeake Bay on the James River. The location of England's first permanent New World settlement, established in 1607, Jamestown served as capital of the Virginia colony until 1699. Archaeological research began in the 1890s, enjoyed federal sponsorship in the 1930s and 1950s, and was revived in the 1990s by two projects, one carried out by the US National Park Service (NPS) with the Colonial Williamsburg Foundation, and the other spearheaded by the Association for the Preservation of Virginia Antiquities (APVA).

Long celebrated as the birthplace of an English-speaking nation, Jamestown is also the birthplace of modern historical archaeology. Excavations began following the 1893 donation of a 9 ha parcel to the APVA, which included the only above-ground trace of seventeenth-century Jamestown, a brick church tower. Here, APVA founder Mary Jeffrey Galt directed archaeological work to inform the reconstruction of the church. In the midst of preparations for the 1907 tercentennial, the nation took its first legislative step in historic preservation by passing the 1906 Antiquities Act to protect federally owned historic resources. The Act granted protection to Jamestown's archaeological resources when 600 ha (excluding APVA property) were acquired for the Colonial National Monument (now Colonial National Historic Park) in 1934.

The major archaeological initiatives sponsored by NPS in the 1930s and 1950s legitimised colonial-period archaeology. When excavations began in 1934, US archaeologists were primarily trained in excavating Native American sites (see **Native Americans**), unaccustomed to the artefacts and **architecture** associated with **English colonialism**. Following the model established by the **restoration** of nearby Williamsburg, Virginia, which relied upon architects to unearth the eighteenth-century capital, the Jamestown project employed separate teams of architects and archaeologists. In 1936, archaeologist and architectural historian J.C. Harrington assumed leadership, unifying the project and setting an example for the excavation and analysis of historic sites and artefacts. Harrington and his team, consisting mainly of African American Civilian Conservation Corps enrollees, discovered fifty-two buildings including brick rowhouses, seventeen wells, brick-, pottery-, and lime-kilns, paved walks, drains, boundary ditches, fence lines and road traces. Excavations were halted by the Second World War.

In 1954, archaeologists John Cotter, Edward Jelks, Bruce Powell, Joel Shiner and Louis Caywood were recruited to spearhead another archaeological initiative at Jamestown, in preparation for the 350th anniversary in 1957. Nine km of trenches were excavated across the town site, unearthing additional brick rowhouses, seven more wells, manufacturing zones and landscape features. In 1958, John Cotter's comprehensive report on Jamestown archaeology was published, interpreting the findings from 1934 to 1956 and providing a reliable guide for future investigations.

In 1992, the NPS implemented the Jamestown Archaeological Assessment (JAA), carried out via a co-operative agreement with the Colonial Williamsburg Foundation, partnered with the College of William and Mary. An interdisciplinary group of researchers performed a holistic evaluation of all cultural resources present upon the publicly owned portion of Jamestown Island. All artefacts, field notes, maps, photographs and reports from previously excavated archaeological features were re-evaluated. Emphasis was placed upon reconstructing the total townscape, with spatial artefact analysis revealing three peaks of development activity, in the 1630s, 1660s and 1680s, related to town-building initiatives. Historical data were culled from public and private documentary, cartographic and pictorial sources, providing a complete reconstruction of property ownership and, with the aid of computerised drafting, a reliable association of structures with their owners.

Limited and directed excavations were undertaken throughout the town site, revisiting sites that had been poorly recorded or understood in the past, also testing **new technologies** such as geophysical surveying methods and environmental **sampling** techniques. The homes and workplaces of ordinary artisans were investigated, while re-examination of Jamestown's rowhouses revealed that they were speculatively built, poorly maintained and seldom inhabited by elites as previously believed. A revised understanding of the capital town, and in particular the haphazard nature of its growth, development and demise in the context of English colonisation and **globalisation**, emerged to guide future research and resource management, while a systematic survey of the island located fifty-eight new sites chronicling Native American activity, seventeenth-century settlement and the establishment of slave-based tobacco plantations in the eighteenth and nineteenth centuries. Geological and **environmental reconstruction** of the island delineated changes in natural resources, with a study of cypress **dendrochronology** pinpointing the drought conditions that exacerbated the adverse conditions faced by early colonists.

In 1994, the Jamestown Rediscovery Project implemented a programme of extensive open-area excavations on the 9 ha APVA property. Rediscovery archaeologists uncovered remains of the 1607 to *c.* 1625 James Fort, formerly thought to have been destroyed by river erosion, including one bulwark, palisade lines, pits, an internal earthfast structure and an associated cellar-set earthfast building. Early colonial human remains were excavated, analysed and displayed with the support of the National Geographic Society. Over half of the 350,000 excavated artefacts date to the early seventeenth century, revealing a material influence from the Low Countries as well as from England, while also reflecting the military nature of life in the fort and hinting at economic relations with Native Americans. Both the JAA and Jamestown Rediscovery projects have actively promoted **public outreach and education** and the NPS and APVA are co-ordinating efforts for joint interpretation of Jamestown and its archaeology for the 2007 anniversary and beyond.

See also: Chesapeake region; contact archaeology;

Further reading

Blanton, D. (2000) 'Drought as a factor in the Jamestown colony, 1607–1612', *Historical Archaeology* 34(4): 74–81.

Cotter, J.L. (1958, reprinted 1994) *Archaeological Investigations at Jamestown Virginia*, Special Publication 32, Richmond: Archaeological Society of Virginia.

Horning, A.J. (1998) 'Journey to Jamestown', *Archaeology* 51(2): 56–63.

—— (1995) '"A verie fit place to erect a great cittie": Comparative contextual analysis of archaeological Jamestown', doctoral dissertation, University of Pennsylvania.

Kelso, W.M. and Jamestown Recovery Team (2000) *Jamestown Rediscovery: Search for the 1607 James Fort*, Charlottesville: University Press of Virginia.

Rehm, K.G. (ed.) (1999) 'Jamestown Island revisited', *Cultural Resource Management* 22(1): 2–23.

AUDREY J. HORNING

L

La Isabella, Dominican Republic

La Isabella was founded by Christopher Columbus on the northern coast of what is now the Dominican Republic in September of 1493. The settlement that he had left on his first voyage had been destroyed by the local Taino Indians. The town was built on a poor harbour, which may reflect either a hasty decision by weary voyagers wanting to put the disappointment of the first settlement behind them or it could indicate an inward focus to the gold-bearing Cibao valley to the south. The 1,500 settlers soon fell to squabbling among themselves and with the local Taino Indians. The location proved such a handicap that within two years the colonists were moving to the southern coast of the island. La Isabella was completely abandoned less than three years later.

The site of Isabella, unlike most of the rest of the sixteenth-century Spanish settlements on Hispaniola, was never lost and in fact lives on as the modern-day village of El Castillo. However, no systematic archaeological work was undertaken there until the late 1980s when the Venezuelan Universidad Nacional Experimental Francisco de Miranda teamed with the Dominican National Park Service and the University of Florida. Work centred on the fortified main town, which housed a church and cemetery, customs house, powder house and Columbus's own walled residence. Across the bay, the unfortified village of Las Coles (Ciudad Marta) was located and several residences and a pottery kiln were excavated.

Excavations recovered a wide variety of fifteenth- and sixteenth-century artefacts and features. The military nature of the settlement is revealed in the fragments of cannon, arquebuses, chain-mail and brigantine armour, sword parts and lead shot recovered from the fortified village. However, the Spaniards also came to settle and trade with the native inhabitants as is evidenced by majolica sherds, wrought **nails**, chamber pots, oil lamps and personal adornments that littered the site. Taino Indian **ceramics** and zemis (religious symbols) were found intermixed with the Spanish material. A cache of mercury and broken crucible fragments belied the gold-prospecting purpose of the colony. Many of the structures were constructed of stone and tapia, packed earth covered with lime plaster.

La Isabella represents Spain's initial foray into colonising the New World. Having no other model, it was patterned wholly after the Old World. Subsequent settlements would try to improve on the model by implementing new ideas in urban planning, intermixing with the local population and making better use of the indigenous resources.

See also: Spanish colonialism

Further reading

Deagan, K.A. and Cruxent, J. (1997) 'Medieval foothold in the Americas', *Archaeology* 50(4): 54–9.

Stahl, A. (1992) 'The coins of La Isabella, 1493–1498', *The Numismatist* 105: 1,399–402.

CHARLES R. EWEN

La Purisima Mission, California, USA

The site of La Purisima Mission, located in present-day Lompoc, California, was established in 1812 by the Spanish missionary Fermin de Lasuen in December 1787. This first mission, now known as Mission Vieja de la Purisima, was destroyed by earthquake in 1812, and a new mission was built approximately 6 km north of the previous location. The mission was part of the Spanish colonial enterprise in California and was one of over twenty missions built along the Pacific Coast.

The ruins of the original mission can still be seen in Lompoc, but, beginning in the 1930s, attention turned towards the second mission, and efforts were begun to restore its dilapidated ruins. Restoration work began in 1934, when the Union Oil Company and the Roman Catholic Church, the then-owners of the site, donated it to the state. The first excavators at the site were members of the Civilian Conservation Corps, who, in the 1930s, explored the Native American barracks and the blacksmith shop. In 1951, a crew, under the direction of Norman Gabel, excavated the northern part of the barracks, but the best-known and most important investigations occurred in 1962, under the direction of James Deetz. Unlike the earlier work, which was largely geared towards the recovery of architectural information, Deetz's research was designed as overtly anthropological. His goals were to learn as much as possible about the material conditions of early nineteenth-century life at a California mission and to collect information about the **acculturation** of the Chumash Indians who were served by the site's missionaries.

Deetz's excavations provided specific information about tanning vats at the mission and the tile water pipes that fed the vats; the blacksmith shop; the Native American barracks; and a dump site near the blacksmith shop. The excavation of seven rooms in the barracks made it possible for him to compare and contrast the findings within each room. These comparisons allowed Deetz to propose some preliminary conclusions about the nature of Chumash acculturation at the mission.

His analysis suggested, for example, that the traditional roles of Chumash men changed more than did female roles. He tracked this change, for the men, from a decrease in chipped stone artefacts – those traditionally associated with hunting, the manufacture of weapons and the dressing of skins – and for the women, the continued presence of basketry and objects associated with milling, two traditional elements of their lives. Deetz also compared the artefacts from the barracks with artefacts collected from a Chumash village located only 38 km away. This comparison showed that the residents of the village had more chipped stone, shell beads, shell ornaments and ground stone artefacts than the natives at the mission, and that the mission dwellers had more **earthenware** and **porcelain**, and more iron, copper, bronze and brass objects than did the village residents. The natives living at the mission were thus deemed to have been more acculturated than the village residents.

Several theoretical problems exist with Deetz's comparisons, most notably that the village dated much earlier than the mission. This disparity means that the differences noticed by Deetz may simply have been related to temporal changes and adaptations rather than to acculturation. Even though this represents a major problem with his conclusions, his research at La Purisima Mission stands today as a pioneering effort to use data from historical archaeology for anthropological purposes.

See also: Mission Santa Clara; mission sites; Spanish colonialism

CHARLES E. ORSER, JR

laboratory methods

Laboratory methods involve all those processes archaeologists must regularly perform with the artefacts and other materials they excavate. The processes include washing, conservation (see **conservation, terrestrial**), cataloguing, drawing and photographing, analysis and storage. Most archaeological projects will have both a field laboratory, for concurrent use with the fieldwork, and a permanent laboratory for final analysis and long-term storage.

The size and duration of an archaeological project will determine the complexity and permanence of the field laboratory. At a minimum, however, every laboratory established in a field camp is equipped with facilities that will permit the washing, initial conservation and cataloguing of the collection. These facilities, and others of a more stationary character, also appear in the permanent laboratory.

The laboratory analysis is the 'hidden' part of archaeological research, seldom recognised as necessary by non-professionals. Laboratory analysis, however, is more time consuming than the fieldwork, and professional archaeology without it would be impossible. It is not too strong to say that archaeology conducted without the benefit of sustained laboratory work is little better than **looting**.

The field laboratory

All excavated materials enter the field laboratory to be washed, inventoried and packaged for transport. The 'washing' of artefacts refers to the removal of earth from the object. The object's material of manufacture will determine the amount and degree of washing because some items made of delicate materials, such as bone, shell and leather, should be washed with extreme caution, if at all. The object of washing is merely to remove the earth to facilitate identification and preservation, not to make the object look like new. Some objects regularly found by historical archaeologists, such as glass **beads** and white-clay smoking pipes (see **pipes, smoking**), may not be completely washed in the field, as it may be difficult to remove the earth from inside the bead's tiny perforation or the pipe stem's small bore. Final washing of these items can be completed in the permanent laboratory or, if possible, completed in the field laboratory. In all cases, however, the washing of artefacts is done with a soft-bristle brush with a minimum of pressure exerted on the artefact. The object is not to harm the specimen in any way.

Archaeologists will occasionally 'block-lift' an artefact from its original location. This process involves the simultaneous removal of the artefact and a bit of the surrounding soil to minimise destruction and to facilitate the recovery of tiny pieces. Technicians will usually remove the earth from around block-lifted artefacts in the field laboratory, though in some cases the work will be completed in the permanent laboratory.

The field laboratory workers will also process the flotation samples. Flotation is a process whereby soil samples that are thought to contain tiny organic materials and artefacts, such as hearths or pits, are agitated in water. Flotation can be accomplished either manually or with the aid of a simple machine made with a large metal or plastic barrel and a supply of running water. The idea behind flotation is that lighter materials (the 'light fraction') will float to the top of the water and can be scooped up with a small-mesh screen, while the heavier materials (the 'heavy fraction') will sink to the bottom. Technicians, in either field or permanent laboratories, will examine the resultant flotation samples, often with a microscope, to determine what materials they contain. This analysis helps archaeologists to reconstruct the subsistence and environmental conditions faced by the residents of a past site. It is not uncommon for historical archaeologists to find small artefacts like glass beads in their flotation samples.

The initial conservation of artefacts is also completed in the field laboratory. Laboratory technicians will begin the preservation of fragile artefacts to facilitate their transport to the permanent laboratory. Field archaeologists with large projects will often employ a full-time, professionally trained conservator if they have reason to believe that they will uncover a large number of significant, fragile materials. This is particularly true when they expect to find significant perishable materials, such as seeds and other organic materials. The conservators will also pack both the delicate and the more stable artefacts for transport or shipping to the permanent laboratory.

'Cataloguing' refers to the process of inventorying and labelling the artefacts found during excavation. Each artefact will be assigned a unique acquisition number that must be written, as small as is legible, on the object with ink. Archaeologists are required by law to follow the procedures outlined by the governmental heritage agency of the countries in which they work. The numbers inscribed on the artefacts are linked to a master finds list that contains all possible information about the object's original provenance, or find spot at the site. These numbers ensure that the precise archaeological location of every specimen can be determined, even after they have been removed for display or prolonged study. Many excavators also use the term 'cataloguing' to refer to the process of completing a catalogue card for every artefact found during excavation. These cards carry the provenance information and a rough, though accurate, drawing of the object, and serve as a lasting record of the artefacts. This part of the cataloguing process is particularly useful if the artefact collection is to be stored at a permanent location beyond easy access by future archaeologists.

The permanent laboratory

The permanent laboratory will be at the archaeologist's home base, either a university or, increasingly, a private consulting firm. The laboratories of historical archaeologists will optimally contain several long tables, have good lighting and provide plenty of work space. All excavated artefacts and other materials are brought to this laboratory for final conservation, analysis, documentation and interpretation.

After all excavated artefacts are brought in from the field, the work of final analysis and interpretation begins. Much of the work that must be performed in the permanent laboratory concerns the 'cross-mending' or assembly of artefacts that were recovered in several pieces. The assembly of broken artefacts can provide information about vessel usage by a household, the way in which an artefact was broken and deposited, and even whether a site was disturbed after it was abandoned. For example, a **pearlware** plate broken into twenty pieces and found across an entire house lot may indicate that the yard was mechanically scraped some time after the plate was deposited. This kind of information is important for understanding the entire history of a site, or what is termed the 'formation processes'.

Cross-mending of sherds can also provide information about the decorative motifs desired by, or available to, the members of a former household. In the case of transfer-printed whiteware vessels, for instance, the assembly of sherds can indicate the presence of particular patterns and

even sets of dinnerware at a site. These patterns can help in dating a site's occupation periods.

The photography and drawing of finds will also occur in the permanent laboratory. The pictures will be used to illustrate archaeological reports, publications and websites, and can also be used for comparative purposes by other archaeologists.

Archaeological laboratories will also contain machines that can be used to conserve artefacts. For example, many laboratories, particularly those associated with underwater archaeology, will contain electrolysis machines that carefully remove rust and concretions from iron objects. More specialised, permanent laboratories will contain other sophisticated conservation facilities.

The permanent laboratory will also contain microscopes, reference books and other research materials needed for the proper identification and interpretation of the finds. The use of out-of-date merchandise catalogues is particularly useful to historical archaeologists when attempting to identify and date mass-produced artefacts.

Further reading

Banning, E.B. (2000) *The Archaeologist's Laboratory: The Analysis of Archaeological Data*, New York: Kluwer Academic/Plenum Press.

CHARLES E. ORSER, JR

Lake Innes Estate, Australia

Situated on the northern coast of New South Wales, **Australia**, the Lake Innes Estate was an early colonial development that depended on unfree labour provided by assigned (convict) servants. Comprising an elite residence and associated facilities mainly constructed in the 1830s, the estate provided a base from which its owner, Major Archibald Clunes Innes, could develop his extensive agro-pastoral and commercial interests in the immediate region, at that time on the edge of European settlement. Born in Scotland in modest circumstances, he had arrived in Australia in 1822 in charge of the guard on a convict ship, gained entry to the highest levels of **Sydney** society and married one of the daughters of Alexander Macquarie, the most senior public servant in New South Wales. Innes and his wife obtained land grants in the Port Macquarie district and, throughout the 1830s and 1840s, lived affluently at Lake Innes House, dispensing generous hospitality to numerous visitors. Innes clearly saw himself as part of an emerging Australian landed aristocracy but the 1840s economic depression, environmental difficulties in the area, unwise investments and an extravagant lifestyle sank him deeply into debt. Also, in New South Wales, the ending of convict assignment to private individuals in 1838 and the abolition of convict transportation in 1840 meant that, henceforth, labour had to be paid for. In the early 1850s, he left the estate to seek paid government employment and, by 1857, he was dead. Lake Innes House and its associated facilities gradually decayed, being unoccupied by the end of the century and a ruin soon after. By the 1990s, it had been extensively vandalised but is now protected by the New South Wales National Parks and Wildlife Service.

The archaeological remains at Lake Innes consist of the substantial brick ruins of the house, stables and servants' accommodation, and the sites of a 'convict' village', a 'home farm', a boathouse, several brickyards and former roads. This extensive complex offers opportunities to investigate archaeological manifestations of socioeconomic differences indicated by historical documentation, differences that ranged from the comfortable life of the Innes family, through a hierarchy of servants (both free and bond) to the most humble convict labourer. Excavations and other research have shown how at one end of the scale the Innes family enjoyed such facilities as flush-toilets with transfer-printed ceramic bowls made by the famous British Wedgwood pottery, while at the other end some of their convict servants lived in earth-floored huts with unglazed windows. The Lake Innes Estate provides, indeed, an Australian version of the **plantation archaeology** that has been studied in other parts of the world into which European settlement expanded.

Further reading

Connah, G. (2001) 'The Lake Innes estate:

Figure 19 High-status brickwork at Lake Innes Estate, Australia
Source: Photo: G. Connah

Privilege and servitude in nineteenth-century Australia', *World Archaeology:* 33: 137–154.
—— (ed.) (1997) *The Archaeology of Lake Innes House: Investigating the Visible Evidence 1993–1995,* Canberra: New South Wales National Parks and Wildlife Service.
—— (1998) 'The archaeology of frustrated ambition: An Australian case study', *Historical Archaeology* 32(2): 7–27.

GRAHAM CONNAH

landscape studies

Landscape has become a significant focus of historical archaeological research, especially in the last two decades. The landscape approach was initially spurred by the seminal work of Henry

Glassie and James Deetz, who showed that the study of spatial relations of buildings and the arrangement of the architectural elements reveal cultural patterns indicative of past ways of thinking. Since this work, the archaeology of the historical landscape has broadened in almost every conceivable direction. From the microscopic analysis of flotation and soil samples to the study of stratigraphic contexts and planting patterns to the formation and design of urban settlements, the reconstruction and interpretation of the landscape offers historical archaeologists a powerful material means to make statements about past cultures.

There are essentially three components to the physical landscape that can be recovered and analysed archaeologically. The broadest, generically cast here as topography, is the form and character of the land itself. Flatness, ruggedness and barrenness, for example, are the sorts of general topographic assessments that can be made of a landscape. At a finer-grain landscape, archaeologists must also consider vegetation. The plants that have grown on archaeological sites and where they were located provide clues to intentional uses (including neglect) of the spaces that formed past living sites. A great deal of data relative to vegetation is gained from seeds, pollen and phytoliths recovered from soil samples and analysed by a growing number of specialists. These resources are proving especially useful in **garden archaeology**, which focuses on the accurate reconstruction of gardens associated with historic houses and yards at many other archaeological sites. The third principal component of the landscape is **architecture**. Houses, outbuildings, fences, roads, paths, waterways, fountains, wells, fields, gardens and yards are all human impacts on land that defined human place and space. The landscape approach to these features, however, begs archaeologists not just to identify and analyse them individually, but also to weave them together as a fabric of related human spaces. Cojoining topography, vegetation and architecture thus creates analysable units out of the archaeological landscape.

Much of historical landscape archaeology focuses on the understanding of the landscape as visual phenomenon. In this sense, landscapes are reconstructed and studied as they were meant to be seen in the past. Emphasis is thus placed on the combination of topographic, vegetation and architectural data into forms that are spatially organised and designed from certain vantage points into views and vistas. Understanding and interpreting these landscapes involves trying to capture the performance of seeing in the past through the reconstruction of the objects that were under gaze.

Perhaps the most well known of these works is Mark Leone's analysis of the William Paca garden in **Annapolis**, Maryland, USA. The Paca garden was a formal landscape consisting of a series of parterres and descending terraces behind Paca's townhouse, built in 1763. The analysis of the topography shows that the terraces of the garden were of unequal widths, allowing the rules of perspective to lead the eye to perceive the terminus of the garden to be further away than it was and, from the rear looking back, for the house to seem larger than it was. Similarly, it was discovered that the size of the garden and the parterres was based on a fixed measure determined by the interior size of the house's parlour. Thus, the formal arrangement was harmoniously ordered to appear correct and unified.

Leone's interpretation of the garden meshed its material features with the social context of William Paca's life in mid-eighteenth-century Annapolis. Taking a Marxian approach, Leone argues that the garden was an ideological manifestation of the developing world view of the Chesapeake elite. Like Paca, many of these elite men were planter-merchants who had dominated the region's political economy for the previous generation. Beginning in the 1760s, however, the British attempted to curb this power through taxation and a stepped-up military presence. Those struggling under the planter aristocracy also began seeking new means to assert themselves. In particular, many participated in the religious Great Awakening led by itinerant preachers in the region's backcountry. Many also found an alternative to forming debt relations with the local merchant-planters by obtaining goods from independent Scottish merchants instead. Each of these factors eroded the authority of the planter-elite, and they responded in ways that they believed would bolster their power. The Paca garden itself was such an effort because in its use of harmony and perspective it presented a unified form based on what were recognised as timeless, natural phenomena. The garden presented to those who saw it that Paca was a master of nature. It was then easy to believe that such a man should be at the head of society, since at that time law and the social order were believed to be guided by similarly natural principles. The whole effort was ideologically designed because the 'nature' that was supposedly discovered in the garden was originally placed there by Paca. Thus, the definition and experience of nature at the Paca garden was really a natural construction serving the political struggles of the elite.

Leone's interpretation has been challenged by many voices in historical archaeology, but the critiques generally focus on Leone's use of ideology rather than on his reconstruction of the garden itself. Critics, that is, have generally accepted the analysis of the garden as a visual phenomenon. A new voice, however, has begun to develop in landscape archaeology that challenges this assumption. This movement is based on a critique of the landscape concept begun in geography and art history in the late 1970s. Through the long-term analysis of the Western landscape tradition, it was found that the landscape took on a particular familiar expression beginning in the seventeenth century. In general, this form was based on the visual experience of the land itself from a single detached vantage point. Typically, the view is framed on its edges and recedes through a sequence of frames towards a fixed point at the back. Originally captured in landscape painting, the landscape view drove the creation of physical forms in gardens and ultimately the definition of parklands in that they represented a 'natural' expression of the cultural norm.

This landscape view has been identified as a modern Western phenomenon intimately associated with Cartesian dualities, in particular the culture–nature dichotomy, and **colonialism**. Culture and nature are divided in the Western landscape tradition because the view and the land are detached, the former being the cultural gaze of the latter. In this sense, landscape was colonisation without a direct engagement. Especially for the urban bourgeoisie, this was a useful cultural adaptation for it allowed them to compete with the landed gentry and remain disengaged with the

intimacies of their growing international accumulation of commodities.

The new voice in landscape archaeology has adopted this critique and attempted to develop new means to interpret the archaeological landscape that approaches the landscape in a non-dichotomous manner. Focusing on the experience of landscape rather than just the landscape-as-seen, the majority of this work to date has been done on the prehistoric landscapes of Europe. However, some initial forays can be found in the study of the historic landscape.

One example of this sort of research is the work on the Virginia landscape by Dell Upton. Identifying his effort as 'imagining the early Virginia landscape', Upton brings a sense of the lived world of landscape to life. It is nice that we are presented with the past imagination rather than just the images, for, as Upton urges, 'a fixed experience of landscape' is not the reality we hope to reconstruct. Rather than just seeing what there is to see, Upton explores the movement of bodies in the landscape of colonial tidewater plantations. This included the approach of visitors to the main houses as well as the movement of family members and slaves. Ultimately, he is able to show how the landscape performed for the planter by articulating various pieces of his world into a unified whole that placed him at the centre and on the top. In a related study Upton urges us to see beyond the articulated landscape produced in the perspective of the planter. Within and between their arranged forms were contested spaces claimed by the others. These spaces included streams, forests and the quarters that were employed by enslaved people to build a distinctive landscape that supported their alterity and resistance.

In a similar vein, Leone has expanded his approach to landscape beyond the just-seen. Analysing the official cityscapes of Annapolis and Baltimore, Maryland, in the late eighteenth and early nineteenth centuries, Leone has identified the relationship between the intended images of the builders and the experience of those living in these places. After the American Revolution, the Maryland State House in Annapolis was refitted with a large dome that stood high above the city. The octagonal structure was built with four rows of windows on each face, which look down at the city in all directions. In the subsequent decades, as the city of Baltimore rose to prominence in Maryland, additional domed structures were built. These domes, unlike the subject-centred gaze of the Paca garden, focused attention on those who could be seen and heard as a result of the dome. These people were the new citizens of the US republic, who with the aid of the domes began to recognise their responsibility to be self-disciplined individuals. The domes worked in this way because they were built using panoptic, or all-seeing-eye, character-istics. Though no one was watching and listening through the windows, the effect was as if one was, because that someone was the individual watching him or herself.

Another example of this recent work is Christo-pher Matthews's study of the landscape as a repository of history. Focusing on the long-term development of the Annapolis landscape from the seventeenth to the twentieth century, Matthews presents a series of stratigraphically layered city-scapes that bear the imprint of the labour and traditions that built them. One of the particular subjects considered by Matthews is the struggle in antebellum Annapolis surrounding the introduction of modernisation and the transition to wage versus enslaved labour. The world that built Annapolis in the colonial period was one of wealthy planters and politicians vying for advantage through competitive consumption. This era passed at the turn of the nineteenth century with the rise of Baltimore and a modern political economy based in international exchange and industrial development. While most histories of Annapolis describe this era as a period of genteel eclipse, Matthews shows that the Annapolis landscape reflected the struggle to reproduce certain essential elements of the *status quo* of the colonial era.

Many of the formal gardens built in the Revolutionary era were turned over to produce cultivation as the city strove to find a place in the modern era. This effort, however, was not without respect to Annapolis's history. Essential to the reproduction of class relations in the new landscape was the continued existence of the town's estates and the production of the landscape through enslaved and household labour. Thus, though certain elements of the way things were done in the city changed in the antebellum era, the city of the 1840s was remarkably similar to the way it was

in the 1790s. The preservation of the landscape as the seat of refined elite households, even as they were incorporated into the regional market system, marked a use of local history to sustain inequality and domination in the town.

The future of historical landscape archaeology will likely follow many of these paths and make new discoveries as the technical and interpretive quest of the built form continues. It will also certainly be the case that the phenomenological approaches finding footing in historical archaeol-ogy will expand with new inquiries into the experience of place from the multi-sensory per-spective of the body. These new paths open up great possibilities for understanding the intimate everyday habits and experiences of the past, which allow historical archaeology to make its most successful contributions to anthropology.

See also: ideology; Marxian approaches

Further reading

Bender, B. (ed.) (1993) *Landscape: Politics and Perspectives*, Oxford: Berg.

Kelso, W.M. and Most, R. (eds) (1990) *Earth Pattern: Essays in Landscape Archaeology*, Charlottesville: University Press of Virginia.

Leone, M.P. (1995) 'A historical archaeology of capitalism', *American Anthropologist* 97: 251–68.

—— (1984) 'Interpreting ideology in historical archaeology: Using the rules of perspective in the William Paca garden in Annapolis, Mary-land', in D. Miller and C. Tilley (eds) *Ideology, Power, and Prehistory*, Cambridge: Cambridge University Press, pp. 25–35.

Matthews, C.N. (1999) 'Context and interpretation: An archaeology of cultural production', *Interna-tional Journal of Historical Archaeology* 3: 261–82.

Miller, N.F. and Gleason, K.L. (eds) (1994) *The Archaeology of Garden and Field*, Philadelphia: University of Pennsylvania Press.

Yamin, R. and Metheny, K.B. (eds) (1996) *Landscape Archaeology: Reading and Interpreting the American Historic Landscape*, Knoxville: University of Tennessee Press.

CHRISTOPHER N. MATTHEWS

language

Acknowledgement and appreciation of information obtained by a language form an important aspect of historical archaeology. Besides its usefulness for analysis and for interpretation of **material culture**, language is a source of social and political organisation, economy, religion, power relationships, gender, sexuality and other topics. It also becomes one of the most complete sources for detailing reconstructions of material culture (taxonomy, function, description and non-material aspects). Some revealing concepts of ethos, **ethnicity**, power relationships among people, between people and institutions, and between various societies may be discovered in language. Admittedly context-dependent, inclusions and modifications resulting from contact with users of other languages should be taken into account. These include encounters at frontiers, **trade** and minorities forcedly introduced into a society. Such interactions on processes actually inscribe complex and multidimensional links that unite peoples in either local or world environments. Historical archaeology requires the availability of sources on the languages of dominant society and on languages of dominated and minority societies. In the bilingual, colonial and post-colonial societies there is a need for interdisciplinarity and a refinement of political sensitiveness. Sociological, anthropological, linguistic and literary strategies should be adopted to enhance the interpretative capacity. The above factors foresee the inclusion of the network theory in archaeology and the sheer disposing of culturalism. A holistic stance should be emphasised in which associations and interactions between male and female agents and their environments are conscious and changeable creations. Words, discourse and language are affected by local, regional and world contacts, and linguistic retention, maintenance, loss and change are important topics. Unbending conservation of language may also lead towards deep ethnocentric societies resentful of integration and exchange.

Dictionaries are involved in fundamental linguistic crystallisations since, as a rule, they contain more data than any other written source. In colonial and post-colonial environments, many dictionaries were prepared by members of the colonising institutions. Rarer still, they were compiled by the natives themselves. Both should be considered as true sources of historical archaeology. If the language of the dictionary is still spoken, contemporary sources should be used to verify changes and nuances. In these cases it is necessary to employ field linguistic studies to solve research problems. Any other written document is a potential source for the study of the language and should be systematically researched. There are numerous cases of dictionary-less dead languages, albeit documented in fragmentary information gathered world-wide by European travellers, chroniclers, state bureaucrats and missionaries. Other sources prepared by natives and political, religious and gender minorities, and those compiled by slaves and free workers, ought to be investigated. In colonial and post-colonial cases, the comparative study of the uses of language may also be possible. Toponymy studies coupled with ancient and contemporary cartography are revealing about space occupation, limitation of boundaries, settlement standards, management strategies, commerce network, ecotone classification and other research items. Linguistic data may be essential for studies in historical archaeology where material culture is not the chief object of analysis. This is the case of collective and individual representations on society, institutions and other practical and symbolical aspects. The more abundant information prepared by elite groups and that compiled by workers, slaves and minorities ought to be researched. In the latter, although with more and more scanty written information as the time period recedes into the past, the need for more thorough searches in archives is imperative.

See also: colonialism; ethnicity

Further reading

Ashcroft, B., Griffiths, G. and Tiffin, H. (1998) *Key Concepts in Post-Colonial Studies*, London: Routledge.

Benson, E. and Conolly, L.W. (eds) (1994) *Encyclopaedia of Post-colonial Literatures in English*, London: Routledge.

Loomba, A. (1998) *Colonialism/Postcolonialism*, London: Routledge.

FRANCISCO NOELLI

L'Anse aux Meadows, Newfoundland, Canada

L'Anse aux Meadows, Newfoundland, Canada, is the site of an eleventh-century Viking colony. Located in 1961 by the Norwegian explorer Helge Ingstad, it is the only known Viking settlement in the New World.

Viking sagas, or written accounts of exploits, told of the existence of a place called 'Vinland' located across the ocean from Iceland and discovered by Leif Eirikson around AD 1000. The writers of the ancient sagas described Vinland as a narrow strip of land with rich forests and meadows, abundant wildlife and, as its name implies, wild grapes.

Scholars debated the location, and, in fact, the very existence of Vinland for many years, and some scholars still do not believe that L'Anse aux Meadows is Vinland. Others, true believers in the ancient sagas, even created an archaeological forgery, the Kensington Rune Stone found in Minnesota in 1898, to substantiate the Viking discovery of the New World long before the arrival of Columbus. This stone exhibited a supposed ancient, Norse inscription and was intended to make the Viking case for New World discovery and also lessen the excitement that had been caused by the 400-year celebration of Columbus's voyage in 1892.

The creation of the Kensington Stone was unnecessary because, in 1960, Ingstad proved that the sagas were correct: the Vikings had indeed visited the New World before Columbus. Near the small village of L'Anse aux Meadows he found the outlines of what he considered to be the remains of ancient Viking houses.

Ingstad and an international team of archaeologists conducted excavations at the site from 1961 to 1968, unearthing the remains of eight Viking 'long houses'. The houses had been constructed of turf in the typical Viking manner and contained artefacts associated with eleventh-century Norse settlements, including iron **nails**, spindles for making yarn, stone lamps and bronze pins. They also discovered a blacksmith's shop complete with anvil, iron fragments and slag.

L'Anse aux Meadows is today a living museum (see **living museums**) managed by the Canadian government, and is a UNESCO World Heritage Site.

CHARLES E. ORSER, JR

leisure

Leisure cuts across time periods and site types as an interest in historical archaeology. It has relevance for understanding subjects such as social divisions and class attitudes, and **children**, and generally for obtaining a better understanding of life in the past. Most commonly, historical archaeologists interpret leisure activities from functionally associated artefacts such as smoking pipes (see **pipes, smoking**), **toys**, musical instruments, tea cups (see **tea/tea ceremony**), **glass bottles** that contained alcoholic beverages and game pieces.

Drinking, smoking and recreational drug use were leisure activities popular in the past just as they are today. Contemporary views of these activities were coloured by ethnic, gender and class biases. Historical archaeology helps to determine the actual extent and impacts of these activities and their meaning for different groups.

Beaudry, Cook and Mrozowski's study of nineteenth-century workers' lives at the **Boott Mills**, Massachusetts, found evidence of drinking and smoking on the part of the female employees. Drinking was discouraged by mill company policy and smoking was of short pipes, strongly associated with the working class. Other leisure activities like card playing and socialising most likely occurred in the backyards. Wylie and Fike's study of opium smoking in the USA also describes illicit consumption, and different attitudes and practices that were based on class and ethnicity.

There are many archaeologically visible sites and activities that can be related to leisure, but not exclusively or without qualification. Historical archaeologists studying gardens (see **garden archaeology**) and **prostitution**, for example, must address the fact that these sites and activities are leisure for some (landowners and clients) but work for others (gardeners and prostitutes). Taverns and inns, sewing and quilting, and gambling are other examples where context becomes very important in interpretation. Taverns can be places of drinking and socialising, and, simultaneously, of job networking and political campaigning. Dominoes or dice, and needles, thread and patches may be associated with relaxation and pleasure by casual game players and participants in church quilting bees, but are tools of the trade for professional gamblers and quilters.

Other studies of leisure in historical archaeology include the activities of US Civil War soldiers in their camps and African American plantation workers. One common theme that has emerged from historical archaeologists' studies of leisure is that people have always made time and artefacts for leisure regardless of limitations.

Further reading

Beaudry, M.C., Cook, L.J. and Mrozowski, S. A. (1991) 'Artifacts and active voices: Material culture as social discourse', in R.H. McGuire and R. Paynter (eds) *The Archaeology of Inequality*, Oxford: Blackwell, pp. 150–91.

Rockman, D.D. and Rothschild, N.A. (1984) 'City tavern, country tavern: An analysis of four colonial sites', *Historical Archaeology* 18(2): 112–21.

Wilkie, L.A. (1994) 'Childhood in the quarters: Playtime at Oakley and Riverlake Plantations', *Louisiana Folklife* 18: 13–20.

Wylie, J. and Fike, R.E. (1993) 'Chinese opium smoking techniques and paraphernalia', in Priscilla Wegars (ed.) *Hidden Heritage: Historical Archaeology of the Overseas Chinese*, Amityville, NY: Baywood, pp. 255–303.

DAVID T. PALMER

Like-a-Fishhook Village, North Dakota, USA

Like-a-Fishhook Village, also known as Fort Berthold Indian Village, was a mid-nineteenth-century Native American village (see **Native Americans**) located on the Missouri River in what is today North Dakota. The occupants of the village were Hidastas, Mandans and Arikaras, three distinct farming cultures who were experiencing increased cultural and health-related pressures because of the spread of smallpox and the presence of people of European descent among them. These cultures probably established the village, composed of a series of semi-subterranean earthlodges in 1845 and covering approximately 16 ha. Prolonged cultural interaction occurred within the village during the forty years of its existence because of the mingling of three distinct Native American cultures along with significant numbers of European American fur traders who built several trading posts near the village. Archaeologists working for the US National Park Service excavated portions of the village in the early 1950s as part of a large archaeological effort in the Missouri River basin in advance of the construction of huge reservoirs along the river.

In keeping with the idea that the village was multicultural, archaeologists found two kinds of dwellings within the village: traditional, round earthlodges of native construction, and square log cabins, undoubtedly modelled on US examples. They also discovered part of the village stockade and a section of Fort Berthold I (built on the north side of the village in 1845 and shortly moved to the south side as the native village expanded). The archaeologists also excavated Fort Berthold II (1858–*c*. 1885). The archaeologists at Like-a--Fishhook Village also recovered a large artefact collection that included materials of both native and European American manufacture. The native items included pottery, lithics and ground stone objects, and the foreign objects included many of the things one would associate with the nineteenth-century fur trade: brass bells, iron pocket knives, iron tools of various sorts, **glass beads** and gun parts and ammunition. In summary, this site provided an excellent opportunity to examine cultural interaction and change in the Upper Mid-west of the USA during a time that the nation was pushing into Native American territory.

See also: contact archaeology

Further reading

Mattes, M. J. (1960) 'Historic sites archaeology on the upper Missouri', in F.H.H. Roberts (ed.) *River Basin Surveys Papers, Bureau of American Ethnology Bulletin 176*, Washington, DC: Government Printing Office, pp. 1–23.

Smith, G.H. (1972) *Like-a-Fishhook Village and Fort Berthold, Garrison Reservoir, North Dakota*, Washington, DC: National Park Service.

CHARLES E. ORSER, JR

linguistic analysis

Linguistic analysis, the examination of language as a social fact, is important to historical archaeologists who endeavour to understand how discourses on ethnic groups are built from **material culture** within specific space and time contexts. Material culture is composed of metacritic signs whose meaning is dispersed in an open network of significants and signifiers. In linguistic analysis, the archaeological record is not merely reduced to its constituent parts, because the analysis makes it possible to discover the non-apparent structure and the principles that compose the parts. Material culture reveals the underlying structure and principles through repetition and, similar to communicative discourse, it fortifies, codifies and reifies the relationships between peoples and between societies.

Linguistic analysis has two main functions in historical archaeology. First is the effort to understand material culture and its significants in both an isolated and an integrated way within social, political, economic and other contexts. The second function is related to social, political, economic and cultural contexts at the individual and the collective level, and at the local, regional and global planes. Linguistic analysis may indicate the complexity of cultural structures that pervade social or political relationships, both within a class or in different classes. This can be, for instance, between masters and slaves, employers and employees, rich and poor. It may reveal how the elite class sees society and how the workers or slaves behold the elites. Linguistic analysis may also exhibit continuity and changes in various aspects of life, including those related to interethnic encounters, wars and barter and exchange networks of interregional and transcontinental trade.

Linguistic analysis may also open the way towards the understanding of subtle differences in class struggles, in the institution of slavery or in the various motifs that engendered war, ethnic conflicts and genocide. It may often be the only tool available to comprehend the hidden messages in historical sources – including official, colonial records – in societies that had no tradition of guarding their data in the same way as the colonisers, even though these societies may have been objectified in chronicles, bureaucratic documents and other written accounts. The same may also apply to groups who were ignored by the elite chroniclers and who remained outside of 'official' history.

See also: ethnicity; historical documents; language

Further reading

Ashcroft, B., Griffiths, G. and Tiffin, H. (1991) *The Empire Writes Back: Theory and Practice in Post-Colonial Literatures*, London: Routledge.

Benson, E. and Conolly, L.W. (eds) (1994) *Encyclopaedia of Post-colonial Literatures in English*, vol. 1, London: Routledge.

Loomba, A. (1998) *Colonialism/Postcolonialism*, London: Routledge.

FRANCISCO NOELLI

living museums

The term 'living museum' refers to a particular kind of history museum that is actively engaged in interpreting the past with the help of costumed actors and authentic or reproduced artefacts from selected periods of time. Living museums can be dedicated to local, regional, national, cultural (ethnic) and historical topics, and some combine several of these topics into their presentations. Living museums are also termed 'open-air' and 'outdoor' museums because, unlike the traditional museum, they tend to incorporate entire houses and yards in their exhibits. Historical archaeology has been intimately involved with many of the living museums now in operation.

The idea for the creation of the living museum is credited to a Swede named Artur Hazelius who, in the late nineteenth century, became alarmed that the Industrial Revolution was rapidly destroying the peaceful and distinctive character of traditional Sweden. His fear of a future devoid of distinct cultural expression (in other words, homogenised through mass production) led him to collect furniture, clothing, tools and many other artefacts that reflected his country's traditional culture. In 1873, he opened the Museum of Scandinavian Folklore (also called the 'Nordic Museum' or 'Nordiska Museet') in Stockholm. As his collection expanded – including the acquisition of whole buildings – Hazelius outgrew his indoor museum. Thus, in 1891, he purchased an old fortification called Skansen, and opened the world's first living, outdoor museum. Today, over a hundred buildings dating from medieval times to the twentieth century are reconstructed at the museum.

Following Hazelius's lead, living museums were soon created throughout the region, including the Frilandsmuseet in Denmark, opened in 1901; the Sandvig Collection at Lillehammer, Norway, opened in 1904; and the Old Town at Aarhus, Denmark, in 1909. These collections were not associated with historical archaeology, but rather drew their inspiration from folklife studies (see **folklore and folklife studies**) and the urge to save the material elements of their traditional lives before they were forever lost to **industrialisation**.

Historical archaeology really became associated with living museums in the USA, beginning in the 1920s with the founding of Colonial Williamsburg, Virginia, in 1926 by John D. Rockefeller. Historical archaeologists involved in the interpretation of Colonial Williamsburg initially dealt mostly with architectural features because their work was instrumental in providing precise detail about the location and description of walls, cellars, gardens, room additions and other features associated with the town's former domestic, commercial, governmental and institutional buildings. Archaeology was equally important, however, for bringing to light the variety of artefacts used by the men and women who called Williamsburg home. Nowhere is the relationship between archaeology and living interpretation more clearly seen at Colonial Williamsburg than at the reconstruction of the slave quarters at **Carter's Grove** Plantation. Historical archaeology has had a major role in providing unique information about the living conditions faced by African American slaves on the plantation and their research has added a tangible, human dimension to the interpretation.

Other outdoor museums in the USA have also benefited from an association with historical archaeology. Some of these museums are Henry Ford's Greenfield Village, Michigan (though the archaeology associated with it was rather crude); Historic Deerfield, Massachusetts; and Old Salem, North Carolina. It is expected that the link between historical archaeology and living museums will continue to be expanded in the future.

Further reading

E.P. Alexander (1996) *Museums in Motion: An Introduction to the History and Functions of Museums*, Walnut Creek, CA: AltaMira Press.

CHARLES E. ORSER, JR

local history

Historical archaeology has contributed greatly to our knowledge of local history, which can be defined as a community's shared heritage. The origins of historical archaeology are found in local history with the start of historic preservation movements in the early twentieth century. During this early period, historical archaeology concentrated on aspects of the famous and wealthy in the past and was primarily used as a 'handmaiden to history', filling in the gaps of time that the written records or oral testimony could not verify. It was not until the civil rights movement of the 1960s and the National Historic Preservation Act of 1966 that a more diverse local history was explored archaeologically. Also, since the 1960s, historical archaeology has no longer been used to just fill in the gaps of history, but has been utilised to critically question the accuracy of historic documents.

Traditionally, archaeology has interpreted local history to the public through **museums** or open-house tours of a site. Since 1980, archaeologists have attempted a more liberal approach of interpreting local history by inviting the public to work collaboratively with academia. The result is a **public archaeology** programme that empowers the community, allowing them to govern their past.

Other archaeologists have used critical theory to interpret local history. Critical theory suggests that the living community should be confronted by their collective heritage. This confrontational approach attempts to make the public critically judge the past and understand the link between the past and their modern culture. Overall, historical archaeology of local history covers specific places, people and events as well as broad national trends and ideas that affect the local community.

In the early twentieth century, some of the first historical archaeology was conducted to clarify local historical events, places and people. This early period, often called the 'humanistic period', was driven by local historic preservation efforts. Examples include the work at **Jamestown**, **Mount Vernon** and Williamsburg, where historical archaeology was used to fill the gaps of history that the written documents did not record, or to help restore razed or deteriorating structures.

The best archaeological example from the early period is Williamsburg, Virginia, a colonial seat of government from 1699 to the end of the American Revolution. After this time, Williamsburg declined in importance as the political power shifted to the new state capital in Richmond. By the early twentieth century, Williamsburg was in economic decay with many of its historic neighbourhoods in disrepair or demolished. In 1926, Reverend Dr W.A.R. Goodwin organised local and national support to begin restoration efforts to return Williamsburg to its colonial glory. Philanthropist John D. Rockefeller, Jr funded the majority of the project, which combined the skills of archaeologists, architects and historians to recreate the historic Williamsburg of the eighteenth century. Starting in the 1930s, archaeologists become used to finding razed building foundations so that they could be restored, but over time the role of archaeologists has become more important in recording the material lives and cultural diversity of the inhabitants of Colonial Williamsburg. By the end of the twentieth century, the colonial past has become alive again with over 500 historic buildings operated as a living museum (see **living museums**), research facility, educational centre and tourist attraction dedicated to preserving and interpreting eighteenth-century Williamsburg.

Historical archaeology was formally recognised as an archaeological discipline in the 1960s with the creation of the **Conference on Historic Site Archaeology** and the **Society for Historical Archaeology**. At this same time, local-history research began to change its research focus from wealthy and famous events and people to a more diverse agenda covering the disenfranchised past. At Williamsburg, for example, archaeologists realised that the entirety of the town's history was not being told, particularly as it pertained to African Americans. Enslaved African Americans first arrived in the **Chesapeake region** at Jamestown in 1619. By the 1770s, over half of all African Americans in the thirteen colonies lived in Virginia or Maryland, and constituted over 50 per cent of the Chesapeake's population. Most people of African descent were slaves working on rural plantations and farms, but urban slavery was also common and slaves worked as domestics and day labourers. A small, free-black population, who lived primarily in urban areas like Williamsburg, was also present in the region.

To enfranchise African American history, interpretive programmes have been started, and archaeology has been a key component to these programmes, usually because few written records are available about the lives of slaves. Archaeological work has included both urban and rural as well as free and enslaved African American sites. Programmes at Williamsburg and the associated **Carter's Grove** Plantation are exemplary in this regard.

Archaeology has also been used to question the accuracy of local history. Local history is based primarily on written records and oral tradition. The accuracy of these records and local lore should not be taken for granted and should be checked using the material record obtained through archaeology. For example, historical archaeology has clarified the quality of diet and health of enslaved African Americans. Planters' diaries often outline food rations given to their enslaved African Americans, and some historians have used these records to argue that enslaved African Americans' diet and heath were extremely poor, lacking in adequate caloric and vitamin intake, and resulting in severe health problems. Archaeological excavations of slave quarters have shown that a slave's diet was not limited to the planter's rations, but encompassed more diverse foods including both wild and domestic animals gathered or hunted in nearby fields and forest, or raised in adjacent gardens or animal pens.

Interpreting local history to the public has a long tradition in archaeology. The traditional method of public archaeology has been in a museum exhibit or a living museum. Several archaeologists have also invited the public to visit their archaeological sites. The traditional ways of interpreting local history to the public can be problematic, however. For example, the archaeologists at the **African Burial Ground** in **New York City** uncovered over 400 individuals of African descent from the colonial period. The public, particularly the descendant community, was not contacted about the presence of this cemetery and the disturbance to it until the project to construct a new federal building was well under way. Members of the African American community were outraged that they were not informed during the planning process and they used political and social leverage to take some control of the project. Ultimately, the descendant community gained ownership of their local history by deciding how, and by whom, the human remains would be excavated, analysed and interpreted.

A less stressful public archaeology programme exists in Alexandria, Virginia, where archaeologists there have assumed a community-friendly approach to interpreting local history. In the 1960s, the city developed an archaeology programme called 'Alexandria Archaeology' to create a partnership between the city's professional archaeologists and the public. The primary goal of this programme has been to research, preserve, collect and interpret local community history. The public is invited to work collaboratively as volunteers with city archaeologists and historians to explore their local heritage through historical research, archaeological excavation, artefact analysis and public interpretation. Since its creation, thousands of volunteers have participated in this programme, empowering the community to control their own heritage as well as raising their historical consciousness.

Historical archaeology has also contributed to local history through its use of critical theory.

Critical theory in historical archaeology suggests that the living community should be confronted by their collective heritage. This approach attempts to make the public critically judge the past and to understand the link between the past and their modern culture. At Colonial Williamsburg, for instance, a confrontational method was used during the re-enactment of a slave auction in 1994. Many in and outside the community were outraged that Williamsburg would recreate such a tragic and brutal event in local history, but by doing so the museum provoked the community to reflect about the past. The slave auction forced the public to think about its local history in a way that emphasised more then just events and people. The auction forced the public to think about the underlying social processes of racism that allowed slavery to exist in Colonial Williamsburg. By understanding the roots of racism, the local community can address the living legacy of racism in modern culture with hopes that they will take an active stance to abolish racism in the future.

Local history is not just about the wealthy or just about enjoyable times. Local history encompasses all that comprises a community's history, including people of all walks of life and events that include wars, plagues, parades and parties, as well as the underlying social discourse and ideologies that drive and structure a community. Local history is our collectively shared heritage that can extend from a city neighbourhood or farmstead to broader lines of national and global heritage.

See also: African American archaeology; history of historical archaeology

Further reading

Baumann, T. (1996) 'Questioning popular history: Knoxville's Perez Dickinson, abolitionist or slave-owner?', *Ohio Valley Historical Archaeology* 11: 6–18.

Chappell, E. (1999) 'Museums and American slavery', in T. Singleton (ed.) *'I, too, am America': Archaeological Studies of African-American Life*, Charlottesville, VA: University Press of Virginia, pp. 240–58.

Cressey, P. (1987) 'Community archaeology in Alexandria, Virginia', in *Conserve Neighborhoods*

69, Washington, DC: National Trust for Historic Preservation, pp. 1–6.

Jameson, J. (ed.) (1997) *Presenting Archaeology to the Public*, Walnut Creek, CA: AltaMira Press.

McDavid, C. and Babson, D. (eds) (1997) 'The realm of politics: Prospects for public participation in African American and plantation archaeology', *Historical Archaeology* 31(3): 1–152.

Potter, P., Jr (1994) *Public Archaeology in Annapolis: A Critical Approach to History in Maryland's Ancient City*, Washington, DC: Smithsonian Institution Press.

TIMOTHY BAUMANN

Longton Hall, Stoke-on-Trent, England

The first commercial production of soft paste **porcelain** in north Staffordshire took place at Longton Hall, in **Stoke-on-Trent**. In 1751, a partnership was formed between London attorney William Jenkinson, potter William Littler and local lawyer William Nicklin. Jenkinson is stated to have 'obtained the art of making porcelain in imitation of china ware' and to be already have been engaged in its manufacture. He himself would have had no practical involvement in the business and it is probable that he employed Littler for a time before the partnership agreement.

Despite the factory's prolific output, it experienced financial difficulties at an early stage and new partners were recruited to raise fresh capital. The financial situation did not improve, however, and in 1760 the partnership broke up and the factory's stock was sold.

Although the factory is poorly documented, Longton Hall porcelain is well represented in modern collections as useful and ornamental wares with underglaze blue painted, overglaze painted and printed decoration. Excavations on the site between 1955 and 1971 have produced further evidence for Longton Hall wares and their manufacture. No examples were found of either the crossed 'Ls' mark or the blue-ground porcelain that have been claimed as Longton Hall features. Teawares (see **tea/tea ceremony**) predominate, mostly with blue-painted decoration. Plain thrown forms are the most common, but there are several

diagnostic moulded types. Sauce boats, dishes, tureens, plates, jugs and cutlery hafts are moulded in a variety of leaf forms. Figure fragments include both the heavy 'snowman' sheep and other subjects, and better quality renderings of musicians and dancers.

The excavated evidence cannot substantiate Bernard Watney's chronology for the Longton Hall wares – early, middle, late – which was based upon the degree of sophistication of modelling and manufacture. However, scientific analysis of the porcelains suggests a possible evolution away from a body containing calcium sulphate (gypsum) and high quantities of flint glass, which has been identified in the 'snowman' figures, to one with less flint glass, greater quantities of limestone and also bone ash.

The excavations revealed the remains of five ovens, at least three of which were in use at the same time. These were a biscuit oven, a glost oven and a small oven for enamel firings. The wide range of saggar types and the unique diversity of kiln furniture highlight concerns for the wares during firing. Both wasters and extant pieces show that warping and collapse were constant problems, arising through poor temperature control within the oven and through the high lead content of the porcelain bodies, which reduced their stability.

Further reading

Barker, D. and Cole, S. (1998) *Digging for Early Porcelain: The Archaeology of Six 18th-Century British Porcelain Factories*, Stoke-on-Trent: City Museum and Art Gallery.

Cherry, J. and Tait, H. (1980) 'Excavations at the Longton Hall porcelain factory, Part II: The kiln furniture', *Post-medieval Archaeology* 14: 1–21.

Tait, H. and Cherry, J. (1978) 'Excavations at the Longton Hall porcelain factory, Part I: The excavation of the factory site', *Post-medieval Archaeology* 12: 1–29.

Watney, B. (1993) 'Excavations at the Longton Hall porcelain manufactory, Part III: The porcelain and other ceramic finds', *Post-medieval Archaeology* 27: 57–109.

—— (1957) *Longton Hall Porcelain*, London: Faber.

DAVID BARKER

looting

The term 'looting' refers to the careless destruction of fragile archaeological contexts and the removal of artefacts for sale. It constitutes one of the most serious concerns of today's archaeology, and the problem is global.

Looting is typically associated with prehistoric, classical, Egyptian, and Mesoamerican archaeology because it is generally the case that the antiquity or rarity of an object will determine its price in the illegal antiquities market. Collectors will typically target sites that contain monumental **architecture** or which have a well-developed and expressive artistic tradition. Sought-after artefacts include statues and figurines of all sorts, objects made of precious metals, items thought valuable because of an association with a famous place or event and whole pottery vessels. The looters' frequent desire to obtain whole pieces of pottery in the USA, and most prominently in the southwest, has led to the archaeologists' appellation 'pot hunters' to describe looters.

The artefacts collected by historical archaeologists are often not rare or desirable enough for artefact hunters to risk stiff penalties to acquire them. This is particularly true for those periods of history that post-date the development of factory-based mass production. Looting can still be a problem for historical archaeology, however. In fact, it is possible that individuals who would not think of looting a prehistoric site – because they believe they have reverence for the past – would think nothing of looting a historic-period site, such as an early nineteenth-century slave plantation. One rationale they may use is that early nineteenth-century sites and artefacts are relatively abundant, and so there is no problem with them conducting a clandestine excavation to recover artefacts for their private collections or for sale to collectors. Many bottle (see **bottles**) collectors regularly engage in the search for and sale of glass bottles, both individually and as members of bottle-hunting clubs. All secret, unscientific excavations, no matter of what magnitude, destroy the invaluable information – both soil layers and the relationships between artefacts – on which archaeologists rely to interpret the past.

Two sites within historical archaeology that are particularly prone to looting are underwater shipwrecks and battlefield sites. Non-archaeologists, undoubtedly influenced by the excited reports of the media, often associate wreck sites with untold riches and the thrill and romance of discovery. Some sport divers may not appreciate that the removal of artefacts from a shipwreck changes the archaeological record forever. Battlefield sites regularly attract looters in search of objects related to important battles or campaigns. The objects sought can include bullets, pieces of muskets and rifles, iron pikes and knives, and accoutrements lost during battle. Potential looters at battlefield sites often use **metal detectors** to locate items that remain among the debris of battles: cannonballs, iron buckles and other objects. The removal of artefacts even from the surface of a battlefield – through illegal excavation – can affect an archaeologist's interpretation of the flow and intensity of battle, the location of military units and the kinds of weapons used.

See also: destruction, site

CHARLES E. ORSER, JR

Lund, Sweden

Lund is a medieval town situated in the county of Skåne in present-day southern Sweden. Before 1658, Skåne was a Danish province. Lund was founded around 990 as part of the Christian state-formation of Denmark. The town was the main royal mint in Denmark from about 1020 to 1377. Lund became the bishop's see for eastern Denmark around 1050 and the archbishop's see for Scandinavia in 1103 or 1104. In the twelfth and early thirteenth centuries, it was the largest and most important town in Scandinavia. The urban area comprised about 100 ha, which was surrounded by an earthen rampart, with a wooden palisade and masonry gates. At the height of its importance, the town housed a cathedral, two monasteries, one nunnery, two friaries, three hospitals and eighteen parish churches. Lund declined in the fourteenth and fifteenth centuries, when the nearby coastal town Malmö became the leading commercial centre for eastern Denmark. At the Reformation, most parish churches and monasteries were pulled down, but Lund retained some importance as a residential city for the local nobility in Skåne. Most of the medieval and early modern town was destroyed in recurring wars between Denmark and Sweden in the seventeenth century. The town was incorporated into the Swedish realm in 1658, and in 1668 a Swedish university was founded in the town. In the eighteenth and nineteenth centuries, Lund was a small Swedish provincial town, and only with the industrialisation from the late nineteenth century and onwards did the town expand beyond its medieval borders.

Archaeology in Lund started in 1890, when the director of the Museum of Cultural History, Georg Karlin, began collecting medieval and post-medieval finds from building sites in the town. In 1905, a specialised archaeologist, Pär-Axel Olsson, was appointed by the museum to take care of excavations and surveys. He began recording remains of the many monuments of the medieval and post-medieval city. More systematic archaeological research was developed by Ragnar Blomqvist, who was in charge of urban archaeology from 1929 to 1968. He studied the local chronology of many artefact types and made several systematic studies of the topography and the settlement of the medieval and post-medieval city. In 1961, the first large-scale excavation was carried out in the town, and since then the archaeological unit of the Museum of Cultural History has been responsible for some thirty major rescue excavations in the medieval town. Partly as a consequence of the long tradition of **urban archaeology** in Lund, **medieval archaeology** was established as a discipline at the University of Lund in 1962.

As a result of 110 years of archaeological activity, Lund has yielded the largest and most varied urban archaeological material in Scandinavia. The layout of the vanished medieval town is today well known. Large parts of the present street net have been dated to the eleventh and early twelfth centuries, whereas all the twenty-seven medieval ecclesiastical institutions have been identified and fairly well dated. About 10,000 graves have been recorded, and some 6,000 of these have been analysed. The settlement structure as well as the building traditions during different parts of the

Middle Ages and the early modern period can be reconstructed in its main outline. The spectrum of artefacts is very broad, including finds of organic material of leather, wood and basketry. The finds include objects from Europe, northern Africa and western Asia, ranging from Greenland to Iran.

The main research issues in the archaeology of Lund have been urban chronology and topography. Questions like the origin of the city and the identification of the ecclesiastical institutions consequently have dominated the research agenda. In recent decades, however, other issues have come into focus. The traditional ideas of urban commercial life have been questioned in archaeological studies of **trade** and handicraft, in which important changes of these activities through the Middle Ages have been underlined. Cultural contacts and cultural processes during the eleventh and twelfth centuries have been studied through the broad and varied spectrum of pottery in Lund. The old questions of urban topography have been redirected towards issues of spatial construction and mental space in the urban settings. By comparing archaeology and written documents it has also been possible to reconstruct the ecclesiastical division of the medieval town and the pattern of ownership in the late medieval and early modern town. Analyses of skeletons have renewed views of **health** and **disease** among the medieval population of the town. Finally, the thick medieval deposits have been the starting point for a methodological debate on the nature of stratigraphy. In summary, it must be underlined that most work has been concerned with the Middle Ages, although a large and varied amounts of post-medieval material is preserved from Lund, including large numbers of pottery and stove tiles. The medieval and post-medieval finds from Lund are exhibited at the Museum of Cultural History in Lund.

Further reading

Arcini, C. (1999) *Health and Disease in Early Lund. Osteo-Pathologic Studies of 3,305 Individuals Buried in the First Cemetery Area of Lund, 990–1536*, Archaeologica Lundensia 8, Lund: Kulturen.

Carelli, P. (forthcoming) 'Building practices and housing culture in medieval Lund: A brief survey', in M. Gläser (ed.) *Kolloqium zur Stadtarch-*

äologie im Hanseraum III: Der Hausbau, Lubeck: Schmidt-Römhild.

—— (1999) 'Exchange of commodities in medieval Lund: Patterns of trade or consumption?', in M. Gläser (ed.) *Kolloqium zur Stadtarchäologie im Hanseraum II: Handel*, Lubeck: Schmidt-Römhild, pp. 469–91.

—— (1997) 'The Past and the Future of Archaeology in Lund', in M. Gläser (ed.) *Kolloqium zur Stadtarchäologie im Hanseraum I: Stand, Aufgaben und Perspektiven*, Lubeck: Schmidt-Römhild, pp. 429–39.

Christensen, T., Larsen, A.-C., Larsson, S. and Vince, A. (1994) 'Early glazed ware from medieval Denmark', *Medieval Ceramics* 18: 67–76.

Magnusson Staaf, B., Eriksdotter G. and Larsson, S. (1996) 'The street as a monument', *Lund Archaeological Review* 1995: 35–51.

Roslund, M. (1997) 'Crumbs from the rich man's table: Byzantine finds in Lund and Sigtuna, c. 980–1260', in H. Andersson, P. Carelli and L. Ersgård (eds) *Visions of the Past: Trends and Traditions in Swedish Medieval Archaeology*, Stockholm: Almqvist and Wicksell International, pp. 239–97.

ANDERS ANDRÉN

makers' marks

Makers' marks on **ceramics** are 'codes' that provide a wealth of information for historical archaeologists, including the names of manufacturers, retailers and importers; the pattern or shape name and number; and information on when, where and for whom the piece was manufactured and how it was marketed.

It is impossible to pinpoint the exact date that potters began to mark their wares. Little is known about pre-1750s marks from Great Britain or the European continent, but, as ceramic production became more industrialised, marking became more common, perhaps for marketing purposes. Little US pottery was marked before 1850, but Chinese **porcelain** was being marked at least as early as the 1300s, during the Ming dynasty.

In his 1988 work on British porcelain, Godden distinguishes between underglaze 'clay marks' and 'overglaze marks'. Clay marks include simple incised or impressed marks indicating the manufacturer. Moulded marks form part of the mould used to shape an item. These marks can be indented or in relief. Applied, or sprigged, marks are applied separately before the ceramic body dries. Underglaze painted or transfer-printed marks are applied before glazing and final firing. Transfer-printed marks are almost always of the same colour as the print on the rest of the vessel. Overglaze marks include simple painted devices, printed marks and lithotransfers/decals (essentially post-1900) and stamps. Marks are usually applied underglaze on **earthenware** and overglaze on porcelain and bone china.

Vessels are usually marked on the base, but marks are occasionally noted on the exterior. Sometimes marks printed on paper labels are applied to the surface of a ceramic item. Forms of marks vary widely, from names, to initials, devices, characters, seals and pattern or other descriptive marks.

Name marks are usually straightforward, but can be misleading. Consider the many 'variations' on the WEDGWOOD mark from the late eighteenth century onward (e.g. J WEDG WOOD), used by companies other than Wedgwood to capitalise on the latter's success. Some name marks relate to the retailer who sold the piece rather than the manufacturer. Initial marks, which consist only of letters, can be difficult to attribute. Device marks are common (e.g. geometric symbols, anchor, Staffordshire knot, the British royal arms, the US eagle) and are often combined with a name mark or initials. Characters and seals are the most common types of Oriental marks. Cushion notes that Chinese marks are groupings of characters (often six) that include the name of the dynasty in power when the piece was produced, the 'reign name' and time period. Seal marks are similar combinations of words written in archaic script. Japanese marks also employ characters, but examples from the late nineteenth century identify the name of the manufacturer.

Pattern or other descriptive marks usually relate to the added pattern on the vessel. Compound marks occasionally occur, where the pattern name and the manufacturer's name or initials occur together, and these tend to date post-1810 in Britain.

Figure 20 Makers' marks

Source: Photos: T. Majewski

Note: All marks are transfer printed and English (Staffordshire), unless otherwise noted. They are as follows, from left to right, by row. Top: 'Andalusia' pattern mark with impressed 'Adams' mark (*c.* 1830s–1840s); US importer's mark (Chauncey Filley), registry mark (18 December 1856) for 'Berlin Swirl' pattern by Mayer & Elliot, Longport and impressed workmen's marks; 'Signing of the Magna Charta' pattern mark in the 'British History' series, manufacturer's name (Jones and Son, 1826–8) incorporated into mark. Middle: 'Views in Mesopotamia' pattern mark, attributed to James Keeling (*c.* 1830); Homer Laughlin mark (1877–*c.* 1900) (blurred print common on US printed marks of this period); American importer's mark (E.A. & S.R Filley) on English-manufactured ware (*c.* 1854). Bottom: composite mark with body and company names, location of manufacture and registry mark (April 14 1866) for 'Nile Shape' (unusual when the mark includes the name of pattern or shape being registered); stamped Homer Laughlin (US) mark with month ('L'), date ('[19]41') and factory ('N 6'); late nineteenth-century J & G Meakin mark incorporating body and company names, with impressed mark containing same information and a workman's mark.

Workmen's marks – numbers, letters or other devices – often were scratched or impressed into the ceramic body before firing. Although these marks indicate information pertinent to the management of the factory where the ceramics were made (e.g. tally marks to pay for piecework, paste composition, vessel size), they generally provide little information as to manufacturer and date. Nonetheless, it is important to recognise them for what they are so as not to confuse them with other types of more informative marks.

Changes in mark styles and content were often made in response to legislation or business practices, and these provide clues to dating. The 1891 US McKinley Tariff Act required that all goods exported to the USA be identified as to country of origin. Thus, inclusion of 'England' in a mark usually indicates a date after 1891, but some potters adopted the convention as early as the 1880s ('Made in England' denotes a twentieth-century date).

Vessels with a 'diamond mark' can be dated to within a few years of their manufacture. The diamond mark was used from 1842 to 1883 to indicate that a particular design was registered with the British Patent Office by the manufacturer (British or otherwise), retailer or wholesaler. Beginning in 1884, the diamond mark was replaced with consecutive registration numbers, usually preceded by 'Rd. No'.

A familiarity with political geography, history and world economic systems is essential for understanding changes in marks from countries such as Japan and Germany. For example, after 1921, use of the word 'Nippon' on Japanese wares was no longer acceptable to the US government as an indicator of country of origin. Research by historical archaeologists working in the western United States, however, indicates that some Japanese companies were using 'Japan' or 'Made in Japan' more than a decade prior to 1921. Some marking conventions may have changed in the industry well in advance of legislative action.

The historical archaeologist's ability to decipher marks is limited by the quantity and quality of reference materials available on manufacturers and their dates of operation and his or her facility in languages other than English. The best 'guides' are compiled using primary materials, particularly company histories and marked pieces. While information is abundant and generally accurate for British and US marks, it is scarce and of uneven quality for marks from other countries. Godden's works are the standard sources for British earthenware and other European porcelain. Barber, Gates and Ormerod, and Lehner focus exclusively on US marks; Cushion provides an overview of marks from the Old World, including China; and the Kowalskys treat US, continental European and British marks. The Kowalskys also compiled a list of eighteenth- through early twentieth-century US and Canadian importers, wholesalers, retailers and auctioneers who handled wares shipped from abroad. If a particular mark or manufacturer is not covered in these sources, analysts should consult specialist literature on a particular ware or manufacturer.

Marks should be 'read' with care. Forging marks has occurred for centuries, and marks frequently contain information designed to mislead the consumer. For example, British manufacturers might christen their ware 'porcelaine opaque', when the ceramic body was neither opaque porcelain nor French in origin. Accurately identified marks, however, are important tools for dating and understanding the context of deposits from historical archaeological sites. **Mean ceramic dating**, in particular, is dependent on using accurately established manufacturing date ranges for specific wares.

See also: dating methods; formula dating

Further reading

Barber, E.A. (1976) *Marks of American Potters*, New York: Feingold & Lewis. [Originally published in 1904.]

Cushion, J.P. (1980) *Handbook of Pottery and Porcelain Marks*, London: Faber & Faber.

Gates, W.T., Jr and Ormerod, D.E. (1982) 'The east Liverpool pottery district: Identification of manufacturers and marks', *Historical Archaeology* 16(1–2): 1–358.

Godden, G.A. (1988) *Encylopaedia of British Porcelain Manufacturers*, London: Barrie & Jenkins.

—— (1964) *Encyclopaedia of British Pottery and Porcelain Marks*, London: Barrie & Jenkins.

Kowalsky, A.A. and Kowalsky, D.E. (1999) *Encyclopedia of Marks on American, English, and European Earthenware, Ironstone, and Stoneware 1780–1980*, Atglen, PA: Schiffer Books.

Lehner, L. (1988) *Lehner's Encyclopedia of U.S. Marks on Pottery, Porcelain & Clay*, Paducah, KY: Collector Books.

TERESITA MAJEWSKI

manor houses

Medieval manors arose from the area of land contributing to the maintenance of the lord's house. The term (from French *manoir* and Latin *maner*) was applied after the eleventh-century Norman Conquest to pre-existing estate forms. Between *c.* 1000–1500, manor houses were an architectural expression of social hierarchy and lordly status.

Early manor houses usually comprised a free-standing ground-floor hall with detached chamber block providing seigneurial accommodation at first-floor level, and a private chapel. These usually developed into a linear range, of timber-frame and/or stone construction, centred on the open hall, with service rooms to the low end and seigneurial quarters to the high end of the hall. From the thirteenth century, higher-status upper halls were often provided at first-floor level (over the ground-floor hall), with access to a chamber block (or solar tower). At the low end of the hall, the typical arrangement of cross-passage, two service rooms and secondary chambers above had developed by the end of the twelfth century. From the early thirteenth century, the main chamber block was commonly attached to the upper end of the hall, producing the standard late medieval English house.

Manor houses are 'polite' buildings, like castles and palaces, but many manor houses share the characteristics of **vernacular architecture**, using regional building materials and construction techniques. As the **architecture** of the lesser elite, manor houses are at the cusp of polite and vernacular architecture.

The late medieval open-hall house (common to manor houses and sub-manorial dwellings) embodied the social relations of the household, centred on the hall, with high-status family rooms at the high end and service rooms at the low end. From the sixteenth century, manor houses had less in common with the houses of those below the elite. The sixteenth-century gentry adopted **Renaissance** ideas, producing greater symmetry of plan and classical architectural detailing. This marked the origins of the **Georgian Order**.

By the thirteenth century, manors are well documented across England as a unit of estate management, with a manorial court (meeting in the hall of the manor house) dealing with by-laws governing petty crime, agricultural practices and tenancy exchanges. From the late sixteenth century, a capitalist property market undermined the continuity of manorial structures. Erosion of customary medieval practices prompted efforts to define the institution of the manor in physical, legal

and moral terms; John Norden (*The Surveior's Dialogue*, 1618) asked whether 'is not every manor a little commonwealth'. However, from *c.* 1600, the term 'manor house' was applied generically to the main house of an estate or village. For the sixteenth and seventeenth centuries it is more appropriate to refer to houses by social group, i.e. gentry houses.

See also: capitalism

Further reading

Cooper, N. (1999) *Houses of the Gentry, 1480–1680*, New Haven: Yale University Press.

Cooper, N. and Majerus, M. (1990) *English Manor Houses*, London: Weidenfeld.

Grenville, J. (1997) *Medieval Housing*, London: Leicester University Press.

Johnson, M.H. (1996) *An Archaeology of Capitalism*, Oxford: Blackwell.

Meirion-Jones, G. and Jones, M. (eds) (1993) *Manorial Domestic Buildings in England and Northern France*, London: Society of Antiquaries of London.

ADRIAN GREEN

maps

Maps, as pictorial representations of physical and cultural landscapes, are an integral part of archaeology. They are used as **historical documents** to provide evidence about past landscapes and the ways in which people organised themselves in place. Maps are cultural artefacts, both produced by the social relations of the day and simultaneously helping to reinforce those social relations. Yet, maps have not often been the subject of critical analysis.

Maps have been produced and used ever since there was a means to record a particular landscape and a need to do so. Historically, maps are made by those in **power** to control the knowledge and image of a place. Locals seldom need to record their landscapes because they already know them intimately. It is the foreigner, the outsider, who wants to lay claim to the land. Once mapped, the land is ready to be occupied and owned (regardless of who was there before).

In the Western world, maps have long been associated with colonisation in two ways: first, in terms of military maps to lay a physical claim; and, second, in terms of cadastral or property maps to lay legal claim and ownership of land. Maps can be best understood in terms of the **material culture** of **colonialism**.

Local or indigenous peoples – native to the landscape mapped by others – may have other means of recording and teaching the next generation about the meaning, significance and **identity** of place. These concepts may be more archaeologically abstract, part of an **oral history**, **folklore** or some other tradition that has either been destroyed as a result of colonialism or is not recognised by the outsiders as a record of place. Few studies focus on modern maps made by indigenous peoples as a form of **resistance** to dominant ideologies and as a way to revitalise cultural and spatial identities.

It is not surprising that in archaeology maps have been recognised as an important tool in the decipherment of past landscapes and social relations of ownership. As documentary evidence, maps have often been used as a control mechanism. Leone and Potter suggest that there have been two ways that documentary and archaeological records are linked: first, one excavates and uses the documentary record to identify the archaeological finds, with the assumption that the documentary record is the 'truth'; or, second, one begins with a history based on the documentary record in order to provide context, and then excavates to fill in gaps or add detail. Neither of these methods is adequate since they imply that the archaeological and documentary records (the maps) are linked and interdependent. It should be possible to regard both maps and what they represent as separate and independent records.

Where differences and inconsistencies occur, the archaeological interpretation is enriched and expanded. In order to compare these two separate records and find ambiguities, each must be sensitively described and analysed. Rather than using map documents as unbiased data, uncritically representing 'how things were', maps ought to be recognised for their potential as artefacts in themselves. They reflect the cultural understandings of the mapmaker. Maps are the product of and reflect the social relations of power, at the same time influencing and perpetuating that social context.

Cartographers and geographers have grappled with the manipulation of information that is represented in maps. The works of J.B. Harley, Mark Monmonier and Dennis Wood are chief among the most critical in deconstructing maps. Maps are based on conventions and symbols that represent a three-dimensional world. While some cartographers may focus on the 'accuracy' of their measurements and the skill of depiction, the act of mapping is always a cultural process. It is based on cultural choices of what is included and named, and what is left off the map. The implications are significant, for the map has become a document 'more real' than the reality of what it is trying to represent. What is on the map 'exists', what is not on the map does not; what is named on the map is significant, what is not named is unimportant to the mapmakers and consequently to the map readers. Every line, colour shading and symbol on the map is chosen to represent some specific feature of the world.

Maps cannot possibly represent a three-dimensional world in a two-dimensional form. Even if a one-to-one scale were possible (although it is not practical), maps would still represent the selection and choice of what is considered important. Mapmakers are influenced by their cultural understanding of the world in which they live. Seeing is a cultural act, contingent on one's cultural perspectives within the complex web of social interactions, understandings and meanings of place and identity.

In a study of maps in **Ireland**, Smith analysed the Ordnance Survey maps of the nineteenth century to explore the colonial perception of the local landscape. In this study it becomes apparent that, while colonial, the map is a site of interaction of many different groups of individuals within society. The map product is the result of many cultural negotiations in which the local sense of place and belonging to the landscape are also encoded in the 'paper landscape'. Future research comparing the traditional idea of maps with indigenous oral maps or 'resistance' maps would add to the discussion of the ideologies of the representation of place.

Further reading

Harvey, J.B. (1989) 'Deconstructing the map', *Cartographica* 26(2): 1–20.

Leone, M. and Potter, P.B. (1988) 'Introduction: Issues in historical archaeology', in M. Leone and P.B. Potter (eds) *The Recovery of Meaning: Historical Archaeology in the Eastern United States*, Washington, DC: Smithsonian Institution Press, pp. 1–22.

Monmonier, M. (1991) *How to Lie with Maps*, Chicago: University of Chicago Press.

Smith, A. (2001) 'Mapping cultural and archaeological meanings: Representing landscapes and pasts in 19th century Ireland', doctoral dissertation, University of Massachusetts, Amherst.

Wood, D. (1992) *The Power of Maps*, New York: Guilford.

ANGÈLE P. SMITH

maritime archaeology

Of the various terms referring to archaeological investigation in and alongside rivers, lakes and seas, 'maritime archaeology' began to gain currency in the 1970s. It found its most eloquent proponent in the late Keith Muckelroy who defined it as: 'The scientific study of the material remains of man and his activities on the sea' (1978: 4). This he distinguished from 'nautical archaeology' with its primary focus on the technology of shipping, and the environmentally specific 'archaeology under water' encompassing investigations carried out in any body of water irrespective of the nature of the site. All these terms, including 'marine archaeology' remain in use, sometimes specific to the definitions offered by Muckelroy, at others with less precision. However, the term 'maritime' has become favoured by many as it is the most inclusive. It entrains aspects that are cultural as well as environmental, metaphysical as well as material and symbolic as well as functional. It includes the prominent interests of water transport technology, trade and exchange, waterborne industries, seafaring, coastal settlements, harbours and waterfronts, ritual and funerary deposits and, arguably, the whole entity that Christer Westerdahl defined as the 'maritime cultural landscape'. This

goes some way beyond the distinct boundaries of the subject defined by Muckelroy. This was partly by design as many, like Sean McGrail, found them too restricting. It has also been an organic process in a research climate where disciplinary boundaries have become increasingly permeable. Maritime research designs now espouse a 'seamless' approach both in terms of environment – submerged, intertidal and coastal – and of source material, be it archaeological, historical, ethnographic, etc. So those 'related objects on the shore' and 'coastal communities' explicitly ruled out by Muckelroy would just as explicitly be ruled in today. Indeed, it is through them that coastal and sea-borne maritime concerns articulate with society at large. Today, then, maritime archaeology is the study of material remains relating to human activities on the seas, interconnected waterways and adjacent locales.

In spite of this broader agenda, maritime archaeology is nevertheless achieving more coherence within the discipline as a whole. This is manifested in its foothold within academia, a growing, world-wide awareness of its problems and potentials in management terms and an increase in substantive publications. In the field, as well as site-specific projects, often initiated as reactions to chance discoveries, there are an increasing number of long-term, interdisciplinary, area-oriented research programmes. In this sense, a reactive nautical archaeology has become a proactive maritime archaeology. For the historical period, this is reflected in concerns with issues such as the development of nation-states, and the ways their capitalist, imperialist and colonial agendas were prosecuted on a global scale. To an extent, this transition reflects the key phases of mainstream archaeological thinking but on a somewhat compressed timescale. Maritime investigations that were 'archaeology' as opposed to artefact salvage began to gather significant momentum in the 1960s, just in time for the cathartic arrival of the **New Archaeology**. Its impact on the maritime sphere was less than dramatic, though it ultimately left an enduring legacy, not least through the work of Keith Muckelroy. Schooled in the theoretical hothouse of 1970s Cambridge, Muckelroy drew his principal inspiration from David Clarke. His outlook was broadly processual and found expression in his interest in formation processes, systems and the use of quantitative data analysis (note the use of the word 'scientific' in his definition). In this he was paralleled by a focus on rigorous recording and analysis of boat finds and in the testing of various forms of 'floating' hypothesis, typified by work in Scandinavia by Ole Crumlin-Pedersen and in Britain by Sean McGrail. Concern with quantifiable data fed through to underwater excavation (see **excavation methods, underwater**) and recording. In the 1970s and early 1980s, a concerted effort was made to transpose Mediterranean advances to more demanding conditions elsewhere. It was reasoned that, if methods were crude, subsequent analysis and interpretation would be similarly limited. Getting one's methodological house in order was also seen as a prerequisite for 'catching up' with land archaeology, gaining academic credibility and reinforcing the distinction between what was archaeology and what was not, i.e. salvage or treasure hunting. Yet this focus on method, quantifiable data and middle-range theory represented a rather selective adoption of the New Archaeology for they were generally pursued within historiographic rather than anthropological frameworks. In the USA, the New Archaeology gained more wholehearted support, finding explicit expression in 'shipwreck anthropology' championed by Richard Gould. This articulated the traditional, particularist versus processual, generalist debate in the context of shipwrecks, shipping and wider society. By the early 1980s, European processual archaeology was being challenged by a contextual approach that advocated a re-engagement with history and agency, and which recognised that material culture is 'meaningfully constituted' and thus 'active' rather than inert. These ideas found immediate favour among those engaged in the large-scale wreck excavations of the time, for these sites, many of them post-medieval, were specific events writ large. In their well-preserved assemblages, often containing thousands of objects, the evidence for individual as well as collective decision-making and action were clearly visible. So too were the symbolic associations of many of the objects and of the vessels themselves. Such high-resolution assemblages demand meticulous recording, which,

while appearing to put general questions on hold, provides a basis for addressing them.

There were of course innovative excavations of other site types such as harbours, crannogs and other settlement sites, but it is the wrecks that raise issues relating to the theory and method of historical archaeology. The preponderance of medieval and early modern wreck investigations initially attracted the same charge made against medieval archaeology: that they were an expensive way of telling us what we already knew. This view assumes primacy of the historical record irrespective of the quality of the data. Analysis then consists of checking the archaeological findings against the historical record to produce 'the identified wreck', 'the identified mystery object', etc. There is no denying that such correlation is fascinating but in essence it is little more than using archaeology to provide physical illustrations for 'real' history. It neither capitalises on the potential of archaeological material nor the synergy between the two sources. A concerted attempt to do so was made in the excavation of the VOC *Amsterdam* (1749). The **Dutch East India Company** (VOC) is one of the best-documented maritime enterprises, while the wreck itself is the best-preserved VOC ship yet found. Here was an opportunity to achieve a more holistic result by interrogating the sources simultaneously. As the archaeology assaulted the archives with new questions, the documents generated questions that the excavators took with them underwater. Far from digging up what was already known, the *Amsterdam* proved to be full of surprises. Historical omissions, inconsistencies and inaccuracies were revealed and, most importantly, explanatory relationships became apparent that would otherwise not have been suspected. To paraphrase Muckelroy: the ship as machine, as an element in a capitalist economic system and as a social unit, was thrown into stark relief.

Through such research programmes, the generalist/particularist debate has effectively been bypassed. Many scholars have sought to actively combine them, exploring approaches influenced by *Annales* historians among others. For example, it would be impossible to understand the complexity of the *Amsterdam* in isolation of the VOC, or of its networks linking European and Oriental societies. The move to the centre ground has not, therefore, been to sit on the theoretical fence but to pursue the best of both processual and post-processual worlds. Maritime archaeology relies on the scientific analysis of the post-depositional processes of site evolution, yet admits no contradiction in seeking to understand the symbolic, as well as functional, meanings of 'active' **material culture** in its pre-depositional and depositional contexts.

As maritime archaeology progressively developed its identity, a recurring question has been whether it is a discipline in its own right or, as Muckelroy saw it, a sub-discipline of archaeology, or simply archaeology. Muckelroy's classification rested largely in his identification of distinct 'maritime cultures'. Whether the culture of any social group can be entirely maritime has been much debated but, ultimately, disciplinary autonomy rests on whether there is a difference in what maritime archaeology can know about the past. Certainly, the degree of preservation common in waterlogged deposits, and the nature of shipwrecks, harbours, waterfronts, coastal settlements, salterns and fish weirs, etc., gives maritime research a distinctive character. It follows that this database will allow certain questions to be addressed more successfully than they might be on the basis of inland remains and vice versa. While this might constitute enough ontological difference to support the status of 'sub-discipline', what we seek to understand remains firmly within the domain of archaeology. Indeed, the future of maritime archaeology lies in its potential, not just for explicating maritime enterprise but in addressing some of archaeology's most fundamental questions: innovation, cultural transmission, the very nature of social change and the trajectory of human affairs. If the past is a foreign country, maritime archaeology offers one of the best ways of reaching it.

See also: processual archaeology; post-processual archaeology

References

Muckelroy, K. (1978) *Maritime Archaeology*, Cambridge: Cambridge University Press.

Further reading

Gawronski, J. (1992) 'Aims and theory of the archae-ology of Dutch East Indiamen', in J. Gawronski, B. Kist and O. Stokvis van Boetzelaer (eds) *Hollandia Compendium*, Amsterdam: Elsevier, pp. 19–31.

Gibbins, D. (1990) 'Analytical approaches in maritime archaeology: A Mediterranean perspective', *Antiquity* 64: 376–89.

Gibbins, D. and Adams, J. (eds) (2001) 'Shipwrecks and maritime archaeology', *World Archaeology* 32: 279–91.

Gould, R. (ed.) (1983) *Shipwreck Anthropology*, Albuquerque: University of New Mexico.

McGrail, S. (ed.) (1984) *Aspects of Maritime Archaeology and Ethnology*, London: National Maritime Museum.

Westerdahl, C. (1992) 'The maritime cultural landscape', *International Journal of Nautical Archaeology* 21(1): 5–14.

JONATHAN ADAMS

Maritime Provinces, the, Canada

Historical archaeology in the Canadian Maritime Provinces of Nova Scotia, New Brunswick and Prince Edward Island has tended to focus on military sites and is only beginning to deal with the complex interaction of Native Mi'kmaqs and Maliseets; the Acadian French, who arrived in the seventeenth century to be dispersed in the eighteenth; their early Scots and English competitors; and various later immigrants including the French fisherfolk of Cape Breton, German Protestants, New England planters, black loyalists and the returning Acadians and Scots highlanders, who repopulated Cape Breton in the nineteenth century.

The emphasis on military archaeology is evident at Fort Anne, in Acadian Port Royal, renamed Annapolis Royal after British occupation in the 1690s. Parks Canada identified a palimpsest of fortifications: the Scots fort of 1629; the defensible habitation of the seventeenth-century merchant Charles d'Aulnay; and eighteenth-century imperial defences. In the 1960s, Norman Barka investigated Fort La Tour, in present-day Saint John, New Brunswick, a civil fort typical of the internecine commercial warfare of the mid-seventeenth century. The **Fortress of Louisbourg** is the best-researched eighteenth-century site in the Atlantic region, if not Canada. Developed as a fortified harbour by the French after the negotiated withdrawal from Newfoundland, in 1713, it became a significant French entrepôt and centre for an important regional fishery until it was obliterated by the British after its fall in 1758. Archaeological research there has focused on the military story and a similar emphasis characterised Parks Canada's investigations of Fort Beausejour, New Brunswick, a French stronghold in the 1750s, and of eighteenth-century British fortifications at Fort Amherst, Prince Edward Island.

More recently, archaeologists in the Maritimes have turned their attention to domestic and commercial matters. Parks Canada returned to Fort Amherst in the 1980s to do an innovative conductivity survey and to excavate an Acadian cellar at Port la Joye. They also located an Acadian farm at the Melanson site, not far from Port Royal, although this remains uninterpreted. David Christianson's excavation of the Belleisle farmstead has yielded information about Acadian life before the expulsion of 1755, as has Parks Canada's excavations at the Roma site in Prince Edward Island. Birgitta Wallace and Rob Ferguson have explored the interconnected commercial, military and fisheries history of eighteenth-century Grassy Island for Parks Canada. The wreck of the *Machault*, a supply ship sunk off New Brunswick en route to Quebec, has provided a fine sample of mid-eighteenth-century **material culture**. Laird Niven's community-sponsored investigations of the black loyalist community at Birchtown opens another new direction for archaeology in the Maritimes.

See also: English colonialism; French colonialism

Further reading

Blanchette, J.-F. (1981) *The Roles of Artifacts in the Study of Foodways in New France 1720–60*, Ottawa: Parks Canada.

Lavoie, M.C. (1987) *Belle Isle Nova Scotia 1680–1755: Acadian Material Life and Economy*, Halifax: Nova Scotia Museum.

Sullivan, C. (1986) *Legacy of the Machault: A Collection of 18th-Century Artifacts*, Ottawa: Parks Canada.

Turnbull, C. J. and Davis, S.A. (1986) *An Archaeological Bibliography of the Maritime Provinces: Works to 1984*, Halifax: The Council of Maritime Premiers' Maritime Committee for Archaeological Cooperation.

PETER E. POPE

maroon sites

The term 'maroon' usually refers to African slaves in the New World who have run away from the sites of their bondage and have created their own settlements, usually in out-of-the-way, difficult-to-reach places. Historical archaeologists have grown increasingly interested in the archaeology of maroons since the early 1990s. Since then, archaeologists have examined the physical remains of maroon settlements in **Brazil**, Cuba, the Dominican Republic, Jamaica and the USA.

Archaeologists have been attracted to maroon sites for at least two important reasons. First, many find maroon sites to be romantic and intriguing places to study because they evoke images of brave slaves openly defying the powerful New World slave regime. In light of the often overwhelming abundance of archaeological research on plantation sites (see **plantation archaeology**), there is something refreshing about investigating the men and women who cast off the shackles of slavery and proclaimed their freedom. In addition, some of the research on maroon sites has probably occurred because archaeologists have discovered that many African Americans, for instance, have grown tired of hearing only about slavery. In other countries, such as Brazil, maroon inhabitants are held in great respect by their descendants, and research often receives popular support.

The second reason that historical archaeologists have shown interest in maroon settlements is more academic and research oriented. Research on maroon sites can provide exciting new information about the resilient and adaptive nature of African culture. Archaeological research at maroon sites can provide both specific and general insights about the social and cultural characteristics of maroon life.

Archaeological research can provide the kind of site-specific information that it can offer for any site: namely, the precise location of the settlement; information about its size; the style and construction methods of its housing; and the dates of its construction, use, and abandonment. Archaeology can also provide unique information about the **material culture** of the people who lived at a maroon site. This tangible information can also provide new understandings of culture contact and the **ethnicity** of the site's residents. If an archaeologist finds that the houses in a maroon community were constructed in both African and Native American styles (see **Native Americans**), then it may be possible to conclude that some cultural mixing occurred there. Artefacts unearthed at a fugitive slave site can also reveal previously unknown information about cultural contacts if, for example, the archaeologist discovered artefacts known to be made in a particular, far-away locale or by a specific people who lived outside the maroon site.

The archaeology of maroon settlements is particularly important for providing anthropological information about the daily lives of its residents. Physical evidence related to power and social relations and the creation and continuation of traditional patterns of economic, political and spiritual life can also be unearthed at maroon sites.

Creolisation is one topic of great concern to anthropologically trained historical archaeologists and its study is particularly well suited to maroon site research. As groups of New World slaves, originally from diverse African cultures, were forced together, they created new cultural expressions that were the result of sharing with and borrowing from other cultural traditions. These new forms of creolised cultures could also include elements from the many European cultures with whom the slaves had regular contact. Archaeology at maroon settlements can provide tangible evidence for the blending of cultures, often in a manner that cannot be duplicated by any other discipline.

Some historians are beginning to question the creolisation thesis, arguing that slaves imported to various parts of the world did not create popula-

tions as diverse as might be supposed. They know, for instance, that some planters, such as the rice growers along the coast of South Carolina, specifically bought men and women from the rice-growing parts of Africa. This targeted slave importation means that people familiar with rice cultivation would tend to live in one slave-holding area. Of course, the creation of rice-growing populations, or others with specific knowledge or talents, does not mean that creolisation did not exist, and for archaeologists it only presents more issues to investigate.

It is likely that archaeological interest in maroon settlements will continue to grow during the early years of the twenty-first century, even though archaeology at maroon sites presents some practical problems. One of the most obvious problems involves finding the sites and, having found them, being able to solve the logistical problems of mounting an archaeological expedition to them. Fugitive slaves usually built their communities in places that are still difficult to reach today, and archaeology at these sites can present significant logistical problems.

See also: African American archaeology; Fort Mose; Nanny Town; Palmares

Further reading

Agorsah, E.K. (1993) 'Archaeology and resistance history in the Caribbean', *African Archaeological Review* 11: 175–95.

Orser, C.E., Jr (1998) 'The archaeology of the African diaspora', *Annual Review of Anthropology* 27: 63–82.

CHARLES E. ORSER, JR

Marquette Mission, Michigan, USA

The Marquette Mission site is a seventeenth-century French mission and an associated Huron Indian village. Historical archaeologists have examined portions of both these settlements.

The site derives its name from Jesuit Father Jacques Marquette, who established the mission and ministered to the **Native Americans** in the region from this base. Marquette built the original mission in 1671 on Mackinac Island (at the western end of Lake Huron), but moved it one year later immediately west to the mainland at today's St Ignace, Michigan. Marquette, who is renowned for his trip down the Mississippi River with Louis Jolliet in 1673, died in 1675 as he was making his way back to the mission. Two years later, his remains were exhumed and reburied at St Ignace in keeping with his wishes. Local priest Father Edward Jacker re-excavated his remains in 1877 and had them reburied on the grounds of the chapel. The mission site was designated a National Historic Landmark in 1960 (see **National Historic Landmarks**).

The area of the mission also included a French trading post, and archaeologists who have excavated around the mission have been interested in understanding the nature of the culture contacts that occurred between the Native Americans and the French settlers in the region. Marquette had purposely established the mission near a village of the Tionontate Huron, who had moved to the St Ignace area around 1670. Archaeologists estimate that between 500–800 people once lived in this village, and their excavations have documented that the village covered 2.4–3.2 ha.

The size of the native village is perhaps not surprising given its location. St Ignace is situated on the southern tip of Michigan's Upper Peninsula at the Straits of Mackinac, a narrow waterway that separates Lake Huron from Lake Michigan. The Straits were thus an important colonial transportation route and strategic location. The French built **Fort Michilimackinac** across the Straits from St Ignace because of the spot's military value.

Archaeologists conducted excavations at the Marquette Mission site in the early 1970s, and again in 1983–6, 1997–8 and 2001. They have excavated over 872 m^2 and have found evidence of longhouses (a characteristic feature of Huron **material culture**), hearths and thousands of artefacts. They have used these artefacts to shed light on Huron **acculturation**. As might be expected, the Native Americans at the Marquette Mission site adapted to using many European objects in their daily lives. As is true of most indigenous peoples, however, their acculturation to European ways was not absolute, and they tenaciously maintained many of their traditions. For instance, the Huron used olive-green bottle glass to fashion traditional arrow points, and they transformed useless brass kettle fragments into spear points and ornamental beads and bracelets. Archaeologist Susan Branstner has convincingly argued that the Huron around the mission site were not prisoners to acculturation. Rather, they relied on conscious decisions about which artefacts to adopt based on their efficiency and availability.

See also: French colonialism

Further reading

Branstner, S.M. (1992) 'Tionontate Huron occupation at the Marquette Mission', in J.A. Walthall and T.E. Emerson (eds) *Calumet and Fleur-de-Lys: Archaeology of Indian and French Contact in the Midcontinent*, Washington: Smithsonian Institution Press, pp. 177–201.

CHARLES E. ORSER, JR

Martin's Hundred, Virginia, USA

The name 'Martin's Hundred' was given to a tract of 8,000 ha assigned to members of the Virginia Company of London calling themselves the 'Society of Martin's Hundred'. After its foundation in 1619, the companys investors sent out the ship *Gift of God* carrying 220 settlers. Due to sickness on board and the resulting loss of leadership, the Martin's Hundred colonists were unable to secure and settle their land until 1620. Located seven miles below **Jamestown**, the tract occupied ten miles of frontage on the north bank of the James River. Its core settlements were extensively excavated between 1976 and 1983.

Named in honour of Sir John Wolstenholme, one of the Society's principal investors, Wolstenholme Towne was laid out in the style of early seventeenth-century plantations in Ulster, Ireland. Two rows of buildings flanked a village green, at one end of which stood a palisaded fort wherein lived governor William Harwood. The James-fronting end of the settlement has been heavily eroded, and the archaeologists estimated that about half the village had been lost to the river. Downstream from the main settlement stood the separately palisaded home of warden John Boyce who is believed to have erected it to secure the acreage on behalf of the Martin's Hundred investors in 1619 pending the arrival of replacement leadership from London. Both the Boyce homestead and the houses of Wolstenholme Towne were destroyed in the widespread Indian attacks of 22 March 1622. From a pre-massacre population of 144, approximately fifty-eight survived, only about twenty-eight of whom returned to re-establish the plantation. Replacement settlers were sent from London aboard the disease-ridden relief ship *Abigail*, but most of those assigned to Martin's Hundred would be dead by the spring of 1623.

Although several small Martin's Hundred farmsteads limped along through the rest of the century to become absorbed into the large tobacco-growing plantation renamed Carter's Grove, the site's dramatic origins were quickly forgotten – save for an incorrectly worded state marker on the highway 3 km distant. In 1969, the Colonial Williamsburg Foundation took possession of the Carter's Grove tract and instructed its archaeology department to conduct a field survey designed to locate eighteenth-century foundations associated with the 1755 mansion. Eighteenth-century remains were scarce, but the testing located several areas of occupation dating from the first half of the previous century. Renewed excavating beginning in 1976 revealed first the layout of William Harwood's post-massacre plantation, then the home of potter Thomas Ward, followed by the plan of what was left of Wolstenholme Towne, and finally that of the earlier Boyce homestead. Together these sites yielded valuable information regarding post-in-the-ground building construction from *c*. 1620–45 as well as of fort building paralleling William Strachey's 1610 description of the palisades at Jamestown.

Large quantities of artefacts were retrieved, conserved and subsequently exhibited, among them the first closed helmets discovered in the New World. Dating as they did to the 1620s they had much to say about munition (run-of-the-mill) armour in use in England in a grey area between the fine suits from the days of Elizabethan chivalry to the much lighter armours of the English Civil

War (1642–6). So little was known that the conservator's discovery that the helmets were secured with brass rivets was first rejected by Tower of London experts as highly unlikely. However, they subsequently, and generously, provided the documentation to prove themselves wrong.

Equally in error were British ecclesiastical historians who refused to believe that common coffins of the 1630s were gabled rather than flat lidded. Evidence for such A-lids was provided by **nails** centrally distributed the length of the skeletons, but it required the opening of several church vaults in England before the Martin's Hundred evidence would be accepted. Two burials associated with the aftermath of the 1622 massacre were without coffins, one victim lying as she had died and the other in a prepared grave. Both, however, provided graphic evidence of Indian ritualistic slaying. The man believed to have been military commander Lieutenant Richard Keene had been felled above the right eye with a sharp instrument deduced to have been an English spade, his skull then crushed from behind with an Indian club. The latter practice had been documented on Roanoke Island, North Carolina, in 1585. In addition, the skull showed scoring resulting from left-side scalping. The second Martin's Hundred victim, a woman, is believed to have met the same fate and to have died in an open rubbish pit outside the Boyce palisade. The contemporaneously published lists of the massacre dead pointed to her only as 'a maide'. The same list included four male servants whose remains were found together in a single grave, one of the men wearing a lone, labourer's nail-studded shoe.

The presence of potter Thomas Ward both before and after the massacre, coupled with the time and site separation provided by the disaster, together yielded much information about the translation of English potting practices and designs to Virginia in the first decades of colonisation. Important among the fragmentary bowls, pipkins, colanders, mugs, chamber pots and the like was a slipware dish dated 1631, the earliest dated piece of US slipware, as well as being among the earliest recorded in England. Pit strata overlying the dated dish were to add cautionary data regarding reliance on dating clay tobacco pipes (see **pipes,**

smoking) on the evidence of their stem bore diameters.

Supported throughout by the National Geographic Society, the Colonial Williamsburg Foundation deemed the Martin's Hundred excavation to be of sufficient public interest to warrant the building of a museum (see **museums**), wherein to tell its story and exhibit its principal artefacts. Built under a hill adjacent to the vestigially reconstructed Wolstenholme Towne site, the museum opened in 1991. A two-volume report and artefact catalogue was published in 2001, at which date several more seventeenth-century sites at Carter's Grove still remained unexcavated.

Further reading

Noël Hume, I. (1979) *Martin's Hundred*, New York: Alfred A. Knopf.

Noël Hume, I. and Noël Hume, A. (2001) *The Archaeology of Martin's Hundred*, 2 vols, Williamsburg: Colonial Williamsburg Foundation.

IVOR NOËL HUME

Marxian approaches

Marxism is a rich intellectual tradition that examines capitalism's fundamental material inequality, probes the historical roots of such inequality and confronts the political significance of all knowledge about the past. Consequently, it harbours many insights that are clearly relevant to historical archaeological theory and practice. Much of the Marxian thinking in historical archaeology, though, somewhat haphazardly borrows from various Marxian concepts, retreats from Marxism's most radical implications or does not acknowledge or even recognise its Marxian roots.

Marxism is 'grand theory'; that is, it forges a comprehensive philosophical framework that explains the fundamental nature of social relations. Archaeologists have often championed universal theories, but Marxism is distinguished by its central intent to transform lived inequality in contemporary society. In contrast to scientifically oriented theories, Marxism almost always rejects facile divisions between analyst and subject of study,

viewing all scholarship as political. Unlike the politicised but eclectic approaches lumped within the rubric of post-processualism, Marxism is a comprehensive philosophy that argues that researchers can know the social world's objective inequalities and contradictions, and formulate activism based on their scholarly insights. Consequently, Marxism occupies a distinctive niche in archaeological thought.

A vast range of thinkers in Karl Marx's wake have borrowed, elaborated and reformulated Marx's assessments of capitalist life. Despite the richness in Marxian approaches, Marxian scholars share a relatively consistent set of insights. Central to these insights is Marxism's emphasis on capitalism's contradictory social relations and tensions. Social scientists often reduce conflict to aberrations in a generally rational if not beneficial socioeconomic system, but Marxism assumes from the outset that conflict and oppression are inherent in capitalism and should be scholars' central focus. Robert Paynter, for instance, argued that historical archaeology must focus on class inequality (see **class, social**), the tensions over material surplus and the capitalist contradictions and crises reflected in commodities. In his advocacy of an archaeology of capitalism, Paynter focused on social organisation and its relationship with resource access in capitalist society. Capitalism is what is known in Marxism as a 'mode of production', one of a range of historically specific sets of social relations that structure resource production, distribution and surplus. The fundamental capitalist distinction is between producers who own the means of production (e.g. tools, materials) and workers who sell their labour for a wage and produce commodities sold by the producer for a profit. Capitalists assume the potential for unending profit, but producers' desire for increasing profit and workers' conflicting interest to secure an equitable share of their labour leads to recurring class crises. Rather than champion an ambiguous definition of class, class in Paynter's formulation is created and reproduced by unequal access to, and control over, strategic resources. Paynter advocated an archaeology that probes why everyday folks adopted certain mass-produced goods at particular moments and how such consumption patterns illuminate class relations in the capitalist cycle of expansion, contraction and crisis. James Delle's comparable study of **coffee** plantations in eastern Jamaica probed how contradictory class relations and socioeconomic crises were negotiated in planters' and enslaved labourers' divergent visions of plantation space. Delle focused on how perceptions of Jamaican plantations were simultaneously shaped by the currents of world-wide capitalist economics, the everyday tension between planters and enslaved labourers, and the contradictions between how capitalists and workers envisioned the same relations and spaces.

Marxism has devoted considerable attention to commodities as symbolically complex entities, a line of thinking that certainly has relevance to archaeological theory; indeed, Marx opened *Capital* pondering commodities' power. Marxism views material meaning as a construction that distorts or masks the social relations surrounding an object's production. In everyday practice, consumers tend to assume that material meaning comes from an individual's contemplation of an object's physical properties (e.g. style, form), but a good's constructed meaning has little or nothing to do with its physical form or an individual's innate taste and aesthetics. Marx referred to this as 'fetishism', arguing that commodities were significant research subjects because they represent the social and labour relations that shaped consumers' socially shared way of seeing both objects and social structure. Some Marxian historical archaeologists have probed how artefacts' meanings reflect the socioeconomic relations of production, dominant exchange values and distinctive consumer symbolism. Charles Orser, for example, advocated a historical archaeology that produces a 'social history of commodities'. Using the example of commodity consumption among enslaved African Americans, Orser argued that archaeologists should use commodities to illuminate the dominant social relations that made both mass production and servitude possible, but archaeologists must also confront the contrasting meanings oppressed consumers like African Americans routinely gave to those goods. Orser's approach attempted to resist reducing all material symbolism to 'false' meanings, instead acknowledging a range of alternative as well as dominant meanings lurking within any

object and changing over time. This appreciation of symbolic variability is not necessarily exclusive to Marxian thinking, but Orser analysed symbolic variation as a product of a historically specific set of class relations. By situating material symbolism within class contradictions, Orser evaded the implication that objects' meanings are shaped by essential cultural identity, dictated by rational market economics, or capable of somehow assuming any symbolism.

Marxism's withering attack on capitalism and focus on dominant structuring mechanisms (e.g. economics) sometimes overshadows its focus on human agency. In most formulations, Marxism probes how the masses articulate shared class exploitation, especially in collective and 'conscious' forms intended to change dominant conditions; from this perspective, individual decision making is meaningless without an appreciation of the conditions shaping that agency. Class consciousness has a range of definitions, but some form of collective class agency is paramount in Marxian definitions of consciousness. Marxism stresses that people's actions and ideas make their conditions even as those conditions shape human agency, a relationship that is central to what is known as the dialectic. Dialectical thinking argues that society cannot be understood without assessing it as a dynamic whole in which all parts (e.g. human agents, production structure) are defined by their contradictory relationships over time. Yet people often view capitalism as stable, placid and timeless, and some historical archaeologists have argued that objects themselves draw attention away from capitalism's vast contradictions. Mark Leone championed the concept of ideology to analyse how material symbolism helps convince people to tolerate oppression. Leone took his central intellectual concept of ideology from Louis Althusser, and his methodology was adapted from Frankfurt school critical theory, primarily critical theorists' belief that self-reflectively exposing historiographic ideologies would lead to working-class 'emancipation'. Althusser defined ideology as unquestioned 'givens' of life that form a class-interested, totalising way of perceiving the world and legitimising inequalities. Yet Althusser was a structural Marxist, and like most structuralists he had little or no interest in history and dialectical change; instead, he espoused a science of human action with a distinct object of study (i.e. modes of production and consciousness). This profoundly complicates ideology, because Althusser argued that social structures – not people – make history; Althusser concluded that Marxism is a 'hard' science that is superior to philosophical, moralising social sciences that separate the basis for human decision making from objective nature. Leone skirted the deterministic inflexibility of Althusser's methodology by turning to critical theory. Critical theorists depicted ideology as a class-interested, totalising illusion. Unlike Althusser, though, the critical theorists were writing in the 1920s and 1930s in the midst of fascism, emergent Nazism and an expanding consumer culture, so they confronted the non-rational aspects of capitalist life and aspired to assertive moral analyses of exploitation and the mechanics of domination. Critical theorists believed that their mission of a contemplative cultural critique directly contrasted with 'objective' science that assumes a division between analyst and object of study.

Leone appropriated critical theory's focus on self-reflection, their interest in scholars' role in the social world and their advocacy of critical history to raise consciousness about ideologies' roots. With Parker Potter and Paul Shackel, Leone argued that archaeology is a practice inevitably structured by contemporary academic and social context. Leone, Potter and Shackel examined how archaeology and history were presented to tourists in Annapolis, Maryland, and concluded that such presentations reproduced contemporary ideologies by divining them in the city's celebrated colonial past. Leone, Potter and Shackel championed a 'critical archaeology' that used mundane and familiar objects to show the 350-year dynamism of modern life and expose how unquestioned contemporary behaviours belied deep-seated historical inequality. For instance, they examined changes in cutlery and ceramic tableware consumption, arguing that the eighteenth-century emergence of table manners was one of many practices designed to distinguish the elite from the working class. Such objects were not simply intended to fortify or display class separations: They also were meant to legitimise inequality by suggesting that elite practices were the 'natural' and 'appropriate' behaviours of

cultured and rational people. Leone, Potter and Shackel focused on how and why the elite cultivated such practices in a moment of class crisis on the eve of the American Revolution, and they concluded that the elite embraced these behaviours to legitimise their precarious control of the revolutionary movement. Leone, Potter and Shackel did not preclude resistance to etiquette, patriotic rhetoric and the like, but their analysis focused most clearly on how dominant ideological practices and beliefs shaped both class domination and all resistance. Subsequently, Leone, Christopher Matthews and Kurt Jordan amplified Leone, Potter and Shackel's earlier definition of critical archaeology by recognising the sway of various forms of resistance. This later framework borrowed the concept of hegemony from Antonio Gramsci and Raymond Williams, giving less credence to dominant ideological production and more to the ever-present tension between dominant and resistant groups. Within a hegemonic society, subordinated groups accept the basic social order of the dominant class; in this perspective, subordinated groups always contest and impact the distribution of power, but they rarely contest its validity and circumstances.

Among critical archaeology's most important insights was that archaeologists are themselves embedded in ideologically influenced state institutions, such as the academy or **cultural-resource management**. Consequently, archaeologists are trained to reproduce dominant ideology, yet they occupy a position from which they can launch attacks upon those very ideologies in practice. Leone, Potter and Shackel argued that in archaeological tours, 'emancipation' – a key, albeit somewhat ambiguous Marxian concept – is oriented toward raising contemporary awareness of inequalities, especially class. Self-reflection itself can be appropriated by any theoretical perspective, and many utterly non-Marxian archaeologists directly borrow from Leone's formulation of critical theory. Marxism, however, points toward creating knowledge that identifies material oppression and in turn forges a subordinated consciousness that resists continued class domination.

Ultimately, historical archaeology has been influenced by Marxian concepts such as class and ideology, Marxism's focus on systemic social contradictions and Marxism's vision of scholarly activism. Yet Marxism presents a profoundly ambitious task linking local experiences and systemic structuring mechanisms, probing complex commodity symbolism in relation to consumer identities and historical socioeconomic cycles, and bridging historical research with contemporary activism. This challenge is compounded by Marxism's demanding, complex and dynamic literature, and caricatures of Marxism as deterministic do little to warm archaeologists to Marxian scholarship. Nevertheless, a modest number of Marxian historical archaeologists have had considerable influence forcing the discipline to consider issues of social inequality, commodification and scholarly practice in historical archaeology.

Further reading

Delle, J.A. (1998) *An Archaeology of Social Space: Analyzing Coffee Plantations in Jamaica's Blue Mountains*, New York: Kluwer Academic/Plenum Press.

Leone, M.P., Matthews, C.N. and Jordan, K.A. (forthcoming) 'Marxist and critical historical archaeology', in T. Majewski and C.E. Orser, Jr (eds) *International Handbook of Historical Archaeology*, New York: Kluwer Academic/Plenum Press.

Leone, M.P., Potter, P.B., Jr, and Shackel, P.A. (1987) 'Toward a critical archaeology', *Current Anthropology* 28: 283–302.

Orser, C.E. (1992) 'Beneath the material surface of things: Commodities, artifacts, and slave plantations', *Historical Archaeology* 26(3): 95–104.

Paynter, R. (1988) 'Steps to an archaeology of capitalism: Material change and class analysis', in M.P. Leone and P.B. Potter, Jr (eds) *The Recovery of Meaning: Historical Archaeology in the Eastern United States*, Washington, DC: Smithsonian Institution Press, pp. 407–33.

PAUL R. MULLINS

Mary Rose, shipwreck

The *Mary Rose*, Henry VIII's warship, was built 1510–11 and sank in July 1545. The surviving hull was raised in 1982 after a monumental programme of archaeology that developed many techniques in underwater excavation (see **excavation methods, underwater**).

The *Mary Rose* had a successful career, serving at times as flagship in Henry's fledgling 'Navy' before capsizing during an engagement with a French invasion fleet off Portsmouth Harbour on the south coast of England. This may have been a result of overloading, overcrowding, poor seamanship and other causes but a survivor told how she keeled over with the wind and the lowest gunports had been left open after firing. As one of the earliest ships to be equipped with lidded ports and guns close to the waterline, the *Mary Rose* marks an important stage in the development of warfare at sea. **Dendrochronology** studies by Dobbs and Bridge have proved that the rebuilds referred to in historical sources were extensive. They included major strengthening of the hull in the 1530s and refits close to the gun ports in the 1540s.

Contemporary salvage attempts failed to raise the vessel and the hull gradually silted up, preserving a substantial proportion of the starboard side. Although early pioneer divers found the wreck in the 1830s, this time capsule of Tudor life was otherwise left alone until historian Alexander McKee started a search in 1965. Under the careful direction of McKee and archaeologist Margaret Rule, investigations proceeded outside the hull until the decision was made to undertake the complete excavation. This took place from 1979 and culminated with the eventful but successful salvage on 11 October 1982. The hull returned to Portsmouth where she has been on public display since 1983, averaging 300,000 visitors per year. The museum exhibits the remarkable selection of objects, which have been designated as one of the United Kingdom's collections of outstanding importance.

The value of the project partly derives from the importance it has to a wide variety of disciplines. For historians, the *Mary Rose* has many associations with Henry VIII whose reign from 1509 to 1547 spans the ship's career and who witnessed the sinking from the shore at Southsea Castle. For naval architects, the ship dates from a revolutionary period in the development of warship design when contemporary hull drawings are not available. For archaeologists, the project has been a seminal moment in the development of **maritime archaeology** and has refined techniques for the conservation of waterlogged wood. Finally, for educationalists and the general public, the surviving hull and contents bring history alive and contribute to lifelong learning with integrity seldom achieved by media or fantasy worlds alone.

Further reading

Dobbs, C.T.C. and Bridge, M. (2000) 'Preliminary results from dendrochronological studies on the *Mary Rose*', in J. Litwin (ed.) *Down the River to the Sea*, Gdansk: Polish Maritime Museum, pp. 257–62.

McKee, A. (1982) *How We Found the Mary Rose*, London: Souvenir.

Mary Rose Trust; major publication in five volumes, in press.

Rule, M.H. (1983) *The Mary Rose: The Excavation and Raising of Henry VIII's Flagship*, second edn, London: Conway Maritime.

CHRISTOPHER DOBBS

material culture

Material culture constitutes for archaeologists the main subject matter of their discipline. Because material culture has a central place in archaeological research, it is perhaps not surprising that archaeologists do not necessarily agree either about what material culture 'means' or how it should be studied.

It may at first seem that 'material culture' refers strictly to artefacts, but archaeologists view material culture in much broader terms. The definition offered by historical archaeologist James Deetz, in his influential *In Small Things Forgotten: The Archaeology of Early American Life*, first published in 1977, suggests the breadth of material culture: it is 'that sector of our physical environment that we modify through culturally determined behavior'. Material culture thus includes artefacts – because artefacts are examples of material culture – but the term really refers to *all* tangible aspects of **culture**. Material culture thus includes landscapes, buildings of all shapes and sizes, formal gardens and even the

patterns a marching band forms on a US football field. Some archaeologists broaden the concept of material culture even further and contend that facial make-up, fingerprints and even body odours constitute examples of material culture. Archaeologists agree, though, that human beings are constantly immersed in a material world, and that human life without material culture is impossible.

The study of material culture is not the sole domain of the archaeologist. Historical architects, museum experts, social and cultural historians, cultural anthropologists, cultural geographers, landscape designers, art historians and folklorists can all possess a strong interest in material culture, and each can bring the strengths and special insights of their disciplines to its study. The analysis of material culture also need not be restricted to the past. Since we are all surrounded by material culture in everything we do, scholars of popular culture, sociologists and political scientists can also examine the impact of material culture on human life.

A brief history of material-culture studies

Material-culture specialist Thomas Schlereth in 1982 provided a concise overview of the history of material-culture studies in the USA from 1876 to 1976. His review presents an excellent way to demonstrate the breadth of material-culture studies as well as the changing emphases of study through the years. It is likely that the history of material-culture study in the USA was duplicated in other parts of world with some minor variations. Schlereth divides the study of material culture into three historical phases: the Age of Collecting (1876–1948), the Age of Description (1948–65) and the Age of Analysis (1965–76). These periods are useful because they have clear relevance to historical archaeology, a field that generally followed the same intellectual trajectory.

Scholars interested in material culture during the years 1876–1948 generally focused their efforts on collecting examples of tangible things to preserve them for future display (such as at the living museum (see **living museums**) at Henry Ford's Greenfield Village) and to hoard them (as treasured objects of art). Many of the collections were composed of objects representing 'high art', while others contained folk-art specimens. In both cases, the collectors – archaeologists, anthropologists, architects and art historians – generally sought to create the collections for the sake of collecting. They usually conducted little or no analysis of the materials they gathered, preferring instead to view the objects merely as the tangible representations of distinct cultures.

Material-culture studies during Schlereth's Age of Description were generally characterised by the scholars' fascination with creating classification schemes that described the objects within their collections. Archaeologists specifically used their collections of excavated and intricately classified material culture to construct regional and continental cultural chronologies. This period saw the rise of institutionalised historical archaeology. In this initial period, pioneering historical archaeologists generally perceived material culture as a form of historical documentation. Historical archaeologists, rather than having to construct cultural chronologies like their colleagues who studied prehistory, used material culture to flesh out the history of particular places and events. They did not have to construct large-scale cultural chronologies from material culture because documentary historians had already illustrated the broad trends of recorded history.

Without question, the most important period in material-culture studies occurred within Schlereth's last period, because it was during the final years of the twentieth century that material-culture specialists, including historical archaeologists, abandoned mere collection and simple classification and began seriously to analyse and interpret material culture. As soon as scholars made the commitment to provide detailed interpretations of material culture, it became clear that many perspectives were possible. The period of analysis continues to the present day, with new ideas constantly being presented.

Interpreting material culture

In *Reading Matter*, Arthur Berger presents a hypothetical situation that amply demonstrates the variation possible in the interpretation of material culture. In his scenario, six scholars have offices that each look down upon a small court-

yard. The scholars are by training a semiotician (someone who studies signs and symbols), an anthropologist, a historian, a psychoanalytic psychologist, a sociologist and a Marxist political scientist. On a picnic table in the centre of the courtyard, the six individuals each see a McDonald's hamburger, some chips and a milkshake. Upon seeing these items, however, each scholar perceives them in a different way. The semiotician sees the items as symbols of US efficiency, modernity and standardisation. They have hidden meanings that extend far beyond just being someone's lunch. The psychologist perceives in the items a need for instant gratification, a desire for community with all other McDonald's patrons and at the same time some measure of depersonalisation and dehumanisation. For the anthropologist, the hamburger, chips and milkshake may have a ritualistic, almost religious, meaning, one that has assumed a prominent place in contemporary US daily life. The golden arches are more than simply a marketing ploy: they are almost religious icons or totems. The sociologist may see the objects as examples of the US youth culture or perhaps elements within a complex socialisation process. The historian may see the objects as the result of a successful corporation's history, and he or she may wonder about the role of the corporation in regional, national and even international politics and economics. And the Marxist political scientist, when looking down at the objects on the table, may see them as examples of blatant exploitation, the dangers inherent in the imposition of corporations into human life, and the role of **ideology** in masking social inequality by promoting the idea that McDonald's, because it is for everyone, reduces class divisions.

Berger's hypothetical picnic table vividly illustrates how scholars from different academic fields can interpret the same pieces of material culture in vastly different ways. And these are certainly not the only interpretations that can be offered. For example, imagine that instead of six scholars trained in different disciplines, six anthropologists looked down at the picnic table. Each of the anthropologists could also perceive the objects differently. A structural-functionalist may see the objects as material manifestations of order and structure, physical things that help the cultural system to function smoothly. A cultural ecologist, on the other hand, may see the hamburger and immediately think about the destruction of the Amazon Rainforest in order to raise beef cattle on gigantic, new ranches. Any six members from the other disciplines would probably also offer six distinct interpretations.

Historical archaeologists are free to choose between different perceptions of material culture, and many distinct ways of interpretation currently exist in the field. Just two examples will illustrate the variation of interpretation possible: the **consumer choice**, and the symbolic interpretations.

Two examples of material-culture analysis in historical archaeology

Like all archaeologists, historical archaeologists uncover artefacts in the course of their excavations. And, also like all other archaeologists, they want to know, as much as is possible, the answers to such questions as how the people who used these objects perceived them, why they had them and how they used them. Two of the most nagging questions in historical archaeology revolve around why people had the things archaeologists find at their former home sites, and what they thought of them.

One of the elements of material culture that separates much historical archaeology from pre-historic and pre-Industrial Revolution archaeology is that many of the items in the post-Industrial Revolution era were mass-produced in factories located far from the places where the objects were used. Also, unlike prehistoric times, people who lived after the Industrial Revolution did not make most or even any of the objects they used everyday. When a historical archaeologist excavates a house site, one of the questions he or she often asks is 'Why these items?' What was it about the articles that made a person in the past purchase them? And, broadening the scope to include other material culture: Why did their house look as it did? Why did they organise their lawn, front yard or garden in the manner they chose? To answer such questions, some of the variables to consider are: availability, price, colour, size and, as discussed below, symbolic value.

Archaeologists can never say for certain what individuals in the past thought was most important

about mass-produced material culture. They do, however, have certain models from which to choose. Archaeologist Terry Klein has enumerated three such models: the socioeconomic model (people in social classes buy what they can afford), the market accessibility model (people buy only what is available) and the changing role of women model (women select most of a family's material culture and they purchase things based on their positions within society and the household). Historical archaeologists have investigated all three models, and no consensus currently exists about which one permits the best interpretation. It is also entirely possible that a completely different model may be more robust than any of the three mentioned.

Archaeologists first turned in earnest to symbolic approaches to material-culture interpretation in the 1980s, and these analyses constitute one of the most fertile areas of research in historical archaeology today. Archaeologists who adopt symbolic analyses point out that material culture has more than merely functional usage. In addition to being useful, material culture can be employed consciously and subconsciously to symbolise certain things. Many archaeologists propose that material culture has a strong social character because it can create relationships, invent categories and enforce boundaries. In other words, material culture is socially active and engaged in the human endeavour.

In an interesting study of colonial **Annapolis**, Maryland, Paul Shackel demonstrates how men and women in one social class (see **class, social**) symbolically used material culture to create distinctions between themselves and people in other classes. They also employed material culture to standardise human behaviour as a way of strengthening the social hierarchy. Much of the symbolising that was enacted occurred in relation to the dinner table, as men and women adopted new rules of etiquette and associated them with the material culture of discipline: napkins, forks, knives and fancy teasets (see **tea/tea ceremony**), as well as the design of place settings and the manners that were deemed appropriate. These tangible manners and their associated artefacts – all examples of material culture – combined with **architecture**, landscape and the social structure of historic

Annapolis to create the material environment in which the people of the city lived.

See also: Chesapeake region; Georgian Order; history of historical archaeology

Further reading

Berger, A.A. (1992) *Reading Matter: Multidisciplinary Perspectives on Material Culture*, New Brunswick, NJ: Transaction.

Dant, T. (1999) *Material Culture in the Social World: Values, Activities, Lifestyles*, Buckingham: Open University Press.

Klein, T.H. and LeeDecker C.H. (eds) (1991) 'Models for the study of consumer behavior', *Historical Archaeology* 25(2): 1–91.

Little, B.J. and Shackel, P.A. (eds) (1992) 'Meaning and uses of material culture', *Historical Archaeology* 26(3): 1–133.

Lubar, S. and Kingery, W.D. (eds) (1993) *History from Things: Essays on Material Culture*, Washington, DC: Smithsonian Institution Press.

Miller, D. (1987) *Material Culture and Mass Consumption*, Oxford: Blackwell.

Schiffer, M.B. (1999) *The Material Life of Human Beings: Artifacts, Behavior, and Communication*, London: Routledge.

Schlereth, T.J. (1982) 'Material culture studies in America, 1876–1976', in T. J. Schlereth (ed.) *Material Culture Studies in America*, Nashville: American Association for State and Local History, 1–75.

CHARLES E. ORSER, JR

Maya archaeology

While archaeology has a history of more than a century in the Maya area, historical archaeology – depending on how it is defined – is only a few decades old. The Maya civilisation had its beginnings some 3,000 years ago and flourished in the region comprising present-day southern Mexico, all of Guatemala and Belize, and western portions of Honduras and El Salvador. Most archaeological attention has been directed to the peak of the civilisation, which dates to the latter half of the first millennium AD and was centred in the northern part of Guatemala. However, the entire area is still populated by Maya peoples who speak the thirty or so languages that make up the Mayan linguistic family.

Archaeologists divide the pre-sixteenth-century occupation of the Maya region into three periods: Pre-classic or Formative, Classic and Post-classic. They also divide the area into two major regions, based on differing culture histories and physiography: the Maya lowlands to the north include the Yucatán Peninsula of Mexico, northern Guatemala and Belize, while the Maya highlands refer to mountainous and piedmont areas of southern Chiapas, Mexico, southern Guatemala and western Honduras and El Salvador.

Maya lowlands

Three kinds of historical archaeology exist in the Maya lowlands: archaeology informed by Classic Maya hieroglyphic texts; archaeology informed by indigenous 'prophetic histories'; and archaeology of sites dating to the contact and colonial period, informed by historic and ethnohistoric writings. While none of these is a genuinely new research direction, their pursuit has greatly intensified, beginning in the 1980s.

If historical archaeology is defined by use of contemporaneous written documents, then the archaeology of the Classic period (*c.* AD 250–950) in the Maya lowlands is increasingly historical. Scholars have known for more than a century that the Maya had complex calendars and a system of hieroglyphic writing appearing in texts carved on stone monuments (called stelae) or painted on various media. These latter include accordion-folded 'books' (codices; sing. codex) made of beaten bark or deerskin; unfortunately, no codices dated to the Classic period survive. For a long time, only the dates of these texts could be read with assurance. In the early 1950s, however, art historian Tatiana Proskouriakoff identified a pattern of dates five years apart on stelae from one site and concluded that the carved texts and images must refer to real historical personages – kings, not gods. About the same time, epigrapher Heinrich Berlin discovered that certain glyphs (now called Emblem Glyphs) were emblematic of certain places, further confirming the historicity of Classic Maya texts. Soon after, Russian scholar Yuri Knorosov determined that the basis of the hieroglyphic writing was phonetic, and now it is known that most texts were in the Ch'olan Mayan language.

Accelerating decipherment of Maya glyphs since the 1980s, particularly by the late Linda Schele and her colleagues, has revealed details of royal visits, births, deaths, alliances, wars, conquests, taking of captives, ritual celebrations and other events. Entire dynasties and royal successions at large civic-ceremonial centres such as Tikal (Guatemala), Palenque (Mexico), Copán (Honduras) and others have been reconstructed. Copán is a particularly striking example, with the longest known inscription – some 2,200 glyphs – carved on the stone steps of its Hieroglyphic Stairway, created in the eighth century. This and other texts have given rise to a strongly historically oriented programme of archaeological excavations at the site.

Classic Maya texts carved into prominently displayed monuments are essentially dynastic propaganda declaimed on stone billboards. Even if the common Maya people were not fully literate, the glyphs have such strong pictographic elements that they are likely to have been widely understood as displays of secular and supernatural powers of the kings. While the new text readings have provided unusually detailed genealogies of Classic-period rulers, the emphasis on dynastic political histories has somewhat limited their utility as a starting point for historical archaeology projects.

A second kind of historical archaeology is based on indigenous Maya concepts of time and traditions known as 'prophetic histories'. The Maya understood the concept of continuous, linear time but also observed recurrent cycles of varying duration, from twenty to 400 years, each with good or bad auguries. Thus, an upcoming 20-year cycle identified by a particular day and month would be not only remembered, but also *predicted* by Maya calendar priests as a time of famine, whereas another cycle might be/have been a time of warfare, or pestilence, or rejoicing, migration, etc. Surviving as oral histories or perhaps written in codices, and referring to events possibly as early as the ninth century AD, these traditions were written after conquest in the Yucatecan Mayan language using Spanish orthography. They are compilations of centuries of historic traditions and priestly prophecies, issued at the end of one cycle and beginning of another. They likely were revised to make the prophecies and the retrodicted histories more closely parallel, and they even contain references to colonial-period events and phenomena, particularly the Roman Catholic religion.

The question archaeologists face is 'Do these documents contain elements of factual history about "pre-historical" people, events and places that can be investigated archaeologically?' Opinions on this question have fluctuated dramatically over the decades, but the increasing decipherment of Classic-period glyphic texts is lending greater credence to some of these histories.

The third component of historical archaeology in the lowlands is the contact, colonial or historical period itself. In the Maya lowlands the contact period could technically be said to begin in the late 1490s, when a shipwrecked sailor from one of Columbus's voyages was washed ashore on the Yucatán Peninsula. It is more appropriately dated several decades later, however, when the Spanish presence became far more evident, for example the founding of Mérida, Yucatán, in 1542. Since about 1990, more and more archaeologists have been addressing themselves to issues of Maya adaptation and **resistance** to Spanish conquest, and the different ways in which colonial history was played out in the area.

Archaeological investigations of the contact and historic periods have been carried out primarily at two kinds of sites: almost incidentally as part of excavations into Post-classic sites occupied when the Spaniards arrived, and at the small, early, open-air mission chapels built in the sixteenth and seventeenth centuries as part of efforts to Christianise the Maya. Many of these mission sites were also sites of earlier Post-classic occupation. Two projects in Belize focused on these small churches: David Pendergast's project at Lamanai (also known as Indian Church) on the New River lagoon in Belize, a Post-classic Maya site that became a Franciscan mission; and Elizabeth Graham's investigation of Tipu, in western Belize near the current border with Guatemala. Excavations at these mission churches revealed many interments, which provide a basis for assessing general health issues among colonial-period Maya populations. One of the problems for historical archaeologists is simply locating these sites, since Spanish geographical descriptions are often vague, the ruins themselves are unremarkable and items of Spanish material culture (olive jars, majolica pottery, metal objects) occur in low frequencies.

Colonial-period lowland Maya house remains occasionally have been mapped, surveyed and excavated as part of these projects, but generally little attention has been devoted to residential structures and artefact assemblages. In addition, agro-industrial plantation and hacienda sites, such as those for sugar, cotton and henequen, other industrial sites (e.g. shipbuilding) and shipwrecks have rarely been the focus of historical archaeological investigation in the northern lowlands.

In the Department of Petén, Guatemala, several archaeological projects, beginning in the 1920s, have attempted to determine the location of Tayasal or 'Taj Itzaj', the island capital of the Itzá Maya. It is now widely agreed by archaeologists and ethnohistorians that Tayasal lies under the present-day capital of Petén, Flores Island in Lake Petén Itzá. Tayasal was the last lowland Maya holdout against Spanish control, falling to an attack by ship in 1697. Although several missions were subsequently established around Lake Petén Itzá and at smaller sites around other nearby lakes, there was very little permanent Spanish settlement in the region for the next two centuries. Only small, rare fragments of Spanish material culture – majolica, gun flints, pipe stems – have been recovered in excavations in Petén.

Maya highlands

Historical archaeology in the Maya highlands has been directed primarily towards the contact and colonial periods, as the Classic and Post-classic cultures lack evidence of significant written records, particularly carved stone, which are so common in the lowlands. Archaeological excavations of colonial-period structures in the Maya highlands have followed the same patterns found at other sites in Latin America: recovery of colonial artefacts in the course of excavations of Post-classic and contact-period sites (e.g. at Utatlan/Gumarcaaj, capital of the K'iche Maya) or during restoration of colonial-period churches and residences.

Guatemalan archaeologists have undertaken

programmes of excavation and restoration in Villa de Santiago de los Caballeros, now known as La Antigua Guatemala. This lovely city, the colonial capital of the country until a devastating earthquake in 1773 forced the capital to be moved to its present location, is now a World Heritage Site. The Convento de Santo Domingo in Antigua has been the focus of archaeological, architectural and historical studies since 1989. Excavations and restoration have taken place in domestic service, residential and liturgico-public areas of the monastery. Research is continuing there as well as in other colonial-period palaces and churches in other highland towns, and addresses issues of cultural patrimony and formation of national identity. The annual symposium on archaeological investigations in Guatemala, held in Guatemala City, which publishes its proceedings, regularly includes one or more sections devoted to colonial archaeology and ethnohistory.

See also: Spanish colonialism

Further reading

Andrews, A.P. (1991) 'The rural chapels and churches of early colonial Yucatán and Belize: An archaeological perspective', in D.H. Thomas (ed.) *Columbian Consequences*, vol. 3, Washington, DC: Smithsonian Institution Press, pp. 355–74.

Fash, W. (1991) *Scribes, Warriors and Kings: The City of Copán and the Ancient Maya*, London: Thames & Hudson.

Lemus Toledo, E. (1996) 'Rescate arqueológico colonial en la Iglesia de Santo Domingo Xenacoj. La arqueología colonial y la identidad nacional', in J.P. Laporte and H.L. Escobedo (eds) *IX Simposio de Investigaciones Arqueológicas en Guatemala, 1995*, Guatemala City: IDAEH, pp. 695–705.

Martin, S. and Grube, N. (2000) *Chronicle of the Maya Kings and Queens: Deciphering the Dynasties of the Ancient Maya*, London: Thames & Hudson.

Pendergast, D.M., Jones, G.D. and Graham, E. (1993) 'Locating Maya lowlands Spanish colonial towns: A case study from Belize', *Latin American Antiquity* 4: 59–73.

Rice, D.S. and Rice, P.M. (1998) 'Settlement continuity and change in the central Petén Lakes region: The case of Zacpetén', in A. Ciudad Ruíz

(ed.) *Anatomía de Una Civilización*, Madrid: Sociedad Española de Estudios Mayas, pp. 207–52.

Rodríguez Giron, Z. (1997) 'Vasijas vidriadas del
Convento Santo Domingo en Antigua Guatemala', in J.P. Laporte and H.L. Escobedo (eds) *X
Simposio de Investigaciones Arqueológicas en Guatemala,
1996*, Guatemala City: IDAEH, pp. 689–717.

PRUDENCE M. RICE

mean ceramic dating

Mean ceramic dating, a kind of **formula dating**,
was invented by Stanley South to provide mean
dates for excavated collections of eighteenth-
century English **ceramics**, including **earthenware**, **stoneware** and **porcelain**. Archaeologists
working in many different historical contexts have
used the dating method since South first presented
it in the early 1970s. Some have even tested the
dating method with post-Columbian Native American pottery (see **Native Americans**). One idea
behind the creation and application of the mean
ceramic dating method is that if it can work with
historically documented sites then it can be used to
provide mean occupation dates for archaeological
sites that are not mentioned in written records.

The formula is based on the idea that mass-
produced ceramics, like many other consumer
goods manufactured during and after the Industrial
Revolution, experience three phases of 'life',
extending from invention and introduction, growth
and popularity, and decline and eventual disuse.
The English manufacturers of eighteenth-century
ceramics documented the life histories of their
wares as a regular business practice because they
had to watch the market for signs of consumer
uninterest. Their recording practices mean that the
introduction, use and discontinuance dates for
many of the most widely used ceramics can be
established by examining **historical documents**.
Having this information readily available, South
found it reasonable to assume that archaeologists
could calculate a single mean date from the
compiled date ranges of all the ceramics found at
any eighteenth-century, British American site. To
obtain the manufacturing information he needed,
South referred to Ivor Noël Hume's authoritative

A Guide to Artifacts of Colonial America (first published
in 1970). Noël Hume was the first director of
excavations at Colonial Williamsburg, Virginia,
and he and his wife Audrey were widely acknowledged, highly respected ceramics experts.

Calculating the mean ceramic date (Y) is a
relatively simply matter. Assuming that the analyst
has identified the ceramic sherds correctly, he or
she then lists in a column the types that appear in
the excavated collection. He or she then establishes
the median manufacturing date for each type of
ceramic from the documentation (or from the
information provided by South or from purely
archaeological information) and records this date
in a second column (called x). A ceramic type with
a known date range of 1700–1800 would have a
median date of 1750. Next, the archaeologist lists
the frequency of each type of ceramics in a third
column (f), and then multiplies the second and
the third columns (the median date by the
frequency, or x times f). The resulting product is
recorded in a fourth column. Once this information is computed and recorded, the mean ceramic
date is computed by simply dividing the sum of the
product in the fourth column by the total number
of sherds in the collection. The formula for doing
this is written as:

$$y = \frac{\Sigma \times (f)}{\Sigma f}$$

South checked the accuracy of the dates he
calculated against the known occupation dates of
several British American sites in the USA, and
discovered that the formula tended to overestimate
the occupation date by just over one year. As a
result, he added a correction of -1.1 years to the
mean date (or in other words he subtracted 1.1
from Y). (He also learned that he could not include
two types of Chinese export porcelain.)

The mean ceramic date obviously provides only
a single date. It does not provide any information,
however, about the variation within the ceramic
collection. For example, if we had a ceramic
collection composed of only two sherds, one with a
median manufacturing date of 1750 and one with a
median date of 1770, then the mean ceramic date
would be 1760. If we had a second collection that

also contained two sherds, but with different manufacturing dates (one with a median date of 1660 and the other a date of 1860), we would still obtain a mean date of 1760, even though the samples are really quite different.

A statistical tool called the 'standard deviation' can be used to measure the 'spread' of the median dates in the collection. This is a powerful addition to the mean ceramic date because the introduction, rise in popularity and eventual decline of ceramic types theoretically approximates a normal or bell-shaped curve. The mean occurs where the curve is at its highest point. After calculating the standard deviation, which involves a few more calculations, it can be added and subtracted from the calculated mean date to derive a more powerful indication of the total dates of the ceramic collection. Thus, instead of receiving one single date, say of 1750, we would obtain a date range (one standard deviation of ten years would yield dates of 1740–60 for the collection).

The mean ceramic dating method found a wide audience in historical archaeology, and many examples appear in the specialist archaeological literature. It is not without its problems, however. It assumes, for instance, that the analyst can accurately identify historic ceramics and that the recorded date ranges are accurate. The method also assumes, somewhat simplistically perhaps, that the marketing and sale of ceramics in the eighteenth century (or for any period for that matter) approximates a normal curve. This idea seems to make great sense, but it is also possible that some ceramics were not produced in keeping with this trajectory.

Further reading

South, S. (1978) 'Pattern recognition in historical archaeology', *American Antiquity* 43: 223–30.
—— (1977) *Method and Theory in Historical Archaeology*, New York: Academic Press.
—— (1972) 'Evolution and horizon as revealed in ceramic analysis in historical archaeology', *The Conference on Historic Site Archaeology Papers 1971* 6: 71–116.

CHARLES E. ORSER, JR

medieval archaeology

Medieval archaeology is a discipline directed towards medieval Europe (*c.* AD 500–1500), which has been represented in most European countries since the 1950s and 1960s. Medieval archaeology shares the fundamental methods with other parts of archaeology, though the sources are sometimes partly different, like masonry houses and thick deposits. The presence of written sources makes the conditions for analysis and interpretation sometimes different from those of prehistoric archaeology. In relation to written sources, medieval archaeology shares the same type of methodological problems as, for instance, **classical archaeology** and US historical archaeology.

The origin of medieval archaeology must be sought in the construction of the concept 'Middle Ages' and in the subsequent medieval studies. The 'Middle Ages' was defined as a special period in European history by Italian humanists in the fifteenth century. They saw the Middle Ages as a period of decline and darkness between antiquity and their own Renaissance. In the second half of the seventeenth century and in the eighteenth century, the 'Middle Ages' became an accepted period name, although it preserved some of its pejorative meaning until the early nineteenth century. Only with the romantic period were the Middle Ages totally reappraised, and became an exemplary period like antiquity had been since the Renaissance. The quest for the Middle Ages became a quest for national **identity**, since medieval studies were part of the romantic and nationalistic movement in Europe after the Napoleonic Wars.

Medieval studies were closely associated with aesthetics in the nineteenth century. Objects of medieval art and craft became obvious exhibits in central museums of 'fine art'. With the Middle Ages as an aesthetic model, historicising styles, such as neo-gothic and neo-romanesque, were created, and at the same time many of the medieval models for these historicising styles were being restored. Several leading architects of the time worked with both restorations and new creations, and some of them also collected their experiences in historical surveys of medieval art and architecture. The practical application of the Middle Ages thus resulted in basic material knowledge of medieval monuments.

The retrieval of medieval artefacts was systematised in the second half of the nineteenth century. Fieldwork was mainly geared to collecting artefacts and compiling inventories of surviving buildings and ruins. In Germany, systematic publication of all historical – especially medieval – monuments began in the 1860s, and, in Denmark, parish-by-parish surveys of both prehistoric and medieval monuments began in 1873. It was also in this phase of systematised medieval studies that the first efforts to establish a professional medieval archaeology can be detected. This is clearest in the work of the Swedish archaeologist Hans Hildebrand (1842–1913), who already in the 1880s claimed that archaeological studies of the Middle Ages had an intrinsic value partly because they could lead to the reinterpretation of medieval texts.

With the breakthrough of modernism in art and architecture around 1900, the historical models in aesthetics were rejected, and the historicising styles lost their significance. At the same time, the view of restoration changed with the recognition of the entire building history of the monuments, including the settings surrounding them. Instead of being aesthetic examples, the monuments began to be viewed as historical documents, which could reflect a long, complex history. Not only important events in the history of the monuments were studied, but also their changing meanings through time. With this shift of perspective, many countries began the publication of historical monuments, describing their entire history.

Systematic archaeological excavations of medieval remains also began around 1900. This work was often a complement to preserved and known environments, in that the excavations concerned vanished or non-functioning sites, such as ruins of churches, monasteries and castles, and towns that had disappeared or been moved. The excavations of ruins often sought to expose the monuments and hence make the past visible and accessible to the public.

In the inter-war years, medieval archaeology underwent a gradual growth, especially as a result of excavations conducted by people with a background in history and art history. The work was intended primarily as a complement to the study of medieval texts. It was considered important to trace the oldest history and topography of individual towns, or to shed light on the building history of individual monuments, but less familiar aspects of the Middle Ages were also studied, such as early urban crafts and the agrarian economy.

Although medieval archaeology existed as a practical activity in the 1920s and 1930s, it was not until after the Second World War that the subject was professionalised and became an academic discipline. In the 1950s and 1960s, archaeological excavations really got under way in surviving medieval settings. That was when excavating archaeology and the architectural documentation of masonry were integrated into a complete stratigraphical analysis of buildings.

The reconstruction and rebuilding of European cities after the Second World War is often pointed out as a decisive factor for the growth of the subject. The large-scale archaeological excavations since the 1950s in many medieval European cities have undoubtedly affected medieval archaeology and its character. More fundamental factors should be sought, however, in changed perspectives on both archaeology and history. Archaeology was no longer viewed as an excavating branch of art history, but rather as an extension of history, while history was increasingly concerned with social and economic history. Medieval archaeology has therefore been heavily influenced by history, and very few medieval archaeologists work with the traditional source material of art history, such as church murals, wooden sculptures, manuscript illustrations and artefacts of gold, silver, enamel and ivory.

The clear link with history means that research in medieval archaeology is traditionally text-bound and thematised according to the self-understanding of the Middle Ages – the doctrine of the four estates of society – in studies concerning the countryside, the towns, the churches and the castles. In addition, there are special studies of artefacts, such as **ceramics**. The thematisation is highly obvious in the internal working groups found in English medieval archaeology: the Deserted Medieval Village Research Group (1952), the Urban Research Committee (1970), the Moated

Sites Research Group (1972), the Churches Committee (1972) and the Medieval Pottery Research Group (1975). A comparable internal specialisation, with separate working groups and conferences, can also be detected in French, German and Scandinavian medieval archaeology. It is also found in handbooks of medieval archaeology from a number of countries.

The interpretative perspective in medieval archaeology has not been very explicit. On the basis of a general idea of complementarity, archaeology has been seen primarily as a method for supplementing contemporary written sources. This perspective has meant that the archaeological interest in the Middle Ages has very different chronological centres of gravity in Europe. In western and southern Europe, the study has mostly concerned the Early Middle Ages, since there are ample written sources from later periods. In northern and eastern Europe, on the other hand, where there are far fewer texts, the whole period has been studied with more equal intensity.

The idea of complementarity has also meant that many medieval archaeological investigations have had the character of detailed studies in relation to a given historical synthesis. Above all, aspects of the Middle Ages that are less well known from texts have been studied. An important area has been settlement, primarily in towns, but also rural settlement. Although churches and castles have been studied as individual monuments, they have often been incorporated in the perspective of settlement archaeology. In the same way, for example, medieval iron production and medieval everyday life have been studied archaeologically, to compensate for the dearth of written sources dealing with these areas.

In the last fifteen years, however, there has been a renewal in the subject, in that the interpretative imperative of the written sources has been questioned. The renewal is particularly noticeable in Scandinavia and Britain, partly due to impulses from anthropologically inspired history, such as the *Annales* school and 'the new cultural history', and partly due to the active integration of the debate in prehistoric archaeology and anthropology into medieval archaeology. The changed character of the discipline has been expressed in two partly different ways.

One reaction has been to write more independent archaeological syntheses about major medieval problems such as farming, the villages, the towns, trade, craft, iron production, coin circulation, the churches and mortuary practices. In this case, the renewal has been stressed by means of an emphasis on the role of archaeology in connection with important problems that have long been debated by historians. In another, more radical approach, the very idea of archaeology as a complement to history has been questioned. Instead of starting with issues raised by historians, several scholars have called for new questions cutting across the traditional thematisation of the medieval archaeology, for instance gender and mental space. This attitude takes its inspiration from post-processual or contextual archaeology with its emphasis on the meaning and active role of artefacts. Yet this inspiration has also functioned as a way to link up with the similar but much older debate about the meaning of **architecture**, which has been part of medieval studies since the inter-war period.

The character of medieval archaeology, as well as the relation between artefact and text, have been discussed intensively in the last fifteen years. However, because of the national fragmentation of the subject, this debate has been divided into different language areas and has thus been conducted more or less independently in, for example, Britain, France, Italy, Germany, Poland and Scandinavia. The viewpoints and perspectives, however, are strikingly parallel. Archaeology has been perceived in all these countries as particularly suitable for the study of areas that are rarely or never mentioned in written sources, such as technology, economy, social conditions and everyday life. Earlier than in other parts of archaeology, medieval archaeologists discovered the French *Annales* historians, since many of them are medieval specialists. Several scholars have pointed approvingly to Fernand Braudel's 'long waves' as suitable objects of archaeological study. Yet there has also been criticism of the concentration of archaeology on economic and social questions. Others, therefore, have argued that material culture is a special dimension in life and that archaeology therefore can just as well study mental and political issues.

The question of the role of texts in archaeological work has been perceived in very different ways. An earlier tradition stressed the given historical background knowledge, and archaeology as a complement to written sources. One reaction to this stance has been to reject written sources in general. This perspective has been particularly clear in the attempts to introduce a 'new medieval archaeology' in the 1980s. In the 1990s, however, different ways of creating a new dialogue between material culture and written sources have been discussed, as part of a more general debate in **contextual historical archaeology**. One new perspective is that all texts are, in a fundamental sense, artefacts and that both forms of expression should be interpreted together. In this way, writing does not have primacy over material culture. Another new idea is that an archaeologist should deliberately look for contradictions between material culture and written sources, thus underlining the uncertain nature of the knowledge of the past.

See also: cathedrals; Christianisation; churches; churchyard archaeology; deserted villages; gender; history of historical archaeology; urban archaeology

Further reading

Andersson, H., Carelli, P. and Ersgård, L. (eds) (1997) *Visions of the Past: Trends and Traditions in Swedish Medieval Archaeology*, Stockholm: Almqvist & Wicksell.

Andersson, H. and Wienberg, J. (eds) (1993) *The Study of Medieval Archaeology*, Stockholm: Almqvist & Wicksell.

Andrén, A. (1998) *Between Artifacts and Texts: Historical Archaeology in Global Perspective*, New York: Plenum Press.

Austin, D. and Alcock, L. (eds) (1990) *From the Baltic to the Black Sea: Studies in Medieval Archaeology*, London: Unwin Hyman.

Clarke, H. (1984) *The Archaeology of Medieval England*, London: British Museum.

Fehring, G.P. (1991) *The Archaeology of Medieval Germany: An Introduction*, London: Routledge.

Hinton, D. (ed.) (1983) *25 Years of Medieval Archaeology*, Sheffield: The Department of Prehistory and Archaeology, University of Sheffield and the Society for Medieval Archaeology.

Moreland, J. (2001) *Archaeology and Text*, London: Duckworth.

ANDERS ANDRÉN

Melbourne, Australia

Melbourne, capital city of Victoria, Australia, was first established in 1835 as a commercial settlement by pastoralists and traders from **Tasmania**. The new arrivals seized land belonging to the Aboriginal Kulin peoples, and erected crude buildings along the banks of the Yarra River, at the head of Port Philip Bay. The settlement, initially known as Bearbrass, was first surveyed in 1837, with a street grid of main roads and lanes imposing a semblance of order on the burgeoning township. Only months after the separation of Victoria as a colony in 1851, the gold rushes brought immigrants flooding into Melbourne on their way to the goldfields. The city's population grew from 125,000 residents in 1861 to 268,000 in 1881, before doubling again in the land boom of the 1880s. A strong manufacturing sector also emerged in the later nineteenth century, centred on clothing, leather goods and food processing, while new railway routes permitted a suburban expansion far beyond the central business district.

Some of the best archaeological evidence for the early years of Melbourne derives from the remains of the *William Salthouse*, wrecked off Point Nepean in 1841. Sailing from Montreal, Canada, it bore a cargo primarily of basic foodstuffs, including wooden casks of flour and salt meat, along with fine French wines to be sold as luxuries.

Within the city of Melbourne, salvage excavations of the Little Lonsdale Street precinct took place in 1987 and 1988. 'Little Lon' emerged in the late 1840s as a hamlet of small timber cottages. As the century progressed, the area became a centre of work as well, with furniture and clothing manufacturers, **prostitution**, engineering, warehouses and small shops. By the 1920s and 1930s, Little Lon had become one of the most cosmopolitan neighbourhoods in Australia, with Chinese, Indian, Syrian, Italian and Irish residents. The community eroded rapidly from the 1940s, however, as the Commonwealth Government began redeveloping the precinct. While conventional historical accounts of Little Lon regarded it as a slum and brothel district, more recent analyses have challenged this interpretation, revealing a complex and dynamic community of working-class immigrants.

As the inner city became more crowded, wealthy residents established stately homes on the semi-rural fringes of Melbourne. The Viewbank homestead, for example, built on a hill above the junction of the Yarra and Plenty rivers, was home to Dr Robert Martin and his family from 1844 until about 1875. Although the homestead was destroyed in the 1920s, the cultural landscape of Viewbank retains many features little changed from the 1840s, with pastured paddocks, hawthorn hedges, solitary eucalypts and European trees in a landscaped garden setting. Excavations at the site recovered interior fittings and domestic items recalling the prominent place of the Martins among Melbourne's mid-nineteenth-century elite.

Further reading

Davison, G. (1978) *The Rise and Fall of Marvellous Melbourne*, Melbourne: Melbourne University Press.

Mayne, A. and Lawrence, S. (1998) 'An ethnography of place: Imagining "Little Lon"', *Journal of Australian Studies* 57: 93–107.

PETER DAVIES

metal detectors

Metal detectors are an inexpensive and effective **remote-sensing** device. Metal detectors can be used to identify sites even when no surface evidence exists. They can help determine site boundaries by establishing the extent of metallic debris associated with an occupation. They can be used to find artefacts that may be easily missed using systematic shovel-testing programmes and can be used to study metallic artefact distribution patterns across a site. They have been used extensively in **battlefield archaeology**, where many of the battle-related artefacts are made of metal.

The detector reacts to the electrical conductivity of objects. The search coil contains a flat, circular coil of wire (antenna) that generates an electromagnetic field. When metallic objects are near this coil, an electrical eddy current is created that is detected by the unit and converted to a visual digital or analogue representation, and/or emitted as an audible signal. The electromagnetic field produced by the search coil penetrates the earth in a cone shape, emanating downward from the coil. The larger the coil, the deeper the buried artefacts that can be detected. Smaller coils are lightweight and easier to use, but penetrate less deeply. Eight-inch and ten-inch coils are popular compromises between the desire for depth and practicality. These coils will reliably detect to a depth of 12 to 14 inches (30 to 35 cm). Smaller coils are useful for precisely locating artefacts, and are most efficient in detecting metallic debris at shallower depths (to about 8 in, 20 cm) than the larger coils. Coils are interchangeable on most machines, and multiple coils can be purchased and used for different purposes, such as for deep searches and to pinpoint targets. For very deep detecting, special, two-coil (double-box) detectors are also available. Their capabilities are limited to finding larger targets or concentrations of metal items at depths around 3 ft (1 m). Specialised detectors that work completely underwater are also available and are important tools in underwater archaeology.

The more expensive models tend to have more elaborate functions and displays, and exhibit a greater range of discrimination as well as sensitivity to certain types of metallic artefacts. However, many detectors can reliably distinguish iron objects from all other metals because iron objects are magnetic as well as good conductors. Many popular detectors have a 'pull-tab' discriminator, tuned so that the machine does not respond to aluminium. Wire, **nails**, bolts and other elongated objects are notorious for giving ambiguous location signals.

Further reading

Connor, M. and Scott, D.D. (1998) 'Metal detector use in archaeology: An introduction', *Historical Archaeology* 32(4): 76–85.

Garrett, C.L. (1985) *The Advanced Handbook on Modern Metal Detectors*, Dallas, TX: Ram Books.

Scott, D.D., Fox, R.A., Connor, M.A. and Harmon, D. (1989) *Archaeological Perspectives on the Battle of the Little Bighorn*, Norman: University of Oklahoma Press.

MELISSA CONNOR

Mexico City, Mexico

Now the largest city in the Americas, Mexico City took its name from its founders, the Mexica Aztecs, who established it as their capital in AD 1325. The modern Mexican flag, with its motif of an eagle resting on a cactus growing from a rock, commemorates the event of the foundation, and Mexica Aztecs called the town 'rock-cactus-place' or, in their language, Tenochtitlán.

Like the modern city that overlies it, Tenochtitlán's urban core focused on a huge plaza, now called the Zócalo. Facing the plaza, to the east, was the palace of the last Aztec emperor, Motecuzoma Xocoyotzin. It lies beneath today's National Palace. To the north of the Zócalo is the Metropolitan Cathedral, on which construction began soon after the Spanish conquest of the Mexica, in AD 1521. The Cathedral's location also maintained a pre-Hispanic function, in that the north side of the ancient plaza was dominated by the ritual precinct of the Great Temple of Tenochtitlán.

The siege that won the Aztec empire for Spain destroyed most of Tenochtitlán, and the ruins of the old capital provided the building material for the new. Not only did the conquering Spaniards delight in building their own palaces over those of the Aztec lords, but they abhorred the devil worship manifested in Aztec monuments, temples and pyramids. Thus was the Great Temple reduced to a pile of rubble and then built over, and its exact location became a matter of speculation.

For 250 years after the conquest, the Spanish colonial capital obliterated its Aztec past. However, in 1790, public-works projects in the Zócalo began to uncover huge sculptures. The intellectual curiosity of the Age of Reason penetrated New Spain, and as antiquities were uncovered throughout the nineteenth century, they were curated at the University of Mexico.

With the twentieth century, further modernisation of the city led to further discoveries in the old heart of Tenochtitlán, with investigations by Leopoldo Batres in 1900 and Manuel Gamio in 1913. In the 1960s and 1970s, excavations for the subway system revealed many Aztec monuments and building fragments – and some whole structures, such as the round temple dedicated to the Aztec wind god, now visible at the Piño Suarez metro station.

The most exciting discoveries, however, were those that revealed the location of the Great Temple itself, and led to its eventual excavation. A chance find in 1978 stirred the Mexican nation's sense of the importance of this ancient pyramid, and with massive popular support it became the focus of an extensive archaeological project, led by Eduardo Matos Moctezuma. The 'Templo Mayor' and its adjacent ritual buildings are now a park, with excellent interpretive museum, in the heart of the city. The Zócalo of Mexico City has, since Aztec times, been bordered by the ritual precinct, but only now, nearly 500 years after the Spanish intrusion, do the important religious structures of the ancient natives and the Spanish colonists together invoke Mexico's strength as a modern mestizo nation.

Further reading

Matos Moctezuma, E. (1994) *The Great Temple of the Aztecs: Treasures of Tenochtitlán*, trans. D. Heyden, London: Thames & Hudson.

SUSAN TOBY EVANS

Middle Colonies, USA

A great deal of historical archaeology has occurred within the states regarded as being within the Middle Atlantic region of the USA. These states – Pennsylvania, New York, New Jersey and Delaware – were known as the 'Middle Colonies' during the colonial era.

Pennsylvania

Historical archaeology in the Middle Colonies began in earnest in the early 1950s. US National Park Service investigations in the newly created Independence National Historical Park in **Philadelphia** and at **Fort Necessity** in south-western Pennsylvania were among the earliest archaeological investigations to focus on historic sites with the intent of answering specifically historical questions, mainly for the purpose of accurate **reconstruction**. At Fort Necessity, a site associated with the French and Indian War, J.C. Harrington recovered information that changed the understanding of the fort's location, size and shape. He went on to write an article entitled 'Historic site archaeology in the United States' that began to define the field of historical archaeology. Jacob Grimm's excavation at Fort Ligonier resulted in one of the earliest publications in historical archaeology, and the Carnegie Museum of Natural History's excavations at Fort Pitt in Pittsburgh provided the basis for reconstruction of the Flag and Music Bastions, which are still found in Point State Park, one of the first parks based in part on archaeological fieldwork.

Most of the early investigations in Independence National Historical Park were conducted by Paul J.F. Schumacher and B. Bruce Powell for the National Park Service. John Cotter became the Regional Archaeologist for the North-east Region of the Park Service in 1957 and from that time until his death in 1999 took an active interest in the historical archaeology of Philadelphia, both inside and outside the park boundaries. Among the early significant investigations inside the park was the effort to find the exact location of Benjamin Franklin's house, first located by Schumacher in 1953 and further delineated by Barbara Liggett in the 1960s. Represented as a ghost structure designed by Robert Venturi, the site, including 'window' views of archaeological foundations as they were found, remains an important component of the park. Also important were the investigations at Carpenters' Court, begun by Schumacher and completed by Powell, that found a cistern, the original privy built by the Carpenters' Company in 1770–1 and Cotter's favorite artefact, a pornographic pipe tamper. Restoration of the *c.* 1790

Bishop White house and its furnishings, also in the park, were in great part based on the results of Schumacher and Powell's work.

Cotter's many University of Pennsylvania field classes – some of the first on historic sites – in the 1960s and 1970s investigated a variety of sites in and outside the city. Students looked for Philadelphia's earliest almshouse in the garden of the Physick House, they worked on the first mint site on 5th Street, explored the workshops at the eighteenth-century Walnut Street Prison and evaluated what needed to be done (but never was) at the Revolutionary War-period Fort Mifflin. They also worked at **Valley Forge**, where archaeological investigations had begun in 1929 with the search for the site of the forge the British destroyed in 1777. In 1962, John Witthoft and J. Duncan Campbell excavated five huts of Maxwell's Brigade, and the Pennsylvania Historical and Museum Commission, along with students from several universities, investigated the encampment of the Virginia Brigade, including seventeen huts.

Historical archaeology in western Pennsylvania also benefited from the training of students. Administered initially by Phil Jack and Ronald Michael, the summer field training programme of the California State College (now California University of Pennsylvania) focused on the Searight and Colley tavern stands erected along the National Road (Route 40), the first major internal improvement built with federal money. Jack and Michael also published their historical research on the nineteenth- and early twentieth-century potteries on the Upper Monongahela River at New Geneva (excavated much later for the US Army Corps of Engineers) and Greensboro. With the approach of the US Bicentennial, the field school focused on Fort Gaddis, a Revolutionary War-period log home and possible frontier fortification (see **fortifications**). Compliance projects in the mid-1970s included excavations at Woodville, a Revolutionary War-period home associated with John and Presley Neville, Revolutionary War veterans and subsequent leaders of south-western Pennsylvania's Federalists. Research at Woodville, a National Historic Landmark, continued into the 1990s and is synthesised in Ronald Carlisle's book *The Story of 'Woodville'*.

The surge of new building in downtown Pittsburgh in the 1980s led to the formation of the Committee on Pittsburgh Archaeology and History (CPAH) and to a number of major urban projects. Verna Cowin and other staff at the Carnegie Museum of Natural History, Section of Anthropology, also mounted a museum exhibit called 'Pieces of the Past' that helped to explain the work of urban archaeologists to the public. Excavations in the city included the University of Pittsburgh's work at the Gateway Center Station of the Pittsburgh Light Rail Transit System and in the Crawford-Roberts Redevelopment Area, located in the heart of the nineteenth-century city's African American Arthursville neighbourhood; the Carnegie Museum of Natural History Section of Anthropology's work at the new PPG corporate headquarters site; GAI Consultants' studies in the city's old warehouse district near 11th Street and their excavation of lift and weigh locks of the Pennsylvania Canal during construction of the East Street Valley Expressway.

In Philadelphia, Barbara Liggett excavated a block at New Market, Philadelphia's second public market; Temple University recorded the transformation of an early residential block (Area F) into a nineteenth-century commercial district and John Milner Associates (JMA) found traces of a seventeenth-century ground surface at Front and Dock Streets. JMA also excavated two cemeteries belonging to the First African Baptist Church in the path of the Vine Street Expressway. While she was the City Archaeologist for Philadelphia, Carmen Weber excavated intact remnants of an eighteenth/early nineteenth-century ship's way on the Delaware River, and Lewis Berger and Associates found remnants of early wharves along the waterfront. Berger archaeologists also found an intact, eighteenth-century ground surface and the remains of several artisan shops at the Arch Street site of the Metropolitan Detention Center in Philadelphia.

Although no archaeology was done when Independence Mall was created in the middle of the twentieth century, investigations in anticipation of new construction and landscaping at the onset of the twenty-first century encountered an extensive intact historic ground surface dating as far back as the contact period, and numerous shaft features.

One of these appeared to be the icehouse built by Robert Morris on the property that served as an executive mansion for the first two presidents of the USA. Analyses of those projects are underway by Kise Straw and Kolodner and JMA in Philadelphia. Lu Ann De Cunzo's investigation of the Magdalen Society of Philadelphia (1800–50) is the only in-depth study in **contextual historical archaeology** done in Pennsylvania.

New York

Much of the early study of the historical archaeology of New York State was done by avocational archaeologists like William Calver and Reginald Bolton, who focused primarily on colonial- and Revolutionary War-period sites. It was only in the late 1960s that these archaeologists were joined by professionals, some of whom worked for the state. Paul Huey and Lois Feister, for example, conducted excavations for many decades on state-owned properties through the Office of Parks, Recreation and Historic Preservation, while others, like Bert Salwen and Robert Schuyler, conducted field schools. However, since the late 1970s, most of the archaeological work in the state has been performed by archaeological consulting firms.

Archaeologists in New York have long been interested in the ways of life of **Native Americans** after their contact with the European invaders. Although they first focused on groups that were members of the Iroquois confederacy, since the 1970s they have also looked at the Mahican and Erie.

Paul Huey's study of Fort Orange in today's Albany remains the classic work on the Dutch colonial period (1625–64/74); more recent studies in Albany have been conducted by Hartgen Archaeological Associates. Important Dutch components were also uncovered in **New York City**, formerly New Amsterdam, by Joel Grossman at the Broad Financial Center and Nan Rothschild and Diana Wall at the Stadt Huys Block. These excavations revealed the extremes to which the Dutch went to recreate their European way of life in their new environment. Meta Janowitz used the results of these excavations in her study of Dutch foodways in New Amsterdam.

Archaeologists in the state have studied many different kinds of sites dating to the English colonial period, including taverns, country estates, farmsteads, colonial villages and even the city itself. Nan Rothschild's book on **New York City** neighbourhoods in the eighteenth century is considered a major contribution to the field. Excavations focusing on the eighteenth-century **almshouses** in New York and Albany have shown the manufacturing activities that the inmates of these institutions undertook: Sherene Baugher's work in New York City shows inmates there made bone **buttons**, while Elizabeth Pena's work at the Dutch Reformed Church almshouse in Albany shows that those inmates made wampum. Archaeologists are also interested in the African presence in colonial New York, a presence that was brought home by the excavations at the **African Burial Ground** in New York City, which is being analysed by Michael Blakey of Howard University.

Much work has focused on military sites associated with the French and Indian and Revolutionary wars. Archaeologists have always paid attention to battlefields and forts, but David Starbuck, in particular, has told the story of how soldiers lived and coped in the field. There has also been interest in sunken colonial ships and boats discovered in Lakes Champlain and George, and off the shore of Long Island. Ships have also been discovered buried in the landfill in New York City, where they were scuttled to hold the landfill in place. The vessels include merchantmen, sloops, double-ended bateaux, schooners, gun-boats, row galleys and even a rare radeau. Before the 1980s, many of these boats were excavated but were not properly conserved and eventually they disintegrated. More recently, goals have been directed towards preservation, with wrecks being recorded and left *in situ*; several underwater preserves have been designated in Lakes Champlain and George. A ship that was excavated at 175 Water Street in New York City in 1982 generated enormous public interest; on a freezing January day, more than 10,000 people lined up to see the ship's excavation. There have also been excavations of the wharves that made up New York City's waterfront in the eighteenth and early nineteenth centuries as well as the uncovering of the terminus of the Erie Canal in

Buffalo, led by Warren Barbour as part of the Inner Harbour project.

Since the 1970s, archaeologists working in New York have become more interested in working in urban areas, work that was inspired by Bert Salwen (the 'father of urban archaeology') who in 1970 discovered the remains of the seventeenth-century stockade in downtown Kingston that had been built under the orders of Peter Stuyvesant. Salwen masterminded the early large-scale excavations in New York as well as encouraging excavations in urban areas throughout the country. Important urban excavations have been done in Buffalo, Binghamton and Albany, as well as in New York City.

The urban projects led to an increased interest in studying the nineteenth century. Focusing particularly on class formation (see **class, social**), studies have taken place in several cities (e.g. the works of Joan Geismar and Diana Wall at middle-class sites, and of Rebecca Yamin at the **Five Points** working-class site, all in New York City, and the work of LuAnn Wurst in Binghamton and Elizabeth Pena in Buffalo), as well as in rural areas. Wall's book on changing gender roles and the formation of the middle class used data from many of the sites that had been excavated in New York City.

New Jersey

The same patriotic fervour that inspired historical archaeological investigations in Williamsburg and **Jamestown**, Virginia, in the 1930s inspired historical archaeology in New Jersey. The US National Park Service conducted excavations at Revolutionary War sites in Morristown, including Fort Nonsense, Jockey Hollow and the New Jersey Brigade encampment (1779–80) in the 1930s, and the sites remain major interpretive centres to this day. As elsewhere, however, it was the **preservation legislation** passed in the 1960s and elaborated in the 1970s that triggered extensive historical investigations in the state. Between 1973 and 1975, Edward Rutsch directed the Great Falls Development Archaeological Project in Paterson, the northern New Jersey city where Alexander Hamilton founded the Society for the Establishing of Useful Manufactures in 1792. In conjunction with a number of construction projects, Rutsch's work included the sites of the Great Locomotive Company's erecting shop, the exterior of the Rogers Locomotive Works erecting shop and the Rogers blacksmith shop, boiler shop and foundry. He also traced and recorded the Lower Raceway in its entirety, portions of the Erie Lackawanna Railroad and the Morris Canal bed. Subsequent projects in Paterson recovered domestic assemblages from the Dublin neighbourhood where many of the workers lived.

Several construction projects in and around New Brunswick required archaeological investigations that recorded remnants of eighteenth-century Dutch and English settlement in the Raritan Valley. While little time was allotted to investigating sites in New Brunswick proper, Raritan Landing, a small port located at the falls of the Raritan River a mile or so above New Brunswick, produced a rich record of a mid-eighteenth-century trading community. Joel Grossman directed data recovery investigations at Raritan Landing in 1979 and Rebecca Yamin used some of the data for her doctoral dissertation on eighteenth-century local trade. In 2000, a consortium of four companies returned to Raritan Landing where they uncovered the remains of what was probably the earliest house (c. 1710), several other houses and shops, a row of about ten warehouses and evidence of the six-month British occupation of the town during the Revolutionary War and of the rebuilding of the community after the war. Earlier archaeological investigations, associated with the building of a housing development at Pluckemin, investigated the site of the continental artillery cantonment of 1778–9.

Archaeological investigations associated with highway construction along the Delaware River near Trenton, in 2000, uncovered even more substantial evidence of New Jersey's eighteenth-century trade. Hunter Research recorded at least two kilns – one for stoneware and one for sugar loaf moulds – that had belonged to William Richards, a Philadelphia merchant who maintained a store and several industrial operations at Trenton and traded in the Caribbean. The foundations of two buildings associated with anadromous fish-processing, one probably for storage and the other for boiling, a process necessary for the manufacture of glue, were also recorded beneath 3 m of fill. Two adjacent circular vaulted structures, each approximately 3 m in diameter, appeared to be commercial bake ovens. This complex of industrial structures plus a variety of shops and large wharves were known as Lamberton (now absorbed into Trenton) and handled most of the area's produce for export from the 1760s to the 1830s.

Another Department of Transportation project, this one near Morristown in northern New Jersey, encountered the remains of an eighteenth-century plantation known as Beverwyck. Archaeological investigations done by McCormick-Taylor recovered assemblages from a farmhouse on the property, a possible distillery, a blacksmith shop and a small structure (6.6 by 7.6 m) believed to be quarters for the enslaved labour force at Beverwyck. This is the only known slave quarter in New Jersey where it is generally believed that slaves lived in the owner's house rather than in separate houses. A concentration of artefacts found in the north-east corner of the structure included buttons, cutlery, a glass bead necklace, a perforated metal disk, coins, two shackles, two seashells and two Revolutionary War military buttons.

Delaware

The earliest primarily historical investigations in Delaware focused on the earliest sites. In the early 1950s, the Sussex County Society for Archaeology and History excavated the seventeenth-century DeVries Palisade (thought to date to 1631) at Lewes, dikes at Pagan Creek and Canary Creek, also at Lewes, and the 'Old House Site', believed to date from the seventeenth century into the eighteenth. Among the early house site investigations by avocational archaeologists was Josh's Cabin, the home of a poor black labourer in New Castle County. Although the purpose of the work was to provide evidence for reconstructing the cabin, the nineteenth-century artefacts found provided information on the African American residents of the site before African Americans were a major focus of archaeological study.

The Hagley Museum carried out several excavations on museum property in the mid-1950s and, in 1968, Hagley staff archaeologist, James Ackerman, excavated the formal gardens of

Eleutherian Mills, the home of E.I. duPont. In the 1970s, the Hagley continued work at mill sites, formal gardens and worker- and management-level housing sites in an area known as Blacksmith Hill. Mills located along both sides of the Brandywine Creek were also studied.

Once Federal legislation was in place, the Delaware Department of Transportation (DELDOT) carried out many of the historical investigations in the state. Among their many projects was the Collins, Geddes Cannery in Lebanon, Kent County. Built in 1869 and destroyed twice by fire, the cannery was the second largest manufacturing industry in Delaware during the nineteenth century. Construction of Wilmington (now Martin Luther King Jr) Boulevard in downtown Wilmington required archaeological investigations on several blocks, some conducted by Lewis Berger and Associates and others by Jay Custer's staff at the University of Delaware. The Christina Gateway Redevelopment Project included the remains of the Old Swedes Church parsonage, which was occupied between 1701 and 1768. The finds suggested that although the clergy claimed to not be adequately compensated for their services, they maintained a comfortable standard of living including such luxuries as expensive Chinese export **porcelain**.

As development pressure increased in the 1980s and 1990s, projects beyond the city limits included sites at small towns that had once been important landings. Thomas Ogle's eighteenth-century tavern, the Mermaid blacksmith shop and the house sites of John Read, William Patterson and Charles Allen, as well as the remains of William Dickson's storehouse, a boat slip, old roadways, fencelines, wells and evidence of nineteenth-century river channelisation, were studied in Christiana, and the archaeological remains of John Darrach's store as well as farm outbuildings, wells and rubbish pits were investigated just south of Smyrna Landing. In addition, numerous farmstead studies in Delaware have contributed to the understanding of changes in the agricultural economy and merchant systems.

The presence of **colonoware pottery** on sites in Wilmington has been connected to the influx of French *émigrés* into the city during the slave revolts in Haiti in the late eighteenth century. Bernard Herman's study of the Thomas Mendenhall house is unusual in that most other late eighteenth-century African American sites cannot be connected to specific people. Post-emancipation African American sites outside of Wilmington show differences in living standards, some just barely at the edge of subsistence and others considerably higher.

See also: African American archaeology; Dutch colonialism; English colonialism

Further reading

Cantwell, A.-M. D. DiZ. Wall (2001) Unearthing Gotham: The archaeology on New York City, New Haven: Yale University Press.

Carlisle, R.C. (1998) *The Story of 'Woodville': The History, Architecture, and Archaeology of a Western Pennsylvania Farm*, Pittsburgh: The Pittsburgh History and Landmarks Foundation.

Catts, W.P. and De Cunzo, L.A. (1993) 'From "white man's garbage" to the study of material culture: A review of historical archaeology in Delaware', *Delaware History* 25(3): 174–99.

Cotter, J.L., Roberts, D.G. and Parrington, M. (1992) *The Buried Past, an Archaeological History of Philadelphia*, Philadelphia: University of Pennsylvania Press.

Rothschild, N.A. (1990) *New York City Neighborhoods: The 18th Century*, New York: Academic Press.

Rutsch, E.S. (1975) '1974 symposium on industrial archaeology, Paterson, New Jersey', *Northeast Historical Archaeology* 4(1/2): 1–94.

Wall, D.D. (1994) *The Archaeology of Gender: Separating the Spheres in Urban America*, New York: Plenum Press.

Yamin, R. (1992/3) 'Local trade in prerevolutionary New Jersey', *Northeast Historical Archaeology* 21–2: 123–36.

REBECCA YAMIN, DIANA DiZEREGA WALL
AND RONALD C. CARLISLE

Millwood Plantation, South Carolina, USA

Millwood Plantation was located on the banks of the Savannah River principally in north-western South Carolina, but a small portion of it was also located across the river in Georgia. James Edward Calhoun, brother-in-law and cousin of the renowned Southern statesman John C. Calhoun, owned the estate from 1832 until his death in 1889. Calhoun was a well-educated Southern gentleman who had served with the famous Stephen H. Long Expedition through the upper US Mid-west in 1823. Millwood was situated in a topographically rugged region, but by 1860 Calhoun had transformed the plantation into a large estate covering over 6,000 ha and housing almost 200 African American slaves. Emancipated slaves continued to live on the estate lands as tenant farmers after Calhoun's death until about 1925, at which time local residents began to use the property as a fishing camp. The site is now under the water of the Richard B. Russell Reservoir.

The site of Millwood Plantation was excavated in 1980 and 1981 under the direction of Charles Orser as part of the large US National Park Service project within the area that would contain the reservoir. Archaeologists recovered almost 62,000 artefacts from inside and immediately around 28 stone building foundations that remained at the site. The structures included three uniformly small, square slave cabins, several houses once inhabited by tenant farmers, a sorghum processing station, a mill building and Calhoun's dwelling.

One of the most important aspects of the research at Millwood Plantation is that it is one of only a handful of large-scale projects to focus on the important period of transition from slavery to tenant farming. Included in this important agricultural shift was a series of significant social transformations as well. One example appears in the changes in the settlement pattern (see **settlement analysis**) at the plantation. Before the American Civil War (1832–61), the agricultural labourers (held in bondage as slaves) lived in nucleated settlements, or quarters, situated relatively close to their places of work. This settlement pattern changed with emancipation, and during a period of great social change (1865–75), both at Millwood and throughout the entire South, the newly freed slaves inhabited smaller, more dispersed, nucleated settlements. The farmers who lived in these small clusters of houses worked in 'squads' under the direction of a 'leader'. These

Figure 21 Late nineteenth-century picture of the central area of Millwood Plantation, South Carolina
Source: Photo: C.E. Orser, Jr

semi-autonomous groups were typically composed of extended families and contained around ten workers. The nucleated, post-war clusters gradually disappeared as freedmen and women sought greater freedom from direct supervision, and they constructed new houses throughout the estate lands.

See also: African American archaeology; plantation archaeology

Further reading

Orser, C.E., Jr (1988) *The Material Basis of the Postbellum Tenant Plantation: Historical Archaeology in the South Carolina Piedmont*, Athens: University of Georgia Press.

Orser, C.E., Jr and Nekola, A.M. (1985) 'Plantation settlement from slavery to tenancy: An example from a Piedmont plantation in South Carolina', in T.A. Singleton (ed.) *The Archaeology of Slavery and Plantation Life*, Orlando: Academic Press, pp. 67–94.

CHARLES E. ORSER, JR

mining archaeology

Mining is the application of human technology to extract from the earth and to refine culturally valuable metals, minerals and other materials. Historically, archaeological evidence of mining occurs as early as the fifth millennium BC and is found in many places throughout the world. The earliest miners gathered naturally occurring metals such as copper, iron and gold, or minerals such as salt. They worked the native metal ores only by heating and hammering or shaping. Later, ancient mining practices involved digging underground shafts and tunnels, and separating metals from rock ores with open hearths, bloomery furnaces and blast furnaces. The mining of metals and minerals played important roles in ancient trading networks and in the development of ancient civilisations' complex societies. Early Mesopotamian gold-mining colonies in Africa, for example, influenced early Egyptian civilisation. Also, later civilisations, such as classical Greece and **Rome**, developed large mines throughout their ancient worlds.

Archaeological studies of mining can be found at least as early as the nineteenth century (in the Reports of the Ancient Mining and Metallurgy Committee of the Royal Anthropological Institute of Great Britain and Northern Ireland). The archaeological study of mining in historical archaeology, however, began not much earlier than the 1980s. Archaeological subjects include mining technology, mining society and culture, and mining landscapes.

The archaeology of mining technology

The study of historical and geographical variability and change in mining technology is an important part of mining archaeology. Ancient mining clearly established the roots of mining technology in the modern world. Mining in medieval Europe built upon this tradition to create a standardised non-industrial mining technology by the sixteenth century that was exported with the European global migration. The technology involved digging an open pit and shallow shafts down to a depth of 100–200 ft to reach the ore. Once underground, the miners dug 'ratholes' to follow the ore body. They carried ore and waste rock out of the underground mines in bags on their backs while climbing up ladders or walking up inclines. Alternatively, they used hand-operated windlasses or animal-powered whims to hoist themselves and materials in and out of the mines. The miners built simple pumping, hoisting, transport and grinding machines from the gear trains, cams, pistons, cylinders and other devices in common use at the time. Spanish colonial miners added to the technology by developing the process of patio amalgamation for recovering silver and gold from ores. Chinese miners in the California gold rush further added to the global non-industrial mining technology by introducing Chinese pumps, bucket bailers on an endless chain driven by an undershot waterwheel, based upon traditional irrigation technology in south **Asia**. The machines were powered mostly with people and animals but also with water and other inanimate sources of power on a small scale.

Mining was among the last of the industries to industrialise, and the Comstock mines of Nevada played a key role in bringing about the change.

The Comstock pattern of deep industrial mining, developed in the 1860s and 1870s, was exported around the world to provide a standardised global technology that is still being used. Early industrial mining technology included highly mechanised and steam-powered pan amalgamation, the factory system and steam engines. As mines deepened, the hand-operated windlasses or animal-powered whims no longer provided the power needed to hoist miners and materials in and out of the mines. Large steam engines provided the solution. Steam engines powered hoists, pumps, stamp mills, air compressors – which operated blowers for ventilation – and mechanical rock drills.

The archaeology of mining technology studies the physical remains of ore extraction and ore beneficiation or upgrading, along with mining-related technologies such as transportation or power or water engineering systems. Ore extraction technologies at archaeological sites include the physical remains of open pits, mine shafts, underground workings, mine waste rock dumps, hoisting systems such as headframes and engines to drive cables, drainage pumps, air compressors for ventilation systems or rock drills, water conveyance and storage systems, ore cars and tracks, and blacksmith shops. Beneficiation or upgrading and refining technologies at archaeological sites may include the physical remains of rock-crushing machines such as stamp mills or ball mills, concentration tables, amalgamation pans, flotation tanks, cyanide-leaching tanks, smelters, blast furnaces, mill tailings and refining furnaces.

Mining archaeologists sometimes focus upon the technologies used to mine and to process metals and minerals. The archaeology of mining technology typically involves the recording of what remains on the surface without excavation. In the USA, several projects of this kind have been done by the **Historic American Engineering Record** (HAER) of the National Park Service. One recent example is the Mariscal Quicksilver Works in Big Bend National Park in west Texas. The Works consisted of a mine and processing plant. It began in 1916 with an inclined retort technology, then switched to a Huettner–Scott furnace technology between 1919 and 1924. The works reopened during the Second World War and used a Gould-type rotary furnace in 1942 and 1943, when it closed for the last time.

HAER projects of this kind are multidisciplinary. Architects and photographers documented the surviving works with measured drawings and photographs. Historians researched the written record. And archaeologists surveyed and documented the physical remains of the workers' settlements. The documents reside in the permanent collection of the US Library of Congress, and many are available on-line.

Some archaeological studies of mining technology, however, have used the techniques of excavation. A good example is David Landon and Timothy Tumberg's archaeological study of the 1850s Iron Trap Rock Mine, a copper ore extraction and beneficiation operation on Michigan's upper peninsula. The excavation of the site of the mine's stamp mill found that copper in the sediments had preserved the remains of two Cornish wooden round buddles. Cornish workers at the mine introduced the round buddles, which were just becoming popular in Cornwall and were virtually unknown in the USA at the time. The design of the buddles reflected the vernacular knowledge of the Cornish immigrants, but they used locally available wood instead of masonry and iron in the buddles' construction.

Another archaeological approach to mining technology is to physically and chemically analyse the material residues of ore processing. Archaeometallurgy is one method. Paul Craddock of the British Museum, for example, studied the residues from ancient iron-working furnaces and found that Africa may be an exception to the widely held view that iron production spread to other world areas from Anatolia some time during the late third millennium BC. An independent origin for African iron production is suggested both by the diversity of the processes used and the presence of quite different types of furnaces.

Social archaeology of mining

Most archaeological studies of mining, however, have explored the social life and culture of miners rather than their technologies. One common research topic is the archaeology of **ethnicity**, nationality, **gender** and other cultural identities that played a major role in the globally constituted mining societies of the modern world. Neville

Ritchie's study of the domestic and landscape **architecture** of overseas Chinese settlements (see **overseas Chinese historical archaeology**) in the goldfields of southern New Zealand is a good example. He found that the buildings typically followed pre-existing Western models and reflected adaptation to local environmental conditions but also retained some traditional Chinese elements. They, for example, used locally available construction materials (e.g. turf, mud bricks and puddled mud, forest trees, canvas, corrugated iron sheets, cobblestones) and places (e.g. rock shelters), and often took advantage of abandoned buildings. They did not have the typical 'high-culture' Chinese architectural elements of upturned eaves, decorative eave brackets, tile roofing and fretwork patterns on fascia boards. The buildings, however, often retained some elements of traditional Chinese rural architecture such as being windowless and having hut shrines, door inscriptions and a chopping block just outside the door.

Another example is Susan Lawrence's study of gender identities at the site of **Dolly's Creek goldfield** in the goldfields of **Australia**. She found that women, although nearly invisible in traditional histories and folk beliefs, played an important role in the culture, society and day-to-day life of this mid-nineteenth-century mining camp. Women and children made up more than half of the camp's population. Both men and women worked the mines and pooled their incomes in domestic households. Many women maintained family farms that raised meat and vegetables for subsistence and cash, and often made it possible to continue mining when it was not profitable. They also dramatically affected the material culture of the camp by introducing the symbols of genteel culture, including decorative tableware, fancy clocks and whitewashed fireplaces.

Another common research topic in the social archaeology of mining is social formations, such as households, local settlements and regional communities. Donald Hardesty's study of the early twentieth-century company town satellite of Reipetown in eastern Nevada is an example. Reipetown society and culture appear to be rather unique. The nearby company towns of Ruth, Kimberly,and McGill, for example, evolved classic industrial

social structures with well-defined occupational and social classes reflected in domestic architecture, town layout, wealth differences and prestige. In contrast, however, archaeological evidence showed no evidence of a class structure in Reipetown, but documentary data and oral testimony show that the settlement occupied a low social status in the social structure of the larger regional community that included the company towns. Visible power and prestige differences were minimal within the Reipetown settlement. No archaeological or other evidence shows significant differences in wealth among the households nor do architectural differences among the houses reflect significant wealth differences. Interestingly enough, despite the documentary evidence and oral testimony of a population dominated by ethnic Greeks, Slavs, Italians, Mexicans and Japanese, the archaeological record of Reipetown spoke not at all about ethnicity and ethnic relationships. There is no evidence of ethnic groups clustering in geographical neighbourhoods, but even more remarkable is the virtual absence, with the exception of a couple of pieces of Japanese ceramic tableware, of artefact markers of ethnicity.

Mining landscapes

Finally, landscape archaeology is another research topic in mining archaeology. Mining transforms natural landscapes in distinctive ways that reflect technology, society and culture, land use practices, responses to landforms and other natural features, and the layout or spatial arrangement of landscape components. Dredging, for example, involves building a large pond upon which the dredge floats and excavates mud, sand and gravel from the bottom of the pond with a large shovel or bucket line. The technology leaves behind a distinctive landscape pattern organised around large serpentine piles of tailings piles and remnants of dredging ponds. Mining landscapes are primary documents of mining's past. Judith Alfrey and Catherine Clark, for example, show how the archaeological sites and monuments in England's Ironbridge Gorge, often called the 'Cradle of the Industrial Revolution', document the process of industrialisation in the coal-mining and iron-making industries.

Further reading

Alfrey, J. and Clark, C. (1993) *The Landscape of Industry: Patterns of Change in the Ironbridge Gorge*, London: Routledge.

Craddock, P. (1996) *Early Metal Mining and Production*, Washington, DC: Smithsonian Institution Press.

Hardesty, D.L. (1988) *The Archaeology of Mining and Miners: A View from the Silver State*, Special Publication 6, Tucson: Society for Historical Archaeology.

Knapp, A.B., Pigott, V. and Herbert, E. (eds) (1998) *Social Approaches to an Industrial Past, the Archaeology and Anthropology of Mining*, London: Routledge.

Landon, D. and Tumberg, T. (1996) 'Archaeological perspectives on the diffusion of technology: An example from the Ohio Trap Rock mine site', *IA: The Journal of the Society for Industrial Archaeology* 22(2): 40–57.

Ritchie, N. (1993) 'Form and adaptation: Nineteenth century Chinese miners' dwellings in southern New Zealand', in P. Wegars (ed.) *Hidden Heritage: Historical Archaeology of the Overseas Chinese*, Amityville, NY: Baywood, pp. 335–73.

DONALD L. HARDESTY

Mission Santa Clara, California, USA

Mission Santa Clara was founded in January 1777 not far from the south end of San Francisco Bay. The eighth Franciscan mission to be built in *Alta California*, it was the first named in honour of a female saint. Santa Clara is unique in the California mission systems as there have been six churches at five different sites. The site of the Franciscan mission lies today on the campus of the Jesuit-operated Santa Clara University which is the only institution of higher education in the USA to stand on a former mission site.

In the sixty years (1777–1837) that marked the existence of Mission Santa Clara de Asís, the mission complex of dormitories, residences, corrals, barns and workshops was moved three times due to flooding and earthquakes. Over this period there were five churches built in distinct locations. The first two complexes and churches (1777–84), stood near the Guadalupe River and were built of wattle-and-daub. Their locations have not been positively identified. Later, churches of adobe construction (1784–1818, 1818–60, 1822–1926) stood on what is today Santa Clara University. Floods, earthquakes, demolition and fires combined to erase these sites.

To date, archaeological and documentary research has positively identified, and begun to reveal, the three Franciscan churches and associated compounds that lie on the modern Jesuit campus. Since 1980, archaeologists from the California Department of Transportation, the Santa Clara University Department of Anthropology and Sociology, and the Archaeology Research Laboratory at Santa Clara University have explored the mission. In addition to a number of Spanish- and Mexican-period rubbish deposits, these projects have identified parts of the 1784–1818 mission quadrangle and cemetery; the 1818–25 church; part of the 1827–51 cemetery; and the mission's *matanza* or slaughter yard. Because of the mission's repeated relocations it has been possible to trace cultural continuity and change within the resident population. Material indicators of continuity include faunal remains of wild game and evidence of the continued use of local plants in the diet and for cordage. Abalone, clam and olivella shells, modified into **beads** and pendants, continued to be deposited in burial contexts. Also, in contexts dating to the first decade of the nineteenth century, there is evidence for the continued use of chert and obsidian for both projectile points and drills.

Prior to the arrival of the Spanish, **ceramics** were unknown in most of California. In a joint project with the Smithsonian Center for Materials Research and Education, Santa Clara University researchers have used neutron activation analysis to study ceramic production and exchange in *Alta California*. This technique has demonstrated that at Mission Santa Clara and at other mission, presidio and pueblo sites both lead-glazed and unglazed coiled and wheel-thrown ceramics were made.

Dietary and DNA analysis, and environmental reconstruction research at Santa Clara is ongoing and continues to reveal new evidence on how the colonial institution of the mission altered the lives of the indigenous peoples of the San Francisco Bay area.

See also: La Purisima Mission; mission sites; Spanish colonialism

Further reading

Hylkema, M. (1995) *Archaeological Investigation at Mission Santa Clara (CA-SCL-30) for the Re-Alignment of Route 82*, Oakland: California Department of Transportation.

Milliken, R.T. (1995) *A Time of Little Choice, the Disintegration of Tribal Culture in the San Francisco Bay Area, 1769–1810*, Menlo Park, CA: Ballena Press.

Shoup, L.H. (1995) *Inigo of Rancho Posolmi: The Life and Times of a Mission Indian and His Land*, Oakland, CA: Archaeological/Historical Consultants.

Skowronek, R.K. (1998) 'Sifting the evidence: Perceptions of life at the Ohlone (Costanoan) missions of Alta California', *Ethnohistory* 45: 45–78.

Skowronek, R.K. and Wizorek, J.C. (1997) 'Archaeology at Santa Clara de Asís: The slow rediscovery of a moveable mission', *Pacific Coast Archaeological Society Quarterly* 33(3): 54–92.

RUSSELL K. SKOWRONEK

mission sites

The interests of both the Church and the Crown were intimately combined in the expansion of European power over the last 500 years. This relationship was manifested through the foundation of Christian missions whose purpose was to convert non-Europeans to Christianity, thus expanding the power of the Church and facilitating control of the converts by the Crown. Missionary activity played a role in the colonial expansion of every European nation, although the degree to which it was integrated into the formal hierarchy of conquest and control varied considerably from nation to nation and century to century. Perhaps the most direct relationship between Church and Crown resulting in the development of large-scale mission systems was the Spanish expansion into the New World. As a result, historical archaeologists

have focused much more attention on Spanish colonial mission sites than on those of other nations. There has been archaeological research at the sites of missions founded by other nations, especially the French in North America, such as the **Marquette Mission** in Michigan. However, mission sites have not become a focus of French colonial archaeology in the same way that they have in the archaeology of **Spanish colonialism**.

Architectural **restoration** is a primary reason for much archaeology at mission sites in the south-western USA, where many of the mission buildings were built of stone, adobe and wood, in a climate that preserved the ruins. Locating lost mission sites is a major focus in the south-east, where mission buildings were usually built of wood, thatch, wattle and daub, and have long since disappeared due to fires, British military attacks, hurricanes and the climate. As a result, much of the literature on mission sites is highly specific, with detailed historical summaries, site plans, artefact descriptions and architectural information intended to assist restoration or confirm the location and layout of the mission site. Synthesis has usually been on a regional level, because contextual differences have limited interregional synthesis. The missions' impacts on **Native Americans** provides one unifying theme.

The Spanish colony of La Florida was a major area of missionary activity. Over 150 missions were established between **Santa Elena** in South Carolina, through coastal Georgia to **St Augustine**, Florida, and north-west from central Florida to Tallahassee. A great deal of archaeological research has been devoted to locating and identifying these sites. The best known of these projects is David Hurst Thomas's search for the site of **Santa Catalina de Guale** on St Catherines Island, Georgia (*c*.1587–1680).

San Luis de Talimali (1656–1704) is at the western end of the Florida mission chain near Tallahassee. Through a combination of broad-scale remote sensing, detailed topographic mapping, auger survey and test pits, the locations of a fortified strong house and fort, Spanish village, central plaza, a large mission church with burials in the nave, *convento*, a large Apalachee Indian council house and an Apalachee chief's house have been found. Council houses were a common feature of

Florida mission sites, but are not found elsewhere in the Spanish borderlands. Large-scale excavations of the church, *convento* and council house in the mission complex, as well as houses in the Spanish village, have revealed a pattern of accommodation and interdependence between the Spanish and the Indians at this site. Bonnie McEwan suggests that the Spanish were able to maintain a highly traditional material life despite the frontier setting, while the Indians also seem to have maintained their traditional culture and generally limited the degree to which Spanish goods were integrated into traditional activities.

In eastern and central Texas, many of the missions were constructed of logs and have long-since disappeared. Hence, the focus of archaeological research has been to relocate these lost sites. Further west, in the area around San Antonio, the mission sites take on the architectural character popularly associated with the Spanish missions. Here is the best-known and most visited mission, San Antonio de Valero (1719), better known as the Alamo. Because of its urban location, archaeological research has been limited, and usually related to urban development. Nonetheless, mission walls and the Native American quarters, along with artefacts and food refuse, have all been examined.

Thomas R. Hester has compared the archaeological evidence from the Indian quarters at San Antonio de Valero with data from excavated Indian quarters at Missions San Juan Capistrano (1731), Concepcion (1731) and San Jose (1721) also in San Antonio, Missions Rosario (1754) and Espiritu Santo (1749) in the Goliad region near the Gulf of Mexico, and Missions San Bernardo (1702) and San Juan Bautista del Rio Grande (1700) near Guerrero, Coahuila, Mexico. He concluded that the mission Indians maintained major elements of their pre-mission material culture throughout the missionisation process. The persistence of chipped stone tools and traditional pottery, despite the presence of imported metal tools and Mexican, Chinese and English **ceramics** is, he believes, indicative of both continuities in traditional hunting and food gathering, and a preference for them over the introduced items. He does acknowledge that

shortages of imported goods may also have been a factor.

Mission San Antonio de Padua de Casas Grandes (1660–86) in Chihuahua, Mexico, was excavated in 1959 by Charles C. Di Peso. The results of the artefact analysis are among the earliest from a mission site to focus on the relationships between the continuity of traditional Native American culture and imported Spanish culture using a quantitative approach. Di Peso divided the entire artefact assemblage from the mission into 'Iberian' or 'indigenous', based on their origin, and then divided each into seven functional categories such as socioreligious goods, food preparation and serving, warfare, hunting and so forth. When compared within functional categories, 'weaving tools' was the only one with no 'Iberian' artefacts, indicating complete continuity in this traditional Native American craft. Food preparation and serving artefacts were almost equally divided between 'Iberian' and 'indigenous', suggesting considerable Indian continuity in these aspects. 'Iberian' artefacts dominated the other groups. Di Peso's results, therefore, also suggest some degree of continuity of traditional material culture among mission Indians.

Completed in 1974, the same years as Di Peso's study was published, Annetta L. Cheek's doctoral dissertation took a more sophisticated approach to artefact analysis from the site of San Xavier del Bac (1692) near Tucson, Arizona, to study the impact of Spanish missionaries on Native American cultures. Excavations at San Xavier del Bac had begun in 1957 and, like most mission excavations, the earlier years of excavation were directed at delineating and dating the construction sequence, with the focus being on the church ruins and adjacent structures. Only a small portion of the site was excavated in 1972–3 specifically for Cheek's study, and was again in, or immediately adjacent to, the church. Cheek recognised that dividing artefacts into either 'Iberian' or 'indigenous' was an oversimplification that masked significant variations. Working from a classification for contact period objects devised by George Quimby and Alexander Spoehr and published in 1951, Cheek devised an artefact **classification** with nine categories. Eight of the categories were for Native American-made artefacts, dependent upon whether each of the form, material and technique of manufacture were European or Indian in origin. The ninth category was for European-made artefacts.

Cheek found that when she applied her classification to the excavated archaeological assemblage from the site, there were too few artefacts in seven of the eight categories of Indian-made artefacts. Collapsing these categories into one produced a tripartite classification of European artefacts, Indian artefacts and Indian-made artefacts in which some aspect of their form, material or method of manufacture was European influenced in some way. This analysis showed that there was increasing influence by non-Indians on the Indians at the mission between approximately 1762 and 1825. There was a decline in aboriginal artefacts from over 90 per cent to less than 75 per cent, and a doubling in the percentage of European-influenced Indian-made artefacts from approximately 3 per cent to over 6 per cent. However, this was less change than Cheek had predicted. As a result, although Native Americans manufactured most of the artefacts recovered, Cheek concluded that the excavated areas were used and occupied almost entirely by Europeans.

Perhaps the earliest published attempt to assess the impact of Spanish missionaries on Native American's material culture was published in 1963 by James Deetz. This work was based on his excavations at mission La Purisima Concepcion (1812) (see **La Purisima Mission**), located north of Santa Barbara in California. The results show the rapid decline in traditional artefacts and their replacement with European artefacts. Further, male-activity artefacts declined far more rapidly than female-activity artefacts. Other researchers excavating at California mission sites have built upon Deetz's conclusions. Robert L. Hoover undertook a multi-year research project at Mission San Antonio de Padua (1771), one of the best-preserved mission complexes in California, located between Santa Barbara and Monterey. A major focus of the research was Native American **acculturation** at the mission using both the classification developed by Quimby and Spoehr, and Deetz's results as a guide.

At Mission Nuestra Senora de la Soledad (1791), located in the Salinas Valley south of Monterey, Paul Farnsworth also focused his research on

Native American acculturation at the mission. Although most of the excavation was in the central complex, including the mission kitchen, mill and blacksmiths, a number of rubbish pits were excavated that resulted from Native American activities at the mission. A rich midden deposit associated with the Indian barracks was also tested.

Following Cheek's analysis in Arizona, and Hoover's research in California, Farnsworth's analysis developed Quimby and Spoehr's classification into ten systematic categories that encompassed both Indian- and European-made artefacts. However, while this was useful for descriptive purposes, he found that a slightly different approach was more useful for studying culture change. This new approach included the recognition that the place of origin, materials and method of manufacture probably had little meaning for the individual using the artefacts; it was more important to understand how they were used, and whether this represented continuity of traditional activities or a change in activities. A European-made or 'hybrid' artefact (combining some aspects of European and traditional elements) could function within Native American culture without requiring any change in meaning, or it could mean something completely new.

Using this approach, Farnsworth compared the artefacts from Deetz's excavations at Mission La Purisima, Hoover's excavations at Mission San Antonio and his own excavations at Mission Soledad. The results showed that in the Indian barracks at each mission, over half of the artefacts could have functioned in traditional activities with no significant change in meaning for the user. Using a series of dated deposits from Mission Soledad, analysis showed that the degree of continuity of traditional activities did not decline steadily the longer the mission operated, as might be expected, but fluctuated. Farnsworth correlated these fluctuations with the changing situation of the missions as they became incorporated into the world economic system. Territorial control and spiritual concerns were replaced by economic motivations. As Native Americans died rapidly from introduced European diseases, more were brought into the mission to increase economic production. Consequently, the degree of Native American cultural continuity fluctuated as each group of Native Americans were brought into the mission.

See also: assimilation; Christianisation; colonialism; creolisation

Further reading

Cheek, A.L. (1974) 'The evidence for acculturation in artifacts: Indians and non-Indians at San Xavier del Bac, Arizona', doctoral dissertation, University of Arizona.

Di Peso, C.C. (1974) *Casas Grandes: A Fallen Trading Center of the Gran Chichimeca*, Dragoon: The Amerind Foundation, pp. 853–959.

Farnsworth, P. (1992) 'Missions, Indians, and cultural continuity', *Historical Archaeology* 26(1): 22–36.

Hester, T.R. (1989) 'Perspectives on the material culture of the mission Indians of the Texas–northeastern Mexico borderlands', in D.H. Thomas (ed.) *Columbian Consequences: Volume 1, Archaeological and Historical Perspectives on the Spanish Borderlands West*, Washington, DC: Smithsonian Institution Press, pp. 213–29.

McEwan, B.G. (ed.) (1993) *The Spanish Missions of La Florida*, Gainesville: University Press of Florida.

Skowronek, R.K. (1998) 'Sifting the evidence: Perceptions of life at the Ohlone (Costanoan) missions of Alta California', *Ethnohistory* 45: 675–708.

PAUL FARNSWORTH

modernity

Modernity is emerging as a major topic of study in historical archaeology, even though not all archaeologists would completely agree on its meaning. The word 'modern' comes from the Latin word *modo*, meaning 'just now'. We can thus think of modernity to be 'our time now'. We are 'modern' while others, either in the past or in less developed parts of the globe, are not modern. This definition, though it makes sense to many people, is inadequate for scholarly purposes because it leaves two major questions unanswered: When did modernity 'begin', and what are its material manifestations?

Historical archaeology is perfectly designed to address both questions as well as others about modernity. Modernity as a subject is so potentially important that some historical archaeologists have argued that it can provide an overarching theme to permit the field to become a fully mature social scientific discipline. A focus on modernity would also make historical archaeology more relevant to scholars working outside archaeology, in such areas as **world systems theory** and **globalisation**.

An initial understanding of modernity can be obtained by imagining that the world is composed of two kinds of people: those who are 'modern' and those who are 'traditional'. Modern men and women are viewed as those people living in the industrial world, in such places as the USA, Canada, Western Europe, Australia and Japan. Traditional men and women, on the other hand, live in all the other places in the world: sub-Saharan Africa, the Arctic, New Guinea and Micronesia.

Such simple characterisations are relatively easy to conceptualise but they are dangerous because they separate individual cultures based on a vague notion of achievement. In other words, the modern/traditional dichotomy makes it easy to imagine that there is something intrinsically 'better' about being 'modern'. To be 'traditional' suggests an unwillingness to become modern or, even worse, an ignorance of the concept itself. People who are modern tend to be idealised as those who invent and innovate, while traditional people are imagined to be conservative and slow to adopt new ways of doing things.

Scholars interested in modernity (and the process of modernisation) have engaged in a fierce debate about the core ideas of modernity and the meanings behind the acceptance and rejection of 'modern' innovations by indigenous peoples. These scholars have generally been arranged into two camps: modernisation theorists and dependency theorists.

Modernisation theorists generally believe that any of the world's peoples can start on the road to modernity, no matter how 'traditional' they may be, if they are given the proper conditions. In their view, traditional peoples must have the economic, political, ideational and social mechanisms to permit them to accept the innovations of the modern world. For instance, the application of high-yield, artificial fertilisers would be of little use to farmers who believe as part of their age-old religion that they must use animal fertilisers to ensure the continuation of their culture. To accept the 'modernisation revolution' the people must have the desire to adopt and adapt, and they must have political leaders who are willing to make a case for change. Modernisation theorists generally promote the infusion of large amounts of foreign capital into 'developing nations' (e.g. those moving from 'traditional' to 'modern') to improve the nation's infrastructure (dams, roads, railway system and telecommunications) as a precondition to accepting full-scale modernisation.

Dependency theorists disagree with the modernisation theorists and argue instead that 'modern' societies only exist because they have exploited traditional societies. They would say, for example, that the bondage of millions of men and women of African descent in the USA helped to ensure the economic success of that nation. Dependency theorists created world systems theory to help explain why some nations were unimaginably wealthy and 'modern' while others were desperately poor and 'traditional'. As part of the same global system, traditional societies (on the 'periphery') used their labour for the benefit of, and sent valuable products to, the modern societies (at the 'core'). To make this system work, Europeans (at the core) had to construct an **ideology** to rationalise it.

Historian Enrique Dussel has argued that the process of modernisation was a distinctly European phenomenon, and that 'Europe' was a mental construct rooted in an ideology of modernity, one in which it was perceived as the centre of the world. Accordingly, modernisation was both rational and irrational at the same time. It was rational because it promoted a sense of achievement and economic emancipation, but it was also irrational because it provided a rationale for mass cultural genocide (i.e. the ends justify the means).

Dussel's understanding has important ramifications for historical archaeologists because it provides myriad topics that can be investigated throughout the world using archaeological methods. These topics include the beginnings of modernity and its historical dynamics across the globe. Dussel says that modernity began when Europeans first perceived their region to be the most developed place on earth. Even though this understanding took root at a time when Europe was composed of a series of small nation-states, Europeans were able to base their unity on their common religious faith and its distinct difference from that of the powerful Middle East. In the face of a gargantuan religious (and cultural) chasm between European Christians and non-European Muslims, Europeans – just beginning their Age of Exploration – began to imagine that they could 'improve' the conditions of the indigenous peoples they encountered by bringing them to modernity. Those peoples who were given the tools of modernity, but who still failed to adopt them, could be justifiably destroyed. Their destruction could be cultural (leading to **assimilation**) or physical (leading to full-scale genocide).

An important element of modernity for historical archaeology is that it provides a theme that historical archaeologists can use to examine the past using both a large scale (to examine the material manifestations of **capitalism**, the elements of culture contact and many other topics) and a small scale (to investigate how capitalism and culture contact affected real men, women and **children** at specific locales). Historical archaeology that can tack back and forth between large topics and their small manifestations seems especially robust and holds great promise for the future.

See also: Dutch colonialism; English colonialism; Portuguese colonialism; Russian colonialism; Spanish colonialism

Further reading

Dussel, E. (1993) 'Eurocentrism and modernity's *Boundary* 2(2): 65–76.
Litvinoff, B. (1991) *1492: The Decline of Medievalism and the Rise of the Modern Age*, New York: Avon.
Orser, C.E., Jr (1996) *A Historical Archaeology of the Modern World*, New York: Plenum Press.

CHARLES E. ORSER, JR

Montarrenti, Italy

In Italy, documents and archaeology reveal an increasingly fortified landscape from the tenth and eleventh centuries AD. The emergence of castles, towers and defended villages relates to a significant redefinition of territory and property, linked to a pronounced imposition of private as opposed to state control. The process is termed *incastellamento* and broadly defines how seigneurial groups – noble families, bishops, even monasteries – concentrated settlers and resources into tightly defended units for both protection and control. Urban centres likewise witnessed the erection of such 'feudal strongholds', notably towers – over 600 in Florence, 900 in **Rome** – although the majority were symbols of status as opposed to active military bases. Many of the urban towers and castles collapsed, were demolished or have since been cleared away; in contrast, however, the rural landscape contains many castles, fortified villages and townships that have their strongest visible roots in this period. However, archaeology indicates in many cases (notably in Alpine regions and in Liguria) origins predating the earliest documentation to *castelli*; indeed, the break-up of Roman control in the fifth century did much to prompt the earliest recourse to hills, either for official military roles, local protection or as refuges; sixth- and seventh-century insecurity did much to reinforce this unstable landscape. A central problem remains securely identifying, dating and defining this sixth- to eighth-century phase, since minimal coin usage, more localised ceramic types, construction in timber and later expansion in stone largely obscure the proto-castle/*incastellamento* epoch.

Montarrenti represents just one example, but a systematically excavated example, of this wider phenomenon of medieval rural upland castle-village settlement in Italy. The site lies 15 km south-west of **Siena** in central Italy, occupying a small horseshoe-shaped hill; when excavations began in 1982, one family still occupied a late medieval tower-house and another such structure had only recently been quitted; two lower houses also remained occupied. Here, as in most incastellated sites there is a spatial and structural division between the seigneurial zone (uppermost unit, often girded by a wall and with at least one tower-

house) and the *borgo* or village, splayed out on the slopes around, and usually protected by a wall. At Montarrenti the *borgo* showed careful planning, its houses organised coherently along the hill contours and skilfully terraced into the bedrock, which offered immediate construction materials. These houses conform to a typical plan, wherein the lower storey contained animal byres and stores, and human space and other storage lay above. Finds from both zones demonstrated an economically healthy community, with the 'workers' possessing a good range of **ceramics**, metal items and coins. There was, nonetheless, a clear material distancing on the part of the lords occupying the upper tower-houses: frescoes reflected a social link with the high culture of Siena; rubbish deposits included sizeable quantities of expensive polychrome glazed ware of the fourteenth century as well as fine glass; while food debris demonstrated the choicer meat cuts filling the elite bellies.

Chronologies are, however, the most revealing aspect of the Montarrenti project: in line with many such sites, the first documentation is much later than that revealed by archaeology. In 1156, the chapel of Saint Lawrence and Saint Andrew is recorded, after which a consistent series of references to people and landed ties occurs, with a settlement peak attested for the fourteenth century. A register of 1317 in fact records the main Sienese landowner at Montarrenti as *Iohannes domini Meschiati*, possessing various of the *borgo* buildings, various units of land, farmsteads and a mill; the register gives an idea of values, but little of the material culture, except confirming the two-storey house form with animal/human division.

The 1982–7 excavations enhanced this detailed picture, but most importantly revealed the deeper roots of the settlement. There were traces of a palisade and of post-built houses that stratigraphically predated the tenth century; a single radiocarbon date for this first timber phase was calculated to the late eighth century. Further, radiocarbon dates of grain deposits relating to the first stone phase pointed to a major (seigneurial?) restructuring of the settlement in 950–1000.

The settlement endured through various changes of hands into the seventeenth century, but by then reduced to a community of just forty-six persons and four farmsteads, and with the castle structures ruinous by the eighteenth century. This shrinkage and decay, in contrast with so many Italian upland sites that leave little scope for extensive archaeological scrutiny, has, as at **Rocca San Silvestro**, been vital in allowing a detailed image of medieval material life to be drawn.

Since Montarrenti, the Siena district has seen full mapping of its archaeology and structural heritage; in the course of this project, additional castle sites have seen archaeological investigation, with integrated documentary analysis. Examples to note are Miranduolo, Serena and San Magno in the Chiusdino district in the south-west of the province, an area of conflict in the tenth–twelfth centuries between the Sienese Gherardeschi family and the bishops of Volterra, linked to the metal/mineral resources of the region. The journal *Archeologia Medievale* forms the key national guide to ongoing research and excavations across Italy on medieval castles, identifying improving abilities to examine and date these common landscape units.

Further reading

Francovich, R. and Hodges, R. (1989) 'Archeologia e storia del villaggio fortificato di Montarrenti (SI): Un caso o un modello?', *Archeologia Medievale* 16: 15–38.

Ginatempo, M. and Giorgi, A. (1996) 'Le fonti documentarie per la storia degli insediamenti medievali in Toscana', *Archeologia Medievale* 23: 7–52.

Nardini, A. (1999) 'L'incastellamento nel territorio di Chiusdino (Siena) tra X e XI secolo. I casi di Miranduolo e Serena', *Archeologia Medievale* 26: 339–51.

Noyé, G. (ed.) (1988) *Structures de l'habitat et occupation du sol dans le pays méditerranéens: les méthodes et l'apport de l'archéologie extensive*, Collections de l'Ecole Française de Rome 105, Publications de la Casa de Velázquez, Série Archéologie, fasc. IX, Rome/Madrid.

Settia, A.A. (1999) *Proteggere e dominare. Fortificazioni e popolamento nell'Italia medievale*, Rome: Laterza.

Toubert, P. (1973) *Les structures du Latium médiéval. Le Latium meridional et la Sabine du IXe siècle à la fin du XIIe siècle*, 2 vols, Rome: Bibliothèques des Ecoles Françaises d'Athènes et de Rome.

Wickham, C. (1985) *Il problema dell'incastellamento nell'Italia centrale*, Florence: All'Insegna del Giglio.

NEIL J. CHRISTIE

Monticello, Virginia, USA

The Monticello of popular memory is the neo-classical mansion whose façade appears on the US nickel, along with the face of its designer, Thomas Jefferson. The real historical Monticello was a 5,000 acre plantation located at the western edge of Virginia's Piedmont. From 1769 to 1826, this complex economic and social community was home not only to Jefferson and his family, but also to scores of enslaved African Americans and their families, whose skills and labour powered Jefferson's agricultural and industrial enterprises.

In excavations conducted during the 1980s, archaeologists investigated the below-ground traces of a terraced vegetable garden, orchards and, most importantly, Mulberry Row, the 1000-ft long street of outbuildings, plantation shops and slave houses that once stood adjacent to the mansion. During this work, thousands of artefacts were recovered, along with the remains of vanished buildings, fences and other landscape features. Fitting these pieces of evidence together into a coherent historical narrative is an ongoing process.

Recent analysis has revealed that the houses constructed along Mulberry Row for enslaved workers in the 1770s had one or two large rooms sharing a single entry. In the 1790s, houses with a smaller single room and independent entry became the norm. This shift apparently represents an increase in the frequency with which slaves could choose their residence partners and live in smaller, family-based groups. This inference is supported by a parallel pattern of change in rectangular sub-floor pits associated with the houses. The earlier large rooms have two sub-floor pits under them, while the later rooms have one or, more frequently, none at all. Current evidence suggests the pits were 'safe-deposit boxes' in which slaves stored personal possessions for safe keeping. Thus, the decline in pit frequency points to a decline in security concerns that would accompany a shift to kin-based housing.

Patterns of change in faunal assemblages also

offer clues about lifeways for Mulberry Row's enslaved residents. Faunal assemblages from the early nineteenth century contain more small wild mammals (possums, raccoons, squirrels) than those from the late eighteenth century. At the same time, once taphonomic differences are accounted for, there are no detectable changes in the quality of meat cuts from domestic mammals that slaves received as part of their provisioned diet. If the provisioned diet remained constant, why would slaves hunt more? A likely answer is a decline in the costs of hunting, which would have accompanied greater mobility across the landscape and increased efficiency in hunting technology (e.g. the use of dogs).

Both archaeologically identifiable changes in housing and diet coincide with important trends in the regional economy. Towards the end of the eighteenth century, Jefferson and many other Chesapeake planters began to supplement their traditional reliance on tobacco with more diversified productive strategies that centred around wheat, but also included small-scale industrial production. The new economic strategy required crop rotations, fertilisers, ploughs, harrows, wagons and mills, and more intensive animal husbandry for manure and ploughing. Slave work regimes became more complex, more dispersed in time and space, and less easily supervised. These changes may have offered enslaved workers greater leverage in negotiating for marginal improvements in their lives. Since 1997, field research at Monticello has begun to reach beyond Mulberry Row to explore these trends and their implications for changes in settlement, land use and the lives of the enslaved field labourers who lived on the four-quarter farms that comprised the agricultural backbone of the plantation.

Further reading

Crader, D.C. (1989) 'Faunal remains from slave quarter sites at Monticello, Charlottesville, Virginia', *Archaeozoologia* 3: 229–36.

Kelso, W.M. (1997) *Archaeology at Monticello*, Charlottesville: Thomas Jefferson Memorial Foundation.

Morgan, P.D. (1998) *Slave Counterpoint: Black Culture in the Eighteenth-century Chesapeake and Low Country*, Chapel Hill: University of North Carolina Press.

Sanford, D. (1995) 'The archaeology of plantation slavery at Thomas Jefferson's Monticello: Context and process in American slave society', doctoral dissertation, University of Virginia.

—— (1994) 'The archaeology of plantation slavery in Piedmont Virginia: Context and process', in P.A. Shackel and B. Little (eds) *Historical Archaeology of the Chesapeake*, Washington, DC: Smithsonian Institution Press, pp. 115–30.

FRASER D. NEIMAN

Moquegua, Peru

Historical archaeology in Moquegua, in far southwestern **Peru**, has focused on the region's wine and brandy agro-industry. Moquegua was established in the late sixteenth century by Spanish settlers moving out of Arequipa, the major colonial city in southern Peru, into the narrow but fertile Moquegua (middle Río Osmore) valley, where they began planting European crops and making wine at their rural haciendas. Distillation of *pisco*, Peruvian grape brandy, probably began in the early eighteenth century. Both products were destined for consumption in the wealthy colonial silver-mining city of Potosí, in present-day Bolivia. Moquegua's viticulture-based economy suffered several boom-and-bust cycles, partly reflecting cycles of the mining industry, and collapsed in the late nineteenth century.

Historical archaeological research in the Moquegua valley began in 1985 with surveys to record the locations of the ruins of the adobe hacienda structures, primarily the gabled storage buildings (*bodegas*) along the valley margins. The Moquegua Bodegas Project undertook mapping of twenty-nine of the 130 identified *bodega* sites, shovel testing at twenty-eight of them and carrying out excavations at four between 1987 and 1989. Industrial portions of the wine haciendas made use of gravity to move quantities of liquid through the stages of wine making and revealed similarities to ancient Roman practices, including use of plastered, sunken grape-crushing vats and huge pithos-like **earthenware** jars. These jars, set in rows into the earthen floors of the structures, were used for fermenting and storing wine, and often bore religious inscriptions and dates on their shoulders. Distillery apparatus was located below and in front of the storage structures. Many sites also had updraft kilns for firing olive jars (see **olive jar**), small, amphora-like earthenware jugs for shipping wine and brandy or for calcining lime. Residential portions of the haciendas included chapels and fragments of tin-enamelled earthenware pottery produced at unknown sites in the Andes, possibly in Cuzco, Peru.

Other historical archaeological studies in Moquegua have been carried out upriver at Torata Alta, a settlement of Lupaqa-speaking Andean peoples at higher elevations around Lake Titicaca, and at spring-fed irrigation systems on the Pacific coast near Ilo, at the mouth of the Río Osmore.

See also: industrial archaeology; Spanish colonialism

Further reading

DeFrance, S.M. (1996) 'Iberian foodways in the Moquegua and Torata Valleys of southern Peru', *Historical Archaeology* 30(3): 20–48.

Rice, P.M. (1996) 'Peru's colonial wine industry and its European background', *Antiquity* 70: 785–800.

—— (1996) 'The archaeology of wine: The wine and brandy haciendas of Moquegua, Peru', *Journal of Field Archaeology* 23: 187–204.

Smith, G.C. (1997) 'Hispanic, Andean, and African influences in the Moquegua Valley of southern Peru', *Historical Archaeology* 31(1): 74–83.

Van Buren, M., Burgi, P. and Rice, P.M. (1993) 'Torata Alta: A late highland settlement in the Osmore drainage', in M. Aldenderfer (ed.) *Domestic Architecture, Ethnicity, and Complementarity in the South-Central Andes*, Iowa City: University of Iowa Press, pp. 136–46.

PRUDENCE M. RICE

mortuary analysis

Archaeologists have been interested in mortuary analysis for many years. Archaeological mortuary analysis usually consists of examinations of the way in which a particular people are interred, the artefacts that accompany them and the spatial arrangement of graves in a cemetery (see **cemeteries**). Archaeologists often collaborate with physical anthropologists in the study of mortuary populations. Physical anthropologists can provide detailed information about the skeleton population itself: how tall the people were, what diseases they may have suffered, how they died and the rates of a people's mortality. Archaeologists are typically more interested in the **material culture** of the burials rather than the physical remains themselves. Some of the issues of concern to archaeologists include what artefacts were buried in the graves, whether coffins and **gravestones** were used, the position of the deceased (on the back or side; flexed or supine) and the directional orientation of the graves in the cemetery.

Archaeologists have learned since the 1960s that they can obtain a great deal of social and cultural information from buried human remains. How a person appears in death may actually reflect how they were perceived in life. It would not be unusual in a hierarchical society, for example, for a king to be interred with more grave goods and with a better coffin and headstone than a pauper. Such one-to-one correlations between life and death are not absolute, however, because it is possible that even some hierarchically organised peoples may choose to bury all their dead in the same fashion.

Historical archaeologists, aided in most cases by documentary evidence of some sort, have provided several important mortuary analyses, and have investigated burial practices among **Native Americans**, African Americans and other peoples. Two examples will serve to illustrate some of the analyses that are possible in historical archaeology.

In the early 1970s, Jerome Handler led a team of anthropologists and archaeologists to **Newton Plantation** in southern Barbados. As part of this study they excavated a portion of the plantation's slave cemetery, which consisted of several low mounds. They removed the remains of 104 individuals interred between about 1660 and 1820.

Handler made an in-depth study of the historical documentation of Barbadian slavery, and was able to make several interesting comparisons between the various burials at the cemetery. One of the most interesting burials was designated Burial 72. This individual was a male about 50 years old at the time of death. He was buried without a coffin lying on his back, and his body was positioned so that his head faced east. The date of burial was probably during the late 1600s or early 1700s.

The most striking aspect of Burial 72 was the grave goods associated with it. Most of the burials at the cemetery had few if any grave accompaniments, with the usual associations being a few **glass beads**, a smoking pipe (see **pipes, smoking**) and perhaps a few nails from the coffin. Burial 72 contained much more: an iron knife, three metal finger rings, three metal bracelets, a short-stemmed, clay smoking pipe and an ornate necklace composed of seven cowrie shells, five drilled fish vertebrae, twenty-one drilled canine teeth, fourteen European-made glass beads, and a large, reddish-orange carnelian bead. This collection of grave goods was so distinctive and so unique within the Newton Plantation cemetery that Handler concluded the man in Burial 72 was probably an important person within the slave community, possibly a healer/diviner.

In another mortuary analysis, Patricia Rubertone examined a cemetery used by the Narragansetts in the seventeenth century. Living in what is today Rhode Island, the Narragansetts felt the brunt of **English colonialism** in New England beginning in 1620, when they met their first Puritans. As part of her mortuary study, Rubertone investigated the meaning of wampum, tiny cylindrical beads cut from shells.

Native Americans traditionally used wampum to cement political alliances and to pay tribute to their more powerful neighbours. As the English in the region grew in number and military strength, they too adopted the custom of requiring wampum as tribute and they began to use the tiny shells as currency. The Narragansett was one group from whom the English demanded tribute. When the Narragansetts discovered that they would be called upon to pay tribute to their new English neighbours, they realised they had several options. They could attack the English, thereby actively resisting the tribute and reasserting their local power; they could try to create political alliances with other tribute-paying natives to present a united front against the English; they could try to talk their way out of paying; or they could simply pay.

Archaeologists who have excavated Narragan-sett village sites and early colonial cemeteries have generally found little wampum in the deposits, and so it would appear that they decided to pay the tribute. If the wampum is not in the Narragansett villages or cemeteries, then it is logical to assume perhaps that it is to be found in the buried deposits of the English settlements, precisely where it would have been paid. However, the actual situation is not so simple because mortuary studies revealed a completely different strategy. When Rubertone investigated a late colonial Narragansett cemetery, she discovered over 2,000 wampum beads. Under the 'rules' of normal **acculturation**, we would expect the amount of wampum associated with Native Americans to decrease over time, as the natives increasingly adopt European customs. However, as Rubertone discovered, the amount of wampum actually increased over time. How could this be so? Among the possible explanations, Rubertone argued that the Narragansetts probably chose to deposit their wampum within the graves of their dead relatives rather than to surrender it to the English interlopers.

Both the Newton Plantation and the Narragansett mortuary studies provided important new interpretations of history. The promise of discovering something entirely new and unexpected about the past is one of the reasons that historical archaeologists are drawn to the fruitful area of mortuary analysis.

Further reading

Handler, J.S. (1997) 'An African-type healer/ diviner and his grave goods: A burial from a plantation slave cemetery in Barbados, West Indies', *International Journal of Historical Archaeology* 1: 91–130.

Handler, J.S. and Lange, F.W. (1978) *Plantation Slavery in Barbados: An Archaeological and Historical Investigation*, Cambridge, MA: Harvard University Press.

Rubertone, P.E. (1989) 'Archaeology, colonialism, and 17th-century Native America: Towards an alternative interpretation', in R. Layton (ed.) *Conflict in the Archaeology of Living Traditions*, London: Unwin Hyman, pp. 32–45.

CHARLES E. ORSER, JR

Mount Vernon, Virginia, USA

Mount Vernon, the home of George Washington, the first president of the USA, is located in northern Virginia about 24 km south of Washington, DC. The estate, originally known as Little Hunting Creek Plantation, was first granted to Washington's great grandfather in 1674. When Lawrence, Washington's older brother, inherited the plantation, he renamed it Mount Vernon in honour of his commanding officer in the British navy, Admiral Edward Vernon. Washington inherited the estate in 1761, and expanded it from 800 ha to almost 3,200 ha. By the time he was finished building the estate, it included five farms and over 300 African American slaves. Washington lived at Mount Vernon until his death in 1799.

The plantation, including the mansion and several outbuildings, is today a historic site that has been restored to its 1799 appearance. The extensive **restoration** project began soon after 1860, the year the Mount Vernon Ladies' Association took possession of the property. Archaeological research at the site was first conducted to aid the reconstruction efforts, and, from the 1930s to the 1950s, archaeologists investigated the mansion, the blacksmith shop, the stercorary (a storehouse for the dung used for fertiliser) and the bowling green. A full-time archaeological programme was instituted at the site in the 1980s, and archaeologists today make major contributions to the restoration efforts and help to build a picture of the daily lives of the men and women who lived on the plantation, including its slaves.

The estate's archaeologists turned their attention in 1999 to the plantation's distillery. Built in 1797 by the Scottish-born farm manager, the distillery was situated near the estate's grist mill, located 4.5 km from the mansion. Historical records indicate that the structure was approximately 23 by 9 m in size with sandstone walls resting on a foundation of river stones. The building was reported to contain five stills, which relied mostly on corn and rye for the distilling process. Only two years after its construction, the distillery produced over 41,000 litres of whiskey.

In 1999, the Mount Vernon archaeologists uncovered a 6 m section of the foundation, and discovered several drains. Since it is possible that the distillers lived in the building, the archaeologists hope eventually to discover artefacts that will reveal how the building's residents lived. In addition, the details of the archaeological research will be used to guide the building's reconstruction.

See also: African American archaeology; plantation archaeology

CHARLES E. ORSER, JR

museums

Archaeology is a vital part of a wide range of museums from national archaeological museums, such as the State Archaeological Museum in Poland, to local town museums, such as the Archaeological Museum in Haarlem, Holland. Archaeological collections, research and exhibits also contribute to thousands of art, history, ethnographic, children's and science museums world-wide. Historical archaeology, in particular, has been an important component of the research, **restoration** and interpretation of heritage sites, such as Empúries, Spain, military sites, such as the Little Bighorn Battlefield, Montana, USA (see **Battle of the Little Bighorn**), living-history museums, such as Sturbridge Village, Massachusetts, and historic house museums, such as Painshill in England, **Carter's Grove** in Williamsburg, Virginia, and Morven in Princeton, New Jersey. Excavations, such as those in **Annapolis** and **St Mary's City**, Maryland, have been interpreted through public education programmes that capitalise on archaeology in-progress to create, in effect, open-air museums. Some sites, such as Pella and Dion in Macedonia, have been enclosed or otherwise preserved to become permanent museums.

Museum collections are not only of value for exhibits, but provide for analysis and comparative study with excavated assemblages. Some museums support the advancement of historical archaeology by sponsoring publications, excavations, symposia and other scholarly activities. Museums can also be a catalyst for community-based archaeology, particularly if the institution already serves as a keeper of people's stories and facilitator of community history projects.

Figure 22 An archaeological 'mini-museum', 'New York Unearthed', located in New York City a few
blocks from Wall Street
Source: Photo: S. Baugher

While the history of museums long precedes the beginnings of historical archaeology, they share common roots. During the Renaissance, the major private collections of Europe were comprised of antiquities excavated, albeit not systematically, from classical sites in Italy, Greece and newly explored exotic locales world-wide. These objects became the basis of national museums founded in the late eighteenth and nineteenth centuries, such as the Louvre and the British Museum. The archaeological artefacts in these museums, while comprising only a small portion of the collection, continued to be prominent signifiers of other cultures and times, and to represent the dominance of these nation-states in the modern world. In the USA, the establishment of the Smithsonian Institution and numerous university museums in the nineteenth century helped to fuel wholesale collecting expeditions to gather objects from indigenous peoples who were perceived as 'vanishing races'. These ethnological and archaeological collections were then displayed in categories derived from prevailing cultural evolutionary models. The centennial celebration in the USA spurred the collecting of colonial artefacts and preservation of significant colonial sites, many of which became historic house museums. With the emerging professionalism of both the museum field and the discipline of archaeology, more museums were founded that included archaeology or, more commonly in Europe, whose missions were solely archaeology.

Historical archaeology has been particularly prominent in the service of municipal and regional museum interpretation because it offers insight into **local history**. Archaeology recovers artefacts that are part of the unique heritage of the people, artefacts that may even become iconic signifiers of that history. These remains may represent a place's origin, such as the town wall preserved at Duisburg's Kultur- und Stadthistorisches Museum in Germany, or be relics of significant events in local history. In some cases whole sites are recreated in museum contexts; for example, the

Gronauer Lock, excavated and disassembled piece by piece, is being installed as a centrepiece of the new Indiana State Museum, Indianapolis.

The heritage of museums is not without its challenge to historical archaeologists today. Despite anthropology's premise of cultural relativism, there is an enduring division in the representation of the human past in history and natural history museums, premised on a separation of Western and non-Western history. As more archaeologists are seeking to collaborate with communities in the design, execution and dissemination of their research, museums can be creative partners in collaborative efforts to do community-based archaeology. The excavations of African American sites in Annapolis by Paul Mullins and Mark Warner combined oral history, community participation in the dig and a jointly curated exhibit of the finds at the nearby Banneker–Douglass Museum. However, in some contexts, museums are so entwined with colonisation, and the structure of their narratives is so foreign, that they are rejected as valid forms of representing the culture. Peter Ucko, for example, has written insightfully on such problems at museums and sites in Zimbabwe. Another aspect of the challenge of museum representation of archaeological material is the conflict between public interpretation and the use of objects originally created for specific purposes. This collision is perhaps most vividly manifest in museums' treatment of human and sacred remains, but also includes fundamental assumptions about what stories are appropriate for public consumption, and museums' assumptions of their audiences' interest in linear chronology. Some museums representing indigenous cultures are using advisory groups and consultants to help determine appropriate and sensitive ways to interpret their pasts, and there is a growing move in museums such as community and tribal museums for the people to curate and present their own heritage.

As a contributor to the research, restoration and interpretation of museums, historical archaeology has been valuable in representing '**ordinary people's culture**', particularly the history of those who have been marginalised or not preserved in the documentary record. Interpretive programmes at sites such as, in the USA, the Little Bighorn, Drayton Hall and Monticello have been transformed by archaeology. For example, at Monticello, where Thomas Jefferson has long been the centrepiece of tour scripts, the **plantation archaeology** of the Mulberry Row slave housing and work areas has been a catalyst for efforts to include a more complete story of those who lived at the site.

Archaeological exhibits have served museums by allowing audiences to observe and understand how the past is known. In addition to public programmes at excavations and historic sites, archaeological methodology has been fodder for public display. When Alexandria Archaeology in Alexandria, Virginia, acquired space in the Torpedo Factory – a munitions plant that had been converted to mixed-use retail and artist space in the 1970s – director Pam Cressey located the lab area near a plate-glass window and made daily artefact processing and analysis accessible to the public. Numerous museums, particularly science and children's museums, have recreated excavations in exhibits that allow the visitors to participate in various ways: finding artefacts by scraping away compressed 'dirt' or sifting through sand; recording evidence by mapping and measuring; and doing analysis such as cross-mending sherds, reconstructing pots and deciphering hieroglyphics. In addition to educating the public about archaeological technique, such museum exhibits also promote awareness of site preservation and raise issues of illegal and unethical cultural-property trafficking.

See also: conservation, terrestrial; public archaeology; repatriation; restoration

Further reading

Gaimster, D. (ed.) (1994) *Museum Archaeology in Europe*, Oxford: Oxbow Books.

Jameson, J.H. (ed.) (1997) *Presenting Archaeology to the Public: Digging for Truths*, Walnut Creek, CA: Alta-Mira Press.

McManus, P.M. (ed.) (1995) *Archaeological Displays and the Public: Museology and Interpretation*, London: Institute of Archaeology, University College London.

Pearce, S.M. (1990) *Archaeological Curatorship*, Washington, DC: Smithsonian Institution Press.

Ucko, P. J. (1994) 'Museums and sites: Cultures of

the past within education, Zimbabwe some ten years on', in P.G. Stone and B.L. Molyneaux (eds) *The Presented Past: Heritage, Museums and Education*, London: Routledge, pp. 237–82.

ELIZABETH KRYDER-REID

N

nails

Nails, usually made of iron, constitute a class of **material culture** that historical archaeologists regularly find in abundance, particularly at sites associated with wooden buildings. Nails can be deposited around buildings during all phases of their lives, from construction to deterioration. Builders frequently lose or discard nails during construction, and after abandonment, as wood-frame buildings fall to ruin, the nails that once held them together become deposited in the soil around the building's foundation.

Historical archaeologists, and also historical architects and restorers, can use nails to help date past buildings. Like many of the artefacts historical archaeologists recover, nails can be dated in a relative way based on their appearance.

Nails have gone through five major design changes, all of which relate to the way in which they are produced. Hand-wrought, or completely hand-made, nails were the earliest nails made. They can be distinguished by their square but tapering cross-section and because their points look flattened when seen from one side but pointed when turned 90°. They have this appearance because the point has been hammered into shape. The heads of hand-wrought nails are uneven because the blacksmith had to make the head by simply pounding on the end of the nail opposite the point. Beginning in the 1790s, manufacturers began to experiment with ways to cut nails from flat, iron stock. The earliest examples still had hand-forged heads, and it was not until the early nineteenth century that manufacturers produced

completely machine-cut nails. After the machine-cut nail, the next design innovation was the 'modern' machine-cut nail, first produced in the early 1830s. The shanks of these nails are generally square in appearance and the heads, when viewed from the top, appear square or rectangular. Machine-cut nails of all types usually have square or slightly curved points. The final improvement in nail design occurred in the mid-nineteenth century when manufacturers first produced the wire nail. This nail, the one we know today, has a round shank and a round head. Each wire nail exhibits 'gripper marks' on the shank just below the head. These tiny parallel indentations indicate where the gripper die grabbed the piece of wire while the machine stamped its head. The points of wire nails are usually sharp and consist of four facets produced by a cutter die.

In the past, just as today, nails were sold according to size, with the size notation being a 'd', representing 'pence'. This convention of designating nail size has roots in the fifteenth century and possibly earlier when nails were sold, for example, for 8 pence per hundred. Carpenters and builders of all kinds use various nail sizes for different tasks, so that a larger nail, perhaps a 30d nail, might be used for framing a building, while a 5d nail might be used for finer work.

In addition to construction nails, manufacturers also produced many kinds of speciality nails. These include horseshoe nails, clinch nails (which curl when used), roofing nails, brads, finishing nails, chair nails and spikes. Some manufacturers also produced nails made of brass, steel, zinc and copper for special purposes, like shoe manufacture.

Further reading

Edwards, J.D. and Wells, T. (1993) *Historic Louisiana Nails: Aids to the Dating of Old Buildings*, Baton Rouge: Department of Geography and Anthropology Louisiana State University.

Nelson, L.H. (1968) 'Nail chronology as an aid to dating old buildings', American Association for State and Local History Technical Leaflet 48, *History News* 24(11): 1–12.

CHARLES E. ORSER, JR

Nanny Town, Jamaica

Nanny Town is a maroon site (see **maroon sites**), located deep in the Blue Mountains of eastern Jamaica, and excavated by Kofi Agorsah in the early 1990s. Nanny Town has long held an important place in the national imagination of Jamaica, as it was home to the legendary Nanny, an African woman, who, in the early eighteenth century, was the leader of a maroon group that evaded the British for years. Nanny is reputed to have been an expert in both the tactics of guerrilla warfare and obeah, the Jamaican version of voodoo; legend has it that she was so powerful that she could catch a bullet in her teeth. Despite her powers, the maroon settlement at Nanny Town was attacked and destroyed by British forces led by a Captain Stoddart in 1734; several hundred maroons were dispersed with the destruction of the town.

Because the history of Nanny Town and its maroon inhabitants is an active part of Jamaican national consciousness, a series of expeditions have been led to the site, some as little more than pilgrimages, others full-fledged archaeological investigations. In the late 1960s, Alan Teulon led a group of Jamaican avocational archaeologists through the eastern Blue Mountains to discover the location of Nanny Town; Anthony Bonner followed this up in the early 1970s with some preliminary excavations. However, serious work on Nanny Town was only initiated in the early 1990s, under the direction of Agorsah, then a professor of archaeology at the University of the West Indies at Mona, Jamaica.

Agorsah's work at Nanny Town recovered an interesting variety of artefacts. Among those recovered were Spanish gold coins from the mid-seventeenth century, wine and medicine **bottles**, tin-glazed **earthenware**, bellarmines, red-clay and white-clay smoking pipes (see **pipes, smoking**), glass and stone **beads**, and locally produced earthenware and terracotta figurines. Some lithic tools, along with the figurines, which seem to be Taino in origin, indicate that there was an indigenous occupation of the site either immediately before, or during, the time that Nanny Town was occupied by the maroons. This opens the possibility that African and Indian peoples coexisted in maroon sites, which was known to have happened historically in other contexts like Hispaniola, Cuba, and the North and South American mainlands, but was previously unknown in Jamaica. It has long been assumed that the indigenous population of Jamaica was eradicated by the Spanish prior to the British conquest in 1655; evidence from Nanny Town suggests otherwise.

While its remoteness has protected Nanny Town from destruction resulting from tourist development – all too common on sites located on or near Jamaica's coasts – Agorsah noted that part of the site had been damaged by recent military activity, probably related to manœuvres associated with the USA-backed cannabis eradication programme, in which military helicopters and other aircraft are used to destroy cannabis fields in Jamaica's remote interior. Only time will tell if Nanny Town will survive as an archaeological site for future generations of archaeologists to explore.

Further reading

Agorsah, E.K. (1994) 'Archaeology of maroon settlements in Jamaica', in E.K. Agorsah (ed.) *Maroon Heritage: Archaeological, Ethnographic, and Historical Perspectives*, Kingston: University of the West Indies Press, pp. 163–87.

Campbell, M.C. (1990) *The Maroons of Jamaica 1655–1796: A History of Resistance, Collaboration, and Betrayal*, Trenton, NJ: African World Press.

JAMES A. DELLE

Nara, Japan

The Nara or Heijo Palace is situated in Nara City in central Japan. The Heijo Palace (Nara Imperial Palace) was a complex consisting of the imperial residence and governmental offices and bureaux. It was built during the Nara Period (AD 710–84) and is surrounded by the sites of aristocrats' mansions, commoners' residences, national markets and temples in the Heijo capital. The capital measured 4.8 km from north to south, and 4.3 km from east to west. The palace was square in plan, being influenced by the Zhang An Palace of Tang dynasty China. The Heijo capital was made up of seventy-two square blocks, eight blocks in the east–west direction and nine blocks in the north–south direction, each block measuring approximately 533 m^2. There was a main avenue in the centre, with thirty-six city blocks on each side of the road. On the east side, there was an additional area, called the Gaikyo, consisting of twelve blocks. To the east of the Gaikyo, Todaiji-Temple is situated, where the Nara-Daibutsu (bronze statue of Buddha) is enshrined.

The Nara National Cultural Properties Research Institute has been excavating Heijo Palace since 1959, and these excavations continue at the present time. Recent excavations at the site of Prince Nagaya mansion nearby, where 100,000 wooden tablets with inscriptions were discovered, attracted great public interest After excavations are completed, the sites are turned into parks with conjectural reconstructions of the buildings that once stood there, or reconstructed foundation platforms with bushes planted to indicate the positions of posts. Artefacts discovered in the course of excavation are exhibited in the Heijo Palace Site Museum. In addition, some archaeological features *in situ* are open for viewing in a modern shelter built over the site. In 1999, this site was designated as a World Heritage Site.

The Nara National Cultural Properties Research Institute is the only national organisation dedicated to researching archaeological sites, architectural structures, gardens and other features on the landscape. The Institute is also responsible for the protection and utilisation of such cultural properties for education in Japanese history under the control of the Japanese Ministry of Education and Science.

Further reading

Barnes, L.G. (1999) *The Rise of Civilization in East Asia: The Archaeology of China, Korea and Japan*, London: Thames & Hudson.

KANAME MAEKAWA

National Historic Landmarks

National Historic Landmarks (NHLs) are places of exceptional value for illustrating and interpreting the heritage of the USA. The Historic Sites Act of 1935 established the NHL programme to identify and protect such places. The Secretary of the US Department of Interior designates properties as NHLs after recommendations by the National Park Service and National Park System Advisory Board, and comments by the public. Potential NHLs are identified through theme studies that compare properties associated with a specific area of history, such as labour history or early contact between **Native Americans** and Europeans. Mission Santa Ines in California, Bethabara in North Carolina, Yuchi Town Site in Alabama, Fort Corchaug in New York and St Mary's City Historic District in Maryland are a few of the NHLs designated for their significance in historical archaeology.

See also: National Register of Historic Places; public archaeology; site significance

BARBARA J. LITTLE

National Register of Historic Places

The National Register of Historic Places is an official list of the USA's cultural resources considered worthy of preservation. National Register documentation is part of a national database available for planning, management, research, education and interpretation. The Register was created through the National Historic Preservation

Act of 1966 (NHPA), which was a response to unfettered development, urban renewal and widespread destruction of historic places after the Second World War. NHPA ensures that historic properties are considered if federal funds or permits are involved in projects. Properties are nominated by states, federal agencies and Indian tribes under four criteria for their association with important: (1) events, (2) persons, (3) **architecture**, art or engineering or (4) information. Archaeological properties, which are almost exclusively nominated under criterion (4), are underrepresented as they make up only about 7 per cent of the listings.

See also: National Historic Landmarks; public archaeology; site significance

BARBARA J. LITTLE

nationalism

In the last two centuries, nationalism has been an important factor in the professionalisation of the study of the past. Nationalism is a political ideology that maintains that nations have the right to self-government. It emerged in the political scene through a series of revolutions, the best known of which is the French Revolution of 1789. Nationalism provoked a break with the *ancien régime*. It allowed the political advance of the middle classes at the expense of the nobility and the monarchy. In addition, a secular language, which at first employed classical imagery, substituted the religious rhetoric dominant until then.

Nationalism sought to express the new political ideology through the argument of the past. Political claims were justified through the allusion to past glories. The deeds of Republican **Rome** were acclaimed when the French king was beheaded, whereas Napoleon directed his attention to Imperial Rome. Ancient Greece was taken as a model of social and political life and Egypt was admired and considered the origin of the two later civilisations. Objects from these three civilisations were brought to the West and displayed in museums to serve as a reference point of excellence against which to measure the progress of 'men' and nations. The need to train curators for the

increasingly numerous museums led to the teaching of archaeology in universities. Popular interest in archaeology also fostered the creation of learned societies and archaeological associations in which archaeology was discussed.

Although, to begin with, the appropriation of the past of the Great Civilisations – Egypt, Greece and Rome – was more significant, interest in the prehistoric and the medieval past soon increased. These periods were instrumental in emphasising the uniqueness of a singular past that formed the basis of the character of a nation. However, it was only from the 1870s that the definition of what was peculiar in each nation began to be crucial. The creation of two new states, Italy and Germany, on the basis of nationalism, made it conceivable for stateless nations to claim political self-government. However, in order to be successful, their political elites had to convince others of the very existence of the nation for whose independence they were bidding. Differences were demonstrated in terms of historical development, **language**, customs, **race** and/or religion. Archaeology and history, therefore, became more instrumental than ever in the political rhetoric. They could demonstrate the reality of the nation by 'proving' when the nation had originated and what had been its historical development. Beyond Europe, however, archaeology was not taken into account in the construction of the national history, given that the white colonisers did not identify with a past protagonised by the natives. Archaeology, therefore, remained in departments and museums of anthropology, the field that studied 'the Primitive Other'.

After playing a crucial role in the peace agreements, nationalism increased its importance after the First World War. More than ever, archaeology had a role in the reinforcement of linguistic, ethnic and racial elements in the construction of a national **identity**. Sets of ancient **material culture** were associated with particular ethnic, racial or linguistic groups, such as the Slavs or the Germans. The term 'culture' became accepted to refer to such groups although it was only defined by V. Gordon Childe in 1929. During the Second World War, archaeology had a definite political role, especially in Germany and Italy. The past was used as a means to justify theories, such as racial superiority and nationalist demands, for example claims on land.

After the armed conflict, archaeologists made an attempt to concentrate on the analysis of the material remains and abandon all involvement with politics. Although this has not been completely achieved, it is clear that archaeologists are now more conscious of the political implications of their endeavours.

Further reading

Atkinson, J.A., Banks, I. and O'Sullivan, J. (eds) (1996) *Nationalism and Archaeology*, Glasgow: Cruithne Press.

Díaz-Andreu, M. and Champion, T. (1996) *Nationalism and Archaeology in Europe*, London: UCL Press.

Kohl, P.L. and Fawcett, C. (eds) (1995) *Nationalism, Politics, and the Practice of Archaeology*, Cambridge: Cambridge University Press.

Meskell, L. (ed.) (1998) *Archaeology under Fire. Nationalism, Politics and Heritage in the Eastern Mediterranean and Middle East*, London: Routledge.

MARGARITA DÍAZ-ANDREU

Native Americans

Historical archaeologists long have been interested in studying the effects of European contact on Native Americans by tracing the appearance and distribution of European objects in native cultures. Although it is an undeniable archaeological fact that items of European material culture made their way into native contexts rapidly with the spread of the European presence throughout the hemisphere, the nature, consequences and extent of cultural change is far more open for debate. The process of post-contact culture change was once viewed by archaeologists largely as one-sided **acculturation**, with elements of native culture being replaced with elements of European culture in ways measurable through changing artefact inventories. To some extent, the larger social and political forces that were propelling Native Americans towards total **assimilation** in the early decades of the twentieth century, following the

1887 Dawes Act, were mirrored by an archaeological record suggesting that traditional native culture was lost long before. However, as the larger field of anthropology has embraced the perspectives of empowerment and acknowledged adaptive responses of indigenous peoples to global imbalances of political and economic power, so too has archaeology replaced simplistic acculturation models with views stressing **resistance** as a positive force in creating ethnic **identity**. Because of its methodological emphasis on integrating archaeology, the documentary record and **oral history**, historical archaeology is a major contributor to the study of the emergence of contemporary Native American groups.

Who are the Native Americans?

The term 'Native American' has several widely used meanings. In the most general terms, Native Americans can be any indigenous people of the Americas living on the North, Central or South American continents. This usage tends to be restricted to discussions of pan-hemispheric indigenous rights and related unification issues for which the largest possible forum is sought. The more specific usage of the term Native American refers to indigenous people within the present area of the USA. The term indigenous has been legally defined by the rulings of the 1990 Native American Graves Protection and Repatriation Act (NAGPRA) to mean people whose cultural origins do not lie beyond the boundaries of the USA. Even more specifically within the USA, 'Native American' refers to those groups that have been federally recognised as sovereign nations and who consequently exist in a government-to-government relationship with the USA. As interpreted by the US Supreme Court in the 1832 case *Worcester v. Georgia*, sovereignty means that Indian nations are distinct political communities with an inherent right to self-government. Self-government extends to tribal or reservation lands and cannot be abridged by state law. However, the Supreme Court stops short of placing Indian nations beyond congressional action and explicitly views them as domestic dependent nations. In legal contexts, the terms Native American, Indian Tribe or Indian Nation are often used compatibly. There are currently more than 300 federally recognised Indian Tribes, with the largest, the Navajo Tribe, covering more than 15 million acres in Arizona, New Mexico and Utah. There are approximately 225 native communities in Alaska also recognised for governmental purposes.

The origins of Native Americans in the western hemisphere date back to at least 12,000 years ago according to well-documented archaeological evidence from Monte Verde in Chile, the Meadow-croft Rockshelter in Pennsylvania and additional sites in Florida and north-western North America. Ongoing research may push dates of original occupation back further and provide better temporal control for the initial waves of human migration into North America. The most accepted scenario for the early peopling of the Americas presents an immediate Siberian or Central Asian origin for the earliest populations, followed by movement (and perhaps exchange) across the Pacific Rim. The lack of fluted projectile points in Siberia and their wide continental distribution in North America by slightly more than 11,000 years ago argues for an early population with non-Siberian origins, say critics who look to fluted projectile point makers of upper palaeolithic cultures in extreme Northern Europe as a possible source. In recent court rulings pertaining to the disposition of the 9,300-year-old Kennewick skeleton, it is clear that human remains of great antiquity are to be considered Native American for the purposes of NAGPRA, whatever their specific biological ancestry proves to be upon scientific analysis. Early people in the Americas, regardless of variability in biological and cultural characteristics, all faced adaptations to the environments of the late Pleistocene geological epoch, when conditions were cooler and generally drier than at present, sea levels lower and surface water availability reduced. Population densities rose during the subsequent Holocene epoch, however, as the more favourable climate resulted in the development of wetland environments and more stable food resources. Although plant domestication occurred independently more than 4,500 years ago in several areas of the hemisphere, most notably Mexico, Peru and eastern North America, the role of population pressure in stimulating the development of Native American agriculture is not clear, nor were sedentism and political complexity dependent on domesticated crops, as demonstrated by examples from gulf-coastal Florida and the north-west coast where maritime cultures flourished amid plentiful marine resources.

The effects of European contact on Native Americans

When Europeans first began colonising the so-called New World in the years after 1492, Native Americans were living in or using virtually every terrestrial and aquatic habitat in the hemisphere and in many cases were exploiting near-shore environments through seafaring technology. Varying scales of political complexity existed, from chiefdoms and kingdoms to bands. The archaeological record demonstrates that political complexity throughout the Americas was unstable and dynamic rather than unilineal and evolutionary. Many large mound centres in south-eastern North America and in Central America had been abandoned centuries before European contact as people dispersed in small family groups throughout the countryside. Political alliances brought people together or broke them apart. Many populations first encountered by Columbus in the Caribbean and by the early conquistadores in south-eastern North America were organised into chiefdoms but lacked nucleated population centres. In fact, the largest mound centre in North America north of Mexico, the Cahokia mound complex near present-day St Louis, Missouri, held perhaps 30,000 people spread across 2,000 acres at its apogee around AD 1100, but was in decline within about 150 years.

Determining the pre-Columbian population of Native America is speculative and problematic at best, and exposes some fundamental methodological problems confronting anthropologists and historical archaeologists who hope to conduct population reconstructions of the contact period. At the root of the problem is the scale and timing of the demographic collapse of native populations following exposure to Europeans. Although the wars of conquest and the harshness of slavery certainly took their toll, death due to the spread of epidemic **disease** appears to be the main culprit in massive depopulation, compounded by lower fertility rates as populations experienced stress.

Influenza, introduced by Columbus's second voyage in 1493 to **La Isabella**, spread throughout Hispaniola within five years. Within twenty years of contact, influenza and smallpox pandemics moved from the Caribbean to the mainland, and measles followed by 1531. Because the transmission of epidemic disease to uninfected populations could precede actual physical contact with Europeans, the method of using historical documents alone to derive direct population estimates is questionable as the populations being documented (and thus entering the historical record) could already have suffered catastrophic population decline. Therefore, there are wide divergences in pre-contact population estimates, with Alfred Kroeber deriving a hemispheric estimate of 8.4 million compared to Henry Dobyns's estimate of 90.4 million based on a depopulation ratio of 20:1. In North America alone, Dobyns places 9.8 million inhabitants at the time of contact.

Archaeological studies of Native American ethnogenesis

The implications of the depopulation of Native America for historical archaeology are profound. If demographic collapse also resulted in a break in the cultural transmission of knowledge and the loss of aboriginal social and cultural diversity, then the notion of direct cultural continuity between the prehistoric past and the ethnohistoric present is challenged. Also called into question is the validity of **ethnographic analogy** as a connecting bridge between prehistory and history. Searching for the archaeological origins of historic period tribes as they passed through the demographic bottleneck of the contact period, and examining the re-emergence of cultural diversity, provide unique problem emphases for historical archaeologists, particularly as such studies emphasise the process of ethnogenesis. Patricia Galloway's study of Choctaw tribal origins places the development of unique Choctaw ethnic identity late in the seventeenth century as four remnant groups coalesced in the face of French and British intrusion into the deep-south region of east-central Mississippi. By the end of the eighteenth century, these related but previously distinct groups were making a new type of curvilinear-incised decorated

pottery and sharing the burial practice of prolonged above-ground exposure and processing of the corpse. Galloway clearly situates Choctaw **ethnicity** as a post-contact cultural phenomenon and states that the very concept of ethnicity cannot be disentangled from the European colonial presence.

Jeffrey Brain's archaeological study of Tunica ethnicity finds that Tunica ethnic identity emerged as an accommodation strategy to intense contact with the French in the eighteenth century, which saw the Tunicas survive through their entrepreneurial skills as middlemen in the colonial trade economy. Settling at various strategic points along trade and communication networks throughout the Yazoo Basin of the Lower Mississippi Valley and ultimately in Mississippi and Louisiana, the Tunica showed, in Brain's terms, a 'corporate adaptability' in keeping just beyond direct French control while remaining key players in the colonial economy. As an indication of Tunica affluence by the mid-eighteenth century, burials contain abundant European items, including **firearms**, European **ceramics** and brass trade kettles.

Although the Choctaw and Tunica cases suggest that Native American ethnicity in the historic period emerged through accommodation and aggregation, the processes of resistance and revitalisation also stimulated the development of cultural identity throughout the post-contact era. Rebellions against colonial authorities, such as the Timucua revolt in the Spanish missions (see **mission sites**) of Florida in 1656 and the Pueblo Revolt of 1680, arose for complex reasons including slights and humiliations to the native power structure, but had the effect of consolidating certain factions around traditional beliefs and practices. Schisms in native society opened up, however, to the extent that traditionalists and progressives became pitted against one another. The tragic culmination of one such schism erupted in the Creek War of 1814 among Creek Indian factions in Alabama. Archaeological investigations of the village of traditionals, known as the Red Sticks, reveals that they favoured the use of native pottery over the commonly available and prestigious European and US ceramics. A similar phenomenon may have occurred some twenty-one years later in Florida during the early years of the Second Seminole War.

Resistance took a less direct form in colonial New England, where Patricia Rubertone's **mortuary analysis** of burials in a seventeenth-century Narragansett cemetery revealed an increase in shell **beads** known as wampum over the amount of wampum interred with earlier burials, coinciding with the escalating interest of the British in exacting tribute from the Narragansett. Rather than pay in wampum, according to Rubertone, the shell beads were simply taken out of circulation as an act of defiance.

The role of historical archaeology in Native American studies

Because the archaeology of Native American cultural development in the 500-plus years following European contact is by definition historical archaeology, historical archaeologists have the opportunity to study the processes of culture change and the emergence of global cultural systems from a humanistic perspective. Archaeological approaches to the formation of tribal identity and ethnogenesis, inasmuch as they are informed by historical sources, tribal traditions and oral histories, can move beyond the level of cultural abstraction to an understanding of how individuals through intentional action can alter or manipulate their material environment. The historical archaeology of Native Americans is not the faceless archaeology of archaeological cultures, but is instead an anthropological history of indigenous people transformed by the modern world.

The relationship of contemporary Native Americans to archaeology ranges from hostile to benign to supportive. Federally recognised tribes can formally participate in the federal cultural-resource management process on tribal lands through their Tribal Historic Preservation Officer. Many tribes routinely undertake archaeological surveys on tribal lands and seek federal-grant funds for cultural-resource projects. Some, like the Mashantucket Pequots of Connecticut and the Makah Indians of Neah Bay in Washington State, have used archaeological results to interpret tribal history and heritage in state-of-the-art tribal museums and cultural centres.

See also: contact archaeology; repatriation

Further reading

Brain, J.P. (1988) *Tunica Archaeology*, Papers of the Peabody Museum of Archaeology and Ethnology, Harvard University, vol. 78, Cambridge, MA: Harvard University Press.

Dobyns, H. (1983) *Their Numbers Became Thinned*, Knoxville: University of Tennessee Press.

Galloway, P. (1995) *Choctaw Genesis, 1500–1700*, Lincoln: University of Nebraska Press.

Rubertone, P.E. (1989) 'Archaeology, colonialism, and seventeenth-century Native America: Towards an alternative interpretation', in R. Layton (ed.), *Conflict in the Archaeology of Living Traditions*, London: Unwin Hyman, pp. 32–45.

Swidler, N., Dongoske, K.E., Anyon, R. and Downer, A.S. (eds) (1997) *Native Americans and Archaeologists: Stepping Stones to Common Ground*, Walnut Creek, CA: AltaMira Press.

Thomas, D.H. (ed.) (1991) *Columbian Consequences II: Archaeological and Historical Perspectives on the Spanish Borderlands East*, Washington, DC: Smithsonian Institution Press.

Washburn, W.E. (ed.) (1988) *Handbook of North American Indians: Volume 4, History of Indian–White Relations*, Washington, DC: Smithsonian Institution Press.

BRENT R. WEISMAN

New Archaeology

The New Archaeology, perhaps more accurately termed **processual archaeology**, was an intellectual movement whose roots were first suggested in US archaeology in 1948 by Walter Taylor and in 1959 by Joseph Caldwell. The true beginnings of the New Archaeology started in the early 1960s, largely with the work of Lewis Binford. The development of the New Archaeology was structurally akin to changes made in other disciplines (e.g. the New History, the New Geography) as scholars of the various disciplines began to examine their forms of argumentation, their explanations and the limits of their data.

The New Archaeology was intimately connected to US historical archaeology in two important ways. First, Binford had obtained personal experience with historical archaeology in 1959 at **Fort Michilimackinac** and he continued to write essays about the field for years afterward. Second, the maturation of historical archaeology during the mid-1970s was directly tied to the principles of the New Archaeology.

See also: history of historical archaeology

CHARLES E. ORSER, JR

New England, USA

The six New England states – Connecticut, Maine, Massachusetts, New Hampshire, Rhode Island and Vermont – have been important to the formation of historical archaeology as a discipline. Research in this region was spurred on by the colonial revival movements of the late nineteenth and early twentieth centuries and the nation's Bicentennial in 1976. Settled early by Europeans and, in large part, densely populated ever since, the New English archaeological record is complex and frustratingly under-explored. In many cases, modern cities and towns overlie much earlier sites. Historical archaeology in New England is undertaken by universities, museums, **cultural-resource management** (CRM) firms, local historical and archaeological societies, state historical preservation agencies, the US National Park Service and the Society for the Preservation of New England Antiquities (SPNEA). Because of the diverse range of groups that conduct historical archaeological research (spanning at least forty years of the modern discipline), there has been no consistent theoretical approach to unify this work. Recently, there has been an emphasis on broader topics such as the examination of **gender**, **race**, **power**, economics and labour relations.

One of the earliest motivations for studying historical sites in New England was to ascertain the first date for European settlement and contact with the Native American population (see **Native Americans**). Despite much research, at present there is no sound scientific evidence to support the notion of a pre-Columbian landing. The docu-

mentary evidence for European exploration of the coast and inland waterways in the sixteenth century has been well studied, and English, French and Dutch colonial settlements were established by the early seventeenth century.

Connecticut

Connecticut was settled in the 1630s by English colonists from Massachusetts Bay Colony after a brief occupation by the Dutch. Connecticut's first settlements were largely rural and agricultural, and in close proximity to the Housatonic, Connecticut and Thames rivers, and along Long Island Sound, where mercantile and shipbuilding communities eventually developed to accommodate trade between Boston and New York and the Caribbean. As a result of this early and even distribution of the population, many of the earliest sites have been either destroyed or overbuilt. In both rural and urban situations, however, particularly since the middle of the eighteenth century, a consistent investment in industrial activities – mills, factories and crafts on every scale – has made **industrial archaeology** very prominent, as seen in the studies of communities like Daniels Village and Phoenixville.

Many of the historical excavations in Connecticut have focused on well-known historical sites, including forts (e.g. Fort Griswold) and individual homes (the Nathan Hale Homestead and the Oliver Ellsworth house). Some notable exceptions include research on Fort Shantok (a Mohegan fortified village with seventeenth- and eighteenth-century occupations) and the Lighthouse site (an eighteenth-century multiracial and multiethnic community). Much of the historical archaeological work in Connecticut is undertaken as CRM, and less frequently by university research, the National Park Service or museums like Old Sturbridge Village, the Mystic Seaport and the Mashantucket Pequot Tribal Nation's Museum and Research Center.

Maine

An abundance of early seventeenth-century French and English sites appears in Maine, established to gain a foothold in North America, particularly along the coast, its islands and on tidal rivers, including the Kennebec and Penobscot. Although historical archaeological research has been undertaken on sites of every period, there is a preponderance of work done on sites dating to before King Philip's War (1675). Government priorities often place emphasis on earlier sites because they are the least well understood and most immediately threatened. Generally speaking, preservation of these sites has been enhanced by a relatively low population density, but they are threatened by recreational development and coastal erosion. The University of Maine, the Maine Bureau of Parks and the Maine Historic Preservation Commission has sponsored and directed most of the research in the state, with a number of non-profit organisations additionally making important contributions.

Early settlement in Maine was rooted in fishing, trade, mission work and in creating a military presence in the northern part of the USA. The French first established a foothold in Maine with the St Croix Colony in 1604. A more permanent installation was created with the stone fort constructed at Pentagoet, dating from 1635–74.

The English followed in 1607, a few months after **Jamestown** was founded, with the establishment of the Popham Colony. Fishing and trade continued to be important components of the English presence, as reflected in sites such as Damariscove Island (as early as 1622), Pemaquid (occupied from 1625 through the eighteenth century), Richmond's Island (1631–45), the Cushnoc Trading Post and the Clark and Lake Company site (1654).

Shipwreck sites (see **shipwrecks**) are also explored and protected by Maine's legislation. One important underwater site is *The Defence* (1779), a US privateer sunk during the Penobscot Expedition.

Massachusetts

Massachusetts had an early interest in the exploration and regulation of historical sites. Although only a small percentage of the undertaken work has been widely published, some CRM firms, university programmes (such as those at Boston University and the University of Massachusetts)

and museums (including Plimouth Plantation, Old Sturbridge Village and Historic Deerfield), and the National Park Service have addressed issues of gender, race and power relations, often extending site and community research to the national and international levels.

Excavations at seventeenth-century English sites in **Plymouth** Colony (including the John Howland, R.M. and Edward Winslow home sites) were also some of the earliest projects in the state. Work in early colonial coastal ports such as Boston (with sites such as the African Meeting House, the Blackstone Block and the sites exposed by the Central Artery/Tunnel construction), Charlestown (the Market Square area), Newbury (at the Spencer–Peirce–Little house) and Salem (including the Narbonne house, the Turner House and Derby Wharf) has provided insights into domestic and public places as well as civic infrastructure. Research in the Connecticut River valley has yielded information on inland colonial sites (including the Thomas Williams house). Excavations at the Emerson Bixby house lot and smithy has revealed some of the complexities of economic and social life in the pre-industrial neighbourhood of Barre Four Corners at the beginning of the Federal period. Research at housing for workers and managers at Lowell textile mills told the story of labour relations negotiated in the US Industrial Revolution. Work on Wellfleet (at the Great Island Tavern), Nantucket and Martha's Vineyard has also illuminated the complex social history arising from whaling and other maritime industries.

New Hampshire

Compared to the rest of New England, historical archaeology took longer to become established as a discipline in New Hampshire. While there were examples of systematic work completed by the late 1960s, it was not until the late 1970s that there was consistently scientific work being undertaken at a wide range of sites, including urban settlements (Strawbery Banke in Portsmouth), very early European fishing settlements (the Isles of Shoals), potteries (including the first professionally excavated example in New England), factories (including the 1780s New England Glassworks) and a religious community (Canterbury Shaker Village).

Because of the high rate of survival of sites, there is much more that can be done. Most sites are not widely published, though work from CRM is on file at the New Hampshire Division of Historical Resources in Concord.

Many of the early excavations were to explore downtown Portsmouth and are part of Strawbery Banke Museum. When the museum opened in 1964, historical archaeology was employed to help with the reconstruction. The wharves at Puddle Dock, the Sherburne house (belonging to an early eighteenth-century merchant) and the Marshall-Toogood pottery (early eighteenth century) are a few of the sites excavated there since.

The Industrial Revolution left a lasting imprint on New Hampshire, particularly because of the river valleys (including the Merrimack, Piscataqua and Androscoggin) that were ideal for powering mills; New Hampshire mills produced textiles, shoes and leather goods, paper, machinery and furniture. The resources in these valleys also provided the raw material for potteries, breweries and quarries.

Rhode Island

Much of the work in Rhode Island has been initiated by researchers at Brown University's Department of Anthropology and its Public Archaeology Laboratory (now a separate entity). Other excavations have been carried out by the National Park Service, state agencies and local historical societies. Many of the sites are individual homesteads; of particular importance is the Mott family house and farm in Portsmouth, where the Quaker family lived continuously from 1639–1895. The Rhode Island Marine Archaeology Project explores the state's shipwrecks, including that of HMS *Cerberus*, a British frigate that was sunk in 1778.

The site at Cocumscussoc, a trading post established by Roger Williams in 1637 in North Kingston, has provided information about the complex relationships between English, Dutch and Native Americans on Naragansett Bay. Similarly, Fort Ninigret, a seventeenth-century fortified site in Charlestown, has revealed information about Native American trade and wampum manufacturing in the historic period.

Sites such as the Roger Williams National Memorial in Providence and the sites at Queen Anne's Square in Newport have contributed to the understanding of urban sites in the eighteenth and nineteenth centuries. There has also been research on sites associated with slavery and freed slaves, and with town farms or asylums.

Vermont

Much of the historical archaeological research in Vermont has focused on sites associated with the American Revolution, some projects initiated at the time of the Bicentennial. One exception, Fort Dummer (1724–60), located near Brattleborough on the Connecticut River, is considered the first English settlement in Vermont and was constructed as an outpost and later utilised as a trading post. Save for work on several blast furnaces, charcoal kilns and lime kilns, there has been very little study of industrial sites in Vermont. Most historical archaeology is undertaken as CRM, with some federal and state-sponsored research, and some excavations, like the 1795 Asa Knight store in Dummerston, by universities and museums.

The bulk of the published academically organised work has been on sites on the banks of, or beneath, the waters of Lake Champlain, a strategic byway since Native American guides first brought Samuel de Champlain there in 1609. The lake was in English hands by 1759, and, in 1776, the Revolution led to the creation of such sites as Mount Independence (in Orwell), the largest military fortification in the north, and the Peter Ferris homestead (1765), which was burned and rebuilt several times during the Revolution.

The Lake Champlain Maritime Museum has excavated and published research on sites such as the wreck of the steamboat *Phoenix* (1814), Benedict Arnold's flagship (1776), the Revolutionary War bridge that spanned from Fort Ticonderoga to Mount Independence, as well as several wrecks from the War of 1812 Battle of Plattsburg Bay. Vermont established the Underwater Historic Preserve System in 1985 to protect these sites at the same time as it makes accommodations for sport divers.

See also: architecture; Boott Mills; capitalism; class, social; contact archaeology; gravestones; living museums; redware; urban archaeology

Further reading

Beaudry, M.C. (1986) 'The archaeology of historical land use in Massachusetts', *Historical Archaeology* 20(2): 38–46.

Bradley, R.L. and Camp, H.B. (1994) *The Forts of Pemaquid, Maine: An Archaeological and Historical Study*, Augusta: The Maine Historic Preservation Commission, the Maine Archaeological Society and the Maine Bureau of Parks and Recreation.

Brown, M.R. (1980) 'A survey of historical archaeology in New England', in P. Benes (ed.) *New England Historical Archeology*, Boston: Boston University, pp. 4–15.

Poirier, D.A. (1999) 'Archaeology of the recent past: An overview of Connecticut historical and industrial archaeology', in K.N. Keegan and W.F. Keegan (eds) *The Archaeology of Connecticut: The Human Era – 11,000 Years Ago to the Present*, Stoors: Bibliopola Press, pp. 52–64.

Starbuck, D.R. (1994) 'Historical archeology in New Hampshire', *The New Hampshire Archeologist* 33/34(1): 81–96.

—— (1994) 'Introduction', *The Journal of Vermont Archaeology* 1: vii–x.

—— (comp.) (1986) 'A bibliography of northeast historical archaeology', *Northeast Historical Archaeology* 15:19–99.

LORINDA B.R. GOODWIN

new technologies

The new technologies of the Industrial Revolution included not only new machinery, but also mechanisms to implement industrial discipline and control workers' behaviours. Prior to the industrial era, people's daily routines were guided by the rhythms of nature. Work began when the sun rose and ended when the sun set. This task orientation meant that the labourer focused his or her energies upon what was necessary. Little demarcation existed between work life and social life, and the work day expanded or contracted according to the nature of the task. The craftsman awoke at sunrise and laboured as long as natural light permitted. The sense of output measured against time was unknown. Craft technologies dominated the manufacturing process with hand tools, simple machines, individual skills, small shops and home productions.

A change in labour practices occurred along with the development of several technological changes. These include (1) the development of iron making, (2) the rise of the steam engine, (3) the mechanisation of textile production and (4) precision machine work. By the end of the eighteenth century, capitalists knew that in order to make industry succeed they had to develop new work practices. Industrialists imposed upon workers a new technology that included high-powered machines, wage labour, factory discipline and surveillance technologies.

Much of the work associated with the new industrial machinery required the deskilling of workers through the process of the division of labour. A division of labour helped to reinforce repetitive, standardised behaviour. Each low-skilled or semi-skilled labourer repeatedly manufactured the same product and each worker could also be easily replaced by other labourers if they did not perform adequately. Production became measured against the time a person laboured rather than the skill of his or her product, or the amount they produced.

One early nineteenth-century account in a southern industry described an 18-year-old boy tending machinery 'who never did a stroke of work in his life previous to [this job]', and later added that 'most of the machines are attended by boys with a few men to supervise and keep the tools in good order'. This new system benefited the manufacturer and came at the expense of the labourer and the craftsman.

Much of the success of north-eastern manufacturing in the first half of the nineteenth century may be attributed to a new technology that included work discipline and the establishment of a corporate paternalism that enforced hierarchy. Because there were few kinship ties among women who came from surrounding farms to work in the cotton factories, it was easy to impose a corporate paternalism upon the labour force. Not only did rules and regulations govern the factory process, but a less explicit discipline existed to standardise and control workers after they left the factory. This new strategy served as a mechanism to ensure profit as well as to extend the corporate influence into domestic, religious and educational aspects of workers' lives.

Industrial capitalists planned many communities in order to standardise the behaviour of workers in the home as well as in the factory. The domestic built environment served as a new technology that served as an essential component of a training ground, which could be used in the manufacturing process. The archaeology at Lowell, Massachusetts, USA, shows us that many boarding houses were constructed with standardised architectural floor plans and façades. All workers received the same size rooms, and had the same types of furnishings. They all ate from the same types of plates and sat on the same types of chairs. The continued reinforcement of discipline trained people in a new work ethic, as a standardised behaviour created a more efficient workplace. It also reinforced the idea that they were interchangeable, and part of a larger working machine.

Managers and/or industrialists often located their houses close to the workers' housing, or within view of the factory or mill. For instance, in **Harpers Ferry**, West Virginia, the superintendent built his quarters on a hill, one of the highest points in Harpers Ferry. He had a commanding view of the factories. Movements on the armoury grounds could be observed from this point, and individuals could be easily located. The presence of these buildings may have given the public the perception of constant surveillance.

Other surveillance technologies developed that regulated the behaviour of workers. Walls, fences and gated entrances allowed for managers and owners to monitor easily the ingress and egress of workers. Guards were often stationed at the gate controlling and monitoring the movement of employees in and out of the armoury. Wider streets and the implementation of a grid town plan facilitated the movement of goods, and allowed for the easier monitoring of the flow of traffic.

The installation of a clock at the factory also allowed for the monitoring of workers' behaviour. Managers expected workers to be in a set place at an exact time. They were expected to labour until they received the signal from the clock. Some industrialists, like Josiah Wedgwood, set the clock a few minutes faster before the work day began, and slowed down the clock a few minutes at the end of the day. Cheating workers out of ten or twenty minutes of work meant higher output for the capitalist.

New, high-precision machineries were introduced into Western culture at an ever increasing rate in the late eighteenth century. Associated with this phenomenon was a set of new technologies, such as deskilling, corporate paternalism and surveillance techniques, which helped to reinforce the development of the industrial era.

Further reading

Gordon, R.B. and Malone, P.M. (1994) *The Texture of Industry: An Archaeological View of the Industrialization of North America*, New York: Oxford University Press.

Hindle, B. and Lubar, S. (1988) *Engines of Change: The American Industrial Revolution, 1790–1860*, Washington, DC: Smithsonian Institution Press.

Mrozowski, S.A., Ziesing, G.H. and Beaudry, M.C. (1996) *Living on the Boott: Historical Archaeology at the Boott Mills Boardinghouses, Lowell, Massachusetts*, Amherst: University of Massachusetts Press.

Shackel, P.A. (1996) *Culture Change and the New Technology: An Archaeology of the Early American Industrial Era*, New York: Plenum Press.

Smith, M.R. (1977) *Harpers Ferry Armory and the New Technology: The Challenge of Change*, Ithaca, NY: Cornell University Press.

PAUL A. SHACKEL

New York City

Whenever archaeologists dig within New York City, they are on the lookout for archaeological sites 'of' the city as well as sites 'in' the city. Archaeology 'of' the city examines the **urbanisation** process of the Europeans, Africans and Asians who settled within the city's boundaries after 1600. However, located 'in' the boundaries of the present-day city's 'geographic place' are Native American sites (see **Native Americans**) that represent thousands of years of history. All but the most recent of these sites are independent of the last four centuries of historical experience and are primarily parts of a separate Native American history of the geographic place now known as New York City. Archaeologists have also excavated sites from the Dutch and English colonial periods and traced the subsequent expansion of the city in the nineteenth and twentieth centuries. New York City **urban archaeology** has focused on the colonial and post-colonial urban development and transformation of a small seventeenth-century frontier fort, Nieuw Amsterdam, into the late nineteenth-/early twentieth-century bustling Port of New York that became the USA's major city. Archaeologists have excavated sites in all of the city's boroughs: Manhattan, Brooklyn, the Bronx, Queens and Staten Island.

In the late nineteenth and early twentieth centuries, most archaeology focused on Native American sites found 'in' the city. Pioneering archaeologists Alanson Skinner, William Calver and Reginald Bolton uncovered numerous Indian sites including camp sites, villages and burial

Figure 23 Excavation of 175 Water Street, New York City
Source: Photo: C. Forster

grounds. Their work inspired later generations of archaeologists to continue to unearth the rich Indian history of New York, including an image of a turtle chipped onto a granite boulder in the Bronx. For historical archaeologists, New York's Native American settlements are a relatively untapped resource, offering interesting comparisons and contrasts to pre-industrial colonial sites.

Early excavations of colonial sites often evolved from the study of Indian sites. In 1890, William Calver was searching for an Indian site when he discovered a 1770s British military encampment in northern Manhattan, in an area known as 'Washington Heights'. In 1925, the 150th anniversary of the Revolutionary War increased public interest in military sites, especially because New York was a major British stronghold during the war. Throughout the twentieth century, historical societies and museums have sponsored excavations at historic sites throughout the city.

In the late 1970s, there was a dramatic increase in archaeological work because of the advent of city, state and federal laws requiring archaeological assessments on publicly funded projects or on development projects receiving discretionary permits. These excavations were undertaken by **cultural-resource management** (CRM) firms. In both the scale and number of projects, New York became the most active city for urban archaeology in the USA, and the city remains the nation's number one centre for urban archaeology. The sites range from farm houses to town houses, from residential to governmental, from sacred to secular.

In 1979, in the city's first major CRM project, archaeologists excavated thousands of seventeenth-century artefacts at the Stadt House site in lower Manhattan. In addition to artefacts and numerous features, they uncovered the partial foundation wall of a tavern (dating to 1670–1706) owned by British Governor Francis Lovelace; an early eighteenth-century well; and the remnants of seventeenth-century Stone Street. These three features were incorporated into the modern plaza of the 85 Broad Street building as the first permanent outdoor archaeological exhibit in New York City.

In 1982, the discovery and excavation of a sunken eighteenth-century merchant ship near Wall Street heightened the public's interest in archaeology, when more than 10,000 people visited the site. Other highly publicised archaeological excavations in the financial and City Hall areas of lower Manhattan uncovered several seventeenth-century Dutch homes; a Dutch warehouse with tems intended for the Native American trade; seventeenth- and eighteenth-century British homes, shops, warehouses and burial grounds; and nineteenth-century homes, including immigrant enclaves such as an infamous slum known as **Five Points**. These excavations took place prior to the construction of modern office towers.

New York City archaeologists have addressed the same range of research questions found within the larger field of historical archaeology, including class (see **class, social**) and status, **ethnicity**, **race** and **gender**. For example, Robert Schuyler's 1970s research on the nineteenth-century free-black settlement of Sandy Ground on Staten Island was the first New York City archaeological study of an African American community. Subsequent studies on other African American sites include the nineteenth-century community of Weeksville in Brooklyn; the eighteenth-century **African Burial Ground** in Manhattan; and 'Seneca Village', a pre-US Civil War integrated community composed of free-black property owners and European immigrants (mainly Irish), destroyed when Central Park was built.

New York City archaeologists have often used the data in CRM reports as starting points and have undertaken additional research on these diverse collections. For example, Diana Wall, in *The Archaeology of Gender*, examines the changing role of nineteenth-century men and women in the homeplace and workplace and provides excellent comparative studies using New York City data. Nan Rothschild, in *New York City Neighborhoods*, analysed neighbourhood formation and change in lower Manhattan using data from several large CRM projects. Over the years, there has been constant and active dissemination of the findings from these excavations through public lectures, museum exhibits, popular magazines and scholarly publications. Every year since 1980, the Professional Archaeologists of New York City (PANYC) have held a public programme to present the latest discoveries and interpretations from city projects. A mini-museum in lower Manhattan, 'New York

Unearthed', is affiliated with the South Street Seaport Museum and provides both a detailed overview of archaeology within the city and specific artefacts from some of the major excavations.

Further reading

Baugher, S. and Wall, D. (1997) 'Ancient and modern united: Archaeological exhibits in urban plazas', in J.H. Jameson, Jr (ed.) *Presenting Archaeology to the Public: Digging for Truths*, Walnut Creek, CA: AltaMira Press, pp. 114–29.

Calver, W. and Bolton, R.P. (1950) *History Written with the Pick and Shovel*, New York: New York Historical Society.

Rothschild, N. (1990) *New York City Neighborhoods*, New York: Academic Press.

Wall, D. (1994) *The Archaeology of Gender: Separating the Spheres in Urban America*, New York: Plenum Press.

SHERENE BAUGHER

New Zealand

The beginnings of historical archaeology in New Zealand can be traced back to six works, published in the 1920s and 1930s, on the redoubts, blockhouses and stockades thrown up by both Maori and European forces during the numerous engagements associated with the New Zealand Wars (1842–72). In method and emphasis they were largely descriptive and historical but at least some of them quite explicitly documented and explained processes of change, notably how Maori fortifications were modified with the introduction of muskets, and to withstand artillery bombardment. However, another forty years were to elapse before the first excavations were conducted on some of these sites and other early European–Maori contact sites in the Bay of Islands.

After such promising beginnings, two reasons can be suggested to account for the hiatus in historical archaeology. In part it results from the overwhelming academic interest in pre-European Maori archaeology in New Zealand, and, perhaps more significantly, it reflects a reliance upon individual research interests, which is reflected in pulses of activity and has come to characterise much subsequent historical archaeology in the country.

Interest in the early historic era resurfaced in the 1960s when prehistorians began to address the impact of colonisation on traditional Maori culture. During this period of 'unconscious historical archaeology', the pattern was dominated by two university-led projects involving excavations on sites associated with Frenchman Marion du Fresne's 1772 visit to the Bay of Islands, and early post-contact sites around the Fiordland Sounds. Simultaneously, in the mid-1960s, the New Zealand Historic Places Trust initiated a major archaeological mitigation project in the Central North Island after much public concern was expressed over the likely impact of the Tongariro Hydro Power Development project on sites in the area. The programme is notable in that it was set up prior to the advent of the first archaeological site protection legislation in 1975.

By the early 1970s, historical archaeology in New Zealand was becoming recognised as a field in its own right. 'Historical archaeology' was used in 1971 for the first time in the title of a publication. However, the late 1970s was to be the real coming of age. Two projects stand out as landmarks. In 1977, Nigel Prickett, in the course of doctoral research, commenced a programme of survey and excavation on British and colonial fortifications associated with the Taranaki Wars in the 1860s. His work is regarded as the first substantial work in historical archaeology in New Zealand.

The same year, a major archaeological mitigation project on the archaeology and history of the goldmining in central Otago was initiated by the Historic Places Trust in response to a major hydro-electric project centred on the Clutha River. Directed by Neville Ritchie, it involved about thirty excavations (twenty-three of them on Chinese sites). An important objective of the ten-year Clutha project, by far the longest archaeological project in New Zealand, was to produce detailed studies of historic material culture that others could build upon. To this end, specific studies were undertaken on European **ceramics**, clay pipes (see **pipes, smoking**), tin wax vesta boxes, **glass** and metal containers, faunal remains and distinctive overseas Chinese artefacts including 'cash'

(Chinese coins), opium paraphernalia, gambling and writing equipment. A pioneering archaeological study of alluvial tailing sites was also undertaken.

The first half of the 1980s was the single most productive period. The emphasis was on getting down to detail, and the work was increasingly funded by government agencies for management, interpretation or mitigation objectives as opposed to university research investigations. Site surveys dominate the early 1980s literature, particularly surveys of mining areas. Over a hundred goldfield surveys have been completed thus far. Similarly major surveys of historic sawmill and logging sites were undertaken, as well as archaeological documentation of the driving dams associated with the unique kauri logging industry in northern New Zealand. This led to major remedial conservation work recently on three of them. For many years, kauri timber was a major export from New Zealand, including huge shipments that were sent to rebuild San Francisco after the 1905 earthquake and fire. The 1980s also saw a boom in urban excavations, particularly in Auckland where approximately one quarter of New Zealand's population lives.

As in the USA, sites associated with New Zealand's 'civil war' (the so-called 'New Zealand Wars') remain a continuing focus for archaeological work. In addition to Prickett's study of the Taranaki War, excavations have been undertaken on several sites associated with the Waikato War, and the later Armed Constabulary sites in the central North Island. More recently, excavations and recording have been extended to coastal defence sites.

Several urban and rural hotel sites have been excavated in various parts of the country as well as excavations on early homesteads, and the Treaty House at Waitangi where the founding document was signed by Maori and European representatives in 1840. Projects on sites associated with recreation include excavations on late nineteenth-century alpine tourist sites in Mount Cook National Park and at Te Wairoa, a mission station and later Anglo-Maori tourist village buried by the eruption of Mt Tarawera in 1886.

In recent times, historical archaeologists have turned their attention to the ephemeral foundations of settlement in New Zealand associated with sealing and whaling, and the 1810 'seal rush from Sydney'. Although sealers are often seen as 'people without history', they were major explorers of the southern ocean, among them being many from the USA, which at the time in the 1790s had the biggest and most dispersed sealing fleet in the world.

Compared with the situation in Australia, underwater archaeology in New Zealand is very much in the formative stage, but there has been one ground-breaking project in recent years that has attracted considerable media attention. This involved the discovery of the ship *Inconstant* in 1996. Wrecked in Wellington harbour in 1849, it was used initially as a floating warehouse, until an earthquake in 1865 left it marooned on dry land. The hull was eventually buried under further reclamation. It has been excavated and is on display in a purpose-built conservation and interpretation space under the high-rise building where it was uncovered.

There have been several projects with an archaeological/engineering orientation in New Zealand including recording and assessment of the rapidly diminishing number of New Zealand railway stations, historic engineering documentation of some of the best of the surviving kauri dams and related sites such as logging trestles, log chutes, rolling roads and tramways, the now defunct coal carbonisation and briquetting industry, and copper mining on Kawau Island, which predates goldmining in New Zealand. Projects on industrial sites include excavations on the Brunner industrial site near Greymouth, the Pollen Pottery and Brickworks in Auckland, the pioneer tanning industry at Pompellier House in the Bay of Islands and several surveys of historic coalfields.

In addition to the work on the mainland, New Zealand archaeologists have been involved in major fieldwork on historic sites on some of the New Zealand-administered sub-Antarctic islands, and in **Antarctica**. While the work in the sub-Antarctic islands has been limited to the failed settlement sites in the Auckland Islands, small test excavations at Cape Evans in 1977, in the New Zealand-administered Ross Dependency, were a forerunner to major and ongoing archaeological,

restoration and conservation projects on the Scott and Shackleton era sites there.

Historical archaeology down under is an admixture of historical archaeology as it has developed in the USA and the more technological industrial-engineering orientation of British industrial archaeology, but at the same time it has developed and maintained a distinctive local character. In New Zealand this stemmed initially from the interest in documenting and explaining changes in the indigenous Maori culture during the historic period and the clash of cultures as evidenced by the New Zealand War sites. It also reflects the strong grounding in anthropological archaeology of most of the New Zealand practitioners. Unlike the situation in the USA and Australia, where historical and prehistoric archaeology have diverged, most New Zealand archaeologists still work in both areas. The attention of Australasian historical archaeologists has been focused increasingly on the sites and material culture of European settlers, and thus they are dealing with local expressions of international processes of colonisation, adaptation and change.

The development of the discipline in New Zealand was reviewed by Smith in 1990. In an associated bibliography he listed 246 publications that he considered were on aspects of historical archaeology in New Zealand. There are about 8,000 recorded European-era sites in New Zealand (out of a total of 54,000) so they comprise about 15 per cent of the total.

During the past decade, there has been a decline in historical archaeological research in New Zealand, reflecting changing academic priorities and funding cuts, a greater emphasis by government departments on remedial conservation rather than survey and excavation, and no individuals embarking on major doctoral projects in historical archaeology. However, the decline has been counteracted to some extent by an increase in co-operative projects with Australian colleagues, most notably in the areas of sealing, whaling and the archaeology of the overseas Chinese. Historical archaeologists in New Zealand and Australia are linked through the **Australasian Society for Historical Archaeology** (ASHA) and its journal *Australasian Historical Archaeology*. This connection has seen an almost exponential increase in the exchange of information and networking between Australasian colleagues, and increasingly with the wider world as more and more Australasian archaeologists go on-line.

Further reading

Ritchie, N.A. (1991) 'An introduction to historical archaeology in New Zealand', *Australian Journal of Historical Archaeology* 9: 3–5.

—— (1986) 'Archaeology and history of the Chinese in southern New Zealand during the nineteenth century', doctoral dissertation, University of Otago, Dunedin.

Smith, I. (1991) 'The development of historical archaeology in New Zealand 1921–1990', *Australian Journal of Historical Archaeology* 9: 6–13.

—— (1990) 'Historical archaeology in New Zealand: A review and bibliography', *New Zealand Journal of Archaeology* 12: 85–119.

NEVILLE A. RITCHIE

Newfoundland and Labrador

The Canadian province of Newfoundland and Labrador was the first American region exploited by Europeans, a significant fact for historical archaeology. Helge and Anna Stine Ingstad identified the only authenticated medieval Norse site in the Americas at **L'Anse aux Meadows**, in northern Newfoundland, and excavated the turf-walled structures there. Further excavation and analysis by Brigetta Wallace for Parks Canada suggest this was Leif's 'booths' of *c.* 1000, the exploratory gateway to Vinland of the Icelandic sagas. It is now a UNESCO World Heritage Site. Across the Strait of Belle Isle at Red Bay, Labrador, where migratory Brigetta whalers hunted whales from 1540–1600, James Tuck directed Memorial University excavations of rendering furnaces, cooperages, camps and cemetery. Robert Grenier directed Parks Canada's nautical team, who excavated boats and a cargo ship lost in 1565. Tuck subsequently excavated **Ferryland**, a colony founded in 1621 by George Calvert on the Avalon Peninsula, recovering as well traces of the sixteenth-century seasonal fisheries and structures

reflecting the growth of settlement through the seventeenth century. Tuck's former students have identified early occupations elsewhere on Newfoundland's original 'English Shore': Steve Mills at Renews; William Gilbert at John Guy's Cupids colony of 1610; Peter Pope on the St John's waterfront; and Roy Skanes in Trinity.

Historical archaeology in Newfoundland initially often concerned military sites. Parks Canada investigated the French fortifications at Castle Hill Placentia, 1693–1713. Parks also sponsored excavation of nineteenth-century fortifications at **Signal Hill** in St John's, by Edward Jelks and, later, Rob Ferguson. The controversial decision to locate a new provincial museum on late eighteenth-century Fort Townshend in St John's required extensive salvage archaeology – work carried out under difficult circumstances by Skanes.

The historical archaeology of the province, with its focus on the industries of the early modern resource periphery, has long since grown beyond military sites. Interest in early settlement has steered researchers away from the 'French Shore', used largely by migratory fishermen from 1504 to 1904. Tuck's Red Bay research touched on a French trading post of *c.* 1700 and the ethnohistorian Ralph Pastore uncovered evidence of French trade at Boyd's Cove, a Beothuk site of 1650–1720, which also yielded evidence that these Native people had become dependent on cold-worked iron scavenged from European sites. Many of the outstanding research questions in the province concern the interaction of the various peoples who have exploited this region, once so rich in maritime resources.

Further reading

Colony of Avalon Foundation (1996–) *Avalon Chronicles* (annual).

Fitzhugh, W.F. and Ward, E.I. (eds) (2000) *Vikings: The North Atlantic Saga*, Washington: Smithsonian Institution Press.

Memorial University of Newfoundland (n.d.) *Newfoundland and Labrador Heritage* (www.heritage.nf.ca).

Pope, P.E. (forthcoming) *Fish into Wine: The Newfoundland Plantation in the Seventeenth Century*, Chapel Hill: University of North Carolina Press.

Tuck, J.A. and Grenier, R. (1989) *Red Bay, Labrador: World Whaling Capital A.D. 1550–1600*, St John's: Atlantic Archaeology.

PETER E. POPE

Newton Plantation, Barbados

Newton Plantation was a slave plantation located in Christ Church parish in southern Barbados, West Indies. Archaeological and ethnohistorical research conducted at the estate constituted one of the first and most extensive anthropological efforts in the early history of **African American archaeology** and **plantation archaeology**.

Barbados, only 415 km^2 in size, was **England**'s first colony in the New World to depend on the cultivation of sugar by slave labour. The small size of the island did not keep the English sugar growers from importing huge numbers of slaves, and by the 1670s, the slave force on the island – of African birth or descent – totalled almost six times the population of all of England's mainland colonies. Sugar production made Barbados the richest English colony and a major destination in the Atlantic slave trade.

Newton Plantation was begun by Samuel Newton some time during the 1650s, just as the island's sugar production was beginning to be established. By the 1670s, Newton was considered to be one of the most important planters on the island, and, in keeping with his economic status, he continued to increase the size of the plantation holdings (two plantations existed in the early years) and to enlarge the number of slaves who worked under his control. By the eighteenth century, only one Newton Plantation remained (the southern of the two), and, when John Newton died in 1794, his descendants obtained ownership of the estate. Archaeological research at the plantation site has focused specifically on the slave period, or from the 1650s to 1834, the date Britain abolished legal bondage.

The initial archaeological research at the site was intended to locate and excavate the remains of the plantation's slave village. The archaeologists, led by anthropologist Jerome S. Handler, found only a small number of artefacts in the area thought to contain the village. With these limited results in hand, the team decided to move to an area thought to contain the slave cemetery. This area indeed contained the cemetery, and the archaeologists discovered skeletal remains from 104 individuals. They have set the date of these interments to the 1660–1820 period.

Research on the skeletal remains has provided significant information about the **material culture** of Barbadian slavery, the health and nutrition of the Newton Plantation slaves and the nature of mortuary customs at the plantation. The research has also yielded information about the social distinctions that operated within the slave population. One burial stood out as especially unique within the site. Handler has interpreted this burial – a 50-year-old male associated with grave items that included an iron knife, metal bracelets and an ornate necklace – as the remains of a traditional slave healer or diviner.

See also: diaspora; mortuary analysis

Further reading

Handler, J.S. (1997) 'An African-type healer/ diviner and his grave goods: A burial from a plantation slave cemetery in Barbados, West Indies', *International Journal of Historical Archaeology* 1: 91–130.

Handler, J.S. and Corruccini, R.S. (1983) 'Plantation slave life in Barbados: A physical anthropological analysis', *Journal of Interdisciplinary History* 14: 65–90.

Handler, J.S. and Lange, F.W. (1978) *Plantation Slavery in Barbados: An Archaeological and Historical Investigation*, Cambridge, MA: Harvard University Press.

CHARLES E. ORSER, JR

non-ferrous metal

In terms of metal artefacts, historical archaeologists typically find an overwhelming number of iron objects, especially at former wooden house sites – typically nails – and at sites associated with agriculture – typically tools of all sorts. Historical archaeologists also find numerous examples of non-ferrous metallic objects. The materials of manufacture of these artefacts are **pewter**, copper, brass, silver, gold and various alloys made during the late nineteenth and early twentieth centuries. An almost countless array of objects manufactured with non-ferrous metals is possible.

Brass, an alloy of copper and zinc, is one of the most commonly found kinds of metal on historical archaeological sites because post-Industrial Revolution manufacturers widely used brass for the production of personal items, such as **buttons** and buckles, as well as for house furnishings, such as candlesticks, drawer pulls and door furniture. Archaeologists usually find abundant examples of brass objects on colonial-period Native American sites (see **Native Americans**) the residents of which were in contact with European and US fur traders. Many natives would often make ornaments and arrow points from pieces of the brass kettles they had received in trade. The **firearms** that they received in trade also contained brass pieces, such as side plates and escutcheon plates, and archaeologists find these objects as well. Cartridges were also made of brass, and many of these contain head stamps, or **makers' marks**, which identify their producers.

Colonial manufacturers widely used pewter, an alloy of tin and lead, to manufacture sturdy tablewares, such as mugs, plates and platters. Precious metals were used for coins and tokens as well as for the fine threads associated with the dress of the wealthy. Tin was of course a commonly used material for the manufacture of cans, and archaeologists who excavate late nineteenth-century logging and mining camps, and early twentieth-century sites of all types frequently discover tin objects. Historical archaeologists also frequently recover lead shot, bullets and pieces of sprue (the refuse from bullet manufacture) at sites associated with firearms.

Non-ferrous artefacts require special handling for cleaning and conservation (see **conservation, terrestrial**). Oftentimes, as in the case of a well-used coin, the archaeologist can actually scrape away the remaining elements of the stamp if the wrong cleaning method is used. For this reason, archaeologists who excavate large amounts of non-ferrous objects, or who have discovered a non-ferrous object that is especially important, will usually employ a conservation specialist.

Further reading

Busch, J. (1981) 'An introduction to the tin can', *Historical Archaeology* 15(1): 95–104.

Noël Hume, I. (1970) *A Guide to Artifacts of Colonial America*, New York: Alfred A. Knopf.

Rock, J.T. (1984) 'Cans in the countryside', *Historical Archaeology* 18(2): 97–111.

Martin, A.S. (1989) 'The role of pewter as missing artifact: Consumer attitudes toward tablewares in late 18th century Virginia', *Historical Archaeology* 23(2): 1–27.

CHARLES E. ORSER, JR

North Africa

Archaeological excavations in North Africa emerged in the late nineteenth and early twentieth centuries as part of the European colonial projects and the development of Orientalist scholarship. For the most part these were French expeditions conducted in the present-day countries of Morocco, Algeria and Tunisia with some Italian excavations in Libya, almost all concentrating on the classical-period cities of the North African littoral. This emphasis on classical urbanism also set the agenda for much of the archaeological work of later, fully historic, periods for which the city has served as the primary locus of archaeological investigation. Attention away from the city, in an effort to answer questions dealing with Islamic-era culture contact, and larger social processes of Islamisation and state formation, has only just begun to take a foothold in the historical archaeology of North Africa.

North Africa only begins to emerge as part of the historical record largely as a result of the Phoenician and later Roman colonisation, which established an impressive network of roads and cities throughout the southern shore of the Mediterranean. Investigations of this process of **urbanisation** and the workings of Roman imperialism often served as ideological support for the new European colonisers who sought to establish what they saw as a similar *mission civilatrice* in the various regions of North Africa. This early archaeological work concentrated most heavily on the great classical cities of Carthage, Leptis Magna, Timgad and Volubilis to mention just a few, as a demonstration of the grandeur and accomplishments of a colonial settler society that had turned the region into an agriculturally productive imperial engine.

Despite the emphasis placed on the classical period during the era of European **colonialism** in North Africa, the early twentieth century also witnessed some limited efforts to conduct archaeological research of the fully historical period beginning with the seventh-century transition of North Africa as a Byzantine domain to one under Arabo-Islamic control. These investigations dovetailed neatly with the questions of urbanism that colleagues of the classical period had begun to outline. Much of the effort of the primarily French archaeologist of various Islamic-period cities throughout North Africa was spent in developing an ideal typical notion of the 'Islamic city'. Indeed, the urban centres of North Africa, both living and ruined, became the prototypes both for understanding Islamic-period urbanism and developing notions of space as fixed by Islamic principles. Such monolithic and essentialising notions of how Islam and the Arab conquests ordered space, particularly urban space, still dominate much of the current debates in understanding the transition of the Middle East from late antiquity to the Islamic period.

North Africa's emergence in the seventh century as part of the *Dar al-Islam* ('the house of Islam'), following the conquests of the Arab armies, was to signal a profound change in the course of this region. Among the most important adjustments were the migration of large numbers of Arabs and other Easterners, and the establishment of Islam and the Arabic language. Even its new Arabic name *al-Magrib* ('the West' or 'where the sun sets') came to symbolise its position within a new geopolitical order that was to be dominated first by the Umayyads, based in Damascus, and then in the eighth century by the Abbasids, whose capital was Baghdad. For the various Berber peoples indigenous to this region, their incorporation within the Islamic world was to have a greater transformative impact on their politics and culture than had their previous contacts with Carthage, Rome, the Vandals and Byzantium. Processes such as 'Islamisation' and 'Arabisation', as well as the emerging political and economic centralisation of an Islamic Empire under various regimes, would bring North Africa into greater structural and cultural connection with other regions of the Near East, especially Egypt, as well as with regions of **West Africa**. With the gradual development of such larger political, economic and cultural ties of trade, empire and Islam, it is impossible to discuss the archaeology of North Africa without reference to its contextualisation within these supraregional social fields. At the same time, it is important not to see the Arab conquest solely in the light of a historical rupture, but to have a clear focus on what remained points of continuity within this region.

It is only since the 1980s that archaeological efforts have begun to move away from the Orientalist fascination with the 'Islamic city' and started to address questions dealing with how North Africa and the peoples who came to inhabit it were integrated as part of the larger Islamic world. These efforts have, to a large extent, not been from the perspective of the imposition of global structuring forces. Rather, they have tended to emphasise the local contexts and build from these the ways in which they articulated with larger regional and supraregional systems. They demonstrate that it is important not to look at North Africa as a monolithic cultural entity – it is hard to imagine that an area extending from the western Egyptian deserts to the Atlantic coast of Morocco ever could be – but rather, that our focus should pay serious attention to the diverse historical developments that shaped this region. This allows opportunity for the examination of the ways in which the culture contacts in North Africa were full of unintended consequences and dialectically shifted the terrain of what the Islamic world was and is.

The first archaeological efforts to offer such an approach to the study of North Africa in the historical period comes with the work of Charles Redman on the medieval site of **Qsar es-Seghir** in northern Morocco. In his monograph stemming from the excavations, *Qsar es-Seghir: An Archaeological View of Medieval Life*, Redman outlines a history of the site, situating it within the context of the local and regional polities, while also demonstrating its significance in the larger history of the beginnings of European colonial expansion under Henry the Navigator of fifteenth-century Portugal. The excavations at Qsar es-Seghir were part of a wider regional archaeological survey and excavation project, which has provided the evidence for other interesting conclusions concerning regional urban settlement. Small-scale excavations and archaeological work at several other Islamic-period cities of Morocco, including Badis, al-Basra and Madinat an-Nakur, have led to the supposition of two distinct urban patterns during the medieval period. The first of these was an Idrisid-period hierarchy of settlements based on a largely agricultural economy, whereas the latter pattern under the more expansive and state-like Almoravid and Almohad dynasties consists of numerous, roughly equal-sized coastal towns and inland capitals serving an economy diversified by the development of long-distance trade. This latter pattern begins to demonstrate how the regions of North Africa have become incorporated into larger trade relations with the greater Islamic world. This was particularly important because of Morocco's connection with the goldfields of West Africa and the influence of the emergent hegemony of the Fatimid Empire in Cairo, which had its start in North Africa.

North Africa's connection to the international movement of bullion was highlighted by a recent find in excavations of the Red Sea port of Ayla (modern Aqaba, Jordan; excavations conducted by Donald Whitcomb) of a traveller's purse containing numerous gold coins, twenty-nine of which were minted in Sijilmasa, Morocco. Interest in the gold trade has prompted excavations of this now ruined city, located on the northern edge of the Sahara desert, conducted by Ronald Messier. From historical accounts it is clear that this city was a northern terminus of a trade route in which manufactured goods of the Islamic world were exchanged for the gold dust and other preciosities of West Africa. While the final results of the excavations still await publication, a picture has begun to develop of North Africa and particularly its most western fringe (present-day Morocco) as deeply integrated in the growing world commerce. This work has the potential to enlighten us about not only the movement of material goods but also other cultural connections between North Africa and other parts of the continent. Muslim traders since the early eighth century have had a profound role in transmitting Arabic, Islam and various sciences into the Sahara and beyond. Timothy Insoll's excavations of Gao, Mali, have demonstrated the degree to which Islam has impacted on these regions tied initially to the Islamic world through their trade with the various polities of North Africa, and later through the importance of the *haj*, the pilgrimage to Mecca.

What should be clear from the archaeological work so far discussed is that scholarly attention has largely remained focused on urban sites. While the terrain of questioning has shifted somewhat from the Orientalist investigations of Islamic urbanism to understanding these sites as situated in multivalent local, regional and global histories and processes, the city remains the primary unit of study. Moreover, the Orientalist tradition is hardly losing ground and in fact dominates much archaeological and restoration work in such contemporary cities as Fez, Algiers, Tunis and Qairouan. It is only in the 1990s that archaeological work in North Africa has stepped beyond the confines of the city and attempted a broader investigation of settlement patterns of the Islamic period. Boone and Benco have given a thorough review of this work and thus it is necessary here only to make a few comments. Most survey work in North Africa has been conducted by classical archaeologists who have, to some degree, extended their analyses to incorporate material from the Islamic period. The results have been paltry, and syntheses that give a clear interpretation of settlement practice of the historical periods utterly lacking. The one exception has been the work of Cressier. By focusing exclusively on the Islamic period in Morocco, his methodology of combining **historical documents**, aerial photography, topographic **maps**, survey, **surface collecting** and soundings has gone a long way in providing a detailed diachronic account of medieval-period settlement. His work has even begun to tackle complex issues dealing with the conflicting and interdependent relationships between immigrating Arab populations, which tended to occupy the new urban foundations, and the local Berber inhabitants practising both pastoralism and agriculture. This turn in North African archaeology from urbanism to settlement patterning, although largely confined to areas of Morocco, has also demonstrated the region's connections with Andalusian Spain. Indeed, even before the Berber Almoravid dynasty had taken over the remains of the collapsed Umayyad Caliphate in the eleventh century, Iberian cultural influences in **architecture**, **ceramics** and other forms of **material culture** and social practice were increasingly prominent. By the eleventh century, the Andalusian influence on style was as important as the tastes and fashions emanating from Fatimid Cairo and further east.

It is fair to conclude that the archaeology of North Africa in the historic periods is very much in its early phases. The volume of research hardly compares to that of other regions of the Middle East, despite the intensification of support for archaeological investigations of these periods. North African archaeology has yet to adequately address questions of culture contact in the Islamic period and develop a clear picture of the intricacies of Berber tribal life and culture, and its adjustments in the face of Arab migrations and the spread of Islam. Understanding the nature of this contact and its dialectical outcomes should emerge as an important contribution for future archaeological work in the region.

See also: contact archaeology; everyday life

Further reading

Benco, N. (1987) *The Early Medieval Pottery Industry at al-Basra, Morocco*, Oxford: BAR.

Boone, J. and Benco, N. (1999) 'Islamic settlement in North Africa and the Iberian Peninsula', *Annual Review of Anthropology* 28: 51–71.

Boone, J., Myers, J.E. and Redman, C.L. (1990) 'Archeological and historical approaches to complex societies: The Islamic states of medieval Morocco', *American Anthropologist* 92: 630–46.

Cressier, (ed) (1992) 'Maroc Saharien et Maroc méditerranéen au moyen âge: le cas des ports de Nul Lamta et de Badis', *Histoire et Archáologie de l'Afrique du Nord: Actes du Ve Colloque International Rèuni dans le Cadre du 115e Congrés National des Sociétés Savants, Avignon, 9–13 Avril 1990*, Paris: CTHS, pp. 393–407.

Messier, R. (1997) 'Rereading medieval sources through multidisciplinary glasses', in M. Le Gall and K. Perkins (eds) *The Maghrib in Question: Essays in History and Historiography*, Austin: University of Texas Press, pp. 174–200.

Redman, C. (1986) *Qsar es-Seghir: An Archaeological View of Medieval Life*, Orlando: Academic Press.

—— (1983) 'Comparative urbanism in the Islamic Far West', *World Archaeology* 14: 355–77.

IAN B. STRAUGHN

olive jar

'Olive jar' is the term used by North American archaeologists for the coarse, wheel-made **earthenware** containers used in Luso-Iberian transatlantic shipping. Perhaps better referred to by their Spanish term, *botija*, these jugs are generally similar in form and function to amphorae used in commerce in the classical Mediterranean civilisations, and even earlier in the ancient Near East. Vessels of interest to historical archaeologists are typically short-necked, high-shouldered jars with tapering bodies and pointed bases, either unglazed or green lead-glazed on the interior, and usually manufactured in southern Spain. Functioning as the tin cans of the sixteenth through eighteenth centuries, olive jars are found in considerable quantities at terrestrial and shipwreck sites.

The primary use of these vessels was to ship liquid or bulk dry goods across the Atlantic. Contents included olive oil (hence the name) and also wine, vinegar, beans, dates, almonds, honey, pitch, soap, etc. Archival sources indicate that vessel names varied by capacity, shape and/or contents, the most common Spanish terms being *botija* or *botijo*, but also *jarra* and *cantaro*. Production of these jars was sometimes established at colonial 'industrial' sites, for example at **Moquegua**, where they were used to transport wine and brandy from the producing haciendas to consumers at the silver mines in what is now Bolivia.

Patterned variations in the size, shape and rim form of olive jars, particularly from known, dated shipwrecks, have been studied as a basis for dating terrestrial sites. One of the earliest of such attempts was John Goggin's pioneering study that distinguished Early (globular, with handles) from more elongate Middle and Late olive jars in four basic forms (A–D). Stephen James's study of more than 600 complete olive jars from two shipwrecks indicated much greater variability in form, and a lack of correlations among glazing, contents and shape. Mitchell Marken's analysis of ceramics from seventeen shipwrecks further illustrated the lack of close correlation between olive jar capacities and Spanish units of measure. Marken noted that more precise dating of terrestrial sites can be achieved by consideration of attributes of both olive jars and Columbia Plain majolica forms.

Further reading

Goggin, J.M. (1960) *The Spanish Olive Jar: An Introductory Study*, Yale University Publications in Anthropology 62, New Haven: Yale University.

James, S.R., Jr (1988) 'A reassessment of the chronological and typological framework of the Spanish olive jar', *Historical Archaeology* 22(1): 43–66.

Marken, M.W. (1994) *Pottery from Spanish Shipwrecks, 1500–1800*, Gainesville: University Press of Florida.

PRUDENCE M. RICE

Ontario, Canada

The development of historical archaeology in Ontario, Canada, parallels its development in other parts of the world. It may be categorised into four distinct stages.

In the first, or 'antiquarian', stage, archaeology was simply used as a means for developing collections: private, public and commercial. It was not perceived as an investigative tool for exploring culture. This stage began during Ontario's earliest period of permanent settlement. During the process of clearing the forests and tilling the land, an intriguing discovery was made – evidence of former human occupation, both prehistoric and historic. At an early date, pioneer archaeologists puzzled over this evidence, but, with limited exceptions, few accounts of these early investigations have survived. John Brant, son of the famous Mohawk Chief Joseph Brant, was reported to have collected artefacts from a burial mound near his home at the head of Lake Ontario, now Burlington. Early Ontario antiquarians followed a pattern established by US colonists, like Charles Willson Peale and Thomas Jefferson, who amassed archaeological and ethnographic collections. British immigrants to Ontario like Thomas Barnett, who established Ontario's first museum in 1827, may have followed the example of John Tradescant of the Ashmolean Museum at Oxford University where Powhatan's mantle is still exhibited. The early antiquarians in Ontario would have also embraced the work of other British and continental archaeologists who studied classical ruins because classical elements are reflected in the architecture, art and other material culture of colonial Upper Canada.

Two British Royal Engineers left a description of their excavation of a mound in Hamilton. They recognised these as being similar to pre-Roman burial mounds in the British Isles.

Many Ontario Iroquoian ossuaries contained historic-period artefacts, such as at the Neutral burial pit in St David's, Ontario, investigated by Frederick Houghton in the late nineteenth century. This research provided much of the first ethnographic material for the collection of the Buffalo (New York) Museum of Science.

Although most of the investigated sites were of native affiliation, an interest in collecting ancient artefacts focused on historic sites as well. Prior to the American Civil War, a thriving tourist industry revolved around War of 1812 battlefields in Ontario. Battlefield sites often hosted observation towers and guided tours, and became subject to Sunday afternoon excavations, as reported on by William Calver and Reginald Bolton in 1950.

By the end of the nineteenth century, a number of historic contact sites had been surveyed in Huronia, including Jesuit missionary and French colonial components. Many of these were reported in the scholarly series published between 1887 until 1928 as appendices to the annual report of the Minister of Education.

The second stage of development, the 'early scientific', was to a large degree centred upon academic institutions and museums. This era was typified by the works of pioneer archaeologists such as David Boyle, W. J. Wintemberg, Norman J. Emerson, Thomas Lee, Frank Ridley, Marian White, Richard S. MacNeish and Walter Kenyon. However, it was Kenneth E. Kidd, described as the 'father of Ontario historical archaeology', who exerted the greatest influence. Kidd's use of the scientific approach was illustrated in *The Excavation of Ste Marie 1* (in 1949), the first formal historical archaeology report prepared in Canada. This publication was followed by his work on the contact-period ossuary of Osossane. With his wife Martha, he devised a classification system using early glass trade **beads** from these sites. The Kidd bead classification system has since gained universal use. Kidd inspired a generation of Ontario archaeologists by establishing the first academic Native Studies and Historical Archaeology programmes offered in Canada.

The third stage is the 'non-*laissez-faire*' stage. The late 1960s and 1970s were years of economic prosperity in Ontario. With prosperity came more recreational activity and a demand for government involvement and development of parks and historic sites. This occurred at all levels of government. Academics were consulted to establish directives and policies for parks that involved **cultural-resource management**. While governments began to establish budgets for the maintenance and management of cultural resources it was recognised in the 1960s that these resources brought with them the obligation of specialised conservation (see **conservation, terrestrial**) and the practice of cultural-resource management became legislated. During this stage, governments attempted to manage these resources 'in-house' using archaeology, not as an academic discipline but as a monitoring technique.

The provincial government created positions for regional archaeologists and staff. They also funded fieldwork including huge projects such as the Big Dig (1970), a massive survey of the Lake Superior region; and employed over one hundred students for salvage excavations at the Draper Site in 1975. A series of provincial publications in archaeology appeared and the studies provided subsidies for the publications of the Ontario Archaeological Society and the Royal Ontario Museum. The increase in archaeological investigation became even greater with the establishment of the Ontario Heritage Act (1974), which created the Ontario Heritage Foundation to oversee and manage heritage properties and the creation of provincial lotteries to pay for them. The Act mandated minimal standards for archaeological performance, creating criteria to regulate the annual issuing of licences to conduct archaeological research. The Act also established a provincial precedent for conducting archaeology as an aspect of cultural-resource management on property owned by the Ontario Heritage Foundation.

Provincial activities were matched only by the federal government. Parks Canada, the custodian of Canada's National Historic Parks, Sites, and Monuments had its headquarters in Ottawa. Until regional headquarters were established, cultural-resource management for the nation was provided from these headquarters. Ottawa was also headquarters for the conservation, curatorial, collections management and **material culture** research facilities. In the 1960s and early 1970s, Parks Canada imported many of its archaeological staff from the UK and the USA. Parks Canada established specialised training in historical archaeology not available in Canadian educational institutions at the time. It was at the national headquarters that planning, research, conservation and interpretation were carried out for Canada's most prestigious historic-period sites, including North America's only Viking site, the John Franklin expeditionary sites and even sixteenth-century Basque whaling sites. The rich resources provided by Parks Canada also fostered and assisted in the development of the then neophyte **Society for Historical Archaeology**.

By the early 1980s, deteriorating economic conditions gave rise to a fourth stage in the development of Ontario historic archaeology, that of 'contract archaeology'. This stage developed as a result of governmental efforts to become more fiscally accountable. The cost of performing archaeological research and field investigations in-house become prohibitive and politically questionable. As a result, governmental agencies began contracting the field and laboratory research to commercial consultants rather than to their own in-house specialists. This practice occurred because of the government-wide downsizing that began in the 1980s. The divesting of archaeological activities was easily justified by a Canadian federal policy, which advocated low-profile nationalism, coupled with a low-priority public attitude regarding cultural elements, during an era when health care and educational issues were of greater concern. Minimum standards were deemed acceptable for the performance of archaeological investigations. Much of the work was initially conducted by academics with institutional affiliations. Between 1980 and 1990, however, a proliferation of consulting firms appeared. Successful archaeology in Ontario required a solid business plan. By 2000, many of the small firms had been replaced by larger consulting firms. The Ontario Heritage Act, mandating archaeological assessment in sensitive locations, greatly promoted the growth of the contract archaeology industry, but economics were often the bottom line in exchange for clearance and investigations at the 'minimum required level'. At the beginning of the twenty-first century, the vast majority of the historical archaeology performed in Ontario was driven by land development pressures rather than by research paradigms. Fortunately, it has been recognised that public resources are still necessary to perform archaeology in circumstances where advanced methods of conservation are required to deal with specialised conditions, such as with the shipwrecks of the *Hamilton* and the *Scourge*.

Academic and avocational archaeology continues at reduced levels, largely due to the withdrawal of public funding in these areas. A review of the Ontario Heritage Act began in the early 1990s. It is difficult to predict future developments in the discipline but inevitably change will continue to occur.

Further reading

Calver, W.L. and Bolton, R.P. (1950) *History Written with Pick and Shovel*, New York: New York Historical Society.

Kidd, K.E. (1953) 'The excavation and historical identification of a Huron ossuary', *American Antiquity* 4: 359–79.

—— (1949) *The Excavation of Ste Marie 1*, Toronto: University of Toronto Press.

Kidd, K.E. and Kidd, M.A. (1970) 'A classification system for glass beads for the use of field archaeologists', in *Canadian Historic Sites: Occasional Papers in Archaeology and History* 1, Ottawa: Department of Indian Affairs and Northern Development, pp. 45–89.

Nelson, D.A. (1983) '*Hamilton* and *Scourge*: Ghost ships of the War of 1812', *National Geographic* 163(3): 289–313.

Upper Canada Herald (1839) 'The *Hamilton* journal', 27 August.

JON K. JOUPPIEN

Opole, Poland

The stronghold of Opole was discovered in 1930 during construction work, and this led to rescue excavations that were directed by Georg Raschke in 1930, 1931 and 1933. Excavations were renewed in 1948 and continued until 1978, led by Rudolf Jamka (1948–51), Włodzimierz Hołubowicz (1952–62), Bogusław Gediga (1963–9, 1977 and 1978). In 1949, the project was incorporated into the millennium programme organised by the Committee for Research on the Origins of the Polish State, which later became the Institute for the History of Material Culture, Polish Academy of Sciences.

The excavations were carried out across an area of 2,300 m^2, around 30 per cent of the total stronghold area. Research techniques on multilayer sites were refined during the excavations. Digging was carried out within the framework of a 100 m^2 grid, which was further divided into 100 squares. Layers 20 cm in thickness (the modern and medieval layers) and 10 cm in thickness (the early medieval ones) were excavated. All the artefacts found were located three-dimensionally.

The chronology of the layers was determined on the basis of the following: stratigraphical analysis, assessment of the speed and process by which layering took place, analysis of archaeological material (typology, analogy), coinage, **dendrochronology** and information from written sources (for the later layers). Nine layers showing separate phases of construction were identified, each of which took 25–40 years to form.

Before the stronghold was built there was a settlement on the island by the River Odra and its arm (the Młynówka). The construction of the stronghold began around AD 990, after the incorporation of Silesia into Polish borders by Mieszko I. The moment the stronghold ceased to function marks the beginning of the castle's construction (1228–1241). The stronghold's rampart was a wood/earth construction that was approximately 10 m wide at the base. The interior was densely packed and it is estimated that 100–160 wooden buildings were contained within. The streets were laid with wood and were 2–4 m wide. Narrow passages, 1 m wide, existed between the buildings. The original layout of the stronghold was observed throughout the entire time it was occupied.

Houses were either of a log-cabin or pale-frame construction. Individual houses were from 9 to over 20 m^2 in area. The interior floors were covered by laths or were of levelled packed earth. The houses were entered from the side of the courtyard or from the side of the passages but never from the street side.

Thousands of artefacts made from organic and non-organic raw materials were registered. They are treated as intrinsic data that allows us to conclude that the following crafts existed at Opole: smithing, goldsmithing, carpentry, coopering, wheelwright's work, pottery making, weaving, shoemaking, stoneworking, saddle making and household work.

In the 1940s, 1950s and 1960s, the archaeological results have often been used for propaganda purposes to emphasise Silesia's attachment to Poland 'since time immemorial'. The intent has been to show its highly civilised Slav character and a cultural development that was free from German influence.

Further reading

Bukowska-Gedigowa, J. and Gediga, B. (1986) *Wczesnośredniowieczny gród na Ostrówku w Opolu*, Wrocław: Ossolineum.

Gediga, B. (1968) 'Early mediaeval Opole and the problem of higher Silesian towns', *Archaeologia Polona* 10: 37–75.

Hołubowicz, W. (1956) *Opole w wiekach X-XII*, Katowice: Śląsk.

Raschke, G. (1931) 'Die Entdeckung des fruehgeschichtlichen Oppeln', *Altschiesien* 3: 261–6.

WŁODZIMIERZ RĄCZKOWSKI

oral history

Oral history offers an alternative database for information regarding the past to historical archaeologists. Oral history refers to the individual memories of persons who have first-hand experience of people, places and events that are collected through an interview process. The quality of, and uses for, oral history in archaeological research are dependent upon a number of factors, including the number of potential informants available, the rapport between interviewer and interviewee, and an understanding on the part of an archaeologist of the strengths and limitations of oral historical sources. While archaeologists once viewed oral history as a means of finding sites or identifying artefacts, by the late 1990s archaeologists had begun to use oral-history interviews as means of understanding class, racial and gender dynamics in past populations.

Like any historical source, oral histories must be interpreted. The information derived through oral history cannot be perceived to be 'factual', but, rather, how an individual, in a given place and time, chooses to remember and convey their understanding of their past. It is necessary for the interviewer to understand why an informant agrees to be interviewed. Informants may view interviews as opportunities to voice previously unheard sides of important events, an opportunity to sanitise historic events or as a means of elevating their family's status. That informants may have such agendas should not weaken the resulting material, but should be considered by those using the information gathered. Interviewers should always include a series of questions whose answers can be verified through other resources, such as additional informants or historical documents, so that the reliability of a given informant can be independently measured later. Generally, it is best if any given information can be confirmed from three independent sources, a process known as 'triangulation'.

Using informants as a means of reconstructing landscapes or remembering the location of buildings has mixed results. Particularly damaging in these kinds of interviews can be any kind of prompting with information from interviewers, since studies have demonstrated that informants may feel the need to incorporate such things into their answers. The processes of memory are such that those specific places that were important to the individual may be remembered, but large spaces in between have been forgotten. Likewise, when using informants to locate lost structures or features, the events most clearly remembered are likely to be those that represent unusual rather than routine occurrences. Often the richest information to be drawn from oral histories is related to an individual's understanding of the social relations that existed between members of their communities.

The greatest constraint of oral historical evidence is the size of the available study population. When investigating time periods longer than fifty years ago, one is limited to a small segment of the population who can provide information for one's study. This sample size becomes progressively narrower as one attempts to study events further removed in time, until first-hand participants are no longer available. Asking descendants of an individual about stories they remember of their grandparents' childhoods may provide some useful insights, but these stories are subject to appear almost as legends.

Oral historical data can also be affected by the rapport an interviewer is able to build with the interviewee. Gender, dialect, age and cultural differences between the interviewer and subject can influence the quality of the data collected. Informants can also be distressed by the presence of tape recorders or video cameras, and often several interviews need to be scheduled before an informant may feel comfortable with an interviewer. One means of circumventing rapport difficulties is to arrange to interview several informants at once. The shared experiences of the informants is comforting to them, but also allows them the freedom to play off one another's memories, resulting in richer dialogues. Archaeologists took this approach while directing excavations in a West Oakland, California, neighbourhood, drawing together individuals of different ethnic and racial backgrounds to discuss their memories of living in a pluralistic community.

Since historical archaeologists are interested in the relationship between material culture and culture, it can be helpful to bring objects to interviews. In a particularly novel approach, Dorothy Washburn, an art historian, in her study of doll play, invited adult women to bring their childhood dolls with them to interviews. Not only was she able to question her informants about their play, and watch physical demonstrations, she was also able to observe their current interactions with these items. She found that the presence of the materials heightened memory, and that recall was much better than with photographs or names of objects. Washburn found that for doll play, which is an arena of activity that involves highly emotive objects (the dolls), the informants had vivid and clear memories of these activities.

While some archaeologists conduct their own oral-history interviews, there are growing numbers of oral-history archives housed in university and public libraries in the USA. Scholars of **African American archaeology** have especially been dependent upon previously published oral histories. During the 1930s and 1940s, the Federal Writer's Project, a New Deal Program, employed writers to interview former slaves. These interviews provide a wealth of information about daily life from the perspective of enslaved African Americans. In his research in South Carolina, Leland Ferguson has demonstrated how the oral histories can be used to understand the broader social-cultural context in which African American artefacts were used.

Further reading

Dunaway, D. and Baum, W. (1996) *Oral History: An Interdisciplinary Anthropology*, Walnut Creek, CA: AltaMira Press.

Perks, R. and Thomson, A. (1998) *The Oral History Reader*, London: Routledge.

Terrill, T. and Hirsch, J. (1978) *Such as Us: Southern Voices of the Thirties*, Chapel Hill: University of North Carolina Press.

Washburn, D. (1997) 'Getting ready: Doll play and real life in American culture, 1900–1980', in A. Martin and J. Garrison (eds) *American Material Culture: The Shape of the Field*, Knoxville: University of Tennessee Press, pp. 105–34.

Vansina, J. (1985) *Oral Tradition as History*, Madison: University of Wisconsin Press.

LAURIE A. WILKIE

ordinary people's culture

The term 'ordinary people's culture' is meant to suggest the ways of life of men, women and **children** who were not part of history's elite classes and who have been all too easy for documentary history to overlook. Historical archaeology is perfectly designed to provide tangible information about these non-elites, and, since the late 1960s a number of its practitioners have been dedicated to investigating the lives of the forgotten, the overlooked and the dispossessed. Some of the topics addressed by historical archaeologists have included what the people ate, how they constructed their homes and yards, the nature of their settlements, the composition of their social structure, how they interacted with one another and with the outside world, how they perceived themselves and were perceived by others, the nature of their **material culture** and how they used it in various social, economic, symbolic and political ways.

Archaeology was for many years largely concerned with the excavation of the rich and the powerful. Archaeologists became world famous for excavating the tombs of pharaohs and the ancient kings of the Maya. These excavations have been widely publicised because they usually occur in exotic settings and yield remarkable finds. In its earliest years, historical archaeology also was associated with history's most powerful and wealthy people, and archaeologists were called upon to excavate the famous places associated with them. Even a brief reflection about the past, however, makes it unavoidably clear that most people in history were not rich, powerful or famous. Most men and women of the past, like most people alive today, led simple lives and had personal histories that were largely unremarkable when viewed on the world's stage. Historical archaeologists still examine famous places associated with well-known people, but, beginning in the 1960s, many of the field's practitioners realised that they possessed excellent investigative tools for examining history's most ordinary people.

As historical archaeology stands at the beginning of the twenty-first century, African American slaves constitute the most prominent 'ordinary people' that have been studied, and archaeologists have made impressive strides in illustrating their daily lives. As the field continues to expand, however, the number of different peoples examined will undoubtedly grow. Even at the start of 2001, the number of diverse people who have been investigated is still remarkable. Two examples from the USA will suffice to demonstrate historical archaeology's interpretive potential in shedding light on history's ordinary folk.

One group of people about which precious little is known are the charcoal burners of the Eureka Charcoal District in central Nevada during the last half of the nineteenth century. The smelting industry around Eureka was centrally important to the economic boom in the region, and the extraction, processing, smelting and refining of ore was a leading-edge, 'modern' technology. To function efficiently, however, this high-tech industry required the assistance of a decidedly low-tech, rural – largely 'traditional' – charcoal industry. Historians have intensively examined the smelting industry, but before the archaeological research of Ronald Reno the carbonari were largely forgotten. Using a combination of **historical documents** and archaeological evidence, Reno presented a

picture of daily life in the charcoal camps. The physical evidence he collected indicated that living conditions were primitive, often consisting of a tent and a mattress, and that hours of work were long, hard and dangerous. Reno noted that whereas the abandoned remains of contemporaneous mining camps in the region are littered with **bottles** and cans, the remains of the charcoal camps contain almost no such containers. This difference suggests that while the area's miners were accepting the more 'modern', mobile lifestyle of Gilded Age America, the charcoal burners retained a more traditional, single-pot pattern of dining. The archaeological deposits at the charcoal camps also contain few if any **earthenware** plates or cups. The lack of these objects suggests that the carbonari ate their meals from large tin cups that, according to a contemporary Sears and Roebuck catalogue, cost only two cents at the time.

In an equally fascinating study, Cheryl Claassen provides insights into the mussel-collecting industry of the Mississippi River watershed. Beginning in the late nineteenth century, men and women who lived in the watershed harvested mussels for two reasons: for high-quality pearls that could sell for thousands of dollars each (from 1860 to 1900), and for the raw materials to manufacture shell **buttons** (from 1891 until about 1950). Most people today know nothing about these activities – though they still continue in the region to some extent – but during the height of the shell-collecting activity, the harvesting and sale of mussels created a boom-town-like atmosphere along the river. Both the pearl and the button industry, of course, required the labour of hundreds of men and women, and Claassen provides a flavour of how these 'ordinary people' lived and worked. The musselers who collected shellfish worked both full time (seasonally and around the year), and part time (spending the rest of their time farming, mining or logging). Men and women both tended the machines that cut buttons from the shells, and employed a technology that had changed little in seven decades. Few African Americans were involved in the button-manufacturing process, and most of the labourers were of Anglo-Saxon heritage. Large numbers of children also worked in button production. Many button factories were located in Iowa and, in the early twentieth century, this state was the scene of intense labour unrest, culminating in a number of work stoppages, including the Muscatine Strike of 1911–12. The workers' concerns revolved around issues of safety, sanitation and wages. Claassen's study does not include the excavation of a mussel collector's home, and though some readers may see her work as non-archaeological, it is important to remember that historical archaeology need not necessarily include excavation. Claassen provides abundant information about the artefacts of both musseling and button production, as well as a thorough **ethnography** of the people's lives, and in the process offers a perfect demonstration of the power of historical archaeology to reveal ordinary people's culture.

See also: African American archaeology; culture; modernity

Further reading

Claassen, C. (1994) 'Washboards, pigtoes, and muckets: Historic musseling in the Mississippi watershed', *Historical Archaeology* 28(2): 1–145.

Reno, R.L. (1996) 'Fuel for the frontier: Industrial archaeology of charcoal production in the Eureka mining district, Nevada, 1869–1891', Nevada, Reno.

CHARLES E. ORSER, JR

Ottoman Empire

The Ottoman Empire (*c.* AD 1300–1923) was one of the major imperial systems of the modern era. During its greatest geographical expanse in the sixteenth century, it included the Balkans, the Middle East and much of North Africa. Historical archaeologists turn to the recent past of this region to examine global exchanges of the modern era outside of European, North American or colonial contexts, often using **world systems theory**. The **consumption** and production of commodities in the Ottoman Empire were linked to global **trade**, and internal transformations in Ottoman state and society.

Ottoman ceramic production in the early period (fourteenth through sixteenth centuries) was tied to trade with the Far East. Chinese export **porcelain** was popular among Ottoman elites. As a result, **ceramics** that combined Chinese design with Turkish metal vessel forms were produced at workshops, such as Iznik in Anatolia. Commissioned by Ottoman and European elites, and sold in the general market-place, these typically blue and white glazed ceramics were distributed throughout the Empire. These wares are good temporal indicators in archaeological contexts. Ottomans had increased access to porcelains after conquests in Egypt and Syria by the Ottoman sultan Selim I (1512–20) secured safe sea trade routes to the Indian Ocean. In the 1990s, Cheryl Haldane and the Institute of Nautical Archaeology–Egypt excavated a seventeenth-century shipwreck in the Red Sea. This ship, with a cargo that included porcelains manufactured in China for Middle Eastern markets, provides evidence for widespread trade routes through the Red Sea in the Ottoman period.

The consumption of tobacco and **coffee** in the later Ottoman period (mid-sixteenth through twentieth centuries) helped entangle the peoples of the region in global exchange networks. Tobacco, a New World crop, was brought through West Africa, then Egypt. Coffee was introduced from Yemen and/or Ethiopia. Although these commodities originated from outside of the Empire, they were quickly accepted by many Ottoman subjects. Uzi Baram examined the consumption of tobacco-pipes (see **pipes, smoking**) and their relationships to global exchange. Pipes are common artefacts found at Ottoman-period sites and represent the global distribution of tobacco. By the nineteenth century, tobacco became a major cash crop produced within the Empire, but its production was largely dominated by Western European interests. The changes in types of tobacco pipes used throughout the empire demonstrate this transformation. While early tobacco pipes were represented by a narrow range of types, the forms diversified in the eighteenth century, at which time forms were more standardised. This corresponded to a period when Western capitalist interests dominated the production and distribution of tobacco and pipes in the region.

Future investigations in the archaeology of the Ottoman Empire should better utilise Ottoman

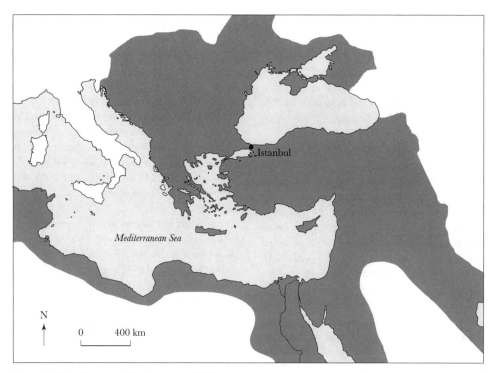

Figure 24 The Ottoman Empire *c.* AD 1700
Source: C. Carroll

documentary sources. This archaeology will probably expand to consider non-elite economic activities and the relationships between the Ottoman state and local communities.

See also: capitalism; commodification; Constantinople; modernity

Further reading

Baram, U. and Carroll, L. (2000) *A Historical Archaeology of the Ottoman Empire: Breaking New Grounds*, New York: Kluwer Academic/Plenum.

LYNDA CARROLL

Oudepost I, South Africa

Oudepost I, or 'Old Post', is a small, stone-walled fortification (see **fortifications**) located on the coast of today's South Africa. The Dutch originally built the outpost in 1669 to establish residence before the French could take possession of the region. Throughout its history, Oudepost was garrisoned by from four to ten men, and had three principal functions: to trade with the local indigenous peoples, to provision ships that stopped there and to report their activities to the Dutch colonial authorities at **Cape Town**. The post operated until 1732, when the Dutch relocated it about 2 km to the north near a better source of water.

Archaeologists Carmel Schrire and Cedric Poggenpoel directed excavations at Oudepost I from 1984 to 1987. When they were finished, they had excavated 17 per cent of the site, and had exposed three structures: an irregularly shaped enclosure (covering about 400 m^2), a long building (measuring almost 20 m by 5 m) and a small, square structure (measuring just under 9 m^2). They discovered that the Dutch had constructed the buildings from the natural rocks they had found on the shore. Schrire and Poggenpoel used the design of the buildings and the artefacts they found inside and around them to interpret their functions. They called the long building the 'lodge' because it contained an abundance of domestic food remains and artefacts, and they designated the irregular building the 'fort' because it contained less food debris, but large numbers of gunflints, lead shot and other objects that can be associated with a military occupation. The function of the small, square building remains a mystery.

The artefacts from the site include both aboriginal and European objects. Analysis revealed that earlier native occupations had occurred at the site and also that Europeans may have visited the site area both before and after the historical documentation suggests. For example, **pipe stem dating** revealed that the thousands of pieces found at the site dated to the 1590–1775 period. An analysis of the faunal remains indicated that the Dutch residents of the site relied heavily on wild animal species, many of which may have been supplied by the local Khoikhoi herders. One remarkable, and particularly human, find was an ostrich shell incised with an image of a palm that grows in South-east Asia, but not in South Africa. Because the Dutch also had outposts in Asia, it is likely that the image was made by a soldier who had seen service in this region, but was later posted to the African coast.

See also: Dutch colonialism; zooarchaeology

Further reading

Schrire, C. (1995) *Digging through Darkness: Chronicles of an Archaeologist*, Charlottesville: University of Virginia Press.
—— (1991) 'The historical archaeology of the impact of colonialism in seventeenth-century South Africa', in L. Falk (ed.), *Historical Archaeology in Global Perspective*, Washington, DC: Smithsonian Institution Press, pp. 69–96.

CHARLES E. ORSER, JR

overseas Chinese historical archaeology

The term 'overseas Chinese historical archaeology' encompasses the historical documentation, archae-ological examination (including surveying, record-ing, **surface collecting**, monitoring and excavating) and analytical interpretation of archae-ological sites outside China that people of Chinese origin or descent once inhabited. Excluded are Manila galleon wreck sites, Native American sites (see **Native Americans**) containing Chinese coins or worked **porcelain** sherds, non-overseas Chinese sites yielding Chinese export porcelain or isolated Chinese artefacts, relic-collector 'excava-tions' of overseas Chinese sites and sport divers' underwater collections of artefacts, although all are certainly of interest.

Adventurous Chinese people have long sought better opportunities abroad, first venturing to places such as Borneo, Formosa, the Dutch East Indies, Malaya and the Philippines. From the mid-nineteenth century onwards, the lure of 'gold', whether as precious metal or wages, attracted them to **Australia** and **New Zealand**; South America, especially Peru; Mexico and Central America; the West Indies, particularly Cuba and Jamaica; Canada; and the western USA. Those locations, and others known through place names or from Lynn Pan's *Encyclopedia of the Overseas Chinese*, thus contain overseas Chinese archaeological sites, most still unexcavated and unrecorded.

Overseas Chinese historical archaeology dates from at least the mid-1950s. It has since become a multidisciplinary field, practised in several coun-tries, whose literature has evolved from simple site reports with 'laundry lists' of artefacts, to complex theoretical analyses placing the overseas Chinese within the cultural and historical contexts of the larger societies to which they immigrated.

Types and time periods of relevant sites vary widely; many have been investigated archaeologi-cally. They include, but are not limited to, an apple-drying industry; blacksmith shops; butcher shops; work camps for charcoal makers, lumber workers and wood choppers, and construction camps for dams, roads and **railways**; ceme-teries and individual gravesites; 'Chinatowns', both isolated and in large urban areas; doctors' offices and herbal-medicine dispensaries; abalone-gathering, shrimping and fishing camps, villages and canneries; gambling halls; market gardens, sometimes terraced; hotels and boarding houses; junks and submerged boats; laundries; mining features, including claims, ditches, dams, reservoirs and stacked rock tailings; opium-smoking establishments; stores; temples; and theatres. Individual components of some sites have included dwellings, cook houses, fireplaces, hearths, forges and pig ovens.

Researchers often first recognise overseas Chinese sites by observing Chinese artefacts on the ground surface. Prior to preparation of a research design for excavation, the investigator conducts extensive 'digging in the documents' to obtain information on the site's Chinese occupants. In the western USA, for example, sources ordinarily consulted include census records, city directories, newspapers, **maps**, mining-claim records, property deeds and leases, court cases, cemetery records and **gravestones**, vital statistics, property assessment and taxing records, **immigration** documents, oral histories (see **oral history**), letters, diaries and photographs (see **photographic information**).

Excavations produce both non-Chinese and Chinese artefacts, the latter manufactured in China, while faunal remains indicate what animals were utilised for food (see **food and foodways**). Archaeologists may discover that an overseas Chinese site has had several phases. Often, particularly with rural mining sites, or buildings in urban areas, non-Chinese were there first, and the Chinese occupation followed. If the site is undisturbed, these phases can generally be distinguished through their artefacts. The main categories of Chinese objects represented usually include utilitarian **ceramics**, table ceramics, **glass** medicine vials, opium-smoking paraphernalia and gambling-related objects.

Unlike many other historic objects, Chinese artefacts are usually not reliable dating indicators (see **dating methods**) for overseas Chinese sites. For example, the most common Chinese coins found archaeologically in the USA date to the reign of Emperor Qianlong (Ch'ien Lung). He ruled from 1736 to 1796, long before large numbers of Chinese began arriving in the USA. Dates for overseas Chinese sites are thus determined by other means, such as historical documentation and datable non-Chinese artefacts.

Hidden Heritage, edited by Priscilla Wegars, surveys research developments through the early 1990s.

Annotated bibliographies in *Northwest Anthropological Research Notes* during 1984, 1985 and 1993 list relevant literature, much of which is housed in the University of Idaho's Asian American Comparative Collection (AACC). Reviews of more recent publications appear in the *Asian American Comparative Collection Newsletter*, and the AACC's website (http://www.uidaho.edu/LS/AACC/) provides information on, or links to, comparative material and standardised terminology.

Today, archaeologists increasingly share their findings with the general public, through books, workshops, conferences, restoration, interpretation, public history and dramatisations. Materials produced by Chinese historical societies and Asian American studies organisations can help archaeologists of non-Chinese descent become sensitive to Chinese culture and concerns, and to recognise, and avoid using, stereotypes such as 'joss house' for temple, 'Chinamen' and 'Orientals' for Chinese people, 'coolies' for labourers, 'Chinese ovens' for Italian bread ovens and 'Chinese tunnels' for sidewalk vaults.

Major projects have taken place only in Australia, Canada, New Zealand and the USA. World-wide, much remains to be accomplished.

Australia

As detailed in Peter Bell's 1996 essay for *Australasian Historical Archaeology*, the examination of overseas Chinese archaeological sites in Australia began in 1982 when Ian Jack and Kate Holmes investigated Ah Toy's garden and habitation on the Palmer Goldfield in Queensland, and Howard Pearce recorded Chinese pig ovens in the Northern Territory's Pine Creek District. Later that decade, both Justin McCarthy and Peter Bell surveyed additional Chinese sites there, Gordon Grimwade studied the Atherton Chinese temple in Queensland and Helen Vivian documented Chinese sites in north-eastern Tasmania. The 1990s saw further studies of the Palmer Goldfield, Scott Mitchell recorded more Northern Territory ovens, Denise Gaughwin assessed Chinese sites in Tasmania, Lindsay Smith surveyed and excavated mining sites at Kiandra, New South Wales, while Justin McCarthy and Jane Lydon excavated urban Chinese sites in Melbourne and **Sydney**, respectively. Indispensable references are Peter Bell, Gordon Grimwade and Neville Ritchie's bibliography, and Paul Macgregor's edited conference proceedings.

Canada

Early overseas Chinese historical archaeology in Canada includes the 1982 excavations of the Kwong Sang Wing building in Barkerville, British Columbia, by Susan Irvine and Pamela Montgomery. During the 1990s, Ying-ying Chen excavated at the Zhigongtang (Chee Kung Tong, Chih Kung T'ang) building there; Gordon Dibb directed a monitoring operation that recovered artefacts from the first Chinese restaurant in Peterborough, Ontario; and Imogene Lim excavated in the Vancouver, British Columbia, Chinatown. In 2000, Sandra Sauer directed excavations at the Wild Horse Creek Chinatown, a goldmining community near Fort Steele, British Columbia.

New Zealand

Overseas Chinese historical archaeology in New Zealand began with the 1977 appointment, for ten years, of Neville Ritchie as archaeologist for the Clutha Valley Development power project, a hydroelectric dam-building scheme centred on the South Island around Cromwell. Surveys of the area affected by reservoir construction identified numerous sites, of which about seventy were related to nineteenth-century Chinese goldmining in Central Otago. Because flooding or other damage would ultimately impact them permanently, Ritchie developed a comprehensive programme to investigate and record the Chinese sites. Between 1978 and 1985, he directed excavations at twenty-one of them, field tested some fifty others and presented the results in his 1986 doctoral thesis. Since Ritchie's work concluded, overseas Chinese archaeological investigation has been mostly confined to student theses and Department of Conservation surveys.

USA

In the early 1950s, M.B. McKusick and C.N. Warren recorded four Chinese sites on San Clemente Island, California. The following decade,

Paul Chace and William Evans documented Chinese railroad labourer camps near Donner Summit, California; Alton Briggs investigated a similar camp in Texas; and James Ayres began directing an urban renewal archaeological salvage project in Tucson, Arizona.

During the 1970s, work in Tucson continued, resulting in artefact studies by John Olsen and by Florence and Robert Lister. Other major projects, at California sites with overseas Chinese components, were Roberta Greenwood's excavations in Ventura; Adrian and Mary Praetzellis's Old Sacramento ceramics research; and George Teague and Lynette Shenk's excavations at Harmony Borax Works. Other significant projects took place in Idaho City, Idaho; Oregon's Applegate Valley; and Lovelock, Nevada.

The 1980s began with Robert Schuyler's *Archaeological Perspectives on Ethnicity in America*; it included four articles on overseas Chinese topics and a bibliography. Major projects in California that decade were George Miller's excavations at Yema-Po, an Alameda County dam construction site; Julia Costello's work at Fiddletown's Chew Kee Store; Allan Pastron, Robert Gross and Donna Garaventa's report on the ceramics from excavations at San Francisco's waterfront; Julia Costello and Mary Maniery's analysis of the Walnut Grove ceramics; Judy Tordoff's work on northern California mining sites; David Felton, Francis Lortie and Peter Schulz's excavations at the Woodland Chinese laundry; and Judy Berryman's investigations of San Clemente Island abalone processing. Other California work included investigations of Marin County shrimp camps, and excavations of Chinatowns or Chinese sites in Los Angeles, Riverside, Sacramento, San Luis Obispo, San Jose and Santa Barbara.

Archaeologists studied overseas Chinese sites in numerous other states. In Idaho, David Sisson investigated Lower Salmon River mining, Darby Stapp excavated at Pierce, Jeffrey Fee researched Chinese gardens in the Payette National Forest and Roderick Sprague directed excavations at Silver City. In Nevada, Donald Hardesty and Eugene Hattori investigated sites associated with Chinese charcoal workers in the Cortez Mining District; in Oregon, John Fagan and Jo Reese focused on the Warrendale Cannery site; and in Texas, Edward

Staski researched early Chinese in El Paso. Other work took place in Phoenix, Arizona; German Gulch, Montana; and elsewhere.

Significant analytical reports focused on the artefacts and food bones from these and other investigations. Jerry Wylie and Richard Fike studied opium-smoking paraphernalia, particularly ceramic opium pipe bowls, while Harvey Steele and Alison Stenger separately performed compositional analyses of Chinese ceramics. To determine Chinese meat preferences, Sherri Gust analysed faunal remains from urban sites, and Julia Longenecker did the same for rural ones. Ruth Ann Sando and David Felton translated and analysed a ledger from a California Chinese-owned store, establishing the Chinese names of ceramic patterns, and quality and price of opium brands.

Some projects lasted into the 1990s and beyond. In California, that decade saw work by Roberta Greenwood on the Los Angeles Metro Rail Project. In Nevada, Sue Fawn Chung, Fred Frampton and Timothy Murphy excavated Carlin's Chinese cemetery; in Hawaii, Conrad Goodwin, Susan Lebo and others separately examined several sites in Honolulu's Chinatown, and, in Wyoming, Dudley Gardner investigated Rock Springs's Chinese community. In Idaho, Ronald James excavated a Snake River placer mining site. Other Idaho investigators also focused on placer mining remains, particularly at Centerville, Idaho City, Leesburg, Pierce and Warren, while excavations inside Idaho City's Pon Yam house yielded well-preserved remains of organic objects including firecrackers and incense sticks. Nevada archaeologists examined the Island Mountain townsite at Gold Creek, while Oregon projects took place in Portland and at the Ah Hee Diggings near Granite. Additional California work included studies of Folsom's Chinese cemetery, laundries in Oakland and Santa Barbara, and San Jose's Woolen Mills Chinatown site.

These and other projects have resulted in numerous site reports. In addition, recent masters' theses of note include Erika Johnson's investigation of Chinese blacksmithing, Nancy Summerlin's analysis of a three-burner wok stove, David Valentine's work on Nevada mining sites and Jeannie Yang's discussion of Oakland laundry workers, while doctoral dissertations have included Paul Chace's on Chinese temple rites in Marysville, California.

Further reading

Bell, P., Grimwade, G. and Ritchie, N. (1993) 'Archaeology of the overseas Chinese in Australia, New Zealand and Papua New Guinea: A select bibliography', *Australasian Society for Historical Archaeology Newsletter* 23(1): Supplement.

Chen, Y.-y. (2001) 'In the colonies of Tang: Historical archaeology of Chinese communities in the North Cariboo District, British Columbia (1860s–1940s)', doctoral dissertation, Simon Fraser University.

Greenwood, R.S. (1996) *Down by the Station: Los Angeles Chinatown, 1880–1933*, Monumenta Archaeologica, 18, Los Angeles: Institute of Archaeology, University of California.

Macgregor, P. (ed.) (1995) *Histories of the Chinese in Australasia and the South Pacific*, Melbourne: Museum of Chinese Australian History.

Pan, L. (ed.) (1999) *The Encyclopedia of the Chinese Overseas*, Cambridge, MA: Harvard University Press.

Ritchie, N.A. (1986) 'Archaeology and history of the Chinese in southern New Zealand during the nineteenth century: A study of acculturation, adaptation, and change', doctoral dissertation, University of Otago.

Wegars, P. (ed.) (1993) *Hidden Heritage: Historical Archaeology of the Overseas Chinese*, Amityville, NY: Baywood.

PRISCILLA WEGARS

P

Padre Island shipwrecks, Texas, USA

Two sixteenth-century Spanish shipwrecks found off the coast of southern Texas constitute the Padre Island shipwrecks. The location of the wrecks first became known in 1967.

History records that fifty-four ships left Spain in 1552 bound for the Spanish colonies in the New World. Sixteen of these vessels were scheduled to land in Mexico, and all of them survived the rough crossing. Other ships in the fleet were not so lucky, experiencing a host of problems, including the loss of the captain-general's ship in mid-Atlantic. Of the sixteen ships bound for Mexico, five were slated to make the return journey, with the remainder, following the conventions of the day, scheduled to be scrapped after landfall. After a year of waiting to leave, four of the ships – the *San Esteban*, the *Espíritu Santo*, the *Santa María de Yciar* and the *San Andrés* – decided to make the journey back across the Atlantic in 1554. They carried with them a cargo estimated by today's value in the millions of dollars (US). Twenty days after leaving port, three of the four vessels sank in a storm off Padre Island; only the *San Andrés* made it to Havana, where it had to be scrapped because of its poor condition. Scholars estimate that between 150 and 200 men lost their lives in the disaster.

A private salvaging company discovered the wreck of the *Espíritu Santo* in 1967 and removed numerous items of historical significance from it, including a solid-gold crucifix, a gold bar, silver disks, cannons and three extremely rare, sixteenth-century astrolabes. After a protracted legal battle with the State of Texas over ownership, the salvors received $313,000 in exchange for the artefacts. The artefacts are considered to be some of the earliest European objects discovered in the New World.

Archaeologists working for the State of Texas began to investigate the remains of the *San Esteban* in 1972. They started with a thorough magnetometer survey, and coupled the field research with an intensive archival project. They recovered hundreds of portable artefacts from the vessel, including anchors, cannons and tools. A number of items of aboriginal manufacture were also included among the finds. The archaeologists also located and documented a section of the keel, making it possible for experts to estimate the overall length of the ship as between 21 and 30 m.

The third ship that sank off Padre Island in 1554 was the *Santa María de Yciar*. Archaeologists believe that the construction of the Port Mansfield Channel destroyed this wreck site in the 1950s.

See also: Spanish colonialism

Further reading

Arnold, J.B., III and Weddle, R.S. (1978) *The Nautical Archaeology of Padre Island: The Spanish Shipwrecks of 1554*, New York: Academic Press.

CHARLES E. ORSER, JR

Palmares, Brazil

Palmares was a maroon settlement (see **maroon sites**) built by runaway African slaves in the backlands of north-eastern Brazil in the present State of Alagoas. Fugitive slaves created the settlement around 1605 in the hills that run parallel to the coast, and it existed until 1694, when the Portuguese finally destroyed it after several attacks. Many scholars have judged Palmares to be the most important maroon settlement in the history of the Atlantic region. Preliminary archaeological investigations were conducted at Palmares in 1992 and 1993 under the direction of Charles Orser and Pedro Funari.

Palmares is widely acknowledged as a significant historical place for several reasons, including:

1 that it was created early in colonial history and existed for many years in open defiance of the European superpowers;
2 at the height of its development (1670–94), it had a population as high as 20,000, the vast majority of whom had run away from the coastal Brazilian sugar plantations, thereby depleting the expensive labour supply;
3 it had a fully developed social and political organisation that incorporated a king and several local rulers;
4 it included as many as ten separate, runaway villages linked together in a complex political, economic and social network that also included several Portuguese settlements on the frontier as well as Native American villages; and
5 the last king of Palmares was Zumbi, a man who is today widely revered as a hero by Afro-Brazilians.

The initial archaeological research at the site was a survey and limited excavation programme intended to determine whether sites associated with Palmares could be discovered at the Sierra de Barriga, a large hill widely reputed to be the location of Macaco, the 'capital' of the 'kingdom'. The archaeological team discovered fourteen distinct sites, ranging in date from the seventeenth to the nineteenth centuries. One site in particular produced a collection of over 250 seventeenth-century artefacts, including unglazed pottery (probably of native manufacture) and tin-glazed earthenware (majolica), probably of either Dutch or Portuguese manufacture. The site also contained areas of burned earth and charcoal. These last finds were significant because **historical documents** indicate that the Portuguese, after their final, successful assault on the Macaco, burned its many structures to make the village uninhabitable in the future.

See also: Dutch colonialism; Portuguese colonialism

Further reading

Funari, P.P.A. (1999) 'Maroon, race, and gender: Palmares material culture and social relations in a runaway settlement', in P.P.A. Funari, M. Hall and S. Jones (eds) *Historical Archaeology: Back from the Edge*, London: Routledge, pp. 308–27.
Orser, C.E., Jr (1994) 'Toward a global historical archaeology: An example from Brazil', *Historical Archaeology* 28(1): 5–22.

CHARLES E. ORSER, JR

palynology

Palynology, a frequent companion to historical archaeology, is literally the study of *pale*, the Greek cognate of the Latin word *pollen*, meaning 'flour or dust'. Palynology is the scientific study of modern and fossil pollen, spores and palynomorphs, such as hystricospheres, dinoflagellates and microforaminifers.

See also: pollen analysis

JAMES SCHOENWETTER

pattern recognition

Pattern recognition, a method used to analyse artefact assemblages, was developed during the formative years of historical archaeology in the 1970s by Stanley South. The analysis technique was a central part of South's influential book *Method and Theory in Historical Archaeology*.

South was one of the most visible proponents of scientifically based historical archaeology, as opposed to more humanist approaches. With its emphasis upon hypothesis testing, problem-oriented research and identifying underlying culture process, scientifically based historical archaeology grew out of the **New Archaeology** in the USA during the 1960s and 1970s. In retrospect, a long-term contribution of the research agenda advanced by South in the late 1970s and early 1980s was the formalisation of historical archaeology as a recognised sub-discipline in archaeology. This maturation period in historical archaeology was also characterised by the standardisation of analysis methods, as illustrated by pattern recognition and **mean ceramic dating**.

Pattern recognition is based upon artefact functional analysis. South developed eight artefact functional categories or groups that correspond to the functional uses of specific artefacts recovered from eighteenth-century sites. The artefact functional categories consist of the Kitchen Group, Architectural Group, Furniture Group, Arms Group, Clothing Group, Personal Group, Tobacco Pipe Group and Activities Group. Each artefact group is further sub-divided by secondary artefact categories, such as ceramics, bottle glass and tableware within the Kitchen Group.

After the artefacts from an excavated site have been identified and catalogued, the objects are then tabulated and placed in the above functional groups by artefact counts. An artefact distribution for the site is then calculated by percentage, resulting in an artefact pattern. The resulting artefact distribution from a specific site is then compared to artefact patterns defined by South to identify how closely an assemblage matches pre-existing functional distributions. The Carolina Artefact Pattern is one of the artefact functional distributions originally defined by South. Containing a predominance of domestic artefacts, especially Kitchen Group items, the Carolina Artefact Pattern is regarded to be functionally indicative of domestic sites occupied during the colonial period.

In general, 80–90 per cent of the artefacts recovered from domestic sites consist of items related to the Kitchen and Architecture groups. The remaining 10–20 per cent of most artefact assemblages are thinly distributed among the remaining six artefact groups. Therefore, Kitchen and Architecture group items are the primary artefacts recovered from most domestic sites. In turn, the other six artefact groups represent secondary categories. A primary benefit of functional analysis is its usefulness in identifying site-specific activities. If one of the six secondary artefact groups is overrepresented in an assemblage, then it is immediately apparent that functionally specific activities occurred at a site or location within a site. For example, the location of a former dwelling at a farmstead will usually contain a distinctive domestic distribution, characterised by a large proportion of Kitchen and Architecture group items. Likewise, a blacksmith shop or tool shed on a house lot would produce metal scrap and tool fragments, indicated functionally by a larger than normal proportion of these items in their respective artefact groups and sub-categories. Consequently, through careful excavation and subsequent analysis of different contexts and spatial locations, the cultural landscape and site-specific activities at historic sites can be effectively reconstructed via functional analysis.

Throughout the 1980s, pattern recognition was used widely among historical archaeologists. An unexpected trend eventually developed during this period that served to undermine functional analysis and the use of pattern recognition. Pattern recognition was based on the assumption of whole culture patterns and the idea that assemblages associated with or produced by similar ethnic, racial and economic groups would produce similar artefact distributions. Conversely, it was also assumed that assemblages associated with dissimilar groups or households would likewise produce mutually exclusive functional distributions. This aspect of scientific historical archaeology articulated by South, which focused upon defining artefact patterns for specific temporal-cultural contexts, inadvertently became the main goal of many archaeological studies in the 1980s, to the point that the activity was eventually questioned by South, in a journal article called 'Whither pattern?' In this article, South emphasised that defining or labelling artefact distributions with pattern descriptors, such as the Carolina Slave Pattern, should not be the primary goal of historical archaeology. Orser, in an article entitled 'On plantations and patterns', likewise critiqued the method in the early 1990s, a few years after South's comments first appeared in the late 1980s.

Perhaps the most relevant criticism of functional analysis identified by Orser is its synchronic and largely atemporal character. Simply put, functional analysis serves to compress and hence eliminate all of the temporal dynamic and variability associated with artefact assemblages. By using functional analysis, all of the temporal variation associated with historical archaeological sites, often encompassing a hundred years or more, is reduced to a single artefact distribution. Orser's criticism of functional analysis was not ignored and, since the 1990s, the method has fallen into disuse among many archaeologists. Ironically, however, although many historical archaeologists stopped using functional analysis, a suitable alternative has yet to be developed or introduced in the discipline. Hence, in many respects, an analytical void was created when functional analysis fell into disuse among the historical archaeological community. After almost a decade since Orser's critique of pattern recognition, many historical archaeologists would probably agree that functional analysis is a useful and indispensable analysis method. It is especially beneficial when it is used for its most relevant and productive purpose – defining functionally based artefact distributions that do not possess pattern labels or are expected to illustrate whole culture patterns. Acknowledging an important point made by Charles Orser, however, functional analysis is limited in its ability to reconstruct or to illustrate diachronic process, which is a fundamental goal of historical archaeology.

Further reading

South, S.A. (1988) 'Whither pattern?', *Historical Archaeology* 22(1): 25–8.
—— (1977) *Method and Theory in Historical Archaeology*, New York: Academic Press.
Orser, C.E., Jr (1990) 'On plantations and patterns', *Historical Archaeology* 23(2): 28–40.

MARK D. GROOVER

pearlware

The contemporary name for the ceramic pearlware (see **ceramics**) was 'china glaze', although Josiah Wedgwood coined the name 'pearl white' for his own pearlware, introduced in 1779. Although credited with inventing pearlware, Wedgwood merely adopted a type of ware already in production. George Miller has shown that 'china glaze' was made in Staffordshire by 1775; thereafter its manufacture increased rapidly.

Pearlware is a lead-glazed **earthenware** similar to **creamware**. It was made from white-firing ball clay from Devon and Dorset, and china clay from Cornwall. Calcined flint strengthened the clay body, which was biscuit fired before decoration and glazing. The liquid glaze was based upon lead oxide, but had a bluish-grey colour derived from minute quantities of cobalt and copper.

Pearlware deliberately imitated Chinese **porcelain**, both in colour and decoration. Early pearlware and creamware forms are interchangeable, but distinctive pearlware types soon emerged. Most significant was the moulded shell edge used predominantly on plates. By *c.* 1810, 'edged' wares – the contemporary term – were the cheapest type of decorated tableware and were widely used throughout the first half of the nineteenth century. The moulded shell edge was normally coloured underglaze in blue, less commonly in green or occasionally in red, brown or yellow. The popularity of edged wares declined steadily from the 1830s as plates with printed decoration became more affordable.

Miller and Hunter have demonstrated how changes in the shell edge moulding can be used for dating. Florid rococo moulding on irregular scalloped rims, sometimes with festoons, was typical from 1775 to *c.* 1810. Around 1800, mouldings evolved with even-scalloped rims, a type that lasted until *c.* 1840. New varieties of moulded edge patterns – not technically shell edges – were introduced around 1820 to counter the fall in prices of edged wares, which began after 1812; they remained in production until the 1840s. Prices continued to fall and edge patterns became more simple. The scallops disappeared between the 1840s and 1860s, and moulded detail declined after the 1850s. Wares of this type survived into the twentieth century with simple blue-painted edges but without moulded detail.

Pearlware was well-suited for decoration. Underglaze painted designs depicting stylised chinoiserie landscapes in cobalt blue were common from 1775 until about 1810. By the 1790s, new 'earth' colours – yellow, orange, brown and red – were introduced to supplement the familiar blue. Brighter 'chrome' colours of pinks and greens were introduced around 1830. Polychrome floral decoration was common on teawares and constituted one of the main exports from Staffordshire to North America during the late eighteenth and early nineteenth centuries. Limited use was made of overglaze painted decoration on teawares from the eighteenth century into the 1820s, but patterns tended to be restricted to simple floral designs. Other types of decoration include sponging, often in conjunction with underglaze painted designs, and metallic lustres in pink, silver and copper.

From the 1780s, underglaze transfer-printed decoration in blue became popular; prints in brown were in use by the 1790s. Initially, designs were inspired by Chinese landscapes, with patterns such as 'Broseley' or 'Two Temples' becoming dominant on teawares. The 'willow pattern', established by the early nineteenth century, was first used solely for tablewares. By about 1810, botanical and European subjects were becoming popular and prints in other colours – green, pink, purple and grey – were introduced in the mid-1820s. Wares with heavy 'flow blue' decoration were particularly associated with the North American market from the 1820s to the 1840s. Printed wares were the most expensive decorated earthenwares of the period, although their price in relation to undecorated wares declined steadily from the end of the eighteenth century.

Slip-decorated pearlwares were widespread. 'Industrial slipwares' or 'factory-made slipwares' were known in their day as 'dipt', 'banded', 'variegated' or 'mocha' wares. Despite their lively and colourful decoration, these were the cheapest decorated hollow wares available. They enjoyed widespread popularity from the 1770s to c. 1900.

Pearlware glaze occurs in varying shades of blue, but a lightening of colour towards white may be seen during the 1820s and 1830s. The transition from pearlware to whiteware is difficult to pinpoint, for blue tints appear in earthenware glazes well into the second half of the nineteenth century. By the early nineteenth century, manufacturers and consumers were no longer making distinctions between the bodies and glazes of their refined earthenwares. Instead, wares were normally listed according to their decoration (i.e. edged, dipped, painted and printed). These terms could refer to creamwares or pearlwares, but it is evident that the majority of the decorated wares were what we would call pearlwares. This contemporary lack of distinction between pearlware and creamware excuses the frequent problems experienced today in distinguishing between the two, and between the contemporary whiteware and **ironstone**. Essentially, all of these common types evolved out of and around each other, and start and end dates are elusive.

Pearlwares include the whole range of tea, table and toilet wares. They were made by all of the major British factories, especially in **Stoke-on-Trent**, Yorkshire, Newcastle-upon-Tyne and Sunderland, South Wales, Scotland and Belfast, and it is difficult to distinguish between the wares of individual centres.

Further reading

Lockett, T.A. and Halfpenny, P.A. (1986) *Creamware and Pearlware*, Stoke-on-Trent: City Museum and Art Gallery.

Miller, G.L. (1991) 'A revised set of CC index values for classification and economic scaling of English ceramics from 1787 to 1880', *Historical Archaeology* 25(1): 1–25.

—— (1987) 'Origins of Josiah Wedgwood's pearlware,' *Northeast Historical Archaeology* 16: 80–92.

Miller, G.L. and Hunter, R.R. (1990) 'English shell edged earthenware: Alias Leeds ware, alias feather edge', in *35th Wedgwood International Seminar*, pp. 107–136.

Miller, G.L., Martin A.S. and Dickinson, N.S. (1994) 'Changing consumption patterns. English ceramics and the American market from 1770 to 1840', in C.E. Hutchins (ed.) *Everyday Life in the Early Republic*, Winterthur: Henry Francis du Pont Winterthur Museum, pp. 219–48.

Sussman, L. (1997) *Mocha, Banded, Cat's Eye, and Other Factory-Made Slipware*, Studies in Northeast Historical Archaeology No. 1, Boston: Council for Northeast Historical Archaeology.

DAVID BARKER

Peru

The modern nation of Peru formed the core of a large Spanish colonial administrative unit, the viceroyalty of Nueva Castilla, initially governed by conquistador Francisco Pizarro. The viceroyalty originally encompassed part of what is now Ecuador in the north through modern Bolivia in the south. Archaeology of the colonial period in this vast area is an underdeveloped field compared to that in other areas of Latin America and has been directed in two ways: towards sites representing the European conquerors and settlers, and towards sites occupied by indigenous populations.

With respect to the archaeology of the Spanish colonial experience, the approach has been largely art historical, with attention centred on the art and architecture of urban elites. Archaeological investigations have been incidental to the architectural restoration of churches, monasteries and residences of colonial elites in all the major colonial cities, with the recovered artefacts – silver, paintings, porcelains, furniture – headed for private or public museums. Examples of note, besides myriad structures in the colonial capital of coastal Lima, include the Iglesia de Santo Domingo/Qoricancha in the Inca capital of **Cuzco** and the Convento de la Recoleta in the beautiful southern city of Arequipa. Elite residential architecture shows clear ties to that of Spain, especially Andalusia, with grand entrances, open central courtyards and second-storey enclosed balconies.

Archaeological investigations of sites occupied by native Andean peoples during the sixteenth century and later typically have been undertaken as adjuncts to large, prehistoric archaeology projects or in the context of ethnohistorical research, especially of the Inca. Methods and theories informing the excavations are primarily those of anthropology. For example, Mary Van Buren's excavations at Torata Alta, near **Moquegua** in southern Peru, were carried out to evaluate an ethnohistorical-ecological model of indigenous 'vertical economies' – producer–trader colonies established at different elevations in the Andes. The site's orthogonal layout indicated a planned settlement and excavations revealed sixteenth- and seventeenth-century occupation. However, was

Torata Alta a pre-conquest colony established for resource procurement or was it a Spanish *reducción*, a resettlement of native peoples? Her studies suggest it could have been both, as the residents were likely Lupaqas from the high elevations around Lake Titicaca. However, they may have lived in the Torata valley for its advantages in the new colonial economy – specifically, escaping forced labour in the silver mines – rather than as an ecological adaptation for resource access.

One problem in the development of historical archaeology in Peru has been the lack of a useful chronology. Most existing chronologies for the Andes are based on critical turning points in history, either secular or ecclesiastical, which may or may not have material correlates recognisable in the archaeological record. One of the first efforts to develop a working chronology came from art historian George Kubler in 1946, who presciently noted another important missing element: intensive study of colonial-period material culture. Like the eologists have been disadvantaged by Spain's refusal-cum-inability to reliably supply its Pacific colonies with the kinds of European goods useful for dating sites in other areas. Also, the colonists' efforts to establish convenient sources of production within the Peruvian viceroyalty, although documented by historians, generally have not been systematically pursued by archaeologists.

Albeit sporadic, archaeological pursuit of colonial manufacturing has been sufficient to suggest that Peru's emerging historical archaeology is an **industrial archaeology** of sorts, focusing on production and trade. The Moquegua Bodegas Project, the first major systematic historical archaeology project in Peru, addressed the development of the valley's wine and brandy agro-industry through mapping and excavations at some of the valley's 130 *bodegas*, or wine hacienda sites. Heather Lechtman's review of metallurgical sites, while primarily directed toward pre-Columbian activity, also included colonial-period mines. The *brea* or tar for caulking wooden ships sailing out of Peru's harbour at Callao (Lima) and for sealing **earthenware** olive jars used in shipping Peruvian wine and brandy may have come from petroleum seeps along the Ecuadorian coast, which have been investigated archaeologically. Excavations of a colonial-period *tambo* or checkpoint along a trade route north of Trujillo indicated probable construction in the eighteenth century. Mary Van Buren's investigations of the silver-mining industry of 'Upper Peru' – Potosí and Porco in modern Bolivia – included excavations at an elite residence in Tarapaya.

As elsewhere, the most commonly recovered artefacts in historical sites in Peru are fragments of pottery, but it is not yet clear when or where imitations of Iberian majolicas – local tin-enamelled earthenwares – began to be produced. Excavations typically reveal a combination of unslipped earthenwares, some showing the mixed traits of **colonoware pottery**, Andean-produced tin--enamelled wares, and imported majolicas (from Spain, Mexico and Panama), porcelains, and later European wares (transfer prints etc.). Potters' guilds are said to have been in existence in Lima by 1577 and a workshop for glazed ware was contracted to be built in Cuzco in 1588. Tin-enamelled pottery from Moquegua's wine haciendas is believed to have been manufactured somewhere in the southern Andes, perhaps in Cuzco or in the Lake Titicaca basin. It is rather poorly made and decorated with green and purplish-brown/black on a very pale green or sharp-yellow ground. Very little blue and white or imported majolica was recovered at these rural sites.

See also: Spanish colonialism

Further reading

Flores Espinoza, I., García Soto, R. and Huertas, V.L. (1981) *Investigación arqueológica-histórica de la Casa Osambela (o de Oquendo) – Lima*, Lima, Peru: Instituto Nacional de Cultura.

Gasco, J., Smith, G.C. and Fournier-García, P. (eds) (1997) *Approaches to the Historical Archaeology of Mexico, Central and South America*, Los Angeles, CA: The Institute of Archaeology.

Jamieson, R. (2000) *Domestic Architecture and Power: The Historical Archaeology of Colonial Ecuador*, New York: Kluwer Academic/Plenum Press.

Van Buren, M. (1999) 'Tarapaya: An elite Spanish residence near colonial Potosí in comparative perspective', *Historical Archaeology* 33(2): 108–22.

—— (1996) 'Rethinking the vertical archipelago:
Ethnicity, exchange, and history in the South Central Andes', *American Anthropologist* 98: 338–51.

PRUDENCE M. RICE

pewter

Pewter is a metal alloy that has tin as its major element. It can also contain copper, lead, antimony and bismuth. A mixture of 80 per cent tin and about 20 per cent copper is reputed to make the best pewter. Eighteenth-century English pewterers referred to the finest pewter by the name 'britannia metal'.

The discovery of pewter antedates written history, and many ancient cultures used it. Pewter was widely used in Europe by the Middle Ages, and colonial Europeans transferred their use of pewter to their colonies, where it was widely used for tableware. The objects typically made from pewter include teapots, candle holders, lamp bases, inkwells, plates, mugs and implements such as ladles and spoons. Like later makers of **ceramics**, individual pewterers stamped their wares with a unique mark that identified their products. For example, Nathaniel Austin, a pewterer and goldsmith in Boston in the 1741–1816 period, marked his wares with 'N AUSTIN' and 'N A'.

Pewter objects dominated the colonial marketplace during the early eighteenth century, but by the end of the century many objects once made of pewter began to be replaced by ceramics. Consumers throughout Britain and British America, eager to own the most modern objects possible, readily replaced their old pewter objects with the new ceramic pieces. Their interest in ceramics exploded with the increased popularity of tea drinking and the accoutrements needed for its consumption (see **tea/tea ceremony**). In addition to decreased demand because of the rise of the powerful ceramics industry, pewterers had the problem that their wares were durable and seldom needed to be replaced. A pewter plate simply did not wear out as easily as ceramics, and it would not break if dropped.

The durability of pewter has a serious ramification for historical archaeology because pewter objects are seldom found in archaeological deposits. Pewter objects frequently appear in **probate inventories** and in other historical records. Pewterers are equally well represented in historical documents, but their workshops seldom contain evidence of their labours because it was easy to clean up after the manufacturing process. So prevalent is the difference between historical records – where pewter is frequently mentioned – and archaeological deposits – where pewter is practically absent – that Ann Smart Martin has justifiably referred to it as the 'missing artefact'.

See also: non-ferrous metal

Further reading

Crossley, D. (1990) *Post-Medieval Archaeology in Britain*, London: Leicester University Press.

Kerfoot, J.B. (1924) *American Pewter*, New York: Bonanza.

Martin, A.S. (1989) 'The role of pewter as missing artifact: Consumer attitudes toward tablewares in late 18th century Virginia', *Historical Archaeology* 23(2): 1–27.

CHARLES E. ORSER, JR

Philadelphia, Pennsylvania, USA

Philadelphia, Pennsylvania, was the largest city in the American colonies in 1765–1810. The Declaration of Independence and Constitution were both adopted in the structure now venerated as Independence Hall, and Philadelphia served as the capital of the USA during the first decade of its existence (1790–1800). Much of the archaeological research conducted in Philadelphia was related to the creation of Independence National Historical Park.

The Walnut Street Prison, constructed in 1775, incorporated reforms such as solitary confinement and segregation between male and female inmates. Excavation of a portion of the 1797 prison workshop by John Cotter revealed remnants of the manufacturing activities documented in historical accounts. Analysis revealed an assemblage that was consistent with the 'Carolina Artefact Pattern' described by Stanley South, indicating that the workshop assemblage was very similar to domestic deposits encountered at the sites of relatively prosperous colonial and early Federal-period inhabitants throughout the Eastern Seaboard.

During the early 1980s, John Milner Associates, in conjunction with Lawrence Angle and Leslie Rankin-Hill, analysed over 140 burials from the First African Baptist Church Burial Ground, providing a detailed view of the living conditions of antebellum free African Americans. The burial ground was first used in 1822. By 1848, the church had dissolved and the cemetery was abandoned, soon to be covered by residential and industrial development. The **human osteology** analysis indicated a highly stressed population with a very low standard of nutritional health. The investigators also noted burial customs such as placing a single coin near the head of the deceased, which may reflect the survival of African mortuary customs.

While most of the archaeology performed at Independence National Historical Park supported traditional reconstructions similar to contemporaneous projects in Williamsburg, Virginia, the Franklin Court project includes innovative presentations of archaeological data. Benjamin Franklin initiated construction of his three-storey house in 1763. Franklin's house was demolished in 1812, and the archaeological and historical data were deemed insufficient to permit an accurate reconstruction. Instead, the architectural firm of Venturi and Rauch designed a 'ghost house', a three-dimensional steel frame that outlines the dimensions of Franklin's house. Some archaeological excavations have been covered with glass portals that allow visitors to examine foundation fragments, wells and privies.

See also: urban archaeology

Further reading

Angel, J.L., Kelley, J.O., Parrington, M. and Pinter, S. (1987) 'Life stresses on the free black community as represented by the First African Baptist Church, Philadelphia, 1823–1841', *American Journal of Physical Anthropology* 7: 213–29.

Cotter, J., Roberts, D.G. and Parrington, M. (1993) *The Buried Past: An Archaeological History of Philadelphia*, Philadelphia: University of Pennsylvania Press.

Cotter, J., Moss, R.W., Gill, B.C. and Kim, J. (1988) *The Walnut Street Prison Workshop*, Philadelphia: The Athenaeum of Philadelphia.

Parrington, M. and Roberts, D.G. (1990) 'Demographic, cultural, and bioanthropological aspects of a nineteenth-century free black population in Philadelphia, Pennsylvania', J.E. Buikstra (ed.) *A Life in Science: Papers in Honor of J. Lawrence Angel*, Kampsville, IL: Center for American Archaeology, pp. 138–70.

Rankin-Hill, L.M. (1997) *A Biohistory of Nineteenth-Century Afro-Americans: The Burial Remains of a Philadelphia Cemetery*, Westport, CT: Bergin & Garvey.

TERRENCE W. EPPERSON

photographic information

Historical archaeologists make abundant use of information contained in photographs. Like all archaeologists, they rely on photography to help document their excavation work. Historical archaeologists researching nineteenth- and twentieth-century sites, however, often have recourse to photographs that are contemporary with the site's period of occupation. Contemporary photographs can contain myriad amounts of important information, including details for the dates of a site's occupation, its usage, the construction methods used for its buildings, the arrangement of the buildings across the site, the environmental setting at different times of year, and so forth.

Aristotle was perhaps the first person known to have anticipated photography, but the first crude camera, the camera obscura, would not appear until many centuries later in the 1500s. It was not until 1826, however, that a French inventor created a way to imprint permanent pictures on a metal plate. The famous daguerreotype was an improvement on this early photographic method, but the first picture reproduced on paper was not made until 1839. Additional photographic improvements, in both equipment and paper, occurred throughout the nineteenth century, increasingly making photography a regular part of Western daily life.

The history of photography means that archaeologists studying the mid- to late nineteenth century and all of the twentieth century may have access to photographs that are directly relevant to the sites and the people they study. Photography can provide information about both **architecture** and **culture**. Much of the information depicted in the photography may be available in no other source.

In terms of architecture, archaeologists conducting investigations at fortification (see **fortifications**) sites often have the advantage of photographic information. Forts are places where important historic events have often occurred and, given their significance, photographers may have left a detailed record documenting how they were built and manned. For example, when Stanley South was investigating the first Fort Moultrie near Charleston, South Carolina, dating from 1776 to 1783, his research, both archaeological and archival, revealed a second (1794–1804) and a third (built in 1808) fort as well. Photographs taken in the 1860s helped South to interpret the design of the third fort and to learn how the three had evolved over time. Similarly, Anton Van Vollenhoven made extensive use of late nineteenth-century photographs in his study of the military fortifications in Pretoria, South Africa.

Archaeologists can also use old photographs for information about the construction of houses and other buildings belonging to men and women who seldom wrote about themselves. Pictures of such **vernacular architecture** are especially meaningful simply because of the lack of other kinds of documentation. For example, images of stone and mud cottages in rural **Ireland** have provided information about general construction techniques and their important regional variations.

Photographic information can also be invaluable in helping to document forgotten ways of life. Archaeologist William Adams made an especially noteworthy use of photographic information in his study of Silcott, Washington. Silcott was a small farming community located on the extreme eastern edge of the State of Washington in the US northwest. Because the dates of Adams's interest were from 1900 to 1930 – a period during which the town underwent significant cultural change – he was able to make expert use of contemporaneous photographic information. His goal in the research was to present a thorough anthropological account of what life had been like in the little town during the early twentieth century. As a result, he was able to use the photographic information for many different purposes: to document the number of buildings in the town during the three decades of his interest and to illustrate their juxtaposition to one another, to show the type of ferry used to transport people and goods across the nearby Snake River and to illustrate the residents' daily activities, such as washing clothes, herding and shearing sheep, and loading hay. Adams was also able to use the photographic collection from Silcott to illustrate family composition, from formal portraits and informal pictures taken outdoors. He also discovered that the photographs could be used to provide functional information about certain artefacts. For example, when examining a photograph of three women washing clothes outdoors, he noticed tin cans used as flower pots in a window in the background. The people's use of tin cans in this way is certainly not unusual or unimaginable, but the photograph documented its use at Silcott during the 1900–30 period. This is a small find to be sure, but it helps to flesh out the historical picture of daily life in the town and to demonstrate visually that individual artefacts can have many uses.

Archaeologists interested in periods both before the invention of the portable camera and after a site's abandonment can also occasionally make use of photography in their studies. It is possible that people may have visited an ancient site for a reason having nothing whatsoever to do with archaeology, but that while they were there they may have inadvertently provided photographic information that an archaeologist may find useful. An archaeologist interested in an ancient earthwork in Europe, for instance, may discover from photographs that the site was an important locale in the 1930s for the worship of the sun. During the investigation of **Millwood Plantation**, in rural South Carolina, a photograph was discovered showing a small group of friends having a Sunday picnic at the long-abandoned site. This picture was intended to provide a record of the good time the friends had that day, but the archaeologists discovered it had a completely different value. Because it showed a standing building in the background, the picture proved that some struc-

tures continued to stand at the site long after its original residents had moved on. A picture postcard from the same period indicated that some of the standing buildings had been used both as picnic shelters and as cabins for people camping at the site.

See also: plantation archaeology

Further reading

Adams, W.H. (1977) *Silcott, Washington: Ethnoarchaeology of a Rural American Community*, Pullman: Laboratory of Anthropology, Washington State University.

South, S. (1974) *Palmetto Parapets: Exploratory Archaeology at Fort Moultrie, South Carolina, 38CH50*, Columbia: Institute of Archaeology and Anthropology, University of South Carolina.

Van Vollenhoven, A.C. (1999) *The Military Fortifications of Pretoria, 1880–1902*, Pretoria: Technikon.

CHARLES E. ORSER, JR

pictorial information

A central goal of historical archaeology is to achieve greater understanding of the recent past. Interpretation in historical archaeology often considers different scales of inquiry. Historical archaeologists strive not only to answer lower-order questions about the people who lived at a site, but also to address higher-order questions related to larger historical trends and archaeological theory. To learn what **everyday life** was like for our forebears, archaeologists begin their research by asking several basic questions, not unlike time detectives or historical reporters: Who were the people who lived at a specific site? When did they live there and for how long? In what kinds of dwellings did they live? What types of household items did they use? In addition to these seemingly simple questions, historical archaeologists also ask more complex 'how' and 'why' questions. These higher-order questions pertain to the processes of culture and historical change that transpired while a site was occupied.

To interpret the archaeological record and gain enhanced understanding of the past, historical archaeologists use a broad range of historical information sources. Property records, inventories of personal possessions owned at the time of death, wills, diaries, family papers and the recollections of informants are examples of primary historical sources scrutinised by historical archaeologists to address lower-order, site-specific questions.

Pictorial information is a valuable type of primary historical document (see **historical documents**) or information source that historical archaeologists rely upon. Visual art is important archaeologically since it was created during the time periods that historical archaeologists investigate. Pictorial information is consequently used to study or contextualise a specific cultural setting or period. For example, the subjects and scenes portrayed by artists help archaeologists understand the architectural styles and construction methods that were used by the former residents of sites during specific time periods. Likewise, pictorial information also helps historical archaeologists identify different types of artefacts.

Representing an ethnographic, visual record of the past, works of art such as paintings, woodcuts and engravings are examples of pictorial information sources. Some of the most prevalent illustrations examined by archaeologists are genre paintings depicting everyday household scenes and public settings. Paintings, sketches and engravings of dwelling interiors – especially kitchens, dining scenes and living areas – are especially useful, since they portray many of the objects recovered archaeologically. Illustrations of taverns and work situations depicting period tools and equipment are also valuable information sources. Formal portraits of individuals are also useful, since they often contain details related to dress, costume and personal adornment.

Ivor Noël Hume and Stanley South are two senior historical archaeologists in the USA who have effectively used pictorial information to interpret artefacts and features encountered during excavations. Noël Hume pioneered this method and has used it as a standard analysis technique since the 1970s. As discussed in the book *Martin's Hundred*, Noël Hume assembled a large collection of pictorial reference information. The images were obtained from diverse sources such as pictures of paintings clipped from magazines, slides, slide catalogues, postcards and picture books. The images were used by Noël Hume to address problems of archaeological interpretation – especially feature and artefact identification.

For example, Noël Hume consulted historical, pictorial sources and successfully identified several puzzling archaeological features encountered at Wolstenholme Towne, a previously unknown early seventeenth-century English settlement near Williamsburg, Virginia. During excavations at the site in the late 1970s, several enclosed compounds were investigated. In two compounds, earthfast timber dwellings were enclosed by lightly constructed fences. An adjacent fort, in contrast, was surrounding by a substantial palisade. In several locations at the site, the fence lines encircling the compounds contained discontinuous segments of a narrow trench. Noël Hume speculated that the odd features were slot trenches used to seat wide wooden planks for slot fences. This hunch was substantiated when Noël Hume and his colleagues located a fifteenth-century woodcut depicting workers raising a slot fence. Likewise, an eighteenth-century sketch located by the research team also depicted a slot fence surrounding a farmhouse. Both of the illustrations independently corroborated archaeological interpretation of the trench features that were encountered at Wolstenholme Towne.

In addition to helping to identify archaeological features and dwelling styles, pictorial information is often used to identify artefacts – especially the former appearance of complete objects based upon archaeologically recovered fragments. Noël Hume, for example, found numerous paintings that contained objects very similar to items recovered from Wolstenholme Towne, ranging from table ceramics to glassware and armour. Similarly, Stanley South effectively used pictorial sources to identify artefacts recovered from **Santa Elena**, a fortified Spanish settlement on the coast of South Carolina that was occupied between the 1560s and 1580s. As presented in his monograph *Spanish Artefacts from Santa Elena*, South relied on sixteenth-century paintings and sketches to help to identify and contextualise archaeologically recovered kitchen items, construction hardware, armour fragments, clothing artefacts and several examples of jewellery.

Although pictorial information is a valuable information source, Noël Hume cautions that, for artefacts, the method should be restricted to identification alone. Artefacts recovered from excavations that are depicted in dated paintings should not be used subsequently to date a site. Although this method is tempting to use, after careful study of different painters Noël Hume concluded that the scenes in many paintings are works of fiction, since they often depict similar individuals, settings and furnishings in slightly modified situations or arrangements. Consequently, household items in paintings, such as table ceramics or glass ware, were often mental visual props of the artist that were used throughout their career. Consequently, depicted objects may have been manufactured much earlier in the formative part of the artist's life than the actual date when the portrait was painted.

See also: historical documents

Further reading

Noël Hume, I. (1982) *Martin's Hundred: The Discovery of a Lost Colonial Virginia Settlement*, New York: Alfred A. Knopf.
South, S.A., Skowronek, R.K. and Johnson, R.E. (1988) *Spanish Artefacts from Santa Elena*, Columbia: South Carolina Institute of Archaeology and Anthropology.

MARK D. GROOVER

pilgrimage sites

The location of pilgrimage shrines is significant for political or economic history, and, for cults. Cults were developed at busy, accessible destinations or along trade routes (e.g. Rome, Mecca), and at natural features (e.g. Benares) or remote sites (e.g. Olympia, Greece; Croagh Patrick, Ireland). The sites tend to evince cycles of development. For instance, in Western Europe, cults of relics boomed *c.* AD 1050–1200, prompting rebuilding of **churches**. In the course of culture change, major shrines were prone to **assimilation** or syncretism (e.g. **Christianisation** of Izamal, Yucatan).

Typical ancillary features include provision for pilgrims' board and lodging. Many routes were provided with improved roads and bridges (e.g. St Ives, Huntingdonshire, **England**) and acquired inns, temples or churches, additional shrines and even castles. Many major shrines attracted secondary cults and monasteries (e.g. Bhubaneswar, India).

See also: Crusades

N. JAMES

pipe stem dating

Pipe stem dating is a kind of **formula dating** and it is wholly unique to historical archaeology. White-clay smoking pipes were commonly made from the mid-sixteenth century to the early twentieth century. A smoking pipe consists of two parts, a small bowl and a long stem. The fragile white-clay pipes broke easily when dropped, leaving many more pieces of stem than bowl. Thus, historical archaeologists regularly find hundreds or even thousands of pipe fragments at their sites. For example, archaeologists excavating at **Fort Michilimackinac**, Michigan, an outpost of eighteenth-century **French colonialism**, collected 5,328 pipe fragments between 1959 and 1966. Almost 82 per cent of these were pipe stem fragments.

In the 1950s, pioneer US historical archaeologist J.C. Harrington examined over 50,000 pipe stems from **Jamestown**, Virginia, a seat of **English colonialism** in North America. Harrington observed that the size of the hole through the stem, or 'bore', appeared to be smaller in later specimens. After measuring 330 stems from colonial sites in Virginia, using a set of drill bits, he discovered that the bores did grow progressively smaller through time. Stems dating from 1620 to 1650 had bores that generally measured 8/64th of an inch (31.7 mm), whereas between 1750 and 1800 most bores were only about 4/64th of an inch (15.9 mm).

In 1961, Lewis Binford realised that Harrington's observations could be converted into a statistical regression formula. With the bore diameter plotted on the X axis and the date on the Y axis, the regression formula will show the precise relationship between bore size and date. The formula devised by Binford is $Y = 1931.85 - 38.26X$, where Y is the mean date to be calculated, 1931.85 is the statistical date that pipe stem bores should theoretically disappear and 38.26 is the number of years that it took for a pipe stem bore to be reduced by 1/64th of an inch (1.6 mm). To obtain X, the mean date of the collection, one must first multiply the number of pipe stems by the number of 64th of an inch in their measurement. Thus, seven stems measuring 6/64th of an inch equals 42, and 35 stems measuring 7/64th of an inch equals 245. After adding all the products together, one must divide by the total number of pipe stems to obtain the mean date of the pipe stems.

Most archaeologists were immediately enthusiastic about Binford's idea, and some began to experiment with the formula itself. Robert Heighton and Kathleen Deagan discovered that the regression line was curved rather than straight. They reasoned that bores reach a minimum diameter and then stay constant after about AD 1800. Lee Hanson also noticed that the regression line was curved, but observed that the slope of the line was greater in the 1620–1725 period than later, meaning that the rate of decrease in bore diameters was greatest in the early period. Another historical archaeologist, Ivor Noël Hume, found that the formula works best with samples of over 900 stems deposited between 1680 and 1760.

CHARLES E. ORSER, JR

pipes, smoking

Smoking pipes can be ubiquitous artefacts on many archaeological sites that were occupied during and after the late sixteenth century. Historical archaeologists have learned that smoking pipes can provide both temporal and cultural information. Smoking pipes consist of two major elements: the bowl and the stem.

People have made smoking pipes from several different kinds of material, including stone; coarse, red clay; and fine, white clay. Stone pipes are usually associated with indigenous peoples and, in the case of many cultures such as **Native Americans**, were used prior to European contact.

In the USA, the red stone pipes made of pipestone (also called catlinite) constitute the famous 'peace pipes'. Native Americans usually made pipes with short stems and Europeans adopted these pipes in the late sixteenth century, just as they were becoming familiar with the habit of smoking tobacco. Beginning in the late sixteenth century, however, the long-stemmed pipe – made of fine, white clay – became widely popular. In the nineteenth century, people often referred to these pipes as 'churchwardens'. Important centres of white-clay pipe manufacture existed in **England**, Holland, **Ireland** and elsewhere. Late eighteenth-century pipe manufacturers produced short-, or 'stub'-stemmed pipes (of **redware**) alongside the long-stemmed varieties.

Pipes can carry information about the relative dates of their manufacture. Studies have shown that pipe bowls became increasingly larger through time as USA-grown tobacco became more plentiful throughout the world. In addition, pipemakers slowly changed the angle of the bowl relative to the stem, so that the angle of the earliest pipes is obtuse, whereas it approximates 90° in the latest pipes. Archaeologists have also developed a **pipe stem dating** method that can be used to provide dates for large collections of stem fragments.

Pipemakers, both indigenous and mass-producing, often included intricate decorations on their pipes. Many Native American and African cultures decorated their pipes with animal motifs, while pipemakers in the USA and Europe regularly used patriotic designs and slogans, geometric patterns, human faces and botanical motifs, such as grapes, trees and shamrocks. Research in the **Chesapeake region** of the USA indicates that both Native Americans and enslaved Africans often etched plain white-clay pipes with designs they found especially meaningful, such as animals and star patterns.

Many pipemakers also stamped their products with **makers' marks**. Archaeologists know, for example, that white-clay pipes marked with 'L E' were probably made by Llewellin Evans, of Bristol, England, from about 1661 to 1686. Makers' marks can appear on the bowl, the stem or the heel, a small, flat projection beneath the base of the bowl. Archaeologists can use these marks to identify the dates of a pipe's manufacture as well as to develop ideas about the marketing and transportation of these mass-produced items.

Further reading

Emerson, M.C. (1994) 'Decorated clay tobacco pipes from the Chesapeake: An African connection', in P.A. Shackel and B.J. Little (eds) *Historical Archaeology of the Chesapeake*, Washington, DC: Smithsonian Institution Press, pp. 35–49.

Mouer, L.D. (1993) 'Chesapeake creoles: The creation of folk culture in colonial Virginia', in T.R. Reinhart and D.J. Pogue (eds) *The Archaeology of 17th-Century Virginia*, Richmond: Archaeological Society of Virginia, pp. 105–66.

Noël Hume, I. (1970) *A Guide to Artifacts of Colonial America*, New York: Alfred A. Knopf.

Walker, I.C. (1977) *Clay Tobacco-Pipes, with Particular Reference to the Bristol Industry*, Ottawa: Parks Canada.

CHARLES E. ORSER, JR

plantation archaeology

The 1492 rediscovery of the New World created fresh opportunities for European nations and individuals to acquire additional wealth. Fertile land and Europe's intense appetite for sugar, tobacco, rice and finally cotton attracted English, Portuguese, Spanish and French farmers, who needed labour to work on plantations. The transatlantic slave trade was established to supply this labour need, but also permanently linked Africa and the New World. Some scholars estimate that between AD 1500 and the mid-nineteenth century nearly 10 million Africans were sold into slavery and brought to the New World. Most of those who survived the Middle Passage, and their descendants, lived and laboured on plantations in the Americas. Because plantations were crucibles in the genesis of African-derived cultures in the New World, the archaeology of plantations has played an important role in documenting the richness and diversity of the African experience outside Africa.

Archaeological data are especially critical since few plantation workers left written accounts of their everyday lives. Thus, plantations have been a major focus of the study of the African **diaspora**, and indeed of US historical archaeology in general. The multidisciplinary anthropological approaches used by US archaeologists in this endeavour incorporate traditional archaeological data with historical, ethnographic, ethnohistoric and architectural data. Primarily, plantation sites in the US South and the Caribbean islands have received the greatest attention. From modest beginnings, searching for vestiges of African traditions in material culture recovered from plantation slave/tenant quarter sites, archaeological research at plantation sites has developed over several decades and branched out to cover several major themes: material aspects of everyday life, ethnic identity, power and resistance, and our relationship with the past.

Material aspects of everyday life

Because most plantation archaeology has been conducted at the location of slave/tenant houses, archaeologists have made tremendous progress in understanding the basic material aspects of daily life in plantation quarters in the analysis and interpretation of house remains, food remains and artefacts reflecting the items used in and around the houses. Through this work, a great deal of variability has been documented for slave/tenant quarters on plantations in the New World. For example, Tom Wheaton and Patrick Garrow suggested that early slave quarters in the Carolina lowcountry and in the Caribbean appear to resemble West African-style wattle and daub houses that were two rooms long and one room wide in the manner of shotgun houses. As housing technology evolved in the New World, plantation housing changed, and slave houses of the late antebellum period superficially appear little different from housing of other ethnic or economic groups. The most common plantation house type for labourers of the late antebellum and postbellum periods in the US South is a one-room wooden, often log, structure with a stick and mud chimney, but frame duplexes were also common.

One burgeoning area of research on plantation housing for slaves and tenants involves the use of root cellars or pits beneath the cabin floors. Some

Figure 25 African American cabins on Pettway Plantation, Alabama, 1937
Source: Photo: Library of Congress

archaeologists believe that these important features reflect West African traditions and were imbued with symbolic or religious significance. Other archaeologists suggest that they were pan-cultural and more strictly utilitarian for the storage of perishable food and other valuable household items. Pit cellars are largely associated with slave houses in the Chesapeake (see **Chesapeake region**) and Upland South, and have not been securely documented in the Deep South or Caribbean. The geographic distribution may reflect differences in soils and climates, but may also reflect specific African cultural roots, temporal trends and the interaction of the degree of control each slave family had over their food and other material goods, the control of rations by the planter and the labour system employed on the plantation.

Faunal remains recovered from plantation slave/tenant houses are used to understand not only what was eaten, but also how food was acquired. Not surprisingly, perhaps, there is abundant evidence of rations in the form of pig bones (usually the lesser cuts like head and feet parts), but also evidence of hunting, trapping and fishing to supplement the monotonous rations of pork, cornmeal and molasses.

Some of the artefacts recovered from slave house contexts initially surprised researchers. Items such as guns and gunflints, slate pencils and eyeglasses go against the traditional view of slaves who were legally banned from possessing firearms and reading, and thus are challenging the traditional ideas about plantation life for slaves and sharecroppers. Other artefacts are pointing to occupational specialities on plantations such as seamstress, healer/conjurer and artisan. Some of these occupational specialities were by planter's design, others by design of the slave/tenant community.

Ethnic identity

Although Charles Fairbanks, the 'father of plantation archaeology', recovered no clear-cut 'African-isms' (artefacts reflecting cultural connections to Africa) in the excavations at coastal Florida and Georgia plantations in the late 1960s, the quest for understanding the relationship between various West African traditions and cultural descendants in the New World continues today. Leland Ferguson recognised the importance of a low-fired, hand-built earthenware (**colonoware pottery**) made and used by enslaved Africans along the Atlantic seaboard. Some small pots recovered from rivers (rather than slave house sites) were found with 'X' or cross marks on the bases that Ferguson believes represents the use of the Bakongo (central African) cosmogram in the New World. In addition to colonowares (including Afro-Caribbean wares), many of the major excavations at slave dwellings have yielded objects that seem to have no obvious utilitarian value. These include pierced coins, hand charms, Chinese coins, crystals, blue **beads** and other artefacts that were likely used as charms or medicines in West African-derived rituals. These dramatic discoveries point to the strong continuity of West and central African cultural traditions on plantations in the New World.

There is an emerging debate concerning whether New World African cultures represent a continuation of African practices and adaptation, or a **creolisation** of many African, European and indigenous New World societies. Given the diversity of the cultures from which African diasporic populations derive, archaeologists are using these special artefacts to make tangible linkages between specific African traditions and those in the New World, and understand the creolised nature of African culture outside Africa.

Power and resistance

The focus on power and resistance on plantations has transformed plantation archaeology by shifting the perception of slaves as cultural pawns to men and women who worked to reclaim as much autonomy as possible. While power was decidedly asymmetrical, the plantation as an economic and social institution involved constant negotiations between planters and slaves/tenants, the unequal participants in the institution. Archaeological investigations are indicating that almost every aspect of everyday life was implicated in the negotiations, including housing, foodways (see **food and foodways**), religious practices, labour and 'free time'.

The planned layout of plantations, and the sizes of big houses versus the slave or tenant houses, provide information about how planters created a landscape of domination. The small, yet snug one-room log cabins that dominated the plantation quarter landscape, were created and used by planters to foster slave/tenant families (who were less likely to resist and run away), yet remind the occupants of their low social position on the plantation. There is some suggestion that slaves/tenants resisted the master's control over the physical structure of the house by creating barriers like rubbish and vegetation that discouraged frequent visits to the quarters by masters and overseers.

Food preparation and procurement were also contested areas. Slaves constantly pushed for rights to hunt, garden and keep small livestock that supplemented, or in some cases replaced, rations. In other words, slaves and tenants wanted to control the source and nature of their food. While negotiating for 'rights' to hunt and garden, at other times slaves/tenants may have more forcefully resisted the constraints of rations by 'stealing' pigs, or meat from the master's smokehouse. Foodways were also influenced by plantation labour patterns, and, as slaves/tenants pushed for a task-based labour system over gang labour, more 'free time' was created for other activities like gardening, hunting and fishing.

The discoveries of artefacts reflecting African-derived spirituality from many plantation sites illustrate that slaves/tenants drew strength from their ancestral African cultural traditions. The hand charms, crystals, pierced coins and other objects are more than just evidence of persistence of African traditions, but also evidence of the slaves' and tenants' efforts to resist the pressures and submit to an inferior status.

Our relationship with the past

One of the most rewarding aspects of plantation archaeology is the realisation in recent years of the role that our work has in modern society. For the most part, plantation archaeology has been conducted by white professionals engaged in interpreting the black past(s) with little regard for the impact of this work on the descendant communities, and no regard for African and African American scholarship. The landmark case of the **African Burial Ground** in **New York City**, excavated in the early 1990s, has led to some changing attitudes, not only among archaeologists, but in African descendant communities, with more emphasis on establishing a dialogue and engaging members of the descendant communities in all aspects of research.

Michael Blakey, analysing the remains from the African Burial Ground in New York, has rightly noted that archaeologists are not just gathering information about the past in their investigations of plantations and other sites associated with Africans and African Americans, but we are also entering a social discourse concerning the relationship between whites and African Americans in the present. An inclusive dialogue to uncover the real identities and histories is necessary to more accurately and sensitively deal with the legacy of plantations and slavery. The stories of Africa, of slavery and plantations, the aftermath of slavery and the quest for equality are stories of heroes with lessons for all, but also painful reminders of the prominence of racism in our society and in our profession. In the special edition of *Historical Archaeology*, edited by Carol McDavid and David Babson in 1997, various archaeologists discuss their struggles with the creation of archaeology in the service of the public that involves the descendant community in the archaeological research of plantations. It is evident in this collection that archaeologists recognise the issues of inclusion and exclusion, but also that solutions are complex because of the racism that pervades the dialogues, and the diversity within and between the descendant communities.

Plantation archaeology has emerged as one of the leading endeavours within historical archaeology. As more sites are excavated, a critical mass of information is being reached that will allow for even more important advances in our understanding of plantation life in the New World.

See also: acculturation; African American archaeology

Further reading

McDavid, C. and Babson, D. (eds) (1997) 'In the realm of politics: Prospects for public participation in plantation archaeology', *Historical Archaeology* 31(3): 1–152.

McKee, L. 'The ideals and realities behind the design and use of nineteenth-century Virginia slave cabins', in A.E. Yentsch and M.C. Beaudry (eds) *The Art and Mystery of Historical Archaeology: Essays in Honor of James Deetz*, Boca Raton: CRC Press, pp. 195–214.

Orser, C.E., Jr (1998) 'The archaeology of the African diaspora', *Annual Review of Anthropology* 27: 63–87.

—— (1988) *The Material Basis of the Postbellum Tenant Plantation: Historical Archaeology in the South Carolina Piedmont*, Athens: University of Georgia Press.

Singleton, T.A. and Bograd, M.D. (eds) (1995) *The Archaeology of the African Diaspora in the Americas: Guides to the Archaeological Literature of the Immigrant Experience in America*, Tucson: The Society for Historical Archaeology.

Wheaton, T. and Garrow, P. (1985) 'Acculturation and the archaeological record in the Carolina lowcountry', in T.A. Singleton (ed.) *The Archaeology of Slavery and Plantation Life*, Orlando: Academic Press, pp. 239–54.

Young, A.L. (1997) 'Risk management strategies among African-American slaves at Locust Grove plantation', *International Journal of Historical Archaeology* 1: 5–37.

AMY L. YOUNG

Plymouth, Massachusetts, USA

Plymouth was a seventeenth-century colony settled by English religious dissenters, or Pilgrims. Excavation of Plymouth Colony domestic sites began with J. Hall's 1864 exploration of the Miles Standish home in Duxbury. In the 1940s, H.H. Hornblower conducted excavations at the R.M. site in Plymouth and the Edward Winslow site in Marshfield; in 1938, S. Strickland at the John Howland site in Kingston; in the 1950s, R.W. Robbins at the John Alden site in Duxbury; and in 1959–66, J.F. Deetz at the Joseph Howland and William Bradford sites in Kingston and Isaac

Allerton and William Bartlett sites in Plymouth. Findings contributed to the interpretation of Pilgrim life at Plimouth Plantation, a living museum (see **living museums**), and to synthetic studies of New England culture and material life by Deetz. Research focused on the transference of traditional culture and its transformation as settlers adapted to new environmental and social conditions. Evidence indicated that houses were timber-framed, single-cell or cross-passage in plan, partially cellared, or post-in-the-ground construction or with sills set on stone foundations. Artefacts recovered included tin-glazed and coarse **earthenware** (from the Low Countries, Iberia, North Devon, the English Midlands and south, as well as locally made) and German **stoneware** in forms for dairying, storage and communal drinking, weaponry and gun parts, utensils, personal objects and building hardware; faunal remains indicate the **consumption** of both domesticated and wild animals, such as deer and bear. In the 1970s, Deetz excavated the 1690–1740 Samuel Smith tavern site at Great Island, in Wellfleet, and portions of the 1792–*c.* 1840 African American settlement at Parting Ways in Plymouth, moving beyond the home sites of the seventeenth-century 'Pilgrim Fathers' of English descent to consider cultural change and ethnic diversity. The Wellfleet tavern assemblage, with high proportions of smoking pipes (see **pipes, smoking**) and drinking vessels, differed markedly from typical domestic assemblages. At Parting Ways, Deetz found the African heritage of the site's occupants expressed in traditional West African architecture, pottery forms, foodways (see **food and foodways**) and mortuary practices (see **mortuary analysis**).

See also: English colonialism

Further reading

Beaudry, M.C. (1984) 'An archaeological perspective on social inequality in seventeenth-century Massachusetts', *American Archaeology* 4(1): 55–60.

Beaudry, M.C. and George, D.C. (1987) 'Old data, new findings: 1940s archaeology at Plymouth reexamined', *American Archaeology* 6(1): 20–30.

Deetz, J. (1968) 'Late man in North America: Archaeology of European Americans', in B. J.

Meggers (ed.) *Anthropological Archaeology in the Americas*, Washington, DC: Anthropological Society of Washington, pp. 121–30.

—— (1960) 'Excavations at the Joseph Howland site (C5), Rocky Nook, Kingston, Massachusetts, 1959: A preliminary report', *Supplement to the Howland Quarterly* 24(2–3): 1–12.

Ekholm, E. and Deetz, J. (1971) 'The Wellfleet tavern site', *Natural History* 80(8): 48–57.

MARY C. BEAUDRY

political economy

Political economy refers to the analysis of social relations based on unequal access to wealth and power. Archaeological analyses of political economy focus on production and exchange of goods and services in prehistoric and historic societies. The political economy is often contrasted to the subsistence economy. The differences between the two lie in their different purposes and internal workings. While the subsistence economy meets household needs for food, clothing and shelter, the political economy attempts to generate income for a ruling elite. The political economy thus mobilises a surplus from the subsistence economy. The surplus is used to finance social, political and religious institutions that, in their more complex forms, are managed by specialised personnel. These institutions are used to support and justify ownership by the ruling elite of productive resources, especially improved agricultural land.

The concept of political economy as a method of scientific inquiry resulted from the invention of **capitalism** in the seventeenth and eighteenth centuries. Historically, *economics* referred to the management of the household economy. When referring to the royal household, the economy was perforce also political. Thus, 'political economy' was originally the study of the problems of the management of the revenues and expenditures of the emerging capitalist nation-states of Western Europe.

The focus of analytical attention of political economy has shifted over the course of the centuries since the inception of the discipline. The mercantilist scholars of the seventeenth century located the origins of wealth in trade surpluses generated through the acquisition of precious metals. They considered government to be an essential part of the economy. James Steuart drew an analogy to Aristotle's family household: 'What oeconomy is in a family, political oeconomy is in a state.' The course of the discipline was redirected by Adam Smith who disagreed that the state ought to act as *pater familias*, as argued by Steuart and other mercantilists. Smith and his followers eschewed the moral and governmental aspects of political economy while developing an interest in matters of marketing and the division of labour. David Ricardo and Karl Marx focused attention on production and the relation of production and distribution to economic growth and class conflict. Marx also emphasised the importance of scientific critique of the relations of production. The influence of Marx thus resulted in the addition of an analysis of social class and a critical perspective to the concerns of political economy. The discipline acquired radical overtones and its practitioners were ostracised as hostile to the existing social order.

As anthropology and archaeology came of age in the early twentieth century, the concept of political economy was seldom used or even debated. More controversial in anthropology was the idea, promoted by the nineteenth-century political economists, that there was a 'world economy' affecting all societies everywhere, no matter how quaint or isolated they might seem. This idea would later be elaborated more completely, and in very different approaches, by historical sociologist Immanuel Wallerstein, political economist Andre Gunder Frank and anthropologist Eric R. Wolf. One of its earliest applications in historical archaeology was in studies of the impact of the world fur trade on indigenous peoples of North America.

As Marxist concepts were revived in the social sciences in the 1960s, the term 'political economy' became prevalent in anthropology in the 1960s, and by the 1970s it became quite commonplace in archaeology, especially in prehistoric archaeology under the aegis of cultural materialism. The concept of political economy has a natural appeal to archaeologists since it directs attention to processes that are both political and economic in nature, bridging both realms of behaviour, allowing holistic analyses of material processes that lead to social and cultural change.

See also: class, social; fur trade archaeology in western Canada; globalisation; Marxian approaches; world(-)systems theory

Further reading

Moore, J.H. (1993) 'Political economy in anthropology', in J.H. Moore (ed.) *The Political Economy of North American Indians*, Norman: University of Oklahoma Press, pp. 3–19.

WILLIAM R. FOWLER, JR

politics in archaeology

Most people would probably not immediately link archaeology with politics, because most people would assume that archaeology – as a scientific, objective practice – would be free of the entanglements and nuances politics and politicians can impose on research. However, politics has been a part of archaeology for a long time, and, beginning in the 1980s, numerous archaeologists began to recognise and examine the connections between archaeology and politics. As part of their discovery, some archaeologists started to investigate the role that politics and political motivations have played in archaeological fieldwork and interpretation, and have even wondered about the role political considerations could play in the future. As part of this study of the underlying, political implications of their discipline, archaeologists realised that archaeological information could be used to promote political agendas, to legitimise history and to oppress or silence indigenous peoples.

Nationalism, as political agenda, has been used by many countries beginning in the early nineteenth century to promote the idea that their citizens have a substantial antiquity in a particular region and to show that the culture had a glorious past at some point in history. Nationalistic arguments can have many goals, including the legitimisation of a nation's occupation of a particular, contested region and the promotion of a sense of cultural and national pride. The idea behind this promotion is that a people are great because of their past and that they belong in a certain place because their ancestors once lived there. Museums around the world are well stocked with exhibits showing the evolution of past cultural greatness, many of which incorporate beautiful works of ancient art executed in intricate detail and using precious metals and stones.

Archaeologists often debate the merits and underlying principles behind nationalistic museum displays and the role of archaeology in promoting a certain message, but most agree that Germany's National Socialists provide one of the most egregious, recent examples of the misuse of archaeological materials to promote a particular political point of view. As they rose to power, the Nazis created a special unit to engage in archaeological research – the SS Ahnenerbe – to promote and give scientific credentials to their racialist beliefs. The group conducted archaeological excavations, produced archaeological fakes and created outlandish theories to support their claims of German superiority and ancient greatness. Other examples, because they are less overt, are more difficult for the public to discern. Ignoring the history of native Australians, **Native Americans** and Africans – the last, for instance, at **Great Zimbabwe** – constitutes instances where archaeology has been used for political purposes. Equally subtle examples derive from the way archaeological history is taught or ignored in public education.

Much early historical archaeology in the USA was conducted with an eye towards legitimising the history of the nation. Excavations at the earliest and most historical sites in the country, often accompanied by extensive physical **reconstruction**, helped to promote the idea that the USA was a legitimate world power, and that it had a rich and colourful history that was worthy of attention.

Historical archaeologists have learned from descendant communities that their archaeological interpretations can have a wide appeal beyond the archaeological profession. Many descendants want to know how their ancestors lived in the past, and wish to understand the material challenges they faced, the triumphs they experienced and the tragedies they suffered. Archaeology can often provide unique insights into these aspects of daily life, but archaeologists doing this research must be willing to accept that some of the men and women

in the community may view the history of past people as *their* history. Such actively engaged descendants may not confront the past in neutral terms and they may not view archaeological interpretations with scientific detachment.

Once political considerations become linked with archaeological research, archaeologists may often face ethical dilemmas over what they can say about the past. A hypothetical example will suffice. Suppose that an indigenous culture somewhere has always been perceived as a peaceful culture and that a significant amount of recorded history indicates that they conducted themselves with constraint, even during the darkest periods of potential conflict with an encroaching imperialist power. Let us suppose further than an archaeologist is engaged in working closely with members of the culture to uncover their history using a series of excavations. During the course of excavation, however, the archaeologist finds irrefutable proof that the ancestors of the culture engaged in mutilating captured children. If the living members of the culture wish to preserve the perception that it has always been peaceful, does the archaeologist publish his or her findings about mutilation? The decision he or she reaches will most certainly have political ramifications of some sort for the culture, for the archaeologist and possibly both.

Politics is a part of modern-day archaeology, and most archaeologists understand this reality. Both pure research projects and **cultural-resource management** efforts around the world frequently receive governmental funding and support. It is possible in many cases that the funding includes certain, often tacit, political arrangements concerning what can be excavated, what interpretations will be tolerated and how the public and scholarly presentations may be organised. The interjection of politics in archaeology does not mean, however, that archaeological research is suspect or unfairly biased. It only means that archaeologists, in addition to all the things they must know to interpret the past, should also be aware of certain political realities that they may possibly confront.

Further reading

Gathercole, P. and Lowenthal, D. (eds) (1990) *The Politics of the Past*, London: Unwin Hyman.

Kohl, P.L. and Fawcett, C. (eds) (1995) *Nationalism, Politics, and the Practice of Archaeology*, Cambridge: Cambridge University Press.

McDavid, C. and Babson, D.W. (eds) (1997) 'In the realm of politics: Prospects for public participation in African-American and plantation archaeology', *Historical Archaeology* 31(3): 1–152.

Trigger, B.G. (1994) 'Alternative archaeologies: Nationalist, colonialist, imperialist', *Man* 19: 355–70.

CHARLES E. ORSER, JR

pollen analysis

Pollen analysis involves the recovery, identification, tabulation and statistical analysis of the pollen and/or spores contained in sediments and soils. Pollen extracted from samples collected at prehistoric and historic sites is analysed to aid in resolving one or more of three kinds of problems: inter- or intra-site relative chronology, identification of palaeoenvironmental conditions, or reconstruction of cultural patterns through evidence of their effects on pollen dispersal and preservation processes.

There are basically two kinds of palynological studies relevant to historical-archaeology research. On the one hand, there are studies of pollen records of equivalent antiquity that are collected from different sorts of cultural or spatial contexts. For example, the pollen data of a suite of samples recovered from floor contexts at a plantation residence may be compared with the data from a suite of floor contexts at contemporary slave cabins to suggest contrasting behaviour patterns. Samples from different geographic positions on the probable surface of an ancient garden may also be compared to provide evidence of planting patterns. On the other hand, there are studies designed to provide evidence of sequential changes in pollen records within a site or the sites of a region. The focus of such studies is explanation of the character and direction of the change(s), their antiquity and their relation to historical records. For example, a pollen sequence may provide evidence of ecosystem changes resulting from human environmental impacts, or provide independent evidence of a historically documented sequence of land use changes. The precise dates attributable to material culture directly associated with pollen samples from historic sites often support very finely resolved and dated pollen sequence chronologies.

The character of historical and anthropological problems investigated at many historic sites encourages multidisciplinary research programmes in which pollen analyses provide a body of information and an interpretive perspective that may be usefully integrated with other forms of research. Reconstruction of a half-century of land use at a historic Nevada locale, for example, integrated the results of analyses of geomorphic-stratigraphic, palynological, macro-floral remains, faunal remains, architectural patterns, material culture and oral and documented histories data. However, sometimes the research question asked is so specific that palynological research is manifestly the most appropriate means of resolving it. Reconstruction of changes in the vegetative landscape of the battlefield at Fort Necessity is an example of this type of study.

Further reading

Faegri, K. and Iverson, J. (1989) *Textbook of Pollen Analysis*, fourth edn, Chichester: John Wiley.

Kelso, G.K. (1994) 'Palynology in historical, rural-landscape studies: Great Meadows, Pennsylvania', *American Antiquity* 59: 359–72.

Pearsall, D.M. (2000) 'Pollen analysis', in *Paleoethnobotany, a Handbook of Procedures*, San Diego: Academic Press, pp. 249–353.

Schoenwetter, J. (1990) 'A method for the application of pollen analysis in landscape archaeology', in W.M. Kelso and R. Most (eds) *Earth Patterns: Essays in Landscape Archaeology*, Charlottesville: University Press of Virginia, pp. 277–96.

Schoenwetter, J. and Hohmann, J.W. (1997) 'Land-use reconstruction at the founding settlement of Las Vegas, Nevada', *Historical Archaeology* 31(4): 41–58.

JAMES SCHOENWETTER

popular culture

Popular culture is a body of widely shared and contested beliefs, practices and objects that presents ordinary social life's extraordinary possibilities. The validation of common folks' lives has been the central thread of popular-culture research since 1958, when Raymond Williams's pronouncement that 'culture is ordinary' succinctly expressed widespread dissatisfaction with the scholarly denigration of everyday life. The 'popular' accents the potentially remarkable dimensions of 'ordinary' practices, such as style, literature and music. In this sense, popular culture mirrors real life, but it is a distorted and selective reflection that presents apparently familiar realities in their most spectacular forms. Victorians, for instance, purchased Chinese-motif plates not because they thirsted for knowledge of Chinese culture but because the 'Orient' evoked wisdom, sensuality, despotism and caricatures that reinforced Western ideologies. Similarly, the exceptional possibilities of everyday life were evoked by the overflowing and exoticised Victorian parlour; the romanticisation of enslaved life in antebellum literature; or even Madonna's titanic bra and attendant hyper-sexualisation.

Popular culture originates in many groups and classes, and emerges from folk culture and commercial discourse alike, but it always has a range of meanings that is a continually unfolding and situationally distinct public product. The particular meanings various individuals and groups favour from this circumscribed range of possibilities reflect their social identity, position in power relations and historical context, so popular culture never assumes a single meaning. Popular culture often is portrayed as opposition to 'mainstream culture', painting the popular as resistant practice by marginalised peoples. Scholars like Dick Hebdige focus on this creative resistance and situate it in relation to capitalism's dominant socioeconomic structures. Thus, the popular illuminates the extremes in the mainstream but is not separable from it: in reactionary and revolutionary ways alike, popular culture appropriates dominant practices, beliefs and objects, and manipulates their prevalent 'mainstream' meaning. Hebdige, for instance, argued that 1970s punk sub-culture modified dominant material styles and social conventions in 'deviant' forms, such as using lavatory chains as clothing accessories, adopting manic and violent public behaviour or adding forbidden symbols (e.g. swastikas) to typical consumer goods. Punk sub-culture was a spectacular deviation that critiqued British class structure even as it aspired to a measure of self-determination in that very society. Hebdige argued that such contradictions ultimately defuse most popular resistance, often when the resistance itself is safely commodified; punk garb, for example, was eventually mass-marketed pre-torn or sans offensive symbols. Popular culture rarely produces radical social change; instead, it insinuates that it will deliver a share of material affluence or symbolic privilege to every member of society.

Popular culture illuminates how we are all ordinary yet desire to be extraordinary, or at least envision extraordinary possibilities within ourselves. Popular-culture scholars tend to focus on spectacular practices, but symbolic variation, resistance and the complexity of everyday life certainly provide productive parallels for historical archaeologists.

Further reading

Hebdige, D. (1979) *Subculture: The Meaning of Style*, New York: Routledge.
Williams, R. (1958) *Culture and Society, 1780–1950*, London: Penguin.

PAUL R. MULLINS

porcelain

Porcelain is a kind of ceramic (see **ceramics**) that is usually finely made, extremely hard and fired at some of the highest temperatures used for ceramics (1250°–1400°C). Porcelain was first made in China between the second and the third centuries AD, and its Asian roots are aptly indicated by the often-used term 'china'. Three major categories of porcelain exist: hard-paste, or 'true' (*pâte dure*); soft-paste, or 'artificial' (*pâte tendre*); and bone china. Each kind of porcelain has slightly different ingredients, though each is generally known for its beauty, with the hard-paste varieties typically thought to be the finest.

Hard-paste porcelain is made from fine clay called 'china clay', or 'kaolin' (from Kao-ling, where the clay was first found in China), and 'china stone' or 'petuntse', a kind of feldspathic rock. Fine kaolin clay deposits only occur in China, east-central Germany and south-west **England**. Hard-paste porcelain can be either unglazed or glazed. Glaze is a thin coat of glassy material usually containing lead, alkaline and petuntse. The glaze, which can be coloured or clear, makes the vessels extremely hard because it fuses with the clay during firing. Unglazed wares are referred to as 'biscuit' or 'bisque'. Unglazed porcelain is often said to resemble white marble.

Porcelain makers decorated their hard-paste porcelain pieces with crackling (tiny cracks that occur during firing), underglaze decorations (hand-painted decorations applied before glazing) and overglaze, hand-painted, enamel decorations (applied after the first firing). The vessels decorated with overglaze painting would be refired, and the raised paint can be felt on the surface of the overglazed vessels.

Soft-paste porcelains were first associated with French manufacturers, but this kind of porcelain has been widely produced elsewhere as well, including England during the eighteenth century. Soft-paste vessels are difficult to distinguish from their hard-paste cousins, even though kaolin and petuntse were not used in the soft-paste wares. To make soft-paste porcelain, potters combined sand, alum, sea salt, soda, nitrate and gypsum into a glassy compound called 'frit'. The clay paste was made by mixing the frit with water and white clay, and firing the vessels at a lower temperature than the hard-paste porcelains. Once fired, the vessels were sprayed with a lead oxide glaze and refired. Some potters decorated their soft-paste wares with gilting, and this decoration would require another firing to fix the design. Soft-paste wares were more fragile than hard-paste wares. Late eighteenth-century English potters were the first to apply transfer-printed designs to their porcelain wares. Transfer printing is the application of intricate designs from an engraved, inked copperplate to the vessel before firing. Potters usually used black, blue,

purple and red colours for their transfer-printed designs.

Bone china has been a standard product of the English porcelain industry since the early nine-teenth century. To make this kind of porcelain, potters mixed the ash from burned animal bones with the china clay and petuntse. They could use as much as 50 per cent ash in the mixture. Josiah Spode II (d. 1827) is often credited with creating the best bone china formula around 1800.

Historical archaeologists frequently find both 'Chinese Export Porcelain' and European varieties at the sites they excavate. The Chinese porcelain will have been made during one of two dynasties: the Ming (1364–1644) or Ch'ing (1644–1912). Much of this porcelain was decorated with blue, underglaze, hand-painted decorations (and often referred to as 'blue and white'), but, by the end of the eighteenth century, Chinese porcelain makers were making overglaze, hand-painted vessels exclusively for export. Patterns incorporating red and gilting were popular.

The porcelain vessels produced in China typically carry **makers' marks** on their bases. These marks can be characters, symbols and slogans, and can be used to identify the dynasty and reign of manufacture.

Historical archaeologists have often considered whether the presence of porcelain at sites can be used to provide information about the socio-economic position or wealth of the site's former inhabitants. Many have assumed that porcelain, being imported from China and finely made, was expensive. For example, archaeologists have un-earthed numerous sherds of Chinese Export Porcelain at many of the home sites at Williams-burg, Virginia, and at the owners' mansions at slave plantations. At three antebellum plantations in South Carolina, archaeologists discovered that imported porcelains accounted for 11, 12 and 14 per cent of the recovered ceramics. Some analysts have argued that porcelains decorated with over-glaze designs were more expensive – and hence indicative of wealth – because they required more steps to manufacture and so were more expensive to import. At Drayton Hall Plantation, a three-storey, eighteenth-century mansion near Charles-ton, South Carolina, for example, overglazed porcelain accounted for 29 per cent of the porcelain present. When the blue underglazed wares were combined with this figure, it was found that the household's ceramic collection included almost 40 per cent Chinese Export Porcelain. Although archaeologists are currently uncertain as to the precise social meaning of porcelain, many are convinced that it must suggest wealth and social identity in some way. It must be remembered, however, that some manufacturers also produced less expensive porcelains for the mass market.

The areal distribution of Chinese Export Porcelain interests historical archaeologists because it occurs in some quantity at a wide range of colonial-period sites. For example, archaeologists have found specimens at Russian–American fur-trading sites in Alaska; the French and British **Fort Michilimackinac** in Michigan; the Dutch **Oudepost I** in South Africa; the Spanish Santa Fe la Vieja; throughout the Islamic **Ottoman Empire** and elsewhere across the world. This multicultural distribution, coupled with the economic, social and ideational meanings of porcelain, makes it an important topic for archaeological study.

Further reading

Leach, B. (1976) *A Potter's Book*, London: Faber & Faber.

Lewis, L.G. (1985) 'The planter class: The archaeological record at Drayton Hall', in T.A. Singleton (ed.) *The Archaeology of Slavery and Plantation Life*, Orlando: Academic Press, pp. 121–40.

Noël Hume, I. (1970) *A Guide to Artifacts of Colonial America*, New York: Alfred A. Knopf.

—— (1969) *Pottery and Porcelain in Colonial Williamsburg's Archaeological Collections*, Williamsburg: Colonial Williamsburg.

Patterson, J.E. (1979) *Porcelain*, New York: Cooper-Hewitt National Design Museum.

CHARLES E. ORSER, JR

Port Essington, Australia

Situated about 200 km north-east of present-day Darwin, **Australia**, Port Essington is a 30-km-long harbour in the Cobourg Peninsula, the northernmost point of the Northern Territory, about 11° south of the equator. Climatically, the environment is dominated by a short summer wet season and a long dry season, resulting in relatively low annual rainfall, high temperatures and a dry tropical vegetation.

Victoria was a garrison of British Royal Marines established at Port Essington in 1838 and abandoned in 1849. It marked the third and longest attempt by the British to establish a military presence on the northern coast of continental Australia during the second quarter of the nineteenth century. The proliferation of places named after the new British monarch led to the settlement being more commonly referred to as Port Essington.

Ostensibly, these settlements were attempts to foster British **trade** in the eastern end of the East Indies Archipelago, but their establishment and maintenance suggest that their primary purpose was to maintain a political presence in a region marked by Dutch colonial expansion and the fear of similar colonising activities by the French and even possibly the Americans. In practice, these settlements were 'limpet ports' on the perimeter of the world's largest continental island, designed to protect British sovereignty of the whole continent. As such, garrisons like Port Essington were characterised by their small size (fewer than sixty men and a very small number of wives), lack of any coherent policy to develop associated civilian settlement or commercial tropical agriculture, lack of attempts to foster regional trade and lack of infrastructure and logistical support. The Victoria settlement was placed, defensively, 20 km inside the harbour entrance; thus, passing vessels using the Torres Strait rarely visited, since it might take several days to beat up against the wind to the settlement. Most of all, it suffered 'the tyranny of distance', being roughly 3,000 km away from Singapore, Swan River (Perth) and **Sydney**, its three closest British administrative centres. Simple logistical requests sent to the colonial Governor in Sydney and then referred to Britain might take several years to be answered.

Excavations undertaken at the settlement in 1966–7 represent the first professional excavation of a European historical site in Australia. While the cultural affinities of the artefacts were British and required researching British sources, the nature of the site demanded theoretical and methodological approaches adapted from North American historic sites. The major theoretical problem to emerge was the effective integration of historical documentary and archaeological data sets in an Australian context, and the associated question of whether archaeology had any more challenging contribution to make to mid-nineteenth-century Australian history than the handmaiden role of domestic description.

Site research recorded and reported on all above-ground architecture and excavations of rubbish dumps, enlisted men's quarters, government store buildings, the small hospital, officers' quarters, magazine, smithy, bakehouse, lime and brick kilns and contemporaneous Aboriginal middens that developed there. The archaeology continually reflected the difficulties of coping with an alien tropical environment, e.g. following widespread destruction by a cyclone, buildings on wooden stumps had their foundations enclosed in rough masonry, which led to termite infestation. Equally, research reflected the improvisation necessary in a settlement supplied with poor quality and inappropriate tools, equipment and stock, and manned by marines without trade skills. The chimneys of five houses of married couples could be seriated according to improvements to building techniques learned during the building of them, which used a chimney design otherwise known only in nineteenth-century west Cornwall, **England**.

Archaeological and documentary evidence highlighted both the extreme isolation and communication problems that beset this small military garrison during its existence. While the site provides an interesting example of **world systems theory** in operation, an analysis of **makers' marks** and ceramic decorative techniques (see **ceramics**) also indicates a time lag in utilitarian British ceramics reaching the settlement. It suffered a high death rate caused by malaria, constant crop failure and lack of necessary Government supplies, including food, clothing and utensils, which were also obtained from infrequent visiting traders and Indonesian fishermen who annually fished for trepang along this coast. More than 200 **porcelain** sherds of Asian manufacture reflect the trade with these visitors.

The settlement was abandoned when the British government decided that perceived threats to its sovereignty of Australia had diminished. Apart from an attempt to run cattle in the area in the 1870s, the region was not subsequently settled and today is part of a National Park.

See also: colonialism; contact archaeology; English colonialism

Further reading

Allen, J. (1978) 'The archaeology of nineteenth century British imperialism: An Australian case study', *World Archaeology* 5: 44–60.

—— (1969) 'Archaeology, and the history of Port Essington', doctoral thesis, Australian National University, Canberra.

—— (1972) 'Port Essington: A successful limpet port', *Australian Historical Studies* 15(59): 341–60.

Blainey, G. (1966) *The Tyranny of Distance*, Melbourne: Sun Books.

Spillett, P.G. (1972) *Forsaken Settlement*, Melbourne: Landsdowne Press.

JIM ALLEN

Port Royal, Jamaica

Port Royal, Jamaica, has been called the most romantic and remarkable city in the western hemisphere, and it is a title many would consider well deserved. The British created Port Royal in 1655 after they had failed to capture Hispaniola from the Spanish. They called the new settlement 'the Point' or 'Point Cagway', but, after the Restoration of the English monarchy in 1660, they renamed the town Port Royal, and the fort – which they had originally named 'Passage Fort', or 'Fort Cromwell' – Fort Charles, after Charles II. The city quickly grew in size, and within British America only Boston outpaced its population. Historians estimate that, in 1692, Port Royal had between 6,500 and 8,000 residents. The busy city numbered among its inhabitants merchants, craftpeople, ship captains, slaves and notorious pirates. The presence

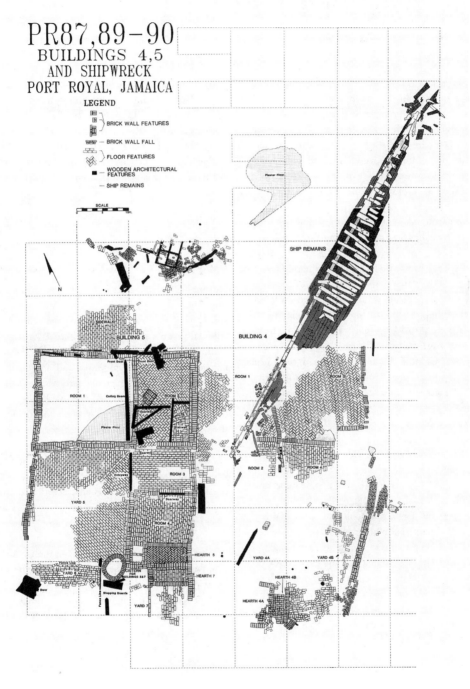

Figure 26 Plan of Buildings 4 and 5, Port Royal, Jamaica
Source: D.L. Hamilton

of the pirates led many to refer to Port Royal as the 'wickedest city in the world'.

The defining moment in the history of the city occurred on 7 June 1692, when a strong earthquake sunk about two-thirds of it, or about 13 ha, into Kingston Harbour. This dramatic event, though devastating to the residents, has been a boon to modern archaeology, and Port Royal is today excavated both as a terrestrial and as an underwater site. In the 1950s, underwater archaeologist Edwin Link discovered a submerged pocket watch, made around 1686, with the hands stopped at the precise moment of the earthquake, 11:43 a.m.

The earthquake has meant that a huge portion of Port Royal lies beneath the water much as it was in 1692. Systematic excavations have occurred, both on land and in the water, from the mid-1960s to the 1990s. Among the thousands of artefacts recovered, archaeologists have completed studies of the smoking pipes (both white- and red-clay types) (see **pipes, smoking**), glass **bottles** and **non-ferrous metal** objects (brass, copper, silver and **pewter**), Chinese Export **porcelain** and iron tools. Given the nature of the finds from the city, some of these studies – such as those involving the pewter objects – are judged to be some of the most complete examinations available. The presence of **makers' marks** on some of the pewter objects allowed archaeologists to identify at least one seventeenth-century pewterer: Simon Benning, who marked his products with a pineapple and the initials 'S B'.

In 1989 and 1990, archaeologists excavated two buildings – named 'Buildings 4 and 5' – in which they found the remains of houses as they looked in 1692, complete with individual, square rooms with brick floors, hearths, sections of plaster and wooden architectural elements. Surprisingly, they also found the remains of a British warship, which they tentatively identified as HMS *Swan*, lying among the building debris.

See also: English colonialism

Further reading

Hamilton, D.L. (1996) 'Historical archaeology on British sites in the seventeenth-century Carib-bean', in H.M. Miller, D.L. Hamilton, N. Honerkamp, S.R. Pendery, P.E. Pope and J.A. Tuck (eds) *The Archaeology of Sixteenth- and Seventeenth-Century British Colonization in the Caribbean, United States and Canada*, Tucson: Society for Historical Archaeology, pp. 3–8.

—— (1992) 'Simon Benning, pewterer of Port Royal', in B. J. Little (ed.) *Text-Aided Archaeology*, Boca Raton: CRC Press, pp. 39–53.

Noël Hume, I. (1968) 'A collection of glass from Port Royal, Jamaica, with some observations on the site, its history, and archaeology', *Historical Archaeology* 2: 5–34.

CHARLES E. ORSER, JR

Portuguese colonialism

During Europe's so-called 'Age of Exploration', the tiny Iberian nation of Portugal was a major superpower that ranked alongside the other great colonial powers of Europe: **England**, Spain, the Netherlands and France. Even though Portugal enjoyed a long period of power and an expansion that covered much of the globe, archaeologists have not examined its colonial sites with the same intensity they have shown for the colonial sites of the other superpowers. The reasons for the paucity of archaeological interest in colonial Portugal is not entirely clear, and the precise reasons for the neglect are probably many and varied. One possibly explanation, however, may derive from the lack of Portuguese settlements in the USA and Great Britain, the countries where historical archaeology was first developed.

The absence of Portuguese sites in the USA that could match **Jamestown**, Virginia, in date and historical significance may have caused the important realm of Portuguese colonial studies to be slow to develop. In addition, the rather late development of historical archaeology in the major Portuguese colonies – **Brazil**, parts of Africa and Asia – has retarded the archaeological investigation of Portuguese colonialism. Even though a great amount of research has not yet been completed, significant progress is being made and the archaeological analysis of Portuguese colonialism is destined to attract greater attention in the future.

Portuguese colonial expansion

Many historians date the beginning of Portuguese colonial expansion with their capture of Ceuta in North Africa in August 1415. This military action changed the course of both Iberian and world history. With the assertion of their national might, the economic tide in Africa shifted from the Muslims to the emerging Portuguese, and the Portuguese empire was founded. They would hold this empire, albeit in various forms, until well into the twentieth century.

The history of Portuguese explorations, conducted in their famous sea-going vessels, is legendary. Only the briefest of outlines serves to illustrate the tiny nation's global reach after Prince Henry the Navigator established the School of Navigation in the far southern city of Sagres in 1415, the same year as the action at Ceuta. In 1488, Bartolomeu Dias rounded the Cape of Good Hope, ten years later Vasco da Gama reached India, in 1500 Cabral found the coast of Brazil and Magellan began his famous circumnavigation in 1519. These colonial developments, carried out during the reign of King Manuel I (1495–1521), solidified Portugal's 'Golden Age', as the tiny nation established colonies throughout Africa, India, Brazil, in the North Atlantic and in Asia.

Historical archaeology in Portugal

Little archaeological work has focused specifically on the Portuguese colonial enterprise, though this situation was beginning to change by the end of the twentieth century. Post-medieval archaeologists in Portugal and historical archaeologists in Portugal's historic colonies are beginning to conduct archaeological research with regularity.

In Portugal itself, post-medieval archaeologists have shown growing interest in **industrial archaeology** and **maritime archaeology**. In the industrial realm, they have investigated mills and the milling process, olive oil factories, urban water-pumping stations, flour mills and factories associated with Portugal's famous cork industry. These studies have documented both the **architecture** and technologies of the industries as well as their individual histories. In one study, Jorge Miranda and João Viegas documented the loca-tions of windmills in one part of Portugal. Their diachronic examination illustrated the changes in technology and the rise and fall of the milling industry from the mid-eighteenth century to the late twentieth century.

In terms of maritime archaeology, the presumed wreck site of the *Nossa Senhora dos Mártires* provides an example of the significant promise of post-medieval archaeology in Portugal. Discovered in 1993 and excavated in 1996, 1997, 1999 and 2000, the wreck site was found at the mouth of the Tagus River at the site of the fortress São Julião da Barra. The Portuguese completed the fortress in the early seventeenth century to protect the mouth of the Tagus – and thus the access to Lisbon – from rapacious English pirates. The Portuguese situated the fortification (see **fortifications**) on the shore, causing the water around it to silt up. Before long, the area around the fortress became a ships' graveyard (see **ships' graveyards**). The *Nossa Senhora dos Mártires* was lost on 15 September 1606 as it was returning to Lisbon after a successful trading expedition to India. Archaeologists have found a large collection of artefacts at the wreck site, including an impressive assemblage of **pewter** examined by Filipe Castro. A wreck site such as the *Nossa Senhora dos Mártires* provides unique insights into topics as diverse as Portuguese shipbuilding techniques to the nature of Portugal's international trade.

Portuguese colonial archaeology

Historical archaeology in the former Portuguese colonies, though not as prominent as the archaeology of other European colonies, is still extremely important. Archaeologists have completed notable studies at fort sites as well as important artefact analyses that document the **material culture** of the colonial Portuguese.

The excavation of forts has occurred in Africa, at the Castelo de São Jorge da Mina in Ghana (built in 1482 and associated with **Elmina**), and at Fort Jesus, Kenya (built in 1593). The excavations at Fort Jesus provide a good indication of the research potential of archaeology at colonial Portuguese military sites.

The Portuguese built Fort Jesus to protect both their possessions in Africa and their trade route to

India. During its history, the Portuguese and the Omani Arabs each controlled the fort several times in turn, but, when the British gained full control of Kenya, they converted the old fortification into a prison. The site was converted into a national park in 1958 and archaeologists began to investigate the site at that time. In 1962, at the end of the research, the fort was opened to the public as a museum.

Fort Jesus is widely considered to represent one of the best examples of sixteenth-century Portuguese military **architecture**. The architect designed it with four irregularly shaped bastions, a main gate extending in a square outward from the curtains and a large, rectangular open parade ground inside. Long barracks were situated along the sides of the parade ground against the wall and a church was built opposite the main gate. The fort's long history, its occupation by two distinct cultures and its architectural intricacies meant that the excavations would be both complicated and rewarding.

As would be expected given the fort's history, the archaeologists uncovered hundreds of artefacts. Included in the sample are ceramic vessels (see **ceramics**) from all over the world, including Portugal (majolica, **redware**), England (**creamware**), China (**porcelain**, **stoneware**), Germany (stoneware) and India (**earthenware**). They also found numerous examples of various kinds of Islamic and local pottery. They identified several different vessel shapes within the collection, including jars, bowls, jugs, plates and water pots. The artefact sample also included many examples of glass **bottles**, glass **beads** of many colours, cannon and cannonballs, personal ornaments (bracelets, rings, pins, pendants), clothing items (buckles), religious medallions, various implements made of brass, copper, iron, ivory, clay and stone, and seventeenth-, eighteenth-, and nineteenth-century coins (Spanish, Portuguese, Persian, Egyptian and English). The excavations at Fort Jesus tangibly illustrated the fort's important role as a trading centre and a place where different cultures came into contact.

The Portuguese never had a lasting colony in North America, but this does not mean that their artefacts were not used there. Archaeologists had found pieces of Portuguese majolica at **Jamestown**, Virginia, for example, and Steven Pendery's study of these tin-glazed earthenwares at seventeenth-century New England sites shows that Portuguese objects, particularly ceramics, were as widely distributed as the ceramics of any other colonial superpower. Archaeologists also frequently find Portuguese majolicas at sites in Brazil, including at slave plantations, colonial towns and settlements, and even at **Palmares**, the fugitive slave kingdom located in the north-east.

Pendery provided a chronology of Portuguese tin-glazed earthenwares for the seventeenth century and showed how eleven different surface decorations were used during a certain part of that century. He also illustrated the vessel forms found in New England, and linked the mention of 'Lisbon ware' in seventeenth-century **probate inventories** with tin-glazed earthenwares. Pendery's research is especially important because in addition to documenting one aspect of Portuguese material culture – which can be used in a comparative manner throughout the Portuguese colonial world – he has also provided a strong impetus for the archaeological analysis of Portuguese colonialism.

Further reading

Hoover, R.L. (1991) 'Oportunidades para Pesquisas na Arqueologia Histórica do Mundo Português', unpublished paper for the XIV Simpósio sobre Tradicões Portuguesas, University of California, Los Angeles.

Kirkman, J.S. (1974) *Fort Jesus: A Portuguese Fortress on the East African Coast*, Oxford: Clarendon.

Menezes, J.L.M. and Rodrigues, M.R.R. (1986) *Fortificações Portuguesas no Nordeste do Brasil: Séculos XVI, XVII e XVIII*, Recife: Pool Editorial.

Miranda, J.A. and Viegas, J.C. (1992) *Moinhos de Vento no Concelho de Oeiras*, Oeiras: Cámara Municipal de Oeiras.

Orser, C.E., Jr (1994) 'Toward a global historical archaeology: An example from Brazil', *Historical Archaeology* 28(1): 5–22.

Palmer, M. (1993) 'A Arqueologia Industrial como Arqueologia Histórica', *Arqueologia Industrial* 1 (2nd series) (1–2): 67–71.

Pendery, S.R. (1999) 'Portuguese tin-glazed earthenware in seventeenth-century New England: A preliminary study', *Historical Archaeology* 33(4): 58–77.

CHARLES E. ORSER, JR

post-medieval archaeology

The term 'post-medieval archaeology' is mainly used in a European context to denote the material study of society in the period spanning the end of the Middle Ages and the onset of industrialisation. Of course, trajectories vary from region to region and the terminal dates for this key technological and cultural phase remain flexible at either end. For instance, much of central and southern Europe was untouched by the spread of the Protestant Reformation, while other areas were slow to industrialise or remained predominantly agricultural economies until the twentieth century. With the foundation of the **Society for Post-medieval Archaeology** in 1966, archaeologists in Britain were the first to identify the period *c.* 1450 to 1750 as one of principal interest, accepting the distinctive character of the epoch, which spans the growth of intercontinental trade and European colonisation, and the impact of printing, the Renaissance, Reformation and gunpowder at one end and the profound social and technological changes delivered by the Enlightenment movement and the development of factory modes of production at the other. However, in recent years it has been those periods of cultural and technological transition between medieval and post-medieval, and post-medieval and modern, which have generated most scholarly interest. The subject is simultaneously beginning to consider the nature of its relationship to those period disciplines with which it interacts, such as medieval or **industrial archaeology**, and to specialist material studies of the post-medieval environment, **churches**, funerary data, **fortifications**, ships, rural landscapes, gardens, **vernacular architecture** and of the various categories of post-medieval domestic artefacts. Post-medieval research agendas must also take into account that so many European post-medieval sites are multi-period in character and that few sites or assemblages can be isolated entirely from preceding or subsequent contexts.

Growth of the discipline

Seen from the outside, European post-medieval archaeology has been perceived as a sub-discipline of historical archaeology, which is limited in its concern with the continuation of indigenous medieval culture. Developments in the subject since its formalisation in the mid-1960s suggest that it has moved far beyond that position and a study of recent conference proceedings illustrates the vibrant nature of current methodological and theoretical debates. Thirty-five years later, post-medieval archaeology is emerging as one of the most dynamic fields of study in global historical archaeology with a prolific publication record, the establishment of regional research frameworks, a strongly embedded network of researchers and practitioners, and growing recognition in university teaching programmes. This new period-discipline, once considered no more than supplemental to the real business of historical research (the 'handmaiden of history' syndrome) is gaining in recognition in its provision of a material and spatial dimension to the study of historical culture. It is rapidly emerging as one of the most advanced in terms of interdisciplinary research and practice, combining archaeological and ethnological fieldwork, artefact studies and scientific analysis with the study of contemporary documentary, cartographic and iconographic sources.

The early years of the discipline in Great Britain and continental Europe were inevitably dominated by the urge to collect data through fieldwork and collections study. The work of early pioneers in post-medieval archaeology can be characterised by an emphasis on recording, characterisation, chronology and attribution with little reference to context or broader cultural questions. Unlike their North American counterparts who stemmed from a training in cultural anthropology, most early British and continental practitioners continued to work in the historical tradition, focusing on chronology and economic data. With the maturity of the discipline, this position has now changed beyond recognition. Today, the archaeology of early modern Europe engages with a wide spectrum of humanities and scientific disciplines, and is principally concerned with the writing of history in its own right. The material dimension offers opportunities both to investigate communities and individuals not represented in the traditional documentary record and to re-evaluate those – often the elites – that are already well represented. In Britain, Martin Biddle's 1959–60 excavations on the site of King Henry VIII's Renaissance palace of Nonsuch in the Surrey countryside were the first to demonstrate publicly the value of an archaeological approach to the lifestyle of an otherwise well-documented European Renaissance monarch. The full layout, architectural scheme and lavish ornamentation of this remarkable building were revealed for the first time, the objects giving meaning to the dry listings of items in contemporary building accounts. Marks and graffiti on architectural fragments indicated that the building was constructed by continental masons with the specialist experience and knowledge base gained while working for Francis I of France. In contrast, excavations during the mid-1970s by the Museum of London of seventeenth-century artisans' tenements at Aldgate on the eastern edge of the City of London revealed vital data on standards of living and dietary habits of one of the poorest working communities living on the edge of the early modern metropolis, a community unknown from contemporary records. Similar case studies illustrating the contribution of archaeological research to key historical narratives can now be found across the continent of Europe where the first regional surveys of post-medieval archaeology are beginning to emerge.

Urban archaeology and material-culture studies

Although so much of the early modern sequence has been lost as a result, post-medieval archaeology has benefited, perhaps more than other period disciplines, from the dramatic post-war development of towns and cities in Europe. The fall of the Iron Curtain in 1990 has generated a further wave of activity in the urban centres of central, Eastern and Baltic Europe as local economies convert to Western models. Archaeological recording on these well-preserved sites has been summarised recently as they are rapidly becoming laboratories for the study of late medieval to early modern urban life on the continent. Meanwhile in Britain, many towns, particularly in south-east **England**, have produced a vast corpus of data for manufacturing and consumer studies. London, as the world's fourth largest city by the end of the seventeenth century, continues to generate most activity. Recently, attention has been turning to investigating those communities and industries lying on the river Thames and in the immediate hinterland of the capital that were caught up in metropolitan expansion after *c.* 1550. The daily life of Londoners from the wealthiest merchants to squatters in the poorest slums can be investigated through the excavated contents of refuse deposits. **Probate inventories** help to enhance the picture for the city's wealthier households. Studies of buildings and housing culture utilise the richness of the visual archival record contained in contemporary maps and plans, and in historical architectural drawings. In London, as elsewhere, material from closely datable, sealed features, such as wells and cesspits, is receiving priority attention. The analysis of domestic assemblages in the context of their associated buildings can provide evidence for variability in the standards of living and nutrition, interior furnishings and personal adornment in households across the capital. Such studies of social topography integrate **ceramics** and other domestic artefacts with buildings evidence and documentary information.

A key emphasis of European **urban archaeology** over the past thirty years has been the study of urban material culture, particularly domestic utensils and fittings. By virtue of their utility at virtually all social levels, their relatively short lifespan, and durability in the ground, ceramics have proved to be the most sensitive sources of information on economic trends, social behaviour patterns and cultural exchange. Although data-rich, pottery catalogues generated by urban archaeology have tended to lack a meaningful synthetic element – bar some exceptions. Today, as the first generation of regional studies emerges, there is greater scope for inter-site and inter-regional comparison. There has also been a welcome tendency to publish production sites, most of which by the seventeenth century are metropolitan in location, the London tin-glazed earthenware industry being a case in point. Outside London, Staffordshire in the North Midlands, particularly the urban conurbation of **Stoke-on-Trent**, formed the centre of a prolific ceramic industry that supplied much of the British Isles, the continent of Europe and North America with refined-body wares throughout the eighteenth to nineteenth centuries. Here the standard of archaeological recording and analysis of production sites and their output provide a model for the discipline. Meanwhile, some of the first synthetic studies of key ceramic industries with international markets, such as the German **stoneware** industry, are being published. In this instance the products, which were traded across Europe and to the New World, have been examined in their widest economic, social and cultural contexts with detailed analyses of technology, distribution, function, iconography and symbolic value.

The archaeology of leisure

An increase in leisure time and in the range of activities and associated structures and artefacts helps us to characterise post-medieval European society. Theatres, gardens, clay tobacco pipes (see **pipes, smoking**) and **coffee** cups, for instance, combine to produce a very different picture of secular activities, relations and mentalities from that of medieval society, whose social calendar was set by the Church. Cities were at the epicentre of the emerging leisure industries of Europe and offered a bewildering array of recreational activities. They also attracted new industries, such as clay-pipe making and specialist catering trades, to service them. The discovery in 1989 of the remains of the Elizabethan **Rose Theatre** and **Globe Theatre** in Southwark, London, both closely associated with William Shakespeare, propelled the archaeology of the post-Middle Ages to the centre-stage of British cultural life, a feat not achieved since the excavations at Nonsuch Palace in the late 1950s. Despite the vast corpus of scholarship on Shakespeare's dramatic work, little was known of the physical setting and staging until these discoveries. Inns, taverns, coaching inns, alehouses and coffee houses had become key features of the urban British scene by the beginning

of the eighteenth century. Recent excavations of eighteenth-century tavern sites in the coaching towns servicing London, such as Guildford and Bagshot in Surrey, and Uxbridge in Middlesex, provide a snapshot of this rich material world that saw the introduction of new products and etiquettes for the consumption of exotic beverages such as coffee and chocolate. Meanwhile, the growing fashion for keeping pets by eighteenth-century middle-class urban households can be seen in a new range of goods designed for that purpose. Finally, the study of the clay tobacco pipe industry has emerged as one of the leading specialisations of post-medieval archaeology across Western and Northern Europe. Regional studies of production and market distributions are well advanced in many areas. With the essential groundwork achieved on chronology and attribution, researchers in the field are now turning to the use of clay pipes for evaluating the social status of consumers.

An embarrassment of riches

The archaeology of the post-Middle Ages is usually defined by the problem of the finds-mountain. Most archaeology of the period has been generated by urban development. For over thirty years, archaeologists have fought to try to bring the sheer quantity of data under control, primarily through detailed recording and characterisation studies. Today, the current trend in the urban sphere is to utilise the information generated by these studies in order to define new archaeological strategies that are more selective in their approach and pursue those topics in need of calibration and further refinement. Meanwhile, international research bodies responsible for leading the discipline, such as the Society for Post-medieval Archaeology, are engaged in a long-term programme of international and interdisciplinary conferences and seminars with associated publications, which deal with key historical questions that help define the period and issues of methodology and disciplinarity. Recent thematic meetings that cut across material specialisations include those on trade and discovery, artefacts from **shipwrecks**, the medieval to early modern transition, the post-medieval to industrial interface and the archaeology of the Reformation. The joint anniversary meeting of the

Society for Post-medieval Archaeology and the **Society for Historical Archaeology** in 1997 provided an opportunity to review thirty years of the development in the discipline. Three decades on from institutional formalisation on both sides of the Atlantic, a number of more critical reviews of post-medieval archaeology are beginning to appear that highlight the challenge facing the subject in reconciling the vision of post-processual approaches (see **post-processual archaeology**) with the rigour of empirical research.

Further reading

Crossley, D. (1990) *Post-Medieval Archaeology in Britain*, Leicester: Leicester University Press.

Egan, G. and Michael, R.L. (eds) (1999) *Old and New Worlds. Historical/Post-medieval Archaeology Papers from the Societies' Joint Conferences at Williamsburg and London 1997 to Mark Thirty Years of Achievement*, Oxford: Oxbow.

Gaimster, D.R.M. (1994) 'The archaeology of post-medieval society, c.1450–1750: Material culture studies in Britain since the war', in B. Vyner (ed.) *Building on the Past. Papers Celebrating 150 Years of the Royal Archaeological Institute*, London: Royal Archaeological Institute, pp. 283–312.

Gaimster, D.R.M. and Stamper, P. (eds) (1997) *The Age of Transition. The Archaeology of English Culture 1400–1600*, Society for Medieval Archaeology Monograph 15, Oxford: Oxbow.

Hook, D.R. and Gaimster, D.R.M (eds) (1995) *Trade and Discovery: the Scientific Study of Artefacts from Post-medieval Europe and Beyond*, Occasional Paper 109, London: British Museum.

Verhaeghe, F. and Otte, M. (eds) *Archéologie des temps modernes*, Liège: Études et Recherches Archéologique de l'Université de Liège 26.

Wilson, J. (1995) *The Archaeology of Shakespeare: The Material Legacy of Shakespeare's Theatre*, Stroud: Alan Sutton.

DAVID R.M. GAIMSTER

post-processual archaeology

Post-processual archaeology developed in the 1980s, largely in reaction to and out of dissatisfac-

tion with the earlier **processual archaeology**. As was true of processual archaeology, historical archaeology played an important role in the formulation of post-processual archaeology. Part of the reason for the impact of historical archaeology in post-processual archaeology was the processual archaeologists' legitimation of historical archaeology with their proposition that all cultural processes, regardless of date, were reasonable topics of analysis.

The tenets of post-processual archaeology

As outlined by English archaeologist Ian Hodder, post-processual archaeology has three important characteristics that set it apart from processual archaeology. First, post-processual archaeologists perceive men, women and **children** as actively engaged in their social worlds. These men and women are more than mere participants in daily life; they are an integral element for constructing society and culture. They negotiate society's rules and they create and maintain social relations within their culture's established norms. Processual archaeologists tend to envision people as being more constrained by their cultures than do post-processual archaeologists. Second, post-processual archaeologists, in accordance with the previous characteristic, tend to focus on the individual, rather than on the broad, behavioural generalisations of the processual archaeologists. Social scientists often refer to an individual's role in social action as 'agency'. Men and women exercise agency when they influence the characteristics and outcomes of certain events. In other words, men and women do not simply wait for their cultures to provide for them; they actively create their own lives on a daily basis. And finally, post-processual archaeologists tend to envision social change as being 'contextual', or, in other words, linked to a specific time and place. Their general conception is that the past cannot be adequately understood without situating its individuals within their social and cultural milieu (in both time and space) as much as is possible.

Some of the elements of 'social action' outlined by Hodder are: belief and action (how individuals experience, understand and therefore shape the world in which they live); material and historical context (the social, cultural, ecological and historical environments in which people live); negotiation (how individuals manipulate and work within their social systems); and material culture (the roles that physical things play in social action to create and maintain social relations as well as personal experience, understanding and perception). Processual archaeologists, on the other hand, tend to imagine that individual cultures are caught up in the grand sweep of cultural evolution and that individuals, though they are obviously important, cannot be truly examined with archaeological evidence.

As may be imagined, not all archaeologists who reject processual archaeology would agree on the precise nature of post-processual archaeology. In fact, its wide-ranging perspectives provide one of its main characteristics. Some may even reject the term 'post-processual' archaeology, claiming that their research is not 'post' anything, but an even newer kind of archaeology than the **New Archaeology**. Still, post-processual archaeology, whatever its name, is a strong force in early twenty-first-century archaeology.

Post-processual historical archaeology

As was true of processual archaeology, historical archaeologists have also had a large impact on post-processual archaeology. In fact, historical archaeology has arguably been as important to the development of post-processual archaeology as any other branch of archaeology. Part of the reason for the widespread use of historical archaeology in post-processual studies undoubtedly involves the broad number of sources available to the historical archaeologist. Many of the topics of most interest to post-processualists, because they concern mind and meaning, are best studied by combining archaeological and historical sources of information. Each kind of source can provide insights not offered by the other, and one of the strengths of historical archaeology is its practitioners' ability to interrelate diverse sources.

Historical archaeologists thus have been instrumental in the formulation and development of post-processual archaeology, particular in the realm of Anglo-American, colonial-period archaeology. Mark Leone, the historical archaeologist who developed a large, multi-year programme of research at **Annapolis**, Maryland, provided an early outline of three kinds of post-processual archaeology, which he termed 'symbolic', 'structural' and 'critical' archaeology.

Leone noted that the three varieties of post-processual archaeology had four general, mutually shared perspectives. These understandings were in agreement with Hodder's view about the nature of post-processual archaeology. The first of the four common viewpoints involves an appreciation for the significance of social action, where individuals have the ability to shape daily history. The second places a strong emphasis on 'meaning', which is intended to indicate that individuals attach various degrees of significance to the daily events that occur during their lifetimes. People do not simply react to their physical and social environments as members of cultures. Rather, they have agency to act within a set of culturally constructed and generally agreed-upon behaviours. A third aspect of post-processual archaeology as outlined by Leone, and perhaps the key element of 'critical archaeology', is the critique of the function and usage of knowledge about the past. Those who refer to themselves as 'critical archaeologists' tend to argue that archaeological knowledge is not necessarily neutral, for one reason, because the way it gets disseminated is through the filter of the archaeologist. Archaeologists excavate archaeological deposits and artefacts, and then are called upon to interpret them. Like all individuals living in active societies, archaeologists experience and interpret the world in different ways and their interpretations may, and perhaps always do, reflect their personalities to some extent. The most glaring examples of the non-academic use of archaeology come from the political world, where archaeological research can be skewed to present a certain national perspective. The final point Leone makes is that post-processual archaeology rejects the positivist position of processual archaeology, by arguing that knowledge is nuanced and not necessarily concrete. Put another way, one person's truth may be another's falsehood. While few practising archaeologists would propose that the past is unknowable – and that as a result the archaeologists' interpretations are merely creative stories – post-processualists accept that the acquisition and acceptance of knowledge rest on many factors, including some relating to class, gender, racial categorisation, economic position and religious and political belief.

Leone's identification of 'symbolic', 'structural' and 'critical' archaeologies, though perhaps somewhat limiting, provides an excellent way to demonstrate the kinds of approaches post-processual historical archaeologists have pursued. An example of each will suffice.

Archaeological examinations of past symbolism are of necessity variable in approach and design because they typically relate to at least two elements: what something is meant to portray, and how people actually perceive the message being sent. It is relatively easy to imagine that people in the past could create and use symbols for many reasons, and so deciphering their meanings in the present can be extremely difficult.

Archaeologist Alasdair Brooks explored the symbolic nature of the invention of myth and tradition by examining nineteenth-century transfer-printed **ceramics** imprinted with images meant to portray a mythic Celtic past. He discovered that early nineteenth-century English potters manufactured dinner plates decorated with Celtic patterns that had names which were consciously invented to symbolise this mythic past. Ceramics with such evocative names as 'Legend of Montrose' (the name of a Walter Scott novel), 'Caledonia' and 'Cambrian' were meant to help establish a Celtic (Scottish) myth throughout the world by being the physical embodiment of that myth. The plates were merely the vehicles by which the myth travelled across the globe wherever the plates were sold. Thus, when archaeologists find transfer-printed ceramics with Celtic patterns at sites in, say, North America, they are forced to consider how the owners of the plates used them to construct their personal understandings of Celtic life. For men and women who had never experienced, and probably would never directly experience, life in the Scottish Highlands, the picture on their dinner plates would become their image of Celtic life, whether or not it was realistic.

Whereas it would have been possible for Brooks to examine the transfer-printed plates merely as historical examples of the kinds of decorations people purchased and used (because they were available), he pushed the analysis into the symbolic

realm. Rather than being content with understanding the functional attributes of the dinner plates alone, he delved beneath the patterns to investigate their symbolic meanings.

Archaeologist James Deetz has been the strongest advocate of a structural approach to archaeological analysis. Structuralism is a complex and formidable body of intellectual thought with roots in French social anthropology. One of its main propositions, however, is that a basic structure exists beneath all human thought and action. This conceptualisation is perhaps best conceived of as being composed of diametrical opposites. For structuralists, an examination of these opposites can reveal much that may not be otherwise readily apparent about human life, including life in the past. To illustrate this point, Deetz examined four classes of everyday material culture related to colonial British American settlements: ceramics, foodways, mortuary contexts and music. Deetz then investigated the binary opposites in eight 'domains': intellect/emotion, private/public, artificial/natural substance, scattered/clustered, extensive/intensive, complex/simple, framed/open and non-symmetry/symmetry. So, for example, for ceramics, the difference in the 'private/public' domain is between individual and corporate utensils (individually used forks and knives, as opposed to a common bowl set in the middle of the table); in the extensive/intensive domain, the distinction is between random, mismatched pieces of ceramics and complete sets. In the mortuary class, the 'scattered/clustered' attribute involves the difference between large cemeteries and family plots.

What this all means for Deetz is that by examining the binary opposites presented by artefacts and other pieces of material culture it is possible to investigate certain elements of Anglo-American life, aspects that may otherwise be hidden from view. The material culture provides a window on the transition of British American culture from the medieval age to the modern era.

Of the three kinds of post-processual archaeology mentioned by Leone, critical archaeology is by far the most controversial. Part of the basis of contention is the belief among critical archaeologists that archaeological knowledge is not neutral. Having made this claim, critical archaeologists feel compelled to explain how they intend to use their data. Critical archaeologists often call their interest in the personal meaning of their interpretations 'reflexivity', which refers to an archaeologist's awareness of how they use the information they have collected and how this usage reflects their personal attitudes, motives and experience. Archaeologists working in Annapolis, Maryland, have largely pioneered the concept of reflexivity within critical archaeology because of their commitment to presenting the archaeological sites as **living museums**. Thus, for example, when Parker Potter discussed the ceramic tablewares found at home sites in Annapolis, his interest was directed both towards agency in the past (how the tablewares were used to promote a particular point of view, much like Brooks's example mentioned above) and agency in the present (how as archaeologists they would seek to interpret the tablewares to the public). Potter reports that fully 90 per cent of the visitors to the Annapolis excavation sites viewed the development of **creamware** in the eighteenth century – and the accompanying use of individual place settings – as a sign that the men and women of historic Annapolis had a growing concern for personal hygiene. Their opinion was almost universal even though no historical evidence exists to suggest that hygiene had anything to do with the invention and marketing of creamware. Still, a relation to hygiene is a meaning that people attach to the ceramic artefacts, perhaps because as modern-day Americans they often think about hygiene and cleanliness. Critical archaeology seeks to mediate between past and present in this manner and at the same time to demonstrate the importance of archaeological interpretations in the present. They would say that an archaeological work in which the archaeologist is not fully cognisant of reflexivity is not an adequate study.

Many varieties of post-processual archaeology exist at the beginning of the twenty-first century, and only a tiny glimpse of the approach is presented here. Post-processual historical archaeology is sure to continue to grow as archaeologists experiment with new approaches and perspectives.

See also: history of historical archaeology; nationalism; politics in archaeology

Further reading

Brooks, A.M. (1997) 'Beyond the fringe: Transfer-printed ceramics and the internationalization of Celtic myth', *International Journal of Historical Archaeology* 1: 39–55.

Deetz, J.F. (1983) 'Scientific humanism and humanistic science: A plea for paradigmatic pluralism in historical archaeology', *Geoscience and Man* 23: 27–34.

Hodder, I. (1985) 'Postprocessual archaeology', in M.B. Schiffer (ed.), *Advances in Archaeological Method and Theory* 8, New York: Academic Press, pp. 1–26.

Leone, M.P. (1986) 'Symbolic, structural, and critical archaeology', in D.J. Meltzer, D.D. Fowler and J.A. Sabloff (eds), *American Archaeology, Past and Future*, Washington, DC: Smithsonian Institution Press, pp. 415–38.

Potter, P.B., Jr (1992) 'Critical archaeology: In the ground and on the street', *Historical Archaeology* 26(3): 117–29.

Shackel, P.A. and Little, B.J. (1992) 'Post-processual approaches to meanings and uses of material culture in historical archaeology', *Historical Archaeology* 26(3): 5–11.

CHARLES E. ORSER, JR

pot hunting

Pot hunting is a term used mostly by US archaeologists to refer to any kind of site **looting**. The term was originally coined because of the propensity of looters to dig into archaeological sites to obtain whole pots that they could then either add to their personal artefact collections or sell to other collectors. Pot hunters, of course, are not only interested in pottery, but whole pottery vessels can sell for extremely high prices in the illegal antiquities market. The term is widely used to refer only to unscrupulous looters and is never used to refer to conscientious avocational archaeologists.

CHARLES E. ORSER, JR

power

Social scientists, including historical archaeologists, have been interested in social power for many years. They have spent considerable time analysing power because it is a multifaceted issue with many historical forms. For historical archaeologists, the milieu of their studies is typically hierarchical, capitalist societies that incorporate many dimensions of power related to socioeconomic class (see **class, social**), racial categorisation, **gender** and many other social variables.

Historical archaeologists who have investigated power have tended to envision it as related to social inequality, where one person or group has 'power over' another person or group or where one person or group has the 'power to' cause something to happen. An individual may have the power to accomplish a task, but he or she may not have the power over others to force them to accomplish the task. Issues of power become even more complex when more than two social actors are considered.

The two sides of social power that archaeologists have investigated are domination and **resistance**. As a person with power attempts to force his or her will on someone whom they perceive to have less power, the person with less power may decide to resist the first person's control. As such, the first person's power is not 'hegemonic' or total. The examination of resistance and domination has been an important focus of much historical archaeology conducted during and after the 1980s.

Slave plantations (see **plantation archaeology**) and factories are two locales in which historical archaeologists have investigated issues of power. Plantations inhabited by agricultural slaves have provided excellent arenas to investigate the dialectical relationship between domination and resistance because of the legal position of slaves. Archaeologists have examined plantation **material culture** and settlement patterns (see **settlement analysis**) to develop clues about past power relationships.

The archaeologists who excavated at the Boott Cotton Mills in Lowell, Massachusetts, provided special insights into past power relations. The managers of the mill maintained a twenty-four-hour control of the largely immigrant work force in the effort to control both factory output and worker lifestyle. Though they banned the consumption of alcohol, the archaeologists discovered eighty-four medicine **bottles** (with the medicine having a high alcohol content) and seventy-two liquor bottles. These finds convinced the archaeologists that the workers were able to resist some of the owners' power and domination, or, in other words, that even workers in a Gilded Age factory were able to take some measure of control of their lives.

Further reading

Beaudry, M.C., Cook, L.J. and Mrozowski, S.A. (1991) 'Artifacts and active voices: Material culture as social discourse', in R.H. McGuire and R. Paynter (eds) *The Archaeology of Inequality*, Oxford: Blackwell, pp. 150–91.

Orser, C.E., Jr (1988) 'Toward a theory of power for historical archaeology: Plantations and space', in M.P. Leone and P.B. Potter, Jr (eds) *The Recovery of Meaning: Historical Archaeology in the Eastern United States*, Washington, DC: Smithsonian Institution Press, pp. 313–43.

Paynter, R. and McGuire, R.H. (1991) 'The archaeology of inequality: Material culture, domination, and resistance', in R.H. McGuire and R. Paynter (eds) *The Archaeology of Inequality*, Oxford: Blackwell, pp. 1–27.

CHARLES E. ORSER, JR

Prague Castle, Czech Republic

Modern Prague has ancient roots as a hill fort that over the centuries has emerged as the centre of the seat of a new and independent government. Today, the city fills a long section of the valley of the Vltava River (Moldau) and, in recent decades, has expanded up onto the surrounding gently rolling upland plateau (460–600 m). Over the centuries, the area of the ancient hill fort has grown into a city-like complex of buildings, including the famous Prague Cathedral at one end, which preserves a spectacular array of structures now largely accessible to the public. More than 1,000 years of history is evident in this museum of a great state.

The earliest stages in the development of this hill fort are only now being revealed. Archaeologists now know that the traditional relations among the many Iron Age villages that were located on defensive hilltops or in other locations throughout the region were strongly influenced by Roman economic and military activities. The decline of Roman influence in this region led to the rise in this region of Bohemia of the early Czech state, during the eighth and ninth centuries, as one of the three great powers in Central Europe (Bohemia, Hungary and Poland). During the eighth century, considerable expansion can be documented for this hilltop settlement overlooking the river that forms the core of Prague Castle. At the end of this period, the Church of the Virgin Mary was erected (c. AD 882–5) at the western end of the settlement. This is only the second Roman Catholic Church-related structure known to have been built in the Czech Republic.

The Great Moravian state was supplanted by the Duchy (Kingdom) of Bohemia in the tenth century, which had its centre in Prague. Bohemia now forms the western province of the Czech Republic. By the tenth century, rapid growth can be documented throughout this area due to the stabilising effects of the early government. This growth is reflected in the urbanisation and development of the entire region, but the record is most clear in the Prague Castle. The Kingdom of Bohemia had a particularly spectacular development during the thirteenth and fourteenth centuries. Included in this period of prosperity was the construction of the Charles Bridge, built in the fourteenth century. Situated directly below the height on which the Prague Castle stands, this is the oldest functioning bridge of the dozen now standing within the city. Unfortunately, soon after, religious and political problems led to Hapsburg control of the area and a long period of economic decline.

Despite the vicissitudes of history, all of these historic periods are reflected in various constructions that are remarkably well preserved within the precinct of the extensive Prague Castle. The modern complex of buildings called the Prague Castle is composed of a series of buildings of various types, some of which date back to the early medieval period. Earlier constructions were of more traditional materials, but stone buildings soon became characteristic of the elaborate architecture

that characterised the castle area. Archaeological investigations have been directed towards the recovery of the early development of the castle since 1911. These excavations, of uniformly high quality, reveal the growth of the original hilltop through encirclement by ever-expanding rings of defensive walls. Within those walls a great cathedral was erected, along with an impressive house for the local bishop. Numerous chapels and other religious edifices were built together with impressive stone buildings housing the royal families, numbers of government offices and the religious leaders. The continuities in functions of these structures are extraordinary. Perhaps most unusual is the survival of numbers of small medieval houses and workshops within this complex. All of these elements combine to make this city within a city an impressive monument to the modern Czech state.

MARSHALL JOSEPH BECKER

preservation legislation

Men and women interested in the preservation and protection of historic monuments, properties and sites have urged their governments to enact legislation that has the specific goal of 'saving the past for the future'. Important historic properties regularly come under attack because of **looting**, vandalism, urban sprawl, poor planning, highway construction, warfare and even programmes of ethnic cleansing meant to erase a culture's history from the landscape. Legislation has been enacted on international, national and local levels. A couple of examples will demonstrate the kinds of legislation enacted.

On the international level, the United Nations Educational, Scientific, and Cultural Organization (UNESCO) has been an important voice in promoting the transnational protection of significant cultural and historical sites. In 1992, it published its *Convention Concerning the Protection of the World Cultural and Natural Heritage*. The framers of this document defined 'cultural heritage' as sites, monuments and groups of buildings that have 'historical, aesthetic, archaeological, scientific, ethnological or anthropological value'. They also created the 'World Heritage List' composed of 'World Heritage Sites'. These are historic properties that are deemed to have special value to the world's cultural history.

Twenty years before this, in 1970, UNESCO hosted a convention in Paris focused on a growing problem in international preservation: the illegal 'import, export and transfer of ownership of cultural property'. This convention specifically mandated measures to help stop the illicit sale of works of art and archaeological artefacts to the world's museums and private collectors. In accordance with this action, other international bodies, such as the European Community (in 1992) and International Council of Museums (in 1995), enacted codes to restrict its members from engaging in the acquisition of illegally obtained objects.

On the national level, the USA developed its first Antiquities Act in 1906 covering 'lands owned or controlled by the Government of the United States'. This Act was followed by the Historic Sites Act of 1935 (providing for the 'preservation of historic American sites, buildings, objects, and antiquities of national significance and for other purposes'), the National Historic Preservation Act of 1966 (establishing 'a program for the preservation of additional historic properties throughout the nation'), 'Executive Order 11593' of 1971 (expanding 'the responsibilities of federal agencies with respect to the purposes of the National Historic Preservation Act') and 36 CFR [Code of Federal Regulations] 60 (establishing the 'basic procedures of nomination to the **National Register of Historic Places**). This body of legislation, and later refinements to it, created a bureaucracy in the USA to deal specifically with cultural and historic properties either on federal land or somehow involving federal monies. One implication of this legislation was the creation of a large **cultural-resource management** focus within US historical archaeology. Many people believe that one deficiency in the legislation is that it does not include historic sites on private property.

Many nations have adopted preservation legislation. For example, the Republic of **Ireland** enacted a National Monuments Act in 1930, a National Monuments (Amendment) Act in 1954 and a National Monuments (Amendment) Act in

1987. These acts established the definition of 'monument' and legislated their guardianship and ownership. Each amendment was intended to refine the provisions of the earlier acts and to respond to current developments and circumstances. For instance, the 1987 amendment restricted the use of detection devices at monument or archaeological areas and established provisions applying to the preservation of shipwreck sites. Such legislation attempts to raise public awareness and appreciation of important cultural and historical sites and properties.

In addition to the federally created legislation, bodies of professional archaeologists have often developed their own rules of conduct. Most of these rules, in addition to setting standards for excavation methods and archaeological reporting, also address the pressing needs of preservation. In Ireland, for example, the Irish Association of Professional Archaeologists has published booklets such as the *Guidelines for Archaeologists* and *The Treatment of Human Remains*. These documents encourage a high level of professionalism among practising archaeologists, and also provide guidelines that add another layer of legislation, albeit with no prosecutorial or legal authority, to the existing statutes.

In addition to national legislation, many local governments have enacted their own laws to govern the protection and use of historic properties. These bodies often work in conjunction with old house societies, **local-history** organisations and concerned citizens to protect sites judged to be of local importance.

See also: heritage management; site significance

Further reading

Hardesty, D.L. and Little, B.J. (2000) *Assessing Site Significance: A Guide for Archaeologists and Historians*, Walnut Creek, CA: AltaMira Press.

Renfrew, C. (2000) *Loot, Legitimacy, and Ownership*, London: Duckworth.

Skeates, R. (2000) *Debating the Archaeological Heritage*, London: Duckworth.

CHARLES E. ORSER, JR

probate inventories

Where they exist, probate inventories often provide historical archaeologists with abundant information and special insights into the past. Probate inventories are lists of a deceased person's belongings at the time of death. Such lists can be extremely detailed, even to the point of enumerating an individual's personal possession on a room-by-room basis. Probate inventories, however, were seldom if ever produced for people at the lowest end of the social ladder.

Historical archaeologists have used probate inventories in two ways: to investigate the correlation between historical documents and archaeological remains, and to assist in site interpretation. Both types of study demonstrate the value of probate inventories to historical archaeology.

Historical archaeologists know that the objects they find buried in the ground do not constitute the entirety of the objects once used by the residents of a particular home site. For example, when she examined a series of probate inventories in Albermarle County, Virginia, dating from 1770 to 1799, Ann Smart Martin learned that **pewter** tablewares were almost always mentioned in the documents. It was clear that pewter objects were widely used in upper-class, late eighteenth-century homes. At the same time, however, archaeologists seldom find pewter objects in their excavations of sites dating to the same period. One reason for the disparity is that pewter dishes do not break when dropped and so they seldom enter the archaeological record in the same way as **ceramics**. Pewter objects are also likely to be handed down as inheritance and will thus be curated as valued pieces. Durability and curation mean that archaeologists will have an inaccurate perception of the use of pewter in past households if they only judge its presence by the number of objects they have excavated.

In other studies, archaeologists have been able to provide more complete interpretations of past sites by linking probate inventories with archaeological information. For example, using probate records and faunal remains from the Mott Farm in Portsmouth, Rhode Island (owned by the same family from 1639 to 1895), zooarchaeologist Joanne Bowen was able to determine how the residents of the farm used their animals. The inventories listed the animals owned by each individual, but provided no information about use. Careful analysis of the bones told her how the animals were used for performing heavy or light tasks, for food and for export. At the nineteenth-century **Millwood Plantation** in South Carolina, an examination of probate records allowed archaeologists to interpret the remains of a brick building foundation with internal, key-hole-shaped, brick structures as an experimental sorghum processor.

See also: zooarchaeology

Further reading

Bowen, J. (1975) 'Probate inventories: An evaluation from the perspective of zooarchaeology and agricultural history at Mott Farm', *Historical Archaeology* 9: 11–25.

Martin, A.S. (1989) 'The role of pewter as missing artifact: Consumer attitudes toward tablewares in late 18th-century Virginia', *Historical Archaeology* 23(2): 1–27.

Orser, C.E., Jr (1985) 'The sorghum industry of a 19th-century cotton plantation in South Carolina', *Historical Archaeology* 19(1): 51–64.

CHARLES E. ORSER, JR

processual archaeology

Processual archaeology, often termed the '**New Archaeology**', was a development in the history of archaeology that was first given expression in the USA, Great Britain and Scandinavia. From these cores, processual archaeology spread throughout the world's archaeological community and became widely practised. Processual archaeology developed in the 1960s, grew to dominate the field in the 1970s and 1980s, and then waned somewhat in the 1990s. At the beginning of the twenty-first century, many archaeologists still consider themselves to be processual archaeologists. Processual archaeology was originally created for use by prehistoric archaeologists, but it had many important ramifications for historical archaeology as well.

The tenets of processual archaeology

The need for processual archaeology developed as young archaeologists in the early 1960s grew tired of the culture-history approach of mainstream archaeology. Archaeologist Walter Taylor recognised in the 1940s that most professional archaeologists spent their time only describing artefacts and the archaeological cultures they represented without working diligently enough to produce explanations of culture process. In other words, these archaeologists were not striving to understand how past cultures actually operated because they were too busy describing what they had excavated. The controversy that developed over description versus explanation was probably most strongly felt in US archaeology because prehistoric archaeology there was so firmly tied to anthropology. Many cultural anthropologists complained that culture-historical archaeologists were contributing nothing to the broader understanding of Native American cultures (see **Native Americans**), with the exception that they could provide detailed catalogues of past Native American **material culture**. For the processual archaeologists, however, this was not enough, and a stronger effort had to be made to transform US archaeology into an anthropological pursuit. The overt identification of US archaeologists with anthropology causes many of them to refer to themselves as 'anthropological archaeologists'. A seminal statement of the need for an overt anthropological archaeology was voiced by Lewis Binford in his article '*Archaeology as anthropology*', which appeared in 1962.

The main tenets of processual archaeology, as they were voiced by Binford early in the formation of this approach, were several and complex. In essence, he argued that:

1 archaeology should adopt an anthropological definition of culture, one that is dynamic and that stresses human adaptation;
2 culture should be viewed as an active, living system of components that permits humans to adapt to cultural changes;
3 archaeologists should have a distinct interest in human behaviour rather than seeking merely to describe the artefacts they have excavated; and

4 archaeologists should understand that individual artefacts can have three main functions:

a 'technomic' – dealing with coping with the physical environment;
b 'sociotechnic' – artefacts that concern the social elements of cultural life; and
c 'ideotechnic' – artefacts that function symbolically.

To develop a truly processual archaeology, one that would involve the excavation of artefacts and other elements of material culture, and from these devise some anthropological understanding, Binford and his colleagues realised that they would have to make archaeology a more 'scientific' discipline. Archaeology would have to be more objective and nomothetic (dealing with broad-scale laws of human behaviour). In addition, archaeologists would have to adopt an explicit scientific methodology that included the creation of hypotheses that they could test during their fieldwork. The testing process would help refine the hypotheses and allow for the creation of new hypotheses. The use of the scientific method would elevate archaeological practice almost to the level of the hard sciences, even though processual archaeologists realised that they did not have the luxury of subjecting past human behaviours to replication or experiment.

Processual historical archaeology

Historical archaeology in the USA was associated with processual archaeology almost from the beginning. The reasons for the companionship of historical and processual archaeology were both personal and academic. For one thing, Lewis Binford had obtained direct, personal experience with historical archaeology when he participated in the 1959 excavation of **Fort Michilimackinac**, an eighteenth-century French and British colonial installation in the USA's upper Great Lakes region. More important, however, was a prominent tenet of processual archaeology. Because processual archaeologists believed that the proper purview of archaeology was the examination of human behaviour, they did not restrict themselves to a particular slice of time. In other words, as anthropological archaeologists they understood that they could investigate sites ranging in date from the earliest prehistoric era to the most recent past. Of course, the most recent past included the sites and people historical archaeologists studied, and processual archaeology thus gave historical archaeology an anthropological legitimacy.

Stanley South has been the most vocal and influential proponent of processual historical archaeology. South promoted historical archaeology as an overtly scientific archaeology based on cultural evolutionism. South's theoretical works have proven extremely important in historical archaeology because he challenged historical archaeologists to conduct their research systematically and with an anthropological perspective. Thus, he did for historical archaeology what Binford did for prehistoric archaeology; he elevated it to a new level of systematic, highly scientific research.

South's scientific historical archaeology is most clearly presented in his widely influential *Method and Theory in Historical Archaeology*, published in 1977. This book was accompanied in the same year by an edited volume, *Research Strategies in Historical Archaeology*. Both books set forth the tenets of a processual historical archaeology and demonstrated the ways in which historical archaeologists could conduct scientific research.

In *Method and Theory in Historical Archaeology* South fully presented his theoretical point of view and explored the methods that would permit him to address various issues involving human behaviour and cultural process. His data consisted of a number of sites, mostly of British American cultural affiliation and eighteenth century in date, that he had investigated in the US South. As part of his scientific goals, he promoted the quantitative study of archaeological remains, and argued that the 'first responsibility' of archaeologists is **pattern recognition**. In other words, South said that archaeologists should look for patterned variability in their archaeological data. In his view, these material-culture patterns would reflect behaviour that was consistent with a culture's norms. Accordingly, he identified in the book the 'Brunswick Pattern of Refuse Disposal' (which involves the spatial distribution of rubbish in a yard area) and the 'Carolina Artefact Pattern' and the 'Frontier Artefact Pattern' (which concern the per cent occurrence of artefacts

within the collections). For example, South defined the 'Carolina Artefact Pattern' as occurring at British American sites where between 51.8 and 69.2 per cent of the artefacts fall into the 'kitchen' group (in which he included **ceramics**, wine and case **bottles**, tumblers, glassware, dishes, forks and anything else that one would normally associate with a kitchen). Conversely, the 'Frontier Artefact Pattern' was characterised by fewer 'kitchen' objects (predicted to fall within 10.2 to 45.0 per cent) but many more 'architecture' artefacts (predicted at between 29.7 and 74.3 per cent). In South's **classification** scheme, **architecture** objects include window glass, **nails**, construction hardware, furniture hardware and anything else related to the building itself.

South's ideas about pattern recognition quickly acquired a strong following among archaeologists, particularly in **cultural-resource management**, where archaeologists were often under pressure to complete their interpretations quickly. The use of quantitative patterns made it possible for them to excavate a site, classify its artefacts, compute the percentages within each category and check them against South's patterns. If they fitted the ranges he identified for each artefact category, then the archaeologists could say that the people at the site were part of a recognised pattern, like the Carolina Artefact Pattern. If, on the other hand, the percentages did not conform to a recognised pattern, the archaeologist could simply create a new pattern. For example, in the 1980s, cultural-resource management archaeologists working in the US South at slave plantation sites (see **plantation archaeology**) created the 'Village Carolina Artefact Pattern' and the 'Carolina Slave Artefact Pattern', as well as several others.

In addition to the pattern concept, South also used in *Method and Theory in Historical Archaeology* the **mean ceramic dating** formula, which he had devised earlier. The formula further showed the value of quantification in historical archaeology.

A study that concretely demonstrates the use of the scientific method in historical archaeology is Kenneth Lewis's *Camden: A Frontier Town*, published in 1976. Camden was a colonial British town in South Carolina. Using the best that scientific archaeology had to offer, Lewis viewed the town as existing within a frontier model of settlement. In other words, to understand the developmental nature of the Camden settlement over time, one had first to understand how frontiers are settled. Frontier settlement of course has broad anthropological and historical implications, and Lewis used them to create his model. After having created the model, and after having fully explored the history of Camden, Lewis proposed a series of hypotheses about its settlement dynamics. He then tested these hypotheses with archaeology, and evaluated them against the model.

Processual historical archaeology was further expanded into **behavioural historical archaeology**, and, at the beginning of the twenty-first century, processual archaeology still has many proponents. From the mid-1980s, however, some archaeologists were beginning to question whether processual archaeology was really doing what it promised. These dissatisfied archaeologists are often referred to as 'post-processual' archaeologists to indicate that they have a different perspective from the processualists. Many historical archaeologists would describe themselves as post-processualists.

See also: behavioural historical archaeology; history of historical archaeology

Further reading

Lewis, K.E. (1976) *Camden: A Frontier Town*, Columbia: Institute of Archaeology and Anthropology, University of South Carolina.

Orser, C.E., Jr (1989) 'On plantations and patterns', *Historical Archaeology* 23(2): 28–40.

South, S. (1977) *Method and Theory in Historical Archaeology*, New York: Academic Press.

—— (ed.) (1977) *Research Strategies in Historical Archaeology*, New York: Academic Press.

CHARLES E. ORSER, JR

prostitution

Prostitution is a topic that most people would not immediately associate with archaeology. Historical archaeology, however, is perfectly suited to provide information about prostitutes because of its ability to examine the daily lives of men and women ignored by mainstream history. The archaeological interest in prostitution developed in the USA as part of a growing interest in **gender** and gender roles. Archaeologist Donna Seifert has provided perhaps the most notable archaeological study of prostitution to date, though future studies are bound to appear.

Seifert, while collaborating on a **cultural-resource management** project, had the opportunity to investigate Washington DC's famous red-light district, called Hooker's Division. In operation from the 1860s to about 1920, the district was situated within walking distance of the White House, the US Capitol and other governmental offices. The area obtained its colourful name during the US Civil War because it was then frequented by soldiers and officers under the command of General Joseph Hooker. During the war period (1861–5), the Division was composed of brothels and saloons, but, from the mid-1860s to the 1880s, it was populated by immigrant and African American, working-class households, among whom the prostitutes lived. During the next few decades, the district was mostly composed of rows of brothels and was almost entirely dedicated to the business of prostitution. Both female- and male-headed households resided in the Division, and many owners of the houses of prostitution also operated other businesses, such as groceries or boarding houses.

The excavations allowed Seifert to examine the differences in the **material culture** of the people who lived in Hooker's Division. Seifert divided the archaeological assemblages into four categories – Early Working Class, Early Prostitute, Late Working Class, Late Prostitute – and examined the differences between them. She discovered that the lives of the Division's working-class residents changed little from 1870 to 1920, but that the material lives of the prostitutes appreciably improved around 1900. She believed that the change represented the prostitutes' increased purchasing power as their trade became more profitable. Clothing was one area of life in which the change was readily apparent. The artefacts indicated that, during the early twentieth century, the clothing of the prostitutes included many fancy objects, such as black-glass **buttons**. In addition, the brothel artefact assemblage also contained more mirror fragments, hair combs and jewellery pieces than the working-class deposits of the same age. The qualitative differences between the prostitute and the working-class collections indicated that the dress of the prostitutes was at a level to which working-class women could only aspire. At the same time, however, the archaeological collections from the brothels also included patent-medicine **bottles** that once contained cures for 'social diseases'.

Seifert's work on prostitution has produced many significant findings. Among them are (1) that historical archaeology really does provide an excellent way to document the daily lives of people typically ignored in written records, and (2) that prostitution provided a mechanism for some women to take control of their own lives.

Further reading

Seifert, D.J. (1994) 'Mrs. Starr's profession', in E.M. Scott (ed.) *Those of Little Note: Gender, Race, and Class in Historical Archaeology*, Tucson: University of Arizona Press, pp. 149–73.

—— (1991) 'Within sight of the White House: The archaeology of working women', *Historical Archaeology* 25(4): 82–108.

CHARLES E. ORSER, JR

pseudo-archaeology

Pseudo-archaeology, sometimes called 'fantastic archaeology' or even 'cult archaeology', refers to a fringe area of archaeology in which its proponents formulate outrageous ideas about the past by reference to actual archaeological sites and remains. Pseudo-archaeologists are typically people who are interested in the past, but who are not content with scientific, reasonable interpretations. Instead, they create interpretations that rest on wild or fantastic propositions. Pseudo-archaeologists are the men and women who write about ancient space aliens visiting the earth, who search for the sunken continent of Atlantis in Antarctica and who claim that the Phoenicians discovered the New World thousands of years before Columbus.

Pseudo-archaeology is usually restricted to prehistoric sites and ancient history because pseudo-archaeologists spend most of their time searching for mystical, lost civilisations that they think existed in antiquity. In this vein, some pseudo-archaeologists argue that the earth is millions of years older than geologists have shown, in an effort to prove that the pyramids of ancient Egypt, the pyramids of the central Mexican jungles and the monuments of South-east **Asia** were all constructed by an ancient, now-lost race of super-intelligent beings. Other pseudo-archaeologists claim that the earth is much younger than the evidence suggests, in an attempt to call evolution into question.

Historical archaeology usually becomes involved when pseudo-archaeologists use colonial-period remains, such as in the north-eastern USA, to argue that North America was visited by ancient Celts, seafaring Egyptians or some other advanced civilisation long before recorded history. As an example, some pseudo-archaeologists claim that the Vikings built the circular, stone Newport Tower in Newport, Rhode Island, as an ancient church. Systematic excavation, however, has definitively shown that the tower was built in the late seventeenth century by Benedict Arnold, the grandfather of the famous American turncoat.

In most cases, pseudo-archaeologists believe in their wild interpretations with an almost religious fervour, and, in fact, some of their ideas do have religious overtones. As a result, professional archaeologists find it extremely difficult, if not impossible, to dissuade them from believing their wild theories, and most archaeologists simply prefer to ignore them. It is true, however, that pseudo-archaeologists dominate the popular media and from their wide exposure promote their outrageous ideas to the general public, who are often persuaded to believe the pseudo-archaeologists' well-crafted stories. Other professional archaeologists, however, believe that they have a responsibility to debunk the pseudo-archaeologists' outlandish interpretations and to promote the truth about the history of past cultures.

Pseudo-archaeologists are known to use intuition, psychic readings and other approaches to locate archaeological sites and to 'understand' the past. Dowsing is one of their favourite techniques that has relevance to historical archaeology. The practice of dowsing, or using 'angle rods' or bent coat hangers to locate buried remains, was introduced to historical archaeology as a sub-surface surveying technique by Ivor Noël Hume, the first archaeologist at Williamsburg, Virginia, in his *Historical Archaeology*, first published in 1969. Dowsing has had a particularly long usage in **England** – where Noël Hume was trained – and dowsers there have been particularly active around the **churches** and **cathedrals** that dot the English countryside. Recent research demonstrates, however, that dowsers are probably merely experiencing a powerful psychological phenomenon called the 'ideomotor effect'. This effect is characterised by involuntary body movements that are caused by an idea or thought rather than by sensory stimulation. Dowsing simply does not survive scientific testing and is not a valid archaeological discovery technique.

Pseudo-archaeology, though it may be interesting, is not simply harmless fun, because it has a dark side as well. Many of the underlying theories used by pseudo-archaeologists, in addition to being terribly outdated, have substantial racist elements. For example, in proposing that **Great Zimbabwe** in Eastern Africa was built by the Phoenicians or that the Lost Tribes of Israel constructed the great earthen mounds of the eastern USA, pseudo-archaeologists imply that the indigenous peoples were not intelligent enough to build these monuments on their own. The image of the lazy, stupid African or Native American helps to support unfortunate stereotypes and offers what appears to be a 'scientific' rationale for their being dominated and oppressed. It is important to remember, also, that much of the theoretical underpinnings of the Nazi ideology were based on the fantastic notion that the German Aryans were the descendants of the people of Atlantis. They believed they were a master race at least partly because of this supposed pedigree.

Further reading

Feder, K.L. (1999) *Frauds, Myths, and Mysteries: Science and Pseudoscience in Archaeology*, third edn, Mountain View, CA: Mayfield.

Harrold, F.B. and Eve, R.A. (eds) (1995) *Cult Archaeology and Creationism: Understanding Pseudo-scientific Beliefs about the Past*, Iowa City: University of Iowa Press.

Wauchope, R. (1962) *Lost Tribes and Sunken Continents: Myth and Method in the Study of American Indians*, Chicago: University of Chicago Press.

Williams, S. (1991) *Fantastic Archaeology: The Wild Side of North American Prehistory*, Philadelphia: University of Pennsylvania Press.

CHARLES E. ORSER, JR

public archaeology

The term 'public archaeology' came into common use in the late 1960s in reference to government-mandated archaeology, usually related to resource management on public land or lands subject to government regulation, and usually supported by public funds. Over the years, its meaning and usage have broadened, and it now describes archaeological research that includes any kind of engagement with the public. This engagement can range from occasional site and laboratory tours to detailed educational programmes, to 'popularised' publications and exhibits, to volunteer opportunities, and to intensive partnerships with descendant groups with specific ties to sites under investigation. These activities are driven by the idea that such interaction is an ethical responsibility on the part of the researcher, an opportunity to spread the news of discoveries and interpretations more widely and a way to gather more information on the sites and topics under study.

Over the last two decades, the proper nature and degree of public engagement has become a source of heated discussion among archaeologists. The point of contention turns on differing models of the archaeologist's role, with one conception seeing the work as simply the gathering and dissemination of what the ground says about the past, versus the view that researchers actually create and inevitably manipulate the archaeological record. In the former, the public's role is to be a relatively passive audience, while the latter conception views the public as active partners with a vital interest in guiding the course of research and interpretation.

Historical archaeology's more broadened acceptance of its responsibility for public engagement had its genesis in the development of publicly open excavations in the 1980s at such historic site museums as Williamsburg, **Monticello** and **Mount Vernon** (all in Virginia) and in cities like Alexandria, Virginia and **Annapolis**, Maryland. Although some of these sites made use of public money, others did not and saw such open excavations as a way to both do research and enhance the museum experience for their paying customers.

Mark Leone and Parker Potter, in their work at Annapolis, sought ways to use public archaeology in that well-preserved colonial capital as more than just another venue for visitors to be exposed to local history. Their programme developed intensive city tours and site interpretation programmes that presented archaeological knowledge as an active force in the present and as a way to instigate social change. Leone and Potter drew on a 'critical theory' approach, with an emphasis on how the current political climate shapes the interpretation of the past in general and archaeological research in particular. Their ambitious goal was to demystify this process for their audience and show how it was used to legitimate the current structure of social, economic and political power. They intended the programming to be provocative and at times confrontational, perhaps defining why it was only a mixed success with visitors. Despite this, their efforts set new standards for interaction between archaeologists and the public, and remain very influential with researchers working at public sites.

Debates over the degree to which historical archaeology should become truly public heated up in the early 1990s with the emerging activism of groups with direct connections with the people and topics under archaeological scrutiny. The efforts by some **Native Americans** to regulate excavations and force **repatriation** and reburial of skeletal material and artefact collections set the stage for similar encounters between historical archaeologists and descendant groups interested in more recent times. In perhaps the most significant example of this, in the early 1990s, members of the African American community in New York City demanded and got extensive control over the excavation and analysis of the **African Burial Ground**, located in mid-town Manhattan. Their efforts limited further disturbance to the burials

and altered the construction plans for the federal office building slated for the site. Community members also took on active definition of the details of the archaeological analysis and distribution of the results, and worked to ensure extensive participation of black scholars in this work.

The confrontations associated with the African Burial Ground project centred on public versus professional control of the research. Researchers who saw the need to maintain a division between the archaeological process and its public audience were categorised as agents of arrogant privilege at best and reactionary racists at worst. Those who advocated making the local community full partners in the project drew criticism for bending to the will of particular political agendas with only peripheral connections to archaeological research. The dichotomy also seemed to require a decision about which takes precedence, the archaeological resource or current public interest. The successes of the New York African Burial Ground Project's educational programmes and the significant findings of the skeletal analysis (conducted under the direction of Michael Blakey at Howard University) clearly validate the struggles and decisions relating to this particular exercise in public archaeology.

At the end of the 1990s, most historical archaeologists have accepted, and many have embraced, an intensified level of engagement with the public in their research projects. To a degree, in the current era of diminishing government support and backlash against land use regulation, promoting 'audience friendly' archaeology has become a survival strategy. This 'public or perish' approach sees public engagement not just as an adjunct to a project, as something taken care of by site tours and newspaper articles, but as having a central role in the research, vital to its success and to continued public support of archaeology.

Acceptance of a truly public approach to archaeological research must begin by seeing the public not just as an audience for archaeology's discoveries and interpretations, but as clients who have some legitimate claims to ownership of the archaeological source material and the products of the research. The stumbling block that remains is how particular researchers choose to channel public access and involvement to their work, and the degree of 'empowerment' they grant to the public. Is providing opportunities for the general public to participate in excavations, to visit sites and to hear about findings and results in timely and non-technical formats enough? Or must archaeologists go further, and allow the public decision-making power over the direction and interpretation of the research?

One recent journal article on the topic (co-authored by this writer) promotes a loosely defined 'public style' of archaeology. This approach first recognises that there are many different segments of the public, from casual site visitors to elementary school students to descendant groups to project volunteers to colleagues both in and outside the discipline of archaeology. These segments are seen as equally important and equally worthy of attention, but with different needs in terms of styles and relative detail of presentation formats and choice of material likely to further engage attention. The public-style approach also emphasises conversations with the public, on and off site, rather than lectures or scripted presentations. Conversations are of course two-way exchanges, depending for success as much on listening as on talking. Hearing what the public has to say about a project provides feedback for the archaeologist, information which serves as a way to gauge whether or not the questions being asked and the interpretations being presented have real significance. The public style of archaeology also emphasises the need to broaden the use of archaeological evidence in museums and other public interpretations of the past. Getting decision makers to use excavated data alongside more traditional sources on the past helps solve an essential dilemma of archaeological research, the challenge of finding lasting ways to get evidence out of the field and into public consciousness.

The conversational tone of the public style of archaeology stands in sharp contrast to the confrontational approach taken in Annapolis and with the New York African Burial Ground Project. The goals (perhaps naive) are to keep archaeological evidence as separate as possible from the turmoil of current politics, to make balanced presentations of findings with clear divisions between evidence and interpretations, to be happy to turn this loose to the public and recognise that they will likely transform the work to fit their own

needs and realities. As with many conversations, the archaeologist and his or her public will have clashing points of view and will not always come to an acceptable consensus. Archaeologists committed to public engagement must trust the public's ability to digest and make the best use of presented evidence and interpretations, much as the public trusts archaeologists to approach the resources under investigation with professionalism, thoroughness and objectivity.

See also: heritage management; museums; politics in archaeology; public outreach and education

Further reading

Jameson, J.H., Jr (ed.) (1997) *Presenting Archaeology to the Public: Digging for Truths*, Walnut Creek, CA: AltaMira Press.

La Roche, C.J. and Blakey, M.L. (1997) 'Seizing intellectual power: The dialogue at the New York African Burial Ground', *Historical Archaeology* 31(3): 84–106.

McGimsey, C.R., III (1972) *Public Archaeology*, New York: Seminar Press.

McKee, L. and Thomas, B.W. (1998) 'Starting a conversation: The public style of archaeology at the Hermitage', *Southeastern Archaeology* 17(1): 133–9.

Potter, P.B. (1994) *Public Archaeology in Annapolis*, Washington, DC: Smithsonian Institution Press.

LARRY McKEE

public outreach and education

The positive value of public outreach and education has been embraced by all sectors of the archaeological community. Through popular publications, programmes encouraging public participation in fieldwork, public presentations, 'archaeology week' events and other types of activities, and an increased interest in on-site interpretation, archaeologists have rallied around the cause of promoting the public benefits of archaeology. Although individual archaeologists and certain well-established archaeological projects long ago brought the public dimension to their efforts, the disciplinary shift to the 'public or perish' philosophy reflects the larger trends of greater accountability of public expenditures and the growth and expansion of the stewardship ethic into the realm of **cultural-resource management**. Through public outreach, archaeologists hope to build a broad base of public support both for basic archaeological research and for the legislative means to protect and preserve archaeological resources. In a global setting, public outreach is often employed to directly connect a people with their past in building a sense of national cultural heritage.

In the USA, the government has taken a leading role in developing public awareness programmes about archaeological resources on federal lands, and has initiated a variety of programmes aimed at reaching multiple audiences. The US National Park Service, the US Army Corps of Engineers, the US Fish and Wildlife Service, the US Forest Service and the US Bureau of Land Management are among the agencies that have developed collaborative projects with schools, universities, volunteers and Indian tribes to accomplish basic archaeological management objectives. Such projects typically include a field component and a follow-up educational packet for dissemination in public schools, including in-service training for teachers. At both the federal and state levels there is a growing interest in using public archaeological sites as outdoor classrooms and in encouraging the direct involvement of government archaeologists with the educational curriculum. There is also a great governmental interest at all levels in fostering creative partnerships with citizen support organisations and other local groups by allowing greater participation in archaeological inventory and preservation activities. The tremendous popularity of archaeology week events reflects the successful collaboration of government, private sector, academic and avocational archaeologists who often work together to co-sponsor public lectures, archaeology fairs, field trips, booklets and videos. More than forty-one states now support archaeology week programmes, which reach an estimated 2 million people annually.

The private sector has also gone public, as portions of contract budgets increasingly are being set aside for public interpretation and education.

Government agencies and private business now realise that public archaeology can be good public relations, and together have supported a proliferation of high-quality archaeological exhibits and a range of educational materials based on archaeological mitigation projects. For their part, university programmes in archaeology must meet the challenge of adequately preparing students for the demands of public archaeology, which include planning and conducting a variety of public outreach activities. The University of Maryland, the University of South Florida and Indiana University are among several US universities to offer formal graduate programmes in public archaeology.

No single phenomenon has facilitated greater outreach than the Internet, through which the many publics of archaeology are linked via electronic webs of communication. Site maps, artefact photographs and interpretations of excavations in progress can be posted on the Web for immediate access to anyone with a computer. Projects such as the Jamestown Rediscovered excavations can reach unlimited numbers of people with their latest findings, and bring results directly to the public without the intervention of the news media. Distribution lists provide rapid dissemination of ideas and controversies, and promote a high level of awareness about archaeological issues. Other websites make primary archaeological data available to the public, such as the US National Park Service's National Archeological Data Base.

With its early emphasis on historic-sites archaeology, historical archaeology has a deep connection to the goals of public outreach and education. Excavations at **Jamestown** and Williamsburg, both in Virginia, were popular tourist destinations in the years when many people thought archaeology could only be found in Egypt, and modern urban excavations in places like **St Augustine**, Florida, and Charleston, South Carolina, continued to draw large crowds in recent years. Although archaeology remains popular at historically dramatic sites like the Little Bighorn Archaeology Project at the scene of Custer's so-called 'Last Stand' (see **Battle of the Little Bighorn**), smaller, more commonplace sites are also attracting public attention. The Delaware Department of Transportation, for example, has effectively incorporated public outreach in the excavation and interpretation of nineteenth-century farmsteads within transportation corridors.

Public outreach and educational initiatives carry messages about the present use of the past, whether hidden or overt. The US National Park Service, like other government agencies, often promotes stewardship themes in an attempt to broaden the feeling of public responsibility for site protection and preservation. Closely related to the steward-ship theme are the various 'lessons of the past' scenarios that promote archaeology's relevance to problems of the modern world. In Canada, the City of Toronto's Archaeological Resource Centre was specifically designed to make the archaeology of the city's past of direct public benefit to the contemporary multicultural population of the city through formal educational programmes. A third message is that the past, as brought into the present through archaeology, can transform the present human experience through the process of self-reflection. This view is most aggressively promoted in the University of Maryland's **Annapolis** project, where archaeology has been used in interpretive programmes to confront traditional historical understandings of the city's colonial heritage.

Although the fate of archaeology in the twenty-first century cannot be foretold, the 'public or perish' adage offers words to the wise.

See also: living museums; public archaeology

Further reading

Ardoun, C.D. (ed.) (1997) *Museums and Archaeology in West Africa*, Washington, DC: Smithsonian Institution Press.

Greengrass, M. (1991) *State Archeology Weeks: Interpreting Archeology for the Public*, Washington, DC: National Park Service.

Haas, D. (1999) *The Federal Archeology Program, 1996–97*, Washington, DC: National Park Service.

Jameson, J.H., Jr (ed.) (1997) *Presenting Archaeology to the Public*, Walnut Creek, CA: AltaMira Press.

Shackel, P.A., Mullins, P.R. and Warner, M.S. (eds) (1998) *Annapolis Pasts: Historical Archaeology in Annapolis*, Knoxville: University of Tennessee Press.

Smith, G.S. and Ehrenhard, J.E. (eds) (1991) *Protecting the Past*, Boca Raton: CRC Press.

Smith, K.C. and McManamon, F.P. (eds) (1991) *Archeology and Education: The Classroom and Beyond*, Washington, DC: National Park Service.

BRENT R. WEISMAN

Puerto Real, Haiti

Located on the northern coast of what is now Haiti, Puerto Real was one of the earliest Spanish settlements to employ a distinctive colonial strategy for the New World. Puerto Real was one of thirteen towns founded across Hispaniola in 1504. Originally envisioned as a mining town, its economy soon turned to slaving as locally available gold and copper deposits proved disappointing. The slave trade declined after the hinterlands of northern Hispaniola and the nearby Bahamas had been depopulated. However, possessing a burgeoning cattle population, the citizens of Puerto Real turned to the hide and tallow trade as their chief source of livelihood.

Unable to compete with the more lucrative trade in gold and silver bullion of the mainland, the merchants of Puerto Real were unable to secure space on the treasure fleets that serviced Spain's colonies in the Circum-Caribbean area. Dealing with foreign smugglers became the only alternative left to the struggling town. The slowly turning wheels of Spanish commerce control eventually forced the abandonment of Puerto Real (and eventually the western third of Hispaniola) in 1578.

The town quickly faded from memory until rediscovered by William Hodges, an avocational archaeologist, in 1974. Realising the significance of his find, Hodges was able to convince the late Charles Fairbanks of the University of Florida to conduct research at the site until 1982. Kathleen Deagan directed research at Puerto Real and the nearby site of En Bas Saline (the alleged site of Columbus's La Navidad) until the Haitian political situation brought all investigations to a halt in 1986.

Initial investigations at the site focused on the central plaza area, where the foundations of two large buildings and a cemetery were uncovered.

Subsequently, a sub-surface survey of the surrounding fields revealed that the city encompassed an area of over 500 m^2 and consisted of fifty-seven individual structures arranged in a grid pattern. Five of these structures were eventually excavated: the two public buildings on the town square, two upper-class residences and a lower-class commercial–residential area.

Puerto Real is one of a handful of sixteenth-century European sites excavated in the New World. Its known early chronology and cultural-contact situation made it an ideal site to test ideas of **creolisation** and **acculturation**. Specifically, early Hispanic colonial adaptive efforts were characterised by the incorporation of locally available elements into the colonist's low-visibility subsistence and technological activities (female oriented), while at the same time maintaining Spanish affiliation in such socially visible activities and elements as clothing, tableware, ornamentation and religious paraphernalia (male oriented). This pattern was established relatively soon after Puerto Real's founding and changed little through time.

See also: Spanish colonialism

Further reading

Deagan, K.A. (1995) *Puerto Real: The Archaeology of a Sixteenth-century Spanish Town in Hispaniola*, Gainesville: University Press of Florida.

Ewen, C.R. (1991) *From Spaniard to Creole: The Archaeology of Cultural Formation at Puerto Real, Haiti*, Tuscaloosa: University of Alabama Press.

CHARLES R. EWEN

Q

Qilakitsoq, Greenland (Eskimo mummies)

In 1972, the graves of six women and two children of the Inuit Thule culture were found in a rock cleft close by the depopulated settlement Qilakitsoq in the Uummannaq district. In 1978, the find of the very well preserved and fully dressed mummies were too well known in the district and the then head of the Greenland National Museum in Nuuk, Jens Rosing, decided to investigate the site and exhume the bodies. The mummies were taken to the Anthropological Laboratory at the University of Copenhagen where intense interdisciplinary research began.

The mummies were radiocarbon dated to the time around AD 1475 and were thus among the oldest preserved bodies in the Arctic. The deceased were buried in two graves. In grave I were three women aged about 20–25, 30 and 45–50, and two children, a baby boy less than 6 months old and an older boy of about 4. In grave II three women of whom the youngest was about 18–22 years old were buried; the other two were about 50. A determination of the HLA-transplantation antigens indicates that one family was buried in each grave. In grave I was the grandmother with her two daughters and two grandchildren, and in grave II two sisters with the daughter of one of the two. The three oldest women could be sibs.

It was impossible to determine if the deceased had died and were buried simultaneously, and it was only possible to state the cause of death with a certain degree of probability in a few cases. The baby boy may have been buried alive together with his deceased mother and his disabled and mentally sick older brother may have died naturally or he may even have been killed due to his handicap. One of the older women in grave II could have died from cancer. Infrared photography disclosed tattooing on the faces of the three older women.

To the Inuit, death is a changeover to another life, and the deceased were well equipped for the journey to their new life in either the sea or in heaven. Besides the clothing they wore, they were provided with seven outer parkas, one inner parka, three pairs of outer trousers, five kamiks (footwear) and seven stockings. The clothing was exquisite. It was made of sealskin, bird and caribou skin with the highest degree of insulation, while at the same time giving the body the opportunity to release surplus heat to avoid dangerous perspiration in the harsh climate of the Arctic.

The mummies are kept at the National Museum and Archives in Nuuk, Greenland.

See also: dress

Further reading

Hart Hansen, J.P. and Gulløv, H.C. (eds) (1989) 'The mummies from Qilakitsoq: Eskimos in the 15th century', in *Man & Society* 12: 1–199.

Hart Hansen, J.P., Meldgaard, J. and Nordqvist, J. (eds) (1991) *The Greenland Mummies*, Washington, D.C.: Smithsonian Intitution Press.

JETTE ARNEBORG

Qsar es-Seghir, Morocco

Qsar es-Seghir ('small fortress') is a medieval Islamic–Portuguese site located in northern Morocco. It lies at the narrowest point between Morocco and Spain on the Strait of Gibraltar. The site was used by Arab and Berber troops in AD 711 to launch their invasion of southern Spain (al-Andalus). Although the early history of the settlement is poorly known, its later political and military history is well documented in medieval Arab chronicles. During the Almoravid conquest of Morocco and Spain (late eleventh and early twelfth centuries), the town served as an important military embarkation point to al-Andalus. Under the Almohad and Merinid dynasties (late twelfth to mid-fifteenth centuries), the town flourished as a commercial entrepôt as trade between Morocco, Spain and the rest of the Mediterranean world intensified. In 1458, as part of the Christian *reconquista* movement, Portuguese troops captured the town, forcing its Muslim inhabitants to leave, and rebuilt the town primarily for military purposes. In 1550, the Portuguese king ordered his troops to abandon the town, effectively bringing its history to a close.

In the 1970s, the site of Qsar es-Seghir became the focus of major archaeological investigations (1974–81) directed by US archaeologist Charles L. Redman. Using the historical record as a framework for archaeological research, Redman and his teams were able to document the transformation of the town's architectural, social and economic organisation from Muslim to Christian Portuguese times.

Archaeologists exposed about 5,000 m^2, or 18 per cent, of the well-preserved 3-ha site and uncovered four occupation phases. At the lowest excavated stratigraphic levels were traces of a probable Almohad mosque, houses with inner courtyards and an enclosure wall. In the following levels, dating to the Marinid period, was evidence of major reconstruction, including a new *hamman* (public bath), central market stalls, new residential structures extending to the town's walls, and rebuilt fortification walls and towers. In upper levels, dating to the early Portuguese period (*c.* 1458–95), the houses were rearranged with smaller rooms and doors leading directly to the street (replacing the typical Islamic bent-axis entryways); other structures were levelled to create a large central plaza; the mosque was converted into a church with Portuguese soldiers buried beneath the nave; the *hamman* was modified into a prison/arsenal; a seaward citadel for military storage and housing was built; and the vertical Islamic fortifications were remodelled to a typical Portuguese style characterised by low sloping walls and a protective moat to thwart cannon artillery. The latter Portuguese levels (*c.* 1495–1550) contained evidence of more diverse commercial activities, such as wine production and blacksmithing, and a more varied population.

The Qsar es-Seghir excavations heralded the beginning of anthropologically oriented, systematic, archaeological research at a historic-period urban site in **North Africa**. The investigations utilised several new approaches, including probability **sampling** to select areas for initial excavation; computer recording and analysis of **material-culture** data; botanical and faunal analysis to reconstruct medieval subsistence patterns; studies of depositional processes; and ethno-archaeological research to aid in archaeological interpretation.

Further reading

Redman, C.L. (1986) *Qsar es-Seghir, an Archaeological View of Medieval Life*, Orlando: Academic Press.

NANCY L. BENCO

R

race

Race is a range of constructed labels applied to subordinate groups in an attempt to rationalise inequality. Race is conventional ideology in the sense that it attempts to legitimise inequalities and construct distinctions of superiority and inferiority by suggesting that one group's dominance is rooted in 'natural', objective differences, such as biology. Race certainly is not 'real' in any essential biological or cultural sense, but race has concrete effects that shape how most people in the colonial and post-colonial worlds define themselves against, support-ing or negotiating racial ideologies. Consequently, while race is utterly constructed and fundamentally oppressive, it is a tangible experience that takes many guises which may be oppressive just as they may foster empowering resistance.

Differences in physical appearance and cultural practice likely always influenced how collectives distinguished each other, but systematic racial ideology emerged in the seventeenth century alongside the Atlantic slave trade and world-wide colonisation. In this historical wake, racism has most explicitly denigrated the African diaspora, but race is not simply a 'false' identity limited to people who are classed black or otherwise outside 'white' European origins. Racial classifications pose tacit oppositions between those being labelled and other social collectives: In the USA, for example, to call someone 'black' is to implicitly outline 'white' identity by defining its opposite. Thus, in racialised Western society, everyone has race whether they recognise it or not.

Very few historical archaeologists approach race as an identity that material culture can empirically illuminate. Instead, race is usually reduced to racism, which is generally considered to be instrumental, consciously inflicted prejudice that was focused on various people classed as non-white in the past. Those archaeologists who do system-atically examine race envision a still-active social framework that is governed by the benefits conferred by whiteness. Whiteness is the notion that a universal, ostensibly white European 'norm' exists as a tacit backdrop against which all cultural, social and material practice can be evaluated. Perceived distance from this ambiguous norm imposed a dimension of racialised tension on all inequality and difference in the colonised world. In a study of plantation landscapes, Terrence Epper-son focused on how racists attempted to appro-priate the products of enslaved African Americans while they simultaneously denied African Amer-icans fundamental citizen rights that were assumed exclusive to whites. In so doing, race oppressed African Americans, yet it also became a target for a distinctive resistance that remains at the heart of contemporary African American culture. Epperson probed the duality of racist tension by examining how enslaved Virginians' quarters adhered to white planters' basic dictates, but enslaved people never-theless maintained modest but important control over interior and shared spaces that shaped collective social activities and identity. Paul Mullins argued that late nineteenth-century consumer culture was also profoundly structured by white racist domination, yet it too was negotiated through myriad forms of resistance. After Emanci-pation, many African Americans purchased mass-produced commodities and endured racialised wage labour without accepting the racist symbolism championed by mass marketers. African Americans purchased symbolically charged 'white' goods like Victorian furnishings, aspiring to – and in circumscribed ways securing – the genteel privileges implied by their consumption. As in Epperson's plantation resistance, racism ensured profound oppression, but African Americans developed modest but meaningful tactics that preserved cultural distinction and eroded racial ideology.

Historical archaeologists studying race stress the contemporary implications of their research. For instance, South African archaeologist Martin Hall argued that archaeology provides a mechanism to dismantle romanticised racist histories. Dominant South African histories paint an idyllic picture of a genteel and calm colonial period in which industrious Europeans arrived and carved out an affluent, cultivated society in a difficult environment. Mainstream histories tend to presume that indigenous South Africans like the Zulu lived in ancestral spaces known under apartheid as homelands. Yet Hall argued that archaeology provides a critical insight into contemporary inequality's roots by revealing an unstable and brutal colonial slave society much like those throughout the European world.

It would be relieving to discover that racism was the scheme of an aberrant white elite or conspiring merchants, but marginalised whites were not duped into becoming racists. Instead, in various ways, whites embraced the power of whiteness as a social 'wage' in place of genuine material and public benefits. In the USA, those 'wages' became increasingly accessible on some scale to European immigrants in the late nineteenth century. Liminal groups were compelled to devise tactics that variously condoned racial marginalisation, protected cultural distinction in the face of racism and negotiated racist stigmatisation so that they could preserve their hopes of sharing in the USA's genuine social and material benefits. Consequently, it is hardly surprising that archaeology reflects that people negotiated racism in many different ways that are far less clear than racial boundaries presume. For instance, Adrian Praetzellis *et al.*'s study of Chinese immigrants exploded the mono-

lithic rubric of 'the Chinese' by identifying a vast range of material conservatism, rapid embrace of consumer goods and many possibilities in between. Robert Paynter also advocated a complex vision of **identity** that acknowledges the centrality of race and the wide range of factors shaping identity. Paynter argued that the colour line is a fundamental feature of Western political economy that portrays various groups as isolated cultures or ethnic collectives. Suggesting the direction race studies will take in historical archaeology, Paynter argued that a sophisticated anthropological vision of identity and race requires an appreciation of the intersection of **culture**, class (see **class, social**) and **ethnicity** in any given context.

See also: African American archaeology; plantation archaeology

Further reading

Epperson, T.W. (1990) 'Race and the disciplines of the plantation', *Historical Archaeology* 24(4): 29–36.

Hall, M. (1988) 'Archaeology under apartheid', *Archaeology* 41(6): 62–4.

Mullins, P.R. (1999) *Race and Affluence: An Archaeology of African America and Consumer Culture*, New York: Kluwer Academic/Plenum Press.

Paynter, R. (1990) 'Afro-Americans in the Massachusetts historical landscape', in D. Lowenthal and P. Gathercole (eds) *Politics of the Past*, London: Unwin Hyman, pp. 49–62.

Praetzellis, A., Praetzellis, M. and Brown, M., III (1987) 'Artifacts as symbols of identity: An example from Sacramento's gold rush era Chinese community', in E. Staski (ed.) *Living in Cities, Current Research in Urban Archaeology*, Tucson: Society for Historical Archaeology, pp. 38–47.

PAUL R. MULLINS

railways

Historical archaeologists have usually not had much interest in railways as such. The study of rail lines, stations and other structures associated with railroads typically fall under the purview of **industrial archaeology**, and industrial archaeologists have produced many significant studies of railways, particularly in Great Britain.

Some historical archaeologists have examined settlements related to railways without specifically studying the railway itself. Archaeologists in the USA, for example, have completed studies of railroad builders, particularly overseas Chinese labourers in the West (see **overseas Chinese historical archaeology**). These studies typically focus on the artefacts present at railroad camps and they may also explore various issues related to the **material culture** of **ethnicity**. Archaeologists in **Australia** have also contributed important studies of railways and the people who built them.

Railways, like other large public works projects (such as canals), provide excellent arenas for archaeological study. It is extremely likely, as historical archaeology expands in the twenty-first century, that archaeologists will provide important investigations of them because they were often directly responsible for increased settlement, national growth, conflicts between newcomers and indigenous people, and labour unrest.

CHARLES E. ORSER, JR

Ravenna, Italy

The city of Ravenna in north-east Italy, formerly a major Adriatic port but now approximately 10 km distant from the coast, is justifiably famous for its remarkable collection of architectural and artistic survivals of late Roman, Ostrogothic and Byzantine date (late fourth to seventh centuries AD). Promoted to imperial capital of the Roman Western Empire in the early fifth century at a period of substantial military upheaval (incursions by Visigoths in Dalmatia and subsequently Italy, covering over a decade; invasions and raids into Gaul and Germany across the Rhine), the city's hosting of emperor, court and metropolitan bishop conditioned monumental investment comprising palaces (imperial and episcopal), cathedral and baptistery, **churches**, monasteries, circus and defences, plus expansion of the port complex of Classe. Sizeable urban growth is thus attested – a rarity in the late Roman West. Its capital status endured the transition to Germanic rule (AD 476 to

Odoacer; AD 493 to the Ostrogothic king Theoderic) and subsequent reconquest of Italy by the East Romans or Byzantines (533–54), and persisted until capture by the Lombards in AD 751. The city's bishop retained prominence and, in the late eighth century, the Frankish king Charlemagne treated Ravenna with significant respect – indeed, he was careful to 'obtain' prized marbles and mosaics for his own capital of Aachen from here and from papal **Rome** in recognition of these cities' imperial pasts. Carolingian and Ottonian kings of Italy did not revive Ravenna as capital, and its medieval and more recent role was not distinguished – leading to the silting of the port and a receded coastline.

Ravenna was among the earliest communes in Italy, and held significance for its university and School of Legal Practice. While never of political and economic substance in the Middle Ages, it remained a point of conflict in the rivalries of the Guelf and Ghibelline families; in the fourteenth century, the Da Polenta family become dominant and hosted the exiled Dante who died in Ravenna in 1321; Dante's remains, honoured across the centuries, were rehoused in a modest tomb built in 1780, close to the ancient church of San Francesco.

Medieval stagnation provided the fortunate circumstances for survival of Ravenna's treasures, ranging from near intact fifth- and sixth-century basilicas and tenth-century bell towers, to magnificent late antique wall and floor mosaics, sarcophagi, plus a remarkable collection of papyri and texts such as Agnellus's ninth-century *Liber Pontificalis ecclesiae Ravennatis*, which provides details of lost inscriptions and insights into contemporary society. Unlike most Italian cities, medieval rebuildings, demolitions and reornamentations have not deprived us of these elements of late antique material expression, allowing us to identify fully the nature of late Roman imperial patronage, the impact of Byzantine art on sixth-century Italy and, perhaps most importantly, the ready assimilation of late antique culture by the Germanic successors of Roman Italy, the Ostrogoths.

Most stunning are the churches of San Vitale and Sant'Apollinare Nuovo, both commenced in the 520s under Gothic rule, and both rededicated from Gothic Arian faith to Catholic rite by the

Byzantines from the 540s. Sant'Apollinare formed the palace church of Theoderic (the palace complex was part excavated in the early twentieth century) and is famous for the processual mosaic friezes above the nave colonnades, one side depicting twenty-two female virgin saints and the three magi paying homage to the Virgin and Child flanked by angels, the other side with twenty-six male martyr saints approaching the enthroned Christ. Between the windows of the clerestory are figures of saints and prophets, and above these are panels depicting Christ's Miracles and Parables, and his Passion and Resurrection. We also see, at the entrance end of the long friezes, images of the fleet base of Classe and of the palace and cityscape of Ravenna. The marblework here and at San Vitale are of exquisite quality, drawing inspiration (and craftsmen) both locally and from Constantinople. An array of fine mosaics also adorns San Vitale, which is best known for two sizeable panels depicting the Byzantine emperor Justinian (527–65) and his entourage (including Bishop Maximian), and the empress Theodora. These relate to the Byzantine reconquest of Ravenna and subsequently of Italy, and the restoration of the Catholic faith. While Ostrogothic in inception, San Vitale in fact owed its construction largely to the banker Julianus Argentarius.

Such wealth derived from Ravenna's capital status and favoured trading networks. Excavations at the port of Classe have, since the 1980s, been invaluable in shifting emphasis from the art to the commodities of late antique life. Vast numbers of finds have been recovered, attesting pan-Mediterranean and wider imports plus a vitality of local production, active well into the seventh century. Subsequently, coinciding with Arab expansion and Byzantine decay in the eastern Mediterranean, serious decline occurs at Classe, matched by a dramatic fall-off in building and maintenance work within Ravenna. We still await full publication of the Classe excavations; however, the annual *Corsi di Studi sull'Arte Ravennate e Bizantina* provide regular discussion on these and on Ravennate church archaeology and art historical studies.

See also: Rome; Siena

Further reading

Bermond Montanari, G. (ed.) (1983) *Ravenna e il porto di Classe. Venti anni di ricerche archeologiche tra Ravenna e Classe*, Bologna: University Press.

Carile, A. (1992) *Storia di Ravenna. Vol. 2.2. Dall'età bizantina all'età ottoniana. Ecclesiologia, cultura e arte*, Venice: Comune di Ravenna.

—— (ed.) (1991) *Storia di Ravenna. Vol. 2.1. Dall'età bizantina all'età ottoniana. Territorio, economia e società*, Venice: Comune di Ravenna.

Christie, N. and Gibson, S. (1988) 'The city walls of Ravenna', *Papers of the British School at Rome* 66: 156–97.

Deichmann, F.W. (1969) *Ravenna: Hauptstadt des spätantiken Abendlandes, I. Geschichte und Monumente*, Wiesbaden: Konrad Theiss.

Gelichi, S. (ed.) (1990) *Storia di Ravenna, Vol. 1: L'evo antico*, Venice: Comune di Ravenna.

Johnson, M. (1988) 'Towards a history of Theoderic's building program', *Dumbarton Oaks Papers* 42: 73–96.

NEIL J. CHRISTIE

reconstruction

Historical archaeologists use the word 'reconstruction' in at least three ways, though they may not necessarily agree on the term's precise meanings. The first refers to the physical reconstruction of buildings and building complexes such as are found at **living museums**. The second and third uses are more theoretical and relate to the development of a mental picture of past daily life using the **material culture** as a guide. 'Historical reconstruction' typically refers to the creation of a picture of the times in which men and women lived, whereas 'social reconstruction' usually refers to the creation of an image of the past social environment of the inhabitants of a site, town or region.

Of the three kinds of reconstruction, only physical reconstructions are relatively static. Historical and social reconstructions will change as new information is gathered and as archaeologists create new ways of investigating and perceiving the past.

Physical reconstruction

Historical archaeologists have maintained a close association with physical reconstruction since the beginning of their discipline. Archaeologists, through excavation, have the ability to uncover past building remains, room additions, cellars and other structural elements that may be otherwise unknown either in historical documents or in living memory. Given the lack of precise information, site interpreters must often rely on archaeological research when they wish to erect a historically accurate building for public exhibit. Archaeologists can provide exact information about building size, dates of construction and abandonment, construction methods, number of rooms and additions, and whether cellars and crawl spaces existed. Site reconstructors need this kind of architectural information to make their buildings conform, as much as is possible, with historical conditions. Physical reconstructions have been particularly important at living museums, but individual examples exist outside museum settings around the world.

Historical reconstruction

The idea that archaeologists should have historical reconstruction as a primary goal of their research extends to the time that archaeologists first realised that they could use artefacts as **historical documents**. This realisation developed in the early nineteenth century among European museum archaeologists when they abandoned their more antiquarian interests in collecting artefacts for their beauty or rarity. The overt interest in historical reconstruction among archaeologists continued to develop throughout the nineteenth century and reached its theoretical and methodological apogee in the mid-twentieth century.

The goal of most prehistoric archaeologists during this period was to reconstruct the history of past cultures by examining their material culture and settlements. The region or culture area were usually their largest subjects of interest. Archaeologists engaged in historical reconstruction quickly discovered that creating prehistoric 'culture histories' was decidedly complex because they were never certain of the precise derivation of particular cultural traits. Prehistoric archaeologists were forced to consider, for example, whether a prehistoric culture used shell-tempered pottery because they had invented it or because they had learned the practice from another culture. Also, if they had learned it from another culture, did they learn it through face-to-face contact or through the movement of the idea only? These kinds of questions are not trivial for prehistorians because they directly relate to a past culture's history. The complexity of such questions made historical reconstruction a difficult and time-consuming proposition that occupied professional archaeologists for many years. At the beginning of the twenty-first century, many archaeologists are still involved in examining the world's culture histories.

Historical archaeologists, of course, do not face the same difficulties as prehistoric archaeologists with historical reconstruction. Because they usually have access to written records of many different kinds, historical archaeologists generally have an easier time reconstructing the histories of the past peoples they study. For example, they can excavate a large, multicomponent site like eighteenth-century Williamsburg, Virginia, and link their archaeological findings with the available historical documentation to provide a fairly complete picture of the history of the town.

With the development of **processual archaeology**, or **New Archaeology**, archaeologists added another kind of historical reconstruction to their list of goals: the reconstruction of extinct lifeways. A focus on the reconstruction of lifeways was an overt effort to promote an explicitly anthropological archaeology, one that could address three levels of past human life: technological, social and ideational. Using an approach based on systems theory, processual archaeologists began to strive towards reconstructions that were both historical and cultural. They usually employed a cultural model rooted in the natural environment, and much of their research, though not all by any means, was dedicated to **environmental reconstruction**.

Social reconstruction

The idea of social reconstruction was also embedded in the precepts of processual archaeology, and many New Archaeologists made significant strides in this area of study. The greatest achievements in the archaeological reconstruction of past societies, however, occurred during the era of **post-processual archaeology**. One reason for the ability of post-processualists to provide more complete images of past social orders undoubtedly derived from their overt focus on individuals and their open interest in such socially relevant topics as **gender**, **ethnicity**, class (see **class, social**) and **race**.

Again, historical archaeologists have been particularly successful in providing thoroughly researched social reconstructions because of the availability of historical documents and sociological information. Documents can exist for the precise site or site complex under study, but they need not necessarily relate to the specific site or even region. In historical archaeology, supporting documents can provide clues about the social milieu in which past men and women lived without being specifically about those people. In other words, a historical archaeologist interested in social reconstruction in colonial South Africa, for example, would not necessarily need to have extant records for the precise site under study. He or she could also use records from the same period of South African history to reconstruct the general characteristics of the social history of the people who once lived at the site under study.

Many of the social reconstructions of historical archaeologists will be complex because of the hierarchical nature of many post-Columbian societies. Given the stratified nature and possible diversity of the sites under study – particularly if they are urban sites – the archaeologist must be conversant with a wide range of topics to provide a plausible social reconstruction. And they, like all archaeologists, must be willing to understand that their reconstructions must change as more information is collected.

See also: history of historical archaeology

CHARLES E. ORSER, JR

redware

Origins

The most common ceramic found around the globe is red earthenware, commonly called 'red-ware'. It has been fashioned from ancient times to the present day from local deposits of red-clay earth found abundantly throughout the world. The earliest known redwares include 'Venus' figures made during the Magdalenian period of the European upper palaeolithic, 17,000 years ago. Probably the earliest true redware ceramics appear in the Near East in the neolithic B archaeological period, 9,000 years ago. Pottery was used in Japan by 5,200 years ago and in China and the New World by about the same time. Earthenware tablets of clay excavated in Mesopotamia are inscribed with the earliest true writing; these cuneiform tax records date back over 5,000 years.

In more recent times, redwares were made in Europe as early as the fourteenth century AD and were in production fairly universally there by the mid-sixteenth century. These utilitarian redwares were so essential to daily life that they were one of the first crafts transplanted to the New World at the time of contact; locally made redwares derived from European models were fashioned as early as 1493 at Los Coles, a site just across the bay from **La Isabella**, Columbus's first settlement.

Technology

Redwares are created from common glacial or alluvial clays that are fired in a kiln at temperatures of up to 1,100 °C, thus forming a somewhat permeable vessel. The clay is first dug, cleaned, kneaded thoroughly to remove air and blend it, and then shaped. Redware pottery has been fashioned in many ways. In post-Columbian North America, much of it has been wheel-thrown, as for most utilitarian redware ceramics from colonial New England. Other techniques include hand forming or modelling clay by pinching, or by pressing into slabs, or by rolling long ropes of clay that were then coiled into shape (as Native North Americans have done); drape moulding by placing a pounded slab of clay over a wooden, clay or plaster form (such as in the making of redware plates from the north-eastern United States); press moulding, a closely related process found in some redware plates from Pennsylvania, North Carolina and Virginia; and slip casting (as seen in early twentieth-century production of US art pottery, as well as in some later redwares). Paste or body clay colour after firing is generally red, brown or buff depending upon the natural presence and amount of iron oxides in the clay. Redwares have endured throughout the centuries, and have coexisted with the creation of more highly fired, and consequently harder, improved earthenwares, stonewares (see **stoneware**) and fine porcelains (see **porcelain**) in China.

Once thrown or formed, an earthenware vessel may be left unglazed. Vessels are more often glazed to make their porous, permeable bodies impervious to liquids. Comparatively, the knowledge of ways to form glazes on pottery dates back to at least 7,000 years ago. For redwares, the discovery of lead-glazing had occurred in the Near East by AD 1100, from where it diffused westward to Europe – probably via travellers and merchants such as Marco Polo (1254–1324) of Venice and Vasco da Gama, who returned from the Far East in 1499. Throughout Europe, powdered, and later liquid, lead oxide glazes were applied to the surface primarily to waterproof redwares. During firing in a kiln, these lead glazes fused with the body of the vessel, thus forming a glasslike, waterproof surface. Lead glazes, normally transparent, could be coloured intentionally by adding metallic oxides such as copper for green, and iron or manganese for brown or black. After about 1740–50, the development of liquid lead oxide glazes resulted in improved, more standardised and streamlined techniques that permitted glazes to be applied more quickly in assembly-line fashion, thereby helping to lower production costs.

Throughout Europe, redwares, like varieties of other ceramic types, could be decorated by piercing, incising or tooling the clay and by applying moulded relief decorations called sprigs prior to firing. Other ornamental effects more often were achieved using coloured slips, or liquid suspensions of clay or other materials in water. Slip decoration on redwares in Europe, Canada and colonial USA was most commonly of white kaolin clay. Occasionally, the kaolin was stained by manganese or copper oxide, to add more colour and create a polychrome effect. Slips were painted, brushed, trailed, swirled or combed onto vessel bodies to create a wide range of surface designs. Trailing, swirling and combing of slips seem to have been practised most frequently in Europe. In the north-eastern USA, potters' kiln samples indicate that painted and brushed slip designs were the dominant methods of slip application. Painted and brushed slip designs could be created more quickly as the process of applying decoration in these methods was less complex. The increased preference for painting and brushing of slip has been interpreted as a development to speed up production techniques. Part-time regional craft production yielded to industrialisation of the skill; semi-skilled labour could quickly and accurately decorate large numbers of ceramic forms with this technique, thus meeting streamlined mass-production goals that accompanied increasing consumption demands fuelling the early Industrial Revolution. This period of **industrialisation** began around 1740 in England with the introduction of the factory system and division of labour. It was not achieved fully in the USA until almost a hundred years later.

Finished vessels were allowed to air dry and then were fired in large oven-like kilns. In the north-eastern USA, the two predominant kiln types – the bottle-shaped and the beehive-shaped updraft kilns – followed traditional English and Germanic prototypes that, in turn, initially derived from Chinese antecedents. Close similarities between traditional European and early colonial kiln hardware also have been demonstrated in the literature.

Socioeconomic considerations

In both Europe and North America, redware ceramics began as highly localised expressions, made on a part-time basis to supply essential utilitarian forms. Vessels related to food storage and preparation dominate assemblages from this period. Most potters' shops were initially run by one or a few men, often related, who were perhaps farmers or shepherds most of the time and potters only occasionally, as needed. As clay was dug or a kiln fired, these part-time crafters might call on their families, neighbours or friends to share the work. No two kiln loads were ever exactly the same, and the quality of much of the output was actually due to a combination of factors, in addition to the skill of the craftsperson: clay content, glaze variations, firing temperature and even the season of the year could affect the colour or appearance of a piece of finished pottery.

As a class of ceramics, redware evolved through time across Europe and in colonial USA. Guilds in sixteenth- and seventeenth-century Europe produced redware varieties, which may be distinguished from one another in ways such as through intentional colourations of lead glazes and the presence or absence of modelled or slip decoration. In spite of specific local and regional differences, considerable contact and interaction among early potters in England, Ireland, Holland, Germany, France, Spain, Italy and seventeenth-century US settlements seems to have occurred. Utilitarian vessel forms from these countries often look quite similar, so much so that the geographic origins of their clays or slips may be distinguished from one another only through chemical or spectroscopic analyses of clay composition or other traits.

By the mid-eighteenth century, redware potters were creating table and teawares in addition to utilitarian forms for storage and food preparation. Tablewares and utilitarian forms remained popular until about 1770, when production declined as consumers turned to increasingly plentiful refined earthenwares such as cream-coloured earthenwares, and to porcelains, to meet their needs. As detrimental health effects of lead glazes were recognised and access increased, through international trade networks, to finer European tablewares such as salt-glazed stonewares and cream-coloured earthenwares, nineteenth-century US redware potters adapted. In some communities redware tablewares and utilitarian forms remained popular until about 1770, when production declined as consumers turned to increasingly plentiful refined earthenwares and porcelains to meet their needs. At this time, many local redware potters ended production. Others, particularly in communities with access to coastal ports and trade networks, successfully made the transition to full-time production. At the start of the Industrial Revolution, many of these potters turned to creating mass-produced vessels such as drain pipes and flower pots that could be produced quickly, in large quantities and at reasonable prices.

Methodological approaches to redware classification

At seventeenth- to eighteenth-century US domestic sites, redwares often comprise upwards of 90 per cent of ceramic assemblages. The intermixture of imported and domestic wares at a site is common and speaks to a crucial need for inexpensive, somewhat durable utilitarian forms. Imported wares may have been desirable economically or socially, but more readily available local supplies usually filled the demand. Through time, forms and functions changed with changing tastes and consumption patterns to include a greater percentage of tablewares to utilitarian wares. In the USA, this shift accompanied a decrease in representation in ceramic assemblages from domestic sites and an increase in percentage of other classes such as improved earthenwares, stonewares and porcelains. These latter wares increase in representation with improvements in technologies such as kiln firing, spurred by the Industrial Revolution and developing world trade networks. Efforts to distinguish domestic from imported redwares and to establish dates of manufacture or deposition for these wares remain a major challenge for historical archaeologists.

In recent decades, historical and archaeological inquiries in Europe and the USA are increasingly identifying specific redware varieties and production periods for European and colonial US kiln sites. As archaeologists gain greater control of the production database, redware varieties may be identified, dated and described more specifically, even to the point of successfully incorporating such technological data into more general ceramic analyses such as the **mean ceramic dating** formula. These data also strengthen and refine alternative classificatory methods such as classifications based on analyses of form and interpretations of vessel functions.

In England, many of the early post-medieval traditions have been named and dated on the basis of their geographic centres of production, such as Wanfried and Astbury slipwares and 'Metropolitan' slipwares of Essex (all of which have fairly clear, red-appearing lead glazes with yellow-appearing white kaolin clay underglaze slip decoration),

North Devon gravel-tempered and sgraffito wares (with greenish yellow lead glaze and kaolin slip) and Buckley redwares (with dark glazes and agate-like clay bodies), all of which had antecedents in earlier, more generalised pottery-making traditions of the Middle Ages. Individual kiln sites for English and US pottery-making centres currently are being carefully excavated in research projects that have the potential to yield valuable descriptive data for supporting more highly refined interpretations of this important, ubiquitous and sparsely defined class of ceramics in the future.

See also: ceramics; creamware; domestic sites; earthenware; England; formula dating; La Isabella; mean ceramic dating; pearlware; porcelain; stoneware; trade; typologies; writing

Further reading

Copeland, R. (1982) *Blue and White Transfer-printed Pottery*, Haverfordwest, Shire.

Hurst, J.G., Neal, D.S. and van Beuningen, H.J.E. (1986) 'Pottery produced and traded in north-west Europe 1350–1650', *Rotterdam Papers VI, a Contribution to Medieval Archaeology*, Museum Boymans-van Beuningen, the Netherlands.

Myers, S.H. (1980) *Handcraft to Industry: Philadelphia Ceramics in the First Half of the Nineteenth Century*, Washington, DC: Smithsonian Institution Press.

Quimby, I.M.G. (ed.) (1973) *Ceramics in America*, Charlottesville: University Press of Virginia.

Rhodes, D. (1973) *Clay and Glazes for the Potter*, revised edn, Radnor, PA: Chilton.

Turnbaugh, S.P. (ed.) (1985) *Domestic Pottery of the Northeastern United States, 1625–1850: Regional Production and World Trade*, Orlando: Academic Press.

Watkins, L.W. (1968) *Early New England Potters and Their Wares*, Cambridge, MA: Harvard University Press.

SARAH PEABODY TURNBAUGH

remote sensing

Archaeologists have an arsenal of remote-sensing techniques they can use to peer beneath the soil without actually excavating. This kind of research is sometimes termed 'sub-surface surveying' because the archaeologist is actually making a survey of what lies beneath the ground's surface. Historical archaeologists use remote-sensing techniques to reveal the presence and locations of walls, cellars, hearths, shipwrecks and many other kinds of human-built artefacts that may exist unseen beneath the surface of the ground and the water.

Archaeologists have adopted high-tech remote-sensing methods for many reasons, but foremost among them are that:

1 archaeological research is expensive and time consuming, and, because archaeologists often only have limited time and funds available, they do not wish to spend their precious resources excavating places that have no potential to produce information;

2 the use of remote sensing allows archaeologists to pin-point the locations of suspected but undiscovered buried and submerged sites within a large area; and

3 because archaeology is a destructive process, archaeologists often wish to preserve an especially important site for later excavation when archaeological techniques may be more sophisticated. In such cases, the precise location of a site can make it easier to protect.

Historical archaeologists can use many kinds of remote sensing, but perhaps the most widely used are **metal detectors**, proton magnetometers, soil resistivity, soil phosphate analysis, ground-penetrating radar and sonar. Each technique has a distinct use, and most archaeologists, unless they are specially trained in the techniques, will generally collaborate with a remote-sensing specialist to ensure the reliability of their results. In almost every terrestrial case, except where it is simply not possible, the archaeologist will first construct a grid over the area to be tested. This grid will usually exist only on paper, but all readings will be taken from the four corners of each individual grid square.

A proton magnetometer is really a sophisticated version of the metal detector. Archaeologists use magnetometers to obtain a series of magnetic readings from the soil. The archaeologist will create a map of the readings, delineating the various 'hot spots', or the places where high readings were obtained. Individuals model of magnetometers, because of their strength, can 'see' further into the ground than others. Archaeologists use proton magnetometers to locate buried and submerged metal objects (such as nails, anchors, chains, spikes and iron tools) and earth magnetised by fire (hearths, burned buildings).

Soil resistivity is a technique in which the archaeologist passes an electrical current underground using at least four metal electrodes pushed into the earth. Different kinds of soil, rocks and human-built features (such as brick walls) retain varying amounts of moisture, and so they have different degrees of resistance to the current. Soil resistivity is particularly useful for locating graves, cellars and other sub-surface features that can be expected to retain different amounts of moisture.

Soil phosphate analysis relies on chemical testing. In soil phosphate analysis, the archaeologist collects a series of small soil samples from beneath the topsoil and then tests each one with chemicals to obtain a reading of the amount of phosphorous present. Everyday human activity adds chemicals such as calcium, nitrogen, carbon and phosphorous to the soil. Of these, only phosphorous is stable over time. The phosphorous content of the soil is important to archaeologists because this chemical is fixed in teeth and bones, it plays a part in human digestion and it occurs in significant amounts in human and animal excreta. Archaeologists can thus use phosphate analysis to discover the former locations of farmyards, privies, fence lines and houses. Soil phosphate analysis is not useful, however, in modern-day pastures because of the widespread presence of animal wastes in the soil.

At the beginning of the twenty-first century, historical archaeologists were beginning to use ground-penetrating (or probing) radar with greater frequency. In this technique, a radar – pulled in a straight line along the ground or towed from a boat – transmits a low-frequency electromagnetic signal into the ground. When the signal encounters an anomaly (a buried wall or a shipwreck, for instance), it sends a signal back to the receiver. Mapping these signals permits an archaeologist to 'read' the size and location of the anomaly. Historical archaeologists have used ground-penetrating radar at a large number of sites. The technique generally does not work well on sites containing a large number of buried rocks and other large, naturally occurring anomalies, and, even in the best case, a trained technician who can decipher the output is required.

Sonar, or SOund Navigation And Ranging, is a complex detection device similar to ground-penetrating radar. The difference is that sonar is used underwater, and that the machine emits a pulse of sound rather than an electromagnetic signal. The sound produces an echo when it strikes an object, such as a submerged ship. The echoes are mapped to reveal the presence of the anomaly.

Archaeologists are also making use of many extremely sophisticated GIS (geographical information systems) applications. These advanced analysis techniques include the analysis of aerial photographs (see **aerial photography**), photogrammetry and digital image processing. Many of these techniques rely on satellite images and airborne thermal scanning, a method that measures the heat differences in the ground surface. Such differences can indicate the presence of buried stone buildings.

Further reading

Arnold, J.B., III (1987) 'Marine magnetometer survey of archaeological materials near Galveston, Texas', *Historical Archaeology* 21(1): 18–47.

Clark, A. (1990) *Seeing beneath the Soil: Prospecting Methods in Archaeology*, London: Batesford.

Kenyon, J.L. and Bevan, B. (1977) 'Ground-penetrating radar and its application to a historical archaeological site', *Historical Archaeology* 11: 48–55.

Scollar, I. (1989) *Archaeological Prospecting, Image Processing, and Remote Sensing*, Cambridge: Cambridge University Press.

CHARLES E. ORSER, JR

Renaissance

In its most common significance, the term 'Renaissance' defines the movement of cultural renewal, starting in Italy, in the fifteenth century, characterised by the rediscovering of models of classic antiquity in sciences, literature and art. The term was adopted by nineteenth-century historio-graphy since the edition in 1860 of *The Civilization of the Renaissance in Italy* by Jacob Burckhardt. The Swiss historian recognised the origin of the modern individual in the social ideology developed by merchant aristocracy in central and northern Italian town states. Valuing work, observation and rational knowledge of nature, it proposed antithetical values to the *ethos* of the feudal warrior aristocracy. Burckhardt's views owe their origins to Voltaire's *Essay on the Customs and Spirit of the Nations*, where the term 'renaissance' described a new age of human history. However, the term was born in the sixteenth-century Italian literature about the visual arts. In Vasari's *Vite* (1550) the word '*rinascita*' indicates the new life of the classical idea of the art as an imitation of nature, appearing in Tuscany since Giotto.

The rediscovering of classical models had as its consequence a new interest in the material evidences of Greek and Roman civilisations. Humanists like Ciriaco D'Ancona, Poggio Braccio-lini and Felice Feliciano collected epigraphs and graphical records of the ancient ruins in their voyages through Italy and eastward. However, this kind of interest was developed above all by the artists. Research about classical remains in Rome and throughout Europe gave birth to a number of sketch notes made mainly by architects like Francesco di Giorgio Martini and Giuliano da Sangallo. The goal of this research was to collect samples to be used in modern works of art – often with the friendly contribution of learned men – to aid in the reconstruction of an ideal image of ancient Rome as it appeared in classical literature. The most relevant examples of this literature are the letter to Pope Leo X, written by Raphael, named *Commissario delle Antichità di Roma* in 1514, helped by Baldassar Castiglione, and the transla-tion of the Vitruvius treatise made for the artist by the humanist Marco Fabio Calvo, assisted by Fra' Giovanni Giocondo, the famous theoretician of classical architecture.

Raphael's dream 'to show the Ancient Rome in drawings' became the aim of some circles of artists, collectors and learned men since the Accademia de' Virtuosi was founded by Claudio Tolomei. This goal was reflected in a number of important publications, and illustrations had a growing

importance thanks to the increasing development of engraving techniques. The better illustrations contributed to the spread of new methods for researching the classical world all over Europe. *Urbis Romae aedificiorum illustrium* by G.B. De'Cava-lieri, published in Florence in 1569, was based on drawings by the architect G.A. Dosio, the collec-tions of Roman statues edited by Cavalieri himself (1560–93), the two plats of Rome by Pirro Ligorio (containing buildings reconstructed from ancient coins) and, above all, the *Speculum Romanae Magnificentiae* (published by Lafrery) ushered in the learned milieu of the age throughout antiquar-ian research.

See also: classical archaeology

Further reading

Burckhardt, J. (1954) *Die Cultur der Renaissance in Italien: ein Versuch* (English trans.: *The Civilization of the Renaissance in Italy: An Essay*), New York: Modern Library.

Di Teodoro, F. (1997) *Raffaello, Baldassar Castiglione e la lettera a Leone X*, Bologna: Nuova Alfa.

Haskell, F. and Penny, N. (1981) *Taste and the Antique: The Lure of Classical Sculpture, 1500–1900*, New Haven: Phaidon.

Lafrery, A. (1544–1602) *Speculum Romanae Magnifi-centiae: omnia fere quaecumque in Urbe monumenta extant...Antonius Lafreri excudit*, Rome: Romae.

Momigliano, A. (1950) 'Ancient history and the antiquarian', *Journal of the Warburg and Courtauld Institutes* 13: 285–315.

Vasari, G. (1963) *Vite de' piu eccellenti architetti, pittori et scultori italiani* (English trans.: *The Lives of the Painters, Sculptors, and Architects*), London: Dent.

Weiss, R. (1988) *The Renaissance Discovery of Classical Antiquity*, Oxford: Oxford University Press.

LUCIANO MIGLIACCIO

repatriation

'Repatriation' refers to the return of cultural property (artefacts and other materials, including human remains) to the indigenous peoples who believe they have cultural and historical connec-tions to the objects and remains. Archaeologists around the world began to wrestle with the many issues surrounding repatriation in the late twentieth century as native peoples started to demand the return of their rightful, cultural property from museums and other repositories. Many archaeologists initially rejected repatriation, believing it was a threat to their scientific and academic freedoms. Others, however, readily accepted it as their duty. As explained by archaeologist Larry Zimmerman – an early proponent of the need for archaeologists to be sensitive to the rights of native peoples – professional archaeology went through four phases concerning repatriation: denial, dialogue, analysis and compromise. These stages were characterised by often vociferous disagreement and debate as archaeologists came to terms with the idea that living men and women – descendants of their 'research subjects' – felt they had a stake in the archaeologist's research. At the beginning of the twenty-first century, most archaeologists have realised that repatriation is the proper course of action and have accepted it.

Repatriation has had the greatest impact on archaeology in the USA, though it is also a significant issue in many other parts of the world, including Australia, New Zealand, Canada and Scandinavia. The situation in the USA provides a good example of how one nation is confronting the issue.

The US Congress passed the National Museum of the American Indian Act as its first repatriation law in 1989. This Act required the Smithsonian Institution to inventory, document and repatriate human remains and grave objects to federally recognised native cultures within the USA. The Congress expanded the law in 1996 to include more classes of artefacts and to establish deadlines for repatriation. The Smithsonian created a Repatriation Office to complete the mandated tasks.

The US Congress followed the National Museum of the American Indian Act with the Native American Graves Protection and Repatriation Act (NAGPRA), signed into law in 1990. This law has had a great impact on archaeology because it supported the right of Native American and Native Hawaiian organisations and descendants to assume custody of human skeletal material, grave objects, items of sacred importance and other cultural

objects. The law places the onus of compliance on all those agencies, museums, and universities that receive federal funding. Curators at these facilities are required to inventory their collections and to ensure that their institutions meet the conditions of the law.

In response to the federal legislation, some indigenous peoples have created their own repatriation offices to ensure the return of their cultural patrimony. For example, in southern California, the Cahuilla Inter-Tribal Repatriation Committee is a consortium of eight tribes who work together on behalf of repatriation.

Further reading

Watkins, J. (2000) *Indigenous Archaeology: American Indian Values and Scientific Practice*, Walnut Creek, CA: AltaMira Press.
Zimmerman, L. (1997) 'Anthropology and responses to the reburial Issue', in T. Biolsi and L. Zimmerman (eds) *Indians and Anthropologists: Vine Deloria Jr. and the Critique of Anthropology*, Tucson: University of Arizona Press, pp. 92–112.

CHARLES E. ORSER, JR

rescue archaeology

Archaeologists generally use the term 'rescue archaeology' to describe excavations that are conducted because a site or area rich in sites is in imminent danger of either being destroyed or of suffering irreparable harm. Rescue, or 'salvage', archaeology is therefore often associated with new construction efforts. **Cultural-resource management** is intended to prevent the need to rescue sites from destruction because planning, surveying and study is designed to precede unintended site discovery. In the best-case scenario, cultural-resource managers will have identified important cultural properties – using a combination of library research and fieldwork – before any significant site devastation can occur.

Rescue archaeology was more common before the passage of the world's **preservation legislation**, but it continues to be practised where the location of precious archaeological remains are unanticipated. Before the legislation was passed, it was not uncommon to see archaeologists literally working just ahead of advancing bulldozers. Antiquities legislation is designed to promote site protection by identifying important sites before they are disturbed.

The need for rescue excavations is especially strong in urban environments because of the intense nature of building there. Before excavation, archaeologists can seldom know with precision what remains may have survived many decades of repeated construction in an area, and so the need for rescue excavation often arises. Numerous examples exist, with the highly significant research at the **African Burial Ground** in **New York City** providing an excellent example. In this particular case, the archaeologists who conducted the preliminary surveying and assessment did not anticipate the survival of the burials within the heart of one of the world's busiest cities. Other rescue excavations have occurred in urban locations throughout the world.

Rescue archaeology is also often practised with underwater remains. Archaeologists may need to conduct emergency excavations when shipwreck sites are discovered by channel dredging, a drop in water level because of drought and by curious sport divers. Rescue excavations in such places are designed to save as much information as possible before the site is either completely destroyed or damaged so completely that examination would be difficult or impossible.

Archaeologists engaged in rescue excavations often find that their research is hurried, and, to compensate, some have adopted special techniques to recover information quickly and efficiently with minimum loss of information. For example, in the mid-twentieth century, some archaeologists employed drag-line bucket devices that could scrape soil from a large area at 5 and 10 cm levels. Although archaeologists engaged in salvage excavations have recovered a great deal of invaluable information, archaeological research is best conducted in situations where it is not necessary to hurry the painstaking excavation process.

See also: site significance

Further reading

Barker, P. (1982) *Techniques of Archaeological Excavation*, second edn, New York: Universe.

CHARLES E. ORSER, JR

resistance

When historical archaeologists use the term 'resistance' they are usually referring to a conscious decision on the part of past men and women to oppose their **domination** by another group or **culture**. Resistance used in this manner is intended to represent a series of social actions that can take various spatial and temporal forms.

The archaeologists' interest in resistance developed in the late twentieth century, largely in reaction to theories of **acculturation**. Acculturation theorists, writing in the early to mid-twentieth century, tended to envision a culture's adoption of foreign cultural traits as something that almost inevitably occurred when the culture came in contact with a technologically more sophisticated culture. The most influential acculturation theorists were US anthropologists who studied the interaction between **Native Americans** and encroaching Europeans and Americans.

Acculturation theory was long a mainstay of historical archaeology because it was first practised in places that had been the scene of colonial-period culture contacts. In the case of North America, the degree of acculturation among Native Americans was often judged by evaluating the relative occurrence of non-indigenous artefacts found in the deposits of their home sites. Large amounts of non-Indian artefacts tended to suggest a great degree of acculturation, whereas small amounts or none at all suggested little or no acculturation.

Beginning in the final decades of the twentieth century, some historical archaeologists became disenchanted with acculturation theory because it did not allow enough decision making on the part of the men and women with whom Europeans and Americans came into contact. In other words, these archaeologists refused to envision indigenous peoples as automatons who merely awaited the arrival of Europeans to obtain a more diverse material culture. Anthropological research was replete with illustrations in which native peoples around the world had the **power** to resist total domination, whether it was economic, technological, political or religious. In keeping with these findings, the goal of much historical archaeology conducted in the last few years of the twentieth century was intended to document the nature of resistance (and domination) using archaeological materials. In the vast number of cases, evidence for resistance existed only within the archaeological record because it was often conducted in a covert manner, involving the continuation of religious practices or the maintenance of a traditional material culture. Authors of **historical documents** may not have written about native resistance, or may have misrepresented or misunderstood it when they did write about it. Archaeology is thus one of the best sources of information about resistance.

At the close of the twentieth century, however, some archaeologists began to question the dominance/resistance paradigm, choosing instead to envision the conflictual interactions between diverse peoples as infinitely complex and deeply nuanced. Some historical archaeologists substituted terms such as 'resistant accommodation' and 'resistant adaptation' to indicate that resistance was not an 'either/or' proposition, but rather an ongoing, often muted process that could have extremely subtle aspects. These archaeologists nevertheless still consider resistance an important topic of study.

Further reading

Colburn, F.D. (ed.) (1989) *Everyday Forms of Peasant Resistance*, Armonk, NY: M.E. Sharpe.

Frazer, B. (ed.) (1999) 'Archaeologies of resistance in Britain and Ireland, parts I and II', *International Journal of Historical Archaeology* 3: 1–125.

McGuire, R.H. and Paynter, R. (eds) (1991) *The Archaeology of Inequality*, Oxford: Blackwell.

CHARLES E. ORSER, JR

restoration

Archaeologists usually use the term 'restoration' in two distinct but related senses: to refer to the restoration of buildings, monuments and yards, and to refer to the restoration of artefacts. In both cases, the archaeologist strives to add a tangible reality to the past by illuminating elements of historical life. The work that archaeologists do in conjunction with restoration helps to tell the story of the past.

Historical archaeology has always been associated with the **reconstruction** of past buildings by providing architectural information that is available in no other source. Reconstruction projects generally occur in situations where a building has been completely removed or is so deteriorated that archaeology is the best means for acquiring structural information. Restoration generally occurs in cases where a building already exists and where the archaeologist is working to provide information about outbuildings, additions and attachments to a standing building, or even information about the kinds of **material culture** used inside the building. Excavations around the exteriors of standing buildings, or even underneath in cellars and basements, can reveal the foundations of forgotten buildings and bring to light the artefacts used inside the building. The excavations at Wetherburn's Tavern in colonial Williamsburg, Virginia, provide an excellent example. In this case, site interpreters used the archaeological information to restore the outbuildings and yards, as well as to furnish the inside of the restored building with the same kinds of objects used during the eighteenth century.

Historical archaeology has also been used to assist with the restoration of formal gardens. Excavation can provide information about the location of various plants, follies and pathways, and can provide specific detail about the spatial design of the garden. Archaeology conducted at the Hermitage Plantation in Tennessee provides an excellent example. President Andrew Jackson lived at the Hermitage, and one of the projects of the Ladies' Hermitage Association was to restore Rachel Jackson's formal garden to its 1840s-era appearance. Archaeological research played a key role in this effort.

During the final years of the twentieth century, some archaeologists began to investigate the idea that site reconstructions and restorations are not necessarily neutral in the messages they convey. Restoration and reconstruction projects are generally dedicated to illustrating how a building or area looked at a particular point in time, and for this reason they must ignore time. No reconstruction, no matter how carefully executed, can be completely successful in representing the entire time span of a building's existence and use. In a thought-provoking examination of Harpers Ferry, West Virginia, Paul Shackel illustrates how the interpreters of this national park used restoration and reconstruction to tell a specific and limited story about the town. The restoration focused on the dramatic years of the US Civil War, and ignored the equally important post-war period, when the town's residents faced significant social and technological changes.

The restoration of artefacts, or finds, generally falls within the realm of conservation (see **conservation, terrestrial**). Highly trained archaeological conservators painstakingly labour to save important artefacts, of all materials, from complete deterioration and destruction. In many cases, the restorationist is employed by a museum, where the eventual goal may be to put the artefact on display for public education. Restoration is necessary so that the public can learn as much as possible from the restored objects. The restoration of fragile materials such as wood and leather require specialised training because the restorer's goal is to stop the artefact's deterioration and to ensure that it does not begin anew.

Further reading

McKee, L. (1996) 'The archaeology of Rachel's Garden', in R. Yamin and K.B. Methey (eds) *Landscape Archaeology: Reading and Interpreting the American Historical Landscape*, Knoxville: University of Tennessee Press, pp. 70–90.

Noël Hume, I. (1969) *Archaeology and Wetherburn's Tavern*, Williamsburg: Colonial Williamsburg Foundation.

Shackel, P.A. (2000) *Archaeology and Created Memory: Public History in a National Park*, New York: Kluwer Academic/Plenum Press.

CHARLES E. ORSER, JR

Richmond Palace, England

Richmond, which was known until 1501 as 'Shene', has seen three successive royal palaces on the same site between the River Thames and what is now Richmond Green. The first was established by Edward III, who died there in 1377. The palace was favoured by Richard II and his queen, Anne of Bohemia, but after she died there in 1394 he had it demolished. The second was begun by Henry V and completed by Henry VI. After a serious fire in 1497, Henry VII rebuilt the palace, and renamed it Richmond after his Earldom in Yorkshire. After Elizabeth I died at Richmond in 1603, the royal residence saw little change, and following a Parliamentary Survey in 1649 most of the palace was pulled down. By the early eighteenth century, few palace buildings survived. Today, the few visible remains include the Gatehouse and the Wardrobe.

During the 1980s and early 1990s, conjectural plans of the Tudor palace were published. These were largely based on contemporary documents and pictures, notably the description by Lancaster Herald (1501), the Parliamentary Survey (1649–50), drawings by Antonis van Wyngaerde (1561–2) and an engraving by Wenceslaus Hollar (1638). The palace had three main courts aligned on an axis at right angles to the Thames. Closest to the river were the Privy Lodgings built around a small central court, beyond which lay the Middle (Fountain) Court and the Great Court. There were also ancillary buildings, gardens and orchards. A moat separated the Privy Lodgings and the Great Orchard from the rest of the palace.

Before the 1990s, remains of the palace had been occasionally observed during building work. For example, renovations in the Wardrobe revealed an oak arch in 1910 and a lath and plaster wall in *c.* 1920, and during the conversion of Trumpeters' House (built 1703–4) in 1951 the entrance to the Middle Court was revealed and demolished. More detailed, but unpublished, surveys were made of a

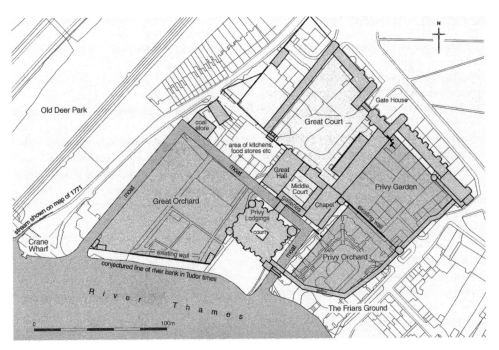

Figure 27 Layout of Richmond Palace, England
Source: R. Cowie

stretch of masonry on the north-east side of the moat in 1944, and of the Gatehouse and the Wardrobe.

The first archaeological excavation on the site, undertaken in 1972 in Old Palace Lane, revealed part of the moat wall. In 1992, five sixteenth-century walls were recorded below ground at the 'Old Palace' next to the Gatehouse. Posts of a jetty, found during a survey of the adjacent Thames foreshore in 1995, were dated by dendrochronology to 1584–5, and identified as part of a wharf that served the palace. In 1997, excavations in the garden of Trumpeters' House revealed structures of late medieval or Tudor date. They included part of a cellar associated with the Privy Lodgings and masonry structures possibly at the rear of the Great Hall. Finds included three fine fragments of architectural terracotta dated to *c.* 1510–40. Most of the demolition debris found on the site probably came from the Privy Lodgings, and included moulded stone in late medieval (perpendicular) forms, suggesting that the building may have incorporated at least part of its medieval precursor.

The publication of a long-lost plan drawn by the Italian architect Costantino de'Servi in about 1611 has provided further information about the exact size and location of the Privy Lodgings and, together with other evidence, has enabled a new overall plan of the palace to be produced.

See also: England

Further reading

Cloake, J. (1995) *Palaces and Parks of Richmond and Kew I: The Palaces of Shene and Richmond*, Chichester: Phillimore.

Cowie, R. and Cloake, J. (2001) 'An archaeological survey of Richmond Palace, Surrey', *Post-medieval Archaeology* 35: 1–50.

Dixon, P. (1975) 'Excavations at Richmond Palace, Surrey', *Post-medieval Archaeology* 9: 103–16.

Eiche, S. (1998) 'Prince Henry's Richmond: The project by Costantino de'Servi', *Apollo* 148: 10–14.

ROBERT COWIE

Rocca San Silvestro, Italy

The Italian medieval mining community of Rocca San Silvestro, located only 3 km inland from Campiglia Marittima on the west coast of central Italy, was established in the late thirteenth century as an industrial village to exploit local copper resources. This village was founded on a particularly high hill in a region noted since antiquity as the 'metallic mountains'. Rocca San Silvestro was the forerunner of mining and other 'company' towns that became common throughout the world by the nineteenth century.

Archaeological evidence indicates that this region had no permanent settlements prior to the building of this specialised industrial village. Prior to constructing this mining community, this region had been exploited for wood, charcoal and wild game since the Etruscan period. The ore extracted was of particularly low grade. The copper produced could compete on the world markets only through availability of cheap fuel sources and low wages. The development of Swedish and other copper mines led to the loss of markets for the copper produced. This small community was in decline by the middle of the fourteenth century and completely abandoned by AD 1450. Thereafter, the ruins were visited primarily by shepherds and their charges, but never reoccupied. The extensive written documentation in this area, which survives from the medieval period, plus the lack of human activity in or around this village, have provided modern researchers with an archaeological treasure. Ricardo Francovich inaugurated a long-term, multidisciplinary study of this archaeological complex that has produced important evidence relating to the beginnings of the Industrial Revolution.

In many respects, the construction of the many stone buildings, including a church, owner's manor house (see **manor houses**), workers' houses and other structures, was based on typical Italian hill towns of the period. However, the buildings at the top and clinging to the sides of this hill were built over a brief period of time rather than accreting in normal village fashion.

The village church that served this community is actually only a very small chapel in which no more than twenty-five people could gather without crowding the limited space. The small churchyard to the west of this small chapel holds the remains of the people who had given life to this community. In death they were buried, one upon the other, in a plot of ground even smaller than the floor of the church. At that time, burials inside churches were limited to the elite, and the owners or operators of this community must have been buried in the cemeteries of the villages from which they had come. Excavations in the cemetery area have provided a great deal of information about customs and social activities among these miners and their families. The analysis of their bones will reveal details of health and nutrition within this early industrial community. Industrial disorders correlated with metals extraction and processing, and lead poisoning in particular, can be studied at this site.

The data from Rocca San Silvestro can be compared with data now available from other central Italian villages of approximately the same date. Of particular interest are other purpose-built villages such as the monastic communities of Anguillara, Farfa and San Vincenzo al Volturno to the south.

MARSHALL JOSEPH BECKER

Rocks, The, Australia

As the port of the British penal colony established in 1788, the Rocks is **Sydney**, Australia's, oldest European, continuously occupied area, and since 1979 has been the subject of intensive historical archaeological investigation. Covering the rocky west side of Sydney Cove, today it occupies an area of 24 ha, managed by the Sydney Harbour Foreshore Authority, defined by the east edge of the Sydney Harbour Bridge, the foreshore and Grosvenor Street to the south.

From the first years of white settlement it was represented by bourgeois observers as the city's underworld slum, but archaeological investigation has challenged such stereotypes. At Lilyvale, Cumberland Street, evidence was found for the homes built by convicts and ex-convicts settling unofficially from the 1790s, using flimsy construction techniques such as wattle-and-daub, with earthen floors, yet furnished with good-quality English **ceramics** and **glass**, while their occupants enjoyed a varied diet. At the Cumberland Street site, households were investigated that in these early decades followed traditional habits such as unspecialised use of domestic and work space, as well as revealing the emergence of modern consumerism and mass production.

This archaeological pattern changes during the nineteenth century, as urbanisation led to over-crowding and poor sanitation, while many moved out along the railway lines in the 1880s, leaving behind the working classes. It remained cosmopolitan, and at Samsons' Cottage, Kendall Lane, evidence was found for a turn-of-the-century Chinese merchant's household, indicating the persistence of traditional identity as well as the use of material culture in communicating with white society. Its strong maritime identity is reflected at sites such as the waterfront Sailors' Home, where communal eating and illegal alcohol consumption were indicated. Evidence for a boarding house run by Mrs Ann Lewis at Jobbins Buildings, Gloucester Street, reveals the crucial role women played in this economy, constructing a 'respectable', private environment.

The outbreak of plague in 1900 prompted 'cleansing' operations and government resumptions, although it remained a close-knit community until the 1970s. As a major tourist destination, interpretive centres such as Susannah Place House Museum, the Sailors Home Visitors Centre and the Museum of Sydney on the site of First Government House explore this rich archaeological resource.

See also: First Government House

Further reading

Gojak, D. and Iacono, N. (1993) 'The archaeology and history of the Sydney Sailors Home, the Rocks, Sydney', *The Bulletin of the Australian Institute for Maritime Archaeology* 17(1): 27–32.

Karskens, G. (1999) *Inside the Rocks: The Archaeology of a Neighbourhood*, Sydney: Hale & Iremonger.

Kelly, M. (1997) *Anchored in a Small Cove: A History and Archaeology of the Rocks, Sydney*, Sydney: Sydney Cove Authority.

Lydon, J. (1999) *Many Inventions: The Chinese in the Rocks 1890–1930*, Melbourne: Monash Publications in History.

—— (1995) 'Boarding-houses in the Rocks: Mrs Ann Lewis' Privy, 1865', *Public History Review* 4: 73–88.

—— (1993) 'Archaeology in the Rocks 1979–1993: From Old Sydney gaol to Mrs Ann Lewis' boarding-house', *Journal of the Australasian Society for Historical Archaeology* 11: 33–42.

JANE LYDON

Rome, Italy

Rome is a veritable storehouse of living historical archaeology. Still, in many parts, girded by the massive third century AD Aurelianic walls (reinforced in the fifth century), its pre-modern interior features an array of antique structures, preserved, adapted, remodelled, restored and imitated. The tendency has long been in archaeology to dwell on the Roman and imperial monuments and to gloss over the medieval and later architectural achievements simply because of the prominence of so many extant and active churches and palazzi; however, a more balanced approach now prevails, active even before the year 2000 Jubilee/Giubileo celebrations, which renewed pilgrimage to, and appreciation of, Rome's ecclesiastical heritage.

In 1897, Rodolfo Lanciani, Professor of Topography at the University of Rome, was able to review in captivating style the wealth of Rome's ancient past as revealed by a spate of major excavations in the heart of the Eternal City since 1872. This work had progressed since the city became the head of a reunified Italy, to such a degree that Lanciani could already view Rome as a glorious archaeological park, celebrating her classical foundations and successes. This past was thus also a public one; indeed, from 1872 the publication of the *Bullettino della Commissione archeologica comunale di Roma* allowed for accessible and stimulating reports. Lanciani recognised a degree of loss, however, of narrow, winding streets in medieval districts of relative shabbiness such as the Ghetto and Regola, duly destroyed to enhance both vision and health; but he also showed an awareness of the Middle Ages, of their value in preserving many of the monuments of the city through reuse and adaptation, in contrast with

Renaissance-period pillaging and removal of materials and art.

The heart of Rome continued to be opened, notably through the works of Giacomo Boni from 1901–6, but at a pace not matched by adequate publication and, progressively, pursued by limited scientific appraisal of anything post-Roman – open-area excavation amid complex layers covering two millennia was an understandable struggle. The photographic record of Thomas Ashby for Rome between 1891 and 1930 offers an invaluable guide to the scale of clearance in a rapidly changing city. Lanciani had observed a doubling of the population between 1870 and 1897 to 400,000 persons; by the 1920s, the population had reached the million, last matched in the reigns of the early emperors.

Mussolini's fascist dream created an even more extended Roman theatre. Between 1926 and 1940, the cutting of roads – new triumphal routes such as the Via del Impero parallel to the ancient Via Sacra – rudely exposed and isolated the Roman monuments, which were then, as in the case of the Mausoleum of Augustus and the relocated Ara Pacis, framed by new-regime monumental palazzi and parks; medieval structures were sacrificed, and even the Roman deposits were only crudely recorded, with exposure and display the main targets. The visible archaeology and setting of early twenty-first-century Rome remains largely that dictated by Mussolini. We should perhaps not be too disdainful of this remodelling; arguably it was no more than the beautifying and imperialising of Rome undertaken by her first emperor, Augustus, at the end of the first century BC.

Between the 1940s and 1970s, new archaeology stuttered, but the efforts of Lugli did much to reappraise Rome's architecture, while Krautheimer initiated a substantial and systematic review of the city's Christian heritage. Since the 1980s, a far more patient and authoritative archaeology has been pursued by scholars such as Carandini, Coarelli, Pensabene and Manacorda, encompassing all periods, and with the medieval and later centuries gaining an increasingly coherent voice from the 1990s through the efforts of Meneghini, Paroli and Delogu, examining in particular ceramic data and papal efforts at urban regeneration. Far more easily now can we observe an evolving urbanism, its ebbs, flows and vicissitudes, and far more can the people of the city be recognised and understood.

As Lanciani proclaimed, 'Rome has always lived, and lived at the expense of the past'; the ancient Romans were extremely conscious of their past and their antiquity, and the Forum and Palatine are showpieces of this layering and exposure of centuries of rule, belief, administration and living. Carandini suggests that the sixth-century BC houses revealed along the Via Sacra in the Forum were in fact occupied by powerful public figures such as Cicero towards the close of the Republic; the Temple of Jupiter Optimus Maximus, like the Regia, both at various times damaged, were always restored to their antique form; and Augustus carefully sited his Palatine house alongside the revered timber 'House of Romulus', itself close to the ancient Temple of Magna Mater. In the fourth and fifth centuries AD, the City Prefect and the emperors were acutely aware of the antiquity and thus sanctity of many of Rome's ancient buildings, even if they then belonged to defunct pagan cults; managing and preserving much of that heritage was deemed essential and is borne out still in the survival of early imperial edifices such as the Pantheon – converted into a church, but this only in the early seventh century.

Building on and respecting the past is also evident in the overlay of structures (see Figure 28). Most instructive is the twelfth-century church of San Clemente, where excavations by Irish Dominican monks from the mid-nineteenth century exposed an early Christian predecessor; this had been maintained throughout the early Middle Ages and then used as a crypt church. However, beneath this, at a depth of 11 m below the present church floor, was preserved part of an early imperial apartment block and granary, the former containing a temple of Mithras; raising and remodelling of the first-century structures in the third century AD are presumed to relate to the creation of a wealthy house or *domus* into which was later inserted the first church to Saint Clement.

The new generation of archaeologists in Rome is striving to make good the gaps caused by the early city archaeologists and to paint whole pictures of space and transformation in the urban centre.

Figure 28 Pantheon, Rome: the best-preserved Roman temple – but with an amalgam of histories
Note: The Agrippa inscription in fact belongs to the Hadrianic (second-century AD) rebuilding of the first-century BC
edifice that was destroyed in the Great Fire of AD 80. Further work is attested on an inscription below, dating
to the early third century. The building reflects Roman innovation in its design and Roman power in the
vast monolithic Egyptian marble columns of the porch. Conversion into the church of S. Maria and Martyres
in the seventh century ensured its survival; medieval and post-medieval accretions (including Bernini's peculiar
twin belfries) have been removed, but the interior boasts the tombs of the artist Raphael (1483–1520) and also of
the Italian monarchy of 1870–1946.
Source: Photo: N.J. Christie

Integrated documentary and archaeological (new
but primarily archival) research has, for example,
shed light on the post-imperial fortunes of the
Forum and Markets of Trajan; still a point of public
oration in the sixth century in the shadow of the
Column of Trajan, sources reveal a persistence in
the forum's monumentality into the ninth century
at least, although the markets by then appear to
have been given over to houses; by the tenth
century, lime burning – attested also in numerous
pockets of the old Forum such as at the Arch of
Severus – signifies removal, stockpiling and burning down of ancient marbles; from the eleventh
century, a church of S. Nicola was created at the
base of the Column, on land belonging to the
monastery of S. Salvatore; around this we hear of
private houses, small gardens and open (ruinous)
spaces – here then we find little attachment to the
Roman past, bar the convenience of walls and

shelter; and for the thirteenth century we find
reference to the imposition of the extant Torre
delle Milizie upon the upper zones of the Markets.
In the Renaissance period the area hosted the
'Alessandrino' quarter, all duly bulldozed under
Mussolini.

For the Palatine, Augenti has likewise pieced
together the shrinking heritage of this sacred zone
after the fifth century, from which time the palace
structures begin to decay, even if still utilised by
Gothic kings and ducal governors in the sixth and
seventh centuries. Here as elsewhere in Rome we
see emerge the conflict between active and inactive
space, and the progressive nucleation of vastly
reduced settlement groups into distinct zones,
largely dictated by Christian basilicas. The Palatine
and Fora appear to have remained points of at least
limited occupation – hinted at previously by the
creation of churches and monasteries, but with the

discovery of eighth- to tenth-century well-to-do houses in the Forum of Nerva now demonstrating a maintained 'prestige' value to this district. In the eleventh to twelfth centuries, the aristocratic Frangipane family even created their own fortified enclave around the Palatine, reusing monuments such as the triumphal arches and the Colosseum as towers and fortresses.

Away from the monumental heart, astonishing results have come from the extremely detailed excavations at the Crypta Balbi under the former churches of Santa Caterina dei Funari (with monastery della Rosa) and San Stanislao dei Polacchi – an evolution fully detailed in a comprehensive museum. This has produced a similar image of Roman public monumentality (Theatre of Balbus) and provision (grain distribution point) followed by decay and redefinition (burials, private structures, hospice, lime burning, workshops, monastic foundation and even a fortified nucleus); again, continuity and/or adaptation of space and walls symbolise the enduring renewal of Rome.

The medieval cityscape now revealed by archaeology and text appears as a fascinating jumble of open and blocked space, with sizeable pockets of human use combined with a vast array of ecclesiastical structures that continued, from early Christian times through to the present century, to attract foreign pilgrims. The contrast of course lies with the bustle of ancient Rome, whose extent, monumentality and confusion are attested even in the fragments of marble plan of the reign of Septimius Severus at the start of the third century AD and recreated in the plastic model at the Museo della Civiltà Romana in Mussolini's administrative Rome (EUR). Neither the map nor model, nor even the fragmented standing remnants of imperial Rome, can in any way do justice to the enormity of the works created under the Republic and the Empire. We can note the city's mass of entertainment structures, most notably the Circus Maximus (capacity $c.$ 200,000, of dimensions 600 × 180 m) and the Colosseum ($c.$ 50,000), the enormous expanse of the public imperial baths (notably those of Diocletian, of $c.$ 380 × 340 m, closely followed by those of Caracalla), the extensive provision of water (recorded in the fourth century as comprising nineteen aqueducts, 1,352

public fountains, 254 reservoirs) and the very feeding and supply of Rome's market and inhabitants (witness the $c.$ 53 million broken-up olive oil amphorae that were dumped over the period AD 140–250 to create the 35-m high, 20,000 m^2 Monte Testaccio). These all provide facts and figures that help picture the city in action, but this can only ever be a crude picture, even alongside the physical evidence of houses, shops and granaries at the old port of Rome, Ostia. Simple mosaic images from Ostia of porters offloading amphorae on their backs from ocean-going vessels to river barges merely hint at the scale of manpower, paid and servile, to allow Rome to function. Aqueducts and bricks likewise tell only vague stories of labour, technology, resources and maintenance.

Little wonder that Rome has always been a honey-pot for tourists and academics alike. While tourists continue the centuries-old admiration of what was, foreign schools and institutes, with their own publications and journals, proliferate to investigate and ruminate further on Rome's vast archaeological, artistic and architectural heritage.

See also: urban archaeology; urbanisation

Further reading

Archeologia a Roma nelle fotografie di Thomas Ashby, 1891–1930 (1989), British School at Rome Archive 2, Naples: Electa.

Archeologia urbana a Roma; il progetto della Crypta Balbi, 5: L'esedra della Crypta Balbi nel medioevo (XI–XV sec.), Florence: All'Insegna del Giglio.

Augenti, A. (1996) *Il Palatino nel Medioevo. Archeologia e topografia (secoli VI–XIII)*, Rome: L'Erma di Bretschneider.

Bianchi, L. (1998) *Case e torri medioevali di Roma*, Rome: L'Erma di Bretschneider.

Coulston, J. and Dodge, H. (eds) (2000) *Ancient Rome: The Archaeology of the Eternal City*, School of Archaeology Monograph 54, Oxford: Oxford University.

Delogu, P. and Paroli, L. (eds) (1993) *La storia economica di Roma nell'alto Medioevo alla luce dei recenti scavi archeologici*, Biblioteca di Archeologia Medievale, 10, Florence: All'Insegna del Giglio.

Krautheimer, R. (1980) *Rome: Profile of a City,*

312–1308, Princeton: Princeton University Press.

Lanciani, R. (1897) *Ancient Rome in the Light of Recent Discoveries*, London: Macmillan.

Meneghini, R. (1993) 'Il Foro e i Mercati di Traiano nel medioevo attraverso le fonti storiche e d'archivio', *Archeologia Medievale* 20: 79–120.

Pani Ermini, L. (ed.) (2000) *Christiana loca. Lo spazio cristiano nella Roma del primo millennio*, Rome: Fratelli Palombi Editori.

NEIL J. CHRISTIE

Rose Theatre, London

The Rose Theatre was the first purpose-built playhouse to be constructed on Bankside, in the part of London known as **Southwark**. Constructed in 1587, the Rose was situated on a plot of land known as the Little Rose Estate, leased by Philip Henslowe (via various other parties) from the parish of St Mildred's in Bread Street. Henslowe entered into a partnership with a man called John Cholmley and the two of them employed a carpenter called John Griggs to build the playhouse.

Records of dramatic production during the first five years of the Rose's existence are scarce but the survival of Philip Henslowe's documents and papers from 1592 onwards (along with the original partnership agreement) provide a unique view of the management and running of a late-Tudor/early-Stuart playhouse. Henslowe's papers (along with those of his son-in-law Edward Alleyn) survive in the archives of Dulwich College in south-east London.

Evidence from documentary and cartographical sources (particularly the maps of John Norden, with his map of 1593 entitled 'Speculum Britanniae' and his panorama of 1600 entitled 'Civitas Londini') has been complemented by archaeological evidence recorded during a **rescue archaeology** excavation, undertaken in 1988–9. Although the entire site of the Rose was not available for excavation, present interpretation of the recorded evidence indicates that the playhouse consisted of two distinct structural phases – an interpretation supported by the documentary and cartographical evidence.

Phase One, built in 1587, appears to have been a building that was an irregular, fourteen-sided polygon with an external diameter of some 22.0 m (72 ft). Parallel foundations provided the base on which an open, timber-framed building, surrounding a central yard, would have been founded. The timber framing would have housed the galleries in which people sat to watch a performance while the open yard would have been where the groundlings stood. The stage projected from the north of the building into the central yard.

Phase Two of the Rose is thought to relate to Henslowe's documented expenditure of 1592 when he records 'suche carges as I have layd owt a bowte my playe howsse'. The expenditure amounts to over one hundred and five pounds and appears to have resulted in an enlargement of the northern half of the building. Eleven years later, Henslowe refused to pay the increased cost for his lease and by 1606 the Surrey and Kent Commissioners for Sewers refer to the Rose as the 'late playhouse'. Evidence of the Rose's destruction was recorded during the on-site archaeological work.

Further reading

Bowsher, J. (1998) *The Rose Theatre: An Archaeological Discovery*, London: Museum of London.

Bowsher, J.M.C. and Blatherwick, S. (1990) 'The structure of the Rose', in F.J. Hildy (ed.) *New Issues in the Reconstruction of Shakespeare's Theatre*, New York: Peter Lang, pp. 55–78.

Foakes, R.A. and Rickert, R.T. (eds) (1961) *Henslowe's Diary*, Cambridge: Cambridge University Press.

Rutter, C.C. (1999) *Documents of the Rose Playhouse*, Manchester: Manchester University Press.

SIMON BLATHERWICK

Ross Female Factory convict site, Tasmania, Australia

From 1803 to 1854, over 74,000 British convicts were transported to the Van Diemen's Land, an island separated from the southern coast of

Australia by the treacherous Bass Straits. Approximately 12,000 of these felons were women, primarily convicted of petty theft of goods stolen from domestic employers. Upon their colonial arrival, most spent time incarcerated within the Female Factory System, a network of women's prisons scattered across the island colony. Named 'factory' as a contraction of the word 'manufactory', these institutions were designed along the model of the British Workhouse System, a nineteenth-century form of public welfare that required standardised rates of labour from inmates to hasten their social and moral salvation from delinquency, idleness and poverty.

Located on the southern edge of the Ross Township in the rural midlands of the island (renamed **Tasmania** in 1855), the Ross Female Factory operated from 1848 through 1854, when Britain ceased convict transportation to Van Diemen's Land. The Ross Factory site was then transferred to civilian management, and experienced a series of municipal and domestic occupations. Gazetted as a historic reserve in 1980, it is now administered through the Tasmanian Parks and Wildlife Service. Both scientific and political values contribute to the significance of the Ross Factory site. Since 1995, the Ross Factory Archaeology Project has studied historical, geophysical and archaeological remains of the Factory. Excavations examined architectural remains and convict-related deposits from the inmate dormitories, solitary cellblock and Assistant Superintendent's quarters.

Results from the Ross Factory Archaeology Project contradicted traditional documentary accounts of **everyday life** within the Australian penal colonies. Archaeological evidence suggested the presence of unique architectural designs at this women's prison. Since this architecture deviates from that of contemporary and well-documented male convict settlements, such as Port Arthur, Sarah Island and Maria Island, these structural differences have been interpreted as material expressions of gender ideology within nineteenth-century institutional sites. Furthermore, archaeological evidence of a black-market trade network was recovered through the Ross Factory Archaeology Project. Comparative historical studies of contemporary male convict settlements are revealing the shadowy presence of an underground sexual

economy throughout the penal colony. Working with data from the Ross Factory Archaeology Project, historians, museum curators, archaeologists and local artists have begun to challenge the traditional images of Australian female convicts as either deceitful whores or as an undifferentiated mass of desperate wretches.

During the 1970s, the Ross Factory site became associated with Australian feminist political activism when a vocal group of heritage professionals, academics and community leaders struggled to improve the visibility of Australian women's history. Their government lobbying and public demonstrations highlighted the absence of women's sites from state and national-heritage register lists. As a result of their powerful efforts, Commonwealth government funds were designated for the acquisition of two female convict sites in Tasmania: the Ross Female Factory, and the first yard of the Cascade Female Factory in Hobart. Thus, the Ross Female Factory site also holds high contemporary-heritage significance as an emblem of Australian feminist political activity.

Further reading

Casella, E.C. (2001) 'Landscapes of punishment and resistance: a female convict settlement in Tasmania', in B. Bender and M. Winer (eds) *Contested Landscapes*: movement, exile and Place, Oxford: Berg Press, pp. 103–120.
—— (1997) 'A large and efficient establishment: Preliminary report of fieldwork at the Ross Female Factory', *Australasian Historical Archaeology* 15: 79–89.
Damousi, J. (1997) *Depraved and Disorderly*, Cambridge: Cambridge University Press.
Daniels, K. (1998) *Convict Women*, St Leonards, New South Wales: Allen & Unwin.
Oxley, D. (1996) *Convict Maids*, Cambridge: Cambridge University Press.

ELEANOR CONLIN CASELLA

Russian colonialism

Russian colonialism, as a topic of historical and archaeological study, encompasses the dynamic eastward expansion of military control, commerce and governmental administration from the Russian heartland west of the Ural Mountains to the eastern shores of Siberia during the late sixteenth and early seventeenth centuries AD. The 3,000-mile advance of Russia's eastern frontier in less than eighty years was driven by a hugely profitable trade in sable, ermine and other sub-Arctic furs from the new territories. The Siberian fur rush was followed by a second pulse of Pacific maritime expansion that centred on the exploration and annexation of Alaska, Russia's first overseas colony. The Russian-American Company (RAC), founded in 1799, administered Alaska as a mercantile monopoly for the Russian Crown until the territory was purchased by the USA in 1867. Russia's Pacific domain, where sea otter, fur seal and fox furs were the most valuable commodities, included dozens of Alaskan outposts as well as stations in the Kurile Islands north of Japan (1828–67) and northern California (Fort Ross, 1812–41). There was even a brief RAC presence in Hawaii (Fort Elisabeth on Kaua'i, 1816–17).

One of the major problems of Russia's colonial enterprise was the great difficulty of supplying its far-flung periphery. The eastern Siberian climate proved too severe for agriculture, so that supplies of flour, beef and other farm produce as well as iron, textiles, glass and ceramics all had to be transported from the Lake Baikal region and the manufacturing city of Irkutsk via a tortuous riverine and overland route. Shipping to Alaska from eastern Siberian ports involved further risk, difficulty and expense. Round-the-world provisioning via Cape Horn, agricultural production in California and purchases of supplies from the Hudson Bay Company in Canada were all attempted, but imported goods were never abundant except at a few major settlements. As a result, colonial Russia depended heavily on Siberian and Alaska Native labour and technologies not only for fur production but also for food supplies, skin clothing, watercraft (kayaks and larger skin boats) and other necessities.

Fur-trade relations with indigenous peoples

Russian expansion across its vast and mostly sub-Arctic colonial territories led to engagement with dozens of different indigenous groups, from the Nenets of western Siberia to the Alutiit and Tlingit of southern Alaska and the Pomo and Coast Miwok of California. Colonial relationships generally followed an exploitative pattern of military conquest followed by forced extraction of Native labour and resources. Beads, iron, tobacco, alcohol and other trade goods were secondary to the threat and application of military force in securing a profitable flow of furs. Fishing, hunting and reindeer-herding peoples in Siberia were forced to hand over hostages and otherwise submit to government authority. They had to supply provisions and pay annual tribute (*iasak*) to the government in the form of sable pelts and other furs. Smallpox and other new diseases decimated local populations.

In southern Alaska, Unangan (Aleut) and Alutiiq hunters were required by the RAC to pursue sea otters each summer in large kayak fleets under Russian command. Women and men not engaged in hunting sea otters were ordered to gather and process food and clothing for company use and redistribution. In addition to these locally produced supplies, hunters and their families were compensated with nominal payments of trade beads, needles, cloth, tobacco and currency. Village chiefs (*toions*) were made responsible for production quotas. Many Native men lost their lives during extended sea otter hunting voyages and villages faced starvation because of the absence of hunters during crucial periods of the annual food harvest. Indigenous populations declined by as much as 75 per cent in some areas due to disease epidemics, malnutrition and social disruption.

The Russian mode of fur production was dramatically different from the system of voluntary commodity exchange that characterised Indian relations in the British and French fur trades (see **fur trade archaeology in western Canada**). Trade relationships were voluntary only in parts of Siberia and 'Russian America' where effective control of indigenous groups was never secured. For example, the Tlingit Indians of south-eastern Alaska, where the Russian colonial capital of Novo-Arkhangelsk (Sitka) was located, were never subjugated. Interior southern and western Alaska also remained beyond the effective control of scattered Russian forts such as Kolmakovskiy

Redoubt, although a low-level trade was conducted. The Chukchi of north-eastern Siberia also successfully resisted Russian control.

Russians on the eastern frontier – an immigrant population that was largely male – were far less numerous than the Native peoples whose territories they entered. These frontiersmen (*promyshlenniki*) commonly formed unions with Siberian and Alaska Native women, and their children were absorbed into a growing creole class (see **creolisation**). Throughout the new territories, the customs, language and religious beliefs of the new dominant culture were gradually accepted. Post-contact generations of creoles served as teachers, managers, explorers and Russian Orthodox clergy. Russian cultural influence, in particular the practice of Russian Orthodoxy, remains strong today throughout former colonial Alaska.

Historical archaeology

The archaeology of Russian colonialism focuses on Russian forts and towns as well as on indigenous settlements. The material evidence of colonial life, from food bone to artefacts and architecture, complements historical data from colonial records and the writings of explorers, traders and Orthodox missionaries. For example, stylistic and distributional analyses of glass beads and ceramics have been used both for dating sites and for interpreting cultural interaction. The complex effects of contact on Native populations and the gradual formation of a class-stratified, multicultural colonial society have been the focus of recent archaeological and historical studies in Russia, Alaska and California. **World systems theory** has been suggested by A.L. Crowell as a model for interpreting the larger economic and social dynamics of the Russian colonies.

In Russia, sixteenth- to nineteenth-century colonial archaeology falls under the category of 'late medieval' studies and includes excavations of towns, forts, settlements and hunting stations representing the period of the Siberian conquest and fur trade. Mangazeia, located above the Arctic Circle between the Ob and Enisei Rivers, was a centre for collecting *iasak* furs from the Ket and Nenets between the mid-1500s and 1643. Excavations by M.I. Belov and colleagues at Mangazeia

produced a wide range of Dutch- and English-made colonial goods, including trade beads from Amsterdam. Investigations of other seventeenth- and eighteenth-century frontier settlements and forts include work by A.P. Okladnikov at Zashiversk and A.P. Artemiev at Albazin and Nerchinsk. Oleg Bychkov's archival and archaeological studies have focused on the lives and material culture of seventeenth-century Russian hunters in Siberia, and documented the Tal'tsinsk glass factory near Irkutsk, founded in 1785. The factory produced beads, bottles, lamps and plate glass for the colonial trade.

Valery Shubin's extensive excavations at the RAC's Kurilorossiia outpost on Urop Island in the Kurile chain, south of the Kamchatka Peninsula (1828–67), uncovered a wooden cabin occupied by Russian *promyshlenniki* and semi-subterranean dwellings that housed Alutiiq sea otter hunters and their families. The multiethnic composition of the personnel at Kurilorosiia, which also included locally indigenous Ainu, is typical of Russian colonial outposts. **Household archaeology** at such sites is ideally suited for examining class and social variations in the colonial population as well as processes of interethnic exchange.

In Alaska, Wendell Oswalt excavated Kolmakovskiy Redoubt on the Kuskokwim River, built by the RAC in 1841 and used by US fur traders until 1917. Large inventories of tools, clothing, household goods, beads and ceramics from well-dated structures inside the fort reflect the lifestyle and commercial operations of interior fur traders during the late Russian period. In general, Russian American settlements of the 1840s and later yield abundant quantities of British ceramics and European-manufactured glass beads, a consequence of the RAC's 1839 supply agreement with the Hudson's Bay Company. Catherine Blee's excavations of mid-century deposits at the capital site of Novo-Arkhangelsk (Sitka) confirm this pattern. At earlier sites such as Three Saints Harbour on Kodiak Island (1784–*c*. 1820), excavated by A.L. Crowell, the low volume and limited variety of trade goods reflect the difficulties of supplying Alaska from Siberia.

Trade goods other than glass beads are limited at most Alaska Native sites even after 1840, a consequence of the Russian emphasis on direct appropriation of indigenous labour as opposed to the large-scale exchange of imported goods for furs. At the Nunakakhnak village site on Kodiak Island, excavated by Richard Knecht, Alutiiq residents of the 1840s were still using large numbers of traditional stone and bone tools after some sixty years of direct Russian rule. A similar pattern has been reported at the Paugvik site in Bristol Bay (AD 1800–70), excavated by Don E. Dumond and James VanStone, and at numerous other Alutiiq, Unangan, Yup'ik, Ahtna and Tlingit sites in southern and western Alaska. The historical archaeology of Russian America thus offers a useful caution against the common assumption that the quantity of trade items in post-contact Native American sites is a straightforward index of the intensity of contact.

Kent Lightfoot and students at the University of California, Berkeley, have carried out ethnohistorical archaeological studies at Fort Ross in northern California. Industries at the fort included agriculture, livestock husbandry, brickmaking and shipbuilding. The workforce included Alaska Native hunters and their families as well as Kashaya Pomo, Coast Miwok and Southern Pomo men and women who worked as agricultural labourers. At the Alaska Native Village Site, located outside the palisade walls, artefact and faunal assemblages reflect a complex blend of Alaska Native, California Native and Russian material cultures and dietary practices, a consequence of interethnic marriage and extensive cultural exchange. Linked Indian settlements in the hinterland of the fort have also been included in the research programme.

Work at Fort Ross, Three Saints Harbour, Kurilorossiia, and other Russian colonial sites illustrates what Lightfoot calls the 'archaeology of pluralism', historical archaeology's potential to illuminate the lifeways of subordinate peoples who received little direct notice in the written records of the colonial era. Class and ethnic stratification of the colonial social order are expressed at these and other Russian colonial sites by spatial segregation (for example, of Russian and Native American workers' quarters from the residences of company mangers) and distinctions in diet, housing and material culture.

See also: acculturation; beads; ceramics; class, social; contact archaeology; ethnicity; glass; Native Americans

Further reading

Crowell, A.L. (1997) *Archaeology and the Capitalist World System: A Study from Russian America*, New York: Plenum.

Gibson, J.R. (1976) *Imperial Russian in Frontier America: The Changing Geography of Supply of Russian America, 1784–1867*, New York: Oxford University Press.

Knecht, R.A. and Jordan, R.H. (1985) 'Nunakakhnak: An historic period Koniag village in Karluk, Kodiak Island, Alaska', *Arctic Anthropology* 22(2): 17–35.

Lightfoot, K.G., Schiff, AM. and Wake, T.A. (eds) (1997) *The Native Alaskan Neighborhood: A Multiethnic Community at Fort Ross*. The Archaeology and Ethnohistory of Fort Ross, California, vol. 2, Berkeley: University of California, Berkeley Archaeological Research Facility.

Oswalt, W.H. (1980) *Kolmakovskiy Redoubt: The Ethnoarchaeology of a Russian Fort in Alaska*, Los Angeles: The Institute of Archaeology, University of California, Los Angeles.

Shubin, V.O. (1990) 'Russian settlements in the Kurile Islands in the 18th and 19th centuries', in R.A. Pierce (ed.) *Russia in North America: Proceedings of the Second International Conference on Russian America, Sitka, Alaska, August 19–22, 1987*, Kingston, Ontario: Limestone Press.

Slezkine, Y. (1994) *Arctic Mirrors: Russia and the Small Peoples of the North*, Ithaca and London: Cornell University Press.

ARON L. CROWELL

S

sampling

Sampling refers to the method and plan an archaeologist will use to acquire information from an archaeological site or region. Archaeologists know that they will seldom if ever have the opportunity to survey or excavate an entire region, and perhaps even an entire individual site, so they must adopt a plan, or 'sampling design', that will provide a certain percentage, or sample, of the area of their interest. Generally, the higher the percentage of the sample, the greater the information from the site. A 50 per cent sample would tend to be more representative of an area's archaeological remains than a 5 per cent sample.

Archaeologists have generated an enormous literature about sampling because it is so central to archaeological practice and because many different, complex strategies exist. No single sampling strategy is good for all cases, and archaeologists must decide which strategy is best suited to their site or area, keeping in mind the amount of time and funds they have available. With the rise of **processual archaeology** in the last decades of the twentieth century, most archaeologists adopted 'probabilistic sampling'. Prior to this, archaeologists commonly used 'non-probabilistic sampling'.

Probabilistic sampling provides information that can be compared using statistics because the sampling units are uniform. Non-probabilistic sampling is not amenable to statistical analysis because it is usually targeted to a particular area within a site or region known to contain archaeological materials. This kind of sampling may be based on an archaeologist's intuition or prior knowledge of an area. Archaeologists involved in **rescue archaeology** often must rely on nonprobabilistic sampling because they do not have the luxury of time to devise a proper probabilistic sampling design.

Archaeologists engaged in probabilistic sampling must first decide on the parameters of their 'data universe'. This universe is the size of the area in which the archaeologist has an interest. A small site may have a data universe of less than 1 ha, whereas an entire region can have a universe than extends for many square kilometres. Archaeologists involved in **cultural-resource management** projects must often devise sampling designs that extend across large regions which are slated to be disturbed by large construction projects, such as dams, new highways and airports. In these cases, the data universe is usually prescribed by the limits of the construction's impact without the archaeologist's input. Archaeologists engaged in pure research efforts must also set the parameters of the data universe, but they will usually do so based on the location of rivers, mountain ranges, ecological zones, other natural features, or on cultural elements, such as a group's territory or range of influence.

After the archaeologist has defined the universe to be covered by the sample, he or she must then set the 'sampling units'. These units can be a series of equally sized squares within a grid (called 'quadrats'), straight lines ('transects') or individual 'spots', where grid co-ordinates meet. The archaeologist will determine the size and shape of the units based on the size of the universe, the time available and several other factors, most of which may be entirely practical. In addition, the units can be designed to correspond to ecological zones or cultural features, such as rooms in a house, or they can be completely arbitrary and cross-cut natural ecozones and cultural realms. Transects can be spaced at regular intervals or staggered in a random manner. Quadrats and spots can also be chosen in a purely random fashion or they can be regularly spaced. Regardless of the method used, the percentage of the total number of units selected for sampling is referred to as the 'sample fraction', and the number of observations is called the 'sample size'.

Sampling in historical archaeology can be somewhat different from sampling in prehistoric archaeology because of the presence of maps and other **historical documents**. These documents, if they are judged to be authentic and generally accurate, can be used to help guide the sampling strategy. Let us suppose, for example, that an archaeologist was interested in conducting a survey within an area that historically was used as a **sugar** plantation region, such as south Louisiana. Historical evidence, from the area under investigation, from the rest of Louisiana and from other sugar-growing regions, indicates that owners of sugar plantations always sited their mansions along a large river near a main road. They also tended to situate their sugar-processing buildings further away from the river. If a historical archaeologist – with limited time and funds – was interested in finding the locations of mansions inhabited by sugar-growing families, it would make little sense to spend time conducting excavations along the backswamp area located some distance from the river. Probabilistic sample units placed away from the river would almost surely yield no information about mansion location. If, however, the archaeologist was interested in locating all possible buildings and industrial works of sugar plantations in south Louisiana (and in the absence of maps), it might make more sense to conduct a probabilistic sampling project throughout the entire region.

In the end, it is the archaeologist's knowledge and experience that guides the use of sampling methods. Large samples, though perhaps the most useful for interpreting history, may be difficult to analyse and require a great deal of curation space.

On the other hand, a sample that is too small may not yield any useful results at all. Historical archaeologists must also balance their knowledge of a region or period of history with the amount of information they hope to gain during survey and excavation. The combination of the methods of scientific archaeology and the knowledge and sensitivity to history is one of the hallmarks of historical archaeology.

Further reading

Hester, T.R., Shafer, H.J. and Feder, K.L. (1997) *Field Methods in Archaeology*, seventh edn, Mountain View: Mayfield.

Mueller, J.W. (ed.) (1975) *Sampling in Archaeology*, Tucson: University of Arizona Press.

Orser, C.E., Jr and Fagan, B.M. (1995) *Historical Archaeology*, New York: HarperCollins.

Sharer, R.J. and Ashmore, W. (1993) *Archaeology: Discovering Our Past*, second edn, Mountain View: Mayfield.

CHARLES E. ORSER, JR

San Luis, Florida, USA

San Luis de Talimali was among the largest and most important **mission sites** in Spanish Florida. Located in present-day Tallahassee, its parishioners were Apalachee Indians who were descendants of the people whose village Hernando de Soto appropriated during the winter of 1539–40. Although these Apalachee remained fiercely hostile to Spaniards throughout the rest of the sixteenth century, by 1608 their attitude changed sufficiently for some principal leaders to render obedience to the Spanish governor and request friars. Unlike native converts in much of Spanish America, religious conversion among the Apalachee appears to have been voluntary.

San Luis was among the first missions to be established when formal Franciscan efforts began in Apalachee in 1633. The mission was moved to its present site in 1656 at the request of Spanish military authorities who placed a blockhouse and small garrison there. Recognised as the capital of western Florida, San Luis was home to a Spanish deputy governor and one of the Apalachee's most powerful chiefs. With the development of ranching, beginning in the 1670s, San Luis also became the site of Florida's only sizeable European community beyond **St Augustine**.

The State of Florida purchased San Luis in 1983, and since that time it has been the focus of full-time archaeological and historical research. The overarching goals have been to examine Spanish colonisation strategies on the frontier, and investigate Apalachee responses to the European intruders. Since the native population was forced to abandon the province at the end of the mission period in 1704, research is also documenting the final episode of the Apalachee in their traditional homeland.

Initial fieldwork at the site consisted of detailed topographical mapping and auger testing. Data from these two surveys were used to generate a series of testable hypotheses about the town site, including the locations of the church complex, fort, Spanish village and Apalachee council house. Since there was no native village on the site prior to the construction of the mission, San Luis provides a unique glimpse into the formation and evolution of a colonial community over nearly three generations. Its most striking feature is the high degree of accommodation of both Apalachee and European town-planning traditions. All public buildings and important residences faced onto the central town plaza. The largest and most important structures, the Apalachee council house and Franciscan church, were situated directly across the central plaza from each other.

The council house served as the centre of political, social, and ritual life for the Apalachee Indians. It was the site of their pre-game ceremonies, public hearings and social events such as dances. Archaeological investigations revealed that the council house at San Luis was a round, thatched building measuring over 120 ft in diameter, making it the largest historical-period native structure found to date in the South-east. Artefacts recovered from the building included native pottery, projectile points, debitage (flintknapping residue) and a modest assortment of European materials. The configuration, construction and materials associated with the Apalachee council

house exhibit little direct evidence of European influence.

Adjacent to the council house on the central plaza was a native leader's residence, presumably the paramount chief's. Materials found in the chief's house were predominantly native in origin, with the exception of large numbers of exotic goods, most notably quartz crystal beads and pendants. Since quartz crystal was thought to possess special powers by many south-eastern natives, the concentration of these objects at the chief's residence may reflect the dual religious and political authority of Apalachee chiefs.

These native structures and their contents reflect the continuance of Apalachee cultural systems during the historical period. Although Spanish military and civil authorities were in residence at San Luis, there is strong documentary and archaeological evidence to suggest that the Apalachee maintained parallel social and political institutions throughout the mission period.

Spaniards living at San Luis were equally conservative and resistant to change. Domestic structures, the church, friary and the fort complex are thoroughly European in design and construction. Spanish dwellings at San Luis were identical to 'common plan' houses in St Augustine, and all structures were built using Spanish measurements and proportional systems. The lucrative export economy and access to exotic goods is evidenced by a relative abundance of imported pottery, foods, jewellery, weaponry and tools. These materials likely served to reinforce the economic and social standing of Spaniards within the community, most of whom were related by blood or marriage to the most prominent Spanish families in St Augustine. Since many introduced domesticates (cattle, hogs, chickens, wheat and fruit trees) were well-suited to the fertile soils of Apalachee, ethnobiologists have suggested that Spaniards living at San Luis enjoyed a more traditional diet than those living in other areas of Spanish Florida.

The most profound cultural changes that can be documented archaeologically at San Luis are the influence of Apalachee women on Hispanic life and native religious conversion. Indian pottery and foodstuffs (particularly maize) have been recovered in large quantities at all Hispanic areas, reflecting the integration of Apalachee women into Spanish lifeways as servants, wives and concubines.

The religious conversion of the native population is evident in the mission cemetery at San Luis, where it is estimated that 900 natives may be buried. All of the Apalachee are interred in a Christian manner in the consecrated floor of the church. Descendants of the Apalachee population from San Luis, currently residing in Louisiana, are the only known survivors of Florida's once numerous aboriginal peoples and have applied for federal recognition based on parish records.

See also: mission sites; Spanish colonialism; St Augustine

Further reading

Hann, J.H. and McEwan, B.G. (1998) *The Apalachee Indians and Mission San Luis*, Gainesville: University Press of Florida.

McEwan, B.G. (ed.) (1993) *The Spanish Missions of La Florida*, Gainesville: University Press of Florida.

Shapiro, G. (1987) 'Archaeology at San Luis: Broad-scale testing, 1984–1985', *Florida Archaeology* 3, Tallahassee: Florida Bureau of Archaeological Research.

BONNIE G. McEWAN

San Vincenzo, Italy

In the Early Middle Ages, monasteries became powerful landholders and agents of innovation and renewal. While monasticism had gained prominence in the later Roman period, a new order was moulded in the earlier sixth century through the figure of Saint Benedict who founded Montecassino in central Italy, and in the late sixth century through Pope Gregory the Great who advertised more widely the Life of Benedict. Under Charlemagne, the Benedictine order became dominant and state support in the form of immunities and land grants made many monasteries rich and the focus of patronage. Montecassino is one of the best known and documented abbeys, although its present form relates to wholesale rebuilding following destruction in the Second World War. Other key central Italian monasteries include

Subiaco (Benedict's first retreat) and Farfa, both of which have seen archaeological investigation.

Best studied, however, is San Vincenzo al Volturno in the Molise province. Unlike Farfa, Subiaco and Montecassino, the early medieval monastic site is no longer active – its abandonment in favour of a smaller complex across the river in the twelfth century has meant that its buried remains (covering about 5 ha) have been accessible for extensive excavations, directed chiefly by Richard Hodges since 1980. The excavations have been informed by texts – notably the twelfth-century *Chronicon*, but including painted and inscribed text found on floor tiles and on the splendid wall paintings that are such a powerful feature of the ninth-century phases at San Vincenzo. Contemporary images such as that of abbot Epiphanius (824–42) in the crypt chapel provide invaluable guides for art historians on early medieval forms, styles and influences. From these we gain a fuller picture of the input of Lombard and Frankish patrons and monks.

The excavations have done far more than identify the Carolingian-period complex. As in other cases, this monastery overlies the remains of a villa that (potentially) held a monastic community in the fifth–sixth centuries, before – as elsewhere in Italy – insecurity caused abandonment (even if burials hint at some level of continuity). The texts record a foundation by three Lombard brothers at the start of the eighth century – an event as yet unproven by archaeology. Fully visible, however, is the massive reworking of the site from the late eighth and early ninth centuries, with a complex plan of crypt church, claustral zone plus the vast church 100 m long – all ornately painted, with images of saints and prophets, and decoration imitating cloths and marbles. The abbey was a rich manuscript production centre, but it also manufactured other commodities such as metalwork, ivories, glass and ceramics, with a series of partially excavated workshops demonstrating the busy industrial lives of the brothers (estimated at about 100 in the later eighth century, rising to perhaps 350 in the ninth). Arrowheads embedded in a workshop door graphically attest the Arab attack of AD 881.

Detailed scrutiny of the monastic charters has reconstructed the evolving landed possessions of the abbey, including (from the tenth century) castles as well as dependent villages and chapels. Field survey has been employed to identify some of these sites that will have provided food and raw materials to the abbey.

Further reading

Balzaretti, R. (1999) 'Review article: San Vincenzo al Volturno. History rewritten?', *Early Medieval Europe* 8: 387–99.

Hodges, R. (1997) *Light in the Dark Ages: The Rise and Fall of San Vincenzo al Volturno*, London: Duckworth.

—— (ed.) (1995) *San Vincenzo al Volturno 2: The 1980–1986 Excavations, Part 2*, Archaeological Monographs 9, London: British School at Rome.

—— (ed.) (1993) *San Vincenzo al Volturno 1: The 1980–1986 Excavations, Part 1*, Archaeological Monographs 7, London: British School at Rome.

NEIL J. CHRISTIE

Santa Catalina de Guale, Georgia, USA

Santa Catalina was a Spanish mission located on St Catherines Island, Georgia, on the east coast of North America. This mission site marked the northernmost extent of Spain's long-term settlements along the Atlantic Ocean. Franciscan missionaries established the mission on St Catherines Island in 1595 near a village of the Guale Indians. The mission was destroyed two years later when the Guale rebelled, but the Spanish re-established it in 1605. The inhabitants of the mission finally abandoned it after a British attack in 1680, and within a few decades the mission was considered 'lost'. Archaeologists from the American Museum of Natural History found the site and have had a sustained archaeological project there since 1977.

The exact location of the Santa Catalina mission was sought by scholars for many years with little success. When the American Museum of Natural History became involved, they used a combination of random **sampling** (in the form of linear transects); randomly placed, hand-excavated test pits; power auger testing; and **remote sensing** (with a proton magnetometer). Historical records were of little help in pinpointing the mission's location.

The Museum began excavation in 1981, and since then they have made several noteworthy findings. For example, they have provided significant detail about the **architecture** of the mission and its related structures through their excavation of two churches (one built before the British attack and one after), a square, shell-covered plaza that probably served as a formal entrance to the church, the cemetery under the church, the friar's complex (composed of two building phases dating before and after the Guale uprising) and two wells belonging to the mission.

The research at Santa Catalina de Guale provides many profound insights into the nature of Spanish colonialism in the south-east USA as well as cultural information about the interaction of **Native Americans** and Spanish missionaries. Some of the most significant information has come from over 400 burials excavated from the floor of the church. These interments were accompanied by a huge array of gravegoods, an assemblage that includes almost thirty-six metal crosses (with various inscriptions and symbols), medallions containing images of important religious figures, smaller medals with similar images, several finger rings with religious inscriptions, a rosary, thousands of **glass beads** (many of which had undoubtedly come from rosaries) and four complete majolica (**earthenware**) vessels. The archaeologists also found several Native American items inside the graves. These objects included projectile points, a rattlesnake shell gorget and numerous shell and stone beads.

In addition to investigating the colonial-period Native American and Spanish settlements, the archaeologists are also examining several pre-contact remains on St Catherines Island. This approach will afford them a rare opportunity to provide a thorough interpretation of the nature of Guale life both before and during their contact with the Spanish missionaries. At the same time, of course, the research also provides unique details about the nature of missionary life in the New World during the sixteenth and seventeenth centuries.

See also: mission sites; Spanish colonialism

Further reading

Larsen, C.S. (1993) 'On the frontier of contact: Mission bioarchaeology in La Florida', in B.G. McEwan (ed.) *The Spanish Missions of La Florida*, Gainesville: University Press of Florida, pp. 322–56.

Thomas, D.H. (1993) 'The archaeology of mission Santa Catalina de Guale: Our first 15 years', in B.G. McEwan (ed.) *The Spanish Missions of La Florida*, Gainesville: University Press of Florida, pp. 1–34.

Thomas, D.H. (1988) 'Saints and soldiers at Santa Catalina: Hispanic designs for colonial America', in M.P. Leone and P.B. Potter, Jr (eds) *The Recovery of Meaning: Historical Archaeology in the Eastern United States*, Washington, DC: Smithsonian Institution Press, pp. 73–140.

CHARLES E. ORSER, JR

Santa Elena, South Carolina, USA

The Spanish built Santa Elena in 1566 as a northern outpost against encroachment by their colonial rivals, the French and the English, and the town served as the capital of Spanish *La Florida* for two decades. Sir Francis Drake's attack on Spanish St Augustine in 1586, in addition to conflicts with local **Native Americans**, caused the Spanish to abandon the town in 1587. The site of Santa Elena was effectively lost until late 1979, when Stanley South determined its exact location. The site is located on Parris Island, South Carolina, just north of Hilton Head Island, in Port Royal Sound.

The Spanish situated Santa Elena just south of an area that had been briefly settled in 1562–3 by a small French force, who had constructed a fort named 'Charlesfort'. In the 1920s, a major stationed at the Marine Corps facility on Parris Island conducted excavations in search of the French fort. When he discovered artefacts and the indications of a moat, he identified them as French and concluded that he had found Charlesfort. Excavating in the same area over sixty years later,

South concluded that the major had actually found Fort San Marcos (1577–87), a Spanish fortification (see **fortifications**) at Santa Elena. South excavated this site for the next several years, and later found the remains of the earlier Fort San Felipe (1572–6), in addition to several elements of the town itself, including five houses (one of which was made in the Native American fashion). The excavation of Fort San Felipe revealed that the Spanish had built it as an earthen fortification with vertical posts set in the ground. They had also used baskets of woven sticks filled with earth and bundles of sticks for the walls. Inside the fort, South and his team discovered the remains of a fortified house, called a *casa fuerte.*

The archaeologists also excavated three wells inside Fort San Felipe, and found inside them numerous botanical remains, including watermelon, squash and persimmon seeds. They also discovered that the Spaniards had used wooden barrels to line the well. Perhaps the most notable artefact they found in the well was the spout of a Chinese export **porcelain** wine ewer dating to the Ming dynasty (1368–1644).

The site of Santa Elena has yielded numerous artefacts. Within the collection are lead musket balls (some with teeth marks on them), a mould for shaping bullets, gun parts, iron points from crossbow arrows and numerous artefacts associated with clothing (**buttons** in the shape of balls, some of which were gold plated; iron buckles; and part of a glass earring). Domestic artefacts include pieces of majolica, glass, copper and silver coins, part of a Maltese cross, gaming disks carved from an **olive jar** and a bone die.

Archaeological research continued at the site throughout the 1990s, and in 1993 South and Chester DePratter discovered a Spanish colonial ceramic kiln that had collapsed with four dozen **redware** vessels inside. This kiln, which they dated to the 1577–87 period, provides a rare glimpse of the manufacture of European-type ceramics in the New World. Significantly, some of the vessels in the kiln resemble Islamic-tradition vessels from North Africa rather than the wares commonly made in the Iberian Peninsula.

See also: fortifications; Spanish colonialism

Further reading

South, S. (1991) *Archaeology at Santa Elena: Doorway to the Past*, Columbia: South Carolina Institute of Archaeology and Anthropology.

—— (1988) 'Santa Elena: Threshold of conquest', in M.P. Leone and P.B. Potter, Jr (eds) *The Recovery of Meaning: Historical Archaeology in the Eastern United States*, Washington, DC: Smithsonian Institution Press, pp. 27–71.

—— (1980) *The Discovery of Santa Elena*, Research Manuscript 165, Columbia: South Carolina Institute of Archaeology and Anthropology.

CHARLES E. ORSER, JR

settlement analysis

The analysis of where people lived – settlement analysis – became a major part of archaeological research during the last half of the twentieth century. Archaeologists realised that understanding the locations of campsites, villages, towns, roads, canals and other elements of human settlement was as important as understanding the artefacts people used within those settlements. Historical archaeologists have been as interested in settlement analysis as prehistorians and many significant studies have been completed.

Scales of analysis

One of the important aspects of settlement analysis is that it can be conducted on several different levels, or scales. An infinite number of ways to define the levels exist, and no one way is inherently more correct than any other. In the mid-1970s, archaeologist David Clarke devised a three-part system of classification that is useful for purposes of illustration. Clarke's 'micro level' existed within structures, so that one level of analysis could be within a house. A historical archaeologist interested in micro-level analysis and examining a seventeenth-century residence might study the arrangement of rooms, the possible placement of furniture within rooms and the location of the building's doors and windows. The focus is within sites at Clarke's 'semi-micro-level'. At this scale, the archaeologists might be interested in the distance between houses, the

arrangement of houses within a village and the placement of pathways and roads within a town. The 'macro-level' is the largest scale Clarke identified. The archaeologist interested in macro-level analysis might investigate the regional pattern of settlement, with focus being on the placement of settlements across an ecological zone or landscape and the distances between the settlements. Clarke, as a prehistorian, did not anticipate that historical archaeologists could be interested in an even larger, 'super macro-level', the global scale. Post-Columbian history is replete with examples of large-scale, long-distance movements of people and commodities, and so some historical archaeologists investigating the past 500 years must often consider extremely large-scale interactions across entire continents.

Analytical methods

The analysis of settlements is made complex because of the many variables that archaeologists can identify within and between settlements. For example, archaeologists must decide what constitutes a 'place' (generally defined as where something is situated), a 'space' (usually conceptualised as the distance *between* places) and a 'boundary' (something that poses limits on a place or space). It is often possible in historical archaeology, because of the existence of **maps** and other **historical documents**, to determine how the people who lived at the site conceptualised space, place and boundaries. Taking the interior of an eighteenth-century fortification (see **fortifications**) as an example, we may well suppose that the buildings inside the fort constituted 'places' and that the distance between them were 'spaces'. The empty parade ground between barracks would qualify as a 'space' under this definition. However, the archaeologist could also go inside the individual buildings and examine the placement of rooms within the officers' quarters, the soldiers' barracks and various special-use buildings. At the same time, the entire fort could also be construed as a 'place' within the landscape (situated in space), and the archaeologist could investigate the placement of forts throughout a region, and examine the distance between them, the distance between forts and indigenous villages, and the placement of forts in relation to woods, rivers, mountains and other environmental features.

Given the theoretical complexity of settlement elements, it is perhaps not surprising that archaeologists have derived complicated methods of analysis and have borrowed concepts and methods from geographers. Many of these methods involve sophisticated statistical measures and considerable computational skills. Scholars have created several complex methods that use various theories, such as network theory and central-place theory, to help them understand the spatial arrangement of human-built features on the earth's surface. Archaeologists intent on settlement analysis must understand the concepts and the methods thoroughly enough to apply them, and, once applied, to understand how to interpret the findings. For instance, because many historical archaeologists study hierarchically arranged societies, they may have reason to use 'central-place theory' in their research. Central-place theory is a model created by German geographer Walter Christaller that assumes hierarchical levels of settlement. It has justifiably generated a complex body of literature. Others engaged in analysing the arrangement of a settlement may use other methods of analysis. An analytical method created by Bill Hillier and Julienne Hanson is based on 'syntax', or the system of spatial relations. In their model, space is merely a physical representation of social relations, and so the spatial and social networks cannot be neatly separated.

Other settlement models used by archaeologists include the 'core–periphery' (or 'centre–periphery') model and the diffusion model. In the core–periphery model, the 'core' is assumed to have certain advantages that help it to grow and stabilise economically and culturally, often at the expense of the periphery. The 'peripheries' lie at various distances away from the cores and typically funnel raw materials and even people (as labourers and consumers) to the cores. The influx of people and goods effectively sustains and builds the core. Scholars from many disciplines including historical archaeology have employed the core–periphery model to describe the geographical distribution and growth of mercantile capitalist organisations across the globe. Diffusion models involve the spread of settlements through space and time, and

it may be said that the core–periphery model is merely a special kind of diffusion model. In the diffusion model, however, no need exists to incorporate social (and spatial) inequality as there is for the core–periphery model. In the diffusionist framework, a culture may spread its settlements across an unoccupied region without opposition or, acting as a core, it may spread its settlements through a periphery's region amid great **resistance**. In either case, time is an important factor because the spread of settlements does not happen without considerable historical elements.

Some insights of settlement analysis

Archaeologists for many years followed the lead of other scholars interested in the spatial arrangement of **material culture** and envisioned settlement as merely functional in its intent and design. In other words, scholars widely believed that people tended to establish their settlements in places that would ensure their survival: near sources of potable water, on high elevations where they would be safe from floods and in environments where they could be assured of a constant supply of food. This understanding is inherently logical because we can well understand that horticulturalist peoples would not choose to live in mountainous zones; they would seek to live where their crops would have the greatest opportunity to grow and mature. Beginning in the late twentieth century, however, many scholars began to question the functionalist interpretation, and started to propose that settlement also had symbolic and ideological elements that were not explicitly related to survival. In such cases, social variables could play a large role in structuring settlements in every scale of analysis. Some have argued, for instance, that social relations of **power** may play a major role in organising a society's settlements, particularly those usually studied by historical archaeologists: large-scale societies with complex social hierarchies.

In an intriguing examination of the naming of streets in late nineteenth-century Stockholm, Sweden, geographer Allen Pred illustrated how the elite elements of Swedish society attempted to create an **ideology** of space in their city. Harried by increasing labour unrest and demands for more widespread franchise, the city's council decided to rename the streets in the city centre. In the mid-1880s, they selected the names from only five, carefully chosen categories: patriotic and historical names, Nordic mythology, famous places near the city, the southern provinces and the northern provinces. They later expanded their list to include famous Swedish authors and those prominent in technology and engineering. Based on their decision and on their ability to make the changes in street names, it may appear that the city council had unlimited power to impose their ideology on the citizens of Stockholm. They symbolised their control through their use of names they thought important. They were undoubtedly surprised to learn, however, that their domination was not complete, because the city's residents responded by referring to the streets with lewd, irreverent and comical names, often intended to embarrass the elites themselves.

A growing number of historical archaeologists, beginning with Mark Leone's analysis of William Paca's garden in **Annapolis**, Maryland, have begun to examine the symbolic nature of past settlement arrangements. These studies have extended settlement analysis in archaeology into new areas of inquiry and have provided significant new insights into past human behaviour.

In the 1990s, historical archaeologist Warren Perry completed an important archaeological study of settlement that stands as an excellent example of the contributions historical archaeologists can make to understanding past human settlements. Perry's research focused on the formation of the Zulu state in south-eastern Africa during the early nineteenth century. He used settlement analysis as a major investigative tool and specifically evaluated the utility of the 'Settler Model', a widely held view that the creation of the Zulu state was based on terrorising and plundering their neighbours, followed by expansion into their territories. Key elements of the model are Mfecane ('the crushing') and Difaqane ('the scattering). In the course of his field and library research, Perry identified fourteen different kinds of sites in his study area: royal residences, food-producing villages, iron-producing sites, African military encampments, extractive and industrial sites, royal grave sites, non-elite burial sites, battlefields, ritual sites, rock shelters, refuge sites, shell middens, pit fall traps and European sites. Perry's careful analysis – rooted in the combination of archaeological data and historical and anthropological information – illustrated that the Settler Model is too simplistic. Instead, the creation of the Zulu state occurred because of a profoundly complex series of events and processes. Perry learned that to understand fully the precise nature of the state's creation required the analysis of settlement along at least three scales: local, regional and global.

The archaeological analysis of settlement will continue to constitute an important focus of research in historical archaeology. As archaeologists develop new tools for analysing spatial arrangement in addition to new ways to interpret their findings, a greater understanding of the relationship between spatial arrangement and social relations will emerge.

See also: garden archaeology; landscape studies; spatial analysis

Further reading

Clarke, D.L. (ed.) (1977) *Spatial Archaeology*, London: Academic Press.

Hillier, B. and Hanson, J. (1984) *The Social Logic of Space*, Cambridge: Cambridge University Press.

Hodder, I. and Orton, C. (1976) *Spatial Analysis in Archaeology*, Cambridge: Cambridge University Press.

Linebaugh, D.W. and Robinson, G.G. (eds) (1994) *Spatial Patternings in Historical Archaeology: Selected Studies of Settlement*, Williamsburg: King and Queen Press, the College of William and Mary.

Orser, C.E., Jr (1996) *A Historical Archaeology of the Modern World*, New York: Plenum.

Perry, W.R. (1999) *Landscape Transformations and the Archaeology of Impact: Social Disruption and State Formation in Southern Africa*, New York: Kluwer Academic/Plenum Press.

Pred, A. (1990) *Making Histories and Constructing Human Geographies: The Local Transformation of Practice, Power Relations, and Consciousness*, Boulder: Westview Press.

CHARLES E. ORSER, JR

Seville Plantation, Jamaica

Located in St Ann's Bay on Jamaica's north coast, Seville Plantation is one of the most thoroughly excavated **sugar** plantation sites in the Caribbean. Now a heritage park administered by the Jamaica National Historical Trust, Seville was the location of Seville Nuevo, the first Spanish settlement on Jamaica's north coast and quite possibly the first location to produce sugar in Jamaica. Following the expulsion of the Spanish from Jamaica by the British in the mid-seventeenth century, a British sugar plantation was established at Seville. The estate operated as an agricultural enterprise for over 200 years; following the abolition of slavery in 1838, the plantation managers augmented their labour force by introducing indentured contract labourers from the Indian sub-continent to work alongside wage labourers emancipated from slavery. In the late nineteenth century, production shifted from sugar to other plantation crops, including pimento, bananas and, eventually, copra.

Upon completion of excavations at nearby Drax Hall Plantation in the late 1980s, Douglas Armstrong initiated a multi-year project at Seville. During the course of his investigations, Armstrong identified two separate villages dating to the era of slavery, the first abandoned *c.* 1760, the second probably occupied at least until emancipation. In examining the artefact collections as well as cartographic data from estate plans, Armstrong determined that the abandonment of the earlier village and the establishment of the second village nearly coincided with a major renovation of the planter's great house. He concluded that both the great house and the first village were likely damaged or destroyed by a tropical storm or hurricane; while the white estate staff were busy supervising the reconstruction of the great house, the enslaved Africans were rebuilding their own community. Armstrong has argued that, under these temporary conditions, the African community may have been more free to design a village plan more suitable to their own needs than the original linear organisation that had been imposed by the whites when the plantation was first established. Further, Armstrong concluded that the original great house was rebuilt from a two-storey to a one-storey house; the later house featured a veranda and an open-floor plan more suitable to the Jamaican climate than the original two-storey house. Armstrong has argued that over the course of several generations, the cultures of both the planters and the enslaved experienced a process of cultural transformation, or ethnogenesis. Armstrong supported his thesis with architectural evidence from the great house, comparative evidence from the differential layouts of the two villages, mortuary evidence recovered from the villages and artefacts recovered from a half-decade of excavations at Seville.

Further reading

Armstrong, D.V. (1999) 'Archaeology and ethno-history of the Caribbean plantation', in T. Singleton (ed.) *'I, too, am America': Archaeological Studies of African-American Life*, Charlottesville: University Press of Virginia, pp. 173–92.
—— (1998) 'Cultural transformation within enslaved laborer communities in the Caribbean', in J.G. Cusick (ed.) *Studies in Culture Contact: Interaction, Change, and Archaeology*, Carbondale: Center for Archaeological Investigations, Southern Illinois University, pp. 378–401.

JAMES A. DELLE

ships' graveyards

Ships' graveyards generally refer to specific geographical areas that have large concentrations of shipwrecks or hulks due to either armed conflict, navigation hazards or abandonment. As a result of changing economic patterns, political and military events or evolving technologies, abandonment of vessels rather than shipwrecks is perhaps the leading cause for the concentration of watercraft in a specific area, with abandonment resulting in prominent collections of hulks that appear as visual ships' graveyards.

With one of the last surviving wooden-ship graveyards, the Port of New York contains within its waters and along its shorelines possibly one of the largest and most diverse collections of abandoned wooden watercraft in existence. Represented by clusters of beached and half-submerged hulks, the vessels represent not only the final century of wooden-ship construction within the USA, but also the emerging technologies such as steam propulsion, all of which were eclipsed by the employment of iron hulls and the diesel engine.

Abandoned, often in groups of similar types of vessels and often in one-time events, hulks often served secondary purposes such as breakwaters or landings, were abandoned after anticipated reuse or were collected for scrapping. The Ferris Ocean Freighter offers a classic example of a vessel type eclipsed by political and economic factors, resulting in its abandonment in large numbers. Ordered to be built in mass quantities by the Emergency Fleet Corporation as a result of the USA entering the First World War, the majority of these wooden freighters were not completely finished at the cessation of the war. Obsolete at the time of construction, most of the vessels were sold as barges or for scrapping. The majority of the fleet ended up in Mallows Bay, Maryland, to be salvaged, while many ended up in large clusters around Staten Island, New York. Others were abandoned along the Texas Coast.

Concentrations of abandoned vessels can also result from humanity's futile efforts to conquer the oceans as in the case of the Falkland Islands. Numerous vessels, including the iron steamship *Great Britain* and the wooden clipper *Snow Squall*, were abandoned in and around Port Stanley after being irreparably damaged, or their crews mentally and physically broken in storms during attempts to round Cape Horn.

The ships' graveyard caused by navigation hazards is exemplified by Diamond Shoals off North Carolina's coast. Known to mariners as the 'Graveyard of the Atlantic', this seaward jutting area of sandbars, where the warm north-bound Gulf Stream and the cold waters of the south-bound Labrador Current meet in a ceaseless turbulence, has claimed countless vessels.

Armed conflict also resulted in several concentrations that are considered ships' graveyards. Perhaps one of the best known is the Japanese Second World War fleet that was sunk in Truk Lagoon, Micronesia. Now a popular site for divers from around the world, it is still visited by relatives who think of it as a memorial to those slain.

See also: maritime archaeology; shipwrecks

STEPHEN R. JAMES, JR

shipwrecks

For thousands of years, ships were some of the most complex artefacts produced by cultures around the globe. Prior to the construction of widespread road and rail networks, ships were a primary means of transport for people joined by oceans, lakes and rivers. While we tend to see bodies of water as separating different groups, in the past the marine environment was a unifying medium that facilitated interaction between settlements and people. Shipwrecks – as the material remains of ships – are therefore important archaeological resources and help illustrate both the technical achievements and interactions of people in the past. Shipwrecks have been studied as archaeological sites for more than a hundred years, and a maturing body of scholarship, techniques and technology has laid the groundwork for emerging contributions of shipwreck archaeology to the larger field of historical archaeology as a whole.

Shipwrecks are but one category of maritime causality site, which spans a continuum from temporary grounding or stranding to catastrophic loss of vessel and crew. Archaeologically, a grounding may be represented by piles of offloaded ballast or jettisoned cargo on the sea floor, while a catastrophic loss may result in the almost complete destruction of a ship with very few material remains – in either case, however, experience has shown that carefully planned and executed archaeological investigation can produce insights into human behaviour and experience in the past.

Contrary to popular notions about shipwrecks, many wrecking events occur over a period of days, or even weeks, with both crew and materials removed from the ship following initial indications of difficulty. After sinking, a ship may deteriorate from a well-integrated machine to its constituent material components through natural forces such as corrosion and cultural forces such as salvage. Typically, as a wreck lies underwater, the rate at which it deteriorates diminishes over time; even in high-energy environments such as surf zones, most wrecks eventually reach an approximate equilibrium with their natural surroundings. When the environment of a wreck is disturbed, either through human actions such as treasure hunting, or natural actions such as a shift in a tidal delta, the wreck may experience additional deterioration until it reaches another approximate equilibrium with the new environmental conditions.

Ethnographic and historical research indicates that seafarers are keenly aware of the changing conditions of risk for different voyages and different weather. In response to this perceived risk, sailors may alter or delay their voyages, change their crews or cargoes and modify their ship or its components – behaviour that will influence the archaeology of a shipwreck. Because many sailors embark on voyages with at least some understanding of the possibility of shipwreck, archaeological distinctions between contexts of intentional and unintentional deposition may be difficult to apply to shipwrecks in many cases. Areas such as the Dry Tortugas in Florida and Yassi Ada in Turkey, for example, are notorious **ships' graveyards** – points of maritime peril – and the extensive assemblage of shipwrecks in these locales needs to be understood not via the concepts of intentional and unintentional deposition, but within a larger regional approach that encompasses both the natural hazards of the area as well as broader social and historical forces that influence voyaging through the area in the first place. Beyond the hazards of a ships' graveyard, it is also the case that extremely low-energy environments such as anchorages often have an extensive collection of shipwrecks caused by the intentional abandonment of ships that have outlived their usefulness. In this case, the concept of intentional deposition may apply, and analytical concepts developed within the larger field of archaeology to explain discard, reuse and recycling of materials can produce worthwhile archaeological interpretations.

Conceptually, it is often useful for archaeologists to distinguish between the remains of a ship and the remains of its cargo. While it is often said that shipwrecks are 'time capsules' where all archaeological materials are approximately contemporaneous, properly speaking this label usually best applies to a ship's cargo. Because many ships are extremely complex and expensive artefacts, they typically have a use-life that stretches into decades. Over the years that a ship is used, it, like other artefacts, will experience wear, modifications and repairs. These alterations of the initial ship's design have material and archaeological correlates that may contribute important insights into larger historical processes at work during the decades of a ship's use. On the other hand, the generally contemporaneous nature of a ship's cargo may be the basis for linking and synchronising the developmental sequences of different artefact classes found in other archaeological contexts such as land excavations.

One conceptual hazard of the time capsule metaphor for shipwrecks is that the wrecking process and subsequent post-depositional forces may scatter the remains of a wreck for hundreds of metres or even kilometres, and thus archaeological materials relevant to an understanding of the wreck may not be close to the largest body of remaining materials. Shipwrecks, therefore, produce the best information about the past when evaluated in the broadest possible historical and archaeological context.

As the archaeological investigation of shipwrecks becomes more sophisticated, data recovered hold increasing promise for land archaeology. At Red Bay, Labrador, underwater archaeologists from Parks Canada worked in concert with land archaeologists to produce fascinating insights into the early Basque whaling industry, which would have been impossible from an examination of the shipwrecks alone. Ships are only part of larger processes that may be represented at other archaeological sites on land and underwater, and it is in concert with historical archaeology, anthropology and history in general that this specialised discipline stands to make its most significant contributions.

See also: conservation, underwater; excavation methods, underwater; maritime archaeology; VOC shipwrecks

Further reading

Delgado, J. (ed.) (1997) *Encyclopedia of Underwater and Maritime Archaeology*, New Haven: Yale University Press.

Gould, R. (2000) *Archaeology and the Social History of Ships*, Cambridge: Cambridge University Press.

—— (ed.) (1983) *Shipwreck Anthropology*, Santa Fe: School of American Research.

Muckelroy, K. (1978) *Maritime Archaeology*, Cambridge: Cambridge University Press.

Redknap, M. (ed.) (1997) *Artefacts from Wrecks: Dated Assemblages from the Late Middle Ages to the Industrial Revolution*, Oxford: Oxbow.

DAVID L. CONLIN AND LARRY E. MURPHY

Siena, Italy

The frantic horse-riding contests of the *palio* in Siena's famed Piazza del Campo mark the long-established ritualised competition between the various *contrade* or districts of the city, represented through Renaissance-style dress, banners and mascots. Supporters and tourists, like the weaving medieval streets of the sprawling city, naturally converge and flow down into the unique scallop-shaped arena framed by high, modernised house frontages and focused on the late thirteenth-century Palazzo Comunale. Ten out of the existing seventeen *contrade* participate in each *palio*, but this is a much reduced figure compared with the fifty-nine medieval districts, each with their own distinct zone and church. Beyond the *palio*, the medieval heritage of the Tuscan city of Siena is extensive and renowned. Most prominent is the cathedral (*duomo*), begun in 1196 and dedicated in 1215, but replanned as an immense structure nearly 100 m in length in which the old *duomo* would have served merely as the transept. The **Black Death** and the loss of perhaps 50 per cent of the urban population curtailed the undertaking, but the skeleton and face survive. The *duomo* interior features floor panels designed by some of the most prominent artists of Siena's medieval floruit. One of the best-known artists is Lorenzetti, whose extended scroll-like images of Good and Bad Government adorn the council room of the Palazzo Comunale. These include stunning detail of house fronts, towers, churches, shops, streets and dress, providing snap-shots against which to compare the archaeology and architecture. Other artists of the Sienese School such as Martini provide images of the evolving cityscape, wherein civic and private towers jostle with bell towers to reflect the upwardly mobile elite. The medieval centuries are likewise marked by more mundane material expression, with Siena the production point for highly successful majolica pottery (primarily four-teenth to fifteenth centuries).

Siena is thus in line with so many Tuscan centres, such as Florence and Pisa, where the twelfth and fourteenth centuries marked an astonishing growth of architectural and artistic expression, responding to expansive Italian participation in trade markets – all brought to life in the later fourteenth-century correspondence and accounts of Francesco di Marco Datini of Prato. The earlier phase relates to the emergence of communes or 'city-republics' in northern and central Italy, essentially self-governing city-states with their own citizen armies (drawn from the territory and also from their *contrade*, then, as now, fiercely loyal to their own banners). Despite the bouts of warfare between centres like Siena, Arezzo, Pisa and Cremona, all saw substantial building programmes – cathedrals, towers, churches, palazzi, piazze – reflecting 'popular' and local elite patronage, investment, display and rivalry.

It is easy therefore to ignore the much older heritage of Siena and other Tuscan cities. Little of Siena's Etruscan township (seventh to third centuries BC) is known, although third- to first-century BC **cemeteries** attest fair prosperity before the creation of the Augustan colony of *Saena Iulia*, itself only patchily understood. *Saena* played no substantial Roman role, but was strong enough to survive the sixth-century warfare in Italy to re-emerge as a bishopric and seat of a Lombard gastald and later Frankish count. As with the majority of Italian towns, the early medieval centuries (sixth to tenth centuries) leave little material trace, although their structural imprint may still be perceived in the configuration of ecclesiastical and market spaces. We await detailed archaeological scrutiny to identify how deep the roots of Siena's churches lie.

Further reading

Francovich, R. (1982) *La ceramica medievale a Siena e nella Toscana meridionale*, Florence: All'Insegna del Giglio.

Origo, I. (1963) *The Merchant of Prato. Daily Life in a Medieval Italian City*, Harmondsworth: Peregrine.

Pietramellara, C. (1980) *Il Duomo di Siena: evoluzioni della forma dalle origini alla fine del Trecento*, Florence: Edam.

Waley, D. (1988) *The Italian City-Republics*, third edn, London: Longman.

NEIL J. CHRISTIE

Signal Hill, Newfoundland, Canada

Signal Hill is an imposing hill situated just northeast of St John's, Newfoundland, on the northern side of the entrance to St John's Harbour. Because of its strategic location, many people, beginning in the early eighteenth century, have used the hill as a signalling station to warn the residents of St John's of approaching ships. French and British forces fought for control of the important hill in 1762, but **fortifications** were not built on the hill until 1795, when a blockhouse was constructed. The British also built three batteries on the hill and used them until the 1860s. In 1870, after the military had withdrawn, the government of Newfoundland converted the empty barracks into hospitals. It was from one of these buildings that Guglielmo Marconi received the first transatlantic wireless signal in 1901. The Canadian government named the area the Signal Hill National Historic Park in 1958. Most of the activity at Signal Hill occurred from 1795 to the mid-nineteenth century, and it is on this period that the archaeology has concentrated.

Edward Jelks, the second president of the **Society for Historical Archaeology**, conducted excavations at Signal Hill in 1965-6. Part of the rationale for his excavations was to find a spot where the government could construct a new visitors' centre that would not disturb or destroy any of the area's historical sites. Jelks and his team conducted excavations at the location of the centre, in the Lower Queen's Battery, the Upper Queen's Battery and Lady's Lookout, an area that contained the hill's highest point. They excavated one structure at the location of the interpretive centre, four in the Lower Queen's Battery, two in the

Upper Queen's Battery and nine at Lady's Lookout. These structures included the 1795 blockhouse, an early nineteenth-century barracks, an 1840s canteen, an 1840s latrine and three possible working floors. The team also mapped and investigated several other structures on the hill.

As may be expected at an important locale, Signal Hill was the scene of abundant activity, and the archaeologists discovered a large collection of artefacts during their excavations. The sample includes English-made fine **earthenware**, **porcelain**, **stoneware**, eleven different styles of white-clay smoking pipes (including specimens impressed with Masonic emblems, nautical designs and Irish-related slogans) (see **pipes, smoking**), pipe stems embossed with the maker's name and city, many types of **buttons** (made of brass, bone, shell and **glass**), iron gun parts and keys, gunflints, slate pencils, coins (ranging in date from a 1799 farthing to a 1943 Canadian penny), jewellery, glass **bottles**, bone dominoes, combs and iron tools.

The archaeology at Signal Hill is important for at least two reasons. First, it helped to document an important period of Newfoundland's history, and, second, it helped to demonstrate the power of historical archaeology to provide unique information about the past at a time when the field was in its earliest, formative stage.

See also: English colonialism; French colonialism

Further reading

Jelks, E.B. (1973) *Archaeological Explorations at Signal Hill, Newfoundland, 1965–1966*, Occasional Papers in Archaeology and History 7, Ottawa: National Historic Sites Service.

CHARLES E. ORSER, JR

site significance

The preservation of archaeological sites and monuments is an important issue in historical archaeology. Preservation strategies often revolve around the concept of *significance*. The concept of site significance partly lies in the idea that important places associated with a people's cultural heritage should be venerated. The concept also lies in the European common-law idea that important antiquities belong to the state, the earliest expression of which appears to be the Swedish Royal Proclamation of 1666. Towards this end, governments began to list, schedule or register important places and to develop criteria for this purpose. Typical examples are the **National Register of Historic Places** in the USA and the English Heritage List. At the international level, UNESCO adopted the Convention Concerning the Protection of the World Cultural and Natural Heritage (World Heritage Convention) in 1972. The convention identifies and lists monuments, groups of buildings and sites that have 'outstanding universal value' and established the World Heritage List. In December 2000, the World Heritage List included 690 sites and monuments such as Hadrian's Wall and Ironbridge Gorge in the UK.

Typically, the listing criteria assess both the significance and the integrity or preservation of a site or monument. The procedures used in the USA are typical. Legal significance in the USA began with the passage of the Historic Sites Act in 1935, which allows the Secretary of the Interior to designate sites important to the cultural heritage of the nation as National Historic Landmarks. Six criteria are used for this purpose. They include association with nationally important historical events or patterns, persons, ideas or ideals, architecture, cultures or ways of life, and information value. The National Historic Preservation Act of 1966 established the National Register of Historic Places. Listed on the National Register are historic properties that are considered to be important to the historical or cultural heritage of the USA at the national, state or local level. Determining eligibility for the National Register follows a series of steps. The first step is to categorise the property as an object, structure, building, site or district. Next, the property is placed within a *historic context* and linked to it by a *property type*. A historic context is a broad historical pattern or event or theme (e.g. peopling places or transforming the environment) that occurred in a particular time period and geographical place, and that is represented by historic properties. A property type is a group of historic properties that hold in common some key physical characteristics or associations with a historic context. If a property belongs to a property type that is strongly associated with and reflects a historic context, it is more likely to be considered significant and, therefore, to be considered eligible for listing on the National Register.

The third step is to evaluate the significance of the property. Four criteria are used to determine whether a historical property is significant enough to be listed on the National Register. A site or monument is significant under Criterion A if it is strongly associated with a historical event that made an important contribution to the broad pattern of national, state or local history. Archaeological sites most often are considered to be significant under this criterion if their physical remains help to interpret or illustrate the historical property associated with the event to the public. Likewise, a site or monument is significant under Criterion B if it is strongly associated with and helps to interpret or illustrate the life of a person who is important in national, state or local history. Archaeological remains are typically not considered to be significant under this criterion unless no other associated properties exist. A site or monument is significant under Criterion C if it is strongly associated with and helps to interpret or illustrate a distinctive architectural or engineering type or pattern or style. Finally, a site or monument is significant under Criterion D if it has yielded or may potentially yield important scientific or scholarly information. Determining what information is important normally requires the development of a research design that stipulates the structure of inquiry within which questions are asked, what questions are important within the structure and the critical data or information requirements of these important questions.

Significance in the USA is not always based upon the four National Register criteria. Some archaeological sites are associated with traditional cultural properties, which are significant because they are associated with important cultural practices or beliefs of a living community. Such practices or beliefs are deeply rooted in the community's history or are important in maintaining the continuing cultural identity of the community. Finally, to be listed or registered, sites and monuments typically have to be well enough preserved or to have retained enough integrity to convey their cultural or historical significance to today's visitor. The National Register of Historic Places in the United States, for example, assesses site integrity with seven criteria. Is the property still associated with its place of importance (location)? Does it retain its original design? Are the materials used in the original property still the same? Does the property reflect workmanship such as a craft? Is the physical setting of the property still the same? Does the property retain the same feeling or sense of its original time and place? Is it strongly associated with its historic context? These criteria have a distinctly architectural bias, reflecting their original development for buildings and structures, but can be applied to archaeological sites and monuments.

Further Reading

Cleere, H. (ed.) (1996) *Archaeological Heritage Management in the Modern World*, London: Routledge.

Hardesty, D. and Little, B. (2000) *Assessing Site Significance: A Guide for Archaeologists and Historians.* Walnut Creek, CA: AltaMira Press.

King, T. (1998) *Cultural Resource Laws and Practice: An Introductory Guide*, Walnut Creek, CA: AltaMira Press.

Little, B., Townsend, J., Seibert, E., Sprinke, J. and Knoerl, J. (2000) *Guidelines for Evaluating and Registering Archeological Properties.* Washington, DC: National Register of Historic Places, National Park Service.

Parker, P. and King, T. (1998) *Guidelines for Evaluating and Documenting Traditional Cultural Properties*, National Register Bulletin 38, Washington, DC: National Register of Historic Places, National Park Service.

DONALD L. HARDESTY

slavery

The historical archaeology of slavery shares elements with, but is not synonymous with, the fields of both **African American archaeology** and **plantation archaeology**. The transatlantic slave trade of the late fifteenth through early nineteenth centuries was the largest forced migration in human history. Although simplistic attempts to identify a distinctive 'slave pattern' in archaeological assemblages have been unsuccessful, historical archaeologists continue to examine the legacy of slavery in many diverse contexts, including the impact on indigenous African cultures, **shipwrecks**, **maroon sites**, modes of domination and resistance, and the transformations and continuities following emancipation. In both Africa and the New World, the public presentation, interpretation and discussion of slavery-related sites is facilitating a long-overdue reckoning with the issues of slavery and **race** by both European- and African-descent people.

The archaeological analysis of slavery is plagued by several conceptual and definitional difficulties. The indiscriminate use of 'slavery' to characterise the diverse forms of human bondage known on all continents throughout the span of recorded history – coupled with strong evocative, metaphorical connotations of the term – restricts its analytical utility and necessitates precise, context-specific definitions. This problem was paradoxically exacerbated by the discourse of both pro- and anti-slavery advocates during the early modern period. The pro-slavery apologists often stressed the perceived similarities between Atlantic colonial slavery and the forms of bondage recorded in the Bible and classical Greek and Roman texts. They also tried to justify their form of slavery by asserting continuity with pre-existing forms of African bondage. Conversely, the abolitionists confounded the issue by contrasting 'slavery' with a very ideological, individualistic definition of 'freedom' that was specific to the emerging forms of capitalism. Finally, because they realise that dehumanisation was an essential element of early modern slavery, the living descendants of enslaved Africans are increasingly resistant to the use of the term 'slave' to describe individual human beings. Recognising that people's identity should not be reduced to their imposed status, many activist scholars prefer the use of terms like 'enslaved labourers' or 'African captives' rather than the term 'slave'.

In his archaeological analysis of landscape transformations in south-eastern Africa, Warren Perry suggests use of the term 'racial commodity slavery' to distinguish European notions of slavery from the wide range of African forms of incorporation. Accordingly, several elements distinguish the racial commodity slavery that characterised the Atlantic colonies of the early modern period from other forms of bond labour. First is the concept of slave as property. Most forms of enslavement were characterised by a tension between viewing the slave as an inferior subject and treating the slave as chattel property. However, under racial commodity slavery, particularly in the English colonies, the enslaved person was viewed almost exclusively as property, contributing to particularly virulent forms of exclusion and dehumanisation. The second distinction was utilisation of the enslaved person almost exclusively as a menial labour source for the production of globally exchanged commodities such as **sugar**, tobacco, **coffee** and cotton. While other systems of bondage utilised the enslaved in a wide range of activities, including soldiers, concubines, craftsmen, family retainers and kin group members, racial commodity slavery's relegation of enslaved to the category of commodity-producing labourer severely limited opportunities for eventual incorporation or emancipation. The third distinction is the global nature of racial commodity slavery, which meant that the enslaver and the enslaved had very different geographical and cultural origins and physical appearances. These differences facilitated the elaboration of the ideology of race and the concomitant assertion of racial inferiority as a purported rationale for enslavement.

Christopher DeCorse and Merrick Posnansky note that historical archaeologists analysing slavery need to be cognisant of African studies. The most obvious issue is the cultural continuities, ruptures and transformations between African origins and emerging New World African American identities. In addition, the transatlantic slave trade had a devastating social and demographic impact on the interior regions that were raided for captives. For example, the defensive hilltop sites and walled settlements that appear during the eighteenth century in Sierra Leone, Liberia and Guinea, and the discontinuities in pottery styles in southern Ghana are all responses to increased slave raiding. Paradoxically, coastal areas directly involved in the captive trade may have experienced relatively

limited cultural disruption. An example of this continuity is the settlement of **Elmina**, Ghana, where DeCorse has conducted extensive excavations. A Portuguese castle was established at this location in 1482, and by the time the settlement was destroyed by British bombardment in 1873 it had over 20,000 inhabitants. Although many of the town's inhabitants traded in African captives and a large number of enslaved people lived within the town, DeCorse's excavations recovered only three artefacts, a shackle and two possible slave burden weights, which were directly related to the slave trade. Although Elmina's inhabitants rapidly adopted many elements of European material culture during the early contact period, DeCorse notes marked continuities in the world view and ideology. Although construction methods and building materials changed, the building plans and spatial configuration remained consistent with indigenous African notions of spatial organisation. Similarly, although Rhenish **stoneware** jugs and Chinese **porcelain** saucers were adopted as grave offerings, the traditional practice of placing burials beneath house floors continued.

A distinctive perspective on the transatlantic slave trade is provided by the analysis and memorialisation of a shipwreck discovered off the Florida Keys in 1973 and identified in 1983 as the English slave ship *Henrietta Marie*. In September of 1699, the *Henrietta Marie* departed from London en route to the West African coast, probably the Calabar region of present-day Nigeria. After obtaining some 250 captives, the vessel sailed to **Port Royal**, Jamaica. Some sixty enslaved individuals died during the Middle Passage, and the remaining 190 men, women and children were auctioned on 18 May 1700. During the return voyage, the *Henrietta Marie* sank in about 30 feet of water in the vicinity of New Ground Reef. Capt. Thomas Chamberlain and a crew of about a dozen perished in the wreck. Since its identification in 1983, the *Henrietta Marie* has provided important data about the transatlantic slave trade. In addition, the memorialisation of the site by the National Association of Black Scuba Divers and the exhibit based on the recovered artefacts has provided an invaluable forum for addressing the continuing legacy of racial commodity slavery. This reckoning is also occurring at other sites such as Elmina

Castle, Ghana; Goree Island, near Dakar, Senegal; the Transatlantic Slavery Gallery in Liverpool, England; and the **African Burial Ground** in **New York City**.

Jerome Handler and his colleagues have examined the issue of slavery through excavation and analysis of the **Newton Plantation** Cemetery in Barbados. This project has analysed the remains of 104 enslaved individuals who were interred in the cemetery between about 1660 and 1820. As was the case with the African Burial Ground in New York City, most of the individuals were buried in the supine position with the head towards the west. Gravegoods, particularly in the later burials, were relatively rare. In most respects, the burial customs were consistent with (but not exclusive to) European Christian customs. However, unlike the African Burial Ground population, most of the Barbados burials did not have coffins. A few of the Barbados burials were remarkable for their associated gravegoods and burial treatment. Handler identified one of the burials as a possible healer/ diviner or medicine man. The man died at about the age of fifty and was buried during the late 1600s or early 1700s. He was interred with the largest and most varied assemblage of African-derived material identified to date in any African descendant site in the New World. The grave goods included: an earthenware clay pipe that is almost certainly of African origin; cowrie shells native to the Indian Ocean; and a carnelian bead hand-crafted in southern India. This burial provides extraordinary evidence of the survival and adaptation of West African spiritual practices in the New World context.

While the discovery of items of African origin within New World sites is very rare, historical archaeologists are becoming increasingly sensitive to the ways in which locally available materials, including manufactured European items, may have been symbolically utilised by enslaved people in ways that were not apparent to the slaveholders. The term 'multivalence' is used to describe items whose meaning and significance are ambiguous and variable, depending upon the cultural context in which they are used. An example of this approach is provided by the multidisciplinary work of Mark Leone and his colleagues in the **Chesapeake region** of the USA. This analysis was

prompted by the discovery of a cache of items enslaved labourers had concealed within the Charles Carroll mansion in Annapolis The cache included quartz crystals, pierced disks, pierced coins, beads, pins, a rounded black pebble and a white potsherd with a blue asterisk painted on the bottom. A systematic analysis of WPA slave narratives and archaeological site reports from throughout the region revealed a consistent pattern whereby these caches were used in a range of African-derived spiritual practices known as conjuring. The fact that these caches date as early as 1702 and are often found within the houses of slaveholders indicates a form of cultural resistance that was invisible to the dominant culture.

Many historical archaeologists are also interested in the cultural transformations and continuities that occurred with the abolition of slavery in the USA and the Caribbean. For example, Douglas Armstrong has examined the spatial transformation of the Drax Hall Plantation, Jamaica, following emancipation in 1838. Although the former slaves, who continued to work on the plantation as labouring tenants, were restricted to the same village area, they dramatically reconfigured their living areas within this restricted space. The former slaves built their new houses closer to the main roads so they no longer had to pass the planter's house when travelling to the fields and sugar works. Similar investigations are being conducted at emancipation-era sites in the USA. According to Armstrong, these spatial reconfigurations reflect transformations in the mode of production operative at the estate as well as in the relationship between the planter and his labour force.

Slavery will undoubtedly continue to be an important research interest for historical archaeologists. Future research will need to be increasingly responsive to the concerns of the African-descent communities and employ nuanced, multidisciplinary and context-specific approaches that eschew simplistic and monolithic conceptions of slavery.

See also: diaspora

Further reading

Armstrong, D.V. (1983) *The Old Village and the Great*

House: An Archaeological and Historical Examination of Drax Hall Plantation, Jamaica, Urbana: University of Illinois Press.

Cottman, M.H. (1999) *The Wreck of the Henrietta Marie: An African-American's Spiritual Journey to Uncover a Sunken Slave Ship's Past*, New York: Harmony.

DeCorse, C.R. (1992) 'Culture contact, continuity, and change on the Gold Coast, A.D. 1400–1900', *African Archaeological Review* 10: 163–96.

Handler, J.S. (1997) 'An African-type healer/diviner and his grave goods: A burial from a plantation slave cemetery in Barbados, West Indies', *International Journal of Historical Archaeology* 1: 91–130.

Leone, M.P. and Fry, G. (1999) 'Conjuring in the big house kitchen: An interpretation of African American belief systems based on the uses of archaeology and folklore sources', *Journal of American Folklore* 112: 372–403.

Perry, W.R. (1999) *Landscape Transformations and the Archaeology of Impact: Social Disruption and State Formation in Southern Africa*, New York: Kluwer Academic/Archaeology', in T.A. Singleton (ed.) *'I, too, am America': Archaeological Studies of African-American Life*, Charlottesville: University Press of Virginia, pp. 21–38.

TERRENCE W. EPPERSON

Society for Historical Archaeology

The Society for Historical Archaeology (SHA) was founded in January 1967 by fourteen professional US archaeologists who were engaged in historical archaeology in some fashion. The first meeting, designated the 'International Conference on Historical Archaeology' was held at Southern Methodist University in Dallas, Texas. Edward Jelks served as the chair of the conference, and John Cotter was elected the Society's first president. The size of the organisation has steadily grown since 1967, and, at the start of the twenty-first century, the Society was the main North American professional organisation for the field.

Membership of the Society is open to anyone interested in the history, anthropology and the interpretation of the past using a combination of archaeological materials and historical records. The Society has traditionally held its annual meeting in January. The conference includes the delivery of professional papers, the holding of public education symposia, educational round-tables and the Society's annual business meeting. The Society's two publications are *Historical Archaeology* (scholarly quarterly) and the *SHA Newsletter* (also a quarterly). The Society also occasionally publishes other works as well.

CHARLES E. ORSER, JR

Society for Post-medieval Archaeology

The Society for Post-medieval Archaeology (SPMA) was founded in **England** in 1967, the same year that the **Society for Historical Archaeology** was founded in the USA. Interest in founding a society dedicated to post-medieval history (originally defined as covering the 1450–1750 period) developed out of the 'Post-medieval Ceramic Research Group' that had been founded about three years earlier by K.J. Barton and John Hurt in Bristol, England. After consideration, the founding members of the Society decided that the focus of the original organisation should be expanded to include non-ceramic topics and that it should be open to everyone interested in post-medieval history, regardless of their professional training.

Post-medieval Archaeology, appearing annually, is the scholarly publication of the Society. The purview of the journal is archaeological research focused on British and colonial history of the post-medieval period. Articles in the journal cover a range of topics, from landscape archaeology to detailed investigations of specific kinds of artefacts. One important aspect of the journal is its thorough catalogue of post-medieval archaeology research conducted each year in Great Britain and **Ireland**.

CHARLES E. ORSER, JR

sociocultural anthropology

Historical archaeology has always shared a rather ambiguous relationship with the broader discipline of anthropology. This situation is due in large measure to early debates concerning whether the field should be a part of history or anthropology. This issue of identity is understandable given the unique association of archaeology with anthropology in the USA. In most parts of the world, archaeology is seen as a separate discipline or as a tool for unearthing a past defined essentially as history. In the USA, the long and fruitful association of archaeology and anthropology stems from a shared concern for the preservation and recovery of Native American history and culture (see **Native Americans**). Greatly influenced by Franz Boas, Americanist anthropology tried to stem the tide of progress that was rapidly eroding Native American society and its archaeological legacy. Unlike their colleagues outside the USA, who saw themselves as comparative sociologists, US anthropologists concentrated on culture itself, and saw it as relatively homogeneous. The behaviour of most Native groups was thought to be influenced or structured by a uniform set of cultural expectations that all members of the group shared. European anthropologists saw societies comprised of several cultural groups. In some respects this is the reason that many historical archaeologists took to European traditions of intellectual thought for inspiration and theory.

Despite these ambiguities, the collaboration between historical archaeologists and cultural anthropologists holds great potential for the study of colonial and post-colonial societies. An example of such work is the collaboration between anthropologist Marshall Sahlins and archaeologist Patrick Kirch in their study of the Anuhulu valley on the Hawaiian island of Oahu. The study draws heavily on documentary evidence concerning land transactions and the results of archaeological survey and excavation to reconstruct the historical landscape. As a result of this collaboration, the history of Anahulu was pushed back to AD 1300 and previous assumptions concerning the antiquity of terraced agriculture were revised to show it dating to the historic period. With this as their framework, Sahlins and Kirch then go on to examine the economic and political history of the valley through the lens of local culture. Using documentary and oral history, they are able to construct portraits of six valley polities whose political and ritual structures were closely linked to the local ecology of each area. The historical anthropology they create is rich, insightful and theoretically challenging.

Another example comes from cultural anthropologist Kathleen Bragdon. Her book, *Native Peoples of Southern New England, 1500–1650*, published in 1996, provides an important synthesis of ethnohistory, historical linguistics, historical ethnography and archaeology. Originally trained as an archaeologist, Bragdon later developed skills as a sociolinguist and cultural anthropologist. The picture Bragdon generates from her impressive research reflects her multifaceted perspective. In a study similar to that conducted by Sahlins and Kirch, Bragdon attempts to link political and cultural development among the native groups of southern New England to three different ecological adaptations. Some groups chose the resource-abundant coastal/estuarine environment, while others centred their economies on river drainages. Still a third set of groups chose the upland areas and relied upon access to lakes for water and lacustrine resources. Based upon this model, she explains why the interior groups developed a heavier reliance on maize horticulture. Drawing on the often overlooked grey literature of **cultural-resource management**, Bragdon provides an important synthesis that chronicles changes in economy, social structure and cosmology over close to 1,000 years of Native American history. Other potential areas for collaboration will no doubt involve studies that focus on the role of material goods as agents of cultural integration and change. In this regard, the work of Jean and John Comaroff, which focuses on colonialism in South Africa, stands out, as does Nicholas Thomas's work in the South Pacific. The Comaroffs provide a series of works that offer a deep and revealing picture of changing notions of identity in colonial South Africa. Among the more noteworthy aspects of their work is their concern for material culture. In particular, they examine the attempts of missionaries to alter the identity of South African women by insisting on their wearing European clothes. This was a common practice in almost all colonial contexts. As anthropologists, the Comaroffs are able to link these practices to cultural perceptions of the body and the way they influenced European–South African interaction and history.

Thomas's study focuses on the South Pacific, but like the Comaroff's he, too, is interested in the role of material culture in shaping changing identities under the weight of colonialism. Thomas's findings echo those of others who have found that European material culture did not alter indigenous culture as much as it was recast to fit that culture.

Further reading

Bragdon, K.J. (1996) *Native Peoples of Southern New England, 1500–1650*, Norman: University of Oklahoma Press.

Comaroff, J. and Comaroff, J. (1997) *The Dialectics of Modernity on a South African Frontier*, Chicago: University of Chicago Press.

—— (1991) *Of Revelation and Revolution, Volume 1: Christianity, Colonialism, and Consciousness in South Africa*, Chicago: University of Chicago Press.

Kirch, P.V. and Sahlins, M. (1992) *Anahulu: The Anthropology of History in the Kingdom of Hawaii, Volume One: Historical Ethnography*, Chicago, University of Chicago Press.

—— (1992) *Anahulu: The Anthropology of History in the Kingdom of Hawaii, Volume Two: Archaeology*, Chicago: University of Chicago Press.

Thomas, N. (1991) *Entangled Objects: Exchange, Material Culture and Colonialism in the Pacific*, Cambridge, MA: Harvard University Press.

STEPHEN A. MROZOWSKI

South Africa

Until the 1980s, archaeologists in South Africa concentrated on the long history of early modern human development and the pre-colonial period. Research into the impact of colonisation on indigenous society was largely confined to measuring declining access to natural resources and collapsing social structures. Cultural historians and restoration architects dealt with the **material culture** of the colonial period, antiquarians

collected historical artefacts or sought evidence of primary events, such as the landing point of **Dutch East India Company** (VOC) commander Jan van Riebeeck, and treasure hunters scoured accessible shipwrecks.

Two posts were established for historical archaeologists at museums in the Cape Province, but this period saw the archaeology of historic sites rather than historical archaeology. From 1976, Hennie N. Vos excavated sites in and around Stellenbosch (founded 1685). Rural town and farm **vernacular architecture** was a strong focus of research associated with the cultural history of Afrikaans-speaking landowners of European origin. Vos outlined architectural developments in Stellenbosch using documentary and archaeological evidence, and his main contribution was to question and dispel 'myths' about old Cape architecture, such as how and when certain elements and features were developed. In **Cape Town**, from 1981, Gabeba Abrahams-Willis carried out archaeological investigations on South African Cultural History Museum properties and was also involved in salvage excavations in the city. She was influential in pointing out the historical archaeological potential of Cape Town through a series of historical map overlays.

In the mid-1980s, theories and methods of historical archaeology were first taught by Martin Hall at the University of Cape Town (UCT). James Deetz lectured in South Africa in 1984 and stimulated a wide appreciation of the place of historical archaeology in academic, museum and **heritage management** institutions as well as the significance of **public archaeology**.

Martin Hall became the first Professor of Historical Archaeology at a South African university in 1991 and has been the most important figure in developing the status of South African historical archaeology. Hall had shifted his focus from a reassessment of the later farming and iron-using communities establishing themselves in southern Africa to the archaeology of **Dutch colonialism** at the Cape of Good Hope. He saw this as a logical move in pursuing his interests in the role of material culture as part of the process of colonisation. The multiple resources incorporated by historical archaeologists, especially the written records, gave him an opportunity to apply new theoretical approaches to the history of colonial expansion in South Africa. In turn, he was a major contributor towards overall theoretical developments in historical archaeology during the 1990s.

Since 1985, a body of researchers have collaborated as the Historical Archaeology Research Group (HARG), based in the Department of Archaeology at UCT. Their work explores areas as diverse as VOC texts, domestic architecture, **oral history**, **fortifications**, **slavery**, household **probate inventories**, **shipwrecks** and Asian **ceramics**. Their contributions also vary from theoretical innovations to establishing **typologies** and producing practical handbooks on artefact analysis.

After the advent of more stringent heritage management legislation in 1999, the expansion of archaeological practice into the modern world resulted from **cultural-resource management** impact assessments on proposed development sites throughout South Africa. Archaeologists at museums in Pretoria, Grahamstown and Pietermaritzburg have increasingly utilised historical-archaeology methods to deal with the range of sites produced by cultural-resource management requirements. Semi-independent archaeology contracts offices have been associated with the University of Cape Town and University of the Witwatersrand since the early 1990s and a handful of individual archaeologists carry out small-scale commissions on a free-lance basis.

Historical archaeology has played an active role in **public archaeology** in South Africa through urban excavations, adult education field schools and programmes for history teachers. As a result of increased government interest in education development, heritage management and cultural tourism after the first democratic elections in South Africa (1994), historical archaeologists became involved in cultural-heritage issues and the archaeology of the dispossessed.

At UCT, Martin Hall established the Multimedia Education Group, using archaeology as a teaching tool, and the Research Unit for the Archaeology of Cape Town (RESUNACT), with an emphasis on the archaeology of the nineteenth and twentieth centuries. The RESUNACT Schools Programme included excavations with teachers and pupils in District Six, a notorious inner-city

area cleared of its inhabitants under apartheid legislation and demolished as a 'slum', and at a Moravian mission (see **mission sites**) village established for landless Khoi and ex-slaves.

Visits and research by Deetz, his students and colleagues, and the connections that were set up as a result, for some years emphasised the North American colonial connection. Closer contacts then developed with European, Australian and other African researchers, particularly for comparative work in nineteenth-century contexts. South Africans also took advantage of the opportunities offered by the Fourth **World Archaeological Congress**, hosted by UCT in 1999, to muster historical archaeologists from around the world.

The written history of coastal South Africa opens with the logs of passing European ships reporting on shipwrecks, sources of fresh water and the state of relations with the local people.

The first permanent European settlement in South Africa was planted by the VOC in 1652 at the 'Cape of Good Hope', half way along the route between the Indies and Europe. It was intended to supply ships and their crews with fresh water, vegetables, fruit and meat and a place to restore their health.

Until recently, the rich hoard of shipwrecks around the 'Cape of Storms' has been the domain of treasure hunters and salvors, though some archaeological investigations were carried out on Portuguese shipwreck and survivor camp sites on the southern Cape and Natal coasts. In the 1990s, systematic excavations supervised by a professional maritime archaeologist took place on the wreck of the VOC *Oosterland* (1697) in Table Bay.

Contact with indigenous hunter-gatherers and nomadic herders (known archaeologically as San and Khoi) was first based on loading fresh water and trading meat for goods such as tobacco, beads and metal. The most comprehensive archaeology of contact between indigenous people and European militia in the late seventeenth century was carried out by Carmel Schrire at Oudepost, a VOC outpost north of Cape Town. The rich documentary sources produced by the Company were combined with the artefacts of daily life left by a small band of unimportant soldiers and their indigenous visitors and, at one stage, murderers.

The Cape was occupied by a varied population of sailors, soldiers and VOC officials of European origins, with slaves of Asian and African origins. Settlers comprised a small group of colonists known as free-burghers and free-blacks ('free' from VOC service contract, or slavery and convict status) and French Huguenot refugees, who were given permission to supply services or granted land to produce fresh food for the Company. Gradually they expanded into the interior where large and small wine, wheat and cattle farms occupied well-watered land while stock farmers spread into the less favourable areas. Studies of outlying farms on the and west coast (Verlorenvlei) revealed distinctive vernacular architectural forms compared to farmsteads on richer soils. Dispossessed of their land, San and Khoi lost their independence and were incorporated as herdsmen and labourers, outlawed to the fringes of an expanding land-hungry colony and even exterminated as vermin.

Yvonne Brink explored the relationship between Company and colonists, and the associated emergence of a mid-eighteenth-century rural style of vernacular architecture. Brink applied a range of approaches, especially from literature and gender theory, to understand how free-burgher farmers responded to Company oppression through the 'language' of **material culture**, for instance in the form of their houses. Brink's innovative theoretical applications emphasised that textual sources and discourses, such as cartography and the rare voices of early colonial women writers, are legitimate and revealing resources for historical archaeologists in South Africa.

Both Company and colonists depended on slave labour for domestic, military, commercial and agricultural purposes. Slaves imported from Africa and Asia soon outnumbered their owners. **Slavery** has been a constant thread running through historical archaeology research in the Cape.

The prestigious estate of Vergelegen near Cape Town (established by the VOC Governor in 1700) was the focus of archaeological work by Ann Markell, Martin Hall and Carmel Schrire. The Slave Lodge and matching outbuildings were revealed to be constructed in a vernacular European style not previously recorded in South Africa – three-aisled structures that could be adapted to various uses including various combina-tions of living–working–food and wine production–storage–stabling.

The discovery of the coffin burial of a woman in the floor of the lodge led to pioneering archaeometrical analyses of historical skeletons. Judith Sealy and her team at UCT demonstrated that isotopic signatures of different skeletal elements indicated a tropical diet in childhood and a fish-rich diet in adulthood. This pattern was interpreted as consistent with the hypothesis that the woman was imported as a slave to the Cape. Glenda Cox then analysed skeletons excavated from unmarked burial grounds in Cape Town (Cobern Street and Fort Knokke). The isotopic analysis of bones from individuals with modified teeth (i.e. first-generation slaves) showed patterning indicating different diets in childhood and adult life.

Antonia Malan incorporated household inventories with family histories of slave owners and slave descendants to recreate colonial domestic life within its architectural framework. She first plotted changing house plans and the use of internal spaces in Cape Town and its hinterland, comparing households of the VOC (1750–95) with the British period (1795–1850). She then focused on the experiences of colonial and slave women, particularly slave and free-black mothers of colonists.

After the decline of the VOC and the takeover of its Asian trading domain by the British in 1795, the Cape became a British Crown Colony and then a minor colonial outpost of Queen Victoria's Empire. By 1815, the colony extended to the Orange River in the north and a disputed eastern frontier on the Fish River, where settler and African farmers met. A group of British settler parties was introduced to form a buffer zone in the volatile border between the colonial and Xhosa cattle pastoralists in 1820.

The interests of Deetz and his students focused on these '1820 Settlers' in the Eastern Cape, in order to track British material culture in global perspective. Patrice Jeppson made a comparative study of imported British **ceramics** used by contemporary mid-nineteenth-century ethnic and social groups at a range of sites – mission hamlets, military fort, elite homestead and town dump in Grahamstown. Margot Winer investigated the community of Salem, combining evidence from excavated artefacts with architectural analysis and

landscape studies to develop a series of patterns of material culture that mirrored unfolding events in the region.

Relations between Khoi–San peoples, African farmers and European settlers in southern Africa in the nineteenth and twentieth centuries form significant sections of archaeological research in the central and northern areas of South Africa. Some projects, such as Garth Sampson's intensive survey of the Seacow Valley (Karoo), though incorporating documentary and ethnographic resources, are not, strictly, based on approaches rooted in historical archaeology. Simon Hall's work on **ethnicity** and the construction of identity within and among southern African 'tribal' groups in the colonial period, however, has been strongly influenced by historical archaeology theory.

Slaves were fully emancipated in 1838. Many ex-slaves from rural areas sought work and shelter in the towns while some found new lives in missions (see **mission sites**). Missionary settlements ranged throughout South Africa from the short-lived village of Schoemansdal (mid-nineteenth century) in the far north, excavated and partially restored as a museum, to Genadendal in the south, focus of a community archaeology programme with local schools. The archaeology of slavery and dispossessed South Africans has been integrated into the South African chapter of the UNESCO/WTO Slave Route Project.

Skilled and unskilled working-class immigrants (see **immigration**) from Britain, colonial administrators, merchants of all sorts and ex-army personnel swelled the population of Cape Town in the nineteenth century. Excavations in areas that developed outside the old boundaries of the town have been conducted on a varied range of housing, from densely packed rows and terraces of rented accommodation to semi-detached cottages, larger villas and houses. These often overlie areas previously used as dumping grounds for urban debris, sources of invaluable comparative collections. Due to poorly developed local industry, consumer goods and mass-produced architectural elements from Britain streamed into South Africa.

Historical archaeology in South Africa includes the **industrial archaeology** of the British Empire, gold and diamond rushes of the 1880s, **industrialisation** and **urbanisation**. As a result of decommissioning of industrial complexes in the Cape and Transvaal, archaeologists had an opportunity to investigate the social, spatial and technological domains of two explosives factories established in the 1890s. These were surveyed and recorded, and, at Modderfontein near Johannesburg, sites in ethnically separated hamlets were excavated. Places like the gas works and original power station in Cape Town, however, were demolished without a full appreciation of their research value for historical archaeologists.

Further reading

Cox, G. and Sealy, J. (1997) 'Investigating identity and life histories: Isotopic analysis and historical documentation of slave skeletons found on the Cape Town foreshore, South Africa', *International Journal of Historical Archaeology* 1: 207–24.

Hall, M. (1993) 'The archaeology of colonial settlement in southern Africa', *Annual Review of Anthropology* 22: 177–200.

—— (1992) 'Small things and the mobile, conflictual fusion of power, fear, and desire', in A.E. Yentsch and M.C. Beaudry (eds) *The Art and Mystery of Historical Archaeology: Essays in Honor of James Deetz*, Boca Raton: CRC Press, pp. 373–400.

Schrire, C. (1995) *Digging through Darkness: Chronicles of an Archaeologist*, Johannesburg: Witwatersrand University Press.

ANTONIA MALAN

South America

The study of archaeology in South America began in the nineteenth century, but historical archaeology in the region has only developed in earnest since the 1980s. Given the history of colonisation of the continent, South American archaeology is usually conceived as being divided into research conducted in Portuguese-speaking **Brazil** and in the Spanish-speaking countries originally colonised by the Spaniards. By the late twentieth century, historical archaeology within Hispanic South America was much more developed in some countries whose self-definition and identity are European, notably Argentina and Uruguay, even though isolated efforts also appeared in other countries. The debates within historical archaeology of Hispanic South America include the definition of the subject, the study of ethnicity and identity, the methodological and theoretical underpinnings of the discipline and the prospectus for future development and unresolved issues.

Archaeology in Hispanic South America has been concerned mostly with prehistory. In the countries with large and impressive remains from pre-colonial empires, such as the Inca, there has been a particularly emphasis on the archaeology of this prestigious past, usually because the state has had a direct interest in fostering the creation of a national identity linked to golden pre-Hispanic times. In countries like **Peru**, Ecuador and to a smaller extent Venezuela and Bolivia, this focus explains a lack of interest in historical archaeology because the use of archaeology for building national identities has traditionally led to the search for the pre-colonial splendour. The historical period and its role in creating the different nations has been left to historians, rather than to historical archaeologists. In countries with less impressive prehistoric remains, such as Uruguay and Argentina, prehistoric archaeology, as an anthropological search for the 'other' – the indigenous inhabitants – is often not considered relevant for building the national identity and the archaeological study of the historical period also lagged behind. In these countries, there has been a growing interest in historical archaeology, particularly after the restoration of civilian control, after several decades of authoritarian rule that inhibited the freedom of scholars to deal with possibly sensitive historical subjects.

Historical archaeology was introduced in Hispanic South America from the USA and there is a common acceptance of the original US definition of historical archaeology as a discipline concerned with the period after the arrival of the Europeans. Historical times are divided in two large divisions: colonial (up to the nineteenth century) and independent or national periods. As historical archaeology deals with a past directly related to the present, its main focus has been the discussion of identity, society and politics.

Ethnicity is a main topic of research. Roman Catholic **mission sites** as well as other historic sites inhabited by Guarani Indians have been actively explored and are a subject particularly relevant to such countries as Argentina, Paraguay and Uruguay. Historical archaeologists interested in this subject are usually conversant with the scientific literature on late prehistoric settlement, as well as on the anthropological and linguistic studies relating to the indigenous Guarani inhabitants. Other ethnic groups in the same area are less well known and studied, even though other indigenous groups – Africans, Europeans and people of mixed descent – lived and interacted with the Guarani. Furthermore, the influence of the Catholic Church is also a factor further blurring the archaeological picture. There has been no emphasis on studying the architectural features of the missions or the pottery found there, or in exploring the possible continuity of prehistoric fabrics and typologies.

There has been a growing interest in the culturally mixed features of the material culture of the historical past. Spanish settlement throughout South America introduced new agricultural and industrial enterprises, coupled with the settlement of Spaniards and African slaves. These migrations substantially altered the indigenous systems of production and subsistence, resulting in new and uniquely mixed material patterns. **Urban archaeology**, developed in several cities and towns, particularly in Argentina and Uruguay, has shown that Spanish chequered city plans were used by the colonisers, with the main administrative and religious buildings in the central square. In these Spanish towns, however, lived Spaniards, Native Indians, Africans and people of mixed heritage. Archaeological studies of the material remains suggest that even though the cities may have been characterised by Spanish material culture – as the grid of the streetscape framed the minds of every town dweller – the inhabitants still used local pottery and cooked a mix of European and local foods.

The general picture of past life, however, is blurred when case studies are carried out, for a variety of situations were possible. The pattern of animal use that developed in the south central Andes in the colonial period, for instance, has been interpreted as more closely parallel to those of the Iberian peninsula than to other areas of Spanish settlement that relied on local resources. Overall, the emphasis on a slave's humanity also created a free black class that filled accepted economic and social roles. Acculturated African slaves, or *ladinos*, were also organised through brotherhoods, and mixed marriages were not exceptional, contributing to producing a mixed society, with a hybrid material culture, varying according to specific, local circumstances. Because case studies are still few in number, difficulty exists when it come to identifying different cultural and social patterns of past life.

Historical archaeology in South America has also been relevant, since the 1980s, to re-evaluating the history of the different countries, becoming meaningful to contemporary debates within society. The archaeological study of the remains of the people who opposed dictatorships and who were killed and buried, usually in unidentified mass graves, has been particularly important. The 'Argentinian Forensic Anthropology Group' is the most active team, with archaeological fieldwork not only in Argentina but in other countries within Latin America and beyond. Thus, it is the only South American archaeological expertise exported outside the continent. The archaeological search for the remains of the 'missing people' has also been important in shifting the traditional focus from society's elites to a much wider focus on the material evidence of both winners and losers, both upper class and ordinary people.

For several decades, the material culture studied and preserved by heritage legislation has been limited to high art, particularly through the efforts of architects. Historical archaeology has been able to produce new evidence – from pottery to skeletal remains – to offer a more complete picture of the past. The forensic study of skeletal remains reached the pages of local and foreign newspapers and news magazines, highlighting a new sociopolitical role for historical archaeology in South America.

There has also been a growing discussion of epistemological issues related to the status of the discipline itself. Archaeology in Hispanic South America has traditionally been considered a part of anthropology, under the influence of the USA. In this context, the first people to deal with historical material culture have generally been architects, art historians and heritage scholars. When historical archaeology developed in the 1980s, prehistorians

and architects were in its forefront, with each group having their own training. This situation led to a divide between the archaeologists used to surveys and excavations – but with little experience with documents and architectural features – and those scholars trained as architects, art historians and heritage students – with a sound knowledge of high style but with little experience with archaeological techniques. In both cases, documentary evidence has been sidelined, resulting in a generally poor use of written evidence. Furthermore, first-hand knowledge of historical theory and discussion tends to be scarce, to the detriment of a comprehensive archaeological study of the historical past.

In this context, there has been a contentious argument about the epistemological status of the discipline. Under the influence of **processual archaeology**, most historical archaeologists consider that archaeology should formulate hypotheses and test them in practice. The role of documents is thus contested, some preferring to consider material and written sources as independent, while others prefer to manage the two types of data alternately, in a complementary manner. The former is usually accused of not paying enough attention to documents, the latter being reproached for not considering the possible contradictions between the two kinds of data and for simply trying to confirm with material remains what documents already state. Beginning in the 1990s, however, post-processual influences began to reach South American historical archaeology, highlighting the idea that documents and artefacts can be interpreted as discourses, rather than as raw evidence to be tested. The debate has been shifting to an understanding that historical archaeology is an independent discipline, more than a handmaiden to history, anthropology or architecture. At the same time, the introduction of discursive approaches is leading to a closer dialogue with several disciplines, whose practitioners are also producing interpretive frameworks for the study of the same subjects.

The prospectus for future development of historical archaeology in South America is linked to its ability to forge a dialogue with related disciplines and to insert itself into the international trends in the discipline. Historical archaeology is still by and large ignored both inside Hispanic South America and on the world stage, even though this situation is changing quickly. Increasingly, there are scholars trained specifically as historical archaeologists in South America, even though the picture is rosier in some countries than in others. Argentina and Uruguay are at the forefront, with most others lagging behind. There are still few translations of major English-language books and papers, inhibiting the diffusion of the current discussions within the discipline, and older culture historical and processual approaches are still to be overcome by more recent discussions.

The main avenues open to the development of historical archaeology are related to its ability to become relevant to both society and the scholarly world, inside and outside the continent. As far as historical archaeology is able to produce interpretations that do not simply confirm established historical facts and ideology, it has a bright future. There is little room for eulogising elite discourses about the past, the traditional stand of high-style approaches, because this is out of tune with national and international trends in historical archaeology.

The most successful historical archaeology of Hispanic South America, the search for the remains of the missing people, points to the features of a relevant discipline in the making: looking for evidence that is meaningful for society, inserted in world debates, which is scholarly and international in outlook at the same time. Its spread from some centres in Argentina and Uruguay to the rest of Hispanic South America depends on how relevant historical archaeology is able to become.

See also: Buenos Aires

Further reading

Bellelli, C. and Tobin, J. (1996) 'Archaeology of the desaparecidos', Society for American Archaeology Bulletin 14: 6–7.

DeFrance, S.D. (1996) 'Iberian foodways in the Moquegua and Torata valleys of southern Peru', Historical Archaeology 30: 20–48.

Funari, P.P.A. (1997) 'Archaeology, history, and historical archaeology in South America', International Journal of Historical Archaeology 1: 189–206.

—— (1996) 'Historical archaeology in Brazil, Uruguay, and Argentina', World Archaeological Bulletin 7: 51–62.

Landers, J. (1997) 'Africans in the Spanish colonies', Historical Archaeology 31: 84–103.

Pedrotta, V. and Gómez Romero, F. (1998) 'An outlook from the Argentinian pampas', International Journal of Historical Archaeology 2: 113–31.

Politis, G. (1995) 'The socio-politics of the development of archaeology in Hispanic South America', in P.J. Ucko (ed.) Theory in Archaeology, a World Perspective, London: Routledge, pp. 197–235.

PEDRO PAULO A. FUNARI

South America, underwater archaeology

South America presents interesting characteristics, from an underwater archaeology research point of view, because its coasts are bathed by the Atlantic and the Pacific oceans. South America also has the world's greatest fluvial network and a considerable number of lakes. However, even with all this potential for the exploration of submerged archaeological sites, it was not until the 1990s that underwater archaeology advanced in some South American countries as a serious branch of archaeology. This outdated reality, when compared to other continents, occurred because of the criminal actions of treasure hunters. As a result, we cannot speak about underwater archaeology in South America without considering the lamentable presence of treasure hunters, exploiters and adventurers.

Most countries are opposed to illegal and criminal destruction of underwater cultural patrimonies, but some South American countries allow the exploitation because of political lobbies, sensationalist appeal and the free access that looters have to underwater archaeological sites. Consequently, the exploring companies do not respect wreck sites that could be considered significant 'time capsules' for exploring the tragic, post-Columbian maritime history of South America.

The root problem in South America rests in the absence of reliable information and professional interest in maritime archaeology. Little if anything is being published about the projects that extract enormous collections from various submerged sites. Treasure hunting recalls the collecting that characterised the early history of archaeology, where archaeologists were directed to 'object fetish' and 'object recovery'. They tended to perceive 'artefacts' as trophies of adventure or illustrations of tragic maritime events. At no time were artefacts collected by systematic excavation. Therefore, we can affirm that in the year 2000 we knew more about the vessels that navigated the ancient Mediterranean than we did about the ones that travelled the seas of the New World.

Beginning in the 1990s, South American countries have been receiving support from UNESCO, ICOMOS and mainly from the United Nations Sea Law Convention, all noted for their policies on underwater archaeological patrimony. Thus, many nations are organising and joining forces, through interchanges and reunions, in the struggle against treasure hunting.

Argentina

In 1978, archaeologist Jorge Fernandéz accomplished the first underwater archaeology in Argentina, after recovering the remains of a canoe in Lake Nahuel Huapi (Bariloche, Province of Rio Negro). Publication of underwater research began in 1980 with the presentation of work by architects Jorge O. Gazaneo, Mabel Scarone, Graciela Di Iorio and Hermann Clinckspoor. Architect Javier Garcia Cano began more systematic research, working with the sloop of war HMS *Swift*. In 1991, the Albenga Foundation – a non-profit organisation dedicated to the preservation of national underwater archaeological sites – was created under the direction of Garcia Cano. In 1995, Albenga, in association with archaeologist Mónica Valentini (director of the underwater-archaeology sector at the Universidade Nacional do Rosário – UNR), initiated a project focused on the remains of Santa Fe La Vieja (1573–1660), a fluvial human settlement. Also in that year, the National Ministry of Culture founded an underwater archaeology programme in the National Institute of Anthro-

pology (INAPL). The programme, directed by archaeologist Dolóres C. Elkin, was dedicated to the research and preservation of the Argentinian underwater cultural patrimony. In 1996, archaeologist Ana María Rocchietti (UNR) initiated a research project at the remains of an early seventeenth-century Native American site (see **Native Americans**) in the Coronda River, called 'La Boca del Arroyo Monje'. In 1997, an underwater project was begun in the harbour of **Buenos Aires**, and, in 1998, the Brozoski Museum collaborated with the INAPL's underwater archaeology group on continued work on the HMS *Swift*, and Albenga, in association with the National Science and Technical University of Norway, conducted geophysical mapping of the San Matías Gulf (Province of Rio Negro). In 1999, archaeologist Adam Hajduk asked Alberga, a non-government organization dedicated to protecting under-worker cultural heritage, to begin a project to examine a number of post-seventeenth-century sites near Lake Nahuel Huapi, and, in 2000, archaeologist Marianos Ramos, of the National University of Luján, working with Alberga, began the underwater and terrestrial 'Vuelta de Obligado' project focusing on an 1845 battlefield.

Brazil

In 1976, divers working under the direction of archaeologist Ullyses Pernambuco de Mello made the first attempt to conduct underwater archaeological research in Brazil. Their research focused on the *Santíssimo Sacramento*, the wreck of a Portuguese galleon that was struck by a storm and sunk in 1668 inside the Baía de Todos os Santos, the harbour of Salvador, Bahia. Unfortunately, the research did not serve to create a methodological approach for underwater archaeology in Brazil. Instead, it served only for the extraction of artefacts and for a historical confirmation of the wreck's location. The archaeologist in charge of the research was not a diver himself, thus making it next to impossible to obtain an organised and systematic study. As a result, the way research was done, instead of stimulating a new scientific research for underwater wreck sites or of generating archaeological underwater research, served mainly to trigger a countrywide boom of amateur divers searching for underwater wrecks and souvenirs. Such conditions spread until the late 1990s.

Back in the late 1970s, the Brazilian underwater cultural patrimony was being officially exploited – though not systematically excavated – through a contradictory government regulation that claimed that 20 per cent of all recovered artefacts should be donated to the Brazilian navy. The rescuer could keep the remaining 80 per cent. So far, the efforts conducted at the *Santíssimo Sacramento*, which resulted in nothing more than an attractive museum, were several shipwrecks that were literally pillaged, including the galleons *Nossa Senhora do Rosário* (1648), *Utrecht* (1648) and *São Paulo* (1652); the vessels *Santa Escolástica* (1701), *Nossa Senhora do Rosário e Santo André* (1737) and *Santo André* (1737); the frigates *Queen* (1800), *Dona Paula* (1827) and *Thetys* (1830); the steamboats *D. Afonso* (1853) and *Príncipe de Astúrias* (1916); and the ship *Aquidabã* (1906).

The policies for permitting the salvage of submersed archaeological patrimony in Brazilian national waters existed until 1986. After 1986, a new regulatory federal law stated that all underwater finds would belong in total to the federal government. This law went directly against the commercial interests of treasure-hunting companies, and they have begun to fight it. Along with this process, it was interesting to observe that the Brazilian authorities, instead of providing the enforcement of the law, merely provided a situation where the underwater patrimony was much more exposed to clandestine pillage because the exploiters would no longer declare any new discoveries.

Only in the 1990s, through work conducted by archaeologist Gilson Rambelli (University of São Paulo's Archaeology and Ethnology Museum), did there emerge a concern for the study of underwater archaeological sites. Rambelli's main objective was to demonstrate to archaeologists that underwater research can be conducted with the same seriousness as terrestrial archaeology, thus giving a proper demonstration against the treasure-hunting lobbyists. Sites then chosen for study – a harbour (Porto Grande de Iguape) and a native/European interethnic site (Toca do Bugio) – broke the traditional specifications of shipwreck sites and opened up a new universe of maritime research that aims to extend archaeological investigations to different water environments. This research programme seeks the comprehension of land–water dynamics, and vice versa, in the period of the European occupation of São Paulo's southern coast (Vale do Ribeira). Other research is being developed in this region on sites including European/Brazilian **fortifications**, prehistoric and historical submersed settlements (in both ocean and land-locked environments) and shipwrecks. Through courses and international interchange, Rambelli and his colleagues have substantially contributed to the formation of a new mentality for archaeology in Brazil, as well as to the beginning of a patrimonial education programme creating awareness and consciousness among sport divers and the general public.

Another important project that deserves mention is the Nau Capitânia Project. This project was conducted to locate the possible underwater site of a 1503 shipwreck, which occurred in the waters surrounding the Archipelago of Fernando de Noronha – 300 mi off the coast of north-east Brazil – and described by Américo Vespúcio in his 'Letter of the Fourth Voyage'. These studies were co-ordinated by historian Marcio Werneck da Cunha and diver Randal Fonseca. After thirteen years of historical research and eight years of collecting data in underwater searches, the project had to be cancelled when the location of the shipwreck site was just about to be confirmed, because of a lack of interest by the authorities.

At the year 2000, the Brazilian National Congress is considering freeing treasure hunters from all legal requirements. This act would run counter to and contradict all international agreements.

Chile

The destructive actions of treasure hunting have caused great damage to the underwater archaeological patrimony in Chile. International co-operation, through the organisation and direction of the International University of San Estanislao de Kosta and archaeologist Pedro Pujante Izquierdo, permitted in March 2000 the Albenga Foundation of Argentina to send specialists to the site of the wreck *San Martin* (a Spanish merchant vessel from

1759), located at Mejillones. This work started a new phase in Chile's archaeology.

Columbia

Underwater archaeology in Columbia is marked by the presence of many international treasure hunters. Efforts got underway, in the year 2000 – through archaeologist Tatiana Villegas Zamora's work and UNESCO's collaboration – to change the public's attitude towards underwater patrimony.

Peru

Protection of the underwater cultural heritage is not considered within Peru's legislation. As a result, the country suffers greatly from the problem of international treasure hunting. With international collaboration, historian Jorge Ortiz Sotelo is working, in the year 2000, to form a local team of underwater archaeology professionals.

Uruguay

Uruguay is a victim of treasure hunting permitted by law. The National Commission of Heritage is attempting to change this reality. Also, the international co-operation for the formation of local specialists has been constant, and will certainly reverse the current situation.

See also: destruction, site; South America

Further reading

Elkin, D. (1998) 'Water: A new field in Argentinean archaeology', in C. Ruppé and J. Barstad (eds) *International Handbook of Underwater Archaeology*, New York: Plenum Press.

García Cano, J. (1997) 'South America', in J. Delgado (ed.) *Encyclopedia of Underwater and Maritime Archaeology*, London: British Museum Press, pp. 395–8.

García Cano, J. and Valentini, M. (forthcoming) 'Arqueología subacuática en una fundación española del siglo XVI: Ruinas de Santa Fe la Vieja, un enfoque metodológico', *Anuario de la Universidad Internacionnal SEK*.

Rambelli, G. (1998) 'A arqueologia subaquática e sua aplicação à arqueologia Brasileira: o exemplo do Baixo Ribeira du Iguape', master's thesis, University of São Paulo.

—— (1997) 'O abandono do patrimônio arqueológico subaquático no Brasil: um problema para a arqueologia Brasileira', *Revista do Museu de Arqueologia e Etnologia da Universidade de São Paulo* 7: 177–80.

GILSON RAMBELLI

Southwark, London, England

A London borough, with its historic core situated at the southern end of London Bridge on the south bank of the River Thames, it was in the 1830s that the borough expanded to its present size. Prior to that expansion the focus of Southwark had been the southern end of the bridgehead, with archaeological evidence pointing to human habitation in Southwark from the mesolithic period onwards.

One of the major factors influencing habitation was the area's natural topography, with early populations settling on the high and dry gravel islands (eyots) that occur along the Thames valley. During the Roman occupation of southern England, the natural topography provided the focus for the first bridge across the Thames, with the settlement that developed around the southern end becoming Southwark. Substantial evidence of Roman occupation has been recorded by archaeologists working within the historic core of Southwark, with evidence of Roman roadside and extramural burial grounds also recorded.

Southwark first appears by name in the *Burghal Hidage* (a list of fortified places) in the early tenth century but is not described in detail until the *Domesday Book* in 1086, although this description is thought to be incomplete. The extent of the eleventh-century settlement is not known although *Domesday* describes Southwark as having a dock, trading shore, fishery and minster.

Throughout the medieval period, Southwark was subject to expansion with its proximity to the city making it particularly attractive to rural nobles and clergy who needed town houses. Of particular note to the history of Southwark is the land-holding of the bishops of Winchester who held a large estate (known as the Liberty of the Clink) to the west of London Bridge. Records of the bishops' estate (held in the Hampshire Record Office) provide a unique picture of life in medieval Southwark.

During the time that the bishops held their estate, part of the area between Bankside and Maiden Lane became known as the Stews – referring to both the freshwater fishponds and the brothels for which the area was notorious. It was in this area, after the Dissolution of the monasteries, that animal-baiting pits and playhouses were developed, to accompany existing attractions. Archaeological excavation, of these two sites in particular, has highlighted the importance of **post-medieval archaeology** in understanding the early modern development of London. The importance of these sites is emphasised by Southwark's association with the development of English literature through connection with Chaucer, Shakespeare and Dickens.

Southwark's proximity to the Thames and therefore to sources of trade meant that it was also home to London's early industrial development, with potteries, shipbuilding, clay-pipe making and **glass** manufacture being among the major industries. That proximity to the Thames now plays a part in Southwark's development for tourism and service industries.

See also: Globe Theatre; pipe stem dating; pipes, smoking; Rose Theatre

Further reading

Carlin, M. (1996) *Medieval Southwark*, London: The Hambledon Press.
Cowan, C. (2000) *Below Southwark: The Archaeological Story*, London: London Borough of Southwark.

SIMON BLATHERWICK

Spanish colonialism

The archaeology of Spanish colonialism is the examination of Spanish and Native American cultures (see **Native Americans**), and the means by which they irrevocably influenced one another. It encompasses the study of cultural landscapes, labour practices, religious indoctrination, miscegenation and social and material traditions, and how these variables shaped the many expressions of Latin American culture found throughout the western hemisphere today.

Spanish colonialism was a highly structured enterprise characterised by formal policies and institutions shaped during Spain's 700-year Reconquest against the Moors. The fall of Granada in 1492, which marked the end of this offensive, was viewed by Queen Isabella and King Ferdinand as a highly symbolic victory over cultural and religious diversity. Colonial expansion was fuelled by the Catholic kings' desire to enlarge their Empire and revenue base, advance the rim of Hispanic Christendom, and to lessen the internal threat to the monarchy posed by the highly trained and powerful military class whose centuries-long obsession with the Reconquest came to an abrupt end.

Forward expansion into the Atlantic had begun in 1477–9 with the appropriation of the Canary Islands. This effort was followed in 1492 when Columbus embarked on what was to become one of the defining events of the millennium. Following patterns well established during the Reconquest, native inhabitants of conquered territories were technically free subjects of the Crown once they accepted Christianity. However, Christianised natives were also required to accept subordination to the King and his colonial representatives. Institutions such as *encomienda* (populated areas commended to worthy individuals by the Crown for a specified period of time) and *repartimiento* (a division of goods, including natives) were legalised means of controlling New World territories and their inhabitants claimed for the Crown.

Most Columbus-era *encomiendas* and *repartimientos* were awarded to successful conquistadors who often financed their own expeditions and viewed these allocations of land and labour as forms of remuneration from the Crown. Other well-established tenets and practices that influenced Spanish colonisation included the notion that civilised people live in fixed, orderly communities; the belief that native populations represented a *tabula rasa* among whom a more perfect spiritual order could be achieved; and the encouragement of intermarriage with natives in order to facilitate religious conversion and Hispanicisation. It is this relationship – both formal and informal – between Spaniards and natives that has dominated the attention of Spanish colonial archaeologists. The focus on European–Indian relations has also distinguished this group of historical archaeologists from others in related fields, including archaeologists studying non-Hispanic colonies, as well as most colonial historians whose primary interest has traditionally been restricted to Europeans in the Americas.

Spaniards were desirous of transplanting those elements of Spanish life which were viewed as necessary to maintaining physical order and cultural identity. The most tangible archaeological manifestations of this intent are the formal Spanish colonial settlements themselves. Many Spanish cities followed a basic gridiron plan, which was subject to modification depending on local topography, water sources and other regional considerations. Although official city-planning ordinances were not codified by King Philip until 1573, this Roman-derived and Renaissance-influenced urban pattern can be observed in varying degrees throughout the Spanish New World beginning in the early sixteenth century. This community pattern belies one aspect of the popular 'Black Legend' rooted in English Protestantism, which attempted to vilify Spaniards. The Black Legend suggested in part that, unlike British colonists, the Spaniards' intention was solely to plunder and exploit, then retreat. The study of Spanish colonial landscapes has provided indisputable evidence that Spaniards intended from the outset to establish permanent communities and maintain them as overseas kingdoms of the Spanish Empire.

The archaeological investigation of Spanish labour practices in the New World reveals the most immediate impact of Spanish colonisation on native populations other than inadvertently introduced pathogens. At Columbus-era sites such as **Puerto Real** (1503–78) on the north coast of present-day Haiti, the impact of this exploitative association was rapid and devastating. Established as a cattle-ranching and slave-trading settlement, research at Puerto Real revealed a rapid replacement of local Taino ceramics (Carrier or Chican-Ostionoid tradition) with those of non-indigenous groups. Africans, in particular, are thought to be responsible for the high increase of Christophe Plain pottery during the colonial occupation. The supplanting of one vigorous ceramic tradition with another is believed to reflect the rapid decimation of the indigenous Taino peoples and their replacement with slave labour from the circum-Caribbean area and directly from Africa during the first decades of Spanish colonisation. Spanish labour practices have also been investigated by historical archaeologists at a wide variety of other sites representing a range of economic enterprises, from a pearl-fishery off the coast of Venezuela, to Peruvian *bodegas* (wineries), to mining operations in Mexico. Through space and time, it is this institutionalised aspect of colonialism that had the most crippling effect on the physical well-being, as well as the social and material order, of the indigenous populations.

Owing largely to forced-labour practices including public-works construction, mining, agriculture and domestic service, native populations became familiar and proficient with a range of Spanish materials. Historical archaeologists have documented the availability of domesticated plants and animals, iron tools, firearms and luxury goods among natives, particularly the leadership element. Gift giving was a common strategy employed by Spaniards to recognise and uphold the authority of native leaders and the institutions they represented. However, since most Hispanic materials recovered from native contexts had aboriginal counterparts and could easily have been incorporated into traditional Indian practices, archaeologists have been unable to document specific technological, subsistence or material changes that fundamentally altered native life.

Religious conversion of the native populations to Catholicism has been a primary focus of investigations at **mission sites**. The importance of missions as an agency of colonisation cannot be overstated. In addition to religious indoctrination, missions often provided the means of relocating nomadic and semi-sedentary native peoples into permanent communities, organising native tribute and labour through their tribal leaders, and establishing a military presence in the hinterland that frequently depended on native allies. Despite a healthy dose of scepticism on the part of some scholars, there is compelling evidence to suggest that many native peoples were sincere in their religious conversion. Archaeological investigations have revealed highly Christianised burial practices among missionised natives throughout the Spanish borderlands and beyond. These native burials are typically extended interments with the hands often folded on the chest, sometimes placed in coffins and located in consecrated cemeteries inside or near mission churches. The non-random distribution of artefacts associated with burials, as well as their placement within mission cemeteries and method of interment, suggests that aboriginal status was reinforced through Christian burial practices. Specifically, the highest ranking natives are believed to be those individuals located near church altars and interred with the most elaborate and greatest quantity of grave goods. The regional variability in religious practices (for example, burials in the south-eastern missions often include objects of both Indian and European origin) is believed by some archaeologists, such as Elizabeth Graham, to reflect the evolving nature of Christianity itself rather than attempts by natives to obscure their true religious beliefs. The most powerful evidence for sincere and lasting religious conversion is the fact that many of the missionised populations did not forsake Christianity when the missions were abandoned by their founders, and many descendants of the missionised Indians remain practising Catholics today.

In addition to mortuary patterning, investigations in mission cemeteries have provided invaluable biocultural details of native life with respect to nutrition, labour, epidemics, and other stresses on the indigenous populations. Clark Spencer Larsen's study of skeletal remains from Guale, Timucuan, and Apalachee missions in Spanish Florida have been particularly illuminating. By comparing prehistoric burial assemblages with those from the missions, Larsen was able to identify an overall decline in the health of the native populations as a consequence of Spanish missionisation. This trend is likely attributable to increased labour demands, changing diet, and exposure to diseases, including those related to increased population density and sedentism.

While labour practices and religious conversion brought about the greatest degree of culture change to native populations, miscegenation (*mes-*

tizaje) likely had the most profound influence on Spanish culture in the New World. Due to shortages of Spanish women in the colonies, it was socially acceptable for Spanish men to marry native women. It was also viewed as a means of civilising the native element and, in those instances where Spaniards married female Indian rulers, a prudent political manœuvre. For native women, intermarriage and interbreeding often represented a form of upward mobility for them and their children since, by Spanish law, *mestizos* (the children of Spaniards and Indians) were exempt from forced labour. This aspect of Spanish colonialism has been an integral part of research in **St Augustine** and elsewhere in the New World. The greatest degree of Indian influence is often found in the least visible areas of daily life such as subsistence and food preparation, which were largely associated with female activities. Hispanic traits were most pronounced in socially visible male-dominated areas including architecture, clothing and weaponry.

In this respect, many of the practices associated with Spanish colonialism were relatively inclusionary. From the very earliest intentional New World settlement at **La Isabella**, Spanish colonial archaeologists have found a level of material, cultural and racial blending unknown at most other European colonies. It is this pattern, which incorporates elements of both Spanish and Indian (and to a lesser degree African) societies, which has been documented archaeologically throughout much of the New World and is recognised by archaeologists today as the Hispanic-American cultural tradition.

See also: San Luis; St Augustine

Further reading

Deagan, K. (ed.) (1995) *Puerto Real: The Archaeology of a Sixteenth-century Spanish Town in Hispaniola*, Gainesville: University Press of Florida.

—— (1983) *Spanish St. Augustine: The Archaeology of a Colonial Creole Community*, New York: Academic Press.

Graham, E. (1998) 'Mission archaeology', *Annual Review of Anthropology* 27: 25–62.

Larsen, C.S. (1993) 'Mission bioarchaeology', in B.G. McEwan (ed.) *The Spanish Missions of La*

Florida, Gainesville: University Press of Florida, pp. 322–56.

McEwan, B.G. (ed.) (1993) *The Spanish Missions of La Florida*, Gainesville: University Press of Florida.

Thomas, D.H. (1991) *Columbian Consequences Vol. 3: The Spanish Borderlands in Pan-American Perspective*, Washington, DC: Smithsonian Institution Press.

—— (1990) *Columbian Consequences Vol. 2: Archaeological and Historical Perspectives on the Spanish Borderlands East*, Washington, DC: Smithsonian Institution Press.

—— (ed.) (1989) *Columbian Consequences Vol. 1: Archaeological and Historical Perspectives on the Spanish Borderlands West*, Washington, DC: Smithsonian Institution Press.

BONNIE G. McEWAN

spatial analysis

Spatial analysis in historical archaeology is concerned with studying relationships between people and space, particularly the ordering, organisation and reorganisation of space for social purposes. Space has been conceptualised in historical archaeology as a category of **material culture** or artefact that can be usefully analysed to understand social, economic and political processes. Furthermore, space not only reflects social action, but also is active in mediating and creating social relations. The scales of spatial analysis in historical archaeology have included region; city, town or village; neighbourhood; site; house lot; and building. Theoretical perspectives range from functionalist, structuralist and behavioural/cognitive approaches to Marxist theory. Within these frameworks, scholars have explored spatial dimensions of change in environment and resource dependence, agricultural practice, town planning, material production, capitalist hierarchies and individual movement, especially as they reflect and structure issues of class, gender, race and ethnic identity.

The application of spatial analysis in historical archaeology is rooted in several disciplinary traditions including prehistoric archaeology, historical geography, cultural ecology and vernacular architecture. Early settlement studies in prehistoric archaeology sought out patterned use of space, particularly at the regional level, viewing these patterns as products of the interaction of environment and technology; they also utilised settlement data for making direct inferences about the social, political and religious organisation of prehistoric cultures. Initial studies of space by historical archaeologists owe some debt to early ideas on the settlement of frontier environments espoused by scholars such as historian Frederick Jackson Turner and geographer John C. Hudson.

Two landmark studies, one on regional settlement dynamics in north-east Missouri, USA, directed by Michael O'Brien, and the other a comprehensive treatment of frontier settlement in South Carolina by Kenneth Lewis, have had significant influences as models for the study of space. O'Brien's adaptive and environmentally oriented model draws on earlier work by Hudson on the patterning of rural settlement along with concepts from prehistorians' study of space, utilising detailed environmental analysis within an economic and sociocultural framework. Lewis framed his study of settlement in South Carolina around the colonial experience, developing a spatial model for analysing the processes of colonialism at the regional level. Looking at the interrelation of frontier and homeland, the development of transportation routes and technologies, the establishment of colonial entrepôts and the hierarchical arrangement of frontier towns and settlements, he suggests a diachronic, evolutionary approach to the examination of colonial space. Lewis demonstrated the dynamic nature of the colonial process, particularly in terms of its spatial implications, with the form, function and meaning of space changing across the region and through time.

Historical archaeologists have moved from the regional study of space to a consideration of more discrete units, such as towns, cities and neighbourhoods, often in association with the study of capitalism. Work in urban areas, notably **Annapolis**, Maryland, has explored a variety of issues relating space to social control. Scholars posit that elites crafted and manipulated town landscapes to define and enhance their social position, and, later, to create sanitised visions of the past. Investigations at the **Boott Mills** complex in Lowell, Massachusetts, have likewise focused on spatial modifications of the industrial landscape and the importance of these spatial realities in the negotiation of power relationships – worker, manager, owner – within a capitalist system. Working in New York City, Nan Rothschild has argued that scholars should examine the city at the neighbourhood level, a more manageable and socially cohesive unit, and has examined ways in which space and place figure in the construction and maintenance of class and ethnic identity.

The interdisciplinary study of vernacular architecture has also contributed to the ways in which historical archaeologists think about space, particularly at the site- or building-specific level. Beginning with folklorist Henry Glassie, these scholars have examined how people conceptualise, move through and use space within the house and surrounding landscape in order to better understand the structuring of class, gender and race relations. For example, cultural historian Dell Upton has argued that only by unfolding the multiple spatial relationships operating on tobacco plantations in the Chesapeake – the differing physical landscapes of planters and slaves – can we understand the dynamics of the master and slave relationship.

Historical archaeologists have also produced a body of scholarship, known as landscape archaeology, which draws on the work of these architectural historians. This approach grew out of early efforts to reconstruct historic gardens, but has since developed into a more generalised concern with larger spatial units termed historic landscapes. Drawing on a wide range of new techniques within environmental archaeology, scholars seek to address the manner in which these landscape units frame, shape and reflect social relations.

The long-term study of plantation systems within historical archaeology has also focused on space and spatial manipulation in terms of understanding power and power relationships. Charles Orser's work in South Carolina draws on Marxist theory and methodology to explore the use of space within a cotton plantation. Orser unwraps the hidden politics of space on this plantation during a critical period in its history, the transition away from the use of slave labour. He suggests that elites used space and spatial relations to craft and

negotiate new social orders that enabled them to retain control of both the land and production. Likewise, James Delle has investigated how British entrepreneurs manipulated space within the colonial plantation system in Jamaica. Delle finds that during periods of crisis within a capitalist system, elites reorganised the spaces of production, and thus the relations of production, in order to secure and maintain their dominant socioeconomic positions.

Finally, the addition of Geographic Information System (GIS) technology to historical archaeology's investigative tool kit has literally changed the way that archaeologists think about and analyse space. GIS has greatly improved the historical archaeologist's ability to describe, analyse, compare and manipulate multiple types of spatially distributed evidence, opening new opportunities for the analysis of space at all scales of study.

See also: vernacular architecture

Further reading

Delle, J.A. (1998) *An Archaeology of Social Space: Analyzing Coffee Plantations in Jamaica's Blue Mountains*, New York: Plenum.

Glassie, H. (1975) *Folk Housing in Middle Virginia: A Structural Analysis of Historic Artifacts*, Knoxville: University of Tennessee Press.

Lewis, K. (1984) *The American Frontier: An Archaeological Study of Settlement Pattern and Process*, New York: Academic Press.

O'Brien, M.J. (1984) *Grassland, Forest, and Historical Settlement: An Analysis of Dynamics in Northeast Missouri*, Lincoln: University of Nebraska Press.

Orser, C.E., Jr (1988) *The Material Basis of the Postbellum Tenant Plantation: Historical Archaeology in the South Carolina Piedmont*, Athens: University of Georgia Press.

Paynter, R. (1982) *Models of Spatial Inequality: Settlement Patterns in Historical Archaeology*, New York: Academic Press.

Upton, D. (1986) 'White and black landscapes in eighteenth-century Virginia', in R.B. St. George (ed.) *Material Life in America, 1600–1860*, Boston: Northeastern University Press, pp. 357–69.

DONALD W. LINEBAUGH

Spitalfields, England

Spitalfields lies about 400m north-east of the walled City of London, alongside the medieval road of Bishopsgate. At the end of the twelfth century, a new hospital, St Mary-without-Bishopsgate, commonly known as St Mary Spital, was founded there. It looked after the sick poor, pilgrims and women in childbirth with the additional aim of looking after the children, up to the age of seven of women who died in childbirth. After its refounding in 1235, it expanded to become the largest medieval hospital in London. It consisted of an infirmary some 60 m long split in two by the church. The infirmary was rebuilt in two storeys in *c.* 1280 when cloisters were built for the Augustinian canons. The sisters who looked after the sick had a timber house in the early years, replaced in stone between 1350 and 1400. The canons also had their own infirmary block, built in about 1400, consisting of an infirmary and a kitchen with a third room attached. The church was expanded in about 1400 when a new Lady Chapel was built at the east end and the south aisle was rebuilt. South of the church lay the cemetery where more than 10,000 skeletons have been excavated including priests buried with their communion set of chalice and paten, benefactors in tombs and with papal bullae, and the inmates of the hospital. Many thousands were buried in pits during a period of serious epidemic in around 1300. In the centre of the cemetery was a charnel house for the storage of bones disturbed in the cemetery and a pulpit for reading sermons at Easter.

In 1539, St Mary Spital was dissolved and the land was sold and became lived on by wealthy minor members of the aristocracy. The owner lived in the old cloister and rented out a fine new house with a gallery and rooms floored in tile and brick on the west side of the old cloister. Buildings on the south side of the old church, which had been demolished, were eventually turned into a fine new brick house for the later owner of the site, the Earl of Bolingbroke. New streets were laid and houses built within the former precincts of the monastery into the middle of the seventeenth century.

The southern part of the precincts was used as an artillery ground by the Gunners of the Tower and the Honourable Artillery Company. The Master Gunner of England had a very fine residence there and large quantities of shot and musket balls illustrate the artillery practice. At around the time of the English Civil War, a practice fort of star-shaped design was constructed in the Artillery Ground.

From the middle of the seventeenth century onwards, the former fields were encroached upon by new housing The artillery ground was sold for new houses in 1682 and Spitalfields Market was founded at around the same time. Many of the houses were inhabited by wealthy Huguenot weavers whose weaving establishments were often, but not always, in cheaper houses elsewhere.

CHRISTOPHER THOMAS

St Augustine, Florida, USA

St Augustine, Florida, is widely recognised for its unique place in history as the oldest continuously occupied city in the USA. The 'ancient city' is also known for having one of the most influential historical archaeology programmes in the country. This research has had an explicit focus on Hispanic colonisation patterns through the study of both the European and native populations associated with the community. Indeed, among the first historical archaeology investigations conducted in St Augustine in the 1930s was that of a historic-period Timucuan Indian cemetery believed to be associated with the mission of Nombre de Dios.

The colonial settlement was founded by Pedro Menéndez de Avilés in 1565 in response to growing concerns over foreign incursions into Spanish America, particularly the founding of France's Fort Caroline, near present-day Jacksonville. Except for the period between 1566 and 1587, when **Santa Elena** was pre-eminent, St Augustine served as the capital of Spanish Florida until 1763 when it was ceded to England under the terms of the Treaty of Paris. In 1784, it was returned to Spain and remained under Spanish control until it became a territory of the USA in 1821. The two distinct episodes of Spanish occupation are identified as the First Spanish (1565–1763) and Second Spanish (1784–1821) periods.

Although many archaeologists have worked in St Augustine through the years, Kathleen Deagan has made the most enduring contribution. Among the most innovative projects undertaken by Deagan was a comprehensive sub-surface investigation of St Augustine and its environs in order to delimit the sixteenth-century occupational area of the town. After testing a broad area with a mechanical soil auger, the excavated materials were analysed and their distribution was plotted. The density of sixteenth-century remains from the area south of the present town plaza suggested the location of the initial colonial settlement. This hypothesis was subsequently verified through excavations that revealed the remains were from habitations rather than secondary refuse. Demonstrated to be an efficient method of delineating occupational boundaries within an urban setting, broad-scale auger surveys have since been replicated on a number of other Spanish colonial sites with equal success.

The archaeological correlates of social variables have been examined through the investigation of eighteenth-century domestic sites for which income, occupation and **ethnicity** were documented. Deagan found a positive correlation between imported Spanish majolica (tin-glazed **earthenware**) and income, and a corresponding negative correlation with native pottery. Other imported materials were also found to have a positive relationship with income and demonstrated a strong relationship between economic status and material patterning. In St Augustine, it was not the types but rather the proportions of materials associated with Spanish dwellings that varied in accordance with status and ethnicity.

The study of ethnicity and **gender** dynamics have been crucial elements of historical archaeology in St Augustine since it was a common practice in the community for Spanish soldiers to marry Indian women. Native influence was most apparent in women's activities with low visibility, such as food procurement and preparation, while materials of European origin were often associated with highly visible male activities, including architecture and military duties. These findings reveal not only those areas where Spaniards incorporated indigenous elements into their lives, but they also underscore the importance of material goods as a means of reinforcing social identification.

Through detailed ceramic analysis, Deagan and her students have also been able to document the decline of the indigenous Timucua population and the influx of other native groups, particularly Guale Indians, into St Augustine. Specifically, the chalky St Johns pottery associated with the Timucuan Indians, which was dominant during the sixteenth century, was gradually supplanted by non-local types. Beginning in the seventeenth century, the most abundant native pottery in St Augustine was the sand- and grit-tempered San Marcos pottery associated with the Guale Indians of the Georgia and South Carolina coastal areas, with whom Spaniards increasingly intermarried.

The overall use of native pottery steadily increased through time in St Augustine, replacing non-majolica imported earthenwares. This is believed to reflect the increasing acceptance of aboriginal food preparation technology as the *criollo* culture evolved. Ethnobiologists studying food remains from St Augustine have corroborated these findings and found Spaniards to be highly resourceful with respect to diet. They readily adopted the indigenous mainstays of corn, beans and squash, introduced plants and animals from the Old World as well as other parts of Spanish America, and continued to import Mediterranean foodstuffs from Spain.

Historical archaeology in St Augustine is providing a social history for a number of groups who are by and large silent in written records. These include not only women and Indians, but also a significant African slave population who escaped from English plantations and found religious sanctuary among the Spaniards. Established in 1738, **Fort Mose** was the first legal free-black town and fort in the present-day USA. Located just two miles north of St Augustine proper, research at the site has added an important new component to our understanding of Spanish colonisation strategies in the Americas.

See also: Fort Mose; Santa Elena; Spanish colonialism

Further reading

Deagan, K. (1983) *Spanish St. Augustine: The*

Archaeology of a Colonial Creole Community, New York: Academic Press.
—— (1981) 'Downtown survey: The discovery of sixteenth-century St. Augustine in an urban area', *American Antiquity* 46: 626–34.
Deagan, K. and MacMahon, D. (1985) *Fort Mose: Colonial America's Black Fortress of Freedom*, Gainesville: University Press of Florida.
Reitz, E. and Scarry. C.M. (1985) *Reconstructing Historic Subsistence with an Example from Sixteenth-century Spanish Florida*, Tucson: Society for Historical Archaeology.

BONNIE G. McEWAN

St Eustatius, Netherlands Antilles

St Eustatius, often called Statia, is a small island (*c.* 8.2 mi^2) located in the northern Caribbean, a part of the Netherlands Antilles. It is the most southerly of the three Dutch Windward Islands group (Saba, St Maarten, St Eustatius). The island was formed by volcanic activity and has three major topographic zones: volcanic hills in the north-west, a large volcano in the south and an agricultural plain in the centre. The west or leeward side is the major anchorage area for ships because the Atlantic side is too rough. St Eustatius has a maritime savannah climate, and the main source of potable water is rainfall collected in cisterns.

The island has almost 300 known archaeological sites, recorded primarily since 1981. There has been little development relative to other Caribbean islands, protecting sites from destruction. No seventeenth-century sites have been located, although scattered artefactual evidence from this period has occasionally been found. Archaeological evidence of plantation housing for enslaved Africans is also lacking (see **plantation archaeology**). Plantations and farms, rural and urban domestic buildings, public buildings, commercial buildings such as warehouses, religious buildings (e.g. synagogues), cemeteries and military **fortifications** are general categories of historic sites located on St Eustatius.

Historical archaeology of St Eustatius is considered to be part of **Caribbean archaeology**. Research topics include plantation sites, **trade**, **slavery** and **colonialism**. A study of Yabba ware ceramics by Barbara Heath found that enslaved Africans on St Eustatius were probably making their own pottery vessels for food preparation and consumption, and other uses.

Although archaeologically known from the Golden Rock site, the native population of the island was not present at the time of Spanish exploration (1493) or the island's initial settlement in 1629. Because of its location, ownership of St Eustatius was violently contested by the Dutch, French and English, changing ownership twenty-two times between 1636 and 1816.

Plantation agriculture was established on St Eustatius by the French in the seventeenth century. Tobacco, cotton, **coffee**, indigo and **sugar** were grown. The island's main economic role as a supplier of European goods and enslaved Africans developed in the seventeenth century. During the American Revolution, the North American trade became very important, with American rebels purchasing arms and ammunition on St Eustatius. The nineteenth century saw the island enter a period of economic and demographic decline.

See also: colonoware pottery

Further reading

Barka, N. (2001) 'Time-lines: Changing settlement patterns on St. Eustatius', in Paul Farnsworth (ed.) *Island Lives: Historical Archaeologies of the Caribbean*, Tuscaloosa: University of Alabama Press, pp. 115–54.
—— (1996) 'Citizens of St. Eustatius 1781: A historical and archaeological study', in R. Paquette and S. Engerman (eds) *The Lesser Antilles in the Age of European Expansion*, Gainesville: University Press of Florida, pp. 223–38.
Heath, B. (1999) 'Yabbas, monkeys, jugs, and jars: An historical context for African-Caribbean pottery on St. Eustatius', in J. Haviser (ed.) *African Sites Archaeology in the Caribbean*, Princeton, Jamaica: Markus Wiener, pp. 196–220.

DAVID T. PALMER

St Mary's City, Maryland, USA

St Mary's City, Maryland, was founded in 1634 by English Roman Catholics seeking the freedom to practise their religion. The idea for the settlement developed in the late 1620s, after George Calvert, Baron of Baltimore, had established his first colony, at **Ferryland**, Newfoundland. Calvert found the weather there too harsh, and began to search for a more southern location for his colony. The Maryland location was chosen, but Calvert died two years before the founding of St Mary's City.

The settlement at St Mary's City was the first European settlement of Maryland and it was the colony's capital from its founding until 1695. At that date, the capital was moved to **Annapolis**, and St Mary's City was eventually abandoned and slowly converted into agricultural land. The State of Maryland created the St Mary's City Restoration Study Commission in 1965, and, after several adjustments of its administration, created the Historic St Mary's City Commission in 1991. St Mary's City has maintained an active and highly successful archaeological programme since 1971.

The archaeologists of St Mary's City have identified over 300 sites within the limits of St Mary's City National Landmark, and they maintain one of the longest operating archaeological field schools in the USA. Excavations at numerous sites have vastly improved our current knowledge of colonial-era **architecture** and **material culture**, and a single excavation project can provide a wealth of new information. For example, excavations at Smith's Townland, a 1 ha tract leased to William Smith in 1666, has revealed the possible location of John Morecroft's house (dating to 1667), an African-American slave cabin (dating to the 1840s) and a pit filled with oyster shells and containing over thirty pieces of moveable type, possibly from William Nuthead's printing press (dating to 1685).

One of the most publicised projects of the St Mary's City archaeologists involved the excavation of three lead coffins buried in the north transept of the Brick Chapel. After the archaeologists had exposed the entire foundation of the chapel in 1990, they used ground-penetrating radar to investigate its floor. Readings from this **remote-sensing** tool indicated a sub-surface disturbance and this is where the archaeologists found the lead

coffins, the first to be investigated in the USA. In 1992, the archaeologists – assisted by a highly trained team equipped with the most sophisticated technology available – began to uncover the coffins. They used special X-ray film, a fibre optics borescope and pumped chilled argon gas into the coffins to help preserve the remains inside. Inside the coffins they found a man, a woman and a child. After careful research and using a process of elimination, the archaeologists decided that the male was Philip Calvert, Chancellor of the colony and the youngest son of George Calvert, and that the woman was Anne Wolsey Calvert, Philip Calvert's first wife. The identity of the child is not known.

See also: Chesapeake region; English colonialism

Further reading

King, J.A. and Chaney, E.E. (1999) 'Lord Baltimore and the meaning of brick architecture in seventeenth-century Maryland', in G. Egan and R.L. Michael (eds) *Old and New Worlds*, Oxford: Oxbow, pp. 51–60.

Miller, H.M. (1999) 'Archaeology and town planning in early British America', in G. Egan and R.L. Michael (eds) *Old and New Worlds*, Oxford: Oxbow, pp. 72–83.

—— (1994) 'The country's house site: An archaeological study of a seventeenth-century domestic landscape', in P.A. Shackel and B.J. Little (eds) *Historical Archaeology of the Chesapeake*, Washington, DC: Smithsonian Institution Press, pp. 65–83.

CHARLES E. ORSER, JR

Stoke-on-Trent, England

Stoke-on-Trent in north Staffordshire, England, is the centre of the British ceramics industry, and is still known today as 'the Potteries'. The modern city is a confederation of six towns, Stoke-upon-Trent, Longton, Hanley, Fenton, Burslem and Tunstall, all of which have a long history of pottery making.

The area owes its industrial development to its natural resources, especially coal and clay. In the north Staffordshire coalfield, coals of varying qualities occur naturally alongside a range of clay types. As well as clays ideal for the making of pottery, there are marls suitable for the manufacture of bricks and tiles, and refractory clays for firebrick.

Pottery has been made in the area since the fourteenth century, growing in scale during the fifteenth and sixteenth centuries, and serving a regional market. By the late seventeenth century, around fifty pottery workshops were producing good-quality slipwares, blackwares, mottled wares, butter pots and brown salt-glazed stonewares. Such wares, through a combination of low price and good quality, came to dominate the coarseware sector of the home market and began to make an impact upon ceramic consumption in the colonies.

The Staffordshire pottery industry was transformed in the years around 1720. Traditional wares using local clays were superseded by new refined earthenwares and stonewares. These involved new production techniques and a reliance upon imported white-firing clays, not available in significant quantities in north Staffordshire. Tea (see **tea/tea ceremony**), **coffee** and tablewares now became the industry's staple products, catering for an expanding middle-class market at home and abroad.

The growing industry was supported by a network of retailers, merchants and carriers who made possible its expansion into continental European, Caribbean (see **Caribbean archaeology**) and North American markets long before the trade was made easier by the opening of the Trent and Mersey canal in 1777. This 93-mile long canal, sponsored by the leading pottery manufacturers, connected the land-locked north Staffordshire towns with the rivers Trent and Mersey, thereby giving access to the North Sea and Europe through the port of Hull, and to the Atlantic through Liverpool.

By the late eighteenth century, pottery from almost 200 Staffordshire factories was coming to dominate the world ceramics market, with **creamware** replacing Chinese porcelains (see **porcelain**) as the tableware of choice in many homes. By 1835, North America overtook Europe as the main market for Staffordshire ceramics, a position that it has retained.

The influence of Stoke-on-Trent upon world ceramics has been considerable. Staffordshire potters have worked in many countries, taking with them manufacturing methods and transmitting styles through the movement of moulds and engraved copper plates. Today, the industry remains dominant in the supply of raw materials and specialist equipment.

See also: creamware; pearlware

Further reading

Greenslade, M.W. and Jenkins, J.G. (eds) (1967) *A History of the County of Stafford*, Oxford: Oxford University Press.

Hawke-Smith, C.F. (1986) *The Making of the Six Towns*, Stoke-on-Trent: City Museum and Art Gallery.

Jenkins, J.G. (ed.) (1963) *A History of the County of Stafford*, Oxford: Oxford University Press.

Weatherill, L. (1971) *The Pottery Trade and North Staffordshire 1660–1760*, Manchester: Manchester University Press.

DAVID BARKER

stoneware

Stoneware is a sophisticated type of ceramic product (see **ceramics**) produced by forcing clay into a specific form, then heating it to its maturation point. At this point, the clay undergoes an irreversible transformation into ceramic. This ceramic is important to historical archaeologists because some stoneware artefacts are highly diagnostic, dateable, and nearly indestructible. Ceramics are often broken and discarded, but preserve over long periods. In addition, stoneware artefacts are usually mundane fragments of everyday life.

Stoneware clays form as feldspathic rock decays. When the clay is deposited at the parent rock, it is a pure, primary clay. Secondary clays collect when they fall out of very still or slow moving bodies of water. The most pure secondary clays are formed in stable marine environments. These deposits become useful when the sea floor is thrust upward and the stratum of pure clay is exposed. When subjected to pressure, clays form into shales. Shale can be used to make stoneware.

Clay is transformed into ceramic by vitrification, where the individual mineral particles begin to melt and become glasslike. Potters also refer to vitrification as 'maturation'. Various clays have different maturation temperatures, which yield different ceramics. Variations in the mineral content of the clay produce these properties. The divisions are summarised below in Table 1.

Table 1 Maturation temperatures of ceramics

Ceramic type	Firing temperature
Terracotta	Below 900°C
Earthenware	900°C–1,200°C
Stoneware	1,200°C–1,350°C
Porcelain	Above 1,300°C

If a clay is heated beyond the point at which it begins to vitrify, the fabric becomes a liquid and the vessel collapses (also called 'slumping'). **Earthenware** clays have a very low vitrification point, and thus they cannot be heated to the same degree as stoneware and **porcelain** clays. Potters add flux and temper to raise or lower the temperature point at which clay begins to vitrify or starts to slump.

Stoneware was developed in **China** during the first century AD, and the technology spread outward. Besides preparing the clay properly, stoneware potters must know how to construct a kiln in which they can fire, maintain and control the sufficient temperature for vitrification. This ceramic was one of the basic pieces of Khmer material culture in Thailand by AD 900. Stoneware technology was established in Germany and France by the twelfth century AD.

Earthenwares remain porous after firing, since the fabric still consists of particulate clays partly vitrified and temper particles. Both stoneware and porcelain clays are totally vitrified during firing. The individual clay particles meld together, creating a glassy and homogeneous fabric. In modern China, potters call this non-porous fabric *Tz'u t'ai*, which includes both stoneware and porcelain. *Tz'u t'ai* excludes earthenwares, which are *Sha t'ai*

('sandy paste'). The chemical purity of porcelain clays produces a translucent fabric, unlike the opaque matrix of stonewares.

Stoneware's vitrified fabric does not require glaze in order to retain liquids. Most vessels were glazed, however, and stoneware fabric will take a metal glaze (such as lead or tin), an alkali glaze (made with wood ash) or a salt glaze (either by direct application or in vapour). A dark brown coating, called Albany Slip, is also common on stoneware made in the USA.

Salt-glazing was invented in Germany in the twelfth century. This technique made stoneware a more competitive product. Lead glazes required pottery to undergo an initial firing to produce a bisque state, then expensive raw materials were applied and additional fuel consumed in a second firing to vitrify the glaze. In addition, lead glazes were known by the sixteenth century to cause illness. The sodium in a salt glaze acts as a flux, which combines with the silica or alumina in the clay fabric to form a glaze that is a part of the ceramic. Since the clay forms into its own glaze, the finish never crazes or flakes like a metal glaze. When salt is introduced in the kiln at temperatures higher than 1,300°C, it vaporises and condenses on all exposed clay surfaces, creating an 'orange-peel' effect. This glaze can be completed in the initial firing, and is inexpensive.

Several regions produced stoneware for distribution in the global economy. Many potteries in China produced stoneware for domestic use and export. Utilitarian brown stoneware is found in most nineteenth-century contexts associated with overseas Chinese populations (see **overseas Chinese historical archaeology**). Both the Rhineland and Westerwald regions of Germany produced salt-glazed wares that were important in the seventeenth and eighteenth centuries. English potteries in Staffordshire reached their peak of salt-glazed stoneware production in the eighteenth century, manufacturing white-bodied, salt-glazed tablewares.

Most stoneware was utilitarian in design: jugs, jars, crocks, plumbing pipe and architectural elements. These are the mundane objects associated with the activities of everyday life, food preparation and storage, sanitation and hygiene, and landscapes and gardens. As such, stonewares were more resistant to the fluctuations of fashion, and the traditions display tremendous continuity through time.

The stoneware potteries were on the cutting edge of the Industrial Revolution, with new manufacturing technologies, increased capitalisation, specialised labour and wage structures, and professionalised management. In addition, many operated sophisticated systems of distribution over the Atlantic and Pacific economies. Stoneware was also a principal medium of the Arts and Crafts and other aesthetic movements opposed to the industrialisation of handicrafts. Even in the late nineteenth and twentieth centuries, amid fully industrialised factories, workers produced folk art and craft-style ceramic objects. Workers in the Grand Ledge Pottery Factory in Michigan, USA, and the Brantford Pottery in Ontario, Canada, sculpted animals and vases for firing along with sewer pipe.

See also: creamware; ironstone

Further reading

Dewhurst, C. (1983) *Grand Ledge Folk Pottery: Traditions at Work*, Ann Arbor: UMI Research Press.

Hillier, B. (1968) *Pottery and Porcelain, 1700–1914, England, Europe, and North America*, New York: Meredith Press.

Ketchum, W.C. (1991) *American Stoneware*, New York: Henry Holt.

Noël Hume, I. (1969) *A Guide to the Artefacts of Colonial America*, New York: Alfred A. Knopf.

Shepard, A.O. (1968) *Ceramics for the Archaeologist*, Washington, DC: The Carnegie Institute of Washington.

TIMOTHY JAMES SCARLETT

stratification, social

Social stratification can be thought of as social inequality that has become 'hardened' or institutionalised within a society. In general, there are two primary schools of thought concerning the nature and origins of social stratification. One views social stratification as based in conflict, either rooted in exploitation or competition within a society. The other, the integrationist view, maintains that stratification is a social mechanism for maintaining order and integration within a society. Archaeologists can uncover these various forms of social stratification when they study, in various contexts, power relations, the development of **capitalism**, **ethnicity** and **race**.

The most immediate conception of social stratification is class stratification explained by Karl Marx and Max Weber. Marx and Weber both fall within a paradigm that considers social stratification to be rooted in social conflict. For Marx, this conflict developed in the differentiation of two classes based on access to economic power, and the exploitation of the working class by the wealthy class of capitalists who own the means of production. In this materialist-historical perspective, economic inequality resulting from relations of production existing in all societies is the root of all class conflict. Societal change occurs when the subordinate class realises its own interests or develops class consciousness, and takes emancipatory action. The development of class consciousness, then, was the goal of the social sciences in the Marxist and neo-Marxist view. In contrast, Weber saw stratification as a product of competition and self-interest in all levels of society. He believed in limited class mobility, and described mechanisms of exclusion and appropriation, by which stratified social groups sought to exclude others and usurp social power from those above them. For Weber, the development of bureaucratic government institutions was vital and necessary in order to curb humankind's natural proclivity to selfishness and competition. As such, domination and social stratification are seen to be inevitable. For this school of thought, the objective of social scientists is to understand human nature and to discover how society can be best treated and managed.

Émile Durkheim's functionalist theory did not thoroughly treat the subjects of inequality and social stratification, although his work was highly influential in archaeology from the 1950s through the 1970s. Durkheim viewed social structures – like class – as necessary in maintaining 'organic solidarity', the smooth functioning society and the management of conflict and other negative influences. A functional position states a structured stratification exists as a necessary institution promoting social order and preventing constant struggle and conflicts. Class conflict is seen as a pathological condition that disrupts a system's equilibrium. The social scientists must study the entire social system and the mechanisms of social control that allow the society to maintain moral integration.

Historical archaeologists have viewed social stratification by using the core–periphery model. The core–periphery model is based on economic (and sociopolitical) domination of outlying areas by central places. The power of the core(s) lies in the ability to control transportation and centralisation of resources, and thereby gain access to resources that is greater and more efficient than that of the peripheries. Because the frontier is peripheral to an economic core, studies of frontiers are a specific subset of core–periphery relationships. Archaeological studies that look at colonisation, frontier farms and plantations all involve the ability of one group to control the resources of another. Robert Paynter's use of the core–periphery model examines the changing role of the USA in a British world system. He traces the Connecticut River Valley's change from periphery in the British system to core of its own national system. Industrialisation of the region was one major factor in its development. By examining the growth of the city of Alexandria, Virginia, in a city-wide context, Pam Cressey and others reveal the differentiation of, and the changing relationships between, core and peripheral economic and social areas within the city. There is an ethnic dimension as well since many of the oppositions are between white and black as well as between rich and poor.

Kathleen Deagan's work on the development of sixteenth- and seventeenth-century **St Augustine** involves the settlement and organisation of a pre-industrial city in a frontier situation. Questions of subsistence, Indian relations, ethnicity, status and settlement hierarchy are complexly interwoven to understand the development of social stratification in this Spanish colony. For instance, Deagan found that Spanish ethnicity among high-status groups, such as the Spanish-born *peninsulares*, is most visible in the public areas. Places that contained lower-status groups, such as *criollos* and *mestizos*, tend to

have a mix of Spanish and other European artefacts.

Randall McGuire's work on the nineteenth-century south-west shows how archaeology can define changing ethnic relationships between Mexican Americans and Anglo-Americans in southern Arizona. In the mid-nineteenth century, both groups appeared assimilated and dependent upon each other. As the Anglos increased their power and access to eastern capital with the introduction of the railroad, the apparent symbiotic existence disappeared and the Anglos became the dominant culture.

Charles Orser describes the power relations created by size and spatial arrangement of plantation housing in a postbellum tenant plantation. Political and economic power, and the inhabitants' tenure correlates with housing size. Distance between buildings may also reflect each resident's relationship to the means of production. Terrence Epperson notes that power relations on plantations were not accomplished by imposing force, but rather the planter used other strategies of control like imposing Euro-American cultural ideals, such as foods (see **food and foodways**), **architecture** and landscape.

Archaeologists need to be sensitive when looking for forms of **domination**, and searching for material manifestations of how African Americans resisted the dominant culture. Some ethnicity studies in historical archaeology identify material symbols of a specific group, while other studies explore the dynamic relationships between ethnic groups and the dominant culture. For instance, Paul Mullins's analysis of consumer choice of African Americans in **Annapolis**, Maryland, shows that material goods found at African American sites reflect their aspiration to achieve civil and consumer citizenship. The use of 'white' **material culture**, such as **ceramics** and table place settings, allowed African Americans to assume the same rights to the goods granted whites. The Annapolis African American assemblages do not represent typical Victorian place settings. They had stylistic disorder and age, while they had very similar functional categories, such as teawares (see **tea/tea ceremony**), when compared with a relatively wealthy white family. The households did not aspire to white dictated styles or project the appearance of assimilation. Most families had a finer set of china and distinctive dining rules reserved for entertaining outsiders.

Consideration of the 'ethnic processes' forces the realisation that there is a great deal of variability within the creation and maintenance of ethnic groups. Group structure and history vary according to cultural context, and economic, political, social and religious circumstances. **Ethnicity**, like ethnic groups themselves, is a changing construct. However, some understandings seem clear. Generally, competition for resources and differential power may encourage either ascription of identity by outsiders or self-determination of group membership or both. Although ethnicity and race are not equivalent, most historical archaeologists have relied upon theoretical treatments of ethnicity for both ethnic groups and racial groups.

Historical archaeologists have also examined social stratification on the industrial landscape. The archaeology at Lowell, Massachusetts, shows how industrial landscapes create and reinforce a hierarchy of power and control over the new industrial town. Stephen Mrozowski and Mary Beaudry explore how the 'mill girls' at Lowell resided in boarding houses that were uniform in size and shape. They were also much smaller than the accommodations allotted the managers. The supervisors' housing, while larger, was also separated from the workers' accommodations. The mills stood within close distance of the living accommodations and could be easily viewed. This architecture, clearly a statement of **power** and stratification, created and reinforced a social hierarchy within a community.

Harpers Ferry, West Virginia, originally developed as a craft town. Workers controlled their means of production. Paul Shackel notes that with the development of the craft industry there was no uniform architectural style. Workers initially designed and built their own houses on government property and the government constructed factories when and where needed. In the 1840s, the armoury underwent major revisions in its labour practices. New rules and regulations reinforced factory discipline. Most of the armoury buildings were unsuited for the implementation of a division of labour, as they lacked architectural and functional unity. The armoury superintendent imposed a grid over the existing town plan and rebuilt the factories so that they had a uniform appearance. The armoury also took control over the workers' housing, enforcing standardised housing facilities. Supervisors had their houses placed on hills overlooking the factories, or they were the largest domestic structures adjacent to the armoury grounds. The threat of surveillance now threatened the workers' freedom. Clearly, a new hierarchy on the landscape helped to reinforce the new wage labour system and the social stratification within the town.

In these industrial landscape cases related to social stratification, it is important to recognise how we see social stratification on the built environment. It is also important to see how people reacted to these inequities. For instance, Robert Paynter (1989) provides an important overview of numerous examples of inequality and **resistance** in various historic and urban contexts. In one case, Michael Nassaney and Marjorie Abel look at the John Russell Cutlery Company in the Connecticut River Valley and describe discontent over the new factor system. They found a large quantity of artefacts related to interchangeable manufacturing along the river bank near the former cutting room and trip hammer shop. These discarded materials consisted of inferior or imperfect manufactured parts. While these workers laboured in a modern factory, Nassaney and Abel suggest that the discarded materials may be a form of defiance against the implementation of the new system. Shackel provides some insight into alternative interpretations and claims that workers' resistance may have been responsible for the creation of anomalies in artefact patterns in the domestic assemblage. He also noticed that a large proportion of industrial-related items found at brewery workers' residences, as well as several cases of arson in a small town brewery, may correspond to workers' discontent over 12–16-hour work days and poor working conditions.

In summary, contemporary views on social stratification maintain that there can be multiple bases or planes of stratification, and that members of a society must navigate many or all of these planes depending on their social situation. Stratification is also subjective. While it is rooted in concrete material conditions, it also depends in large part on the perceptions of those inside and outside of particular social groups. Groups must have, and their members must recognise, criteria for determining and signalling group inclusion and exclusion. Finally, social stratification must be maintained; part of this maintenance is the constant legitimation of some individuals' differential access to social, economic or political power through existing educational structures, the mass media and other opinion-influencing agencies. All of these aspects can be approached through archaeological research that is sensitive to the subjectivities of class, race, gender and ethnicity, and there are many elements of stratification that have yet to be approached by historical archaeologists.

Further reading

Durkheim, É. (1964) *The Division of Labor in Society*, New York: Free Press.

Marx, K. (1973) *Capital*, New York: International Publishers.

Mrozowski, S.A., Ziesing, G.H. and Beaudry, M.C. (1996) *Living on the Boott: Historical Archaeology at the Boott Mills Boardinghouses, Lowell, Massachusetts*, Amherst: University of Massachusetts Press.

Mullins, P.R. (1999) *Race and Affluence: An Archaeology of African America and Consumer Culture*, New York: Kluwer Academic/Plenum Publishers.

Paynter, R. (1989) 'The archaeology of equality and inequality', *Annual Review of Anthropology* 18: 369–99.

Shackel, P.A. (1996) *Culture Change and the New Technology: An Archaeology of the Early American Industrial Era*, New York: Plenum Press.

Weber, M. (1978) 'Class, status, party', in *Economy and Society*, vol. 2, Berkeley: University of California Press, pp. 927–39.

PAUL A. SHACKEL AND MATTHEW PALUS

stratification, soil

Archaeological sites are composed of stratification, which is the formation through time of layers of soil, walls, postholes and other forms of stratigraphic units into a physical mass, which is buried, above ground or both. Archaeological stratigraphy is the science by which stratification is unravelled and every unit is placed in its correct position in a sequence of relative time. Such stratigraphic sequences can be illustrated in a universal manner by the use of the **Harris matrix**.

As stratification is an incidental by-product of living, it is an unbiased record of the past and therein lies its supreme value to archaeological studies. Stratification is the essence of archaeology and its sequences are the unbiased testing patterns against which all archaeological research from excavations must be tested. Laws of stratification control its study and its units are placed in a relative time, or stratigraphic, sequence by answering the fundamental question of which unit of a given two was created first. Stratigraphic sequences are recovered by careful stratigraphic excavation and recorded by attention to the two forms of stratification, the deposit unit and the interface unit, documented respectively in section drawings and in topographical plans. The study of artefact content from deposit units determines the relationships of the stratigraphic sequences to absolute, or calendar, time.

The most important stratigraphic law is the Law of Superposition, which states generally that of any two stratigraphic units, that which is underneath was made first. The physical disposition of the units of stratification is the evidence by which, through the application of stratigraphic laws, those units may be placed in position relative to each other in time, and thus the development of the site may be recreated on paper. Created over a period of absolute time, the stratigraphic sequence on the site is first and foremost understood in terms of relative time. Absolute time is seen by means of a calendar and relative time sequences are illustrated in Harris matrix diagrams.

The physical disposition of stratification can only be properly recovered by stratigraphic excavation. That method was developed intensively in the 1960s, primarily in the context of historical archaeology, and it was revolutionised by the invention of the Harris matrix in 1973. Stratigraphic excavation means that units of stratification are removed in the reverse order to that in which they were created, so that the latest, or youngest, units on a site are recorded and excavated before those that preceded them. Stratigraphic excavation means that units must be excavated and recorded by their shapes as found and that they should not be removed by arbitrary levels of a given thickness. Such arbitrary excavation makes it impossible to recover the unbiased stratigraphic sequence, as it destroys the original physical dimensions of the units upon which sequential determinations rely completely.

There are two types of stratigraphic unit, one having mass or a physical presence, and the other being the surface of the mass or a surface in its own right, such as a ditch. The first are generically called layers or contexts; the latter are features or interfaces. The first can be excavated; the second can only be recorded. The units of mass are illustrated in section drawings. The line, or interfacial, units appear in sections but can only be fully documented by contour plans. The mass deposits represent the disuse periods on a site, while the interfacial units are the periods of its use. The last usually represent greater periods of elapsed time than the periods of deposit. The concepts of disuse and use represent the duality of archaeological stratification and they are reflected in sections through stratification and by the successive surfaces of the site, which people used in the course of daily living. Stratigraphic excavation and recording recover the physical dimensions of a site (sections/depth; plans/area) as well as evidence for the relative time of the stratigraphic sequence (Harris matrix/time).

The duality of stratification is further reflected in the disposition of portable artefacts. Surfaces, having no mass, contain no artefacts; these are found in the deposits below the surfaces. Having determined the stratigraphic sequence in relative time, the archaeologist will use artefacts found in the deposits to assign absolute dates to the units of that sequence. This is a difficult task, as artefacts, unlike units of stratification, can be moved and deposited without losing their original integrity. Artefacts cannot be taken at face value, as some may be residual in the ground; that is to say, they may have been contemporary with an earlier deposit, which was destroyed to make the one in which they were found. They may be contaminated, or later than the creation of the deposit, having been introduced into it by a later activity that cannot be observed in the stratification.

After testing the artefacts against the stratigraphic sequence, the archaeologist may determine which are contemporary, more or less, with the creation in absolute time of the deposit in which they were discovered. By such a contemporary status, artefacts may give a date after which (*terminus post quem*) the deposit was formed and also a date before which its formation ceased (*terminus ante quem*).

Once the artefact dating is completed, the data are applied to the stratigraphic units, which may be grouped thereby into phases and periods of site development. Contour and surface plans are then drawn to reflect the revised chronological arrangements, and the evolution of the site through absolute time can thereby be recreated. The advent in the 1990s of geographic information systems for computerised mapping made the easy production of such plans universally possible and represents a major revolution in stratigraphic studies.

See also: dating methods

Further reading

Harris, E.C. (1989) *Principles of Archaeological Stratigraphy*, London: Academic Press.
Harris, E.C., Brown, M.B., III and Brown, G.J. (eds) (1993) *Practices of Archaeological Stratigraphy*, London: Academic Press.

EDWARD CECIL HARRIS

sugar

Sugar was the most significant tropical commodity produced in the Caribbean (see **Caribbean archaeology**) with enslaved African labour; rum and molasses are important by-products. Sugar was introduced into the Caribbean as early as the first quarter of the sixteenth century, becoming the dominant crop by the early eighteenth century. By far the vast majority of enslaved Africans transported to the New World were brought to labour on sugar plantations in the Caribbean, mainland **South America** (particularly **Brazil**) and later the Gulf Coast of North America. The political landscapes of sugar plantations generally included great houses inhabited by plantation owners, overseers' houses, industrial works to process sugar cane into a transportable form and slave quarters. Much of Caribbean archaeology has focused on excavating the industrial works and slave quarters associated with sugar plantations.

Further reading

Mintz, S. (1985) *Sweetness and Power: The Place of Sugar in Modern History*, New York: Viking.

JAMES A. DELLE

surface collecting

Surface collecting is a surveying method that archaeologists sometimes use to find sites. The method simply involves the inspection of the ground for artefacts and other evidence of past human habitation. In some cases, past men and women may have left artefacts directly on the ground surface and they may never have been buried; in other cases, the artefacts will have been buried but have worked their way to the surface through a number of processes. In the case of buried sites, archaeologists will use the objects found on the surface to infer what may lie underneath.

As is true of all methods of archaeological **sampling**, many ways exist to conduct surface collecting. Archaeologists can walk along linear transects and simply examine the ground within their view, or they can select square 'quadrats' from a grid and then examine the ground in these defined areas. Archaeologists engaged in **cultural-resource management** projects often use surface collecting because it is cost effective and relatively rapid to perform. In addition, many of the projects on which they work involve the scraping of the topsoil, in effect leaving a new surface ready for inspection. Cultural-resource management archaeologists usually employ a probabilistic sampling design intended to provide statistically useful information. Many avocational archaeologists also rely on surface collecting to locate sites and artefacts, but their surveys are

usually non-probabilistic, meaning that they use their prior knowledge and experience to decide exactly where to look for artefacts. Their samples would not be available for statistical analysis.

Surface-collecting surveys are best conducted where the ground has recently been ploughed or where a large area has been disturbed, such as for the grading for a new road bed. In other locations, such as pastures or grassy yards, no surface indications of what lies underneath may be obvious and so surface collecting is not possible. For this reason, archaeologists do not always use surface collecting and they must rely on other **remote-sensing** methods.

Surface collecting is not always the best way to determine the nature and extent of buried archaeological sites. To use it effectively to infer what is buried, an archaeologist must be completely conversant with the 'site formation processes' at work in the area. Site formation processes, as defined by Michael Schiffer, consist of all the cultural and natural processes that can affect archaeological sites during and after their occupation. For example, a surface collection of artefacts from an area known to have suffered repeated, serious flooding would probably not provide any useful information about sites buried in the immediate area because the artefacts could have been transported great distances by the water. Similarly, animals can carry and displace artefacts, and frost can change the distribution of objects as well. Humans in the past can also affect what future archaeologists may locate on the ground surface. Non-archaeologists can remove artefacts selectively from sites they discover, leaving an inaccurate view of the remains underneath. Residents of modern houses can move old 'trash' away from their homes, thereby upsetting the integrity of any future surface collection.

See also: destruction, site

Further reading

Hester, T.R., Shafer, H.J. and Feder, K.L. (1997) *Field Methods in Archaeology*, seventh edn, Mountain View: Mayfield.

Schiffer, M.B. (1987) *Formation Processes of the*

Archaeological Record, Albuquerque: University of New Mexico Press.

CHARLES E. ORSER, JR

Sydney, Australia

As the first site of European settlement in Australia following the arrival of the First Fleet in 1788, intensive historical archaeological investigation of early Sydney since the 1970s has addressed issues such as the city's development, exchange between colonists and Aboriginal people, the experience of convicts and other emigrant groups, and the emergence of a distinctive local identity. Historical archaeology was first taught in Australia from 1974 at the University of Sydney, initiating investigation of the colony's past at sites such as the Old Sydney Burial Ground, Hyde Park (convict) Barracks and Old Sydney Gaol. The first major project to capture public attention was the 1983 excavation of the site of **First Government House**, establishing the public value of colonial archaeological heritage.

The New South Wales Heritage Act (1977) integrated historical archaeology into the planning framework, facilitating the development of a substantial archaeological community. Separate legislation has governed Aboriginal archaeology, producing a research dichotomy. However, in the political context of reconciliation, since the mid-1990s, this has been addressed by an emerging interest in evidence for Aboriginal life in Sydney before and after colonisation. Sites such as Moore's Wharf in Millers Point and Angel Place, on the former Tank Stream, which fed Sydney Cove, possibly indicate coexistence.

Investigation of earliest settlement by whites has revealed the rapid degradation of the environment, indicated for example by extreme soil erosion and the disappearance of local oyster beds due to water pollution. By the 1820s, specialised districts had emerged, and archaeological evidence reveals very different experiences of settlers, contrasting the elite circumstances of the Governor at First Government House, the comfortable if makeshift dwellings of aspiring ex-convicts in the **Rocks**, the resistance to control expressed by convicts at Hyde Park Barracks, the prosperity of the emancipist Hill family in Pitt Street, the town's south, and the attempts at respectability of 'currency' (Australian-born) laundress Catherine Lindsay, who established a household in the dairying and manufacturing outskirts of the Brickfields.

In the city's west, investigation of convict huts at the colony's agricultural settlement at Parramatta, established by 1789, has revealed their meagre material circumstances. Parramatta Park, run by the National Parks and Wildlife Service, conserves the former 'Government Domain', a rich cultural landscape containing Old Government House and associated remains of the farming settlement, including a dairying precinct and evidence for early cultivation.

Local industrial development and its social consequences during the nineteenth and early twentieth centuries has been explored through sites such as Paddy's Market in Darling Harbour, the Grace Brothers site and University Hall in Glebe, and the Central Sugar Refinery Site in Pyrmont. Public interest in Sydney's archaeological heritage plays an important role in urban planning, as demonstrated by the 1998 campaign to preserve the Conservatorium of Music site, once within the First Government House grounds.

Further reading

Connah, G. (1988) *The Archaeology of Australia's History*, Cambridge: Cambridge University Press.
Museum of Sydney (1996) *Sites – Nailing the Debate: Archaeology and Interpretation in Museums*, Sydney: Historic Houses Trust of New South Wales.

JANE LYDON

T

Tasmania, Australia

Named Van Diemen's Land until 1855, Tasmania, the second Australian colony, was founded in 1803 to protect British territorial interests in the Southern Ocean, and to accommodate rising numbers of transported British felons. The island colony renamed itself Tasmania to discourage association with its infamous 'convict stain' after cessation of British transportation in 1854. Emphasising its new economic base in primary extraction and agricultural industries, Tasmania recast itself as a quiet, rural and dignified outpost of British culture.

This self-consciously reconstructed identity has patterned the development of historical archaeology within Tasmania. Funded through a combination of industry and government grants, the vast majority of Tasmanian work has focused on sites related to rural, industrial or convict heritage. Since the late 1970s, Tasmanian historical archaeology has evolved as a speciality field within four types of cultural-heritage management projects.

First, regional surveys have been completed for numerous urban districts, most notably Hobart, Launceston, Sorrell, Strahan, Glenorchy and Clarence. As urban planning documents, these reports emphasised architectural and historic resources associated with early colonial settlement. However, they also include sub-surface archaeological zoning plans to guide future development projects.

Tasmanian rural and industrial heritage surveys have incorporated historical archaeology on a more explicit level. During the 1990s, Parks and Wildlife Service projects identified traditional recreational and pastoral uses of the Central Plateau region, and surveyed sites associated with the nineteenth-century hops, sealing and whaling industries. Regional historic site inventories have also been completed for Tasmanian forested areas. Co-ordinated through the Forestry Commission, this research has examined archaeological places associated with the timber, mining and pastoral industries. Finally, the Queen Victoria Museum and Art Gallery commissioned a multi-volume report on places related to the apple industry, one of Tasmania's original horticultural industries.

Thematic research in Tasmanian historical archaeology has occurred through both academic and management-oriented projects. Since the mid-1970s, a large corpus of archaeological research has studied British convict sites and penal settlements. Although the majority of this work focused on Port Arthur and the surrounding Tasman Peninsula, other archaeological projects have studied male convict probation stations along the Midlands Road, the Sarah Island and Maria Island penal settlements, and the Female Factory convict prisons at Georgetown, Cascades and Ross. Following excavation of the mid-nineteenth-century Aboriginal settlement at **Wybalenna**, Flinders Island, contact-period Aboriginal sites have been documented by the Tasmanian Parks and Wildlife Service and the Tasmanian Aboriginal Land Council for heritage management purposes.

Finally, three major urban excavations have been undertaken in Hobart by Austral Archaeology Pty. Ltd. In 1993, work on the former Blundstone Boot Factory in central Hobart revealed evidence of *c.* 1820s and 1858 period residential and commercial site use. Their 1994 excavation of McLaren's Hotel site recovered remains of an 1830s era tavern and several conjoined cottages. During July 1998, Austral excavated within the working-class Wapping district of Hobart. Multiple nineteenth-century occupation levels were located, containing well-preserved structural evidence and intact yard deposits dated from *c.* 1820. Reports on these excavations are owned by the various client organisations.

ELEANOR CONLIN CASELLA

tea/tea ceremony

The origin of tea drinking in **China** and Japan is buried in antiquity, but it is thought that tea became a daily beverage during the third century BC. Tea drinking became an obsession with Europeans beginning in 1610, when the ships of the **Dutch East India Company** first brought it to the continent. Though the precise date is unknown, scholars think that tea did not reach **England** until the 1650s. Queen Anne is credited with making tea drinking an institution when she decided, in the early eighteenth century, to drink it rather than ale for breakfast. Before long, tea became a fixed part of the English diet and tea drinking soon had its own ceremony and a **material culture**. Tea drinkers had to have vessels – cups, saucers and pots – that could both withstand the boiling temperature without breaking down and also be worthy of display during the ceremony. The old coarse **earthenware** vessels were wholly unsuitable. In addition to ceramic (see **ceramics**) and silver vessels, numerous other special artefacts were also required to drink tea in the proper manner: tea canister, sugar bowl, creamer, sugar tongs or spoon, tea spoons, tea strainer, waste bowl and tray.

The tea ceremony needed a special set of artefacts but it also involved a special time of day (the afternoon) and a unique etiquette. The proper accoutrements had to be laid out in a prescribed way on the tea table, the utensils had to be manipulated in a certain way and the finest silver or Chinese export **porcelain** teaset had to be used

and displayed. Tea drinking became an institution of the wealthy and the ceremony became a way of making and cementing social contacts. Tea was popular, however, and it did not take long for tea drinking to diffuse through the entire English population and to become a commonplace activity within all social classes (see **class, social**).

Historical archaeologists have explored the tea ceremony because of its material associations and its obvious social characteristics. Archaeologists who unearth pieces of teasets are forced to wonder about their social implications.

Diana diZerega Wall, in her research in **New York City**, has provided some of the most interesting studies of the tea ceremony. Studying the half-century after the American Revolution (from *c.* 1780 to *c.* 1830), Wall examined the excavated teawares that had been used by three sets of households (dating to *c.* 1790, *c.* 1805 and *c.* 1820). In investigating the changes that occurred during this period, she discovered that teawares, like many ceramic objects, were social actors. City dwellers used their teawares to offer tea both to their families and to others, and, over time, they changed the decorations on their vessels from Chinese landscapes to floral patterns. Though this shift may seem minor, Wall believed that it may indicate the feminisation of the afternoon tea ceremony, an event the urban middle class was beginning to practise. As such, the pieces of ceramic teasets found during excavation are silent reminders of social change.

See also: feminist archaeology; gender; urbanisation

Further reading

Roth, R. (1961) 'Tea drinking in 18th-century America: Its etiquette and equipage', in *United States National Museum Bulletin 225, Contributions from the Museum of History and Technology*, Washington, DC: Smithsonian Institution, pp. 61–91.

South, S. (1977) *Method and Theory in Historical Archaeology*, New York: Academic Press.

Wall, D.D. (1994) *The Archaeology of Gender: Separating the Spheres of Urban America*, New York: Plenum Press.

—— (1994) 'Family dinners and social teas:

Ceramics and domestic rituals', in C.E. Hutchins (ed.) *Everyday Life in the Early Republic*, Winterthur: Henry Francis du Pont Winterthur Museum, pp. 249–83.

CHARLES E. ORSER, JR

Teotihuacan, Mexico

By AD 600, Teotihuacan, the capital of the state of the same name north of modern Mexico City, was the largest city in the Americas, with up to 200,000 residents. According to William Sanders, who directed a regional survey of the surrounding valley, Teotihuacan drew its power from control of a regional irrigation system. The city also controlled the production and distribution of artefacts from Mexico's only green obsidian source at nearby Pachuca. An expansionist state, Teotihuacan traded with Matacapan on the Gulf of Mexico, Monte Alban in Oaxaca and the Maya area, at both Tikal and Kaminaljuyu near Guatemala City. Sanders argues the Teotihuacan military conquered Kaminaljuyu to control the nearby El Chayal obsidian outcrop used by the Classic Maya, as well as chocolate in the Soconusco area of Chiapas. Teotihuacan influence, through trade, alliances or conquest, is evident throughout Mesoamerica between AD 400 and 700 by the occurrence of Pachuca obsidian, Teotihuacan **architecture** and cylinder vessels with slab feet. One building at Tikal and the public buildings at Kaminaljuyu were in Teotihuacan style.

Teotihuacan was laid out in a grid around AD 1. The Avenue of the Dead formed the main north–south axis more than six km in length and oriented 15° 25' east of true north. With an east–west street, the city was divided into quarters and covered 20 km². Monumental architecture lined the street, including the Pyramid of the Moon at the north end, the Pyramid of the Sun nearby along the east side and the Temple of Quetzacoatl (the feathered serpent). The Pyramid of the Sun is 215 m long and 60 m high. Architecture was the distinctive 'talud-tablero' style of alternating sloping and vertical blocks on building façades. The city was densely settled with people living in apartment compounds associated with kin-based craft production.

From modest beginnings as a village, Teotihuacan flourished between AD 1 and 750, when it was burned and abandoned. The ethnic group and language of the people are unknown and the city was unoccupied at the time of the sixteenth-century Spanish conquest of Central America. During the Teotihuacan Mapping Project directed by Rene Millon, the city was mapped and surface-collected with an enormous database computerised by George Cowgill. Other work includes excavations at the Temple of Quetzacoatl (where 200 young men had been sacrificed in the building's dedication) by Cabrera Castro and others, excavations of an Oaxaca enclave by Michael Spence and consolidation and restoration by the Mexican government. Historical archaeology in the surrounding valley by Thomas Charlton includes a study of majolica ceramics by Donna Seifert.

Further reading

Cabrera C.R., Sugiyami, S. and Cowgill, G. (1991) 'The Templo de Quetzacoatl project at Teotihuacan', *Ancient Mesoamerica* 2: 77–92.

Millon, R. (1973) *Urbanization of Teotihuacan, Mexico, Volume 1, The Teotihuacan Map, Part 1, Text*, Austin: University of Texas Press.

Sanders, W.T. and Michels, J. (1977) *Teotihuacan and Kaminaljuyu: A Study in Prehistoric Culture Contact*, University Park: Pennsylvania State University Press.

HEATHER McKILLOP

terminus ante quem

In archaeological parlance, the term *terminus ante quem* (the date before which), or TAQ, is used as a relative dating technique for soil deposits based on the dates of the artefacts they contain. The term is regularly used in archaeology, but it was formally introduced to historical archaeology by Ivor Noël Hume, the British-trained excavator of Williamsburg, Virginia.

The concept is easily understood. Suppose a historical archaeologist locates a soil layer that is bisected by a dry-laid stone wall. During excavation, the archaeologists discover tucked inside the wall a coin bearing the date 1813. Based on this information, the archaeologists can assign a *terminus ante quem* to the soil layer of 1813. They know, based on the date of the coin, that it was deposited before 1813, otherwise the wall could not cut through it.

The concept can also be used in conjunction with the known manufacturing-date ranges of artefacts, such as decorated **ceramics** or **glass bottles**, and with dates derived from other sources. The *terminus ante quem* is useful to historical archaeologists because they can often determine it from the known manufacturing dates of artefacts.

See also: terminus post quem

CHARLES E. ORSER, JR

terminus post quem

Terminus post quem, or TPQ, is a term used by archaeologists to indicate the date of a soil layer or feature based on its association with artefacts. The term, which means 'the date after which', is widely used in archaeology, but Ivor Noël Hume, the excavator of Williamsburg, Virginia, introduced the term to historical archaeology.

Like the ***terminus ante quem***, the concept of *terminus post quem* rests on the idea that archaeological features can be dated by reference to artefacts within or near them. For example, let us suppose that an archaeologist finds two soil layers, one directly on top of the other. In the lower of the two, he or she discovers a coin bearing the date 1853. In the absence of any disturbances of the soil layers, the archaeologist can assign a *terminus post quem* of 1853 to the upper soil layer. He or she knows that it could not date before 1853 because coins were not minted bearing that date until 1853. The upper soil layer, however, could date to any time after 1853.

CHARLES E. ORSER, JR

toys

Toys are a ubiquitous and often little discussed component of historical archaeological sites – particularly those sites that date to the mid-nineteenth century and beyond. Marbles, broken dolls, toy teasets and fragments of die-cast metal toys are among the most commonly recovered examples. Toys can be chronologically diagnostic components of archaeological assemblages. Marbles, based on material and form of manufacture, can be used to date deposits. Likewise, hairstyles on moulded porcelain-head dolls are chronologically distinct. Far more useful than their role in dating, however, is the potential for toys to be used in studies of gender, class, racial and ethnic identities, in contexts where toys were used by **children**, as well as in contexts where they were not used.

When associated with the activities of children, toys can provide insight into the construction and indoctrination of class, racial and gendered identities. With the separation of the domestic and business spheres of women's and men's activities in the nineteenth century, childhood, and what it was to be a child, were redefined within the middle class. Toys that encouraged gender-specific play became the norm. **Porcelain**, or 'china', dolls that encouraged attention to both fashion and mothering and children, and doll-sized teasets that encouraged familiarity with hosting and etiquette were popular for girls. Dolls reinforced beauty ideals, with pale white skin, fair hair and blue eyes being common attributes. Dolls of colour that were not meant to depict specific stereotypes did not become commonly available until the late 1920s. In contrast, boys were more likely to be given toys that involved mechanics (particularly transportation-related objects) and were tied to current events. In the USA, after 1865, as individual gun ownership and the glamorisation of the frontier became more fashionable, toys guns became increasingly popular. For instance, the 1894 Montgomery Ward catalogue includes a number of toy cannons, bows and arrows, guns, tin soldiers and Buffalo Bill-themed toys. Musical instruments, educational games and marbles remain genderless toys.

While many of the toys recovered by archaeologists were used by children, there are important examples of toys that were used by adults in non-play situations. One of the more evocative examples of this is Larry McKee's interpretation of doll hands/arms recovered from the slave quarters of the **Hermitage Plantation**. McKee has suggested that these items may have been used as protective charms by enslaved African Americans, much as the metal-hand charms from the site appear to have been. Less dramatic was the common practice of putting a small 'Frozen Charlotte' doll into a teapot prior to filling it with hot water. The small toy was supposed to limit the possibility of the hot water cracking the teapot because the Frozen Charlotte would break instead. Adult women of the middle and upper classes throughout the nineteenth century would collect fashion dolls from Paris. Thus, the presence of toys at an archaeological site no way definitively indicates the presence of children.

Further reading

Prichett, J. and Pastron, A. (1980) 'Ceramic dolls as chronological indicators: Implications from a San Francisco dump site', in A.E. Ward (ed.) *Forgotten Places and Things: Archaeological Perspectives on American History*, Albuquerque: Center for Anthropological Studies, pp. 321–34.

LAURIE A. WILKIE

trade

Studying trade and its attendant physical manifestations, such as the location of trade (e.g. forts), transportation facilities (especially trails) and commodities of exchange, provide historical archaeologists with increased understanding of interaction among different social and economic groups. The fur trade that ensued almost immediately at first contact between Europeans and native people has been a major focus of historical archaeology. Much of this effort has been directed at the excavation of the forts from which trade ensued, although there has been growing interest in recent years in native sites associated with the fur trade. Following this latter focus, archaeologists can pursue questions of **culture** contact and culture change by examining the types of goods selected and possibly modified within the native cultural domain. For example, Daniel Rogers in his 1990 study of Arikara contact with Europeans through the northern plains fur

trade illustrated the need to understand the existing native cognitive and cosmological structures, which often determined whether or not a European trade good would be acceptable.

The study of trade removes a strictly narrow focus on the local setting of an archaeological site and compels the researcher to understand how that site functioned in a much broader array of economic, social and political spheres. In part, Immanuel Wallerstein's **world-systems theory** provided this impetus within archaeology, particularly in the 1980s. One of the classic historical archaeological studies of how the local trade and exchange process was grounded in a much larger trading network was William Adams's work at Silcott, a small farming community in southeastern Washington. Adams combined archaeological, historical and ethnographic approaches to examine how this small town was linked into an increasing rank of regional, national and international trade networks.

Trade can be productively linked with the study of status in the archaeological record, particularly within the area of **consumer choice**. A group's social or economic status may affect how easily it can access goods through the trade network; for example, in a nineteenth-century Puerto Rico barrio, upper-status residents had access to a wider range of goods produced outside the Spanish realm than did lower-status occupants. Distance from major markets may have an effect on whether or not certain goods were used for status display; **ceramics** were frequently employed in some urban sites for this purpose. This use of ceramics as status indicators seems to break down in rural settings where trade networks are attenuated.

Further reading

Adams, W.H. (1976) 'Trade networks and interaction spheres: A view from Silcott', *Historical Archaeology* 10: 99–112.

Joseph, J.W. and Bryne, S.C. (1992) 'Socio-economics and trade in Viejo San Juan, Puerto Rico: Observations from the Ballaja Archaeological Project', *Historical Archaeology* 26(1): 45–58.

Miller, G.L. and Hurry, S.D. (1983) 'Ceramic supply in an economically isolated frontier community: Portage County of the Ohio

Western Reserve 1800–1825', *Historical Archaeology* 17(2): 80–92.

Rogers, J.D. (1990) *Objects of Change: The Archaeology and History of Arikara Contact with Europeans*, Washington, DC: Smithsonian Institution Press.

Wallerstein, I. (1979) *Capitalist World-Economy: Essays*, New York: Cambridge University Press.

MARGARET A. KENNEDY

transitional periods

When archaeologists think about long-term history, they usually divide it into a series of 'periods'. They realise that these periods are somewhat arbitrary and only useful for analytical purposes. Nobody seriously believes, for example, that the final year of the period of US history referred to as 'antebellum', (that is, before the US Civil War, or 1860) was completely different from the first year of the war, 1861. Similarly, the last year of the war cannot really be distinguished, in archaeological terms, from the first year of the 'postbellum' era (1866). The artefacts men and women used in the antebellum period did not mysteriously disappear in 1861 to be replaced by 'war-era' artefacts, and those of the war years did not disappear in favour of 'postbellum' artefacts. Even so, historical archaeologists investigating this historical period do divide history into three 'periods' for purposes of analysis. While the artefacts may not appear remarkably different, history tells us that several important events had occurred, including the emancipation of millions of African American slaves, the political maintenance of the union of states and the beginning of war and the start of peace. In this example, the war years constitute a transitional period, and the division of time into discrete epochs makes it possible to compare the three periods of US history.

Transitional periods may be difficult for archaeologists to identify because they can be of extremely short duration (perhaps only a few days) or their effects can be ephemeral (represented by the construction of a temporary shelter on a windswept beach). But even so, transitional periods are important to archaeology because they represent times of cultural change. The word 'transition' is meant to suggest this change.

Historical archaeologists around the world examine many different kinds of transitional periods. Some of these have global significance, whereas others are limited to a small region. Two of the most important transitional periods that historical archaeologists are currently studying involve the cultural interactions and transformations that occurred when European explorers and colonialists came into contact with indigenous peoples, and the transition between the medieval and the modern periods of European history.

The interaction and exchange between indigenous peoples and foreign invaders/settlers have been a staple of archaeological research for years. Archaeologists have examined the process of contact in many places, including those involving the Roman Empire, the explorations of the **Vikings** into Northern Europe and North America, the incursions of the Spanish into Mesoamerica and the Caribbean (see **Caribbean archaeology**), the Portuguese efforts in **Asia** and **South America** and so forth.

A second, and emerging, important area of research in historical archaeology concerns the transition from medievalism to modernism. This period of history is extremely important to our understanding of today's world, and historical archaeology can do much to illustrate the historical and cultural dimensions of this important transition.

See also: colonialism; Dutch colonialism; English colonialism; French colonialism

Further reading

Dyson, S.L. (ed.) (1985) *Comparative Studies in the Archaeology of Colonialism*, BAR International Series 233, Oxford: BAR.

Gaimster, D. and Stamper, P. (ed.) (1997) *The Age of Transition: The Archaeology of English Culture, 1400–1600*, Oxford: Oxbow.

Johnson, M. (1996) *An Archaeology of Capitalism*, Oxford, Blackwell.

CHARLES E. ORSER, JR

typologies

Typologies are systems of **classification** that researchers use to organise archaeological data. Artefacts are grouped into descriptive types on the basis of attributes, or observable characteristics. These characteristics may be material, technological, functional, formal or stylistic and are selected according to their relevance to the questions asked by a researcher. Historical archaeologists are fortunate in having access to the documentary record that provides a window on the classificatory systems employed by people in the past. Also known as a **folk typology**, such a system helps a researcher to understand how artefacts were named and used by the very people whose remains they are. Typologies provide standardised descriptions of artefacts and allow assemblages to be quantified, enabling comparison between artefacts and assemblages over space and time.

A typology is a hierarchically organised system of classification that groups artefacts according to their varying degrees of similarity. Often in historical archaeology, artefacts are initially sorted into groups or classes based on their constituent material, like **ceramics** or **glass**. These broad classes are then sub-divided into types according to more specific attributes chosen by the archaeologist. The class ceramics, for example, may be divided by such distinguishing characteristics as the specific ceramic material, creating type groupings like coarse **earthenware**, **porcelain** and **stoneware**. These groups may further be broken down on the basis of characteristics like decorative style or vessel form. Certain attributes may be more relevant than others, depending on the issues a researcher is attempting to address. An archaeologist interested in examining the role of ceramics in foodways would, for example, be better served by a typology based on vessel form and function than one based on the decorative style or production methods of the ceramics. Typological systems, however, are not mutually exclusive and different typologies of the same objects may be needed to reveal the range of information about the past available from the artefacts.

The familiarity of many historical objects gives historical archaeologists an advantage in identifying and interpreting excavated artefacts. Further, access to **historical documents** like encyclopedias, **probate inventories**, patent and production records make historical typologies epistemologically different from those employed in prehistoric archaeology. Because external documentary sources like the written record and art help identify the forms and uses of historic artefacts, robust and meaningful functional typologies can be constructed for their identification and analysis. The forms, functions, techniques of manufacture, provenance and price of many historical artefacts are documented. Such evidence allows historical archaeologists to construct typologies that recognise the attributes and employ the nomenclature used by past peoples. A system that has successfully integrated archaeological artefacts and the historical record is the Potomac Typological System, or POTS, developed by Mary Beaudry and four of her colleagues. POTS is a typology of ceramics found on British colonial sites in the Chesapeake area of Maryland and Delaware. This system is based on probate inventories and other historical documents, like the anonymous mid-eighteenth-century work *The Complete Appraiser*, which was intended to provide names and descriptions of common items for contemporary probate-inventory takers. POTS links excavated vessel shapes to terms used in these documents. Organised first by vessel form and then by vessel function, this typology uses seventeenth- and eighteenth-century vessel names and provides a standardised system for identifying individual vessels and their uses. This, in turn, allows ceramic assemblages to be quantified, enabling researchers in this geographic area not only to describe excavated objects and assemblages but also to interpret the past behaviour and cultural processes they represent.

While folk typologies found in documents can help archaeologists to understand how artefacts were named and used in the past, however, they may not be wholly relevant to present issues of interest to researchers. The distinction made between flatwares and hollowwares by potters in the seventeenth century, for example, may not be the most useful way to categorise ceramic vessels for a present-day analysis of ceramic importation in colonial settings. In addition, more than one folk typology may have been used simultaneously in the past. The groupings used in a typology, then, may not necessarily replicate an original folk typology.

Further, even with the aid of historical documents, historical archaeologists should maintain a critical approach to the relation of form and function, recognising the flexibility of functional groups. The multifunctionality of objects is well illustrated in Elizabeth Scott's examination of vessel functions suggested in eighteenth- and nineteenth-century cookbook instructions, in which drinking vessels were used to cut dough and 'sallad dishes' served as butter plates.

While artefact types encompass a range of variation, creating typologies is necessary for organising archaeological data and quantifying artefact assemblages. Typologies provide a means of systematising artefact description and identification, and create a standardised nomenclature for historical objects. Such standardisation allows archaeologists to examine the similarities and differences between artefacts and between archae-ological collections. Typologies, then, are not the final goal of archaeological research, but instead are the starting point from which to proceed to the analysis and interpretation of the material record.

Further reading

Beaudry, M.C., Long, J., Miller, H.M., Neiman, F.D. and Stone, G.W. (1983) 'A vessel typology for early Chesapeake ceramics: The Potomac typological system', *Historical Archaeology* 17(1): 18–43.

Scott, E.M. (1997) '"A little gravy in the dish and onions in a tea cup": What cookbooks reveal about material culture', *International Journal of Historical Archaeology* 1: 131–55.

Walker, I.C. (1967) 'Historic archaeology: Methods and principles', *Historical Archaeology* 1: 23–34.

STACEY C. JORDAN

U

urban archaeology

Urban archaeology includes all research by archaeologists in and about cities. The distinctive nature of urban settings makes it necessary for them to apply creative methods and theory. Urban archaeology is both more challenging and more rewarding than other kinds of archaeology. It is more expensive and more difficult, but it also can result in greater public awareness and support. It is not the case that urban development results in the wholesale destruction of the archaeological record. Urban archaeology can, therefore, be a rewarding undertaking. It is also a necessary endeavour, because certain important issues can only be studied in cities.

Defining urban archaeology is not as straightforward as it might at first appear. For decades there has been a dichotomy between those who view it as archaeology *in* cities versus those who view it as archaeology *of* cities. The former definition encompasses any and all archaeological research that happens to occur in an urban setting. Those who hold this definition treat cities as distinctive environments (such as river valleys or tropical rain forests) requiring the application of a specific set of methods, regardless of what materials are being sought and what research is being pursued. The latter involves the archaeological study of urban phenomena *per se*. Those who argue for this definition treat cities as both environment and the subject of study.

For good reasons, most historical archaeologists define urban archaeology as archaeology of cities.

Figure 29 View of excavation of seventeenth-century Hanover Square, Manhattan, New York City
Source: Photo: C. Forster

No matter how historical archaeology is conceptualised, it is indisputable that **urbanisation** and the development of writing are significantly linked in global culture history. Some exceptions notwithstanding, cities and documents co-occur most of the time, and there is a good functionalist explanation for this co-occurrence. The administrative challenges of complex societies, with large, dense population centres, almost always require written records.

This is a complicated issue that will not be dealt with here. It is also somewhat irrelevant so far as a definition of urban archaeology is concerned, given the fact that archaeology *of* cities is actually a subset of archaeology *in* cities. The latter definition is more inclusive, and thus more appropriate when a number of important methodological concerns are considered. Probably the most important involves the degree to which integrity of archaeological resources is maintained in urban settings, whether these resources are related to urban phenomena or not. After several decades of urban archaeology it is now apparent that urban development does not often lead to the destruction of the archaeological record. Indeed, the processes of urbanisation often enhance preservation.

History of urban archaeology

Urban archaeology has its early roots in **classical archaeology**. European explorers and scholars since the Renaissance have focused on ancient cities of the Mediterranean and Near Eastern regions (e.g. Pompeii, Hissarlik). The archaeology conducted in these early times was nothing like its more modern counterpart, of course, and recognisable urban archaeology does not emerge until the twentieth century. It emerges first in Europe and subsequently in North America, largely in response to the rapid urban development of the last few decades, and the dangers to the archaeological record this development was thought to entail.

The founders of modern urban archaeology emerge after the Second World War with a call for more frequent and rigorous archaeological research in cities. A number of influential works (e.g. *Archeology in Megalopolis* by Bert Salwen) appear shortly thereafter, followed by a flood of articles, books and especially contract archaeology reports.

The distinctive nature of urban archaeology

Urban archaeology can be viewed as a distinctive archaeological endeavour in a number of signifi-

cant ways. Methodological distinctions derive from the unique environment in which fieldwork is conducted (archaeology in the city). Theoretical distinctions exist because there are important research issues that can only be explored in urban settings (archaeology of the city).

Fieldwork in cities is both more challenging and more rewarding than fieldwork elsewhere. Survey and **sampling** strategies, necessary to determine the nature and extent of the urban archaeological record, must be sophisticated given the nature of cities and the demands of modern archaeology. Cities are very large sites that exhibit vast material and behavioural variability. They are by definition concentrations of human activity and experience. The quantity of **material culture** and data recoverable is enormous. In addition, the urban landscape often imposes a degree of arbitrariness regarding which portions of the resource are accessible. The challenge is to design opportunistic yet appropriate survey and sampling strategies.

Urban excavation is also a challenge. Any urban archaeological excavation is bound to be more expensive than any comparably sized project in a non-urban area. Urban archaeological deposits commonly exhibit very complex stratigraphy, and can be found remarkably deep below the surface. What results is slower-than-normal excavation because of both research requirements and safety concerns. The potentially great volume of material recovered confounds the situation.

Adding to the expense is the frequent need to rent laboratory facilities in high-priced urban neighbourhoods, or to transport artefacts on a regular basis to facilities far removed from the project area. Providing housing for workers is also expensive.

Urban archaeology is more disruptive to the non-archaeological community than other archaeology. It is a rare urban archaeological project that does not cost a large number of people outside the archaeological community either money or time. Municipal officials and other citizens often respond to expenses and delays with puzzlement ('Why is archaeology necessary?'), annoyance ('We have more important things to do, and you're getting in the way'), and outright resentment ('You're excavating in my parking space!'). Such potential conflicts seldom arise outside of cities, and for this reason urban archaeologists sometimes envy colleagues working in remote locales.

Urban archaeology is highly visible. The public is ubiquitous around urban archaeological sites, creating a number of public relations and security challenges. Urban archaeologists must confront the puzzlement, annoyance and resentment discussed above on a daily basis. They must also deal with a wide range of other public responses to their work, from simple curiosity to mindless vandalism and treasure hunting. Complicating all of these various public interactions is the prospect of liability if someone gets hurt or even inconvenienced in a manner they decide justifies litigation.

Public visibility is not all negative, however. Indeed, the conspicuousness of urban archaeology is also one of its greatest rewards. The potential to increase public awareness, education and support is always high in a place where many people live and work on a regular basis. The challenge is to exploit this potential by dedicating resources to **public outreach and education** efforts (e.g. guided tours, demonstrations, public lectures, the use of volunteers, visits to local schools and well-co-ordinated interactions with the media).

Both the challenges and opportunities of urban archaeology make it essential that great effort goes into creating a sound research design as the initial step in any project. Many urban archaeologists appreciate this necessity. Research designs reflect knowledge of the issues to be explored along with an understanding of the urban environment in which the work is conducted. The research designs allow projects to proceed smoothly and on schedule despite the multiple, diverse demands that are imposed from various external sources.

Cities are complex entities that have been studied by a variety of scholars, and the value of interdisciplinary co-operation has been recognised by urban archaeologists. Many research designs incorporate the contributions of experts from various fields, and collaboration with these experts is an expected, integral part of the research undertaking.

Topics studied by urban archaeologists

Those who do archaeology in cities recognise the potential to study any research issue in urban settings. It is nevertheless obvious that most urban archaeological research involves phenomena that are unique to cities, and it is this research that is described here.

An important topic of research among urban archaeologists is urbanisation, the general processes related to the emergence and development of cities. Logically, emphasis is given to the spatial and material characteristics of urbanisation. The patterned ways in which these characteristics have changed through time during the course of urbanisation is a major theoretical concern. Recognising how the spatial and material patterns reflect behavioural and cultural reality is a major methodological challenge.

The diachronic nature of urban archaeology permits a number of models of urbanisation to be empirically evaluated. These models, suggested by urban geographers, planners and others, are often modified or even rejected outright by urban archaeologists. The classic, functionalist models of urban development (e.g. Park, Burgess, Sjoberg) have been questioned with empirical, archaeological evidence, for example. Additionally, more humanistic arguments that urbanisation cannot be measured or understood quantitatively (e.g. Mumford, Toynbee) have been disputed. Urban archaeologists are making significant, scholarly contributions to urbanisation studies, from a unique and (until recently) neglected perspective.

Another topic studied by many urban archaeologists is **ethnicity**. Cities are concentrations of many ethnic groups. It is reasonable to conclude that ethnic identity is more meaningful in cities because of the frequent and intensive contact between these groups. Such identity can be maintained for generations and, as a result, ethnic group-specific behavioural, cultural and material patterns are potentially highly visible.

Urban archaeologists who study ethnicity sometimes find it useful to focus on architectural variation. Cities are concentrations of architectural forms that date to the past and the present. Many of these are above ground, making fieldwork less expensive and time consuming than would be the case if excavation was required. **Architecture** is relatively permanent and well preserved, compared to other parts of the archaeological record, and architectural constructs often reflect ethnic-group identification as well as distinctive ethnic-group behavioural patterns.

Recognising and documenting ethnicity in the archaeological record nevertheless remains a problematic exercise. A primary reason for this is the inability to differentiate material markers of ethnicity from material markers of other social identifications, especially socioeconomic ones. Indeed, it is often argued that economic class (see **class, social**) is more apparent in the archaeological record than ethnicity, and thus more fruitfully explored by the methods of urban archaeology.

Since cities are concentrations of diverse people participating in complex social systems, it follows that a wide range of socioeconomic statuses and roles will be represented within them. As was the case with ethnicity, therefore, the investigation of socioeconomic interaction is a primary concern of urban archaeologists.

Environmental issues are also given special consideration by urban archaeologists. Cities have profound impacts on their environmental settings and, in turn, environmental conditions play a critical role in shaping urban characteristics. Urban archaeologists have made important contributions to understanding this complementary relationship. In part because of the work of urban archaeologists, it is now abundantly clear that cities are not in any way detached from the environmental setting they occupy, a popular and sometimes scholarly misconception. In fact, cities might be more dependent on the environment for support and even survival, because of the high density of people and great diversity of activities they contain.

Further reading

Dickens, R.S., Jr (ed.) (1982) *Archaeology of Urban America: The Search for Pattern and Process*, New York: Academic Press.

Staski, E. (ed.) (1987) *Living in Cities: Research in Urban Archaeology*, Tucson: Society for Historical Archaeology.

—— (1982) 'Advances in urban archaeology', in M.B. Schiffer (ed.) *Advances in Archaeological Method and Theory, Vol. 5*, New York: Academic Press, pp. 97–149.

Ucko, P.J., Tringham, R. and Dimbleby, G.W. (eds) (1972) *Man, Settlement and Urbanism*, London: Duckworth.

EDWARD STASKI

urbanisation

When archaeologists use the term 'urbanisation' they are typically referring to the process in which humans began to settle in particular locales and constructed socially complex communities inhabited by large numbers of people. Many archaeologists restrict the term to the study of the earliest known cities, but 'urbanisation' need not be used in such a limited fashion because the process of urbanisation continues to this day. Men and women are still learning how to negotiate urban spaces and how to live surrounded by hundreds, perhaps even millions, of people they do not know but with whom they are in contact. Some people use the term 'civilisation' to be largely synonymous with 'urbanisation', although 'civilisation' is a highly charged and contested term that many archaeologists use only sparingly if at all. Historical archaeologists working on the process of urbanisation conduct **urban archaeology**.

Depending upon one's perspective, the development of cities is either one of the greatest achievements of human history or a profound curse, the effects of which are just beginning to place severe stress on society. The process of urbanisation has created an environment in which humans have invented untold services and have developed significant technological marvels. Urbanisation has also brought overcrowding, burgeoning crime and urban blight.

Archaeologists were quick to recognise the historical and cultural importance of cities, and some of the world's most celebrated excavations have occurred within ancient urban areas. Some of the most remarkable urban centres that have been the focus of archaeological research include: in **South America**, Machu Picchu, **Cuzco**, Tiwanaku and **Huánuco Pampa**; in Mesopotamia and the Near East, Eridu, Uruk, Mohenjo-Daro, Harappa, Çatal Hüyük and Jericho; in South-east Asia, **Angkor**; and in Europe, **Rome** and London.

The characteristics of urbanisation

Each historic city has its own unique character, **culture** and history, but archaeologists have been intent on understanding what they can collectively reveal about the process of urbanization. V. Gordon Childe was one of the first archaeologists to provide criteria in which the growth of cities could be understood. Writing in the 1930s, Childe termed the development of cities the 'urban revolution' and the name stuck for many years.

In Childe's scheme, once people settled down and began to raise dependable crops, their development of metallurgy created a new class of metal-working specialists. Because these craft-people laboured on a full-time basis, they were not able to grow their own crops. Leaders with authority had to redistribute the farmers' surplus crops to the metal workers, to keep them fit for work. Food production increased as the farmers further sophisticated their agricultural techniques, and, with more abundant food, the population increased. A larger population meant a greater social stratification, and this hierarchical structure led to the invention of economically based social classes. Writing was required as long-distance trade developed, and powerful religious and political leaders rose to supreme power and solidified their authority through the redistribution of foodstuffs and other materials. These same leaders had impressive monuments built to honour themselves and their ancestors.

Childe's scenario was unquestioned for many years, but archaeologists began to question his view of urbanisation in the 1960s. Much of the discontent centred on the idea that his model of urbanisation did not emphasise the actual *process* of urbanisation. Rather, he merely gave a sequential, historical point of view.

Archaeologists in the 1960s were striving to create a **New Archaeology**, a **processual archaeology** that had explanation as one of its overt goals. Childe's outdated trait list approach to urbanisation (where certain characteristics would indicate the presence or absence of a city) was largely discarded. Beginning in the 1960s and continuing into the twenty-first century, archaeologists emphasised various factors that could account for urbanisation, including the role of the environment, the development of irrigation systems that would ensure the growth of crops and thereby ensure urban population expansion, the institution of long-distance trade and the development of transnational markets, and the rise of a powerful elite class of rulers who managed the development of cities using various means.

In almost every case, ancient urbanisation is accompanied by the rise of the 'state'. Archaeologists engaged in the investigation of urbanisation generally conflate urbanisation with the rise of states because the two exist in tandem in history. Large, socially complex state-level societies needed cities in which to house their large populations and to express the strength of the polity. Peoples organised in non-state organisations simply did not have the population to require urbanisation.

Urbanisation and historical archaeology

Most historical archaeologists investigate state-level societies in one form or another. This is particularly true for those archaeologists studying the global cultural interactions that occurred during the past 500 years and which included an urban dimension, as well as those engaged in investigating the transition in Europe, Asia and elsewhere from medieval towns to modern cities. Historical archaeologists can examine urbanisation from many different perspectives and can employ an almost endless collection of theoretical lenses, but three examples will serve to demonstrate the nature of some of the research on urbanisation in historical archaeology.

England has provided an excellent arena in which to examine the growth of urban centres, and many archaeologists have studied various aspect of urbanisation there. In one study, John Schofield investigated the housing of London during the 1400–1600 period. Unlike many previous research-ers who examined only the housing of the elite, he focused on houses of the 'middling' social class (see **class, social**), a group that was much more numerous within the city than elites. His specific interest was in the changes the emerging middle class made to the designs and uses of the interiors of their homes and the **architecture** they employed. The changes that Schofield observed during the two centuries of his interest allowed him to see the process of urbanisation in action. He learned, for example, that non-elite members of society were influential throughout the period in affecting the architecture used for personal residences. This finding runs counter to much scholarship on the history of architecture because many scholars imbue a society's elites with the power to influence the ways in which buildings are designed, built and used. The gentry lived in cities and were influential to be sure, but they were not the only people who could induce urban, architectural change. Schofield also learned that some of the developments in housing were uniquely urban, meaning that they were not affected by the more numerous rural house designs. The development of the first-floor hall located near the street represents one urban innovation. He also discovered that new building forms only emerged at the end of the sixteenth century as elite families grew in wealth and prominence, and solidified their power in urban centres.

In another study, Daniel Schávelzon investigated the creation and growth of Buenos Aires, Argentina, a city that he describes as being 'at the end of the world'. Schávelzon charted the creation of the city, from the very beginning of the process of urbanisation in Argentina to the city's condition in 2000, as one of the largest cities in the Americas with a population of over 8 million. Addressing one of the core issues of urbanisation, Schávelzon investigated how a major urban centre like Buenos Aires could survive and even prosper given its initial, tentative settlement of 1536. Life was so precarious in this early settlement – with hunger prevalent and mortality high – that the settlers burned the town and shifted their interest to Asunción, a town that had the advantage of a safe harbour. A harbour was important because the colonial Spanish could use it as a point of embarkation for future expeditions. Asunción would remain the focus of Spanish expansion in Argentina until 1580. Buenos Aires was founded in that year in its current location at the mouth of the Rio de la Plata.

Schávelzon showed how the population of the city exploded after 1850, and how the residents became enmeshed in the expanding global marketplace. Coarse **earthenware** ceramics made by Africans living in Argentina and **creamware**

pieces manufactured in England provided mute testimony both to the multiculturalism of the city and to the reach of market goods manufactured in distant factories. Buenos Aires, as a major port city, received regular shipments from the UK, the USA, France, Sweden, the Netherlands, Denmark, Spain, Belgium, Russia and elsewhere. The city grew in size as the population increased and the city's outside business contacts expanded. The urban, residential architecture used in the city ranged from simple two-room houses to large, multi-room structures with interior patios and attached stores and houses for rent.

In a third important study, Joan Geismar explored a topic that is central to modern urbanisation but which is seldom mentioned: the deposition of human waste. Everyone today knows that the process of urbanisation, whether in the far distant past or today, brings with it the problem of waste disposal. Archaeologists excavating urban sites typically find large numbers of artefacts simply because so many people lived in small areas for so many years. Before the advent of efficient sewer systems, urban dwellers had recourse only to privies or outhouses, and urban archaeologists find them in cities throughout the world. The first known sewage system appeared at Mohenjo-Daro (dated to 2500 BC), but the adoption of such systems was not uniform across the globe.

Archaeologists like to locate privies because they often serve as time capsules for the men, women and **children** who used them. People with limited space, such as urban dwellers, would often toss their refuse down the same hole they used for their daily toilet. People with something to hide, such as a drinking problem, might throw things down the hole to conceal them, and children could have dropped items down the privy hole as practical jokes or simply for sport. In any case, privies often provide superb archaeological deposits.

While excavating privies in **New York City**, Joan Geismar observed that waste matter was either entirely missing from several of them or was just barely present. Conducting research on this interesting cultural phenomenon, she discovered that the filling of privies was a major problem in the growth of urbanisation. In cities, unlike in rural areas, privy pits could only be moved a certain number of times before landowners simply ran out of room. As a result, an industry developed around the cleaning of urban privies. Waste materials were usually removed from urban privies at night and so the term 'night soil' became a useful euphemism. The first vacuum machine to remove night soil (a large, cylindrical tank mounted on wagon wheels) was patented in December 1850. This invention spurred the growth of an industry committed to efficient disposal, with the eventual outcome being the creation of indoor plumbing. One element of the late nineteenth- and early twentieth-century privy-cleaning industry is that the removed waste materials were often sold to outlying farmers for fertiliser.

See also: Spanish colonialism

Further reading

Geismar, J. H. (1993) 'Where is night soil? Thoughts on an urban privy', *Historical Archaeology* 27(2): 57–70.

Schávelzon, D. (2000) *The Historical Archaeology of Buenos Aires: A City at the End of the World*, New York: Kluwer Academic/Plenum Press.

Schofield, J. (1997) 'Urban housing in England, 1400–1600', in D. Gaimster and P. Stamper (eds) *The Age of Transition: The Archaeology of English Culture, 1400–1600*, Oxford: Oxbow, pp. 127–44.

CHARLES E. ORSER, JR

US Civil War archaeology

US Civil War archaeology focuses on developing through archaeological research a broader understanding of the most influential event in nineteenth-century US history. Historical archaeologists assert that excavation and analysis of Civil War period sites:

1 can provide a different perspective on the conflict from historic documents;
2 can substantiate or refute historic documents and historical interpretations of the war;
3 in some cases may be the only method of documenting unrecorded war events; and
4 provide tangible evidence of the war's impact.

Further, excavation of Civil War sites expands an anthropological understanding of war. Typically, Civil War archaeologists study sites related to military activities; however, the broader effects of the war on US society and the landscape are also examined. Therefore, US Civil War archaeology may be defined as archaeological research at any site where questions regarding the war, or its influence, are asked.

US Civil War archaeology as a recognisable specialisation within the discipline of historical archaeology emerged in the late 1970s from earlier particularistic examinations of **fortifications**, arsenals, batteries, redoubts, entrenchments, lines or other remains of military engineering, mostly at battlefields owned by the US government and protected by the US National Park Service. Usually these excavations were brief, brought about by park development, and necessarily had limited objectives such as documenting construction techniques and collecting military material culture for display. Reports of these efforts were largely descriptive but serve today to assist archaeologists as a comparative database for future work. Meanwhile, excavations at these types of military features continue and are expanding knowledge about the technology of nineteenth-century warfare. Civil War archaeologists can use this basic data to examine questions such as the differences between Union and Confederate war technologies, and the possible changes in these technologies resulting from evolving battlefield tactics.

The study of deployment and manœuvre on Civil War battlefields was difficult prior to the 1980s because traditional archaeological survey methods did not allow for wide-scale analysis of the vast and fluid nineteenth-century battlefield. However, systematic metal detector survey and global positioning system (GPS) recording of military features, with post-processing into geographical information system (GIS) data layers, are revolutionising this aspect of Civil War archaeology. Archaeologists were at first reluctant to use **metal detectors** as they were negatively associated with relic hunters. However, Douglas D. Scott and Richard Allan Fox Jr's careful metal detector survey of the post-Civil War **Battle of the Little Bighorn**, Montana, legitimised metal detector use in professional archaeology and also provided a theoretical perspective that has become *de rigueur* in battlefield study. In his analysis of battlefield manœuvre, Fox developed a stability/disintegration model contending that as human behaviour is patterned so is battlefield manœuvre. Stability and disintegration of military units can be mapped by carefully recording the provenance of expended cartridges and bullets. This theory and method have been successfully adapted at Civil War battlefields such as Monroe's Crossroads, North Carolina. Secondly, GPS and GIS mapping technology have allowed an expanded view and analysis of Civil War battlefields and are also an excellent step in battlefield preservation. Archaeologists can now map Civil War skirmish lines and entrenchments for examination of battlefield tactics. The US National Park Service's American Battlefield Protection Program has taken significant steps in refining this methodology.

Some of the most fruitful studies in Civil War archaeology have been at non-battlefield sites such as campgrounds, prisons and towns. James B. Legg and Steven D. Smith's 1987 excavations of the 1863–4 winter encampment surrounding the 55th Massachusetts Volunteers and 1st North Carolina Coloured Infantry cemetery (see **cemeteries**) provided evidence of the lives and deaths of African American soldiers isolated on Folly Island near Charleston, South Carolina. Forensic examination of the soldiers recovered from the cemetery indicated great strength, the result of hard labour during their former lives as slaves. Other camp excavations have documented Camp Nelson, Kentucky, and Camp Allegheny, West Virginia. Joel W. Grossman's archaeological examination of the West Point Foundry in Cold Spring, New York, led to the uncovering of wartime espionage. John W. Walker's and Guy Prentice's excavations at Andersonville Prison, Georgia, are examples of efforts to understand prison life and prison construction. **Urban archaeology** at **Harpers Ferry**, West Virginia, has provided a broad historical perspective of a town and armoury destroyed by war.

In 1991, historical archaeologists gathered at the annual meeting of the **Society for Historical Archaeology** in an all-day symposium focused on the archaeology of Civil War sites. This seminal event led to the publication of the 1994 book *Look to the Earth: Historical Archaeology and the American Civil War*, edited by Clarence R. Geier, Jr and Susan E. Winter. The symposium and the book have done much to direct the course of Civil War archaeology studies through the 1990s. Importantly, they demonstrate the range and potential of archaeology to go beyond the traditional reliance on historic documents for the study of the Civil War.

See also: battlefield archaeology

Further reading

Fox, R.A. (1993) *Archaeology, History, and Custer's Last Battle: The Little Big Horn Reexamined*, Norman: University of Oklahoma Press.

Geier, Clarence R. and Potter, Stephen R. (eds) (2000) *Archaeological Perspectives on the American Civil War*, Gainesville: University Press of Florida.

Geier, C.R. and Winter, S.E. (eds) (1994) *Look to the Earth: Historical Archaeology and the American Civil War*, Knoxville: University of Tennessee Press.

Scott, D.D. and Hunt, W.J. (1998) *The Civil War Battlefield at Monroe's Crossroads, Fort Bragg, North Carolina: A Historical Archeological Perspective*, Tallahassee, FL: National Park Service.

Shackel, P.A. and Winter, S.E. (eds) (1994) 'An archaeology of Harpers Ferry's commercial and residential district', *Historical Archaeology* 28(4): 1–121.

Smith, S.D. (1993) *Whom We Would Never More See: History and Archaeology Recover the Lives and Deaths of African American Civil War Soldiers on Folly Island, South Carolina*, Columbia: South Carolina Department of Archives and History.

STEVEN D. SMITH

USA, western

The western USA extends from the Rocky Mountains westward to the Pacific Ocean and covers several geographically distinct regions, the most prominent of which are California, the south-west, the Pacific north-west, the Great Basin and the Rocky Mountains. What is considered to be the 'historic period' begins at different times in these regions. In the Great Basin, for example, it begins with the exploration of Jedadiah Smith in 1827 but begins much earlier in

California and the south-west with the first Spanish travellers through the region in the 1500s. The history of archaeology in western America begins as early as the 1870s, mostly in the south-west. Historical archaeology, however, is much later, originating in the 1960s and not of much interest to archaeologists until the 1980s. California is the most active of all the regions of western America in the late twentieth century.

Typical historical-sites research in western America includes the study of **Spanish colonialism**, the fur trade and associated **English colonialism** and **Russian colonialism**, the overseas Chinese (see **overseas Chinese historical archaeology**), overland trails and emigration, **industrial archaeology** and **urban archaeology**. There is much regional variation, however, in the importance of each of these topics. Spanish colonial archaeology, for example, dominates the regions of California and the south-west. In the Pacific north-west, the archaeology of the fur trade and Russian and English colonial archaeology are more common. Also, historical archaeology in the Great Basin and the Rocky Mountains is much more oriented towards industrial archaeology and overland emigration.

Spanish colonial archaeology

Historical archaeology in two of the regions, the American south-west and California, holds much in common and, for this reason, will be discussed together. The archaeology of the Spanish colonial period dominates both regions. Typical research topics include the economics and politics of Spanish missions and presidios, and their impact upon indigenous peoples. Julia Costello, for example, combined documentary and archaeological data to portray the economic life of the Franciscan missions of Alta California between 1790 and 1835. She found that economics varied considerably from one mission to another and that the political autonomy resulting from the Mexican War of Independence in 1810 caused even more divergence. In addition, the data suggested that the agricultural success of missions depended more on local history than on ecological patterns. Finally, Costello found that the living conditions of the Indian labour force at the missions were not positively correlated with the mission's economic success.

In another example of Spanish colonial archaeology in the region, Jack Williams uses archaeological data from three presidios in Arizona to test two competing hypotheses of the world system relationships (see **world(-)systems theory**) between Spain and New Spain. One hypothesis, first proposed by sociologist Immanuel Wallerstein, is that New Spain had been a full-blown economic and political dependency of Spain since the sixteenth century. The other hypothesis, put forth by historian Fernand Braudel, contends that New Spain and Spain enjoyed more or less equal economic and political relationships until the early nineteenth-century wars of liberation. To test the hypotheses with archaeological data, Williams uses Wallerstein's argument that world system peripheries have high percentages of the 'essential goods' of everyday life such as tableware, food and clothing that come from core regions. Thus, Wallerstein's model would show high percentages of imported essential goods in New Spain after the sixteenth century. In contrast, Braudel's model would not show high percentages of imported essential goods until after the beginning of the Republic Period in 1822. Williams found that the percentage of essential goods coming from outside the region is low in the three presidios that he tested, suggesting that they were self-sufficient. Braudel's model, therefore, is supported.

The fur trade and European settlement

Archaeological studies similar to those on Spanish colonisation have been done on the fur trade and English and Russian colonisation in the Pacific north-west and California. Both the Russian settlement at Fort Ross, California, and the English settlement at Fort Vancouver, British Columbia, for example, have been the subject of extensive archaeological research. Aron Crowell gives a good example of this type of study. He explored the lives of eighteenth-century Russian American fur traders at the site of an outpost at Three Saints Harbour in southern Alaska. They were not isolated but were integrated into a world system that provided food, housing materials such as iron nails and personal items. He found imported trade items such as

English pottery, Chinese **porcelain**, **glass beads** and Russian vodka, which they exchanged for furs with indigenous peoples.

Industrial archaeology

Industrial archaeology is another important research topic in the western USA. Archaeological studies of the technology, society, culture and landscapes of mining, logging, water engineering and transportation are the most common. The advent of modern historic preservation laws and policies in the 1960s, an explosion of new mining activity in the region in the 1970s and 1980s, and the large amount of public land in the area combined to produce many of the studies. Typical studies explore the physical remains of mines and mining camps, sawmills and logging camps, and other work camps such as temporary railroad and water engineering construction camps. A.E. Rogge and others, for example, studied several work camps associated with the construction of the Theodore Roosevelt Dam on the Salt River in central Arizona in the first decade of the twentieth century. Among other things, they found archaeological evidence of Apache work camps. The evidence included the remains of wickiups, metal buckets and cans that had been punctured with nails to make strainers for brewing corn beer, grills made with woven wire for roasting ash bread and metal wash basins and buckets that had been ritually smashed and slashed with an axe or a hatchet.

A key theme of industrial archaeology in the western USA is **mining archaeology**, especially the archaeology of precious-metal mining rushes, which played an important role in the history of the western USA. The California Gold Rush, for example, attracted a global labour migration, which led to the explosive growth of California after 1849 and stimulated a number of other rushes in others parts of the west, including the Comstock silver rush in the Great Basin about a decade later. Archaeological studies of the gold rush have helped document the event and the social and cultural changes that followed. The Klondike and Alaskan Gold Rush at the beginning of the twentieth century is another example of an archaeologically well-studied mining rush.

Overseas Chinese archaeology

Another research theme in the historical archaeology of the western USA is the overseas Chinese (see **overseas Chinese historical archaeology**). The California Gold Rush played a major role in the first significant Chinese immigration to the western US in the 1850s. Major studies of urban overseas Chinese have resulted from urban development projects in several cities in the US west, including Los Angeles, Sacramento, Tucson and El Paso. In addition, archaeological studies of rural Chinese settlements have been done in mining districts throughout the western USA. The key research topics include technology, subsistence, architecture, landscapes, geomancy or *feng shui* and social and cultural change.

Roberta Greenwood notes the possible widespread occurrence of *feng shui* in the US west but cautions against its uncritical use in interpretation. Sanborn fire insurance maps of Chinese urban settlements in California, for example, often show that they did not conform to *feng shui* principles because of adaptations to local economic and political conditions. Thus, Chinese settlements often were found either in areas with low land prices or on the outskirts of towns where they were forced to reside by the dominant white population.

Overseas Chinese landscapes include the terraced garden, which has been recorded in the US west as well as in Canada and **New Zealand**, often in association with mining activities. Archaeological studies have provided the best evidence of the landform, which often substantially changed the patterning of vegetation as well as landforms of local-scale ecosystems. Jeffrey Fee, for example, documents Chinese terraced gardens on the South Fork of the Salmon River in Idaho. The garden terraces typically appear on mountain slopes as a series of steps engineered to make the most efficient use of space. They vary in size, shape, slope and elevation. Archaeological remains on the terraces, such as pollen, macrofossils, ditches and artefacts, provide information about the cultigens grown in the gardens, Chinese gardening practices, engineering of the terraces and the lifestyles of the gardeners.

Urban archaeology

Urban archaeology is another important research topic in the western USA. **Consumer choice** is a common focus of the research. Susan Henry, for example, found foodway differences among urban socioeconomic classes in late nineteenth- and early twentieth-century Phoenix based upon the relative cost of ceramic tableware and meat cuts. She conducted archaeological studies of fifteen domestic households with different occupations that could be ranked by class or other socioeconomic status. Henry found that the relative cost of ceramic tableware and butchered cuts of meat recovered from the households generally tracked the social rank of households; however, the correlation was fairly low, suggesting that the specific histories of households also played a role.

Overland trails and emigration

Finally, the archaeology of overland trails and emigration is an important research topic in the western USA. The earliest trails, such as the Santa Fe Trail, opened in the 1500s and have been the subject of archaeological studies. Other archaeological studies have gathered information from campsites associated with trails of exploration such as the Lewis and Clark Trail and the routes of mining rushes such as the Gold Rush trails to Alaska. Also, the way stations along the Pony Express Trail have been the subject of a number of archaeological studies. Perhaps the most famous of the trails, however, are associated with the US westward emigration in the nineteenth century. The time period from 1841 to 1865, for example, saw the emigration of more than 300,000 people along the Oregon and California trails into the western USA.

Archaeological studies of overland emigration include Donald Hardesty's work at the two mountain camps of the ill-fated Donner Party in the Sierra Nevada Mountains. The excavation found a wide range of US material culture from the 1840s time period. They include, among other things, sprig-painted and shell-edged ceramic tableware; gothic cathedral pickle bottles; firearms paraphernalia such as gunflints, percussion caps, musket balls; clothing and personal gear such as buttons, beads, jewellery, tobacco pipes and a Roman Catholic religious medal; two 1830s coins; hand tools; and wagon hardware. The excavation also recovered animal bone remains, most of which are butchered oxen bones but which also include horse or mule, bear and human bone fragments. No evidence of cannibalism, however, was found. The excavation found the remains of one log cabin at the largest camp, but no evidence of a mass burial of the Donner Party dead, long reputed to be in the floor of the cabin, and it also relocated the site of the second camp, where the Donner family spent the winter of 1846–7.

Further reading

Costello, J.G. (1992) 'Not peas in a pod: Documenting diversity among the California missions', in B. Little (ed.) *Text-Aided Archaeology*, Boca Raton, FL: CRC Press, pp. 67–81.

Crowell, A.L. (1997) *Archaeology and the Capitalist World System: A Study from Russian America*, New York: Plenum.

Hardesty, D.L. (1997) *The Archaeology of the Donner Party*, Reno: University of Nevada Press.

Henry, S.L. (1987) 'Factors influencing consumer behavior in turn-of-the-century Phoenix, Arizona', in S.M. Spencer-Wood (ed.) *Consumer Choice in Historical Archaeology*, New York: Plenum Press, pp. 359–82.

Rogge, A.E., McWatters, D.L., Keane, M. and Emanuel, R. (1995) *Raising Arizona's Dams: Daily Life, Danger, and Discrimination in the Dam Construction Camps of Central Arizona, 1890s–1940s*, Tucson: University of Arizona Press.

Wegars, P. (ed.) (1993) *Hidden Heritage: Historical Archaeology of the Overseas Chinese*, Amityville, NY: Baywood.

Williams, J. (1992) 'The archaeology of underdevelopment and the military frontier of northern New Spain', *Historical Archaeology* 26(1): 7–21.

DONALD L. HARDESTY

utopian communities

People interested in moving out of a society's mainstream sometimes create utopian communities composed of like-minded individuals. The settlements created are usually fairly small in size and located some distance from major population centres. Their residents seek to make the towns as self-contained as possible because they wish to separate themselves from society at large. Religion constitutes one the greatest reasons for the creation of utopian communities. People holding special beliefs may wish to segregate themselves from a society whose dominant members hold different religious beliefs, from a political or economic system that they find evil or misguided, or from social environments within which they may be persecuted. One important characteristic of utopian communities is that their members usually seek to create what they consider to be a perfect society along the lines promoted by their religious or political beliefs. Utopian leaders seek to make their communities shining examples to the rest of the world.

Utopian communities appear throughout the world, but one particular place they have been especially prominent is the mid-western region of the USA. The rise in utopianism in the early nineteenth century coincided with the opening of the spacious land west of the Appalachian Mountains. The rolling hills, rich farmland and wooded riverbanks provided an appealing environment for utopianists, especially once the **Native Americans** had been dispossessed. Utopianists quickly founded settlements such as Zoar, Ohio; Watervliet, Ohio; Pleasant Hill, Kentucky; and Amana, Iowa.

Historical archaeologists have only conducted limited research within abandoned and still extant utopian communities. They have investigated New Harmony, Indiana (settled in 1814 by the Harmony Society and sold in 1824 to Robert Owen's English utopianists); Bishop Hill, Illinois (settled in 1846 by the Bishop Hill Colony, a group of Swedish religious dissenters who opposed state Christianity); and Nauvoo, Illinois (settled in 1839 by the Church of Jesus Christ of Latter-Day Saints, or Mormons). Much of the archaeological research conducted at these sites has been intended to assist with the **reconstruction** of buildings that can be used for interpretive and museum purposes.

Utopian communities provide historical archaeologists with an excellent arena in which to examine the relationship between religious beliefs, communal ideals and **material culture**. For example, at the New Harmony, Indiana, settlement, George Rapp, the community's founder, designed a concentric hedge called the Labyrinth. Navigating this complicated piece of landscape architecture was the only amusement allowed to the sedate Rappites. The deeper meaning of the maze, however, was intended to convince the community's residents that heaven (the centre of the design) was only reached after a difficult journey (the trip through the Labyrinth). In Bishop Hill, Illinois, archaeologists have been able to investigate communal living by excavating the colony's dormitories.

Further reading

Leone, M.P. and Silberman, N.A. (1995) *Invisible America: Unearthing Our Hidden History*, New York: Henry Holt.

CHARLES E. ORSER, JR

Valley Forge, Pennsylvania, USA

Valley Forge, Pennsylvania, is located about 10 km north-west of Philadelphia on the south bank of the Schuykill River. The locale was made famous during the winter of 1777–8 when elements of the Continental Army camped there. Local historians first developed an interest in preserving the site in the nineteenth century, and in 1893 the State of Pennsylvania named it a state park. In 1977, the site became a National Historical Park administered by the US National Park Service. Historical archaeologists conducted excavations at Valley Forge in the 1960s (under the direction of John Cotter, a pioneer US historical archaeologist), and in the 1970s, in accordance with the Park Service's planned interpretive programme.

Residing in a series of rough huts, the US Continental soldiers, lead by General George Washington, endured a harsh winter and stayed at the site until mid-June 1778. The army was a revolutionary force that was to stand against the British Army barracked in Philadelphia and under the command of Sir William Howe. The task faced by Washington and his officers while at Valley Forge was to mould the Continental soldiers into a coherent fighting force that could fight against the British with some measure of competence, training and self-assurance. Their efforts in this regard have become legendary in US **ideology**.

Historical records indicate that the soldiers built their huts themselves and that the typical hut size was only about 4.8 by 5.5 m. Twelve men were expected to live in each hut, but only half that many officers were assigned to each structure.

Officers above the rank of colonel either built log structures or lived in approved farmhouses nearby. As part of their encampment, the soldiers also constructed a hospital hut, storerooms, slaughterhouses and bake ovens.

Historical archaeologists substantiated the size of the huts, their spatial arrangement and the artefacts inside them. Not surprisingly, they discovered that the huts were not uniformly made. Excavated examples ranged in size from 2 by 2.3 m to 3.6 by 3.8 m. They learned also that the soldiers had excavated the floors to depths of between 20 and 45 cm. Most of the huts had simple fireplaces (made of sticks and mud or stones), but they were not consistently placed within the huts. One excavated hut had no fireplace at all.

As one may imagine, many of the artefacts the archaeologists recovered were those that would be expected at an eighteenth-century military encampment: lead musket balls, gunflints, assorted gun parts, various iron tools and military buckles. The excavated animal bones, however, provide a unique glimpse into the nature of the soldiers' diet during that difficult winter. The majority of excavated bones were from domestic cows, with sheep and pig bones being present but less frequent. Other species also possibly consumed include deer, snapping turtle, goat, rabbit, squirrel and unidentified fish.

See also: zooarchaeology

Further reading

Parrington, M., Schenck, H. and Thibaut, J. (1984)

'The material world of the Revolutionary War soldier at Valley Forge', in D.G. Orr and D.G. Crozier (eds), *The Scope of Historical Archaeology: Essays in Honor of John L. Cotter*, Philadelphia: Laboratory of Anthropology, Temple University, pp. 125–61.

CHARLES E. ORSER, JR

VERENIGDE OOSTINDISCHE COMPAGNIE (VOC) *see* Dutch East India Company

vernacular architecture

The term 'vernacular architecture' is used to signify that portion of the built environment which contains buildings and other structures constructed with the use of traditional knowledge rather than formal, architectural training. A simple cabin built in the woods by frontier settlers would constitute an example of vernacular architecture; a grand state-house erected in a major city is an example of formal **architecture**. Other terms used interchangeably with vernacular architecture help to indicate the humble nature of this kind of building: traditional architecture, folk architecture and folk housing. Vernacular architecture is part of a people's **everyday life**, with the knowledge of specific building techniques and designs typically being handed down through the generations. Vernacular architecture was not typically learned from books or instructional tracts because folk architecture is designed in ways that are consistent with 'the way things have always been done'. Examples of vernacular architecture include the houses of English peasants and African slaves in Brazil, Native American wigwams and longhouses (see **Native Americans**), miners' cabins in the US West and any other kind of architecture that is based on tradition rather than formally outlined rules.

Figure 30 An example of vernacular architecture near Beaufort, South Carolina, 1938
Source: Library of Congress

Historical architects, folklorists, **material culture** specialists, museum personnel, cultural geographers and anthropologists have all pursued the study of vernacular architecture. Historical archaeologists, because they study both below- and aboveground examples of material culture, have also examined vernacular architecture, both as standing buildings and as their buried remains.

Some examples of vernacular architecture

Archaeologists play an important role in the study of how men and women construct their houses and other buildings. North American archaeologists, for instance, have provided abundant information about the sizes, construction techniques and designs of prehistoric- and historic-period architecture. Archaeological descriptions of Iroquois and Huron longhouses in New York State and Ontario, Anazasi and Zuni pueblos in Arizona and New Mexico, and Arikara and Hidasta earthlodges in North and South Dakota, among others, have significantly enriched our knowledge of traditional, indigenous building techniques before and during the arrival of Europeans. Archaeologists have provided the same kind of information for cultures around the world, and their research helps to write the history of ancient vernacular architecture.

Historical archaeologists have also vastly increased our knowledge of vernacular architecture. Important studies abound and are far too numerous to mention here. The following four examples, however, will provide an idea of the kinds of information historical archaeologists provide through their research efforts.

Working at **Puerto Real**, Haiti, Kathleen Deagan and her team of archaeologists investigated a place they termed Locus 39, an area they thought represented a residential zone within the sixteenth-century Spanish settlement. Deagan's archaeologists located and uncovered a large portion of a building in this locale. This structure covered an area larger than 24 m east to west and 7 m north to south. Portions of the walls appeared to have been supported by wooden posts, whereas others were made of masonry. The building contained three rooms: one on the east end, made of masonry and measuring 7 m wide with an undetermined length, and an adjacent room immediately to the west that measured 7 m^2 and may have had an interior, wooden room divider. A third room was situated adjacent to the second room. The archaeologists did not think that this third room was enclosed but it may have been roofed. Their excavations showed that the posts for the walls had been set inside narrow trenches and that at their bases they may have been surrounded by stone and masonry sills to retard decay. As an example of the conservative nature of traditional building, vernacular architects in Haiti still use this technique today.

While conducting excavations elsewhere in the Caribbean (see **Caribbean archaeology**), at Drax Hall Plantation in Jamaica, Douglas Armstrong was able to document the vernacular architecture of the African slaves and their descendants who resided at the estate. The plantation was continuously inhabited from 1760 to the 1920s, but in his excavations Armstrong was able to isolate two examples of vernacular architecture, one from the slave period (1760–1810) and one from the free-labourer period (1840–1925). Excavations revealed that the slave-period house measured 4.5 by 9 m in size and contained three linearly arranged rooms, distinguished by their flooring material. The floors were all that remained of the dwellings. The room on the north end had a floor made of limestone blocks, whereas the room in the middle had a floor of smaller limestone rocks, brick and marl. The room on the southern end only had a dirt floor. The structure's builders had included three doors, two of which were opposite one another and led to the middle room, but the third led to the dirt-floor room. Interestingly, Armstrong discovered that the excavated house from the free-labourer period was, with minor variation, a copy of the slave house. Only the size of the floor stones and a slightly larger central room distinguished the free-labourers' cottage from the slave cabin. Other than these small differences, the vernacular architecture at Drax Hall seemed to follow the same tradition of building. These two buildings again speak to the tenacity of traditional building methods.

The vernacular architecture of Australia's European period, as explained by Graham Connah, represents the mixing of several cultural traditions. In particular, the construction of earthen structures (often referred to as 'earthfast' building) has been influenced by English, Irish, German, Italian and Mexican construction methods One wall-construction method Connah illustrated is called pisé. In pisé construction, the builders design a set of flat, wooden forms that are the desired width of the wall to be built. With the forms prepared, they pour slightly moistened loamy mud into them and compact the mud with a steel ramming tool, much like those still used today. The builders remove the frames, leaving the standing wall. The compacting action creates a strong wall that in the proper environment can last for decades.

In a study of vernacular architecture among the Tiv in south-central Nigeria, S. Oluwole Ogundele shows that the building method in Tivland is rooted in tradition. Using a combination of archaeological surveying and **ethnoarchaeology**, Ogundele documented how the Tiv construct their buildings, which are circular in shape. They use a stick and a length of rope to inscribe the size of the house on the ground. Once this is done they excavate a foundation trench to a depth of about 20–30 cm. Then they begin to construct the wall using adobe (sun-dried clay) blocks that average about 19 cm^2 in size. They build the walls to an average height of about 2 m. The diameter of the houses ranges from 4 to almost 10 m. Once the walls are finished, the workers begin to construct the conical roof, which is composed of a wooden frame covered with palm fronds. Ogundele's field research indicates that the Tiv had used this style of architecture since before the presence of written history in the area. The ancient Tiv built their houses on the sides or tops of hills. The only real modifications they made involved the terrain, so that a house on the side of a hill would have to have walls of unequal heights to accommodate the slope and still provide for a level building.

The essentially conservative nature of vernacular architecture is not meant to suggest that traditional cultures are static and unchanging. All cultures change no matter where they are located and when in time they existed. Vernacular architecture changed along with the rest of culture, but because buildings can be fairly permanent (or at least long lasting) they can appear to be static examples of culture. The illusory permanence of architecture is one reason that scholars who study folk building often examine several buildings within a region.

Some ways of understanding vernacular architecture

As long as scholars have been investigating the world's vernacular architecture they have wondered about the mindsets of the people who built them. Why did they use circular rather than square buildings? Why did they adopt a conical roof rather than one with straight sides? Why did some cultures place their buildings on linear streets while others situated their structures in what appears to be a haphazard fashion? Did folk builders even think about their designs or were the layouts merely the result of endless years of tradition?

Such questions are extremely important because historical archaeologists must do more than simply uncover examples of buried vernacular architecture. As anthropologists and historians they must seek to provide explanations for the 'why' of the designs. Of course, providing these answers is not easy and those who have offered explanations have found that their views are not always accepted by others. The following brief examples illustrate three approaches to interpreting vernacular architecture.

In a now-classic study, folklorist Henry Glassie studied the folk housing in two counties in Virginia, just east of Charlottesville. His goal was to explain the 'theory' behind the architecture in this region by recourse to structuralism. One of the tenets of structuralism – a mainstay of much theoretical reasoning in **sociocultural anthropology** during the 1970s – was to discover the hidden, underlying structure of culture. Structuralists believe that they can learn the basic rules of a culture's deep structure by examining its many components, including vernacular architecture. Structuralists often refer to this structure in linguistic terms and refer to the rules as a 'grammar'. In the case of folk architecture, the rules of building a house – the location of its rooms, the pitch of its roof, the location of its porch and so forth – fit together like the parts of a sentence. Just as with language, native speakers know where to put the nouns and the verbs without consciously thinking about it. Thus, in Virginia, Glassie sought to learn the grammar of vernacular building. To accomplish this goal, he generated several architectural rules, beginning with Rule I.A.: 'Selection of the Geometric Entity', which was a square. In other words, the basic unit of building in Virginia was a square; everything began with it. Further rules involved the placement of windows, the presence of fireplaces, the ways of positioning partitions and so forth.

Glassie believed that knowledge of these rules would permit him to understand how folk builders constructed any building within that part of Virginia. These rules would make it possible to understand the different designs as a series of individual components. Using this system, Glassie could also examine the transformations of the designs – from one type of house (using one set of components) to another (using a different set) over time.

In another study of vernacular architecture, Matthew Johnson used and refined Glassie's approach. Examining fifteenth- through seventeenth-century houses in Suffolk, **England** (north-east of London), Johnson used Glassie's structuralist notion of 'grammar' but added an updated twist. Johnson noted that Glassie had failed to ground the logic of his grammar in the everyday cultural experiences of the people who produced the folk architecture. Though some basis for the universality of structural rules imagined by the structuralists may exist, Johnson said that the foundation of an architectural grammar may lie within the society's social inequalities or the ideological roots of the social hierarchy. In other words, Johnson argued for a more contextualised approach that provided more historical grounding for the grammar. At the same time, he believed that Glassie had not paid enough attention to historical change when considering vernacular architecture. Thus, Johnson's version of structuralism was a historical or contextual one.

In another study, Ross Jamieson explored the vernacular architecture of fifteenth-century Ecuador, a region then being entered and inhabited by Spanish colonialists. Working in the highland region, Jamieson investigated the relationship between architecture and colonial **power**. Rather than rely on any notion of structural rules, he approached vernacular architecture through the lens of social power In other words, vernacular architecture does not just 'happen'; it appears within a social network. Vernacular architecture reflects a whole series of complex social relations, most of which involve some degree of social power. Thus, for Jamieson the issue is to discover the meaning of the architectural patterns in terms of the social hierarchy and the interaction between Spanish colonialists and indigenous people. Like Johnson's approach this is a highly contextual understanding of how vernacular architecture and a people's sociocultural situation interact and are enmeshed.

See also: African American archaeology; architecture; Caribbean archaeology; Spanish colonialism

Further reading

Armstrong, D.V. (1990) *The Old Village and the Great House: An Archaeological and Historical Examination of Drax Hall Plantation, St. Ann's Bay, Jamaica*, Urbana: University of Illinois Press.

Connah, G. (1993) *The Archaeology of Australia's History*, Cambridge: Cambridge University Press.

Deagan, K. and Reitz, E.J. (1995) 'Merchants and cattlemen: The archaeology of a commercial structure at Puerto Real', in K. Deagan (ed.) *Puerto Real: The Archaeology of a Sixteenth-Century Spanish Town in Hispaniola*, Gainesville: University Press of Florida, pp. 231–84.

Glassie, H. (1975) *Folk Housing in Middle Virginia: A Structural Analysis of Historic Artifacts*, Knoxville: University of Tennessee Press.

Jamieson, R.W. (2000) *Domestic Architecture and Power: The Historical Archaeology of Colonial Ecuador*, New York: Kluwer Academic/Plenum Press.

Johnson, M. (1993) *Housing Culture: Traditional Architecture in an English Landscape*, Washington, DC: Smithsonian Institution Press.

Ogundele, S.O. (1998) 'Aspects of indigenous Tiv architecture: Past and present', in K.W. Wesler (ed.) *Historical Archaeology in Nigeria*, Trenton, NJ: Africa World Press, pp. 259–72.

CHARLES E. ORSER, JR

Vikings

The Vikings were northern Scandinavians whose homeland was Denmark, Norway, Finland and Sweden. They were skilled at sea travel and navigation, and they are widely known for their armed campaigns throughout Northern Europe. The height of power and influence is termed the 'Viking Age' and extends from the late 700s to about 1100. Before their **power** waned, they had either briefly visited or had built settlements in Russia, Italy, Spain, Britain and **Ireland**, Iceland, Greenland and even North America. The Vikings have come down in history as warlike, violent plunderers, but present-day researchers – relying partly on archaeological information – are now demonstrating that the Vikings were not so single-minded. In addition to their success in war, they were also careful settlers, creative innovators and dedicated farmers.

Archaeologists have conducted numerous excavations at sites throughout the Viking world. These studies have added flesh to our knowledge about this important culture. For example, excavations in the Bjäresjö region in southern Sweden have provided important information about Viking farming. Here, men and women living in settlements composed of four to six dwellings worked agricultural fields about 2–4 ha in size. From these fields they harvested rye, barley and emmer wheat. Archaeologists estimate that these crops provided the Bjäresjö people with about 50 per cent of their diet. They supplemented these cereals with nuts, fish, cattle, sheep, pigs, horses and eggs.

Other significant excavations of Viking sites have occurred in Ireland, where the Vikings arrived in the 800s. Excavations at Fishamble Street/Wood Quay, Dublin, and in Bakehouse Lane, Waterford, have documented the physical nature of Viking colonisation. Archaeologists unearthed evidence of at least fourteen eleventh-century house plots in Dublin. These houses were roughly rectangular in design and ranged in size from 3.2 by 3.8 m to 6 by 8 m. Preservation (see **preservation legislation**) at this site was remarkable because of its waterlogged condition, and archaeologists were able to recover woollen garments, leather shoes, carved bone, coins, **ceramics** and thousands of other pieces of **material culture**. In addition to documenting the nature of Viking Age material culture, the artefacts also reveal that the Vikings in Dublin mixed freely with the local men and women, and in effect created a Hiberno-Norse settlement. Similarly impressive excavations at Coppergate, York, **England**, have recovered thousands of artefacts from this important Viking settlement and using these materials, archaeologists continue to rewrite Viking history.

See also: Fyrkat; L'Anse aux Meadows

Further reading

Barry, T.B. (1987) *The Archaeology of Medieval Ireland*, London: Routledge.
Olson, E.G.A. (1991) 'The agrarian landscape of Viking Age farmers at Bjäresjö', in B.E. Berglund (ed.) *The Cultural Landscape During 6000 Years in Southern Sweden*, Copenhagen: Munksgaard International, pp. 190–3.

CHARLES E. ORSER, JR

VOC shipwrecks

Sunken ships of the **Dutch East India Company** or VOC are relatively new sources of information for the research of Dutch expansion and seventeenth- and eighteenth-century intercontinental trade and industry. The study of these VOC wrecks is essentially based on an integrative historical and archaeological approach applying data from both material and written sources. Through interdisciplinary integration, the analysis of an individual vessel contributes to a deeper understanding of both the practical organisation of the shipping activities of the VOC, and the functioning of the company in a wider socio-economic and cultural context.

Archaeology of VOC shipwrecks started in the early 1960s, coinciding with the explosive development of underwater archaeology. Technical innovations in diving resulted in high performance and publicly available diving gear. This stimulated a massive exploration of the underwater world. Sunken ships became targets for scientists, tourists and businessmen. From the beginning, VOC wrecks were a category of historic shipwrecks that

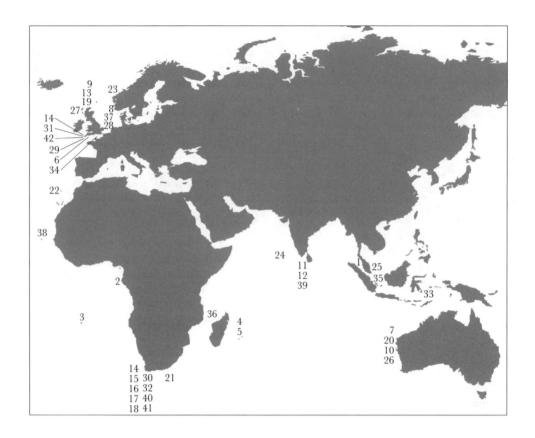

Figure 31 Sites of located and excavated VOC-wrecks (in chronological order)
(J. Gawronski, 2001)

1 Nassau, 1606, Malacca, Malaysia Middelburg, 1606
2 Mauritius, 1609, Gabon
3 Witte Leeuw, 1613, St Helena
4 Banda, 1615, Mauritius
5 Geunieerde Provinciën, 1615, Mauritius
6 Campen, 1627, Isle of Wight, UK
7 Batavia, 1629, Houtman Abrolhos Is, W Australia
8 Rob, 1640, Texel, Netherlands
9 Lastdrager, 1653, Shetland Is, UK
10 Vergulde Draeck, 1656, W Australia
11 Avondster, 1659, Galle, Sri Lanka
12 Hercules, 1661, Galle, Sri Lanka
13 Kennemerland, 1664, Shetland Is, UK
14 Princesse Maria, 1686, Scilly Is, UK
15 Dageraad, 1694, Robben I, S Africa
16 Oosterland, 1697, Cape Town, S Africa
17 Huis te Kraaijenstein, 1698, Cape Peninsula, S Africa
18 Meresteyn, 1702, Saldanha Bay, S Africa
19 Liefde, 1711, Shetland Is, UK
20 Zuytdorp, 1713, W Australia
21 Bennebroek, 1713, Ciskei, S Africa

22 Slot ter Hooghe, 1724, Porto Santo, Madeira
23 Akerendam, 1725, Alesund, Norway
24 Ravenstein, 1726, Ari Atoll, Maldives
25 Risdam, 1727, Mersing, Malaysia
26 Zeewyk, 1727, Houtman Abrolhos Is, W Australia
27 Adelaar, 1728, Barra, Outer Hebrides, UK
28 Vliegent Hart, 1735, Schooneveld, Flushing, Netherlands
29 Boot, 1738, Prawl Point, South Devon, UK
30 Vis, 1740, Table Bay, S Africa
31 Hollandia, 1743, Scilly Is, UK
32 Reijgersdaal, 1747, Cape Town, S Africa
33 Nieuwekerke, 1748, Tukangbesi Is, Sulawesi, Indonesia
34 Amsterdam, 1749, Hastings, UK
35 Geldermalsen, 1752, Riau Archipelago, Indonesia
36 Bredenhof, 1753, Mozambique
37 Buitenzorg, 1760, Wadden Sea, Netherlands
38 Leimuiden, 1770, Cape Verde Is
39 Geinwens, 1775, Galle, Sri Lanka
40 Nieuw Rhoon, 1776, Cape Town, S Africa
41 Middelburg, 1781, Saldanha Bay, S Africa
42 Zeelelie, 1795, Scilly Is, UK

attracted special interest, both for their historical significance and their commercial value because of bullion or **porcelain** treasure.

During its two centuries of existence, the VOC probably built around 1,600 ships. Half of this number was produced in **Amsterdam**. The most important shipping facility of the VOC was created in the 1660s on an artificial island in the eastern part of the city's harbour front, called Oostenburg. Here, a large-scale and fully developed complex for the construction, supplying, equipping and reception of fleets was realised in only five years. The scale, layout, buildings and installations, labour differentiation (170 functions) and personnel size (200 staff and 1,100 workmen) made Oostenburg a utilitarian facility with early industrial features. The Amsterdam shipyard had a production rate of three to five ships per year, culminating in seven ships in the 1740s. Standardisation of equipment and supplies made it possible annually to dispatch fleets of up to fifteen ships from Amsterdam to **Asia**, half of the total annual fleet. The total number of shipping movements on the intercontinental route amounted to more than 8,000 voyages (4,789 outward bound and 3,401 inward bound), not taking into account the intensive traffic of VOC ships in the intra-Asiatic trade. In a period of 200 years, approximately 250 ships (105 outward bound and 141 inward bound vessels) were lost; in other words, about 3 per cent of all voyages had a fatal end.

Some fifty VOC wrecks have been located and excavated in Europe, Africa, Asia and **Australia**. These sites cover the entire VOC period and date from 1606 (the *Nassau* and the *Middelburg*, Straits of Malacca) to 1795 (the *Zeelelie*, Scilly Isles). This number is continually increasing, particularly as a result of ongoing commercial projects, mostly in African and Asian waters. These discoveries lead generally to salvage and destruction rather than systematic documentation and excavation. Nevertheless, despite their attraction to salvors, a fair number of sites have been investigated in a sound archaeological manner. Other factors contributing to qualitative variation in the material record are the shipwrecking event, which affected the integrity of the vessel, and the diversity of natural conditions. The sites are widely spread over the globe, in environments varying from the cold Atlantic to the tropical Indian Ocean.

From a material (archaeological) point of view, VOC ships represent rich and complex assemblages composed of many thousands of artefacts and designed for many different purposes. Essentially, such ships can be characterised as the company's multifunctional tool for establishing a world-wide network of trade and industry. They created a bridge between Europe and Asia, as part of an intricate economic and political system, which led to technological, commercial and cultural exchange on a global scale. VOC ships acted as military platforms with guns and soldiers; they carried cargo and provisions for the overseas settlements as part of an economic trade and supply system; they were floating villages accommodating crews of over 300 men with a ranked social structure and differentiated labour; they were the post office and the bank of the company, transporting documents and currency. In fact, they represent a microcosm of the VOC, expressed in a material and three-dimensional way.

VOC wrecks are a specific category of research subject. In terms of site formation processes, shipwrecks are sharply defined in time, and offer, when dated, a material complex of secure chronological precision. Due to their particular historical background (belonging to a bureaucratic trading company), archival references are available for archaeological research. The application of written sources from the companies archive enabled the fine-tuning of the classification of material culture and the interpretation of archaeological contexts from these shipwrecks. Specific material-oriented research in the archives helps to identify artefacts, but also helps the investigator to select records, such as bookkeeping journals or instructions, which may contain particular information on certain aspects of material reality.

The further study of the administration of the company gives a better insight into the production side of the enterprise. Integrative historical and archaeological studies of certain VOC wrecks, such as the *Hollandia* and the *Amsterdam*, have especially contributed to the development of analytical approaches for examining the (pre-) industrial nature and **modernity** of the company's production system and organisation. The complex relationships of the company with its suppliers and its work force, together with the larger technological, socioeconomic and cultural systems in which the VOC functioned, have become important new subjects for study, combining data on ships, infrastructure and administration, obtained both by excavation and archival research.

Further reading

Delgado, J.P. (ed.) (1997) *Encyclopaedia of Underwater and Maritime Archaeology*, London: British Museum Press.

Gawronski, J. (1998) 'The underwater heritage of the Dutch East India Company (VOC): Aspects of historical-archaeological studies of VOC-shipwrecks, in G. Volpe (ed.) *Archeologia Subacquea.*

Come opera l'archeologo. Storie delle acque, Firenze: Edizioni All'Insegna del Giglio, pp. 409–24.

—— (1997) 'The *Hollandia* and the *Amsterdam*: Ships and the economic network of the VOC in Amsterdam around 1750', in D.C. Lakey (ed.) *Underwater Archaeology 1997*, Tucson: Society for Historical Archaeology, pp. 1–8.

Kist, J.B. (1992) 'Integrating archaeological and historical records in Dutch East India Company research', in D.H. Keith and T.L. Carrell (eds) *Underwater Archaeological Proceedings from the Society for Historical Archaeology Conference 1992*, Tucson: Society for Historical Archaeology, pp. 53–7.

JERZY GAWRONSKI

VOC *see* Dutch East India Company

Wales

The Principality of Wales is perhaps the least known and understood part of the UK, and the profile of *archaeoleg hanesyddol Gymreig* (Welsh historical archaeology) in the wider historical-archaeology community has inevitably suffered as a result. If truth be told, '*archaeoleg hanesyddol*' is itself a neologism of sorts, as historical archaeology in Wales has, in the past, almost always taken place within the interlocking and closely related contexts of post-medieval and **industrial archaeology**. As a whole, the growth of post-medieval archaeology in Wales has often closely paralleled developments in **England** and the rest of Britain, but there are undoubtedly themes and issues that are particularly important to historical archaeology as practised in Wales. Prominent among these important issues are language and industry. Indeed, the industrial transformation of Wales is undoubtedly the single most important factor in the development of this small nation in the post-medieval period.

Social context

Given Wales's somewhat low international profile, a brief description of the post-medieval context in Wales is necessary. In the search for arbitrary divisions, the post-medieval period in Wales may be said to begin with the Act of Union of 1536, which fully incorporated Wales into the English state. The Act also removed formal recognition from the Welsh language, necessitating the formation of a Welsh ruling class fluent in English.

Crucially, however, parliament soon permitted the use of Welsh in church services, which gave the language a respectability and legal status denied to the other Celtic languages of Britain and Ireland. Ultimately, while Wales stands as an early example of English post-medieval imperialism, it never became the proving ground for British colonialism that some have identified in Ireland.

Despite a vibrant and important local culture, Wales remained a linguistically isolated, largely agricultural society marginal to the growing British Empire for most of the next two centuries. From the mid-eighteenth century, everything would change. John Davies's monumental *History of Wales* stresses that while change occurs in all periods, the years between 1770 and 1850 wrought fundamental shifts in Wales. The population doubled in two generations, the proportion of the population dependent on the land plummeted, land transportation links radically improved and the internal distribution of the population shifted dramatically. These changes were wrought by the vital importance of Welsh industry to the British Empire, particularly the massive coalfields of south Wales, but also the slate mines and other industries of both north and south. Yet the stresses wrought by industrialisation arguably saved the distinctive identity of Wales. Unlike the Irish, Scots and other emigrant groups studied in historical archaeology, the opportunities presented by the Welsh Industrial Revolution removed the pressure to emigrate. While some of the population did leave for the New World, the typical Welsh pattern was one of internal migration, particularly to the coalfields. In proportion to population, Welsh migrants to the

USA were four times less numerous than the English, seven times less numerous than the Scots and twenty-six times less numerous than the Irish. Yet ironically, within the radicalisation and social ferment that grew out of industrial Wales, the distinctive Welsh language and culture began to erode; where the overwhelming majority of the population in the eighteenth century spoke Welsh, by 1901, the proportion had fallen to 50 per cent. Today, only 20 per cent of the people of Wales speak the language of their fathers as their first language.

Post-medieval archaeology

The early years of Welsh post-medieval archaeology closely mirror developments in England, which is unsurprising given that the **Society for Post-medieval Archaeology** is a national British organisation. Many of the same problems and issues presented themselves to the early post-medievalists on either side of the border. Certainly, the importance of finds studies and the concept of period continuity that characterised early English post-medieval archaeology also occur in Wales. In Wales, the work of John Lewis stands out in particular in this regard, and his contributions to the study of medieval and later pottery in Wales, and indeed in the rest of Britain, cannot be understated. Lewis was also one of the few British archaeologists to engage with Jenkins's challenge to study the way of life of communities unaffected by large-scale industrialisation. His study of the folk traditions and social background of the Ewenny potteries remains an important landmark in this regard. Traditional post-medieval research issues of landscape development and rural architecture, such as Smith's important survey of the *Houses of the Welsh Countryside*, have also featured strongly in Wales – although studies of urbanisation were undoubtedly hindered by the lack of large early post-medieval centres within the Principality.

The themes explored by recent post-medieval archaeology in Wales make more sense within the sociohistorical context described earlier. Research in north Pembrokeshire, directed by Harold Mytum, has engaged with a more overtly theoretical agenda. Of particular note is Mytum's study of language and cultural identity on Pembrokeshire

gravestones. Mytum identified pedimented gravestones in nineteenth-century north Pembrokeshire that convey elements of class identity, cultural identity and highly specific cultural identities. The **material culture** of cottages and farms, particularly pottery and **architecture**, has also been part of this ongoing Pembrokeshire research, which has often served to increase our understanding of the geographically isolated rural poor of Wales.

Industrial archaeology

Whatever the contributions of post-medieval archaeology in understanding the sociocultural life of the rural poor, no survey of historical archaeology in Wales can escape the central role of **industrial archaeology** in understanding the recent Welsh past. One figure stands out as an evangelical figure in the early development of Welsh industrial archaeology: David Morgan Rees. It was Rees's arrival at the Department of Industry at the National Museum (of Wales) in 1959 that served as the catalyst in the development of the Welsh sub-discipline. As Briggs has noted, Rees's achievement was to encourage both the recording and responsible preservation of the industrial past in a nation whose attitude towards that past could be ambivalent; when the Snowdonia National Park was created, the historically important Blaenau Ffestiniog slate mines were deliberately excluded as an 'ugly' scar on north Wales's most famous natural landscape. Rees's 1975 volume *The Industrial Archaeology of Wales*, with its list of over 500 'key sites', remains the concrete foundation upon which industrial archaeology in the Principality rests.

Wales, and indeed the world, owes Rees and those who followed him, such as W. Gerwyn Thomas and Douglas Hague, an inordinate favour. If the Industrial Revolution is the central event in the development of the modern West, then Wales is the testing ground in which that revolution was perfected, and Wales was the furnace that fired the British Empire. The growth of the coal industry went hand in hand with the growth of the iron industry, which in turn went hand in hand with the expansion of the railways. In 1830, 40 per cent of British pig iron was produced in south Wales. By the 1870s, a third of British export coal came from the south Wales coalfields. In 1860, fifteen of the eighteen copper works in the UK were in Wales – more than half of these in the Tawe valley alone.

Most of these aspects of the Welsh industrial past have indeed been examined by heritage organisations, local councils and individual industrial archaeologists. An incomplete list of examples would include Dyfed and Clwyd County Councils' surveys of lead mines, the National Trust's survey of industrial sites at Aberglaslyn, the Merthyr Tydfil Heritage Trust's important work in the unofficial capital of industrial Wales and the restoration of the Melingriffith water pump near Cardiff. Furthermore, despite the Blaenau Ffestiniog slate mine oversight, the three National Parks in Wales have often taken a proactive role in preserving the industrial past. Nor has the social side of industrial archaeology been overlooked, as evidenced by Lowe's work on nineteenth-century workers' housing. Finally, the Royal Commission for Ancient and Historical Monuments (Wales), in conjunction with *Cadw* (the Welsh heritage body) has set up the *Panel Archaeoleg Ddiwydiannol Cymru*, the Welsh Industrial Archaeology Panel, which has played an important role in maximising the sub-discipline's occasionally scarce resources.

If very little Welsh industrial archaeology could be described as theory-informed, then the sheer number of industrial sites in Wales must be offered in mitigation. With so much of the threatened past to record, theory is a luxury few Welsh industrial archaeologists have been able to afford. Once the task of recording the industrial remains is more complete, a more theory-informed approach will also develop. It is also likely that there will be more of an engagement between archaeologists examining the urban, industrial, rural and agricultural pasts. Despite its undoubted achievements, only through a holistic approach to the past can *archaeoleg hanesyddol Gymreig* develop and grow. However, there is little doubt that Welsh historical archaeology will develop methodological and theoretical structures that will permit the examination of specifically Welsh issues within specifically Welsh contexts.

Further reading

Briggs, C.S. (ed.) (1992) *The Welsh Industrial Heritage:*

A Review, London: Council for British Archaeology.

Davies, J. (1993) *A History of Wales*, Harmondsworth: Allen Lane.

Lewis, J.M. (1982) *The Ewenny Potteries*, Cardiff: National Museum of Wales.

Mytum, H.C. (1999) 'Welsh cultural identity in nineteenth-century Pembrokeshire: The pedimented headstone as graveyard monument', in S. Tarlow and S. West (eds) *The Familiar Past? Archaeologies of Later Historical Britain*, London: Routledge, pp. 215–30.

Rees, D.M. (1975) *The Industrial Archaeology of Wales*, Newton Abbot: David and Charles.

Smith, P. (1975) *Houses of the Welsh Countryside*, London: Royal Commission on Ancient and Historical Monuments in Wales.

Vyner, B. and Wrathmell, S. (eds) (1987) *Medieval and Later Pottery in Wales; Presented to J.M. Lewis*, Cardiff: University College.

ALASDAIR M. BROOKS

Wapping, England

Wapping, to the east of the City of London, was in the centre of London's docklands from the fifteenth century onwards. Two main sites of the historic period have been archaeologically investigated: the burial ground of the church of St John Wapping and the Hermitage Pothouse at Hermitage Basin.

The parish of St John Wapping was created in 1694 and the new church was built in 1760. The churchyard formed the basis of the archaeological investigation and was divided into three areas. There was a communal burial vault in the northeast corner of the site, a series of ten family burial vaults along the southern boundary wall of the site and interments in the main part of the burial area. Many of the burials were in lead coffins, particularly those in the family vaults, with coffin plates. Although no access was available to the skeletal material, 126 individuals could be identified from their coffin plates. The documentary sources for the parish are extensive and a complete set of parish burial registers survives. These give age, address and, in some cases, cause of death. By comparing the registers with the archaeological evidence and the other available evidence, including wills and trade directories, vestry minutes and churchwarden accounts, conclusions can be drawn about the buried population and the history and familial relationships of those within the ground can be traced. It was clear that the different areas of the churchyard were occupied by slightly different groups and that the most affluent members of the local community wanted to be buried in their own private vaults.

The Hermitage Pothouse was indicated by documentary evidence to be at the head of the former Hermitage Dock and was in production from *c.* 1665 to *c.* 1773. The pottery produced is known as tin-glazed ware, or sometimes delftware after the major production centre (Delft) in the Low Countries. Wapping was the one factory established on the north bank of the Thames, but in common with all the other factories was close to the river.

Three kilns were excavated; two of a type normally associated with the manufacture of stoneware and earthenware but at the Hermitage Pothouse used to manufacture tin-glazed ware. The third was represented by a firebox type associated with a rectangular tin-glaze kiln.

During its lifetime the pothouse site would have produced quantities of ceramic waste and it is this that was recovered from this excavation. Although only a very small percentage of the total waste material discarded, there are a number of traits and trends to be observed among the assemblage. There is a minor portion of typical late seventeenth-century forms such as caudle cups and chargers, whereas the larger portion of the material is typical of the eighteenth century, producing forms such as punch bowls, flat-base plates and recessed-base plates. The excavation provided a first range of pottery forms from this pothouse, which was previously only known from documentary evidence.

ADRIAN MILES

West Africa

West Africa is poorly known archaeologically. Although there are a few, notable exceptions, regional chronologies, artefact sequences and basic culture histories are lacking for many areas. The first archaeological work, primarily by amateur Europeans, dates to the late nineteenth and early twentieth centuries. In some areas, professional archaeologists have focused greater attention on the study of Stone Age or early Iron Age traditions, but the archaeology of historically known populations has been of increasing importance, particularly during the post-colonial period. Since the 1960s, an increasing amount of research has been done on sites or on topics that relate to transformations and events that are known, at least in part, though documentary sources or oral traditions. However, the term 'historical archaeology' is generally not used, the research that falls within this rubric often being subsumed under 'ethnohistory', '**ethnoarchaeology**' or late Iron Age archaeology. In the sense that non-archaeological sources often provide limited information, the term 'protohistoric' is sometimes used, particularly in Francophone countries, to describe much of the last 1,000 years of the West African past.

West Africa is here considered to extend south of the Tropic of Cancer and west of Cameroon and Chad, bounded by the Atlantic Ocean in the south and west. This is an arbitrary division, as culture contacts and trade have long connected West Africa with regions to the north and east. The vast area considered here incorporates a tremendous range of climatic diversity, ranging from some of the driest areas of the world in the north to tropical rain forests in the south. A wide range of cultural traditions, languages, sociopolitical organisations and historical patterns mirrors this environmental diversity.

Although the historic period may be considered to begin with the advent of documentary accounts, written sources are quite limited for many parts of West Africa until the late nineteenth or twentieth centuries. Indigenous writing systems did emerge in some areas, most notably in Liberia, Nigeria and Cameroon. However, these systems appear in the late nineteenth or twentieth centuries and are quite restricted in terms of their distribution and the amount of information they provide. The primary documentary sources for most of West Africa are descriptions and travel accounts by outsiders. Because of the paucity of information sometimes provided by the documentary record, researchers have often turned to the archaeological record, oral traditions and ethnographic data to supplement interpretations of the past.

Contacts between the people of West Africa and literate populations to the north, and with Europeans on the coast, have been important in providing documentary records, as well as the source of change and transformation in social, political and economic conditions. The earliest documentary sources for West Africa, which date to early in the second millennium AD, are by Arab travellers who provide brief descriptions of some of the civilisations and principal settlements of the savannah and Sahel.

Archaeological research has been undertaken on some of the sites known through Arabic sources such as Koumbi-Saleh, Tegaoust and Azugi in Mauritania, Jenne-jeno, Gao-Sané and Tombouctou in present-day Mali, and Azelik and Marandet in Niger. These data enhance the limited details provided by written accounts of some of the early West African states. Koumbi-Saleh in southern Mauritania is believed to have been the capital of ancient Ghana, which emerged as the principal state in the western Sahel by AD 1000. Oral traditions of the Soninke people refer to the town of Koumbi, which is said to have been the capital of an ancient empire. The Arab traveller Al Bekri described the capital of Ghana in 1067. He refers to a large settlement consisting of two towns, one occupied by Muslim Arab traders and the other an indigenous African town that included the palace of the King. Archaeological study of Koumbi-Saleh uncovered a town consistent with these limited accounts, including the remains of two discrete occupation areas. One settlement area has Islamic tombs and multi-storeyed stone buildings, while the second site, located nearby, lacks these features. The latter area may have been the royal town of al-Ghala where the non-Muslim King of Ghana lived.

Sites associated with ancient Mali have also been investigated. Mali was one of the states that rose to prominence following the decline of ancient Ghana. Mali reached its apogee in the thirteenth and fourteenth centuries, when it extended over parts of Mali, Senegal, Gambia, Mauritania and Guinea. This area includes the fertile lands of the inland Niger Delta, as well as the goldfields of the upper Niger River. Modern-day *griot*, or professional praise singers, still sing stories about ancient Mali and its rulers. Mali is also known through limited Arabic sources. Mansa Musa, ruler of Mali between 1312 and 1337, spent and gave away so much gold during his pilgrimage to Mecca in 1324 that currencies were devalued. Mansa Musa became widely known and 'Rex Melly', or the King of Mali, appears on Angelino Dulcert's 1339 map of Africa.

The exact extent and location of Mali remains uncertain. Some sites, including Jenne-jeno and Gao-Sané, have produced exotic trade items such as Chinese **porcelain**, imported **beads** and **glass** from Mameluke Egypt that attest to Mali's contacts with North Africa. Tombs at Gao-Sané have produced royal epigraphs that complement the scant travel accounts. Work has also been undertaken at Niani, a possible capital of ancient Mali. Located in modern Guinea, Niani corresponds to some aspects of the capital mentioned in documentary sources. Yet excavations at the site suggest the settlement was occupied between AD 600 and 1000, abandoned and reoccupied during the sixteenth and seventeenth centuries, suggesting the settlement was not occupied during Mali's apogee.

The uncertainty in locating the capitals of ancient Ghana and Mali underscore the limited information provided by Arabic sources. Even during the latter half of the second millennium AD, documentary sources often provide only brief and, at times, contradictory information. The value of the sources that are available is enhanced by increasing information on archaeological sites and the settlement patterns of the surrounding regions, the large majority of which are unmentioned in written sources. Excavations and regional surveys of the Senegal River Basin, the inland Niger Delta and parts of Ghana, Nigeria and Cameroon have started to uncover regional changes in social, political and economic organisation that have occurred.

The Europeans arrived on the West African coast in the fifteenth century. The Portuguese reached the mouth of Pra River in modern Ghana in 1471 and the coast of Nigeria by the end of the century. In the following centuries, the Dutch, British, Swedes, Danes, French, Germans and

Americans competed for trade. European sources provide comparatively detailed information for some areas, such as coastal Senegal and Ghana. Yet African–European interactions were primarily limited to the coast and its immediate hinterland until the late nineteenth and twentieth centuries when colonial governments extended control over the interior. Prior to that time period, European contact with the majority of the peoples of West Africa was limited and European accounts of African populations non-existent.

Few archaeological projects have been undertaken on sites occupied by Europeans and African settlements directly associated with European outposts. Much of the research that has been done has focused on the history and plans of the European trade posts and fortifications, and their restoration, not on the archaeological record. Many of the sites that have received attention were outposts that were important during the Atlantic trade, including the forts of Goreé Island off the Senegal coast, Bunce Island in the Sierra Leone estuary, the European forts of coastal Ghana and Ouidah in the Republic of Benin.

The African trading settlements at **Elmina**, Ghana, and Savi in the Republic of Benin have been excavated. Elmina is significant as the site of the first and largest European fort in sub-Saharan Africa. Founded by the Portuguese in 1482 next to an existing African settlement, Castelo de São Jorge da Mina emerged as the centre for Portuguese trade in the region. It then became the centre of Dutch trade after the castle's capture by the Dutch in 1637. Archaeological work has concentrated on the African town site, exposing a variety of structures and a diversity of trade materials dating from the fifteenth to the nineteenth centuries. Savi was the capital town of the Hueda state, which was an important trading entrepôt in the late seventeenth and early eighteenth centuries. Savi remained unallied with any one European power. Dutch, English, French and Portuguese trade posts were located next to the Hueda palace, and the African rulers carefully structured African–European relations. Research at both Elmina and Savi underscore the ways in which an increasingly European-centred global economy was locally articulated.

In contrast to the coastal trading sites, much more archaeological research has been carried out on settlements in the West African interior. While many of these date to the last 500 years, documents frequently provide little or no information and in many instances oral traditions are also limited. As is the case for the period pre-dating the Atlantic trade, archaeological data provide a principal source of information. Changes in the archaeological record can be examined in light of a general historical context provided by non-archaeological sources. In particular, archaeological data has been used to evaluate the consequences and impacts of the Atlantic slave trade and a global economy. Changes dating to the period of the Atlantic trade include transformations in settlement patterns, the appearance of fortified towns and radical change in indigenous industries. Archaeological data also serve as a means of examining the subsistence patterns, technology and everyday lifeways that are poorly represented in other source material.

Further reading

DeCorse, C.R. (2001) *An Archaeology of Elmina: Africans and Europeans on the Gold Coast, 1400–1900*, Washington, Smithsonian Institution Press.

—— (ed.) (2000) *West Africa during the Atlantic Slave Trade: Archaeological Perspective*, London: Leicester University Press.

Insoll, T. (1996) *Islam, Archaeology and History: Gao Region (Mali) ca. AD 900–1250*, New York: Oxford University Press.

McIntosh, S.K. (1994) 'Changing perceptions of West Africa's past: Archaeological research since 1988, *Journal of Archaeological Research* 2: 165–98.

CHRISTOPHER R. DeCORSE

whaling

Before the commercial exploitation of petroleum in the mid-nineteenth century, whaling provided the oil used for domestic and municipal lighting, and for the lubrication of machinery.

Whaling also provided whalebone, or baleen, a springy cartilage used in women's fashions. Whaling was of tremendous economic significance, and it was also an important catalyst for exploration and colonisation. Historical and underwater archaeologists in many parts of the world have become involved in the study of whaling sites.

The earliest whaling sites studied are in Red Bay, Newfoundland, where sixteenth-century Basques set up shore stations and hunted whale species that frequented the shallow coastal waters during the summer months. On shore, archaeologists have excavated the sites of crew quarters, tryworks or furnaces and a cemetery (see **cemeteries**). Underwater sites excavated include that of the galleon *San Juan* and a smaller open whaleboat. The Basques stopped going to Canada around 1600, but, as the Basque fishery was closing, British and Dutch whalers began whaling at Spitsbergen in the high Arctic. They too used shore stations and ships moored in bays, and archaeologists have found extensive remains of their stations.

The first English-speaking settlers in New England hunted the abundant whales along their shores into the eighteenth century. Archaeological sites associated with whaling from that period are related to on-shore services such as taverns and townships where the whalers lived. In the nineteenth century, New Bedford, Massachusetts, prospered by servicing the great US deep-sea, or pelagic, whaling fleets. Sites managed by the US National Parks Service include businesses like chandlers, who supplied the fleets, and those like candle makers, who processed the whale oil. Other shore sites associated with the US pelagic whalers can be found around the world, including the Azores Islands, the islands of the South Pacific and Paita, Peru, where the Americans established resupply and provisioning bases. In many cases these supplied the large British and French pelagic fleets as well. Among the sites investigated by archaeologists are the wrecks of whaling ships at the island of Pohnpei, Micronesia, which are being studied by Suzanne Scott Finney.

While other nations were pursuing pelagic whaling, in Australia and New Zealand shore and bay whaling were revived. Most of the shore stations have been recorded, and a few have been excavated. The Archaeology of Whaling in Southern Australia and New Zealand (AWSANZ) is an international collaborative project between terrestrial and underwater archaeologists that is integrating existing studies and carrying out additional survey and excavation. One whaling ship, the *Litherland*, has also been excavated in Australia. Archaeologists from Australia, New Zealand and South Africa have also recorded whaling stations in the sub-Antarctic, including those on Macquarie, Heard and Marion Islands. In the later nineteenth century, whalers began to exploit the west coast of North America, and archaeologists have worked on sites in San Diego and Alaska.

Further reading

Lawrence, S. and Staniforth, M. (eds) (1998), *The Archaeology of Whaling in Southern Australia and New Zealand*, Canberra: Brolga Press for the Australasian Society for Historical Archaeology and the Australian Institute for Maritime Archaeology.

Tuck, J.A. and Grenier, R. (1989), *Red Bay, Labrador: World Whaling Capital A.D. 1550-1600*, St John's, Newfoundland: Atlantic Archaeology.

SUSAN LAWRENCE

Wharram Percy, England

Research from 1948 to 1990 made Wharram Percy the best-known deserted village (see **deserted villages**) in Britain and Ireland. The antiquity and complexity of the site surprised archaeologists and helped to alert them to evidence elsewhere. The site comprises 10 ha of earthworks and a church (see **churches**), now partly ruined, and is surrounded by the vestigial earthworks of fields. These features date from *c.* AD 1100–1500. The village was planned in two rows along a lane beside a stream. The rows comprise five blocks of tofts and crofts, amounting to about thirty domestic plots. Beside one block lay a larger building, interpreted as a manor house (see **manor houses**); a separate group of more complicated earthworks is thought to represent a later manor. The church and priest's house occupied a distinct platform. The stream was dammed to power a mill and make a fish pond.

Extensive excavations revealed successive methods of medieval and post-medieval house construction in timber and masonry – the latter more common later. Ordinary houses and ancillary structures were investigated as well as the bigger ensembles of the putative manors. The church was examined with attention to the structural sequence (beginning in the tenth century), some 600 graves, 1,000 skeletons and memorials. All the excavations showed complicated successions of building with varying forms and orientations.

The site was not always fully occupied. Some of it was quarried in the late 1200s and almost half of it was abandoned in the 1300s, probably in conjunction with a change from arable farming to herding, although one of the manorial sites was given over to new houses. The researchers' initial expectations of greater antiquity were amply confirmed when two houses of the mid-first millennium were found as well as finds, in other locations, from the eighth century. There were at least five houses in the Roman period; and there was occupation in the preceding Iron Age too. Certain boundaries were maintained through most of the entire history. Wharram Percy was largely abandoned when the farming regime was committed more exclusively to herding. However, a farm was built in the 1770s and part of it then converted into cottages, the church was used to the mid-1900s and now the site is a minor visitor attraction.

The research was undertaken by volunteers in short summer seasons. Many archaeologists contributed and the evolving methodology proved influential throughout Britain. Open-area excavation was gradually adopted. Latterly, more refined **aerial photography** was carried out and methods of extensive ground survey were developed in order to provide context in the surrounding landscape. Documentary research was integrated with the fieldwork: there was mention of the place in 1086 (the Domesday survey) and manorial and ecclesiastical records helped to account for subsequent development at the site and other settlements in the parish.

See also: gravestones; historical documents; medieval archaeology

Further reading

Beresford, M. and Hurst, J. (1990) *Wharram Percy: Deserted Medieval Village*, London: B.T. Batsford.

N. JAMES

windmills

By the beginning of the twenty-first century, historical archaeologists had not paid much attention to the study of windmills, called molinology. This lack of research, however, does not mean that the examination of windmills is unimportant. On the contrary, the study of windmills and windmill technology has an important potential to provide significant new information about many important topics, including technological change, the daily lives of millers and milling families, the interaction between millers and farmers, the rationale behind the locations of mills, the rise and fall of milling and other important historical and anthropological questions. In places with long milling traditions, these topics can link medieval and post-medieval periods, and provide for studies with considerable time depth. Much of the study of mills has occurred within **industrial archaeology**.

In 1989, Jorge Miranda and João Viegas completed an important study of windmills in Portugal, in a region just west of Lisbon. Miranda and Viegas conducted a study of windmills in a three-parish region in the Oeiras area and documented the numbers of standing, ruined and abandoned mills. In the best tradition of historical archaeology, they were sensitive to the significance of each mill's date of construction and history, and they provided detailed information about the mills' historical and cultural contexts. They also carefully documented the construction techniques and the technology used within each mill in the region.

Miranda and Viegas were not content with simply providing the raw data for the mills they examined. Instead, they moved to a second level of analysis – the regional scale – and explored the locations of the mills in relation to several cultural and natural features in the area, including the distances to railroads, population centres and water courses. They also provided several temporal scales, charting the locations of mills in 1850, 1900, 1930 and 1989. This diachronic examination made it possible for them to study the rise and fall of milling as well as its cultural significance in the region. They demonstrated that the peak of mill usage in this area was around 1850. The area's mills experienced a rapid decline after this date, and, in the five decades between 1850 and 1900, mill usage had fallen off a full 77 per cent.

Several aspects of the decline of milling are worthy of detailed consideration by historical archaeologists. One of the most important features of the decline – in addition to the disuse of the technology itself – is the social impact of each mill's closure. Historical archaeologists who conduct research on the regional scale, as did Miranda and Viegas in Portugal, have the opportunity to demonstrate how mills were connected and whether the closure of one mill affected the closure of others. In other words, rather than seeing the mills merely as individual examples of a certain kind of technology – which indeed they were – analysts can link mills together in social, political and economic networks. In the region studied by Miranda and Viegas, the distribution of mills in 1850 indicates that they were stretched out along the major north-to-south running rivers. Ecological factors undoubtedly played a role in guiding the placement of windmills, but the clustered arrangements of mills in Oeiras seems to suggest some sort of intentional grouping that may have had more to do with the social networks of the people associated with the mills rather with simple geography.

Further reading

Miranda, J.A. and Viegas, J.C. (1992) *Moinhos de Vento no Concelho de Oeiras*, Oeiras: Câmar Municipal de Oeiras.

CHARLES E. ORSER, JR

Witte Leeuw, shipwreck

The *Witte Leeuw* was a ship of the **Dutch East India Company**, or VOC, that was built in *c.* 1610 in **Amsterdam** and was sunk in 1613 off St Helena. The *Witte Leeuw* dates from the early period of the Dutch East India trade. The ship was homeward bound with a cargo of Asian products reflecting the commercial and cultural interests of the early European explorers. This site is particularly important as it yielded the most extensive shipwrecked collection of early seventeenth-century Wan Li **porcelain**.

The *Witte Leeuw* left Amsterdam in January 1610 for Bantam in Indonesia. In the following three years, the ship took part in several commercial and military expeditions to the Moluccas and the Philippines capturing Spanish cargo ships. Back in Bantam, a cargo of cloves, nutmeg and pepper was taken on board before the ship sailed to Europe in 1613. Apart from spices, 1,317 diamonds are also mentioned on the cargo list. During an engagement with Portuguese ships off St Helena, the *Witte Leeuw* and her entire crew were lost, as one of the two stern cannon – bronze 24-pounders – blew up.

The shipwreck was discovered in 1976 by shipwreck explorer Robert Sténuit during an underwater archaeological expedition, sponsored by Henri Delauze of Comex, France. The site was located in Jamestown Bay at a depth of 33 m, buried in 3 m of mud, at about 250 m from the coast in a heavily contaminated area used as anchorage for nearly 400 years. During a five-month campaign, the wreck was only partially excavated and recorded. The excavation yielded some unexpected results, however. Several cannon, among which was the remaining 24-pounder sternpiece, shed light on the armament of early VOC ships. A series of rare shells from East Indonesia appeared to be a unique early seventeenth-century naturalist collection and illustrated the start of scientific research of Asian nature and culture by European explorers.

Most of the finds consisted of fragments of blue and white export porcelain. These ceramics were damaged by the explosion. No mention is made of the purchase of porcelain in the existing cargo manifests. The porcelain in the wreck was probably acquired privately at Bantam from Chinese merchants; this would explain the presence of a number of Chinese artefacts among the finds. Another possibility is that the porcelain was a prize taken from one of the Spanish ships captured in the Philippines. The bulk of the collection consisting of porcelain sherds was acquired by the Rijksmuseum in Amsterdam to prevent dispersal of the archaeological complex, as most of the complete items were destined for auction. The ceramics from the *Witte Leeuw* became the focus of an extensive restoration and conservation project that enabled a detailed study of late Wan Li porcelain intended for the European market in the earliest period of the West European porcelain trade.

Further reading

Pijl-Ketel, C. van der (1982) *The Ceramic Load of the Witte Leeuw (1613)*, Amsterdam: Rijksmuseum.
Sténuit, R. (1978) 'The sunken treasure of St Helena', *National Geographic Magazine* 154(4): 562–76.

JERZY GAWRONSKI AND BAS KIST

women in historical archaeology

Women have played a role in historical archaeology since its inception, but it has taken several decades for their numbers and prominence in the field to approach being on a par with that of men. Even at the beginning of the twenty-first century, some would argue that women face obstacles that men do not in carving out a successful career in the field.

The Society for Historical Archaeology (SHA) formed in 1967 with 207 members, thirty-five of whom were women. This group of female pioneers in historical archaeology included women such as Margaret Kimball Brown and Kathleen Gilmore, whose contributions to the field are noteworthy. The career trajectories of these two women of the founding members of the founding group of historical archaeologists are instructive in a number of ways, especially when contrasted with the experiences of women who have entered the field in the past two decades.

Gilmore first attempted to pursue a career as a geologist, encountering both prejudice and discrimination in a male-dominated field. She completed a Ph.D. in archaeology in 1973 at Southern Methodist University after raising four daughters; her research focused on Spanish missions in east-central Texas. In the early 1970s, Gilmore became an adjunct professor at the University of North Texas and soon was acknowledged as an expert in Spanish colonial archaeology. She was the first woman elected to the Executive Board of the Society for Historical Archaeology (in 1974), became its first female president in 1978 and in 1995 was the first woman to receive the SHA's J.C. Harrington Medal, awarded for lifetime achievement in historical archaeology.

Margaret Kimball Brown's career paralleled Gilmore's in some ways; she, too, was a founding member of SHA while still a graduate student; in 1971 she published an important monograph on glass from **Fort Michilimackinac**, an eighteenth-century French fort and trading post in Michigan. Her dissertation, completed in 1973 at Michigan State University, addressed culture contact in the early French territory of Illinois; in the ensuing years Brown's expertise in French colonial archaeology grew as she focused her energies on excavation at sites such as Kaskaskia Village and on publication of monograph site reports and books about life in the Illinois territory. Despite 'flying under the radar', in part because of the obstacles she faced as a woman, like Gilmore, Brown, who worked for the Illinois Department of Conservation and as Site Manager of the Cahokia Mounds State Historic Site, was a mentor to innumerable young archaeologists and influenced many to choose a career in historical archaeology and ethnohistory.

Gilmore and Brown both carved out careers in historical archaeology when there were few places to study the subject and even fewer teachers of the subject who were willing to serve as sponsors and mentors for aspiring females. Despite setbacks and lack of female role models, both have made substantive contributions to the field that reflect their passion for the subject. Women who followed them have benefited from their efforts and example, and have tended to find far better conditions in which to study and work. Kathleen Deagan, for instance, is one of the most prominent of several women who studied with the late Charles Fairbanks of the University of Florida; like Gilmore and Brown, Deagan has devoted her career to solid fieldwork and to obtaining an in-depth knowledge of a particular colonial culture and has produced a steady flow of influential publications. Though she is based at the Florida Museum of Natural History, she has trained many of the current and upcoming generations of historical archaeologists in the field and in the classroom. Indeed, Deagan's remarkable contributions to our understanding of the process of ethnogenesis in La Florida, the region of the US South-east and the Caribbean colonised by Spain, especially her work in St Augustine, Florida, was acknowledged and celebrated by the SHA with a special Award of Merit in 1992.

By the early 1990s, feminist perspectives had sufficiently penetrated archaeology to bring about interest in women and gender as research topics in historical archaeology as well as an explicit concern for equity issues within the field. Publications devoted to both areas of inquiry ensued and both areas of investigation have had a significant impact on practice and theory. A handful of equity studies, for instance, examined the frequency of women's publication within the Society's journal, topics women published on and citation practices, in addition to women's participation in the SHA as officers and members of the editorial board. Preliminary results indicated that, while women published less often than men, there were other reasons for this than discrimination against them, and a wider study of women's experiences in the field was recommended.

In 1991, the SHA took a bold step in surveying its membership to elicit information that would provide a profile of the overall membership and to pinpoint members' gender and equity concerns. This move was in part prompted by the formation in the 1980s of an active Women's Caucus within the SHA that increased communication among women historical archaeologists. As a result, it became clear that what individuals often perceived as personal experiences and conditions within the field were shared by others, but, in order for remedies to be found, accurate information was needed. The SHA survey produced hard data on the demographics of the membership, workplace issues and relative success among both women and men in professional activities like publication, research funding, etc. Some discrepancies highlighted by the results of the survey were immediately targeted by the SHA and today the active role the SHA took in reforming its election and publishing practices are obvious in many ways.

For instance, only three women served as SHA President between 1978 (when Gilmore was the first woman president) and 1990, but since then the presidency has been filled by women on six additional occasions, and women's representation on the Executive Board has steadily been at parity with that of men; the editorial advisory board has also increased its female membership. The widening range of opportunities has encouraged increasing numbers of women students to complete their degrees and find employment in the field. Perhaps most importantly, the number of publications by women has increased exponentially, both in the form of journal articles (not just in *Historical Archaeology* but also in the *International Journal of Historical Archaeology*, the *Australasian Journal of Historical Archaeology*, etc.) and major books. Women have been instrumental in promoting the growth of historical archaeology outside of North America. Professor Judy Birmingham of the University of Sydney is often referred to as the 'mother of Australian historical archaeology' and, apart from initiating many Ph.D. students into the field, has done innovative work in both urban and contact archaeology in that continent. Carmel Schire, of Rutgers University (USA) brought James Deetz to Cape Town in the early 1980s to inspire archaeologists to undertake colonial archaeology, with the result that the University of Cape Town now has a highly active historical archaeology unit. At Sheffield University, David Crossley trained many women students in 'post-medieval' archaeology, and his Ph.D. student Marilyn Palmer is one of only a few women holding a lectureship in this subject anywhere in the UK. (Recently in the UK the phrase 'historical archaeology' has been promulgated as a substitute for 'post-medieval archaeology' and applied to Roman and medieval periods, resulting in what may be perceived as an expansion of 'historical archaeology' within the UK, albeit with scant additional attention paid to the time periods (sixteenth to twentieth centuries) that historical archaeologists in other parts of the world tend to focus on. Whether this redefinition produces an improved standing for women in UK university posts is not readily apparent.)

Women may still be in a minority in tenured academic posts or chairs in historical archaeology (this is less true in North America than elsewhere), but in truth there are still relatively few full-time, tenure-track jobs for historical archaeologists. Numbers of women students in historical archaeology remain high, however, and women now readily find employments in federal and state agencies that carry out archaeological activities, as well as in museums and historical organisations.

The growth of archaeological heritage management in the USA and throughout the world has
brought about a dramatic shift in archaeology as a
whole, providing unparalleled opportunities for
women in private-sector employment; many women work for archaeological consultancies and
some have established their own successful businesses as consulting archaeologists.

Careers for women in historical archaeology
now are varied and full of options; surely
institutionalised inequalities remain, but it is no
longer inevitable, or nearly so, that women
historical archaeologists will labour for a lifetime
with little recognition of their impact on the field.
Women historical archaeologists can now achieve
prominence, ascend to senior posts and exercise
authority and influence on the field as a whole.
Today, women historical archaeologists are active
and influential in all areas of the discipline:
research and publication; fieldwork and site survey;
education and public outreach; heritage management; conservation; museum-based curation and
exhibition design; database management and
digital media production. What may be most
significant is the fact that women historical
archaeologists, through their substantive research,
reason and intuition, continue to make long-lasting
contributions to the emergent understanding of the
multifarious manifestations and effects of European
expansion and cultural interaction throughout the
globe.

Further reading

Beaudry, M.C. (1994) 'Cowgirls with the blues? A
  study of women's publication and the citation of
  women's work in historical archaeology', in C.P.
  Claassen (ed.) *Women in Archaeology*, Philadelphia:
  University of Pennsylvania Press, pp. 138–58.
—— (1994) 'Women historical archaeologists:
  Who's counting?', in M.C. Nelson, S.M. Nelson
  and A. Wylie (eds) *Equity Issues for Women in
  Archaeology*, Archaeological Papers of the Amer-
  ican Anthropological Association No. 5, Wash-
  ington, DC, pp. 225–8.
Chester, H., Rothschild, N.A. and Wall, D. (1994)
  'Women in historical archaeology: The SHA
  survey', in M.C. Nelson, S.M. Nelson and A.
  Wylie (eds) *Equity Issues for Women in Archaeology*,
  Archaeological Papers of the American Anthropological Association No. 5, Washington, DC,
  pp. 213–18.
Scott, E.M. (ed.) (1994) *Those of Little Note: Gender,
  Race, and Class in Historical Archaeology*, Tucson:
  University of Arizona Press.
Seifert, D.J. (ed.) (1991) 'Gender in historical
  archaeology', *Historical Archaeology* 25(4) (theme
  issue).
Spencer-Wood, S. (1994) 'The historical archaeology women's caucus and the SHA committee
  on gender issues', in M.C. Nelson, S.M. Nelson
  and A. Wylie (eds) *Equity Issues for Women in
  Archaeology*, Archaeological Papers of the Amer-
  ican Anthropological Association No. 5, Washington, DC, pp. 219–24.
Victor, K.L. and Beaudry, M.C. (1992) 'Women's
  participation in prehistoric and historical archaeology: A comparative look at the journals
  American Antiquity and *Historical Archaeology*', in
  C.P. Claassen (ed.) *Exploring Gender through Archaeology: Selected Papers from the 1991 Boone Conference*,
  Monographs in World Archaeology No. 11,
  Madison, WI: The Prehistory Press, pp. 11–21.

MARY C. BEAUDRY

World Archaeological Congress

The World Archaeological Congress (WAC) was
founded in Southampton, **England**, in September
1986. The organisation was created because of a
significant disagreement within the International
Union of Prehistoric and Protohistoric Sciences
(IUPPS) over academic freedom and apartheid in
South Africa. As one might imagine, given the
passions raised about apartheid throughout the
world, the creation of the WAC was controversial
and complex. To summarise, however, a main issue
that brought about its creation revolved around
whether South African scholars should be allowed
to participate in IUPPS conferences or whether
they should be banned from attending. Those who
wished to include South Africans in the conference
argued that many of the affected scholars had
actually fought against apartheid. They did not
support the discriminatory actions of their government, and it was not their fault, they said, that their

government acted contrary to their wishes. Those on the other side of the argument countered that only through such bold actions as banning important scholars from high-profile international scientific conferences would the South African government understand the international cost of their actions.

The WAC has been a leader in promoting the involvement of descendant communities in archaeological research and in making archaeologists understand that living peoples are not merely objects of study. The WAC was also an early proponent of the respect by archaeologists of human remains and the need for **repatriation**.

As a truly international organisation, the WAC is represented by senior and junior representatives from all continents. It does not publish a scholarly journal, but it does print a bulletin and a newsletter. In addition, the organisation has a history of publishing collections of papers delivered at their congresses and inter-congresses.

Further reading

Ucko, P. (1987) *Academic Freedom and Apartheid: The Story of the World Archaeological Congress*, London: Duckworth.

CHARLES E. ORSER, JR

world(-)systems theory

World systems theory is part of a global perspective for examining the connections and contacts between past peoples, many of whom were separated by great differences in **culture** and by vast geographic distance. World systems theory is not a coherent body of thought, but its practitioners generally share the same beliefs, including a hesitation to accept the isolation of indigenous peoples usually classified as 'nations' and 'tribes'; an emphasis on social relations to account for the connections between individuals; and an understanding that social, economic and political processes help to explain the nature of the relationships between peoples.

World systems theory developed as part of the intellectual effort to understand **modernity**.

World-systems theory (with a hyphen) is identified with historical sociologist Immanuel Wallerstein, while world systems theory (with no hyphen) is associated with political economist Andre Gunder Frank. Historical archaeologists regularly use the works of both scholars.

According to Wallerstein, world-systems theory provides a perspective for understanding the 'modern world system' that has been developing since the sixteenth century. This system has three main features: a single, expanding economy rooted in **capitalism**; multiple state-level cultures that are superpowers and who are engaged in worldwide exploration and colonisation; and social relations that at their very foundation embody the interactions between capitalists (owners) and labourers (workers).

Historical archaeologists are drawn to world systems theory because of its explicit interest in long-range connections between vastly different peoples. Many historical archaeologists, having discovered thousands of non-native artefacts at post-AD 1500 sites, have wondered how the objects came to be there. The presence of artefacts such as English **ceramics** at sites as far apart as **South Africa** and Alaska, and tiny glass **beads** from Venetian factories at Native American sites throughout North America (see **Native Americans**), demonstrates the importance of past trade networks that linked together diverse peoples into a common system. Using world systems theory as a model for this interaction helps historical archaeologists to place the people whose history and culture they study in a series of contexts, extending from local to international levels.

World-systems theorists generally envision the world as being divided into 'cores', 'peripheries' and 'semi-peripheries'. Cores are the places from which production and capital emanate, while peripheries are the places dependent on or exploited by the cores. Those places that are intermediate between the two are termed 'semi-peripheries'. For historical archaeologists, the colonial European superpowers constitute cores, while the peripheries are the places they colonized in North America, **South America**, Africa and Asia. Semi-peripheries include places like Eastern Europe that, while not as developed as the cores, were not exactly peripheries either.

World-systems theorists focus their attention on the post-AD 1500 period because of their strong interest in capitalism. They see the capitalist economy as a central, structuring force in modern history. Not all scholars agree that capitalism deserves special consideration, however. These scholars, led largely by Andre Gunder Frank, argue that world systems have existed for at least 5,000 years. Frank used archaeological information from ancient sites in Western and Central Asia to argue that cores and peripheries, and the unequal social relations they foster, have operated since the Bronze Age.

Historical archaeologist Aron Crowell used world-systems theory in his study of the late eighteenth-century Russian fur trade in Alaska. Adopting the core–periphery framework, Crowell sought to understand the nature of the social relations between Native American groups and Russian American fur traders. He was specifically interested in the manner in which Russians adapted to the American frontier, the ways in which they constructed a stratified, colonial society far from their homeland and the nature of their interactions with native men and women. When studied in conjunction with **historical documents**, the artefacts and architectural remains excavated from the Three Saints Harbour site in southern Alaska provided a picture of the fur traders' daily life. Crowell's use of world-systems theory allowed him to understand the broad contexts of the traders' consumption habits, the nature of their housing and the differences between the diets of high- and low-ranked traders. When considering their housing, for example, Crowell found that the fur traders' connections with the world-system helped them to survive. They used locally available materials to build their houses, but relied on imported iron to make **nails** and other pieces of hardware. Without their access to the world system they would not have been able to obtain the iron stock need to make iron tools and other objects. At the same time, the traders imported huge amounts of ceramics from England and **porcelain** from China, glass beads from Russian, Chinese and European factories, and vodka from Moscow. World-systems theory allowed Crowell to show that the site at Three Saints Harbour was not an isolated outpost. It was one

small element of a large, international system that brought goods to Alaska and kept the fur traders there in touch with the outside world.

See also: fur trade archaeology in western Canada; vernacular architecture

Further reading

Chase-Dunn, C. and Hall, T.D. (1997) *Rise and Demise: Comparing World-Systems*, Boulder: Westview.

Crowell, A.L. (1997) *Archaeology and the Capitalist World System: A Study from Russian America*, New York: Plenum.

Frank, A.G. (1993) 'Bronze Age world system cycles', *Current Anthropology* 34: 383–429.

Frank, A.G. and Gills, B.K. (eds) (1993) *The World-System: Five Hundred Years or Five Thousand?*, London: Routledge.

Kardulias, P.N. (1999) *World-Systems Theory in Practice: Leadership, Production, and Exchange*, Lanham, MD: Rowman & Littlefield.

Wallerstein, I. (1980) *The Modern World System II: Mercantilism and Consolidation of the European World-Economy, 1600–1750*, New York: Academic Press.

—— (1974) *The Modern World System I: Capitalist Agriculture and the Origins of the European World-Economy in the Sixteenth Century*, New York: Academic Press.

CHARLES E. ORSER, JR

Worthy Park, Jamaica

Worthy Park was a large sugar plantation located in eastern Jamaica, approximately 35 km northwest of Kingston. The plantation operated from 1670 to 1975. The significance of Worthy Park to historical archaeologists stems not from archaeological research but rather from the careful investigation of the history and **culture** of its African slave community by historian Michael Craton. Historical archaeologists who have studied slavery in both the Caribbean, the US South and elsewhere have often looked to Craton's ethnohistory both for inspiration and for an example of how to construct a sensitive and deeply contextual understanding of slave life during the plantation period.

English planters came to the Worthy Park area in the late seventeenth century as part of an expanding interest in plantation-style agriculture conducted with the labour of enslaved men and women of African birth and descent. The expansion of the sugar trade corresponded with the growing interest in tea drinking in Europe (see **tea/tea ceremony**), and the Caribbean islands provided superb places to cultivate sugar. Enslaved Africans would provide the labour.

Hundreds of slaves toiled at Worthy Park, and, given the richness of the historical information, Craton was able to chart the slave community's demographic profile from 1783 to 1838. Craton was also able to investigate the slaves' rates of mortality and fertility, and their life expectancy; the diseases that affected them; the medicines they used; the jobs they held; and the way they created and maintained some sense of social cohesion. The records also allowed Craton to examine the slaves' social system and to use biographies of individual slaves to put a human face on bondage. He was also able to investigate the important transition from slave to free wage labour during the 1834–46 period, an issue that archaeologist Douglas Armstrong was also able to pursue using excavations at Drax Hall Plantation, another Jamaican estate.

Craton's work on the Worthy Park slave community was situated within the burgeoning field of social history that began in earnest in the 1970s. Historians at this time were discovering the value of anthropological insights, just as anthropologists were re-establishing their links with historical analysis. Ethnohistory was one outcome of this cross-disciplinary understanding. Many historical archaeologists working in this period were also profoundly influenced by the work of social historians, particularly as the historians' research pertained to slave communities. Craton's work specifically had an impact on the historical archaeology being practised at slave plantation sites.

See also: African American archaeology; Caribbean archaeology; history of historical archaeology; plantation archaeology; vernacular architecture

Further reading

Craton, M. (1978) *Searching for the Invisible Man: Slaves and Plantation Life in Jamaica*, Cambridge, MA: Harvard University Press.

CHARLES E. ORSER, JR

writing

'Historical archaeology' – whether viewed as the archaeology of modern capitalism or as 'text-aided' archaeology in any period – is defined by its use of both written records and archaeological materials. A common theme in programmatic statements on historical archaeology is the 'gap' between archaeological and textual records, and the ways in which this gap can be a productive space. Archaeological data can 'fill in' details about the past (on the lives of non-elites, for example) that are not recorded in written documents. Alternatively, when both written and archaeological evidence exists on the same topic, the 'gap' between what written texts say about the past and what is attested in the archaeological record can be used to reconsider specific claims in text-based histories.

Assumptions about a 'gap' between writing and **material culture**, however, raise questions of categorisation. 'Writing' is often assumed to be a self-evident, cross-cultural phenomenon: a method of recording information by visible marks. Definitions of writing vary as to whether or not these marks need to relate directly to the spoken word. The assumption that 'true' writing must be based on spoken language has been prevalent in nineteenth- and twentieth-century theories, which posit 'writing' as a cross-cultural category. These theories have often been evolutionary and hierarchical in approach. Thus, so-called 'picture writing', with little relation to spoken language, is placed at the bottom of a unitary developmental sequence of 'writing'. Alphabetic writing, which textualises sound at the level of the phoneme, is placed at the summit of that developmental sequence. Evolutionary assumptions, again presuming that 'writing' is a transparent cross-cultural category, have also shaped theories that claim that 'writing' is a practice whose presence marks a 'gap' between oral and literate cultures. These theories have suggested that major changes in cognition occur when the so-called savage mind learns to read.

Other approaches to 'writing', however, focus less on universal definitions and more on how writing is conceptualised and produced in particular times and places. Such focused studies have revealed that societies do not necessarily have an independent category of 'writing'. Writing may, instead, be understood as part of a larger field of cultural practices – such as painting, weaving, seeing, counting or remembering. Such broader conceptual fields may therefore link 'writing' to other material practices. For example, the organisational and material structure of written documents may be linked to the patterns of cloth, or to the arrangement of buildings in the landscape. Furthermore, attention to the ways in which texts are used in particular times and places has revealed the frequency of 'recitation literacy', in which texts are made available to a wider audience by being read aloud. Finally, focused studies of the histories of writing in particular places have refuted the picture-to-alphabet trajectory proposed by evolutionary models. In sum, culturally focused studies of 'writing' have blurred the gaps between writing and material culture, between oral and literate societies, and between the assumed evolutionary stages in the 'history' of writing's development.

Evolutionary legacies

One common approach to theorising writing in the nineteenth and twentieth centuries has been evolutionary. From Edward Tylor and Isaac Taylor in the nineteenth century to Ignace Gelb, David Diringer and John DeFrancis in the twentieth, the same basic history of writing has been repeated over and over, with slight variations and varying neologisms. This constructed history assumes that 'true writing' records the spoken word as closely as possible, and is based on a division of speech into the smallest possible units of sound. 'True writing' is posited as something achieved over time, through a series of stages. Such models claim that writing first develops from pictorial representations that have little or no direct relationship to spoken language. Such 'ideographic' writing systems are followed by 'logographic' systems, in which written marks represent whole words. In turn, syllabic systems allow an even more precise parsing of the sound units of speech. And, finally, the 'most efficient' form of writing arises: the alphabet.

There are a number of problems with these evolutionary models of writing's history. Despite being evolutionary, these theories are ahistoric. Although these models claim to chart the development of scripts over time, actual considerations of specific histories of writing systems reveal that writing traditions do not necessarily begin with pictures and end with an alphabet. Piotr Michalowski points out that in the Near East – the source of our earliest information on the 'origins' of writing – no clear linear evolution from pictorially based to sound-based writing has been attested. Rather, a multiplicity of different written practices, with varying relations to speech, was constantly being developed and lost throughout Mesopotamia. The history of writing in Mesopotamia therefore reveals a complex picture of the contemporaneous coexistence of different types of writing. Michalowski argues that this complex coexistence is better understood when, rather than assuming an abstract evolutionary drive towards alphabetic sound recording, one considers the particular purposes to which particular writing traditions were being used. Is a society using writing to record tribute information or prayers?

In addition to their historical inaccuracy, evolutionary views of writing are problematically marked, in a number of ways, by the nineteenth-century capitalist environment in which they have their origins. As was common in visions of social evolution in the nineteenth century, the cultural practices of the West (in this case, alphabetic writing) were assumed to be an ideal end-of-time goal. All other social practices from other parts of the globe were viewed as inferior, undeveloped. Evolutionary histories of a number of practices were therefore fabricated so that their history ended in the West. Models of writing that place the alphabet and the close representation of the spoken word at the summit of writing's achievement continue this tradition of Eurocentrism. In addition, the influences of bureaucratic assumptions (linked to the increasing textualisation of capitalist life) are revealed in descriptions of the alphabet as the most 'efficient' and 'accurate' form of writing possible. That desires of 'efficiency' in writing need to be placed in a specifically bureaucratic cultural context is suggested by the ninth edition (1888) of the *Encyclopaedia Britannica*. Unlike the eighth and tenth editions, this edition does not have an entry for 'writing'. Instead, it has an entry for 'writing machines', focused on a number of mechanisms (carbon paper, lithographic printers, typewriters) by which documents may be reproduced. The page devoted to these devices repeatedly emphasises the speed with which these various appliances can produce and duplicate written documents.

The interface between the written and the oral

Evolutionary assumptions also mark a tradition of studying writing that proposes a 'gap' between 'oral' and 'literate' societies. In the early 1960s, a number of writers – Eric Havelock, Jack Goody and Ian Watt – proposed that the arrival of literacy in a society had profound cognitive effects. These arguments repeated Lewis Henry Morgan's nineteenth-century claims in *Ancient Society*, in which the invention of writing marked the great leap from barbarism to civilisation. As with evolutionary models of writing's history, these studies are based on little, or problematic, uses of evidence – problems that have been critiqued by John Halverson. A noted exception to work in this tradition is Elizabeth Eisenstein's studies of the social and cognitive implications of the shift to print literacy in Early Modern Europe. Unlike Goody, who tries to create a universal model for the impact of literacy based on problematic claims about its consequences in classical Greece, Eisenstein limits her arguments to a more richly documented period. She is thus better able to consider the multiple social contexts, and consequences, for the impact of print literacy on a particular time and place.

Other contextually grounded studies of the interface between the written and the oral in the 1980s and 1990s have revealed the ways in which written texts are linked to oral recitation. Eric Havelock, despite his continued emphasis on the revolutionary cognitive impacts of the alphabet, introduced the concept of 'recitation literacy' to describe the classical Greek practice of reading written texts aloud. The practice of 'recitation literacy' therefore blurs a sharp division between 'oral' and 'written' culture, because it allows a number of individuals (who may or may not read or write themselves) to become familiar with the contents of a written document. Recitation literacy is cross-culturally an extremely common practice. M.T. Clanchy has studied the relations between oral testimony and written texts in early medieval English society. He points out an initial mistrust of purely written evidence: written documents needed to be read aloud in order to be accepted as socially legitimate forms of knowledge. A number of studies of Mesoamerican writing have stressed the importance of recitation literacy in pre-Columbian societies, and have highlighted the ties between oral performance and elite power. In other words, theories of a universal 'gap' between orality and literacy become problematic once the actual uses of texts in specific times and places are considered.

'Writing' as material culture

Another 'gap' that becomes problematic once the specific social uses of written documents are considered is the categorical separation of writing from material culture. Writing, of course, is a material practice: it uses tools, it inscribes physical surfaces, it requires specific bodily skills to produce and, when placed on non-perishable materials, it can be excavated as part of the archaeological record. A number of studies have tried to blur the boundaries between text and material culture.

One approach in using 'text as material culture' considers inscribed monuments as archaeologically recovered objects. Kathleen Morrison and Mark Lycett's study of monumental inscriptions in the environs of Vijayanagara combines considerations of what inscribed monuments say, and who they were created by and addressed to, with their spatial distributions and contexts in the landscape. Morrison and Lycett consider how historical knowledge drawn from monumental texts is like other forms of archaeological knowledge, in that it is influenced by the parameters of data recovery. Where a text is located affects the possibility of its archaeological discovery, and reflects its original audiences and patrons. Another approach to text as material culture considers the physical and formal parallels between written documents and other material practices. Matthew Johnson demonstrates how the conceptual ordering of a European feudal document can be related to the spatial divisions of the feudal landscape to which it refers. Barbara Little has considered the similarities and differences between printed documents and other patterns of social and spatial divisions in eighteenth- and nineteenth-century Maryland.

Finally, studies of writing as material culture have explored emic understandings of what 'writing' is. Such studies reveal that the modern Western category of 'writing' may inhibit richer understandings of material practices in other times and places. Scholarship on Mesoamerican 'writing' has repeatedly revealed indigenous associations between this form of material production and acts of painting, weaving, counting and seeing. M.T. Clanchy's research on the adoption of writing as a social practice in early medieval England reveals how 'writing' was initially viewed not as a self-sufficient practice in and of itself, but was instead integrated into a pre-existing set of practices of remembering based on material objects. Thus, early uses of written documents emphasised their materiality: written labels were created for the more traditional material objects of memory; written documents were given oversized wax seals in order to make them more physically substantial.

See also: Chesapeake region

Further reading

Boone, E. and Mignolo, W. (1994) *Writing Without Words: Alternative Literacies in Mesoamerica and the Andes*, Durham: Duke University Press.

Clanchy, M.T. (1979) *From Memory to Written Record: England 1066–1307*, Cambridge: Harvard University Press.

Eisenstein, E.L. (1983) *The Printing Revolution in Early Modern Europe*, Cambridge, MA: Cambridge University Press.

Johnson, M.H. (1996) *An Archaeology of Capitalism*, Oxford: Blackwell.

Little, B.J. (1992) 'Explicit and implicit meanings in material culture and print culture', *Historical Archaeology* 26: 85–94.

Michalowski, P. (1990) 'Early Mesopotamian communicative systems: Art, literature, and writing', in A.C. Gunder (ed.), *Investigating Artistic Environ-*

ments in the Ancient Near-east, Washington, DC: Arthur M. Sackler Gallery, pp. 53–70.

Morrison, K.D and Lycett, M.T. (1997) 'Inscriptions as artifacts: Precolonial south India and the analysis of texts, *Journal of Archaeological Method and Theory* 4: 215–37.

BYRON HAMANN

Wybalenna, Tasmania, Australia

Wybalenna, on tiny Flinders Island, about 64 km off the north-eastern coast of Tasmania, was home to hundreds of Tasmanian men, women and **children** from 1835 to 1847. The British authorities called the settlement an 'aboriginal establishment on Flinders Island', but it was in truth a prison camp where the Tasmanians were interned.

Historical archaeologist Judy Birmingham excavated the aboriginal internment camp in the 1970s. She focused part of her attention on the ways in which the Tasmanians accepted or rejected English attempts to transform them into Europeans. Using an 1838 map of the site, Birmingham and her team were able to identify a military barracks, a hospital and surgeon's quarters, a smithy, the chaplain's residence, the commander's home and the small cottages of the Tasmanian internees.

Birmingham was able to excavate five of the Tasmanians' cabins. The builders of the camp had created these five cottages as a linear row of single-room units. Her excavations revealed that two small cottages (measuring about 3.7 by 4.4 m) appeared on either side of a larger cabin (measuring 4.6 by 5 m). The builders had constructed the cottages with brick and stone walls, and brick floors. These cottages were almost the exact size of contemporary slave cabins in the US South and the Caribbean (see **Caribbean archaeology**).

Excavations further revealed that the people at the camp used a large array of objects manufactured in Europe, including white-clay smoking pipes (see **pipes, smoking**), English **ceramics** and **glass** vessels, and bone **buttons**. At the same time, however, the discovery of sandstone pounding tools and snail shells pierced for stringing indicate that the **acculturation** of the Tasmanians was not complete. In a demonstration of the complexity of social change and acculturation, Birmingham learned that the men and women living in the five cottages were not equally 'Europeanised'. In other words, the acculturation of the native Tasmanians at Wybalenna was not uniform. She was able to substantiate this interpretation by comparing the artefacts from each cottage. For example, when she compared the clay pipes from Cottage 7 with those from Cottage 8 (two of the smaller cabins), she learned that Cottage 7 was associated with twenty-six pipe fragments whereas Cottage 8 was associated with over twice that number. The same distribution occurred with other artefacts as well.

The research at Wybalenna is important for at least two reasons. In the first place it provides new information about the native Tasmanians, men and women whom it has been all too easy to dismiss from orthodox history. Birmingham's careful research documents how these indigenous peoples were treated by the invading, though more powerful, foreigners and how they were interned simply for being themselves. Second, the Wybalenna research provides an example of one of the most important contributions to knowledge historical archaeologists can make: the documentation of cultures that have been overlooked, forgotten or ignored.

Further reading

Birmingham, J. (1992) *Wybalenna: The Archaeology of Cultural Accommodation in Nineteenth Century Tasmania*, Sydney: Australian Society for Historical Archaeology.

CHARLES E. ORSER, JR

Z

zooarchaeology

Zooarchaeology is the study of animal remains from archaeological sites. Animal, or faunal, remains may be from both vertebrates (bones and eggshell) and invertebrates (skeleton/exoskeleton fragments and outer shells). Although preservation conditions do not often allow complete recovery of animal remains, zooarchaeological analysis can provide evidence of many of the foods that were consumed; methods of food preparation; hunting, fishing, gathering, purchasing and other food-procurement activities; ethnic affiliation and socio-economic position of persons at a site; refuse disposal patterns; animal husbandry practices; and uses of non-food animal products. Given the temporal depth of many historical and post-medieval archaeological sites (see **post-medieval archaeology**), zooarchaeologists also may see change through time in any of these aspects.

Zooarchaeologists identify the bone and shell from archaeological sites using comparative osteological collections. In addition to counting and weighing the fragments, they made calculations to estimate the minimum number of individuals of each species represented in the faunal assemblage, and the amount of meat each may have contributed to the diet. Any butchering marks on the bones (from cutting, chopping and sawing) are noted so that, when possible, one may reconstruct butchering methods. Several criteria are used to determine the age of an animal at death; this knowledge provides some indication of the season of the year when the animal was eaten (and therefore the season when the bones/shell were

deposited and the site occupied) as well as some idea of livestock management practices and culling of animals.

Zooarchaeologists working on historical and post-medieval sites have the advantage of being able to use archival documents and **oral history** in combination with the archaeological evidence. Such contemporary documents as cookbooks, newspaper food advertisements, hotel menus, store account ledgers, personal diaries and correspondence, and military records provide evidence of food preferences, means of preparation, cost and availability of foods in different locations, and distribution of foods within a region or society.

Historical archaeologists often examine the archaeological evidence for cultural change or continuity, especially in the context of European contact and colonisation. Zooarchaeology contributes to this endeavour, particularly with evidence for changes in diet on the part of both European colonisers and native groups, and, conversely, with evidence for a continuation of those Old World European and native diets. Elizabeth Reitz examined animal remains from the sixteenth-century Spanish settlements of **St Augustine**, Florida, and **Santa Elena**, in what is now South Carolina. She found that Spanish colonists continued some aspects of an Old World Iberian meat diet but also utilised new meat resources. They continued to raise the European livestock that could survive in the very different climate and environment of the south-eastern coast of North America, but they also adopted Native American patterns of animal use (see **Native Americans**), adding new foods to their diet. There were variations in diet among the

Spanish colonists, as well, which could be correlated with differences in wealth or ethnicity; for example, households that included Native American women were those with the greatest use of local wild resources.

At a later colonial site, the eighteenth-century fur-trading settlement of **Fort Michilimackinac** in what is now northern Michigan, Elizabeth Scott was able to use zooarchaeological evidence to associate particular households with residents of several economic and ethnic groups based on differences in diet. British elite military officers maintained as close to an Old World English diet as possible, the only notable change being the addition of a large quantity of local fish. French-Canadian traders changed their Old World diets to a greater degree, incorporating many local wild animals and relying less on domestic livestock. Finally, the animal remains from the household of a German-Jewish fur trader indicate that, when he became financially able to do so, he chose to eat a more kosher diet, greatly reducing the amount of pork and virtually eliminating wild mammals and birds from his diet.

Another topic often addressed by zooarchaeologists working with historical sites is the difference that an urban or rural setting makes in the availability and use of animal resources by peoples in the past. David Landon revealed how the foods utilised in seventeenth- and eighteenth-century Boston were very similar to those utilised in the surrounding rural communities. By the late eighteenth and early nineteenth centuries, with the beginnings of industrialisation and expansion of market-oriented production, farmers became increasingly specialised towards production for the urban market and urban markets grew larger and more centralised.

Cynthia Price analysed animal remains from the early nineteenth-century (c. 1820s–c. 1850s) occupation of the Widow Harris site, a small Euro-American farmstead in the foothills of the eastern Ozarks in Missouri, USA. She used photographs (see **photographic information**), **oral-history** interviews, ethnohistory and folklore to better understand the cultural behaviour that had resulted in the particular distribution of animal remains at the site. Different butchering, preparation and consumption practices were followed for small animals (such as squirrels) and large animals (such as hogs). The bones from these animals entered the archaeological record at different stages in those activities, and at different locations on the farmstead.

See also: colonialism; contact archaeology; food and foodways; Spanish colonialism

Further reading

Crabtree, P.J. (1990) 'Zooarchaeology and complex societies: Some uses of faunal analysis for the study of trade, social status, and ethnicity', in M.B. Schiffer (ed.) *Archaeological Method and Theory*, 2, Tucson: University of Arizona Press, pp. 155–205.

Landon, D.B. (1996) 'Feeding colonial Boston: A zooarchaeological study', *Historical Archaeology* 30(1): 1–153.

Price, C.R. (1985) 'Patterns of cultural behavior and intra-site distributions of faunal remains at the Widow Harris site', *Historical Archaeology* 19(2): 40–56.

Reitz, E.J. and Scarry, C.M. (1985) *Reconstructing Historic Subsistence with an Example from Sixteenth Century Spanish Florida*, Tucson: Society for Historical Archaeology.

Scott, E.M. (1996) 'Who ate what? Archaeological food remains and cultural diversity', in E.J. Reitz, L.A. Newsom and S.J. Scudder (eds) *Case Studies in Environmental Archaeology*, New York: Plenum Press, pp. 339–56.

ELIZABETH M. SCOTT

Index